Avizandum Statutes on

Scots Commercial and Consumer Law
2026–2027

24th edition

AVIZANDUM STATUTES

Avizandum Statutes are designed specifically to provide undergraduates at Scottish universities with legislation and, where appropriate, other core materials in a readily accessible format. All materials have been selected on the basis of their relevance to university courses and appear in updated form. The lack of annotation and commentary means that the volumes are ideal for use in examinations.

Volumes in the series:

Jonathan Hardman and Claudia Paduano (eds), *Avizandum Statutes on Scots Commercial and Consumer Law 2026–2027, 24th edition* (2026)

Jane Mair (ed), *Avizandum Statutes on Scots Family Law 2026–2027, 24th edition* (2026)

Andrew J M Steven and Scott Wortley (eds), *Avizandum Statutes on Scots Property, Trusts and Succession Law 2026–2027, 23rd edition* (2026)

Navraj Singh Ghaleigh (ed), *Avizandum Statutes on Scots Public Law, 6th edition* (2026)

Rachel McPherson (ed), *Avizandum Statutes on Scots Criminal Law and Evidence* (2026)

Laura J Macgregor and Lorna Richardson (eds), *Avizandum Legislation on the Scots Law of Obligations, 10th edition* (2025)

Elizabeth B Crawford and Janeen M Carruthers (eds), *Avizandum Legislation on International Private Law, 5th edition* (2020)

https://edinburghuniversitypress.com/series-avizandum-statutes

Avizandum Statutes on

Scots Commercial and Consumer Law

2026–2027

24th edition

Editors

Jonathan Hardman LLB (Hons), DipLP, LLM, PhD
Senior Lecturer in Company and Commercial Law, University of Edinburgh

and

Claudia Paduano LLB (Hons), LLM, PhD
Lecturer in Commercial Law, University of Glasgow

EDINBURGH
University Press

Edinburgh University Press is one of the leading university presses in the UK. Publishing new research in the arts and humanities, EUP connects people and ideas to inspire creative thinking, open new perspectives and shape the world we live in. For more information, visit www.edinburghuniversitypress.com.

First published 2003
24th edition published 2026

Edinburgh University Press Ltd
13 Infirmary Street
Edinburgh EH1 1LT

Typeset in 9/10 pt, Palatino
by Deanta Global Publishing Services, Chennai, India
Printed and bound in the UK using 100% renewable electricity by CPI Group (UK) Ltd

A CIP record for this book is available from the British Library

ISBN 978 1 3995 7220 0 (paperback)
ISBN 978 1 3995 7222 4 (webready PDF)
ISBN 978 1 3995 7221 7 (epub)

EDITORS' PREFACE

Welcome to the 24th edition of *Avizandum Statutes on Scots Commercial and Consumer Law*, and our first as editors. It is our pleasure to take over the editorship of this important collection of statutes. We would particularly like to thank the diligent editorial work of our predecessor, Alisdair MacPherson, and those who came before him. As ever, the book contains relevant legislation for students on commercial or business law courses in Scotland. The material may also be of value to others seeking a compilation of key legislation in the areas covered.

The biggest change from last year's edition has been the updating of the Limited Partnership Act 1907 to reflect changes enacted by the Economic Crime and Corporate Transparency Act 2023. The substantive reforms to partnerships are expected to take effect by the end of 2026 or in the near future. Therefore, this edition includes the reforms. *Italics* have been used for those legislative provisions that have been included but are not yet in force as at 10 April 2026.

At the time that updates were submitted, a number of changes to various acts were pending but not yet in force. Without clarity on when the changes would take effect, we decided to not include them in this edition. These include:

- changes pending to the Consumer Rights Act 2015 arising under the Digital Markets, Competition and Consumers Act 2024 (e.g. sections 36, 37, 50 and 90);
- changes to the Bankruptcy (Scotland) Act 2016 arising under:
  - the Economic Crime and Corporate Transparency Act 2023 (section 17);
  - the Bankruptcy and Diligence (Scotland) Act 2024 (section 22);
  - the Judicial Factors Act 2025 (sections 25, 88, 98, 99, 100, 107 and a new 129ZA); and
  - the Employment Rights Act 2025 (schedules 3 and 8); and
- changes to the Consumer Contracts (Information, Cancellation and Additional Charges) Regulations 2013 arising under the Digital Competition and Consumers Act 2024.

Similarly, the Digital Assets (Scotland) Bill had been passed by the Scottish Parliament but had not yet received Royal Assent when this manuscript was submitted.

The present volume has been updated to 10 April 2026 but, as noted above, it has been possible to include some changes which will take effect shortly. Amendments to legislation as originally enacted are indicated using […].

We would like to thank Edinburgh University Press, and especially Laura Quinn, for their help in preparing this volume. If you have any suggestions as to what future editions of this statute book should include, please feel free to email us at jonathan.hardman@ed.ac.uk and claudia.paduano@glasgow.ac.uk.

Jonathan Hardman
University of Edinburgh

Claudia Paduano
University of Glasgow
April 2026

CONTENTS

PART I
STATUTES

COMPENSATION ACT 1592
(RPS 1592/4/83; APS III, 573)

Oure Souerane Lord and estaitis of parliament statutis and Ordanis that ony debt de liquido ad liquidum instantlie verifiet be wreit or aith of the partie befoir the geving of decreit be admittit be all Jugis within this realme be way of exceptioun bot nocht eftir the geving thairof in the suspensioun or in reductioun of the same decreit.

DILIGENCE ACT 1661*
(RPS 1661/1/433; APS VII, 317, c 344)

[A]ll compriseings deduced . . . befor the first effectuall compriseing or after but within yeer and day of the same Shall come in pari passu together [. . .].

* As applied to adjudications by Adjudications Act 1672 (RPS 1672/6/55; APS VIII, 93, c 45).

LIFE ASSURANCE ACT 1774
(14 Geo 3, c 48)

1 No Insurance to be made on the lives of persons having no interest, &c
From and after the passing of this Act no insurance shall be made by any person or persons, bodies politick or corporate, on the life or lives of any person, or persons, or on any other event or events whatsoever, wherein the person or persons for whose use, benefit, or on whose account such policy or policies shall be made, shall have no interest, or by way of gaming or wagering; and every assurance made contrary to the true intent and meaning hereof shall be null and void to all intents and purposes whatsoever.

2 No policies on lives without inserting the persons names, &c
And it shall not be lawful to make any policy or policies on the life or lives of any person or persons, or other event or events, without inserting in such policy or policies the person or persons name or names interested therein, or for whose use, benefit, or on whose account such policy is so made or underwrote.

3 How much may be recovered where the insured hath interest in lives
And in all cases where the insured hath interest in such life or lives, event or events, no greater sum shall be recovered or received from the insurer or insurers than the amount of value of the interest of the insured in such life or lives, or other event or events.

4 Not to extend to insurances on ships, goods, &c
Provided always, that nothing herein contained shall extend or be construed to extend to insurances bona fide made by any person or persons on ships, goods, or merchandises, but every such insurance shall be as valid and effectual in the law as if this Act had not been made.

MERCANTILE LAW AMENDMENT (SCOTLAND) ACT 1856
(19 & 20 Vict, c 60)

8 Cautioners not to be entitled to benefit of discussion
Where any person shall become bound as cautioner for any principal debtor, it shall not be necessary for the creditor to whom such cautionary obligation shall be granted, before calling on the cautioner for payment of the debt to which such cautionary obligation refers, to discuss or do diligence against the principal debtor, as now required by law; but it shall be competent to such creditor to proceed against the principal debtor and the said cautioner, or against either of them, and to use all action or diligence against both or either of them which is competent according to the law of Scotland: Provided always, that nothing herein contained shall prevent any cautioner from stipulating in the instrument of caution that the creditor shall be bound before proceeding against him to discuss and do diligence against the principal debtor.

9 Discharge of one cautioner, to operate as a discharge to all
Where two or more parties shall become bound as cautioners for any debtor, any discharge granted by the creditor in such debt or obligation to any one of such cautioners without the consent of the other cautioners shall be deemed and taken to be a discharge granted to all the cautioners; but nothing herein contained shall be deemed to extend to the case of a cautioner consenting to the discharge of a co-cautioner who may have become bankrupt.

TITLES TO LAND CONSOLIDATION (SCOTLAND) ACT 1868
(31 & 32 Vict, c 101)

59 Unnecessary to libel and conclude for decree of special adjudication
Whereas it is inconvenient in practice to libel and conclude for general adjudication of lands as the alternative only of special adjudication, in terms of an Act of the Parliament of Scotland passed in the year one thousand six hundred and seventy-two: It shall not be necessary to libel or conclude for special adjudication, and it shall be lawful to libel and conclude and decern for general adjudication without such alternative, anything in the said last-recited Act of the Parliament of Scotland, or in any other Act or Acts of the Parliament of Scotland or of Great Britain or of the United Kingdom of Great Britain and Ireland, to the contrary notwithstanding.

[62 Effect of a decree of adjudication or sale
In all cases a decree of adjudication whether for debt or in implement, or a decree of constitution and adjudication whether for debt or in implement, if duly obtained in the form prescribed by this Act, or obtained, if prior to the commencement of this Act, in the form then in use, or a decree of declarator and adjudication, or a decree of sale, shall, except in the case where the subjects contained in the decree of adjudication, or of constitution and adjudication, or of declarator and adjudication, are heritable securities, be held equivalent to and shall have the legal operation and effect of a conveyance in ordinary form of the lands therein contained granted in favour of the adjudger or purchaser by the ancestor of such apparent heir, or by the owner or proprietor in trust or otherwise, and whether in life or deceased, of the lands adjudged, or by the seller of the lands sold, although [under legal disability by reason of nonage] or [mental or other incapacity] and it shall be lawful and competent to such adjudger or purchaser to complete [title by recording the decree as a conveyance or by using the decree as a midcouple or link of title.]

[155 Date on which inhibition takes effect
(1) An inhibition has effect from the beginning of the day on which it is registered unless the circumstances referred to in subsection (2) below apply.

(2) Those circumstances are—

(a) a notice of inhibition is registered in the Register of Inhibitions;

(b) the schedule of inhibition is served on the debtor after that notice is registered; and

(c) the inhibition is registered before the expiry of the period of 21 days beginning with the day on which the notice is registered.

(3) In those circumstances the inhibition has effect from the beginning of the day on which the schedule of inhibition is served.

(4) A notice of inhibition must be in (or as nearly as may be in) the form prescribed.]

157 No inhibition to have effect against acquirenda, unless in case of heir under entail or other indefeasible title

No inhibition to be recorded from and after the thirty-first day of December one thousand eight hundred and sixty-eight shall have any force or effect as against any lands to be acquired by the person or persons against whom such inhibition is used after the date of recording such inhibition, or of recording the previous notice thereof prescribed by this Act, as the case may be: Provided always, that where such inhibition is used against a person or persons who shall thereafter succeed to any lands which, at the date of recording the inhibition or previous notice thereof, as the case may be, were destined to such person or persons by a deed of entail, or by a similar indefeasible title, then and in that case such inhibition shall affect the said person or persons in so far as regards the lands so destined, and to which he or they shall succeed as aforesaid, but no further.

159 Litigiosity not to begin before date of registration of notice of summons

[(1)] It shall be competent to register in the general register of inhibitions a notice of any signeted summons of reduction of any conveyance or deed of or relating to lands, and in the register of adjudications a notice of any signeted summons of adjudication or of constitution and adjudication combined [. . .] in implement, which notice shall [be in (or as nearly as may be in) the form prescribed]; and no summons of reduction, constitution, adjudication, or constitution and adjudication combined, shall have any effect in rendering litigious the lands to which such summons relates, except from and after the date of the registration of such notice.

[(2) A notice registered under subsection (1) on or after the date on which section 67 of the Land Registration etc (Scotland) Act 2012 (asp 5) (warrant to place a caveat) comes into force shall not have any effect in rendering litigious any land a title sheet for which is comprised in the Land Register of Scotland or in placing in bad faith any person acquiring such land.]

[159A Registration of notice of summons of action of reduction

(1) This section applies where a pursuer raises an action of reduction of a conveyance or deed of or relating to lands granted in breach of an inhibition.

(2) The pursuer shall, as soon as is reasonably practicable after the summons in the action is signeted—

(a) register a notice of that signeted summons in accordance with section 159 of this Act; and

(b) [. . .] record in the Register of Sasines a copy of that notice.

(3) Where a decree of reduction is not obtained in the action to which the notice relates, the pursuer shall, as soon as is reasonably practicable—

(a) register in the Register of Inhibitions; and

(b) [. . .] record in the Register of Sasines,

a discharge of that notice in (or as nearly as may be in) the form prescribed.

[(4) This section does not apply in relation to lands for which there is a title sheet in the Land Register of Scotland.]]

WRITS EXECUTION (SCOTLAND) ACT 1877
(40 & 41 Vict, c 40)

1 Extracts of writs registered in Books of Council and Session to have, in certain cases, warrant for execution. Form of warrant of execution inserted in extracts of all protests, &c

In all extracts of writs, deeds, or other documents which contain a clause of registration for preservation and execution, and which are registered in the register of deeds and probative writs and protests in the Books of Council and Session in Scotland, the keeper or assistant keeper of the said register shall insert a warrant for execution in the form, or as nearly as may be in the form, of the Schedule to this Act annexed.

The warrants for execution inserted in the extracts of all protests of bills, promissory notes or bankers notes, or certificates of judgment registered for execution under the Judgments Extension Act, 1868, shall be as nearly as may be in the form of the said Schedule to this Act annexed.

2 Extracts of writs registered in Sheriff Court Books to have warrant of execution in certain cases

In all extracts of writs, deeds, or other documents which contain a clause of registration for preservation and execution, and which are registered in the Sheriff Court Books of any county in Scotland, and in all extracts of protests of bills, promissory notes, or bankers notes registered in the Sheriff Court Books, the sheriff clerk shall insert a warrant of execution in the form, or as nearly as may be in the form, of the Schedule to this Act annexed.

[3 Power to execute diligence by virtue of warrant

The warrant inserted in an extract of a document registered in the Books of Council and Session or in sheriff court books which contains an obligation to pay a sum of money shall have the effect of authorising—

(a) in relation to an ordinary debt within the meaning of the Debtors (Scotland) Act 1987, the charging of the debtor to pay to the creditor within the period specified in the charge the sum specified in the extract and any interest accrued on the sum and, in the event of failure to make such payment within that period, the execution of an earnings arrestment, a money attachment] and the [attachment] of articles belonging to the debtor and, if necessary for the purpose of executing the [money attachment or] [attachment], the opening of shut and lockfast places;

(b) in relation to an ordinary debt within the meaning of the Debtors (Scotland) Act 1987, an arrestment other than an arrestment of the debtor's earnings in the hands of his employer; and

[(ba) in relation to an ordinary debt within the meaning of the Debtors (Scotland) Act 1987, inhibition against the debtor;]

(c) if the document is a maintenance order within the meaning of the Debtors (Scotland) Act 1987, a current maintenance arrestment in accordance with Part III of that Act.]

. . .

5 Extracts of deeds registered in the Books of Council and Session, and Register of Sasines, to be authenticated

Extracts of all writs, deeds, or other documents of what nature soever, which may be registered in the Books of Council and Session, shall be equivalent to the registered writs, deeds, or other documents themselves, except where any writ, deed, or other document so registered shall be offered to be improven, and such extracts shall be signed on the last page thereof, by the keeper or assistant keeper of the register of deeds and probative writs and protests in the Books of Council and Session; and extracts of all writs registered in and issued from the office of the

General Register of Sasines shall be signed, on the last page thereof, by the keeper of the said register, or by a deputy duly commissioned by him to that effect, and no further signature on any other page of such extracts shall be necessary. But each sheet of all such extracts shall [bear] an office seal or stamp [. . .] of the said keepers; provided that it shall be necessary and sufficient in the case of marginal additions occurring in any extract that the same shall be authenticated by the signature of the officer certifying such extract.

6 Writs registered in the Register of Sasines for preservation only may afterwards be registered for preservation and execution

Where any writ containing in gremio thereof a procuratory or clause of registration for preservation and execution shall have been registered in the General Register of Sasines [. . .] for preservation but not for execution, it shall be competent to present for registration in the said register an extract of such registered writ [with, written on the extract, a statement to the effect] that such extract is to be registered for preservation and execution; and it shall be lawful to register such extract accordingly, and to issue one or more extracts thereof, with warrant of execution in terms (mutatis mutandis) of Schedule B. annexed to the Land Registers (Scotland) Act 1868, and every such warrant of execution shall have all the like force and effect as any warrant of execution issued in terms of the twelfth section of the said last-mentioned Act; and in making such subsequent registration it shall not be necessary to engross ad longum in the said register the extract so presented, but the registration thereof may be effected by the insertion of a memorandum of such extract in the appropriate division or divisions of said register, setting forth the volume of the register, and the folio or folios of such volume in which said original writ is engrossed, and the insertion of such memorandum shall be deemed equivalent to the full engrossment in the division or divisions of the register in which such memorandum shall be entered as aforesaid of the extract so presented for registration.

7 After transmission of volumes of records of Books of Council and Session to the Lords Clerk Register, the deputy keeper of records may issue extracts of any deeds recorded in said volumes and authenticate the same as well as other extracts

Whereas [. . .] the volumes of records of the Books of Council and Session are, along with the warrants thereof, periodically transmitted by the keeper of the register of deeds and probative writs and protests in the Books of Council and Session, to the Lord Clerk Register or his deputies; be it enacted, that the deputy keeper of the records or any officer holding a commission to that effect from the Lord Clerk Register may, at any time, issue extracts one or more of any writ, deed, or other document registered in said volumes of records transmitted as aforesaid, in the same or in a similar form to the extracts of such writs, deeds, or other documents which might have been issued previous to such transmission. And all such extracts and the warrants of execution therein contained shall have all the like force and effect as any extract from the Books of Council and Session, made and issued previous to such transmission, or as any warrant of execution contained in or appended to such extract; and in all extracts issued as aforesaid, and also in all extracts issued of writs contained in any record in the custody of the Lord Clerk Register, it shall be sufficient that the last page thereof shall be signed by the said deputy keeper of the records or by any officer duly commissioned by the Lord Clerk Register to that effect, and no further signature on any other page of such extracts shall be necessary, but each sheet of all such extracts shall [bear] an office seal or stamp [. . .] of the Lord Clerk Register; provided that it shall be necessary and sufficient in the case of marginal additions occurring in any such extract that the same shall be authenticated by the signature of the officer certifying such extract.

8 Commencement and extent of Act
This Act shall take effect from and after the first day of October one thousand eight hundred and seventy-seven, and shall apply to Scotland only.

BILLS OF EXCHANGE ACT 1882
(45 & 46 Vict, c 61)

PART I
PRELIMINARY

1 Short title
This Act may be cited as the Bills of Exchange Act 1882.

2 Interpretation of terms
In this Act, unless the context otherwise requires,—

'Acceptance' means an acceptance completed by delivery or notification.

'Action' includes counter claim and set off.

'Banker' includes a body of persons whether incorporated or not who carry on the business of banking.

'Bankrupt' includes any person whose estate is vested in a trustee or assignee under the law for the time being in force relating to bankruptcy.

'Bearer' means the person in possession of a bill or note which is payable to bearer.

'Bill' means bill of exchange, and 'note' means promissory note.

'Delivery' means transfer of possession, actual or constructive, from one person to another.

'Holder' means the payee or indorsee of a bill or note who is in possession of it, or the bearer thereof.

'Indorsement' means an indorsement completed by delivery.

'Issue' means the first delivery of a bill or note, complete in form to a person who takes it as a holder.

'Person' includes a body of persons whether incorporated or not.

['Postal operator' has the meaning given by [section 27 of the Postal Services Act 2011].]

'Value' means valuable consideration.

'Written' includes printed, and 'writing' includes print.

PART II
BILLS OF EXCHANGE

Form and interpretation

3 Bill of exchange defined

(1) A bill of exchange is an unconditional order in writing, addressed by one person to another, signed by the person giving it, requiring the person to whom it is addressed to pay on demand or at a fixed or determinable future time a sum certain in money to or to the order of a specified person, or to bearer.

(2) An instrument which does not comply with these conditions, or which orders any act to be done in addition to the payment of money, is not a bill of exchange.

(3) An order to pay out of a particular fund is not unconditional within the meaning of this section; but an unqualified order to pay, coupled with (a) an indication of a particular fund out of which the drawee is to reimburse himself or a

particular account to be debited with the amount, or (b) a statement of the transaction which gives rise to the bill, is unconditional.

(4) A bill is not invalid by reason—

(a) That it is not dated;

(b) That it does not specify the value given, or that any value has been given therefor;

(c) That it does not specify the place where it is drawn or the place where it is payable.

4 Inland and foreign bills

(1) An inland bill is a bill which is or on the face of it purports to be (a) both drawn and payable within the British Islands, or (b) drawn within the British Islands upon some person resident therein. Any other bill is a foreign bill.

For the purposes of this Act 'British Islands' means any part of the United Kingdom of Great Britain and Ireland, the islands of Man, Guernsey, Jersey, Alderney, and Sark, and the islands adjacent to any of them being part of the dominions of Her Majesty.

(2) Unless the contrary appear on the face of the bill the holder may treat it as an inland bill.

5 Effect where different parties to bill are the same person

(1) A bill may be drawn payable to, or to the order of, the drawer; or it may be drawn payable to, or to the order of, the drawee.

(2) Where in a bill drawer and drawee are the same person, or where the drawee is a fictitious person or a person not having capacity to contract, the holder may treat the instrument, at his option, either as a bill of exchange or as a promissory note.

6 Address to drawee

(1) The drawee must be named or otherwise indicated in a bill with reasonable certainty.

(2) A bill may be addressed to two or more drawees whether they are partners or not, but an order addressed to two drawees in the alternative or to two or more drawees in succession is not a bill of exchange.

7 Certainty required as to payee

(1) Where a bill is not payable to bearer, the payee must be named or otherwise indicated therein with reasonable certainty.

(2) A bill may be made payable to two or more payees jointly, or it may be made payable in the alternative to one of two, or one or some of several payees. A bill may also be made payable to the holder of an office for the time being.

(3) Where the payee is a fictitious or non-existing person the bill may be treated as payable to bearer.

8 What bills are negotiable

(1) When a bill contains words prohibiting transfer, or indicating an intention that it should not be transferable, it is valid as between the parties thereto, but is not negotiable.

(2) A negotiable bill may be payable either to order or to bearer.

(3) A bill is payable to bearer which is expressed to be so payable, or on which the only or last indorsement is an indorsement in blank.

(4) A bill is payable to order which is expressed to be so payable, or which is expressed to be payable to a particular person, and does not contain words prohibiting transfer or indicating an intention that it should not be transferable.

(5) Where a bill, either originally or by indorsement, is expressed to be payable to the order of a specified person, and not to him or his order, it is nevertheless payable to him or his order at his option.

9 Sum payable

(1) The sum payable by a bill is a sum certain within the meaning of this Act, although it is required to be paid—

(a) With interest.

(b) By stated instalments.

(c) By stated instalments, with a provision that upon default in payment of any instalment the whole shall become due.

(d) According to an indicated rate of exchange or according to a rate of exchange to be ascertained as directed by the bill.

(2) Where the sum payable is expressed in words and also in figures, and there is a discrepancy between the two, the sum denoted by the words is the amount payable.

(3) Where a bill is expressed to be payable with interest, unless the instrument otherwise provides, interest runs from the date of the bill, and if the bill is undated from the issue thereof.

10 Bill payable on demand

(1) A bill is payable on demand—

(a) Which is expressed to be payable on demand, or at sight, or on presentation; or

(b) In which no time for payment is expressed.

(2) Where a bill is accepted or indorsed when it is overdue, it shall, as regards the acceptor who so accepts, or any indorser who so indorses it, be deemed a bill payable on demand.

11 Bill payable at a future time

A bill is payable at a determinable future time within the meaning of this Act which is expressed to be payable—

(1) At a fixed period after date or sight.

(2) On or at a fixed period after the occurrence of a specified event which is certain to happen, though the time of happening may be uncertain.

An instrument expressed to be payable on a contingency is not a bill, and the happening of the event does not cure the defect.

12 Omission of date in bill payable after date

Where a bill expressed to be payable at a fixed period after date is issued undated, or where the acceptance of a bill payable at a fixed period after sight is undated, any holder may insert therein the true date of issue or acceptance, and the bill shall be payable accordingly.

Provided that (1) where the holder in good faith and by mistake inserts a wrong date, and (2) in every case where a wrong date is inserted, if the bill subsequently comes into the hands of a holder in due course the bill shall not be avoided thereby, but shall operate and be payable as if the date so inserted had been the true date.

13 Ante-dating and post-dating

(1) Where a bill or an acceptance or any indorsement on a bill is dated, the date shall, unless the contrary be proved, be deemed to be the true date of the drawing, acceptance, or indorsement, as the case may be.

(2) A bill is not invalid by reason only that it is ante-dated or post-dated, or that it bears date on a Sunday.

14 Computation of time of payment

Where a bill is not payable on demand the day on which it falls due is determined as follows:

[(1) The bill is due and payable in all cases on the last day of the time of payment as fixed by the bill or, if that is a non-business day, on the succeeding business day.]

(2) Where a bill is payable at a fixed period after date, after sight, or after the happening of a specified event, the time of payment is determined by excluding the day from which the time is to begin to run and by including the day of payment.

(3) Where a bill is payable at a fixed period after sight, the time begins to run from the date of the acceptance if the bill be accepted, and from the date of noting or protest if the bill be noted or protested for non-acceptance, or for non-delivery.

(4) The term 'month' in a bill means a calendar month.

15 Case of need

The drawer of a bill and any indorser may insert therein the name of a person to whom the holder may resort in case of need, that is to say, in case the bill is dishonoured by non-acceptance or non-payment. Such person is called the referee in case of need. It is in the option of the holder to resort to the referee in case of need or not as he may think fit.

16 Optional stipulations by drawer or indorser

The drawer of a bill, and any indorser, may insert therein an express stipulation—

(1) Negativing or limiting his own liability to the holder;

(2) Waiving as regards himself some or all of the holder's duties.

17 Definition and requisites of acceptance

(1) The acceptance of a bill is the signification by the drawee of his assent to the order of the drawer.

(2) An acceptance is invalid unless it complies with the following conditions, namely:

(a) It must be written on the bill and be signed by the drawee. The mere signature of the drawee without additional words is sufficient.

(b) It must not express that the drawee will perform his promise by any other means than the payment of money.

18 Time for acceptance

A bill may be accepted—

(1) Before it has been signed by the drawer, or while otherwise incomplete;

(2) When it is overdue, or after it has been dishonoured by a previous refusal to accept, or by non-payment;

(3) When a bill payable after sight is dishonoured by non-acceptance, and the drawee subsequently accepts it, the holder, in the absence of any different agreement, is entitled to have the bill accepted as of the date of first presentment to the drawee for acceptance.

19 General and qualified acceptance

(1) An acceptance is either (a) general, or (b) qualified.

(2) A general acceptance assents without qualification to the order of the drawer. A qualified acceptance in expressed terms varies the effect of the bill as drawn.

In particular an acceptance is qualified which is—

(a) conditional, that is to say, which makes payment by the acceptor dependent on the fulfilment of a condition therein stated;

(b) partial, that is to say, an acceptance to pay part only of the amount for which the bill is drawn;

(c) local, that is to say, an acceptance to pay only at a particular specified place;

An acceptance to pay at a particular place is a general acceptance, unless it expressly states that the bill is to be paid there only and not elsewhere:

(d) qualified as to time;

(e) the acceptance of some one or more of the drawees, but not of all.

20 Inchoate instruments

(1) Where a simple signature on a blank paper is delivered by the signer in order that it may be converted into a bill, it operates as a prima facie authority to fill it up as a complete bill for any amount [. . .] using the signature for that of the drawer, or the acceptor, or an indorser; and, in like manner, when a bill is wanting in any material particular, the person in possession of it has a prima facie authority to fill up the omission in any way he thinks fit.

(2) In order that any such instrument when completed may be enforceable against any person who became a party thereto prior to its completion, it must be filled up within a reasonable time, and strictly in accordance with the authority given. Reasonable time for this purpose is a question of fact.

Provided that if any such instrument after completion is negotiated to a holder in due course it shall be valid and effectual for all purposes in his hands and he may enforce it as if it had been filled up within a reasonable time and strictly in accordance with the authority given.

21 Delivery

(1) Every contract on a bill, whether it be the drawer's, the acceptor's, or an indorser's is incomplete and revocable, until delivery of the instrument in order to give effect thereto.

Provided that where an acceptance is written on a bill, and the drawee gives notice to or according to the directions of the person entitled to the bill that he has accepted it, the acceptance then becomes complete and irrevocable.

(2) As between immediate parties, and as regards a remote party other than a holder in due course, the delivery—

(a) in order to be effectual must be made either by or under the authority of the party drawing, accepting, or indorsing, as the case may be:

(b) may be shown to have been conditional or for a special purpose only, and not for the purpose of transferring the property in the bill.

But if the bill be in the hands of a holder in due course a valid delivery of the bill by all parties prior to him so as to make them liable to him is conclusively presumed.

(3) Where a bill is no longer in the possession of a party who has signed it as drawer, acceptor, or indorser, a valid and unconditional delivery by him is presumed until the contrary is proved.

Capacity and authority of parties

22 Capacity of parties

(1) Capacity to incur liability as a party to a bill is co-extensive with capacity to contract.

Provided that nothing in this section shall enable a corporation to make itself liable as drawer, acceptor, or indorser of a bill unless it is competent to do so under the law for the time being in force relating to corporations.

(2) Where a bill is drawn or indorsed by an infant, minor, or corporation having no capacity or power to incur liability on a bill, the drawing or indorsement entitles the holder to receive payment of the bill, and to enforce it against any other party thereto.

23 Signature essential to liability

No person is liable as drawer, indorser, or acceptor of a bill who has not signed it as such: Provided that

(1) Where a person signs a bill in a trade or assumed name, he is liable thereon as if he had signed it in his own name:

(2) The signature of the name of a firm is equivalent to the signature by the person so signing of the names of all persons liable as partners in that firm.

24 Forged or unauthorised signature

Subject to the provisions of this Act, where a signature on a bill is forged or placed thereon without the authority of the person whose signature it purports to be, the forged or unauthorised signature is wholly inoperative, and no right to retain the bill or to give a discharge therefor or to enforce payment thereof against any party thereto can be acquired through or under that signature, unless the party against whom it is sought to retain or enforce payment of the bill is precluded from setting up the forgery or want of authority.

Provided that nothing in this section shall affect the ratification of an unauthorised signature not amounting to a forgery.

25 Procuration signatures

A signature by procuration operates as notice that the agent has but a limited authority to sign, and the principal is only bound by such signature if the agent in so signing was acting within the actual limits of his authority.

26 Person signing as agent or in representative capacity

(1) Where a person signs a bill as drawer, indorser, or acceptor, and adds words to his signature, indicating that he signs for or on behalf of a principal, or in a representative character, he is not personally liable thereon; but the mere addition to his signature of words describing him as an agent, or as filling a representative character, does not exempt him from personal liability.

(2) In determining whether a signature on a bill is that of the principal or that of the agent by whose hand it is written, the construction most favourable to the validity of the instrument shall be adopted.

The consideration for a bill

27 Value and holder for value

(1) Valuable consideration for a bill may be constituted by,—

(a) Any consideration sufficient to support a simple contract;

(b) An antecedent debt or liability. Such a debt or liability is deemed valuable consideration whether the bill is payable on demand or at a future time.

(2) Where value has at any time been given for a bill the holder is deemed to be a holder for value as regards the acceptor and all parties to the bill who became parties prior to such time.

(3) Where the holder of a bill has a lien on it, arising either from contract or by implication of law, he is deemed to be a holder for value to the extent of the sum for which he has a lien.

28 Accommodation bill or party

(1) An accommodation party to a bill is a person who has signed a bill as drawer, acceptor, or indorser, without receiving value therefor, and for the purpose of lending his name to some other person.

(2) An accommodation party is liable on the bill to a holder for value; and it is immaterial whether, when such holder took the bill, he knew such party to be an accommodation party or not.

29 Holder in due course

(1) A holder in due course is a holder who has taken a bill, complete and regular on the face of it, under the following conditions, namely,

(a) That he became the holder of it before it was overdue, and without notice that it had been previously dishonoured, if such was the fact;

(b) That he took the bill in good faith and for value, and that at the time the bill was negotiated to him he had no notice of any defect in the title of the person who negotiated it.

(2) In particular the title of a person who negotiates a bill is defective within

the meaning of this Act when he obtained the bill, or the acceptance thereof, by fraud, duress or force and fear, or other unlawful means, or for an illegal consideration, or when he negotiates it in breach of faith, or under such circumstances as amount to a fraud.

(3) A holder (whether for value or not), who derives his title to a bill through a holder in due course, and who is not himself a party to any fraud or illegality affecting it, has all the rights of that holder in due course as regards the acceptor and all parties to the bill prior to that holder.

30 Presumption of value and good faith

(1) Every party whose signature appears on a bill is prima facie deemed to have become a party thereto for value.

(2) Every holder of a bill is prima facie deemed to be a holder in due course; but if in an action on a bill it is admitted or proved that the acceptance, issue, or subsequent negotiation of the bill is affected with fraud, duress, or force and fear, or illegality, the burden of proof is shifted, unless and until the holder proves that, subsequent to the alleged fraud or illegality, value has in good faith been given for the bill.

Negotiation of bills

31 Negotiation of bill

(1) A bill is negotiated when it is transferred from one person to another in such a manner as to constitute the transferee the holder of the bill.

(2) A bill payable to bearer is negotiated by delivery.

(3) A bill payable to order is negotiated by the indorsement of the holder completed by delivery.

(4) Where the holder of a bill payable to his order transfers it for value without indorsing it, the transfer gives the transferee such title as the transferor had in the bill, and the transferee in addition acquires the right to have the indorsement of the transferor.

(5) Where any person is under obligation to indorse a bill in a representative capacity, he may indorse the bill in such terms as to negative personal liability.

32 Requisites of a valid indorsement

An indorsement in order to operate as a negotiation must comply with the following conditions, namely:—

(1) It must be written on the bill itself and signed by the indorser. The simple signature of the indorser on the bill, without additional words, is sufficient.

An indorsement written on an allonge, or a 'copy' of a bill issued or negotiated in a country where 'copies' are recognised, is deemed to have been written on the bill itself.

(2) It must be an indorsement of the entire bill. A partial indorsement, that is to say, an indorsement which purports to transfer to the indorsee a part only of the amount payable, or which purports to transfer the bill to two or more indorsees severally, does not operate as a negotiation of the bill.

(3) Where a bill is payable to the order of two or more payees or indorsees who are not partners all must indorse, unless the one indorsing has authority to indorse for the others.

(4) Where, in a bill payable to order, the payee or indorsee is wrongly designated, or his name is mis-spelt, he may indorse the bill as therein described, adding, if he thinks fit, his proper signature.

(5) Where there are two or more indorsements on a bill, each indorsement is deemed to have been made in the order in which it appears on the bill, until the contrary is proved.

(6) An indorsement may be made in blank or special. It may also contain terms making it restrictive.

33 Conditional indorsement
Where a bill purports to be indorsed conditionally the condition may be disregarded by the payer, and payment to the indorsee is valid whether the condition has been fulfilled or not.

34 Indorsement in blank and special indorsement
(1) An indorsement in blank specifies no indorsee, and a bill so indorsed becomes payable to bearer.
(2) A special indorsement specifies the person to whom, or to whose order, the bill is to be payable.
(3) The provisions of this Act relating to a payee apply with the necessary modifications to an indorsee under a special indorsement.
(4) When a bill has been indorsed in blank, any holder may convert the blank indorsement into a special indorsement by writing above the indorser's signature a direction to pay the bill to or to the order of himself or some other person.

35 Restrictive indorsement
(1) An indorsement is restrictive which prohibits the further negotiation of the bill or which expresses that it is a mere authority to deal with the bill as thereby directed and not a transfer of ownership thereof, as, for example, if a bill be indorsed 'Pay D. only', or 'Pay D. for the account of X.,' or 'Pay D. or order for collection.'
(2) A restrictive indorsement gives the indorsee the right to receive payment of the bill and to sue any party thereto that his indorser could have sued, but gives him no power to transfer his rights as indorsee unless it expressly authorises him to do so.
(3) Where a restrictive indorsement authorises further transfer, all subsequent indorsees take the bill with the same rights and subject to the same liabilities as the first indorsee under the restrictive indorsement.

36 Negotiation of overdue or dishonoured bills
(1) Where a bill is negotiable in its origin it continues to be negotiable until it has been (a) restrictively indorsed or (b) discharged by payment or otherwise.
(2) Where an overdue bill is negotiated, it can only be negotiated subject to any defect of title affecting it at its maturity, and thenceforward no person who takes it can acquire or give a better title than that which the person from whom he took it had.
(3) A bill payable on demand is deemed to be overdue within the meaning and for the purposes of this section, when it appears on the face of it to have been in circulation for an unreasonable length of time. What is an unreasonable length of time for this purpose is a question of fact.
(4) Except where an indorsement bears date after the maturity of the bill, every negotiation is prima facie deemed to have been effected before the bill was overdue.
(5) Where a bill which is not overdue has been dishonoured any person who takes it with notice of the dishonour takes it subject to any defect of title attaching thereto at the time of dishonour, but nothing in this sub-section shall affect the rights of a holder in due course.

37 Negotiation of bill to party already liable thereon
Where a bill is negotiated back to the drawer, or to a prior indorser or to the acceptor, such party may, subject to the provisions of this Act, reissue and further negotiate the bill, but he is not entitled to enforce payment of the bill against any intervening party to whom he was previously liable.

38 Rights of the holder
The rights and powers of the holder of a bill are as follows:
(1) He may sue on the bill in his own name:

(2) Where he is a holder in due course, he holds the bill free from any defect of title of prior parties, as well as from mere personal defences available to prior parties among themselves, and may enforce payment against all parties liable on the bill:

(3) Where his title is defective (a) if he negotiates the bill to a holder in due course, that holder obtains a good and complete title to the bill, and (b) if he obtains payment of the bill the person who pays him in due course gets a valid discharge for the bill.

General duties of the holder

39 When presentment for acceptance is necessary

(1) Where a bill is payable after sight, presentment for acceptance is necessary in order to fix the maturity of the instrument.

(2) Where a bill expressly stipulates that it shall be presented for acceptance, or where a bill is drawn payable elsewhere than at the residence or place of business of the drawee, it must be presented for acceptance before it can be presented for payment.

(3) In no other case is presentment for acceptance necessary in order to render liable any party to the bill.

(4) Where the holder of a bill, drawn payable elsewhere than at the place of business or residence of the drawee, has not time, with the exercise of reasonable diligence, to present the bill for acceptance before presenting it for payment on the day that it falls due, the delay caused by presenting the bill for acceptance before presenting it for payment is excused, and does not discharge the drawer and the indorsers.

40 Time for presenting bill payable after sight

(1) Subject to the provisions of this Act, when a bill payable after sight is negotiated, the holder must either present it for acceptance or negotiate it within a reasonable time.

(2) If he do not do so, the drawer and all indorsers prior to that holder are discharged.

(3) In determining what is a reasonable time within the meaning of this section, regard shall be had to the nature of the bill, the usage of trade with respect to similar bills, and the facts of the particular case.

41 Rules as to presentment for acceptance and excuses for non-presentment

(1) A bill is duly presented for acceptance which is presented in accordance with the following rules:

(a) The presentment must be made by or on behalf of the holder to the drawee or to some person authorised to accept or refuse acceptance on his behalf at a reasonable hour on a business day and before the bill is overdue:

(b) Where a bill is addressed to two or more drawees, who are not partners, presentment must be made to them all, unless one has authority to accept for all, then presentment may be made to him only:

(c) Where the drawee is dead, presentment may be made to his personal representative:

(d) Where the drawee is bankrupt, presentment may be made to him or to his trustee:

(e) Where authorised by agreement or usage, a presentment through [a postal operator] is sufficient.

(2) Presentment in accordance with these rules is excused, and a bill may be treated as dishonoured by non-acceptance—

(a) Where the drawee is dead or bankrupt, or is a fictitious person or a person not having capacity to contract by bill:

(b) Where, after the exercise of reasonable diligence, such presentment cannot be effected:

(c) Where although the presentment has been irregular, acceptance has been refused on some other ground.

(3) The fact that the holder has reason to believe that the bill, on presentment, will be dishonoured does not excuse presentment.

42 Non-acceptance

(1) When a bill is duly presented for acceptance and is not accepted within the customary time, the person presenting it must treat it as dishonoured by nonacceptance. If he do not, the holder shall lose his right of recourse against the drawer and indorsers.

43 Dishonour by non-acceptance and its consequences

(1) A bill is dishonoured by non-acceptance—

(a) when it is duly presented for acceptance, and such an acceptance as is prescribed by this Act is refused or cannot be obtained; or

(b) when presentment for acceptance is excused and the bill is not accepted.

(2) Subject to the provisions of this Act when a bill is dishonoured by nonacceptance an immediate right of recourse against the drawer and indorsers accrues to the holder, and no presentment for payment is necessary.

44 Duties as to qualified acceptances

(1) The holder of a bill may refuse to take a qualified acceptance, and if he does not obtain an unqualified acceptance may treat the bill as dishonoured by non-acceptance.

(2) Where a qualified acceptance is taken, and the drawer or an indorser has not expressly or impliedly authorised the holder to take a qualified acceptance, or does not subsequently assent thereto, such drawer or indorser is discharged from his liability on the bill.

The provisions of this sub-section do not apply to a partial acceptance, whereof due notice has been given. Where a foreign bill has been accepted as to part, it must be protested as to the balance.

(3) When the drawer or indorser of a bill receives notice of a qualified acceptance, and does not within a reasonable time express his dissent to the holder he shall be deemed to have assented thereto.

45 Rules as to presentment for payment

Subject to the provisions of this Act a bill must be duly presented for payment. If it be not so presented the drawer and indorsers shall be discharged.

A bill is duly presented for payment which is presented in accordance with the following rules:—

(1) Where the bill is not payable on demand, presentment must be made on the day it falls due.

(2) Where the bill is payable on demand then, subject to the provisions of this Act, presentment must be made within a reasonable time after its issue in order to render the drawer liable, and within a reasonable time after its indorsement, in order to render the indorser liable.

In determining what is a reasonable time, regard shall be had to the nature of the bill, the usage of trade with regard to similar bills, and the facts of the particular case.

(3) Presentment must be made by the holder or by some person authorised to receive payment on his behalf at a reasonable hour on a business day, at the proper place as hereinafter defined, either to the person designated by the bill as payer, or to some person authorised to pay or refuse payment on his behalf if with the exercise of reasonable diligence such person can there be found.

(4) A bill is presented at the proper place:—

(a) Where a place of payment is specified in the bill and the bill is there presented.

(b) Where no place of payment is specified, but the address of the drawee or acceptor is given in the bill, and the bill is there presented.

(c) Where no place of payment is specified and no address given, and the bill is presented at the drawee's or acceptor's place of business if known, and if not, at his ordinary residence if known.

(d) In any other case if presented to the drawee or acceptor wherever he can be found, or if presented at his last known place of business or residence.

(5) Where a bill is presented at the proper place, and after the exercise of reasonable diligence no person authorised to pay or refuse payment can be found there, no further presentment to the drawee or acceptor is required.

(6) Where a bill is drawn upon, or accepted by two or more persons who are not partners, and no place of payment is specified, presentment must be made to them all.

(7) Where the drawee or acceptor of a bill is dead, and no place of payment is specified, presentment must be made to a personal representative, if such there be, and with the exercise of reasonable diligence he can be found.

(8) Where authorised by agreement or usage a presentment through [a postal operator] is sufficient.

46 Excuses for delay or non-presentment for payment

(1) Delay in making presentment for payment is excused when the delay is caused by circumstances beyond the control of the holder, and not imputable to his default, misconduct, or negligence. When the cause of delay ceases to operate presentment must be made with reasonable diligence.

(2) Presentment for payment is dispensed with,—

(a) Where, after the exercise of reasonable diligence presentment, as required by this Act, cannot be effected.

The fact that the holder has reason to believe that the bill will, on presentment, be dishonoured, does not dispense with the necessity for presentment.

(b) Where the drawee is a fictitious person.

(c) As regards the drawer where the drawee or acceptor is not bound, as between himself and the drawer, to accept or pay the bill, and the drawer has no reason to believe that the bill would be paid if presented.

(d) As regards an indorser, where the bill was accepted or made for the accommodation of that indorser, and he has no reason to expect that the bill would be paid if presented.

(e) By waiver of presentment, express or implied.

47 Dishonour by non-payment

(1) A bill is dishonoured by non-payment (a) when it is duly presented for payment and payment is refused or cannot be obtained, or (b) when presentment is excused and the bill is overdue and unpaid.

(2) Subject to the provisions of this Act, when a bill is dishonoured by nonpayment, an immediate right of recourse against the drawer and indorsers accrues to the holder.

48 Notice of dishonour and effect of non-notice

Subject to the provisions of this Act, when a bill has been dishonoured by nonacceptance or by non-payment, notice of dishonour must be given to the drawer and each indorser, and any drawer or indorser to whom such notice is not given is discharged; Provided that—

(1) Where a bill is dishonoured by non-acceptance, and notice of dishonour is not given, the rights of the holder in due course subsequent to the omission, shall not be prejudiced by the omission.

(2) Where a bill is dishonoured by non-acceptance and due notice of dishonour is given, it shall not be necessary to give notice of a subsequent dishonour by nonpayment unless the bill shall in the meantime have been accepted.

49 Rules as to notice of dishonour

Notice of dishonour in order to be valid and effectual must be given in accordance with the following rules:—

(1) The notice must be given by or on behalf of the holder, or by or on behalf of an indorser who, at the time of giving it, is himself liable on the bill.

(2) Notice of dishonour may be given by an agent either in his own name, or in the name of any party entitled to give notice whether that party be his principal or not.

(3) Where the notice is given by or on behalf of the holder, it enures for the benefit of all subsequent holders and all prior indorsers who have a right of recourse against the party to whom it is given.

(4) Where notice is given by or on behalf of an indorser entitled to give notice as herein-before provided, it enures for the benefit of the holder and all indorsers subsequent to the party to whom notice is given.

(5) The notice may be given in writing or by personal communication, and may be given in any terms which sufficiently identify the bill, and intimate that the bill has been dishonoured by non-acceptance or non-payment.

(6) The return of a dishonoured bill to the drawer or an indorser is, in point of form, deemed a sufficient notice of dishonour.

(7) A written notice need not be signed, and an insufficient written notice may be supplemented and validated by verbal communication. A misdescription of the bill shall not vitiate the notice unless the party to whom the notice is given is in fact misled thereby.

(8) Where notice of dishonour is required to be given to any person, it may be given either to the party himself, or to his agent in that behalf.

(9) Where the drawer or indorser is dead, and the party giving notice knows it, the notice must be given to a personal representative if such there be, and with the exercise of reasonable diligence he can be found.

(10) Where the drawer or indorser is bankrupt, notice may be given either to the party himself or to the trustee.

(11) Where there are two or more drawers or indorsers who are not partners, notice must be given to each of them, unless one of them has authority to receive such notice for the others.

(12) The notice may be given as soon as the bill is dishonoured and must be given within a reasonable time thereafter.

In the absence of special circumstances notice is not deemed to have been given within a reasonable time, unless—

(a) where the person giving and the person to receive notice reside in the same place, the notice is given or sent off in time to reach the latter on the day after the dishonour of the bill.

(b) where the person giving and the person to receive notice reside in different places, the notice is sent off on the day after the dishonour of the bill, if there be a post at a convenient hour on that day, and if there be no such post on that day then by the next post thereafter.

(13) Where a bill when dishonoured is in the hands of an agent, he may either himself give notice to the parties liable on the bill, or he may give notice to his principal. If he gives notice to his principal, he must do so within the same time as if he were the holder, and the principal upon receipt of such notice has himself the same time for giving notice as if the agent had been an independent holder.

(14) Where a party to a bill receives due notice of dishonour, he has after the receipt of such notice the same period of time for giving notice to antecedent parties that the holder has after the dishonour.

(15) Where a notice of dishonour is duly addressed and posted, the sender is deemed to have given due notice of dishonour, notwithstanding any miscarriage by the [postal operator concerned].

50 Excuses for non-notice and delay

(1) Delay in giving notice of dishonour is excused where the delay is caused by circumstances beyond the control of the party giving notice, and not imputable to his default, misconduct, or negligence. When the cause of delay ceases to operate the notice must be given with reasonable diligence.

(2) Notice of dishonour is dispensed with—

(a) When, after the exercise of reasonable diligence, notice as required by this Act cannot be given to or does not reach the drawer or indorser sought to be charged:

(b) By waiver express or implied. Notice of dishonour may be waived before the time of giving notice has arrived, or after the omission to give due notice:

(c) As regards the drawer in the following cases, namely, (1) where drawer and drawee are the same person, (2) where the drawee is a fictitious person or a person not having capacity to contract, (3) where the drawer is the person to whom the bill is presented for payment, (4) where the drawee or acceptor is as between himself and the drawer under no obligation to accept or pay the bill, (5) where the drawer has countermanded payment:

(d) As regards the indorser in the following cases, namely, (1) where the drawee is a fictitious person or a person not having capacity to contract and the indorser was aware of the fact at the time he indorsed the bill, (2) where the indorser is the person to whom the bill is presented for payment,

(3) where the bill was accepted or made for his accommodation.

51 Noting or protest of bill

(1) Where an inland bill has been dishonoured it may, if the holder think fit, be noted for non-acceptance or non-payment, as the case may be; but it shall not be necessary to note or protest any such bill in order to preserve the recourse against the drawer or indorser.

(2) Where a foreign bill, appearing on the face of it to be such, has been dishonoured by non-acceptance it must be duly protested for non-acceptance and where such a bill, which has not been previously dishonoured by non-acceptance, is dishonoured by non-payment it must be duly protested for non-payment. If it be not so protested the drawer and indorsers are discharged. Where a bill does not appear on the face of it to be a foreign bill, protest thereof in the case of dishonour is unnecessary.

(3) A bill which has been protested for non-acceptance may be subsequently protested for non-payment.

(4) Subject to the provisions of this Act, when a bill is noted or protested, [it may be noted on the day of its dishonour and must be noted not later than the next succeeding business day]. When a bill has been duly noted, the protest may be subsequently extended as of the date of the noting.

(5) Where the acceptor of the bill becomes bankrupt or insolvent or suspends payment before it matures, the holder may cause the bill to be protested for better security against the drawer and indorsers.

(6) A bill must be protested at the place where it is dishonoured: Provided that—

(a) When a bill is presented through [a postal operator], and returned by post dishonoured, it may be protested at the place to which it is returned and on the day of its return if received during business hours, and if not received during business hours, then not later than the next business day:

(b) When a bill drawn payable at the place of business or residence of some person other than the drawee, has been dishonoured by non-acceptance, it must be protested for non-payment at the place where it is expressed to be payable, and no further presentment for payment to, or demand on, the drawee is necessary.

(7) A protest must contain a copy of the bill, and must be signed by the notary making it, and must specify—

(a) The person at whose request the bill is protested:

(b) The place and date of protest, the cause or reason for protesting the bill, the demand made, and the answer given, if any, or the fact that the drawee or acceptor could not be found.

[(7A) In subsection (7) 'notary' includes a person who, for the purposes of the Legal Services Act 2007, is an authorised person in relation to any activity which constitutes a notarial activity (within the meaning of that Act).]

(8) Where a bill is lost or destroyed, or is wrongly detained from the person entitled to hold it, protest may be made on a copy or written particulars thereof.

(9) Protest is dispensed with by any circumstance which would dispense with notice of dishonour. Delay in noting or protesting is excused when the delay is caused by circumstances beyond the control of the holder, and not imputable to his default, misconduct, or negligence. When the cause of delay ceases to operate the bill must be noted or protested with reasonable diligence.

52 Duties of holder as regards drawee or acceptor

(1) When a bill is accepted generally presentment for payment is not necessary in order to render the acceptor liable.

(2) When by the terms of a qualified acceptance presentment for payment is required, the acceptor, in the absence of an express stipulation to that effect, is not discharged by the omission to present the bill for payment on the day that it matures.

(3) In order to render the acceptor of a bill liable it is not necessary to protest it, or that notice of dishonour should be given to him.

(4) [Subject to Part 4A (presentment by electronic means)] where the holder of a bill presents it for payment, he shall exhibit the bill to the person from whom he demands payment, and when a bill is paid the holder shall forthwith deliver it up to the party paying it.

Liabilities of parties

53 Funds in hands of drawee

(1) *[Does not apply to Scotland.]*

(2) In Scotland, where the drawee of a bill [other than a cheque] has in his hands funds available for the payment thereof, the bill operates as an assignment of the sum for which it is drawn in favour of the holder, from the time when the bill is presented to the drawee.

54 Liability of acceptor

The acceptor of a bill, by accepting it—

(1) Engages that he will pay it according to the tenor of his acceptance:

(2) Is precluded from denying to a holder in due course:

(a) The existence of the drawer, the genuineness of his signature, and his capacity and authority to draw the bill;

(b) In the case of a bill payable to drawer's order, the then capacity of the drawer to indorse, but not the genuineness or validity of his indorsement;

(c) In the case of a bill payable to the order of a third person, the existence of the payee and his then capacity to indorse, but not the genuineness or validity of his indorsement.

55 Liability of drawer or indorser

(1) The drawer of a bill by drawing it—

(a) Engages that on due presentment it shall be accepted and paid according to its tenor, and that if it be dishonoured he will compensate the holder or any indorser who is compelled to pay it, provided that the requisite proceedings on dishonour be duly taken;

(b) Is precluded from denying to a holder in due course the existence of the payee and his then capacity to indorse.

(2) The indorser of a bill by indorsing it—

(a) Engages that on due presentment it shall be accepted and paid according to its tenor, and that if it be dishonoured he will compensate the holder or a subsequent indorser who is compelled to pay it, provided that the requisite proceedings on dishonour be duly taken;

(b) Is precluded from denying to a holder in due course the genuineness and regularity in all respects of the drawer's signature and all previous indorsements;

(c) Is precluded from denying to his immediate or a subsequent indorsee that the bill was at the time of his indorsement a valid and subsisting bill, and that he had then a good title thereto.

56 Stranger signing bill liable as indorser

Where a person signs a bill otherwise than as drawer or acceptor, he thereby incurs the liabilities of an indorser to a holder in due course.

57 Measure of damages against parties to dishonoured bill

Where a bill is dishonoured, the measure of damages, which shall be deemed to be liquidated damages, shall be as follows:

(1) The holder may recover from any party liable on the bill, and the drawer who has been compelled to pay the bill may recover from the acceptor, and an indorser who has been compelled to pay the bill may recover from the acceptor or from the drawer, or from a prior indorser—

(a) The amount of the bill:

(b) Interest thereon from the time of presentment for payment if the bill is payable on demand, and from the maturity of the bill in any other case:

(c) The expenses of noting, or, when protest is necessary, and the protest has been extended, the expenses of protest.

[. . .]

(3) Where by this Act interest may be recovered as damages, such interest may, if justice require it, be withheld wholly or in part, and where a bill is expressed to be payable with interest at a given rate, interest as damages may or may not be given at the same rate as interest proper.

58 Transferor by delivery and transferee

(1) Where the holder of a bill payable to bearer negotiates it by delivery without indorsing it, he is called a 'transferor by delivery'.

(2) A transferor by delivery is not liable on the instrument.

(3) A transferor by delivery who negotiates a bill thereby warrants to his immediate transferee being a holder for value that the bill is what it purports to be, that he has a right to transfer it, and that at the time of the transfer he is not aware of any fact which renders it valueless.

Discharge of bill

59 Payment in due course

(1) A bill is discharged by payment in due course by or on behalf of the drawee or acceptor.

'Payment in due course' means payment made at or after the maturity of the bill to the holder thereof in good faith and without notice that his title to the bill is defective.

(2) Subject to the provisions herein-after contained, when a bill is paid by the drawer or an indorser it is not discharged; but

(a) Where a bill payable to, or to the order of, a third party is paid by the drawer, the drawer may enforce payment thereof against the acceptor, but may not re-issue the bill.

(b) Where a bill is paid by an indorser, or where a bill payable to drawer's order is paid by the drawer, the party paying it is remitted to his former rights as regards the acceptor or antecedent parties, and he may, if he thinks fit, strike out his own subsequent indorsements, and again negotiate the bill.

(3) Where an accommodation bill is paid in due course by the party accommodated the bill is discharged.

60 Banker paying demand draft whereon indorsement is forged

When a bill payable to order on demand is drawn on a banker, and the banker on whom it is drawn pays the bill in good faith and in the ordinary course of business, it is not incumbent on the banker to show that the indorsement of the payee or any subsequent indorsement was made by or under the authority of the person whose indorsement it purports to be, and the banker is deemed to have paid the bill in due course, although such indorsement has been forged or made without authority.

61 Acceptor the holder at maturity

When the acceptor of a bill is or becomes the holder of it at or after its maturity, in his own right, the bill is discharged.

62 Express waiver

(1) When the holder of a bill at or after its maturity absolutely and unconditionally renounces his rights against the acceptor the bill is discharged.

The renunciation must be in writing, unless the bill is delivered up to the acceptor.

(2) The liabilities of any party to a bill may in like manner be renounced by the holder before, at, or after its maturity; but nothing in this section shall affect the rights of a holder in due course without notice of the renunciation.

63 Cancellation

(1) Where a bill is intentionally cancelled by the holder or his agent, and the cancellation is apparent thereon, the bill is discharged.

(2) In like manner any party liable on a bill may be discharged by the intentional cancellation of his signature by the holder or his agent. In such case any indorser who would have had a right of recourse against the party whose signature is cancelled, is also discharged.

(3) A cancellation made unintentionally, or under a mistake, or without the authority of the holder is inoperative; but where a bill or any signature thereon appears to have been cancelled the burden of proof lies on the party who alleges that the cancellation was made unintentionally, or under a mistake, or without authority.

64 Alteration of bill

(1) Where a bill or acceptance is materially altered without the assent of all parties liable on the bill, the bill is avoided except as against a party who has himself made, authorised, or assented to the alteration, and subsequent indorsers.

Provided that,

Where a bill has been materially altered, but the alteration is not apparent, and the bill is in the hands of a holder in due course, such holder may avail himself of the bill as if it had not been altered, and may enforce payment of it according to its original tenor.

(2) In particular the following alterations are material, namely, any alteration of the date, the sum payable, the time of payment, the place of payment, and where a bill has been accepted generally, the addition of a place of payment without the acceptor's assent.

Acceptance and payment for honour

65 Acceptance for honour supra protest

(1) Where a bill of exchange has been protested for dishonour by nonacceptance, or protested for better security, and is not overdue, any person, not being a party already liable thereon, may, with the consent of the holder, intervene and accept the bill supra protest, for the honour of any party liable thereon, or for the honour of the person for whose account the bill is drawn.

(2) A bill may be accepted for honour for part only of the sum for which it is drawn.

(3) An acceptance for honour supra protest in order to be valid must—

(a) be written on the bill, and indicate that it is an acceptance for honour;

(b) be signed by the acceptor for honour.

(4) Where an acceptance for honour does not expressly state for whose honour it is made, it is deemed to be an acceptance for the honour of the drawer.

(5) Where a bill payable after sight is accepted for honour, its maturity is calculated from the date of the noting for non-acceptance, and not from the date of the acceptance for honour.

66 Liability of acceptor for honour

(1) The acceptor for honour of a bill by accepting it engages that he will, on due presentment, pay the bill according to the tenor of his acceptance, if it is not paid by the drawee, provided it has been duly presented for payment, and protested for non-payment, and that he receives notice of these facts.

(2) The acceptor for honour is liable to the holder and to all parties to the bill subsequent to the party for whose honour he has accepted.

67 Presentment to acceptor for honour

(1) Where a dishonoured bill has been accepted for honour supra protest, or contains a reference in case of need, it must be protested for non-payment before it is presented for payment to the acceptor for honour, or referee in case of need.

(2) Where the address of the acceptor for honour is in the same place where the bill is protested for non-payment, the bill must be presented to him not later than the day following its maturity; and where the address of the acceptor for honour is in some place other than the place where it was protested for nonpayment, the bill must be forwarded not later than the day following its maturity for presentment to him.

(3) Delay in presentment or non-presentment is excused by any circumstances which would excuse delay in presentment for payment or non-presentment for payment.

(4) When a bill of exchange is dishonoured by the acceptor for honour it must be protested for non-payment by him.

68 Payment for honour supra protest

(1) Where a bill has been protested for non-payment any person may intervene and pay it supra protest for the honour of any party liable thereon, or for the honour of the person for whose account the bill is drawn.

(2) Where two or more persons offer to pay a bill for the honour of different parties, the person whose payment will discharge most parties to the bill shall have the preference.

(3) Payment for honour supra protest, in order to operate as such and not as a mere voluntary payment, must be attested by a notarial act of honour which may be appended to the protest or form an extension of it.

(4) The notarial act of honour must be founded on a declaration made by the payer for honour, or his agent in that behalf, declaring his intention to pay the bill for honour, and for whose honour he pays.

(5) Where a bill has been paid for honour, all parties subsequent to the party for whose honour it is paid are discharged, but the payer for honour is subrogated

for, and succeeds to both the rights and duties of, the holder as regards the party for whose honour he pays, and all parties liable to that party.

(6) The payer for honour on paying to the holder the amount of the bill and the notarial expenses incidental to its dishonour is entitled to receive both the bill itself and the protest. If the holder do not on demand deliver them up he shall be liable to the payer for honour in damages.

(7) Where the holder of a bill refuses to receive payment supra protest he shall lose his right of recourse against any party who would have been discharged by such payment.

Lost instruments

69 Holder's right to duplicate of lost bill

Where a bill has been lost before it is overdue, the person who was the holder of it may apply to the drawer to give him another bill of the same tenor, giving security to the drawer if required to indemnify him against all persons whatever in case the bill alleged to have been lost shall be found again.

If the drawer on request as aforesaid refuses to give such duplicate bill, he may be compelled to do so.

70 Action on lost bill

In any action or proceeding upon a bill, the court or a judge may order that the loss of the instrument shall not be set up, provided an indemnity be given to the satisfaction of the court or judge against the claims of any other person upon the instrument in question.

Bill in a set

71 Rules as to sets

(1) Where a bill is drawn in a set, each part of the set being numbered and containing a reference to the other parts, the whole of the parts constitute one bill.

(2) Where the holder of a set indorses two or more parts to different persons, he is liable on every such part, and every indorser subsequent to him is liable on the part he has himself indorsed as if the said parts were separate bills.

(3) Where two or more parts of a set are negotiated to different holders in due course, the holder whose title first accrues is as between such holders deemed the true owner of the bill; but nothing in this sub-section shall affect the rights of a person who in due course accepts or pays the part first presented to him.

(4) The acceptance may be written on any part, and it must be written on one part only.

If the drawee accepts more than one part, and such accepted parts get into the hands of different holders in due course, he is liable on every such part as if it were a separate bill.

(5) When the acceptor of a bill drawn in a set pays it without requiring the part bearing the acceptance to be delivered up to him, and that part at maturity is outstanding in the hands of a holder in due course, he is liable to the holder thereof.

(6) Subject to the preceding rules, where any one part of a bill drawn in a set is discharged by payment or otherwise, the whole bill is discharged.

Conflict of laws

72 Rules where laws conflict

Where a bill drawn in one country is negotiated, accepted, or payable in another, the rights, duties, and liabilities of the parties thereto are determined as follows:

(1) The validity of a bill as regards requisites in form is determined by the law of the place of issue, and the validity as regards requisites in form of the supervening contracts, such as acceptance, or indorsement, or acceptance supra protest, is determined by the law of the place where such contract was made.

Provided that—

(a) Where a bill is issued out of the United Kingdom it is not invalid by reason only that it is not stamped in accordance with the law of the place of issue:

(b) Where a bill, issued out of the United Kingdom, conforms, as regards requisites in form, to the law of the United Kingdom, it may, for the purpose of enforcing payment thereof, be treated as valid as between all persons who negotiate, hold, or become parties to it in the United Kingdom.

(2) Subject to the provisions of this Act, the interpretation of the drawing, indorsement, acceptance, or acceptance supra protest of a bill, is determined by the law of the place where such contract is made.

Provided that where an inland bill is indorsed in a foreign country the indorsement shall as regards the payer be interpreted according to the law of the United Kingdom.

(3) The duties of the holder with respect to presentment for acceptance or payment and the necessity for or sufficiency of a protest or notice of dishonour, or otherwise, are determined by the law of the place where the act is done or the bill is dishonoured.

[. . .]

(5) Where a bill is drawn in one country and is payable in another, the due date thereof is determined according to the law of the place where it is payable.

PART III
CHEQUES ON A BANKER

73 Cheque defined

A cheque is a bill of exchange drawn on a banker payable on demand. Except as otherwise provided in this Part, the provisions of this Act applicable to a bill of exchange payable on demand apply to a cheque.

74 Presentment of cheque for payment

Subject to the provisions of this Act—

(1) Where a cheque is not presented for payment within a reasonable time of its issue, and the drawer or the person on whose account it is drawn had the right at the time of such presentment as between him and the banker to have the cheque paid and suffers actual damage through the delay, he is discharged to the extent of such damage, that is to say, to the extent to which such drawer or person is a creditor of such banker to a larger amount than he would have been had such cheque been paid.

(2) In determining what is a reasonable time regard shall be had to the nature of the instrument, the usage of trade and of bankers, and the facts of the particular case.

(3) The holder of such cheque as to which such drawer or person is discharged shall be a creditor, in lieu of such drawer or person, of such banker to the extent of such discharge, and entitled to recover the amount from him.

[74A Presentment of cheque for payment: alternative place of presentment

Where the banker on whom a cheque is drawn—

(a) has by notice published in the London, Edinburgh and Belfast Gazettes specified an address at which cheques drawn on him may be presented, and

(b) has not by notice so published cancelled the specification of that address, the cheque is also presented at the proper place if it is presented there.]

[. . .]

75 Revocation of banker's authority

The duty and authority of a banker to pay a cheque drawn on him by his customer are determined by—

(1) Countermand of payment:

(2) Notice of the customer's death.

[. . .]

Crossed cheques

76 General and special crossings defined

(1) Where a cheque bears across its face an addition of—

(a) The words 'and company' or any abbreviation thereof between two parallel transverse lines either with or without the words 'not negotiable'; or

(b) Two parallel transverse lines simply, either with or without the words 'not negotiable';

that addition constitutes a crossing, and the cheque is crossed generally.

(2) Where a cheque bears across its face an addition of the name of a banker, either with or without the words 'not negotiable', that addition constitutes a crossing, and the cheque is crossed specially and to that banker.

77 Crossing by drawer or after issue

(1) A cheque may be crossed generally or specially by the drawer.

(2) Where a cheque is uncrossed, the holder may cross it generally or specially.

(3) Where a cheque is crossed generally, the holder may cross it specially.

(4) Where a cheque is crossed generally or specially, the holder may add the words 'not negotiable'.

(5) Where a cheque is crossed specially, the banker to whom it is crossed may again cross it specially to another banker for collection.

(6) Where an uncrossed cheque, or a cheque crossed generally is sent to a banker for collection, he may cross it specially to himself.

78 Crossing a material part of cheque

A crossing authorised by this Act is a material part of the cheque; it shall not be lawful for any person to obliterate or, except as authorised by this Act, to add to or alter the crossing.

79 Duties of banker as to crossed cheques

(1) Where a cheque is crossed specially to more than one banker except when crossed to an agent for collection being a banker, the banker on whom it is drawn shall refuse payment thereof.

(2) Where the banker on whom a cheque is drawn which is so crossed nevertheless pays the same, or pays a cheque crossed generally otherwise than to a banker, or if crossed specially otherwise than to the banker to whom it is crossed, or his agent for collection being a banker, he is liable to the true owner of the cheque for any loss he may sustain owing to the cheque having been so paid.

Provided that where a cheque is presented for payment which does not at the time of presentment appear to be crossed, or to have had a crossing which had been obliterated, or to have been added to or altered otherwise than as authorised by this Act, the banker paying the cheque in good faith and without negligence shall not be responsible or incur any liability, nor shall the payment be questioned by reason of the cheque having been crossed, or of the crossing having been obliterated on having been added to or altered otherwise than as authorised by this Act, and of payment having been made otherwise than to a banker or to the banker to whom the cheque is or was crossed, or to his agent for collection being a banker as the case may be.

80 Protection to banker and drawer where cheque is crossed

Where the banker, on whom a crossed cheque [(including a cheque which under section 81A below or otherwise is not transferable)] is drawn in good faith and without negligence pays it, if crossed generally to a banker, and if crossed specially, to the banker to whom it is crossed, or his agent for collection being a banker, the banker paying the cheque, and, if the cheque has come into the hands of the payee, the drawer, shall respectively be entitled to the same rights and be placed in the same position as if payment of the cheque had been made to the true owner thereof.

81 Effect of crossing on holder
Where a person takes a crossed cheque which bears on it the words 'not negotiable', he shall not have and shall not be capable of giving a better title to the cheque than that which the person from whom he took it had.

[81A Non-transferable cheques
(1) Where a cheque is crossed and bears across its face the words 'account payee' or 'a/c payee', either with or without the words 'only', the cheque shall not be transferable, but shall only be valid as between the parties thereto.
(2) A banker is not to be treated for the purposes of section 80 above as having been negligent by reason only of his failure to concern himself with any purported indorsement of a cheque which under subsection (1) above or otherwise is not transferable.]

[. . .]

PART IV
PROMISSORY NOTES

83 Promissory note defined
(1) A promissory note is an unconditional promise in writing made by one person to another signed by the maker, engaging to pay, on demand or at a fixed or determinable future time, a sum certain in money, to, or to the order of, a specified person or to bearer.
(2) An instrument in the form of a note payable to maker's order is not a note within the meaning of this section unless and until it is indorsed by the maker.
(3) A note is not invalid by reason only that it contains also a pledge of collateral security with authority to sell or dispose thereof.
(4) A note which is, or on the face of it purports to be, both made and payable within the British Islands is an inland note. Any other note is a foreign note.

84 Delivery necessary
A promissory note is inchoate and incomplete until delivery thereof to the payee or bearer.

85 Joint and several notes
(1) A promissory note may be made by two or more makers, and they may be liable thereon jointly, or jointly and severally according to its tenor.
(2) Where a note runs 'I promise to pay' and is signed by two or more persons it is deemed to be their joint and several note.

86 Note payable on demand
(1) Where a note payable on demand has been indorsed, it must be presented for payment within a reasonable time of the indorsement. If it be not so presented the indorser is discharged.
(2) In determining what is a reasonable time, regard shall be had to the nature of the instrument, the usage of trade, and the facts of the particular case.
(3) Where a note payable on demand is negotiated, it is not deemed to be overdue for the purpose of affecting the holder with defects of title of which he had no notice, by reason that it appears that a reasonable time for presenting it for payment has elapsed since its issue.

87 Presentment of note for payment
(1) Where a promissory note is in the body of it made payable at a particular place, it must be presented for payment at that place in order to render the maker liable. In any other case, presentment for payment is not necessary in order to render the maker liable.
(2) Presentment for payment is necessary in order to render the indorser of a note liable.

(3) Where a note is in the body of it made payable at a particular place, presentment at that place is necessary in order to render an indorser liable; but when a place of payment is indicated by way of memorandum only, presentment at that place is sufficient to render the indorser liable, but a presentment to the maker elsewhere, if sufficient in other respects, shall also suffice.

[(4) This section is subject to Part 4A (presentment by electronic means).]

88 Liability of maker

The maker of a promissory note by making it—

(1) Engages that he will pay it according to its tenor;

(2) Is precluded from denying to a holder in due course the existence of the payee and his then capacity to indorse.

89 Application of Part II to notes

(1) Subject to the provisions in this part and, except as by this section provided, the provisions of this Act relating to bills of exchange apply, with the necessary modifications, to promissory notes.

(2) In applying those provisions the maker of a note shall be deemed to correspond with the acceptor of a bill, and the first indorser of a note shall be deemed to correspond with the drawer of an accepted bill payable to drawer's order.

(3) The following provisions as to bills do not apply to notes; namely, provisions relating to—

(a) Presentment for acceptance;
(b) Acceptance;
(c) Acceptance supra protest;
(d) Bills in a set.

(4) Where a foreign note is dishonoured, protest thereof is unnecessary.

[PART 4A

PRESENTMENT OF CHEQUES AND OTHER INSTRUMENTS BY ELECTRONIC MEANS

89A Presentment of instruments by electronic means

(1) Presentment for payment of an instrument to which this section applies may be effected by provision of an electronic image of both faces of the instrument, instead of by presenting the physical instrument, if the person to whom presentment is made accepts the presentment as effective.

This is subject to regulations under subsection (2) and to section 89C.

(2) The Treasury may by regulations prescribe circumstances in which sub section (1) does not apply.

(3) Regulations under subsection (2) may in particular prescribe circumstances by reference to—

(a) descriptions of instrument;
(b) arrangements under which presentment is made;
(c) descriptions of persons by or to whom presentment is made;
(d) descriptions of persons receiving payment or on whose behalf payment is received.

(4) Where presentment for payment is made under subsection (1)—

(a) any requirement—

(i) that the physical instrument must be exhibited, presented or delivered on or in connection with presentment or payment (including after presentment or payment or in connection with dishonour for non-payment), or

(ii) as to the day, time or place on or at which presentment of the physical instrument may be or is to be made, and

(b) any other requirement which is inconsistent with subsection (1),
does not apply.

(5) Subsection (4) does not affect any requirement as to the latest time for presentment.

(6) References in subsections (4) and (5) to a requirement are to a requirement or prohibition, whether imposed by or under any enactment, by a rule of law or by the instrument in question.

(7) Where an instrument is presented for payment under this section—

(a) any banker providing the electronic image,

(b) any banker to whom it is provided, and

(c) any banker making payment of the instrument as a result of provision of the electronic image,

are subject to the same duties in relation to collection and payment of the instrument as if the physical instrument had been presented.

This is subject to any provision made by or under this Part.

89B Instruments to which section 89A applies

(1) Subject to subsection (2), section 89A applies to—

(a) a cheque, or

(b) any other bill of exchange or any promissory note or other instrument—

(i) which appears to be intended by the person creating it to enable a person to obtain payment from a banker indicated in it of the sum so mentioned,

(ii) payment of which requires the instrument to be presented, and

(iii) which, but for section 89A, could not be presented otherwise than by presenting the physical instrument.

(2) Section 89A does not apply to any banknote (within the meaning given in section 208 of the Banking Act 2009) [or to anything that is an electronic trade document for the purposes of the Electronic Trade Documents Act 2023 (see section 2 of that Act)].

(3) The reference in subsection (1) to the person creating an instrument is—

(a) in the case of a bill of exchange, a reference to the drawer;

(b) in the case of a promissory note, a reference to the maker.

(4) For the purposes of subsection (1)(b)(i) an indication may be by code or number and need not indicate that payment is intended to be obtained from the banker.

89C Banker's obligation in relation to accepting physical instrument for presentment

Provision of an electronic image of an instrument does not constitute presentment of the instrument under section 89A if the arrangements between—

(a) the banker authorised to collect payment of the instrument on behalf of a customer, and

(b) that customer,

do not permit the customer to pay in the physical instrument but instead require an electronic image to be provided (whether to that banker or to any other person).

89D Copies of instruments and evidence of payment

(1) The Treasury may by regulations make provision for—

(a) requiring a copy of an instrument paid as a result of presentment under section 89A to be provided, on request, to the creator of the instrument by the banker who paid the instrument;

(b) a copy of an instrument provided in accordance with the regulations to be evidence of receipt by a person identified in accordance with the regulations of the sum payable by the instrument.

(2) Regulations under subsection (1)(a) may in particular—

(a) prescribe the manner and form in which a copy is to be provided;

(b) require the copy to be certified to be a true copy of the electronic image provided to the banker making the payment on presentment under section 89A;

(c) provide for the copy to be accompanied by prescribed information;

(d) require any copy to be provided free of charge or permit charges to be made for the provision of copies in prescribed circumstances.

(3) The reference in subsection (1)(a) to the creator of the instrument is—

(a) in the case of a bill of exchange, a reference to the drawer;

(b) in the case of a promissory note, a reference to the maker.

89E Compensation in cases of presentment by electronic means

(1) The Treasury may by regulations make provision for the responsible banker to compensate any person for any loss of a kind specified by the regulations which that person incurs in connection with electronic presentment or purported electronic presentment of an instrument.

(2) In this section 'electronic presentment or purported electronic presentment of an instrument' includes—

(a) presentment of an instrument to which section 89A applies under that section;

(b) presentment of any other instrument by any means involving provision of an electronic image by which it may be presented for payment;

(c) purported presentment for payment by any means involving provision of an electronic image of an instrument that may not be presented for payment in that way;

(d) provision, in purported presentment for payment, of—

(i) an electronic image that purports to be, but is not, an image of a physical instrument (including an image that has been altered electronically), or

(ii) an electronic image of an instrument which has no legal effect; or

(e) provision, in presentment or purported presentment for payment, of an electronic image which has been stolen.

(3) In this section, the 'responsible banker', in relation to electronic presentment or purported electronic presentment of an instrument, means—

(a) the banker who is authorised to collect payment of the instrument on a customer's behalf, or

(b) if the holder of the instrument is a banker, that banker.

(4) In this section—

(a) references to an instrument include references to an instrument which has no legal effect (whether because it has been fraudulently altered or created, or because it has been discharged, or otherwise);

(b) in relation to an electronic image which is not an image of a physical instrument, references to the instrument are to a purported instrument (of which it purports to be an image); and

(c) in relation to an instrument which is not a bill of exchange or promissory note, references to the holder are to the payee or indorsee of the instrument who is in possession of it or, if it is payable to bearer, the person in possession of it.

(5) Regulations under this section may in particular make provision for—

(a) the responsible banker to be required to pay compensation irrespective of fault;

(b) the amount of compensation to be reduced by virtue of anything done, or any failure to act, by the person to whom compensation is payable.

(6) Nothing in this section or regulations under it is to be taken to—

(a) prevent the responsible banker claiming a contribution from any other person, or

(b) affect any remedy available to the responsible banker in contract or otherwise.

(7) Except so far as regulations under this section provide expressly, nothing in this section or regulations under it is to be taken to affect any liability of the responsible banker which exists apart from this section or any such regulations.

89F Supplementary

(1) Regulations under this Part may—

(a) include incidental, supplementary and consequential provision;

(b) make transitory or transitional provision or savings;

(c) make different provision for different cases or circumstances or for different purposes;

(d) make provision subject to exceptions.

(2) The power to make regulations under this Part is exercisable by statutory instrument.

(3) An instrument containing—

(a) regulations under section 89A or 89D, or

(b) the first regulations to be made under section 89E, may not be made unless a draft of the instrument has been laid before, and approved by resolution of, each House of Parliament.

(4) An instrument containing any other regulations under section 89E is subject to annulment in pursuance of a resolution of either House of Parliament.

(5) For the purposes of this Part, a banker collects payment of an instrument on behalf of a customer by—

(a) receiving payment of the instrument for the customer, or

(b) receiving payment of the instrument for the banker (but not as holder), having—

(i) credited the customer's account with the amount of the instrument, or

(ii) otherwise given value to the customer in respect of the instrument.

(6) Section 89E(4) applies for the purposes of subsection (5) in its application to section 89E.]

PART V
SUPPLEMENTARY

90 Good faith

A thing is deemed to be done in good faith, within the meaning of this Act, where it is in fact done honestly, whether it is done negligently or not.

91 Signature

(1) Where, by this Act, any instrument or writing is required to be signed by any person, it is not necessary that he should sign it with his own hand, but it is sufficient if his signature is written thereon by some other person by or under his authority.

(2) In the case of a corporation, where, by this Act, any instrument or writing is required to be signed, it is sufficient if the instrument or writing be sealed with the corporate seal.

But nothing in this section shall be construed as requiring the bill or note of a corporation to be under seal.

92 Computation of time

Where, by this Act, the time limited for doing any act or thing is less than three days, in reckoning time, non-business days are excluded.

'Non-business days' for the purposes of this Act mean—

(a) [Saturday,] Sunday, Good Friday, Christmas Day;

(b) A bank holiday under [the Banking and Financial Dealings Act 1971];

(c) A day appointed by Royal proclamation as a public fast or thanksgiving day;

[(d) A day declared by an order under section 2 of the Banking and Financial Dealings Act 1971 to be a non-business day.]

Any other day is a business day.

93 When noting equivalent to protest

For the purposes of this Act, where a bill or note is required to be protested within a specified time or before some further proceeding is taken, it is sufficient that the bill has been noted for protest before the expiration of the specified time or the taking of the proceeding; and the formal protest may be extended at any time thereafter as of the date of the noting.

94 Protest when notary not accessible

[(1)] Where a dishonoured bill or note is authorised or required to be protested, and the services of a notary cannot be obtained at the place where the bill is dishonoured, any householder, or substantial resident of the place may, in the presence of two witnesses, give a certificate, signed by them, attesting to the dishonour of the bill, and the certificate shall in all respects operate as if it were a formal protest of the bill.

The form given in Schedule 1 to this Act may be used with necessary modifications, and if used shall be sufficient.

[(2) In subsection (1) 'notary' includes a person who, for the purposes of the Legal Services Act 2007, is an authorised person in relation to any activity which constitutes a notarial activity (within the meaning of that Act).]

95 Dividend warrants may be crossed

The provisions of this Act as to crossed cheques shall apply to a warrant for payment of dividend.

[. . .]

97 Savings

(1) The rules in bankruptcy relating to bills of exchange, promissory notes, and cheques, shall continue to apply thereto notwithstanding anything in this Act contained.

(2) The rules of common law including the law merchant, save in so far as they are inconsistent with the express provisions of this Act, shall continue to apply to bills of exchange, promissory notes, and cheques.

(3) Nothing in this Act or in any repeal effected thereby shall affect—

(a) [. . .] any law or enactment for the time being in force relating to the revenue:

(b) The provisions of the Companies Act, 1862, or Acts amending it, or any Act relating to joint stock banks or companies:

(c) The provisions of any Act relating to or confirming the privileges of the Bank of England or the Bank of Ireland respectively:

(d) The validity of any usage relating to dividend warrants, or the indorse ments thereof.

98 Saving of summary diligence in Scotland

Nothing in this Act or in any repeal effected thereby shall extend or restrict, or in any way alter or affect the law and practice in Scotland in regard to summary diligence.

99 Construction with other Acts, etc

Where any Act or document refers to any enactment repealed by this Act, the Act or document shall be construed, and shall operate as if it referred to the corresponding provisions of this Act.

100 Parole evidence allowed in certain judicial proceedings in Scotland

In any judicial proceeding in Scotland, any fact relating to a bill of exchange, bank cheque, or promissory note, which is relevant to any question of liability thereon, may be proved by parole evidence: Provided that this enactment shall not in any way affect the existing law and practice whereby the party who is, according to the tenor of any bill of exchange, bank cheque, or promissory note, debtor to the holder in the amount thereof, may be required, as a condition of obtaining a sist of diligence, or suspension of a charge, or threatened charge, to make such consignation, or to find such caution as the court or judge before whom the cause is depending may require. [. . .]

SCHEDULES

FIRST SCHEDULE

Section 94

Form of protest which may be used when the services of a notary cannot be obtained

Know all men that I, *A. B.* [householder], of in the county of in the United Kingdom, at the request of *C. D.*, there being no notary public available, did on the day of 188 at______________________ demand payment [*or* acceptance] of the bill of exchange hereunder written, from *E. F.*, to which demand he made answer [state answer, if any] wherefore I now, in the presence of *G. H.* and *J. K.* do protest the said bill of exchange.

(Signed) A. B.
G. H. } *Witnesses*
J. K.

N.B.—The bill itself should be annexed, or a copy of the bill and all that is written thereon should be underwritten.

FACTORS ACT 1889
(52 & 53 Vict, c 45)

Preliminary

1 Definitions

For the purposes of this Act—

(1) The expression 'mercantile agent' shall mean a mercantile agent having in the customary course of his business as such agent authority either to sell goods or to consign goods for the purpose of sale, or to buy goods, or to raise money on the security of goods:

(2) A person shall be deemed to be in possession of goods or of the documents of title to goods, where the goods or documents are in the actual custody or are held by any other person subject to his control or for him or on his behalf:

(3) The expression 'goods' shall include wares and merchandise:

(4) The expression 'document of title' shall include any bill of lading, dock warrant, warehouse-keeper's certificate, and warrant or order for the delivery of goods, and any other document used in the ordinary course of business as proof of the possession or control of goods, or authorising or purporting to authorise, either by endorsement or by delivery, the possessor of the document to transfer or receive goods thereby represented:

(5) The expression 'pledge' shall include any contract pledging, or giving a lien or security on, goods, whether in consideration of an original advance or of any further or continuing advance or of any pecuniary liability:

(6) The expression 'person' shall include any body of persons corporate or unincorporated.

Dispositions by mercantile agents

2 Powers of mercantile agent with respect to disposition of goods

(1) Where a mercantile agent is, with the consent of the owner, in possession of goods or of the documents of title to goods, any sale, pledge, or other disposition of the goods, made by him when acting in the ordinary course of business of a

mercantile agent, shall, subject to the provisions of this Act, be as valid as if he were expressly authorised by the owner of the goods to make the same; provided that the person taking under the disposition acts in good faith, and has not at the time of the disposition notice that the person making the disposition has not authority to make the same.

(2) Where a mercantile agent has, with the consent of the owner, been in possession of goods or of the documents of title to goods, any sale, pledge, or other disposition, which would have been valid if the consent had continued, shall be valid notwithstanding the determination of the consent; provided that the person taking under the disposition has not at the time thereof notice that the consent has been determined.

(3) Where a mercantile agent has obtained possession of any documents of title to goods by reason of his being or having been, with the consent of the owner, in possession of the goods represented thereby, or of any other documents of title to the goods, his possession of the first-mentioned documents shall, for the purposes of this Act, be deemed to be with the consent of the owner.

(4) For the purposes of this Act the consent of the owner shall be presumed in the absence of evidence to the contrary.

Dispositions by sellers and buyers of goods

8 Disposition by seller remaining in possession

Where a person, having sold goods, continues, or is, in possession of the goods or of the documents of title to the goods, the delivery or transfer by that person, or by a mercantile agent acting for him, of the goods or documents of title under any sale, pledge, or other disposition thereof, or under any agreement for sale, pledge, or other disposition thereof, to any person receiving the same in good faith and without notice of the previous sale, shall have the same effect as if the person making the delivery or transfer were expressly authorised by the owner of the goods to make the same.

9 Disposition by buyer obtaining possession

Where a person, having bought or agreed to buy goods, obtains with the consent of the seller possession of the goods or the documents of title to the goods, the delivery or transfer, by that person or by a mercantile agent acting for him, of the goods or documents of title under any sale, pledge, or other disposition thereof, or under any agreement for sale, pledge, or other disposition thereof, to any person receiving the same in good faith and without notice of any lien or other right of the original seller in respect of the goods, shall have the same effect as if the person making the delivery or transfer were a mercantile agent in possession of the goods or documents of title with the consent of the owner.

[For the purposes of this section—

(i) the buyer under a conditional sale agreement shall be deemed not to be a person who has bought or agreed to buy goods, and

(ii) 'conditional sale agreement' means an agreement for the sale of goods which is a consumer credit agreement within the meaning of the Consumer Credit Act 1974 under which the purchase price or part of it is payable by instalments, and the property in the goods is to remain in the seller (notwithstanding that the buyer is to be in possession of the goods) until such conditions as to the payment of instalments or otherwise as may be specified in the agreement are fulfilled.]

PARTNERSHIP ACT 1890
(53 & 54 Vict, c 39)

Nature of partnership

1 Definition of partnership

(1) Partnership is the relation which subsists between persons carrying on a business in common with a view of profit.

(2) But the relation between members of any company or association which is—

[(a) Registered under the Companies Act 2006,] or

(b) Formed or incorporated by or in pursuance of any other Act of Parliament or letters patent, or Royal Charter

[. . .]

is not a partnership within the meaning of this Act.

2 Rules for determining existence of partnership

In determining whether a partnership does or does not exist, regard shall be had to the following rules:

(1) joint tenancy, tenancy in common, joint property, common property, or part ownership does not of itself create a partnership as to anything so held or owned, whether the tenants or owners do or do not share any profits made by the use thereof.

(2) The sharing of gross returns does not of itself create a partnership, whether the persons sharing such returns have or have not a joint or common right or interest in any property from which or from the use of which the returns are derived.

(3) The receipt by a person of a share of the profits of a business is prima facie evidence that he is a partner in the business, but the receipt of such a share, or of a payment contingent on or varying with the profits of a business, does not of itself make him a partner in the business; and in particular—

(a) The receipt by a person of a debt or other liquidated amount by instalments, or otherwise out of the accruing profits of a business does not of itself make him a partner in the business or liable as such:

(b) A contract for the remuneration of a servant or agent of a person engaged in a business by a share of the profits of the business does not of itself make the servant or agent a partner in the business or liable as such:

(c) A person being the widow [, widower, surviving civil partner] or child of a deceased partner, and receiving by way of annuity a portion of the profits made in the business in which the deceased person was a partner, is not by reason only of such receipt a partner in the business or liable as such:

(d) The advance of money by way of loan to a person engaged or about to engage in any business on a contract with that person that the lender shall receive a rate of interest varying with the profits, or shall receive a share of the profits arising from carrying on the business, does not of itself make the lender a partner with the person or persons carrying on the business or liable as such. Provided that the contract is in writing, and signed by or on behalf of all the parties thereto:

(e) A person receiving by way of annuity or otherwise a portion of the profits of a business in consideration of the sale by him of the goodwill of the business is not by reason only of such receipt a partner in the business or liable as such.

3 Postponement of rights of person lending or selling in consideration of share of profits in case of insolvency

In the event of any person to whom money has been advanced by way of loan upon such a contract as is mentioned in the last foregoing section, or of any buyer of a goodwill in consideration of a share of the profits of the business, being adjudged a bankrupt, entering into an arrangement to pay his creditors less than [100p] in the pound, or dying in insolvent circumstances, the lender of the loan shall not be entitled to recover anything in respect of the loan, and the seller of the goodwill shall not be entitled to recover anything in respect of the share of profits contracted for, until the claims of the other creditors of the borrower or buyer for valuable consideration in money or money's worth have been satisfied.

4 Meaning of firm

(1) Persons who have entered into partnership with one another are for the purposes of this Act called collectively a firm, and the name under which their business is carried on is called the firm-name.

(2) In Scotland a firm is a legal person distinct from the partners of whom it is composed, but an individual partner may be charged on a decree or diligence directed against the firm, and on payment of the debts is entitled to relief pro rata from the firm and its other members.

[*(3) In relation to a limited partnership registered under the Limited Partnerships Act 1907, subsection (2) applies only if the limited partnership was registered by the registrar for Scotland.*]

Relations of partners to persons dealing with them

5 Power of partner to bind the firm

Every partner is an agent of the firm and his other partners for the purpose of the business of the partnership; and the acts of every partner who does any act for carrying on in the usual way business of the kind carried on by the firm of which he is a member bind the firm and his partners, unless the partner so acting has in fact no authority to act for the firm in the particular matter, and the person with whom he is dealing either knows that he has no authority, or does not know or believe him to be a partner.

6 Partners bound by acts on behalf of firm

An act or instrument relating to the business of the firm done or executed in the firm-name, or in any other manner showing an intention to bind the firm, by any person thereto authorised, whether a partner or not, is binding on the firm and all the partners.

Provided that this section shall not affect any general rule of law relating to the execution of deeds or negotiable instruments.

7 Partner using credit of firm for private purposes

Where one partner pledges the credit of the firm for a purpose apparently not connected with the firm's ordinary course of business, the firm is not bound, unless he is in fact specially authorised by the other partners; but this section does not affect any personal liability incurred by an individual partner.

8 Effect of notice that firm will not be bound by acts of partner

If it has been agreed between the partners that any restriction shall be placed on the power of any one or more of them to bind the firm, no act done in contravention of the agreement is binding on the firm with respect to persons having notice of the agreement.

9 Liability of partners

Every partner in a firm is liable jointly with the other partners, and in Scotland severally also, for all debts and obligations of the firm incurred while he is a partner; and after his death his estate is also severally liable in a due course of administration for such debts and obligations, so far as they remain unsatisfied, but subject in England or Ireland to the prior payment of his separate debts.

10 Liability of the firm for wrongs

Where, by any wrongful act or omission of any partner acting in the ordinary course of the business of the firm, or with the authority of his co-partners, loss or injury is caused to any person not being a partner in the firm, or any penalty is incurred, the firm is liable therefor to the same extent as the partner so acting or omitting to act.

11 Misapplication of money or property received for or in custody of the firm
In the following cases; namely—

(a) Where one partner acting within the scope of his apparent authority receives the money or property of a third person and misapplies it; and

(b) Where a firm in the course of its business receives money or property of a third person, and the money or property so received is misapplied by one or more of the partners while it is in the custody of the firm;

the firm is liable to make good the loss.

12 Liability for wrongs joint and several
Every partner is liable jointly with his co-partners and also severally for everything for which the firm while he is a partner therein becomes liable under either of the two last preceding sections.

13 Improper employment of trust-property for partnership purposes
If a partner, being a trustee, improperly employs trust property in the business or on the account of the partnership, no other partner is liable for the trust-property to the persons beneficially interested therein.

Provided as follows:—

(1) This section shall not affect any liability incurred by any partner by reason of his having notice of a breach of trust; and

(2) Nothing in this section shall prevent trust money from being followed and recovered from the firm if still in its possession or under its control.

14 Persons liable by 'holding out'

(1) Every one who by words spoken or written or by conduct represents himself, or who knowingly suffers himself to be represented, as a partner in a particular firm, is liable as a partner to anyone who has on the faith of any such representation given credit to the firm, whether the representation has or has not been made or communicated to the person so giving credit by or with the knowledge of the apparent partner making the representation or suffering it to be made.

(2) Provided that where after a partner's death the partnership business is continued in the old firm-name, the continued use of that name or of the deceased partner's name as part thereof shall not of itself make his executors' or administrators' estate or effects liable for any partnership debts contracted after his death.

15 Admissions and representations of partners
An admission or representation made by any partner concerning the partnership affairs, and in the ordinary course of its business, is evidence against the firm.

16 Notice to acting partner to be notice to the firm
Notice to any partner who habitually acts in the partnership business of any matter relating to partnership affairs operates as a notice to the firm, except in the case of a fraud on the firm committed by or with the consent of that partner.

17 Liabilities of incoming and outgoing partners

(1) A person who is admitted as a partner into an existing firm does not thereby become liable to the creditors of the firm for anything done before he became a partner.

(2) A partner who retires from a firm does not thereby cease to be liable for partnership debts or obligations incurred before his retirement.

(3) A retiring partner may be discharged from any existing liabilities, by an agreement to that effect between himself and the members of the firm as newly constituted and the creditors, and this agreement may be either express or inferred, as a fact from the course of dealing between the creditors and the firm as newly constituted.

18 Revocation of continuing guaranty by change in firm
A continuing guaranty or cautionary obligation given either to a firm or to a third person in respect of the transactions of a firm is, in the absence of agreement to the contrary, revoked as to future transactions by any change in the constitution of the firm to which, or of the firm in respect of the transactions of which, the guaranty or obligation was given.

Relations of partners to one another

19 Variation by consent of terms of partnership
The mutual rights and duties of partners, whether ascertained by agreement or defined by this Act, may be varied by the consent of all the partners, and such consent may be either express or inferred from a course of dealing.

20 Partnership property
(1) All property and rights and interests in property originally brought into the partnership stock or acquired, whether by purchase or otherwise, on account of the firm or for the purposes and in the course of the partnership business, are called in this Act partnership property, and must be held and applied by the partners exclusively for the purposes of the partnership and in accordance with the partnership agreement.

(2) Provided that the legal estate or interest in any land, or in Scotland [of . . .] any heritable estate, which belongs to the partnership shall devolve according to the nature and tenure thereof, and the general rules of law thereto applicable, but in trust, so far as necessary, for the persons beneficially interested in the land under this section.

(3) Where co-owners of an estate or interest in any land, or in Scotland of any heritable estate, not being itself partnership property, are partners as to profits made by the use of that land or estate, and purchase other land or estate out of the profits to be used in like manner, the land or estate so purchased belongs to them, in the absence of an agreement to the contrary, not as partners but as co-owners for the same respective estates and interests as are held by them in the land or estate first mentioned at the date of the purchase.

21 Property bought with partnership money
Unless the contrary intention appears, property bought with money belonging to the firm is deemed to have been bought on account of the firm.

22 Conversion into personal estate of land held as partnership property
Where land or any heritable interest therein has become partnership property, it shall, unless the contrary intention appears, be treated as between the partners (including the representatives of a deceased partner), and also as between the heirs of a deceased partner and his executors or administrators, as personal or moveable and not real or heritable estate.

23 *[Does not apply to Scotland]*

24 Rules as to interests and duties of partners subject to special agreement
The interests of partners in the partnership property and their rights and duties in relation to the partnership shall be determined, subject to any agreement express or implied between the partners, by the following rules:

(1) All the partners are entitled to share equally in the capital and profits of the business, and must contribute equally towards the losses whether of capital or otherwise sustained by the firm.

(2) The firm must indemnify every partner in respect of payments made and personal liabilities incurred by him—

(a) In the ordinary and proper conduct of the business of the firm; or,

(b) In or about anything necessarily done for the preservation of the business or property of the firm.

(3) A partner making, for the purpose of the partnership, any actual payment or advance beyond the amount of capital which he has agreed to subscribe, is entitled to interest at the rate of five per cent. per annum from the date of the payment or advance.

(4) A partner is not entitled, before the ascertainment of profits, to interest on the capital subscribed by him.

(5) Every partner may take part in the management of the partnership business.

(6) No partner shall be entitled to remuneration for acting in the partnership business.

(7) No person may be introduced as a partner without the consent of all existing partners.

(8) Any difference arising as to ordinary matters connected with the partnership business may be decided by a majority of the partners, but no change may be made in the nature of the partnership business without the consent of all existing partners.

(9) The partnership books are to be kept at the place of business of the partnership (or the principal place, if there is more than one), and every partner may, when he thinks fit, have access to and inspect and copy any of them.

25 Expulsion of partner

No majority of the partners can expel any partner unless a power to do so has been conferred by express agreement between the partners.

26 Retirement from partnership at will

(1) Where no fixed term has been agreed upon for the duration of the partnership, any partner may determine the partnership at any time on giving notice of his intention so to do to all the other partners.

(2) Where the partnership has originally been constituted by deed, a notice in writing, signed by the partner giving it, shall be sufficient for this purpose.

27 Where partnership for term is continued over, continuance on old terms presumed

(1) Where a partnership entered into for a fixed term is continued after the term has expired, and without any express new agreement, the rights and duties of the partners remain the same as they were at the expiration of the term, so far as is consistent with the incidents of a partnership at will.

(2) A continuance of the business by the partners or such of them as habitually acted therein during the term, without any settlement or liquidation of the partnership affairs, is presumed to be a continuance of the partnership.

28 Duty of partners to render accounts, &c

Partners are bound to render true accounts and full information of all things affecting the partnership to any partner or his legal representatives.

29 Accountability of partners for private profits

(1) Every partner must account to the firm for any benefit derived by him without the consent of the other partners from any transaction concerning the partnership, or from any use by him of the partnership property name or business connexion.

(2) This section applies also to transactions undertaken after a partnership has been dissolved by the death of a partner, and before the affairs thereof have been completely wound up, either by any surviving partner or by the representatives of the deceased partner.

30 Duty of partner not to compete with firm

If a partner, without the consent of the other partners, carries on any business of the same nature as and competing with that of the firm, he must account for and pay over to the firm all profits made by him in that business.

31 Rights of assignee of share in partnership

(1) An assignment by any partner of his share in the partnership, either absolute or by way of mortgage or redeemable charge, does not, as against the other partners, entitle the assignee, during the continuance of the partnership, to interfere in the management or administration of the partnership business or affairs, or to require any accounts of the partnership transactions, or to inspect the partnership books, but entitles the assignee only to receive the share of profits to which the assigning partner would otherwise be entitled, and the assignee must accept the account of profits agreed to by the partners.

(2) In the case of a dissolution of the partnership, whether as respects all the partners or as respects the assigning partner, the assignee is entitled to receive the share of the partnership assets to which the assigning partner is entitled as between himself and the other partners, and, for the purpose of ascertaining that share, to an account as from the date of the dissolution.

Dissolution of partnership, and its consequences

32 Dissolution by expiration or notice

Subject to any agreement between the partners a partnership is dissolved—

(a) If entered into for a fixed term, by the expiration of that term:

(b) If entered into for a single adventure or undertaking, by the termination of that adventure or undertaking:

(c) If entered into for an undefined time, by any partner giving notice to the other or others of his intention to dissolve the partnership.

In the last-mentioned case the partnership is dissolved as from the date mentioned in the notice as the date of dissolution, or, if no date is so mentioned, as from the date of the communication of the notice.

33 Dissolution by bankruptcy, death, or charge

(1) Subject to any agreement between the partners, every partnership is dissolved as regards all partners by the death or bankruptcy of any partner.

(2) A partnership may, at the option of the other partners, be dissolved if any partner suffers his share of the partnership property to be charged under this Act for his separate debt.

34 Dissolution by illegality of partnership

A partnership is in every case dissolved by the happening of any event which makes it unlawful for the business of the firm to be carried on or for the members of the firm to carry it on in partnership.

35 Dissolution by the Court

On application by a partner the Court may decree a dissolution of the partnership in any of the following cases:

[*(a) When a partner has a mental disorder within the meaning of section 328 of the Mental Health (Care and Treatment) (Scotland) Act 2003 or section 305 of the Mental Capacity Act (Northern Ireland) 2016 (as the case may be):*]

(b) When a partner, other than the partner suing, becomes in any other way permanently incapable of performing his part of the partnership contract:

(c) When a partner, other than the partner suing, has been guilty of such conduct as, in the opinion of the Court, regard being had to the nature of the business, is calculated to prejudicially affect the carrying on of the business:

(d) When a partner, other than the partner suing, wilfully or persistently commits a breach of the partnership agreement, or otherwise so conducts himself in matters relating to the partnership business that it is not reasonably practicable for the other partner or partners to carry on the business in partnership with him:

(e) When the business of the partnership can only be carried on at a loss:

(f) Whenever in any case circumstances have arisen which, in the opinion of the Court, render it just and equitable that the partnership be dissolved.

36 Rights of persons dealing with firm against apparent members of firm

(1) Where a person deals with a firm after a change in its constitution he is entitled to treat all apparent members of the old firm as still being members of the firm until he has notice of the change.

(2) An advertisement in the London Gazette as to a firm whose principal place of business is in England or Wales, in the Edinburgh Gazette as to a firm whose principal place of business is in Scotland, and in the [Belfast Gazette] as to a firm whose principal place of business is in Ireland, shall be notice as to persons who had not dealings with the firm before the date of the dissolution or change so advertised.

(3) The estate of a partner who dies, or who becomes bankrupt, or of a partner who, not having been known to the person dealing with the firm to be a partner, retires from the firm, is not liable for partnership debts contracted after the date of the death, bankruptcy, or retirement respectively.

37 Right of partners to notify dissolution

On dissolution of a partnership or retirement of a partner any partner may publicly notify the same, and may require the other partner or partners to concur for that purpose in all necessary or proper acts, if any, which cannot be done without his or their concurrence.

38 Continuing authority of partners for purposes of winding up

After the dissolution of a partnership the authority of each partner to bind the firm, and the other rights and obligations of the partners, continue notwithstanding the dissolution so far as may be necessary to wind up the affairs of the partnership, and to complete transactions begun but unfinished at the time of the dissolution [, and in relation to any prosecution of the partnership by virtue of section 1 of the Partnerships (Prosecution) (Scotland) Act 2013], but not otherwise.

Provided that the firm is in no case bound by the acts of a partner who has become bankrupt; but this proviso does not affect the liability of any person who has after the bankruptcy represented himself or knowingly suffered himself to be represented as a partner of the bankrupt.

39 Rights of partners as to application of partnership property

On the dissolution of a partnership every partner is entitled, as against the other partners in the firm, and all persons claiming through them in respect of their interests as partners, to have the property of the partnership applied in payment of the debts and liabilities of the firm, and to have the surplus assets after such payment applied in payment of what may be due to the partners respectively after deducting what may be due from them as partners to the firm; and for that purpose any partner or his representatives may on the termination of the partnership apply to the Court to wind up the business and affairs of the firm.

40 Apportionment of premium where partnership prematurely dissolved

Where one partner has paid a premium to another on entering into a partnership for a fixed term, and the partnership is dissolved before the expiration of that term otherwise than by the death of a partner, the Court may order the repayment of the premium, or of such part thereof as it thinks just, having regard to the terms of the partnership contract and to the length of time during which the partnership has continued; unless

(a) the dissolution is, in the judgment of the Court, wholly or chiefly due to the misconduct of the partner who paid the premium, or

(b) the partnership has been dissolved by an agreement containing no provision for a return of any part of the premium.

41 Rights where partnership dissolved for fraud or misrepresentation
Where a partnership contract is rescinded on the ground of fraud or misrepresentation of one of the parties thereto, the party entitled to rescind is, without prejudice to any other right, entitled—

(a) to a lien on, or right of retention of, the surplus of the partnership assets, after satisfying the partnership liabilities, for any sum of money paid by him for the purchase of a share in the partnership and for any capital contributed by him, and is

(b) to stand in the place of the creditors of the firm for any payments made by him in respect of the partnership liabilities, and

(c) to be indemnified by the person guilty of the fraud or making the representation against all the debts and liabilities of the firm.

42 Right of outgoing partner in certain cases to share in profits made after dissolution

(1) Where any member of a firm has died or otherwise ceased to be a partner, and the surviving or continuing partners carry on the business of the firm with its capital or assets without any final settlement of accounts as between the firm and the outgoing partner or his estate, then, in the absence of any agreement to the contrary, the outgoing partner or his estate is entitled at the option of himself or his representatives to such share of the profits made since the dissolution as the Court may find to be attributable to the use of his share of the partnership assets, or to interest at the rate of five per cent. per annum on the amount of his share of the partnership assets.

(2) Provided that where by the partnership contract an option is given to surviving or continuing partners to purchase the interest of a deceased or outgoing partner, and that option is duly exercised, the estate of the deceased partner, or the outgoing partner or his estate, as the case may be, is not entitled to any further or other share of profits; but if any partner assuming to act in exercise of the option does not in all material respects comply with the terms thereof, he is liable to account under the foregoing provisions of this section.

43 Retiring or deceased partner's share to be a debt
Subject to any agreement between the partners, the amount due from surviving or continuing partners to an outgoing partner or the representatives of a deceased partner in respect of the outgoing or deceased partner's share is a debt accruing at the date of the dissolution or death.

44 Rule for distribution of assets on final settlement of accounts
In settling accounts between the partners after a dissolution of partnership, the following rules shall, subject to any agreement, be observed:

(a) Losses, including losses and deficiencies of capital, shall be paid first out of profits, next out of capital, and lastly, if necessary, by the partners individually in the proportion in which they were entitled to share profits:

(b) The assets of the firm including the sums, if any, contributed by the partners to make up losses or deficiencies of capital, shall be applied in the following manner and order:

1 In paying the debts and liabilities of the firm to persons who are not partners therein:

2 In paying to each partner rateably what is due from the firm to him for advances as distinguished from capital:

3 In paying to each partner rateably what is due from the firm to him in respect of capital:

4 The ultimate residue, if any, shall be divided among the partners in the proportion in which the profits are divisible.

Supplemental

45 Definitions of 'court' and 'business'
In this Act, unless the contrary intention appears—
The expression 'court' includes every court and judge having jurisdiction in the case:
The expression 'business' includes every trade, occupation or profession.

46 Saving for rules of equity and common law
The rules of equity and of common law applicable to partnership shall continue in force except so far as they are inconsistent with the express provisions of this Act.

47 Provision as to bankruptcy in Scotland
(1) In the application of this Act to Scotland the bankruptcy of a firm or of an individual shall mean sequestration under the Bankruptcy (Scotland) Acts, and also in the case of an individual the issue against him of a decree of cessio bonorum.
(2) Nothing in this Act shall alter the rules of the law of Scotland relating to the bankruptcy of a firm or of the individual partners thereof.

[. . .]

50 Short title
This Act may be cited as the Partnership Act 1890.

FACTORS (SCOTLAND) ACT 1890
(53 & 54 Vict, c 40)

1 Application of 52 & 53 Vict c 45 to Scotland
Subject to the following provisions, the Factors Act, 1889, shall apply to Scotland—
(1) The expression 'lien' shall mean and include right of retention; the expression 'vendor's lien' shall mean and include any right of retention competent to the original owner or vendor; and the expression 'set off' shall mean and include compensation.
(2) In the application of section five of the recited Act, a sale, pledge, or other disposition of goods shall not be valid unless made for valuable consideration.

MARINE INSURANCE ACT 1906
(6 Edw 7, c 41)

Marine insurance

1 Marine insurance defined

A contract of marine insurance is a contract whereby the insurer undertakes to indemnify the assured, in manner and to the extent thereby agreed, against marine losses, that is to say, the losses incident to marine adventure.

2 Mixed sea and land risks

(1) A contract of marine insurance may, by its express terms, or by usage of trade, be extended so as to protect the assured against losses on inland waters or on any land risk which may be incidental to any sea voyage.

(2) Where a ship in course of building, or the launch of a ship, or any adventure analogous to marine adventure, is covered by a policy in the form of a marine policy, the provisions of this Act, in so far as applicable, shall apply thereto; but, except as by this section provided, nothing in this Act shall alter or affect any rule of law applicable to any contract of insurance other than a contract of marine insurance as by this Act defined.

3 Marine adventure and maritime perils defined

(1) Subject to the provisions of this Act, every lawful marine adventure may be the subject of a contract of marine insurance.

(2) In particular there is a marine adventure where—

(a) Any ship goods or other moveables are exposed to maritime perils. Such property is in this Act referred to as 'insurable property';

(b) The earning or acquisition of any freight, passage money, commission, profit, or other pecuniary benefit, or the security for any advances, loan or disbursements, is endangered by the exposure of insurable property to maritime perils;

(c) Any liability to a third party may be incurred by the owner of, or other person interested in or responsible for, insurable property, by reason of maritime perils.

'Maritime perils' means the perils consequent on, or incidental to, the navigation of the sea, that is to say, perils of the seas, fire, war perils, pirates, rovers, thieves, captures, seisures, restraints, and detainments of princes and peoples, jettisons, barratry, and any other perils, either of the like kind or which may be designated by the policy.

Insurable interest

4 Avoidance of wagering or gaming contracts

(1) Every contract of marine insurance by way of gaming or wagering is void.

(2) A contract of marine insurance is deemed to be a gaming or wagering contract—

(a) Where the assured has not an insurable interest as defined by this Act, and the contract is entered into with no expectation of acquiring such an interest; or

(b) Where the policy is made 'interest or no interest', or 'without further proof of interest than the policy itself', or 'without benefit of salvage to the insurer', or subject to any other like term:

Provided that, where there is no possibility of salvage, a policy may be effected without benefit of salvage to the insurer.

5 Insurable interest defined

(1) Subject to the provisions of this Act, every person has an insurable interest who is interested in a marine adventure.

(2) In particular a person is interested in a marine adventure where he stands in any legal or equitable relation to the adventure or to any insurable property at risk therein, in consequence of which he may benefit by the safety or due arrival of insurable property, or may be prejudiced by its loss, or damage thereto, or by the detention thereof, or may incur liability in respect thereof.

6 When interest must attach

(1) The assured must be interested in the subject-matter insured at the time of the loss though he need not be interested when the insurance is effected:

Provided that where the subject-matter is insured 'lost or not lost', the assured may recover although he may not have acquired his interest until after the loss, unless at the time of effecting the contract of insurance the assured was aware of the loss, and the insurer was not.

(2) Where the assured has no interest at the time of the loss, he cannot acquire interest by any act or election after he is aware of the loss.

7 Defeasible or contingent interest

(1) A defeasible interest is insurable, as also is a contingent interest.

(2) In particular, where the buyer of goods has insured them, he has an insurable interest, notwithstanding that he might, at his election, have rejected the goods, or have treated them as at the seller's risk, by reason of the latter's delay in making delivery or otherwise.

8 Partial interest

A partial interest of any nature is insurable.

9 Re-insurance

(1) The insurer under a contract of marine insurance has an insurable interest in his risk, and may re-insure in respect of it.

(2) Unless the policy otherwise provides, the original assured has no right or interest in respect of such re-insurance.

10 Bottomry

The lender of money on bottomry or respondentia has an insurable interest in respect of the loan.

11 Master's and seamen's wages

The master or any member of the crew of a ship has an insurable interest in respect of his wages.

12 Advance freight

In the case of advance freight, the person advancing the freight has an insurable interest, in so far as such freight is not repayable in case of loss.

13 Charges of insurance

The assured has an insurable interest in the charges of any insurance which he may effect.

14 Quantum of interest

(1) Where the subject-matter insured is mortgaged, the mortgagor has an insurable interest in the full value thereof, and the mortgagee has an insurable interest in respect of any sum due or to become due under the mortgage.

(2) A mortgagee, consignee, or other person having an interest in the subjectmatter insured may insure on behalf and for the benefit of other persons interested as well as for his own benefit.

(3) The owner of insurable property has an insurable interest in respect of the full value thereof, notwithstanding that some third person may have agreed, or be liable, to indemnify him in case of loss.

15 Assignment of interest

Where the assured assigns or otherwise parts with his interest in the subject-matter insured, he does not thereby transfer to the assignee his rights under the contract of insurance, unless there be an express or implied agreement with the assignee to that effect.

But the provisions of this section do not affect a transmission of interest by operation of law.

Insurable value

16 Measure of insurable value

Subject to any express provision or valuation in the policy, the insurable value of the subject-matter insured must be ascertained as follows:—

(1) In insurance on ship, the insurable value is the value, at the commencement of the risk, of the ship, including her outfit, provisions and stores for the officers and crew, money advanced for seamen's wages, and other disbursements (if any) incurred to make the ship fit for the voyage or adventure contemplated by the policy, plus the charges of insurance upon the whole.

The insurable value, in the case of a steamship, includes also the machinery, boilers, and coals and engine stores if owned by the assured, and, in the case of a ship engaged in a special trade, the ordinary fittings requisite for that trade.

(2) In insurance on freight, whether paid in advance or otherwise, the insurable value is the gross amount of freight at the risk of the assured, plus the charges of insurance.

(3) In insurance on goods or merchandise, the insurable value is the prime cost of the property insured, plus the expenses of and incidental to shipping and the charges of insurance upon the whole.

(4) In insurance on any other subject-matter, the insurable value is the amount at the risk of the assured when the policy attaches, plus the charges of insurance.

Disclosure and representations

17 Insurance is uberrimae fidei

A contract of marine insurance is a contract based upon the utmost good faith [. . .].

[. . .]

21 When contract is deemed to be concluded

A contract of marine insurance is deemed to be concluded when the proposal of the assured is accepted by the insurer, whether the policy be then issued or not; and, for the purpose of showing when the proposal was accepted, reference may be made to the slip or covering note or other customary memorandum of the contract. [. . .]

The policy

22 Contract must be embodied in policy

Subject to the provisions of any statute, a contract of marine insurance is inadmissible in evidence unless it is embodied in a marine policy in accordance with this Act. The policy may be executed and issued either at the time when the contract is concluded, or afterwards.

23 What policy must specify

A marine policy must specify—

(1) The name of the assured, or of some person who effects the insurance on his behalf.

[. . .]

24 Signature of insurer

(1) A marine policy must be signed by or on behalf of the insurer, provided that in the case of a corporation the corporate seal may be sufficient, but nothing in

this section shall be construed as requiring the subscription of a corporation to be under seal.

(2) Where a policy is subscribed by or on behalf of two or more insurers, each subscription, unless the contrary be expressed, constitutes a distinct contract with the assured.

25 Voyage and time policies

(1) Where the contract is to insure the subject-matter 'at and from', or from one place to another or others, the policy is called a 'voyage policy', and where the contract is to insure the subject-matter for a definite period of time the policy is called a 'time policy'. A contract for both voyage and time may be included in the same policy.

[. . .]

26 Designation of subject-matter

(1) The subject-matter insured must be designated in a marine policy with reasonable certainty.

(2) The nature and extent of the interest of the assured in the subject-matter insured need not be specified in the policy.

(3) Where the policy designates the subject-matter insured in general terms, it shall be construed to apply to the interest intended by the assured to be covered.

(4) In the application of this section regard shall be had to any usage regulating the designation of the subject-matter insured.

27 Valued policy

(1) A policy may be either valued or unvalued.

(2) A valued policy is a policy which specifies the agreed value of the subjectmatter insured.

(3) Subject to the provisions of this Act, and in the absence of fraud, the value fixed by the policy is, as between the insurer and the assured, conclusive of the insurable value of the subject intended to be insured, whether the loss be total or partial.

(4) Unless the policy otherwise provides, the value fixed by the policy is not conclusive for the purpose of determining whether there has been a constructive total loss.

28 Unvalued policy

An unvalued policy is a policy which does not specify the value of the subjectmatter insured, but, subject to the limit of the sum insured, leaves the insurable value to be subsequently ascertained, in the manner herein-before specified.

29 Floating policy by ship or ships

(1) A floating policy is a policy which describes the insurance in general terms, and leaves the name of the ship or ships and other particulars to be defined by subsequent declaration.

(2) The subsequent declaration or declarations may be made by indorsement on the policy, or in other customary manner.

(3) Unless the policy otherwise provides, the declarations must be made in the order of dispatch or shipment. They must, in the case of goods, comprise all consignments within the terms of the policy, and the value of the goods or other property must be honestly stated, but an omission or erroneous declaration may be rectified even after loss or arrival, provided the omission or declaration was made in good faith.

(4) Unless the policy otherwise provides, where a declaration of value is not made until after notice of loss or arrival, the policy must be treated as an unvalued policy as regards the subject-matter of that declaration.

30 Construction of terms in policy

(1) A policy may be in the form in the First Schedule to this Act.

(2) Subject to the provisions of this Act, and unless the context of the policy otherwise requires, the terms and expressions mentioned in the First Schedule to this Act shall be construed as having the scope and meaning in that schedule assigned to them.

31 Premium to be arranged

(1) Where an insurance is effected at a premium to be arranged, and no arrangement is made, a reasonable premium is payable.

(2) Where an insurance is effected on the terms that an additional premium is to be arranged in a given event, and that event happens but no arrangement is made, then a reasonable additional premium is payable.

Double insurance

32 Double insurance

(1) Where two or more policies are effected by or on behalf of the assured on the same adventure and interest or any part thereof, and the sums insured exceed the indemnity allowed by this Act, the assured is said to be over-insured by double insurance.

(2) Where the assured is over-insured by double insurance—

(a) The assured, unless the policy otherwise provides, may claim payment from the insurers in such order as he may think fit, provided that he is not entitled to receive any sum in excess of the indemnity allowed by this Act;

(b) Where the policy under which the assured claims is a valued policy, the assured must give credit as against the valuation for any sum received by him under any other policy without regard to the actual value of the subject-matter insured;

(c) Where the policy under which the assured claims is an unvalued policy he must give credit, as against the full insurable value, for any sum received by him under any other policy.

(d) Where the assured receives any sum in excess of the indemnity allowed by this Act, he is deemed to hold such sum in trust for the insurers, according to their right of contribution among themselves.

Warranties, etc

33 Nature of warranty

(1) A warranty, in the following sections relating to warranties, means a promissory warranty, that is to say, a warranty by which the assured undertakes that some particular thing shall or shall not be done, or that some condition shall be fulfilled, or whereby he affirms or negatives the existence of a particular state of facts.

(2) A warranty may be express or implied.

(3) A warranty, as above defined, is a condition which must be exactly complied with, whether it be material to the risk or not. [. . .]

[. . .]

35 Express warranties

(1) An express warranty may be in any form of words from which the intention to warrant is to be inferred.

(2) An express warranty must be included in, or written upon, the policy, or must be contained in some document incorporated by reference into the policy.

(3) An express warranty does not exclude an implied warranty, unless it be inconsistent therewith.

36 Warranty of neutrality

(1) Where insurable property, whether ship or goods, is expressly warranted neutral, there is an implied condition that the property shall have a neutral char-

acter at the commencement of the risk, and that, so far as the assured can control the matter, its neutral character shall be preserved during the risk.

(2) Where a ship is expressly warranted 'neutral' there is also an implied condition that, so far as the assured can control the matter, she shall be properly documented, that is to say, that she shall carry the necessary papers to establish her neutrality, and that she shall not falsify or suppress her papers, or use simulated papers. If any loss occurs through breach of this condition, the insurer may avoid the contract.

37 No implied warranty of nationality

There is no implied warranty as to the nationality of a ship, or that her nationality shall not be changed during the risk.

38 Warranty of good safety

Where the subject-matter insured is warranted 'well' or 'in good safety' on a particular day, it is sufficient if it be safe at any time during that day.

39 Warranty of seaworthiness of ship

(1) In a voyage policy there is an implied warranty that at the commencement of the voyage the ship shall be seaworthy for the purpose of the particular adventure insured.

(2) Where the policy attaches while the ship is in port, there is also an implied warranty that she shall, at the commencement of the risk, be reasonably fit to encounter the ordinary perils of the port.

(3) Where the policy relates to a voyage which is performed in different stages, during which the ship requires different kinds of or further preparation or equipment, there is an implied warranty that at the commencement of each stage the ship is seaworthy in respect of such preparation or equipment for the purposes of that stage.

(4) A ship is deemed to be seaworthy when she is reasonably fit in all respects to encounter the ordinary perils of the seas of the adventure insured.

(5) In a time policy there is no implied warranty that the ship shall be seaworthy at any stage of the adventure, but where, with the privity of the assured, the ship is sent to sea in an unseaworthy state, the insurer is not liable for any loss attributable to unseaworthiness.

40 No implied warranty that goods are seaworthy

(1) In a policy on goods or other moveables there is no implied warranty that the goods or moveables are seaworthy.

(2) In a voyage policy on goods or other moveables there is an implied warranty that at the commencement of the voyage the ship is not only seaworthy as a ship, but also that she is reasonably fit to carry the goods or other moveables to the destination contemplated by the policy.

41 Warranty of legality

There is an implied warranty that the adventure insured is a lawful one, and that, so far as the assured can control the matter, the adventure shall be carried out in a lawful manner.

The voyage

42 Implied condition as to commencement of risk

(1) Where the subject-matter is insured by a voyage policy 'at and from' or 'from' a particular place, it is not necessary that the ship should be at that place when the contract is concluded, but there is an implied condition that the adventure shall be commenced within a reasonable time, and that if the adventure be not so commenced the insurer may avoid the contract.

(2) The implied condition may be negatived by showing that the delay was

caused by circumstances known to the insurer before the contract was concluded, or by showing that he waived the condition.

43 Alteration of port of departure
Where the place of departure is specified by the policy, and the ship instead of sailing from that place sails from any other place, the risk does not attach.

44 Sailing for different destination
Where the destination is specified in the policy, and the ship, instead of sailing for that destination, sails for any other destination, the risk does not attach.

45 Change of voyage
(1) Where, after the commencement of the risk, the destination of the ship is voluntarily changed from the destination contemplated by the policy, there is said to be a change of voyage.
(2) Unless the policy otherwise provides, where there is a change of voyage, the insurer is discharged from liability as from the time of the change, that is to say, as from the time when the determination to change it is manifested; and it is immaterial that the ship may not have left the course of voyage contemplated by the policy when the loss occurs.

46 Deviation
(1) Where a ship, without lawful excuse, deviates from the voyage contemplated by the policy, the insurer is discharged from liability as from the time of deviation, and it is immaterial that the ship may have regained her route before any loss occurs.
(2) There is a deviation from the voyage contemplated by the policy—
(a) Where the course of the voyage is specifically designated by the policy, and that course is departed from; or
(b) Where the course of the voyage is not specifically designated by the policy, but the usual and customary course is departed from.
(3) The intention to deviate is immaterial; there must be a deviation in fact to discharge the insurer from his liability under the contract.

47 Several ports of discharge
(1) Where several ports of discharge are specified by the policy, the ship may proceed to all or any of them, but, in the absence of any usage or sufficient cause to the contrary, she must proceed to them, or such of them as she goes to, in the order designated by the policy. If she does not there is a deviation.
(2) Where the policy is to 'ports of discharge', within a given area, which are not named, the ship must, in the absence of any usage or sufficient cause to the contrary, proceed to them, or such of them as she goes to, in their geographical order. If she does not there is a deviation.

48 Delay in voyage
In the case of a voyage policy, the adventure insured must be prosecuted throughout its course with reasonable dispatch, and, if without lawful excuse it is not so prosecuted, the insurer is discharged from liability as from the time when the delay becomes unreasonable.

49 Excuses for deviation or delay
(1) Deviation or delay in prosecuting the voyage contemplated by the policy is excused—
(a) Where authorised by any special term in the policy; or
(b) Where caused by circumstances beyond the control of the master and his employer; or
(c) Where reasonably necessary in order to comply with an express or implied warranty; or

(d) Where reasonably necessary for the safety of the ship or subject-matter insured; or

(e) For the purpose of saving human life, or aiding a ship in distress where human life may be in danger; or

(f) Where reasonably necessary for the purpose of obtaining medical or surgical aid for any person on board the ship; or

(g) Where caused by the barratrous conduct of the master or crew, if barratry be one of the perils insured against.

(2) When the cause excusing the deviation or delay ceases to operate, the ship must resume her course, and prosecute her voyage, with reasonable dispatch.

Assignment of policy

50 When and how policy is assignable

(1) A marine policy is assignable unless it contains terms expressly prohibiting assignment. It may be assigned either before or after loss.

(2) Where a marine policy has been assigned so as to pass the beneficial interest in such policy, the assignee of the policy is entitled to sue thereon in his own name; and the defendant is entitled to make any defence arising out of the contract which he would have been entitled to make if the action had been brought in the name of the person by or on behalf of whom the policy was effected.

(3) A marine policy may be assigned by indorsement thereon or in other customary manner.

51 Assured who has no interest cannot assign

Where the assured has parted with or lost his interest in the subject-matter insured, and has not, before or at the time of so doing, expressly or impliedly agreed to assign the policy, any subsequent assignment of the policy is inoperative:

Provided that nothing in this section affects the assignment of a policy after loss.

The premium

52 When premium payable

Unless otherwise agreed, the duty of the assured or his agent to pay the premium, and the duty of the insurer to issue the policy to the assured or his agent, are concurrent conditions, and the insurer is not bound to issue the policy until payment or tender of the premium.

53 Policy effected through broker

(1) Unless otherwise agreed, where a marine policy is effected on behalf of the assured by a broker, the broker is directly responsible to the insurer for the premium, and the insurer is directly responsible to the assured for the amount which may be payable in respect of losses, or in respect of returnable premium.

(2) Unless otherwise agreed, the broker has, as against the assured, a lien upon the policy for the amount of the premium and his charges in respect of effecting the policy; and, where he has dealt with the person who employs him as a principal, he has also a lien on the policy in respect of any balance on any insurance account which may be due to him from such person, unless when the debt was incurred he had reason to believe that such person was only an agent.

54 Effect of receipt on policy

Where a marine policy effected on behalf of the assured by a broker acknowledges the receipt of the premium, such acknowledgement is, in the absence of fraud, conclusive as between the insurer and the assured, but not as between the insurer and broker.

Loss and abandonment

55 Included and excluded losses

(1) Subject to the provisions of this Act, and unless the policy otherwise provides, the insurer is liable for any loss proximately caused by a peril insured against, but, subject as aforesaid, he is not liable for any loss which is not proximately caused by a peril insured against.

(2) In particular,—

(a) The insurer is not liable for any loss attributable to the wilful misconduct of the assured, but, unless the policy otherwise provides, he is liable for any loss proximately caused by a peril insured against, even though the loss would not have happened but for the misconduct or negligence of the master or crew;

(b) Unless the policy otherwise provides, the insurer on ship or goods is not liable for any loss proximately caused by delay, although the delay be caused by a peril insured against.

(c) Unless the policy otherwise provides, the insurer is not liable for ordinary wear and tear, ordinary leakage and breakage, inherent vice or nature of the subject-matter insured, or for any loss proximately caused by rats or vermin, or for any injury to machinery not proximately caused by maritime perils.

56 Partial and total loss

(1) A loss may be either total or partial. Any loss other than a total loss, as hereinafter defined, is a partial loss.

(2) A total loss may be either an actual total loss, or a constructive total loss.

(3) Unless a different intention appears from the terms of the policy, an insurance against total loss includes a constructive, as well as an actual, total loss.

(4) Where the assured brings an action for a total loss and the evidence proves only a partial loss, he may, unless the policy otherwise provides, recover for a partial loss.

(5) Where goods reach their destination in specie, but by reason of obliteration of marks, or otherwise, they are incapable of identification, the loss, if any, is partial, and not total.

57 Actual total loss

(1) Where the subject-matter insured is destroyed, or so damaged as to cease to be a thing of the kind insured, or where the assured is irretrievably deprived thereof, there is an actual total loss.

(2) In the case of an actual total loss no notice of abandonment need be given.

58 Missing ship

Where the ship concerned in the adventure is missing, and after the lapse of a reasonable time no news of her has been received, an actual total loss may be presumed.

59 Effect of transhipment, etc

Where, by a peril insured against, the voyage is interrupted at any intermediate port or place, under such circumstances as, apart from any special stipulation in the contract of affreightment, to justify the master in landing and re-shipping the goods or other moveables, or in transhipping them, and sending them on to their destination, the liability of the insurer continues, notwithstanding the landing or transhipment.

60 Constructive total loss defined

(1) Subject to any express provision in the policy, there is a constructive total loss where the subject-matter insured is reasonably abandoned on account of its total loss appearing to be unavoidable, or because it could not be preserved from actual total loss without an expenditure which would exceed its value when the expenditure had been incurred.

(2) In particular, there is a constructive total loss—

(i) Where the assured is deprived of the possession of his ship or goods by a peril insured against, and (a) it is unlikely that he can recover the ship or goods, as the case may be, or (b) the cost of recovering the ship or goods, as the case may be, would exceed their value when recovered; or

(ii) In the case of damage to a ship, where she is so damaged by a peril insured against that the cost of repairing the damage would exceed the value of the ship when repaired.

In estimating the cost of repairs, no deduction is to be made in respect of general average contributions to those repairs payable by other interests, but account is to be taken of the expense of future salvage operations and of any future general average contributions to which the ship would be liable if repaired; or

(iii) In the case of damage to goods, where the cost of repairing the damage and forwarding the goods to their destination would exceed their value on arrival.

61 Effect of constructive total loss

Where there is a constructive total loss the assured may either treat the loss as a partial loss, or abandon the subject-matter insured to the insurer and treat the loss as if it were an actual total loss.

62 Notice of abandonment

(1) Subject to the provisions of this section, where the assured elects to abandon the subject-matter insured to the insurer, he must give notice of the abandonment. If he fails to do so the loss can only be treated as a partial loss.

(2) Notice of abandonment may be given in writing, or by word of mouth, or partly in writing and partly by word of mouth, and may be given in terms which indicate the intention of the assured to abandon his insured interest in the subject-matter insured unconditionally to the insurer.

(3) Notice of abandonment must be given with reasonable diligence after the receipt of reliable information of the loss, but where the information is of a doubtful character the assured is entitled to a reasonable time to make inquiry.

(4) Where notice of abandonment is properly given, the rights of the assured are not prejudiced by the fact that the insurer refuses to accept the abandonment.

(5) The acceptance of an abandonment may be either express or implied from the conduct of the insurer. The mere silence of the insurer after notice is not an acceptance.

(6) Where a notice of abandonment is accepted the abandonment is irrevocable. The acceptance of the notice conclusively admits liability for the loss and the sufficiency of the notice.

(7) Notice of abandonment is unnecessary where, at the time when the assured receives information of the loss, there would be no possibility of benefit to the insurer if notice were given to him.

(8) Notice of abandonment may be waived by the insurer.

(9) Where an insurer has re-insured his risk, no notice of abandonment need be given by him.

63 Effect of abandonment

(1) Where there is a valid abandonment the insurer is entitled to take over the interest of the assured in whatever may remain of the subject-matter insured, and all proprietary rights incidental thereto.

(2) Upon the abandonment of a ship, the insurer thereof is entitled to any freight in course of being earned, and which is earned by her subsequent to the casualty causing the loss, less the expenses of earning it incurred after the casualty; and, where a ship is carrying the owner's goods, the insurer is entitled to a

reasonable remuneration for the carriage of them subsequent to the casualty causing the loss.

Partial losses (including salvage and general average and particular charges)

64 Particular average loss

(1) A particular average loss is a partial loss of the subject-matter insured, caused by a peril insured against, and which is not a general average loss.

(2) Expenses incurred by or on behalf of the assured for the safety or preservation of the subject-matter insured, other than general average and salvage charges, are called particular charges. Particular charges are not included in particular average.

65 Salvage charges

(1) Subject to any express provision in the policy, salvage charges incurred in preventing a loss by perils insured against may be recovered as a loss by those perils.

(2) 'Salvage charges' means the charges recoverable under maritime law by a salvor independently of contract. They do not include the expenses of services in the nature of salvage rendered by the assured or his agents, or any person employed for hire by them, for the purpose of averting a peril insured against. Such expenses, where properly incurred, may be recovered as particular charges or as a general average loss, according to the circumstances under which they were incurred.

66 General average loss

(1) A general average loss is a loss caused by or directly consequential on a general average act. It includes a general average expenditure as well as a general average sacrifice.

(2) There is a general average act where any extraordinary sacrifice or expenditure is voluntarily and reasonably made or incurred in the time of peril for the purpose of preserving the property imperilled in the common adventure.

(3) Where there is a general average loss, the party on whom it falls is entitled, subject to the conditions imposed by maritime law, to a rateable contribution from the other parties interested, and such contribution is called a general average contribution.

(4) Subject to any express provision in the policy, where the assured has incurred a general average expenditure, he may recover from the insurer in respect of the proportion of the loss which falls upon him; and, in the case of a general average sacrifice, he may recover from the insurer in respect of the whole loss without having enforced his right of contribution from the other parties liable to contribute.

(5) Subject to any express provision in the policy, where the assured has paid, or is liable to pay, a general average contribution in respect of the subject insured, he may recover therefor from the insurer.

(6) In the absence of express stipulation, the insurer is not liable for any general average loss or contribution where the loss was not incurred for the purpose of avoiding, or in connexion with the avoidance of, a peril insured against.

(7) Where ship, freight, and cargo, or any two of those interests, are owned by the same assured, the liability of the insurer in respect of general average losses or contributions is to be determined as if those subjects were owned by different persons.

Measure of indemnity

67 Extent of liability of insurer for loss

(1) The sum which the assured can recover in respect of a loss on a policy by which he is insured, in the case of an unvalued policy to the full extent of the

insurable value, or in the case of a valued policy to the full extent of the value fixed by the policy, is called the measure of indemnity.

(2) Where there is a loss recoverable under the policy, the insurer, or each insurer if there be more than one, is liable for such proportion of the measure of indemnity as the amount of his subscription bears to the value fixed by the policy in the case of a valued policy, or to the insurable value in the case of an unvalued policy.

68 Total loss

Subject to the provisions of this Act and to any express provision in the policy, where there is a total loss of the subject-matter insured,—

(1) If the policy be a valued policy, the measure of indemnity is the sum fixed by the policy.

(2) If the policy be an unvalued policy, the measure of indemnity is the insurable value of the subject-matter insured.

69 Partial loss of ship

Where a ship is damaged, but not totally lost, the measure of indemnity, subject to any express provision in the policy, is as follows:—

(1) Where the ship has been repaired, the assured is entitled to the reasonable cost of the repairs, less the customary deductions, but not exceeding the sum insured in respect of any one casualty.

(2) Where the ship has been only partially repaired, the assured is entitled to the reasonable cost of such repairs, computed as above, and also to be indemnified for the reasonable depreciation, if any, arising from the unrepaired damage, provided that the aggregate amount shall not exceed the cost of repairing the whole damage, computed as above.

(3) Where the ship has not been repaired, and has not been sold in her damaged state during the risk, the assured is entitled to be indemnified for the reasonable depreciation arising from the unrepaired damage, but not exceeding the reasonable cost of repairing such damage, computed as above.

70 Partial loss of freight

Subject to any express provision in the policy, where there is a partial loss of freight, the measure of indemnity is such proportion of the sum fixed by the policy in the case of a valued policy, or of the insurable value in the case of an unvalued policy, as the proportion of freight lost by the assured bears to the whole freight at the risk of the assured under the policy.

71 Partial loss of goods, merchandise, etc

Where there is a partial loss of goods, merchandise, or other moveables, the measure of indemnity, subject to any express provision in the policy, is as follows:—

(1) Where part of the goods, merchandise, or other moveables insured by a valued policy is totally lost, the measure of indemnity is such proportion of the sum fixed by the policy as the insurable value of the part lost bears to the insurable value of the whole, ascertained as in the case of an unvalued policy.

(2) Where part of the goods, merchandise, or other moveables insured by an unvalued policy is totally lost, the measure of indemnity is the insurable value of the part lost, ascertained as in the case of total loss.

(3) Where the whole or any part of the goods or merchandise insured has been delivered damaged at its destination, the measure of indemnity is such proportion of the sum fixed by the policy in the case of a valued policy, or of the insurable value in the case of an unvalued policy, as the difference between the gross sound and damaged values at the place of arrival bears to the gross sound value.

(4) 'Gross value' means the wholesale price or, if there be no such price, the estimated value, with, in either case, freight, landing charges, and duty paid beforehand; provided that, in the case of goods or merchandise customarily sold in

bond, the bonded price is deemed to be the gross value. 'Gross proceeds' means the actual price obtained at a sale where all charges on sale are paid by the sellers.

72 Apportionment of valuation

(1) Where different species of property are insured under a single valuation, the valuation must be apportioned over the different species in proportion to their respective insurable values, as in the case of an unvalued policy. The insured value of any part of a species is such proportion of the total insured value of the same as the insurable value of the part bears to the insurable value of the whole, ascertained in both cases as provided by this Act.

(2) Where a valuation has to be apportioned, and particulars of the prime cost of each separate species, quality, or description of goods cannot be ascertained, the division of the valuation may be made over the net arrived sound values of the different species, qualities, or descriptions of goods.

73 General average contributions and salvage charges

(1) Subject to any express provision in the policy, where the assured has paid, or is liable for, any general average contribution, the measure of indemnity is the full amount of such contribution, if the subject-matter liable to contribution is insured for its full contributory value; but, if such subject-matter be not insured for its full contributory value, or if only part of it be insured, the indemnity payable by the insurer must be reduced in proportion to the under insurance, and where there has been a particular average loss which constitutes a deduction from the contributory value, and for which the insurer is liable, that amount must be deducted from the insured value in order to ascertain what the insurer is liable to contribute.

(2) Where the insurer is liable for salvage charges the extent of his liability must be determined on the like principle.

74 Liabilities to third parties

Where the assured has effected an insurance in express terms against any liability to a third party, the measure of indemnity, subject to any express provision in the policy, is the amount paid or payable by him to such third party in respect of such liability.

75 General provisions as to measure of indemnity

(1) Where there has been a loss in respect of any subject-matter not expressly provided for in the foregoing provisions of this Act, the measure of indemnity shall be ascertained, as nearly as may be, in accordance with those provisions, in so far as applicable to the particular case.

(2) Nothing in the provisions of this Act relating to the measure of indemnity shall affect the rules relating to double insurance, or prohibit the insurer from disproving interest wholly or in part, or from showing that at the time of the loss the whole or any part of the subject-matter insured was not at risk under the policy.

76 Particular average warranties

(1) Where the subject-matter insured is warranted free from particular average, the assured cannot recover for a loss of part, other than a loss incurred by a general average sacrifice, unless the contract contained in the policy be apportionable; but, if the contract be apportionable, the assured may recover for a total loss of any apportionable part.

(2) Where the subject-matter insured is warranted free from particular average, either wholly or under a certain percentage, the insurer is nevertheless liable for salvage charges, and for particular charges and other expenses properly incurred pursuant to the provisions of the suing and labouring clause in order to avert a loss insured against.

(3) Unless the policy otherwise provides, where the subject-matter is warranted

free from particular average under a specified percentage, a general average loss cannot be added to a particular average loss to make up the specified percentage.

(4) For the purpose of ascertaining whether the specified percentage has been reached, regard shall be had only to the actual loss suffered by the subject-matter insured. Particular charges and the expenses of and incidental to ascertaining and proving the loss must be excluded.

77 Successive losses

(1) Unless the policy otherwise provides, and subject to the provisions of this Act, the insurer is liable for successive losses, even though the total amount of such losses may exceed the sum insured.

(2) Where, under the same policy, a partial loss, which has not been repaired or otherwise made good, is followed by a total loss, the assured can only recover in respect of the total loss:

Provided that nothing in this section shall affect the liability of the insurer under the suing and labouring clause.

78 Suing and labouring clause

(1) Where the policy contains a suing and labouring clause, the engagement thereby entered into is deemed to be supplementary to the contract of insurance, and the assured may recover from the insurer any expenses properly incurred pursuant to the clause, notwithstanding that the insurer may have paid for a total loss, or that the subject-matter may have been warranted free from particular average, either wholly or under a certain percentage.

(2) General average losses and contributions and salvage charges, as defined by this Act, are not recoverable under the suing and labouring clause.

(3) Expenses incurred for the purpose of averting or diminishing any loss not covered by the policy are not recoverable under the suing and labouring clause.

(4) It is the duty of the assured and his agents, in all cases, to take such measures as may be reasonable for the purpose of averting or minimising a loss.

Rights of insurer on payment

79 Right of subrogation

(1) Where the insurer pays for a total loss, either of the whole, or in the case of goods of any apportionable part, of the subject-matter insured, he thereupon becomes entitled to take over the interest of the assured in whatever may remain of the subject-matter so paid for, and he is thereby subrogated to all the rights and remedies of the assured in and in respect of that subject-matter as from the time of the casualty causing the loss.

(2) Subject to the foregoing provisions, where the insurer pays for a partial loss, he acquires no title to the subject-matter insured, or such part of it as may remain, but he is thereupon subrogated to all rights and remedies of the assured in and in respect of the subject-matter insured as from the time of the casualty causing the loss, in so far as the assured has been indemnified, according to this Act, by such payment for the loss.

80 Right of contribution

(1) Where the assured is over-insured by double insurance, each insurer is bound, as between himself and the other insurers, to contribute rateably to the loss in proportion to the amount for which he is liable under his contract.

(2) If any insurer pays more than his proportion of the loss, he is entitled to maintain an action for contribution against the other insurers, and is entitled to the like remedies as a surety who has paid more than his proportion of the debt.

81 Effect of under insurance

Where the assured is insured for an amount less than the insurable value or, in the case of a valued policy, for an amount less than the policy valuation, he is deemed to be his own insurer in respect of the uninsured balance.

Return of premium

82 Enforcement of return

Where the premium or a proportionate part thereof is, by this Act, declared to be returnable,—

(a) If already paid, it may be recovered by the assured from the insurer; and

(b) If unpaid, it may be retained by the assured or his agent.

83 Return by agreement

Where the policy contains a stipulation for the return of the premium, or a proportionate part thereof, on the happening of a certain event, and that event happens, the premium, or, as the case may be, the proportionate part thereof, is thereupon returnable to the assured.

84 Return for failure of consideration

(1) Where the consideration for the payment of the premium totally fails, and there has been no fraud or illegality on the part of the assured or his agents, the premium is thereupon returnable to the assured.

(2) Where the consideration for the payment of the premium is apportionable and there is a total failure of any apportionable part of the consideration, a proportionate part of the premium is, under the like conditions, thereupon returnable to the assured.

(3) In particular—

(a) Where the policy is void, or is avoided by the insurer as from the commencement of the risk, the premium is returnable, provided that there has been no fraud or illegality on the part of the assured; but if the risk is not apportionable, and has once attached, the premium is not returnable;

(b) Where the subject-matter insured, or part thereof, has never been imperilled, the premium, or, as the case may be, a proportionate part thereof, is returnable:

Provided that where the subject-matter has been insured 'lost or not lost' and has arrived in safety at the time when the contract is concluded, the premium is not returnable unless, at such time, the insurer knew of the safe arrival.

(c) Where the assured has no insurable interest throughout the currency of the risk, the premium is returnable, provided that this rule does not apply to a policy effected by way of gaming or wagering;

(d) Where the assured has a defeasible interest which is terminated during the currency of the risk, the premium is not returnable;

(e) Where the assured has over-insured under an unvalued policy, a proportionate part of the premium is returnable;

(f) Subject to the foregoing provisions, where the assured has over-insured by double insurance, a proportionate part of the several premiums is returnable:

Provided that, if the policies are effected at different times, and any earlier policy has at any time borne the entire risk, or if a claim has been paid on the policy in respect of the full sum insured thereby, no premium is returnable in respect of that policy, and when the double insurance is effected knowingly by the assured no premium is returnable.

Mutual insurance

85 Modification of Act in case of mutual insurance

(1) Where two or more persons mutually agree to insure each other against marine losses there is said to be a mutual insurance.

(2) The provisions of this Act relating to the premium do not apply to mutual

insurance, but a guarantee, or such other arrangement as may be agreed upon, may be substituted for the premium.

(3) The provisions of this Act, in so far as they may be modified by the agreement of the parties, may in the case of mutual insurance be modified by the terms of the policies issued by the association, or by the rules and regulations of the association.

(4) Subject to the exceptions mentioned in this section, the provisions of this Act apply to a mutual insurance.

Supplemental

86 Ratification by assured

Where a contract of marine insurance is in good faith effected by one person on behalf of another, the person on whose behalf it is effected may ratify the contract even after he is aware of a loss.

87 Implied obligations varied by agreement or usage

(1) Where any right, duty, or liability would arise under a contract of marine insurance by implication of law, it may be negatived or varied by express agreement or by usage, if the usage be such as to bind both parties to the contract.

(2) The provisions of this section extend to any right, duty, or liability declared by this Act which may be lawfully modified by agreement.

88 Reasonable time, etc, a question of fact

Where by this Act any reference is made to reasonable time, reasonable premium, or reasonable diligence, the question what is reasonable is a question of fact.

89 Slip as evidence

Where there is a duly stamped policy, reference may be made, as heretofore, to the slip or covering note, in any legal proceeding.

90 Interpretation of terms

In this Act, unless the context or subject-matter otherwise requires,—

'Action' includes counter-claim and set off:

'Freight' includes the profit derivable by a shipowner from the employment of his ship to carry his own goods or moveables, as well as freight payable by a third party, but does not include passage money:

'Moveables' means any moveable tangible property, other than the ship, and includes money, valuable securities, and other documents:

'Policy' means a marine policy.

91 Savings

(1) Nothing in this Act, or in any repeal effected thereby, shall affect—

(a) The provisions of the Stamp Act 1891, or any enactment for the time being in force relating to the revenue;

(b) The provisions of the Companies Act 1862, or any enactment amending or substituted for the same;

(c) The provisions of any statute not expressly repealed by this Act.

(2) The rules of the common law including the law merchant, save in so far as they are inconsistent with the express provisions of this Act, shall continue to apply to contracts of marine insurance.

[. . .]

94 Short title

This Act may be cited as the Marine Insurance Act 1906.

SCHEDULES

SCHEDULE 1
FORM OF POLICY

Section 30

Be it known that .. .. .. as well in .. .. own name as for and in the name and names of all and every other person or persons to whom the same doth, may, or shall appertain, in part or in all doth make assurance and cause .. .. and them, and every of them, to be insured lost or not lost, at and from .. ..

Upon any kind of goods and merchandises, and also upon the body, tackle, apparel, ordnance, munition, artillery, boat, and other furniture, of and in the good ship or vessel called the .. .. whereof is master under God, for this present voyage, ... or whosoever else shall go for master in the said ship, or by whatsoever other name or names the said ship, or the master thereof, is or shall be named or called; beginning the adventure upon the said goods and merchandises from the loading thereof aboard the said ship, ... upon the said ship, ... etc and so shall continue and endure, during her abode there, upon the said ship, etc. And further, until the said ship, with all her ordnance, tackle, apparel, etc, and goods and merchandises whatsoever shall be arrived at .. .. upon the said ship, etc, until she hath moored at anchor for twenty-four hours in good safety; and upon the goods and merchandises, until the same be there discharged and safely landed. And it shall be lawful for the said ship, etc, in this voyage, to proceed and sail to and touch and stay at any ports or places whatsoever without prejudice to this insurance. The said ship, etc, goods and merchandises, etc, for so much as concerns the assured by agreement between the assured and assurers in this policy, are and shall be valued at .. ..

Touching the adventures and perils which we the assurers are contented to bear and do take upon us in this voyage: they are of the seas, men of war, fire, enemies, pirates, rovers, thieves, jettisons, letters of mart and countermart, surprisals, takings at sea, arrests, restraints, and detainments of all kings, princes, and people, of what nation, condition, or quality soever, barratry of the master and mariners, and of all other perils, losses, and misfortunes, that have or shall come to the hurt, detriment, or damage of the said goods and merchandises, and ship, etc, or any part thereof. And in case of any loss or misfortune it shall be lawful to the assured, their factors, servants and assigns, to sue, labour, and travel for, in and about the defence, safeguards, and recovery of the said goods and merchandises, and ship, etc, or any part thereof, without prejudice to this insurance; to the charges whereof we, the assurers, will contribute each one according to the rate and quantity of his sum herein assured. And it is especially declared and agreed that no acts of the insurer or insured in recovering, saving, or preserving the property insured shall be considered as a waiver, or acceptance of abandonment. And it is agreed by us, the insurers, that this writing or policy of assurance shall be of as much force and effect as the surest writing or policy of assurance heretofore made in Lombard Street, or in the Royal Exchange, or elsewhere in London. And so we, the assurers, are contented, and do hereby promise and bind ourselves, each one for his own part, our heirs, executors, and goods to the assured, their executors, administrators, and assigns, for the true performance of the premises, confessing ourselves paid the consideration due unto us for this assurance by the assured, at and after the rate of .. ..

In Witness whereof we, the assurers, have subscribed our names and sums assured in London.

N.B.—Corn, fish, salt, fruit, flour, and seed are warranted free from average, unless general, or the ship be stranded—sugar, tobacco, hemp, flax, hides and skins are warranted free from average, under five pounds per cent, and all other goods, also the ship and freight, are warranted free from average, under three pounds per cent unless general, or the ship be stranded.

Rules for construction of policy

The following are the rules referred to by this Act for the construction of a policy in the above or other like form, where the context does not otherwise require:—

1 Where the subject-matter is insured 'lost or not lost', and the loss has occurred before the contract is concluded, the risk attaches, unless at such time the assured was aware of the loss, and the insurer was not.

2 Where the subject-matter is insured 'from' a particular place, the risk does not attach until the ship starts on the voyage insured.

3 (a) Where a ship is insured 'at and from' a particular place, and she is at that place in good safety when the contract is concluded, the risk attaches immediately.

(b) If she be not at that place when the contract is concluded, the risk attaches as soon as she arrives there in good safety, and, unless the policy otherwise provides, it is immaterial that she is covered by another policy for a specified time after arrival.

(c) Where chartered freight is insured 'at and from' a particular place, and the ship is at that place in good safety when the contract is concluded the risk attaches immediately. If she be not there when the contract is concluded, the risk attaches as soon as she arrives there in good safety.

(d) Where freight, other than chartered freight, is payable without special conditions and is insured 'at and from' a particular place, the risk attaches pro rata as the goods or merchandise are shipped; provided that if there be cargo in readiness which belongs to the shipowner, or which some other person has contracted with him to ship, the risk attaches as soon as the ship is ready to receive such cargo.

4 Where goods or other moveables are insured 'from the loading thereof', the risk does not attach until such goods or moveables are actually on board, and the insurer is not liable for them while in transit from shore to ship.

5 Where the risk on goods or other moveables continues until they are 'safely landed', they must be landed in the customary manner and within a reasonable time after arrival at the port of discharge, and if they are not so landed the risk ceases.

6 In the absence of any further license or usage, the liberty to touch and stay 'at any port or place whatsoever' does not authorise the ship to depart from the course of her voyage from the port of departure to the port of destination.

7 The term 'perils of the seas' refers only to fortuitous accidents or casualties of the seas. It does not include the ordinary action of the winds and waves.

8 The term 'pirates' includes passengers who mutiny and rioters who attack the ship from the shore.

9 The term 'thieves' does not cover clandestine theft or a theft committed by anyone of the ship's company, whether crew or passengers.

10 The term 'arrests, etc, of kings, princes, and people' refers to political or executive acts, and does not include a loss caused by riot or by ordinary judicial process.

11 The term 'barratry' includes every wrongful act wilfully committed by the master or crew to the prejudice of the owner, or, as the case may be, the charterer.

12 The term 'all other perils' includes only perils similar in kind to the perils specifically mentioned in the policy.

13 The term 'average unless general' means a partial loss of the subject-matter insured other than a general average loss, and does not include 'particular charges'.

14 Where the ship has stranded, the insurer is liable for the excepted losses, although the loss is not attributable to the stranding, provided that when the stranding takes place the risk has attached and, if the policy be on goods, that the damaged goods are on board.

15 The term 'ship' includes the hull, materials and outfit, stores and provisions for the officers and crew, and, in the case of vessels engaged in a special trade, the ordinary fittings requisite for the trade, and also, in the case of a steamship, the machinery, boilers, and coals and engine stores, if owned by the assured.

16 The term 'freight' includes the profit derivable by a shipowner from the employment of his ship to carry his own goods or moveables, as well as freight payable by a third party, but does not include passage money.

17 The term 'goods' means goods in the nature of merchandise, and does not include personal effects or provisions and stores for use on board. In the absence of any usage to the contrary, deck cargo and living animals must be insured specifically, and not under the general denomination of goods.

LIMITED PARTNERSHIPS ACT 1907
(7 Edw 7, c 24)

3 Interpretation of terms

[*(1)*] In the construction of this Act the following words and expressions shall have the meanings respectively assigned to them in this section, unless there be something in the subject or context repugnant to such construction:—

[*'authorised corporate service provider' has the same meaning as in the Companies Act 2006 (see section 1098A of that Act);*]

[*'body corporate' has the same meaning as in the Companies Acts (see section 1173 of the Companies Act 2006);*]

[*'corporate managing officer' means a managing officer that is a legal entity;*]

[*'the court' has the same meaning as in the Companies Acts (see section 1156 of the Companies Act 2006);*]

'Firm,' 'firm name,' and 'business' have the same meanings as in the Partnership Act 1890;

[*'the Gazette' means—*

(a) as respects limited partnerships registered in England and Wales, the London Gazette,

(b) as respects limited partnerships registered in Scotland, the Edinburgh Gazette, and

(c) as respects limited partnerships registered in Northern Ireland, the Belfast Gazette;]

'General partner' shall mean any partner who is not a limited partner as defined by this Act.

[*'legal entity' means a body corporate or other entity that (in each case) is a legal person under the law by which it is governed;*]

[*'limited partnership' means a firm that is registered as a limited partnership under this Act (for the only circumstances in which a firm can cease to be registered as a limited partnership under this Act while remaining a firm see section 26 (voluntary deregistration));*]

[*'managing officer'—*

(a) in relation to a company, means a director or shadow director;

(b) in relation to a legal entity the affairs of which are managed by some or all of its members, means one of those members;

(c) in relation to any other legal entity, means an officer of the entity whose functions correspond to that of a director of a company;]

['Private fund limited partnership' means a limited partnership that is designated under section 8(2) as a private fund limited partnership;]

[*'the register of limited partnerships' means the records kept by the registrar under section 1080 of the Companies Act 2006 relating to limited partnerships;*]

[*'service address' has the same meaning as in the Companies Acts (see section 1141(1) and (2) of the Companies Act 2006).*]

[*(2) For the purposes of the definition of 'managing officer' in subsection (1), 'director' and 'shadow director' have the same meanings as in the Companies Acts (see sections 250 and 251 of the Companies Act 2006).*

(3) In this section 'the Companies Acts' has the meaning given by section 2(1) of the Companies Act 2006.]

[*(4) Section 1125 of the Companies Act 2006 (meaning of 'daily default fine') applies for the purpose of any provision made by this Act as it applies for the purposes of provisions of the Companies Acts.*]

4 Definition and constitution of limited partnership

(1) [. . .] Limited partnerships may be formed in the manner and subject to the conditions by this Act provided.

(2) A limited partnership [. . .] must consist of one or more persons called general partners, who shall be liable for all debts and obligations of the firm [*(including debts and obligations incurred in accordance with section 38 of the Partnership Act 1890)*], and one or more persons to be called limited partners [. . .]

[(2A) Each limited partner in a limited partnership that is not a private fund limited partnership shall, at the time of entering into the partnership, contribute to the partnership a sum or sums as capital or property valued at a stated amount, and shall not be liable for the debts or obligations of the firm [*(including debts and obligations incurred in accordance with section 38 of the Partnership Act 1890)*] beyond the amount so contributed.

(2B) A limited partner in a private fund limited partnership—

(a) is under no obligation to contribute any capital or property to the partnership unless otherwise agreed between the partners, and

(b) is not liable for the debts or obligations of the firm [*(including debts or obligations incurred in accordance with section 38 of the Partnership Act 1890)*] beyond the amount of the partnership property which is available to the general partners to meet such debts or obligations.]

(3) [Subject to subsection (3A), a limited partner] shall not during the continuance of the partnership, either directly or indirectly, draw out or receive back any part of his contribution, and if he does so draw out or receive back any such part shall be liable for the debts and obligations of the firm up to the amount so drawn out or received back.

[(3A) In the case of a limited partner in a private fund limited partnership—

(a) where the limited partnership was registered on or after 6th April 2017, subsection (3) does not apply;

(b) where the limited partnership was registered before 6th April 2017, subsection (3) applies only in relation to the amount of any contribution made by the limited partner when the limited partnership was not a private fund limited partnership.]

(4) A body corporate may be a limited partner.

5 Registration of limited partnership required

Every limited partnership must be registered as such in accordance with the provisions of this Act [. . .].

[*Application of other laws to limited partnerships*]

6 Modifications of general law in case of limited partnerships

(1) A limited partner shall not take part in the management of the partnership business, and shall not have power to bind the firm:

Provided that a limited partner may by himself or his agent at any time inspect the books of the firm and examine into the state and prospects of the partnership business, and may advise with the partners thereon.

If a limited partner takes part in the management of the partnership business he shall be liable for all debts and obligations of the firm [*(including debts and obligations incurred in accordance with section 38 of the Partnership Act 1890)*] incurred while he so takes part in the management as though he were a general partner.

[(1A) Section 6A (actions by limited partners) makes provision supplementing subsection (1).]

(2) A limited partnership shall not be dissolved by the death [. . .] of a limited partner, and the lunacy of a limited partner shall not be a ground for dissolution of the partnership by the court unless the lunatic's share cannot be otherwise ascertained and realised.

[*(2A) A limited partnership shall not be dissolved under section 33(1) of the Partnership Act 1890 by the bankruptcy of a partner.*

(2B) A limited partnership is dissolved if—

(a) it ceases to have any general partners,

(b) it ceases to have any limited partners, or

(c) each general partner is either insolvent or disqualified under the directors disqualification legislation (see section 8J(3)), irrespective of whether they became insolvent or disqualified before or after this subsection comes into force.]

[. . .]

[[*(3A) If a limited partnership is dissolved at a time when the partnership has at least one general partner who is—*

(a) solvent, and

(b) not disqualified under the directors disqualification legislation,

the general partners at that time who are solvent and are not so disqualified must either wind up the partnership's affairs or take all reasonable steps to ensure that its affairs are wound up by a person who is not a partner at that time.

(3B) If a limited partnership is dissolved at a time when the partnership does not have a general partner who is—

(a) solvent, and

(b) not disqualified under the directors disqualification legislation,

the limited partners at that time who are solvent must take all reasonable steps to ensure that the partnership's affairs are wound up by a person who is not a limited partner at that time.

(3BA) For enforcement of the duties under subsections (3A) and (3B) see section 29.]

[. . .]

(3D) Subsections (3A) and (3B) have effect subject to any order of the court as to the winding up of the affairs of the partnership.]

[. . .]

(5) Subject to any agreement expressed or implied between the partners—

(a) Any difference arising as to ordinary matters connected with the partnership business may be decided by a majority of the general partners;

(b) A limited partner may, with the consent of the general partners, assign his share in the partnership, and upon such an assignment the assignee shall become a limited partner with all the rights of the assignor;

(c) The other partners shall not be entitled to dissolve the partnership by reason of any limited partner suffering his share to be charged for his separate debt;

(d) A person may be introduced as a partner without the consent of the existing limited partners;

(e) A limited partner shall not be entitled to dissolve the partnership by notice.

[(f) A limited partner in a private fund limited partnership is not subject to the duties in—

(i) section 28 of the Partnership Act 1890(3) (duty of partners to render accounts, etc), or

(ii) section 30 of that Act (duty of partner not to compete with firm).]

[(6) Section 36(1) of the Partnership Act 1890 (rights of persons dealing with firm against apparent members of firm) does not apply where a partner in a private fund limited partnership ceases to be a member of the firm.]

[6A [. . .] actions by limited partners

[*(A1) A limited partner in a limited partnership is not to be regarded as taking part in the management of the partnership business for the purposes of section 6(1) merely because the limited partner appoints a person to wind up the limited partnership pursuant to section 6(3B).*]

(1) A limited partner in a private fund limited partnership is not to be regarded as taking part in the management of the partnership business for the purposes of section 6(1) merely because the limited partner takes any action listed in subsection (2).

(2) The actions are—

(a) taking part in a decision about—

(i) the variation of, or waiver of a term of, the partnership agreement or associated documents;

(ii) whether the general nature of the partnership business should change;

(iii) whether a person should become or cease to be a partner;

(iv) whether the partnership should end or the term of the partnership should be extended;

[. . .]

(c) enforcing an entitlement under the partnership agreement, provided that the entitlement does not involve a limited partner taking part in the management of the partnership business;

(d) entering into, or acting under, a contract with the other partners in the partnership, provided that the contract does not require, or the action under the contract does not involve, a limited partner taking part in the management of the partnership business;

(e) providing surety or acting as guarantor for the partnership;

(f) approving the accounts of the partnership;

(g) reviewing or approving a valuation of the partnership's assets;

(h) discussing the prospects of the partnership business;

(i) consulting or advising with a general partner or any person appointed to manage or advise the partnership about the affairs of the partnership or about its accounts;

(j) taking part in a decision regarding changes in the persons responsible for the day-to-day management of the partnership;

(k) acting, or authorising a representative to act, as a director, member, employee, officer or agent of, or a shareholder or partner in—

(i) a general partner in the partnership; or

(ii) another person appointed to manage or advise the partnership in relation to the affairs of the partnership,

provided that this does not involve a limited partner taking part in the management of the partnership business or authorising a representative to take any action that would involve taking part in the management of the partnership business if taken by a limited partner;

(l) appointing or nominating a person to represent the limited partner on a committee, authorising such a person to take any action in that capacity that would not involve taking part in the management of the partnership business if taken by the limited partner, or revoking such an appointment or nomination;

(m) taking part in a decision about how the partnership should exercise any right as an investor in another collective investment scheme as defined in section 8D(4) ('master fund'), provided that the partnership's exercise of the right would not cause the partnership to be liable for the debts or obligations of the master fund beyond the amount contributed, or agreed to be contributed, by the partnership to the master fund;

(n) taking part in a decision approving or authorising an action proposed to be taken by a general partner or another person appointed to manage the partnership, including in particular a proposal in relation to—

(i) the disposal of all or part of the partnership business or the acquisition of another business by the partnership;

(ii) the acquisition or disposal of a type of investment or a particular investment by the partnership;

(iii) the exercise of the partnership's rights in respect of an investment;

(iv) the participation by a limited partner in a particular investment by the partnership;

(v) the incurring, extension, variation or discharge of debt by the partnership;

(vi) the creation, extension, variation or discharge of any other obligation owed by the partnership.

(3) The fact that a decision that affects or relates to a private fund limited partnership involves an actual or potential conflict of interest is not of itself a reason to regard a limited partner in the partnership who takes part in the decision as taking part in the management of the partnership business for the purposes of section 6(1).

(4) Nothing in this section—

(a) limits the circumstances in which a limited partner in a [. . .] limited partnership is not to be regarded as taking part in the management of the partnership business;

[. . .]

[*(5) Nothing in subsections (1) to (3) affects the circumstances in which a limited partner in a limited partnership that is not a private fund limited partnership may be regarded as taking part in the management of the partnership business.*]

7 Law as to private partnerships to apply where not excluded by this Act
Subject to the provisions of this Act, the Partnership Act 1890, and the rules of equity and of common law applicable to partnerships, except so far as they are inconsistent with the express provisions of the last-mentioned Act, shall apply to limited partnerships.

[*7A Application of company law*

(1) The Secretary of State may by regulations—

(a) make provision in relation to limited partnerships that corresponds or is similar to any provision relating to companies or other corporations made by or under, or capable of being made under, any Act;

(b) provide for any such provision which would otherwise have effect in relation to limited partnerships not to apply to them or to apply to them with such modifications as appear appropriate.

(2) Regulations under subsection (1) may amend or repeal provision made by this Act, the Partnership Act 1890 or the Companies Act 2006.

(3) The provision which may be made by regulations under subsection (1) by virtue of section 38(1) includes provision amending, repealing or revoking provision made by or under any Act, whenever passed or made.

(4) Regulations under subsection (1) are subject to the negative resolution procedure if they only make provision that corresponds or is similar to provision made or capable of being made by regulations subject to the negative resolution procedure.

(5) Any other regulations under subsection (1) are subject to the affirmative resolution procedure.]

[8 Duty to register [and designate]

[(1)] The registrar shall register a limited partnership if an application is made to the registrar in accordance with section 8A.]

[(2) The registrar must designate a limited partnership on the register as a private fund limited partnership if an application for such designation is made to the registrar in accordance with section 8D.]

[8A Application for registration

(1) An application for registration must—

(a) specify the firm name, complying with section 8B, under which the limited partnership is to be registered,

[*(aa) specify the intended address of the limited partnership's registered office, which must be an appropriate address within the meaning given by section 8E(2),*

(ab) specify which of the addresses mentioned in section 8E(2)(c) the intended address is,]

[*(ac) specify the intended registered email address of the limited partnership, which must be an appropriate email address within the meaning given by section 8H(2),*]

(b) contain the details listed in subsection (2) [or (3)],

(c) be [. . .] authenticated by or on behalf of each [proposed] partner, and

(d) be made to the registrar for the part of the United Kingdom in which the principal place of business of the limited partnership is to be situated.

[*(1A) An application for registration of a limited partnership which specifies that the intended address of its registered office is an address mentioned in section 8E(2)(c)(iv) must be accompanied by a statement by the authorised corporate service provider confirming that the address is the authorised corporate service provider's address.*]

[*(1B) The application must also contain a statement that none of the proposed general partners is disqualified under the directors disqualification legislation (see subsection (8)).*]

(2) [Except in the case of an application that is accompanied by an application for designation as a private fund limited partnership, the required] details are—

[*(a) the intended general nature of the limited partnership's business,*]

(b) the [required information about each proposed] general partner,

(c) the [required information about each proposed] limited partner,

(d) the amount of the capital contribution of each [proposed] limited partner (and whether the contribution is paid in cash or in another specified form),

(e) the address of the proposed principal place of business of the limited partnership, and

(f) the term (if any) for which the limited partnership is to be entered into (beginning with the date of registration).]

[*(2A) The details referred to in subsection (2)(a) about the general nature of the partnership business may be given by reference to one or more categories of any system of classifying business activities prescribed by regulations made by the Secretary of State for the purposes of this section.*]

[(3) In the case of an application that is accompanied by an application for designation as a private fund limited partnership, the required details are—

(a) the [required information about each proposed] general partner,

(b) the [required information about each proposed] limited partner, and

(c) the address of the proposed principal place of business of the limited partnership.]

[*(3A) For the required information about a proposed general partner or a proposed limited partner see Part 2 of the Schedule.*]

[(4) An application for registration of a limited partnership whose principal place of business is to be situated in Scotland must contain a statement of initial significant control.

(5) The statement of initial significant control must—

(a) state whether, on registration, there will be any person who will count as either a registrable person or a registrable relevant legal entity in relation to the limited partnership for the purposes of regulation 10 of the Scottish Partnerships PSC Regulations (duty to investigate and obtain information),

(b) include the required particulars of any person identified under paragraph (a), and

(c) if there is no person identified under paragraph (a), state that fact.

(6) It is not necessary to include under subsection (5)(b) the date on which a person becomes a registrable person or a registrable relevant legal entity in relation to the limited partnership.

(7) If the statement of initial significant control includes required particulars of a registrable person, it must also contain a statement that those particulars are included with the knowledge of that individual.

(8) In this section—

[*'disqualified under the directors disqualification legislation'—*

(a) in relation to a statement about a person delivered to the registrar for England and Wales or Scotland, means that the person falls within any of the entries in the first column of Part 1 of the table in section 159A of the Companies Act 2006;

(b) in relation to a statement about a person delivered to the registrar for Northern Ireland, means that the person falls within any of the entries in the first column of Part 2 of that table;]

'the Scottish Partnerships PSC Regulations' means the Scottish Partnerships (Register of People with Significant Control) Regulations 2017;

'registrable person', 'registrable relevant legal entity' and 'required particulars' have the same meaning as in the Scottish Partnerships PSC Regulations.]

[*(9) Regulations under subsection (2A) are subject to the negative resolution procedure.*]

[8B Name of limited partnership

(1) This section sets out conditions which must be satisfied by the firm name of a limited partnership as specified in the application for registration.

(2) The name must end with—

(a) the words 'limited partnership' (upper or lower case, or any combination), or

(b) the abbreviation 'LP' (upper or lower case, or any combination, with or without punctuation).

(3) But if the principal place of business of a limited partnership is to be in Wales, its firm name may end with—

(a) the words 'partneriaeth cyfyngedig' (upper or lower case, or any combination), or

(b) the abbreviation 'PC' (upper or lower case, or any combination, with or without punctuation).]

[8C Certificate of registration [and certificate of designation as a private fund limited partnership]

(1) On registering a limited partnership the registrar shall issue a certificate of registration.

(2) The certificate must be—

(a) signed by the registrar, or

(b) authenticated with the registrar's seal.

(3) The certificate must state—

(a) the firm name of the limited partnership given in the application for registration,

(b) the limited partnership's registration number,

(c) the date of registration, and

(d) that the limited partnership is registered as a limited partnership under this Act.

(4) The certificate is conclusive evidence that a limited partnership came into existence on the date of registration.]

[(5) If a limited partnership is designated on the register as a private fund limited partnership, the registrar must issue a certificate of designation as a private fund limited partnership.

(6) The certificate must be signed by the registrar or authenticated with the registrar's seal.

(7) The certificate must state—

(a) the firm name and registration number of the limited partnership,

(b) the date of designation as a private fund limited partnership, and

(c) that the limited partnership is designated as a private fund limited partnership under this Act.

(8) A certificate of designation as a private fund limited partnership is conclusive evidence that the limited partnership was designated as a private fund limited partnership on the date of designation.

(9) If a limited partnership is designated as a private fund limited partnership at the same time as it is registered, the registrar may issue a combined certificate instead of issuing separate certificates under subsections (1) and (5), and that combined certificate—

(a) must be signed by the registrar or authenticated with the registrar's seal,
(b) must state the particulars mentioned in subsections (3) and (7), and
(c) is conclusive evidence that—
(i) a limited partnership came into existence on the date of registration, and
(ii) the limited partnership was designated as a private fund limited partnership on the date of registration.]

[8D Application for designation as a private fund limited partnership

(1) An application for designation as a private fund limited partnership may be made with an application for registration under section 8A or at any time after a limited partnership has been registered.

(2) An application for designation as a private fund limited partnership must—
(a) specify the firm name of the partnership;
(b) specify the address of the partnership's principal place of business or proposed principal place of business;
(c) in the case of an application made after the firm is registered as a limited partnership, specify the limited partnership's registration number and the date of registration;
(d) include confirmation by a general partner that the partnership meets the private fund conditions;
(e) be [. . .] authenticated by or on behalf of each general partner; and
(f) be made to the registrar.

(3) The private fund conditions are that the partnership—
(a) is constituted by an agreement in writing, and
(b) is a collective investment scheme.

(4) In subsection (3) 'collective investment scheme' has the same meaning as in Part 17 of the Financial Services and Markets Act 2000 (see section 235 of that Act), ignoring any order made under section 235(5) of that Act (8).]

[. . .]

10 Advertisement in Gazette of statement of general partner becoming a limited partner and of assignment of share of limited partner

(1) Notice of any arrangement or transaction under which any person will cease to be a general partner in any firm [that is not a private fund limited partnership], and will become a limited partner in that firm, or under which the share of a limited partner in a firm [that is not a private fund limited partnership] will be assigned to any person, shall be forthwith advertised in the Gazette, and until notice of the arrangement or transaction is so advertised the arrangement or transaction shall, for the purposes of this Act, be deemed to be of no effect.

[(1A) Notice of any arrangement or transaction under which any person will cease to be a general partner in a private fund limited partnership shall be forthwith advertised in the Gazette.

(1B) Where a person deals with a private fund limited partnership after an arrangement or transaction of the type referred to in subsection (1A), that person is entitled to treat the person who is ceasing to be a general partner as still being a general partner of the firm until the person has notice of the arrangement or transaction.

(1C) Advertisement of a notice in accordance with subsection (1A) is notice to a person dealing with the firm for the purpose of subsection (1B).]

[Notification of other changes in partnerships

10A Duty to notify registrar of other changes in partnerships

(1) The general partners in a limited partnership must give notice to the registrar of any change mentioned in subsection (2).

(2) The changes are—

(a) in the case of any limited partnership, changes to—

(i) the firm name, or

(ii) the address of the principal place of business of the limited partnership;

(b) in the case of a limited partnership that is not a private fund limited partnership, changes to—

(i) the general nature of the limited partnership's business, or

(ii) the term or character of the limited partnership.

(3) The notice must specify the date on which the change occurred.

(4) A notice under subsection (2)(b)(i) may specify the change to the general nature of the partnership business by reference to one or more categories of any system of classifying business activities prescribed by regulations made by the Secretary of State under section 8A(2A).

(5) A notice under this section must be given within the period of 14 days beginning with the day on which the change occurs.

10B Notification of other changes occurring before registration

(1) The general partners in a limited partnership must give notice to the registrar if, on registration of the limited partnership, the address of the principal place of business of the limited partnership is different to that contained in the application for registration under section 8A.

(2) The general partners in a limited partnership that is not a private fund limited partnership must give notice to the registrar if, on registration of the limited partnership, any of the following details are different to those contained in the application for registration under section 8A—

(a) the general nature of the limited partnership's business,

(b) the term of the limited partnership,

(c) the amount of the capital contribution of a limited partner, or

(d) the form of the capital contribution of a limited partner.

(3) A notice under subsection (1) must specify the address of the principal place of business of the limited partnership.

(4) A notice under subsection (2)(a)—

(a) must specify the general nature of the limited partnership's business, and

(b) may do so by reference to one or more categories of any system of classifying business activities prescribed by regulations made by the Secretary of State under section 8A(2A).

(5) A notice under subsection (2)(b), (c) or (d) must specify the details mentioned in the paragraph under which the notice is given.

(6) A notice under this section must be given within the period of 14 days beginning with the day on which the limited partnership was registered.

10C Failure to notify other changes in partnerships

(1) If the general partners fail to comply with section 10A or 10B an offence is committed by each general partner who is in default.

(2) But where the general partner is a legal entity, it does not commit an offence as a general partner in default unless one of its managing officers is in default.

(3) Where any such offence is committed by a general partner that is a legal entity, or any such offence is by virtue of this subsection committed by a managing officer that is a legal entity, any managing officer of the legal entity who is in default also commits the offence if—

(a) the managing officer is an individual, or

(b) the managing officer is a legal entity and one of its managing officers is in default.

(4) A person guilty of an offence under this section is liable on summary conviction—

(a) in England and Wales, to a fine;

(b) in Scotland or Northern Ireland, to a fine not exceeding level 5 on the standard scale and, for continued contravention, a daily default fine not exceeding one-tenth of level 5 on the standard scale.

(5) A general partner or managing officer is 'in default' for the purposes of this section if they authorise or permit, participate in, or fail to take all reasonable steps to prevent, the contravention.]

[*Confirmation statements*

10D Duty to deliver confirmation statements

(1) The general partners in a limited partnership must, within the period of 14 days after each review period, deliver to the registrar a statement (a 'confirmation statement') confirming that any information required by subsection (2) is being delivered at the same time as the confirmation statement.

(2) The information that must be delivered at the same time as the confirmation statement is—

(a) a notice of any notifiable change in respect of which a notice under section 8N, 8R, 8S or 10A has not been delivered,

(b) a notice under section 8F if—

(i) the limited partnership's registered office is not at an appropriate address within the meaning given by section 8E(2) when the confirmation statement is made, and

(ii) the limited partnership has not given a notice under section 8F that is awaiting registration by the registrar,

(c) a notice under section 8I if—

(i) the limited partnership's registered email address is not at an appropriate email address within the meaning given by section 8H(2) when the confirmation statement is made, and

(ii) the limited partnership has not given a notice under section 8I that is awaiting registration by the registrar,

(d) a notice under section 8L(1) by each general partner that—

(i) is a legal entity,

(ii) has a registered officer who does not meet the requirements in section 8K(1)(a) to (c), and

(iii) has not given a notice under section 8L(1) that is awaiting registration by the registrar, and

(e) if any general partner that is a legal entity has one or more corporate managing officers—

(i) for which the named contact is not an individual who is a managing officer of the corporate managing officer, and

(ii) in respect of which the general partner has not given a notice under section 8L(2) that is awaiting registration by the registrar, a notice under section 8L(2) by each such general partner in respect of each such corporate managing officer.

(3) For the purposes of this section, each of the following is a review period—

(a) where the limited partnership was registered before this section comes fully into force, the period—

(i) beginning with the date of the limited partnership's registration, and

(ii) ending with the period of 6 months beginning when this section comes fully into force;

(b) where the limited partnership was registered after this section comes fully into force, the period of 12 months beginning with the date of the limited partnership's registration;

(c) each period of 12 months beginning with the day after the end of the previous review period.

(4) But a review period may be shortened by the general partners—

(a) notifying the registrar of the shortened review period, and

(b) delivering the confirmation statement within the period of 14 days after that shortened review period.

(5) For the purpose of making a confirmation statement, the general partners in a limited partnership are entitled to assume that information that has been delivered to the registrar has been properly delivered unless the registrar has notified the limited partnership otherwise.

(6) In this section a 'notifiable change' means a change mentioned in section 8N(1), 8R(1), 8S(1) to (3) or 10A(2) that occurred during the review period.

10E Power to amend matters to be confirmed in confirmation statement

(1) The Secretary of State may by regulations make further provision about the matters that must be confirmed in a confirmation statement delivered under section 10D(1).

(2) The regulations may—

(a) amend or repeal the provisions of section 10D, and

(b) provide for exceptions from the requirements of that section as it has effect from time to time.

(3) Regulations under this section are subject to the affirmative resolution procedure.

10F Failure to deliver confirmation statement

(1) If the general partners fail to comply with section 10D(1) an offence is committed by each general partner who is in default.

(2) But where the general partner is a legal entity, it does not commit an offence as a general partner in default unless one of its managing officers is in default.

(3) Where any such offence is committed by a general partner that is a legal entity, or any such offence is by virtue of this subsection committed by a managing officer that is a legal entity, any managing officer of the legal entity also commits the offence if—

(a) the managing officer is an individual who is in default, or

(b) the managing officer is a legal entity that is in default and one of its managing officers is in default.

(4) A person guilty of an offence under this section is liable on summary conviction—

(a) in England and Wales, to a fine;

(b) in Scotland or Northern Ireland, to a fine not exceeding level 5 on the standard scale and, for continued contravention, a daily default fine not exceeding one-tenth of level 5 on the standard scale.

(5) The contravention continues until such time as the general partners have delivered the statement required by section 10D(1).

(6) A general partner or managing officer is 'in default' for the purposes of this section if they authorise or permit, participate in, or fail to take all reasonable steps to prevent, the contravention.]

[Power for HMRC to obtain accounts

10G Power for HMRC to obtain accounts

(1) HMRC may by notice in writing require the general partners in a limited partnership to—

(a) prepare accounts in accordance with regulations made by the Secretary of State for the purposes of this paragraph;

(b) deliver those accounts to HMRC, together with—

(i) an auditor's report prepared in accordance with regulations made by the Secretary of State for the purposes of this sub-paragraph;

(ii) such supporting evidence as may be required by regulations made by the Secretary of the State for the purposes of this sub-paragraph.

(2) A requirement under this section may specify—

(a) the period to which the accounts must relate;

(b) the form and manner in which the documents are to be delivered;

(c) the period within which they are to be delivered.

(3) HMRC may by notice in writing extend a period specified in a requirement under this section.

(4) If the general partners in a limited partnership fail to comply with a requirement under this section an offence is committed by each general partner who is in default.

(5) But where the general partner is a legal entity, it does not commit an offence as a general partner in default unless one of its managing officers is in default.

(6) Where any such offence is committed by a general partner that is a legal entity, or any such offence is by virtue of this subsection committed by a managing officer that is a legal entity, any managing officer of the legal entity also commits the offence if—

(a) the managing officer is an individual who is in default, or

(b) the managing officer is a legal entity that is in default and one of its managing officers is in default.

(7) A person guilty of an offence under this section is liable—

(a) on conviction on indictment, to imprisonment for a term not exceeding two years or a fine (or both);

(b) on summary conviction—

(i) in England and Wales, to imprisonment for a term not exceeding the general limit in a magistrates' court or a fine (or both);

(ii) in Scotland, to imprisonment for a term not exceeding 12 months or a fine not exceeding the statutory maximum (or both) and, for continued contravention, a daily default fine not exceeding one-fifth of the statutory maximum;

(iii) in Northern Ireland, to imprisonment for a term not exceeding 6 months or a fine not exceeding the statutory maximum (or both) and, for continued contravention, a daily default fine not exceeding one-fifth of the statutory maximum.

(8) A general partner or managing officer is 'in default' for the purposes of this section if they authorise or permit, participate in, or fail to take all reasonable steps to prevent, the contravention.

(9) In this section 'HMRC' means the Commissioners for His Majesty's Revenue and Customs.

(10) Regulations under this section are subject to the affirmative resolution procedure.]

[. . .]

[The registrar]

[15 The registrar

(1) The registrar of companies is the registrar of limited partnerships.

(2) In this Act—

(a) references to the registrar in relation to the registration of a limited partnership are to the registrar to whom the application for registration is to be made (see section 8A(1)(d));

(b) references to registration in a particular part of the United Kingdom are to registration by the registrar for that part of the United Kingdom;

[(ba) references to the registrar in relation to an application for designation of a limited partnership as a private fund limited partnership made with an application for registration are to the registrar to whom the application for registration is to be made (see section 8A(1)(d));]

(c) references to the registrar in relation to any other matter relating to a limited partnership are to the registrar for the part of the United Kingdom in which the partnership is registered.]

[The register of limited partnerships

16 Inspection and copies of the register of limited partnerships

(1) Any person may—

(a) inspect the register of limited partnerships;

(b) require a copy of any material on the register of limited partnerships that is available for inspection.

(2) The right of inspection extends to the originals of documents delivered to the registrar in hard copy form if, and only if, the record kept by the registrar of the contents of the

document is illegible or unavailable (see section 1083(1) of the Companies Act 2006 for provision about the retention of hard copies by the registrar).

(3) The registrar may specify the form and manner in which an application is to be made for inspection or a copy.

(4) The registrar may determine the form and manner in which the copies are to be provided.

(5) Section 1091 of the Companies Act 2006 (certification of copies), and any regulations made under it, apply in relation to copies provided under this section as they apply in relation to the copies provided as mentioned in that section.

(6) This section has effect subject to section 16A and 16B.]

[16A *Material not available for public inspection*

(1) The registrar must not make the following material available for public inspection, so far as it forms part of the register of limited partnerships—

(a) any application or other document delivered to the registrar under section 8G, 8Q or 8W (changes of addresses by registrar) other than an order or direction of the court;

(b) so much of any document delivered to the registrar as is required to contain—

(i) a limited partnership's registered email address,

(ii) the email address of the named contact for a general partner's managing officer,

(iii) protected date of birth information, or

(iv) protected residential address information;

(c) so much of any statement delivered to the registrar under any of the following provisions as is required to confirm that an individual is an individual whose identity is verified (within the meaning of section 1110A of the Companies Act 2006)—

section 8A(1F)(b);

section 8L(3)(a) or (b);

section 8R(7)(b);

(d) any statement delivered to the registrar by virtue of section 33(3) (documents to be delivered by authorised corporate service providers);

(e) any statement or other document delivered to the registrar by virtue of section 1067A of the Companies Act 2006 (delivery of documents: identity verification and authorised corporate service providers);

(f) any statement made in accordance with regulations made by virtue of section 1082(2)(c) of the Companies Act 2006 (statement of unique identifier);

(g) any document provided to the registrar under section 1092A of the Companies Act 2006 (power to require further information);

(h) any record of the information contained in a document or part of a document that is unavailable because of any of the previous paragraphs of this subsection;

(i) any e-mail address, identification code or password deriving from a document delivered for the purpose of authorising or facilitating electronic filing procedures or providing information by telephone;

(j) any other material excluded from public inspection by or under any other enactment.

(2) The registrar need not retain material to which subsection (1) applies for longer than appears to the registrar reasonably necessary for the purposes for which the material was delivered to the registrar.

(3) In this section—

'protected date of birth information' means information as to the day of the month (but not the month or year) on which—

(a) a partner was born, or

(b) a general partner's registered officer was born;

'protected residential address information' means information as to the usual residential address of—

(a) a partner,

(b) a general partner's registered officer, or

(c) the named contact for a general partner's managing officer.

(4) Information about a partner, registered officer or named contact does not cease to be protected date of birth information or protected residential address information when they cease to be a partner, registered officer or named contact.

(5) The restrictions on making information available for public inspection imposed by subsection (1)(h) and (i) do not affect the availability for public inspection of the same information contained in material derived from another description of document (or part of a document) in relation to which the relevant restriction does not apply.

(6) In this section 'registered officer' and 'named contact' have the meanings given by section 8K(4) and (5).]

[16B *Records relating to dissolved or deregistered limited partnerships*

(1) This section applies where a limited partnership is dissolved or deregistered under section 26.

(2) The registrar need not make any information contained in records relating to the limited partnership available for public inspection at any time after the end of the period of 20 years beginning with the date on which the limited partnership is dissolved or deregistered.

(3) The registrar of companies for England and Wales may, at any time after the period of two years beginning with the date on which the limited partnership is dissolved or deregistered, direct that any records relating to the limited partnership that are held by the registrar are to be removed to the Public Record Office.

(4) The registrar of companies for Northern Ireland may, at any time after the period of two years beginning with the date on which the limited partnership is dissolved or deregistered, direct that any records relating to the limited partnership that are held by the registrar are to be removed to the Public Record Office of Northern Ireland.

(5) Records in respect of which a direction is given under subsection (3) or (4) are to be disposed of under the enactments relating to the Public Record Office or, as the case may be, the Public Record Office of Northern Ireland.]

[*Restriction on disclosure of information by registrar*

16C *Restriction on disclosure of information by registrar*

(1) The registrar must not disclose protected date of birth information or protected residential address information except—

(a) in accordance with subsection (2) or (3),

(b) in accordance with section 16E (disclosure of protected residential address information under court order), or

(c) as permitted by section 1110F of the Companies Act 2006 (general powers of disclosure by the registrar).

(2) The registrar may disclose protected date of birth information or protected residential address information if the same information is required to be made available for public inspection as a result of being contained in a document, part of a document or record to which section 16A(1) does not apply.

(3) The registrar may disclose protected date of birth information or protected residential address information to a credit reference agency.

(4) The Secretary of State may make provision by regulations specifying conditions for the disclosure of protected date of birth information or protected residential address information in accordance with subsection (3).

(5) The Secretary of State may make provision by regulations requiring the registrar, on application, to refrain from disclosing protected date of birth information or protected residential address information to a credit reference agency.

(6) Regulations under subsection (5) may make provision of the kind referred to in section 243(5) to (6A) of the Companies Act 2006.

(7) In this section—

'credit reference agency' means a person carrying on a business comprising the provision of information relevant to the financial standing of individuals, being information collected by the agency for that purpose;

'protected date of birth information' has the meaning given by section 16A(3);
'protected residential address information' has the meaning given by section 16A(3).
(8) Regulations under this section are subject to the negative resolution procedure.]

[Restriction on use or disclosure of information by partners

16D Restriction on use or disclosure of information by partners

(1) A limited partner must not—

(a) use or disclose protected residential address information, except for communicating with the individual concerned, or

(b) use or disclose protected date of birth information.

(2) A general partner must not use or disclose protected residential address information, except—

(a) for communicating with the individual concerned,

(b) in order to comply with any requirement of this Act as to information to be sent to the registrar, or

(c) in accordance with section 16E (disclosure of residential address information under court order).

(3) A general partner must not use or disclose protected date of birth information except in order to comply with any requirement of this Act as to information to be sent to the registrar.

(4) Subsections (1), (2) and (3) do not prohibit any use or disclosure of protected date of birth information or protected residential address information with the consent of the individual concerned.

(5) If a partner uses or discloses information in contravention of subsection (1), (2) or (3) an offence is committed by—

(a) the partner, and

(b) if the partner is a legal entity, any of its managing officers who is in default.

(6) A person guilty of an offence under this section is liable on summary conviction—

(a) in England and Wales, to a fine;

(b) in Scotland or Northern Ireland, to a fine not exceeding level 5 on the standard scale and, for continued contravention, a daily default fine not exceeding one-tenth of level 5 on the standard scale.

(7) A managing officer is 'in default' for the purposes of this section if they authorise or permit, participate in, or fail to take all reasonable steps to prevent, the contravention.

(8) But a corporate managing officer does not commit an offence as a managing officer in default unless one of its managing officers is in default.

(9) Where any such offence is committed by a corporate managing officer the managing officer in question also commits the offence (subject to subsection (8)).

(10) In this section—

'protected date of birth information' has the meaning given by section 16A(3);
'protected residential address information' has the meaning given by section 16A(3).]

[Disclosure of protected residential address information under court order

16E Disclosure of protected residential address information under court order

(1) The court may make an order for the disclosure of protected residential address information by the appropriate limited partnership or by the registrar if—

(a) there is evidence that service of documents at a service address other than the individual's usual residential address is not effective to bring them to the notice of the individual, or

(b) it is necessary or expedient for the information to be provided in connection with the enforcement of an order or decree of the court, and the court is otherwise satisfied that it is appropriate to make the order.

(2) An order for disclosure by the registrar may be made only if—

(a) the appropriate limited partnership does not have the protected residential address information, or

(b) the appropriate limited partnership was dissolved.

(3) The order may be made on the application of a liquidator, creditor or partner of the appropriate limited partnership, or any other person appearing to the court to have a sufficient interest.

(4) The order must specify the persons to whom, and purposes for which, disclosure is authorised.

(5) In this section—

'appropriate limited partnership'—

(a) in relation to protected residential address information about a partner in a limited partnership means that limited partnership;

(b) in relation to protected residential address information about a registered officer of a general partner in a limited partnership means that limited partnership;

(c) in relation to protected residential address information about a named contact for the managing officer of a general partner in a limited partnership means that limited partnership;

'named contact' has the meaning given by section 8K(5);

'protected residential address information' has the meaning given by section 16A(3);

'registered officer' has the meaning given by section 8K(4).]

[*Dissolution, revival and deregistration*

18 *Duty to notify registrar of dissolution*

(1) A person who is a general partner in a limited partnership at a time when it is dissolved must notify the registrar of the dissolution within the period of 14 days beginning with the day on which the person becomes aware of its dissolution.

(2) A person who is a limited partner in a limited partnership at a time when it is dissolved must, if there are no general partners at that time, notify the registrar of the dissolution within the period of 14 days beginning with the day on which the person becomes aware of its dissolution.

(3) But no notice is required under subsection (1) or (2) if

(a) the limited partnership is dissolved under section 19(6) (dissolution on publication of notice in Gazette),

(b) another person has notified the registrar of the dissolution under subsection (1) or (2), or

(c) a dissolution notice under section 19 is published before the end of the period of 14 days mentioned in subsection (1) or (2).

(4) If a person fails to comply with subsection (1) or (2) an offence is committed by—

(a) the person, and

(b) if the person is a legal entity, any of its managing officers who is in default.

(5) A person guilty of an offence under this section is liable on summary conviction—

(a) in England and Wales, to a fine;

(b) in Scotland or Northern Ireland, to a fine not exceeding level 5 on the standard scale and, for continued contravention, a daily default fine not exceeding one-tenth of level 5 on the standard scale.

(6) A managing officer is 'in default' for the purposes of this section if they authorise or permit, participate in, or fail to take all reasonable steps to prevent, the contravention.

(7) But a corporate managing officer does not commit an offence as a managing officer in default unless one of its managing officers is in default.

(8) Where any such offence is committed by a corporate managing officer the managing officer in question also commits the offence (subject to subsection (7)).]

[. . .]

CONVEYANCING (SCOTLAND) ACT 1924
(14 & 15 Geo 5, c 27)

44 General Register of Inhibitions and Register of Adjudications to be combined; limitation of effect of entries therein

(1) The General Register of Inhibitions and Interdictions and the Register of Adjudications shall be combined, and the Keeper thereof shall keep only one register for inhibitions, interdictions, adjudications, reductions, and notices of litigiosity, and such register shall be called the Register of Inhibitions and Adjudications; and a reference in any public, general or local Act to the General Register of Inhibitions or the Register of Adjudications shall be deemed to mean and include such Register of Inhibitions and Adjudications.

(2)(a) No action whether raised before or after the commencement of this Act relating to land or to a lease or to a heritable security, shall be deemed to have had or shall have the effect of making such land, lease or heritable security litigious, unless and until [—

(i)] a notice relative to such action in or as nearly as may be in the form of Schedule RR annexed to the Titles to Land Consolidation (Scotland) Act, 1868, shall have been or shall be registered in the Register of Inhibitions and Adjudications in the manner provided by section one hundred and fifty-nine of that Act [; or

(ii) a notice of an application under section 8 of the Law Reform (Miscellaneous Provisions)(Scotland) Act 1985 has been registered in the said register.]

(b) No decree in any action of adjudication of land or of a lease or of a heritable security, whether pronounced before or after the commencement of this Act, and no abbreviate of any such decree shall be deemed to have had or to have any effect in making such land, lease or heritable security litigious.

[(2A) A notice registered under subsection (2)(a)(i) of this section on or after the date on which section 67 of the Land Registration etc (Scotland) Act 2012 (asp 5) (warrant to place a caveat) comes into force shall not have any effect in rendering—

(a) any land or lease for which there is a title sheet in the Land Register of Scotland, or

(b) any heritable security the particulars of which are entered in a title sheet in that register,

litigious or in placing in bad faith any person acquiring such land, lease or heritable security.]

(3)(a) All inhibitions and all notices of litigiosity registered in terms of section one hundred and fifty-nine of the Titles to Land Consolidation (Scotland) Act, 1868, subsisting at the commencement of this Act shall prescribe and be of no effect on the lapse of five years after such commencement or at such earlier date as they would prescribe according to the present law and practice; and all [. . .] [, notices of litigiosity and notices of applications under section 8 of the Law Reform (Miscellaneous Provisions)(Scotland) Act 1985] which relate to land or to a lease or to a heritable security and which shall be first registered after the commencement of this Act, shall prescribe and be of no effect on the lapse of five years from the date on which the same shall respectively take effect: Provided that in no case shall litigiosity be pleadable or be founded on to any effect after the expiry of six months from and after final decree is pronounced in the action creating such litigiosity.

[(aa) all inhibitions shall cease to have effect on the lapse of five years from the date on which they take effect.]

(b) From and after the commencement of this Act interdiction, whether judicial or voluntary, shall be incompetent, and any interdiction which is legally operative at such commencement shall remain legally operative for not longer than the period of five years thereafter.

(4) [. . .]

(c) No deed, decree, instrument or writing granted or expede by a person whose estates have been sequestrated under the Bankruptcy (Scotland) Act, 1856, or the Bankruptcy (Scotland) Act, 1913 [or the Bankruptcy (Scotland) Act 1985 or the Bankruptcy (Scotland) Act 2016], or the heirs, executors, successors or assignees of such person relative to any land or lease or heritable security belonging to such person at the date of such sequestration or subsequently acquired by him shall be challengeable or denied effect on the ground of such sequestration if such deed, decree, instrument or writing shall have been granted or expede, or shall come into operation at a date when the effect of recording [(a)] the abbreviate provided for under section forty-four of the said Act of 1913, as amended by this Act, shall have expired in terms of the said section as amended as aforesaid [; or (b) under subsection (1)(a) of section 14 of the Bankruptcy (Scotland) Act 1985 [or (1)(a) of section 26 of the Bankruptcy (Scotland) Act 2016] the certified copy of an order shall have expired by virtue of subsection (3) of [the said section 14 or (4) of the said section 26]], unless the trustee in such sequestration shall before the recording of such deed, decree, instrument or writing in the appropriate Register of Sasines have completed his title to such land, lease or heritable security by recording the same in such register [or have recorded a memorandum in such register [in the form provided by Schedule O to this Act]] Provided always, in the case of sequestrations awarded under the Bankruptcy (Scotland) Act, 1856, that the provisions of this section shall not apply to any deed, decree, instrument or writing dated within five years after the commencement of this Act.

(5) The provisions of this section shall not affect the ranking of adjudgers inter se, or any real right obtained in virtue of a decree of adjudication, or in virtue of a decree pronounced in an action creating litigiosity, or by a trustee in bankruptcy, if such right has been completed by the recording in the appropriate Register of Sasines of any deed, decree, abbreviate, or instrument necessary to effect the completion of such right.

(6) Section one hundred and fifty-nine of the Titles to Land Consolidation (Scotland) Act, 1868, and sections sixteen and seventeen of the Land Registers (Scotland) Act, 1868, [. . .] are hereby amended in accordance with this section, and section forty-two of the Conveyancing (Scotland) Act, 1874, and Schedule J thereto annexed, are hereby repealed.

CURRENCY AND BANK NOTES ACT 1954
(2 & 3 Eliz 2, c 12)

1 Issue and recall of bank notes by Bank of England

(1) The Bank of England may issue bank notes of such denominations as the Treasury may approve and shall not issue any other bank notes, and any bank notes issued under this section may be put into circulation in Scotland and Northern Ireland as well as in England and Wales.

(2) All bank notes issued under this section shall be legal tender in England and Wales, and all such notes of denominations of less than five pounds shall be legal tender in Scotland and Northern Ireland.

(3) Bank notes shall be payable only at the head office of the Bank of England unless expressly made payable also at some other place.

(4) The holder of bank notes of any denominations shall be entitled, on a demand made by him during office hours at the head office of the Bank of England or, in the case of notes payable also at some place other than the head office, either at the head office or at that other place, to receive in exchange for the notes bank notes of such lower denominations, being bank notes which for the time being are legal tender in the United Kingdom or in England and Wales, as he may specify.

(5) The Bank of England shall have power, on giving not less than one month's notice in the London, Edinburgh and Belfast Gazettes, to call in any bank notes on payment of the face value thereof, and any such notes with respect to which a notice has been given under this subsection shall on the expiration of the notice cease to be legal tender.

(6) All bank notes which, immediately before the commencement of this Act, were legal tender in the United Kingdom, or were legal tender in England and Wales subject to the provisions of section six of the Bank of England Act 1833 (under which five-pound notes were not legal tender by the Bank of England), shall be deemed to have been issued under this section and shall be legal tender accordingly in the United Kingdom or, as the case may be, in England and Wales.

CHEQUES ACT 1957
(5 & 6 Eliz 2, c 36)

1 Protection of bankers paying unindorsed or irregularly indorsed cheques, etc

(1) Where a banker in good faith and in the ordinary course of business pays a cheque drawn on him which is not indorsed or is irregularly indorsed, he does not in doing so, incur any liability by reason only of the absence of, or irregularity in indorsement, and he is deemed to have paid it in due course.

(2) Where a banker in good faith and in the ordinary course of business pays any such instrument as the following namely—

(a) a document issued by a customer of his which, though not a bill of exchange, is intended to enable a person to obtain payment from him of the sum mentioned in the document;

(b) a draft payable on demand drawn by him upon himself, whether payable at the head office or some other office of his bank; he does not, in so doing, incur any liability by reason only of the absence of, or irregularity in, indorsement, and the payment discharges the instrument.

2 Rights of bankers collecting cheques not indorsed by holders

A banker who gives value for, or has a lien on, a cheque payable to order which the holder delivers to him for collection without indorsing it, has such (if any) rights as he would have had if, upon delivery, the holder had indorsed it in blank.

3 Unindorsed cheques as evidence of payment

[(1)] An unindorsed cheque which appears to have been paid by the banker on whom it is drawn is evidence of the receipt by the payee of the sum payable by the cheque.

[(2) For the purposes of subsection (1) above, a copy of a cheque to which that subsection applies is evidence of the cheque if—

(a) the copy is made by the banker in whose possession the cheque is after presentment and,

(b) it is certified by him to be a true copy of the original.]

4 Protection of bankers collecting payment of cheques, etc

(1) Where a banker, in good faith and without negligence—

(a) receives payment for a customer of an instrument to which this section applies; or

(b) having credited a customer's account with the amount of such an instrument, receives payment thereof for himself;

and the customer has no title, or a defective title, to the instrument, the banker does not incur any liability to the true owner of the instrument by reason only of having received payment thereof.

(2) This section applies to the following instruments, namely:—

(a) cheques [(including cheques which under section 81A(1) of the Bills of Exchange Act 1882 or otherwise are not transferable)];

(b) any document issued by a customer of a banker which, though not a bill of exchange, is intended to enable a person to obtain payment from that banker of the sum mentioned in the document;

(c) any document issued by a public officer is intended to enable a person to obtain payment from the Paymaster General or the Queen's and Lord Treasurer's Remembrancer of the sum mentioned in the document but is not a bill of exchange;

(d) any draft payable on demand drawn by a banker upon himself whether payable at the head office or some other office of his bank.

(3) A banker is not to be treated for the purposes of this section as having been negligent by reason only of his failure to concern himself with absence of, or irregularity in, indorsement of an instrument.

5 Application of certain provisions of Bills of Exchange Act, 1882, to instruments not being bills of exchange

The provisions of the Bills of Exchange Act, 1882, relating to crossed cheques shall, so far as applicable, have effect in relation to instruments (other than cheques) to which the last foregoing section applies as they have effect in relation to cheques.

6 Construction, saving and repeal

(1) This Act shall be construed as one with the Bills of Exchange Act, 1882.

(2) The foregoing provisions of this Act do not make negotiable any instrument which, apart from them, is not negotiable.

[. . .]

HIRE-PURCHASE ACT 1964
(1964, c 53)

[PART III
TITLE TO MOTOR VEHICLES ON HIRE-PURCHASE OR CONDITIONAL SALE

27 Protection of purchasers of motor vehicles

(1) This section applies where a motor vehicle has been bailed or (in Scotland) hired under a hire-purchase agreement, or has been agreed to be sold under a conditional sale agreement, and, before the property in the vehicle has become vested in the debtor, he disposes of the vehicle to another person.

(2) Where the disposition referred to in subsection (1) above is to a private purchaser, and he is a purchaser of the motor vehicle in good faith without notice of the hire-purchase or conditional sale agreement (the 'relevant agreement') that disposition shall have effect as if the creditor's title to the vehicle has been vested in the debtor immediately before that disposition.

(3) Where the person to whom the disposition referred to in subsection (1) above is made (the 'original purchaser') is a trade or finance purchaser, then if the person who is the first private purchaser of the motor vehicle after that disposition (the 'first private purchaser') is a purchaser of the vehicle in good faith without notice of the relevant agreement, the disposition of the vehicle to the first private purchaser shall have effect as if the title of the creditor to the vehicle had been vested in the debtor immediately before he disposed of it to the original purchaser.

(4) Where, in a case within subsection (3) above—

(a) the disposition by which the first private purchaser becomes a purchaser of the motor vehicle in good faith without notice of the relevant agreement is itself a bailment or hiring under a hire-purchase agreement, and

(b) the person who is the creditor in relation to that agreement disposes of the vehicle to the first private purchaser, or a person claiming under him, by transferring to him the property in the vehicle in pursuance of a provision in the agreement in that behalf, the disposition referred to in paragraph (b) above (whether or not the person to whom it is made is a purchaser in good faith without notice of the relevant agreement) shall as well as the disposition referred to in paragraph (a) above, have effect as mentioned in subsection (3) above.

(5) The preceding provisions of this section apply—

(a) notwithstanding anything in [section 21 of the Sale of Goods Act 1979] (sale of goods by a person not the owner), but

(b) without prejudice to the provisions of the Factors Acts (as defined by [section 61(1) of the said Act of 1979]) or any other enactment enabling the apparent owner of goods to dispose of them as if he were the true owner.

(6) Nothing in this section shall exonerate the debtor from any liability (whether criminal or civil) to which he would be subject apart from this section; and, in a case where the debtor disposes of the motor vehicle to a trade or finance purchaser, nothing in this section shall exonerate—

(a) that trade or finance purchaser, or

(b) any other trade or finance purchaser who becomes a purchaser of the vehicle and is not a person claiming under the first private purchaser,

from any liability (whether criminal or civil) to which he would be subject apart from this section.

28 Presumptions relating to dealings with motor vehicles

(1) Where in any proceedings (whether criminal or civil) relating to a motor vehicle it is proved—

(a) that the vehicle was bailed or (in Scotland) hired under a hire-purchase agreement, or was agreed to be sold under a conditional sale agreement, and

(b) that a person (whether a party to the proceedings or not) became a private purchaser of the vehicle in good faith without notice of the hire-purchase or conditional sale agreement (the 'relevant agreement'), this section shall have effect for the purposes of the operation of section 27 of this Act in relation to those proceedings.

(2) It shall be presumed for those purposes unless the contrary is proved, that the disposition of the vehicle to the person referred to in subsection (1)(b) above (the 'relevant purchaser') was made by the debtor.

(3) If it is proved that that disposition was not made by the debtor, then it shall be presumed for those purposes, unless the contrary is proved—

(a) that the debtor disposed of the vehicle to a private purchaser purchasing in good faith without notice of the relevant agreement, and

(b) that the relevant purchaser is or was a person claiming under the person to whom the debtor so disposed of the vehicle.

(4) If it is proved that the disposition of the vehicle to the relevant purchaser was not made by the debtor, and that the person to whom the debtor disposed of the vehicle (the 'original purchaser') was a trade or finance purchaser, then it shall be presumed for those purposes, unless the contrary is proved—

(a) that the person who, after the disposition of the vehicle to the original purchaser, first became a private purchaser of the vehicle was a purchaser in good faith without notice of the relevant agreement, and

(b) that the relevant purchaser is or was a person claiming under the original purchaser.

(5) Without prejudice to any other method of proof, where in any proceedings a party thereto admits a fact, that fact shall, for the purposes of this section, be taken as against him to be proved in relation to those proceedings.

29 Interpretation of Part III

(1) In this Part of this Act—

'conditional sale agreement' means an agreement for the sale of goods under which the purchase price or part of it is payable by instalments, and the property in the goods is to remain in the seller (notwithstanding that the buyer is to be in possession of the goods) until such conditions as to the payment of instalments or otherwise as may be specified in the agreement are fulfilled;

'creditor' means the person by whom goods are bailed or (in Scotland) hired under a hire-purchase agreement or as the case may be, the seller under a conditional sale agreement, or the person to whom his rights and duties have passed by assignment or operation of law;

'disposition' means any sale or contract of sale (including a conditional sale agreement), any bailment or (in Scotland) hiring under a hire-purchase agreement and any transfer of the property in goods in pursuance of a provision in that behalf contained in a hire-purchase agreement, and includes any transaction purporting to be a disposition (as so defined), and 'dispose of' shall be construed accordingly;

'hire-purchase agreement' means an agreement, other than a conditional sale agreement, under which—

(a) goods are bailed or (in Scotland) hired in return for periodical payments by the person to whom they are bailed or hired, and

(b) the property in the goods will pass to that person if the terms of the agreement are complied with and one or more of the following occurs—

(i) the exercise of an option to purchase by that person,

(ii) the doing of any other specified act by any party to the agreement,

(iii) the happening of any other specified events; and

'motor vehicle' means a mechanically propelled vehicle intended or adapted for use on roads to which the public has access.

(2) In this Part of this Act 'trade or finance purchaser' means a purchaser who, at the time of the disposition made to him, carries on a business which consists, wholly or partly—

(a) of purchasing motor vehicles for the purpose of offering or exposing them for sale, or

(b) of providing finance by purchasing motor vehicles for the purpose of bailing or (in Scotland) hiring them under hire-purchase agreements or agreeing to sell them under conditional sale agreements,

and 'private purchaser' means a purchaser who, at the time of the disposition made to him, does not carry on any such business.

(3) For the purposes of this Part of this Act a person becomes a purchaser of a motor vehicle if, and at the time when, a disposition of the vehicle is made to him; and a person shall be taken to be a purchaser of a motor vehicle without notice of a hire-purchase agreement or conditional sale agreement if, at the time of the disposition made to him, he has no actual notice that the vehicle is or was the subject of any such agreement.

(4) In this Part of this Act the 'debtor' in relation to a motor vehicle which has been bailed or hired under a hire-purchase agreement, or, as the case may be, agreed to be sold under a conditional sale agreement, means the person who at the material time (whether the agreement has before that time been terminated or not) either—

(a) is the person to whom the vehicle is bailed or hired under that agreement, or

(b) is, in relation to the agreement, the buyer,

including a person who at that time is, by virtue of section 130(4) of the Consumer Credit Act 1974 treated as a bailee or (in Scotland) a custodier of the vehicle.

(5) In this Part of this Act any reference to the title of the creditor to a motor vehicle which has been bailed or (in Scotland) hired under a hire-purchase agreement or agreed to be sold under a conditional sale agreement, and is disposed of by the debtor, is a reference to such title (if any) to the vehicle as, immediately before that disposition, was vested in the person who then was the creditor in relation to the agreement.]

CARRIAGE OF GOODS BY ROAD ACT 1965
(1965, c 37)

1 Convention to have force of law

Subject to the following provisions of this Act, the provisions of the Convention on the Contract for the International Carriage of Goods by Road (in this Act referred to as 'the Convention'), as set out in the Schedule to this Act, shall have the force of law in the United Kingdom so far as they relate to the rights and liabilities of persons concerned in the carriage of goods by road under a contract to which the Convention applies.

2 Designation of High Contracting Parties

(1) Her Majesty may by Order in Council from time to time certify who are the High Contracting Parties to the Convention and in respect of what territories they are respectively parties.

(2) An Order in Council under this section shall, except so far as it has been superseded by a subsequent Order, be conclusive evidence of the matters so certified.

3 Power of court to take account of other proceedings

(1) A court before which proceedings are brought to enforce a liability which is limited by article 23 in the Schedule to this Act may at any stage of the proceedings make any such order as appears to the court to be just and equitable in view of the provisions of the said article 23 and of any other proceedings which have

been, or are likely to be, commenced in the United Kingdom or elsewhere to enforce the liability in whole or in part.

(2) Without prejudice to the preceding subsection, a court before which proceedings are brought to enforce a liability which is limited by the said article 23 shall, where the liability is, or may be, partly enforceable in other proceedings in the United Kingdom or elsewhere, have jurisdiction to award an amount less than the court would have awarded if the limitation applied solely to the proceedings before the court, or to make any part of its award conditional on the result of any other proceedings.

4 Registration of foreign judgments

(1) Subject to the next following subsection, Part I of the Foreign Judgments (Reciprocal Enforcement) Act 1933 (in this section referred to as 'the Act of 1933') shall apply whether or not it would otherwise have so applied, to any judgment which—

(a) has been given in any such action as is referred to in paragraph 1 of article 31 in the Schedule to this Act, and

(b) has been so given by any court or tribunal of a territory in respect of which one of the High Contracting Parties other than the United Kingdom, is a party to the Convention, and

(c) has become enforceable in that territory.

(2) In the application of Part I of the Act of 1933 in relation to any such judgment as is referred to in the preceding subsection, section 4 of that Act shall have effect with the omission of subsections (2) and (3).

(3) The registration, in accordance with Part I of the Act of 1933, of any such judgment as is referred to in subsection (1) of this section shall constitute, in relation to that judgment compliance with the formalities for the purposes of paragraph 3 of article 31 in the Schedule to this Act.

5 Contribution between carriers

(1) Where a carrier under a contract to which the Convention applies is liable in respect of any loss or damage for which compensation is payable under the Convention, nothing in [section 1 of the Civil Liability (Contribution) Act 1978] or section 3(2) of the Law Reform (Miscellaneous Provisions) (Scotland) Act 1940 shall confer on him any right to recover contribution in respect of that loss or damage from any other carrier who, in accordance with article 34 in the Schedule to this Act, is a party to the contract of carriage.

(2) The preceding subsection shall be without prejudice to the operation of article 37 in the Schedule to this Act.

6 Actions against High Contracting Parties

Every High Contracting Party to the Convention shall, for the purpose of any proceedings brought in a court in the United Kingdom in accordance with the provisions of article 31 in the Schedule to this Act to enforce a claim in respect of carriage undertaken by that Party, be deemed to have submitted to the jurisdiction of that court, and accordingly rules of court may provide for the manner in which any such action is to be commenced and carried on; but nothing in this section shall authorise the issue of execution, or in Scotland the execution of diligence, against the property of any High Contracting Party.

7 Arbitrations

(1) Any reference in the preceding provisions of this Act to a court includes a reference to an arbitration tribunal acting by virtue of article 33 in the Schedule to this Act.

(2) For the purposes of article 32 in the Schedule to this Act, as it has effect (by virtue of the said article 33) in relation to arbitrations,—

[(a) as respects England and Wales and Northern Ireland, the provisions of

section 14(3) to (5) of the Arbitration Act 1996 (which determine the time at which an arbitration is commenced) apply;]

(c) as respects Scotland, an arbitration shall be deemed to be commenced when one party to the arbitration serves on the other party or parties a notice requiring him or them to appoint an arbiter or to agree to the appointment of an arbiter or, where the arbitration agreement provides that the reference shall be to a person named or designated in the agreement, requiring him or them to submit the dispute to the person so named or designated.

8 Resolution of conflicts between Conventions on carriage of goods

(1) If it appears to Her Majesty in Council that there is any conflict between the provisions of this Act (including the provisions of the Convention as set out in the Schedule to this Act) and any provisions relating to the carriage of goods for reward by land, sea or air contained in—

(a) any other Convention which has been signed or ratified by or on behalf of Her Majesty's Government in the United Kingdom before the passing of this Act, or

(b) any enactment of the Parliament of the United Kingdom giving effect to such a Convention,

Her Majesty may by Order in Council make such provision as may seem to her to be appropriate for resolving that conflict by amending or modifying this Act or any such enactment.

(2) Any statutory instrument made by virtue of this section shall be subject to annulment in pursuance of a resolution of either House of Parliament.

[8A Amendments consequential on revision of Convention

(1) If at any time it appears to Her Majesty in Council that Her Majesty's Government in the United Kingdom have agreed to any revision of the Convention, Her Majesty may by Order in Council make such amendment of—

[(a) this Act; and]

(c) section 5(1) of the Carriage by Air and Road Act 1979, as appear to Her to be appropriate in consequence of the revision.

(2) In the preceding subsection 'revision' means an omission from, addition to or alteration of the Convention and includes replacement of the Convention or part of it by another Convention.

(3) An Order in Council under this section shall not be made unless a draft of the Order has been laid before Parliament and approved by a resolution of each House of Parliament. [. . .]

9 Application to British possessions, etc

Her Majesty may by Order in Council direct that this Act shall extend, subject to such exceptions, adaptations and modifications as may be specified in the Order, to—

(a) the Isle of Man;

(b) any of the Channel Islands;

(c) any colony.

10 Application to Scotland

In its application to Scotland, the Schedule to this Act shall have effect as if—

(a) any reference therein to a plaintiff included a reference to a pursuer;

(b) any reference therein to a defendant included a reference to a defender; and

(c) any reference to security for costs included a reference to caution for expenses.

11 [*Applies to Northern Ireland*]

12 Orders in Council

An Order in Council made under any of the preceding provisions of this Act may contain such transitional and supplementary provisions as appear to Her Majesty to be expedient and may be varied or revoked by a subsequent Order in Council made under that provision.

13 Application to Crown
This Act shall bind the Crown.

14 Short title, interpretation and commencement
(1) This Act may be cited as the Carriage of Goods by Road Act 1965.
(2) The persons who, for the purposes of this Act, are persons concerned in the carriage of goods by road under a contract to which the Convention applies are—
(a) the sender,
(b) the consignee,
(c) any carrier who, in accordance with article 34 in the Schedule to this Act or otherwise, is a party to the contract of carriage,
(d) any person for whom such a carrier is responsible by virtue of article 3 in the Schedule to this Act,
(e) any person to whom the rights and liabilities of any of the persons referred to in paragraphs (a) to (d) of this subsection have passed (whether by assignment or assignation or by operation of law).
(3) Except in so far as the context otherwise requires, any reference in this Act to an enactment shall be construed as a reference to that enactment as amended or extended by or under any other enactment.
(4) This Act shall come into operation on such day as Her Majesty may by Order in Council appoint; but nothing in this Act shall apply in relation to any contract for the carriage of goods by road made before the day so appointed.

SCHEDULE

CONVENTION ON THE CONTRACT FOR THE INTERNATIONAL CARRIAGE OF GOODS BY ROAD (CMR)

Section 1

CHAPTER I

Scope of application

Article 1
1 This Convention shall apply to every contract for the carriage of goods by road in vehicles for reward, when the place of taking over of the goods and the place designated for delivery, as specified in the contract, are situated in two different countries, of which at least one is a contracting country, irrespective of the place of residence and the nationality of the parties.
2 For the purposes of this Convention, 'vehicles' means motor vehicles, articulated vehicles, trailers and semi-trailers as defined in article 4 of the Convention on Road Traffic dated 19th September 1949.
3 This Convention shall apply also where carriage coming within its scope is carried out by States or by governmental institutions or organisations.
4 This Convention shall not apply:
(a) to carriage performed under the terms of any international postal convention;
(b) to funeral consignments;
(c) to furniture removal.
5 The Contracting Parties agree not to vary any of the provisions of this Convention by special agreements between two or more of them, except to make it inapplicable to their frontier traffic or to authorise the use in transport operations entirely confined to their territory of consignment notes representing a title to the goods.

Article 2

1 Where the vehicle containing the goods is carried over part of the journey by sea, rail, inland waterways or air, and except where the provisions of article 14 are applicable, the goods are not unloaded from the vehicle, this Convention shall nevertheless apply to the whole of the carriage. Provided that to the extent that it is proved that any loss, damage or delay in delivery of the goods which occurs during the carriage by the other means of transport was not caused by an act or omission of the carrier by road, but by some event which could only have occurred in the course of and by reason of the carriage by that other means of transport, the liability of the carrier by road shall be determined not by this Convention but in the manner in which the liability of the carrier by the other means of transport would have been determined if a contract for the carriage of the goods alone had been made by the sender with the carrier by the other means of transport in accordance with the conditions prescribed by law for the carriage of goods by that means of transport. If, however, there be no such prescribed conditions, the liability of the carrier by road shall be determined by this Convention.

2 If the carrier by road is also himself the carrier by the other means of transport, his liability shall also be determined in accordance with the provisions of paragraph 1 of this article, but as if, in his capacities as carrier by road and as carrier by the other means of transport, he were two separate persons.

CHAPTER II

Persons for whom the carrier is responsible

Article 3

For the purposes of this Convention the carrier shall be responsible for the acts and omissions of his agents and servants and of any other persons of whose services he makes use for the performance of the carriage, when such agents, servants or other persons are acting within the scope of their employment, as if such acts or omissions were his own.

CHAPTER III

Conclusion and performance of the contract of carriage

Article 4

The contract of carriage shall be confirmed by the making out of a consignment note. The absence, irregularity or loss of the consignment note shall not affect the existence or the validity of the contract of carriage which shall remain subject to the provisions of this Convention.

Article 5

1 The consignment note shall be made out in three original copies signed by the sender and by the carrier. These signatures may be printed or replaced by the stamps of the sender and the carrier if the law of the country in which the consignment note has been made out so permits. The first copy shall be handed to the sender, the second shall accompany the goods and the third shall be retained by the carrier.

2 When the goods which are to be carried have to be loaded in different vehicles, or are of different kinds or are divided into different lots, the sender or the carrier shall have the right to require a separate consignment note to be made out for each vehicle used, or for each kind or lot of goods.

Article 6

1 The consignment note shall contain the following particulars:

(a) the date of the consignment note and the place at which it is made out;
(b) the name and address of the sender;
(c) the name and address of the carrier;

(d) the place and the date of taking over of the goods and the place designated for delivery;

(e) the name and address of the consignee;

(f) the description in common use of the nature of the goods and the method of packing, and, in the case of dangerous goods, their generally recognised description;

(g) the number of packages and their special marks and numbers;

(h) the gross weight of the goods or their quantity otherwise expressed;

(i) charges relating to the carriage (carriage charges, supplementary charges, customs duties and other charges incurred from the making of the contract to the time of delivery);

(j) the requisite instructions for Customs and other formalities;

(k) a statement that the carriage is subject, notwithstanding any clause to the contrary, to the provisions of this Convention.

2 Where applicable, the consignment note shall also contain the following particulars:

(a) a statement that transhipment is not allowed;

(b) the charges which the sender undertakes to pay;

(c) the amount of 'cash on delivery' charges;

(d) a declaration of the value of the goods and the amount representing special interest in delivery;

(e) the sender's instructions to the carrier regarding insurance of the goods;

(f) the agreed time-limit within which the carriage is to be carried out;

(g) a list of documents handed to the carrier.

3 The parties may enter in the consignment note any other particulars which they deem useful.

Article 7

1 The sender shall be responsible for all expenses, loss and damage sustained by the carrier by reason of the inaccuracy or inadequacy of:

(a) the particulars specified in article 6, paragraph 1, (b), (d), (e), (f), (g), (h) and (j);

(b) the particulars specified in article 6, paragraph 2;

(c) any other particulars or instructions given by him to enable the consignment note to be made out or for the purpose of their being entered therein.

2 If, at the request of the sender, the carrier enters in the consignment note the particulars referred to in paragraph 1 of this article, he shall be deemed, unless the contrary is proved to have done so on behalf of the sender.

3 If the consignment note does not contain the statement specified in article 6, paragraph 1(k), the carrier shall be liable for all expenses, loss and damage sustained through such omission by the person entitled to dispose of the goods.

Article 8

1 On taking over the goods, the carrier shall check:

(a) the accuracy of the statements in the consignment note as to the number of packages and their marks and numbers, and

(b) the apparent condition of the goods and their packaging.

2 Where the carrier has no reasonable means of checking the accuracy of the statements referred to in paragraph 1(a) of this article, he shall enter his reservations in the consignment note together with the grounds on which they are based. He shall likewise specify the grounds for any reservations which he makes with regard to the apparent condition of the goods and their packaging. Such reservations shall not bind the sender unless he has expressly agreed to be bound by them in the consignment note.

3 The sender shall be entitled to require the carrier to check the gross weight of the goods or their quantity otherwise expressed. He may also require the contents

of the packages to be checked. The carrier shall be entitled to claim the cost of such checking. The result of the checks shall be entered in the consignment note.

Article 9

1 The consignment note shall be prima facie evidence of the making of the contract of carriage, the conditions of the contract and the receipt of the goods by the carrier.

2 If the consignment note contains no specific reservations by the carrier, it shall be presumed, unless the contrary is proved, that the goods and their packaging appeared to be in good condition when the carrier took them over and that the number of packages, their marks and numbers corresponded with the statements in the consignment note.

Article 10

The sender shall be liable to the carrier for damage to persons, equipment or other goods, and for any expenses due to defective packing of the goods, unless the defect was apparent or known to the carrier at the time when he took over the goods and he made no reservations concerning it.

Article 11

1 For the purposes of the Customs or other formalities which have to be completed before delivery of the goods, the sender shall attach the necessary documents to the consignment note or place them at the disposal of the carrier and shall furnish him with all the information which he requires.

2 The carrier shall not be under any duty to enquire into either the accuracy or the adequacy of such documents and information. The sender shall be liable to the carrier for any damage caused by the absence, inadequacy or irregularity of such documents and information, except in the case of some wrongful act or neglect on the part of the carrier.

3 The liability of the carrier for the consequences arising from the loss or incorrect use of the documents specified in and accompanying the consignment note or deposited with the carrier shall be that of an agent, provided that the compensation payable by the carrier shall not exceed that payable in the event of loss of the goods.

Article 12

1 The sender has a right to dispose of the goods, in particular by asking the carrier to stop the goods in transit, to change the place at which delivery is to take place or to deliver the goods to a consignee other than the consignee indicated in the consignment note.

2 This right shall cease to exist when the second copy of the consignment note is handed to the consignee or when the consignee exercises his right under article 13, paragraph 1; from that time onwards the carrier shall obey the orders of the consignee.

3 The consignee shall, however, have the right of disposal from the time when the consignment note is drawn up, if the sender makes an entry to that effect in the consignment note.

4 If in exercising his right of disposal the consignee has ordered the delivery of the goods to another person, that other person shall not be entitled to name other consignees.

5 The exercise of the right of disposal shall be subject to the following conditions:

(a) that the sender or, in the case referred to in paragraph 3 of this article, the consignee who wishes to exercise the right produces the first copy of the consignment note on which the new instructions to the carrier have been entered and indemnifies the carrier against all expenses, loss and damage involved in carrying out such instructions;

(b) that the carrying out of such instructions is possible at the time when the instructions reach the person who is to carry them out and does not either interfere with the normal working of the carrier's undertaking or prejudice the senders or consignees of other consignments;

(c) that the instructions do not result in a division of the consignment.

6 When, by reason of the provisions of paragraph 5(b) of this article, the carrier cannot carry out the instructions which he receives he shall immediately notify the person who gave him such instructions.

7 A carrier who has not carried out the instructions given under the conditions provided for in this article, or who has carried them out without requiring the first copy of the consignment note to be produced, shall be liable to the person entitled to make a claim for any loss or damage caused thereby.

Article 13

1 After arrival of the goods at the place designated for delivery, the consignee shall be entitled to require the carrier to deliver to him, against a receipt, the second copy of the consignment note and the goods. If the loss of the goods is established or if the goods have not arrived after the expiry of the period provided for in article 19, the consignee shall be entitled to enforce in his own name against the carrier any rights arising from the contract of carriage.

2 The consignee who avails himself of the rights granted to him under paragraph 1 of this article shall pay the charges shown to be due on the consignment note, but in the event of dispute on this matter the carrier shall not be required to deliver the goods unless security has been furnished by the consignee.

Article 14

1 If for any reason it is or becomes impossible to carry out the contract in accordance with the terms laid down in the consignment note before the goods reach the place designated for delivery, the carrier shall ask for instructions from the person entitled to dispose of the goods in accordance with the provisions of article 12.

2 Nevertheless, if circumstances are such as to allow the carriage to be carried out under conditions differing from those laid down in the consignment note and if the carrier has been unable to obtain instructions in reasonable time from the person entitled to dispose of the goods in accordance with the provisions of article 12, he shall take such steps as seem to him to be in the best interests of the person entitled to dispose of the goods.

Article 15

1 Where circumstances prevent delivery of the goods after their arrival at the place designated for delivery, the carrier shall ask the sender for his instructions. If the consignee refuses the goods the sender shall be entitled to dispose of them without being obliged to produce the first copy of the consignment note.

2 Even if he has refused the goods, the consignee may nevertheless require delivery so long as the carrier has not received instructions to the contrary from the sender.

3 When circumstances preventing delivery of the goods arise after the consignee, in exercise of his rights under article 12, paragraph 3, has given an order for the goods to be delivered to another person, paragraphs 1 and 2 of this article shall apply as if the consignee were the sender and that other person were the consignee.

Article 16

1 The carrier shall be entitled to recover the cost of his request for instructions and any expenses entailed in carrying out such instructions, unless such expenses were caused by the wrongful act or neglect of the carrier.

2 In the cases referred to in article 14, paragraph 1, and in article 15, the carrier may immediately unload the goods for account of the person entitled to dispose of them and thereupon the carriage shall be deemed to be at an end. The carrier shall then hold the goods on behalf of the person so entitled. He may however entrust

them to a third party, and in that case he shall not be under any liability except for the exercise of reasonable care in the choice of such third party. The charges due under the consignment note and all other expenses shall remain chargeable against the goods.

3 The carrier may sell the goods, without awaiting instructions from the person entitled to dispose of them, if the goods are perishable or their condition warrants such a course, or when the storage expenses would be out of proportion to the value of the goods. He may also proceed to the sale of the goods in other cases if after the expiry of a reasonable period he has not received from the person entitled to dispose of the goods instructions to the contrary which he may reasonably be required to carry out.

4 If the goods have been sold pursuant to this article, the proceeds of sale, after deduction of the expenses chargeable against the goods, shall be placed at the disposal of the person entitled to dispose of the goods. If these charges exceed the proceeds of sale, the carrier shall be entitled to the difference.

5 The procedure in the case of sale shall be determined by the law or custom of the place where the goods are situated.

CHAPTER IV
Liability of the carrier

Article 17

1 The carrier shall be liable for the total or partial loss of the goods and for damage thereto occurring between the time when he takes over the goods and the time of delivery, as well as for any delay in delivery.

2 The carrier shall however be relieved of liability if the loss, damage or delay was caused by the wrongful act or neglect of the claimant, by the instructions of the claimant given otherwise than as the result of a wrongful act or neglect on the part of the carrier, by inherent vice of the goods or through circumstances which the carrier could not avoid and the consequences of which he was unable to prevent.

3 The carrier shall not be relieved of liability by reason of the defective condition of the vehicle used by him in order to perform the carriage, or by reason of the wrongful act or neglect of the person from whom he may have hired the vehicle or of the agents or servants of the latter.

4 Subject to article 18, paragraphs 2 to 5 the carrier shall be relieved of liability when the loss or damage arises from the special risks inherent in one or more of the following circumstances:

(a) use of open unsheeted vehicles, when their use has been expressly agreed and specified in the consignment note;

(b) the lack of, or defective condition of packing in the case of goods which, by their nature, are liable to wastage or to be damaged when not packed or when not properly packed;

(c) handling, loading, stowage or unloading of the goods by the sender, the consignee or person acting on behalf of the sender or consignee;

(d) the nature of certain kinds of goods which particularly exposes them to total or partial loss or to damage, especially through breakage, rust, decay, desiccation, leakage, normal wastage, or the action of moth or vermin;

(e) insufficiency or inadequacy of marks or numbers on the packages;

(f) the carriage of livestock.

5 Where under this article the carrier is not under any liability in respect of some of the factors causing the loss, damage or delay, he shall only be liable to the extent that those factors for which he is liable under this article have contributed to the loss, damage or delay.

Article 18

1 The burden of proving that loss, damage or delay was due to one of the causes specified in article 17, paragraph 2, shall rest upon the carrier.

2 When the carrier establishes that in the circumstances of the case, the loss or damage could be attributed to one or more of the special risks referred to in article 17, paragraph 4, it shall be presumed that it was so caused. The claimant shall however be entitled to prove that the loss or damage was not, in fact, attributable either wholly or partly to one of these risks.

3 This presumption shall not apply in the circumstances set out in article 17, paragraph 4(a), if there has been an abnormal shortage, or a loss of any package.

4 If the carriage is performed in vehicles specially equipped to protect the goods from the effects of heat, cold, variations in temperature or the humidity of the air, the carrier shall not be entitled to claim the benefit of article 17, paragraph 4(d) unless he proves that all steps incumbent on him in the circumstances with respect to the choice, maintenance and use of such equipment were taken and that he complied with any special instructions issued to him.

5 The carrier shall not be entitled to claim the benefit of article 17, paragraph 4(f), unless he proves that all steps normally incumbent on him in the circumstances were taken and that he complied with any special instructions issued to him.

Article 19

Delay in delivery shall be said to occur when the goods have not been delivered within the agreed time-limit or when, failing an agreed time-limit, the actual duration of the carriage having regard to the circumstances of the case, and in particular, in the case of partial loads, the time required for making up a complete load in the normal way, exceeds the time it would be reasonable to allow a diligent carrier.

Article 20

1 The fact that the goods have not been delivered within thirty days following the expiry of the agreed time-limit, or if there is no agreed time-limit, within sixty days from the time when the carrier took over the goods, shall be conclusive evidence of the loss of the goods, and the person entitled to make a claim may thereupon treat them as lost.

2 The person so entitled may, on receipt of compensation for the missing goods, request in writing that he shall be notified immediately should the goods be recovered in the course of the year following the payment of compensation. He shall be given a written acknowledgement of such request.

3 Within the thirty days following receipt of such notification, the person entitled as aforesaid may require the goods to be delivered to him against payment of the charges shown to be due on the consignment note and also against refund of the compensation he received less any charges included therein but without prejudice to any claims to compensation for delay in delivery under article 23 and, where applicable, article 26.

4 In the absence of the request mentioned in paragraph 2 or of any instructions given within the period of thirty days specified in paragraph 3, or if the goods are not recovered until more than one year after the payment of compensation, the carrier shall be entitled to deal with them in accordance with the law of the place where the goods are situated.

Article 21

Should the goods have been delivered to the consignee without collection of the 'cash on delivery' charge which should have been collected by the carrier under the terms of the contract of carriage, the carrier shall be liable to the sender for compensation not exceeding the amount of such charge without prejudice to his right of action against the consignee.

Article 22

1 When the sender hands goods of a dangerous nature to the carrier, he shall inform the carrier of the exact nature of the danger and indicate, if necessary, the precautions to be taken. If this information has not been entered in the consignment note, the burden of proving, by some other means, that the carrier knew the exact nature of the danger constituted by the carriage of the said goods shall rest upon the sender or the consignee.

2 Goods of a dangerous nature which, in the circumstances referred to in paragraph 1 of this article, the carrier did not know were dangerous, may, at any time or place, be unloaded, destroyed or rendered harmless by the carrier without compensation; further, the sender shall be liable for all expenses, loss or damage arising out of their handing over for carriage or of their carriage.

Article 23

1 When, under the provisions of this Convention, a carrier is liable for compensation in respect of total or partial loss of goods, such compensation shall be calculated by reference to the value of the goods at the place and time at which they were accepted for carriage.

2 The value of the goods shall be fixed according to the commodity exchange price or, if there is no such price, according to the current market price, or, if there is no commodity exchange price or current market price, by reference to the normal value of goods of the same kind and quality.

[3 Compensation shall not, however, exceed 8.33 units of account per kilogram of gross weight short.]

4 In addition, the carriage charges, Customs duties and other charges incurred in respect of the carriage of the goods shall be refunded in full in case of total loss and in proportion to the loss sustained in case of partial loss, but no further damages shall be payable.

5 In the case of delay, if the claimant proves that damage has resulted therefrom the carrier shall pay compensation for such damage not exceeding the carriage charges.

6 Higher compensation may only be claimed where the value of the goods or a special interest in delivery has been declared in accordance with articles 24 and 26.

[7 The unit of account mentioned in this Convention is the Special Drawing Right as defined by the International Monetary Fund. The amount mentioned in paragraph 3 of this article shall be converted into the national currency of the State of the Court seised of the case on the basis of the value of that currency on the date of judgment or the date agreed upon by the Parties.]

Article 24

The sender may, against payment of a surcharge to be agreed upon, declare in the consignment note a value for the goods exceeding the limit laid down in article 23, paragraph 3, and in that case the amount of the declared value shall be substituted for that limit.

Article 25

1 In case of damage, the carrier shall be liable for the amount by which the goods have diminished in value, calculated by reference to the value of the goods fixed in accordance with article 23, paragraphs 1, 2 and 4.

2 The compensation may not, however, exceed:

(a) if the whole consignment has been damaged, the amount payable in the case of total loss;

(b) if part only of the consignment has been damaged, the amount payable in the case of loss of the part affected.

Article 26

1 The sender may, against payment of a surcharge to be agreed upon, fix the amount of a special interest in delivery in the case of loss or damage or of the

agreed time-limit being exceeded, by entering such amount in the consignment note.

2 If a declaration of a special interest in delivery has been made, compensation for the additional loss or damage proved may be claimed, up to the total amount of the interest declared, independently of the compensation provided for in articles 23, 24 and 25.

Article 27

1 The claimant shall be entitled to claim interest on compensation payable. Such interest, calculated at five per centum per annum, shall accrue from the date on which the claim was sent in writing to the carrier or, if no such claim has been made, from the date on which legal proceedings were instituted.

2 When the amounts on which the calculation of the compensation is based are not expressed in the currency of the country in which payment is claimed, conversion shall be at the rate of exchange applicable on the day and at the place of payment of compensation.

Article 28

1 In cases where, under the law applicable, loss, damage or delay arising out of carriage under this Convention gives rise to an extra-contractual claim, the carrier may avail himself of the provisions of this Convention which exclude his liability or which fix or limit the compensation due.

2 In cases where the extra-contractual liability for loss, damage or delay of one of the persons for whom the carrier is responsible under the terms of article 3 is in issue, such person may also avail himself of the provisions of this Convention which exclude the liability of the carrier or which fix or limit the compensation due.

Article 29

1 The carrier shall not be entitled to avail himself of the provisions of this chapter which exclude or limit his liability or which shift the burden of proof if the damage was caused by his wilful misconduct or by such default on his part as, in accordance with the law of the court or tribunal seised of the case, is considered as equivalent to wilful misconduct.

2 The same provision shall apply if the wilful misconduct or default is committed by the agents or servants of the carrier or by any other persons of whose services he makes use for the performance of the carriage, when such agents, servants or other persons are acting within the scope of their employment. Furthermore, in such a case such agents, servants or other persons shall not be entitled to avail themselves, with regard to their personal liability, of the provisions of this chapter referred to in paragraph 1.

CHAPTER V

Claims and actions

Article 30

1 If the consignee takes delivery of the goods without duly checking their condition with the carrier or without sending him reservations giving a general indication of the loss or damage, not later than the time of delivery in the case of apparent loss or damage and within seven days of delivery, Sundays and public holidays excepted, in the case of loss or damage which is not apparent, the fact of his taking delivery shall be prima facie evidence that he has received the goods in the condition described in the consignment note. In the case of loss or damage which is not apparent the reservations referred to shall be made in writing.

2 When the condition of the goods has been duly checked by the consignee and the carrier, evidence contradicting the result of this checking shall only be admissible in the case of loss or damage which is not apparent and provided that

the consignee has duly sent reservations in writing to the carrier within seven days, Sundays and public holidays excepted, from the date of checking.

3 No compensation shall be payable for delay in delivery unless a reservation has been sent in writing to the carrier, within twenty-one days from the time that the goods were placed at the disposal of the consignee.

4 In calculating the time-limits provided for in this article the date of delivery, or the date of checking, or the date when the goods were placed at the disposal of the consignee, as the case may be, shall not be included.

5 The carrier and the consignee shall give each other every reasonable facility for making the requisite investigations and checks.

Article 31

1 In legal proceedings arising out of carriage under this Convention, the plaintiff may bring an action in any court or tribunal of a contracting country designated by agreement between the parties and, in addition, in the courts or tribunals of a country within whose territory:

(a) the defendant is ordinarily resident, or has his principal place of business, or the branch or agency through which the contract of carriage was made, or

(b) the place where the goods were taken over by the carrier or the place designated for delivery is situated,

and in no other courts or tribunals.

2 Where in respect of a claim referred to in paragraph 1 of this article an action is pending before a court or tribunal competent under that paragraph, or where in respect of such a claim a judgment has been entered by such a court or tribunal no new action shall be started between the same parties on the same grounds unless the judgment of the court or tribunal before which the first action was brought is not enforceable in the country in which the fresh proceedings are brought.

3 When a judgment entered by a court or tribunal of a contracting country in any such action as is referred to in paragraph 1 of this article has become enforceable in that country, it shall also become enforceable in each of the other contracting States, as soon as the formalities required in the country concerned have been complied with. These formalities shall not permit the merits of the case to be reopened.

4 The provisions of paragraph 3 of this article shall apply to judgments after trial, judgments by default and settlements confirmed by an order of the court, but shall not apply to interim judgments or to awards of damages, in addition to costs against a plaintiff who wholly or partly fails in his action.

5 Security for costs shall not be required in proceedings arising out of carriage under this Convention from nationals of contracting countries resident or having their place of business in one of those countries.

Article 32

1 The period of limitation for an action arising out of carriage under this Convention shall be one year. Nevertheless, in the case of wilful misconduct, or such default as in accordance with the law of the court or tribunal seised of the case, is considered as equivalent to wilful misconduct, the period of limitation shall be three years. The period of limitation shall begin to run:

(a) in the case of partial loss, damage or delay in delivery, from the date of delivery;

(b) in the case of total loss, from the thirtieth day after the expiry of the agreed time-limit or where there is no agreed time-limit from the sixtieth day from the date on which the goods were taken over by the carrier;

(c) in all other cases, on the expiry of a period of three months after the making of the contract of carriage.

The day on which the period of limitation begins to run shall not be included in the period.

2 A written claim shall suspend the period of limitation until such date as the carrier rejects the claim by notification in writing and returns the documents attached thereto. If a part of the claim is admitted the period of limitation shall start to run again only in respect of that part of the claim still in dispute. The burden of proof of the receipt of the claim, or of the reply and of the return of the documents, shall rest with the party relying upon these facts. The running of the period of limitation shall not be suspended by further claims having the same object.

3 Subject to the provisions of paragraph 2 above, the extension of the period of limitation shall be governed by the law of the court or tribunal seised of the case. That law shall also govern the fresh accrual rights of action.

4 A right of action which has become barred by lapse of time may not be exercised by way of counter-claim or set-off.

Article 33

The contract of carriage may contain a clause conferring competence on an arbitration tribunal if the clause conferring competence on the tribunal provides that the tribunal shall apply this Convention.

CHAPTER VI

Provisions relating to carriage performed by successive carriers

Article 34

If carriage governed by a single contract is performed by successive road carriers, each of them shall be responsible for the performance of the whole operation, the second carrier and each succeeding carrier becoming a party to the contract of carriage, under the terms of the consignment note, by reason of his acceptance of the goods and the consignment note.

Article 35

1 A carrier accepting the goods from a previous carrier shall give the latter a dated and signed receipt. He shall enter his name and address on the second copy of the consignment note. Where applicable, he shall enter on the second copy of the consignment note and on the receipt reservations of the kind provided for in article 8, paragraph 2.

2 The provisions of article 9 shall apply to the relations between successive carriers.

Article 36

Except in the case of a counter-claim or a set-off raised in an action concerning a claim based on the same contract of carriage, legal proceedings in respect of liability for loss, damage or delay may only be brought against the first carrier, the last carrier or the carrier who was performing that portion of the carriage during which the event causing the loss, damage or delay occurred; an action may be brought at the same time against several of these carriers.

Article 37

A carrier who has paid compensation in compliance with the provisions of this Convention, shall be entitled to recover such compensation, together with interest thereon and all costs and expenses incurred by reason of the claim, from the other carriers who have taken part in the carriage, subject to the following provisions:

(a) the carrier responsible for the loss or damage shall be solely liable for the compensation whether paid by himself or by another carrier;

(b) when the loss or damage has been caused by the action of two or more carriers, each of them shall pay an amount proportionate to his share of liability; should it be impossible to apportion the liability, each carrier shall be liable in proportion to the share of the payment for the carriage which is due to him;

(c) if it cannot be ascertained to which carriers liability is attributable for the loss or damage, the amount of the compensation shall be apportioned between all the carriers as laid down in (b) above.

Article 38
If one of the carriers is insolvent, the share of the compensation due from him and unpaid by him shall be divided among the other carriers in proportion to the share of the payment for the carriage due to them.

Article 39
1 No carrier against whom a claim is made under articles 37 and 38 shall be entitled to dispute the validity of the payment made by the carrier making the claim if the amount of the compensation was determined by judicial authority after the first mentioned carrier had been given due notice of the proceedings and afforded an opportunity of entering an appearance.
2 A carrier wishing to take proceedings to enforce his right of recovery may make his claim before the competent court or tribunal of the country in which one of the carriers concerned is ordinarily resident, or has his principal place of business or the branch or agency through which the contract of carriage was made. All the carriers concerned may be made defendants in the same action.
3 The provisions of article 31, paragraphs 3 and 4 shall apply to judgments entered in the proceedings referred to in articles 37 and 38.
4 The provisions of article 32 shall apply to claims between carriers. The period of limitation shall, however, begin to run either on the date of the final judicial decision fixing the amount of compensation payable under the provisions of this Convention, or, if there is no such judicial decision, from the actual date of payment.

Article 40
Carriers shall be free to agree among themselves on provisions other than those laid down in articles 37 and 38.

CHAPTER VII
Nullity of stipulations contrary to the Convention

Article 41
1 Subject to the provisions of article 40, any stipulation which would directly or indirectly derogate from the provisions of this Convention shall be null and void. The nullity of such a stipulation shall not involve the nullity of the other provisions of the contract.
2 In particular, a benefit of insurance in favour of the carrier or any other similar clause, or any clause shifting the burden of proof shall be null and void.

[Chapter VIII deals with the coming into force of the Convention, the settlement of disputes between the high contracting parties and related matters.]

CARRIAGE OF GOODS BY SEA ACT 1971
(1971, c 19)

1 Application of Hague Rules as amended

(1) In this Act, 'the Rules' means the International Convention for the unification of certain rules of law relating to bills of lading signed at Brussels on 25th August 1924, as amended by the Protocol signed at Brussels on 23rd February 1968 [and by the protocol signed at Brussels on 21st December 1979].

(2) The provisions of the Rules, as set out in the Schedule to this Act, shall have the force of law.

(3) Without prejudice to subsection (2) above, the said provisions shall have effect (and have the force of law) in relation to and in connection with the carriage of goods by sea in ships where the port of shipment is a port in the United Kingdom, whether or not the carriage is between ports in two different States within the meaning of Article X of the Rules.

(4) Subject to subsection (6) below, nothing in this section shall be taken as applying anything in the Rules to any contract for the carriage of goods by sea, unless the contract expressly or by implication provides for the issue of a bill of lading or any similar document of title.

[. . .]

(6) Without prejudice to Article X(c) of the Rules, the Rules shall have the force of law in relation to—

(a) any bill of lading if the contract contained in or evidenced by it expressly provides that the Rules shall govern the contract, and

(b) any receipt which is a non-negotiable document marked as such if the contract contained in or evidenced by it is a contract for the carriage of goods by sea which expressly provides that the Rules are to govern the contract as if the receipt were a bill of lading, but subject, where paragraph (b) applies, to any necessary modifications and in particular with the omission in Article III of the Rules of the second sentence of paragraph 4 and of paragraph 7.

(7) If and so far as the contract contained in or evidenced by a bill of lading or receipt within paragraph (a) or (b) of subsection (6) above applies to deck cargo or live animals, the Rules as given the force of law by that subsection shall have effect as if Article I(c) did not exclude deck cargo and live animals.

In this subsection 'deck cargo' means cargo which by the contract of carriage is stated as being carried on deck and is so carried.

[1A Conversion of special drawing rights into sterling

(1) For the purposes of Article IV of the Rules the value on a particular day of one special drawing right shall be treated as equal to such a sum in sterling as the International Monetary Fund have fixed as being the equivalent of one special drawing right—

(a) for that day; or

(b) if no sum has been so fixed for that day, for the last day before that day for which a sum has been so fixed.

(2) A certificate given by or on behalf of the Treasury stating—

(a) that a particular sum in sterling has been fixed as aforesaid for a particular day; or

(b) that no sum has been so fixed for a particular day and that a particular sum in sterling has been so fixed for a day which is the last day for which a sum has been so fixed before the particular day,

shall be conclusive evidence of those matters for the purposes of subsection (1) above;

and a document purporting to be such a certificate shall in any proceedings be received in evidence and, unless the contrary is proved, be deemed to be such a certificate.

(3) The Treasury may charge a reasonable fee for any certificate given in

pursuance of subsection (2) above, and any fee received by the Treasury by virtue of this subsection shall be paid into the Consolidated Fund.]

2 Contracting States, etc

(1) If Her Majesty by Order in Council certifies to the following effect, that is to say, that for the purposes of the Rules—

(a) a State specified in the Order is a contracting State, or is a contracting State in respect of any place or territory so specified; or

(b) any place or territory specified in the Order forms part of a State so specified (whether a contracting State or not),

the Order shall, except so far as it has been superseded by a subsequent Order, be conclusive evidence of the matters so certified.

(2) An Order in Council under this section may be varied or revoked by a subsequent Order in Council.

3 Absolute warranty of seaworthiness not to be implied in contracts to which Rules apply

There shall not be implied in any contract for the carriage of goods by sea to which the Rules apply by virtue of this Act any absolute undertaking by the carrier of the goods to provide a seaworthy ship.

4 Application of Act to British possessions, etc

(1) Her Majesty may by Order in Council direct that this Act shall extend, subject to such exceptions, adaptations and modifications as may be specified in the Order, to all or any of the following territories, that is—

(a) any colony (not being a colony for whose external relations a country other than the United Kingdom is responsible),

(b) any country outside Her Majesty's dominions in which Her Majesty has jurisdiction in right of Her Majesty's Government of the United Kingdom.

(2) An Order in Council under this section may contain such transitional and other consequential and incidental provisions as appear to Her Majesty to be expedient, including provisions amending or repealing any legislation about the carriage of goods by sea forming part of the law of any of the territories mentioned in paragraphs (a) and (b) above.

(3) An Order in Council under this section may be varied or revoked by a subsequent Order in Council.

5 Extension of application of Rules to carriage from ports in British possessions, etc

(1) Her Majesty may by Order in Council provide that section 1(3) of this Act shall have effect as if the reference therein to the United Kingdom included a reference to all or any of the following territories, that is—

(a) the Isle of Man;

(b) any of the Channel Islands specified in the Order;

(c) any colony specified in the Order (not being a colony for whose external relations a country other than the United Kingdom is responsible);

[. . .]

(e) any country specified in the Order, being a country outside Her Majesty's dominions in which Her Majesty has jurisdiction in right of Her Majesty's Government of the United Kingdom.

(2) An Order in Council under this section may be varied or revoked by a subsequent Order in Council.

6 Supplemental

(1) This Act may be cited as the Carriage of Goods by Sea Act 1971.

(2) It is hereby declared that this Act extends to Northern Ireland.

(3) The following enactments shall be repealed, that is—

(a) the Carriage of Goods by Sea Act 1924,

(b) section 12(4)(a) of the Nuclear Installations Act 1965,

and without prejudice to section [17(2)(a) of the Interpretation Act 1978], the reference to the said Act of 1924 in section 1(1)(i)(ii) of the Hovercraft Act 1968 shall include a reference to this Act.

[(4) It is hereby declared that for the purposes of Article VIII of the Rules section 186 of the Merchant Shipping Act 1995 (which entirely exempts shipowners and others in certain circumstances for loss of, or damage to, goods) is a provision relating to limitation of liability.]

(5) This Act shall come into force on such day as Her Majesty may by Order in Council appoint, and, for the purposes of the transition from the law in force immediately before the day appointed under this subsection to the provisions of this Act, the Order appointing the day may provide that those provisions shall have effect subject to such transitional provisions as may be contained in the Order.

SCHEDULE

THE HAGUE RULES AS AMENDED BY THE BRUSSELS PROTOCOL 1968

Article I

In these Rules the following words are employed, with the meanings set out below:—

(a) 'Carrier' includes the owner or the charterer who enters into a contract of carriage with a shipper.

(b) 'Contract of carriage' applies only to contracts of carriage covered by a bill of lading or any similar document of title, in so far as such document relates to the carriage of goods by sea, including any bill of lading or any similar document as aforesaid issued under or pursuant to a charter party from the moment at which such bill of lading or similar document of title regulates the relations between a carrier and a holder of the same.

(c) 'Goods' includes goods, wares, merchandise, and articles of every kind whatsoever except live animals and cargo which by the contract of carriage is stated as being carried on deck and is so carried.

(d) 'Ship' means any vessel used for the carriage of goods by sea.

(e) 'Carriage of goods' covers the period from the time when the goods are loaded on to the time they are discharged from the ship.

Article II

Subject to the provisions of Article VI, under every contract of carriage of goods by sea the carrier, in relation to the loading, handling, stowage, carriage, custody, care and discharge of such goods, shall be subject to the responsibilities and liabilities, and entitled to the rights and immunities hereinafter set forth.

Article III

(1) The carrier shall be bound before and at the beginning of the voyage to exercise due diligence to—

(a) Make the ship seaworthy.

(b) Properly man, equip and supply the ship.

(c) Make the holds, refrigerating and cool chambers, and all other parts of the ship in which goods are carried, fit and safe for their reception, carriage and preservation.

(2) Subject to the provisions of Article IV, the carrier shall properly and carefully load, handle, stow, carry, keep, care for, and discharge the goods carried.

(3) After receiving the goods into his charge the carrier or the master or agent of the carrier shall, on demand of the shipper, issue to the shipper a bill of lading showing among other things—

(a) The leading marks necessary for identification of the goods as the same are furnished in writing by the shipper before the loading of such goods starts, provided such marks are stamped or otherwise shown clearly upon the goods if uncovered, or on the cases or coverings in which such goods are contained, in such a manner as should ordinarily remain legible until the end of the voyage.

(b) Either the number of packages or pieces, or the quantity, or weight, as the case may be, as furnished in writing by the shipper.

(c) The apparent order and condition of the goods.

Provided that no carrier, master or agent of the carrier shall be bound to state or show in the bill of lading any marks, number, quantity, or weight which he has reasonable ground for suspecting not accurately to represent the goods actually received, or which be has had no reasonable means of checking.

(4) Such a bill of lading shall be prima facie evidence of the receipt by the carrier of the goods as therein described in accordance with paragraph 3(a), (b) and (c). However, proof to the contrary shall not be admissible when the bill of lading has been transferred to a third party acting in good faith.

(5) The shipper shall be deemed to have guaranteed to the carrier the accuracy at the time of shipment of the marks, number, quantity and weight, as furnished by him, and the shipper shall indemnify the carrier against all loss, damages and expenses arising or resulting from inaccuracies in such particulars. The right of the carrier to such indemnity shall in no way limit his responsibility and liability under the contract of carriage to any person other than the shipper.

(6) Unless notice of loss or damage and the general nature of such loss or damage be given in writing to the carrier or his agent at the port of discharge before or at the time of the removal of the goods into the custody of the person entitled to delivery thereof under the contract of carriage, or, if the loss or damage be not apparent, within three days, such removal shall be prima facie evidence of the delivery by the carrier of the goods as described in the bill of lading.

The notice in writing need not be given if the state of the goods has, at the time of their receipt, been the subject of joint survey or inspection.

Subject to paragraph *6bis* the carrier and the ship shall in any event be discharged from all liability whatsoever in respect of the goods, unless suit is brought within one year of their delivery or of the date when they should have been delivered. This period may, however, be extended if the parties so agree after the cause of action has arisen.

In the case of any actual or apprehended loss or damage the carrier and the receiver shall give all reasonable facilities to each other for inspecting and tallying the goods.

(*6bis*) An action for indemnity against a third person may be brought even after the expiration of the year provided for in the preceding paragraph if brought within the time allowed by the law of the court seised of the case. However, the time allowed shall be not less than three months, commencing from the day when the person bringing such action for indemnity has settled the claim or has been served with process in the action against himself.

(7) After the goods are loaded the bill of lading to be issued by the carrier, master, or agent of the carrier, to the shipper shall, if the shipper so demands, be a 'shipped' bill of lading, provided that if the shipper shall have previously taken up any document of title to such goods, he shall surrender the same as against the issue of the 'shipped' bill of lading, but at the option of the carrier such document of title may be noted at the port of shipment by the carrier, master, or agent with the name or names of the ship or ships upon which the goods have been shipped and the date or dates of shipment, and when so noted if it shows the particulars mentioned in paragraph 3 of Article III, shall for the purpose of this article be deemed to constitute a 'shipped' bill of lading.

(8) Any clause, covenant, or agreement in a contract of carriage relieving the carrier or the ship from liability for loss or damage to, or in connection with, goods arising from negligence, fault, or failure in the duties and obligations provided in

this article or lessening such liability otherwise than as provided in these Rules, shall be null and void and of no effect. A benefit of insurance in favour of the carrier or similar clause shall be deemed to be a clause relieving the carrier from liability.

Article IV

(1) Neither the carrier nor the ship shall be liable for loss or damage arising or resulting from unseaworthiness unless caused by want of due diligence on the part of the carrier to make the ship seaworthy, and to secure that the ship is properly manned, equipped and supplied, and to make the holds, refrigerating and cool chambers and all other parts of the ship in which goods are carried fit and safe for their reception, carriage and preservation in accordance with the provisions of paragraph 1 of Article III. Whenever loss or damage has resulted from unseaworthiness the burden of proving the exercise of due diligence shall be on the carrier or other person claiming exemption under this article.

(2) Neither the carrier nor the ship shall be responsible for loss or damage arising or resulting from—

(a) Act, neglect, or default of the master, mariner, pilot, or the servants of the carrier in the navigation or in the management of the ship.

(b) Fire, unless caused by the actual fault or privity of the carrier.

(c) Perils, dangers and accidents of the sea or other navigable waters.

(d) Act of God.

(e) Act of war.

(f) Act of public enemies.

(g) Arrest or restraint of princes, rulers or people, or seizure under legal process.

(h) Quarantine restrictions.

(i) Act or omission of the shipper or owner of the goods, his agent or representative.

(j) Strikes or lockouts or stoppage or restraint of labour from whatever cause, whether partial or general.

(k) Riots and civil commotions.

(l) Saving or attempting to save life or property at sea.

(m) Wastage in bulk or weight or any other loss or damage arising from inherent defect, quality or vice of the goods.

(n) Insufficiency of packing.

(o) Insufficiency or inadequacy of marks.

(p) Latent defects not discoverable by due diligence.

(q) Any other cause arising without the actual fault or privity of the carrier, or without the fault or neglect of the agents or servants of the carrier, but the burden of proof shall be on the person claiming the benefit of this exception to show that neither the actual fault or privity of the carrier nor the fault or neglect of the agents or servants of the carrier contributed to the loss or damage.

(3) The shipper shall not be responsible for the loss or damage sustained by the carrier or the ship arising or resulting from any cause without the act, fault or neglect of the shipper, his agents or his servants.

(4) Any deviation in saving or attempting to save life or property at sea or any reasonable deviation shall not be deemed to be an infringement or breach of these Rules or of the contract of carriage, and the carrier shall not be liable for any loss or damage resulting therefrom.

(5)(a) Unless the nature and value of such goods have been declared by the shipper before shipment and inserted in the bill of lading, neither the carrier nor the ship shall in any event be or become liable for any loss or damage to or in connection with the goods in an amount exceeding [666.67 units of account] per package or unit or [2 units of account per kilogramme] of gross weight of the goods lost or damaged, whichever is the higher.

(b) The total amount recoverable shall be calculated by reference to the value of such goods at the place and time at which the goods are discharged from the ship in accordance with the contract or should have been so discharged.

The value of the goods shall be fixed according to the commodity exchange price, or, if there be no such price, according to the current market price, or, if there be no commodity exchange price or current market price, by reference to the normal value of goods of the same kind and quality.

(c) Where a container, pallet or similar article of transport is used to consolidate goods, the number of packages or units enumerated in the bill of lading as packed in such article of transport shall be deemed the number of packages or units for the purpose of this paragraph as far as these packages or units are concerned. Except as aforesaid such article of transport shall be considered the package or unit.

[(d) The unit of account mentioned in this Article is the special drawing right as defined by the International Monetary Fund. The amounts mentioned in subparagraph (a) of this paragraph shall be converted into national currency on the basis of the value of that currency on a date to be determined by the law of the court seised of the case.]

(e) Neither the carrier nor the ship shall be entitled to the benefit of the limitation of liability provided for in this paragraph if it is proved that the damage resulted from an act or omission of the carrier done with intent to cause damage, or recklessly and with knowledge that damage would probably result.

(f) The declaration mentioned in sub-paragraph (a) of this paragraph, if embodied in the bill of lading, shall be prima facie evidence, but shall not be binding or conclusive on the carrier.

(g) By agreement between the carrier, master or agent of the carrier and the shipper other maximum amounts than those mentioned in sub-paragraph (a) of this paragraph may be fixed, provided that no maximum amount so fixed shall be less than the appropriate maximum mentioned in that sub-paragraph.

(h) Neither the carrier nor the ship shall be responsible in any event for loss or damage to, or in connection with, goods if the nature or value thereof has been knowingly mis-stated by the shipper in the bill of lading.

(6) Goods of an inflammable, explosive or dangerous nature to the shipment whereof the carrier, master or agent of the carrier has not consented with knowledge of their nature and character, may at any time before discharge be landed at any place, or destroyed or rendered innocuous by the carrier without compensation and the shipper of such goods shall be liable for all damages and expenses directly or indirectly arising out of or resulting from such shipment. If any such goods shipped with such knowledge and consent shall become a danger to the ship or cargo, they may in like manner be landed at any place, or destroyed or rendered innocuous by the carrier without liability on the part of the carrier except to general average, if any.

Article IV bis

(1) The defences and limits of liability provided for in these Rules shall apply in any action against the carrier in respect of loss or damage to goods covered by a contract of carriage whether the action be founded in contract or in tort.

(2) If such an action is brought against a servant or agent of the carrier (such servant or agent not being an independent contractor), such servant or agent shall be entitled to avail himself of the defences and limits of liability which the carrier is entitled to invoke under these Rules.

(3) The aggregate of the amounts recoverable from the carrier, and such servants and agents, shall in no case exceed the limit provided for in these Rules.

(4) Nevertheless, a servant or agent of the carrier shall not be entitled to avail himself of the provisions of this article, if it is proved that the damage resulted

from an act or omission of the servant or agent done with intent to cause damage or recklessly and with knowledge that damage would probably result.

Article V

A carrier shall be at liberty to surrender in whole or in part all or any of his rights and immunities or to increase any of his responsibilities and obligations under these Rules, provided such surrender or increase shall be embodied in the bill of lading issued to the shipper. The provisions of the Rules shall not be applicable to charter parties, but if bills of lading are issued in the case of a ship under a charter party they shall comply with the terms of these Rules. Nothing in these Rules shall be held to prevent the insertion in a bill of lading of any lawful provisions regarding general average.

Article VI

Notwithstanding the provisions of the preceding articles, a carrier, master or agent of the carrier and a shipper shall in regard to any particular goods be at liberty to enter into any agreement in any terms as to the responsibility and liability of the carrier for such goods, and as to the rights and immunities of the carrier in respect of such goods, or his obligation as to seaworthiness, so far as this stipulation is not contrary to public policy, or the care or diligence of his servants or agents in regard to the loading, handling, stowage, carriage, custody, care and discharge of the goods carried by sea, provided that in this case no bill of lading has been or shall be issued and that the terms agreed shall be embodied in a receipt which shall be a non-negotiable document and shall be marked as such.

Any agreement so entered into shall have full legal effect.

Provided that this article shall not apply to ordinary commercial shipment made in the ordinary course of trade, but only to other shipments where the character or condition of the property to be carried or the circumstances, terms and conditions under which the carriage is to be performed are such as reasonably to justify a special agreement.

Article VII

Nothing herein contained shall prevent a carrier or a shipper from entering into any agreement, stipulation, condition, reservation or exemption as to the responsibility and liability of the carrier or the ship for the loss or damage to, or in connection with, the custody and care and handling of goods prior to the loading on, and subsequent to the discharge from, the ship on which the goods are carried by sea.

Article VIII

The provisions of these Rules shall not affect the rights and obligations of the carrier under any statute for the time being in force relating to the limitation of the liability of owners of sea-going vessels.

Article IX

These rules shall not affect the provisions of any international Convention or national law governing liability for nuclear damage.

Article X

The provisions of these Rules shall apply to every bill of lading relating to the carriage of goods between ports in two different States if:

(a) the bill of lading is issued in a contracting State, or

(b) the carriage is from a port in a contracting State, or

(c) the contract contained in or evidenced by the bill of lading provides that these Rules or legislation of any State giving effect to them are to govern the contract, whatever may be the nationality of the ship, the carrier, the shipper, the consignee, or any other interested person.

[The last two paragraphs of this article require contracting States to apply the Rules to

bills of lading mentioned in the article and authorise them to apply the Rules to other bills of lading.]

[Articles XI to XVI deal with the coming into force of the Convention, procedure for ratification, accession and denunciation and the right to call for a fresh conference to consider amendments to the Rules contained in the Convention.]

COINAGE ACT 1971
(1971, c 24)

2 Legal tender

(1) Gold coins shall be legal tender for payment of any amount, but shall not be legal tender if their weight has become less than that specified in Schedule 1 to this Act, or in the proclamation under which they are made, as the least current weight.

(1A) Subject to any provision made by proclamation under section 3 of this Act, coins of cupro-nickel, silver or bronze shall be legal tender as follows—

(a) coins of cupro-nickel or silver of denominations of more than 10 pence, for payment of any amount not exceeding £10;

(b) coins of cupro-nickel or silver of denominations of not more than 10 pence, for payment of any amount not exceeding £5;

(c) coins of bronze, for payment of any amount not exceeding 20 pence.

(1B) Other coins, if made current by a proclamation under section 3 of this Act, shall be legal tender in accordance with the provision made by that proclamation or by any later proclamation made under that section.

(2) References in [subsection (1A)] of this section to coins of any denomination include references to coins treated as being of such a denomination by virtue of a proclamation made in pursuance of section 15(5) of the Decimal Currency Act 1969; and silver coins of the Queen's Maundy money issued before 15th February 1971 shall be treated for the purposes of this section as being denominated in the same number of new pence as the number of pence in which they were denominated.

(3) In this section 'coins' means coins made by the Mint in accordance with this Act and not called in by proclamation under section 3 of this Act.

UNSOLICITED GOODS AND SERVICES ACT 1971
(1971, c 30)

[. . .]

2 Demands and threats regarding payment

(1) A person who, not having reasonable cause to believe there is a right to payment, in the course of any trade or business makes a demand for payment, or asserts a present or prospective right to payment, for what he knows are unsolicited goods sent (after the commencement of this Act) to another person with a view to his acquiring them [for the purposes of his trade or business], shall be guilty of an offence and on summary conviction shall be liable to a fine not exceeding [level 4 on the standard scale].

(2) A person who, not having reasonable cause to believe there is a right to payment, in the course of any trade or business and with a view to obtaining any payment for what he knows are unsolicited goods sent as aforesaid—

(a) threatens to bring any legal proceedings; or

(b) places or causes to be placed the name of any person on a list of defaulters or debtors or threatens to do so; or

(c) invokes or causes to be invoked any other collection procedure or threatens to do so, shall be guilty of an offence and shall be liable on summary conviction to a fine not exceeding [level 5 on the standard scale].

3 Directory entries

[(1) A person ('the purchaser') shall not be liable to make any payment, and shall be entitled to recover any payment made by him, by way of charge for including or arranging for the inclusion in a directory of an entry relating to that person or his trade or business, unless—

(a) there has been signed by the purchaser or on his behalf an order complying with this section,

(b) there has been signed by the purchaser or on his behalf a note complying with this section of his agreement to the charge and before the note was signed, a copy of it was supplied, for retention by him, to him or a person acting on his behalf,

(c) there has been transmitted by the purchaser or a person acting on his behalf an electronic communication which includes a statement that the purchaser agrees to the charge and the relevant condition is satisfied in relation to that communication, [or

(d) the charge arises under a contract in relation to which the conditions in section 3B(1) (renewed and extended contracts) are met.]

(2) A person shall be guilty of an offence punishable on summary conviction with a fine not exceeding [level 5 on the standard scale] if, in a case where a payment in respect of a charge would [. . .] be recoverable from him in accordance with the terms of subsection (1) above, he demands payment, or asserts a present or prospective right to payment, of the charge or any part of it, without knowing or having reasonable cause to believe [that—

(a) the entry to which the charge relates was ordered in accordance with this section,

(b) a proper note of the agreement has been duly signed, or

(c) the requirements set out in subsection (1)(c) [or (d)] above have been met.]

(3) For the purposes of [this section—

(a)] an order for an entry in a directory must be made by means of an order form or other stationery belonging to the [purchaser, which may be sent electronically but which must bear his name and address (or one or more of his addresses)]; and

[b] the note [of a person's agreement to a charge must—

(i) specify the particulars set out in Part 1 of the Schedule to the Regulatory Reform (Unsolicited Goods and Services Act 1971) (Directory Entries and Demands for Payment) Order 2005, and

(ii) give reasonable particulars of the entry in respect of which the charge would be payable].

[(3A) In relation to an electronic communication which includes a statement that the purchaser agrees to a charge for including or arranging the inclusion in a directory of any entry, the relevant condition is that—

(a) before the electronic communication was transmitted the information referred to in subsection (3B) below was communicated to the purchaser, and

(b) the electronic communication can readily be produced and retained in a visible and legible form.

(3B) that information is—

(a) the following particulars—

(i) the amount of the charge;

(ii) the name of the directory or proposed directory;

(iii) the name of the person producing the directory;

(iv) the geographic address at which that person is established;

(v) if the directory is or is to be available in printed form, the proposed date of publication of the directory or of the issue in which the entry is to be included;

(vi) if the directory or the issue in which the entry is to be included is to be put on sale, the price at which it is to be offered for sale and the minimum number of copies which are to be available for sale;

(vii) if the directory or the issue in which the entry is to be included is to be distributed free of charge (whether or not it is also to be put on sale), the minimum number of copies which are to be so distributed;

(viii) if the directory is or is to be available in a form other than in printed form, adequate details of how it may be accessed; and

(b) reasonable particulars of the entry in respect of which the charge would be payable.

(3C) In this section 'electronic communication' has the same meaning as in the Electronic Communications Act 2000.]

[. . .]

[3B Renewed and extended contracts

(1) The conditions referred to in section 3(1)(d) above are met in relation to a contract ('the new contract') if—

(a) a person ('the purchaser') has entered into an earlier contract ('the earlier contract') for including or arranging for the inclusion in a particular issue or version of a directory ('the earlier directory') of an entry ('the earlier entry') relating to him or his trade or business;

(b) the purchaser was liable to make a payment by way of a charge arising under the earlier contract for including or arranging for the inclusion of the earlier entry in the earlier directory;

(c) the new contract is a contract for including or arranging for the inclusion in a later issue or version of a directory ('the later directory') of an entry ('the later entry') relating to the purchaser or his trade or business;

(d) the form, content and distribution of the later directory is materially the same as the form, content and distribution of the earlier directory;

(e) the form and content of the later entry is materially the same as the form and content of the earlier entry;

(f) if the later directory is published other than in electronic form—

(i) the earlier directory was the last, or the last but one, issue or version of the directory to be published before the later directory, and

(ii) the date of publication of the later directory is not more than 13 months after the date of publication of the earlier directory;

(g) if the later directory is published in electronic form, the first date on which the new contract requires the later entry to be published is not more than the relevant period after the last date on which the earlier contract required the earlier entry to be published;

(h) if it was a term of the earlier contract that the purchaser renew or extend the contract—

(i) before the start of the new contract the relevant publisher has given notice in writing to the purchaser containing the information set out in Part 3 of the Schedule to the Regulatory Reform (Unsolicited Goods and Services Act 1971) (Directory Entries and Demands for Payment) Order 2005; and

(ii) the purchaser has not written to the relevant publisher withdrawing his agreement to the renewal or extension of the earlier contract within the period of 21 days starting when he receives the notice referred to in sub-paragraph (i); and

(i) if the parties to the earlier contract and the new contract are different—

(i) the parties to both contracts have entered into a novation agreement in respect of the earlier contract; or

(ii) the relevant publisher has given the purchaser the information set out in Part 4 of the Schedule to the Regulatory Reform (Unsolicited Goods and Services Act 1971) (Directory Entries and Demands for Payment) Order 2005.

(2) For the purposes of subsection (1)(d) and (e), the form, content or distribution of the later directory, or the form or content of the later entry, shall be taken to be materially the same as that of the earlier directory or the earlier entry (as the case may be), if a reasonable person in the position of the purchaser would—

(a) view the two as being materially the same; or

(b) view that of the later directory or the later entry as being an improvement on that of the earlier directory or the earlier entry.

(3) For the purposes of subsection (1)(g) 'the relevant period' means the period of 13 months or (if shorter) the period of time between the first and last dates on which the earlier contract required the earlier entry to be published.

(4) For the purposes of subsection (1)(h) and (i) 'the relevant publisher' is the person with whom the purchaser has entered into the new contract.

(5) The information referred to in subsection (1)(i)(ii) must be given to the purchaser prior to the conclusion of the new contract.]

4 Unsolicited publications

(1) A person shall be guilty of an offence if he sends or causes to be sent to another person any book, magazine or leaflet (or advertising material for any such publication) which he knows or ought reasonably to know is unsolicited and which describes or illustrates human sexual techniques.

(2) A person found guilty of an offence under this section shall be liable on summary conviction to a fine not exceeding [level 5 on the standard scale].

(3) A prosecution for an offence under this section shall not in England and Wales be instituted except by, or with the consent of, the Director of Public Prosecutions.

5 Offences by corporations

(1) Where an offence under this Act which has been committed by a body corporate is proved to have been committed with the consent or connivance of, or to be attributable to any neglect on the part of, any director, manager, secretary, or other similar officer of the body corporate, or of any person who was purporting to act in any such capacity, he as well as the body corporate shall be guilty of that offence and shall be liable to be proceeded against and punished accordingly.

(2) Where the affairs of a body corporate are managed by its members, this section shall apply in relation to the acts or defaults of a member in connection with his functions of management as if he were a director of the body corporate.

6 Interpretation

(1) In this Act, unless the context or subject matter otherwise requires,—

'acquire' includes hire;

'send' includes deliver, and 'sender' shall be construed accordingly;

'unsolicited' means, in relation to goods sent to any person, that they are sent without any prior request made by him or on his behalf.

[(2) For the purposes of this Act any invoice or similar document stating the amount of any payment shall be regarded as asserting a right to the payment unless it complies with the conditions set out in Part 2 of the Schedule to the Regulatory Reform (Unsolicited Goods and Services Act 1971) (Directory Entries and Demands for Payment) Order 2005.]

[(3) Nothing in section 3 or 3B affects the rights of any consumer under the Consumer Contracts (Information, Cancellation and Additional Charges) Regulations 2013.]

7 Citation, commencement and extent

(1) This Act may be cited as the Unsolicited Goods and Services Act 1971.

(2) This Act shall come into force at the expiration of three months beginning with the day on which it is passed.

(3) This Act does not extend to Northern Ireland.

SUPPLY OF GOODS (IMPLIED TERMS) ACT 1973
(1973, c 13)

8 Implied terms as to title

[(1) In every [relevant hire-purchase agreement], other than one to which subsection (2) below applies, there is—

(a) an implied term on the part of the creditor that he will have a right to sell the goods at the time when the property is to pass; and

(b) an implied term that—

(i) the goods are free, and will remain free until the time when the property is to pass, from any charge or encumbrance not disclosed or known to the person to whom the goods are bailed or (in Scotland) hired before the agreement is made, and

(ii) that person will enjoy quiet possession of the goods except so far as it may be disturbed by any person entitled to the benefit of any charge or encumbrance so disclosed or known.

(2) In a [relevant hire-purchase agreement], in the case of which there appears from the agreement or is to be inferred from the circumstances of the agreement an intention that the creditor should transfer only such title as he or a third person may have, there is—

(a) an implied term that all charges or encumbrances known to the creditor and not known to the person to whom the goods are bailed or hired have been disclosed to that person before the agreement is made; and

(b) an implied term that neither—

(i) the creditor; nor

(ii) in a case where the parties to the agreement intend that any title which may be transferred shall be only such title as a third person may have, that person; nor

(iii) anyone claiming through or under the creditor or that third person otherwise than under a charge or encumbrance disclosed or known to the person to whom the goods are bailed or hired, before the agreement is made; will disturb the quiet possession of the person to whom the goods are bailed or hired.

(3) As regards England and Wales and Northern Ireland, the term implied by subsection (1)(a) above is a condition and the terms implied by subsections (1)(b), (2)(a) and (2)(b) above are warranties.]

9 Bailing or hiring by description

[(1) Where under a [relevant hire-purchase agreement] goods are bailed or (in Scotland) hired by description, there is an implied term that the goods will correspond with the description, and if under the agreement the goods are bailed or hired by reference to a sample as well as a description, it is not sufficient that the bulk of the goods corresponds with the sample if the goods do not also correspond with the description.

(1A) As regards England and Wales and Northern Ireland, the term implied by subsection (1) above is a condition.

(2) Goods shall not be prevented from being bailed or hired by description by reason only that, being exposed for sale, bailment or hire, they are selected by the person to whom they are bailed or hired.]

10 Implied undertakings as to quality or fitness

[(1) Except as provided by this section and section 11 below and subject to the provisions of any other enactment, including any enactment of the Parliament of

Northern Ireland or the Northern Ireland Assembly, there is no implied term as to the quality or fitness for any particular purpose of goods bailed or (in Scotland) hired under a [relevant hire-purchase agreement].

(2) Where the creditor bails or hires goods under a [relevant hire-purchase agreement] in the course of a business, there is an implied term that the goods supplied under the agreement are of satisfactory quality.

(2A) For the purposes of this Act, goods are of satisfactory quality if they meet the standard that a reasonable person would regard as satisfactory, taking account of any description of the goods, the price (if relevant) and all the other relevant circumstances.

(2B) For the purposes of this Act, the quality of goods includes their state and condition and the following (among others) are in appropriate cases aspects of the quality of goods—

(a) fitness for all the purposes for which goods of the kind in question are commonly supplied,

(b) appearance and finish,

(c) freedom from minor defects,

(d) safety, and

(e) durability.

(2C) The term implied by subsection (2) above does not extend to any matter making the quality of goods unsatisfactory—

(a) which is specifically drawn to the attention of the person to whom the goods are bailed or hired before the agreement is made,

(b) where that person examines the goods before the agreement is made, which that examination ought to reveal, or

(c) where the goods are bailed or hired by reference to a sample, which would have been apparent on a reasonable examination of the sample.

[. . .]

(3) Where the creditor bails or hires goods under a [relevant hire-purchase agreement] in the course of a business and the person to whom the goods are bailed or hired, expressly or by implication, makes known—

(a) to the creditor in the course of negotiations conducted by the creditor in relation to the making of the [relevant hire-purchase agreement], or

(b) to a credit-broker in the course of negotiations conducted by that broker in relation to goods sold by him to the creditor before forming the subject matter of the [relevant hire-purchase agreement],

any particular purpose for which the goods are being bailed or hired, there is an implied term that the goods supplied under the agreement are reasonably fit for that purpose, whether or not that is a purpose for which such goods are commonly supplied, except where the circumstances show that the person to whom the goods are bailed or hired does not rely, or that it is unreasonable for him to rely, on the skill or judgment of the creditor or credit-broker.

(4) An implied term as to quality or fitness for a particular purpose may be annexed to a [relevant hire-purchase agreement] by usage.

(5) The preceding provisions of this section apply to a [relevant hire-purchase agreement] made by a person who in the course of a business is acting as agent for the creditor as they apply to an agreement made by the creditor in the course of a business, except where the creditor is not bailing or hiring in the course of a business and either the person to whom the goods are bailed or hired knows that fact or reasonable steps are taken to bring it to the notice of that person before the agreement is made.

(6) In subsection (3) above and this subsection—

(a) 'credit-broker' means a person acting in the course of a business of credit brokerage;

(b) 'credit brokerage' means the effecting of introductions of individuals desiring to obtain credit—

(i) to persons carrying on any business so far as it relates to the provision of credit, or

(ii) to other persons engaged in credit brokerage.

(7) As regards England and Wales and Northern Ireland, the terms implied by subsections (2) and (3) above are conditions.

[. . .]

11 Samples

[(1) Where under a [relevant hire-purchase agreement] goods are bailed or (in Scotland) hired by reference to a sample, there is an implied term—

(a) that the bulk will correspond with the sample in quality; and

(b) that the person to whom the goods are bailed or hired will have a reasonable opportunity of comparing the bulk with the sample; and

(c) that the goods will be free from any defect, making their quality unsatisfactory, which would not be apparent on reasonable examination of the sample.

(2) As regards England and Wales and Northern Ireland, the term implied by subsection (1) above is a condition.]

[12 Exclusion of implied terms

An express term does not negative a term implied by this Act unless inconsistent with it.]

[12A Remedies for breach of [relevant hire-purchase agreement] as respects Scotland

(1) Where in a [relevant hire-purchase agreement] the creditor is in breach of any term of the agreement (express or implied), the person to whom the goods are hired shall be entitled—

(a) to claim damages, and

(b) if the breach is material, to reject any goods delivered under the agreement and treat it as repudiated.

[. . .]

(4) This section applies to Scotland only.]

[. . .]

15 Supplementary

[(1) In sections 8 to 14 above and this section—

'business' includes a profession and the activities of any government department (including a Northern Ireland department), [or local or public authority];

'buyer' and 'seller' includes a person to whom rights and duties under a conditional sale agreement have passed by assignment or operation of law;

'conditional sale agreement' means an agreement for the sale of goods under which the purchase price or part of it is payable by instalments, and the property in the goods is to remain in the seller (notwithstanding that the buyer is to be in possession of the goods) until such conditions as to the payment of instalments or otherwise as may be specified in the agreement are fulfilled;

['consumer sale' has the same meaning as in section 55 of the Sale of Goods Act 1979 (as set out in paragraph 11 of Schedule 1 to that Act)];

'creditor' means the person by whom the goods are bailed or (in Scotland) hired under a hire-purchase agreement or the person to whom his rights and duties under the agreement have passed by assignment or operation of law; and

'hire-purchase agreement' means an agreement, other than conditional sale agreement, under which—

(a) goods are bailed or (in Scotland) hired in return for periodical payments by the person to whom they are bailed or hired, and

(b) the property in the goods will pass to that person if the terms of the agreement are complied with and one or more of the following occurs—

(i) the exercise of an option to purchase by that person,

(ii) the doing of any other specified act by any party to the agreement,

(iii) the happening of any other specified event.

[and a hire-purchase agreement is relevant if it is not a contract to which Chapter 2 of Part 1 of the Consumer Rights Act 2015 applies;]

[. . .]

(4) Nothing in sections 8 to 13 above shall prejudice the operation of any other enactment including any enactment of the Parliament of Northern Ireland or the Northern Ireland Assembly or any rule of law whereby any term, other than one relating to quality or fitness, is to be implied in any [relevant hire-purchase agreement].]

CONSUMER CREDIT ACT 1974
(1974, c 39)

[. . .]

PART II
CREDIT AGREEMENTS, HIRE AGREEMENTS AND LINKED TRANSACTIONS

8 Consumer credit agreements

(1) A [consumer] credit agreement is an agreement between an individual ('the debtor') and any other person ('the creditor') by which the creditor provides the debtor with credit of any amount.

[. . .]

[(3) A consumer credit agreement is a regulated credit agreement within the meaning of this Act if it—

(a) is a regulated credit agreement for the purposes of Chapter 14A of Part 2 of the Regulated Activities Order; and

(b) [if entered into on or after 21st March 2016,] is not an agreement the purpose of which is the acquisition or retention, by an individual acting for purposes outside those of any trade, business or profession carried on by the individual, of property rights in land or in an existing or projected building.]

[(3A) A reference in paragraph (3)(b) to any land or building—

(a) in relation to an agreement entered into before [IP completion day], is a reference to any land or building in the United Kingdom or within the territory of an EEA State;

(b) in relation to an agreement entered into on or after [IP completion day], is a reference to any land or building in the United Kingdom.]

[(4) Subsection (1) does not apply in relation to an agreement that is a green deal plan (see instead section 189B).]

9 Meaning of credit

(1) In this Act 'credit' includes a cash loan, and any other form of financial accommodation.

(2) Where credit is provided otherwise than in sterling it shall be treated for the purposes of this Act as provided in sterling of an equivalent amount.

(3) Without prejudice to the generality of subsection (1), the person by whom goods are bailed or (in Scotland) hired to an individual under a hire-purchase agreement shall be taken to provide him with fixed-sum credit to finance the transaction of an amount equal to the total price of the goods less the aggregate of the deposit (if any) and the total charge for credit.

(4) For the purposes of this Act, an item entering into the total charge for credit shall not be treated as credit even though time is allowed for its payment.

10 Running-account credit and fixed-sum credit

(1) For the purposes of this Act—

(a) running-account credit is a facility under a [consumer] credit agreement whereby the debtor is enabled to receive from time to time (whether in his own person, or by another person) from the creditor or a third party cash, goods and services (or any of them) to an amount or value such that, taking into account payments made by or to the credit of the debtor, the credit limit (if any) is not at any time exceeded; and

(b) fixed-sum credit is any other facility under a [consumer] credit agreement whereby the debtor is enabled to receive credit (whether in one amount or by instalments).

(2) In relation to running-account credit, 'credit limit' means, as respects any period, the maximum debit balance which, under the credit agreement, is allowed to stand on the account during that period, disregarding any term of the agreement allowing that maximum to be exceeded merely temporarily.

(3) For the purposes of [any provision of this Act that specifies an amount of credit (except section 17(1)(a))], running-account credit shall be taken not to exceed the amount specified in [that provision] ('the specified amount') if—

(a) the credit limit does not exceed the specified amount; or

(b) whether or not there is a credit limit, and if there is, notwithstanding that it exceeds the specified amount,—

(i) the debtor is not enabled to draw at any one time an amount which, so far as (having regard to section 9(4)) it represents credit, exceeds the specified amount, or

(ii) the agreement provides that, if the debit balance rises above a given amount (not exceeding the specified amount), the rate of the total charge for credit increases or any other condition favouring the creditor or his associate comes into operation, or

(iii) at the time the agreement is made it is probable, having regard to the terms of the agreement and any other relevant considerations, that the debit balance will not at any time rise above the specified amount.

11 Restricted-use credit and unrestricted-use credit

(1) A restricted-use credit agreement is a regulated consumer credit agreement—

(a) to finance a transaction between the debtor and the creditor, whether forming part of that agreement or not, or

(b) to finance a transaction between the debtor and a person (the 'supplier') other than the creditor, or

(c) to refinance any existing indebtedness of the debtor's, whether to the creditor or another person, and 'restricted-use credit' shall be construed accordingly.

(2) An unrestricted-use credit agreement is a regulated consumer credit agreement not falling within subsection (1), and 'unrestricted-use credit' shall be construed accordingly.

(3) An agreement does not fall within subsection (1) if the credit is in fact provided in such a way as to leave the debtor free to use it as he chooses, even though certain uses would contravene that or any other agreement.

(4) An agreement may fall within subsection (1)(b) although the identity of the supplier is unknown at the time the agreement is made.

12 Debtor-creditor-supplier agreements

A debtor-creditor-supplier agreement is a regulated consumer credit agreement being—

(a) a restricted-use credit agreement which falls within section 11(1)(a), or

(b) a restricted-use credit agreement which falls within section 11(1)(b) and is made by the creditor under pre-existing arrangements, or in contemplation of future arrangements, between himself and the supplier, or

(c) an unrestricted-use credit agreement which is made by the creditor under pre-existing arrangements between himself and a person (the 'supplier') other than the debtor in the knowledge that the credit is to be used to finance a transaction between the debtor and the supplier.

13 Debtor-creditor agreements

A debtor-creditor agreement is a regulated consumer credit agreement being—

(a) a restricted-use credit agreement which falls within section 11(1)(b) but is not made by the creditor under pre-existing arrangements, or in contemplation of future arrangements, between himself and the supplier, or

(b) a restricted-use credit agreement which falls within section 11(1)(c), or

(c) an unrestricted-use credit agreement which is not made by the creditor under pre-existing arrangements between himself and a person (the 'supplier') other than the debtor in the knowledge that the credit is to be used to finance a transaction between the debtor and the supplier.

14 Credit-token agreements

(1) A credit-token is a card, check, voucher, coupon, stamp, form, booklet or other document or thing given to an individual by a person carrying on a consumer credit business, who undertakes—

(a) that on the production of it (whether or not some other action is also required) he will supply cash, goods and services (or any of them) on credit, or

(b) that where, on the production of it to a third party (whether or not any other action is also required), the third party supplies cash, goods and services (or any of them), he will pay the third party for them (whether or not deducting any discount or commission), in return for payment to him by the individual.

(2) A credit-token agreement is a regulated agreement for the provision of credit in connection with the use of a credit-token.

(3) Without prejudice to the generality of section 9(1), the person who gives to an individual an undertaking falling within subsection (1)(b) shall be taken to provide him with credit drawn on whenever a third party supplies him with cash, goods or services.

(4) For the purposes of subsection (1), use of an object to operate a machine provided by the person giving the object or a third party shall be treated as the production of the object to him.

15 Consumer hire agreements

(1) A consumer hire agreement is an agreement made by a person with an individual (the 'hirer') for the bailment or (in Scotland) the hiring of goods to the hirer, being an agreement which—

(a) is not a hire-purchase agreement, and

(b) is capable of subsisting for more than three months, [. . .].

[(2) A consumer hire agreement is a regulated agreement within the meaning of this Act if it is a regulated consumer hire agreement for the purposes of Chapter 14B of Part 2 of the Regulated Activities Order.]

[. . .]

17 Small agreements

(1) A small agreement is—

[(a) a regulated consumer credit agreement for credit not exceeding £50, other than—

(i) a hire-purchase agreement,

(ii) a conditional sale agreement, or

(iii) a regulated deferred payment credit agreement; or]

(b) a regulated consumer hire agreement which does not require the hirer to make payments exceeding [£50], being an agreement which is either unsecured or secured by a guarantee or indemnity only (whether or not the guarantee or indemnity is itself secured).

[(2) For the purposes of paragraph (a) of subsection (1), running-account credit shall be taken not to exceed the amount specified in that paragraph if the credit limit does not exceed that amount.]

(3) Where—

(a) two or more small agreements are made at or about the same time between the same parties, and

(b) it appears probable that they would instead have been made as a single agreement but for the desire to avoid the operation of provisions of this Act which would have applied to that single agreement but, apart from this subsection, are not applicable to the small agreements,

this Act applies to the small agreements as if they were regulated agreements other than small agreements.

(4) If, apart from this subsection, subsection (3) does not apply to any agreements but would apply if, for any party or parties to any of the agreements, there were substituted an associate of that party, or associates of each of those parties, as the case may be, then subsection (3) shall apply to the agreements.

18 Multiple agreements

(1) This section applies to an agreement (a 'multiple agreement') if its terms are such as—

(a) to place a part of it within one category of agreement mentioned in this Act, and another part of it within a different category of agreement so mentioned, or within a category of agreement not so mentioned, or

(b) to place it, or a part of it, within two or more categories of agreement so mentioned.

(2) Where a part of an agreement falls within subsection (1), that part shall be treated for the purposes of this Act as a separate agreement.

(3) Where an agreement falls within subsection (1)(b), it shall be treated as an agreement in each of the categories in question, and this Act shall apply to it accordingly.

(4) Where under subsection (2) a part of a multiple agreement is to be treated as a separate agreement, the multiple agreement shall (with any necessary modifications) be construed accordingly; and any sum payable under the multiple agreement, if not apportioned by the parties, shall for the purposes of proceedings in any court relating to the multiple agreement be apportioned by the court as may be requisite.

(5) In the case of an agreement for running-account credit, a term of the agreement allowing the credit limit to be exceeded merely temporarily shall not be treated as a separate agreement or as providing fixed-sum credit in respect of the excess.

(6) This Act does not apply to a multiple agreement so far as the agreement relates to goods if under the agreement payments are to be made in respect of the goods in the form of rent (other than a rentcharge) issuing out of land.

19 Linked transactions

(1) A transaction entered into by the debtor or hirer, or a relative of his, with any other person ('the other party'), except one for the provision of security, is a linked transaction in relation to an actual or prospective regulated agreement (the 'principal agreement') of which it does not form part if—

(a) the transaction is entered into in compliance with a term of the principal agreement; or

(b) the principal agreement is a debtor-creditor-supplier agreement and the transaction is financed, or to be financed, by the principal agreement; or

(c) the other party is a person mentioned in subsection (2), and a person so mentioned initiated the transaction by suggesting it to the debtor or hirer, or his relative, who enters into it—

(i) to induce the creditor or owner to enter into the principal agreement, or

(ii) for another purpose related to the principal agreement, or

(iii) where the principal agreement is a restricted-use credit agreement, for a purpose related to a transaction financed, or to be financed, by the principal agreement.

(2) The persons referred to in subsection (1)(c) are—

(a) the creditor or owner, or his associate;

(b) a person who, in the negotiation of the transaction, is represented by a credit-broker who is also a negotiator in antecedent negotiations for the principal agreement;

(c) a person who, at the time the transaction is initiated, knows that the principal agreement has been made or contemplates that it might be made.

(3) A linked transaction entered into before the making of the principal agreement has no effect until such time (if any) as that agreement is made.

(4) Regulations may exclude linked transactions of the prescribed description from the operation of subsection (3).

[20 Total charge for credit

In this Act, the 'total charge for credit' has the meaning given by the Regulated Activities Order for the purposes of Chapter 14A of Part 2 of that Order.]

PART V
ENTRY INTO CREDIT OR HIRE AGREEMENTS

Preliminary matters

55 Disclosure of information

(1) Regulations may require specified information to be disclosed in the prescribed manner to the debtor or hirer before a regulated agreement [, other than a regulated deferred payment credit agreement,] is made.

[(2) If regulations under subsection (1) are not complied with, the agreement is enforceable against the debtor or hirer on an order of the court only (and for these purposes a retaking of goods or land to which the agreement relates is an enforcement of the agreement).]

[. . .]

[55C Copy of draft consumer credit agreement

(1) Before a regulated consumer credit agreement, other than an excluded agreement, is made, the creditor must, if requested, give to the debtor without delay a copy of the prospective agreement (or such of its terms as have at that time been reduced to writing).

(2) Subsection (1) does not apply if at the time the request is made, the creditor is unwilling to proceed with the agreement.

(3) A breach of the duty imposed by subsection (1) is actionable as a breach of statutory duty.

(4) For the purposes of this section an agreement is an excluded agreement if it is—

(a) an agreement secured on land,

(b) an agreement under which a person takes an article in pawn,

(c) an agreement under which the creditor provides the debtor with credit which exceeds £60,260 [and which is not a residential renovation agreement], or

(d) an agreement entered into by the debtor wholly or predominantly for the purposes of a business carried on, or intended to be carried on, by him.

[(5) Article 60C(5) and (6) of the Regulated Activities Order applies for the purposes of subsection 4(d).]

[(6) This section does not apply to a regulated deferred payment credit agreement.]

56 Antecedent negotiations

(1) In this Act 'antecedent negotiations' means any negotiations with the debtor or hirer—

(a) conducted by the creditor or owner in relation to the making of any regulated agreement, or

(b) conducted by a credit-broker in relation to goods sold or proposed to be sold by the credit-broker to the creditor before forming the subject-matter of a debtor-creditor-supplier agreement within section 12(a), or

(c) conducted by the supplier in relation to a transaction financed or proposed to be financed by a debtor-creditor-supplier agreement within section 12(b) or (c), and 'negotiator' means the person by whom negotiations are so conducted with the debtor or hirer.

(2) Negotiations with the debtor in a case falling within subsection (1)(b) or (c) shall be deemed to be conducted by the negotiator in the capacity of agent of the creditor as well as in his actual capacity.

(3) An agreement is void if, and to the extent that, it purports in relation to an actual or prospective regulated agreement—

(a) to provide that a person acting as, or on behalf of, a negotiator is to be treated as the agent of the debtor or hirer, or

(b) to relieve a person from liability for acts or omissions of any person acting as, or on behalf of, a negotiator.

(4) For the purposes of this Act, antecedent negotiations shall be taken to begin when the negotiator and the debtor or hirer first enter into communication (including communication by advertisement), and to include any representations made by the negotiator to the debtor or hirer and any other dealings between them.

57 Withdrawal from prospective agreement

(1) The withdrawal of a party from a prospective regulated agreement shall operate to apply this Part to the agreement, any linked transaction and any other thing done in anticipation of the making of the agreement as it would apply if the agreement were made and then cancelled under section 69.

(2) The giving to a party of a written or oral notice which, however expressed, indicates the intention of the other party to withdraw from a prospective regulated agreement operates as a withdrawal from it.

(3) Each of the following shall be deemed to be the agent of the creditor or owner for the purpose of receiving a notice under subsection (2)—

(a) a credit-broker or supplier who is the negotiator in antecedent negotiations, and

(b) any person who, in the course of a business carried on by him, acts on behalf of the debtor or hirer in any negotiations for the agreement.

(4) Where the agreement, if made, would not be a cancellable agreement, subsection (1) shall nevertheless apply as if the contrary were the case.

58 Opportunity for withdrawal from prospective land mortgage

(1) Before sending to the debtor or hirer, for his signature, an unexecuted agreement in a case where the prospective regulated agreement is to be secured on land (the 'mortgaged land'), the creditor or owner shall give the debtor or hirer a copy of the unexecuted agreement which contains a notice in the prescribed form indicating the right of the debtor or hirer to withdraw from the prospective agreement, and how and when the right is exercisable, together with a copy of any other document referred to in the unexecuted agreement.

(2) Subsection (1) does not apply to—

(a) a restricted-use credit agreement to finance the purchase of the mortgaged land, or

(b) an agreement for a bridging loan in connection with the purchase of the mortgaged land or other land.

59 Agreement to enter future agreement void

(1) An agreement is void if, and to the extent that, it purports to bind a person to enter as debtor or hirer into a prospective regulated agreement.

(2) Regulations may exclude from the operation of subsection (1) agreements such as are described in the regulations.

Making the agreement

60 Form and content of agreements

(1) The [Treasury] shall make regulations as to the form and content of documents embodying regulated agreements, [other than regulated deferred payment credit agreements,] and the regulations shall contain such provisions as appear to [them] appropriate with a view to ensuring that the debtor or hirer is made aware of—

(a) the rights and duties conferred or imposed on him by the agreement,

(b) the amount and rate of the total charge for credit (in the case of a consumer credit agreement),

(c) the protection and remedies available to him under this Act, and

(d) any other matters which, in the opinion of the [Treasury], it is desirable for him to know about in connection with the agreement.

(2) Regulations under subsection (1) may in particular—

(a) require specified information to be included in the prescribed manner in documents, and other specified material to be excluded;

(b) contain requirements to ensure that specified information is clearly brought to the attention of the debtor or hirer, and that one part of a document is not given insufficient or excessive prominence compared with another.

(3) If, on an application made to the [FCA] by a person carrying on a consumer credit business or a consumer hire business, it appears to the [FCA] impracticable for the applicant to comply with any requirement of regulations under subsection (1) in a particular case, [it] may, by notice to the applicant direct that the requirement be waived or varied in relation to such agreements, and subject to such conditions (if any), as [it] may specify, and this Act and the regulations shall have effect accordingly.

(4) The [FCA] shall give a notice under subsection (3) only if [it] is satisfied that to do so would not prejudice the interests of debtors or hirers.

[(5) An application may be made under subsection (3) only if it relates to—

(a) a consumer credit agreement secured on land,

(b) a consumer credit agreement under which a person takes an article in pawn,

(c) a consumer credit agreement under which the creditor provides the debtor with credit which exceeds £60,260 [and which is not a residential renovation agreement],

(d) a consumer credit agreement entered into by the debtor wholly or predominantly for the purposes of a business carried on, or intended to be carried on, by him, or

(e) a consumer hire agreement.

[(6) Article 60C(5) and (6) of the Regulated Activities Order applies for the purposes of subsection (5)(d).]

61 Signing of agreement

(1) A regulated agreement is not properly executed unless—

(a) a document in the prescribed form itself containing all the prescribed terms and conforming to regulations under section 60(1) is signed in the prescribed manner both by the debtor or hirer and by or on behalf of the creditor or owner, and

(b) the document embodies all the terms of the agreement, other than implied terms, and

(c) the document is, when presented or sent to the debtor or hirer for signature, in such a state that all its terms are readily legible.

(2) In addition, where the agreement is one to which section 58(1) applies, it is not properly executed unless—

(a) the requirements of section 58(1) were complied with, and

(b) the unexecuted agreement was sent, for his signature, to the debtor or hirer [by an appropriate method] not less than seven days after a copy of it was given to him under section 58(1), and

(c) during the consideration period, the creditor or owner refrained from approaching the debtor or hirer (whether in person, by telephone or letter, or in any other way) except in response to a specific request made by the debtor or hirer after the beginning of the consideration period, and

(d) no notice of withdrawal by the debtor or hirer was received by the creditor or owner before the sending of the unexecuted agreement.

(3) In subsection (2)(c), 'the consideration period' means the period beginning with the giving of the copy under section 58(1) and ending—

(a) at the expiry of seven days after the day on which the unexecuted agreement is sent, for his signature, to the debtor or hirer, or

(b) on its return by the debtor or hirer after signature by him, whichever first occurs.

(4) Where the debtor or hirer is a partnership or an unincorporated body of persons, subsection (1)(a) shall apply with the substitution for 'by the debtor or hirer' of 'by or on behalf of the debtor or hirer'.

[(5) This section does not apply to a regulated deferred payment credit agreement.]

[61A Duty to supply copy of executed consumer credit agreement

(1) Where a regulated consumer credit agreement, other than an excluded agreement, has been made, the creditor must give a copy of the executed agreement, and any other document referred to in it, to the debtor.

(2) Subsection (1) does not apply if—

(a) a copy of the unexecuted agreement (and of any other document referred to in it) has already been given to the debtor, and

(b) the unexecuted agreement is in identical terms to the executed agreement.

(3) In a case referred to in subsection (2), the creditor must inform the debtor in writing—

(a) that the agreement has been executed,

(b) that the executed agreement is in identical terms to the unexecuted agreement a copy of which has already been given to the debtor, and

(c) that the debtor has the right to receive a copy of the executed agreement if the debtor makes a request for it at any time before the end of the period referred to in section 66A(2).

(4) Where a request is made under subsection (3)(c) the creditor must give a copy of the executed agreement to the debtor without delay.

(5) If the requirements of this section are not observed, the agreement is not properly executed.

(6) For the purposes of this section, an agreement is an excluded agreement if it is—

(a) a cancellable agreement, or

(b) an agreement—

(i) secured on land,

(ii) under which the creditor provides the debtor with credit which exceeds £60,260, or

(iii) entered into by the debtor wholly or predominantly for the purposes of a business carried on, or intended to be carried on, by him,

unless the creditor or a credit intermediary has complied with or purported to comply with regulation 3(2) of the Consumer Credit (Disclosure of Information) Regulations 2010.

[(6A) An agreement is not an excluded agreement by virtue of subsection (6)(b)(ii) if it is a residential renovation agreement.]

[(7) Article 60C(5) and (6) of the Regulated Activities Order applies for the purposes of subsection (6)(b)(iii).

[(7A) This section does not apply to a regulated deferred payment credit agreement.]

(8) In this section, 'credit intermediary' means a person who in the course of business—

(a) carries on any of the activities specified in article 36A(1)(d) to (f) of the Regulated Activities Order for a consideration that is or includes a financial consideration, and

(b) does not do so as a creditor.]]

[61B Duty to supply copy of overdraft agreement

(1) Where an authorised business overdraft agreement or an authorised nonbusiness overdraft agreement has been made, a document containing the terms of the agreement must be given to the debtor.

(2) The creditor must provide the document referred to in subsection (1) to the debtor before or at the time the agreement is made unless—

(a) the creditor has provided the debtor with the information referred to in regulation 10(3) of the Consumer Credit (Disclosure of Information) Regulations 2010, in which case it [may] be provided after the agreement is made,

(b) the creditor has provided the debtor with the information referred to in regulation 10(3)(c), (e), (f), (h) and (k) of those Regulations, in which case it must be provided immediately after the agreement is made, or

(c) the agreement is an agreement of a description referred to in regulation 10(4)(b) of those Regulations, in which case it must be provided immediately after the agreement is made.

(3) If the requirements of this section are not observed, the agreement is enforceable against the debtor on an order of the court only (and for these purposes a retaking of goods or land to which the agreement relates is an enforcement of the agreement).]

62 Duty to supply copy of unexecuted agreement [: excluded agreement]

(1) If [in the case of a regulated agreement which is an excluded agreement] the unexecuted agreement is presented personally to the debtor or hirer for his signature, but on the occasion when he signs it the document does not become an executed agreement, a copy of it, and of any other document referred to in it, must be there and then delivered to him.

(2) If the unexecuted agreement is sent to the debtor or hirer for his signature, a copy of it, and of any other document referred to in it, must be sent to him at the same time.

(3) A regulated agreement [which is an excluded agreement] is not properly executed if the requirements of this section are not observed.

[(4) In this section, 'excluded agreement' has the same meaning as in section 61A.]

63 Duty to supply copy of executed agreement [: excluded agreements]

(1) If [in the case of a regulated agreement which is an excluded agreement] the unexecuted agreement is presented personally to the debtor or hirer for his signature, and on the occasion when he signs it the document becomes an executed agreement, a copy of the executed agreement, and of any other document referred to in it, must be there and then delivered to him.

(2) A copy of the executed agreement, and of any other document referred to in it, must be given to the debtor or hirer within the seven days following the making of the agreement unless—

(a) subsection (1) applies, or

(b) the unexecuted agreement was sent to the debtor or hirer for his signature and, on the occasion of his signing it, the document became an executed agreement.

(3) In the case of a cancellable agreement, a copy under subsection (2) must be sent [by an appropriate method].

(4) In the case of a credit-token agreement, a copy under subsection (2) need not be given within the seven days following the making of the agreement if it is given before or at the time when the credit-token is given to the debtor.

(5) A regulated agreement [which is an excluded agreement] is not properly executed if the requirements of this section are not observed.

[(6) In this section, 'excluded agreement' has the same meaning as in section 61A.]

64 Duty to give notice of cancellation rights

(1) In the case of a cancellable agreement, a notice in the prescribed form indicating the right of the debtor or hirer to cancel the agreement, how and when that right is exercisable, and the name and address of a person to whom notice of cancellation may be given,—

(a) must be included in every copy given to the debtor or hirer under section 62 or 63, and

(b) except where section 63(2) applied, must also be sent [by an appropriate method] to the debtor or hirer within the seven days following the making of the agreement.

(2) In the case of a credit-token agreement, a notice under subsection (1)(b) need not be sent [by an appropriate method] within the seven days following the making of the agreement if either—

(a) it is sent [by an appropriate method] to the debtor or hirer before the credit-token is given to him, or

(b) it is sent [by an appropriate method] to him together with the credit-token.

(3) Regulations may provide that except where section 63(2) applied a notice sent under subsection (1)(b) shall be accompanied by a further copy of the executed agreement, and of any other document referred to in it.

(4) Regulations may provide that subsection (1)(b) is not to apply in the case of agreements such as are described in the regulations, being agreements made by a particular person, if—

(a) on an application by that person to the [FCA], the [FCA] has determined that, having regard to—

(i) the manner in which antecedent negotiations for agreements with the applicant of that description are conducted, and

(ii) the information provided to debtors or hirers before such agreements are made, the requirement imposed by subsection (1)(b) can be dispensed with without prejudicing the interests of debtors or hirers, and

(b) any conditions imposed by the [FCA] in making the determination are complied with.

(5) A cancellable agreement is not properly executed if the requirements of this section are not observed.

65 Consequences of improper execution

(1) An improperly-executed regulated agreement is enforceable against the debtor or hirer on an order of the court only.

(2) A retaking of goods or land to which a regulated agreement relates is an enforcement of the agreement.

66 Acceptance of credit-tokens

(1) The debtor shall not be liable under a credit-token agreement for use made of the credit-token by any person unless the debtor had previously accepted the credit-token, or the use constituted an acceptance of it by him.

(2) The debtor accepts a credit-token when—

(a) it is signed, or

(b) a receipt for it is signed, or

(c) it is first used,

either by the debtor himself or by a person who, pursuant to the agreement, is authorised by him to use it.

[Withdrawal from certain agreements]

[66A Withdrawal from consumer credit agreement

(1) The debtor under a regulated consumer credit agreement, other than an excluded agreement, may withdraw from the agreement, without giving any reason, in accordance with this section.

(2) To withdraw from an agreement under this section the debtor must give oral or written notice of the withdrawal to the creditor before the end of the period of 14 days beginning with [the day after] the relevant day.

(3) For the purposes of subsection (2) the relevant day is whichever is the latest of the following—

(a) the day on which the agreement is made;

(b) where the creditor is required to inform the debtor of the credit limit under the agreement, the day on which the creditor first does so;

(c) in the case of an agreement to which section 61A (duty to supply copy of executed consumer credit agreement) applies, the day on which the debtor receives a copy of the agreement under that section or on which the debtor is informed as specified in subsection (3) of that section;

(d) in the case of an agreement to which section 63 (duty to supply copy of executed agreement: excluded agreements) applies, the day on which the debtor receives a copy of the agreement under that section.

(4) Where oral notice under this section is given to the creditor it must be given in a manner specified in the agreement.

(5) Where written notice under this section is given by facsimile transmission or electronically—

(a) it must be sent to the number or electronic address specified for the purpose in the agreement, and

(b) where it is so sent, it is to be regarded as having been received by the creditor at the time it is sent (and section 176A does not apply).

(6) Where written notice under this section is given in any other form—

(a) it must be sent by post to, or left at, the postal address specified for the purpose in the agreement, and

(b) where it is sent by post to that address, it is to be regarded as having been received by the creditor at the time of posting (and section 176 does not apply).

(7) Subject as follows, where the debtor withdraws from a regulated consumer credit agreement under this section—

(a) the agreement shall be treated as if it had never been entered into, and

(b) where an ancillary service relating to the agreement is or is to be provided by the creditor, or by a third party on the basis of an agreement between the third party and the creditor, the ancillary service contract shall be treated as if it had never been entered into.

(8) In the case referred to in subsection (7)(b) the creditor must without delay notify any third party of the fact that the debtor has withdrawn from the agreement.

(9) Where the debtor withdraws from an agreement under this section—

(a) the debtor must repay to the creditor any credit provided and the interest accrued on it (at the rate provided for under the agreement), but

(b) the debtor is not liable to pay to the creditor any compensation, fees or charges except any non-returnable charges paid by the creditor to a public administrative body.

(10) An amount payable under subsection (9) must be paid without undue delay and no later than the end of the period of 30 days beginning with the day

after the day on which the notice of withdrawal was given (and if not paid by the end of that period may be recovered by the creditor as a debt).

(11) Where a regulated consumer credit agreement is a conditional sale, hirepurchase or credit-sale agreement and—

(a) the debtor withdraws from the agreement under this section after the credit has been provided, and

(b) the sum payable under subsection (9)(a) is paid in full by the debtor,

title to the goods purchased or supplied under the agreement is to pass to the debtor on the same terms as would have applied had the debtor not withdrawn from the agreement.

(12) In subsections (2), (4), (5), (6) and (9)(a) references to the creditor include a person specified by the creditor in the agreement.

(13) In subsection (7)(b) the reference to an ancillary service means a service that relates to the provision of credit under the agreement and includes in particular an insurance or payment protection policy.

(14) For the purposes of this section, an agreement is an excluded agreement if it is—

(a) an agreement for credit exceeding £60,260 [, other than a residential renovation agreement],

(b) an agreement secured on land,

(c) a restricted-use credit agreement to finance the purchase of land, or

(d) an agreement for a bridging loan in connection with the purchase of land.]

Cancellation of certain agreements within cooling-off period

67 Cancellable agreements

[(1) Subject to subsection (2)] a regulated agreement may be cancelled by the debtor or hirer in accordance with this Part if the antecedent negotiations included oral representations made when in the presence of the debtor or hirer by an individual acting as, or on behalf of, the negotiator, unless—

(a) the agreement is secured on land, or is a restricted-use credit agreement to finance the purchase of land or is an agreement for a bridging loan in connection with the purchase of land, or

(b) the unexecuted agreement is signed by the debtor or hirer at premises at which any of the following is carrying on any business (whether on a permanent or temporary basis)—

(i) the creditor or owner;

(ii) any party to a linked transaction (other than the debtor or hirer or a relative of his);

(iii) the negotiator in any antecedent negotiations.

[(2) This section does not apply where section 66A applies.]

68 Cooling-off period

The debtor or hirer may serve notice of cancellation of a cancellable agreement between his signing of the unexecuted agreement and—

(a) the end of the fifth day following the day on which he received a copy under section 63(2) or a notice under section 64(1)(b), or

(b) if (by virtue of regulations made under section 64(4)) section 64(1)(b) does not apply, the end of the fourteenth day following the day on which he signed the unexecuted agreement.

69 Notice of cancellation

(1) If within the period specified in section 68 the debtor or hirer under a cancellable agreement serves on—

(a) the creditor or owner, or

(b) the person specified in the notice under section 64(1), or

(c) a person who (whether by virtue of subsection (6) or otherwise) is the agent of the creditor or owner,

a notice (a 'notice of cancellation') which, however expressed and whether or not conforming to the notice given under section 64(1), indicates the intention of the debtor or hirer to withdraw from the agreement, the notice shall operate—

(i) to cancel the agreement, and any linked transaction, and

(ii) to withdraw any offer by the debtor or hirer, or his relative, to enter into a linked transaction.

(2) In the case of a debtor-creditor-supplier agreement for restricted-use credit financing—

(a) the doing of work or supply of goods to meet an emergency, or

(b) the supply of goods which, before service of the notice of cancellation, had by the act of the debtor or his relative become incorporated in any land or thing not comprised in the agreement or any linked transaction,

subsection (1) shall apply with the substitution of the following for paragraph (i)—

'(i) to cancel only such provisions of the agreement and any linked transaction as—

(aa) relate to the provision of credit, or

(bb) require the debtor to pay an item in the total charge for credit, or

(cc) subject the debtor to any obligation other than to pay for the doing of the said work, or the supply of the said goods.'

(3) Except so far as is otherwise provided, references in this Act to the cancellation of an agreement or transaction do not include a case within subsection (2).

(4) Except as otherwise provided by or under this Act, an agreement or transaction cancelled under subsection (1) shall be treated as if it had never been entered into.

(5) Regulations may exclude linked transactions of the prescribed description from subsection (1)(i) or (ii).

(6) Each of the following shall be deemed to be the agent of the creditor or owner for the purpose of receiving a notice of cancellation—

(a) a credit-broker or supplier who is the negotiator in antecedent negotiations, and

(b) any person who, in the course of a business carried on by him, acts on behalf of the debtor or hirer in any negotiations for the agreement.

[(7) Whether or not it is actually received by him, a notice of cancellation sent to a person shall be deemed to be served on him—

(a) in the case of a notice sent by post, at the time of posting, and

(b) in the case of a notice transmitted in the form of an electronic communication in accordance with section 17A(1), at the time of the transmission.]

70 Cancellation: recovery of money paid by debtor or hirer

(1) On the cancellation of a regulated agreement, and of any linked transaction,—

(a) any sum paid by the debtor or hirer, or his relative, under or in contemplation of the agreement or transaction, including any item in the total charge for credit, shall become repayable, and

(b) any sum, including any item in the total charge for credit, which but for the cancellation is, or would or might become, payable by the debtor or hirer, or his relative, under the agreement or transaction shall cease to be, or shall not become, so payable, and

(c) in the case of a debtor-creditor-supplier agreement falling within section 12(b), any sum paid on the debtor's behalf by the creditor to the supplier shall become repayable to the creditor.

(2) If, under the terms of a cancelled agreement or transaction, the debtor or hirer, or his relative, is in possession of any goods, he shall have a lien on them for

any sum repayable to him under subsection (1) in respect of that agreement or transaction, or any other linked transaction.

(3) A sum repayable under subsection (1) is repayable by the person to whom it was originally paid, but in the case of a debtor-creditor-supplier agreement falling within section 12(b) the creditor and the supplier shall be under a joint and several liability to repay sums paid by the debtor, or his relative, under the agreement or under a linked transaction falling within section 19(1)(b) and accordingly, in such a case, the creditor shall be entitled, in accordance with rules of court, to have the supplier made a party to any proceedings brought against the creditor to recover any such sums.

(4) Subject to any agreement between them, the creditor shall be entitled to be indemnified by the supplier for loss suffered by the creditor in satisfying his liability under subsection (3), including costs reasonably incurred by him in defending proceedings instituted by the debtor.

(5) Subsection (1) does not apply to any sum which, if not paid by a debtor, would be payable by virtue of section 71, and applies to a sum paid or payable by a debtor for the issue of a credit-token only where the credit-token has been returned to the creditor or surrendered to a supplier.

(6) If the total charge for credit includes an item in respect of a fee or commission charged by a credit-broker, the amount repayable under subsection (1) in respect of that item shall be the excess over [£5] of the fee or commission.

(7) If the total charge for credit includes any sum payable or paid by the debtor to a credit-broker otherwise than in respect of a fee or commission charged by him, that sum shall for the purposes of subsection (6) be treated as if it were such a fee or commission.

(8) So far only as is necessary to give effect to section 69(2), this section applies to an agreement or transaction within that subsection as it applies to a cancelled agreement or transaction.

71 Cancellation: repayment of credit

(1) Notwithstanding the cancellation of a regulated consumer credit agreement, other than a debtor-creditor-supplier agreement for restricted-use credit, the agreement shall continue in force so far as it relates to repayment of credit and payment of interest.

(2) If, following the cancellation of a regulated consumer credit agreement, the debtor repays the whole or a portion of the credit—

(a) before the expiry of one month following service of the notice of cancellation, or

(b) in the case of a credit repayable by instalments, before the date on which the first instalment is due,

no interest shall be payable on the amount repaid.

(3) If the whole of a credit repayable by instalments is not repaid on or before the date specified in subsection (2)(b), the debtor shall not be liable to repay any of the credit except on receipt of a request in writing in the prescribed form, signed by or on behalf of the creditor, stating the amounts of the remaining instalments (recalculated by the creditor as nearly as may be in accordance with the agreement and without extending the repayment period), but excluding any sum other than principal and interest.

(4) Repayment of a credit, or payment of interest, under a cancelled agreement shall be treated as duly made if it is made to any person on whom, under section 69, a notice of cancellation could have been served, other than a person referred to in section 69(6)(b).

72 Cancellation: return of goods

(1) This section applies where any agreement or transaction relating to goods, being—

(a) a restricted-use debtor-creditor-supplier agreement, a consumer hire agreement, or a linked transaction to which the debtor or hirer under any regulated agreement is a party, or

(b) a linked transaction to which a relative of the debtor or hirer under any regulated agreement is a party,

is cancelled after the debtor or hirer (in a case within paragraph (a)) or the relative (in a case within paragraph (b)) has acquired possession of the goods by virtue of the agreement or transaction.

(2) In this section—

(a) 'the possessor' means the person who has acquired possession of the goods as mentioned in subsection (1),

(b) 'the other party' means the person from whom the possessor acquired possession, and

(c) 'the pre-cancellation period' means the period beginning when the possessor acquired possession and ending with the cancellation.

(3) The possessor shall be treated as having been under a duty throughout the pre-cancellation period—

(a) to retain possession of the goods, and

(b) to take reasonable care of them.

(4) On the cancellation, the possessor shall be under a duty, subject to any lien to restore the goods to the other party in accordance with this section, and meanwhile to retain possession of the goods and take reasonable care of them.

(5) The possessor shall not be under any duty to deliver the goods except at his own premises and in pursuance of a request in writing signed by or on behalf of the other party and served on the possessor either before, or at the time when, the goods are collected from those premises.

(6) If the possessor—

(a) delivers the goods (whether at his own premises or elsewhere) to any person on whom, under section 69, a notice of cancellation could have been served (other than a person referred to in section 69(6)(b)), or

(b) sends the goods at his own expense to such a person, he shall be discharged from any duty to retain the goods or deliver them to any person.

(7) Where the possessor delivers the goods as mentioned in subsection (6)(a), his obligation to take care of the goods shall cease; and if he sends the goods as mentioned in subsection (6)(b), he shall be under a duty to take reasonable care to see that they are received by the other party and not damaged in transit, but in other respects his duty to take care of the goods shall cease.

(8) Where, at any time during the period of 21 days following the cancellation, the possessor receives such a request as is mentioned in subsection (5), and unreasonably refuses or unreasonably fails to comply with it, his duty to take reasonable care of the goods shall continue until he delivers or sends the goods as mentioned in subsection (6), but if within that period he does not receive such a request his duty to take reasonable care of the goods shall cease at the end of that period.

(9) The preceding provisions of this section do not apply to—

(a) perishable goods, or

(b) goods which by their nature are consumed by use and which, before the cancellation, were so consumed, or

(c) goods supplied to meet an emergency, or

(d) goods which, before the cancellation, had become incorporated in any land or thing not comprised in the cancelled agreement or a linked transaction.

(10) Where the address of the possessor is specified in the executed agreement, references in this section to his own premises are to that address and no other.

(11) Breach of a duty imposed by this section is actionable as a breach of statutory duty.

73 Cancellation: goods given in part-exchange

(1) This section applies on the cancellation of a regulated agreement where, in antecedent negotiations, the negotiator agreed to take goods in part-exchange (the 'part-exchange goods') and those goods have been delivered to him.

(2) Unless, before the end of the period of ten days beginning with the date of cancellation, the part-exchange goods are returned to the debtor or hirer in a condition substantially as good as when they were delivered to the negotiator, the debtor or hirer shall be entitled to recover from the negotiator a sum equal to the part-exchange allowance (as defined in subsection (7)(b)).

(3) In the case of a debtor-creditor-supplier agreement within section 12(b), the negotiator and the creditor shall be under a joint and several liability to pay to the debtor a sum recoverable under subsection (2).

(4) Subject to any agreement between them, the creditor shall be entitled to be indemnified by the negotiator for loss suffered by the creditor in satisfying his liability under subsection (3), including costs reasonably incurred by him in defending proceedings instituted by the debtor.

(5) During the period of ten days beginning with the date of cancellation, the debtor or hirer, if he is in possession of goods to which the cancelled agreement relates, shall have a lien on them for—

(a) delivery of the part-exchange goods, in a condition substantially as good as when they were delivered to the negotiator; or

(b) a sum equal to the part-exchange allowance;

and if the lien continues to the end of that period it shall thereafter subsist only as a lien for a sum equal to the part-exchange allowance.

(6) Where the debtor or hirer recovers from the negotiator or creditor, or both of them jointly, a sum equal to the part-exchange allowance, then, if the title of the debtor or hirer to the part-exchange goods has not vested in the negotiator, it shall so vest on the recovery of that sum.

(7) For the purposes of this section—

(a) the negotiator shall be treated as having agreed to take goods in partexchange if, in pursuance of the antecedent negotiations, he either purchased or agreed to purchase those goods or accepted or agreed to accept them as part of the consideration for the cancelled agreement, and

(b) the part-exchange allowance shall be the sum agreed as such in the antecedent negotiations or, if no such agreement was arrived at, such sum as it would have been reasonable to allow in respect of the part-exchange goods if no notice of cancellation had been served.

(8) In an action brought against the creditor for a sum recoverable under subsection (2), he shall be entitled, in accordance with rules of court, to have the negotiator made a party to the proceedings.

Exclusion of certain agreements from Part V

74 Exclusion of certain agreements from Part V

[(1) Except as provided in subsections (1A) to (2), this Part does not apply to—

(a) a non-commercial agreement,

(b) a debtor-creditor agreement enabling the debtor to overdraw on a current account,

(c) a debtor-creditor agreement to finance the making of such payments arising on, or connected with, the death of a person as may be prescribed, or

(d) a small debtor-creditor-supplier agreement for restricted-use credit.

(1A) Section 56 (antecedent negotiations) applies to a non-commercial agreement.

(1B) Where an agreement that falls within subsection (1)(b) is an authorised business overdraft agreement the following provisions apply—

[. . .]
(b) section 56 (antecedent negotiations);
(c) section 60 (regulations on form and content of agreements);
(d) section 61B (duty to supply copy of overdraft agreement).

(1C) Where an agreement that falls within subsection (1)(b) is an authorised non-business overdraft agreement the following provisions apply—
(a) section 55 (regulations on disclosure of information);
[. . .]
(c) section 55C (copy of draft consumer credit agreement);
(d) section 56 (antecedent negotiations);
(e) section 60 (regulations on form and content of agreements);
(f) section 61B (duty to supply copy of overdraft agreement).

(1D) Where an agreement that falls within subsection (1)(b) would be an authorised non-business overdraft agreement but for the fact that the credit is not repayable on demand or within three months the following provisions apply—
(a) section 55 (regulations on disclosure of information);
[. . .]
(d) section 55C (copy of draft consumer credit agreement);
(e) section 56 (antecedent negotiations);
(f) section 60 (regulations on form and content of agreements);
(g) section 61 (signing of agreement);
(h) section 61A (duty to supply copy of executed agreement);
(i) section 66A (withdrawal from consumer credit agreement).

(1E) In the case of an agreement that falls within subsection (1)(b) but does not fall within subsection (1B), (1C) or (1D), section 56 (antecedent negotiations) applies.

(1F) The following provisions apply to a debtor-creditor agreement to finance the making of such payments arising on, or connected with, the death of a person as may be prescribed—
(a) section 55 (regulations on disclosure of information);
[. . .]
(d) section 55C (copy of draft consumer credit agreement);
(e) section 56 (antecedent negotiations);
(f) section 60 (regulations on form and content of agreements);
(g) section 61 (signing of agreement);
(h) section 61A (duty to supply copy of executed agreement);
(i) section 66A (withdrawal from consumer credit agreement).]

[(2) The following provisions apply to a small debtor-creditor-supplier agreement for restricted-use credit—
(a) section 55 (regulations on disclosure of information);
(b) section 56 (antecedent negotiations);
(c) section 66A (withdrawal from consumer credit agreement).]

[(2A) In the case of an agreement to which Part 2 or 3 of the Consumer Contracts (Information, Cancellation and Additional Charges) Regulations 2013 applies, the reference in subsection (2) to a small agreement is to be read as if in section 17(1)(a) and (b) '£42' were substituted for '£50'.]

(3) [Subsection (1)(c) applies] only where the [FCA] so determines, and such a determination—
(a) may be made subject to such conditions as the [FCA] thinks fit, and
(b) shall be made only if the [FCA] is of opinion that it is not against the interests of debtors.

[. . .]

(4) If any term of an agreement falling within subsection [(1)(d)] is expressed in writing, regulations under section 60(1) shall apply to that term (subject to section 60(3)) as if the agreement were a regulated agreement not falling within subsection [(1)(d)].

[. . .]

PART VI
MATTERS ARISING DURING CURRENCY OF CREDIT OR HIRE AGREEMENTS

75 Liability of creditor for breaches by supplier

(1) If the debtor under a debtor-creditor-supplier agreement falling within section 12(b) or (c) has, in relation to a transaction financed by the agreement, any claim against the supplier in respect of a misrepresentation or breach of contract, he shall have a like claim against the creditor, who, with the supplier, shall accordingly be jointly and severally liable to the debtor.

(2) Subject to any agreement between them, the creditor shall be entitled to be indemnified by the supplier for loss suffered by the creditor in satisfying his liability under subsection (1), including costs reasonably incurred by him in defending proceedings instituted by the debtor.

(3) Subsection (1) does not apply to a claim—

(a) under a non-commercial agreement,

(b) so far as the claim relates to any single item to which the supplier has attached a cash price not exceeding [£100] or more than [£30,000], or

[(c) under a debtor-creditor-supplier agreement for running-account credit—

(i) which provides for the making of payments by the debtor in relation to specified periods which, in the case of an agreement which is not secured on land, do not exceed three months, and

(ii) which requires that the number of payments to be made by the debtor in repayments of the whole amount of the credit provided in each such period shall not exceed one.]

(4) This section applies notwithstanding that the debtor, in entering into the transaction, exceeded the credit limit or otherwise contravened any term of the agreement.

(5) In an action brought against the creditor under subsection (1) he shall be entitled, in accordance with rules of court, to have the supplier made a party to the proceedings.

[75A Further provision for liability of creditor for breaches by supplier

(1) If the debtor under a linked credit agreement has a claim against the supplier in respect of a breach of contract the debtor may pursue that claim against the creditor where any of the conditions in subsection (2) are met.

(2) The conditions in subsection (1) are—

(a) that the supplier cannot be traced,

(b) that the debtor has contacted the supplier but the supplier has not responded,

(c) that the supplier is insolvent, or

(d) that the debtor has taken reasonable steps to pursue his claim against the supplier but has not obtained satisfaction for his claim.

(3) The steps referred to in subsection (2)(d) need not include litigation.

(4) For the purposes of subsection (2)(d) a debtor is to be deemed to have obtained satisfaction where he has accepted a replacement product or service or other compensation from the supplier in settlement of his claim.

(5) In this section 'linked credit agreement' means a regulated consumer credit agreement which serves exclusively to finance an agreement for the supply of specific goods or the provision of a specific service and where—

(a) the creditor uses the services of the supplier in connection with the preparation or making of the credit agreement, or

(b) the specific goods or provision of a specific service are explicitly specified in the credit agreement.

(6) This section does not apply where—

(a) the cash value of the goods or service is £30,000 or less,

(b) the linked credit agreement is for credit which exceeds £60,260 [and is not a residential renovation agreement], or

(c) the linked credit agreement is entered into by the debtor wholly or predominantly for the purposes of a business carried on, or intended to be carried on, by him.

[(7) Article 60C(5) and (6) of the Regulated Activities Order applies for the purposes of subsection (6)(c).]

[(8) This section does not apply to an agreement secured on land.]]

76 Duty to give notice before taking certain action

(1) The creditor or owner is not entitled to enforce a term of a regulated agreement by—

(a) demanding earlier payment of any sum, or

(b) recovering possession of any goods or land, or

(c) treating any right conferred on the debtor or hirer by the agreement as terminated, restricted or deferred,

except by or after giving the debtor or hirer not less than seven days' notice of his intention to do so.

(2) Subsection (1) applies only where—

(a) a period for the duration of the agreement is specified in the agreement, and

(b) that period has not ended when the creditor or owner does an act mentioned in subsection (1),

but so applies notwithstanding that, under the agreement, any party is entitled to terminate it before the end of the period so specified.

(3) A notice under subsection (1) is ineffective if not in the prescribed form.

(4) Subsection (1) does not prevent a creditor from treating the right to draw on any credit as restricted or deferred and taking such steps as may be necessary to make the restriction or deferment effective.

(5) Regulations may provide that subsection (1) is not to apply to agreements described by the regulations.

(6) Subsection (1) does not apply to a right of enforcement arising by reason of any breach by the debtor or hirer of the regulated agreement.

[(7) This section does not apply to a regulated deferred payment credit agreement.]

77 Duty to give information to debtor under fixed-sum credit agreement

(1) The creditor under a regulated agreement for fixed-sum credit, within the prescribed period after receiving a request in writing to that effect from the debtor and payment of a fee of [£1], shall give the debtor a copy of the executed agreement (if any) and of any other document referred to in it, together with a statement signed by or on behalf of the creditor showing, according to the information to which it is practicable for him to refer,—

(a) the total sum paid under the agreement by the debtor;

(b) the total sum which has become payable under the agreement by the debtor but remains unpaid, and the various amounts comprised in that total sum, with the date when each became due; and

(c) the total sum which is to become payable under the agreement by the debtor, and the various amounts comprised in that total sum, with the date, or mode of determining the date, when each becomes due.

(2) If the creditor possesses insufficient information to enable him to ascertain the amounts and dates mentioned in subsection (1)(c), he shall be taken to comply with that paragraph if his statement under subsection (1) gives the basis on which, under the regulated agreement, they would fall to be ascertained.

[(2A) Subsection (2B) applies if the regulated agreement is a green deal plan [. . .].

(2B) The duty imposed on the creditor by subsection (1) may be discharged by another person acting on the creditor's behalf.]

(3) Subsection (1) does not apply to—

(a) an agreement under which no sum is, or will or may become, payable by the debtor, or

(b) a request made less than one month after a previous request under that subsection relating to the same agreement was complied with.

(4) If the creditor under an agreement fails to comply with subsection (1)—

(a) he is not entitled, while the default continues, to enforce the agreement [. . .]

(5) This section does not apply to a non-commercial agreement [or to a regulated deferred payment credit agreement].

[77A Statements to be provided in relation to fixed-sum credit agreements

[(1) The creditor under a regulated agreement for fixed-sum credit must give the debtor statements under this section.

(1A) The statements must relate to consecutive periods.

(1B) The first such period must begin with either—

(a) the day on which the agreement is made, or

(b) the day the first movement occurs on the debtor's account with the creditor relating to the agreement.

(1C) No such period may exceed a year.

(1D) For the purposes of subsection (1C), a period of a year which expires on a non-working day may be regarded as expiring on the next working day.

(1E) Each statement under this section must be given to the debtor before the end of the period of thirty days beginning with the day after the end of the period to which the statement relates.]

(2) Regulations may make provision about the form and content of statements under this section.

[(2A) Subsection (2B) applies if the regulated agreement is a green deal plan [. . .].

(2B) Any duty imposed on the creditor by this section may be discharged by another person acting on the creditor's behalf.]

(3) The debtor shall have no liability to pay any sum in connection with the preparation or the giving to him of a statement under this section.

(4) The creditor is not required to give the debtor any statement under this section once the following conditions are satisfied—

(a) that there is no sum payable under the agreement by the debtor; and

(b) that there is no sum which will or may become so payable.

(5) Subsection (6) applies if at a time before the conditions mentioned in subsection (4) are satisfied the creditor fails to give the debtor—

(a) a statement under this section within the period mentioned in subsection [(1E)]. [. . .]

(6) Where this subsection applies in relation to a failure to give a statement under this section to the debtor—

(a) the creditor shall not be entitled to enforce the agreement during the period of non-compliance;

(b) the debtor shall have no liability to pay any sum of interest to the extent calculated by reference to the period of non-compliance or to any part of it; and

(c) the debtor shall have no liability to pay any default sum which (apart from this paragraph)—

(i) would have become payable during the period of non-compliance; or

(ii) would have become payable after the end of that period in connection with a breach of the agreement which occurs during that period (whether or not the breach continues after the end of that period).

(7) In this section 'the period of non-compliance' means, in relation to a failure to give a statement under this section to the debtor, the period which—

(a) begins immediately after the end of the period mentioned in [. . .] subsection (5); and

(b) ends at the end of the day on which the statement is given to the debtor or on which the conditions mentioned in subsection (4) are satisfied, whichever is earlier.

(8) This section does not apply [in relation to—

(a) a non-commercial agreement,

(b) a small agreement, or

(c) a regulated deferred payment credit agreement.]

[(9) This section does not apply where the holder of a current account overdraws on the account without a pre-arranged overdraft or exceeds a pre-arranged overdraft limit.]

[77B Fixed-sum credit agreement: statement of account to be provided on request

(1) This section applies to a regulated consumer credit agreement—

(a) which is for fixed-sum credit,

(b) which is of fixed duration,

(c) where the credit is repayable in instalments by the debtor, and

(d) which is not an excluded agreement.

(2) Upon a request from the debtor, the creditor must as soon as reasonably practicable give to the debtor a statement in writing which complies with subsections (3) to (5).

(3) The statement must include a table showing the details of each instalment owing under the agreement as at the date of the request.

(4) Details to be provided under subsection (3) must include—

(a) the date on which the instalment is due,

(b) the amount of the instalment,

(c) any conditions relating to payment of the instalment, and

(d) a breakdown of the instalment showing how much of it is made up of capital repayment, interest payment and other charges.

(5) Where the rate of interest is variable or the charges under the agreement may be varied, the statement must also indicate clearly and concisely that the information in the table is valid only until the rate of interest or charges are varied.

(6) The debtor may make a request under subsection (2) at any time that the agreement is in force unless a previous request has been made less than a month before and has been complied with.

(7) The debtor shall have no liability to pay any sum in connection with the preparation or the giving of a statement under this section.

[(7A) Subsection (7B) applies if the regulated agreement is a green deal plan [. . .].

(7B) The duty imposed on the creditor by this section may be discharged by another person acting on the creditor's behalf.]

(8) A breach of the duty imposed by this section is actionable as a breach of statutory duty.

(9) For the purposes of this section, an agreement is an excluded agreement if it is—

(a) an agreement secured on land,

(b) an agreement under which a person takes an article in pawn,

(c) an agreement under which the creditor provides the debtor with credit which exceeds £60,260 [and which is not a residential renovation agreement], or

(d) an agreement entered into by the debtor wholly or predominantly for the purpose of a business carried on, or intended to be carried on, by him.

[(10) Article 60C(5) and (6) of the Regulated Activities Order applies for the purposes of subsection (9)(d).]]

[(11) This section does not apply to a regulated deferred payment credit agreement.]

78 Duty to give information to debtor under running-account credit agreement

(1) The creditor under a regulated agreement for running-account credit, within the prescribed period after receiving a request in writing to that effect from

the debtor and payment of a fee of [£1], shall give the debtor a copy of the executed agreement (if any) and of any other document referred to in it, together with a statement signed by or on behalf of the creditor showing, according to the information to which it is practicable for him to refer,—

(a) the state of the account, and

(b) the amount, if any, currently payable under the agreement by the debtor to the creditor, and

(c) the amounts and due dates of any payments which, if the debtor does not draw further on the account, will later become payable under the agreement by the debtor to the creditor.

[(1A) Where a request under subsection (1) also amounts to a request under regulation 49 of the Payment Services Regulations 2017 (information during period of contract), subsection (1) applies as if the words 'and payment of a fee of £1' were omitted.]

(2) If the creditor possesses insufficient information to enable him to ascertain the amounts and dates mentioned in subsection (1)(c), he shall be taken to comply with that paragraph if his statement under subsection (1) gives the basis on which, under the regulated agreement, they would fall to be ascertained.

(3) Subsection (1) does not apply to—

(a) an agreement under which no sum is, or will or may become, payable by the debtor, or

(b) a request made less than one month after a previous request under that subsection relating to the same agreement was complied with.

(4) Where running-account credit is provided under a regulated agreement, the creditor shall give the debtor statements in the prescribed form, and with the prescribed contents—

(a) showing according to the information to which it is practicable for him to refer, the state of the account at regular intervals of not more than twelve months, and

(b) where the agreement provides, in relation to specified periods, for the making of payments by the debtor, or the charging against him of interest or any other sum, showing according to the information to which it is practicable for him to refer the state of the account at the end of each of those periods during which there is any movement in the account.

[(4A) Regulations may require a statement under subsection (4) to contain also information in the prescribed terms about the consequences of the debtor—

(a) failing to make payments as required by the agreement; or

(b) only making payments of a prescribed description in prescribed circumstances.]

(5) A statement under subsection (4) shall be given within the prescribed period after the end of the period to which the statement relates.

(6) If the creditor under an agreement fails to comply with subsection (1)—

(a) he is not entitled, while the default continues, to enforce the agreement

[. . .]

(7) This section does not apply to a non-commercial agreement, and subsections [(4) to (5)] do not apply to a small agreement.

[78A Duty to give information to debtor on change of rate of interest

(1) Where the rate of interest charged under a regulated consumer credit agreement, other than an excluded agreement, is to be varied, the creditor must inform the debtor in writing of the matters mentioned in subsection (3) before the variation can take effect.

(2) But subsection (1) does not apply where—

(a) the agreement provides that the creditor is to inform the debtor in writing periodically of the matters mentioned in subsection (3) in relation to any variation, at such times as may be provided for in the agreement,

(b) the agreement provides that the rate of interest is to vary according to a reference rate,

(c) the reference rate is publicly available,

(d) information about the reference rate is available on the premises of the creditor, and

(e) the variation of the rate of interest results from a change to the reference rate.

(3) The matters referred to in subsections (1) and (2)(a) are—

(a) the variation in the rate of interest,

(b) the amount of any payments that are to be made after the variation has effect, if different, expressed as a sum of money where practicable, and

(c) if the number or frequency of payments changes as a result of the variation, the new number or frequency.

(4) In the case of an agreement mentioned in subsection (5) this section applies as follows—

(a) the obligation in subsection (1) only applies if the rate of interest increases, and

(b) subsection (3) is to be read as if paragraphs (b) and (c) were omitted.

(5) The agreements referred to in subsection (4) are—

(a) an authorised business overdraft agreement,

(b) an authorised non-business overdraft agreement, or

(c) an agreement which would be an authorised non-business overdraft agreement but for the fact that the credit is not repayable on demand or within three months.

(6) For the purposes of this section an agreement is an excluded agreement if it is—

(a) a debtor-creditor agreement arising where the holder of a current account overdraws on the account without a pre-arranged overdraft or exceeds a pre-arranged overdraft limit, or

(b) an agreement secured on land.]

79 Duty to give hirer information

(1) The owner under a regulated consumer hire agreement, within the prescribed period after receiving a request in writing to that effect from the hirer and payment of a fee of [£1], shall give to the hirer a copy of the executed agreement and of any other document referred to in it, together with a statement signed by or on behalf of the owner showing, according to the information to which it is practicable for him to refer, the total sum which has become payable under the agreement by the hirer but remains unpaid and the various amounts comprised in that total sum, with the date when each became due.

(2) Subsection (1) does not apply to—

(a) an agreement under which no sum is, or will or may become, payable by the hirer, or

(b) a request made less than one month after a previous request under that subsection relating to the same agreement was complied with.

(3) If the owner under an agreement fails to comply with subsection (1)—

(a) he is not entitled, while the default continues, to enforce the agreement [. . .]

(4) This section does not apply to a non-commercial agreement.

80 Debtor or hirer to give information about goods

(1) Where a regulated agreement, other than a non-commercial agreement, requires the debtor or hirer to keep goods to which the agreement relates in his possession or control, he shall, within seven working days after he has received a request in writing to that effect from the creditor or owner, tell the creditor or owner where the goods are.

(2) If the debtor or hirer fails to comply with subsection (1), and the default continues for 14 days, he commits an offence.

[. . .]

82 Variation of agreements

(1) Where, under a power contained in a regulated agreement, the creditor or owner varies the agreement, the variation shall not take effect before notice of it is given to the debtor or hirer in the prescribed manner.

[(1A) Subsection (1) does not apply to a variation in the rate of interest charged under an agreement not secured on land (see section 78A).

(1B) Subsection (1) does not apply to a variation in the rate of interest charged under an agreement secured on land if—

(a) the agreement falls within subsection (1D), and

(b) the variation is a reduction in the rate.

(1C) Subsection (1) does not apply to a variation in any other charge under an agreement if—

(a) the agreement falls within subsection (1D), and

(b) the variation is a reduction in the charge.

(1D) The agreements referred to in subsections (1B) and (1C) are—

(a) an authorised business overdraft agreement,

(b) an authorised non-business overdraft agreement, or

(c) an agreement which would be an authorised non-business overdraft agreement but for the fact that the credit is not repayable on demand or within three months.

(1E) Subsection (1) does not apply to a debtor-creditor agreement arising where the holder of a current account overdraws on the account without a prearranged overdraft or exceeds a pre-arranged overdraft limit.]

(2) Where an agreement (a 'modifying agreement') varies or supplements an earlier agreement, the modifying agreement shall for the purposes of this Act be treated as—

(a) revoking the earlier agreement, and

(b) containing provisions reproducing the combined effect of the two agreements, and obligations outstanding in relation to the earlier agreement shall accordingly be treated as outstanding instead in relation to the modifying agreement.

[(2A) Subsection (2) does not apply if [the earlier agreement or] the modifying agreement is an exempt agreement [. . .].]

[(2B) Subsection (2) does not apply if the modifying agreement varies—

(a) the amount of the repayment to be made under the earlier agreement, or

(b) the duration of the agreement,

as a result of the discharge of part of the debtor's indebtedness under the earlier agreement by virtue of section 94(3).]

(3) If the earlier agreement is a regulated agreement but (apart from this subsection) the modifying agreement is not then, [unless the modifying agreement is—

(a) for running account credit; or

(b) an exempt agreement [. . .], it shall be treated as a regulated agreement.]

(4) If the earlier agreement is a regulated agreement for running-account credit, and by the modifying agreement the creditor allows the credit limit to be exceeded but intends the excess to be merely temporary, Part V (except section 56) shall not apply to the modifying agreement.

(5) If—

(a) the earlier agreement is a cancellable agreement, and

(b) the modifying agreement is made within the period applicable under section 68 to the earlier agreement,

then, whether or not the modifying agreement would, apart from this subsection, be a cancellable agreement, it shall be treated as a cancellable agreement in respect of which a notice may be served under section 68 not later than the end of the period applicable under that section to the earlier agreement.

[(5A) Subsection (5) does not apply where the modifying agreement is an exempt agreement [. . .].]

(6) Except under subsection (5), a modifying agreement shall not be treated as a cancellable agreement.

[(6A) If—

(a) the earlier agreement is an agreement to which section 66A (right of withdrawal) applies, and

(b) the modifying agreement is made within the period during which the debtor may give notice of withdrawal from the earlier agreement (see section 66A(2)),

then, whether or not the modifying agreement would, apart from this subsection, be an agreement to which section 66A applies, it shall be treated as such an agreement in respect of which notice may be given under subsection (2) of that section within the period referred to in paragraph (b) above.

(6B) Except as provided for under subsection (6A) section 66A does not apply to a modifying agreement.]

(7) This section does not apply to a non-commercial agreement [or to a regulated deferred payment credit agreement].

[(8) In this section, an 'exempt agreement' means an agreement which is an exempt agreement for the purposes of Chapter 14A of Part 2 of the Regulated Activities Order by virtue of article 60C(2) (regulated mortgage contracts and regulated home purchase plans) or article 60D (exemption relating to the purchase of land for non-residential purposes) of that Order.]

[. . .]

83 Liability for misuse of credit facilities

(1) The debtor under a regulated consumer credit agreement shall not be liable to the creditor for any loss arising from use of the credit facility by another person not acting, or to be treated as acting, as the debtor's agent.

(2) This section does not apply to a non-commercial agreement, or to any loss in so far as it arises from misuse of an instrument to which section 4 of the Cheques Act 1957 applies.

84 Misuse of credit-tokens

(1) Section 83 does not prevent the debtor under a credit-token agreement from being made liable to the extent of [£35] (or the credit limit if lower) for loss to the creditor arising from use of the credit-token by other persons during a period beginning when the credit-token ceases to be in the possession of any authorised person and ending when the credit-token is once more in the possession of an authorised person.

(2) Section 83 does not prevent the debtor under a credit-token agreement from being made liable to any extent for loss to the creditor from use of the credit-token by a person who acquired possession of it with the debtor's consent.

(3) Subsections (1) and (2) shall not apply to any use of the credit-token after the creditor has been given oral or written notice that it is lost or stolen, or is for any other reason liable to misuse.

[(3A) Subsections (1) and (2) shall not apply to any use, in connection with a distance contract (other than an excepted contract), of a card which is a credittoken.

(3B) In subsection (3A), 'distance contract' and 'excepted contract' have the meanings given in the Consumer Protection (Distance Selling) Regulations 2000.

(3C) Subsections (1) and (2) shall not apply to any use, in connection with a distance contract within the meaning of the Financial Services (Distance Marketing) Regulations 2004, of a card which is a credit-token.

(3D) In subsection (3C), 'distance contract' and 'excepted contract' have the meanings given in the Financial Services (Distance Marketing) Regulations 2004.]

(4) Subsections (1) and (2) shall not apply unless there are contained in the credit-token agreement in the prescribed manner particulars of the name, address and telephone number of a person stated to be the person to whom notice is to be given under subsection (3).

(5) Notice under subsection (3) takes effect when received, but where it is given orally, and the agreement so requires, it shall be treated as not taking effect if not confirmed in writing within seven days.

(6) Any sum paid by the debtor for the issue of the credit-token to the extent (if any) that it has not been previously offset by use made of the credittoken, shall be treated as paid towards satisfaction of any liability under subsection (1) or (2).

(7) The debtor, the creditor, and any person authorised by the debtor to use the credit-token, shall be authorised persons for the purposes of subsection (1).

(8) Where two or more credit-tokens are given under one credit-token agreement, the preceding provisions of this section apply to each credit-token separately.

85 Duty on issue of new credit-tokens

(1) Whenever, in connection with a credit-token agreement, a credit-token (other than the first) is given by the creditor to the debtor, the creditor shall give the debtor a copy of the executed agreement (if any) and of any other document referred to in it.

(2) If the creditor fails to comply with this section—

(a) he is not entitled, while the default continues, to enforce the agreement

[. . .]

(3) This section does not apply to a small agreement.

86 Death of debtor or hirer

(1) The creditor or owner under a regulated agreement is not entitled, by reason of the death of the debtor or hirer, to do an act specified in paragraphs (a) to (e) of section 87(1) if at the death the agreement is fully secured.

(2) If at the death of the debtor or hirer a regulated agreement is only partly secured or is unsecured, the creditor or owner is entitled, by reason of the death of the debtor or hirer, to do an act specified in paragraphs (a) to (e) of section 87(1) on an order of the court only.

(3) This section applies in relation to the termination of an agreement only where—

(a) a period for its duration is specified in the agreement, and

(b) that period has not ended when the creditor or owner purports to terminate the agreement,

but so applies notwithstanding that, under the agreement, any party is entitled to terminate it before the end of the period so specified.

(4) The section does not prevent the creditor from treating the right to draw on any credit as restricted or deferred, and taking such steps as may be necessary to make the restriction or deferment effective.

(5) This section does not affect the operation of any agreement providing for payment of sums—

(a) due under the regulated agreement, or

(b) becoming due under it on the death of the debtor or hirer,

out of the proceeds of a policy of assurance on his life.

(6) For the purposes of this section an act is done by reason of the death of the debtor or hirer if it is done under a power conferred by the agreement which is—

(a) exercisable on his death, or

(b) exercisable at will and exercised at any time after his death.

PART VII
DEFAULT AND TERMINATION

[Information sheets

[86A [FCA] to prepare information sheets on arrears and default

(1) The [FCA shall prepare and issue], an arrears information sheet and a default information sheet.

(2) The arrears information sheet shall include information to help debtors and hirers who receive notices under section 86B or 86C.

(3) The default information sheet shall include information to help debtors and hirers who receive default notices.

(4) Regulations may make provision about the information to be included in an information sheet.

(5) An information sheet takes effect for the purposes of this Part at the end of the period of three months beginning with the day on which [it is issued] [or on such later date as the FCA may specify in relation to the information sheet].

[(6) If the FCA revises an information sheet after it has been issued, it shall issue the revised information sheet.]

(7) A revised information sheet takes effect for the purposes of this Part at the end of the period of three months beginning with the day on which [it is issued] [or on such later date as the FCA may specify in relation to the information sheet].]

[Sums in arrears and default sums

[86B Notice of sums in arrears under fixed-sum credit agreements etc

(1) This section applies where at any time the following conditions are satisfied—

(a) that the debtor or hirer under an applicable agreement is required to have made at least two payments under the agreement before that time;

(b) that the total sum paid under the agreement by him is less than the total sum which he is required to have paid before that time;

(c) that the amount of the shortfall is no less than the sum of the last two payments which he is required to have made before that time;

(d) that the creditor or owner is not already under a duty to give him notices under this section in relation to the agreement; and

(e) if a judgment has been given in relation to the agreement before that time, that there is no sum still to be paid under the judgment by the debtor or hirer.

(2) The creditor or owner—

(a) shall, within the period of 14 days beginning with the day on which the conditions mentioned in subsection (1) are satisfied, give the debtor or hirer a notice under this section; and

(b) after the giving of that notice, shall give him further notices under this section at intervals of not more than six months.

(3) The duty of the creditor or owner to give the debtor or hirer notices under this section shall cease when either of the conditions mentioned in subsection (4) is satisfied; but if either of those conditions is satisfied before the notice required by subsection (2)(a) is given, the duty shall not cease until that notice is given.

(4) The conditions referred to in subsection (3) are—

(a) that the debtor or hirer ceases to be in arrears;

(b) that a judgment is given in relation to the agreement under which a sum is required to be paid by the debtor or hirer.

(5) For the purposes of subsection (4)(a) the debtor or hirer ceases to be in arrears when—

(a) no [payments], which he has ever failed to [make] under the agreement when required, [are] still owing;

(b) no default sum, which has ever become payable under the agreement in connection with his failure to pay any sum under the agreement when required, is still owing;

(c) no sum of interest, which has ever become payable under the agreement in connection with such a default sum, is still owing; and

(d) no other sum of interest, which has ever become payable under the agreement in connection with his failure to pay any sum under the agreement when required, is still owing.

(6) A notice under this section shall include a copy of the current arrears information sheet under section 86A.

(7) The debtor or hirer shall have no liability to pay any sum in connection with the preparation or the giving to him of a notice under this section.

(8) Regulations may make provision about the form and content of notices under this section.

(9) In the case of an applicable agreement under which the debtor or hirer must make all payments he is required to make at intervals of one week or less, this section shall have effect as if in subsection (1)(a) and (c) for 'two' there were substituted 'four'.

(10) If an agreement mentioned in subsection (9) was made before the beginning of the relevant period, only amounts resulting from failures by the debtor or hirer to make payments he is required to have made during that period shall be taken into account in determining any shortfall for the purposes of subsection (1)(c).

(11) In subsection (10) 'relevant period' means the period of 20 weeks ending with the day on which the debtor or hirer is required to have made the most recent payment under the agreement.

[(11A) This section does not apply to a regulated deferred payment credit agreement.]

[(12) In this section 'applicable agreement' means an agreement which falls within subsection (12A) or (12B).

(12A) An agreement falls within this subsection if—

(a) it is a regulated agreement for fixed-sum credit; and

(b) it is not—

(i) a non-commercial agreement;

(ii) a small agreement; or

(iii) a green deal plan [. . .].

(12B) An agreement falls within this subsection if—

(a) it is a regulated consumer hire agreement; and

(b) it is neither a non-commercial agreement nor a small agreement.]

[(13) In this section—

(a) 'payments' in relation to an applicable agreement which is a regulated agreement for fixed-sum credit means payments to be made at predetermined intervals provided for under the terms of the agreement; and

(b) 'payments' in relation to an applicable agreement which is a regulated consumer hire agreement means any payments to be made by the hirer in relation to any period in consideration of the bailment or hiring to him of goods under the agreement.]]

[86C Notice of sums in arrears under running-account credit agreements

(1) This section applies where at any time the following conditions are satisfied—

(a) that the debtor under an applicable agreement is required to have made at least two payments under the agreement before that time;

(b) that the last two payments which he is required to have made before that time have not been made;

(c) that the creditor has not already been required to give a notice under this section in relation to either of those payments; and

(d) if a judgment has been given in relation to the agreement before that time, that there is no sum still to be paid under the judgment by the debtor.

(2) The creditor shall, no later than the end of the period within which he is next required to give a statement under section 78(4) in relation to the agreement, give the debtor a notice under this section.

(3) The notice shall include a copy of the current arrears information sheet under section 86A.

(4) The notice may be incorporated in a statement or other notice which the creditor gives the debtor in relation to the agreement by virtue of another pro vision of this Act.

(5) The debtor shall have no liability to pay any sum in connection with the preparation or the giving to him of the notice.

(6) Regulations may make provision about the form and content of notices under this section.

(7) In this section 'applicable agreement' means an agreement which—

(a) is a regulated agreement for running-account credit; and

(b) is neither a non-commercial agreement nor a small agreement.

[(8) In this section 'payments' means payments to be made at predetermined intervals provided for under the terms of the agreement.]]

[86D Failure to give notice of sums in arrears

(1) This section applies where the creditor or owner under an agreement is under a duty to give the debtor or hirer notices under section 86B but fails to give him such a notice—

(a) within the period mentioned in subsection (2)(a) of that section; or

(b) within the period of six months beginning with the day after the day on which such a notice was last given to him.

(2) This section also applies where the creditor under an agreement is under a duty to give the debtor a notice under section 86C but fails to do so before the end of the period mentioned in subsection (2) of that section.

(3) The creditor or owner shall not be entitled to enforce the agreement during the period of non-compliance.

(4) The debtor or hirer shall have no liability to pay—

(a) any sum of interest to the extent calculated by reference to the period of non-compliance or to any part of it; or

(b) any default sum which (apart from this paragraph)—

(i) would have become payable during the period of non-compliance; or

(ii) would have become payable after the end of that period in connection with a breach of the agreement which occurs during that period (whether or not the breach continues after the end of that period).

(5) In this section 'the period of non-compliance' means, in relation to a failure to give a notice under section 86B or 86C to the debtor or hirer, the period which—

(a) begins immediately after the end of the period mentioned in (as the case may be) subsection (1)(a) or (b) or (2); and

(b) ends at the end of the day mentioned in subsection (6).

(6) That day is—

(a) in the case of a failure to give a notice under section 86B as mentioned in subsection (1)(a) of this section, the day on which the notice is given to the debtor or hirer;

(b) in the case of a failure to give a notice under that section as mentioned in subsection (1)(b) of this section, the earlier of the following—

(i) the day on which the notice is given to the debtor or hirer;

(ii) the day on which the condition mentioned in subsection (4)(a) of that section is satisfied;

(c) in the case of a failure to give a notice under section 86C, the day on which the notice is given to the debtor.]

[86E Notice of default sums

(1) This section applies where a default sum becomes payable under a regulated agreement by the debtor or hirer.

(2) The creditor or owner shall, within the prescribed period after the default sum becomes payable, give the debtor or hirer a notice under this section.

(3) The notice under this section may be incorporated in a statement or other notice which the creditor or owner gives the debtor or hirer in relation to the agreement by virtue of another provision of this Act.

(4) The debtor or hirer shall have no liability to pay interest in connection with the default sum to the extent that the interest is calculated by reference to a period occurring before the 29th day after the day on which the debtor or hirer is given the notice under this section.

(5) If the creditor or owner fails to give the debtor or hirer the notice under this section within the period mentioned in subsection (2), he shall not be entitled to enforce the agreement until the notice is given to the debtor or hirer.

(6) The debtor or hirer shall have no liability to pay any sum in connection with the preparation or the giving to him of the notice under this section.

(7) Regulations may—

(a) provide that this section does not apply in relation to a default sum which is less than a prescribed amount;

(b) make provision about the form and content of notices under this section.

(8) This section does not apply [in relation to—

(a) a non-commercial agreement,

(b) a small agreement, or

(c) a regulated deferred payment credit agreement.]

[86F Interest on default sums

(1) This section applies where a default sum becomes payable under a regulated agreement by the debtor or hirer.

(2) The debtor or hirer shall only be liable to pay interest in connection with the default sum if the interest is simple interest.]]

Default notices

87 Need for default notice

(1) Service of a notice on the debtor or hirer in accordance with section 88 (a 'default notice') is necessary before the creditor or owner can become entitled, by reason of any breach by the debtor or hirer of a regulated agreement,—

(a) to terminate the agreement, or

(b) to demand earlier payment of any sum, or

(c) to recover possession of any goods or land, or

(d) to treat any right conferred on the debtor or hirer by the agreement as terminated, restricted or deferred, or

(e) to enforce any security.

(2) Subsection (1) does not prevent the creditor from treating the right to draw upon any credit as restricted or deferred, and taking such steps as may be necessary to make the restriction or deferment effective.

(3) The doing of an act by which a floating charge becomes fixed is not enforcement of a security.

(4) Regulations may provide that section (1) is not to apply to agreements described by the regulations.

[(5) Subsection (1)(d) does not apply in a case referred to in section 98A(4) (termination or suspension of debtor's right to draw on credit under open-end agreement).]

[(6) This section does not apply to a regulated deferred payment credit agreement.]

88 Contents and effect of default notice

(1) The default notice must be in the prescribed form and specify—

(a) the nature of the alleged breach;

(b) if the breach is capable of remedy, what action is required to remedy it and the date before which that action is to be taken;

(c) if the breach is not capable of remedy, the sum (if any) required to be paid as compensation for the breach, and the date before which it is to be paid.

(2) A date specified under subsection (1) must not be less than [14] days after the date of service of the default notice, and the creditor or owner shall not take action such as is mentioned in section 87(1) before the date so specified or (if no requirement is made under subsection (1)) before those [14] days have elapsed.

(3) The default notice must not treat as a breach failure to comply with a provision of the agreement which becomes operative only on breach of some other provision, but if the breach of that other provision is not duly remedied or compensation demanded under subsection (1) is not duly paid, or (where no requirement is made under subsection (1)) if the [14] days mentioned in subsection (2) have elapsed, the creditor or owner may treat the failure as a breach and section 87(1) shall not apply to it.

(4) The default notice must contain information in the prescribed terms about the consequences of failure to comply with it [and any other prescribed matters relating to the agreement].

[(4A) The default notice must also include a copy of the current default information sheet under section 86A.]

(5) A default notice making a requirement under subsection (1) may include a provision for the taking of action such as is mentioned in section 87(1) at any time after the restriction imposed by subsection (2) will cease, together with a statement that the provision will be ineffective if the breach is duly remedied or the compensation duly paid.

89 Compliance with default notice

If before the date specified for that purpose in the default notice the debtor or hirer takes the action specified under section 88(1)(b) or (c) the breach shall be treated as not having occurred.

Further restriction of remedies for default

90 Retaking of protected hire-purchase etc goods

(1) At any time when—

(a) the debtor is in breach of a regulated hire-purchase or a regulated conditional sale agreement relating to goods, and

(b) the debtor has paid to the creditor one-third or more of the total price of the goods, and

(c) the property in the goods remains in the creditor,

the creditor is not entitled to recover possession of the goods from the debtor except on an order of the court.

(2) Where under a hire-purchase or conditional sale agreement the creditor is required to carry out any installation and the agreement specifies, as part of the total price, the amount to be paid in respect of the installation (the 'installation charge') the reference in subsection (1)(b) to one-third of the total price shall be construed as a reference to the aggregate of the installation charge and one-third of the remainder of the total price.

(3) In a case where—

(a) subsection (1)(a) is satisfied, but not subsection (1)(b), and

(b) subsection (1)(b) was satisfied on a previous occasion in relation to an earlier agreement, being a regulated hire-purchase or regulated conditional sale agreement, between the same parties, and relating to any of the goods comprised in the later agreement (whether or not other goods were also included),

subsection (1) shall apply to the later agreement with the omission of paragraph (b).

(4) If the later agreement is a modifying agreement, subsection (3) shall apply with the substitution, for the second reference to the later agreement, of a reference to the modifying agreement.

(5) Subsection (1) shall not apply, or shall cease to apply, to an agreement if the debtor has terminated, or terminates, the agreement.

(6) Where subsection (1) applies to an agreement at the death of the debtor, it shall continue to apply (in relation to the possessor of the goods) until the grant of probate or administration, or (in Scotland) confirmation (on which the personal representative would fall to be treated as the debtor).

(7) Goods falling within this section are in this Act referred to as 'protected goods'.

91 Consequences of breach of s 90

If goods are recovered by the creditor in contravention of section 90—

(a) the regulated agreement, if not previously terminated, shall terminate, and

(b) the debtor shall be released from all liability under the agreement, and shall be entitled to recover from the creditor all sums paid by the debtor under the agreement.

92 Recovery of possession of goods or land

(1) Except under an order of the court, the creditor or owner shall not be entitled to enter any premises to take possession of goods subject to a regulated hirepurchase agreement, regulated conditional sale agreement or regulated consumer hire agreement.

(2) At any time when the debtor is in breach of a regulated conditional sale agreement relating to land, the creditor is entitled to recover possession of the land from the debtor, or any person claiming under him, on an order of the court only.

(3) An entry in contravention of subsection (1) or (2) is actionable as a breach of statutory duty.

93 Interest not to be increased on default

The debtor under a regulated consumer credit agreement shall not be obliged to pay interest on sums which, in breach of the agreement, are unpaid by him at a rate—

(a) where the total charge for credit includes an item in respect of interest, exceeding the rate of that interest, or

(b) in any other case, exceeding what would be the rate of the total charge for credit if any items included in the total charge for credit by virtue of [rules made by the FCA under paragraph (2)(d) of article 60M of the Regulated Activities Order] were disregarded.

[93A Summary diligence not competent in Scotland

Summary diligence shall not be competent in Scotland to enforce payment of a debt due under a regulated agreement or under any security related thereto.]

Early payment by debtor

94 Right to complete payments ahead of time

(1) The debtor under a regulated consumer credit agreement is entitled at any time, by notice to the creditor and the payment to the creditor of all amounts payable by the debtor to him under the agreement [and any amount which the creditor claims under section 95A(2)] [or section 95B(2)] (less any rebate allowable under section 95), to discharge the debtor's indebtedness under the agreement.

(2) A notice under subsection (1) may embody the exercise by the debtor of any option to purchase goods conferred on him by the agreement, and deal with any other matter arising on, or in relation to, the termination of the agreement.

[(3) The debtor under a regulated consumer credit agreement, other than an agreement secured on land, is entitled at any time to discharge part of his indebtedness by taking the steps in subsection (4).

(4) The steps referred to in subsection (3) are as follows—

(a) he provides notice to the creditor,

(b) he pays to the creditor some of the amount payable by him to the creditor under the agreement before the time fixed by the agreement, and

(c) he makes the payment—

(i) before the end of the period of 28 days beginning with the day following that on which notice under paragraph (a) was received by the creditor, or

(ii) on or before any later date specified in the notice.

(5) Where a debtor takes the steps in subsection (4) his indebtedness shall be discharged by an amount equal to the sum of the amount paid and any rebate allowable under section 95 less any amount which the creditor claims under section 95A(2) [or section 95B(2)].

(6) A notice—

(a) under subsection (1), other than a notice relating to a regulated consumer credit agreement secured on land, or

(b) under subsection (4)(a),

need not be in writing.]

95 Rebate on early settlement

(1) Regulations may provide for the allowance of a rebate of charges for credit to the debtor under a regulated consumer credit agreement where, under section 94, on refinancing, on breach of the agreement, or for any other reason, his indebtedness is discharged [or is discharged in part] or becomes payable before the time fixed by the agreement, or any sum becomes payable by him before the time so fixed.

(2) Regulations under subsection (1) may provide for calculation of the rebate by reference to any sums paid or payable by the debtor or his relative under or in connection with the agreement (whether to the creditor or some other person), including sums under linked transactions and other items in the total charge for credit.

[95A Compensatory amount

(1) This section applies where—

(a) a regulated consumer credit agreement, other than an agreement secured on land, provides for the rate of interest on the credit to be fixed for a period of time, and

(b) under section 94 the debtor discharges all or part of his indebtedness during that period.

(2) The creditor may claim an amount equal to the cost which the creditor has incurred as a result only of the debtor's indebtedness being discharged during that period if—

(a) the amount of the payment under section 94 exceeds £8,000 or, where more than one such payment is made in any 12 month period, the total of those payments exceeds £8,000,

(b) the agreement is not a debtor-creditor agreement enabling the debtor to overdraw on a current account, and

(c) the amount of the payment under section 94 is not paid from the proceeds of a contract of payment protection insurance.

(3) The amount in subsection (2)—

(a) must be fair,

(b) must be objectively justified, and

(c) must not exceed whichever is the higher of—

(i) the relevant percentage of the amount of the payment under section 94, and

(ii) the total amount of interest that would have been paid by the debtor under the agreement in the period from the date on which the debtor makes the payment under section 94 to the date fixed by the agreement for the discharge of the indebtedness of the debtor.

(4) In subsection (3)(c)(i) 'relevant percentage' means—

(a) 1%, where the period from the date on which the debtor makes the payment under section 94 to the date fixed by the agreement for the discharge of the indebtedness of the debtor is more than one year, or

(b) 0.5%, where that period is equal to or less than one year.]

[95B Compensatory amount: green deal finance

(1) This section applies where—

(a) a regulated consumer credit agreement provides for the rate of interest on the credit to be fixed for a period of time ('the fixed rate period'),

(b) the agreement is a green deal plan [. . .] which is of a duration specified for the purposes of this section in regulations, and

(c) under section 94 the debtor discharges all or part of his indebtedness during the fixed rate period.

(2) The creditor may claim an amount equal to the cost which the creditor has incurred as a result only of the debtor's indebtedness being discharged during the fixed rate period if—

(a) the amount of the payment under section 94 is not paid from the proceeds of a contract of payment protection insurance, and

(b) such other conditions as may be specified for the purposes of this section in regulations are satisfied.

(3) The amount in subsection (2)—

(a) must be fair,

(b) must be objectively justified,

(c) must be calculated by the creditor in accordance with provision made for the purposes of this section in regulations, and

(d) must not exceed the total amount of interest that would have been paid by the debtor under the agreement in the period from the date on which the debtor makes the payment under section 94 to the date fixed by the agreement for the discharge of the indebtedness of the debtor.

(4) If a creditor could claim under either section 95A or this section, the creditor may choose under which section to claim.]

96 Effect on linked transactions

(1) Where for any reason the indebtedness of the debtor under a regulated consumer credit agreement is discharged before the time fixed by the agreement, he, and any relative of his, shall at the same time be discharged from any liability under a linked transaction, other than a debt which has already become payable.

(2) Subsection (1) does not apply to a linked transaction which is itself an agreement providing the debtor or his relative with credit.

(3) Regulations may exclude linked transactions of the prescribed description from the operation of subsection (1).

97 Duty to give information

(1) The creditor under a regulated consumer credit agreement, within the prescribed period after he has received a request [. . .] to that effect from the debtor, shall give the debtor a statement in the prescribed form indicating, according to the information to which it is practicable for him to refer, the amount of the payment required to discharge the debtor's indebtedness under the agreement, together with the prescribed particulars showing how the amount is arrived at.

(2) Subsection (1) does not apply to a request made less than one month after a previous request under that subsection relating to the same agreement was complied with.

[(2A) A request under subsection (1) need not be in writing unless the agreement is secured on land.]

(3) If the creditor fails to comply with subsection (1)—

(a) he is not entitled, while the default continues, to enforce the agreement

[. . .]

[(4) This section does not apply to a regulated deferred payment credit agreement.]

[97A Duty to give information on partial repayment

(1) Where a debtor under a regulated consumer credit agreement—

(a) makes a payment by virtue of which part of his indebtedness is discharged under section 94, and

(b) at the same time or subsequently requests the creditor to give him a statement concerning the effect of the payment on the debtor's indebtedness,

the creditor must give the statement to the debtor before the end of the period of seven working days beginning with the day following that on which the creditor receives the request.

(2) The statement shall be in writing and shall contain the following particulars—

(a) a description of the agreement sufficient to identify it,

(b) the name, postal address and, where appropriate, any other address of the creditor and the debtor,

(c) where the creditor is claiming an amount under section 95A(2) [or section 95B(2)], that amount and the method used to determine it,

(d) the amount of any rebate to which the debtor is entitled—

(i) under the agreement, or

(ii) by virtue of section 95 where that is higher,

(e) where the amount of the rebate mentioned in paragraph (d)(ii) is given, a statement indicating that this amount has been calculated having regard to the Consumer Credit (Early Settlement) Regulations 2004,

(f) where the debtor is not entitled to any rebate, a statement to this effect,

(g) any change to—

(i) the number, timing or amount of repayments to be made under the agreement, or

(ii) the duration of the agreement,

which results from the partial discharge of the indebtedness of the debtor, and

(h) the amount of the debtor's indebtedness remaining under the agreement at the date the creditor gives the statement.]

[(3) This section does not apply to a regulated deferred payment credit agreement.]

Termination of agreements

98 Duty to give notice of termination (non-default cases)

(1) The creditor or owner is not entitled to terminate a regulated agreement except by or after giving the debtor or hirer not less than seven days' notice of the termination.

(2) Subsection (1) applies only where—

(a) a period for the duration of the agreement is specified in the agreement, and

(b) that period has not ended when the creditor or owner does an act mentioned in subsection (1),

but so applies notwithstanding that, under the agreement, any party is entitled to terminate it before the end of the period so specified.

(3) A notice under subsection (1) is ineffective if not in the prescribed form.

(4) Subsection (1) does not prevent a creditor from treating the right to draw on any credit as restricted or deferred and taking such steps as may be necessary to make the restriction or deferment effective.

(5) Regulations may provide that subsection (1) is not to apply to agreements described by the regulations.

(6) Subsection (1) does not apply to the termination of a regulated agreement by reason of any breach by the debtor or hirer of the agreement.

[(7) This section does not apply to a regulated deferred payment credit agreement.]

[98A Termination etc of open-end consumer credit agreements

(1) The debtor under a regulated open-end consumer credit agreement, other than an excluded agreement, may by notice terminate the agreement, free of charge, at any time, subject to any period of notice not exceeding one month provided for by the agreement.

(2) Notice under subsection (1) need not be in writing unless the creditor so requires.

(3) Where a regulated open-end consumer credit agreement, other than an excluded agreement, provides for termination of the agreement by the creditor—

(a) the termination must be by notice served on the debtor, and

(b) the termination may not take effect until after the end of the period of two months, or such longer period as the agreement may provide, beginning with the day after the day on which notice is served.

(4) Where a regulated open-end consumer credit agreement, other than an excluded agreement, provides for termination or suspension by the creditor of the debtor's right to draw on credit—

(a) to terminate or suspend the right to draw on credit the creditor must serve a notice on the debtor before the termination or suspension or, if that is not practicable, immediately afterwards,

(b) the notice must give reasons for the termination or suspension, and

(c) the reasons must be objectively justified.

(5) Subsection (4)(a) and (b) does not apply where giving the notice—

(a) is prohibited by [[an assimilated] obligation], or

(b) would, or would be likely to, prejudice—

(i) the prevention or detection of crime,

(ii) the apprehension or prosecution of offenders, or

(iii) the administration of justice.

(6) An objectively justified reason under subsection (4)(c) may, for example, relate to—

(a) the unauthorised or fraudulent use of credit, or

(b) a significantly increased risk of the debtor being unable to fulfil his obligation to repay the credit.

(7) Subsections (1) and (3) do not affect any right to terminate an agreement for breach of contract.

(8) For the purposes of this section an agreement is an excluded agreement if it is—

(a) an authorised non-business overdraft agreement,

(b) an authorised business overdraft agreement,

(c) a debtor-creditor agreement arising where the holder of a current account overdraws on the account without a pre-arranged overdraft or exceeds a pre-arranged overdraft limit, or

(d) an agreement secured on land.]

99 Right to terminate hire-purchase etc agreements

(1) At any time before the final payment by the debtor under a regulated hirepurchase or regulated conditional sale agreement falls due, the debtor shall be entitled to terminate the agreement by giving notice to any person entitled or authorised to receive the sums payable under the agreement.

(2) Termination of an agreement under subsection (1) does not affect any liability under the agreement which has accrued before the termination.

(3) Subsection (1) does not apply to a conditional sale agreement relating to land after the title to the land has passed to the debtor.

(4) In the case of a conditional sale agreement relating to goods, where the property in the goods, having become vested in the debtor, is transferred to a

person who does not become the debtor under the agreement, the debtor shall not thereafter be entitled to terminate the agreement under subsection (1).

(5) Subject to subsection (4), where a debtor under a conditional sale agreement relating to goods terminates the agreement under this section after the property in the goods has become vested in him, the property in the goods shall thereupon vest in the person (the 'previous owner') in whom it was vested immediately before it became vested in the debtor:

Provided that if the previous owner has died, or any other event has occurred whereby that property, if vested in him immediately before that event, would thereupon have vested in some other person, the property shall be treated as having devolved as if it had been vested in the previous owner immediately before his death or immediately before that event, as the case may be.

100 Liability of debtor on termination of hire-purchase etc agreement

(1) Where a regulated hire-purchase or regulated conditional sale agreement is terminated under section 99 the debtor shall be liable, unless the agreement provides for a smaller payment, or does not provide for any payment, to pay to the creditor the amount (if any) by which one-half of the total price exceeds the aggregate of the sums paid and the sums due in respect of the total price immediately before the termination.

(2) Where under a hire-purchase or conditional sale agreement the creditor is required to carry out any installation and the agreement specifies, as part of the total price, the amount to be paid in respect of the installation (the 'installation charge') the reference in subsection (1) to one-half of the total price shall be construed as a reference to the aggregate of the installation charge and one-half of the remainder of the total price.

(3) If in any action the court is satisfied that a sum less than the amount specified in subsection (1) would be equal to the loss sustained by the creditor in consequence of the termination of the agreement by the debtor, the court may make an order for the payment of that sum in lieu of the amount specified in subsection (1).

(4) If the debtor has contravened an obligation to take reasonable care of the goods or land, the amount arrived at under subsection (1) shall be increased by the sum required to recompense the creditor for that contravention, and subsection (2) shall have effect accordingly.

(5) Where the debtor, on the termination of the agreement, wrongfully retains possession of goods to which the agreement relates, then, in any action brought by the creditor to recover possession of the goods from the debtor, the court, unless it is satisfied that having regard to the circumstances it would not be just to do so, shall order the goods to be delivered to the creditor without giving the debtor an option to pay the value of the goods.

101 Right to terminate hire agreement

(1) The hirer under a regulated consumer hire agreement is entitled to terminate the agreement by giving notice to any person entitled or authorised to receive the sums payable under the agreement.

(2) Termination of an agreement under subsection (1) does not affect any liability under the agreement which has accrued before the termination.

(3) A notice under subsection (1) shall not expire earlier than eighteen months after the making of the agreement, but apart from that the minimum period of notice to be given under subsection (1), unless the agreement provides for a shorter period, is as follows.

(4) If the agreement provides for the making of payments by the hirer to the owner at equal intervals, the minimum period of notice is the length of one interval or three months, whichever is less.

(5) If the agreement provides for the making of such payments at differing in-

tervals, the minimum period of notice is the length of the shortest interval or three months, whichever is less.

(6) In any other case, the minimum period of notice is three months.

(7) This section does not apply to—

(a) any agreement which provides for the making by the hirer of payments which in total (and without breach of the agreement) exceed [£1,500] in any year, or

(b) any agreement where—

(i) goods are bailed or (in Scotland) hired to the hirer for the purposes of a business carried on by him, or the hirer holds himself out as requiring the goods for those purposes, and

(ii) the goods are selected by the hirer, and acquired by the owner for the purposes of the agreement at the request of the hirer from any person other than the owner's associate, or

(c) any agreement where the hirer requires, or holds himself out as requiring, the goods for the purpose of bailing or hiring them to other persons in the course of a business carried on by him.

(8) If, on an application made to the [FCA] by a person carrying on a consumer hire business, it appears to the [FCA] that it would be in the interest of hirers to do so, [it] may [. . .] direct that [, subject to such conditions (if any) as it may specify, this section shall not apply to consumer hire agreements made by the applicant; and this Act shall have effect accordingly].

[(8A) If it appears to the [FCA] that it would be in the interest of hirers to do so, it may [. . .] direct that, subject to such conditions (if any) as it may specify, this section shall not apply to a consumer hire agreement if the agreement falls within a specified description; and this Act shall have effect accordingly.]

(9) In the case of a modifying agreement, subsection (3) shall apply with the substitution for 'the making of the agreement' of 'the making of the original agreement'.

102 Agency for receiving notice of rescission

(1) Where the debtor or hirer under a regulated agreement claims to have a right to rescind the agreement, each of the following shall be deemed to be the agent of the creditor or owner for the purpose of receiving any notice rescinding the agreement which is served by the debtor or hirer—

(a) a credit-broker or supplier who was the negotiator in antecedent negotiations, and

(b) any person who, in the course of a business carried on by him, acted on behalf of the debtor or hirer in any negotiations for the agreement.

(2) In subsection (1) 'rescind' does not include—

(a) service of a notice of cancellation, or

(b) termination of an agreement under section 99 or 101 or by the exercise of a right or power in that behalf expressly conferred by the agreement.

103 Termination statements

(1) If an individual (the 'customer') serves on any person (the 'trader') a notice—

(a) stating that—

(i) the customer was the debtor or hirer under a regulated agreement described in the notice, and the trader was the creditor or owner under the agreement, and

(ii) the customer has discharged his indebtedness to the trader under the agreement, and

(iii) the agreement has ceased to have any operation; and

(b) requiring the trader to give the customer a notice, signed by or on behalf of the trader, confirming that those statements are correct, the trader shall, within the prescribed period after receiving the notice, either comply with it or serve on the customer a counter-notice stating that, as the case may be, he disputes the correctness of the notice or asserts that the customer is not indebted to him under the agreement.

(2) Where the trader disputes the correctness of the notice he shall give particulars of the way in which he alleges it to be wrong.

(3) Subsection (1) does not apply in relation to any agreement if the trader has previously complied with that subsection on the service of a notice under it with respect to that agreement.

(4) Subsection (1) does not apply to a non-commercial agreement [or to a regulated deferred payment credit agreement].

[. . .]

[(6) A breach of the duty imposed by subsection (1) is actionable as a breach of statutory duty.]

104 Goods not to be treated as subject to landlord's hypothec in Scotland

Goods comprised in a hire-purchase agreement or goods comprised in a conditional sale agreement which have not become vested in the debtor shall not be treated in Scotland as subject to the landlord's hypothec—

(a) during the period between the service of a default notice in respect of the goods and the date on which the notice expires or is earlier complied with; or

(b) if the agreement is enforceable on an order of the court only, during the period between the commencement and termination of an action by the creditor to enforce the agreement.

PART VIII
SECURITY

General

105 Form and content of securities

(1) Any security provided in relation to a regulated agreement shall be expressed in writing.

(2) Regulations may prescribe the form and content of documents ('security instruments') to be made in compliance with subsection (1).

(3) Regulations under subsection (2) may in particular—

(a) require specified information to be included in the prescribed manner in documents, and other specified material to be excluded;

(b) contain requirements to ensure that specified information is clearly brought to the attention of the surety, and that one part of a document is not given insufficient or excessive prominence compared with another.

(4) A security instrument is not properly executed unless—

(a) a document in the prescribed form, itself containing all the prescribed terms and conforming to regulations under subsection (2), is signed in the prescribed manner by or on behalf of the surety, and

(b) the document embodies all the terms of the security, other than implied terms, and

(c) the document, when presented or sent for the purpose of being signed by or on behalf of the surety, is in such state that its terms are readily legible, and

(d) when the document is presented or sent for the purpose of being signed by or on behalf of the surety there is also presented or sent a copy of the document.

(5) A security instrument is not properly executed unless—

(a) where the security is provided after, or at the time when, the regulated agreement is made, a copy of the executed agreement, together with a copy of any other document referred to in it, is given to the surety at the time the security is provided, or

(b) where the security is provided before the regulated agreement is made, a copy of the executed agreement, together with a copy of any other document referred to in it, is given to the surety within seven days after the regulated agreement is made.

(6) Subsection (1) does not apply to a security provided by the debtor or hirer.

(7) If—

(a) in contravention of subsection (1) a security is not expressed in writing, or

(b) a security instrument is improperly executed,

the security, so far as provided in relation to a regulated agreement, is enforceable against the surety on an order of the court only.

(8) If an application for an order under subsection (7) is dismissed (except on technical grounds only) section 106 (ineffective securities) shall apply to the security.

(9) Regulations under section 60(1) shall include provision requiring documents embodying regulated agreements also to embody any security provided in relation to a regulated agreement by the debtor or hirer.

106 Ineffective securities

Where, under any provision of this Act, this section is applied to any security provided in relation to a regulated agreement, then, subject to section 177 (saving for registered charges)—

(a) the security, so far as it is so provided, shall be treated as never having effect;

(b) any property lodged with the creditor or owner solely for the purposes of the security as so provided shall be returned by him forthwith;

(c) the creditor or owner shall take any necessary action to remove or cancel an entry in any register, so far as the entry relates to the security as so provided; and

(d) any amount received by the creditor or owner on realisation of the security shall, so far as it is referable to the agreement, be repaid to the surety.

107 Duty to give information to surety under fixed-sum credit agreement

(1) The creditor under a regulated agreement for fixed-sum credit in relation to which security is provided, within the prescribed period after receiving a request in writing to that effect from the surety and payment of a fee of [£1], shall give to the surety (if a different person from the debtor)—

(a) a copy of the executed agreement (if any) and of any other document referred to in it;

(b) a copy of the security instrument (if any); and

(c) a statement signed by or on behalf of the creditor showing, according to the information to which it is practicable for him to refer,—

(i) the total sum paid under the agreement by the debtor,

(ii) the total sum which has become payable under the agreement by the debtor but remains unpaid, and the various amounts comprised in that total sum, with the date when each became due, and

(iii) the total sum which is to become payable under the agreement by the debtor, and the various amounts comprised in that total sum, with the date, or mode of determining the date, when each becomes due.

(2) If the creditor possesses insufficient information to enable him to ascertain the amounts and dates mentioned in subsection (1)(c)(iii), he shall be taken to comply with that sub-paragraph if his statement under subsection (1)(c) gives the basis on which, under the regulated agreement, they would fall to be ascertained.

(3) Subsection (1) does not apply to—

(a) an agreement under which no sum is, or will or may become, payable by the debtor, or

(b) a request made less than one month after a previous request under that subsection relating to the same agreement was complied with.

(4) If the creditor under an agreement fails to comply with subsection (1)—

(a) he is not entitled, while the default continues, to enforce the security, so far as provided in relation to the agreement [. . .]

(5) This section does not apply to a non-commercial agreement.

108 Duty to give information to surety under running-account credit agreement

(1) The creditor under a regulated agreement for running-account credit in relation to which security is provided, within the prescribed period after receiving a request in writing to that effect from the surety and payment of a fee of [£1], shall give to the surety (if a different person from the debtor)—

(a) a copy of the executed agreement (if any) and of any other document referred to in it;

(b) a copy of the security instrument (if any); and

(c) a statement signed by or on behalf of the creditor showing, according to the information to which it is practicable for him to refer,—

(i) the state of the account, and

(ii) the amount if any, currently payable under the agreement by the debtor to the creditor, and

(iii) the amounts and due dates of any payments which, if the debtor does not draw further on the account, will later become payable under the agreement by the debtor to the creditor.

(2) If the creditor possesses insufficient information to enable him to ascertain the amounts and dates mentioned in subsection (1)(c)(iii), he shall be taken to comply with that sub-paragraph if his statement under subsection (1)(c) gives the basis on which, under the regulated agreement, they would fall to be ascertained.

(3) Subsection (1) does not apply to—

(a) an agreement under which no sum is, or will or may become, payable by the debtor, or

(b) a request made less than one month after a previous request under that subsection relating to the same agreement was complied with.

(4) If the creditor under an agreement fails to comply with subsection (1)—

(a) he is not entitled, while the default continues, to enforce the security, so far as provided in relation to the agreement [. . .]

(5) This section does not apply to a non-commercial agreement.

109 Duty to give information to surety under consumer hire agreement

(1) The owner under a regulated consumer hire agreement in relation to which security is provided, within the prescribed period after receiving a request in writing to that effect from the surety and payment of a fee of [£1], shall give to the surety (if a different person from the hirer)—

(a) a copy of the executed agreement and of any other document referred to in it;

(b) a copy of the security instrument (if any); and

(c) a statement signed by or on behalf of the owner showing, according to the information to which it is practicable for him to refer, the total sum which has become payable under the agreement by the hirer but remains unpaid and the various amounts comprised in that total sum, with the date when each became due.

(2) Subsection (1) does not apply to—

(a) an agreement under which no sum is, or will or may become, payable by the hirer, or

(b) a request made less than one month after a previous request under that subsection relating to the same agreement was complied with.

(3) If the owner under an agreement fails to comply with subsection (1)—

(a) he is not entitled, while the default continues, to enforce the security, so far as provided in relation to the agreement [. . .]

(4) This section does not apply to a non-commercial agreement.

110 Duty to give information to debtor or hirer

(1) The creditor or owner under a regulated agreement, within the prescribed period after receiving a request in writing to that effect from the debtor or hirer and payment of a fee of [£1], shall give the debtor or hirer a copy of any security instrument executed in relation to the agreement after the making of the agreement.

(2) Subsection (1) does not apply to—

(a) a non-commercial agreement, or

(b) an agreement under which no sum is, or will or may become, payable by the debtor or hirer, or

(c) a request made less than one month after a previous request under subsection (1) relating to the same agreement was complied with.

(3) If the creditor or owner under an agreement fails to comply with subsection (1)—

(a) he is not entitled, while the default continues, to enforce the security (so far as provided in relation to the agreement) [. . .]

111 Duty to give surety copy of default etc notice

(1) When a default notice or a notice under section 76(1) or 98(1) is served on a debtor or hirer, a copy of the notice shall be served by the creditor or owner on any surety (if a different person from the debtor or hirer).

(2) If the creditor or owner fails to comply with subsection (1) in the case of any surety, the security is enforceable against the surety (in respect of the breach or other matter to which the notice relates) on an order of the court only.

[. . .]

113 Act not to be evaded by use of security

(1) Where a security is provided in relation to an actual or prospective regulated agreement, the security shall not be enforced so as to benefit the creditor or owner, directly or indirectly, to an extent greater (whether as respects the amount of any payment or the time or manner of its being made) than would be the case if the security were not provided and any obligations of the debtor or hirer, or his relative, under or in relation to the agreement were carried out to the extent (if any) to which they would be enforced under this Act.

(2) In accordance with subsection (1), where a regulated agreement is enforceable on an order of the court or the [FCA] only, any security provided in relation to the agreement is enforceable (so far as provided in relation to the agreement) where such an order has been made in relation to the agreement, but not otherwise.

(3) Where—

(a) a regulated agreement is cancelled under section 69(1) or becomes subject to section 69(2), or

(b) a regulated agreement is terminated under section 91, or

(c) in relation to any agreement an application for an order under section [65(1) or 124(1) or a notice under section 28A of the Financial Services and Markets Act 2000] is dismissed (except on technical grounds only), or

(d) a declaration is made by the court under section 142(1) (refusal of enforcement order) as respects any regulated agreement,

section 106 shall apply to any security provided in relation to the agreement.

(4) Where subsection (3)(d) applies and the declaration relates to a part only of the regulated agreement, section 106 shall apply to the security only so far as it concerns that part.

(5) In the case of a cancelled agreement, the duty imposed on the debtor or hirer by section 71 or 72 shall not be enforceable before the creditor or owner has discharged any duty imposed on him by section 106 (as applied by subsection (3)(a)).

(6) If the security is provided in relation to a prospective agreement or transaction, the security shall be enforceable in relation to the agreement or transaction only after the time (if any) when the agreement is made; and until that time the person providing the security shall be entitled, by notice to the creditor or owner, to require that section 106 shall thereupon apply to the security.

(7) Where an indemnity [or guarantee] is given in a case where the debtor or hirer is a minor, or [an indemnity is given in a case where he] is otherwise not of full capacity, the reference in subsection (1) to the extent to which his obligations would be enforced shall be read in relation to the indemnity [or guarantee] as a reference to the extent to which [those obligations] would be enforced if he were of full capacity.

(8) Subsections (1) and (3) also apply where a security is provided in relation to an actual or prospective linked transaction, and in that case—

(a) references to the agreement shall be read as references to the linked transaction, and

(b) references to the creditor or owner shall be read as references to any person (other than the debtor or hirer, or his relative) who is a party, or prospective party, to the linked transaction.

Pledges

114 Pawn-receipts

(1) At the time he receives the article, a person who takes any article in pawn under a regulated agreement shall give to the person from whom he receives it a receipt in the prescribed form (a 'pawn-receipt').

(2) A person who takes any article in pawn from an individual whom he knows to be, or who appears to be and is, a minor commits an offence.

(3) This section and sections [117] to 122 do not apply to—

(a) a pledge of documents of title [or of bearer bonds], or

(b) a non-commercial agreement.

[. . .]

116 Redemption period

(1) A pawn is redeemable at any time within six months after it was taken.

(2) Subject to subsection (1), the period within which a pawn is redeemable shall be the same as the period fixed by the parties for the duration of the credit secured by the pledge, or such longer period as they may agree.

(3) If the pawn is not redeemed by the end of the period laid down by subsections (1) and (2) (the 'redemption period'), it nevertheless remains redeemable until it is realised by the pawnee under section 121 except where under section 120(1)(a) the property in it passes to the pawnee.

(4) No special charge shall be made for redemption of a pawn after the end of the redemption period, and charges in respect of the safe keeping of the pawn shall not be at a higher rate after the end of the redemption period than before.

117 Redemption procedure

(1) On surrender of the pawn-receipt, and payment of the amount owing, at any time when the pawn is redeemable, the pawnee shall deliver the pawn to the bearer of the pawn-receipt.

(2) Subsection (1) does not apply if the pawnee knows or has reasonable cause to suspect that the bearer of the pawn-receipt is neither the owner of the pawn nor authorised by the owner to redeem it.

(3) The pawnee is not liable to any person in tort or delict for delivering the pawn where subsection (1) applies, or refusing to deliver it where the person demanding delivery does not comply with subsection (1) or, by reason of subsection (2), subsection (1) does not apply.

118 Loss etc of pawn-receipt

(1) A person (the 'claimant') who is not in possession of the pawn-receipt but claims to be the owner of the pawn, or to be otherwise entitled or authorised to redeem it, may do so at any time when it is redeemable by tendering to the pawnee in place of the pawn-receipt—

(a) a statutory declaration made by the claimant in the prescribed form, and with the prescribed contents, or

(b) where the pawn is security for fixed-sum credit not exceeding [£75] or running-account credit on which the credit limit does not exceed [£75], and the pawnee agrees, a statement in writing in the prescribed form, and with the prescribed contents, signed by the claimant.

(2) On compliance by the claimant with subsection (1), section 117 shall apply as if the declaration or statement were the pawn-receipt, and the pawn-receipt itself shall become inoperative for the purposes of section 117.

119 Unreasonable refusal to deliver pawn

(1) If a person who has taken a pawn under a regulated agreement refuses without reasonable cause to allow the pawn to be redeemed, he commits an offence.

(2) On the conviction in England and Wales of a pawnee under subsection (1) where the offence does not amount to theft, [Chapter 3 of Part 7 of the Sentencing Code (restitution orders)] shall apply as if the pawnee had been convicted of stealing the pawn.

(3) On the conviction in Northern Ireland of a pawnee under subsection (1) where the offence does not amount to theft, section 27 (orders for restitution) of the Theft Act (Northern Ireland) 1969, and any provision of the Theft Act (Northern Ireland) 1969 relating to that section, shall apply as if the pawnee had been convicted of stealing the pawn.

120 Consequence of failure to redeem

(1) If at the end of the redemption period the pawn has not been redeemed—

(a) notwithstanding anything in section 113, the property in the pawn passes to the pawnee where—

[(i) the redemption period is six months,

(ii) the pawn is security for fixed-sum credit not exceeding £75 or runningaccount credit on which the credit limit does not exceed £75, and

(iii) the pawn was not immediately before the making of the regulated consumer credit agreement a pawn under another regulated consumer credit agreement in respect of which the debtor has discharged his indebtedness in part under section 94(3); or]

(b) in any other case the pawn becomes realisable by the pawnee.

(2) Where the debtor or hirer is entitled to apply to the court for a time order under section 129, subsection (1) shall apply with the substitution, for 'at the end of the redemption period' of 'after the expiry of five days following the end of the redemption period'.

121 Realisation of pawn

(1) When a pawn has become realisable by him, the pawnee may sell it, after giving to the pawnor (except in such cases as may be prescribed) not less than the

prescribed period of notice of the intention to sell, indicating in the notice the asking price and such other particulars as may be prescribed.

(2) Within the prescribed period after the sale takes place, the pawnee shall give the pawnor the prescribed information in writing as to the sale, its proceeds and expenses.

(3) Where the net proceeds of sale are not less than the sum which, if the pawn had been redeemed on the date of the sale, would have been payable for its redemption, the debt secured by the pawn is discharged and any surplus shall be paid by the pawnee to the pawnor.

(4) Where subsection (3) does not apply, the debt shall be treated as from the date of sale as equal to the amount by which the net proceeds of sale fall short of the sum which would have been payable for the redemption of the pawn on that date.

(5) In this section the 'net proceeds of sale' is the amount realised (the 'gross amount') less the expenses (if any) of the sale.

(6) If the pawnor alleges that the gross amount is less than the true market value of the pawn on the date of sale, it is for the pawnee to prove that he and any agents employed by him in the sale used reasonable care to ensure that the true market value was obtained, and if he fails to do so subsections (3) and (4) shall have effect as if the reference in subsection (5) to the gross amount were a reference to the true market value.

(7) If the pawnor alleges that the expenses of the sale were unreasonably high, it is for the pawnee to prove that they were reasonable, and if he fails to do so subsections (3) and (4) shall have effect as if the reference in subsection (5) to expenses were a reference to reasonable expenses.

122 Order in Scotland to deliver pawn

(1) As respects Scotland where—

(a) a pawn is either—

(i) an article which has been stolen, or

(ii) an article which has been obtained by fraud, and a person is convicted of any offence in relation to the theft or, as the case may be, the fraud; or

(b) a person is convicted of an offence under section 119(1), the court by which that person is so convicted may order delivery of the pawn to the owner or the person otherwise entitled thereto.

(2) A court making an order under subsection (1)(a) for delivery of a pawn may make the order subject to such conditions as to payment of the debt secured by the pawn as it thinks fit.

Negotiable instruments

123 Restrictions on taking and negotiating instruments

(1) A creditor or owner shall not take a negotiable instrument, other than a bank note or cheque, in discharge of any sum payable—

(a) by the debtor or hirer under a regulated agreement, or

(b) by any person as surety in relation to the agreement.

(2) The creditor or owner shall not negotiate a cheque taken by him in discharge of a sum payable as mentioned in subsection (1) except to a banker (within the meaning of the Bills of Exchange Act 1882).

(3) The creditor or owner shall not take a negotiable instrument as security for the discharge of any sum payable as mentioned in subsection (1).

(4) A person takes a negotiable instrument as security for the discharge of a sum if the sum is intended to be paid in some other way, and the negotiable instrument is to be presented for payment only if the sum is not paid in that way.

(5) This section does not apply where the regulated agreement is a noncommercial agreement.

(6) The [Treasury] may by order provide that this section shall not apply

where the regulated agreement has a connection with a country outside the United Kingdom.

124 Consequences of breach of s 123

(1) After any contravention of section 123 has occurred in relation to a sum payable as mentioned in section 123(1)(a), the agreement under which the sum is payable is enforceable against the debtor or hirer on an order of the court only.

(2) After any contravention of section 123 has occurred in relation to a sum payable by any surety, the security is enforceable on an order of the court only.

(3) Where an application for an order under subsection (2) is dismissed (except on technical grounds only) section 106 shall apply to the security.

125 Holders in due course

(1) A person who takes a negotiable instrument in contravention of section 123(1) or (3) is not a holder in due course, and is not entitled to enforce the instrument.

(2) Where a person negotiates a cheque in contravention of section 123(2), his doing so constitutes a defect in his title within the meaning of the Bills of Exchange Act 1882.

(3) If a person mentioned in section 123(1)(a) and (b) ('the protected person') becomes liable to a holder in due course of an instrument taken from the protected person in contravention of section 123(1) or (3), or taken from the protected person and negotiated in contravention of section 123(2), the creditor or owner shall indemnify the protected person in respect of that liability.

(4) Nothing in this Act affects the rights of the holder in due course of any negotiable instrument.

Land mortgages

126 Enforcement of land mortgages

[(1)] A land mortgage securing a regulated agreement [or a regulated mortgage contract (within the meaning of the Regulated Activities Order)] is enforceable (so far as provided in relation to the agreement) on an order of the court only.

[(2) Subject to section 140A(5) (unfair relationships between creditors and debtors), for the purposes of subsection (1) and Part 9 (judicial control), a regulated mortgage contract which would, but for article 60C(2) of the Financial Services and Markets Act 2000 (Regulated Activities) Order 2001, be a regulated agreement is to be treated as if it were a regulated agreement.]

PART IX
JUDICIAL CONTROL

Enforcement of certain regulated agreements and securities

127 Enforcement orders in cases of infringement

(1) In the case of an application for an enforcement order under—

[(za) section 55(2) (disclosure of information), or]

[(zb) section 61B(3) (duty to supply copy of overdraft agreement), or]

(a) section 65(1) (improperly executed agreements), or

(b) section 105(7)(a) or (b) (improperly executed security instruments), or

(c) section 111(2) (failure to serve copy of notice on surety), or

(d) section 124(1) or (2) (taking of negotiable instrument in contravention of section 123),

the court shall dismiss the application if, but [. . .] only if, it considers it just to do so having regard to—

(i) prejudice caused to any person by the contravention in question, and the degree of culpability for it; and

(ii) the powers conferred on the court by subsection (2) and sections 135 and 136.

(2) If it appears to the court just to do so, it may in an enforcement order reduce or discharge any sum payable by the debtor or hirer, or any surety, so as to compensate him for prejudice suffered as a result of the contravention in question.

[. . .]

128 Enforcement orders on death of debtor or hirer

The court shall make an order under section 86(2) if, but only if, the creditor or owner proves that he has been unable to satisfy himself that the present and future obligations of the debtor or hirer under the agreement are likely to be discharged.

Extension of time

129 Time orders

(1) [Subject to subsection (3) below,] if it appears to the court just to do so—

(a) on an application for an enforcement order; or

(b) on an application made by a debtor or hirer under this paragraph after service on him of—

(i) a default notice, or

(ii) a notice under section 76(1) or 98(1); or

[(bza) on an application made by a debtor under this paragraph after the creditor has informed the debtor of the creditor's intention—

(i) to enforce a term of a regulated deferred payment credit agreement by—

(aa) demanding earlier payment of any sum,

(bb) treating any right conferred on the debtor by the agreement as terminated, restricted or deferred, or

(ii) to terminate a regulated deferred payment credit agreement, or]

[(ba) on an application made by a debtor or hirer under this paragraph after he has been given a notice under section 86B or 86C; or]

(c) in an action brought by a creditor or owner to enforce a regulated agreement or any security, or recover possession of any goods or land to which a regulated agreement relates,

the court may make an order under this section (a 'time order').

(2) A time order shall provide for one or both of the following, as the court considers just—

(a) the payment by the debtor or hirer or any surety of any sum owed under a regulated agreement or a security by such instalments, payable at such times, as the court having regard to the means of the debtor or hirer and any surety, considers reasonable;

(b) the remedying by the debtor or hirer of any breach of a regulated agreement (other than non-payment of money) within such period as the court may specify.

[(3) Where in Scotland a time to pay direction or a time order has been made in relation to a debt, it shall not thereafter be competent to make a time order in relation to the same debt.]

[129A Debtor or hirer to give notice of intent etc to creditor or owner

(1) A debtor or hirer may make an application under section 129(1)(ba) in relation to a regulated agreement only if—

(a) following his being given the notice under section 86B or 86C, he gave a notice within subsection (2) to the creditor or owner; and

(b) a period of at least 14 days has elapsed after the day on which he gave that notice to the creditor or owner.

(2) A notice is within this subsection if it—

(a) indicates that the debtor or hirer intends to make the application;

(b) indicates that he wants to make a proposal to the creditor or owner in relation to his making of payments under the agreement; and

(c) gives details of that proposal.]

130 Supplemental provisions about time orders

(1) Where in accordance with rules of court an offer to pay any sum by instalments is made by the debtor or hirer and accepted by the creditor or owner, the court may in accordance with rules of court make a time order under section 129(2)(a) giving effect to the offer without hearing evidence of means.

(2) In the case of a hire-purchase or conditional sale agreement only, a time order under section 129(2)(a) may deal with sums which, although not payable by the debtor at the time the order is made, would if the agreement continued in force become payable under it subsequently.

(3) A time order under section 129(2)(a) shall not be made where the regulated agreement is secured by a pledge if, by virtue of regulations made under section 76(5), 87(4) or 98(5), service of a notice is not necessary for enforcement of the pledge.

(4) Where, following the making of a time order in relation to a regulated hire-purchase or conditional sale agreement or a regulated consumer hire agreement, the debtor or hirer is in possession of the goods, he shall be treated (except in the case of a debtor to whom the creditor's title has passed) as a bailee or (in Scotland) a custodier of the goods under the terms of the agreement, notwithstanding that the agreement has been terminated.

(5) Without prejudice to anything done by the creditor or owner before the commencement of the period specified in a time order made under section 129(2)(b) ('the relevant period'),—

(a) he shall not while the relevant period subsists take in relation to the agreement any action such as is mentioned in section 87(1);

(b) where—

(i) a provision of the agreement ('the secondary provision') becomes operative only on breach of another provision of the agreement ('the primary provision'), and

(ii) the time order provides for the remedying of such a breach of the primary provision within the relevant period,

he shall not treat the secondary provision as operative before the end of that period;

(c) if while the relevant period subsists the breach to which the order relates is remedied it shall be treated as not having occurred.

(6) On the application of any person affected by a time order, the court may vary or revoke the order.

[Interest

[130A Interest payable on judgment debts etc

(1) If the creditor or owner under a regulated agreement wants to be able to recover from the debtor or hirer post-judgment interest in connection with a sum that is required to be paid under a judgment given in relation to the agreement (the 'judgment sum'), he—

(a) after the giving of that judgment, shall give the debtor or hirer a notice under this section (the 'first required notice'); and

(b) after the giving of the first required notice, shall give the debtor or hirer further notices under this section at intervals of not more than six months.

(2) The debtor or hirer shall have no liability to pay post-judgment interest in connection with the judgment sum to the extent that the interest is calculated by reference to a period occurring before the day on which he is given the first required notice.

(3) If the creditor or owner fails to give the debtor or hirer a notice under this section within the period of six months beginning with the day after the day on which such a notice was last given to the debtor or hirer, the debtor or hirer shall have no liability to pay post-judgment interest in connection with the judgment sum to the extent that the interest is calculated by reference to the whole or to a part of the period which—

(a) begins immediately after the end of that period of six months; and

(b) ends at the end of the day on which the notice is given to the debtor or hirer.

(4) The debtor or hirer shall have no liability to pay any sum in connection with the preparation or the giving to him of a notice under this section.

(5) A notice under this section may be incorporated in a statement or other notice which the creditor or owner gives the debtor or hirer in relation to the agreement by virtue of another provision of this Act.

(6) Regulations may make provision about the form and content of notices under this section.

(7) This section does not apply in relation to post-judgment interest which is required to be paid by virtue of any of the following—

(a) section 4 of the Administration of Justice (Scotland) Act 1972;

(b) Article 127 of the Judgments Enforcement (Northern Ireland) Order 1981;

(c) section 74 of the County Courts Act 1984.

(8) This section does not apply in relation to a non-commercial agreement or to a small agreement.

(9) In this section 'post-judgment interest' means interest to the extent calculated by reference to a period occurring after the giving of the judgment under which the judgment sum is required to be paid.]]

Protection of property pending proceedings

131 Protection orders

The court, on application of the creditor or owner under a regulated agreement, may make such orders as it thinks just for protecting any property of the creditor or owner, or property subject to any security, from damage or depreciation pending the determination of any proceedings under this Act, including orders restricting or prohibiting use of the property or giving directions as to its custody.

Hire and hire-purchase etc agreements

132 Financial relief for hirer

(1) Where the owner under a regulated consumer hire agreement recovers possession of goods to which the agreement relates otherwise than by action, the hirer may apply to the court for an order that—

(a) the whole or part of any sum paid by the hirer to the owner in respect of the goods shall be repaid, and

(b) the obligation to pay the whole or part of any sum owed by the hirer to the owner in respect of the goods shall cease,

and if it appears to the court just to do so, having regard to the extent of the enjoyment of the goods by the hirer, the court shall grant the application in full or in part.

(2) Where in proceedings relating to a regulated consumer hire agreement the court makes an order for the delivery to the owner of goods to which the agreement relates the court may include in the order the like provision as may be made in an order under subsection (1).

133 Hire-purchase etc agreements: special powers of court

(1) If, in relation to a regulated hire-purchase or conditional sale agreement, it appears to the court just to do so—

(a) on an application for an enforcement order or time order; or

(b) in an action brought by the creditor to recover possession of goods to which the agreement relates,

the court may—

(i) make an order (a 'return order') for the return to the creditor of goods to which the agreement relates;

(ii) make an order (a 'transfer order') for the transfer to the debtor of the creditor's title to certain goods to which the agreement relates ('the transferred goods'), and the return to the creditor of the remainder of the goods.

(2) In determining for the purposes of this section how much of the total price has been paid ('the paid-up sum'), the court may—

(a) treat any sum paid by the debtor, or owed by the creditor, in relation to the goods as part of the paid-up sum;

(b) deduct any sum owed by the debtor in relation to the goods (otherwise than as part of the total price) from the paid-up sum,

and make corresponding reductions in amounts so owed.

(3) Where a transfer order is made, the transferred goods shall be such of the goods to which the agreement relates as the court thinks just; but a transfer order shall be made only where the paid-up sum exceeds the part of the total price referable to the transferred goods by an amount equal to at least one-third of the unpaid balance of the total price.

(4) Notwithstanding the making of a return order or transfer order, the debtor may at any time before the goods enter the possession of the creditor, on payment of the balance of the total price and the fulfilment of any other necessary conditions, claim the goods ordered to be returned to the creditor.

(5) When, in pursuance of a time order or under this section, the total price of goods under a regulated hire-purchase agreement or regulated conditional sale agreement is paid and any other necessary conditions are fulfilled, the creditor's title to the goods vests in the debtor.

(6) If, in contravention of a return order or transfer order, any goods to which the order relates are not returned to the creditor, the court, on the application of the creditor, may—

(a) revoke so much of the order as relates to those goods, and

(b) order the debtor to pay the creditor the unpaid portion of so much of the total price as is referable to those goods.

(7) For the purposes of this section, the part of the total price referable to any goods is the part assigned to those goods by the agreement or (if no such assignment is made) the part determined by the court to be reasonable.

134 Evidence of adverse detention in hire-purchase etc cases

(1) Where goods are comprised in a regulated hire-purchase agreement, regulated conditional sale agreement or regulated consumer hire agreement, and the creditor or owner—

(a) brings an action or makes an application to enforce a right to recover possession of the goods from the debtor or hirer, and

(b) proves that a demand for the delivery of the goods was included in the default notice under section 88(5), or that, after the right to recover possession of the goods accrued but before the action was begun or the application was made, he made a request in writing to the debtor or hirer to surrender the goods,

then, for the purposes of the claim of the creditor or owner to recover possession of the goods, the possession of them by the debtor or hirer shall be deemed to be adverse to the creditor or owner.

(2) In subsection (1) 'the debtor or hirer' includes a person in possession of the goods at any time between the debtor's or hirer's death and the grant of probate or administration, or (in Scotland) confirmation.

(3) Nothing in this section affects a claim for damages for conversion or (in Scotland) for delict.

Supplemental provisions as to orders

135 Power to impose conditions, or suspend operation of order

(1) If it considers it just to do so, the court may in an order made by it in relation to a regulated agreement include provisions—

(a) making the operation of any term of the order conditional on the doing of specified acts by any party to the proceedings;

(b) suspending the operation of any term of the order either—

(i) until such time as the court subsequently directs, or

(ii) until the occurrence of a specified act or omission.

(2) The court shall not suspend the operation of a term requiring the delivery up of goods by any person unless satisfied that the goods are in his possession or control.

(3) In the case of a consumer hire agreement, the court shall not so use its powers under subsection (1)(b) as to extend the period for which, under the terms of the agreement, the hirer is entitled to possession of the goods to which the agreement relates.

(4) On the application of any person affected by a provision included under subsection (1), the court may vary the provision.

136 Power to vary agreements and securities

(1) The court may in an order made by it under this Act include such provision as it considers just for amending any agreement or security in consequence of a term of the order.

[. . .]

[Unfair relationships

[140A Unfair relationships between creditors and debtors

(1) The court may make an order under section 140B in connection with a credit agreement if it determines that the relationship between the creditor and the debtor arising out of the agreement (or the agreement taken with any related agreement) is unfair to the debtor because of one or more of the following—

(a) any of the terms of the agreement or of any related agreement;

(b) the way in which the creditor has exercised or enforced any of his rights under the agreement or any related agreement;

(c) any other thing done (or not done) by, or on behalf of, the creditor (either before or after the making of the agreement or any related agreement).

(2) In deciding whether to make a determination under this section the court shall have regard to all matters it thinks relevant (including matters relating to the creditor and matters relating to the debtor).

(3) For the purposes of this section the court shall (except to the extent that it is not appropriate to do so) treat anything done (or not done) by, or on behalf of, or in relation to, an associate or a former associate of the creditor as if done (or not done) by, or on behalf of, or in relation to, the creditor.

(4) A determination may be made under this section in relation to a relationship notwithstanding that the relationship may have ended.

(5) An order under section 140B shall not be made in connection with a credit agreement which is an exempt agreement [for the purposes of Chapter 14A of Part 2 of the Regulated Activities Order by virtue of article 60C(2) of that Order (regulated mortgage contracts and regulated home purchase plans)].]

[(6) An order under section 140B shall not be made in connection with a credit agreement entered into under the Bounce Back Loan Scheme.

(7) In subsection (6) 'the Bounce Back Loan Scheme' means the scheme of that name operated from 4 May 2020 by the British Business Bank plc on behalf of the Secretary of State.]

[140B Powers of court in relation to unfair relationships

(1) An order under this section in connection with a credit agreement may do one or more of the following—

(a) require the creditor, or any associate or former associate of his, to repay (in whole or in part) any sum paid by the debtor or by a surety by virtue of the agreement or any related agreement (whether paid to the creditor, the associate or the former associate or to any other person);

(b) require the creditor, or any associate or former associate of his, to do or not to do (or to cease doing) anything specified in the order in connection with the agreement or any related agreement;

(c) reduce or discharge any sum payable by the debtor or by a surety by virtue of the agreement or any related agreement;

(d) direct the return to a surety of any property provided by him for the purposes of a security;

(e) otherwise set aside (in whole or in part) any duty imposed on the debtor or on a surety by virtue of the agreement or any related agreement;

(f) alter the terms of the agreement or of any related agreement;

(g) direct accounts to be taken, or (in Scotland) an accounting to be made, between any persons.

(2) An order under this section may be made in connection with a credit agreement only—

(a) on an application made by the debtor or by a surety;

(b) at the instance of the debtor or a surety in any proceedings in any court to which the debtor and the creditor are parties, being proceedings to enforce the agreement or any related agreement; or

(c) at the instance of the debtor or a surety in any other proceedings in any court where the amount paid or payable under the agreement or any related agreement is relevant.

(3) An order under this section may be made notwithstanding that its effect is to place on the creditor, or any associate or former associate of his, a burden in respect of an advantage enjoyed by another person.

(4) An application under subsection (2)(a) may only be made—

(a) in England and Wales, to the county court;

(b) in Scotland, to the sheriff court;

(c) in Northern Ireland, to the High Court (subject to subsection (6)).

(5) In Scotland such an application may be made in the sheriff court for the district in which the debtor or surety resides or carries on business.

(6) In Northern Ireland such an application may be made to the county court if the credit agreement is an agreement under which the creditor provides the debtor with—

(a) fixed-sum credit not exceeding £15,000; or

(b) running-account credit on which the credit limit does not exceed £15,000.

(7) Without prejudice to any provision which may be made by rules of court made in relation to county courts in Northern Ireland, such rules may provide that an application made by virtue of subsection (6) may be made in the county court for the division in which the debtor or surety resides or carries on business.

(8) A party to any proceedings mentioned in subsection (2) shall be entitled, in accordance with rules of court, to have any person who might be the subject of an order under this section made a party to the proceedings.

(9) If, in any such proceedings, the debtor or a surety alleges that the relationship between the creditor and the debtor is unfair to the debtor, it is for the creditor to prove to the contrary.]

[140C Interpretation of ss 140A and 140B

(1) In this section and in sections 140A and 140B 'credit agreement' means any agreement between an individual (the 'debtor') and any other person (the 'creditor') by which the creditor provides the debtor with credit of any amount.

(2) References in this section and in sections 140A and 140B to the creditor or to the debtor under a credit agreement include—

(a) references to the person to whom his rights and duties under the agreement have passed by assignment or operation of law;

(b) where two or more persons are the creditor or the debtor, references to any one or more of those persons.

(3) The definition of 'court' in section 189(1) does not apply for the purposes of sections 140A and 140B.

(4) References in sections 140A and 140B to an agreement related to a credit agreement (the 'main agreement') are references to—

(a) a credit agreement consolidated by the main agreement;

(b) a linked transaction in relation to the main agreement or to a credit agreement within paragraph (a);

(c) a security provided in relation to the main agreement, to a credit agreement within paragraph (a) or to a linked transaction within paragraph (b).

(5) In the case of a credit agreement which is not a regulated consumer credit agreement, for the purposes of subsection (4) a transaction shall be treated as being a linked transaction in relation to that agreement if it would have been such a transaction had that agreement been a regulated consumer credit agreement.

(6) For the purposes of this section and section 140B the definitions of 'security' and 'surety' in section 189(1) apply (with any appropriate changes) in relation to—

(a) a credit agreement which is not a consumer credit agreement as if it were a consumer credit agreement; and

(b) a transaction which is a linked transaction by virtue of subsection (5).

(7) For the purposes of this section a credit agreement (the 'earlier agreement') is consolidated by another credit agreement (the 'later agreement') if—

(a) the later agreement is entered into by the debtor (in whole or in part) for purposes connected with debts owed by virtue of the earlier agreement; and

(b) at any time prior to the later agreement being entered into the parties to the earlier agreement included—

(i) the debtor under the later agreement; and

(ii) the creditor under the later agreement or an associate or a former associate of his.

(8) Further, if the later agreement is itself consolidated by another credit agreement (whether by virtue of this subsection or subsection (7)), then the earlier agreement is consolidated by that other agreement as well.]

[. . .]

Miscellaneous

141 Jurisdiction and parties

(1) In England and Wales the county court shall have jurisdiction to hear and determine—

(a) any action by the creditor or owner to enforce a regulated agreement or any security relating to it;

(b) any action to enforce any linked transaction against the debtor or hirer or his relative,

and such an action shall not be brought in any other court.

(2) Where an action or application is brought in the High Court which, by virtue of this Act, ought to have been brought in the county court it shall not be treated as improperly brought, but shall be transferred to the county court.

[(3) In Scotland the sheriff court shall have jurisdiction to hear and determine any action referred to in subsection (1) and such an action shall not be brought in any other court.

(3A) Subject to subsection (3B) an action which is brought in the sheriff court by virtue of subsection (3) shall be brought only in one of the following courts, namely—

(a) the court for the place where the debtor or hirer is domiciled (within the meaning of section 41 or 42 of the Civil Jurisdiction and Judgments Act 1982);

(b) the court for the place where the debtor or hirer carries on business; and

(c) where the purpose of the action is to assert, declare or determine proprietary or possessory rights, or rights of security, in or over moveable property, or to obtain authority to dispose of moveable property, the court for the place where the property is situated.

(3B) Subsection (3A) shall not apply—

(a) where rule 3 of Schedule 8 to the said Act of 1982 applies; or

(b) where the jurisdiction of another court has been prorogated by an agreement entered into after the dispute has arisen.]

(4) In Northern Ireland the county court shall have jurisdiction to hear and determine any action or application falling within subsection (1).

(5) Except as may be provided by rules of court, all the parties to a regulated agreement, and any surety, shall be made parties to any proceedings relating to the agreement.

142 Power to declare rights of parties

(1) Where under any provision of this Act a thing can be done by a creditor or owner on an enforcement order only, and either—

(a) the court dismisses (except on technical grounds only) an application for an enforcement order, or

(b) where no such application has been made or such an application has been dismissed on technical grounds only an interested party applies to the court for a declaration under this subsection,

the court may if it thinks just make a declaration that the creditor or owner is not entitled to do that thing, and thereafter no application for an enforcement order in respect of it shall be entertained.

(2) Where—

(a) a regulated agreement or linked transaction is cancelled under section 69(1), or becomes subject to section 69(2), or

(b) a regulated agreement is terminated under section 91, and an interested party applies to the court for a declaration under this subsection, the court may make a declaration to that effect.

143, 144 [*Apply to Northern Ireland*]

PART X
ANCILLARY CREDIT BUSINESSES

Definitions

145 Types of ancillary credit business

(1) An ancillary credit business is any business so far as it comprises or relates to—

(a) credit brokerage,

(b) debt-adjusting,

(c) debt-counselling,

(d) debt-collecting,

[(da) debt administration;

(db) the provision of credit information services, or]

(e) the operation of a credit reference agency.

[(2) 'Credit brokerage' means the carrying on of an activity of the kind specified by article 36A(1)(a) to (c) of the Regulated Activities Order (credit broking), disregarding the effect of paragraph (2) of that article.]

[. . .]

[(5) 'Debt adjusting' means the carrying on of an activity of the kind specified by article 39D of that Order (debt adjusting).

(6) 'Debt-counselling' means the carrying on of an activity of the kind specified by article 39E of that Order (debt-counselling).

(7) 'Debt-collecting' means the carrying on of an activity of the kind specified by article 39F of that Order (debt-collecting).

(7A) 'Debt administration' means the carrying on of an activity of the kind specified by article 39G of that Order (debt administration), disregarding the effect of paragraph (3) of that article.

(7B) A person ('P') provides credit information services if P carries on, by way of business, an activity of the kind specified by article 89A(1) or (2) of that Order (providing credit information services).

(8) A person ('P') operates a credit reference agency if P carries on, by way of business, an activity of the kind specified by article 89B of that Order (providing credit references).]

[. . .]

153 Definition of canvassing off trade premises (agreements for ancillary credit services)

(1) An individual (the 'canvasser') canvasses off trade premises the services of a person carrying on an ancillary credit business if he solicits the entry of another individual (the 'consumer') into an agreement for the provision to the consumer of those services by making oral representations to the consumer, or any other individual, during a visit by the canvasser to any place (not excluded by subsection (2)) where the consumer, or that other individual as the case may be, is, being a visit—

(a) carried out for the purpose of making such oral representations to individuals who are at that place, but

(b) not carried out in response to a request made on a previous occasion.

(2) A place is excluded from subsection (1) if it is a place where (whether on a permanent or temporary basis)—

(a) the ancillary credit business is carried on, or

(b) any business is carried on by the canvasser or the person whose employee or agent the canvasser is, or by the consumer.

154 Prohibition of canvassing certain ancillary credit services off trade premises

It is an offence to canvass off trade premises the services of a person carrying on a business of credit-brokerage, debt-adjusting [, debt-counselling or the provision of credit information services].

155 Right to recover brokerage fees

(1) [Subject to subsection (2A)] the excess over [£5] of a fee or commission for his services charged by a credit-broker to an individual to whom this subsection applies shall cease to be payable or, as the case may be, shall be recoverable by the individual if the introduction does not result in his entering into a relevant agreement within the six months following the introduction (disregarding any agreement which is cancelled under section 69(1) or becomes subject to section 69(2)).

(2) Subsection (1) applies to an individual who sought an introduction for a purpose which would have been fulfilled by his entry into—

(a) a regulated agreement, or

(b) in the case of an individual [desiring to obtain credit to finance the acquisition or provision of a dwelling occupied or to be occupied by that individual or a relative of that individual], an agreement for credit secured on land,

[(c) a credit agreement which is an exempt agreement for the purposes of Chapter 14A of Part 2 of the Regulated Activities Order, or

(d) an agreement which is not a regulated credit agreement or a regulated consumer hire agreement but which would be such an agreement if the law applicable to the agreement were the law of a part of the United Kingdom.]

[(2A) But subsection (1) does not apply where—

(a) the fee or commission relates to the effecting of an introduction of a kind mentioned in [article 36E of the Regulated Activities Order (activities in relation to certain agreements relating to land)]; and

(b) the person charging that fee or commission is an authorised person or an appointed representative, within the meaning of the Financial Services and Markets Act 2000.]

(3) An agreement is a relevant agreement for the purposes of subsection (1) in relation to an individual if it is an agreement such as is referred to in subsection (2) in relation to that individual.

(4) In the case of an individual desiring to obtain credit under a consumer credit agreement, any sum payable or paid by him to a credit-broker otherwise than as a fee or commission for the credit-broker's services shall for the purposes of subsection (1) be treated as such a fee or commission if it enters, or would enter, into the total charge for credit.

[. . .]

Credit reference agencies

157 Duty to disclose name etc of agency

[(A1) Where a creditor under a prospective regulated agreement, other than an excluded agreement, decides not to proceed with it on the basis of information obtained by the creditor from a credit reference agency, the creditor must, when informing the debtor of the decision—

(a) inform the debtor that this decision has been reached on the basis of information from a credit reference agency, and

(b) provide the debtor with the particulars of the agency including its name, address and telephone number.]

(1) [In any other case,] a creditor, owner or negotiator, within the prescribed period after receiving a request in writing to that effect from the debtor or hirer, shall give him notice of the name and address of any credit reference agency from which the creditor, owner or negotiator has, during the antecedent negotiations, applied for information about his financial standing.

(2) Subsection (1) does not apply to a request received more than 28 days after the termination of the antecedent negotiations, whether on the making of the regulated agreement or otherwise.

[(2A) A creditor is not required to disclose information under this section if such disclosure—

(a) contravenes [the UK GDPR],

(b) is prohibited by [[an assimilated] obligation],

(c) would create or be likely to create a serious risk that any person would be subject to violence or intimidation, or

(d) would, or would be likely to, prejudice—

(i) the prevention or detection of crime,

(ii) the apprehension or prosecution of offenders, or

(iii) the administration of justice.]

(3) If the creditor, owner or negotiator fails to comply with subsection [(A1) or] (1) he commits an offence.

[(4) For the purposes of subsection (A1) an agreement is an excluded agreement if it is—

(a) a consumer hire agreement, or

(b) an agreement secured on land.]

158 Duty of agency to disclose filed information

(1) A credit reference agency, within the prescribed period after receiving,—

(a) [a request in writing to that effect from a consumer], and

(b) such particulars as the agency may reasonably require to enable them to identify the file, and

(c) a fee of [£2],

shall give the consumer a copy of the file relating to [it] kept by the agency.

(2) When giving a copy of the file under subsection (1), the agency shall also give the consumer a statement in the prescribed form of [the consumer's] rights under section 159.

(3) If the agency does not keep a file relating to [the consumer] it shall give the consumer notice of that fact, but need not return any money paid.

(4) If the agency contravenes any provision of this section it commits an offence.

[(4A) In this section 'consumer' means—

(a) a partnership consisting of two or three persons not all of whom are bodies corporate; or

(b) an unincorporated body of persons which does not consist entirely of bodies corporate and is not a partnership.]

(5) In this Act 'file', in relation to an individual, means all the information about him kept by a credit reference agency, regardless of how the information is stored, and 'copy of the file', as respects information not in plain English, means a transcript reduced into plain English.

159 Correction of wrong information

[(1) Any individual (the 'objector') given—

(a) information under [Article 15(1) to (3) of the [UK GDPR] (confirmation of processing, access to data and safeguards for third country transfers)] by a credit reference agency, or

(b) information under section 158,

who considers that an entry in his file is incorrect, and that if it is not corrected he is likely to be prejudiced, may give notice to the agency requiring it either to remove the entry from the file or amend it.]

(2) Within 28 days after receiving a notice under subsection (1), the agency shall by notice inform the [objector] that it has—

(a) removed the entry from the file, or

(b) amended the entry, or

(c) taken no action,

and if the notice states that the agency has amended the entry it shall include a copy of the file so far as it comprises the amended entry.

(3) Within 28 days after receiving a notice under subsection (2), or where no such notice was given, within 28 days after the expiry of the period mentioned in subsection (2), the [objector] may, unless he has been informed by the agency that it has removed the entry from his file, serve a further notice on the agency requiring it to add to the file an accompanying notice of correction (not exceeding 200 words) drawn up by the [objector], and include a copy of it when furnishing information included in or based on that entry.

(4) Within 28 days after receiving a notice under subsection (3), the agency, unless it intends to apply to the [the relevant authority] under subsection (5), shall by notice inform the [objector] that it has received the notice under subsection (3) and intends to comply with it.

(5) If—

(a) the [objector] has not received a notice under subsection (4) within the time required, or

(b) it appears to the agency that it would be improper for it to publish a notice of correction because it is incorrect, or unjustly defames any person, or is frivolous or scandalous, or is for any other reason unsuitable, the [objector] or, as the case may be, the agency may, in the prescribed manner and on payment of [the prescribed fee], apply to [the relevant authority], who may make such order on the application as he thinks fit.

(6) If a person to whom an order under this section is directed fails to comply with it within the period specified in the order he commits an offence.

[(7) The Information Commissioner may vary or revoke any order made by him under this section.

(8) In this section 'the relevant authority' means—

(a) where the objector is a partnership or other unincorporated body of persons, the [FCA], and

(b) in any other case, the Information Commissioner.]

160 Alternative procedure for business consumers

(1) The [FCA], on an application made by a credit reference agency, may direct that this section shall apply to the agency if [it] is satisfied—

(a) that compliance with section 158 in the case of consumers who carry on a business would adversely affect the service provided to its customers by the agency, and

(b) that, having regard to the methods employed by the agency and to any other relevant factors, it is probable that consumers carrying on a business would not be prejudiced by the making of the direction.

(2) Where an agency to which this section applies receives a request, particulars and a fee under section 158(1) from a consumer who carries on a business and section 158(3) does not apply, the agency, instead of complying with section 158, may elect to deal with the matter under the following subsections.

(3) Instead of giving the consumer a copy of the file, the agency shall within the prescribed period give notice to the consumer that it is proceeding under this section, and by notice give the consumer such information included in or based on entries in the file as the [FCA] may direct, together with a statement in the prescribed form of the consumer's rights under subsections (4) and (5).

(4) If within 28 days after receiving the information given [to the consumer] under subsection (3), or such longer period as the [FCA] may allow, the consumer—

(a) gives notice to the [FCA] that [the consumer] is dissatisfied with the information, and

(b) satisfies the [FCA] that [the consumer] has taken such steps in relation to the agency as may be reasonable with a view to removing the cause of [the consumer's] dissatisfaction, and

(c) pays the [FCA] [the prescribed fee],

the [FCA] may direct the agency to give the [FCA] a copy of the file, and the [FCA] may disclose to the consumer such of the information on the file as the [FCA] thinks fit.

(5) Section 159 applies with any necessary modifications to information given to the consumer under this section as it applies to information given under section 158.

(6) If an agency making an election under subsection (2) fails to comply with subsection (3) or (4) it commits an offence.

[(7) In this section 'consumer' has the same meaning as in section 158.]

[. . .]

PART XI
ENFORCEMENT OF ACT

161 Enforcement authorities

(1) The following authorities ('enforcement authorities') have a duty to enforce this Act and regulations made under it—

[. . .]

(b) in Great Britain, the local weights and measures authority,

(c) in Northern Ireland, the Department of Commerce for Northern Ireland.

[(1A) Subsection (1) does not limit any function of the FCA in relation to the enforcement of this Act or regulations made under it.]

[(1B) For the investigatory powers available to a local weights and measures authority or the Department of Enterprise, Trade and Investment in Northern Ireland for the purposes of the duty in subsection (1), see Schedule 5 to the Consumer Rights Act 2015.]

[. . .]

(3) Every local weights and measures authority shall, whenever the [FCA] requires, report to [it] in such form and with such particulars as [it] requires on the exercise of their functions under this Act.

[. . .]

[. . .]

166 Notification of convictions and judgments to [FCA]

Where a person is convicted of an offence or has a judgment given against him by or before any court in the United Kingdom and it appears to the court—

(a) having regard to the functions of the [FCA under the Financial Services and Markets Act 2000 or] this Act, that the conviction or judgment should be brought to the [FCA's] attention, and

(b) that it may not be brought to [its] attention unless arrangements for that purpose are made by the court,

the court may make such arrangements notwithstanding that the proceedings have been finally disposed of.

167 Penalties

(1) An offence under a provision of this Act specified in column 1 of Schedule 1 is triable in the mode or modes indicated in column 3, and on conviction is punishable as indicated in column 4 (where a period of time indicates the maximum term of imprisonment, and a monetary amount indicates the maximum fine, for the offence in question).

[. . .]

168 Defences

(1) In any proceedings for an offence under this Act it is a defence for the person charged to prove—

(a) that his act or omission was due to a mistake, or to reliance on information supplied to him, or to an act or omission by another person, or to an accident or some other cause beyond his control, and

(b) that he took all reasonable precautions and exercised all due diligence to avoid such an act or omission by himself or any person under his control.

(2) If in any case the defence provided by subsection (1) involves the allegation that the act or omission was due to an act or omission by another person or to reliance on information supplied by another person, the person charged shall not, without leave of the court, be entitled to rely on that defence unless, within a period ending seven clear days before the hearing, he has served on the prosecutor a notice giving such information identifying or assisting in the identification of that other person as was then in his possession.

169 Offences by bodies corporate

Where at any time a body corporate commits an offence under this Act with the consent or connivance of, or because of neglect by, any individual, the individual commits the like offence if at that time—

(a) he is a director, manager, secretary or similar officer of the body corporate, or

(b) he is purporting to act as such an officer, or

(c) the body corporate is managed by its members of whom he is one.

170 No further sanctions for breach of Act

(1) A breach of any requirement made (otherwise than by any court) by or under this Act shall incur no civil or criminal sanction as being such a breach, except to the extent (if any) expressly provided by or under this Act [or by or under the Financial Services and Markets Act 2000 by virtue of an order made under section 107 of the Financial Services Act 2012].

(2) In exercising [its] functions under this Act the [FCA] may take account of any matter appearing to [it] to constitute a breach of a requirement made by or under this Act, whether or not any sanction for that breach is provided by or under this Act and, if it is so provided, whether or not proceedings have been brought in respect of the breach.

(3) Subsection (1) does not prevent the grant of an injunction, or the making of an order of certiorari, mandamus or prohibition or as respects Scotland the grant of an interdict or of an order under [section 45 of the Court of Session Act 1988] (order for specific performance of statutory duty).

171 Onus of proof in various proceedings

(1) If an agreement contains a term signifying that in the opinion of the parties section 10(3)(b)(iii) does not apply to the agreement, it shall be taken not to apply unless the contrary is proved.

(2) It shall be assumed in any proceedings, unless the contrary is proved, that when a person initiated a transaction as mentioned in section 19(1)(c) he knew the principal agreement had been made, or contemplated that it might be made.

[. . .]

(4) In proceedings brought by the creditor under a credit-token agreement—

(a) it is for the creditor to prove that the credit-token was lawfully supplied to the debtor, and was accepted by him, and

(b) if the debtor alleges that any use made of the credit-token was not authorised by him, it is for the creditor to prove either—

(i) that the use was so authorised, or

(ii) that the use occurred before the creditor had been given notice under section 84(3).

(5) In proceedings under section 50(1) in respect of a document received by a minor at any school or other educational establishment for minors, it is for the person sending it to him at that establishment to prove that he did not know or suspect it to be such an establishment.

(6) In proceedings under section 119(1) it is for the pawnee to prove that he had reasonable cause to refuse to allow the pawn to be redeemed.

[. . .]

172 Statements by creditor or owner to be binding

(1) A statement by a creditor or owner is binding on him if given under—

section 77(1),
section 78(1),
section 79(1),
section 97(1),
section 107(1)(c),
section 108(1)(c), or
section 109(1)(c).

(2) Where a trader—

(a) gives a customer a notice in compliance with section 103(1)(b), or

(b) gives a customer a notice under section 103(1) asserting that the customer is not indebted to him under an agreement, the notice is binding on the trader.

(3) Where in proceedings before any court—

(a) it is sought to reply on a statement or notice given as mentioned in subsection (1) or (2), and

(b) the statement or notice is shown to be incorrect, the court may direct such relief (if any) to be given to the creditor or owner from the operation of subsection (1) or (2) as appears to the court to be just.

173 Contracting-out forbidden

(1) A term contained in a regulated agreement or linked transaction, or in any other agreement relating to an actual or prospective regulated agreement or linked transaction, is void if, and to the extent that, it is inconsistent with a provision for the protection of the debtor or hirer or his relative or any surety contained in this Act or in any regulation made under this Act.

(2) Where a provision specifies the duty or liability of the debtor or hirer or his relative or any surety in certain circumstances, a term is inconsistent with that provision if it purports to impose, directly or indirectly, an additional duty or liability on him in those circumstances.

(3) Notwithstanding subsection (1), a provision of this Act under which a thing may be done in relation to any person on an order of the court or the [FCA] only shall not be taken to prevent its being done at any time with that person's consent given at that time, but the refusal of such consent shall not give rise to any liability.

PART XII
SUPPLEMENTAL

[. . .]

[174A Powers to require provision of information or documents etc

(1) Every power conferred on a relevant authority by or under this Act (however expressed) to require the provision or production of information or documents includes the power—

(a) to require information to be provided or produced in such form as the authority may specify, including, in relation to information recorded otherwise than in a legible form, in a legible form;

(b) to take copies of, or extracts from, any documents provided or produced by virtue of the exercise of the power;

(c) to require the person who is required to provide or produce any information or document by virtue of the exercise of the power—

(i) to state, to the best of his knowledge and belief, where the information or document is;

(ii) to give an explanation of the information or document;

(iii) to secure that any information provided or produced, whether in a document or otherwise, is verified in such manner as may be specified by the authority;

(iv) to secure that any document provided or produced is authenticated in such manner as may be so specified;

(d) to specify a time at or by which a requirement imposed by virtue of paragraph (c) must be complied with.

(2) Every power conferred on a relevant authority by or under this Act (however expressed) to inspect or to seize documents at any premises includes the power to take copies of, or extracts from, any documents inspected or seized by virtue of the exercise of the power.

(3) But a relevant authority has no power under this Act—

(a) to require another person to provide or to produce,

(b) to seize from another person, or

(c) to require another person to give access to premises for the purposes of the inspection of, any information or document which the other person would be entitled to refuse to provide or produce in proceedings in the High Court on the grounds of legal professional privilege or (in Scotland) in proceedings in the Court of Session on the grounds of confidentiality of communications.

(4) In subsection (3) 'communications' means—

(a) communications between a professional legal adviser and his client;

(b) communications made in connection with or in contemplation of legal proceedings and for the purposes of those proceedings.

[(5) In this section, 'relevant authority' means an enforcement authority or an officer of an enforcement authority.]]

175 Duty of persons deemed to be agents

Where under this Act a person is deemed to receive a notice or payment as agent of the creditor or owner under a regulated agreement, he shall be deemed to be under a contractual duty to the creditor or owner to transmit the notice, or remit the payment, to him forthwith.

176 Service of documents

(1) A document to be served under this Act by one person ('the server') on another person ('the subject') is to be treated as properly served on the subject if dealt with as mentioned in the following subsections.

(2) The document may be delivered or sent [by an appropriate method] to the subject, or addressed to him by name and left at his proper address.

(3) For the purposes of this Act, a document sent by post to, or left at, the address last known to the server as the address of a person shall be treated as sent by post to, or left at, his proper address.

(4) Where the document is to be served on the subject as being the person having any interest in land, and it is not practicable after reasonable inquiry to ascertain the subject's name or address, the document may be served by—

(a) addressing it to the subject by the description of the person having that interest in the land (naming it), and

(b) delivering the document to some responsible person on the land or affixing it, or a copy of it, in a conspicuous position on the land.

(5) Where a document to be served on the subject as being a debtor, hirer or surety, or as having any other capacity relevant for the purposes of this Act, is served at any time on another person who—

(a) is the person last known to the server as having that capacity, but

(b) before that time had ceased to have it, the document shall be treated as having been served at that time on the subject.

(6) Anything done to a document in relation to a person who (whether to the knowledge of the server or not) has died shall be treated for the purposes of subsection (5) as service of the document on that person if it would have been so treated had he not died.

[(7) The following enactments shall not be construed as authorising service on the Public Trustee (in England and Wales) or the Probate Judge (in Northern Ireland) of any document which is to be served under this Act—

section 9 of the Administration of Estates Act 1925;

section 3 of the Administration of Estates Act (Northern Ireland) 1955.]

(8) References in the preceding subsections to the serving of a document on a person include the giving of the document to that person.

[176A Electronic transmission of documents

(1) A document is transmitted in accordance with this subsection if—

(a) the person to whom it is transmitted agrees that it may be delivered to him by being transmitted to a particular electronic address in a particular electronic form,

(b) it is transmitted to that address in that form, and

(c) the form in which the document is transmitted is such that any information in the document which is addressed to the person to whom the document is transmitted is capable of being stored for future reference for an appropriate period in a way which allows the information to be reproduced without change.

(2) A document transmitted in accordance with subsection (1) shall, unless the contrary is proved, be treated for the purposes of this Act, except section 69, as having been delivered on the working day immediately following the day on which it is transmitted.

(3) In this section, 'electronic address' includes any number or address used for the purposes of receiving electronic communications.]

177 Saving for registered charges

(1) Nothing in this Act affects the rights of a creditor in a heritable security who—

(a) became the creditor under a transfer for value without notice of any defect in the title arising (apart from this section) by virtue of this Act; or

(b) derives title from such a creditor.

(2) Nothing in this Act affects the operation of section 41 of the Conveyancing (Scotland) Act 1924 (protection of purchasers), or of that section as applied to standard securities by section 32 of the Conveyancing and Feudal Reform (Scotland) Act 1970.

(3) Subsection (1) does not apply to a creditor carrying on [a consumer credit business, a consumer hire business or a business of debt-collecting or debt administration].

(4) Where, by virtue of subsection (1), a land mortgage is enforced which apart from this section would be treated as never having effect, the original creditor or owner shall be liable to indemnify the debtor or hirer against any loss thereby suffered by him.

(5) [*Substitutes subsections (1) to (3) for Scotland.*]

(6) [*Applies to Northern Ireland.*]

178 Local Acts

The [Treasury] or the Department of Commerce for Northern Ireland may by order make such amendments or repeals of any provision of any local Act as appears to the [Treasury] or, as the case may be, the Department, necessary or expedient in consequence of the replacement by this Act of the enactments relating to pawnbrokers and moneylenders.

Regulations, orders, etc

179 Power to prescribe form etc of secondary documents

(1) Regulations may be made as to the form and content of credit-cards, trading-checks, receipts, vouchers and other documents or things issued by creditors, owners or suppliers under or in connection with regulated agreements or by other persons in connection with linked transactions, and may in particular—

(a) require specified information to be included in the prescribed manner in documents, and other specified material to be excluded;

(b) contain requirements to ensure that specified information is clearly brought to the attention of the debtor or hirer, or his relative, and that one part of a document is not given insufficient or excessive prominence compared with another.

(2) If a person issues any document or thing in contravention of regulations under subsection (1) then, as from the time of the contravention but without prejudice to anything done before it, this Act shall apply as if the regulated agreement had been improperly executed by reason of a contravention of regulations under section 60(1).

180 Power to prescribe form etc of copies

(1) Regulations may be made as to the form and content of documents to be issued as copies of any executed agreement, security instrument or other document referred to in this Act, and may in particular—

(a) require specified information to be included in the prescribed manner in any copy, and contain requirements to ensure that such information is clearly brought to the attention of a reader of the copy;

(b) authorise the omission from a copy of certain material contained in the original, or the inclusion of such material in condensed form.

(2) A duty imposed by any provision of this Act [. . .] to supply a copy of any document—

(a) is not satisfied unless the copy supplied is in the prescribed form and conforms to the prescribed requirements;

(b) is not infringed by the omission of any material, or its inclusion in condensed form, if that is authorised by regulations;

and references in this Act to copies shall be construed accordingly.

(3) Regulations may provide that a duty imposed by this Act to supply a copy of a document referred to in an unexecuted agreement or an executed agreement shall not apply to documents of a kind specified in the regulations.

181 Power to alter monetary limits etc

(1) The [Treasury] may by order made by statutory instrument amend, or further amend, any of the following provisions of this Act so as to reduce or increase a sum mentioned in that provision, namely, sections [. . .], 17(1), [. . .] [. . .], 70(6), 75(3)(b), 77(1), 78(1), 79(1), 84(1), 101(7)(a), 107(1), 108(1), 109(1), 110(1), [. . .] [. . .], 140B(6), 155(1) and 158(1).

(2) An order under subsection (1) amending section [. . .], 17(1), [. . .] [. . .], 75(3)(b) [. . . or 140B(6)] shall be of no effect unless a draft of the order has been laid before and approved by each House of Parliament.

182 Regulations and orders

(1) Any power of the [Treasury] to make regulations or orders under this Act, except the power conferred by sections [. . .] 181 and 192 shall be exercisable by statutory instrument subject to annulment in pursuance of a resolution of either House of Parliament.

[. . .]

(2) Where a power to make regulations or orders is exercisable by the [Treasury] by virtue of this Act, regulations or orders made in the exercise of that power may—

(a) make different provision in relation to different cases or classes of case, and

(b) exclude certain cases or classes of case, and

(c) contain such transitional provision as the [Treasury] thinks fit.

(3) Regulations may provide that specified expressions, when used as described by the regulations, are to be given the prescribed meaning, notwithstanding that another meaning is intended by the person using them.

(4) Any power conferred on the [Treasury] by this Act to make orders includes power to vary or revoke an order so made.

183 Determinations etc by [FCA]

[(1) The [FCA] may vary or revoke any determination made, or direction given, by it under this Act.

[. . .]

Interpretation

184 Associates

[(1) A person is an associate of an individual if that person is—

(a) the individual's husband or wife or civil partner,
(b) a relative of—
(i) the individual, or
(ii) the individual's husband or wife or civil partner, or
(c) the husband or wife or civil partner of a relative of—
(i) the individual, or
(ii) the individual's husband or wife or civil partner.]

(2) A person is an associate of any person with whom he is in partnership, and of the husband or wife [or civil partner] or a relative of any individual with whom he is in partnership.

(3) A body corporate is an associate of another body corporate—

(a) if the same person is a controller of both, or a person is a controller of one and persons who are his associates, or he and persons who are his associates, are controllers of the other; or

(b) if a group of two or more persons is a controller of each company, and the groups either consist of the same persons or could be regarded as consisting of the same persons by treating (in one or more cases) a member of either group as replaced by a person of whom he is an associate.

(4) A body corporate is an associate of another person if that person is a controller of it or if that person and persons who are his associates together are controllers of it.

(5) In this section 'relative' means brother, sister, uncle, aunt, nephew, niece, lineal ancestor or lineal descendant, references to a husband or wife include a former husband or wife and a reputed husband or wife, [and references to a civil partner include a former civil partner] [and a reputed civil partner]; and for the purposes of this subsection a relationship shall be established as if any illegitimate child, stepchild or adopted child of a person [were the legitimate child of the relationship in question].

185 Agreement with more than one debtor or hirer

(1) Where an actual or prosective regulated agreement has two or more debtors or hirers (not being a partnership or an unincorporated body of persons)—

(a) anything required by or under this Act to be done to or in relation to the debtor or hirer shall be done to or in relation to each of them; and

(b) anything done under this Act by or on behalf of one of them shall have effect as if done by or on behalf of all of them.

[. . .]

[(2) Notwithstanding subsection (1)(a), where credit is provided under an agreement to two or more debtors jointly, in performing his duties—

(a) in the case of fixed-sum credit, under section 77A, or

(b) in the case of running-account credit, under section 78(4),

the creditor need not give statements to any debtor who has signed and given to him a notice (a 'dispensing notice') authorising him not to comply in the debtor's case with section 77A or (as the case may be) 78(4).

(2A) A dispensing notice given by a debtor is operative from when it is given to the creditor until it is revoked by a further notice given to the creditor by the debtor.

(2B) But subsection (2) does not apply if (apart from this subsection) dispensing notices would be operative in relation to all of the debtors to whom the credit is provided.

(2C) Any dispensing notices operative in relation to an agreement shall cease to have effect if any of the debtors dies.

(2D) A dispensing notice which is operative in relation to an agreement shall be operative also in relation to any subsequent agreement which, in relation to the earlier agreement, is a modifying agreement.]

(3) Subsection (1)(b) does not apply for the purposes of section 61(1)(a) [. . .].

(4) Where a regulated agreement has two or more debtors or hirers (not being a partnership or an unincorporated body of persons), section 86 applies to the death of any of them.

(5) An agreement for the provision of credit, or the bailment or (in Scotland) the hiring of goods, to two or more persons jointly where—

(a) one or more of those persons is an individual, and

(b) one or more of them is [not an individual],

is a consumer credit agreement or consumer hire agreement if it would have been one had they all been individuals; and [each person within paragraph (b)] shall accordingly be included among the debtors or hirers under the agreement.

(6) Where subsection (5) applies, references in this Act to the signing of any document by the debtor or hirer shall be construed in relation to a body corporate [within paragraph (b) of that subsection] as referring to a signing on behalf of the body corporate.

186 Agreement with more than one creditor or owner

Where an actual or prospective regulated agreement has two or more creditors or owners, anything required by or under this Act to be done to, or in relation to, or by, the creditor or owner shall be effective if done to, or in relation to, or by, any one of them.

187 Arrangements between creditor and supplier

(1) A consumer credit agreement shall be treated as entered into under preexisting arrangements between a creditor and a supplier if it is entered into in accordance with, or in furtherance of, arrangements previously made between persons mentioned in subsection (4)(a), (b) or (c).

(2) A consumer credit agreement shall be treated as entered into in contemplation of future arrangements between a creditor and a supplier if it is entered into in the expectation that arrangements will subsequently be made between persons mentioned in subsection (4)(a), (b) or (c) for the supply of cash, goods and services (or any of them) to be financed by the consumer credit agreement.

(3) Arrangements shall be disregarded for the purposes of subsection (1) or (2) if—

(a) they are arrangements for the making, in specified circumstances, of payments to the supplier by the creditor, and

(b) the creditor holds himself out as willing to make, in such circumstances, payments of the kind to suppliers generally.

[(3A) Arrangements shall also be disregarded for the purposes of subsections (1) and (2) if they are arrangements for the electronic transfer of funds from a current account at a bank within the meaning of the Bankers' Books Evidence Act 1879.]

(4) The persons referred to in subsections (1) and (2) are—

(a) the creditor and the supplier;

(b) one of them and an associate of the other's;

(c) an associate of one and an associate of the other's.

(5) Where the creditor is an associate of the supplier's, the consumer credit agreement shall be treated, unless the contrary is proved, as entered into under pre-existing arrangements between the creditor and the supplier.

[187A Definition of 'default sum'

(1) In this Act 'default sum' means, in relation to the debtor or hirer under a regulated agreement, a sum (other than a sum of interest) which is payable by him under the agreement in connection with a breach of the agreement by him.

(2) But a sum is not a default sum in relation to the debtor or hirer simply because, as a consequence of his breach of the agreement, he is required to pay it earlier than he would otherwise have had to.]

188 Examples of use of new terminology

(1) Schedule 2 shall have effect for illustrating the use of terminology employed in this Act.

(2) The examples given in Schedule 2 are not exhaustive.

(3) In the case of conflict between Schedule 2 and any other provision of this Act, that other provision shall prevail.

(4) The [Treasury] may by order amend Schedule 2 by adding further examples or in any other way.

189 Definitions

(1) In this Act, unless the context otherwise requires—

'advertisement' includes every form of advertising, whether in a publication, by television or radio, by display of notices, signs, labels, showcards or goods, by distribution of samples, circulars, catalogues, price lists or other material, by exhibition of pictures, models or films, or in any other way, and references to the publishing of advertisements shall be construed accordingly;

[. . .]

'ancillary credit business' has the meaning given by section 145(1);

'antecedent negotiations' has the meaning given by section 56;

[. . .]

['appropriate method' means—

(a) post, or

(b) transmission in the form of an electronic communication [in accordance with section 176A(1)].]

'assignment', in relation to Scotland, means assignation;

'associate' shall be construed in accordance with section 184;

['authorised business overdraft agreement' means a debtor-creditor agreement which provides authorisation in advance for the debtor to overdraw on a current account, where the agreement is entered into by the debtor wholly or predominantly for the purposes of the debtor's business (see subsection (2A));

'authorised non-business overdraft agreement' means a debtor-creditor agreement which provides authorisation in advance for the debtor to overdraw on a current account where—

(a) the credit must be repaid on demand or within three months, and

(b) the agreement is not entered into by the debtor wholly or predominantly for the purposes of the debtor's business (see subsection (2A));]

[. . .]

'bill of sale' has the meaning given by section 4 of the Bills of Sale Act 1878 or, for Northern Ireland, by section 4 of the Bills of Sale (Ireland) Act 1879;

['building society' means a building society within the meaning of the Building Societies Act 1986;]

'business' includes profession or trade, and references to a business apply subject to subsection (2);

'cancellable agreement' means a regulated agreement which, by virtue of section 67, may be cancelled by the debtor or hirer;

'canvass' shall be construed in accordance with sections 48 and 153;

'cash' includes money in any form;

'charity' means as respects England and Wales a charity registered under [the Charities Act [2011]] or an exempt charity (within the meaning of that Act), and as respects Northern Ireland an institution or other organisation established for charitable purposes only ('organisation' including any persons administering a trust and 'charitable' being construed in the same way as if it were contained in the Income Tax Acts) [, and as respects Scotland a body entered in the Scottish Charity Register];

'conditional sale agreement' means an agreement for the sale of goods or land under which the purchase price or part of it is payable by instalments, and the property in the goods or land is to remain in the seller (notwithstanding that the buyer is to be in possession of the goods or land) until such conditions as to the payment of instalments or otherwise as may be specified in the agreement are fulfilled;

'consumer credit agreement' has the meaning given by section 8, and includes a consumer credit agreement which is cancelled under section 69(1), or becomes subject to section 69(2), so far as the agreement remains in force;

['consumer credit business' means any business being carried on by a person so far as it comprises or relates to—

(a) the provision of credit by him, or

(b) otherwise his being a creditor,

under regulated consumer credit agreements];

'consumer hire agreement' has the meaning given by section 15;

['consumer hire business' means any business being carried on by a person so far as it comprises or relates to—

(a) the bailment or (in Scotland) the hiring of goods by him, or

(b) otherwise his being an owner,

under regulated consumer hire agreements;]

'controller', in relation to a body corporate, means a person—

(a) in accordance with whose directions or instructions the directors of the body corporate or of another body corporate which is its controller (or any of them) are accustomed to act, or

(b) who, either alone or with any associate or associates, is entitled to exercise, or control the exercise of, one third or more of the voting power at any general meeting of the body corporate or of another body corporate which is its controller;

'copy' shall be construed in accordance with section 180;

[. . .]

'court' means in relation to England and Wales the county court, in relation to Scotland the sheriff court and in relation to Northern Ireland the High Court or the county court;

'credit' shall be construed in accordance with section 9;

'credit-broker' means a person carrying on a business of credit-brokerage;

'credit-brokerage' has the meaning given by section 145(2);

['credit information services' [is to be read in accordance with] section 145(7B);]

['credit intermediary' has the meaning given by section 160A;]

'credit limit' has the meaning given by section 10(2);

'creditor' means [(except in relation to green deal plans: see instead section 189B(2))] the person providing credit under a consumer credit agreement or the person to whom his rights and duties under the agreement have passed by assignment or operation of law, and in relation to a prospective consumer credit agreement, includes the prospective creditor;

'credit reference agency' [is to be read in accordance with] section 145(8);

'credit-sale agreement' means an agreement for the sale of goods, under which the purchase price or part of it is payable by instalments, but which is not a conditional sale agreement;

'credit-token' has the meaning given by section 14(1);

'credit-token agreement' means a regulated agreement for the provision of credit in connection with the use of a credit-token;

'debt-adjusting' has the meaning given by section 145(5);

['debt administration' has the meaning given by section 145(7A);] 'debt-collecting' has the meaning given by section 145(7);

'debt-counselling' has the meaning given by section 145(6);

'debtor' means [(except in relation to green deal plans: see instead section 189B(3))] the individual receiving credit under a consumer credit agreement or the person to whom his rights and duties under the agreement have passed by assignment or operation of law, and in relation to a prospective consumer credit agreement includes the prospective debtor;

'debtor-creditor agreement' has the meaning given by section 13;

'debtor-creditor-supplier agreement' has the meaning given by section 12;

'default notice' has the meaning given by section 87(1);

['default sum' has the meaning given by section 187A;]

'deposit' means [. . .] any sum payable by a debtor or hirer by way of deposit or downpayment, or credited or to be credited to him on account of any deposit or downpayment, whether the sum is to be or has been paid to the creditor or owner or any other person, or is to be or has been discharged by a payment of money or a transfer or delivery of goods or by any other means;

['documents' includes information recorded in any form;]

[. . .]

'electric line' has the meaning given by [the Electricity Act 1989] or, for Northern Ireland the Electricity Supply (Northern Ireland) Order 1972;

['electronic communication' means an electronic communication within the meaning of the Electronic Communications Act 2000 (c 7).]

'embodies' and related words shall be construed in accordance with subsection (4);

'enforcement authority' has the meaning given by section 161(1);

'enforcement order' means an order under section 65(1), 105(7)(a) or (b), 111(2) or 124(1) or (2);

'executed agreement' means a document, signed by or on behalf of the parties, embodying the terms of a regulated agreement, or such of them as have been reduced to writing;

[. . .]

['FCA' means the Financial Conduct Authority;]

'finance' means to finance wholly or partly, and 'financed' and 'refinanced' shall be construed accordingly;

'file' and 'copy of the file' have the meanings given by section 158(5);

'fixed-sum credit' has the meaning given by section 10(1)(b);

'friendly society' means a society registered [or treated as registered under the Friendly Societies Act 1974 or the Friendly Societies Act 1992];

'future arrangements' shall be construed in accordance with section 187;

[. . .]

[. . .]

'give' means deliver or send [by an appropriate method] to;

'goods' has the meaning given by [section 61(1) of the Sale of Goods Act 1979];

['green deal plan' has the meaning given by section 1 of the Energy Act 2011;]

[. . .]

'High Court' means Her Majesty's High Court of Justice, or the Court of Session in Scotland or the High Court of Justice in Northern Ireland;

'hire-purchase agreement' means an agreement, other than a conditional sale agreement, under which—

(a) goods are bailed or (in Scotland) hired in return for periodical payments by the person to whom they are bailed or hired, and

(b) the property in the goods will pass to that person if the terms of the agreement are complied with and one or more of the following occurs—

(i) the exercise of an option to purchase by that person,

(ii) the doing of any other specified act by any party to the agreement,

(iii) the happening of any other specified event;

'hirer' means the individual to whom goods are bailed or (in Scotland) hired under a consumer hire agreement, or the person to whom his rights and duties under the agreement have passed by assignment or operation of law, and in relation to a prospective consumer hire agreement includes the prospective hirer;

['individual' includes—

(a) a partnership consisting of two or three persons not all of whom are bodies corporate; and

(b) an unincorporated body of persons which does not consist entirely of bodies corporate and is not a partnership.]

'installation' means—

(a) the installing of any electric line or any gas or water pipe,

(b) the fixing of goods to the premises where they are to be used, and the alteration of premises to enable goods to be used on them,

(c) where it is reasonably necessary that goods should be constructed or erected on the premises where they are to be used, any work carried out for the purpose of constructing or erecting them on those premises;

[. . .]

'judgment' includes an order or decree made by any court;

'land' includes an interest in land, and in relation to Scotland includes heritable subjects of whatever description;

'land improvement company' means an improvement company as defined by section 7 of the improvement of Land Act 1899;

'land mortgage' includes any security charged on land;

[. . .]

'linked transaction' has the meaning given by section 19(1);

'local authority', in relation to England [. . .], means [. . .] a county council, a London borough council, a district council, the Common Council of the City of London, or the Council of the Isles of Scilly, [in relation to Wales means a county council or a county borough council,] and in relation to Scotland, means a [council constituted under section 2 of the Local Government etc (Scotland) Act 1994], and, in relation to Northern Ireland, means a district council;

'modifying agreement' has the meaning given by section 82(2);

'mortgage', in relation to Scotland, includes any heritable security;

'multiple agreement' has the meaning given by section 18(1);

'negotiator' has the meaning given by section 56(1);

'non-commercial agreement' means a consumer credit agreement or a consumer hire agreement not made by the creditor or owner in the course of a business carried on by him;

'notice' means notice in writing;

'notice of cancellation' has the meaning given by section 69(1);

[. . .]

['open-end' in relation to a consumer credit agreement, means of no fixed duration;]

'owner' means a person who bails or (in Scotland) hires out goods under a consumer hire agreement or the person to whom his rights and duties under the agreement have passed by assignment or operation of law, and in relation to a prospective consumer hire agreement, includes the prospective bailor or person from whom the goods are to be hired;

'pawn' means any article subject to a pledge;

'pawn-receipt' has the meaning given by section 114;

'pawnee' and 'pawnor' include any person to whom the rights and duties of the original pawnee or the original pawnor, as the case may be, have passed by assignment or operation of law;

'payment' includes tender;

[. . .]

'pledge' means the pawnee's rights over an article taken in pawn;

'prescribed' means prescribed by regulations made by the Secretary of State;

'pre-existing arrangements' shall be construed in accordance with section 187;

'principal agreement' has the meaning given by section 19(1);

'protected goods' has the meaning given by section 90(7);

[. . .]

'redemption period' has the meaning given by section 116(3);

[. . .]

['regulated agreement' means a consumer credit agreement which is a regulated agreement (within the meaning of section 8(3)) or a consumer hire agreement which is a regulated agreement (within the meaning of section 15(2));]

['regulated deferred payment credit agreement' means an agreement—

(a) which meets each of the conditions set out in article 60F(2)(a) to (d) (exempt agreements: exemptions relating to number of repayments to be made) of the Regulated Activities Order; and

(b) to which article 60F(7A) of that Order applies;]

['Regulated Activities Order' means the Financial Services and Markets Act 2000 (Regulated Activities) Order 2001;]

'regulations' means regulations made by the [Treasury];

'relative', except in section 184, means a person who is an associate by virtue of section 184(1);

'representation' includes any condition or warranty, and any other statement or undertaking, whether oral or in writing;

['residential renovation agreement' means a consumer credit agreement [entered into on or after 21st March 2016]—

(a) which is unsecured; and

(b) the purpose of which is the renovation of residential property, as described in Article 2(2a) of Directive 2008/48/EC of the European Parliament and of the Council of 23rd April 2008 on credit agreements for consumers.]

'restricted-use credit agreement' and 'restricted-use credit' have the meanings given by section 11(1);

'rules of court', in relation to Northern Ireland means, in relation to the High Court, rules made under section 7 of the Northern Ireland Act 1962, and, in relation to any other court, rules made by the authority having for the time being power to make rules regulating the practice and procedure in that court;

'running-account credit' shall be construed in accordance with section 10;

'security', in relation to an actual or prospective consumer credit agreement or consumer hire agreement, or any linked transaction, means a mortgage, charge, pledge, bond, debenture, indemnity, guarantee, bill, note or other right provided by the debtor or hirer, or at his request (express or implied), to secure the carrying out of the obligations of the debtor or hirer under the agreement;

'security instrument' has the meaning given by section 105(2);

'serve on' means deliver or send [by an appropriate method] to;

'signed' shall be construed in accordance with subsection (3);

'small agreement' has the meaning given by section 17(1), and 'small' in relation to an agreement within any category shall be construed accordingly;

[. . .]

[. . .]

'supplier' has the meaning given by section 11(1)(b) or 12(c) or 13(c) or, in relation to an agreement falling within section 11(1)(a), means the creditor, and includes a person to whom the rights and duties of a supplier (as so defined) have passed by assignment or operation of law, or (in relation to a prospective agreement) the prospective supplier;

'surety' means the person by whom any security is provided, or the person to whom his rights and duties in relation to the security have passed by assignment or operation of law;

'technical grounds' shall be construed in accordance with subsection (5);

'time order' has the meaning given by section 129(1);

['total charge for credit' has the meaning given by section 20];

'total price' means the total sum payable by the debtor under a hire-purchase agreement or a conditional sale agreement, including any sum payable on the exercise of an option to purchase, but excluding any sum payable as a penalty or as compensation or damages for a breach of the agreement;

['the UK GDPR' has the same meaning as in Parts 5 to 7 of the Data Protection Act 2018 (see section 3(10) and (14) of that Act);]

[. . .]

'unexecuted agreement' means a document embodying the terms of a prospective regulated agreement, or such of them as it is intended to reduce to writing;

[. . .]

'unrestricted-use credit agreement' and 'unrestricted-use credit' have the meanings given by section 11(2);

'working day' means any day other than—

(a) Saturday or Sunday,

(b) Christmas Day or Good Friday,

(c) a bank holiday within the meaning given by section 1 of the Banking and Financial Dealings Act 1971.

[(1A) In sections [. . .], 70(4), 73(4) and 75(2) [. . .] 'costs', in relation to proceedings in Scotland, means expenses.]

(2) A person is not to be treated as carrying on a particular type of business merely because occasionally he enters into transactions belonging to a business of that type.

[(2A) For the purpose of the definitions of 'authorised business overdraft agreement' and 'authorised non-business overdraft agreement' [article 60C(5) and (6) of the Regulated Activities Order applies.]]

(3) Any provision of this Act requiring a document to be signed is complied with by a body corporate if the document is sealed by that body.

This subsection does not apply to Scotland.

(4) A document embodies a provision if the provision is set out either in the document itself or in another document referred to in it.

(5) An application dismissed by the court [. . .] shall, if the court [. . .] so certifies, be taken to be dismissed on technical grounds only.

(6) Except in so far as the context otherwise requires, any reference in this Act to an enactment shall be construed as a reference to that enactment as amended by or under any other enactment, including this Act.

(7) In this Act, except where otherwise indicated—

(a) a reference to a numbered Part, section or Schedule is a reference to the Part or section of, or the Schedule to, this Act so numbered, and

(b) a reference in a section to a numbered subsection is a reference to the subsection of that section so numbered, and

(c) a reference in a section, subsection or Schedule to a numbered paragraph is a reference to the paragraph of that section, subsection or Schedule so numbered.

[. . .]

191 [*Applies to Northern Ireland*]

193 Short title and extent

(1) This Act may be cited as the Consumer Credit Act 1974.

(2) This Act extends to Northern Ireland.

SCHEDULES

[. . .]

SCHEDULE 1. PROSECUTION AND PUNISHMENT OF OFFENCES

Section 167

1 *Section*	2 *Offence*	3 *Mode of prosecution*	4 *Imprisonment or fine*
[. . .]	[. . .]	[. . .]	[. . .]
49(1)	. . . Canvassing debtor-creditor agreements off trade premises.	(a) Summarily. (b) On indictment.	[The prescribed sum.] 1 year or a fine or both.
49(2)	. . . Soliciting debtor-creditor agreements during visits made in response to previous oral requests.	(a) Summarily. (b) On indictment.	[The prescribed sum.] 1 year or a fine or both.
50(1)	. . . Sending circulars to minors.	(a) Summarily. (b) On indictment.	[The prescribed sum.] 1 year or a fine or both.
[. . .]	[. . .]	[. . .]	[. . .]
[. . .]	[. . .]	[. . .]	[. . .]
[. . .]	[. . .]	[. . .]	[. . .]
80(2)	. . . Failure to tell creditor or owner whereabouts of goods.	[. . .]	[Level 3 on the standard scale.]
[. . .]	[. . .]	[. . .]	[. . .]
114(2)	. . . Taking pledges from minors.	(a) Summarily. (b) On indictment.	[The prescribed sum.] 1 year or a fine or both.
[. . .]	[. . .]	[. . .]	[. . .]
119(1)	. . . Unreasonable refusal to allow pawn to be redeemed.	Summarily.	[Level 4 on the standard scale.]
154	. . . Canvassing ancillary credit services of trade premises.	(a) Summarily. (b) On indictment.	[The prescribed sum.] 1 year or a fine or both.
157(3)	. . . Refusal to give name etc of credit reference agency.	Summarily.	[Level 4 on the standard scale.]
158(4)	. . . Failure of credit reference agency to disclose filed information.	Summarily.	[Level 4 on the standard scale.]
159(6)	. . . Failure of credit reference agency to correct information.	Summarily.	[Level 4 on the standard scale.]
160(6)	. . . Failure of credit reference agency to comply with section 160(3) or (4).	Summarily.	[Level 4 on the standard scale.]
[. . .]	[. . .]	[. . .]	[. . .]
[. . .]	*[. . .]*	*[. . .]*	*[. . .]*

SCHEDULE 2
EXAMPLES OF USE OF NEW TERMINOLOGY

Section 188(1)

PART I
LIST OF TERMS

Term	*Defined in section*	*Illustrated by examples(s)*
Advertisement	189(1)	2
[. . .]		
Antecedent negotiations	56	1, 2, 3, 4
Cancellable agreement	67	4
Consumer credit agreement	8	5, 6, 7, 15, 19, 21
Consumer hire agreement	15	20, 24
Credit	9	16, 19, 21
Credit-broker	189(1)	2
Credit limit	10(2)	6, 7, 19, 22, 23
Creditor	189(1)	1, 2, 3, 4
Credit-sale agreement	189(1)	5
Credit-token	14	3, 14, 16
Credit-token agreement	14	3, 14, 16, 22
Debtor-creditor agreement	13	8, 16, 17, 18
Debtor-creditor-supplier agreement	12	8, 16
Fixed-sum credit	10	9, 10, 17, 23
Hire-purchase agreement	189(1)	10
Individual	189(1)	19, 24
Linked transaction	19	11
Modifying agreement	82(2)	24
Multiple agreement	18	16, 18
Negotiator	56(1)	1, 2, 3, 4
[. . .]		
Pre-existing arrangements	187	8, 21
Restricted-use credit	11	10, 12, 13, 14, 16
Running-account credit	10	15, 16, 18, 23
Small agreement	17	16, 17, 22
Supplier	189(1)	3, 14
Total charge for credit	20	5, 10
Total price	189(1)	10
Unrestricted-use credit	11	8, 12, 16, 17, 18

PART II
EXAMPLES

Example 1

Facts Correspondence passes between an employee of a money-lending company (writing on behalf of the company) and an individual about the terms on which the company would grant him a loan under a regulated agreement.

Analysis The correspondence constitutes antecedent negotiations falling within section 56(1)(a), the money-lending company being both creditor and negotiator.

Example 2

Facts Representations are made about goods in a poster displayed by a shopkeeper near the goods, the goods being selected by a customer who has read the poster and then sold by the shopkeeper to a finance company introduced by him (with whom he has a business relationship). The goods are disposed of by the finance company to the customer under a regulated hire-purchase agreement.

Analysis The representations in the poster constitute antecedent negotiations falling within section 56(1)(b), the shopkeeper being the credit-broker and negotiator and the finance company being the creditor. The poster is an advertisement and the shopkeeper is the advertiser.

Example 3

Facts Discussions take place between a shopkeeper and a customer about goods the customer wishes to buy using a credit-card issued by the D Bank under a regulated agreement.

Analysis The discussions constitute antecedent negotiations falling within section 56(1)(c), the shopkeeper being the supplier and negotiator and the D Bank the creditor. The credit-card is a credit-token as defined in section 14(1), and the regulated agreement under which it was issued is a credit-token agreement as defined in section 14(2).

Example 4

Facts Discussions take place and correspondence passes between a secondhand car dealer and a customer about a car, which is then sold by the dealer to the customer under a regulated conditional sale agreement. Subsequently, on a revocation of that agreement by consent, the car is resold by the dealer to a finance company introduced by him (with whom he has a business relationship), who in turn dispose of it to the same customer under a regulated hire-purchase agreement.

Analysis The discussions and correspondence constitute antecedent negotiations in relation both to the conditional sale agreement and the hire-purchase agreement. They fall under section 56(1)(a) in relation to the conditional sale agreement, the dealer being the creditor and the negotiator. In relation to the hirepurchase agreement they fall within section 56(1)(b), the dealer continuing to be treated as the negotiator but the finance company now being the creditor. Both agreements are cancellable if the discussions took place when the individual conducting the negotiations (whether the 'negotiator' or his employee or agent) was in the presence of the debtor, unless the unexecuted agreement was signed by the debtor at trade premises (as defined in section 67(b)). If the discussions all took place by telephone however, or the unexecuted agreement was signed by the debtor on trade premises (as so defined) the agreements are not cancellable.

Example 5

Facts E agrees to sell to F (an individual) an item of furniture in return for 24 monthly instalments of £10 payable in arrear. The property in the goods passes to F immediately.

Analysis This is a credit-sale agreement (see definition of 'credit-sale agreement' in section 189(1)). The credit provided amounts to £240 less the amount which [constitutes the total charge for credit (within the meaning given by section 20)]. (This amount is required to be deducted by section 9(4).) Accordingly the agreement falls within section 8(2) and is a consumer credit agreement.

Example 6

Facts The G Bank grants H (an individual) an unlimited over-draft, with an increased rate of interest on so much of any debit balance as exceeds £2,000.

Analysis Although the overdraft purports to be unlimited, the stipulation for increased interest above £2,000 brings the agreement within section 10(3)(b)(ii) and it is a consumer credit agreement.

Example 7

Facts J is an individual who owns a small shop which usually carries a stock worth about £1,000. K makes a stocking agreement under which he undertakes to provide on short-term credit the stock needed from time to time by J without any specified limit.

Analysis Although the agreement appears to provide unlimited credit, it is probable, having regard to the stock usually carried by J, that his indebtedness to K will not at any time rise above £5,000. Accordingly the agreement falls within section 10(3)(b)(iii) and is a consumer credit agreement.

Example 8

Facts U, a moneylender, lends £500 to V (an individual) knowing he intends to use it to buy office equipment from W. W introduced V to U, it being his practice to introduce customers needing finance to him. Sometimes U gives W a commission for this and sometimes not. U pays the £500 direct to V.

Analysis Although this appears to fall under section 11(1)(b), it is excluded by section 11(3) and is therefore (by section 11(2)) an unrestricted-use credit agreement. Whether it is a debtor-creditor agreement (by section 13(c)) or a debtorcreditor-supplier agreement (by section 12(c)) depends on whether the previous dealings between U and W amount to 'pre-existing arrangements', that is whether the agreement can be taken to have been entered into 'in accordance with, or in furtherance of' arrangements previously made between U and W, as laid down in section 187(1).

Example 9

Facts A agrees to lend B (an individual) £4,500 in nine monthly instalments of £500.

Analysis This is a cash loan and is a form of credit (see section 9 and definition of 'cash' in section 189(1)). Accordingly it falls within section 10(1)(b) and is fixedsum credit amounting to £4,500.

Example 10

Facts C (in England) agrees to bail goods to D (an individual) in return for periodical payments. The agreement provides for the property in the goods to pass to D on payment of a total of £7,500 and the exercise by D of an option to purchase. The sum of £7,500 includes a down-payment of £1,000. It also includes an amount which, according to regulations made under section 20(1), constitutes a total charge for credit of £1,500.

Analysis This is a hire-purchase agreement with a deposit of £1,000 and a total price of £7,500 (see definitions of 'hire-purchase agreement', 'deposit' and 'total price' in section 189(1)). By section 9(3), it is taken to provide credit amounting to £7,500 – (£1,500 + £1,000), which equals £5,000. Under section 8(2), the agreement is therefore a consumer credit agreement, and under sections 9(3) and 11(1) it is a restricted-use credit agreement for fixed-sum credit. A similar result would follow if the agreement by C had been a hiring agreement in Scotland.

Example 11

Facts X (an individual) borrows £500 from Y (Finance). As a condition of the granting of the loan X is required—

(a) to execute a second mortgage on his house in favour of Y (Finance), and
(b) to take out a policy of insurance on his life with Y (Insurances).

In accordance with the loan agreement, the policy is charged to Y (Finance) as collateral security for the loan. The two companies are associates within the meaning of section 184(3).

Analysis The second mortgage is a transaction for the provision of security and accordingly does not fall within section 19(1), but the taking out of the insurance policy is a linked transaction falling within section 19(1)(a). The charging of the policy is a separate transaction (made between different parties) for the provision of security and again is excluded from section 19(1). The only linked transaction is therefore the taking out of the insurance policy. If X had not been required by the loan agreement to take out the policy, but it had been done at the suggestion of Y (Finance) to induce them to enter into the loan agreement, it would have been a linked transaction under section 19(1)(c)(i) by virtue of section 19(2)(a).

Example 12

Facts The N Bank agrees to lend O (an individual) £2,000 to buy a car from P. To make sure the loan is used as intended, the N Bank stipulates that the money must be paid by it direct to P.

Analysis The agreement is a consumer credit agreement by virtue of section 8(2). Since it falls within section 11(1)(b), it is a restricted-use credit agreement, P being the supplier. If the N Bank had not stipulated for direct payment to the supplier, section 11(3) would have operated and made the agreement into one for unrestricted-use credit.

Example 13

Facts Q, a debt-adjuster, agrees to pay off debts owed by R (an individual) to various moneylenders. For this purpose the agreement provides for the making of a loan by Q to R in return for R's agreeing to repay the loan by instalments with interest. The loan money is not paid over to R but retained by Q and used to pay off the money lenders.

Analysis This is an agreement to refinance existing indebtedness of the debtor's, and if the loan by Q does not exceed £5,000 is a restricted-use credit agreement falling within section 11(1)(c).

Example 14

Facts On payment of £1, S issues to T (an individual) a trading check under which T can spend up to £20 at any shop which has agreed, or in future agrees, to accept S's trading checks.

Analysis The trading check is a credit-token falling within section 14(1)(b). The credit-token agreement is a restricted-use credit agreement within section 11(1)(b), any shop in which the credit-token is used being the 'supplier'. The fact that further shops may be added after the issue of the credit-token is irrelevant in view of section 11(4).

Example 15

Facts A retailer L agrees with M (an individual) to open an account in M's name and, in return for M's promise to pay a specified minimum sum into the account each month and to pay a monthly charge for credit, agrees to allow to be debited to the account, in respect of purchases made by M from L, such sums as will not increase the debit balance at any time beyond the credit limit, defined in the agreement as a given multiple of the specified minimum sum.

Analysis This agreement provides credit falling within the definition of running-account credit in section 10(1)(a). Provided the credit limit is not over £5,000, the agreement falls within section 8(2) and is a consumer credit agreement for running-account credit.

Example 16

Facts Under an unsecured agreement, A (Credit), an associate of the A Bank, issues to B (an individual) a credit-card for use in obtaining cash on credit from A (Credit), to be paid by branches of the A Bank (acting as agent of A (Credit)), or goods or cash from suppliers or banks who have agreed to honour credit-cards issued by A (Credit). The credit limit is £30.

Analysis This is a credit-token agreement falling within section 14(1)(a) and (b). It is a regulated consumer credit agreement for running-account credit. Since the credit limit does not exceed £30, the agreement is a small agreement. So far as the agreement relates to goods it is a debtor-creditor-supplier agreement within section 12(b), since it provides restricted-use credit under section 11(1)(b). So far as it relates to cash it is a debtor-creditor agreement within section 13(c) and the credit it provides is unrestricted-use credit. This is therefore a multiple agreement. In that the whole agreement falls within several of the categories of agreement mentioned in this Act, it is, by section 18(3), to be treated as an agreement in each of those categories. So far as it is a debtor-creditor-supplier agreement providing restricted-use credit it is, by section 18(2), to be treated as a separate agreement; and similarly so far as it is a debtor-creditor agreement providing unrestricted-use credit. (See also Example 22.)

Example 17

Facts The manager of the C Bank agrees orally with D (an individual) to open a current account in D's name. Nothing is said about overdraft facilities. After maintaining the account in credit for some weeks, D draws a cheque in favour of E for an amount exceeding D's credit balance by £20. E presents the cheque and the Bank pay it.

Analysis In drawing the cheque D, by implication, requests the Bank to grant him an overdraft of £20 on its usual terms as to interest and other charges. In deciding to honour the cheque, the Bank by implication accept the offer. This constitutes a regulated small consumer credit agreement for unrestricted-use, fixed sum credit. It is a debtor-creditor agreement, and falls within section 74(1)(b) [. . .] (Compare Example 18.)

Example 18

Facts F (an individual) has had a current account with the G Bank for many years. Although usually in credit, the account has been allowed by the Bank to become overdrawn from time to time. The maximum such overdraft has been is about £1,000. No explicit agreement has ever been made about overdraft facilities. Now, with a credit balance of £500, F draws a cheque for £1,300.

Analysis It might well be held that the agreement with F (express or implied) under which the Bank operate his account includes an implied term giving him the right to overdraft facilities up to say £1,000. If so, the agreement is a regulated consumer credit agreement for unrestricted-use, running-account credit. It is a debtor-creditor agreement, and falls within section 74(1)(b) [. . .]. It is also a multiple agreement, part of which (i.e. the part not dealing with the overdraft), as referred to in section 18(1)(a), falls within a category of agreement not mentioned in this Act. (Compare Example 17.)

Example 19

Facts H (a finance house) agrees with J (a partnership of individuals) to open an unsecured loan account in J's name on which the debit balance is not to exceed £7,000 (having regard to payments into the account made from time to time by J). Interest is to be payable in advance on this sum, with provision for yearly adjustments. H is entitled to debit the account with interest, a 'setting-up' charge, and other charges. Before J has an opportunity to draw on the account it is initially debited with £2,250 for advance interest and other charges.

Analysis This is a personal running-account credit agreement (see sections 8(1) and 10(1)(a), and definition of 'individual' in section 189(1)). By section 10(2) the credit limit is £7,000. By section 9(4) however the initial debit of £2,250, and any other charges later debited to the account by H, are not to be treated as credit even though time is allowed for their payment. Effect is given to this by section 10(3). Although the credit limit of £7,000 exceeds the amount (£5,000) specified in section 8(2) as the maximum for a consumer credit agreement, so that the agreement is not within section 10(3)(a), it is caught by section 10(3)(b)(i). At the beginning J can effectively draw (as credit) no more than £4,750, so the agreement is a consumer credit agreement.

Example 20

Facts K (in England) agrees with L (an individual) to bail goods to L for a period of three years certain at £2,000 a year, payable quarterly. The agreement contains no provision for the passing of the property in the goods to L.

Analysis This is not a hire-purchase agreement (see paragraph (b) of the definition of that term in section 189(1)), and is capable of subsisting for more than three months. Paragraphs (a) and (b) of section 15(1) are therefore satisfied, but paragraph (c) is not. The payments by L must exceed £5,000 if he conforms to the agreement. It is true that under section 101 L has a right to terminate the agreement on giving K three months' notice expiring not earlier than eighteen months after the making of the agreement, but that section applies only where the agreement is a regulated consumer hire agreement apart from the section (see subsection (1)). So the agreement is not a consumer hire agreement, though it would be if the hire charge were say £1,500 a year, or there were a 'break' clause in it operable by either party before the hire charges exceeded £5,000. A similar result would follow if the agreement by K had been a hiring agreement in Scotland.

Example 21

Facts The P Bank decides to issue cheque cards to its customers under a scheme whereby the bank undertakes to honour cheques of up to £30 in every case where the payee has taken the cheque in reliance on the cheque card, whether the customer has funds in his account or not. The P Bank writes to the major retailers advising them of this scheme and also publicises it by advertising. The Bank issues a cheque card to Q (an individual), who uses it to pay by cheque for goods costing £20 bought by Q from R, a major retailer. At the time, Q has £500 in his account at the P Bank.

Analysis The agreement under which the cheque card is issued to Q is a consumer credit agreement even though at all relevant times Q has more than £30 in his account. This is because Q is free to draw out his whole balance and then use the cheque card, in which case the Bank has bound itself to honour the cheque. In other words the cheque card agreement provides Q with credit, whether he avails himself of it or not. Since the amount of the credit is not subject to any express limit, the cheque card can be used any number of times. It may be presumed however that section 10(3)(b)(iii) will apply. The agreement is an unrestricted-use debtor-creditor agreement (by section 13(c)). Although the P Bank wrote to R informing R of the P Bank's willingness to honour any cheque taken by R in reliance on a cheque card, this does not constitute pre-existing arrangements as mentioned in section 13(c) because section 187(3) operates to prevent it. The agreement is not a credit-token agreement within section 14(1)(b) because payment by the P Bank to R, would be a payment of the cheque and not a payment for the goods.

Example 22

Facts The facts are as in Example 16. On one occasion B uses the credit-card in a way which increases his debit balance with A (Credit) to £40. A (Credit) writes to B agreeing to allow the excess on that occasion only, but stating that it must be paid off within one month.

Analysis In exceeding his credit limit B, by implication, requests A (Credit) to allow him a temporary excess (compare Example 17). A (Credit) is thus faced by B's action with the choice of treating it as a breach of contract or granting his implied request. He does the latter. If he had done the former, B would be treated as taking credit to which he was not entitled (see section 14(3)) and, subject to the terms of his contract with A (Credit), would be liable to damages for breach of contract. As it is, the agreement to allow the excess varies the original credit-token agreement by adding a new term. Under section 10(2), the new term is to be disregarded in arriving at the credit limit, so that the credit-token agreement at no time ceases to be a small agreement. By section 82(2) the later agreement is deemed to revoke the original agreement and contain provisions reproducing the combined effect of the two agreements. By section 82(4), this later agreement is exempted from Part V (except section 56).

Example 23

Facts Under an oral agreement made on 10th January, X (an individual) has an overdraft on his current account at the Y bank with a credit limit of £100. On 15th February, when his overdraft stands at £90, X draws a cheque for £25. It is the first time that X has exceeded his credit limit, and on 16th February the bank honours the cheque.

Analysis The agreement of 10th January is a consumer credit agreement for running-account credit. The agreement of 15th–16th February varies the earlier agreement by adding a term allowing the credit limit to be exceeded merely temporarily. By section 82(2) the later agreement is deemed to revoke the earlier agreement and reproduce the combined effect of the two agreements. By section 82(4), Part V of this Act (except section 56) does not apply to the later agreement. By section 18(5), a term allowing a merely temporary excess over the credit limit is not to be treated as a separate agreement, or as providing fixed-sum credit. The whole of the £115 owed to the bank by X on 16th February is therefore runningaccount credit.

Example 24

Facts On 1st March 1975 Z (in England) enters into an agreement with A (an unincorporated body of persons) to bail to A equipment consisting of two components (component P and component Q). The agreement is not a hire-purchase agreement and is for a fixed term of 3 years, so paragraphs (a) and (b) of section 15(1) are both satisfied. The rental is payable monthly at a rate of £2,400 a year, but the agreement provides that this is to be reduced to £1,200 a year for the remainder of the agreement if at any time during its currency A returns component Q to the owner Z. On 5th May 1976 A is incorporated as A Ltd, taking over A's assets and liabilities. On 1st March 1977, A Ltd returns component Q. On 1st January 1978, Z and A Ltd agree to extend the earlier agreement by one year, increasing the rental for the final year by £250 to £1,450.

Analysis When entered into on 1st March 1975, the agreement is a consumer hire agreement. A falls within the definition of 'individual' in section 189(1) and if A returns component Q before 1st May 1976 the total rental will not exceed £5,000 (see section 15(1)(c)). When this date is passed without component Q having been returned it is obvious that the total rental must now exceed £5,000. Does this mean that the agreement then ceases to be a consumer hire agreement? The answer is no, because there has been no change in the terms of the agreement, and without such a change the agreement cannot move from one category to the other. Similarly, the fact that A's rights and duties under the agreement pass to a body corporate on 5th May 1976 does not cause the agreement to cease to be a consumer hire agreement (see definition of 'hirer' in section 189(1)).

The effect of the modifying agreement of 1st January 1978 is governed by section 82(2), which requires it to be treated as containing provisions reproducing the combined effect of the two actual agreements, that is to say as providing that—

(a) obligations outstanding on 1st January 1978 are to be treated as outstanding under the modifying agreement;

(b) the modifying agreement applies at the old rate of hire for the months of January and February 1978, and

(c) for the year beginning 1st March 1978 A Ltd will be the bailee of component P at a rental of £1,450.

The total rental under the modifying agreement is £1,850. Accordingly the modifying agreement is a regulated agreement. Even if the total rental under the modifying agreement exceeded £5,000 it would still be regulated because of the provisions of section 82(3).

UNFAIR CONTRACT TERMS ACT 1977
(1977, c 50)

PART II
AMENDMENT OF LAW FOR SCOTLAND

15 Scope of Part II

(1) This Part of this Act [. . .] is subject to Part III of this Act and does not affect the validity of any discharge or indemnity given by a person in consideration of the receipt by him of compensation in settlement of any claim which he has.

(2) Subject to subsection (3) below, sections 16 [and 17] of this Act apply to any contract only to the extent that the contract—

(a) relates to the transfer of the ownership or possession of goods from one person to another (with or without work having been done on them);

(b) constitutes a contract of service or apprenticeship;

(c) relates to services of whatever kind, including (without prejudice to the foregoing generality) carriage, deposit and pledge, care and custody, mandate, agency, loan and services relating to the use of land;

(d) relates to the liability of an occupier of land to persons entering upon or using that land;

(e) relates to a grant of any right or permission to enter upon or use land not amounting to an estate or interest in the land.

(3) Notwithstanding anything in subsection (2) above, sections 16 *[and 17]*—

(a) do not apply to any contract to the extent that the contract—

(i) is a contract of insurance (including a contract to pay an annuity on human life);

(ii) relates to the formation, constitution or dissolution of any body corporate or unincorporated association or partnership;

(b) apply to—

a contract of marine salvage or towage; a charter party of a ship or hovercraft;
a contract for the carriage of goods by ship or hovercraft; or
a contract to which subsection (4) below relates,

only to the extent that—

(i) both parties deal or hold themselves out as dealing in the course of a business (and then only in so far as the contract purports to exclude or restrict liability for breach of duty in respect of death or personal injury);

[. . .]

(4) This subsection relates to a contract in pursuance of which goods are carried by ship or hovercraft and which either—

(a) specifies ship or hovercraft as the means of carriage over part of the journey to be covered; or

(b) makes no provision as to the means of carriage and does not exclude ship or hovercraft as that means,

in so far as the contract operates for and in relation to the carriage of the goods by that means.

16 Liability for breach of duty

(1) [Subject to subsection (1A) below,] where a term of a contract [, or a provision of a notice given to persons generally or to particular persons,] purports to exclude or restrict liability for breach of duty arising in the course of any business or from the occupation of any premises used for business purposes of the occupier, that term [or provision]—

(a) shall be void in any case where such exclusion or restriction is in respect of death or personal injury;

(b) shall, in any other case, have no effect if it was not fair and reasonable to incorporate the term in the contract [or, as the case may be, if it is not fair and reasonable to allow reliance on the provision].

[(1A) Nothing in paragraph (b) of subsection (1) above shall be taken as implying that a provision of a notice has effect in circumstances where, apart from that paragraph, it would not have effect.]

(2) Subsection (1)(a) above does not affect the validity of any discharge and indemnity given by a person, on or in connection with an award to him of compensation for pneumoconiosis attributable to employment in the coal industry, in respect of any further claim arising from his contracting that disease.

(3) Where under subsection (1) above a term of a contract [or a provision of a notice] is void or has no effect, the fact that a person agreed to, or was aware of, the term [or provision] shall not of itself be sufficient evidence that he knowingly and voluntarily assumed any risk.

[(4) This section does not apply to—

(a) a term in a consumer contract, or

(b) a notice to the extent that it is a consumer notice,

(but see the provision made about such contracts and notices in sections 62 and 65 of the Consumer Rights Act 2015).]

17 Control of unreasonable exemptions in [. . .] standard form contracts

(1) Any term of a contract which is [. . .] a standard form contract shall have no effect for the purpose of enabling a party to the contract—

(a) who is in breach of a contractual obligation, to exclude or restrict any liability of his to the [. . .] customer in respect of the breach;

(b) in respect of a contractual obligation, to render no performance, or to render a performance substantially different from that which the [. . .] customer reasonably expected from the contract;

if it was not fair and reasonable to incorporate the term in the contract.

(2) In this section 'customer' means a party to a standard form contract who deals on the basis of written standard terms of business of the other party to the contract who himself deals in the course of a business.

[(3) This section does not apply to a term in a consumer contract (but see the provision made about such contracts in section 62 of the Consumer Rights Act 2015).]

[. . .]

20 Obligations implied by law in sale and hire-purchase contracts

(1) Any term of a contract which purports to exclude or restrict liability for breach of the obligations arising from—

(a) section 12 of the Sale of Goods Act [1979] (seller's implied undertakings as to title etc);

(b) section 8 of the Supply of Goods (Implied Terms) Act 1973 (implied terms as to title in hire-purchase agreements),

shall be void.

[(1A) Any term of a contract which purports to exclude or restrict liability for breach of the obligations arising from—

(a) section 13, 14 or 15 of the 1979 Act (seller's implied undertakings as to conformity of goods with description or sample, or as to their quality or fitness for a particular purpose);

(b) section 9, 10 or 11 of the 1973 Act (the corresponding things in relation to hire purchase),

shall have effect only if it was fair and reasonable to incorporate the term in the contract.

(1B) This section does not apply to a consumer contract (but see the provision made about such contracts in section 31 of the Consumer Rights Act 2015).]

[. . .]

21 Obligations implied by law in other contracts for the supply of goods

(1) Any term of a contract to which this section applies purporting to exclude or restrict liability for breach of an obligation [such as is referred to in subsection (3) below shall have no effect if it was not fair and reasonable to incorporate the term in the contract.]

(2) This section applies to any contract to the extent that it relates to any such matter as is referred to in section 15(2)(a) of this Act, but does not apply to—

(a) a contract of sale of goods or a hire-purchase agreement; or

(b) a charterparty of a ship or hovercraft [. . .]

(3) An obligation referred to in this subsection is an obligation incurred under a contract in the course of a business and arising by implication of law from the nature of the contract which relates—

(a) to the correspondence of goods with description or sample, or to the quality or fitness of goods for any particular purpose; or

(b) to any right to transfer ownership or possession of goods, or to the enjoyment of quiet possession of goods.

[(3A) Notwithstanding anything in the foregoing provisions of this section, any term of a contract which purports to exclude or restrict liability for breach of the obligations arising under section 11B of the Supply of Goods and Services Act 1982 (implied terms about title, freedom from encumbrances and quiet possession in certain contracts for the transfer of property in goods) shall be void.]

[(3B) This section does not apply to a consumer contract (but see the provision made about such contracts in section 31 of the Consumer Rights Act 2015).]

[. . .]

[. . .]

23 Evasion by means of secondary contract

Any term of any contract shall be void which purports to exclude or restrict, or has the effect of excluding or restricting—

(a) the exercise, by a party to any other contract, of any right or remedy which arises in respect of that other contract in consequence of breach of duty, or of obligation, liability for which could not by virtue of the provisions of this Part of this Act be excluded or restricted by a term of that other contract;

(b) the application of the provisions of this Part of this Act in respect of that or any other contract.

24 The 'reasonableness' test

(1) In determining for the purposes of this Part of this Act whether it was fair and reasonable to incorporate a term in a contract, regard shall be had only to the circumstances which were, or ought reasonably to have been, known to or in the contemplation of the parties to the contract at the time the contract was made.

(2) In determining for the purposes of section 20 or 21 of this Act whether it was fair and reasonable to incorporate a term in a contract, regard shall be had in particular to the matters specified in Schedule 2 to this Act; but this sub-section shall not prevent a court or arbiter from holding in accordance with any rule of law, that a term which purports to exclude or restrict any relevant liability is not a term of the contract.

[(2A) In determining for the purposes of this Part of this Act whether it is fair and reasonable to allow reliance on a provision of a notice (not being a notice having contractual effect), regard shall be had to all the circumstances obtaining when the liability arose or (but for the provision) would have arisen.]

(3) Where a term in a contract [or a provision of a notice] purports to restrict liability to a specified sum of money, and the question arises for the purposes of this Part of this Act whether it was fair and reasonable to incorporate the term in the contract [or whether it is fair and reasonable to allow reliance on the provision], then, without prejudice to subsection (2) above [in the case of a term in a contract], regard shall be had in particular to—

(a) the resources which the party seeking to rely on that term [or provision] could expect to be available to him for the purpose of meeting the liability should it arise;

(b) how far it was open to that party to cover himself by insurance.

(4) The onus of proving that it was fair and reasonable to incorporate a term in a contract [or that it is fair and reasonable to allow reliance on a provision of a notice] shall lie on the party so contending.

25 Interpretation of Part II

(1) In this Part of this Act—

'breach of duty' means the breach—

(a) of any obligation, arising from the express or implied terms of a contract, to take reasonable care or exercise reasonable skill in the performance of the contract;

(b) of any common law duty to take reasonable care or exercise reasonable skill;

(c) of the duty of reasonable care imposed by section 2(1) of the Occupiers' Liability (Scotland) Act 1960;

'business' includes a profession and the activities of any government department or local or public authority;

[. . .]

['consumer contract' has the same meaning as in the Consumer Rights Act 2015 (see section 61);

'consumer notice' has the same meaning as in the Consumer Rights Act 2015 (see section 61);]

'goods' has the same meaning as in the Sale of Goods Act [1979];

'hire-purchase agreement' has the same meaning as in section 189(1) of the Consumer Credit Act 1974;

['notice' includes an announcement, whether or not in writing, and any other communication or pretended communication;]

'personal injury' includes any disease and any impairment of physical or mental condition.

[. . .]

(2) In relation to any breach of duty or obligation, it is immaterial for any purpose of this Part of this Act whether the act or omission giving rise to that breach was inadvertent or intentional or whether liability for it arises directly or vicariously.

(3) In this Part of this Act, any reference to excluding or restricting any liability includes—

(a) making the liability or its enforcement subject to any restrictive or onerous conditions;

(b) excluding or restricting any right or remedy in respect of the liability, or subjecting a person to any prejudice in consequence of his pursuing any such right or remedy;

(c) excluding or restricting any rule of evidence or procedure;

[. . .]

but does not include an agreement to submit any question to arbitration.

(5) In section 15 [, 16, 20 and] 21 of this Act, any reference to excluding or restricting liability for breach of any obligation or duty shall include a reference to excluding or restricting the obligation or duty itself.

PART III
PROVISIONS APPLYING TO WHOLE OF UNITED KINGDOM

26 International supply contracts

(1) The limits imposed by this Act on the extent to which a person may exclude or restrict liability by reference to a contract term do not apply to liability arising under such a contract as is described in subsection (3) below.

(2) The terms of such a contract are not subject to any requirement of reasonableness under section 3 [. . .]: and nothing in Part II of this Act shall require the incorporation of the terms of such a contract to be fair and reasonable for them to have effect.

(3) Subject to subsection (4), that description of contract is one whose characteristics are the following—

(a) either it is a contract of sale of goods or it is one under or in pursuance of which the possession or ownership of goods passes, and

(b) it is made by parties whose places of business (or, if they have none, habitual residences) are in the territories of different States (the Channel Islands and the Isle of Man being treated for this purpose as different States from the United Kingdom).

(4) A contract falls within subsection (3) above only if either—

(a) the goods in question are, at the time of the conclusion of the contract, in the course of carriage, or will be carried, from the territory of one State to the territory of another; or

(b) the acts constituting the offer and acceptance have been done in the territories of different States; or

(c) the contract provides for the goods to be delivered to the territory of a state other than that within whose territory those acts were done.

27 Choice of law clauses

(1) Where the [law applicable to] a contract is the law of any part of the United Kingdom only by choice of the parties (and apart from that choice would be the law of some country outside the United Kingdom) sections 2 to 7 and 16 to 21 of this Act do not operate as part [of the law applicable to the contract].

(2) This Act has effect notwithstanding any contract term which applies or purports to apply the law of some country outside the United Kingdom, where [. . .]—

(a) the term appears to the court, or arbitrator or arbiter to have been imposed wholly or mainly for the purpose of enabling the party imposing it to evade the operation of this Act; [. . .]

29 Saving for other relevant legislation

(1) Nothing in this Act removes or restricts the effect of, or prevents reliance upon, any contractual provision which—

(a) is authorised or required by the express terms or necessary implication of an enactment; or

(b) being made with a view to compliance with an international agreement to which the United Kingdom is a party, does not operate more restrictively than is contemplated by the agreement.

(2) A contract term is to be taken—

(a) for the purposes of Part I of this Act, as satisfying the requirement of reasonableness; and

(b) for those of Part II, to have been fair and reasonable to incorporate,

if it is incorporated or approved by, or incorporated pursuant to a decision or ruling of, a competent authority acting in the exercise of any statutory jurisdiction or function and is not a term in a contract to which the competent authority is itself a party.

(3) In this section—

'competent authority' means any court, arbitrator or arbiter, government department or public authority;

'enactment' means any legislation (including subordinate legislation) of the United Kingdom or Northern Ireland and any instrument having effect by virtue of such legislation; and

'statutory' means conferred by an enactment.

. . .

SCHEDULE 2
'GUIDELINES' FOR APPLICATION OF REASONABLENESS TEST

Sections 11(2) and 24(2)

The matters to which regard is to be had in particular for the purposes of sections [6(1A), 7(1A) and (4),] 20 and 21 are any of the following which appear to be relevant—

(a) the strength of the bargaining positions of the parties relative to each other, taking into account (among other things) alternative means by which the customer's requirements could have been met;

(b) whether the customer received an inducement to agree to the terms, or in accepting it had an opportunity of entering into a similar contract with other persons, but without having to accept similar terms;

(c) whether the customer knew or ought reasonably to have known of the existence and extent of the term (having regard, among other things, to any customs of the trade and any previous course of dealing between the parties);

(d) where the term excludes or restricts any relevant liability if some condition is not complied with, whether it was reasonable at the time of the contract to expect that compliance with that condition would be practicable;

(e) whether the goods were manufactured, processed or adapted to the special order of the customer.

SALE OF GOODS ACT 1979
(1979, c 54)

PART I
CONTRACTS TO WHICH ACT APPLIES

1 Contracts to which Act applies

(1) This Act applies to contracts of sale of goods made on or after (but not to those made before) 1 January 1894.

(2) In relation to contracts made on certain dates, this Act applies subject to the modification of certain of its sections as mentioned in Schedule 1 below.

(3) Any such modification is indicated in the section concerned by a reference to Schedule 1 below.

(4) Accordingly, where a section does not contain such a reference, this Act applies in relation to the contract concerned without such modification of the section.

[(5) Certain sections or subsections of this Act do not apply to a contract to which Chapter 2 of Part 1 of the Consumer Rights Act 2015 applies.

(6) Where that is the case it is indicated in the section concerned.]

PART II
FORMATION OF THE CONTRACT

Contract of sale

2 Contract of sale

(1) A contract of sale of goods is a contract by which the seller transfers or agrees to transfer the property in goods to the buyer for a money consideration, called the price.

(2) There may be a contract of sale between one part owner and another.

(3) A contract of sale may be absolute or conditional.

(4) Where under a contract of sale the property in the goods is transferred from the seller to the buyer the contract is called a sale.

(5) Where under a contract of sale the transfer of the property in the goods is to take place at a future time or subject to some condition later to be fulfilled the contract is called an agreement to sell.

(6) An agreement to sell becomes a sale when the time elapses or the conditions are fulfilled subject to which the property in the goods is to be transferred.

3 Capacity to buy and sell

(1) Capacity to buy and sell is regulated by the general law concerning capacity to contract and to transfer and acquire property.

(2) Where necessaries are sold and delivered [. . .] to a person who by reason of mental incapacity or drunkenness is incompetent to contract, he must pay a reasonable price for them.

(3) In subsection (2) above 'necessaries' means goods suitable to the condition in life of the [. . .] person concerned and to his actual requirements at the time of the sale and delivery.

Formalities of contract

4 How contract of sale is made

(1) Subject to this and any other Act, a contract of sale may be made in writing (either with or without seal), or by word of mouth, or partly in writing and partly by word of mouth, or may be implied from the conduct of the parties.

(2) Nothing in this section affects the law relating to corporations.

Subject matter of contract

5 Existing or future goods

(1) The goods which form the subject of a contract of sale may be either existing goods, owned or possessed by the seller, or goods to be manufactured or acquired by him after the making of the contract of sale, in this Act called future goods.

(2) There may be a contract for the sale of goods the acquisition of which by the seller depends on a contingency which may or may not happen.

(3) Where by a contract of sale the seller purports to effect a present sale of future goods, the contract operates as an agreement to sell the goods.

6 Goods which have perished

Where there is a contract for the sale of specific goods, and the goods without the knowledge of the seller have perished at the time when a contract is made, the contract is void.

7 Goods perishing before sale but after agreement to sell

Where there is an agreement to sell specific goods and subsequently the goods, without any fault on the part of the seller or buyer, perish before the risk passes to the buyer, the agreement is avoided.

The price

8 Ascertainment of price

(1) The price in a contract of sale may be fixed by the contract, or may be left to be fixed in a manner agreed by the contract, or may be determined by the course of dealing between the parties.

(2) Where the price is not determined as mentioned in subsection (1) above the buyer must pay a reasonable price.

(3) What is a reasonable price is a question of fact dependent on the circumstances of each particular case.

9 Agreement to sell at valuation

(1) Where there is an agreement to sell goods on the terms that the price is to be fixed by the valuation of a third party, and he cannot or does not make the valuation, the agreement is avoided; but if the goods or any part of them have been delivered to and appropriated by the buyer he must pay a reasonable price for them.

(2) Where the third party is prevented from making the valuation by the fault of the seller or buyer, the party not at fault may maintain an action for damages against the party at fault.

[Implied terms etc]

10 Stipulations about time

(1) Unless a different intention appears from the terms of the contract, stipulations as to time of payment are not of the essence of a contract of sale.

(2) Whether any other stipulation as to time is or is not of the essence of the contract depends on the terms of the contract.

(3) In a contract of sale 'month' prima facie means calendar month.

11 [*Does not apply to Scotland.*]

12 Implied terms about title, etc

(1) In a contract of sale, other than one to which subsection (3) below applies, there is an implied [term] on the part of the seller that in the case of a sale he has a right to sell the goods, and in the case of an agreement to sell he will have such a right at the time when the property is to pass.

(2) In a contract of sale, other than one to which subsection (3) below applies, there is also an implied [term] that—

(a) the goods are free, and will remain free until the time when the property is to pass, from any charge or encumbrance not disclosed or known to the buyer before the contract is made, and

(b) the buyer will enjoy quiet possession of the goods except so far as it may be disturbed by the owner or other person entitled to the benefit of any charge or encumbrance so disclosed or known.

(3) This subsection applies to a contract of sale in the case of which there appears from the contract or is to be inferred from its circumstances an intention that the seller should transfer only such title as he or a third person may have.

(4) In a contract to which subsection (3) above applies there is an implied [term] that all charges or encumbrances known to the seller and not known to the buyer have been disclosed to the buyer before the contract is made.

(5) In a contract to which subsection (3) above applies there is also an implied [term] that none of the following will disturb the buyer's quiet possession of the goods, namely—

(a) the seller;

(b) in a case where the parties to the contract intend that the seller should transfer only such title as a third person may have, that person;

(c) anyone claiming through or under the seller or that third person otherwise than under a charge or encumbrance disclosed or known to the buyer before the contract is made.

[(5A) As regards England and Wales and Northern Ireland, the term implied by subsection (1) above is a condition and the terms implied by subsections (2), (4) and (5) above are warranties.]

(6) Paragraph 3 of Schedule 1 below applies in relation to a contract made before 18 May 1973.

[(7) This section does not apply to a contract to which Chapter 2 of Part 1 of the Consumer Rights Act 2015 applies (but see the provision made about such contracts in section 17 of that Act).]

13 Sale by description

(1) Where there is a contract for the sale of goods by description, there is an implied [term] that the goods will correspond with the description.

[(1A) As regards England and Wales and Northern Ireland, the term implied by subsection (1) above is a condition.]

(2) If the sale is by sample as well as by description it is not sufficient that the bulk of the goods corresponds with the sample if the goods do not also correspond with the description.

(3) A sale of goods is not prevented from being a sale by description by reason only that, being exposed for sale or hire, they are selected by the buyer.

(4) Paragraph 4 of Schedule 1 below applies in relation to a contract made before 18 May 1973.

[(5) This section does not apply to a contract to which Chapter 2 of Part 1 of the Consumer Rights Act 2015 applies (but see the provision made about such contracts in section 11 of that Act).]

14 Implied terms about quality or fitness

(1) Except as provided by this section and section 15 below and subject to any other enactment, there is no implied [term] about the quality or fitness for any particular purpose of goods supplied under a contract of sale.

[(2) Where the seller sells goods in the course of a business, there is an implied term that the goods supplied under the contract are of satisfactory quality.

(2A) For the purposes of this Act, goods are of satisfactory quality if they meet the standard that a reasonable person would regard as satisfactory, taking account of any description of the goods, the price (if relevant) and all the other relevant circumstances.

(2B) For the purposes of this Act, the quality of goods includes their state and condition and the following (among others) are in appropriate cases aspects of the quality of goods—

(a) fitness for all the purposes for which goods of the kind in question are commonly supplied,

(b) appearance and finish,

(c) freedom from minor defects,

(d) safety, and

(e) durability.

(2C) The term implied by subsection (2) above does not extend to any matter making the quality of goods unsatisfactory—

(a) which is specifically drawn to the buyer's attention before the contract is made,

(b) where the buyer examines the goods before the contract is made, which that examination ought to reveal, or

(c) in the case of a contract for sale by sample, which would have been apparent on a reasonable examination of the sample.]

[...]

(3) Where the seller sells goods in the course of a business and the buyer, expressly or by implication, makes known—

(a) to the seller, or

(b) where the purchase price or part of it is payable by instalments and the goods were previously sold by a credit-broker to the seller, to that credit-broker, any particular purpose for which the goods are being bought,

there is an implied [term] that the goods supplied under the contract are reasonably fit for that purpose, whether or not that is a purpose for which such goods are commonly supplied, except where the circumstances show that the buyer does not rely, or that it is unreasonable for him to rely, on the skill or judgment of the seller or credit-broker.

(4) An implied [term] about quality or fitness for a particular purpose may be annexed to a contract of sale by usage.

(5) The preceding provisions of this section apply to a sale by a person who in the course of a business is acting as agent for another as they apply to a sale by a principal in the course of a business, except where that other is not selling in the course of a business and either the buyer knows that fact or reasonable steps are taken to bring it to the notice of the buyer before the contract is made.

[(6) As regards England and Wales and Northern Ireland, the terms implied by subsections (2) and (3) above are conditions.]

(7) Paragraph 5 of Schedule 1 below applies in relation to a contract made on or after 18 May 1973 and before the appointed day, and paragraph 6 in relation to one made before 18 May 1973.

(8) In subsection (7) above and paragraph 5 of Schedule 1 below references to the appointed day are to the day appointed for the purposes of those provisions by an order of the Secretary of State made by statutory instrument.

[(9) This section does not apply to a contract to which Chapter 2 of Part 1 of the Consumer Rights Act 2015 applies (but see the provision made about such contracts in sections 9, 10 and 18 of that Act).]

Sale by sample

15 Sale by sample

(1) A contract of sale is a contract for sale by sample where there is an express or implied term to that effect in the contract.

(2) In the case of a contract for sale by sample there is an implied [term]—

(a) that the bulk will correspond with the sample in quality;

[. . .]

(c) that the goods will be free from any defect, making their quality unsatisfactory, which would not be apparent on reasonable examination of the sample.

[(3) As regards England and Wales and Northern Ireland, the term implied by subsection (2) above is a condition.]

(4) Paragraph 7 of Schedule 1 below applies in relation to a contract made before 18 May 1973.

[(5) This section does not apply to a contract to which Chapter 2 of Part 1 of the Consumer Rights Act 2015 applies (but see the provision made about such contracts in sections 13 and 18 of that Act).]

Miscellaneous

15A [*Does not apply to Scotland.*]

[15B Remedies for breach of contract as respects Scotland

(1) Where in a contract of sale the seller is in breach of any term of the contract (express or implied), the buyer shall be entitled—

(a) to claim damages, and

(b) if the breach is material, to reject any goods delivered under the contract and treat it as repudiated.

[(1A) Subsection (1) does not apply to a contract to which Chapter 2 of Part 1 of the Consumer Rights Act 2015 applies (but see the provision made about such contracts in sections 19 to 22 of that Act).]

[. . .]

(3) This section applies to Scotland only.]

PART III

EFFECTS OF THE CONTRACT

Transfer of property as between seller and buyer

16 Goods must be ascertained

[Subject to section 20A below] where there is a contract for the sale of unascertained goods no property in the goods is transferred to the buyer unless and until the goods are ascertained.

17 Property passes when intended to pass

(1) Where there is a contract for the sale of specific or ascertained goods the property in them is transferred to the buyer at such time as the parties to the contract intend it to be transferred.

(2) For the purpose of ascertaining the intention of the parties regard shall be had to the terms of the contract, the conduct of the parties and the circumstances of the case.

18 Rules for ascertaining intention

Unless a different intention appears, the following are rules for ascertaining the intention of the parties as to the time at which the property in the goods is to pass to the buyer.

Rule 1.—Where there is an unconditional contract for the sale of specific goods in a deliverable state the property in the goods passes to the buyer when the contract is made, and it is immaterial whether the time of payment or the time of delivery, or both, be postponed.

Rule 2.—Where there is a contract for the sale of specific goods and the seller is bound to do something to the goods for the purpose of putting them into a deliverable state, the property does not pass until the thing is done and the buyer has notice that it has been done.

Rule 3.—Where there is a contract for the sale of specific goods in a deliverable state but the seller is bound to weigh, measure, test, or do some other act or thing with reference to the goods for the purpose of ascertaining the price, the property does not pass until the act or thing is done and the buyer has notice that it has been done.

Rule 4.—When goods are delivered to the buyer on approval or on sale or return or other similar terms the property in the goods passes to the buyer:—

(a) when he signifies his approval or acceptance to the seller or does any other act adopting the transaction;

(b) if he does not signify his approval or acceptance to the seller but retains the goods without giving notice of rejection, then, if a time has been fixed for the return of the goods, on the expiration of that time, and, if no time has been fixed, on the expiration of a reasonable time.

Rule 5.—(1) Where there is a contract for the sale of unascertained or future goods by description, and goods of that description and in a deliverable state are unconditionally appropriated to the contract, either by the seller with the assent of the buyer or by the buyer with the assent of the seller, the property in the goods then passes to the buyer; and the assent may be express or implied, and may be given either before or after the appropriation is made.

(2) Where, in pursuance of the contract, the seller delivers the goods to the buyer or to a carrier or other bailee or custodier (whether named by the buyer or

not) for the purpose of transmission to the buyer, and does not reserve the right of disposal, he is to be taken to have unconditionally appropriated the goods to the contract.

[(3) Where there is a contract for the sale of a specified quantity of unascertained goods in a deliverable state forming part of a bulk which is identified either in the contract or by subsequent agreement between the parties and the bulk is reduced to (or to less than) that quantity, then, if the buyer under that contract is the only buyer to whom goods are then due out of the bulk—

(a) the remaining goods are to be taken as appropriated to that contract at the time when the bulk is so reduced; and

(b) the property in those goods then passes to that buyer.

(4) Paragraph (3) above applies also (with the necessary modifications) where a bulk is reduced to (or to less than) the aggregate of the quantities due to a single buyer under separate contracts relating to that bulk and he is the only buyer to whom goods are then due out of that bulk.]

19 Reservation of right of disposal

(1) Where there is a contract for the sale of specific goods or where goods are subsequently appropriated to the contract, the seller may, by the terms of the contract or appropriation, reserve the right of disposal of the goods until certain conditions are fulfilled; and in such a case, notwithstanding the delivery of the goods to the buyer, or to a carrier or other bailee or custodier for the purpose of transmission to the buyer, the property in the goods does not pass to the buyer until the conditions imposed by the seller are fulfilled.

(2) Where goods are shipped, and by the bill of lading the goods are deliverable to the order of the seller or his agent, the seller is prima facie to be taken to reserve the right of disposal.

(3) Where the seller of goods draws on the buyer for the price, and transmits the bill of exchange and bill of lading to the buyer together to secure acceptance or payment of the bill of exchange, the buyer is bound to return the bill of lading if he does not honour the bill of exchange, and if he wrongfully retains the bill of lading the property in the goods does not pass to him.

20 [Passing of risk]

(1) Unless otherwise agreed, the goods remain at the seller's risk until the property in them is transferred to the buyer, but when the property in them is transferred to the buyer the goods are at the buyer's risk whether delivery has been made or not.

(2) But where delivery has been delayed through the fault of either buyer or seller the goods are at the risk of the party at fault as regards any loss which might not have occurred but for such fault.

(3) Nothing in this section affects the duties or liabilities of either seller or buyer as a bailee or custodier of the goods of the other party.

[(4) This section does not apply to a contract to which Chapter 2 of Part 1 of the Consumer Rights Act 2015 applies (but see the provision made about such contracts in section 29 of that Act).]

[20A Undivided shares in goods forming part of a bulk

(1) This section applies to a contract for the sale of a specified quantity of unascertained goods if the following conditions are met—

(a) the goods or some of them form part of a bulk which is identified either in the contract or by subsequent agreement between the parties; and

(b) the buyer has paid the price for some or all of the goods which are the subject of the contract and which form part of the bulk.

(2) Where this section applies, then (unless the parties agree otherwise), as soon as the conditions specified in paragraphs (a) and (b) of subsection (1) above are met or at such later time as the parties may agree—

(a) property in an undivided share in the bulk is transferred to the buyer; and
(b) the buyer becomes an owner in common of the bulk.

(3) Subject to subsection (4) below, for the purposes of this section, the undivided share of a buyer in a bulk at any time shall be such share as the quantity of goods paid for and due to the buyer out of the bulk bears to the quantity of goods in the bulk at that time.

(4) Where the aggregate of the undivided shares of buyers in a bulk determined under subsection (3) above would at any time exceed the whole of the bulk at that time, the undivided share in the bulk of each buyer shall be reduced proportionately so that the aggregate of the undivided shares is equal to the whole bulk.

(5) Where a buyer has paid the price for only some of the goods due to him out of a bulk, any delivery to the buyer out of the bulk shall, for the purposes of this section, be ascribed in the first place to the goods in respect of which payment has been made.

(6) For the purpose of this section payment of part of the price for any goods shall be treated as payment for a corresponding part of the goods.]

[20B Deemed consent by co-owner to dealings in bulk goods

(1) A person who has become an owner in common of a bulk by virtue of section 20A above shall be deemed to have consented to—

(a) any delivery of goods out of the bulk to any other owner in common of the bulk, being goods which are due to him under his contract;

(b) any dealing with or removal, delivery or disposal of goods in the bulk by any other person who is an owner in common of the bulk in so far as the goods fall within that co-owner's undivided share in the bulk at the time of the removal, dealing, delivery or disposal.

(2) No cause of action shall accrue to anyone against a person by reason of that person having acted in accordance with paragraph (a) or (b) of subsection (1) above in reliance on any consent deemed to have been given under that subsection.

(3) Nothing in this section or section 20A above shall—

(a) impose an obligation on a buyer of goods out of a bulk to compensate any other buyer of goods out of that bulk for any shortfall in the goods received by that other buyer;

(b) affects any contractual arrangement between buyers of goods out of a bulk for adjustments between themselves; or

(c) affect the rights of any buyer under his contract.]

Transfer of title

21 Sale by person not the owner

(1) Subject to this Act, where goods are sold by a person who is not their owner, and who does not sell them under the authority or with the consent of the owner, the buyer acquires no better title to the goods than the seller had, unless the owner of the goods is by his conduct precluded from denying the seller's authority to sell.

(2) Nothing in this Act affects—

(a) the provisions of the Factors Acts or any enactment enabling the apparent owner of goods to dispose of them as if he were their true owner;

(b) the validity of any contract of sale under any special common law or statutory power of sale or under the order of a court of competent jurisdiction.

22 [Does not apply to Scotland.]

23 Sale under voidable title

When the seller of goods has a voidable title to them, but his title has not been avoided at the time of the sale, the buyer acquires a good title to the goods, provided he buys them in good faith and without notice of the seller's defect of title.

24 Seller in possession after sale

Where a person having sold goods continues or is in possession of the goods, or of the documents of title to the goods, the delivery or transfer by that person, or by a mercantile agent acting for him, of the goods or documents of title under any sale, pledge, or other disposition thereof, to any person receiving the same in good faith and without notice of the previous sale, has the same effect as if the person making the delivery or transfer were expressly authorised by the owner of the goods to make the same.

25 Buyer in possession after sale

(1) Where a person having bought or agreed to buy goods obtains, with the consent of the seller, possession of the goods or the documents of title to the goods, the delivery or transfer by that person, or by a mercantile agent acting for him, of the goods or documents of title, under any sale, pledge, or other disposition thereof, to any person receiving the same in good faith and without notice of any lien or other right of the original seller in respect of the goods, has the same effect as if the person making the delivery or transfer were a mercantile agent in possession of the goods or documents of title with the consent of the owner.

(2) For the purposes of subsection (1) above—

(a) the buyer under a conditional sale agreement is to be taken not to be a person who has bought or agreed to buy goods, and

(b) 'conditional sale agreement' means an agreement for the sale of goods which is a consumer credit agreement within the meaning of the Consumer Credit Act 1974 under which the purchase price or part of it is payable by instalments, and the property in the goods is to remain in the seller (notwithstanding that the buyer is to be in possession of the goods) until such conditions as to the payment of instalments or otherwise as may be specified in the agreement are fulfilled.

(3) Paragraph 9 of Schedule 1 below applies in relation to a contract under which a person buys or agrees to buy goods and which is made before the appointed day.

(4) In subsection (3) above and paragraph 9 of Schedule 1 below references to the appointed day are to the day appointed for the purposes of those provisions by an order of the Secretary of State made by statutory instrument.

26 Supplementary to sections 24 and 25

In sections 24 and 25 above 'mercantile agent' means a mercantile agent having in the customary course of his business as such agent authority either—

(a) to sell goods, or
(b) to consign goods for the purpose of sale, or
(c) to buy goods, or
(d) to raise money on the security of goods.

PART IV
PERFORMANCE OF THE CONTRACT

27 Duties of seller and buyer

It is the duty of the seller to deliver the goods, and of the buyer to accept and pay for them, in accordance with the terms of the contract of sale.

28 Payment and delivery are concurrent conditions

Unless otherwise agreed, delivery of the goods and payment of the price are concurrent conditions, that is to say, the seller must be ready and willing to give possession of the goods to the buyer in exchange for the price and the buyer must be ready and willing to pay the price in exchange for possession of the goods.

29 Rules about delivery

(1) Whether it is for the buyer to take possession of the goods or for the seller to send them to the buyer is a question depending in each case on the contract, express or implied, between the parties.

(2) Apart from any such contract, express or implied, the place of delivery is the seller's place of business if he has one, and if not, his residence; except that, if the contract is for the sale of specific goods, which to the knowledge of the parties when the contract is made are in some other place, then that place is the place of delivery.

(3) Where under the contract of sale the seller is bound to send the goods to the buyer, but no time for sending them is fixed, the seller is bound to send them within a reasonable time.

[(3A) Subsection (3) does not apply to a contract to which Chapter 2 of Part 1 of the Consumer Rights Act 2015 applies (but see the provision made about such contracts in section 28 of that Act).]

(4) Where the goods at the time of sale are in the possession of a third person, there is no delivery by seller to buyer unless and until the third person acknowledges to the buyer that he holds the goods on his behalf; but nothing in this section affects the operation of the issue or transfer of any document of title to goods.

(5) Demand or tender of delivery may be treated as ineffectual unless made at a reasonable hour, and what is a reasonable hour is a question of fact.

(6) Unless otherwise agreed, the expenses of and incidental to putting the goods into a deliverable state must be borne by the seller.

30 Delivery of wrong quantity

(1) Where the seller delivers to the buyer a quantity of goods less than he contracted to sell, the buyer may reject them, but if the buyer accepts the goods so delivered he must pay for them at the contract rate.

(2) Where the seller delivers to the buyer a quantity of goods larger than he contracted to sell, the buyer may accept the goods included in the contract and reject the rest, or he may reject the whole.

. . .

[(2C) Subsections (2A) and (2B) above do not apply to Scotland.

(2D) Where the seller delivers a quantity of goods—

(a) less than he contracted to sell, the buyer shall not be entitled to reject the goods under subsection (1) above,

(b) larger than he contracted to sell, the buyer shall not be entitled to reject the whole under subsection (2) above,

unless the shortfall or excess is material.

(2E) Subsection (2D) above applies to Scotland only.]

(3) Where the seller delivers to the buyer a quantity of goods larger than he contracted to sell and the buyer accepts the whole of the goods so delivered he must pay for them at the contract rate.

[. . .]

(5) This section is subject to any usage of trade, special agreement, or course of dealing between the parties.

[(6) This section does not apply to a contract to which Chapter 2 of Part 1 of the Consumer Rights Act 2015 applies (but see the provision made about such contracts in section 25 of that Act).]

31 Instalment deliveries

(1) Unless otherwise agreed, the buyer of goods is not bound to accept delivery of them by instalments.

(2) Where there is a contract for the sale of goods to be delivered by stated instalments, which are to be separately paid for, and the seller makes defective deliveries in respect of one or more instalments, or the buyer neglects or refuses to take

delivery of or pay for one or more instalments, it is a question in each case depending on the terms of the contract and the circumstances of the case whether the breach of contract is a repudiation of the whole contract or whether it is a severable breach giving rise to a claim for compensation but not to a right to treat the whole contract as repudiated.

[(3) This section does not apply to a contract to which Chapter 2 of Part 1 of the Consumer Rights Act 2015 applies (but see the provision made about such contracts in section 26 of that Act).]

32 Delivery to carrier

(1) Where, in pursuance of a contract of sale, the seller is authorised or required to send the goods to the buyer, delivery of the goods to a carrier (whether named by the buyer or not) for the purpose of transmission to the buyer is prima facie deemed to be delivery of the goods to the buyer.

(2) Unless otherwise authorised by the buyer, the seller must make such contract with the carrier on behalf of the buyer as may be reasonable having regard to the nature of the goods and the other circumstances of the case; and if the seller omits to do so, and the goods are lost or damaged in course of transit, the buyer may decline to treat the delivery to the carrier as a delivery to himself or may hold the seller responsible in damages.

(3) Unless otherwise agreed, where goods are sent by the seller to the buyer by a route involving sea transit, under circumstances in which it is usual to insure, the seller must give such notice to the buyer as may enable him to insure them during their sea transit, and if the seller fails to do so, the goods are at his risk during such sea transit.

[(4) This section does not apply to a contract to which Chapter 2 of Part 1 of the Consumer Rights Act 2015 applies (but see the provision made about such contracts in section 29 of that Act).]

33 Risk where goods are delivered at distant place

[(1)] Where the seller of goods agrees to deliver them at his own risk at a place other than that where they are when sold, the buyer must nevertheless (unless otherwise agreed) take any risk of deterioration in the goods necessarily incident to the course of transit.

[(2) This section does not apply to a contract to which Chapter 2 of Part 1 of the Consumer Rights Act 2015 applies (but see the provision made about such contracts in section 29 of that Act).]

34 Buyer's right of examining the goods

[(1)] [Unless otherwise agreed, when the seller tenders delivery of goods to the buyer, he is bound on request to afford the buyer a reasonable opportunity of examining the goods for the purpose of ascertaining whether they are in conformity with the contract and, in the case of a contract for sale by sample, of comparing the bulk with the sample.]

[(2) Nothing in this section affects the operation of section 22 (time limit for short-term right to reject) of the Consumer Rights Act 2015.]

35 Acceptance

(1) The buyer is deemed to have accepted the goods [subject to subsection (2) below—

(a) when he intimates to the seller that he has accepted them, or

(b) when the goods have been delivered to him and he does any act in relation to them which is inconsistent with the ownership of the seller.

(2) Where goods are delivered to the buyer, and he has not previously examined them, he is not deemed to have accepted them under subsection (1) above until he has had a reasonable opportunity of examining them for the purpose—

(a) of ascertaining whether they are in conformity with the contract, and

(b) in the case of a contract for sale by sample, of comparing the bulk with the sample.

[. . .]

(4) The buyer is also deemed to have accepted the goods when after the lapse of a reasonable time he retains the goods without intimating to the seller that he has rejected them.

(5) The questions that are material in determining for the purposes of subsection (4) above whether a reasonable time has elapsed include whether the buyer has had a reasonable opportunity of examining the goods for the purpose mentioned in subsection (2) above.

(6) The buyer is not by virtue of this section deemed to have accepted the goods merely because—

(a) he asks for, or agrees to, their repair by or under an arrangement with the seller, or

(b) the goods are delivered to another under a sub-sale or other disposition.

(7) Where the contract is for the sale of goods making one or more commercial units, a buyer accepting any goods included in a unit is deemed to have accepted all the goods making the unit; and in this subsection 'commercial unit' means a unit division of which would materially impair the value of the goods or the character of the unit.

(8)] Paragraph 10 of Schedule 1 below applies in relation to a contract made before 22 April 1967 or (in the application of this Act to Northern Ireland) 28 July 1967.

[(9) This section does not apply to a contract to which Chapter 2 of Part 1 of the Consumer Rights Act 2015 applies (but see the provision made about such contracts in section 21 of that Act).]

[35A Right of partial rejection

(1) If the buyer—

(a) has the right to reject the goods by reason of a breach on the part of the seller that affects some or all of them, but

(b) accepts some of the goods, including, where there are any goods unaffected by the breach, all such goods,

he does not by accepting them lose his right to reject the rest.

(2) In the case of a buyer having the right to reject an instalment of goods, subsection (1) above applies as if references to the goods were references to the goods comprised in the instalment.

(3) For the purposes of subsection (1) above, goods are affected by a breach if by reason of the breach they are not in conformity with the contract.

(4) This section applies unless a contrary intention appears in, or is to be implied from, the contract.]

[(5) This section does not apply to a contract to which Chapter 2 of Part 1 of the Consumer Rights Act 2015 applies (but see the provision made about such contracts in section 21 of that Act).]

36 Buyer not bound to return rejected goods

[(1)] Unless otherwise agreed, where goods are delivered to the buyer, and he refuses to accept them, having the right to do so, he is not bound to return them to the seller, but it is sufficient if he intimates to the seller that he refuses to accept them.

[(2) This section does not apply to a contract to which Chapter 2 of Part 1 of the Consumer Rights Act 2015 applies (but see the provision made about such contracts in section 20 of that Act).]

37 Buyer's liability for not taking delivery of goods

(1) When the seller is ready and willing to deliver the goods, and requests the

buyer to take delivery, and the buyer does not within a reasonable time after such request take delivery of the goods, he is liable to the seller for any loss occasioned by his neglect or refusal to take delivery, and also for a reasonable charge for the care and custody of the goods.

(2) Nothing in this section affects the rights of the seller where the neglect or refusal of the buyer to take delivery amounts to a repudiation of the contract.

PART V
RIGHTS OF UNPAID SELLER AGAINST THE GOODS

Preliminary

38 Unpaid seller defined

(1) The seller of goods is an unpaid seller within the meaning of this Act—

(a) when the whole of the price has not been paid or tendered;

(b) when a bill of exchange or other negotiable instrument has been received as conditional payment, and the condition on which it was received has not been fulfilled by reason of the dishonour of the instrument or otherwise.

(2) In this Part of this Act 'seller' includes any person who is in the position of a seller, as, for instance, an agent of the seller to whom the bill of lading has been indorsed, or a consignor or agent who has himself paid (or is directly responsible for) the price.

39 Unpaid seller's rights

(1) Subject to this and any other Act, notwithstanding that the property in the goods may have passed to the buyer, the unpaid seller of goods, as such, has by implication of law—

(a) a lien on the goods or right to retain them for the price while he is in possession of them;

(b) in the case of the insolvency of the buyer, a right of stopping the goods in transit after he has parted with the possession of them;

(c) a right of re-sale as limited by this Act.

(2) Where the property in goods has not passed to the buyer, the unpaid seller has (in addition to his other remedies) a right of withholding delivery similar to and coextensive with his rights of lien or retention and stoppage in transit where the property has passed to the buyer.

[. . .]

Unpaid seller's lien

41 Seller's lien

(1) Subject to this Act, the unpaid seller of goods who is in possession of them is entitled to retain possession of them until payment or tender of the price in the following cases:—

(a) where the goods have been sold without any stipulation as to credit;

(b) where the goods have been sold on credit but the term of credit has expired;

(c) where the buyer becomes insolvent.

(2) The seller may exercise his lien or right of retention notwithstanding that he is in possession of the goods as agent or bailee or custodier for the buyer.

42 Part delivery

Where an unpaid seller has made part delivery of the goods, he may exercise his lien or right of retention on the remainder, unless such part delivery has been made under such circumstances as to show an agreement to waive the lien or right of retention.

43 Termination of lien

(1) The unpaid seller of goods loses his lien or right of retention in respect of them—

(a) when he delivers the goods to a carrier or other bailee or custodier for the purpose of transmission to the buyer without reserving the right of disposal of the goods;

(b) when the buyer or his agent lawfully obtains possession of the goods;

(c) by waiver of the lien or right of retention.

(2) An unpaid seller of goods who has a lien or right of retention in respect of them does not lose his lien or right of retention by reason only that he has obtained judgment or decree for the price of the goods.

Stoppage in transit

44 Right of stoppage in transit

Subject to this Act, when the buyer of goods becomes insolvent the unpaid seller who has parted with the possession of the goods has the right of stopping them in transit, that is to say, he may resume possession of the goods as long as they are in course of transit, and may retain them until payment or tender of the price.

45 Duration of transit

(1) Goods are deemed to be in course of transit from the time when they are delivered to a carrier or other bailee or custodier for the purpose of transmission to the buyer, until the buyer or his agent in that behalf takes delivery of them from the carrier or other bailee or custodier.

(2) If the buyer or his agent in that behalf obtains delivery of the goods before their arrival at the appointed destination, the transit is at an end.

(3) If, after the arrival of the goods at the appointed destination, the carrier or other bailee or custodier acknowledges to the buyer or his agent that he holds the goods on his behalf and continues in possession of them as bailee or custodier for the buyer or his agent, the transit is at an end, and it is immaterial that a further destination for the goods may have been indicated by the buyer.

(4) If the goods are rejected by the buyer, and the carrier or other bailee or custodier continues in possession of them, the transit is not deemed to be at an end, even if the seller has refused to receive them back.

(5) When goods are delivered to a ship chartered by the buyer it is a question depending on the circumstances of the particular case whether they are in the possession of the master as a carrier or as agent to the buyer.

(6) Where the carrier or other bailee or custodier wrongfully refuses to deliver the goods to the buyer or his agent in that behalf, the transit is deemed to be at an end.

(7) Where part delivery of the goods has been made to the buyer or his agent in that behalf, the remainder of the goods may be stopped in transit, unless such part delivery has been made under such circumstances as to show an agreement to give up possession of the whole of the goods.

46 How stoppage in transit is effected

(1) The unpaid seller may exercise his right of stoppage in transit either by taking actual possession of the goods or by giving notice of his claim to the carrier or other bailee or custodier in whose possession the goods are.

(2) The notice may be given either to the person in actual possession of the goods or to his principal.

(3) If given to the principal, the notice is ineffective unless given at such time and under such circumstances that the principal, by the exercise of reasonable diligence, may communicate it to his servant or agent in time to prevent a delivery to the buyer.

(4) When notice of stoppage in transit is given by the seller to the carrier or

other bailee or custodier in possession of the goods, he must re-deliver the goods to, or according to the directions of, the seller; and the expenses of the re-delivery must be borne by the seller.

Re-sale etc by buyer

47 Effect of sub-sale etc by buyer

(1) Subject to this Act, the unpaid seller's right of lien or retention or stoppage in transit is not affected by any sale or other disposition of the goods which the buyer may have made, unless the seller has assented to it.

(2) Where a document of title to goods has been lawfully transferred to any person as buyer or owner of the goods, and that person transfers the document to a person who takes it in good faith and for valuable consideration, then—

(a) if the last-mentioned transfer was by way of sale the unpaid seller's right of lien or retention or stoppage in transit is defeated; and

(b) if the last-mentioned transfer was made by way of pledge or other disposition for value, the unpaid seller's right of lien or retention or stoppage in transit can only be exercised subject to the rights of the transferee.

Rescission: and re-sale by seller

48 Rescission: and re-sale by seller

(1) Subject to this section, a contract of sale is not rescinded by the mere exercise by an unpaid seller of his right of lien or retention or stoppage in transit.

(2) Where an unpaid seller who has exercised his right of lien or retention or stoppage in transit re-sells the goods, the buyer acquires a good title to them as against the original buyer.

(3) Where the goods are of a perishable nature, or where the unpaid seller gives notice to the buyer of his intention to re-sell, and the buyer does not within a reasonable time pay or tender the price, the unpaid seller may re-sell the goods and recover from the original buyer damages for any loss occasioned by his breach of contract.

(4) Where the seller expressly reserves the right of re-sale in case the buyer should make default, and on the buyer making default re-sells the goods, the original contract of sale is rescinded but without prejudice to any claim the seller may have for damages.

[. . .]

PART VI
ACTIONS FOR BREACH OF THE CONTRACT

Seller's remedies

49 Action for price

(1) Where, under a contract of sale, the property in the goods has passed to the buyer and he wrongfully neglects or refuses to pay for the goods according to the terms of the contract, the seller may maintain an action against him for the price of the goods.

(2) Where, under a contract of sale, the price is payable on a day certain irrespective of delivery and the buyer wrongfully neglects or refuses to pay such price, the seller may maintain an action for the price, although the property in goods has not passed and the goods have not been appropriated to the contract.

(3) Nothing in this section prejudices the right of the seller in Scotland to recover interest on the price from the date of tender of the goods, or from the date on which the price was payable, as the case may be.

50 Damages for non-acceptance

(1) Where the buyer wrongfully neglects or refuses to accept and pay for the goods, the seller may maintain an action against him for damages for nonacceptance.

(2) The measure of damages is the estimated loss directly and naturally resulting in the ordinary course of events, from the buyer's breach of contract.

(3) Where there is an available market for the goods in question the measure of damages is prima facie to be ascertained by the difference between the contract price and the market or current price at the time or times when the goods ought to have been accepted or (if no time was fixed for acceptance) at the time of the refusal to accept.

Buyer's remedies

51 Damages for non-delivery

(1) Where the seller wrongfully neglects or refuses to deliver the goods to the buyer, the buyer may maintain an action against the seller for damages for nondelivery.

(2) The measure of damages is the estimated loss directly and naturally resulting, in the ordinary course of events, from the seller's breach of contract.

(3) Where there is an available market for the goods in question the measure of damages is prima facie to be ascertained by the difference between the contract price and the market or current price of the goods at the time or times when they ought to have been delivered or (if no time was fixed) at the time of the refusal to deliver.

[(4) This section does not apply to a contract to which Chapter 2 of Part 1 of the Consumer Rights Act 2015 applies (but see the provision made about such contracts in section 19 of that Act).]

52 Specific performance

(1) In any action for breach of contract to deliver specific or ascertained goods the court may, if it thinks fit, on the plaintiff's application, by its judgment or decree direct that the contract shall be performed specifically, without giving the defendant the option of retaining the goods on payment of damages.

(2) The plaintiff's application may be made at any time before judgment or decree.

(3) The judgment or decree may be unconditional, or on such terms and conditions as to damages, payment of the price and otherwise as seem just to the court.

(4) The provisions of this section shall be deemed to be supplementary to, and not in derogation of, the right of specific implement in Scotland.

[(5) This section does not apply to a contract to which Chapter 2 of Part 1 of the Consumer Rights Act 2015 applies (but see the provision made about such contracts in section 19 of that Act).]

53 [*Does not apply to Scotland.*]

[53A Measure of damages as respects Scotland

(1) The measure of damages for the seller's breach of contract is the estimated loss directly and naturally resulting, in the ordinary course of events, from the breach.

(2) Where the seller's breach consists of the delivery of goods which are not of the quality required by the contract and the buyer retains the goods, such loss as aforesaid is prima facie the difference between the value of the goods at the time of delivery to the buyer and the value they would have had if they had fulfilled the contract.

[(2A) This section does not apply to a contract to which Chapter 2 of Part 1 of the Consumer Rights Act 2015 applies (but see the provision made about such contracts in section 19 of that Act).]

(3) This section applies to Scotland only.]

Interest, etc

54 Interest, etc

[(1)] Nothing in this Act affects the right of the buyer or the seller to recover interest or special damages in any case where by law interest or special damages may be recoverable, or to recover money paid where the consideration for the payment of it has failed.

[(2) This section does not apply to a contract to which Chapter 2 of Part 1 of the Consumer Rights Act 2015 applies (but see the provision made about such contracts in section 19 of that Act.]

PART VII
SUPPLEMENTARY

55 Exclusion of implied terms

(1) Where a right, duty or liability would arise under a contract of sale of goods by implication of law, it may (subject to the Unfair Contract Terms Act 1977) be negatived or varied by express agreement, or by the course of dealing between the parties, or by such usage as binds both parties to the contract.

[(1A) Subsection (1) does not apply to a contract to which Chapter 2 of Part 1 of the Consumer Rights Act 2015 applies (but see the provision made about such contracts in section 31 of that Act).]

(2) An express [term] does not negative a [term] implied by this Act unless inconsistent with it.

(3) Paragraph 11 of Schedule 1 below applies in relation to a contract made on or after 18 May 1973 and before 1 February 1978, and paragraph 12 in relation to one made before 18 May 1973.

56 Conflict of laws

Paragraph 13 of Schedule 1 below applies in relation to a contract made on or after 18 May 1973 and before 1 February 1978, so as to make provision about conflict of laws in relation to such a contract.

57 Auction sales

(1) Where goods are put up for sale by auction in lots, each lot is prima facie deemed to be the subject of a separate contract of sale.

(2) A sale by auction is complete when the auctioneer announces its completion by the fall of the hammer, or in other customary manner; and until the announcement is made any bidder may retract his bid.

(3) A sale by auction may be notified to be subject to a reserve or upset price, and a right to bid may also be reserved expressly by or on behalf of the seller.

(4) Where a sale by auction is not notified to be subject to a right to bid by or on behalf of the seller, it is not lawful for the seller to bid himself or to employ any person to bid at the sale, or for the auctioneer knowingly to take any bid from the seller or any such person.

(5) A sale contravening subsection (4) above may be treated as fraudulent by the buyer.

(6) Where, in respect of a sale by auction, a right to bid is expressly reserved (but not otherwise) the seller or any one person on his behalf may bid at the auction.

58 Payment into court in Scotland

[(1)] In Scotland where a buyer has elected to accept goods which he might have rejected, and to treat a breach of contract as only giving rise to a claim for damages, he may, in an action by the seller for the price, be required, in the discretion of the court before which the action depends, to consign or pay into court the price of the goods, or part of the price, or to give other reasonable security for its due payment.

[(2) This section does not apply to a contract to which Chapter 2 of Part 1 of the Consumer Rights Act 2015 applies (but see the provision made about such contracts in section 27 of that Act).]

59 Reasonable time a question of fact

Where a reference is made in this Act to a reasonable time the question what is a reasonable time is a question of fact.

60 Rights etc enforceable by action

Where a right, duty or liability is declared by this Act, it may (unless otherwise provided by this Act) be enforced by action.

61 Interpretation

(1) In this Act, unless the context or subject matter otherwise requires,—

'action' includes counterclaim and set-off, and in Scotland condescendence and claim and compensation;

['bulk' means a mass or collection of goods of the same kind which—

(a) is contained in a defined space or area; and

(b) is such that any goods in the bulk are interchangeable with any other goods therein of the same number or quantity;]

'business' includes a profession and the activities of any government department (including a Northern Ireland department) or local or public authority;

'buyer' means a person who buys or agrees to buy goods;

[. . .]

'contract of sale' includes an agreement to sell as well as a sale;

'credit-broker' means a person acting in the course of a business of credit brokerage carried on by him, that is a business of effecting introductions of individuals desiring to obtain credit—

(a) to persons carrying on any business so far as it relates to the provision of credit, or

(b) to other persons engaged in credit brokerage;

'defendant' includes in Scotland defender, respondent, and claimant in a multiplepoinding;

'delivery' means voluntary transfer of possession from one person to another; [except that in relation to sections 20A and 20B above it includes such appropriation of goods to the contract as results in property in the goods being transferred to the buyer;]

'document of title to goods' has the same meaning as it has in the Factors Acts;

'Factors Acts' means the Factors Act 1889, the Factors (Scotland) Act 1890, and any enactment amending or substituted for the same;

'fault' means wrongful act or default;

'future goods' means goods to be manufactured or acquired by the seller after the making of the contract of sale;

'goods' includes all personal chattels other than things in action and money, and in Scotland all corporeal moveables except money; and in particular 'goods' includes emblements, industrial growing crops, and things attached to or forming part of the land which are agreed to be severed before sale or under the contract of sale; [and includes an undivided share in goods;]

'plaintiff' includes pursuer, complainer, claimant in a multiplepoinding and defendant or defender counter-claiming;

[. . .]

'property' means the general property in goods, and not merely a special property;

[. . .]

'sale' includes a bargain and sale as well as a sale and delivery;

'seller' means a person who sells or agrees to sell goods;

'specific goods' means goods identified and agreed on at the time a contract of sale is made; [and includes an undivided share, specified as a fraction or percentage, of goods identified and agreed on as aforesaid;]

'warranty' (as regards England and Wales and Northern Ireland) means an agreement with reference to goods which are the subject of a contract of sale, but collateral to the main purpose of such contract, the breach of which gives rise to a claim for damages, but not to a right to reject the goods and treat the contract as repudiated.

[. . .]

(3) A thing is deemed to be done in good faith within the meaning of this Act when it is in fact done honestly, whether it is done negligently or not.

(4) A person is deemed to be insolvent within the meaning of this Act if he has either ceased to pay his debts in the ordinary course of business or he cannot pay his debts as they become due, [. . .]

(5) Goods are in a deliverable state within the meaning of this Act when they are in such a state that the buyer would under the contract be bound to take delivery of them.

[. . .]

(6) As regards the definition of 'business' in subsection (1) above, paragraph 14 of Schedule 1 below applies in relation to a contract made on or after 18 May 1973 and before 1 February 1978, and paragraph 15 in relation to one made before 18 May 1973,

62 Savings: rules of law etc

(1) The rules in bankruptcy relating to contracts of sale apply to those contracts, notwithstanding anything in this Act.

(2) The rules of the common law, including the law merchant, except in so far as they are inconsistent with the provisions of [legislation including this Act and the Consumer Rights Act 2015], and in particular the rules relating to the law of principal and agent and the effect of fraud, misrepresentation, duress or coercion, mistake, or other invalidating cause, apply to contracts for the sale of goods.

(3) Nothing in this Act or the Sale of Goods Act 1893 affects the enactments relating to bills of sale, or any enactment relating to the sale of goods which is not expressly repealed or amended by this Act or that.

(4) The provisions of this Act about contracts of sale do not apply to a transaction in the form of a contract of sale which is intended to operate by way of mortgage, pledge, charge, or other security.

(5) Nothing in this Act prejudices or affects the landlord's right of hypothec [. . .] in Scotland.

64 Short title and commencement

(1) This Act may be cited as the Sale of Goods Act 1979.

(2) This Act comes into force on 1 January 1980.

SUPPLY OF GOODS AND SERVICES ACT 1982
(1982, c 29)

[PART IA
SUPPLY OF GOODS AS RESPECTS SCOTLAND

Contracts for the transfer of property in goods

[11A The contracts concerned

(1) In this Act in its application to Scotland a ['relevant contract for the transfer of goods'] means a contract under which one person transfers or agrees to transfer to another the property in goods, other than an excepted contract [, and other than a contract to which Chapter 2 of Part 1 of the Consumer Rights Act 2015 applies].

(2) For the purposes of this section an excepted contract means any of the following—

(a) a contract of sale of goods;

(b) a hire-purchase agreement;

[. . .]

(d) a transfer or agreement to transfer for which there is no consideration;

(e) a contract intended to operate by way of mortgage, pledge, charge or other security.

(3) For the purposes of this Act in its application to Scotland a contract is a [relevant contract for the transfer of goods] whether or not services are also provided or to be provided under the contract, and (subject to subsection (2) above) whatever is the nature of the consideration for the transfer or agreement to transfer.]

[11B Implied terms about title, etc

(1) In a [relevant contract for the transfer of goods], other than one to which subsection (3) below applies, there is an implied term on the part of the transferor that in the case of a transfer of the property in the goods he has a right to transfer the property and in the case of an agreement to transfer the property in the goods he will have such a right at the time when the property is to be transferred.

(2) In a [relevant contract for the transfer of goods], other than one to which subsection (3) below applies, there is also an implied term that—

(a) the goods are free, and will remain free until the time when the property is to be transferred, from any charge or encumbrance not disclosed or known to the transferee before the contract is made, and

(b) the transferee will enjoy quiet possession of the goods except so far as it may be disturbed by the owner or other person entitled to the benefit of any charge or encumbrance so disclosed or known.

(3) This subsection applies to a [relevant contract for the transfer of goods] in the case of which there appears from the contract or is to be inferred from its circumstances an intention that the transferor should transfer only such title as he or a third person may have.

(4) In a contract to which subsection (3) above applies there is an implied term that all charges or encumbrances known to the transferor and not known to the transferee have been disclosed to the transferee before the contract is made.

(5) In a contract to which subsection (3) above applies there is also an implied term that none of the following will disturb the transferee's quiet possession of the goods, namely—

(a) the transferor;

(b) in a case where the parties to the contract intend that the transferor should transfer only such title as a third person may have, that person;

(c) anyone claiming through or under the transferor or that third person otherwise than under a charge or encumbrance disclosed or known to the transferee before the contract is made.]

(6) [*amends Unfair Contract Terms Act 1977*]

[11C Implied terms where transfer is by description

(1) This section applies where, under a [relevant contract for the transfer of goods], the transferor transfers or agrees to transfer the property in the goods by description.

(2) In such a case there is an implied term that the goods will correspond with the description.

(3) If the transferor transfers or agrees to transfer the property in the goods by reference to a sample as well as by description it is not sufficient that the bulk of the goods corresponds with the sample if the goods do not also correspond with the description.

(4) A contract is not prevented from falling within subsection (1) above by reason only that, being exposed for supply, the goods are selected by the transferee.]

[11D Implied terms about quality or fitness

(1) Except as provided by this section and section 11E below and subject to the provisions of any other enactment, there is no implied term about the quality or fitness for any particular purpose of goods supplied under a [relevant contract for the transfer of goods].

(2) Where, under such a contract, the transferor transfers the property in goods in the course of a business, there is an implied term that the goods supplied under the contract are of satisfactory quality.

(3) For the purposes of this section and section 11E below, goods are of satisfactory quality if they meet the standard that a reasonable person would regard as satisfactory, taking account of any description of the goods, the price (if relevant) and all the other relevant circumstances.

[. . .]

(4) The term implied by subsection (2) above does not extend to any matter making the quality of goods unsatisfactory—

(a) which is specifically drawn to the transferee's attention before the contract is made,

(b) where the transferee examines the goods before the contract is made, which that examination ought to reveal, or

(c) where the property in the goods is, or is to be, transferred by reference to a sample, which would have been apparent on a reasonable examination of the sample.

(5) Subsection (6) below applies where, under a [relevant contract for the transfer of goods], the transferor transfers the property in goods in the course of a business and the transferee, expressly or by implication, makes known—

(a) to the transferor, or

(b) where the consideration or part of the consideration for the transfer is a sum payable by instalments and the goods were previously sold by a creditbroker to the transferor, to that credit-broker,

any particular purpose for which the goods are being acquired.

(6) In that case there is (subject to subsection (7) below) an implied term that the goods supplied under the contract are reasonably fit for the purpose, whether or not that is a purpose for which such goods are commonly supplied.

(7) Subsection (6) above does not apply where the circumstances show that the transferee does not rely, or that it is unreasonable for him to rely, on the skill or judgment of the transferor or credit-broker.

(8) An implied term about quality or fitness for a particular purpose may be annexed by usage to a [relevant contract for the transfer of goods].

(9) The preceding provisions of this section apply to a transfer by a person who in the course of a business is acting as agent for another as they apply to a transfer by a principal in the course of a business, except where that other is not transferring in the course of a business and either the transferee knows that fact or

reasonable steps are taken to bring it to the transferee's notice before the contract concerned is made.

[. . .]]

[11E Implied terms where transfer is by sample

(1) This section applies where, under a [relevant contract for the transfer of goods], the transferor transfers or agrees to transfer the property in the goods by reference to a sample.

(2) In such a case there is an implied term—

(a) that the bulk will correspond with the sample in quality;

(b) that the transferee will have a reasonable opportunity of comparing the bulk with the sample; and

(c) that the goods will be free from any defect, making their quality unsatisfactory, which would not be apparent on reasonable examination of the sample.

(3) For the purposes of this section a transferor transfers or agrees to transfer the property in goods by reference to a sample where there is an express or implied term to that effect in the contract concerned.]

[11F Remedies for breach of contract

(1) Where in a [relevant contract for the transfer of goods] a transferor is in breach of any term of the contract (express or implied), the other party to the contract (in this section referred to as 'the transferee') shall be entitled—

(a) to claim damages; and

(b) if the breach is material, to reject any goods delivered under the contract and treat it as repudiated.

[. . .]]

Contracts for the hire of goods

[11G The contracts concerned

(1) In this Act in its application to Scotland a '[relevant contract for the hire of goods'] means a contract under which one person ('the supplier') hires or agrees to hire goods to another, other than [a hire-purchase agreement] [and other than a contract to which Chapter 2 of Part 1 of the Consumer Rights Act 2015 applies].

[. . .]

(3) For the purposes of this Act in its application to Scotland a contract is a [relevant contract for the hire of goods] whether or not services are also provided or to be provided under the contract, and [. . .] whatever is the nature of the consideration for the hire or agreement to hire.]

[11H Implied terms about right to transfer possession etc

(1) In a [relevant contract for the hire of goods] there is an implied term on the part of the supplier that—

(a) in the case of a hire, he has a right to transfer possession of the goods by way of hire for the period of the hire; and

(b) in the case of an agreement to hire, he will have such a right at the time of commencement of the period of the hire.

(2) In a [relevant contract for the hire of goods] there is also an implied term that the person to whom the goods are hired will enjoy quiet possession of the goods for the period of the hire except so far as the possession may be disturbed by the owner or other person entitled to the benefit of any charge or encumbrance disclosed or known to the person to whom the goods are hired before the contract is made.

(3) The preceding provisions of this section do not affect the right of the supplier to repossess the goods under an express or implied term of the contract.]

[11I Implied terms where hire is by description

(1) This section applies where, under a [relevant contract for the hire of goods], the supplier hires or agrees to hire the goods by description.

(2) In such a case there is an implied term that the goods will correspond with the description.

(3) If under the contract the supplier hires or agrees to hire the goods by reference to a sample as well as by description it is not sufficient that the bulk of the goods corresponds with the sample if the goods do not also correspond with the description.

(4) A contract is not prevented from falling within subsection (1) above by reason only that, being exposed for supply, the goods are selected by the person to whom the goods are hired.]

[11J Implied terms about quality or fitness

(1) Except as provided by this section and section 11K below and subject to the provisions of any other enactment, there is no implied term about the quality or fitness for any particular purpose of goods hired under a [relevant contract for the hire of goods].

(2) Where, under such a contract, the supplier hires goods in the course of a business, there is an implied term that the goods supplied under the contract are of satisfactory quality.

(3) For the purposes of this section and section 11K below, goods are of satisfactory quality if they meet the standard that a reasonable person would regard as satisfactory, taking account of any description of the goods, the consideration for the hire (if relevant) and all the other relevant circumstances.

[. . .]

(4) The term implied by subsection (2) above does not extend to any matter making the quality of goods unsatisfactory—

(a) which is specifically drawn to the attention of the person to whom the goods are hired before the contract is made, or

(b) where that person examines the goods before the contract is made, which that examination ought to reveal; or

(c) where the goods are hired by reference to a sample, which would have been apparent on reasonable examination of the sample.

(5) Subsection (6) below applies where, under a [relevant contract for the hire of goods], the supplier hires goods in the course of a business and the person to whom the goods are hired, expressly or by implication, makes known—

(a) to the supplier in the course of negotiations conducted by him in relation to the making of the contract; or

(b) to a credit-broker in the course of negotiations conducted by that broker in relation to goods sold by him to the supplier before forming the subject matter of the contract,

any particular purpose for which the goods are being hired.

(6) In that case there is (subject to subsection (7) below) an implied term that the goods supplied under the contract are reasonably fit for that purpose, whether or not that is a purpose for which such goods are commonly supplied.

(7) Subsection (6) above does not apply where the circumstances show that the person to whom the goods are hired does not rely, or that it is unreasonable for him to rely, on the skill or judgment of the hirer or credit-broker.

(8) An implied term about quality or fitness for a particular purpose may be annexed by usage to a relevant contract for the hire of goods.

(9) The preceding provisions of this section apply to a hire by a person who in the course of a business is acting as agent for another as they apply to a hire by a principal in the course of a business, except where that other is not hiring in the course of a business and either the person to whom the goods are hired knows

that fact or reasonable steps are taken to bring it to that person's notice before the contract concerned is made.

[. . .]]

[11K Implied terms where hire is by sample

(1) This section applies where, under a [relevant contract for the hire of goods], the supplier hires or agrees to hire the goods by reference to a sample.

(2) In such a case there is an implied term—

(a) that the bulk will correspond with the sample in quality; and

(b) that the person to whom the goods are hired will have a reasonable opportunity of comparing the bulk with the sample; and

(c) that the goods will be free from any defect, making their quality unsatisfactory, which would not be apparent on reasonable examination of the sample.

(3) For the purposes of this section a supplier hires or agrees to hire goods by reference to a sample where there is an express or implied term to that effect in the contract concerned.]

Exclusion of implied terms, etc

[11L Exclusion of implied terms etc

(1) Where a right, duty or liability would arise under a [relevant contract for the transfer of goods] or a [relevant contract for the hire of goods] by implication of law, it may (subject to subsection (2) below and the 1977 Act) be negatived or varied by express agreement, or by the course of dealing between the parties, or by such usage as binds both parties to the contract.

(2) An express term does not negative a term implied by the preceding provisions of this Part of this Act unless inconsistent with it.

(3) Nothing in the preceding provisions of this Part of this Act prejudices the operation of any other enactment or any rule of law whereby any term (other than one relating to quality or fitness) is to be implied in a [relevant contract for the transfer of goods] or a [relevant contract for the hire of goods].]

[. . .]

DEBTORS (SCOTLAND) ACT 1987
(1987, c 18)

PART I
EXTENSION OF TIME TO PAY DEBTS

Time to pay directions on granting decree

1 Time to pay directions

(1) Subject to subsections (3) to (5) below and to section 14 of this Act, [on an application by the debtor,] the court [or the First-tier Tribunal], on granting decree for payment of any principal sum of money [shall, if satisfied that it is reasonable in all the circumstances to do so, and having regard in particular to the matters mentioned in subsection (1A) below,] direct that any sum decerned for in the decree (including any interest claimed in pursuance of subsections (6) and (7) below) or any expenses in relation to which the decree contains a finding as to liability or both such sum and such expenses shall be paid—

(a) by such instalments, commencing at such time after the date of intimation by the creditor to the debtor of an extract of the decree containing the direction, payable at such intervals; or

(b) as a lump sum at the end of such period following intimation as mentioned in paragraph (a) above,

as the court [or the First-tier Tribunal] may specify in the direction.

[(1A) The matters referred to in subsection (1) above are—

(a) the nature of and reasons for the debt in relation to which decree is granted;

(b) any action taken by the creditor to assist the debtor in paying that debt;

(c) the debtor's financial position;

(d) the reasonableness of any proposal by the debtor to pay that debt; and

(e) the reasonableness of any refusal by the creditor of, or any objection by the creditor to, any proposal by the debtor to pay that debt.]

(2) A direction under subsection (1) above shall be known as a 'time to pay direction'.

(3) Where a court [or the First-tier Tribunal] grants a decree which contains a finding as to liability for expenses but does not at the same time make a time to pay direction, then (whether or not the decree also decerns for payment of the expenses), it shall not at any time thereafter be competent for the court [or the First-tier Tribunal] to make a time to pay direction in relation to those expenses.

(4) Where a court [or the First-tier Tribunal] grants a decree which contains a finding as to liability for expenses and makes a time to pay direction in relation to those expenses but—

(a) does not decern for payment of the expenses; or

(b) decerns for payment of the expenses as taxed by the auditor of court [or auditor of the Court of Session] but does not specify the amount of those expenses,

in relation to so much of the time to pay direction as relates to the expenses, the reference in subsection (1) above to the date of intimation of an extract of the decree containing the direction shall be treated as a reference to the date of intimation of an extract of a decree decerning for payment of the expenses, being an extract specifying their amount.

(5) It shall not be competent for the court [or the First-tier Tribunal] to make a time to pay direction—

(a) where the sum of money (exclusive of any interest and expenses) decerned for exceeds [£25,000] or such amount as may be prescribed in regulations made by the Lord Advocate;

(b) where the decree contains an award of a capital sum on divorce or on the granting of a declarator of nullity of marriage;

(c) in connection with a maintenance order;

[(cc) in connection with a liability order within the meaning of the Child Support Act 1991;]

(d) in an action by or on behalf of [the Commissioners for Her Majesty's Revenue and Customs] for payment of any sum recoverable [under or by virtue of any enactment or under a contract settlement];

[(da) in an action by or on behalf of Revenue Scotland for payment of any sum recoverable under or by virtue of the Revenue Scotland and Tax Powers Act 2014 (asp 16) or any other enactment in respect of a devolved tax, under a contract settlement or under a settlement agreement,]

[. . .]

(f) in an action for payment of—

[. . .]

(ii) car tax due under the Car Tax Act 1983.

[. . .]

(6) Without prejudice to section 2(5) of this Act, interest payable under a decree containing a time to pay direction (other than interest awarded as a specific sum in the decree) shall not be recoverable by the creditor except in accordance with subsection (7) below.

(7) A creditor who wishes to recover interest to which subsection (6) above applies shall serve a notice on the debtor, not later than the date prescribed by Act of Sederunt [or the First-tier Tribunal for Scotland Housing and Property Chamber (Procedure) Regulations 2017] occurring—

(a) in the case of a direction under subsection (1)(a) above, before the date when the last instalment of the debt concerned (other than such interest) is payable under the direction;

(b) in the case of a direction under subsection (1)(b) above, before the end of the period specified in the direction,

stating that he is claiming such interest and specifying the amount of the interest claimed.

(8) Any sum paid by a debtor under a time to pay direction shall not be ascribed to interest claimed in pursuance of subsections (6) and (7) above until the debt concerned (other than such interest) has been discharged.

[(8A) In paragraph (d) of subsection (5) above, 'contract settlement' means an agreement made in connection with any person's liability to make a payment to the Commissioners for Her Majesty's Revenue and Customs under or by virtue of any enactment.]

[(8B) In paragraph (da) of subsection (5)—

'contract settlement' means any agreement made in connection with any person's liability to make a payment to Revenue Scotland under or by virtue of the Revenue Scotland and Tax Powers Act 2014 (asp 16) or any other enactment in respect of a devolved tax,

'devolved tax' has the meaning given by section 80A(4) of the Scotland Act 2012 (c 46),

'settlement agreement' has the meaning given by section 246(1) of the Revenue Scotland and Tax Powers Act 2014 (asp 16).]

[. . .]

2 Effect of time to pay direction on diligence

(1) While a time to pay direction is in effect, it shall not be competent—

(a) to serve a charge for payment; or

(b) to commence or execute any of the following diligences—

(i) an arrestment and action of furthcoming or sale;

(ii) [an attachment;]

(iii) an earnings arrestment;

(iv) an adjudication for debt;

[(v) a money attachment;]

[(vi) a land attachment;
(vii) a residual attachment]
to enforce payment of the debt concerned.

(2) While a time to pay direction is in effect an arrestment used on the dependence of the action or in security of the debt concerned shall remain in effect—

(a) if it has not been recalled; and

(b) to the extent that it has not been restricted under subsection (3) below,

but, while the direction is in effect, it shall not be competent to commence an action of furthcoming or sale following on such an arrestment.

[(2A) Where the arrestment which remains in effect as mentioned in subsection (2) above is an arrestment such as is mentioned in subsection (1) of section 73J of this Act, while the time to pay direction is in effect—

(a) it shall not be competent to release funds under subsection (2) of that section; and

(b) the period during which the direction is in effect shall be disregarded for the purposes of determining whether the period mentioned in subsection (3) of that section has expired.]

[(2B) While a time to pay direction is in effect an interim attachment shall remain in effect—

(a) if it has not been recalled; or

(b) to the extent that it has not been restricted under subsection (3) below.]

(3) The court [or the First-tier Tribunal] may, on making a time to pay direction, recall or restrict [an interim attachment or] an arrestment of the kind described in subsection (2) above.

(4) If [an interim attachment or] an arrestment of the kind described in subsection (2) above is in effect, the court [or the First-tier Tribunal] may order that the making of a time to pay direction and the recall or restriction of the [interim attachment or] arrestment shall be subject to the fulfilment by the debtor of such conditions within such period as the court [or the First-tier Tribunal] thinks fit; and, where the court [or the First-tier Tribunal] so orders, it shall postpone granting decree until such fulfilment or the end of that period, whichever is the earlier.

(5) Where a time to pay direction is recalled or ceases to have effect, otherwise than—

(a) under section 12(2)(a) of this Act; or

(b) by reason of the debt concerned being paid or otherwise extinguished,

the debt in so far as it remains outstanding and interest thereon, whether or not awarded as a specific sum in the decree, shall, subject to any enactment or rule of law to the contrary, become enforceable by any diligence mentioned in subsection (1)(b) above.

[(5A) Where—

(a) a time to pay direction is recalled or ceases to have effect as mentioned in subsection (5) above; and

(b) an arrestment such as is mentioned in section 73J(1) of this Act is in effect,

the clerk of court [, sheriff clerk or, in relation to time to pay directions made by the First-tier Tribunal, a member of administration staff of the First-tier Tribunal] shall intimate the fact of that recall or cessation to the arrestee.]

3 Variation and recall of time to pay direction and arrestment

(1) The court which granted a decree [, or the First-tier Tribunal, where it has made an order,] containing a time to pay direction may, on an application by the debtor or the creditor—

(a) vary or recall the direction if it is satisfied that it is reasonable [in all the circumstances] to do so; or

(b) if [an interim attachment or] an arrestment in respect of the debt concerned is in effect, recall or restrict the [interim attachment or] arrestment.

(2) If [an interim attachment or] an arrestment in respect of the debt concerned is in effect, the court [or the First-tier Tribunal] may order that any variation, recall or restriction under subsection (1) above shall be subject to the fulfilment by the debtor of such conditions as the court [or the First-tier Tribunal] thinks fit.

(3) The clerk of court [, sheriff clerk or, in relation to time to pay directions made by the First-tier Tribunal, a member of administration staff of the First-tier Tribunal] shall as soon as is reasonably practicable intimate a variation under subsection (1) above to the debtor and to the creditor, and the variation shall come into effect on the date of such intimation.

4 Lapse of time to pay direction

(1) If, on the day on which an instalment payable under a time to pay direction becomes due, there remains unpaid a sum, due under previous instalments, of not less than the aggregate of 2 instalments, the direction shall cease to have effect.

(2) If at the end of the period of 3 weeks immediately following the day on which the last instalment payable under a time to pay direction becomes due, any part of the debt concerned remains outstanding, the direction shall cease to have effect.

(3) If any sum payable under a time to pay direction under section 1(1)(b) of this Act remains unpaid 24 hours after the end of the period specified in the direction, the direction shall cease to have effect.

(4) Where—

(a) a decree for payment of a principal sum of money contains a finding as to liability for expenses and decree for payment of the expenses is subsequently granted; and

(b) a time to pay direction is made in relation to both the principal sum and the expenses,

if under subsections (1) to (3) above the direction ceases to have effect in relation to the sum payable under either of the decrees, the direction shall also cease to have effect in relation to the sum payable under the other decree.

Time to pay orders following charge or diligence

5 Time to pay orders

(1) Subject to section 14 of this Act, this section applies to a debt due under a decree or other document in respect of which—

(a) a charge for payment has been served on the debtor;

(b) an arrestment has been executed; or

(c) an action of adjudication for debt has been commenced.

(2) Subject to subsections (4) and (5) below, the sheriff [or the First-tier Tribunal] [, on an application by the debtor, shall, if satisfied that it is reasonable in all the circumstances to do so, and having regard in particular to the matters mentioned in subsection (2A) below,] make an order that a debt to which this section applies (including any interest claimed in pursuance of subsections (6) and (7) below) so far as outstanding, shall be paid—

(a) by such instalments, commencing at such time after the date of intimation in accordance with section 7(4) of this Act [. . .] to the debtor of the order under this subsection, payable at such intervals; or

(b) as a lump sum at the end of such period following intimation as mentioned in paragraph (a) above,

as the sheriff may specify in the order.

[(2A) The matters referred to in subsection (2) above are—

(a) the nature of and reasons for the debt in relation to which the order is sought;

(b) any action taken by the creditor to assist the debtor in paying that debt;

(c) the debtor's financial position;

(d) the reasonableness of any proposal by the debtor to pay that debt; and

(e) the reasonableness of the objection by the creditor to the offer by the debtor to pay that debt.]

(3) An order under subsection (2) above shall be known as a 'time to pay order'.

(4) It shall not be competent for the sheriff [or the First-tier Tribunal] to make a time to pay order—

(a) where the amount of the debt outstanding at the date of the making of the application under subsection (2) above (exclusive of any interest) exceeds [£10,000] or such amount as may be prescribed in regulations made by the Lord Advocate;

(b) where, in relation to the debt, a time to pay direction or a time to pay order has previously been made (whether such direction or order is in effect or not);

[. . .]

(d) in relation to a debt including any sum recoverable by or on behalf of [the Commissioners of Her Majesty's Revenue and Customs [under or by virtue of any enactment or under a contract settlement]];

[(da) in relation to a debt including any sum recoverable by or on behalf of Revenue Scotland under or by virtue of the Revenue Scotland and Tax Powers Act 2014 (asp 16) or any other enactment in respect of a devolved tax, under a contract settlement or under a settlement agreement,]

[. . .]

(f) in relation to a debt including—

[. . .]

(ii) car tax due under the Car Tax Act 1983.

[. . .]

(5) Where in respect of a debt to which this section applies—

(a) [articles belonging to the debtor have been attached and notice of an auction given under section 27(4) of the Debt Arrangement and Attachment (Scotland) Act 2002 (asp 17) but no auction has yet taken place;]

[(aa) money owned by the debtor has been attached and removed;]

(b) moveable property of the debtor has been arrested and in respect of the arrested property—

(i) a decree in an action of furthcoming has been granted but has not been enforced; or

(ii) a warrant of sale has been granted but the warrant has not been executed;

(c) a decree in an action of adjudication for debt has been granted and the creditor has, with the debtor's consent or acquiescence, entered into possession of any property adjudged by the decree or has obtained a decree of maills and duties, or a decree of removing or ejection, in relation to any such property.

(d) property owned by the debtor has been attached by residual attachment and a satisfaction order under section 136(2) of the 2007 Act has been made but not yet executed,]

it shall not be competent for the sheriff [or the First-tier Tribunal] to make a time to pay order in respect of that debt until the diligence has been completed or has otherwise ceased to have effect.

[(5A) Where, in respect of a debt to which this section applies, an arrestment such as is mentioned in subsection (1) of section 73J of this Act has been executed, the sheriff [or the First-tier Tribunal] may make a time to pay order in respect of that debt only if less than 8 weeks of the period mentioned in subsection (3) of that section have expired.]

(6) Without prejudice to section 9(12) of this Act, interest payable under a decree for payment of a debt in respect of which a time to pay order has been made (other than interest awarded as a specific sum in the decree) shall not be recoverable by the creditor except in accordance with subsection (7) below.

(7) A creditor who wishes to recover interest to which subsection (6) above applies shall serve a notice on the debtor not later than the date prescribed by Act of Sederunt [or by rules made under section 68 or paragraph 4 of schedule 9 of the Tribunals (Scotland) Act 2014] occurring—

(a) in the case of an order under subsection (2)(a) above, before the date when the last instalment of the debt (other than such interest) is payable under the order;

(b) in the case of an order under subsection (2)(b) above, before the end of the period specified in the order,

stating that he is claiming such interest and specifying the amount of the interest claimed.

(8) Any sum paid by a debtor under a time to pay order shall not be ascribed to interest claimed in pursuance of subsections (6) and (7) above until the debt concerned (other than such interest) has been discharged.

[(8A) In paragraph (d) of subsection (4) above, 'contract settlement' means an agreement made in connection with any person's liability to make a payment to the Commissioners for Her Majesty's Revenue and Customs under or by virtue of any enactment.]

[(8B) In paragraph (da) of subsection (4)—

'contract settlement' means any agreement made in connection with any person's liability to make a payment to Revenue Scotland under or by virtue of the Revenue Scotland and Tax Powers Act 2014 (asp 16) or any other enactment in respect of a devolved tax,

'devolved tax' has the meaning given by section 80A(4) of the Scotland Act 2012 (c 46),

'settlement agreement' has the meaning given by section 246(1) of the Revenue Scotland and Tax Powers Act 2014 (asp 16).]

[. . .]

6 Application for time to pay order

(1) An application for a time to pay order shall specify, to the best of the debtor's knowledge, the amount of the debt outstanding as at the date of the making of the application and shall include an offer to pay it—

(a) by specified instalments, payable at specified intervals; or

(b) as a lump sum at the end of a specified period.

(2) The [. . .] duty under section 96(2)(b) of this Act [on the sheriff clerk or, in relation to time to pay directions made by the First-tier Tribunal, a member of administration staff of the First-tier Tribunal] to assist the debtor in the completion of certain forms shall, in relation to a form of application for a time to pay order, consist of a duty to assist him in the completion of the form in accordance with proposals for payment made by the debtor.

(3) On receipt of an application for a time to pay order, the sheriff [or the Firsttier Tribunal] shall, if the application is properly made and unless it appears [. . .] that the making of a time to pay order would not be competent, make an interim order sisting diligence as provided for in section 8(1) of this Act.

(4) The sheriff [or the First-tier Tribunal] may, where the debtor is unable to furnish the necessary information, make an order requiring the creditor, within such period as may be specified therein, to furnish to the sheriff [or the First-tier Tribunal] such particulars of the decree or other document under which the debt is payable as may be prescribed by Act of Sederunt [or rules made under section 68 or paragraph 4 of schedule 9 of the Tribunals (Scotland) Act 2014].

(5) If a creditor fails to comply with an order under subsection (4) above the sheriff [or the First-tier Tribunal] may, after giving the creditor an opportunity to make representations, make an order recalling or extinguishing any existing diligence, and interdicting the creditor from executing diligence, for the recovery of the debt.

(6) Where the sheriff [or the First-tier Tribunal] makes an interim order under subsection (3) above, the sheriff clerk [or, in relation to time to pay directions made by the First-tier Tribunal, a member of administration staff of the First-tier Tribunal] shall as soon as is reasonably practicable—

(a) serve a copy of the application for the time to pay order on the creditor informing him that he may object to the granting of the application within a period of 14 days after the date of service;

[(b) serve on—

(i) the creditor; and

(ii) where an arrestment such as is mentioned in section 73J(1) of this Act is in effect, the arrestee,

a copy of the interim order; and

(c) serve on the creditor a copy of any order under subsection (4) above.]

7 Disposal of application

(1) If no objection is made in pursuance of section 6(6)(a) of this Act, the sheriff [or the First-tier Tribunal] shall make a time to pay order in accordance with the application.

(2) If such an objection is made, the sheriff [or the First-tier Tribunal] shall not dispose of the application without first—

(a) giving the debtor an opportunity to make representations; and

(b) if agreement is not reached as to whether a time to pay order should be made or as to its terms, giving the parties an opportunity to be heard.

(3) Where the sheriff [or the First-tier Tribunal] refuses to make a time to pay order, he shall recall any interim order under section 6(3) of this Act.

(4) The sheriff clerk [or, in relation to time to pay directions made by the Firsttier Tribunal, a member of administration staff of the First-tier Tribunal] shall as soon as is reasonably practicable—

(a) intimate the decision of the sheriff [or the First-tier Tribunal] on an application for a time to pay order (including any recall of an interim order under subsection (3) above) to the debtor [the creditor and, where an arrestment such as is mentioned in section 73J(1) of this Act is in effect, the arrestee]; and

(b) if the sheriff [or the First-tier Tribunal] has made a time to pay order, inform the creditor of the date when he intimated that fact to the debtor.

8 Effect of interim order on diligence

(1) While an interim order under section 6(3) of this Act is in effect it shall not be competent in respect of the debt—

[(za) to attach in execution of the decree any articles which have been attached by interim attachment;]

(a) [to give, in relation to any articles which have been attached, notice of an auction under section 27(4) of the Debt Arrangement and Attachment (Scotland) Act 2002 (asp 17);]

[(aa) to execute a money attachment;]

(b) to execute an earnings arrestment;

(c) [subject to subsection (1A) below,] where an arrestment of property belonging to the debtor (other than an arrestment of earnings in the hands of his employer) has been executed before or after the making of the interim order, to commence an action of furthcoming or sale, or to grant decree in any such action which has already been commenced, in pursuance of that arrestment;

(d) to commence an action of adjudication for debt or, if such an action has already been commenced, to take any steps other than the registration of a notice of litigiosity in connection with the action, the obtaining and extracting of a decree in the action, the registration of an abbreviate of adjudication and the completion of title to property adjudged by the decree,

[*(e) subject to subsection (1C) below, to apply, under section 130(1) of the 2007 Act, for a residual attachment order*].

[(1A) Where the arrestment mentioned in subsection (1)(c) above is an arrestment such as is mentioned in subsection (1) of section 73J of this Act, while the interim order is in effect—

(a) it shall not be competent to release funds under subsection (2) of that section; and

(b) the period during which the order is in effect shall be disregarded for the purposes of determining whether the period mentioned in subsection (3) of that section has expired.

(1B) Where, before the interim order is made—

(a) a notice of land attachment is registered, it shall not be competent to take any steps other than—

(i) serving, under subsection (5) of section 83 of the 2007 Act, a copy of that notice; and

(ii) registering, under subsection (6) of that section, a certificate of service; or

(b) a land attachment is created, it shall not be competent to make, under section 97(2) of the 2007 Act, an order granting a warrant for sale of the attached land.

(1C) Where, before the interim order is made, a residual attachment order has been made, it shall not be competent—

(a) to take any steps other than serving, under section 133(1) of the 2007 Act, a schedule of residual attachment; or

(b) to make, under section 136(2) of the 2007 Act, a satisfaction order.]

(2) An interim order under section 6(3) of this Act shall come into effect on intimation to the creditor under section 6(6)(b) of this Act and shall remain in effect until intimation of the sheriff's [or the First-tier Tribunal's] decision on the application for a time to pay order is made to the debtor and the creditor under section 7(4)(a) of this Act.

[. . .]

9 Effect of time to pay order on diligence

(1) While a time to pay order is in effect, it shall not be competent—

(a) to serve a charge for payment; or

(b) to commence or execute any of the following diligences—

(i) an arrestment and action of furthcoming or sale;

[(ii) an attachment;]

(iii) an earnings arrestment;

(iv) an adjudication for debt;

[(v) a money attachment;]

to enforce payment of the debt concerned.

(2) On making a time to pay order, the sheriff in respect of the debt—

(a) shall make an order recalling any existing earnings arrestment;

(b) where the debt is being enforced by a conjoined arrestment order, shall—

(i) if he, or another sheriff sitting in the same sheriff court, made the conjoined arrestment order, vary it so as to exclude the debt or, where no other debt or maintenance is being enforced by the order, recall the order;

(ii) if a sheriff sitting in another sheriff court made the conjoined arrestment order, require intimation of the time to pay order to be made to a sheriff sitting there who shall so vary or, as the case may be, recall the conjoined arrestment order;

(c) [where a notice of land attachment has been registered under section 83(1)(c) of the 2007 Act, shall make an order prohibiting the taking of any steps other than—

(i) the serving, under subsection (5) of that section, of a copy of the notice; and

(ii) the registration, under subsection (6) of that section, of a certificate of service;

[(ca) where a residual attachment order has been made under section 132(2) of the 2007 Act, shall make an order prohibiting the taking of any steps other than the serving, under section 133(1) of the 2007 Act, of a schedule of residual attachment;

(cb) may make an order recalling an interim attachment;]

(d) may make an order recalling [an attachment];

(e) may make an order recalling or restricting any arrestment other than an arrestment of the debtor's earnings in the hands of his employer.

[(2A) On making a time to pay order, the First-tier Tribunal in respect of the debt—

(a) must make an order recalling any existing earnings arrestment,

(b) where the debt is being enforced by a conjoined arrestment order, must—

(i) if the First-tier Tribunal Housing and Property Chamber made the conjoined arrestment order, vary it so as to exclude the debt or, where no other debt or maintenance is being enforced by the order, recall the order,

(ii) if either—

(aa) another Chamber of the First-tier Tribunal, or

(bb) a sheriff sitting in the sheriff court,

made the conjoined arrestment order, require intimation of the time to pay order to be made to the other Chamber or to the sheriff who must so vary or, as the case may be, recall the conjoined arrestment order,

(c) where a notice of land attachment has been registered under section 83(1)(c) of the 2007 Act, must make an order prohibiting the taking of any steps other than—

(i) the serving, under subsection (5) of that section, of a copy of the notice, and

(ii) the registration, under subsection (6) of that section, of a certificate of service,

(d) where a residual attachment order has been made under section 132(2) of the 2007 Act, must make an order prohibiting the taking of any steps other than the serving, under section 133(1) of the 2007 Act, of a schedule of residual attachment,

(e) may make an order recalling an interim attachment,

(f) may make an order recalling an attachment,

(g) may make an order recalling or restricting any arrestment other than an arrestment of the debtor's earnings in the hands of the debtor's employer.]

(3) If [an interim attachment, an attachment] or such an arrestment as is mentioned in subsection (2)(e) above is in effect, the sheriff [or the First-tier Tribunal] may order that the making of a time to pay order [, the recall of the interim attachment or the attachment] or the recall or restriction of the arrestment shall be subject to the fulfilment by the debtor of such conditions as the sheriff [or the First-tier Tribunal] thinks fit.

(4) [Subject to subsection (4A) below,] where the sheriff [or the First-tier Tribunal] does not exercise the powers conferred [. . .] by subsection [(2)(cb), (d) or (e)] above to recall a diligence, [the sheriff or the First-tier Tribunal] shall order that no further steps shall be taken by the creditor in the diligence concerned other than, in the case of [an attachment, making a report of attachment under section 17 of the Debt Arrangement and Attachment (Scotland) Act 2002 (asp 17) or applying for an order under section 20(1) of that Act.]

[(4A) Where, in relation to an arrestment such as is mentioned in subsection (1) of section 73J of this Act, the sheriff [or the First-tier Tribunal] does not exercise the power conferred [. . .] by subsection (2)(e) above to recall that arrestment, [the sheriff or that tribunal] shall make an order—

(a) prohibiting, while the time to pay order is in effect, the release of funds under subsection (2) of section 73J of this Act; and

(b) providing that the period during which the time to pay order is in effect shall be disregarded for the purposes of determining whether the period mentioned in subsection (3) of that section has expired.]

(5) Any order made under subsection (2) or (4) above shall specify the diligence in relation to which it is made.

(6) The sheriff [or the First-tier Tribunal] shall not make an order under subsection [(2)(cb), (d) or (e)] above without first giving the creditor an opportunity to make representations.

(7) The sheriff clerk [or, in relation to time to pay directions made by the Firsttier Tribunal, a member of administration staff of the First-tier Tribunal] shall, at the same time as [intimation is made] under section 7(4)(a) of this Act—

(a) intimate any order under subsection (2) or (4) above to the debtor and the creditor and the order shall come into effect on such intimation being made to the creditor;

(b) intimate any order under subsection (2)(a) or (b) above to the employer [; and

(c) where any order under subsection (4A) above is made in relation to an arrestment such as is mentioned in section 73J(1) of this Act is in effect, intimate that order to the arrestee.]

(8) While an order under subsection (4) above is in effect it shall not be competent [. . .]—

(a) [to sell articles which have been attached (other than by virtue of section 20(1) or 22(3) of the Debt Arrangement and Attachment (Scotland) Act (asp 17);]

(b) [to grant] a decree of furthcoming or sale of arrested property.

(9) For the purposes of section [24 of the Debt Arrangement and Attachment (Scotland) Act 2002 (asp 17)], the period during which an order under subsection (4) above is in effect shall be disregarded in calculating the period during which [an attachment] to which the order applies remains in effect.

(10) Where, before the making of a time to pay order in respect of a debt, a charge to pay that debt has been served—

(a) if the period for payment specified in the charge has not expired, the charge shall lapse on the making of the order;

(b) if that period has expired, nothing in the time to pay order nor in any order under this section shall affect retrospectively the effect of the charge in the constitution of apparent insolvency within the meaning of section [16 of the Bankruptcy (Scotland) Act 2016].

(11) If, when a time to pay order in relation to a debt is made, any diligence enforcing it is in effect which is not specified in an order under subsection (2) or (4) above, the diligence shall remain in effect unless and until it is recalled under section 10(4) of this Act.

(12) Where a time to pay order is recalled or ceases to have effect, otherwise than—

(a) under section 12(2)(a) of this Act; or

(b) by the debt payable under the order being paid or otherwise extinguished,

the debt in so far as it remains outstanding (including interest thereon, whether or not awarded as a specific sum in the decree) shall, subject to any enactment or rule of law to the contrary, become enforceable by any diligence mentioned in subsection (1)(b) above; and, notwithstanding section [25 of the Debt Arrangement and Attachment (Scotland) Act 2002 (asp 17)], in this subsection 'diligence' includes, where the debt was, immediately before the time to pay order was made, being enforced by [an attachment] in any premises, [another attachment] in those premises.

10 Variation and recall of time to pay order and arrestment

(1) The sheriff [or the First-tier Tribunal] may, on an application by the debtor or the creditor—

(a) vary or recall a time to pay order if [the sheriff or the Tribunal] is satisfied that it is reasonable [in all the circumstances] to do so; or

(b) if [an interim attachment, an attachment] or an arrestment in respect of the debt is in effect, recall [the attachment] or recall or restrict the arrestment.

(2) If [an interim attachment, an attachment] or an arrestment in respect of the debt is in effect, the sheriff [or the First-tier Tribunal] may order that any variation, recall or restriction under subsection (1) above shall be subject to the fulfilment by the debtor of such conditions as the sheriff [or the First-tier Tribunal] thinks fit.

(3) The sheriff clerk [or, in relation to time to pay directions made by the Firsttier Tribunal, a member of administration staff of the First-tier Tribunal] shall as soon as is reasonably practicable intimate a variation under subsection (1) above to the debtor and to the creditor, and the variation shall come into effect on the date of such intimation.

(4) Where, after a time to pay order has been made, it comes to the knowledge of the sheriff [or the First-tier Tribunal] that the debt to which the order applies is being enforced by any of the diligences mentioned in section 9(1)(b) of this Act which was in effect when the time to pay order was made, the sheriff [or the Firsttier Tribunal], after giving all interested parties an opportunity to be heard, may make—

(a) an order recalling the time to pay order; or

(b) any of the orders mentioned in subsection (2) or (4) of section 9 of this Act; and that section shall, subject to any necessary modifications, apply for the purposes of an order made under this paragraph as it applies for the purposes of an order made under either of those subsections.

11 Lapse of time to pay order

(1) If, on the day on which an instalment payable under a time to pay order becomes due, there remains unpaid a sum, due under previous instalments, of not less than the aggregate of 2 instalments, the order shall cease to have effect.

(2) If at the end of the period of 3 weeks immediately following the day on which the last instalment payable under a time to pay order becomes due, any part of the debt payable under the order remains outstanding, the order shall cease to have effect.

(3) If any sum payable under a time to pay order under section 5(2)(b) of this Act remains unpaid 24 hours after the end of the period specified in the order, the order shall cease to have effect.

Miscellaneous

12 Sequestration and insolvency

(1) While a time to pay direction or a time to pay order is in effect, the creditor shall not be entitled to found on the debt concerned in presenting, or in concurring in the presentation of, a petition for the sequestration of the debtor's estate.

(2) A time to pay direction or a time to pay order shall cease to have effect—

(a) on the granting of an award of sequestration of the debtor's estate;

(b) on the granting by the debtor of a voluntary trust deed whereby his estate is conveyed to a trustee for the benefit of his creditors generally; or

(c) on the entering by the debtor into a composition contract with his creditors.

13 Saving of creditor's rights and remedies

(1) No right or remedy of a creditor to enforce his debt shall be affected by—

(a) a time to pay direction;

(b) a time to pay order; or

(c) an interim order under section 6(3) of this Act,

except as expressly provided in this Part of this Act.

(2) The recall—

(a) on the making of a time to pay direction or an order under section 3(1) of this Act, of an arrestment; or

(b) on the making of a time to pay order or an order under section 10(1) of this Act, of an arrestment or [an attachment],

shall not prevent the creditor therein from being ranked by virtue of that arrestment or [attachment] pari passu under paragraph [1 of Schedule 7 of the Bankruptcy (Scotland) Act 2016] on the proceeds of any other arrestment or [attachment].

14 Circumstances where direction or order not competent or no longer effective

(1) It shall be competent to make a time to pay direction or a time to pay order only in relation to a debtor who is an individual and only if, and to the extent that, the debtor is liable for payment of the debt concerned in either or both of the following capacities—

(a) personally;

(b) as a tutor of an individual or as a judicial factor loco tutoris, curator bonis or judicial factor loco absentis on an individual's estate.

(2) A time to pay direction or a time to pay order shall cease to have effect on the death of the debtor or on the transmission of the obligation to pay the debt concerned during his lifetime to another person.

(3) Where a time order for the payment by instalments of a sum owed under a regulated agreement or a security has been made under section 129(2)(a) of the Consumer Credit Act 1974 it shall not thereafter be competent to make a time to pay direction or a time to pay order in relation to that sum.

15 Interpretation of Part I

(1) In this Part of this Act—

['2007 Act' means the Bankruptcy and Diligence etc (Scotland) Act 2007,]

'adjudication for debt' does not include—

(a) an adjudication on a *debitum fundi*; [. . .]

['the First-tier Tribunal' means the First-tier Tribunal for Scotland Housing and Property Chamber.]

(2) In sections 1 to 4 of this Act—

'the court' means the Court of Session or the sheriff;

'the debt concerned' means the sum or expenses in respect of which a time to pay direction is made.

['decree', where the context requires or permits, includes an order made by the First-tier Tribunal.]

(3) In sections 5 to 14 of this Act—

'debt' means the sum due by a debtor under a decree or other document (including any interest thereon and any expenses decerned for), and any expenses of diligence used to recover such sum which are chargeable against the debtor, but does not include—

(a) any sum due under an order of court in criminal proceedings;

(b) maintenance, whether due at the date of application for the time to pay order or not, or any capital sum awarded on divorce or on the granting of a declarator of nullity of marriage or any other sum due under a decree awarding maintenance or such a capital sum; or

(c) any fine imposed—

(i) for contempt of court;

(ii) under any enactment, for professional misconduct; or

(iii) for failure to implement an order under section 91 of the Court of Session Act 1868 (orders for specific performance of statutory duty);

'decree or other document' means—

(a) a decree of the Court of Session or the sheriff;

[(aa) a summary warrant;]

(b) an extract of a document which is registered for execution in the Books of Council and Session or the sheriff court books;

(c) an order or determination which by virtue of any enactment is enforceable as if it were an extract registered decree arbitral bearing a warrant for execution issued by the sheriff;

(d) a civil judgment granted outside Scotland by a court, tribunal or arbiter which by virtue of any enactment or rule of law is enforceable in Scotland; and

(e) a document or settlement which by virtue of an Order in Council made under section 13 of the Civil Jurisdiction and Judgments Act 1982 is enforceable in Scotland,

but does not include a maintenance order [, a liability order within the meaning of the Child Support Act 1991] [. . .];

'sheriff'—

(a) in relation to a debt constituted by decree granted by a sheriff, means that sheriff or another sheriff sitting in the same sheriff court;

(b) in any other case, means the sheriff having jurisdiction—

(i) in the place where the debtor is domiciled;

(ii) if the debtor is not domiciled in Scotland, in a place in Scotland where he carries on business; or

(iii) if the debtor does not carry on business in Scotland, in a place where he has property which is not exempt from diligence;

and, for the purposes of sub-paragraphs (i) and (ii) above, the debtor's domicile shall be determined in accordance with section 41 of the Civil Jurisdiction and Judgments Act 1982.

[PART 1A
DILIGENCE ON THE DEPENDENCE

Availability of diligence on the dependence

[15A Diligence on the dependence of action

(1) Subject to subsection (2) below and to sections 15C to 15F of this Act, the Court of Session or the sheriff may grant warrant for diligence by—

(a) arrestment; or

(b) inhibition,

on the dependence of an action.

(2) Warrant for—

(a) arrestment on the dependence of an action is competent only where the action contains a conclusion for payment of a sum other than by way of expenses; and

(b) inhibition on the dependence is competent only where the action contains—

(i) such a conclusion; or

(ii) a conclusion for specific implement of an obligation to convey heritable property to the creditor or to grant in the creditor's favour a real right in security, or some other right, over such property.

(3) In this Part of this Act, 'action' includes, in the sheriff court—

(a) a summary cause;

[(b) a simple procedure case (within the meaning of section 72(9) of the Courts Reform (Scotland) Act 2014); and]

(c) a summary application,

and references to 'summons', 'conclusion' and to cognate expressions shall be construed accordingly.]

[15B Diligence on the dependence of petition

(1) Subject to subsection (2) below and to sections 15C to 15F of this Act, the Court of Session may grant warrant for diligence by—

(a) arrestment; or

(b) inhibition,

on the dependence of a petition.

(2) Warrant for—

(a) arrestment on the dependence of a petition is competent only where the petition contains a prayer for payment of a sum other than by way of expenses; and

(b) inhibition on the dependence is competent only where the petition contains—

(i) such a prayer; or

(ii) a prayer for specific implement of an obligation to convey heritable property to the creditor or to grant in the creditor's favour a real right in security, or some other right, over such property.

(3) The provisions of this Act (other than section 15A), of any other enactment and of any rule of law relating to diligence on the dependence of actions shall, in so far as is practicable and unless the contrary intention appears, apply to petitions in relation to which it is competent to grant warrant for such diligence and to the parties to them as they apply to actions and to parties to them.]

[15C Diligence on the dependence to secure future or contingent debts

(1) It shall be competent for the court to grant warrant for diligence on the dependence where the sum concluded for is a future or contingent debt.

(2) In this section and in sections 15D to 15M of this Act, the 'court' means the court before which the action is depending.]

Application for diligence on the dependence

[15D Application for diligence on the dependence

(1) A creditor may, at any time during which an action is in dependence, apply to the court for warrant for diligence by—

(a) arrestment; or

(b) inhibition,

on the dependence of the action.

(2) An application under subsection (1) above shall—

(a) be in (or as nearly as may be in) the form prescribed by Act of Sederunt;

(b) subject to subsection (3) below, be intimated to and provide details of—

(i) the debtor; and

(ii) any other person having an interest;

(c) state whether the creditor is seeking the grant, under section 15E(1) of this Act, of warrant for diligence on the dependence in advance of a hearing on the application under section 15F of this Act; and

(d) contain such other information as the Scottish Ministers may by regulations prescribe.

(3) An application under subsection (1) above need not be intimated where the creditor is seeking the grant, under section 15E(1) of this Act, of warrant in advance of a hearing on the application under section 15F of this Act.

(4) The court, on receiving an application under subsection (1) above, shall—

(a) subject to section 15E of this Act, fix a date for a hearing on the application under section 15F of this Act; and

(b) order the creditor to intimate that date to—

(i) the debtor; and

(ii) any other person appearing to the court to have an interest.]

[15E Grant of warrant without a hearing

(1) The court may, if satisfied as to the matters mentioned in subsection (2) below, make an order granting warrant for diligence on the dependence without a hearing on the application under section 15F of this Act.

(2) The matters referred to in subsection (1) above are—

(a) that the creditor has a prima facie case on the merits of the action;

(b) that there is a real and substantial risk enforcement of any decree in the action in favour of the creditor would be defeated or prejudiced by reason of—

(i) the debtor being insolvent or verging on insolvency; or

(ii) the likelihood of the debtor removing, disposing of, burdening, concealing or otherwise dealing with all or some of the debtor's assets,

were warrant for diligence on the dependence not granted in advance of such a hearing; and

(c) that it is reasonable in all the circumstances, including the effect granting warrant may have on any person having an interest, to do so.

(3) The onus shall be on the creditor to satisfy the court that the order granting warrant should be made.

(4) Where the court makes an order granting warrant for diligence on the dependence without a hearing on the application under section 15F of this Act, the court shall—

(a) fix a date for a hearing under section 15K of this Act; and

(b) order the creditor to intimate that date to—

(i) the debtor; and

(ii) any other person appearing to the court to have an interest.

(5) Where a hearing is fixed under subsection (4)(a) above, section 15K of this Act shall apply as if an application had been made to the court for an order under that section.

(6) Where the court refuses to make an order granting a warrant without a hearing under section 15F of this Act and the creditor insists in the application, the court shall—

(a) fix a date for such a hearing on the application; and

(b) order the creditor to intimate that date to—

(i) the debtor; and

(ii) any other person appearing to the court to have an interest.]

[15F Hearing on application

(1) At the hearing on an application for warrant for diligence on the dependence, the court shall not make any order without first giving—

(a) any person to whom intimation of the date of the hearing was made; and

(b) any other person the court is satisfied has an interest, an opportunity to be heard.

(2) The court may, if satisfied as to the matters mentioned in subsection (3) below, make an order granting warrant for diligence on the dependence.

(3) The matters referred to in subsection (2) above are—

(a) that the creditor has a prima facie case on the merits of the action;

(b) that there is a real and substantial risk enforcement of any decree in the action in favour of the creditor would be defeated or prejudiced by reason of—

(i) the debtor being insolvent or verging on insolvency; or

(ii) the likelihood of the debtor removing, disposing of, burdening, concealing or otherwise dealing with all or some of the debtor's assets,

were warrant for diligence on the dependence not granted; [. . .]

(c) that it is reasonable in all the circumstances, including the effect granting warrant may have on any person having an interest, to do so[; and

(d) where the debtor is an individual, that the creditor has provided the debtor with a debt advice and information package.]

(4) The onus shall be on the creditor to satisfy the court that the order granting warrant should be made.

(5) Where the court makes an order granting or, as the case may be, refusing warrant for diligence on the dependence, the court shall order the creditor to intimate that order to—

(a) the debtor; and

(b) any other person appearing to the court to have an interest.

(6) Where the court makes an order refusing warrant for diligence on the dependence, the court may impose such conditions (if any) as it thinks fit.

(7) Without prejudice to the generality of subsection (6) above, those conditions may require the debtor—

(a) to consign into court such sum; or

(b) to find caution or to give such other security,

as the court thinks fit.]

[(8) In this section and in section 15K, 'debt advice and information package' means the debt advice and information package referred to in section 10(5) of the Debt Arrangement and Attachment (Scotland) Act 2002.]

Execution before service

[15G Execution of diligence before service of summons

(1) This section applies where diligence by—

(a) arrestment; or

(b) inhibition,

on the dependence of an action is executed before service of the summons on the debtor.

(2) Subject to subsection (3) below, if the summons is not served on the debtor before the end of the period of 21 days beginning with the day on which the diligence is executed, the diligence shall cease to have effect.

(3) The court may, on the application of the creditor, make an order extending the period referred to in subsection (2) above.

(4) In determining whether to make such an order the court shall have regard to—

(a) the efforts of the creditor to serve the summons within the period of 21 days; and

(b) any special circumstances preventing or obstructing service within that period.]

Restriction on property attached

[15H Sum attached by arrestment on dependence

(1) The court may, subject to subsection (2) below, when granting warrant for arrestment on the dependence, limit the sum which may be attached to funds not exceeding such amount as the court may specify.

(2) The maximum amount which the court may specify under subsection (1) above shall be the aggregate of—

(a) the principal sum concluded for;

(b) a sum equal to 20 per cent of that sum or such other percentage as the Scottish Ministers may, by regulations, prescribe;

(c) a sum equal to 1 year's interest on the principal sum at the judicial rate; and

(d) any sum prescribed under subsection (3) below.

(3) The Scottish Ministers may, by regulations, prescribe a sum which appears to them to be reasonable having regard to the expenses likely to be—

(a) incurred by a creditor; and

(b) chargeable against a debtor,

in executing an arrestment on the dependence.

(4) For the avoidance of doubt, section 73F of this Act applies to any sum attached under this section.]

[15J Property affected by inhibition on dependence

Where the court grants warrant for diligence by inhibition on the dependence—

(a) in a case where the action is brought for specific implement of an obligation—

(i) to convey heritable property to the creditor;

(ii) to grant in the creditor's favour a real right in security over such property; or

(iii) to grant some other right over such property,

the court shall limit the property inhibited to that particular property; and

(b) in any other case, the court may limit the property inhibited to such property as the court may specify.]

Recall etc of diligence on the dependence

[15K Recall or restriction of diligence on dependence

(1) This section applies where warrant is granted for diligence on the dependence.

(2) The debtor and any person having an interest may apply to the court for an order—

(a) recalling the warrant;

(b) restricting the warrant;

(c) if an arrestment or inhibition has been executed in pursuance of the warrant—

(i) recalling; or

(ii) restricting,

that arrestment or inhibition;

(d) determining any question relating to the validity, effect or operation of the warrant; or

(e) ancillary to any order mentioned in paragraphs (a) to (d) above.

(3) An application under subsection (2) above shall—

(a) be in (or as nearly as may be in) the form prescribed by Act of Sederunt; and

(b) be intimated to—

(i) the creditor; and

(ii) any other person having an interest.

(4) At the hearing on the application under subsection (2) above, the court shall not make any order without first giving—

(a) any person to whom intimation of the application was made; and

(b) any other person the court is satisfied has an interest, an opportunity to be heard.

(5) Where the court is satisfied that the warrant is invalid it—

(a) shall make an order—

(i) recalling the warrant; and

(ii) if an arrestment or inhibition has been executed in pursuance of the warrant, recalling that arrestment or inhibition; and

(b) may make an order ancillary to any order mentioned in paragraph (a) above.

[(5A) Where subsection (5B) applies and the court is satisfied that the creditor has not provided the debtor with a debt advice and information package it—

(a) must make an order—

(i) recalling the warrant, and

(ii) if an arrestment or inhibition has been executed in pursuance of the warrant, recalling that arrestment or inhibition, and

(b) may make an order ancillary to any order mentioned in paragraph (a).

(5B) This subsection applies where—

(a) the debtor is an individual, and

(b) the hearing is a hearing fixed under section 15E(4)(a).]

(6) Where the court is satisfied that an arrestment or inhibition executed in pursuance of the warrant is incompetent, it—

(a) shall make an order recalling that arrestment or inhibition; and

(b) may make an order ancillary to any such order.

(7) Subject to subsection (8) below, where the court is satisfied that the warrant is valid but that—

(a) an arrestment or inhibition executed in pursuance of it is irregular or ineffective; or

(b) it is reasonable in all the circumstances, including the effect granting warrant may have had on any person having an interest, to do so,

the court may make any order such as is mentioned in subsection (2) above.

(8) If no longer satisfied as to the matters mentioned in subsection (9) below, the court—

(a) shall make an order such as is mentioned in subsection (5)(a) above; and

(b) may make an order such as is mentioned in subsection (5)(b) above.

(9) The matters referred to in subsection (8) above are—

(a) that the creditor has a prima facie case on the merits of the action;

(b) that there is a real and substantial risk enforcement of any decree in the action in favour of the creditor would be defeated or prejudiced by reason of—

(i) the debtor being insolvent or verging on insolvency; or

(ii) the likelihood of the debtor removing, disposing of, burdening, concealing or otherwise dealing with all or some of the debtor's assets; and

(c) that it is reasonable in all the circumstances, including the effect granting warrant may have had on any person having an interest, for the warrant or, as the case may be, any arrestment or inhibition executed in pursuance of it to continue to have effect.

(10) The onus shall be on the creditor to satisfy the court that no order under subsection (5), [(5A),] (6), (7) or (8) above should be made.

(11) In granting an application under subsection (2) above, the court may impose such conditions (if any) as it thinks fit.

(12) Without prejudice to the generality of subsection (11) above, the court may impose conditions which require the debtor—

(a) to consign into court such sum; or

(b) to find such caution or to give such other security, as the court thinks fit.

(13) Where the court makes an order under this section, the court shall order the debtor to intimate that order to—

(a) the creditor; and

(b) any other person appearing to the court to have an interest.

(14) This section applies irrespective of whether warrant for diligence on the dependence is obtained, or executed, before this section comes into force.]

[15L Variation of orders and variation or recall of conditions

(1) Where—

(a) an order restricting warrant for diligence on the dependence is made under section 15K(7); or

(b) a condition is imposed by virtue of—

(i) section 15F(6); or

(ii) section 15K(11),

of this Act, the debtor may apply to the court for variation of the order or, as the case may be, variation or removal of the condition.

(2) An application under subsection (1) above shall—

(a) be in (or as nearly as may be in) the form prescribed by Act of Sederunt; and

(b) be intimated to—

(i) the creditor; and

(ii) any other person having an interest.

(3) At the hearing on the application under subsection (1) above, the court shall not make any order without first giving—

(a) any person to whom intimation of the application was made; and

(b) any other person the court is satisfied has an interest, an opportunity to be heard.

(4) On an application under subsection (1) above, the court may if it thinks fit—

(a) vary the order; or

(b) vary or remove the condition.

(5) Where the court makes an order varying the order or, as the case may be, varying or removing the condition, the court shall order the debtor to intimate that order to—

(a) the creditor; and

(b) any other person appearing to the court to have an interest.]

General and miscellaneous

[15M Expenses of diligence on the dependence

(1) Subject to subsection (3)(a) below, a creditor shall be entitled to such expenses as the creditor incurs—

(a) in obtaining warrant for diligence on the dependence; and

(b) where an arrestment or inhibition is executed in pursuance of the warrant, in so executing the arrestment or inhibition.

(2) Subject to subsection (3)(b) below, a debtor shall be entitled, where—

(a) warrant for diligence on the dependence is granted; and

(b) the court is satisfied that the creditor was acting unreasonably in applying for it,

to the expenses incurred in opposing that warrant.

(3) The court may modify or refuse—

(a) such expenses as are mentioned in subsection (1) above if it is satisfied that—

(i) the creditor was acting unreasonably in applying for the warrant; or

(ii) such modification or refusal is reasonable in all the circumstances and having regard to the outcome of the action; and

(b) such expenses as are mentioned in subsection (2) above if it is satisfied as to the matter mentioned in paragraph (a)(ii) above.

(4) Subject to subsections (1) to (3) above, the court may make such finding as it thinks fit in relation to such expenses as are mentioned in subsections (1) and (2) above.

(5) Expenses incurred as mentioned in subsection (1) and (2) above in obtaining or, as the case may be, opposing an application for warrant shall be expenses of process.

(6) Subsections (1) to (5) above are without prejudice to any enactment or rule of law as to the recovery of expenses chargeable against a debtor as are incurred in executing an arrestment or inhibition on the dependence of an action.]

[15N Application of this Part to admiralty actions

This Part of this Act (other than sections 15H, 15J and 15M) shall apply, in so far as not inconsistent with the provisions of Part V of the Administration of Justice Act 1956 (c 46)(admiralty jurisdiction and arrestment of ships), to an arrestment on the dependence of an admiralty action as it applies to any other arrestment on the dependence.]]

[PART 3A

ARRESTMENT AND ACTION OF FURTHCOMING

[73A Arrestment and action of furthcoming to proceed only on decree or document of debt

(1) Arrestment and action of furthcoming or sale shall be competent only in execution of—

(a) subject to subsection (2) below, a decree; or
(b) a document of debt.

(2) Arrestment and action of furthcoming or sale in execution of a summary warrant shall be competent only if—

(a) the debtor has been charged to pay the debt due by virtue of the summary warrant; and
(b) the period for payment specified in the charge has expired without payment being made.

(3) Any rule of law, having effect immediately before the coming into force of this section, as to the decrees or documents on which arrestment and action of furthcoming or sale can proceed shall, in so far as inconsistent with this section, cease to have effect.

(4) In this Part of this Act—

'decree' means—

(a) a decree of the Court of Session, of the High Court of Justiciary or of the sheriff;
(b) a decree of the Court of Teinds;
(c) a summary warrant;
(d) a civil judgment granted outside Scotland by a court, tribunal or arbiter which by virtue of any enactment or rule of law is enforceable in Scotland;
(e) an order or determination which by virtue of any enactment is enforceable as if it were an extract registered decree arbitral bearing a warrant for execution issued by the sheriff;
(f) a warrant granted, in criminal proceedings, for enforcement by civil diligence; or
(g) a liability order within the meaning of section 33(2) of the Child Support Act 1991 (c 48),

being a decree, warrant, judgment, order or determination which, or an extract of which, authorises arrestment and action of furthcoming or sale; and

'document of debt' means—

(a) a document registered for execution in the Books of Council and Session or the sheriff court books;
(b) a document or settlement which by virtue of an Order in Council under section 13 of the Civil Jurisdiction and Judgments Act 1982 (c 27) is enforceable in Scotland,

[. . .] or

(d) a maintenance arrangement (within the meaning of Article 3(e) of the Hague Convention) which is registered in the sheriff court under the Hague Convention,]

[being a document, settlement, instrument or arrangement] which, or an extract of which, authorises arrestment and action of furthcoming or sale.

(5) The Scottish Ministers may, by order, modify the definitions of 'decree' and 'document of debt' in subsection (4) above so as to—

(a) add or remove types of decree or document to or, as the case may be, from those referred to in that provision; or
(b) vary any of the descriptions of the types of decree or document there referred to.]

[73B Schedule of arrestment to be in prescribed form

(1) This section applies where a creditor arrests in execution of—

(a) a decree and the creditor has not executed an arrestment on the dependence of the action; or
(b) a document of debt.

(2) The schedule of arrestment used in executing the arrestment shall be in (or as nearly as may be in) the form prescribed by the Scottish Ministers by regulations.]

[73C Arrestment on the dependence followed by decree

(1) This section applies where a creditor obtains a decree (in this Part of this Act referred to as a 'final decree') in an action on the dependence of which the creditor has executed an arrestment.

(2) The creditor shall, as soon as reasonably practicable, serve a copy of that final decree, in (or as nearly as may be in) the form prescribed by Act of Sederunt, on the arrestee.]

[73E Funds attached

(1) Subsections (2) to (5) below apply—

(a) where a creditor arrests in execution of—

(i) a decree and the creditor has not executed an arrestment on the dependence of the action; or

(ii) a document of debt; and

(b) only to the extent that the arrestee holds funds due to the debtor the value of which, at the time the arrestment is executed, is or can be ascertained (whether or not that arrestee also holds other moveable property of the debtor).

(2) Subject to subsection (4) below and to section 73F of this Act, the funds mentioned in subsection (1)(b) above attached by the arrestment shall be the lesser of—

(a) the sum due by the arrestee to the debtor; or

(b) the aggregate of—

(i) the principal sum, in relation to which the decree or document is executed, owed by the debtor to the creditor;

(ii) any judicial expenses chargeable against the debtor by virtue of the decree;

(iii) the expenses of executing the arrestment;

(iv) interest on the principal sum up to and including the date of service of the schedule of arrestment;

(v) the interest on the principal sum which would be accrued in the period of 1 year beginning with the day after the date mentioned in sub-paragraph (iv) above;

(vi) any interest on the expenses of executing the arrestment which is chargeable against the debtor; and

(vii) any sum prescribed under subsection (3) below.

(3) The Scottish Ministers may, by regulations, prescribe a sum which appears to them to be reasonable having regard to the average expenses likely to be incurred and chargeable against a debtor in a typical action of furthcoming.

(4) Where—

(a) the arrestee holds both funds due to and other moveable property of the debtor; and

(b) the sum mentioned in paragraph (b) of subsection (2) above exceeds the sum mentioned in paragraph (a) of that subsection,

the arrestment shall, in addition to the funds equal to the sum mentioned in that paragraph (a), attach the whole moveable property so held.

(5) Except as provided for in subsection (4) above, an arrestment to which this section applies shall not attach any moveable property of the debtor other than the sum attached under subsection (2) above.

(6) Where, in a case to which subsections (2) to (5) above apply—

(a) in addition to the funds mentioned in subsection (1)(b) above, the arrestee holds funds due to the debtor the value of which is not or cannot be ascertained; and

(b) the sum mentioned in paragraph (a) of subsection (2) above exceeds the sum mentioned in paragraph (b) of that subsection,

the arrestment shall not attach any of the funds mentioned in paragraph (a) above.]

[73F Protection of minimum balance in certain bank accounts

(1) Subject to subsection (2) below, this section applies where—

(a) a creditor arrests—

(i) in pursuance of a warrant granted for diligence on the dependence of an action; or

(ii) in execution of a decree or document of debt;

(b) the arrestment attaches funds standing to the credit of a debtor in an account held by a bank or other financial institution; and

(c) the debtor is an individual.

(2) This section does not apply where the account is—

(a) held in the name of a company, a limited liability partnership, a partnership or an unincorporated association; or

(b) operated by the debtor as a trading account.

(3) The arrestment shall—

(a) in a case where the sum standing to the credit of the debtor exceeds the sum [of £1,000], attach only the balance above that sum; and

(b) in any other case, attach no funds.

(4) [. . .]

(5) In subsection (1) above, 'bank or other financial institution' means—

(a) the Bank of England;

(b) a person who has permission under [Part 4A] of the Financial Services and Markets Act 2000 (c 8) to accept deposits;

(c) an EEA firm of the kind mentioned in paragraph 5(b) of Schedule 3 to that Act which has permission under paragraph 15 of that schedule (as a result of qualifying for authorisation under paragraph 12 of that schedule) to accept deposits; or

(d) a person who is exempt from the general prohibition in respect of accepting deposits as a result of an exemption order made under section 38(1) of that Act,

and the expressions in this definition shall be read with section 22 of that Act, any relevant order made under that section and Schedule 2 to that Act.

(6) The Scottish Ministers may, by regulations—

(a) modify subsection (2) above so as to—

(i) add or remove types of account to or, as the case may be, from those referred to in that paragraph; or

(ii) vary any of the descriptions of the types of account there referred to; [. . .]

[(aa) vary the protected minimum sum mentioned in subsection (3)(a), and]

(b) modify the definition of 'bank or other financial institution' in subsection (5) above so as to—

(i) add or remove types of financial institution to or, as the case may be, from those referred to in that provision; or

(ii) vary any of the descriptions of the types of institution there referred to.]

[73G Arrestee's duty of disclosure

(1) This section applies where a creditor arrests—

(a) in pursuance of a warrant granted for diligence on the dependence of an action; or

(b) in execution of a decree or document of debt.

(2) The arrestee shall, before the expiry of the period mentioned in subsection (3) below, send to the creditor in (or as nearly as may be in) the form prescribed by the Scottish Ministers by regulations, the information mentioned in subsection (4) below.

(3) The period referred to in subsection (2) above is the period of 3 weeks beginning with the day on which the arrestment is executed.

(4) The information referred to in subsection (2) above is—
(a) where any property, other than funds due to the debtor, is attached—
(i) the nature of that property; and
(ii) the value of it in so far as known to the arrestee; and
(b) where any such funds are attached, the nature and value of those funds.
(5) The arrestee shall, at the same time as sending, under subsection (2) above, the information to the creditor, send a copy of it to—
(a) the debtor; and
(b) in so far as known to the arrestee, any person—
(i) who owns or claims to own attached property; or
(ii) to whom attached funds are or are claimed to be due,
solely or in common with the debtor.]

[73H Failure to disclose information

(1) Where an arrestee fails without reasonable excuse to send the prescribed form under section 73G(2) of this Act, the sheriff may, on the application of the creditor, make an order requiring the arrestee to pay to the creditor—
(a) the sum due to the creditor by the debtor; or
(b) the sum mentioned in section 73F(4) of this Act,
whichever is the lesser.
(2) Where the arrestee fails to send the prescribed form in relation to an arrestment on the dependence of an action, the sheriff—
(a) may not make an order under subsection (1) above until the creditor has served a copy of the final decree under section 73C(2) above; and
(b) may deal with the failure as a contempt of court.
(3) Where a sum is paid by virtue of an order under subsection (1) above—
(a) the debt owed by the debtor to the creditor shall be reduced by that sum; and
(b) the arrestee shall not be entitled to recover that sum from the debtor.
(4) An arrestee aggrieved by an order under subsection (1) above may, before the expiry of the period of 2 weeks beginning with the day on which the order is made, appeal, on point of law only, to the sheriff principal, whose decision shall be final.]

[73J Automatic release of arrested funds

(1) This section applies where—
(a) a creditor—
(i) obtains a final decree in an action on the dependence of which the creditor has executed an arrestment; or
(ii) arrests in execution of a decree or document of debt; and
(b) the arrestment attaches funds which are due to the debtor (whether or not it also attaches other moveable property of the debtor).
(2) Subject to section 73L of this Act, the arrestee—
(a) shall, on the expiry of the period mentioned in subsection (3) below, release to the creditor, from the attached funds, a sum calculated in accordance with section 73K of this Act; and
(b) may, where a mandate authorises the arrestee to do so, release that sum before the expiry of that period.
(3) The period referred to in subsection (2) above is the period of 14 weeks beginning with the date of service of a copy of the final decree under section 73C(2) of this Act or, as the case may be, the date of service of the schedule of arrestment.
(4) In this section and in sections 73K to 73P of this Act, references to funds or sums due to or by any person do not include references to funds or sums due in respect of future or contingent debts.]

[73K Sum released under section 73J(2)

The sum released under section 73J(2) of this Act is the lowest of—

(a) the sum attached by the arrestment;

(b) the sum due by the arrestee to the debtor; or

(c) the aggregate of—

(i) the principal sum, in relation to which the decree or document is executed or, as the case may be, which is decerned for in the final decree, owed by the debtor to the creditor;

(ii) any judicial expenses chargeable against the debtor by virtue of the decree or final decree;

(iii) the expenses of executing the arrestment;

(iv) interest on the principal sum up to and including the date of service of the schedule of arrestment or, as the case may be, the date of the final decree;

(v) the interest on the principal sum which would be accrued in the period beginning with the day after the date mentioned in sub-paragraph (iv) above and ending on the day on which the funds are released under section 73J(2) of this Act; and

(vi) any interest on the expenses of executing the arrestment which is chargeable against the debtor.]

[73L Circumstances preventing automatic release

(1) No funds may be released under section 73J(2) of this Act where—

(a) a person mentioned in subsection (2) below applies, by notice of objection, to the sheriff under section 73M(1) of this Act;

(b) the debtor applies to the sheriff under section 73Q(2) of this Act;

(c) an action of multiplepoinding is raised in relation to the funds attached by the arrestment; or

(d) the arrestment is—

(i) recalled;

(ii) restricted; or

(iii) otherwise ceases to have effect.

(2) The persons referred to in subsection (1)(a) above are—

(a) the debtor;

(b) the arrestee; and

(c) any other person to whom the funds are due solely or in common with the debtor (in this section and in sections 73M and 73N of this Act, the 'third party').]

[73M Notice of objection

(1) Where section 73J of this Act applies—

(a) the debtor;

(b) the arrestee; or

(c) a third party,

may, by notice of objection, apply to the sheriff for an order recalling or restricting the arrestment.

(2) The notice of objection referred to in subsection (1) above shall—

(a) be in (or as nearly as may be in) the form prescribed by Act of Sederunt;

(b) be given to the persons mentioned in subsection (3) below before the expiry of the period of 4 weeks beginning with the date of service of a copy of the final decree under section 73C(2) of this Act or, as the case may be, the date of service of the schedule of arrestment; and

(c) specify one or more of the grounds of objection mentioned in subsection (4) below.

(3) The persons referred to in subsection (2)(b) above are—

(a) the creditor;

(b) the sheriff clerk;

(c) the debtor or, as the case may be, the arrestee; and

(d) in so far as known to the person objecting, any third party.

(4) The grounds of objection referred to in subsection (2)(c) above are—

(a) the warrant in execution of which the arrestment was executed is invalid;

(b) the arrestment has been executed incompetently or irregularly;

(c) the funds attached are due to the third party solely or in common with the debtor.

(5) Where a person applies by notice of objection under subsection (1) above, that person may not, subject to subsection (6) below, raise—

(a) an action of multiplepoinding; or

(b) subject to subsection (7) below, any other proceedings,

in relation to the funds attached.

(6) Subsection (5) above is without prejudice to the right of the person—

(a) to enter any such action or proceedings raised by any other person; and

(b) to raise such an action or proceedings where the sheriff makes, under section 73N(5) of this Act, an order sisting the proceedings on the objection.

(7) A debtor who applies by notice of objection under subsection (1) above may apply to the sheriff under section 73Q(2) of this Act and, in such a case, the sheriff may deal with both applications at one hearing.]

[73N Hearings following notice of objection

(1) Subject to subsection (5) below, before the expiry of the period of 8 weeks beginning with the day on which an application by notice of objection is made under section 73M(1) of this Act, the sheriff shall hold a hearing to determine the objection.

(2) At the hearing under subsection (1) above, the sheriff shall not make any order without first giving—

(a) the creditor;

(b) the arrestee;

(c) the debtor; and

(d) any third party, an opportunity to be heard.

(3) Where the sheriff upholds the objection, the sheriff may make an order recalling or restricting the arrestment.

(4) Where the sheriff rejects the objection, the sheriff may make an order requiring a sum determined in the order to be released to the creditor—

(a) in a case where the period mentioned in section 73J(3) of this Act has not expired, on the expiry of that period; or

(b) in any other case, as soon as reasonably practicable after the date on which the order is made.

(5) Where—

(a) the sheriff is satisfied that it is more appropriate for the matters raised at the hearing to be dealt with by—

(i) an action of multiplepoinding; or

(ii) other proceedings,

raised in relation to the funds attached; or

(b) at any time before a decision is made under subsections (3) or (4) above, such an action is or other proceedings are raised,

the sheriff shall make an order sisting the proceedings on the objection.

(6) The sheriff may make such other order as the sheriff thinks fit.

(7) Where the sheriff makes an order under this section, the sheriff shall order the person who objected to intimate that order to such of the persons mentioned in subsection (2) above as the sheriff thinks fit.

(8) A person aggrieved by a decision of the sheriff under this section may, before the expiry of the period of 14 days beginning with the day on which the decision is made, appeal, on point of law only, to the sheriff principal, whose decision shall be final.]

[73P Arrestee not liable for funds released in good faith

Where an arrestee releases funds under section 73J(2) of this Act in good faith but—

(a) the warrant in execution of which the arrestment was executed is invalid; or

(b) the arrestment was incompetently or irregularly executed,

the arrestee is not liable to the debtor or to any other person having an interest in the funds for damages for patrimonial loss caused by the release of funds.]

[73Q Application for release of property where arrestment unduly harsh

(1) This section applies where—

(a) a creditor—

(i) obtains final decree in an action on the dependence of which the creditor executed an arrestment; or

(ii) arrests in execution of a decree or document of debt; and

(b) the arrestment attaches funds due to or other moveable property of the debtor.

(2) The debtor may apply to the sheriff for an order—

(a) providing that the arrestment ceases to have effect in relation to—

(i) the funds or other property attached; or

(ii) so much of those funds or that property as the sheriff specifies; and

(b) requiring the arrestee to release the funds or property to the debtor.

(3) An application under subsection (2) above shall be—

(a) in (or as nearly as may be in) the form prescribed by Act of Sederunt;

(b) made at any time during which the arrestment has effect; and

(c) intimated to—

(i) the creditor;

(ii) the arrestee; and

(iii) any other person appearing to have an interest.]

[73R Hearing on application under section 73Q for release of property

(1) At the hearing on an application under section 73Q(2) of this Act, the sheriff shall not make any order without first giving—

(a) the creditor;

(b) the arrestee; and

(c) any other person appearing to the court to have an interest, an opportunity to be heard.

(2) Subject to subsection (3) below, if the sheriff is satisfied that the arrestment is unduly harsh—

(a) to the debtor; or

(b) where the debtor is an individual, to any person such as is mentioned in subsection (4) below,

the sheriff shall make an order such as is mentioned in section 73Q(2) of this Act.

(3) Before making an order under subsection (2) above the sheriff shall have regard to all the circumstances including, in a case where the debtor is an individual and funds are attached—

(a) the source of those funds; and

(b) where the source of those funds is or includes earnings, whether an earnings arrestment, current maintenance arrestment or conjoined arrestment order is in effect in relation to those earnings.

(4) The persons referred to in subsection (2)(b) above are—

(a) a spouse of the debtor;

(b) a person living together with the debtor as husband and wife;

(c) a civil partner of the debtor;

(d) a person living with the debtor in a relationship which has the characteristics of the relationship between a husband and wife except that the person and the debtor are of the same sex;

(e) a child of the debtor under the age of 16 years, including—

(i) a stepchild; and

(ii) any child brought up or treated by the debtor or any person mentioned in paragraph (b), (c) or (d) above as a child of the debtor or, as the case may be, that person.

(5) Where the sheriff refuses to make an order under subsection (2) above, the sheriff may, in a case where funds are attached, make an order requiring a sum determined in the order to be released to the creditor—

(a) in a case where the period mentioned in section 73J(3) of this Act has not expired, on the expiry of that period; or

(b) in any other case, as soon as reasonably practicable after the date on which the order is made.

(6) Where the sheriff makes an order under this section, the sheriff shall order the debtor to intimate that order to the persons mentioned in subsection (1) above.

(7) A person aggrieved by a decision of the sheriff under this section may, before the expiry of the period of 14 days beginning with the day on which the decision is made, appeal, on point of law only, to the sheriff principal, whose decision shall be final.]

[73S Mandate to be in prescribed form

(1) A mandate authorising an arrestee to pay over any funds or hand over other property attached by an arrestment shall be in (or as nearly as may be in) the form prescribed by the Scottish Ministers by regulations.

(2) A mandate which is not in (or as nearly as may be in) the prescribed form is invalid.

(3) Where—

(a) a mandate is invalid by virtue of subsection (2) above; but

(b) the arrestee pays over funds or hands over other property in accordance with that mandate,

the arrestee is not liable to the debtor or to any other person having an interest in the funds or property for damages for patrimonial loss caused by paying over the funds or handing over the property provided the arrestee acted in good faith.]

[73T Arrestment of ships etc

For the avoidance of doubt, this Part of this Act does not apply to the arrestment of a ship, cargo or other maritime property.]]

PART VI

WARRANTS FOR DILIGENCE AND CHARGES FOR PAYMENT

. . .

88 Warrants for diligence: special cases

(1) This section applies where a creditor has acquired by assignation intimated to the debtor, confirmation as executor, or otherwise a right to—

(a) a decree;

(b) an obligation contained in a document an extract of which, after the document has been registered in the Books of Council and Session or in sheriff court books, may be obtained containing warrant for execution;

(c) an order or determination which by virtue of any enactment is enforceable as if it were an extract registered decree arbitral bearing a warrant for execution issued by a sheriff,

either directly or through a third party from a person in whose favour the decree, order or determination was granted or who was the creditor in the obligation contained in the document.

(2) Where this section applies, the creditor who has acquired a right as

mentioned in subsection (1) above may apply to the appropriate clerk for a warrant having the effect of authorising the execution at the instance of that creditor of any diligence authorised by an extract of the decree or document or by the order or determination, as the case may be.

(3) The applicant under subsection (2) above shall submit to the appropriate clerk—

(a) an extract of the decree or of the document registered as mentioned in subsection (1)(b) above or a certified copy of the order or determination; and

(b) the assignation (along with evidence of its intimation to the debtor), confirmation as executor or other document establishing the applicant's right.

(4) The appropriate clerk shall grant the warrant applied for under subsection (2) above if he is satisfied that the applicant's right is established.

(5) Where—

(a) a charge has already been served in pursuance of the decree, order, determination or registered document; and

(b) the applicant under subsection (2) above submits with his application the certificate of execution of the charge in addition to the documents mentioned in subsection (3) above,

a warrant granted under subsection (4) above shall authorise the execution at the instance of the applicant of diligence in pursuance of that charge.

(6) For the purposes of this section, 'the appropriate clerk' shall be—

(a) in the case of a decree granted by the Court of Session or a document registered (whether before or after such acquisition) in the Books of Council and Session, a clerk of court of the Court of Session;

(b) in the case of a decree granted by the High Court of Justiciary, a clerk of Justiciary;

(c) in the case of a decree granted by a sheriff or a document registered (whether before or after such acquisition) in the books of a sheriff court, the sheriff clerk of that sheriff court;

(d) in the case of such an order or determination as is mentioned in subsection (1)(c) above, any sheriff clerk.

89 Abolition of letters of horning, horning and poinding, poinding, and caption

The granting of letters of horning, letters of horning and poinding, letters of poinding and letters of caption shall cease to be competent.

90 Provisions relating to charges for payment

(1) [. . .] the execution of [. . .] an earnings arrestment shall not be competent unless a charge for payment has been served on the debtor and the period for payment specified in the charge has expired without payment being made.

[(1A) The following subsections of this section apply to any case where it is competent to execute diligence only if a charge for payment has been served on the debtor.]

[. . .]

(3) The period for payment specified in any charge for payment served in pursuance of a warrant for execution shall be 14 days if the person on whom it is served is within the United Kingdom and 28 days if he is outside the United Kingdom or his whereabouts are unknown.

(4) Any such charge shall be in the form prescribed by Act of Sederunt or Act of Adjournal.

(5) Subject to subsection (6) below, where any such charge has been served, it shall not be competent to execute [diligence] by virtue of that charge more than 2 years after the date of such service.

(6) A creditor may reconstitute his right to execute [diligence] by the service of a further charge for payment.

(7) No expenses incurred in the service of a further charge for payment within the period of 2 years after service of the first charge shall be chargeable against the debtor.

(8) Registration of certificates of execution of charges for payment in a register of hornings shall cease to be competent.

91 Enforcement of certain warrants and precepts of sheriff anywhere in Scotland

(1) The following may be executed anywhere in Scotland—

(a) a warrant for execution contained in an extract of a decree granted by a sheriff;

(b) a warrant for execution inserted in an extract of a document registered in sheriff court books;

(c) a summary warrant;

(d) a warrant of a sheriff for arrestment on the dependence of an action or in security;

(e) a precept (issued by a sheriff clerk) of arrestment in security of a liquid debt the term of payment of which has not arrived.

(2) A warrant or precept mentioned in subsection (1) above may be executed by a sheriff officer of—

(a) the court which granted it; or

(b) the sheriff court district in which it is to be executed.

PART VII

MISCELLANEOUS AND GENERAL

. . .

94 Ascription of sums recovered by diligence or while diligence is in effect

(1) This section applies to any sums recovered by any of the following diligences—

[. . .]

(b) an earnings arrestment;

(c) an arrestment and action of furthcoming or sale; or

(d) a conjoined arrestment order in so far as it enforces an ordinary debt,

or paid to account of the sums recoverable by the diligence while the diligence is in effect.

(2) A sum to which this section applies shall be ascribed to the following in the order in which they are mentioned—

(a) the expenses already incurred in respect of—

(i) the diligence;

(ii) any previous diligence the expenses of which are chargeable against and recoverable from the debtor under section 93(5) of this Act;

(iii) the execution of a current maintenance arrestment;

(b) any interest, due under the decree or other document on which the diligence proceeds, which has accrued at the date of execution of the [. . .] earnings arrestment or arrestment, or in the case of an ordinary debt included in a conjoined arrestment order which has accrued at the date of application under section 60(2) or 62(5) of this Act;

(c) any sum (including any expenses) due under the decree or other document, other than any expenses or interest mentioned in paragraphs (a) and (b) above.

[95A Prescription of arrestment

(1) Subject to subsection (2) below, an arrestment which is not insisted in prescribes—

(a) where it is on the dependence of an action, at the end of the period of 3 years beginning with the day on which a final interlocutor is obtained by the creditor for payment of all or part of a principal sum concluded for; or

(b) where it is in execution of an extract decree or other extract registered document relating to a due debt, at the end of the period of 3 years beginning with the day on which the arrestment is executed.

(2) Where the arrestment secures or enforces a future or contingent debt due to the creditor, it prescribes, if not insisted in, at the end of the period of 3 years beginning on the day on which the debt becomes due.

(3) In a case where—

(a) a time to pay direction;

(b) an interim order under section 6(3) of this Act; or

(c) a time to pay order,

has been made, there shall be disregarded, in computing the period at the end of which the arrestment prescribes, the period during which the time to pay direction, interim order or time to pay order is in effect.

(4) Nothing in this section shall apply to an earnings arrestment, a current maintenance arrestment or a conjoined arrestment order.

(5) Subsections (1) to (3) above apply irrespective of whether the arrestment is executed, or warrant for it obtained, before this section comes into force.

(6) For the purposes of subsection (1)(a) above, a final interlocutor is obtained when an interlocutor cannot be recalled or altered and is not subject to review.]

102 Procedure in diligence proceeding on extract of registered document etc

(1) The Court of Session may by Act of Sederunt—

(a) regulate and prescribe the procedure and practice in; and

(b) prescribe the form of any document to be used in, or for the purposes of, diligence of a kind specified in subsection (2) below.

(2) The diligences referred to in subsection (1) above are diligences proceeding—

(a) on an extract of a document which has been registered for execution in the Books of Council and Session or in sheriff court books; or

(b) on an order or a determination which by virtue of any enactment is to be treated as if it were so registered.

[SCHEDULE 2 Section 49

(Schedule 2 substituted by SSI 2024/293)

[TABLE A: DEDUCTIONS FROM WEEKLY EARNINGS

Net earnings	*Deduction**
Not exceeding £172.61	Nil
Exceeding £172.61 but not exceeding £345.22	£2.30 or 15% of earnings exceeding £172.61, whichever is the greater
Exceeding £345.22 but not exceeding £575.37	£25.89 plus 20% of earnings exceeding £345.22
Exceeding £575.37 but not exceeding £863.06	£71.92 plus 25% of earnings exceeding £575.37
Exceeding £863.06	£143.84 plus 50% of earnings exceeding £863.06

TABLE B: DEDUCTIONS FROM MONTHLY EARNINGS

Net earnings	*Deduction**
Not exceeding £750.00	Nil
Exceeding £750.00 but not exceeding £1,500.00	£10.00 or 15% of earnings exceeding £750.00, whichever is the greater
Exceeding £1,500.00 but not exceeding £2,500.00	£112.50 plus 20% of earnings exceeding £1,500.00
Exceeding £2,500.00 but not exceeding £3,750.00	£312.50 plus 25% of earnings exceeding £2,500.00
Exceeding £3,750.00	£625.00 plus 50% of earnings exceeding £3,750.00

TABLE C: DEDUCTIONS FROM DAILY EARNINGS

Net earnings	*Deduction**
Not exceeding £24.66	Nil
Exceeding £24.66 but not exceeding £49.32	£0.33 or 15% of earnings exceeding £24.66, whichever is the greater
Exceeding £49.32 but not exceeding £82.19	£3.70 plus 20% of earnings exceeding £49.32
Exceeding £82.19 but not exceeding £123.29	£10.27 plus 25% of earnings exceeding £82.19
Exceeding £123.29	£20.55 plus 50% of earnings exceeding £123.29

* When applying a percentage the calculation should be done to two decimal places of a penny and the result rounded to the nearest whole penny, with an exact half penny being rounded down]]

CONSUMER PROTECTION ACT 1987
(1987, c 43)

PART I
PRODUCT LIABILITY

1 Purpose and construction of Part I

(1) This Part [was enacted] for the purpose of making such provision as [was] necessary in order to comply with the product liability Directive and shall be construed accordingly.

(2) In this Part, except in so far as the context otherwise requires—

[. . .]

'dependant' and 'relative' have the same meaning as they have in, respectively, the Fatal Accidents Act 1976 and the [Damages (Scotland) Act 2011];

'producer', in relation to a product, means—

(a) the person who manufactured it;

(b) in the case of a substance which has not been manufactured but has been won or abstracted, the person who won or abstracted it;

(c) in the case of a product which has not been manufactured, won or abstracted but essential characteristics of which are attributable to an industrial or other process having been carried out (for example, in relation to agricultural produce), the person who carried out that process;

'product' means any goods or electricity and (subject to subsection (3) below) includes a product which is comprised in another product, whether by virtue of being a component part or raw material or otherwise; and

'the product liability Directive' means the Directive of the Council of the European Union, dated 25th July 1985, (No 85/374/EEC) on the approximation of the laws, regulations and administrative provisions of the member States concerning liability for defective products.

(3) For the purposes of this Part a person who supplies any product in which products are comprised, whether by virtue of being component parts or raw materials or otherwise, shall not be treated by reason only of his supply of that product as supplying any of the products so comprised.

2 Liability for defective products

(1) Subject to the following provisions of this Part, where any damage is caused wholly or partly by a defect in a product, every person to whom subsection (2) below applies shall be liable for the damage.

(2) This subsection applies to—

(a) the producer of the product;

(b) any person who, by putting his name on the product or using a trade mark or other distinguishing mark in relation to the product, has held himself out to be the producer of the product;

(c) any person who has imported the product into [the United Kingdom] in order, in the course of any business of his, to supply it to another.

(3) Subject as aforesaid, where any damage is caused wholly or partly by a defect in a product, any person who supplied the product (whether to the person who suffered the damage, to the producer of any product in which the product in question is comprised or to any other person) shall be liable for the damage if—

(a) the person who suffered the damage requests the supplier to identify one or more of the persons (whether still in existence or not) to whom subsection (2) above applies in relation to the product;

(b) that request is made within a reasonable period after the damage occurs and at a time when it is not reasonably practicable for the person making the request to identify all those persons; and

(c) the supplier fails, within a reasonable period after receiving the request, either to comply with the request or to identify the person who supplied the product to him.

[. . .]

(5) Where two or more persons are liable by virtue of this Part for the same damage, their liability shall be joint and several.

(6) This section shall be without prejudice to any liability arising otherwise than by virtue of this Part.

3 Meaning of 'defect'

(1) Subject to the following provisions of this section, there is a defect in a product for the purposes of this Part if the safety of the product is not such as persons generally are entitled to expect; and for those purposes 'safety', in relation to a product, shall include safety with respect to products comprised in that product and safety in the context of risks of damage to property, as well as in the context of risks of death or personal injury.

(2) In determining for the purposes of subsection (1) above what persons generally are entitled to expect in relation to a product all the circumstances shall be taken into account, including—

(a) the manner in which, and purposes for which, the product has been marketed, its get-up, the use of any mark in relation to the product and any instructions for, or warnings with respect to, doing or refraining from doing anything with or in relation to the product;

(b) what might reasonably be expected to be done with or in relation to the product; and

(c) the time when the product was supplied by its producer to another;

and nothing in this section shall require a defect to be inferred from the fact alone that the safety of a product which is supplied after that time is greater than the safety of the product in question.

4 Defences

(1) In any civil proceedings by virtue of this Part against any person ('the person proceeded against') in respect of a defect in a product it shall be a defence for him to show—

(a) that the defect is attributable to compliance with any requirement imposed by or under any enactment or with any [assimilated] obligation; or

(b) that the person proceeded against did not at any time supply the product to another; or

(c) that the following conditions are satisfied, that is to say—

(i) that the only supply of the product to another by the person proceeded against was otherwise than in the course of a business of that person's; and

(ii) that section 2(2) above does not apply to that person or applies to him by virtue only of things done otherwise than with a view to profit; or

(d) that the defect did not exist in the product at the relevant time; or

(e) that the state of scientific and technical knowledge at the relevant time was not such that a producer of products of the same description as the product in question might be expected to have discovered the defect if it had existed in his products while they were under his control; or

(f) that the defect—

(i) constituted a defect in a product ('the subsequent product') in which the product in question had been comprised; and

(ii) was wholly attributable to the design of the subsequent product or to compliance by the producer of the product in question with instructions given by the producer of the subsequent product.

(2) In this section 'the relevant time', in relation to electricity, means the time at which it was generated, being a time before it was transmitted or distributed, and in relation to any other product, means—

(a) if the person proceeded against is a person to whom subsection (2) of section 2 above applies in relation to the product, the time when he supplied the product to another;

(b) if that subsection does not apply to that person in relation to the product, the time when the product was last supplied by a person to whom that subsection does apply in relation to the product.

5 Damage giving rise to liability

(1) Subject to the following provisions of this section, in this Part 'damage' means death or personal injury or any loss of or damage to any property (including land).

(2) A person shall not be liable under section 2 above in respect of any defect in a product for the loss of or any damage to the product itself or for the loss of or any damage to the whole or any part of any product which has been supplied with the product in question comprised in it.

(3) A person shall not be liable under section 2 above for any loss of or damage to any property which, at the time it is lost or damaged, is not—

(a) of a description of property ordinarily intended for private use, occupation or consumption; and

(b) intended by the person suffering the loss or damage mainly for his own private use, occupation or consumption.

(4) No damages shall be awarded to any person by virtue of this Part in respect of any loss of or damage to any property if the amount which would fall to be so awarded to that person, apart from this subsection and any liability for interest, does not exceed £275.

. . .

(8) Subsections (5) to (7) above shall not extend to Scotland.

6 Application of certain enactments etc

(1) Any damage for which a person is liable under section 2 above shall be deemed to have been caused—

(a) for the purposes of the Fatal Accidents Act 1976, by that person's wrongful act, neglect or default;

(b) for the purposes of section 3 of the Law Reform (Miscellaneous Provisions) (Scotland) Act 1940 (contribution among joint wrongdoers), by that person's wrongful act or negligent act or omission;

(c) for the purposes of [sections 3 to 6 of the Damages (Scotland) Act 2011] (rights of relatives of a deceased), by that person's act or omission, and

(d) for the purposes of Part II of the Administration of Justice Act 1982 (damages for personal injuries, etc—Scotland), by an act or omission giving rise to liability in that person to pay damages.

(2) Where—

(a) a person's death is caused wholly or partly by a defect in a product, or a person dies after suffering damage which has been so caused;

(b) a request such as mentioned in paragraph (a) of subsection (3) of section 2 above is made to a supplier of the product by that person's personal representatives or, in the case of a person whose death is caused wholly or partly by the defect, by any dependant or relative of that person; and

(c) the conditions specified in paragraphs (b) and (c) of that subsection are satisfied in relation to that request,

this Part shall have effect for the purposes of the Law Reform (Miscellaneous Provisions) Act 1934, the Fatal Accidents Act 1976 and the [Damages (Scotland) Act 2011] as if liability of the supplier to that person under that subsection did not depend on that person having requested the supplier to identify certain persons or on the said conditions having been satisfied in relation to a request made by that person.

(3) Section 1 of the Congenital Disabilities (Civil Liability) Act 1976 shall have effect for the purposes of this Part as if—

(a) a person were answerable to a child in respect of an occurrence caused wholly or partly by a defect in a product if he is or has been liable under section 2 above in respect of any effect of the occurrence on a parent of the child, or would be so liable if the occurrence caused a parent of the child to suffer damage;

(b) the provisions of this Part relating to liability under section 2 above applied in relation to liability by virtue of paragraph (a) above under the said section 1; and

(c) subsection (6) of the said section 1 (exclusion of liability) were omitted.

(4) Where any damage is caused partly by a defect in a product and partly by the fault of the person suffering the damage, the Law Reform (Contributory Negligence) Act 1945 and section 5 of the Fatal Accidents Act 1976 (contributory negligence) shall have effect as if the defect were the fault of every person liable by virtue of this Part for the damage caused by the defect.

(5) In subsection (4) above 'fault' has the same meaning as in the said Act of 1945.

(6) Schedule 1 to this Act shall have effect for the purpose of amending the Limitation Act 1980 and the Prescription and Limitation (Scotland) Act 1973 in their application in relation to the bringing of actions by virtue of this Part.

(7) It is hereby declared that liability by virtue of this Part is to be treated as liability in tort for the purposes of any enactment conferring jurisdiction on any court with respect to any matter.

(8) Nothing in this Part shall prejudice the operation of section 12 of the Nuclear Installations Act 1965 (rights to compensation for certain breaches of duties confined to rights under that Act).

7 Prohibition on exclusions from liability

The liability of a person by virtue of this Part to person who has suffered damage caused wholly or partly by a defect in a product, or to a dependant or relative of such a person, shall not be limited or excluded by any contract term, by any notice or by any other provision.

[. . .]

9 Application of Part I to Crown

(1) Subject to subsection (2) below, this Part shall bind the Crown.

(2) The Crown shall not, as regards the Crown's liability by virtue of this Part, be bound by this Part further than the Crown is made liable in tort or in reparation under the Crown Proceedings Act 1947, as that Act has effect from time to time.

PART II
CONSUMER SAFETY

[. . .]

11 Safety regulations

(1) The Secretary of State may by regulations under this section ('safety regulations') make such provision as he considers appropriate [. . .] for the purpose of securing—

(a) that goods to which this section applies are safe;

(b) that goods to which this section applies which are unsafe, or would be unsafe in the hands of persons of a particular description, are not made available to persons generally or, as the case may be, to persons of that description, and

(c) that appropriate information is, and inappropriate information is not, provided in relation to goods to which this section applies.

(2) Without prejudice to the generality of subsection (1) above, safety regulations may contain provision—

(a) with respect to the composition or contents, design, construction, finish or packing of goods to which this section applies, with respect to standards for such goods and with respect to other matters relating to such goods;

(b) with respect to the giving, refusal, alteration or cancellation of approvals of such goods, of descriptions of such goods or of standards for such goods;

(c) with respect to the conditions that may be attached to any approval given under the regulations;

(d) for requiring such fees as may be determined by or under the regulations to be paid on the giving or alteration of any approval under the regulations and on the making of an application for such an approval or alteration;

(e) with respect to appeals against refusals, alterations and cancellations of approvals given under the regulations and against the conditions contained in such approvals;

(f) for requiring goods to which this section applies to be approved under the regulations or to conform to the requirements of the regulations or to descriptions or standards specified in or approved by or under the regulations;

(g) with respect to the testing or inspection of goods to which this section applies (including provision for determining the standards to be applied in carrying out any test or inspection);

(h) with respect to the ways of dealing with goods of which some or all do not satisfy a test required by or under the regulations or a standard connected with a procedure so required;

(i) for requiring a mark, warning or instruction or any other information relating to goods to be put on or to accompany the goods or to be used or provided in some other manner in relation to the goods, and for securing that inappropriate information is not given in relation to goods either by means of misleading marks or otherwise;

(j) for prohibiting persons from supplying, or from offering to supply, agreeing to supply, exposing for supply or possessing for supply, goods to which this section applies and component parts and raw materials for such goods;

(k) for requiring information to be given to any such person as may be determined by or under the regulations for the purpose of enabling that person to exercise any function conferred on him by the regulations.

(3) Without prejudice as aforesaid, safety regulations may contain provision—

(a) for requiring persons on whom functions are conferred by or under section 27 below to have regard, in exercising their functions so far as relating to any provision of safety regulations, to matters specified in a direction issued by the Secretary of State with respect to that provision;

(b) for securing that a person shall not be guilty of an offence under section 12 below unless it is shown that the goods in question do not conform to a particular standard;

(c) for securing that proceedings for such an offence are not brought in England and Wales except by or with the consent of the Secretary of State or the Director of Public Prosecutions;

(d) for securing that proceedings for such an offence are not brought in Northern Ireland except by or with consent of the Secretary of State or the Director of Public Prosecutions for Northern Ireland;

(e) for enabling a magistrates' court in England and Wales or Northern Ireland to try an information or, in Northern Ireland, a complaint in respect of such an offence if the information was laid or the complaint made within twelve months from the time when the offence was committed;

(f) for enabling summary proceedings for such an offence to be brought in Scotland at any time within twelve months from the time when the offence was committed; and

(g) for determining the persons by whom, and the manner in which, anything required to be done by or under the regulations is to be done.

(4) Safety regulations shall not provide for any contravention of the regulations to be an offence.

(5) Where the Secretary of State proposes to make safety regulations it shall be his duty before he makes them—

(a) to consult such organisations as appear to him to be representative of interests substantially affected by the proposal;

(b) to consult such other persons as he considers appropriate; and

(c) in the case of proposed regulations relating to goods suitable for use at work to consult [the Health and Safety Executive] in relation to the application of the proposed regulations to Great Britain;

but the preceding provisions of this subsection shall not apply in the case of regulations which provide for the regulations to cease to have effect at the end of a period of not more than twelve months beginning with the day on which they come into force and which contain a statement that it appears to the Secretary of State that the need to protect the public requires that the regulations should be made without delay.

(6) The power to make safety regulations shall be exercisable by statutory instrument subject to annulment in pursuance of a resolution of either House of Parliament and shall include power—

(a) to make different provision for different cases; and

(b) to make such supplemental, consequential and transitional provision as the Secretary of State considers appropriate.

(7) This section applies to any goods other than—

(a) growing crops and things comprised in land by virtue of being attached to it;

(b) water, food, feeding stuff and fertiliser;

(c) gas which is, is to be or has been supplied by a person authorised to supply it by or under [section 7A of the Gas Act 1986 (licensing of gas suppliers and gas shippers) or paragraph 5 of Schedule 2A to that Act (supply to very large customers an exception to prohibition on unlicensed activities)];

(d) controlled drugs and licensed medicinal products;

[(e) medical devices].

12 Offences against the safety regulations

(1) Where safety regulations prohibit a person from supplying or offering or agreeing to supply any goods or from exposing or possessing any goods for supply that person shall be guilty of an offence if he contravenes the prohibition.

(2) Where safety regulations require a person who makes or processes any goods in the course of carrying on a business—

(a) to carry out a particular test or use a particular procedure in connection with the making or processing of the goods with a view to ascertaining whether the goods satisfy any requirements of such regulations; or

(b) to deal or not to deal in a particular way with a quantity of the goods of which the whole or part does not satisfy such a test or does not satisfy standards connected with such a procedure,

that person shall be guilty of an offence if he does not comply with the requirement.

(3) If a person contravenes a provision of safety regulations which prohibits or requires the provision, by means of a mark or otherwise, of information of a particular kind in relation to goods, he shall be guilty of an offence.

(4) Where safety regulations require any person to give information to another for the purpose of enabling that other to exercise any function, that person shall be guilty of an offence if—

(a) he fails without reasonable cause to comply with the requirement; or

(b) in giving the information which is required of him—

(i) he makes any statement which he knows is false in a material particular; or

(ii) he recklessly makes any statement which is false in a material particular.

(5) A person guilty of an offence under this section shall be liable on summary conviction to imprisonment for a term not exceeding six months or to a fine not exceeding level 5 on the standard scale or to both.

13 Prohibition notices and notices to warn

(1) The Secretary of State may—

(a) serve on any person a notice ('a prohibition notice') prohibiting that person, except with the consent of the Secretary of State, from supplying, or from offering to supply, agreeing to supply, exposing for supply or possessing for supply, any relevant goods which the Secretary of State considers are unsafe and which are described in the notice;

(b) serve on any person a notice ('a notice to warn') requiring that person at his own expense to publish, in a form and manner and on occasions specified in the notice, a warning about any relevant goods which the Secretary of State considers are unsafe, which that person supplies or has supplied and which are described in the notice.

(2) Schedule 2 to this Act shall have effect with respect to prohibition notices and notices to warn, and the Secretary of State may by regulations make provision specifying the manner in which information is to be given to any person under that Schedule.

(3) A consent given by the Secretary of State for the purposes of a prohibition notice may impose such conditions on the doing of anything for which the consent is required as the Secretary of State considers appropriate.

(4) A person who contravenes a prohibition notice or a notice to warn shall be guilty of an offence and liable on summary conviction to imprisonment for a term not exceeding six months or to a fine not exceeding level 5 on the standard scale or to both.

(5) The power to make regulations under subsection (2) above shall be exercisable by statutory instrument subject to annulment in pursuance of a resolution of either House of Parliament and shall include power—

(a) to make different provision for different cases; and

(b) to make such supplemental, consequential and transitional provision as the Secretary of State considers appropriate.

(6) In this section 'relevant goods' means—

(a) in relation to a prohibition notice, any goods to which section 11 above applies; and

(b) in relation to a notice to warn, any goods to which that section applies or any growing crops or things comprised in land by virtue of being attached to it.

[(7) A notice may not be given under this section in respect of any aspect of the safety of goods, or any risk or category of risk associated with goods, concerning which provision is contained in the General Product Safety Regulations 2005.]

14 Suspension notices

(1) Where an enforcement authority has reasonable grounds for suspecting that any safety provision has been contravened in relation to any goods, the authority may serve a notice ('suspension notice') prohibiting the person on whom it is served, for such period ending not more than six months after the date of the notice as is specified therein, from doing any of the following things without the consent of the authority, that is to say, supplying the goods, offering to supply them, agreeing to supply them or exposing them for supply.

(2) A suspension notice served by an enforcement authority in respect of any goods shall—

(a) describe the goods in a manner sufficient to identify them;

(b) set out the grounds on which the authority suspects that a safety provision has been contravened in relation to the goods, and

(c) state that, and the manner in which, the person on whom the notice is served may appeal against the notice under section 15 below.

(3) A suspension notice served by an enforcement authority for the purpose of prohibiting a person for any period from doing the things mentioned in subsection (1) above in relation to any goods may also require that person to keep the authority informed of the whereabouts throughout that period of any of those goods in which he has an interest.

(4) Where a suspension notice has been served on any person in respect of any goods, no further such notice shall be served on that person in respect of the same goods unless—

(a) proceedings against that person for an offence in respect of a contravention in relation to the goods of a safety provision (not being an offence under this section); or

(b) proceedings for the forfeiture of the goods under section 16 or 17 below, are pending at the end of the period specified in the first-mentioned notice.

(5) A consent given by an enforcement authority for the purposes of subsection (1) above may impose such conditions on the doing of anything for which the consent is required as the authority considers appropriate.

(6) Any person who contravenes a suspension notice shall be guilty of an offence and liable on summary conviction to imprisonment for a term not exceeding six months or to a fine not exceeding level 5 on the standard scale or to both.

(7) Where an enforcement authority serves a suspension notice in respect of any goods, the authority shall be liable to pay compensation to any person having an interest in the goods in respect of any loss or damage caused by reason of the service of the notice if—

(a) there has been no contravention in relation to the goods of any safety provision; and

(b) the exercise of the power is not attributable to any neglect or default by that person.

(8) Any disputed question as to the right to or the amount of any compensation payable under this section shall be determined by arbitration or, in Scotland, by a single arbiter appointed, failing agreement between the parties, by the sheriff.

15 Appeals against suspension notices

(1) Any person having an interest in any goods in respect of which a suspension notice is for the time being in force may apply for an order setting aside the notice.

(2) An application under this section may be made—

(a) to any magistrates' court in which proceedings have been brought in England and Wales or Northern Ireland—

(i) for an offence in respect of a contravention in relation to the goods of any safety provision; or

(ii) for the forfeiture of the goods under section 16 below;

(b) where no such proceedings have been so brought, by way of complaint to a magistrates' court; or

(c) in Scotland, by summary application to the sheriff.

(3) On an application under this section to a magistrates' court in England and Wales or Northern Ireland the court shall make an order setting aside the suspension notice only if the court is satisfied that there has been no contravention in relation to the goods of any safety provision.

(4) On an application under this section to the sheriff he shall make an order setting aside the suspension notice only if he is satisfied that at the date of making the order—

(a) proceedings for an offence in respect of a contravention in relation to the goods of any safety provision; or

(b) proceedings for the forfeiture of the goods under section 17 below, have not been brought or, having been brought, have been concluded.

(5) Any person aggrieved by an order made under this section by a magistrates' court in England and Wales or Northern Ireland, or by a decision of such a court not to make such an order, may appeal against that order or decision—

(a) in England and Wales, to the Crown Court;

(b) in Northern Ireland, to the county court;

and an order so made may contain such provision as appears to the court to be appropriate for delaying the coming into force of the order pending the making and determination of any appeal (including any application under section 111 of the Magistrates' Courts Act 1980 or Article 146 of the Magistrates' Courts (Northern Ireland) Order 1981 (statement of case)).

16 [*Does not apply to Scotland.*]

17 Forfeiture: Scotland

(1) In Scotland a sheriff may make an order for forfeiture of any goods in relation to which there has been a contravention of a safety provision—

(a) on an application by the procurator-fiscal made in the manner specified in [section 134 of the Criminal Procedure (Scotland) Act 1995]; or

(b) where a person is convicted of any offence in respect of any such contravention, in addition to any other penalty which the sheriff may impose.

(2) The procurator-fiscal making an application under subsection (1)(a) above shall serve on any person appearing to him to be the owner of, or otherwise to have an interest in, the goods to which the application relates a copy of the application, together with a notice giving him the opportunity to appear at the hearing of the application to show cause why the goods should not be forfeited.

(3) Service under subsection (2) above shall be carried out, and such service may be proved, in the manner specified for citation of an accused in summary proceedings under the [Criminal Procedure (Scotland) Act 1995].

(4) Any person upon whom notice is served under subsection (2) above and any other person claiming to be the owner of, or otherwise to have an interest in, goods to which an application under this section relates shall be entitled to appear at the hearing of the application to show cause why the goods should not be forfeited.

(5) The sheriff shall not make an order following an application under subsection (1)(a) above—

(a) if any person on whom notice is served under subsection (2) above does not appear, unless service of the notice on that person is proved; or

(b) if no notice under subsection (2) above has been served, unless the court is satisfied that in the circumstances it was reasonable not to serve notice on any person.

(6) The sheriff shall make an order under this section only if he is satisfied that there has been a contravention in relation to those goods of a safety provision.

(7) For the avoidance of doubt it is declared that the sheriff may infer for the purposes of this section that there has been a contravention in relation to any goods of a safety provision if he is satisfied that any such provision has been contravened in relation to any goods which are representative of those goods (whether by reason of being of the same design or part of the same consignment or batch or otherwise).

(8) Where an order for the forfeiture of any goods is made following an application by the procurator-fiscal under subsection (1)(a) above, any person who

appeared, or was entitled to appear, to show cause why goods should not be forfeited may, within twenty-one days of the making of the order, appeal to the High Court by Bill of Suspension on the ground of an alleged miscarriage of justice; [and section 182(5)(a) to (e) of the Criminal Procedure (Scotland) Act 1995 shall apply to an appeal under this subsection as it applies to a stated case under Part X of that Act].

(9) An order following an application under subsection (1)(a) above shall not take effect—

(a) until the end of the period of twenty-one days beginning with the day after the day on which the order is made; or

(b) if an appeal is made under subsection (8) above within that period, until the appeal is determined or abandoned.

(10) An order under subsection (1)(b) above shall not take effect—

(a) until the end of the period within which an appeal against the order could be brought under the Criminal Procedure (Scotland) Act 1995; or

(b) if an appeal is made within that period, until the appeal is determined or abandoned.

(11) Subject to subsection (12) below, goods forfeited under this section shall be destroyed in accordance with such directions as the sheriff may give.

(12) If he thinks fit the sheriff may direct that the goods be released, to such person as he may specify, on condition that that person does not supply those goods to any other person otherwise than as mentioned in section 46(7)(a) or (b) below.

18 Power to obtain information

(1) If the Secretary of State considers that, for the purpose of deciding whether—

(a) to make, vary or revoke any safety regulations; or

(b) to serve, vary or revoke a prohibition notice; or

(c) to serve or revoke a notice to warn,

he requires information which another person is likely to be able to furnish, the Secretary of State may serve on the other person a notice under this section.

(2) A notice served on any person under this section may require that person—

(a) to furnish to the Secretary of State, within a period specified in the notice, such information as is so specified;

(b) to produce such records as are specified in the notice at a time and place so specified and to permit a person appointed by the Secretary of State for the purpose to take copies of the records at that time and place.

(3) A person shall be guilty of an offence if he—

(a) fails, without reasonable cause, to comply with a notice served on him under this section; or

(b) in purporting to comply with a requirement which by virtue of paragraph (a) of subsection (2) above is contained in such a notice—

(i) furnishes information which he knows is false in a material particular; or

(ii) recklessly furnishes information which is false in a material particular.

(4) A person guilty of an offence under subsection (3) above shall—

(a) in the case of an offence under paragraph (a) of that subsection, be liable on summary conviction to a fine not exceeding level 5 on the standard scale; and

(b) in the case of an offence under paragraph (b) of that subsection be liable—

(i) on conviction on indictment, to a fine,

(ii) on summary conviction, to a fine not exceeding the statutory maximum.

19 Interpretation of Part II

(1) in this Part—

'controlled drug' means a controlled drug within the meaning of the Misuse of Drugs Act 1971;

'feeding stuff' and 'fertiliser' have the same meaning as in Part IV of the Agriculture Act 1970;

'food' does not include anything containing tobacco but, subject to that, has the same meaning as in the [Food Safety Act 1990] or, in relation to Northern Ireland, the same meaning as in the [the Food Safety (Northern Ireland) Order 1991];

'licensed medicinal product' means—

(a) any medicinal product within the meaning of the Medicines Act 1968 in respect of which a product licence within the meaning of that Act is for the time being in force;

(b) any other article or substance in respect of which any such licence is for the time being in force in pursuance of an order under section 104 or 105 of that Act (application of Act to other articles and substances); [or

(c) a veterinary medicinal product that has a marketing authorisation under the Veterinary Medicines Regulations 2006.]

['medical device' has the same meaning as in Part 4 of the Medicines and Medical Devices Act 2021;]

'safe', in relation to any goods, means such that there is no risk, or no risk apart from one reduced to a minimum, that any of the following will (whether immediately or after a definite or indefinite period) cause the death of, or any personal injury to, any person whatsoever, that is to say—

(a) the goods;

(b) the keeping, use or consumption of the goods;

(c) the assembly of any of the goods which are, or are to be, supplied unassembled;

(d) any emission or leakage from the goods or, as a result of the keeping, use or consumption of the goods, from anything else; or

(e) reliance on the accuracy of any measurement, calculation or other reading made by or by means of the goods,

and [. . .] 'unsafe' shall be construed accordingly;

'tobacco' includes any tobacco product within the meaning of the Tobacco Products Duty Act 1979 and any article or substance containing tobacco and intended for oral or nasal use.

(2) In the definition of 'safe' in subsection (1) above, references to the keeping, use or consumption of any goods are references to—

(a) the keeping, use or consumption of the goods by the persons by whom, and in all or any of the ways or circumstances in which, they might reasonably be expected to be kept, used or consumed; and

(b) the keeping, use or consumption of the goods either alone or in conjunction with other goods in conjunction with which they might reasonably be expected to be kept, used or consumed.

[. . .]

PART IV
ENFORCEMENT OF PARTS II AND III

27 Enforcement

(1) Subject to the following provisions of this section—

(a) it shall be the duty of every weights and measures authority in Great Britain to enforce within their area the safety provisions [. . .]; and

(b) it shall be the duty of every district council in Northern Ireland to enforce within their area the safety provisions.

(2) The Secretary of State may by regulations—

(a) wholly or partly transfer any duty imposed by subsection (1) above on a weights and measures authority or a district council in Northern Ireland to such other person who has agreed to the transfer as is specified in the regulations;

(b) relieve such an authority or council of any such duty so far as it is exercisable in relation to such goods as may be described in the regulations.

(3) The power to make regulations under subsection (2) above shall be exercisable by statutory instrument subject to annulment in pursuance of a resolution of either House of Parliament and shall include power—

(a) to make different provision for different cases; and

(b) to make such supplemental, consequential and transitional provision as the Secretary of State considers appropriate.

[(3A) For the investigatory powers available to a person for the purposes of the duty imposed by subsection (1), see Schedule 5 to the Consumer Rights Act 2015 (as well as section 29).]

(4) Nothing in this section shall authorise any weights and measures authority, or any person on whom functions are conferred by regulations under subsection (2) above, to bring proceedings in Scotland for an offence.

[. . .]

29 Powers of search etc

(1) Subject to the following provisions of this Part, a duly authorised officer of an enforcement authority may at any reasonable hour and on production, if required, of his credentials exercise [the power conferred by subsection (4)].

[. . .]

(4) If the officer has reasonable grounds for suspecting that any goods are manufactured or imported goods which have not been supplied in the United Kingdom since they were manufactured or imported he may—

(a) for the purpose of ascertaining whether there has been any contravention of any safety provision in relation to the goods, require any person carrying on a business, or employed in connection with a business, to produce any records relating to the business;

(b) for the purpose of ascertaining (by testing or otherwise) whether there has been any such contravention, seize and detain the goods;

(c) take copies of, or of any entry in, any records produced by virtue of paragraph (a) above.

[. . .]

(7) If and to the extent that it is reasonably necessary to do so to prevent a contravention of any safety provision [. . .], the officer may, for the purpose of exercising his power under subsection (4) [. . .] above to seize any goods [. . .]—

(a) require any person having authority to do so to open any container or to open any vending machine; and

(b) himself open or break open any such container or machine where a requirement made under paragraph (a) above in relation to the container or machine has not been complied with.

[. . .]

30 Provisions supplemental to s 29

(1) An officer seizing any goods [. . .] under section [29(4)] above shall inform the following persons that the goods [. . .] have been so seized, that is to say—

(a) the person from whom they are seized; and

(b) in the case of imported goods seized on any premises under the control of the Commissioners of Customs and Excise, the importer of those goods (within the meaning of the Customs and Excise Management Act 1979).

(2) If a justice of the peace—

(a) is satisfied by any written information on oath that there are reasonable grounds for believing either—

(i) that any [. . .] records which any officer has power to inspect under section [29(4)] above are on any premises and that their inspection is likely to disclose evidence that there has been a contravention of any safety provision [. . .]; or

(ii) that such a contravention has taken place, is taking place or is about to take place on any premises; and

(b) is also satisfied by any such information either—

(i) that admission to the premises has been or is likely to be refused and that notice of intention to apply for a warrant under this subsection has been given to the occupier; or

(ii) that an application for admission, or the giving of such a notice, would defeat the object of entry or that the premises are unoccupied or that the occupier is temporarily absent and it might defeat the object of the entry to await his return, the justice may by warrant under his hand, which shall continue in force for a period of one month, authorise any officer of an enforcement authority to enter the premises, if need be by force.

(3) An officer entering any premises by virtue of [. . .] a warrant under subsection (2) above may take with him such other persons and such equipment as may appear to him necessary.

(4) On leaving any premises which a person is authorised to enter by a warrant under subsection (2) above, that person shall, if the premises are unoccupied or the occupier is temporarily absent, leave the premises as effectively secured against trespassers as he found them.

(5) If any person who is not an officer of an enforcement authority purports to act as such under section [29(4)] above of this section he shall be guilty of an offence and liable on summary conviction to a fine not exceeding level 5 on the standard scale.

(6) Where any goods seized by an officer under section [29(4)] above are submitted to a test, the officer shall inform the persons mentioned in subsection (1) above of the result of the test and, if—

(a) proceedings are brought for an offence in respect of a contravention in relation to the goods of any safety provision [. . .] or for the forfeiture of the goods under section 16 or 17 above, or a suspension notice is served in respect of any goods; and

(b) the officer is requested to do so and it is practicable to comply with the request, the officer shall allow any person who is a party to the proceedings or, as the case may be, has an interest in the goods to which the notice relates to have the goods tested.

(7) The Secretary of State may by regulations provide that any test of goods seized under section [29(4)] above by an officer of an enforcement authority shall—

(a) be carried out at the expense of the authority in a manner and by a person prescribed by or determined under the regulations; or

(b) be carried out either as mentioned in paragraph (a) above or by the authority in a manner prescribed by the regulations.

(8) The power to make regulations under subsection (7) above shall be exercisable by statutory instrument subject to annulment in pursuance of a resolution of either House of Parliament and shall include power—

(a) to make different provision for different cases; and

(b) to make such supplemental, consequential and transitional provisions as the Secretary of State considers appropriate.

(9) In the application of this section to Scotland, the reference in subsection (2) above to a justice of the peace shall include a reference to a sheriff and the references to written information on oath shall be construed as references to evidence on oath.

(10) In the application of this section to Northern Ireland, the references in subsection (2) above to any information on oath shall be construed as references to any complaint on oath.

31 Power of customs officer to detain goods

(1) A customs officer may, for the purpose of facilitating the exercise by an enforcement authority or officer of such an authority of any functions conferred on the authority or officer by or under Part II of this Act, or by [section 29(4) of this Act or Schedule 5 to the Consumer Rights Act 2015] in its application for the purposes of the safety provisions, seize any imported goods and detain them for not more than two working days.

(2) Anything seized and detained under this section shall be dealt with during the period of its detention in such manner as the Commissioners of Customs and Excise may direct.

(3) In subsection (1) above the reference to two working days is a reference to a period of forty-eight hours calculated from the time when the goods in question are seized but disregarding so much of any period as falls on a Saturday or Sunday or on Christmas Day, Good Friday or a day which is a bank holiday under the Banking and Financial Dealings Act 1971 in the part of the United Kingdom where the goods are seized.

(4) In this section and section 32 below 'customs officer' means any officer within the meaning of the Customs and Excise Management Act 1979.

32 Obstruction of authorised officer

(1) Any person who—

(a) intentionally obstructs any officer of an enforcement authority who is acting in pursuance of [section 29(4)] or any customs officer who is [acting in pursuance of section 31]; or

(b) intentionally fails to comply with any requirements made of him by any officer of an enforcement authority under [section 29(4)], or

(c) without reasonable cause fails to give any officer of an enforcement authority who is so acting any other assistance or information which the officer may reasonably require of him for the purposes of the exercise of the officer's functions under [section 29(4)],

shall be guilty of an offence and liable on summary conviction to a fine not exceeding level 5 on the standard scale.

(2) A person shall be guilty of an offence if, in giving any information which is required of him by virtue of subsection (1)(c) above—

(a) he makes any statement which he knows is false in a material particular, or

(b) he recklessly makes a statement which is false in a material particular.

(3) A person guilty of an offence under subsection (2) above shall be liable—

(a) on conviction on indictment to a fine;

(b) on summary conviction, to a fine not exceeding the statutory maximum.

33 Appeals against detention of goods

(1) Any person having an interest in any goods which are for the time being detained under [section 29(4)] by an enforcement authority or by an officer of such an authority may apply for an order requiring the goods to be released to him or to another person.

(2) An application under this section may be made—

(a) to any magistrates' court in which proceedings have been brought in England and Wales or Northern Ireland—

(i) for an offence in respect of a contravention in relation to the goods of any safety provision [. . .]; or

(ii) for the forfeiture of the goods under section 16 above;

(b) where no such proceedings have been so brought, by way of complaint to a magistrates' court; or

(c) in Scotland, by summary application to the sheriff [. . .].

(3) On an application under this section to a magistrates' court or to the sheriff, an order requiring goods to be released shall be made only if the court or sheriff is satisfied—

(a) that proceedings—

(i) for an offence in respect of a contravention in relation to the goods of any safety provision [. . .]; or

(ii) for the forfeiture of the goods under section 16 or 17 above,

have not been brought or, having been brought, have been concluded without the goods being forfeited; and

(b) where no such proceedings have been brought, that more than six months have elapsed since the goods were seized.

(4) *[Does not apply to Scotland.]*

34 Compensation for seizure and detention

(1) Where an officer of an enforcement authority exercises any power under section [29(4)] above to seize and detain goods, the enforcement authority shall be liable to pay compensation to any person having an interest in the goods in respect of any loss or damage caused by reason of the exercise of the power if—

(a) there has been no contravention in relation to the goods of any safety provision [. . .]; and

(b) the exercise of the power is not attributable to any neglect or default by that person [. . .].

(2) Any disputed question as to the right to or the amount of any compensation payable under this section shall be determined by arbitration or, in Scotland, by a single arbiter appointed, failing agreement between the parties, by the sheriff.

35 Recovery of expenses of enforcement

(1) This section shall apply where a court—

(a) convicts a person of an offence in respect of a contravention in relation to any goods of any safety provision [. . .]; or

(b) makes an order under section 16 or 17 above for the forfeiture of any goods [. . .].

(2) The court may (in addition to any other order it may make as to costs or expenses) order the person convicted or, as the case may be, any person having an interest in the goods to reimburse an enforcement authority for any expenditure which has been or may be incurred by that authority—

(a) in connection with any seizure or detention of the goods by or on behalf of the authority; or

(b) in connection with any compliance by the authority with directions given by the court for the purposes of any order for the forfeiture of the goods.

PART V
MISCELLANEOUS AND SUPPLEMENTAL

36 [*Amends Health and Safety at Work etc Act 1974*]

37 [Power of Commissioners for Revenue and Customs to disclose information]

(1) If they think it appropriate to do so for the purpose of facilitating the exercise by any person to whom subsection (2) below applies of any function conferred on that person by or under Part II of this Act, or by or under Part IV of this Act in its application for the purposes of the safety provisions, [the Commissioners for Her Majesty's Revenue and Customs] may authorise the disclosure to that person of any information obtained [or held] for the purposes of the exercise by [Her Majesty's Revenue and Customs] of their functions in relation to imported goods.

(2) This subsection applies to an enforcement authority and to any officer of an enforcement authority.

(3) A disclosure of information made to any person under subsection (1) above shall be made in such manner as may be directed by [the Commissioners for Her Majesty's Revenue and Customs] and may be made through such persons acting on behalf of that person as may be so directed.

(4) Information may be disclosed to a person under subsection (1) above whether or not the disclosure of the information has been requested by or on behalf of that person.

[. . .]

39 Defence of due diligence

(1) Subject to the following provisions of this section, in proceedings against any person for an offence to which this section applies it shall be a defence for that person to show that he took all reasonable steps and exercised all due diligence to avoid committing the offence.

(2) Where in any proceedings against any person for such an offence the defence provided by subsection (1) above involves an allegation that the commission of the offence was due—

(a) to the act or default of another; or

(b) to reliance on information given by another,

that person shall not, without the leave of the court, be entitled to rely on the defence unless, not less than seven clear days before the hearing of the proceedings, he has served a notice under subsection (3) below on the person bringing the proceedings.

(3) A notice under this subsection shall give such information identifying or assisting in the identification of the person who committed the act or default or gave the information as is in the possession of the person serving the notice at the time he serves it.

(4) It is hereby declared that a person shall not be entitled to rely on the defence provided by subsection (1) above by reason of his reliance on information supplied by another, unless he shows that it was reasonable in all the circumstances for him to have relied on the information, having regard in particular—

(a) to the steps which he took, and those which might reasonably have been taken, for the purpose of verifying the information, and

(b) to whether he had any reason to disbelieve the information.

(5) This section shall apply to an offence under section [. . .] 12(1), (2) or (3), 13(4) [, or 14(6)] above.

40 Liability of persons other than principal offender

(1) Where the commission by any person of an offence to which section 39 above applies is due to an act or default committed by some other person in the course of any business of his, the other person shall be guilty of the offence and

may be proceeded against and punished by virtue of this subsection whether or not proceedings are taken against the first-mentioned person.

(2) Where a body corporate is guilty of an offence under this Act (including where it is so guilty by virtue of subsection (1) above) in respect of any act or default which is shown to have been committed with the consent or connivance of, or to be attributable to any neglect on the part of, any director, manager, secretary or other similar officer of the body corporate or any person who was purporting to act in any such capacity he, as well as the body corporate, shall be guilty of that offence and shall be liable to be proceeded against and punished accordingly.

(3) Where the affairs of a body corporate are managed by its members, subsection (2) above shall apply in relation to the acts and defaults of a member in connection with his functions of management as if he were a director of the body corporate.

41 Civil proceedings

(1) An obligation imposed by safety regulations shall be a duty owed to any person who may be affected by a contravention of the obligation and, subject to any provisions to the contrary in the regulations and to the defences and other incidents applying to actions for breach of statutory duty, a contravention of any such obligation shall be actionable accordingly.

(2) This Act shall not be construed as conferring any other right of action in civil proceedings, apart from the right conferred by virtue of Part I of this Act, in respect of any loss or damage suffered in consequence of a contravention of a safety provision [. . .].

(3) Subject to any provision to the contrary in the agreement itself, an agreement shall not be void or unenforceable by reason only of a contravention of a safety provision [. . .].

(4) Liability by virtue of subsection (1) above shall not be limited or excluded by any contract term, by any notice or (subject to the power contained in subsection (1) above to limit or exclude it in safety regulations) by any other provision.

(5) Nothing in subsection (1) above shall prejudice the operation of section 12 of the Nuclear Installations Act 1965 (rights to compensation for certain breaches of duties confined to rights under that Act).

(6) In this section 'damage' includes personal injury and death.

42 Reports etc

(1) It shall be the duty of the Secretary of State at least once in every five years to lay before each House of Parliament a report on the exercise during the period to which the report relates of the functions which under Part II of this Act, or under Part IV of this Act in its application for the purposes of the safety provisions, are exercisable by the Secretary of State, weights and measures authorities, district councils in Northern Ireland and persons on whom functions are conferred by regulations made under section 27(2) above.

(2) The Secretary of State may from time to time prepare and lay before each House of Parliament such other reports on the exercise of those functions as he considers appropriate.

(3) Every weights and measures authority, every district council in Northern Ireland and every person on whom functions are conferred by regulations under subsection (2) of section 27 above shall, whenever the Secretary of State so directs, make a report to the Secretary of State on the exercise of the functions exercisable by that authority or council under that section or by that person by virtue of any such regulations.

(4) A report under subsection (3) above shall be in such form and shall contain such particulars as are specified in the direction of the Secretary of State.

(5) The first report under subsection (1) above shall be laid before each House

of Parliament not more than five years after the laying of the last report under section 8(2) of the Consumer Safety Act 1978.

43 Financial provisions

(1) There shall be paid out of money provided by Parliament—

(a) any expenses incurred or compensation payable by a Minister of the Crown or Government department in consequence of any provision of this Act; and

(b) any increase attributable to this Act in the sums payable out of money so provided under any other Act.

(2) Any sums received by a Minister of the Crown or Government department by virtue of this Act shall be paid into the Consolidated Fund.

44 Service of documents etc

(1) Any documents required or authorised by virtue of this Act to be served on a person may be so served—

(a) by delivering it to him or by leaving it at his proper address or by sending it by post to him at that address; or

(b) if the person is a body corporate, by serving it in accordance with paragraph (a) above on the secretary or clerk of that body; or

(c) if the person is a partnership, by serving it in accordance with that paragraph on a partner or on a person having control or management of the partnership business.

(2) For the purposes of subsection (1) above, and for the purposes of section 7 of the Interpretation Act 1978 (which relates to the service of documents by post) in its application to that subsection, the proper address of any person on whom a document is to be served by virtue of this Act shall be his last known address except that—

(a) in the case of service on a body corporate or its secretary or clerk, it shall be the address of the registered or principal office of the body corporate;

(b) in the case of service on a partnership or a partner or a person having the control or management of a partnership business, it shall be the principal office of the partnership; and for the purposes of this subsection the principal office of a company registered outside the United Kingdom or of a partnership carrying on business outside the United Kingdom is its principal office within the United Kingdom.

(3) The Secretary of State may by regulations make provision for the manner in which any information is to be given to any person under any provision of Part IV of this Act.

(4) Without prejudice to the generality of subsection (3) above regulations made by the Secretary of State may prescribe the person, or manner of determining the person, who is to be treated for the purposes of section [. . .] 30 above as the person from whom goods were [. . .] seized where the goods were [. . .] seized from a vending machine.

(5) The power to make regulations under subsection (3) or (4) above shall be exercisable by statutory instrument subject to annulment in pursuance of a resolution of either House of Parliament and shall include power—

(a) to make different provision for different cases; and

(b) to make such supplemental, consequential and transitional provision as the Secretary of State considers appropriate.

45 Interpretation

(1) In this Act, except in so far as the context otherwise requires—

'aircraft' includes gliders, balloons and hovercraft;

'business' includes a trade or profession and the activities of a professional or trade association or of a local authority or other public authority;

'conditional sale agreement', 'credit-sale agreement' and 'hire-purchase agreement' have the same meanings as in the Consumer Credit Act 1974 but as if in the definitions in that Act 'goods' had the same meaning as in this Act;

'contravention' includes a failure to comply and cognate expressions shall be construed accordingly;

'enforcement authority' means the Secretary of State, any other Minister of the Crown in charge of a Government department, any such department and any authority, council or other person on whom functions under this Act are conferred by or under section 27 above;

'gas' has the same meaning as in Part I of the Gas Act 1986;

'goods' includes substances, growing crops and things comprised in land by virtue of being attached to it and any ship, aircraft or vehicle;

'information' includes accounts, estimates and returns;

'magistrates' court', in relation to Northern Ireland, means a court of summary jurisdiction;

'modifications' includes additions, alterations and omissions, and cognate expressions shall be construed accordingly;

'motor vehicle' has the same meaning as in [the Road Traffic Act 1988];

'notice' means a notice in writing;

'notice to warn' means a notice under section 13(1)(b) above;

'officer', in relation to an enforcement authority, means a person authorised in writing to assist the authority in carrying out its functions under or for the purposes of the enforcement of any of the safety provisions or of any of the provisions made by or under Part III of this Act;

'personal injury' includes any disease and any other impairment of a person's physical or mental condition;

'premises' includes any place and any ship, aircraft or vehicle;

'prohibition notice' means a notice under section 13(1)(a) above;

'records' includes any books or documents and any records in non-documentary form;

'safety provision' means [. . .] any provision of safety regulations, a prohibition notice or a suspension notice;

'safety regulations' means regulations under section 11 above;

'ship' includes any boat and any other description of vessel used in navigation;

'subordinate legislation' has the same meaning as in the Interpretation Act 1978;

'substance' means any natural or artificial substance, whether in solid, liquid or gaseous form or in the form of a vapour, and includes substances that are comprised in or mixed with other goods;

'supply' and cognate expressions shall be construed in accordance with section 46 below;

'suspension notice' means a notice under section 14 above.

(2) Except in so far as the context otherwise requires, references in this Act to a contravention of a safety provision shall, in relation to any goods, include references to anything which would constitute such a contravention if the goods were supplied to any person.

(3) References in this Act to any goods in relation to which any safety provision has been or may have been contravened shall include references to any goods which it is not reasonably practicable to separate from any such goods.

[. . .]

(5) In Scotland, any reference in this Act to things comprised in land by virtue of being attached to it is a reference to moveables which have become heritable by accession to heritable property.

46 Meaning of 'supply'

(1) Subject to the following provisions of this section, references in this Act to supplying goods shall be construed as references to doing any of the following, whether as principal or agent, that is to say—

(a) selling, hiring out or lending the goods;
(b) entering into a hire-purchase agreement to furnish the goods;
(c) the performance of any contract for work and materials to furnish the goods;
(d) providing the goods in exchange for any consideration [. . .] other than money;
(e) providing the goods in or in connection with the performance of any statutory function; or
(f) giving the goods as a prize or otherwise making a gift of the goods;

and, in relation to gas or water, those references shall be construed as including references to providing the service by which the gas or water is made available for use.

(2) For the purposes of any reference in this Act to supplying goods, where a person ('the ostensible supplier') supplies goods to another person ('the customer') under a hire-purchase agreement, conditional sale agreement or credit-sale agreement or under an agreement for the hiring of goods (other than a hire-purchase agreement) and the ostensible supplier—

(a) carries on the business of financing the provision of goods for others by means of such agreements; and
(b) in the course of that business acquired his interest in the goods supplied to the customer as a means of financing the provision of them for the customer by a further person ('the effective supplier'),

the effective supplier and not the ostensible supplier shall be treated as supplying the goods to the customer.

(3) Subject to subsection (4) below, the performance of any contract by the erection of any building or structure on any land or by the carrying out of any other building works shall be treated for the purposes of this Act as a supply of goods in so far as, but only in so far as, it involves the provision of any goods to any person by means of their incorporation into the building, structure or works.

(4) Except for the purposes of, and in relation to, notices to warn [. . .], references in this Act to supplying goods shall not include references to supplying goods comprised in land where the supply is effected by the creation or disposal of an interest in the land.

(5) Except in Part I of this Act references in this Act to a person's supplying goods shall be confined to references to that person's supplying goods in the course of a business of his, but for the purposes of this subsection it shall be immaterial whether the business is a business of dealing in the goods.

(6) For the purposes of subsection (5) above goods shall not be treated as supplied in the course of a business if they are supplied, in pursuance of an obligation arising under or in connection with the insurance of the goods, to the person with whom they were insured.

(7) Except for the purposes of, and in relation to, prohibition notices or suspension notices, references in [Part 2 or Part 4] of this Act to supplying goods shall not include—

(a) references to supplying goods where the person supplied carries on a business of buying goods of the same description as those goods and repairing or reconditioning them,
(b) references to supplying goods by a sale of articles as scrap (that is to say, for the value of materials included in the articles rather than for the value of the articles themselves).

(8) Where any goods have at any time been supplied by being hired out or lent to any person, neither a continuation or renewal of the hire or loan (whether on the same or different terms) nor any transaction for the transfer after that time of any interest in the goods to the person to whom they were hired or lent shall be treated for the purposes of this Act as a further supply of the goods to that person.

(9) A ship, aircraft or motor vehicle shall not be treated for the purposes of this

Act as supplied to any person by reason only that services consisting in the carriage of goods or passengers in that ship, aircraft or vehicle, or in its use for any other purpose, are provided to that person in pursuance of an agreement relating to the use of the ship, aircraft or vehicle for a particular period or for particular voyages, flights or journeys.

47 Savings for certain privileges

(1) Nothing in this Act shall be taken as requiring any person to produce any records if he would be entitled to refuse to produce those records in any proceedings in any court on the ground that they are the subject of legal professional privilege or, in Scotland, that they contain a confidential communication made by or to an advocate or solicitor in that capacity, or as authorising any person to take possession of any records which are in the possession of a person who would be so entitled.

(2) Nothing in this Act shall be construed as requiring a person to answer any question or give any information if to do so would incriminate that person or that person's spouse [or civil partner].

48 [*Minor and consequential amendments and repeals*]

49 [*Northern Ireland*]

50 Short title, commencement and transitional provision

(1) This Act may be cited as the Consumer Protection Act 1987.

(2) This Act shall come into force on such day as the Secretary of State may by order made by statutory instrument appoint, and different days may be so appointed for different provisions or for different purposes.

. . .

SCHEDULE 2

PROHIBITION NOTICES AND NOTICES TO WARN

Section 13

PART I

PROHIBITION NOTICES

1 A prohibition notice in respect of any goods shall—

(a) state that the Secretary of State considers that the goods are unsafe;

(b) set out the reasons why the Secretary of State considers that the goods are unsafe;

(c) specify the day on which the notice is to come into force; and

(d) state that the trader may at any time make representations in writing to the Secretary of State for the purpose of establishing that the goods are safe.

2—(1) If representations in writing about a prohibition notice are made by the trader to the Secretary of State, it shall be the duty of the Secretary of State to consider whether to revoke the notice and—

(a) if he decides to revoke it, to do so;

(b) in any other case, to appoint a person to consider those representations, any further representations made (whether in writing or orally) by the trader about the notice and the statements of any witnesses examined under this Part of this Schedule.

(2) Where the Secretary of State has appointed a person to consider representations about a prohibition notice, he shall serve a notification on the trader which—

(a) states that the trader may make oral representations to the appointed person for the purpose of establishing that the goods to which the notice relates are safe; and

(b) specifies the place and time at which the oral representations may be made.

(3) The time specified in a notification served under sub-paragraph (2) above shall not be before the end of the period of twenty-one days beginning with the day on which the notification is served, unless the trader otherwise agrees.

(4) A person on whom a notification has been served under sub-paragraph (2) above or his representative may, at the place and time specified in the notification—

(a) make oral representations to the appointed person for the purpose of establishing that the goods in question are safe; and

(b) call and examine witnesses in connection with representations.

3—(1) Where representations in writing about a prohibition notice are made by the trader to the Secretary of State at any time after a person has been appointed to consider representations about that notice, then, whether or not the appointed person has made a report to the Secretary of State, the following provisions of this paragraph shall apply instead of paragraph 2 above.

(2) The Secretary of State shall, before the end of the period of one month beginning with the day on which he receives the representations, serve a notification on the trader which states—

(a) that the Secretary of State has decided to revoke the notice, has decided to vary it or, as the case may be, has decided neither to revoke nor to vary it; or

(b) that, a person having been appointed to consider representations about the notice, the trader may, at a place and time specified in the notification, make oral representations to the appointed person for the purpose of establishing that the goods to which the notice relates are safe.

(3) The time specified in a notification served for the purposes of sub-paragraph (2)(b) above shall not be before the end of the period of twenty-one days beginning with the day on which the notification is served, unless the trader otherwise agrees or the time is the time already specified for the purposes of paragraph 2(2)(b) above.

(4) A person on whom a notification has been served for the purposes of sub-paragraph (2)(b) above or his representative may, at the place and time specified in the notification—

(a) make oral representations to the appointed person for the purpose of establishing that the goods in question are safe; and

(b) call and examine witnesses in connection with the representations.

4—(1) Where a person is appointed to consider representations about a prohibition notice, it shall be his duty to consider—

(a) any written representations made by the trader about the notice, other than those in respect of which a notification is served under paragraph 3(2)(a) above;

(b) any oral representations made under paragraph 2(4) or 3(4) above; and

(c) any statements made by witnesses in connection with the oral representations, and after considering any matters under this paragraph, to make a report (including recommendations) to the Secretary of State about the matters considered by him and the notice.

(2) It shall be the duty of the Secretary of State to consider any report made to him under sub-paragraph (1) above and, after considering the report, to inform the trader of his decision with respect to the prohibition notice to which the report relates.

5—(1) The Secretary of State may revoke or vary a prohibition notice by serving on the trader a notification stating that the notice is revoked or, as the case may be, is varied as specified in the notification.

(2) The Secretary of State shall not vary a prohibition notice so as to make the effect of the notice more restrictive for the trader.

(3) Without prejudice to the power conferred by section 13(2) of this Act, the service of a notification under sub-paragraph (1) above shall be sufficient to satisfy

the requirement of paragraph 4(2) above that the trader shall be informed of the Secretary of State's decision.

PART II
NOTICES TO WARN

6—(1) If the Secretary of State proposes to serve a notice to warn on any person in respect of any goods, the Secretary of State, before he serves the notice shall serve on that person a notification which—

(a) contains a draft of the proposed notice;

(b) states that the Secretary of State proposes to serve a notice in the form of the draft on that person;

(c) states that the Secretary of State considers that the goods described in the draft are unsafe;

(d) sets out the reasons why the Secretary of State considers that those goods are unsafe; and

(e) states that that person may make representations to the Secretary of State for the purpose of establishing that the goods are safe if, before the end of the period of fourteen days beginning with the day on which the notification is served, he informs the Secretary of State—

(i) of his intention to make representations; and

(ii) whether the representations will be made only in writing or both in writing and orally.

(2) Where the Secretary of State has served a notification containing a draft of a proposed notice to warn on any person, he shall not serve a notice to warn on that person in respect of the goods to which the proposed notice relates unless—

(a) the period of fourteen days beginning with the day on which the notification was served expires without the Secretary of State being informed as mentioned in sub-paragraph (1)(e) above;

(b) the period of twenty-eight days beginning with that day expires without any written representations being made by that person to the Secretary of State about the proposed notice; or

(c) the Secretary of State has considered a report about the proposed notice by a person appointed under paragraph 7(1) below.

7—(1) Where a person on whom a notification containing a draft of a proposed notice to warn has been served—

(a) informs the Secretary of State as mentioned in paragraph 6(1)(e) above before the end of the period of fourteen days beginning with the day on which the notification was served; and

(b) makes written representations to the Secretary of State about the proposed notice before the end of the period of twenty-eight days beginning with that day, the Secretary of State shall appoint a person to consider those representations, any further representations made by that person about the draft notice and the statements of any witnesses examined under this Part of this Schedule.

(2) Where—

(a) the Secretary of State has appointed a person to consider representations about a proposed notice to warn; and

(b) the person whose representations are to be considered has informed the Secretary of State for the purposes of paragraph 6(1)(e) above that the representations he intends to make will include oral representations,

the Secretary of State shall inform the person intending to make the representations of the place and time at which oral representations may be made to the appointed person.

(3) Where a person on whom a notification containing a draft of a proposed notice to warn has been served is informed of a time for the purposes of subparagraph (2) above, that time shall not be—

(a) before the end of the period of twenty-eight days beginning with the day on which the notification was served; or

(b) before the end of the period of seven days beginning with the day on which that person is informed of the time.

(4) A person who has been informed of a place and time for the purposes of sub-paragraph (2) above or his representative may, at that place and time—

(a) make oral representations to the appointed person for the purpose of establishing that the goods to which the proposed notice relates are safe; and

(b) call and examine witnesses in connection with the representations.

8—(1) Where a person is appointed to consider representations about a proposed notice to warn, it shall be his duty to consider—

(a) any written representations made by the person on whom it is proposed to serve the notice; and

(b) in a case where a place and time has been appointed under paragraph 7(2) above for oral representations to be made by that person or his representative, any representations so made and any statements made by witnesses in connection with those representations,

and, after considering those matters to make a report (including recommendations) to the Secretary of State about the matters considered by him and the proposal to serve the notice.

(2) It shall be the duty of the Secretary of State to consider any report made to him under sub-paragraph (1) above, and after considering the report, to inform the person on whom it was proposed that a notice to warn should be served of his decision with respect to the proposal.

(3) If at any time after serving a notification on a person under paragraph 6 above the Secretary of State decides not to serve on that person either the proposed notice to warn or that notice with modifications, the Secretary of State shall inform that person of the decision, and nothing done for the purposes of any of the preceding provisions of this Part of this Schedule before that person was so informed shall—

(a) entitle the Secretary of State subsequently to serve the proposed notice or the notice with modifications; or

(b) require the Secretary of State, or any person appointed to consider representations about the proposed notice, subsequently to do anything in respect of, or in consequence of, any such representations.

(4) Where a notification containing a draft of a proposed notice to warn is served on a person in respect of any goods, a notice to warn served on him in consequence of a decision made under sub-paragraph (2) above shall either be in the form of the draft or shall be less onerous than the draft.

9 The Secretary of State may revoke a notice to warn by serving on the person on whom the notice was served a notification stating that the notice is revoked.

PART III
GENERAL

10—(1) Where in a notification served on any person under this Schedule the Secretary of State has appointed a time for the making of oral representations or the examination of witnesses, he may, by giving that person such notification as the Secretary of State considers appropriate, change that time to a later time or appoint further times at which further representations may be made or the examination of witnesses may be continued; and paragraphs 2(4), 3(4) and 7(4) above shall have effect accordingly.

(2) For the purposes of this Schedule the Secretary of State may appoint a person (instead of the appointed person) to consider any representations or statements, if the person originally appointed, or last appointed under this sub-

paragraph, to consider those representations or statements has died or appears to the Secretary of State to be otherwise unable to act.

11 In this Schedule—

'the appointed person' in relation to a prohibition notice or a proposal to serve a notice to warn, means the person for the time being appointed under this Schedule to consider representations about the notice or, as the case may be, about the proposed notice;

'notification' means a notification in writing;

'trader', in relation to a prohibition notice, means the person on whom the notice is or was served.

CARRIAGE OF GOODS BY SEA ACT 1992
(1992, c 50)

1 Shipping documents etc to which Act applies

(1) This Act applies to the following documents, that is to say—

(a) any bill of lading;

(b) any sea waybill; and

(c) any ship's delivery order.

(2) References in this Act to a bill of lading—

(a) do not include references to a document which is incapable of transfer either by indorsement or, as a bearer bill, by delivery without indorsement; but

(b) subject to that, do include references to a received for shipment bill of lading.

(3) References in this Act to a sea waybill are references to any document which is not a bill of lading but—

(a) is such a receipt for goods as contains or evidences a contract for the carriage of goods by sea; and

(b) identifies the person to whom delivery of the goods is to be made by the carrier in accordance with that contract.

(4) References in this Act to a ship's delivery order are references to any document which is neither a bill of lading nor a sea waybill but contains an undertaking which—

(a) is given under or for the purposes of a contract for the carriage by sea of the goods to which the document relates, or of goods which include those goods; and

(b) is an undertaking by the carrier to a person identified in the document to deliver the goods to which the document relates to that person.

[. . .]

2 Rights under shipping documents

(1) Subject to the following provisions of this section, a person who becomes—

(a) the lawful holder of a bill of lading;

(b) the person who (without being an original party to the contract of carriage) is the person to whom delivery of the goods to which a sea waybill relates is to be made by the carrier in accordance with that contract; or

(c) the person to whom delivery of the goods to which a ship's delivery order relates is to be made in accordance with the undertaking contained in the order,

shall (by virtue of becoming the holder of the bill or, as the case may be, the person to whom delivery is to be made) have transferred to and vested in him all rights of suit under the contract of carriage as if he had been a party to that contract.

(2) Where, when a person becomes the lawful holder of a bill of lading, possession of the bill no longer gives a right (as against the carrier) to possession of the

goods to which the bill relates, that person shall not have any rights transferred to him by virtue of subsection (1) above unless he becomes the holder of the bill—

(a) by virtue of a transaction effected in pursuance of any contractual or other arrangements made before the time when such a right to possession ceased to attach to possession of the bill; or

(b) as a result of the rejection to that person by another person of goods or documents delivered to the other person in pursuance of any such arrangements.

(3) The rights vested in any person by virtue of the operation of subsection (1) above in relation to a ship's delivery order—

(a) shall be so vested subject to the terms of the order; and

(b) where the goods to which the order relates form a part only of the goods to which the contract of carriage relates, shall be confined to rights in respect of the goods to which the order relates.

(4) Where, in the case of any document to which this Act applies—

(a) a person with any interest or right in or in relation to goods to which the document relates sustains loss or damage in consequence of a breach of the contract of carriage; but

(b) subsection (1) above operates in relation to that document so that rights of suit in respect of that breach are vested in another person,

the other person shall be entitled to exercise those rights for the benefit of the person who sustained the loss or damage to the same extent as they could have been exercised if they had been vested in the person for whose benefit they are exercised.

(5) Where rights are transferred by virtue of the operation of subsection (1) above in relation to any document, the transfer for which that subsection provides shall extinguish any entitlement to those rights which derives—

(a) where that document is a bill of lading, from a person's having been an original party to the contract of carriage; or

(b) in the case of any document to which this Act applies, from the previous operation of that subsection in relation to that document;

but the operation of that subsection shall be without prejudice to any rights which derive from a person's having been an original party to the contract contained in, or evidenced by, a sea waybill and, in relation to a ship's delivery order, shall be without prejudice to any rights deriving otherwise than from the previous operation of that subsection in relation to that order.

3 Liabilities under shipping documents

(1) Where subsection (1) of section 2 of this Act operates in relation to any document to which this Act applies and the person in whom rights are vested by virtue of that subsection—

(a) takes or demands delivery from the carrier of any of the goods to which the document relates;

(b) makes a claim under the contract of carriage against the carrier in respect of any of those goods; or

(c) is a person who, at a time before those rights were vested in him, took or demanded delivery from the carrier of any of those goods,

that person shall (by virtue of taking or demanding delivery or making the claim or, in a case falling within paragraph (c) above, of having the rights vested in him) become subject to the same liabilities under that contract as if he had been a party to that contract.

(2) Where the goods to which a ship's delivery order relates form a part only of the goods to which the contract of carriage relates, the liabilities to which any person is subject by virtue of the operation of this section in relation to that order shall exclude liabilities in respect of any goods to which the order does not relate.

(3) This section, so far as it imposes liabilities under any contract on any person, shall be without prejudice to the liabilities under the contract of any person as an original party to the contract.

4 Representations in bills of lading

A bill of lading which—

(a) represents goods to have been shipped on board a vessel or to have been received for shipment on board a vessel; and

(b) has been signed by the master of the vessel or by a person who was not the master but had the express, implied or apparent authority of the carrier to sign bills of lading,

shall, in favour of a person who has become the lawful holder of the bill, be conclusive evidence against the carrier of the shipment of the goods or, as the case may be, of their receipt for shipment.

5 Interpretation etc

(1) In this Act—

'bill of lading', 'sea waybill' and 'ship's delivery order' shall be construed in accordance with section 1 above;

'the contract of carriage'—

(a) in relation to a bill of lading or sea waybill, means the contract contained in or evidenced by that bill or waybill; and

(b) in relation to a ship's delivery order, means the contract under or for the purposes of which the undertaking contained in the order is given;

'holder', in relation to a bill of lading, shall be construed in accordance with subsection (2) below;

'information technology' includes any computer or other technology by means of which information or other matter may be recorded or communicated without being reduced to documentary form.

[. . .]

(2) References in this Act to the holder of a bill of lading are references to any of the following persons, that is to say—

(a) a person with possession of the bill who, by virtue of being the person identified in the bill, is the consignee of the goods to which the bill relates;

(b) a person with possession of the bill as a result of the completion, by delivery of the bill, of any indorsement of the bill or, in the case of a bearer bill, of any other transfer of the bill;

(c) a person with possession of the bill as a result of any transaction by virtue of which he would have become a holder falling within paragraph (a) or (b) above had not the transaction been effected at a time when possession of the bill no longer gave a right (as against the carrier) to possession of the goods to which the bill relates;

and a person shall be regarded for the purposes of this Act as having become the lawful holder of a bill of lading wherever he has become the holder of the bill in good faith.

(3) References in this Act to a person's being identified in a document include references to his being identified by a description which allows for the identity of the person in question to be varied, in accordance with the terms of the document, after its issue; and the reference in section 1(3)(b) of this Act to a document's identifying a person shall be construed accordingly.

(4) Without prejudice to sections 2(2) and 4 above, nothing in this Act shall preclude its operation in relation to a case where the goods to which a document relates—

(a) cease to exist after the issue of the document; or

(b) cannot be identified (whether because they are mixed with other goods or for any other reason);

and references in this Act to the goods to which a document relates shall be construed accordingly.

(5) The preceding provisions of this Act shall have effect without prejudice to the application, in relation to any case, of the rules (the Hague-Visby Rules) which for the time being have the force of law by virtue of section 1 of the Carriage of Goods by Sea Act 1971.

6 Short title, repeal, commencement and extent

(1) This Act may be cited as the Carriage of Goods by Sea Act 1992.

(2) The Bills of Lading Act 1855 is hereby repealed.

(3) This Act shall come into force at the end of the period of two months beginning with the day on which it is passed; but nothing in this Act shall have effect in relation to any document issued before the coming into force of this Act.

(4) This Act extends to Northern Ireland.

CONTRACT (SCOTLAND) ACT 1997
(1997, c 34)

1 Extrinsic evidence of additional contract term etc

(1) Where a document appears (or two or more documents appear) to comprise all the express terms of a contract or unilateral voluntary obligation, it shall be presumed, unless the contrary is proved, that the document does (or the documents do) comprise all the express terms of the contract or unilateral voluntary obligation.

(2) Extrinsic oral or documentary evidence shall be admissible to prove, for the purposes of subsection (1) above, that the contract or unilateral voluntary obligation includes additional express terms (whether or not written terms).

(3) Notwithstanding the foregoing provisions of this section, where one of the terms in the document (or in the documents) is to the effect that the document does (or the documents do) comprise all the express terms of the contract or unilateral voluntary obligation, that term shall be conclusive in the matter.

(4) This section is without prejudice to any enactment which makes provision as respects the constitution, or formalities of execution, of a contract or unilateral voluntary obligation.

2 Supersession

(1) Where a deed is executed in implement, or purportedly in implement, of a contract, an unimplemented, or otherwise unfulfilled, term of the contract shall not be taken to be superseded by virtue only of that execution or of the delivery and acceptance of the deed.

(2) Subsection (1) above is without prejudice to any agreement which the parties to a contract may reach (whether or not an agreement incorporated into the contract) as to supersession of the contract.

3 Damages for breach of contract of sale

Any rule of law which precludes the buyer in a contract of sale of property from obtaining damages for breach of that contract by the seller unless the buyer rejects the property and rescinds the contract shall cease to have effect.

4 Short title, extent etc

. . .

(3) Section 1 of this Act applies only for the purposes of proceedings commenced on or after, and sections 2 and 3 only as respects contracts entered into on or after, the date on which this Act comes into force.

. . .

ELECTRONIC COMMUNICATIONS ACT 2000
(2000, c 7)

PART II
FACILITATION OF ELECTRONIC COMMERCE, DATA STORAGE, ETC

7 Electronic signatures and related certificates

(1) In any legal proceedings—

(a) an electronic signature incorporated into or logically associated with a particular electronic communication or particular electronic data, and

(b) the certification by any person of such a signature,

shall each be admissible in evidence in relation to any question as to the authenticity of the communication or data or as to the integrity of the communication or data.

(2) For the purposes of this section an electronic signature is so much of anything in electronic form as—

(a) is incorporated into or otherwise logically associated with any electronic communication or electronic data; and

[(b) purports to be used by the individual creating it to sign.]

(3) For the purposes of this section an electronic signature incorporated into or associated with a particular electronic communication or particular electronic data is certified by any person if that person (whether before or after the making of the communication) has made a statement confirming that—

(a) the signature,

(b) a means of producing, communicating or verifying the signature, or

(c) a procedure applied to the signature,

is (either alone or in combination with other factors) a valid means of [signing] [. . .]

[7A Electronic seals and related certificates

(1) In any legal proceedings—

(a) an electronic seal incorporated into or logically associated with a particular electronic communication or particular electronic data, and

(b) the certification by any person of such a seal,

shall each be admissible in evidence in relation to any question as to the authenticity of the communication or data, the integrity of the communication or data, or both.

(2) For the purposes of this section an electronic seal is so much of anything in electronic form as—

(a) is incorporated into or otherwise logically associated with electronic communication or electronic data; and

(b) purports to ensure the origin and integrity of the communication or data.

(3) For the purposes of this section an electronic seal incorporated into or associated with a particular electronic communication or particular electronic data is certified by any person if that person (whether before or after the making of the communication) has made a statement confirming that—

(a) the seal,

(b) a means of producing, communicating or verifying the seal, or

(c) a procedure applied to the seal,

is (either alone or in combination with other factors) a valid means of ensuring the origin of the communication or data, the integrity of the communication or data, or both.]

[7B Electronic time stamps and related certificates

(1) In any legal proceedings—

(a) an electronic time stamp incorporated into or logically associated with a particular electronic communication or particular electronic data, and

(b) the certification by any person of such a time stamp,

shall each be admissible in evidence in relation to any question as whether the communication or data existed at the time the electronic time stamp was incorporated into or logically associated with such communication or data.

(2) For the purposes of this section an electronic time stamp is so much of anything in electronic form as—

(a) is incorporated into or otherwise logically associated with any electronic communication or electronic data; and

(b) purports to bind electronic communication or electronic data to a particular time establishing evidence that such data existed at that time.

(3) For the purposes of this section an electronic time stamp incorporated into or associated with a particular electronic communication or particular electronic data is certified by any person if that person (whether before or after the making of the communication) has made a statement confirming that—

(a) the time stamp,

(b) a means of producing, communicating or verifying the time stamp, or

(c) a procedure applied to the time stamp,

is (either alone or in combination with other factors) a valid means of establishing whether the communication or data existed at a particular point in time.]

[7C Electronic documents and related certificates

(1) In any legal proceedings an electronic document shall be admissible in evidence in relation to any question as to the authenticity of an electronic transaction.

(2) For the purposes of this section an electronic document is anything stored in electronic form, including text or sound, and visual or audiovisual recording.]

[7D Electronic registered delivery service and related certificates

(1) In any legal proceedings, any electronic communication or electronic data sent and received using an electronic registered delivery service shall be admissible in evidence.

(2) For the purposes of this section an electronic registered delivery service is a service which—

(a) provides for the transmission of data between third parties by electronic means;

(b) provides evidence relating to the handling of the transmitted data, including proof of sending and receiving the data; and

(c) protects transmitted data against the risk of loss, theft, damage or unauthorised alterations.]

LIMITED LIABILITY PARTNERSHIPS ACT 2000
(2000, c 12)

Introductory

1 Limited liability partnerships

(1) There shall be a new form of legal entity to be known as a limited liability partnership.

(2) A limited liability partnership is a body corporate (with legal personality separate from that of its members) which is formed by being incorporated under this Act; and—

(a) in the following provisions of this Act (except in the phrase 'oversea limited liability partnership'), and

(b) in any other enactment (except where provision is made to the contrary or the context otherwise requires),

references to a limited liability partnership are to such a body corporate.

(3) A limited liability partnership has unlimited capacity.

(4) The members of a limited liability partnership have such liability to contribute to its assets in the event of its being wound up as is provided for by virtue of this Act.

(5) Accordingly, except as far as otherwise provided by this Act or any other enactment, the law relating to partnerships does not apply to a limited liability partnership.

(6) The Schedule (which makes provision about the names and registered offices of limited liability partnerships) has effect.

Incorporation

2 Incorporation document etc

(1) For a limited liability partnership to be incorporated—

(a) two or more persons associated for carrying on a lawful business with a view to profit must have subscribed their names to an incorporation document,

[(b) the incorporation document or a copy of it must have been delivered to the registrar, and]

(c) there must have been so delivered a statement [. . .], made by either a solicitor engaged in the formation of the limited liability partnership or anyone who subscribed his name to the incorporation document, that the requirement imposed by paragraph (a) has been complied with.

(2) The incorporation document must—

[. . .]

(b) state the name of the limited liability partnership,

(c) state whether the registered office of the limited liability partnership is to be situated in England and Wales, in Wales [, in Scotland or in Northern Ireland],

(d) state the address of that registered office, [which must be an appropriate address,]

[(da) state the intended registered email address of the limited liability partnership, which must be an appropriate email address,]

[(e) give the required [information about] each of the persons who are to be members of the limited liability partnership on incorporation,

[(ea) in the case of each individual named as a member, state that the individual's identity is verified within the meaning of section 1110A of the Companies Act 2006 (meaning of 'identity is verified'),]

[(eb) state that no person who is named as a member is disqualified under the directors disqualification legislation,]

(f) either specify which of those persons are to be designated members or state that every person who from time to time is a member of the limited liability partnership is a designated member,] [and]

[(g) include a statement of initial significant control].

[(2ZA) The required information mentioned in subsection (2)(e) is the information mentioned in sections 167J and 167K of the Companies Act 2006 as applied to limited liability partnerships by regulation 17A of the 2009 Regulations.]

[(2ZB) Where any of the persons named as members would be disqualified under the directors disqualification legislation but for the permission of a court to act, the incorporation document must include a statement to that effect, in respect of each of them, specifying—

(a) the person's name,

(b) the court by which permission is given, and

(c) the date on which permission was given.

(2ZC) Where any of the persons named as members would be disqualified under the directors disqualification legislation by virtue of section 11A of the Company Directors Disqualification Act 1986 or Article 15A of the Company Directors Disqualification (Northern Ireland) Order 2002 (designated persons under sanctions legislation) but for the authority of a licence of the kind mentioned in that section or Article, the incorporation document must include a statement to that effect, in respect of each of them, specifying—

(a) the person's name, and

(b) the date on which the licence was issued and by whom it was issued.]

[. . .]

(3) If a person makes a false statement under subsection (1)(c) which he—

(a) knows to be false, or

(b) does not believe to be true, he commits an offence.

(4) A person guilty of an offence under subsection (3) is liable—

(a) on summary conviction, to imprisonment for a period not exceeding six months or a fine not exceeding the statutory maximum, or to both, or

(b) on conviction on indictment, to imprisonment for a period not exceeding two years or a fine, or to both.

[(5) In this section—

'appropriate address' means an address at which, in the ordinary course of events—

(a) a document addressed to the limited liability partnership, and delivered there by hand or by post, would be expected to come to the attention of a person acting on behalf of the limited liability partnership, and

(b) the delivery of documents there is capable of being recorded by the obtaining of an acknowledgement of delivery;

'appropriate email address' means an email address to which, in the ordinary course of events, emails sent by the registrar would be expected to come to the attention of a person acting on behalf of the limited liability partnership.]

[*'disqualified under the directors disqualification legislation' has the meaning given in section 159A(2) of the Companies Act 2006, as applied to limited liability partnerships by regulation 17ZC of the 2009 Regulations;*

'permission of the court to act' means permission of a court under provision mentioned in column 2 of the table in section 159A(2) of that Act, as so applied.]

3 Incorporation by registration

[(1) The registrar, if satisfied that the requirements of section 2 are complied with, shall—

(a) register the documents delivered under that section, and

(b) give a certificate that the limited liability partnership is incorporated.]

[(1A) The certificate must state—

(a) the name and registered number of the limited liability partnership,

(b) the date of its incorporation, and

(c) whether the limited liability partnership's registered office is situated in England and Wales (or in Wales), in Scotland or in Northern Ireland.]

(2) The registrar may accept the statement delivered under paragraph (c) of subsection (1) of section 2 as sufficient evidence that the requirement imposed by paragraph (a) of that subsection has been complied with.

(3) The certificate shall either be signed by the registrar or be authenticated by his official seal.

(4) The certificate is conclusive evidence that the requirements of section 2 are complied with and that the limited liability partnership is incorporated by the name specified in the incorporation document.

Membership

4 Members

(1) On the incorporation of a limited liability partnership its members are the persons who subscribed their names to the incorporation document (other than any who have died or been dissolved).

(2) Any other person may become a member of a limited liability partnership by and in accordance with an agreement with the existing members.

[(2A) Subsections (1) and (2) are subject to section 159A(1) of the Companies Act 2006, as applied to limited liability partnerships by regulation 17ZC of the 2009 Regulations.]

(3) A person may cease to be a member of a limited liability partnership (as well as by death or dissolution) in accordance with an agreement with the other members or, in the absence of agreement with the other members as to cessation of membership, by giving reasonable notice to the other members.

(4) A member of a limited liability partnership shall not be regarded for any purpose as employed by the limited liability partnership unless, if he and the other members were partners in a partnership, he would be regarded for that purpose as employed by the partnership.

[4A Minimum membership for carrying on business

(1) This section applies where a limited liability partnership carries on business without having at least two members, and does so for more than 6 months.

(2) A person who, for the whole or any part of the period that it so carries on business after those 6 months—

(a) is a member of the limited liability partnership, and

(b) knows that it is carrying on business with only one member,

is liable (jointly and severally with the limited liability partnership) for the payment of the limited liability partnership's debts contracted during the period or, as the case may be, that part of it.]

5 Relationship of members etc

(1) Except as far as otherwise provided by this Act or any other enactment, the mutual rights and duties of the members of a limited liability partnership, and the mutual rights and duties of a limited liability partnership and its members, shall be governed—

(a) by agreement between the members, or between the limited liability partnership and its members, or

(b) in the absence of agreement as to any matter, by any provision made in relation to that matter by regulations under section 15(c).

(2) An agreement made before the incorporation of a limited liability partnership between the persons who subscribe their names to the incorporation document may impose obligations on the limited liability partnership (to take effect at any time after its incorporation).

6 Members as agents

(1) Every member of a limited liability partnership is the agent of the limited liability partnership.

(2) But a limited liability partnership is not bound by anything done by a member in dealing with a person if—

(a) the member in fact has no authority to act for the limited liability partnership by doing that thing, and

(b) the person knows that he has no authority or does not know or believe him to be a member of the limited liability partnership.

(3) Where a person has ceased to be a member of a limited liability partnership, the former member is to be regarded (in relation to any person dealing with the limited liability partnership) as still being a member of the limited liability partnership unless—

(a) the person has notice that the former member has ceased to be a member of the limited liability partnership, or

(b) notice that the former member has ceased to be a member of the limited liability partnership has been delivered to the registrar.

(4) Where a member of a limited liability partnership is liable to any person (other than another member of the limited liability partnership) as a result of a wrongful act or omission of his in the course of the business of the limited liability partnership or with its authority, the limited liability partnership is liable to the same extent as the member.

7 Ex-members

(1) This section applies where a member of a limited liability partnership has either ceased to be a member or—

(a) has died,

(b) has become bankrupt or had his estate sequestrated or has been wound up,

(c) has granted a trust deed for the benefit of his creditors, or

(d) has assigned the whole or any part of his share in the limited liability partnership (absolutely or by way of charge or security).

(2) In such an event the former member or—

(a) his personal representative,

(b) his trustee in bankruptcy [, the trustee or interim trustee in the sequestration, under the Bankruptcy (Scotland) Act 2016, of the former member's estate or the former member's] liquidator,

(c) his trustee under the trust deed for the benefit of his creditors, or

(d) his assignee,

may not interfere in the management or administration of any business or affairs of the limited liability partnership.

(3) But subsection (2) does not affect any right to receive an amount from the limited liability partnership in that event.

8 Designated members

(1) If the incorporation document specifies who are to be designated members—

(a) they are designated members on incorporation, and

(b) any member may become a designated member by and in accordance with an agreement with the other members,

and a member may cease to be a designated member in accordance with an agreement with the other members.

(2) But if there would otherwise be no designated members, or only one, every member is a designated member.

(3) If the incorporation document states that every person who from time to time is a member of the limited liability partnership is a designated member, every member is a designated member.

(4) A limited liability partnership may at any time deliver to the registrar—

(a) notice that specified members are to be designated members, or

(b) notice that every person who from time to time is a member of the limited liability partnership is a designated member,

and, once it is delivered, subsection (1) (apart from paragraph (a)) and subsection (2), or subsection (3), shall have effect as if that were stated in the incorporation document.

[. . .]

(6) A person ceases to be a designated member if he ceases to be a member.

[. . .]

Regulations

14 Insolvency and winding up

(1) Regulations shall make provision about the insolvency and winding up of limited liability partnerships by applying or incorporating, with such modifications as appear appropriate, [—

(a) in relation to a limited liability partnership registered in Great Britain, Parts [A1] to 4, 6 and 7 of the Insolvency Act 1986;

(b) in relation to a limited liability partnership registered in Northern Ireland, Parts [1A] to 5 and 7 of the Insolvency (Northern Ireland) Order 1989, and so much of Part 1 of that Order as applies for the purposes of those Parts.]

(2) Regulations may make other provision about the insolvency and winding up of limited liability partnerships, and provision about the insolvency and winding up of oversea limited liability partnerships, by—

(a) applying or incorporating, with such modifications as appear appropriate, any law relating to the insolvency or winding up of companies or other corporations which would not otherwise have effect in relation to them, or

(b) providing for any law relating to the insolvency or winding up of companies or other corporations which would otherwise have effect in relation to them not to apply to them or to apply to them with such modifications as appear appropriate.

(3) In this Act 'oversea limited liability partnership' means a body incorporated or otherwise established outside [the United Kingdom] and having such connection with [the United Kingdom], and such other features, as regulations may prescribe.

15 Application of company law etc

Regulations may make provision about limited liability partnerships and oversea limited liability partnerships (not being provision about insolvency or winding up) by—

(a) applying or incorporating, with such modifications as appear appropriate, any law relating to companies or other corporations which would not otherwise have effect in relation to them,

(b) providing for any law relating to companies or other corporations which would otherwise have effect in relation to them not to apply to them or to apply to them with such modifications as appear appropriate, or

(c) applying or incorporating, with such modifications as appear appropriate, any law relating to partnerships.

DEBT ARRANGEMENT AND ATTACHMENT (SCOTLAND) ACT 2002
(2002, asp 17)

PART 1
THE DEBT ARRANGEMENT SCHEME

1 Debt arrangement scheme

This Part of this Act constitutes a scheme (to be known as the 'debt arrangement scheme') under which [persons] may arrange for their debts to be paid under debt payment programmes.

2 Debt payment programmes

(1) A debt payment programme is a programme which provides for the payment of money owed by a debtor.

[(1A) Subsection (1) above is subject to any provision in regulations made under section 7A(1) below.]

(2) The Scottish Ministers may, on an application by a debtor, approve any debt payment programme set out in the application.

(3) Such an application [. . .] shall—

(a) specify, to the best of the debtor's knowledge and belief, in relation to each debt which the debtor is proposing to be paid under the debt payment programme—

(i) the amount outstanding;

(ii) the creditor to whom the debt is due; and

(iii) the period for which the debt has been due;

(b) set out the arrangements under which those debts are, in accordance with the provisions of the programme, to be paid, in particular specifying—

(i) the amounts which the debtor proposes to pay under the programme;

(ii) the proposed regularity of those payments;

(iii) the manner in which those payments are to be made; and

(iv) the manner in which, and period over which, each of the debts included in the programme is to be paid;

(c) specify the name and address of the person (the 'payments distributor') who is to—

(i) receive payments from the debtor; and

(ii) pay, on behalf of the debtor, the debts included in the programme, in accordance with the provisions of the programme; and

(d) contain such other information (including information relating to the debtor's financial circumstances), and be in such form, as may be prescribed.

(4) Such an application shall, subject to any contrary provision in regulations made under section 7(1) [or 7A(1)] below, incorporate the consent, indicated in the prescribed form, of all the debtor's creditors.

(5) A person's name and address shall not be specified in an application for approval of a debt payment programme as a payments distributor unless that person has been approved by the Scottish Ministers as a person suitable to carry out the functions of a payments distributor.

3 Money advice

(1) A debtor is not entitled to make an application for the approval, or the variation, of a debt payment programme unless the debtor has obtained the advice of a money adviser in relation to—

(a) the debtor's financial circumstances;

(b) the effect of the proposed programme or, as the case may be, the proposed variation of the programme; and

(c) the preparation of the application.

(2) Such an application shall—

(a) contain a [. . .] declaration by the money adviser who provided the advice referred to in subsection (1) above that such advice has been given; and

(b) specify the name and address of the money adviser.

[(3) Subsections (1) and (2) above are subject to any contrary provision in regulations made under section 7(1) below.]

4 Effect of debt payment programmes

(1) Where a debt payment programme has been approved or varied, the debts specified in the application for the approval or, as the case may be, the variation shall be paid in accordance with the programme.

(2) It is not competent—

(a) to serve a charge for payment in respect of; or

(b) [subject to subsection (2A),] to commence or execute any diligence to enforce payment of; or

[(c) to commit a debtor to prison under section 4 of the Civil Imprisonment (Scotland) Act 1882, except for the purposes of section 40A of the Child Support Act 1991, in respect of,]

any debt owed by a debtor who has debts which are being paid under an approved debt payment programme.

[(2A) Despite subsection (2)(b), it is competent to—

(a) auction an attached article where—

(i) notice has been given to the debtor under section 27(4) below; or

(ii) an article has been removed, or notice of removal has been given, under section 53 below;

(b) implement a decree of furthcoming;

(c) implement a decree or order for sale of a ship (or a share of it) or cargo.

[. . .]

(3) A creditor is not entitled to found on any debt owed by such a debtor in presenting, or concurring in the presentation of, a petition for the sequestration of the debtor's estate.

(4) There is to be disregarded, for the purposes of the exercise by a creditor of any rights to enforce a debt or remedies to like effect, any period during which the debtor's debts were subject to an approved debt payment programme.

(5) The debts referred to in subsections (2) to (4) above are restricted to—

(a) those to which the debtor's debt payment programme relates; and

(b) any other debts owed to creditors who have been given notice, in the prescribed form, of the approval of the debt payment programme.

5 Variation of debt payment programmes

(1) The Scottish Ministers may, on an application by the debtor or by any creditor, approve the variation of a debt payment programme.

(2) The Scottish Ministers may not consider an application for approval of a variation under subsection (1) above unless—

(a) where the application is made by the debtor, a copy of the application has been given to each creditor who is owed a debt which is being paid under the debt payment programme; or

(b) where the application is made by a creditor, a copy of the application has been given to the debtor and to each other creditor who is owed such a debt.

(3) Such an application may seek the variation of any condition which is attached to the approval of the programme or, as the case may be, a previous variation of the programme.

(4) An application for the variation of a debt payment programme shall—

(a) contain such information, and be in such form, as may be prescribed;

[. . .]

6 Deduction from earnings

(1) Where an approved debt payment programme requires sums to be paid to the payments distributor by way of deduction of the debtor's earnings from employment, the debtor shall provide an instruction, in the prescribed form, to the person by whom the debtor is employed to make—

(a) deductions from the debtor's earnings; and

(b) payments of the amounts deducted to the payments distributor, in accordance with the provisions of the debt payment programme.

(2) It is the duty of the employer to comply with any instruction so provided.

7 Debt payment programmes: power to make further provision

(1) The Scottish Ministers may, by regulations, make such further provision as they think fit in connection with—

(a) applications for the approval, or for the variation, of debt payment programmes;

(b) the manner in which such programmes are to operate, including conditions with which debtors, creditors, payments distributors or money advisers must comply;

(c) the effect of such programmes; and

(d) the effect of the failure of an employer to comply with the duty under section 6(2) above.

(2) The regulations may, in particular, make provision about—

(a) the class of person who may or may not make an application for the approval, or the variation, of a debt payment programme;

(b) the class of debt in respect of which such an application may or may not be made;

[(ba) circumstances in which some or all of the functions of a money adviser under section 3 above may instead be carried out by an approved intermediary;

(bb) circumstances in which a debtor is entitled to make an application for the approval, or the variation, of a debt payment programme where the debtor has not obtained advice under section 3(1) above;

(bc) the manner in which—

(i) the seeking of the consent of creditors to applications for approval of debt payment programmes; or

(ii) the making of such applications,

affects the rights and remedies of creditors or other third parties.]

[(bd) the method of assessing the amount of a debtor's assets, income, liabilities and expenditure in considering applications for the approval, or the variation, of a debt payment programme;]

(c) the matters to which the Scottish Ministers are to have regard in determining whether to approve such an application;

(d) the conditions which may or may not be attached to an approval of such an application;

(e) circumstances in which such an application will not be approved;

(f) appeals against determinations by the Scottish Ministers on such applications;

(g) circumstances in which the consent for the purposes of section 2(4) above of a creditor or creditors generally may be dispensed with;

(h) circumstances in which a creditor may object to—

(i) the dispensation of the creditor's consent; or

(ii) the approval of such an application, and the manner in which such objection may be made;

(i) the remitting of any such application in respect of which a creditor has made an objection to the sheriff for determination;

(j) the manner in which a debt payment programme may be varied;

(k) the priority in which debts are to be paid under a debt payment programme;

(l) the ingathering and sale or other disposal of assets and the distribution to creditors of amounts so realised;

(m) the period for which a debt payment programme is to remain in operation;

(n) circumstances in which, and the procedure under which, any such period can, in relation to a particular debt payment programme, be shortened or extended;

(o) circumstances in which a debt payment programme is to cease to have effect;

(p) subject to section 4 above, the manner in which a debt payment programme affects the rights or remedies of a creditor or other third party;

(q) circumstances in which creditors are to notify debtors of the right to make such an application and the effect of the failure of a creditor to provide that notice;

(r) the class of person who may act as a payments distributor;

(s) the class of person who may act as a money adviser;

[(sa) the class of person who may act as an approved intermediary;]

(t) the functions of a payments distributor;

(u) the functions of a money adviser;

[(ua) the functions of an approved intermediary;]

[(ub) the remuneration of the payments distributors and money advisers;]

(v) the establishment and maintenance by the Scottish Ministers of a register of debt payment programmes and applications for the approval, and variation, of such programmes;

(w) the information which is to be kept in such a register;

(x) the manner in which that information is to be kept and in which it, or any part of it, is to be made available to the public; and

(y) the determination, and charging, by the Scottish Ministers of fees in respect of—

(i) the consideration of applications for the approval, or the variation, of a debt payment programme; and

(ii) the provision of information recorded in the register of debt payment programmes.

(3) The regulations may also—

(a) make different provision in relation to such different types of debtors, debts or other matters as may be described by the Scottish Ministers;

(b) provide that such different provision is to have effect only for such period as is specified by the Scottish Ministers; and

(c) provide that, on the expiry of that period, the Scottish Ministers may determine that the different provision to which they relate is to—

(i) continue to have effect without limit of time;

(ii) continue to have effect for such further period as may be determined by the Scottish Ministers; or

(iii) cease to have effect.

(4) The regulations may also modify any enactment (including this Act), instrument or document for the purposes of making such further provision as is mentioned in subsection (1) above.

[7A Debt payment programmes: power to make provision about debt relief

(1) The Scottish Ministers may, by regulations, make such further provision as they think fit in connection with debt payment programmes for the purposes of—

(a) enabling such programmes to provide for the payment of part only of money owed by debtors; and

(b) on the completion of such programmes or otherwise, enabling any liability of debtors to pay any part of such money owed as is outstanding to be discharged.

(2) The regulations may, in particular, make provision about—

(a) the minimum proportion or percentage of debts which shall be paid under such debt payment programmes;

(b) without prejudice to section 7(2)(h) to (j) above, the consent of creditors for the purposes of section 2(4) above (including the circumstances in which consent by a majority by number or in value shall be sufficient);

(c) the effect of such programmes on debtors' liabilities for interest, fees, penalties and other charges in relation to debts being paid under such programmes;

(d) the effect of such programmes on the rights of creditors to charge interest, fees, penalties or other charges in relation to debts being paid under such programmes;

(e) circumstances in which, on completion of such programmes or otherwise, any liability of debtors to pay—

(i) part of any debts as are outstanding; or

(ii) any interest, fees, penalties or other charges in relation to such debts,

is to be discharged.

(3) Subsections (3) and (4) of section 7 above apply for the purposes of regulations under this section as they apply for the purposes of regulations under subsection (1) of that section.]

8 Functions of the Scottish Ministers

(1) The Scottish Ministers may by order provide that their functions under this Part of this Act may be performed on their behalf by such other person as may be specified in the order.

(2) Such an order does not allow regulations under this Part of this Act or any further order under this section to be made by any person other than the Scottish Ministers.

(3) Such an order may make different provision for different functions.

9 Interpretation of Part

(1) In this Part of this Act—

['approved intermediary' means any person, not being a money adviser, who has been approved by the Scottish Ministers as a person who may give advice to a debtor for the purposes of section 3(1) above.]

'money adviser' means any person who has been approved by the Scottish Ministers as a person who may give advice to a debtor for the purposes of section 3(1) above; and

'prescribed' means prescribed by regulations made by the Scottish Ministers.

[. . .]

[PART 1A
INTERIM ATTACHMENT

Interim attachment

[9A Interim attachment

(1) Subject to sections 9B to 9E below, the court may grant warrant for diligence by attachment of corporeal moveable property owned (whether alone or in common) by the debtor on the dependence of an action (such attachment is to be known as interim attachment).

(2) Warrant for interim attachment is competent only where an action contains a conclusion for payment of a sum other than by way of expenses.

(3) This Part of this Act shall apply to petitions in the Court of Session and to parties to them as it applies to actions and to parties to them.

(4) In this Part of this Act—

'action' includes, in the sheriff court—

(a) a summary cause;

[(b) a simple procedure case (within the meaning of section 72(9) of the Courts Reform (Scotland) Act 2014); and]

(c) a summary application,

and references to 'summons', 'conclusion' and to cognate expressions shall be construed accordingly;

'court' means—

(a) the court before which the action is in dependence; or

(b) where, by virtue of section 9L(1)(a) below, the interim attachment has effect after the creditor obtains a final interlocutor for payment, the court which granted that interlocutor;

'creditor' means the party who concludes for payment and who seeks, obtains or executes warrant for interim attachment;

'debtor' means the party against whom the conclusion for payment is addressed; and expressions used in this Part of this Act have, unless the context otherwise requires, the same meanings as those expressions have in Part 2 of this Act.]

[9B Articles exempt from interim attachment

It is not competent to attach by interim attachment—

(a) any article within a dwellinghouse;

(b) any article which, by virtue of section 11 below, it is not competent to attach;

(c) a mobile home which is the only or principal residence of a person other than the debtor;

(d) any article of a perishable nature or which is likely to deteriorate substantially and rapidly in condition or value; or

(e) where the debtor is engaged in trade, any article acquired by the debtor—

(i) to be sold by the debtor (whether or not after adaptation); or

(ii) as a material for a process of manufacturing for sale by the debtor, in the ordinary course of that trade.]

Application for interim attachment

[9C Application for warrant for interim attachment

(1) A creditor may, at any time during which an action is in dependence, apply to the court for warrant for interim attachment.

(2) An application under subsection (1) above shall—

(a) be in (or as nearly as may be in) the form prescribed by Act of Sederunt;

(b) subject to subsection (3) below, be intimated to and provide details of—

(i) the debtor; and

(ii) any other person having an interest;

(c) state whether the creditor is seeking the grant, under section 9D(1) below, of warrant for interim attachment in advance of a hearing on the application under section 9E below; and

(d) contain such other information as the Scottish Ministers may by regulations prescribe.

(3) An application under subsection (1) above need not be intimated where the creditor is seeking the grant, under section 9D(1) below, of warrant in advance of a hearing on the application under section 9E below.

(4) The court, on receiving an application under subsection (1) above, shall—

(a) subject to section 9D below, fix a date for a hearing on the application under section 9E below; and

(b) order the creditor to intimate that date to—

(i) the debtor; and

(ii) any other person appearing to the court to have an interest.]

[9D Grant of warrant without a hearing

(1) The court may, if satisfied as to the matters mentioned in subsection (2) below, make an order granting warrant for interim attachment without a hearing on the application under section 9E below.

(2) The matters referred to in subsection (1) above are—

(a) that the creditor has a prima facie case on the merits of the action;

(b) that there is a real and substantial risk enforcement of any decree in the action in favour of the creditor would be defeated or prejudiced by reason of—

(i) the debtor being insolvent or verging on insolvency; or

(ii) the likelihood of the debtor removing, disposing of, burdening, concealing or otherwise dealing with all or some of the debtor's assets,

were warrant for interim attachment not granted in advance of such a hearing; and

(c) that it is reasonable in all the circumstances, including the effect granting warrant may have on any person having an interest, to do so.

(3) The onus shall be on the creditor to satisfy the court that the order granting warrant should be made.

(4) Where the court makes an order granting warrant for interim attachment without a hearing on the application under section 9E below, the court shall—

(a) fix a date for a hearing under section 9M below; and

(b) order the creditor to intimate that date to—

(i) the debtor; and

(ii) any other person appearing to the court to have an interest.

(5) Where a hearing is fixed under subsection (4)(a) above, section 9M (except

subsection (11)) below shall apply as if an application had been made to the court for an order under that section.

(6) Where the court refuses to make an order granting warrant without a hearing under section 9E below and the creditor insists in the application, the court shall—

(a) fix a date for such a hearing on the application; and

(b) order the creditor to intimate that date to—

(i) the debtor; and

(ii) any other person appearing to the court to have an interest.]

[9E Hearing on application

(1) At the hearing on an application for warrant for interim attachment, the court shall not make any order without first giving—

(a) any person to whom intimation of the date of the hearing was made; and

(b) any other person appearing to the court to have an interest, an opportunity to be heard.

(2) The court may, if satisfied as to the matters mentioned in subsection (3) below, make an order granting warrant for interim attachment.

(3) The matters referred to in subsection (2) above are—

(a) that the creditor has a prima facie case on the merits of the action;

(b) that there is a real and substantial risk enforcement of any decree in the action in favour of the creditor would be defeated or prejudiced by reason of—

(i) the debtor being insolvent or verging on insolvency; or

(ii) the likelihood of the debtor removing, disposing of, burdening, concealing or otherwise dealing with all or some of the debtor's assets,

were warrant for interim attachment not granted; and

(c) that it is reasonable in all the circumstances, including the effect granting warrant may have on any person having an interest, to do so.

(4) The onus shall be on the creditor to satisfy the court that the order granting warrant should be made.

(5) Where the court makes an order granting or, as the case may be, refusing warrant for interim attachment, the court shall order the creditor to intimate that order to—

(a) the debtor; and

(b) any other person appearing to the court to have an interest.

(6) Where the court makes an order refusing warrant for interim attachment, the court may impose such conditions (if any) as it thinks fit.

(7) Without prejudice to the generality of subsection (6) above, those conditions may require the debtor—

(a) to consign into court such sum; or

(b) to find caution or to give such other security,

as the court thinks fit.]

Execution of interim attachment

[9F Execution of interim attachment

(1) Sections 12, 13, 15 and (subject to subsection (6) below) 17 below apply to execution of an interim attachment as they apply to execution of an attachment.

(2) The officer shall, immediately after executing an interim attachment, complete a schedule such as is mentioned in subsection (3) below (in this Part of this Act, a 'schedule of interim attachment').

(3) The schedule of interim attachment—

(a) shall be—

(i) in (or as nearly as may be in) the form prescribed by Act of Sederunt; and

(ii) signed by the officer; and

(b) shall specify—

(i) the articles attached; and
(ii) their value, so far as ascertainable.

(4) The officer shall—
(a) give a copy of the schedule of interim attachment to the debtor; or
(b) where it is not practicable to do so—
(i) give a copy of the schedule to a person present at the place where the interim attachment was executed; or
(ii) where there is no such person, leave a copy of the schedule at that place.

(5) References in this Part of this Act to the day on which an interim attachment is executed are references to the day on which the officer complies with subsection (4) above.

(6) The application of section 17 below shall be subject to the following modifications—
(a) subsections (3)(b) and (4) shall not apply;
(b) in subsections (1), (5) and (6), the references to the sheriff shall be construed as references to the court; and
(c) in subsection (6)(b), the reference to the sheriff clerk shall, in the case of an action in the Court of Session, be construed as a reference to the clerk of the court.]

[9G Execution of interim attachment before service

(1) This section applies where an interim attachment is executed before the service of the summons on the debtor.

(2) Subject to subsection (3) below, if the summons is not served on the debtor before the end of the period of 21 days beginning with the day on which the interim attachment is executed, the attachment shall cease to have effect.

(3) The court may, on the application of the creditor, make an order extending the period referred to in subsection (2) above.

(4) In determining whether to make such an order the court shall have regard to—
(a) the efforts of the creditor to serve the summons within the period of 21 days; and
(b) any special circumstances preventing or obstructing service within that period.]

Interim attachment: further procedure

[9H Order for security of attached articles

(1) The court may, on an application, at any time after articles have been attached—
(a) by the creditor;
(b) the officer; or
(c) the debtor,
make an order for the security of any of the attached articles.

(2) An application for an order under subsection (1) above shall—
(a) be in (or as nearly as may be in) the form prescribed by Act of Sederunt; and
(b) be intimated—
(i) where it is made by the creditor or the officer, to the debtor;
(ii) where it is made by the debtor, to the creditor and the officer.

(3) At the hearing on the application under subsection (1) above, the court shall not make any order without first giving—
(a) any person to whom intimation of the application was made; and
(b) any other person the court is satisfied has an interest,
an opportunity to be heard.]

Interim attachment: effects

[9J Unlawful acts after interim attachment

Section 21 (except subsections (3) and (15)) below applies to an interim attachment as it applies to an attachment with the following modifications—

(a) in subsections (10) and (11), the references to the sheriff shall be construed as references to the court; and

(b) in subsection (12), the references to sections 51 and 54(1) below shall be of no effect.]

[9K Articles belonging to or owned in common by a third party

(1) Where—

(a) a third party claims to own an article attached by interim attachment; and

(b) the court, on the application of the third party, makes an order stating that it is satisfied that the claim is valid,

the interim attachment of that article shall cease to have effect.

(2) Where—

(a) a third party claims to own an article attached by interim attachment in common with the debtor;

(b) the court, on the application of the third party, makes an order stating that it is satisfied—

(i) that the claim is valid; and

(ii) that the continued attachment of the article would be unduly harsh to the third party,

the interim attachment of that article shall cease to have effect.

(3) Subsection (2) of section 34 below applies where a third party makes an application for the purposes of subsection (1)(b) above as it applies where a third party makes an application for the purposes of subsection (1)(b)(ii) of that section.

(4) Where the attachment of an article ceases, by virtue of an order under subsection (1) or (2) above, to have effect, the officer may attach other articles which are owned by the debtor and kept at the place at which the original interim attachment was executed.]

[9L Duration of interim attachment

(1) An interim attachment shall, unless recalled, have effect only until—

(a) subject to subsections (2), (4) and (7) below, where—

(i) the creditor obtains a final interlocutor for payment of all or part of a principal sum concluded for in the action on the dependence of which warrant for interim attachment was granted;

(ii) the creditor obtains a final interlocutor in the creditor's favour in respect of another remedy concluded for in that action; or

(iii) the final interlocutor is of absolvitor or dismissal and the court grants decree under and for the purposes of section 9Q(1)(b) below,

the expiry of the period of 6 months after the action is disposed of;

(b) where—

(i) the final interlocutor is of absolvitor or dismissal; and

(ii) no decree under and for the purposes of section 9Q(1)(b) below is granted,

the granting of that interlocutor; or

(c) the creditor consents, by virtue of subsection (3) below, to the interim attachment ceasing to have effect in relation to every article attached.

(2) An interim attachment shall have effect in relation to a specific article only until the article is attached by the creditor in execution of any such final interlocutor or decree as is mentioned in subsection (1)(a) above.

(3) The creditor may at any time consent in writing to the interim attachment

ceasing to have effect in relation to a specific article attached; and the attachment shall cease to have effect when that consent is notified to the court.

(4) The court may, on an application by the creditor, extend the period mentioned in subsection (1)(a) above but only if—

(a) the application is made before the expiry of the period mentioned in that subsection; and

(b) the court is satisfied that exceptional circumstances make it reasonable to grant the application.

(5) An application under subsection (4) above shall—

(a) be in (or as nearly as may be in) the form prescribed by Act of Sederunt; and

(b) be intimated by the creditor to—

(i) the debtor; and

(ii) any other person having an interest.

(6) The court shall order the creditor to intimate any decision under subsection (4) above disposing of the application under that subsection to—

(a) the debtor; and

(b) any other person appearing to the court to have an interest.

(7) Where such an application is made but not disposed of before the date on which the interim attachment would, but for this subsection, cease to have effect, the interim attachment shall continue to have effect until the application is disposed of.

(8) In calculating the period mentioned in subsection (1)(a) above, any period during which—

(a) a time to pay direction under section 1(1) of the Debtors (Scotland) Act 1987 (c 18); or

(b) an order under—

(i) section 6(3) of that Act (interim order sisting diligence); or

(ii) section 9(4) of that Act (diligence sisted if not recalled on making of time to pay order),

is in effect shall be disregarded.

(9) For the purposes of subsection (1) above—

(a) a final interlocutor is obtained when an interlocutor—

(i) cannot be recalled or altered; and

(ii) is not subject to review; and

(b) an action is disposed of on the date on which the final interlocutor mentioned in paragraph (a) of that subsection is obtained unless, on a later date, the creditor obtains a final interlocutor for expenses in the action, in which case it is disposed of on that later date.]

Recall etc of interim attachment

[9M Recall or restriction of interim attachment

(1) This section applies where warrant is granted for interim attachment.

(2) The debtor and any person having an interest may apply to the court for an order—

(a) recalling the warrant;

(b) restricting the warrant;

(c) if an interim attachment has been executed in pursuance of the warrant—

(i) recalling; or

(ii) restricting, that attachment;

(d) determining any question relating to the validity, effect or operation of the warrant; or

(e) ancillary to any order mentioned in paragraphs (a) to (d) above.

(3) An application under subsection (2) above shall—

(a) be in (or as nearly as may be in) the form prescribed by Act of Sederunt; and

(b) be intimated to—

(i) the creditor; and

(ii) any other person having an interest.

(4) At the hearing on the application under subsection (2) above, the court shall not make any order without first giving—

(a) any person to whom intimation of the application was made; and

(b) any other person the court is satisfied has an interest,

an opportunity to be heard.

(5) Where the court is satisfied that the warrant is invalid it—

(a) shall make an order—

(i) recalling the warrant; and

(ii) if interim attachment has been executed in pursuance of the warrant, recalling that interim attachment; and

(b) may make an order ancillary to any order mentioned in paragraph (a) above.

(6) Where the court is satisfied that an interim attachment executed in pursuance of the warrant is incompetent, it—

(a) shall make an order recalling the interim attachment; and

(b) may make an order ancillary to any such order.

(7) Subject to subsection (8) below, where the court is satisfied that the warrant is valid but that—

(a) an interim attachment executed in pursuance of it is irregular or ineffective; or

(b) it is reasonable in all the circumstances, including the effect granting warrant may have had on any person having an interest, to do so,

the court may, subject to subsection (11) below, make any order such as is mentioned in subsection (2) above.

(8) If no longer satisfied as to the matters mentioned in subsection (9) below, the court—

(a) shall make an order such as is mentioned in subsection (5)(a) above; and

(b) may make an order such as is mentioned in subsection (5)(b) above.

(9) The matters referred to in subsection (8) above are—

(a) that the creditor has a prima facie case on the merits of the action;

(b) that there is a real and substantial risk enforcement of any decree in the action in favour of the creditor would be defeated or prejudiced by reason of—

(i) the debtor being insolvent or verging on insolvency; or

(ii) the likelihood of the debtor removing, disposing of, burdening, concealing or otherwise dealing with all or some of the debtor's assets; and

(c) that it is reasonable in all the circumstances, including the effect granting warrant may have had on any person having an interest, for the warrant or, as the case may be, any interim attachment executed in pursuance of it to continue to have effect.

(10) The onus shall be on the creditor to satisfy the court that no order under subsection (5), (6), (7) or (8) above should be made.

(11) Where—

(a) by virtue of section 9L(1)(a) above, the interim attachment continues to have effect after the creditor obtains a final interlocutor for payment; and

(b) the period of six months mentioned in that paragraph has not expired,

the court shall not make an order under subsection (7) above.

(12) In granting an application under subsection (2) above, the court may impose such conditions (if any) as it thinks fit.

(13) Without prejudice to the generality of subsection (12) above, those conditions may require the debtor—

(a) to consign into court such sum; or

(b) to find such caution or to give such other security,

as the court thinks fit.

(14) Where the court makes an order under this section, the court shall order the debtor to intimate that order to—

(a) the creditor; and

(b) any other person appearing to the court to have an interest.]

[9N Variation of orders and variation or recall of conditions

(1) Where—

(a) an order restricting warrant for interim attachment is made under section 9M(7) above; or

(b) a condition is imposed under—

(i) section 9E(6) above; or

(ii) section 9M(12) above,

the debtor may apply to the court for variation of the order or, as the case may be, variation or removal of the condition.

(2) An application under subsection (1) above shall—

(a) be in (or as nearly as may be in) the form prescribed by Act of Sederunt; and

(b) be intimated to—

(i) the creditor; and

(ii) any other person having an interest.

(3) At the hearing on the application under subsection (1) above, the court shall not make any order without first giving—

(a) any person to whom intimation of the application was made; and

(b) any other person the court is satisfied has an interest,

an opportunity to be heard.

(4) On an application under subsection (1) above, the court may if it thinks fit—

(a) vary the order; or

(b) vary or remove the condition.

(5) Where the court makes an order varying the order or, as the case may be, varying or removing the condition, the court shall order the debtor to intimate that order to—

(a) the creditor; and

(b) any other person appearing to the court to have an interest.]

General and miscellaneous provisions

[9P Expenses of interim attachment

(1) Subject to subsection (3)(a) below, a creditor shall be entitled to the expenses incurred—

(a) in obtaining warrant for interim attachment; and

(b) where an interim attachment is executed in pursuance of the warrant, in so executing that attachment.

(2) Subject to subsection (3)(b) below, a debtor shall be entitled, where—

(a) warrant for interim attachment is granted; and

(b) the court is satisfied that the creditor was acting unreasonably in applying for it,

to the expenses incurred in opposing that warrant.

(3) The court may modify or refuse—

(a) such expenses as are mentioned in subsection (1) above if it is satisfied that—

(i) the creditor was acting unreasonably in applying for the warrant; or

(ii) such modification or refusal is reasonable in all the circumstances and having regard to the outcome of the action; and

(b) such expenses as are mentioned in subsection (2) above if it is satisfied as to the matter mentioned in paragraph (a)(ii) above.

(4) Subject to subsections (1) to (3) above, the court may make such findings as it thinks fit in relation to such expenses as are mentioned in subsections (1) and (2) above.

(5) Expenses incurred as mentioned in subsections (1) and (2) above in obtaining or, as the case may be, opposing an application for warrant shall be expenses of process.]

[9Q Recovery of expenses of interim attachment

(1) Subject to subsection (4) below, any expenses chargeable against the debtor which are incurred in executing an interim attachment shall be recoverable only by attachment—

(a) in execution of a decree granted by virtue of—

(i) the conclusion for payment in the action on the dependence of which the warrant for interim attachment was granted; or

(ii) another conclusion in the creditor's favour in that action; or

(b) where the final interlocutor in the action is of absolvitor or dismissal, in execution of a decree granted under and for the purposes of this subsection.

(2) Where any such expenses cease to be recoverable in pursuance of subsection (1) above, they cease to be chargeable against the debtor.

(3) Subsection (4) below applies where interim attachment is—

(a) recalled under section 2(3), 3(1)(b), 9(2)(cb) or 10(1)(b) of the 1987 Act in relation to a time to pay direction or order;

(b) in effect immediately before the date of sequestration (within the meaning of the Bankruptcy (Scotland) Act [2016]) of the debtor's estate;

(c) in effect immediately before the appointment of an administrator under Part II of the Insolvency Act 1986 (c 45);

(d) in effect against property of the debtor immediately before a floating charge attaches all or part of that property under section 53(7)(attachment on appointment of receiver by holder of charge) or 54(6)(attachment on appointment of receiver by court) of the 1986 Act;

(e) in effect immediately before the commencement of the winding up, under Part IV or V of the 1986 Act, of the debtor; or

(f) rendered unenforceable by virtue of the creditor entering into a composition contract or acceding to a trust deed for creditors or by virtue of the subsistence of a protected trust deed within the meaning of Schedule [4 of the 2016] Act.

(4) Where this subsection applies—

(a) the expenses of the interim attachment which were chargeable against the debtor remain so chargeable; and

(b) if the debtor's obligation to pay the expenses is not discharged under or by virtue of the time to pay direction or order, sequestration, appointment, receivership, winding up, composition contract or trust deed for creditors,

those expenses are recoverable in pursuance of subsection (1) above.]

[9R Ascription of sums recovered while interim attachment is in effect

(1) This section applies where—

(a) any amounts are—

(i) secured by an interim attachment; and

(ii) while the attachment is in effect, paid to account of the amounts recoverable from the debtor; and

(b) that interim attachment ceases to have effect.

(2) Such amounts shall be ascribed to the following in the order in which they are mentioned—

(a) the expenses incurred in—

(i) obtaining warrant for; and

(ii) executing,

the interim attachment;

(b) any interest which has accrued, in relation to a sum due under a decree granted by virtue of the conclusion in relation to which warrant for interim attachment was granted, as at the date of execution;

(c) any sum due under that decree together with such interest as has accrued after that date.

(3) Where an interim attachment is followed by an attachment in execution of a decree granted by virtue of the conclusion in relation to which the warrant for the interim attachment was granted, section 41 below shall apply to amounts to which this section applies as it applies to amounts to which that section applies.]

[9S Ranking of interim attachment

For the purposes of any enactment or rule of law as to ranking or preference—

(a) where—

(i) an interim attachment has been executed; and

(ii) the creditor has, without undue delay, obtained an interlocutor for payment of all or part of the sum concluded for,

that interim attachment shall be treated as if it were an attachment by virtue of section 10 below of the property attached, executed when the interim attachment was executed; and

(b) where an interim attachment has ceased to have effect in relation to any article by virtue of section 9L(2) above, the attachment of the article in question shall be taken to have been executed when the interim attachment was executed.]]

PART 2
ATTACHMENT

Attachment

10 Attachment

(1) There shall be a form of diligence over corporeal moveable property for recovery of money owed; it is to be known as attachment.

(2) Attachment is exigible only in execution of a decree or document of debt and only upon property owned (whether alone or in common) by the debtor.

(3) Attachment is competent only where—

[(a) the debtor has been charged to pay the debt;

(b) the period for payment specified in the charge has expired without payment being made; and

(c) where the debtor is an individual, the creditor has, no earlier than 12 weeks before taking any steps to execute the attachment, provided the debtor with a debt advice and information package.]

[. . .]

(5) In this section—

[. . .]

'debt advice and information package' means a document or bundle of documents containing such information (including information regarding the availability of money advice within the debtor's locality), and in such form, as the Scottish Ministers may determine;

'decree' means—

(a) a decree of the Court of Session, of the High Court of Justiciary or of the sheriff;
(b) a decree of the Court of Teinds;
(c) a summary warrant;
(d) a civil judgment granted outside Scotland by a court, tribunal or arbiter which by virtue of any enactment or rule of law is enforceable in Scotland;
(e) an order or determination which by virtue of any enactment is enforceable as if it were an extract registered decree arbitral bearing a warrant for execution issued by the sheriff;
(f) a warrant granted, in criminal proceedings, for enforcement by civil diligence;
(g) an order under section 114 of the Companies Clauses Consolidation (Scotland) Act 1845 (c 17);
(h) a determination under section 46 of the Harbours, Docks and Piers Clauses Act 1847 (c 27); or
(i) a liability order within the meaning of section 33(2) of the Child Support Act 1991 (c 48),

being a decree, warrant, judgment, order or determination which, or an extract of which, authorises attachment; and

'document of debt' means—

(a) a document registered for execution in the Books of Council and Session or the sheriff court books;
(b) a document or settlement which by virtue of an Order in Council made under section 13 of the Civil Jurisdiction and Judgments Act 1982 (c 27) is enforceable in Scotland,
[[(c) a court settlement or authentic instrument (within the meaning of Article 3 of the Hague Convention) which is registered in the sheriff court under the Hague Convention;] or
(d) a maintenance arrangement (within the meaning of Article 3 of the Hague Convention) which is registered in the sheriff court under the Hague Convention,]

[being a document, bill, settlement, instrument or arrangement] which, or an extract of which, authorises attachment.

['the Hague Convention' means the Convention on the International Recovery of Child Support and other forms of Family Maintenance done at The Hague on 23rd November 2007.

[. . .]]

(6) The Scottish Ministers may by order modify the definitions of 'decree' and 'document of debt' in subsection (5) above so as to—
(a) add or remove types of decree or document to or, as the case may be, from those referred to in that provision; or
(b) vary any of the descriptions of the types of decree or document there referred to.

(7) In this Act, references to attaching are references to the execution of attachment.

11 Articles exempt from attachment

(1) It is not competent to attach—
(a) any implements, tools of trade, books or other equipment reasonably required for the use of the debtor in the practice of the debtor's profession, trade or business and not exceeding in aggregate value £1,000 or such amount as may be prescribed in regulations made by the Scottish Ministers;
(b) any vehicle, the use of which is so reasonably required by the debtor, not exceeding in value [£1,000] or such amount as may be prescribed in regulations made by the Scottish Ministers;
(c) a mobile home which is the debtor's only or principal residence;
(d) any tools or other equipment reasonably required for the purpose of keeping

in good order and condition any garden or yard adjacent to, or associated with, a dwellinghouse in which the debtor resides;

[(e) any money.]

(2) The Scottish Ministers may by regulations modify subsection (1) above so as to—

(a) add or remove types of articles to or, as the case may be, from those referred to in that provision; or

(b) vary any of the descriptions of the types of articles there referred to.

[(3) It is not competent to attach cargo which it is competent to arrest by virtue of section 47C of the Administration of Justice Act 1965 (c 46) (competence of arresting cargo.)]*

[(3) In subsection (1)(e) above, 'money' has the same meaning as in section 175 of the Bankruptcy and Diligence etc (Scotland) Act 2007 (asp 3).]*

12 Times when attachment is not competent

(1) It is not competent to execute an attachment on—

(a) a Sunday;

(b) a day which is a public holiday in the area in which the attachment is to be executed; or

(c) such other day as may be prescribed by Act of Sederunt.

(2) The execution of an attachment shall not—

(a) begin before 8 am or after 8 pm; or

(b) be continued after 8 pm,

unless the officer has obtained prior authority from the sheriff for such commencement or continuation.

13 Presumption of ownership

(1) An officer may, when executing an attachment, proceed on the assumption that the debtor owns, solely or in common with a third party, any article which is in the possession of the debtor.

(2) The officer shall, before attaching any article, make enquiries of any person who is present at the place at which the article is situated as to the ownership of the article (and in particular shall enquire as to whether there is any person who owns the article in common with the debtor).

(3) The officer may not proceed on the assumption mentioned in subsection (1) above where the officer knows or ought to know that the contrary is the case.

(4) The officer is not precluded from relying on that assumption by reason only of one or both of the following circumstances—

(a) that the article belongs to a class which is commonly held under a hire, hire-purchase or conditional sale agreement or on some other limited title of possession;

(b) that an assertion has been made that the article is not owned by the debtor.

[13A Schedule of attachment

(1) The officer must, immediately after executing an attachment, complete a schedule such as is mentioned in subsection (2) below (in this section, the 'attachment schedule').

(2) An attachment schedule—

(a) must be in (or as nearly as may be in) the form prescribed by Act of Sederunt; and

(b) must specify—

(i) the articles attached; and

(ii) their value, so far as ascertainable.

(3) The officer must—

(a) give a copy of the attachment schedule to the debtor; or

(b) where it is not practicable to do so—

(i) give a copy of the schedule to a person present at the place where the attachment was executed; or

(ii) where there is no such person, leave a copy of it at that place.

(4) An attachment is executed on the day on which the officer complies with subsection (3) above.]

Attachment of articles kept outwith dwellinghouses etc

14 Procedure for attachment of articles kept outwith dwellinghouses etc

Sections 15 to [19A] below apply only in relation to the attachment of articles which are—

(a) kept outwith a dwellinghouse; or

(b) mobile homes which are not the only or principal residence of the debtor.

15 [Valuation]

(1) An officer may open shut and lockfast places for the purposes of executing an attachment.

(2) When executing an attachment the officer shall, subject to subsection (3) below, value the articles being attached at the price which they are likely to fetch if sold on the open market.

(3) Where the officer considers that an article is such that a valuation by a professional valuer or other suitably skilled person is appropriate, the officer shall arrange for such a valuation and a valuation so arranged shall proceed on the basis set out in subsection (2) above.

16 Attachment of mobile homes

(1) Where a mobile home which is the only or principal residence of a person other than the debtor has been attached—

(a) the officer shall give notice to that other person of that fact; and

(b) the sheriff may, on an application by the debtor or that other person, order that the attachment of the mobile home is to cease to have effect.

(2) The sheriff—

(a) shall consider any application for an order under subsection (1) above which is made before the date which is 14 days after the date on which the mobile home is attached; and

(b) may, on cause shown, consider any such application which is made at any time after that date but before the date on which the attached mobile home is auctioned.

17 Report of attachment

(1) The officer shall, within 14 days of the execution of an attachment (or such longer period as the sheriff on cause shown may allow on application by the officer), make to the sheriff a report of the attachment.

(2) A report made under subsection (1) above shall—

(a) be in the form prescribed by Act of Sederunt; and

(b) be signed by the officer.

(3) Such a report shall specify—

(a) whether any person, in response to enquiries made under section 13(2) above, asserted that any attached article is not owned by the debtor (or is owned in common by the debtor and a third party);

(b) whether any attached article has been redeemed under section 18(1) below.

(4) Such a report need not be made in respect of any article or vehicle which has been sold in pursuance of an order made under section 20(1)(b) or, as the case may be, 22(3) below.

(5) The sheriff may refuse to receive such a report on the ground that it has not been made and signed in accordance with subsections (1) and (2) above.

(6) If the sheriff so refuses—

(a) the attachment to which the report relates is to cease to have effect; and

(b) the sheriff clerk shall intimate the refusal to—

(i) the debtor; and

(ii) if another person is in possession of the attached articles, that person.

18 Redemption

(1) Subject to any order made under section 20(1)(b) below, the debtor is entitled, within 14 days of the date on which an article is attached, to redeem that article.

(2) The amount for which such an article may be redeemed is the value fixed under subsection (2) or (3) of section 15 above.

(3) The officer shall, on receiving payment from the debtor for the redemption of an attached article, grant a receipt in the form prescribed by Act of Sederunt to the debtor.

(4) The attachment of the article is, on the grant of such a receipt, to cease to have effect.

(5) Where an article is redeemed after the officer has made a report under section 17(1) above in respect of the attachment, the officer shall report the redemption as soon as is reasonably practicable to the sheriff.

19 Removal and auction of attached articles

(1) [An officer] may, after the report of attachment has been received by the sheriff—

(a) make arrangements for the auction of the attached articles; and

(b) on the date specified in the notice given under section 27(4) below, remove the attached articles from the place at which they are kept.

(2) The officer may open shut and lockfast places for the purpose of so removing the attached articles.

(3) The officer may not remove any vehicle in respect of which an application for an order under subsection (1) or (3) of section 22 below has been made but not disposed of.

(4) The officer may remove to the place at which the auction is to be held such attached articles as, if sold at their values fixed under subsection (2) or, as the case may be, (3) of section 15 above, would realise in aggregate the sum recoverable at the time of the auction.

(5) The remaining attached articles will cease to be subject to attachment.

(6) An attached article shall not, subject to any order made under section 20(1)(b) or 22(3) below, be auctioned before the date which is 7 days after the date on which the article is removed by the officer from the place at which it was attached.

[19A Urgent removal of attached articles

(1) The officer may at any time remove an attached article without notice if—

(a) the officer considers it necessary for—

(i) the security; or

(ii) the preservation of the value,

of the article; and

(b) there is insufficient time to obtain an order under section 20(1)(a) below.

(2) The officer shall remove an article under subsection (1) above—

(a) to the nearest convenient premises of the debtor or the person in possession of the articles; or

(b) if—

(i) no such premises are available; or

(ii) the officer considers such premises to be unsuitable,

to the nearest suitable secure premises.

(3) Subsections (2) and (6) of section 19 above shall apply to this section as they apply to that section.]

Attachment: further procedure

20 Order for security of articles or sale of articles which are perishable etc

(1) The sheriff may, on an application by the creditor, the officer or the debtor, at any time after articles have been attached make an order—

(a) for the security of any of the attached articles;

(b) in relation to any of the articles which are of a perishable nature or which are likely to deteriorate substantially and rapidly in condition or value, for the creditor or the officer to make arrangements for their immediate sale and for any proceeds of the sale to be consigned in court.

(2) An application for an order under subsection (1) above—

(a) by the creditor or the officer, shall be intimated by the creditor or, as the case may be, the officer to the debtor;

(b) by the debtor, shall be intimated to the creditor and the officer, [—

(i) who attached articles; or

(ii) who is authorised to arrange the auction,]

at the time when it is made.

(3) A decision of the sheriff to make an order under subsection (1)(b) above shall not be subject to appeal.

(4) Any sum consigned in court in pursuance of an order made under subsection (1)(b) above shall, where an attachment ceases to have effect before the auction of attached articles is held, be paid to the creditor to the extent necessary to meet the sum recoverable, any surplus thereof being paid to the debtor.

21 Unlawful acts after attachment

(1) The debtor or person in possession of an attached article shall not move it from the place at which it was attached.

(2) If an article is so moved—

(a) the debtor or, as the case may be, the person in possession of the attached articles is acting in breach of the attachment; and

(b) the sheriff may, on an application by the creditor or by the officer, by order authorise the attachment of other articles which are owned by the debtor and kept at the place at which the original attachment was executed.

(3) Subsection (1) above does not apply in relation to any vehicle in respect of which an application for an order under subsection (1) or (3) of section 22 below has been made but not disposed of.

(4) The debtor shall not sell, make a gift of or otherwise relinquish ownership of any attached article.

(5) If an attached article is so sold, gifted or otherwise disposed of the debtor is acting in breach of the attachment.

(6) Any person who wilfully damages or destroys any article which that person knows has been attached is acting in breach of the attachment.

(7) Where an attached article is stolen, the debtor shall give notice to the creditor and the officer [—

(i) who attached articles; or

(ii) who is authorised to arrange the auction,]

of that fact and of any related claim which the debtor makes, or intends to make, under a contract of insurance.

(8) Any debtor who fails to give notice as required by subsection (7) above is acting in breach of the attachment.

(9) Any act which is, under subsection (2), (5), (6) or (8) above, a breach of the attachment may be dealt with as a contempt of court.

(10) Where attached articles are damaged, destroyed or stolen the sheriff, on an application by the creditor or by the officer, may by order authorise—

(a) the attachment of other articles which are owned by the debtor and kept at the place at which the original attachment was executed;

(b) the revaluation of any damaged article in accordance with subsection (2) or (3) of section 15 above.

(11) Where the debtor or any third party who knows that an article is attached—

(a) moves it from the place at which the attachment was executed, and it is—

(i) damaged, destroyed, lost or stolen; or

(ii) acquired from or through the debtor or, as the case may be, the third party by another person without knowledge of the attachment and for value; or

(b) wilfully damages or destroys it,

the sheriff may order the debtor or, as the case may be, the third party to consign the sum set out in subsection (12) below in court.

(12) That sum is—

(a) where the article has been damaged but not so damaged as to make it worthless, a sum equal to the difference between the value of the article fixed under subsection (2) or (3) of section 15 above or, as the case may be, under section 51 or 54(1) below and the value of the article so damaged; or

(b) in any other case, a sum equal to the value of the article as fixed under subsection (2) or (3) of section 15 above or, as the case may be, under section 51 or 54(1) below.

(13) For the purposes of subsection (12)(a) above, the officer shall, subject to subsection (14) below, value a damaged article at the price which it is likely to fetch if sold in that condition on the open market.

(14) Where the officer considers that a damaged article is such that a valuation by a professional valuer or other suitably skilled person is appropriate, the officer shall arrange for such a valuation and a valuation so arranged shall proceed on the basis set out in subsection (13) above.

(15) Any sum consigned in court in pursuance of an order made under subsection (11) above shall, where the attachment of a damaged article ceases to have effect before it is auctioned, be paid to the creditor to the extent necessary to meet the sum recoverable, any surplus thereof being paid to the debtor.

22 Release of vehicle from attachment

(1) The sheriff may, on an application by the debtor and on being satisfied that the auction of any vehicle which has been attached would be unduly harsh in the circumstances, make an order—

(a) providing that the attachment of the vehicle is to cease to have effect; and

(b) where the vehicle has been removed by the officer from the place at which it was attached, requiring the officer to return the vehicle to that place.

(2) The sheriff may not make an order under subsection (1) above unless the value of the vehicle (as fixed under subsection (2) or (3) of section 15 above) does not exceed £1,000 or such other amount as may be prescribed in regulations made by the Scottish Ministers.

(3) Where the value (as fixed under subsection (2) or (3) of section 15 above) of an attached vehicle does exceed £1,000 or, as the case may be, such other prescribed amount the sheriff may, on an application by the debtor and on being satisfied that the auction of any vehicle which has been attached would be unduly harsh in the circumstances, make an order requiring the officer to—

(a) make arrangements for the immediate sale of the vehicle;

(b) pay to the debtor from any proceeds of such sale the sum of £1,000 (or such lesser amount as the sheriff may specify); and

(c) consign any surplus remaining in court.

(4) Where the amount realised on the sale of a vehicle in pursuance of an order

has been made under subsection (3) above is less than the amount which the officer is required by that order to pay to the debtor, the order shall be deemed to have required the officer to pay the amount realised only.

(5) Where the officer is unable to sell the vehicle in pursuance of an order made under subsection (3) above within 14 days of the date on which the order was made, the attachment of that vehicle is to cease to have effect.

(6) The sheriff may consider an application for an order under subsection (1) or (3) above only where it is made within 14 days of the date on which the vehicle is attached.

23 Appeals against valuation

(1) Where the sheriff is satisfied that the aggregate of the values of attached articles fixed under section 15(2) or (3) above or, as the case may be, section 51 or 54(1) below is substantially below the aggregate of the prices which they are likely to fetch if sold on the open market, the sheriff may, on or before the day which immediately precedes the day on which the articles are to be auctioned, order that the attachment is to cease to have effect.

(2) The sheriff may make an order under subsection (1) above on the application of the debtor or on the sheriff's own accord.

(3) The sheriff shall not make such an order without first giving the debtor and the creditor—

(a) an opportunity to make representations; and

(b) if either party wishes to be heard, an opportunity to be heard.

24 Duration of attachment

(1) An attachment shall, subject to subsections (6), (7) and (8) below, have effect only until—

(a) the earlier of—

(i) the date which is six months after the date on which the article is attached; and

(ii) the date which is 28 days after the date on which the attached article is removed by the officer from the place at which it was attached; or

(b) such other date as may be specified in an order made under subsection (2) or section 29(4)(b) below or in an exceptional attachment order.

(2) Where the sheriff is satisfied—

(a) that, if the date on which an attachment is to cease to have effect were to be substituted with a later date, the debtor is likely to comply with an agreement between the creditor and the debtor for the payment of the sum recoverable by instalments or otherwise; or

(b) that the auction of the attached articles cannot take place before the date on which the attachment is to cease to have effect due to circumstances for which the creditor cannot be held responsible and that the attachment ceasing to have effect on that date would prejudice the creditor,

the sheriff may, on an application by the creditor or by the officer, by order provide that the attachment is to remain in effect until such later date as the sheriff considers reasonable in the circumstances.

(3) Where the period for which an attachment is to have effect is extended by an order made under subsection (2) above, an application may be made for another order under that subsection so as to further extend that period.

(4) The sheriff may consider an application for an order under subsection (2) above only where it is made during the period in respect of which an extension is being sought.

(5) A decision of the sheriff on such an application shall be intimated to the debtor by the sheriff clerk.

(6) Where such an application is made but not disposed of before the date on which the attachment in respect of which it is made would, but for this subsection,

cease to have effect, the attachment shall continue to have effect until the application is disposed of.

(7) Where such an application is—

(a) made on the ground referred to in paragraph (a) of subsection (2) above; and

(b) refused by the sheriff within 14 days of the date on which the attachment in respect of which it is made would, but for this subsection, cease to have effect,

the attachment shall continue to have effect until the date which is 14 days after the date of the refusal.

(8) Where—

(a) arrangements for an auction of attached articles are, under section 29(1) below, cancelled; and

(b) the agreement in respect of which the cancellation is made is breached by the debtor,

the period which begins with the date on which the report of agreement was made under section 29(3) below and which ends with the date on which the debtor breaches the agreement is to be disregarded in determining the date on which the attachment is, under subsection (1) above, to cease to have effect.

25 Second attachment at same place

(1) Subject to—

(a) section 9(12) (which provides that a debt which remains outstanding on the recall or cessation of a time to pay order may be enforced by certain diligences) of the Debtors (Scotland) Act 1987 (c 18);

(b) any order made under subsection (2)(b) or (10)(a) of section 21 above; and

(c) sections 34(3) and 35(4) below,

where articles are attached (or are purported to be attached) at any place, it is not competent to attach other articles kept at that place to enforce the same debt unless those other articles are brought to that place after the execution of the first attachment.

(2) It is not competent to attach any article in respect of which an attachment has—

(a) previously been executed in enforcement of the same debt; and

(b) ceased, by virtue of section 16, 18(4), 22(1), 34(1), 35(3), 55(2) or 56(4) of this Act, to have effect.

26 Invalidity and cessation of attachment

(1) Where, at any time before the auction of an article which has been or purports to have been attached, the sheriff is satisfied that—

(a) the attachment has ceased to have effect; or, as the case may be

(b) the purported attachment is invalid (by reason of the attachment being incompetent or otherwise),

the sheriff shall make an order declaring that to be the case and may make such consequential order as appears to the sheriff to be necessary in the circumstances.

(2) An order under subsection (1) above may be made on an application by the debtor or on the sheriff's own initiative.

(3) Where such an order is made on the sheriff's own initiative, the sheriff clerk shall intimate the order to the debtor.

(4) The sheriff shall not make an order under subsection (1) above without first giving the debtor and the creditor—

(a) an opportunity to make representations; and

(b) if either party wishes to be heard, an opportunity to be heard.

(5) Where—

(a) an order is made under subsection (1) above; and

(b) [an officer] has removed the article from the place at which it was, or purported to be, attached, the officer shall return the article to the place from which it was removed.

(6) The sheriff shall give reasons for a refusal to grant an order under subsection (1) above.

Auction of attached articles

27 Notice of public auction

(1) The auction of attached articles shall, subject to subsections (2) and (3) below, be by public auction held in an auction room.

(2) If it is impractical to hold the auction of an attached article in an auction room the auction may be held at such other place (other than the debtor's dwellinghouse) as the officer considers appropriate.

(3) The auction of other articles which have been attached together with an article which is to be auctioned at a place other than an auction room may, if the officer considers it appropriate (having had regard, in particular, to the expenses which are likely to be incurred in connection with the auction), also be held at that other place.

(4) The officer [. . .] shall give notice to the debtor and to any other person in possession of the attached articles of—

(a) the date on which the auction is to be held;

(b) the location of the auction room or, as the case may be, the other place at which the auction is to be held; and

(c) where sections 15 to 19 above apply in relation to the attached articles, the date arranged for the removal of those attached articles from the place at which they are kept.

(5) The officer shall advertise the auction by public notice.

28 Alteration of arrangements for removal or auction

(1) Subject to subsection (2) below and without prejudice to section 29(4) below, the creditor or the officer is not, after notice has been given under section 27(4) above to the debtor, entitled to arrange—

(a) a new date for the auction; or

(b) where [sections 15 to 19A] above apply in relation to the attached articles, a new date for the removal of those articles from the place where they are kept.

(2) Where, for any reason for which neither the creditor nor the officer is responsible, it is not possible—

(a) for the auction to be held on the date specified in the notice given under section 27(4) above; or

(b) for the attached articles to be removed from the place where they are kept on the date so specified,

the creditor may instruct the officer to arrange a new date for the auction or, as the case may be, a new date for the removal and the officer shall intimate the new date to the debtor and to any other person in possession of the attached articles.

(3) A new date arranged under subsection (2) above shall not in any case be fewer than 7 days after the date of intimation under that subsection.

29 Cancellation of auctions

(1) The officer may, for the purposes of enabling the sum recoverable to be paid in accordance with an agreement between the creditor and the debtor, cancel arrangements for an auction of attached articles.

(2) The officer may not cancel the arrangements for such an auction on more than two occasions.

(3) Where an auction has been cancelled the officer shall—

(a) make to the sheriff a report of the agreement reached; and

(b) arrange for the return of any attached articles which have been removed for auction to the place from which they were removed.

(4) The sheriff, if satisfied on an application by the creditor that the debtor is in

breach of any agreement which has been reported under subsection (3) above, may by order provide—

(a) if the arrangements for the auction of the attached articles can still be implemented in accordance with the provisions of this Part and Part 3 of this Act, that the officer may resume making arrangements for the auction in accordance with those provisions;

(b) if for any reason for which neither the creditor nor the officer is responsible arrangements for the auction cannot be implemented in accordance with those provisions, that the provisions of this Part and Part 3 of this Act which prevent such implementation are not to apply for the purposes of the attachment and auction of those articles.

(5) The sheriff shall not make an order under subsection (4) above without first giving the debtor—

(a) an opportunity to make representations; and

(b) if the debtor so wishes, an opportunity to be heard.

30 Auction

(1) The officer shall attend the auction and maintain a record of the attached articles which are sold.

(2) Such a record shall specify the amount for which each attached article is sold.

(3) The officer shall be accompanied at the auction by another person who shall witness the proceedings.

(4) Any attached article exposed for sale in the auction may be purchased by—

(a) any creditor, including the creditor on whose behalf the article was attached;

(b) a third party who owns the attached article in common with the debtor.

31 Disposal of proceeds of auction

(1) The officer shall, subject to section [24 (further provision as regards the effect of sequestration on diligence) of the Bankruptcy (Scotland) Act 2016], dispose of the proceeds of the auction by—

(a) retaining such amount as necessary to meet the fees and outlays of the officer;

(b) paying to the creditor the remainder of the proceeds of auction so far as necessary to meet the sum recoverable; and

(c) paying to the debtor any surplus remaining.

[(1A) Where an article is sold at the auction at a price below the value of the article, the difference between that price and that value shall, prior to the proceeds of the auction being disposed of under subsection (1) above, be credited against the sum recoverable.

(1B) Where—

(a) an article to which subsection (1A) above applies has been damaged and revalued under section 21(10)(b) above;

(b) the damage was not caused by the fault of the debtor; and

(c) no sum has been consigned into court by a third party under section 21(11) above,

the revaluation shall be disregarded for the purposes of subsection (1A) above.]

(2) Where the sum recoverable is not realised by the proceeds of auction and any article remains unsold after being exposed for auction—

(a) ownership of the article shall, without prejudice to the rights of any third party, pass to the creditor; and

(b) the value of that article shall be credited against the sum recoverable.

(3) Where the value of unsold articles exceeds the amount of the sum recoverable which remains outstanding, subsection (2) above shall operate only in relation to such of those articles which have, in aggregate, the value which is nearest to the amount which remains outstanding.

(4) The references in subsections [(1A),] (2)(b) and (3) above to the value of an article are references to the value of the article as fixed under subsection (2) or (3) of section 15 above or, as the case may be, section 51 or 54(1) below.

(5) Where the creditor does not uplift an article within 3 working days after the day on which the auction is held the ownership of the article shall revert to the person who owned the article before the operation of subsection (2)(a) above.

(6) For the purposes of this section—

'proceeds of auction' include any amount—

(a) consigned in court in pursuance of an order made under section 21(11), 20(1)(b), 22(3) or 50(5) of this Act;

(b) received by the officer in respect of a transfer, under section 35(2) below, of the debtor's interest in any article owned in common by the debtor and a third party,

but do not include any amount which the officer is required to pay to the debtor in pursuance of an order under section 22(3) above; and

'working day' means a day which is not—

(a) a Saturday;
(b) a Sunday;
(c) New Year's Day;
(d) 2nd January;
(e) Good Friday;
(f) Easter Monday;
(g) Christmas Day;
(h) Boxing Day; or
(i) any other day which is a public holiday in the area in which the auction is held.

32 Report of auction

(1) The officer who arranged the auction shall, within the period of 14 days after the date on which the auction is held, make to the sheriff a report in the form prescribed by Act of Sederunt (a 'report of auction').

(2) A report of auction shall—

(a) specify—
(i) any attached articles which have been sold;
(ii) the amount for which they have been sold;
(iii) any attached articles which remain unsold;
[(iiia) any sums paid by the debtor to account of the sum recoverable;]
(iv) any chargeable expenses;
(v) any surplus paid to the debtor; and
(vi) any balance due by or to the debtor;

(b) refer to any article in respect of which—
(i) an attachment has, under section 34(1) below or in pursuance of an order made under section 35(3) below, ceased to have effect;
(ii) the debtor's interest has, under section 35(2) below, transferred to a third party;

(c) contain a declaration by the officer that all the information contained within it is, to the best of the officer's knowledge, true; and

(d) be signed by the officer and the witness who attended the auction.

(3) If the officer—

(a) without reasonable excuse makes a report of auction after the expiry of the period mentioned in subsection (1) above; or

(b) wilfully refuses to make, or delays making, a report of auction after the expiry of that period,

the sheriff may make an order providing that the officer is liable for the chargeable expenses, either in whole or in part.

(4) An order made under subsection (3) above does not prejudice the right of the sheriff to report the matter to the Court of Session or the sheriff principal under section 79(1)(b) (investigation of alleged misconduct by a messenger-at-arms or sheriff officer) of the Debtors (Scotland) Act 1987 (c 18).

33 Audit of report of auction

(1) The sheriff shall remit the report of auction to the auditor of court who shall—

(a) tax the chargeable expenses;

(b) certify the balance due by or to the debtor following the auction; and

(c) make a report to the sheriff.

(2) The auditor of court shall not alter the report of auction without first providing all interested persons an opportunity to make representations.

(3) The auditor of court shall not charge a fee in respect of the report made under subsection (1)(c) above.

(4) On receipt of a report made under subsection (1)(c) above the sheriff shall make an order—

(a) declaring the balance due by or to the debtor, as certified by the auditor of court;

(b) declaring such a balance after making modifications to the balance so certified; or

(c) where the sheriff is satisfied that there has been a substantial irregularity in the execution of the attachment (other than the timing of the report of auction), declaring the attachment and auction to be void.

(5) An order made under subsection (4)(c) above may make such consequential provision as the sheriff thinks fit.

(6) An order made under subsection (4)(c) above shall not affect the title of a person to any article acquired by that person at the auction, or subsequently, in good faith.

(7) The sheriff may not make an order under subsection (4)(b) or (c) above without first

[(a) giving—

(i) the debtor;

(ii) the creditor; and

(iii) any third party who claims ownership (whether alone or in common with the debtor) of any attached article,

an opportunity to make representations; or

(b) holding a hearing.]

(8) The sheriff clerk shall intimate the sheriff's order under subsection (4) above to the [persons mentioned in subsection (7)(a) above].

General and miscellaneous provisions

34 Articles belonging to a third party

(1) Where at any time before an attached article is auctioned—

(a) a third party claims to own the article; and

(b) either—

(i) the officer is satisfied that the claim is valid and neither the debtor nor any other person in possession of the article disputes the claim; or

(ii) the sheriff, on an application by the third party, makes an order stating that the sheriff is [satisfied that the claim is valid],

the attachment of that article is to cease to have effect.

(2) The making of an application to the sheriff for the purposes of subsection (1)(b)(ii) above does not preclude the third party making the application from taking any other proceedings for the recovery of an article which is owned by the third party.

(3) Where the attachment of an article ceases, under subsection (1) above, to

have effect, the officer may attach other articles which are owned by the debtor and kept at the place at which the original attachment was executed.

35 Articles in common ownership

(1) Articles which are owned in common by a debtor and a third party may be attached and disposed of in satisfaction of the debts of the debtor.

(2) Where at any time before an attached article is auctioned—

(a) a third party claims to own the article in common with the debtor;

(b) either—

(i) the officer is satisfied that the claim is valid; or

(ii) the sheriff, on an application by the third party, makes an order stating that the sheriff is so satisfied; and

(c) the third party pays to the officer a sum equal to the value of the debtor's interest in the article,

the debtor's interest in the article shall transfer to the third party.

(3) Where the sheriff is satisfied—

(a) that an article which has been removed from the place at which it was attached is owned in common by the debtor and a third party; and

(b) that the auction of the article would be unduly harsh to the third party in the circumstances,

the sheriff may, on an application by the third party before the attached article is auctioned, order that the attachment of that article is to cease to have effect.

(4) Where—

(a) the debtor's interest in an article owned in common by the debtor and a third party is, under subsection (2) above, transferred to the third party; or

(b) the attachment of an article which is so owned ceases, in pursuance of an order made under subsection (3) above, to have effect,

the officer may attach other articles which are owned by the debtor and kept at the place at which the original attachment was executed.

36 Procedure where articles in common ownership are sold at auction

(1) This subsection applies where—

(a) a third party claimed, before an attached article was auctioned, to own the article in common with the debtor;

(b) the debtor's interest in the article has not transferred to the third party under section 35(2) above;

(c) the attachment of the article has not, by virtue of an order made under section 35(3) above, ceased to have effect;

(d) the third party's interest in the article has, following the auction of the article, been transferred to another person; and

(e) either—

(i) the third party's claim is, after that transfer of interest, admitted by the creditor and the debtor; or

(ii) where the third party's claim is not so admitted, the sheriff, on an application by the third party after that transfer of interest, is satisfied that the claim is valid.

(2) Where subsection (1) above applies, the creditor shall—

(a) where the article has been sold at the auction, pay to the third party the fraction of the proceeds of the sale of the article which corresponded to the third party's interest in the article; or

(b) where the ownership of the article has passed to the creditor under section 31(2)(a) above, pay to the third party the fraction of the value of the article which corresponded to the third party's interest in the article.

(3) The reference in subsection (2)(b) above to the value of an article is a reference to the value of the article as fixed under subsection (2) or (3) of section 15 above or, as the case may be, section 51 or 54(1) below.

37 Attachment terminated by payment or tender of full amount owing

An attachment is to cease to have effect if the sum recoverable is—

(a) paid to the creditor, the officer or any other person who has authority to receive payment on behalf of the creditor; or

(b) tendered to any of those persons and the tender is not accepted within a reasonable time.

38 Assistance to debtor

The sheriff clerk shall, if requested by the debtor—

(a) provide the debtor with information as to the procedures available to him under any provision of this Part or Part 3 of this Act; and

(b) assist the debtor in the completion of any form required in connection with any proceedings under any provision of this Part or Part 3 of this Act,

but the sheriff clerk shall not be liable for any error or omission by him in performing the duties imposed on him by this section.

39 Expenses chargeable in relation to attachment etc

(1) Schedule 1 to this Act has effect for the purposes of determining the liability, as between the creditor and the debtor, for expenses incurred in serving a charge and in the process of attachment and auction.

(2) The Scottish Ministers may by order modify that schedule so as to—

(a) add or remove types of expenses to or, as the case may be, from those referred to in that schedule; or

(b) vary any of the descriptions of the types of expenses there referred to.

40 Recovery from debtor of expenses of attachment

(1) Subject to subsections (2) and (4) below, any expenses chargeable against the debtor which are incurred in an attachment (including the service of the charge preceding it and the auction following it) are recoverable from the debtor by the attachment concerned but not by any other legal process, and any such expenses which have not been recovered by the time the attachment and auction is completed will cease to be chargeable against the debtor.

(2) The sheriff shall grant decree for payment of—

(a) any expenses awarded by the sheriff against the debtor in favour of the creditor under paragraph 4 or 7 of schedule 1 to this Act; or

(b) any additional sum of expenses awarded by the sheriff against the debtor in favour of the creditor under paragraph 5 of that schedule.

(3) Subsection (4) below applies where an attachment is—

(a) recalled under [section 9(2)(d) or (10)(b)] (effect of time to pay order on diligence) of the Debtors (Scotland) Act 1987 (c 18) in relation to a time to pay order;

(b) in effect immediately before the date of sequestration (within the meaning of the Bankruptcy (Scotland) Act [2016]) of the debtor's estate;

(c) in effect immediately before the [appointment of an administrator] under Part II of the Insolvency Act 1986 (c 45);

(d) in effect against property of the debtor immediately before a floating charge attaches to all or part of that property under section 53(7) (attachment on appointment of receiver by holder of charge) or 54(6) (attachment on appointment of receiver by court) of that Act of 1986;

(e) in effect immediately before the commencement of the winding up, under Part IV or V of that Act of 1986, of the debtor; or

(f) rendered unenforceable by virtue of the creditor entering into a composition contract or acceding to a trust deed for creditors or by virtue of the subsistence of a protected trust deed within the meaning of Schedule [4 of the Bankruptcy (Scotland) Act [2016].

(4) Where this subsection applies—

(a) the expenses of the attachment which were chargeable against the debtor remain so chargeable; and

(b) if the debtor's obligation to pay the expenses is not discharged under or by virtue of the time to pay order, sequestration, [appointment], receivership, winding up, composition contract or trust deed for creditors, those expenses are recoverable by further attachment.

41 Ascription of sums recovered by attachment or while attachment is in effect

(1) This section applies to any amounts recovered by an attachment or paid to account of the amounts recoverable by the attachment while the attachment is in effect.

(2) An amount to which this section applies shall be ascribed to the following in the order in which they are mentioned—

(a) the expenses already incurred in respect of—

(i) the attachment;

[(ia) any previous interim attachment the expenses of which are chargeable against and recoverable from the debtor under section 9Q(1)(a) of this Act;]

(ii) any previous diligence the expenses of which are chargeable against and recoverable from the debtor under section 40(4) above or section 93(5) of the Debtors (Scotland) Act 1987 (c 18);

(b) any interest, due under the decree or other document of debt on which the attachment proceeds, which has accrued at the date of execution of the attachment;

(c) any sum (including any expenses) due under the decree or other document of debt, other than any expenses or interest mentioned in paragraphs (a) and (b) above.

42 Restriction on fees payable by debtor

No fees shall be payable by a debtor in connection with—

(a) any application by the debtor;

(b) objections by the debtor to an application by any other person; or

(c) a hearing held,

under any provision of this Part or Part 3 of this Act, to any officer of any office or department connected with the Court of Session or the sheriff court the expenses of which are paid wholly or partly out of the Scottish Consolidated Fund.

43 [repealed]

44 [Amending provision]

45 Interpretation of this Part and Parts 3 and 4

In this Part and in Parts 3 and 4 of this Act—

'chargeable expenses' means expenses chargeable against the debtor in accordance with this Part of this Act;

'dwellinghouse' does not include—

(a) a garage, even although it forms part of the structure or building which consists of or includes the dwellinghouse; or

(b) other structures or buildings used in connection with the dwellinghouse, but does include a mobile home or other place used as a dwelling;

'exceptional attachment order' has the meaning given by section 47(1) below;

'mobile home' means a caravan, houseboat or other moveable structure used as a dwelling;

'non-essential assets' has the meaning given by schedule 2 to this Act;

'officer' means the officer of court appointed by a creditor;

'sum recoverable' means the debt in respect of which the attachment is executed together with any interest thereon and any chargeable expenses; and

'summary warrant' means a summary warrant granted under, or by virtue of, any enactment.

PART 3
ATTACHMENT OF ARTICLES KEPT IN DWELLINGHOUSES: SPECIAL PROCEDURE

46 Restriction on attachment of articles kept in dwellinghouses

Articles kept in a dwellinghouse may be attached but only—

(a) in pursuance of an exceptional attachment order; and

(b) otherwise in accordance with this Part of this Act.

47 Exceptional attachment order

(1) The sheriff may, on an application by the creditor and on being satisfied that there are exceptional circumstances, order that an attachment of non-essential assets of the debtor's kept in any dwellinghouse specified in the application may take place; such an order shall be called an 'exceptional attachment order'.

(2) An exceptional attachment order shall—

(a) authorise the attachment, removal and auction of non-essential assets of the debtor's which are, at the time when an attachment is executed in pursuance of the order, kept in any dwellinghouse specified in the application for the order;

(b) specify a period during which the order is to be executed; and

(c) empower the officer to open shut and lockfast places for the purpose of executing the order.

(3) In considering whether to make such an order the sheriff shall have regard to the matters set out in subsection (4) below.

(4) Those matters are—

(a) the nature of the debt (and, in particular, whether the debt incurred relates to any tax or duty or to any trade or business carried on by the debtor);

(b) whether the debtor resides in the dwellinghouse specified in the application;

(c) whether the debtor carries on a trade or business in that dwellinghouse;

(d) whether money advice has been given to the debtor;

(e) whether any direction made under section 1 (time to pay directions) of the Debtors (Scotland) Act 1987 (c 18), or order made under section 5 (time to pay orders) of that Act, in respect of the debt, or any other debt, has lapsed under section 4 (lapse of time to pay directions) or, as the case may be, section 11 (lapse of time to pay orders), of that Act of 1987;

(f) any agreement between the debtor and creditor for the settlement of the debt;

(g) any declaration or representation made, or document lodged, by or on behalf of the debtor which relates to—

(i) the existence of any non-essential assets owned by the debtor;

(ii) where they exist, their value; or

(iii) the debtor's financial circumstances [; and

(h) whether an application by the debtor for approval of a debt payment programme under Part 1 of this Act has been refused or approved, and if approved, whether that programme has been varied, or is revoked or completed.]

(5) Before deciding whether to make an exceptional attachment order, the sheriff may make—

(a) an order for a visit to the debtor by a person specified in the order for the purposes of giving money advice to the debtor; or

(b) such other order as the sheriff thinks fit.

(6) The Scottish Ministers may by order modify subsection (4) above so as to—

(a) add or remove matters to or, as the case may be, from those referred to in that subsection; or

(b) vary any of the descriptions of the matters there referred to.

48 Exceptional circumstances

(1) The reference in section 47(1) above to the sheriff being satisfied that there are exceptional circumstances is to be regarded as a reference to the sheriff being satisfied—

(a) that the creditor has taken reasonable steps to negotiate (or seek to negotiate) a settlement of the debt;

(b) that the creditor has executed, or so far as it is reasonable to do so has attempted to execute—

(i) an arrestment and action of furthcoming or sale; and

(ii) an earnings arrestment, in order to secure payment of the debt;

(c) that there is a reasonable prospect that the sum recovered from an auction of the debtor's non-essential assets would be at least equal to the aggregate of the following—

(i) a reasonable estimate of any chargeable expenses; and

(ii) £100 or such other amount as may be specified by order made by the Scottish Ministers; and

(d) that, having had regard to the matters set out in section 47(4) above and any other matters which the sheriff considers appropriate, it would be reasonable in the circumstances to grant the exceptional attachment order.

(2) For the purposes of subsection (1)(b) above, a creditor who has not proceeded with the diligences referred to in that subsection on the ground that so proceeding would be unlikely to recover the aggregate of—

(a) a reasonable estimate of the expenses likely to be incurred by the creditor in exercising the diligences; and

(b) £100 or such other amount as may be specified by order made by the Scottish Ministers, is to be treated as having attempted to execute those diligences in so far as it is reasonable to do so.

49 Power of entry

(1) Notwithstanding the authorisation in an exceptional attachment order to open shut and lockfast places, the officer shall not enter a dwellinghouse to execute the order unless the officer—

(a) at the intended time of entry, is satisfied as to the condition set out in subsection (2) below; or

(b) has, at least 4 days before the intended date of entry, served notice on the debtor setting out that intention and specifying that date.

(2) That condition is that there appears to the officer to be a person present who—

(a) is aged 16 years or over; and

(b) is not, because of the person's age, knowledge of English, mental illness, mental or physical disability or otherwise, unable to understand the consequences of the procedure being carried out.

(3) Where the sheriff is satisfied that the requirement of service under subsection (1)(b) above is likely to prejudice the execution of the order the sheriff may, on an application by the officer, dispense with that requirement.

(4) An application for a dispensation under subsection (3) above need not be intimated to the debtor.

50 Unlawful acts before attachment

(1) It shall be regarded as a breach of an exceptional attachment order—

(a) for the debtor or any other person who knows that the order has been made to, without the consent of the sheriff, move any article which forms part of the debtor's non-essential assets from the dwellinghouse in which it is kept; or

(b) for the debtor, without the consent of the sheriff, to sell, make a gift of or otherwise relinquish ownership of any such article,

before an attachment is executed in pursuance of the order.

(2) Any person who—

(a) knows that an exceptional attachment order has been made; and

(b) before an attachment is executed in pursuance of the order, wilfully damages or destroys any article which forms part of the debtor's non-essential assets,

shall be regarded as acting in breach of the order.

(3) Where, at any time after an exceptional attachment order has been made, an article which forms part of the debtor's non-essential assets is stolen, the debtor shall give notice to the creditor, the officer and the sheriff who granted the order of that fact and of any related claim which the debtor makes, or intends to make, under a contract of insurance.

(4) Any failure by the debtor to give notice as required by subsection (3) above is to be regarded as acting in breach of the order.

(5) Where a debtor or any third party who knows that an exceptional attachment order has been made and that an article forms part of the debtor's nonessential assets—

(a) moves it from the dwellinghouse in which it is kept before an attachment is executed in pursuance of the order, and it is—

(i) damaged, destroyed, lost or stolen; or

(ii) acquired from or through the debtor or, as the case may be, the third party by another person without knowledge of order and for value; or

(b) wilfully damages or destroys it,

the sheriff may order the debtor or, as the case may be, the third party to consign the sum set out in subsection (6) below in court.

(6) That sum shall be—

(a) where the article has been damaged but not so damaged as to make it worthless, a sum equal to the difference between the value of the article before it was damaged and the value of the article so damaged; or

(b) where the damaged article is worthless, a sum equal to the value of the article before it was so damaged.

(7) Any reference in subsection (6) above to the value of an article is a reference to the officer's best estimate of the amount which the article is or, as the case may be, was likely to realise on sale by auction.

(8) Any sum consigned in court in pursuance of an order made under subsection (5) above shall, where that order ceases to have effect before an auction is held in execution of the order, be paid to the creditor to the extent necessary to meet the sum recoverable, any surplus thereof being paid to the debtor.

51 Valuation

When executing an attachment in pursuance of an exceptional attachment order the officer shall value the articles being attached at the price which they are likely to fetch if sold on the open market.

52 Articles with sentimental value

(1) An officer may not, in executing an exceptional attachment order, attach any articles which the officer considers likely to be of sentimental value to the debtor.

(2) Subsection (1) above applies only where the aggregate of the values of articles considered likely to be of that type (as fixed by the officer under section 51 above) does not exceed £150 or such other amount as may be prescribed in regulations made by the Scottish Ministers.

53 Removal of articles attached in dwellinghouse

(1) The officer shall, unless the officer considers it impractical to do so, immediately remove any article which is attached in execution of an exceptional attachment order from the dwellinghouse in which it is attached.

(2) If an article is not immediately removed from the dwellinghouse in which it is attached, the officer shall give notice to the debtor and to any other person in

possession of the article of the date arranged for the removal of the article from that dwellinghouse.

(3) The officer may remove from the dwellinghouse only such attached articles as, if sold at their values fixed under section 51 above, would realise in aggregate the sum recoverable.

54 Professional valuation

(1) The officer may, if the officer considers it appropriate, arrange for an attached article to be valued by a professional valuer or other suitably skilled person.

(2) Any such valuer or other person shall value an attached article at the price which it is likely to fetch if sold on the open market.

(3) If such a valuer or other person values an attached article at an amount other than the amount at which that article was valued by the officer when executing the attachment, the officer shall notify the debtor of the value arrived at by the valuer or other person.

55 Release of articles from attachment

(1) An article attached in execution of an exceptional attachment order shall not, subject to any order made under section 20(1)(b) above, be auctioned before the date which is 7 days after the date on which the article was removed by the officer from the dwellinghouse in which it was attached.

(2) The sheriff may, on an application by the debtor, make an order—

(a) providing that the attachment of an article attached in execution of an exceptional attachment order is to cease to have effect; and

(b) requiring the officer to return the article to the dwellinghouse at which it was attached.

(3) Where the sheriff is satisfied that—

(a) the attachment of an article is not competent; or

(b) the auction of an attached article would be unduly harsh in the circumstances,

the sheriff shall grant an order under subsection (2) above in respect of the article.

(4) Where the sheriff is satisfied that—

(a) articles likely to be of sentimental value to the debtor were kept in a dwellinghouse when an exceptional attachment order was executed in the dwellinghouse;

(b) those articles are likely to realise, on sale by auction, an aggregate amount not exceeding £150 or such other amount as may be prescribed in regulations made under section 52(2) above; and

(c) an article of that type has been attached in execution of the exceptional attachment order, the sheriff shall grant an order under subsection (2) above in respect of the attached article.

(5) The sheriff may consider an application for an order under subsection (2) above only where it is made during the period in which the article which is subject of the application may not, by virtue of subsection (1) above, be auctioned.

56 Redemption

(1) Subject to any order made under section 20(1)(b) above, the debtor is entitled, within 7 days of the date on which an article is attached, to redeem that article.

(2) The amount for which such an article may be redeemed is the value fixed under section 51 or 54(1) above.

(3) The officer shall, on receiving payment from the debtor for the redemption of an attached article, grant a receipt in the form prescribed by Act of Sederunt to the debtor.

(4) The attachment of the article is, on the grant of such a receipt, to cease to have effect.

57 Appeals

(1) An appeal made against any decision of a sheriff made under or for the purposes of this Part or, where the appeal relates to the attachment of articles kept in a dwellinghouse, under or for the purposes of Part 2 of this Act may be made only—

(a) to the sheriff principal;

(b) with the leave of the sheriff; and

(c) on a point of law.

(2) The decision of the sheriff principal on such an appeal is final.

PART 4
ABOLITION OF POINDINGS AND WARRANT SALES

58 Abolition of poindings and warrant sales

(1) It is not, subject to section 59 below, competent to enforce payment of a debt by poinding or warrant sale; and any enactment or rule of law allowing such enforcement shall cease to have effect.

(2) The following provisions of the Debtors (Scotland) Act 1987 (c 18) are repealed—

(a) Part II;

(b) section 74(2);

(c) Schedule 1; and

(d) Schedule 5.

59 Savings

(1) The provisions set out in subsection (5) below continue to have effect in relation to a poinding in respect of which a warrant sale has been completed before 30 December 2002 as if sections 58(2) above and 61 below had not come into force.

(2) Subject to subsection (3) below, those provisions also continue to have that effect in relation to a poinding executed before that date in respect of which a warrant sale has not been completed before that date.

(3) The saving provided for in subsection (2) above—

(a) has effect only if the poinding was executed at a place other than a dwellinghouse; and

(b) continues to have effect after 31 March 2003 only if a warrant sale is completed in respect of the poinding on or before that date.

(4) A summary warrant which, before 30 December 2002, authorised a poinding and sale in accordance with Schedule 5 to the Debtors (Scotland) Act 1987 (c 18) is to be treated on and after that date as authorising an attachment.

(5) The provisions referred to in subsections (1) and (2) above are—

(a) paragraph 24 of Schedule 7 to the Bankruptcy (Scotland) Act 1985 (c 66);

(b) the provisions of the Act of 1987 mentioned in section 58(2) above; and

(c) the provisions of the Act of 2002 mentioned in paragraph 29 of schedule 3 to this Act.

PART 5
MISCELLANEOUS AND GENERAL

60 Application of this Act to sequestration for rent and arrestment

[. . .]

(2) It is not competent for [the landlord's] hypothec to arise in any article—

(a) of the type described in section 11(1);

[. . .]

(3) An arrestment (other than an arrestment of a debtor's earnings in the hands of the debtor's employer) of any article of the type mentioned in paragraph (a) or (b) of subsection (2) above is incompetent.

[. . .]

[60A Electronic signatures

(1) This section applies where—

(a) a report or declaration under this Act requires to be signed; and

(b) provision is made by virtue of this Act or any other enactment permitting the report or declaration to be an electronic communication.

(2) Where the report or declaration is an electronic communication, the requirement is satisfied by a certified electronic signature.

(3) Subsection (2) above is to be read in accordance with section 7(2) and (3) of the Electronic Communications Act 2000 (c7) (electronic signatures and certification).]

61 [*Minor and consequential amendments and repeals*]

62 [*Regulations and orders*]

63 Crown application

This Act binds the Crown acting in its capacity as a creditor or employer.

64 Short title and commencement

(1) This Act may be cited as the Debt Arrangement and Attachment (Scotland) Act 2002.

(2) Subject to subsections (3) and (4) below, this Act (except this section and sections 43 and 62 above) comes into force on 30 December 2002.

. . .

SCHEDULE 2
NON-ESSENTIAL ASSETS

1 For the purposes of Part 3 of this Act, 'non-essential assets' are, subject to paragraph 2 below, corporeal moveable property of the debtor's which is kept in a dwellinghouse.

2 None of the following is a non-essential asset for the purposes of Part 3 of this Act—

(a) an article specified in paragraph 3 below;

(b) an article described in paragraph 4 below; and

(c) an article the attachment of which is (by virtue of section 11(1) above or otherwise) incompetent.

3 The articles referred to in paragraph 2(a) above are—

(a) clothing reasonably required for the use of the debtor or any member of the debtor's household;

(b) implements, tools of trade, books or other equipment reasonably required for the use of any member of the debtor's household in the practice of such member's profession, trade or business, not exceeding in aggregate value £1,000 or such other amount as may be prescribed in regulations made by the Scottish Ministers;

(c) medical aids or medical equipment reasonably required for the use of the debtor or any member of the debtor's household;

(d) books or other articles reasonably required for the education or training of the debtor or any member of the debtor's household not exceeding in aggregate value £1,000 or such other amount as may be prescribed in regulations made by the Scottish Ministers;

(e) articles reasonably required for the care or upbringing of a child who is a member of the debtor's household;

(f) toys for the use of any child who is a member of the debtor's household.

4 The articles referred to in paragraph 2(b) above are the following so far as they are reasonably required, at the time of the attachment, for the use of the debtor or a member of the debtor's household—

(a) beds or bedding;

(b) household linen;

(c) chairs or settees;
(d) tables;
(e) food;
(f) lights or light fittings;
(g) heating appliances;
(h) curtains;
(i) floor coverings;
(j) furniture, equipment or utensils used for storing, cooking or eating food;
(k) refrigerators;
(l) articles used for cleaning, drying, mending, or pressing clothes;
(m) articles used for cleaning the dwellinghouse;
(n) furniture used for storing—
(i) clothing, bedding or household linen;
(ii) articles used for cleaning the dwellinghouse; or
(iii) utensils used for cooking or eating food;
(o) articles used for safety in the dwellinghouse;
(p) tools used for maintenance or repair of the dwellinghouse or of household articles;
(q) computers and accessory equipment;
(r) microwave ovens;
(s) radios;
(t) telephones;
(u) televisions.

5 The Scottish Ministers may by regulations modify paragraph 4 above so as to—
(a) add or remove types of articles to or, as the case may be, from those referred to in that paragraph; or
(b) vary any of the descriptions of the types of articles there referred to.

. . .

BANKRUPTCY AND DILIGENCE ETC (SCOTLAND) ACT 2007
(2007, asp 3)

PART 5
INHIBITION

Creation

146 Certain decrees and documents of debt to authorise inhibition without need for letters of inhibition

(1) Inhibition in execution is competent to enforce—
(a) payment of a debt constituted by a decree or document of debt;
(b) subject to subsection (2) below, an obligation to perform a particular act (other than payment) contained in a decree.

(2) Inhibition under subsection (1)(b) above is competent only if the decree is a decree—
(a) in an action containing an alternative conclusion or crave for payment of a sum other than by way of expenses; or
(b) for specific implement of an obligation to convey heritable property to the creditor or to grant in the creditor's favour a real right in security, or some other right, over such property.

(3)–(5) [*amending provisions*]

(6) It is not competent for the Court of Session to grant letters of inhibition.

(7) In a case where inhibition is executed under subsection (1)(b) above—
(a) sections 165 and 166 of this Act do not apply; and
(b) sections 158, 159, 160 and 163 of this Act have effect as if references to a 'debtor' or 'creditor' were references to the debtor or creditor in the obligation.

(8) In this Part—

'decree' has the meaning given by section 221 of this Act, except that paragraphs (c), (g) and (h) of the definition of 'decree' in that section do not apply; and

'document of debt' has the meaning given by section 221 of this Act.

(9) The Scottish Ministers may by order modify the definitions of 'decree' and 'document of debt' in subsection (8) above by—

(a) adding types of decree or document to;

(b) removing types of decree or document from; or

(c) varying the description of,

the types of decree or document to which those definitions apply.

147 Provision of debt advice and information package when executing inhibition

Where the debtor is an individual, a schedule of inhibition served in execution of an inhibition under section 146(1) of this Act (other than an inhibition such as is mentioned in section 146(2)(b)) must be accompanied with a debt advice and information package.

148 Registration of inhibition

(1) An inhibition is registered only by registering—

(a) the schedule of inhibition; and

(b) the certificate of execution of the inhibition,

in the Register of Inhibitions.

(2) References in any enactment to registering or, as the case may be, recording an inhibition must, unless the context otherwise requires, be construed as references to registration in accordance with subsection (1) above.

(3) The—

(a) schedule of inhibition; and

(b) certificate of execution of the inhibition,

must be in (or as nearly as may be in) the form prescribed by the Scottish Ministers by regulations.

[148A Register of Inhibitions: electronic signature of documents

(1) This section applies in relation to a document which is required or permitted to be registered or recorded in the Register of Inhibitions.

(2) An electronic signature fulfils any requirement (however expressed) that the document be signed in order to be registered or recorded in the Register.

(3) Any requirement (however expressed) that the document be given to the Keeper in order to be registered or recorded in the Register may be fulfilled by transmitting it to the Keeper electronically.

(4) For the purposes of subsection (3), the document must be transmitted by a means (and in a form) which is specified on the Keeper's website as being acceptable for those purposes.

(5) In this section—

'document' includes a copy of a document,

'electronic signature' is to be construed in accordance with section 7(2) of the Electronic Communications Act 2000, but includes a version of an electronic signature which is reproduced on a paper document,

'the Keeper' means the Keeper of the Registers of Scotland,

'the Keeper's website' means the website maintained by, or on behalf of, the Keeper of the Registers of Scotland.]

149 [Amends Titles to Land Consolidation (Scotland) Act 1868.]

Effect

150 Property affected by inhibition

(1) Subject to section 153 of this Act, inhibition may affect any heritable property.

(2) Any enactment or rule of law by virtue of which inhibition may affect other property ceases to have effect.

(3) For the purposes of subsection (1) above and section 157 of the 1868 Act, a person acquires property at the beginning of the day on which the deed conveying or otherwise granting a real right in the property is delivered to that person.

151 Effect on inhibition to enforce obligation when alternative decree granted

Where—

(a) an inhibition is executed to enforce a decree such as is mentioned in section 146(2)(a) of this Act; and

(b) decree is subsequently granted in terms of the alternative conclusion or crave mentioned in that section,

the inhibition continues to have effect for the purposes of enforcing payment of the debt constituted by that subsequent decree.

152 Effect of conversion of limited inhibition on the dependence to inhibition in execution

[(1)] [Subject to subsection (2) below,] where—

(a) a creditor obtains a decree for payment of all or part of a principal sum concluded or craved for in proceedings on the dependence of which warrant for inhibition was granted; and

(b) the warrant was limited to specified property by virtue of section 15J(b) of the 1987 Act (property affected by inhibition on dependence),

[any inhibition on the dependence which, on decree, becomes an inhibition in execution of that decree, is no longer limited to that property].

[(2) Subsection (1) above has effect from the beginning of the day on which—

(a) an extract of the decree (or a copy of the interlocutor certified by the clerk of court); and

(b) a notice in (or as nearly as may be in) the form set out in the Schedule to the Bankruptcy and Diligence etc (Scotland) Act 2007 (Inhibition) Order 2009,

are registered in the Register of Inhibitions.]

153 Property affected by inhibition to enforce obligation to convey heritable property

Where a decree such as is mentioned in section 146(2)(b) of this Act is granted, any inhibition executed to enforce that decree is limited to the property to which the decree relates.

154 Inhibition not to confer a preference in ranking

(1) An inhibition does not confer any preference in any—

(a) sequestration;

(b) insolvency proceedings; or

(c) other process in which there is ranking.

(2) Subsection (1) above does not affect any preference claimed in—

(a) a sequestration;

(b) insolvency proceedings; or

(c) any other process,

where the inhibition has effect before this section comes into force.

(3) For the avoidance of doubt, in this section, 'other process' includes the process, under section 27(1) of the Conveyancing and Feudal Reform (Scotland) Act 1970 (c 35), of applying the proceeds of sale where a creditor in a standard security has effected a sale of the security subjects.

(4) In this section, 'insolvency proceedings' means—

(a) winding up;

(b) receivership;

(c) administration; and

(d) proceedings in relation to a company voluntary arrangement,

within the meaning of the Insolvency Act 1986 (c 45).

Termination

...

157 Inhibition terminated by payment of full amount owing

(1) This section applies where—

(a) an inhibition executed to enforce payment of a debt has effect; and

(b) a sum is paid, in respect of the debt constituted by the decree or document of debt authorising the inhibition, to the creditor, [an officer of court] or any other person who has authority to receive payment on behalf of the creditor.

(2) Where the sum paid amounts to the sum of—

(a) the debt (including any interest due under the decree or document of debt);

(b) the expenses incurred by the creditor in executing an inhibition (referred to in this section and in sections 165 and 166 as the 'inhibition expenses'); and

(c) the expenses of discharging the inhibition,

the inhibition ceases to have effect.

(3) Any rule of law to the effect that an inhibition ceases to have effect on payment or tender of the debt constituted by the decree or document of debt is abolished.

(4) This section and sections 165 and 166 of this Act do not apply to an inhibition on the dependence of an action.

158 Inhibition terminated by compliance with obligation to perform

Where—

(a) an inhibition executed to enforce an obligation to perform a particular act (other than payment) contained in a decree has effect; and

(b) the debtor has complied with the decree, the inhibition ceases to have effect.

159 Termination of inhibition when property acquired by third party

(1) Notwithstanding section 160 of this Act, an inhibition ceases to have effect (and is treated as never having had effect) in relation to property if a person acquires the property (or a right in the property) in good faith and for adequate consideration.

(2) For the purposes of subsection (1) above, a person acquires property (or a right in the property) when the deed conveying (or granting the right in) the property is delivered to the person.

(3) An acquisition under subsection (1) above may be from the inhibited debtor or any other person who has acquired the property or right (regardless of whether that person acquired in good faith or for value).

(4) For the purposes of subsection (1) above, a person is presumed to have acted in good faith if the person—

(a) is unaware of the inhibition; and

(b) has taken all reasonable steps to discover the existence of an inhibition affecting the property.

Breach

160 Breach of inhibition

An inhibited debtor breaches the inhibition when the debtor delivers a deed—

(a) conveying; or

(b) otherwise granting a right in,

property over which the inhibition has effect to a person other than the inhibiting creditor.

161 Prescription of right to reduce transactions in breach of inhibition

For the avoidance of doubt, section 8(1) of the Prescription and Limitation (Scotland) Act 1973 (c 52) (extinction of certain rights relating to property by prescriptive period of 20 years) applies to the right of an inhibitor to have a deed granted in breach of an inhibition reduced.

163 Reduction of lease granted in breach of inhibition

(1) This section applies where an inhibited debtor grants a lease of property affected by the inhibition.

(2) A lease which, on the date an action of reduction of the lease is raised, has an unexpired duration of not less than 5 years is reducible.

(3) A lease which, on the date an action of reduction of the lease is raised, has an unexpired duration of less than 5 years may be reduced only if the Court of Session is satisfied that it would be fair and reasonable in all the circumstances to do so.

(4) In calculating the unexpired duration of a lease for the purposes of subsections (2) and (3) above—

(a) any provision in the lease (however expressed) enabling the lease to be terminated earlier than the date on which the lease would otherwise terminate must be disregarded; and

(b) where the lease includes provision (however expressed) requiring the landlord to renew it, the duration of any such renewed lease must be added to the duration of the original lease.

General and miscellaneous

[. . .]

165 Expenses of inhibition

(1) Subject to subsection (3) below, the inhibition expenses are chargeable against the debtor.

(2) Inhibition expenses are recoverable from the debtor by land attachment or residual attachment executed for the purpose of enforcing payment of the debt to which the inhibition relates but not by any other legal process.

(3) Where a creditor has executed an inhibition, the expenses of only one further inhibition in relation to the debt to which the first inhibition relates are chargeable against the debtor as inhibition expenses.

(4) For the purposes of a sequestration or other process in which there is ranking, the inhibition expenses must be treated as part of the debt constituted by the decree or document of debt authorising the inhibition.

166 Ascription

(1) This section applies where—

(a) an inhibition has effect; and

(b) any sums are paid to account of the sums recoverable from the debtor by virtue of the decree or document of debt authorising the inhibition.

(2) Such sums must be ascribed to the following in the order in which they are mentioned—

(a) the expenses which are chargeable against the debtor incurred in respect of any diligence (other than the inhibition) authorised by the decree or document of debt;

(b) the inhibition expenses;

(c) any interest which has accrued, at the date on which the inhibition takes effect, on the debt constituted by the decree or document of debt;

(d) the debt constituted by the decree or document of debt together with such interest as has accrued after the date on which the inhibition takes effect.

168 Inhibition effective against judicial factor

(1) Notwithstanding the appointment of a judicial factor on a debtor's estate, an inhibition has effect.

(2) But subsection (1) above does not apply in a case where—

(a) a judicial factor is appointed under section 11A of the Judicial Factors (Scotland) Act 1889 (c 39) (application for judicial factor on deceased person's estate); and

(b) the inhibition was effective against the debtor prior to the debtor's death.

PART 11
MAILLS AND DUTIES, SEQUESTRATION FOR RENT AND LANDLORD'S HYPOTHEC

Landlord's hypothec and sequestration for rent

208 Abolition of sequestration for rent and restriction of landlord's hypothec

(1) The diligence of sequestration for rent is abolished and any enactment or rule of law enabling an action of sequestration for rent to be raised ceases to have effect.

(2) Notwithstanding that abolition, the landlord's hypothec—

(a) continues, subject to subsections (3) to (9) below, as a right in security over corporeal moveable property kept in or on the subjects let; and—

(b) ranks accordingly in any—

(i) sequestration;

(ii) insolvency proceedings; or

(iii) other process in which there is ranking,

in respect of that property.

(3) The landlord's hypothec no longer arises in relation to property which is kept—

(a) in a dwellinghouse;

(b) on agricultural land; or

(c) on a croft.

(4) It no longer arises in relation to property which is owned by a person other than the tenant.

(5) Property which is acquired by a person from the tenant—

(a) in good faith; or

(b) where the property is acquired after an interdict prohibiting the tenant from disposing of or removing items secured by the hypothec has been granted in favour the landlord, in good faith and for value,

ceases to be subject to the hypothec upon acquisition by the person.

(6) Subsection (5)(b) above does not affect the tenant's liability for breach of the interdict.

(7) Where property is owned in common by the tenant and a third party, any right of hypothec arises only to the extent of the tenant's interest in that property.

(8) The landlord's hypothec—

(a) is security for rent due and unpaid only; and

(b) subsists for so long as that rent remains unpaid.

(9) Any enactment or rule of law relating to the landlord's hypothec ceases to have effect in so far as it is inconsistent with subsections (2) to (8) above.

(10) Subsections (1) to (3), (8) and (9) above do not affect an action of sequestration for rent brought before this section comes into force.

(11) Subsection (3) above does not affect a landlord's right of hypothec which arose before and subsists on the coming into force of this section.

(12) In subsection (2) above, 'insolvency proceedings' means—

(a) winding up;

(b) receivership;

(c) administration; and

(d) proceedings in relation to a company voluntary arrangement,

within the meaning of the Insolvency Act 1986 (c 45).

(13) In subsection (3) above—

'agricultural land' has the same meaning as in section 1(2) of the Agricultural Holdings (Scotland) Act 1991 (c 55);

'croft' has the same meaning as in section 3(1) of the Crofters (Scotland) Act 1993 (c 44); and 'dwellinghouse' includes—

(a) a mobile home or other place used as a dwelling; and

(b) any other structure or building used in connection with the dwelling-house.

THIRD PARTIES (RIGHTS AGAINST INSURERS) ACT 2010 (2010, c 10)

Transfer of rights to third parties

1 Rights against insurer of insolvent person etc

(1) This section applies if—

(a) a relevant person incurs a liability against which that person is insured under a contract of insurance, or

(b) a person who is subject to such a liability becomes a relevant person.

(2) The rights of the relevant person under the contract against the insurer in respect of the liability are transferred to and vest in the person to whom the liability is or was incurred (the 'third party').

(3) The third party may bring proceedings to enforce the rights against the insurer without having established the relevant person's liability; but the third party may not enforce those rights without having established that liability.

(4) For the purposes of this Act, a liability is established only if its existence and amount are established; and, for that purpose, 'establish' means establish—

(a) by virtue of a declaration under section 2 or a declarator under section 3,

(b) by a judgment or decree,

(c) by an award in arbitral proceedings or by an arbitration, or

(d) by an enforceable agreement.

(5) In this Act—

(a) references to an 'insured' are to a person who incurs or who is subject to a liability to a third party against which that person is insured under a contract of insurance;

(b) references to a 'relevant person' are to a person within sections 4 to 7 [(and see also paragraph 1A of Schedule 3)];

(c) references to a 'third party' are to be construed in accordance with subsection (2);

(d) references to 'transferred rights' are to rights under a contract of insurance which are transferred under this section.

2 *[Does not apply to Scotland]*

3 Establishing liability in Scotland

(1) This section applies where a person (P)—

(a) claims to have rights under a contract of insurance by virtue of a transfer under section 1, but

(b) has not yet established the insured's liability which is insured under that contract.

(2) P may bring proceedings against the insurer for either or both of the following—

(a) a declarator as to the insured's liability to P;

(b) a declarator as to the insurer's potential liability to P.

(3) Where proceedings are brought under subsection (2)(a) the insurer may rely on any defence on which the insured could rely if those proceedings were proceedings brought against the insured in respect of the insured's liability to P.

(4) Subsection (3) is subject to section 12(1).

(5) Where the court grants a declarator under this section, the effect of which is that the insurer is liable to P, the court may grant the appropriate decree against the insurer.

(6) Where a person applying for a declarator under subsection (2)(b) is entitled or required, by virtue of the contract of insurance, to do so in an arbitration, that person may also apply in the same arbitration for a declarator under subsection (2)(a).

(7) In the application of this section to an arbitration, subsection (5) is to be read as if ' tribunal ' were substituted for 'court' and ' make the appropriate award ' for 'grant the appropriate decree'.

(8) When bringing proceedings under subsection (2)(a), P may also make the insured a defender to those proceedings.

(9) If (but only if) the insured is a defender to proceedings under this section (whether by virtue of subsection (8) or otherwise), a declarator under subsection (2) binds the insured as well as the insurer.

(10) In this section, the reference to the insurer's potential liability to P is a reference to the insurer's liability in respect of the insured's liability to P, if established.

Relevant persons

4 Individuals

(1) An individual is a relevant person if any of the following is in force in respect of that individual in England and Wales—

[. . .]

(b) an administration order made under Part 6 of the County Courts Act 1984,

(c) an enforcement restriction order made under Part 6A of that Act,

(d) subject to subsection (4), a debt relief order made under Part 7A of the Insolvency Act 1986,

(e) a voluntary arrangement approved in accordance with Part 8 of that Act, or

(f) a bankruptcy order made under Part 9 of that Act.

(2) An individual is a relevant person if [either] of the following is in force in respect of [the individual's estate] in Scotland—

(a) an award of sequestration made [by virtue of section 2 or 5 of the Bankruptcy (Scotland) Act 2016], or

(b) a protected trust deed within the meaning of that Act.

[. . .]

(3) An individual is a relevant person if any of the following is in force in respect of that individual in Northern Ireland—

(a) an administration order made under Part 6 of the Judgments Enforcement (Northern Ireland) Order 1981 (SI 1981/226 (NI 6)),

(b) a deed of arrangement registered in accordance with Chapter 1 of Part 8 of the Insolvency (Northern Ireland) Order 1989 (SI 1989/2405 (NI 19)),

[(ba) subject to subsection (4), a debt relief order made under Part 7A of that Order,]

(c) a voluntary arrangement approved under Chapter 2 of Part 8 of that Order, or

(d) a bankruptcy order made under Part 9 of that Order.

(4) If an individual is a relevant person by virtue of subsection (1)(d) [or (3)(ba)], that person is a relevant person for the purposes of section 1(1)(b) only.

(5) Where an award of sequestration made [by virtue of section 2 or 5 of the Bankruptcy (Scotland) Act 2016] is recalled or reduced, any rights which were transferred under section 1 as a result of that award are re-transferred to and vest in the person who became a relevant person as a result of the award.

[. . .]

5 Individuals who die insolvent

(1) An individual who dies insolvent is a relevant person for the purposes of section 1(1)(b) only.

(2) For the purposes of this section an individual (D) is to be regarded as having died insolvent if, following D's death—

(a) D's estate falls to be administered in accordance with an order under section 421 of the Insolvency Act 1986 or Article 365 of the Insolvency (Northern Ireland) Order 1989 (SI 1989/2405 (NI 19)),

(b) an award of sequestration is made [by virtue of section 2 or 5 of the Bankruptcy (Scotland) Act 2016] in respect of D's estate and the award is not recalled or reduced, or

(c) a judicial factor is appointed under section 11A of the Judicial Factors (Scotland) Act 1889 in respect of D's estate and the judicial factor certifies that the estate is absolutely insolvent within the meaning of the Bankruptcy (Scotland) Act [2016].

(3) Where a transfer of rights under section 1 takes place as a result of an insured person being a relevant person by virtue of this section, references in this Act to an insured are, where the context so requires, to be read as references to the insured's estate.

6 Corporate bodies etc

[(1) A body corporate or unincorporated body is a relevant person if a compromise or arrangement between the body and its creditors (or a class of them) is in force, having been sanctioned in accordance with section 899 [or 901F] of the Companies Act 2006.]

(2) A body corporate or an unincorporated body is a relevant person if, in England and Wales or Scotland—

(a) a voluntary arrangement approved in accordance with Part 1 of the Insolvency Act 1986 is in force in respect of it,

[(b) the body is in administration under Schedule B1 to that Act,]

(c) there is a person appointed in accordance with Part 3 of that Act who is acting as receiver or manager of the body's property (or there would be such a person so acting but for a temporary vacancy),

(d) the body is, or is being, wound up voluntarily in accordance with Chapter 2 of Part 4 of that Act,

(e) there is a person appointed under section 135 of that Act who is acting as provisional liquidator in respect of the body (or there would be such a person so acting but for a temporary vacancy), or

(f) the body is, or is being, wound up by the court following the making of a winding-up order under Chapter 6 of Part 4 of that Act or Part 5 of that Act.

(3) A body corporate or an unincorporated body is a relevant person if, in Scotland—

(a) an award of sequestration has been made [by virtue of section 6 of the Bankruptcy (Scotland) Act 2016] in respect of the body's estate, and the body has not been discharged under that Act,

(b) the body has been dissolved and an award of sequestration has been made [by virtue of] that section in respect of its estate, [or]

(c) a protected trust deed within the meaning of the Bankruptcy (Scotland) Act [2016] is in force in respect of the body's estate.

[. . .]

(4) A body corporate or an unincorporated body is a relevant person if, in Northern Ireland—

(a) a voluntary arrangement approved in accordance with Part 2 of the Insolvency (Northern Ireland) Order 1989 (SI 1989/2405 (NI 19)) is in force in respect of the body,

[(b) the body is in administration under Schedule B1 to that Order,]

(c) there is a person appointed in accordance with Part 4 of that Order who is acting as receiver or manager of the body's property (or there would be such a person so acting but for a temporary vacancy),

(d) the body is, or is being, wound up voluntarily in accordance with Chapter 2 of Part 5 of that Order,

(e) there is a person appointed under Article 115 of that Order who is acting as provisional liquidator in respect of the body (or there would be such a person so acting but for a temporary vacancy), or

(f) the body is, or is being, wound up by the court following the making of a winding-up order under Chapter 6 of Part 5 of that Order or Part 6 of that Order.

[(4A) A body corporate or unincorporated body is a relevant person if it is in insolvency under Part 2 of the Banking Act 2009.

(4B) A body corporate or unincorporated body is a relevant person if it is in administration under relevant sectoral legislation as defined in Schedule A1.]

(5) A body within [subsection (1)] is not a relevant person in relation to a liability that is transferred to another body by the order sanctioning the compromise or arrangement.

(6) Where a body is a relevant person by virtue of [subsection (1)], section 1 has effect to transfer rights only to a person on whom the compromise or arrangement is binding.

(7) Where an award of sequestration made [by virtue of section 6 of the Bankruptcy (Scotland) Act 2016] is recalled or reduced, any rights which were transferred under section 1 as a result of that award are re-transferred to and vest in the person who became a relevant person as a result of the award.

[. . .]

(9) In this section—

(a) a reference to a person appointed in accordance with Part 3 of the Insolvency Act 1986 includes a reference to a person appointed under section 101 of the Law of Property Act 1925;

(b) a reference to a receiver or manager of a body's property includes a reference to a receiver or manager of part only of the property and to a receiver only of the income arising from the property or from part of it;

(c) for the purposes of subsection (3) 'body corporate or unincorporated body' includes any entity, other than a trust, the estate of which may be sequestrated [by virtue of section 6 of the Bankruptcy (Scotland) Act 2016];

(d) a reference to a person appointed in accordance with Part 4 of the Insolvency (Northern Ireland) Order 1989 (SI 1989/2405 (NI 19)) includes a reference to a person appointed under section 19 of the Conveyancing Act 1881.

[6A Corporate bodies etc that are dissolved

(1) A body corporate or unincorporated body is a relevant person if the body has been dissolved, subject to the exceptions in subsections (2) and (3).

(2) The body is not a relevant person by virtue of subsection (1) if, since it was dissolved (or, if it has been dissolved more than once, since it was last dissolved), something has happened which has the effect that the body is treated as not having been dissolved or as no longer being dissolved.

(3) Subsection (1) applies to a partnership only if it is a body corporate.

(4) For the purposes of this section, 'dissolved' means dissolved under the law of England and Wales, Scotland or Northern Ireland (whether or not by a process referred to as dissolution).]

7 Scottish trusts

(1) A trustee of a Scottish trust is, in respect of a liability of that trustee that falls to be met out of the trust estate, a relevant person if—

(a) an award of sequestration has been made [by virtue of section 6 of the Bankruptcy (Scotland) Act 2016] in respect of the trust estate, and the trust has not been discharged under that Act, or

(b) a protected trust deed within the meaning of that Act is in force in respect of the trust estate.

[. . .]

(2) Where an award of sequestration made [by virtue of section 6 of the Bankruptcy (Scotland) Act 2016] is recalled or reduced any rights which were transferred under section 1 as a result of that award are re-transferred to and vest in the person who became a relevant person as a result of the award.

[. . .]

(4) In this section 'Scottish trust' means a trust the estate of which may be sequestrated [by virtue of section 6 of the Bankruptcy (Scotland) Act 2016].

Transferred rights: supplemental

8 Limit on rights transferred

Where the liability of an insured to a third party is less than the liability of the insurer to the insured (ignoring the effect of section 1), no rights are transferred under that section in respect of the difference.

9 Conditions affecting transferred rights

(1) This section applies where transferred rights are subject to a condition (whether under the contract of insurance from which the transferred rights are derived or otherwise) that the insured has to fulfil.

(2) Anything done by the third party which, if done by the insured, would have amounted to or contributed to fulfilment of the condition is to be treated as if done by the insured.

(3) The transferred rights are not subject to a condition requiring the insured to provide information or assistance to the insurer if that condition cannot be fulfilled because the insured is—

(a) an individual who has died,

(b) a body corporate that has been dissolved; [or

(c) an unincorporated body other than a partnership, that has been dissolved.]

(4) A condition requiring the insured to provide information or assistance to the insurer does not include a condition requiring the insured to notify the insurer of the existence of a claim under the contract of insurance.

(5) The transferred rights are not subject to a condition requiring the prior discharge by the insured of the insured's liability to the third party.

(6) In the case of a contract of marine insurance, subsection (5) applies only to the extent that the liability of the insured is a liability in respect of death or personal injury.

(7) In this section—

'contract of marine insurance' has the meaning given by section 1 of the Marine Insurance Act 1906;

[. . .]

'personal injury' includes any disease and any impairment of a person's physical or mental condition.

[(8) For the purposes of this section—

(a) 'dissolved' means dissolved under the law of England and Wales, Scotland or Northern Ireland (whether or not by a process referred to as dissolution), and

(b) a body has been dissolved even if, since it was dissolved, something has happened which has the effect that (but for this paragraph) the body is treated as not having been dissolved or as no longer being dissolved.]

10 Insurer's right of set off

(1) This section applies if—

(a) rights of an insured under a contract of insurance have been transferred to a third party under section 1,

(b) the insured is under a liability to the insurer under the contract ('the insured's liability'), and

(c) if there had been no transfer, the insurer would have been entitled to set off the amount of the insured's liability against the amount of the insurer's own liability to the insured.

(2) The insurer is entitled to set off the amount of the insured's liability against the amount of the insurer's own liability to the third party in relation to the transferred rights.

Provision of information etc

11 Information and disclosure for third parties

Schedule 1 (information and disclosure for third parties) has effect.

Enforcement of transferred rights

12 Limitation and prescription

(1) Subsection (2) applies where a person brings proceedings for a declaration under section 2(2)(a), or for a declarator under section 3(2)(a), and the proceedings are started or, in Scotland, commenced—

(a) after the expiry of a period of limitation applicable to an action against the insured to enforce the insured's liability, or of a period of prescription applicable to that liability, but

(b) while such an action is in progress.

(2) The insurer may not rely on the expiry of that period as a defence unless the insured is able to rely on it in the action against the insured.

(3) For the purposes of subsection (1), an action is to be treated as no longer in progress if it has been concluded by a judgment or decree, or by an award, even if there is an appeal or a right of appeal.

(4) Where a person who has already established an insured's liability to that person brings proceedings under this Act against the insurer, nothing in this Act is to be read as meaning—

(a) that, for the purposes of the law of limitation in England and Wales, that person's cause of action against the insurer arose otherwise than at the time when that person established the liability of the insured,

(b) that, for the purposes of the law of prescription in Scotland, the obligation in respect of which the proceedings are brought became enforceable against the insurer otherwise than at that time, or

(c) that, for the purposes of the law of limitation in Northern Ireland, that person's cause of action against the insurer arose otherwise than at the time when that person established the liability of the insured.

13 Jurisdiction within the United Kingdom

(1) Where a person (P) domiciled in a part of the United Kingdom is entitled to bring proceedings under this Act against an insurer domiciled in another part, P may do so in the part where P is domiciled or in the part where the insurer is domiciled (whatever the contract of insurance may stipulate as to where proceedings are to be brought).

(2) The following provisions of the Civil Jurisdiction and Judgments Act 1982 (relating to determination of domicile) apply for the purposes of subsection (1)—

(a) section 41(2), (3), (5) and (6) (individuals);

(b) section 42(1), (3), (4) and (8) (corporations and associations);

(c) section 45(2) and (3) (trusts);

(d) section 46(1), (3) and (7) (the Crown).

(3) In Schedule 5 to that Act (proceedings excluded from general provisions as to allocation of jurisdiction within the United Kingdom) at the end add—

'11' *Proceedings by third parties against insurers*
Proceedings under the Third Parties (Rights against Insurers) Act 2010.'

Enforcement of insured's liability

14 Effect of transfer on insured's liability

(1) Where rights in respect of an insured's liability to a third party are transferred under section 1, the third party may enforce that liability against the insured only to the extent (if any) that it exceeds the amount recoverable from the insurer by virtue of the transfer.

(2) Subsection (3) applies if a transfer of rights under section 1 occurs because the insured person is a relevant person by virtue of—

(a) section 4(1)(a) or (e), (2)(b) or (3)(b) or (c),

(b) [section 6(1)], (2)(a), (3)(c) or (4)(a), or

(c) section 7(1)(b).

(3) If the liability is subject to the arrangement, trust deed or compromise by virtue of which the insured is a relevant person, the liability is to be treated as subject to that arrangement, trust deed or compromise only to the extent that the liability exceeds the amount recoverable from the insurer by virtue of the transfer.

[. . .]

(6) For the purposes of this section the amount recoverable from the insurer does not include any amount that the third party is unable to recover as a result of—

(a) a shortage of assets on the insurer's part, in a case where the insurer is a relevant person, or

(b) a limit set by the contract of insurance on the fund available to meet claims in respect of a particular description of liability of the insured.

(7) Where a third party is eligible to make a claim in respect of the insurer's liability under or by virtue of rules made under Part 15 of the Financial Services and Markets Act 2000 (the Financial Services Compensation Scheme)—

(a) subsection (6)(a) applies only if the third party has made such a claim, and

(b) the third party is to be treated as being able to recover from the insurer any amount paid to, or due to, the third party as a result of the claim.

Application of Act

15 Reinsurance

This Act does not apply to a case where the liability referred to in section 1(1) is itself a liability incurred by an insurer under a contract of insurance.

16 Voluntarily-incurred liabilities

It is irrelevant for the purposes of section 1 whether or not the liability of the insured is or was incurred voluntarily.

17 Avoidance

(1) A contract of insurance to which this section applies is of no effect in so far as it purports, whether directly or indirectly, to avoid or terminate the contract or alter the rights of the parties under it in the event of the insured—

(a) becoming a relevant person, or

(b) dying insolvent (within the meaning given by section 5(2)).

(2) A contract of insurance is one to which this section applies if the insured's rights under it are capable of being transferred under section 1.

18 Cases with a foreign element

Except as expressly provided, the application of this Act does not depend on whether there is a connection with a part of the United Kingdom; and in particular it does not depend on—

(a) whether or not the liability (or the alleged liability) of the insured to the third party was incurred in, or under the law of, England and Wales, Scotland or Northern Ireland;

(b) the place of residence or domicile of any of the parties;

(c) whether or not the contract of insurance (or a part of it) is governed by the law of England and Wales, Scotland or Northern Ireland;

(d) the place where sums due under the contract of insurance are payable.

Supplemental

[19 Power to change the meaning of 'relevant person'

(1) The Secretary of State may by regulations make provision adding or removing circumstances in which a person is a 'relevant person' for the purposes of this Act, subject to subsection (2).

(2) Regulations under this section may add circumstances only if, in the Secretary of State's opinion, the additional circumstances—

(a) involve actual or anticipated dissolution of a body corporate or an unincorporated body,

(b) involve actual or anticipated insolvency or other financial difficulties for an individual, a body corporate or an unincorporated body, or

(c) are similar to circumstances for the time being described in sections 4 to 7.

(3) Regulations under this section may make provision about—

(a) the persons to whom, and the extent to which, rights are transferred under section 1 in the circumstances added or removed by the regulations (the 'affected circumstances'),

(b) the re-transfer of rights transferred under section 1 where the affected circumstances change, and

(c) the effect of a transfer of rights under section 1 on the liability of the insured in the affected circumstances.

(4) Regulations under this section which add or remove circumstances involving actual or anticipated dissolution of a body corporate or unincorporated body may change the cases in which the following provisions apply so that they include or exclude cases involving that type of dissolution or any other type of dissolution of a body—

(a) section 9(3) (cases in which transferred rights are not subject to a condition requiring the insured to provide information or assistance to the insurer), and

(b) paragraph 3 of Schedule 1 (notices requiring disclosure).

(5) Regulations under this section which add circumstances may provide that section 1 of this Act applies in cases involving those circumstances in which either or both of the following occurred in relation to a person before the day on which the regulations come into force—

(a) the circumstances arose in relation to the person;

(b) a liability against which the person was insured under an insurance contract was incurred.

(6) Regulations under this section which—

(a) add circumstances, and

(b) provide that section 1 of this Act applies in a case involving those circumstances in which both of the events mentioned in subsection (5)(a) and (b) occurred in relation to a person before the day on which the regulations come into force,

must provide that, in such a case, the person is to be treated for the purposes of this Act as not having become a relevant person until that day or a later day specified in the regulations.

(7) Regulations under this section which remove circumstances may provide that section 1 of this Act does not apply in cases involving those circumstances in which one of the events mentioned in subsection (5)(a) and (b) (but not both) occurred in relation to a person before the day on which the regulations come into force.

(8) Regulations under this section may—

(a) include consequential, incidental, supplementary, transitional, transitory or saving provision,

(b) make different provision for different purposes, and

(c) make provision by reference to an enactment as amended, extended or applied from time to time,

(and subsections (3) to (7) are without prejudice to the generality of this subsection).

(9) Regulations under this section may amend an enactment, whenever passed or made, including this Act.

(10) Regulations under this section are to be made by statutory instrument.

(11) Regulations under this section may not be made unless a draft of the statutory instrument containing the regulations has been laid before, and approved by a resolution of, each House of Parliament.]

[19A Interpretation

(1) The references to enactments in sections 4 to 7 [. . .], [Schedule A1 and paragraph 3(2)(b)] of Schedule 1 are to be treated as including references to those enactments as amended, extended or applied by another enactment, whenever passed or made, unless the contrary intention appears.

(2) In this Act, 'enactment' means an enactment contained in, or in an instrument made under, any of the following—

(a) an Act;

(b) an Act or Measure of the National Assembly for Wales;

(c) an Act of the Scottish Parliament;

(d) Northern Ireland legislation.]

20 Amendments, transitionals, repeals, etc

(1) Schedule 2 (amendments) has effect.

(2) Schedule 3 (transitory, transitional and saving provisions) has effect.

(3) Schedule 4 (repeals and revocations) has effect.

21 Short title, commencement and extent

(1) This Act may be cited as the Third Parties (Rights against Insurers) Act 2010.

(2) This Act comes into force on such day as the Secretary of State may by order made by statutory instrument appoint.

(3) This Act extends to England and Wales, Scotland and Northern Ireland, subject as follows.

(4) Section 2 and paragraphs 3 and 4 of Schedule 1 do not extend to Scotland.

(5) Section 3 extends to Scotland only.

(6) Any amendment, repeal or revocation made by this Act has the same extent as the provision to which it relates.

SCHEDULES

[SCHEDULE A1
ADMINISTRATION UNDER RELEVANT SECTORAL LEGISLATION

For the purposes of section 6(4B)—

(a) a body is in administration under relevant sectoral legislation if the appointment of an administrator of the body under an enactment listed below has effect, and

(b) the body does not cease to be in administration merely because an administrator vacates office (by reason of resignation, death or otherwise) or is removed from office.

List of Enactments

Aviation

Chapter 1 of Part 1 of the Transport Act 2000

Energy

Chapter 3 of Part 3 of the Energy Act 2004
Chapter 5 of Part 2 of the Energy Act 2011
Part 2 of the Energy Act (Northern Ireland) 2011 (c 6 (NI))

Financial Services

Part 2 of the Insolvency Act 1986 (as it has effect by virtue of section 249 of the Enterprise Act 2002), as applied by Schedule 15A to the Building Societies Act 1986
Part 3 of the Insolvency (Northern Ireland) Order 1989 (as it has effect by virtue of article 4 of the Insolvency (Northern Ireland) Order 2005, as applied by Schedule 15A to the Building Societies Act 1986
Part 3 of the Banking Act 2009
Investment Bank Special Administration Regulations 2011 Part 6 of the Financial Services (Banking Reform) Act 2013
[Payment and Electronic Money Institution Insolvency Regulations 2021]

Postal Services

Part 4 of the Postal Services Act 2011

Railways

Part 1 of the Railways Act 1993
Chapter 7 of Part 4 of the Greater London Authority Act 1999

Water and sewerage

Chapter 2 of Part 2 of the Water Industry Act 1991
Chapter 2 of Part 3 of the Water and Sewerage Services (Northern Ireland) Order 2006]

SCHEDULE 1
INFORMATION AND DISCLOSURE FOR THIRD PARTIES

Notices requesting information

1—(1) If a person (A) reasonably believes that—

(a) another person (B) has incurred a liability to A, and

(b) B is a relevant person,

A may, by notice in writing, request from B such information falling within sub paragraph (3) as the notice specifies.

(2) If a person (A) reasonably believes that—

(a) a liability has been incurred to A,

(b) the person who incurred the liability is insured against it under a contract of insurance,

(c) rights of that person under the contract have been transferred to A under section 1, and

(d) there is a person (C) who is able to provide information falling within sub-paragraph (3),

A may, by notice in writing, request from C such information falling within that sub-paragraph as the notice specifies.

(3) The following is the information that falls within this sub-paragraph—

(a) whether there is a contract of insurance that covers the supposed liability or might reasonably be regarded as covering it;

(b) if there is such a contract—

(i) who the insurer is;

(ii) what the terms of the contract are;

(iii) whether the insured has been informed that the insurer has claimed not to be liable under the contract in respect of the supposed liability;

(iv) whether there are or have been any proceedings between the insurer and the insured in respect of the supposed liability and, if so, relevant details of those proceedings;

(v) in a case where the contract sets a limit on the fund available to meet claims in respect of the supposed liability and other liabilities, how much of it (if any) has been paid out in respect of other liabilities;

(vi) whether there is a fixed charge to which any sums paid out under the contract in respect of the supposed liability would be subject.

(4) For the purpose of sub-paragraph (3)(b)(iv), relevant details of proceedings are—

(a) in the case of court proceedings—

(i) the name of the court;

(ii) the case number;

(iii) the contents of all documents served in the proceedings in accordance with rules of court or orders made in the proceedings, and the contents of any such orders;

(b) in the case of arbitral proceedings or, in Scotland, an arbitration—

(i) the name of the arbitrator;

(ii) information corresponding with that mentioned in paragraph (a)(iii).

(5) In sub-paragraph (3)(b)(vi), in its application to Scotland, 'fixed charge' means a fixed security within the meaning given by section 47(1) of the Bankruptcy and Diligence etc (Scotland) Act 2007 (asp 3).

(6) A notice given by a person under this paragraph must include particulars of the facts on which that person relies as entitlement to give the notice.

Provision of information where notice given under paragraph 1

2—(1) A person (R) who receives a notice under paragraph 1 must, within the period of 28 days beginning with the day of receipt of the notice—

(a) provide to the person who gave the notice any information specified in it that R is able to provide;

(b) in relation to any such information that R is not able to provide, notify that person why R is not able to provide it.

(2) Where—

(a) a person (R) receives a notice under paragraph 1,

(b) there is information specified in the notice that R is not able to provide because it is contained in a document that is not in R's control,

(c) the document was at one time in R's control, and

(d) R knows or believes that it is now in another person's control,

R must, within the period of 28 days beginning with the day of receipt of the notice, provide the person who gave the notice with whatever particulars R can as to the nature of the information and the identity of that other person.

(3) If R fails to comply with a duty imposed on R by this paragraph, the person who gave R the notice may apply to court for an order requiring R to comply with the duty.

(4) No duty arises by virtue of this paragraph in respect of information as to which a claim to legal professional privilege or, in Scotland, to confidentiality as between client and professional legal adviser could be maintained in legal proceedings.

[Paragraphs 3 and 4 do not apply to Scotland.]

Avoidance

5 A contract of insurance is of no effect in so far as it purports, whether directly or indirectly—

(a) to avoid or terminate the contract or alter the rights of the parties under it in the event of a person providing information, or giving disclosure, that the person is required to provide or give by virtue of a notice under paragraph 1 or 3, or

(b) otherwise to prohibit, prevent or restrict a person from providing such information or giving such disclosure.

Other rights to information etc

6 Rights to information, or to inspection of documents, that a person has by virtue of paragraph 1 or 3 are in addition to any such rights as the person has apart from that paragraph.

Interpretation

7 For the purposes of this Schedule—

(a) a person is able to provide information only if—

(i) that person can obtain it without undue difficulty from a document that is in that person's control, or

(ii) where that person is an individual, the information is within that person's knowledge;

(b) a document is in a person's control if it is in that person's possession or if that person has a right to possession of it or to inspect or take copies of it.

SCHEDULE 3
TRANSITORY, TRANSITIONAL AND SAVING PROVISIONS

1—(1) Section 1(1)(a) applies where the insured became a relevant person before, as well as when the insured becomes such a person on or after, commencement day.

(2) Section 1(1)(b) applies where the liability was incurred before, as well as where it is incurred on or after, commencement day.

2 Until the coming into force of section 47(1) of the Bankruptcy and Diligence etc (Scotland) Act 2007 (asp 3), the reference to that provision in paragraph 1(5) of Schedule 1 is to be read as a reference to section 486(1) of the Companies Act 1985.

3 Despite its repeal by this Act, the Third Parties (Rights against Insurers) Act 1930 continues to apply in relation to—

(a) cases where the event referred to in subsection (1) of section 1 of that Act and the incurring of the liability referred to in that subsection both happened before commencement day;

(b) cases where the death of the deceased person referred to in subsection (2) of that section happened before that day.

4 Despite its repeal by this Act, the Third Parties (Rights against Insurers) Act (Northern Ireland) 1930 continues to apply in relation to—

(a) cases where the event referred to in subsection (1) of section 1 of that Act and the incurring of the liability referred to in that subsection both happened before commencement day;

(b) cases where the death of the deceased person referred to in subsection (2) of that section happened before that day.

5 In this Schedule 'commencement day' means the day on which this Act comes into force.

CONSUMER INSURANCE (DISCLOSURE AND REPRESENTATIONS) ACT 2012
(2012, c 6)

Main definitions

1 Main definitions

In this Act—

'consumer insurance contract' means a contract of insurance between—

(a) an individual who enters into the contract wholly or mainly for purposes unrelated to the individual's trade, business or profession, and

(b) a person who carries on the business of insurance and who becomes a party to the contract by way of that business (whether or not in accordance with permission for the purposes of the Financial Services and Markets Act 2000);

'consumer' means the individual who enters into a consumer insurance contract, or proposes to do so;

'insurer' means the person who is, or would become, the other party to a consumer insurance contract.

Pre-contract and pre-variation information

2 Disclosure and representations before contract or variation

(1) This section makes provision about disclosure and representations by a consumer to an insurer before a consumer insurance contract is entered into or varied.

(2) It is the duty of the consumer to take reasonable care not to make a misrepresentation to the insurer.

(3) A failure by the consumer to comply with the insurer's request to confirm or amend particulars previously given is capable of being a misrepresentation for the purposes of this Act (whether or not it could be apart from this subsection).

(4) The duty set out in subsection (2) replaces any duty relating to disclosure or representations by a consumer to an insurer which existed in the same circumstances before this Act applied.

[. . .]

3 Reasonable care

(1) Whether or not a consumer has taken reasonable care not to make a misrepresentation is to be determined in the light of all the relevant circumstances.

(2) The following are examples of things which may need to be taken into account in making a determination under subsection (1)—

(a) the type of consumer insurance contract in question, and its target market,

(b) any relevant explanatory material or publicity produced or authorised by the insurer,

(c) how clear, and how specific, the insurer's questions were,

(d) in the case of a failure to respond to the insurer's questions in connection with the renewal or variation of a consumer insurance contract, how clearly the insurer communicated the importance of answering those questions (or the possible consequences of failing to do so),

(e) whether or not an agent was acting for the consumer.

(3) The standard of care required is that of a reasonable consumer: but this is subject to subsections (4) and (5).

(4) If the insurer was, or ought to have been, aware of any particular characteristics or circumstances of the actual consumer, those are to be taken into account.

(5) A misrepresentation made dishonestly is always to be taken as showing lack of reasonable care.

Qualifying misrepresentations

4 Qualifying misrepresentations: definition and remedies

(1) An insurer has a remedy against a consumer for a misrepresentation made by the consumer before a consumer insurance contract was entered into or varied only if—

(a) the consumer made the misrepresentation in breach of the duty set out in section 2(2), and

(b) the insurer shows that without the misrepresentation, that insurer would not have entered into the contract (or agreed to the variation) at all, or would have done so only on different terms.

(2) A misrepresentation for which the insurer has a remedy against the consumer is referred to in this Act as a 'qualifying misrepresentation'.

(3) The only such remedies available are set out in Schedule 1.

5 Qualifying misrepresentations: classification and presumptions

(1) For the purposes of this Act, a qualifying misrepresentation (see section 4(2)) is either—

(a) deliberate or reckless, or

(b) careless.

(2) A qualifying misrepresentation is deliberate or reckless if the consumer—

(a) knew that it was untrue or misleading, or did not care whether or not it was untrue or misleading, and

(b) knew that the matter to which the misrepresentation related was relevant to the insurer, or did not care whether or not it was relevant to the insurer.

(3) A qualifying misrepresentation is careless if it is not deliberate or reckless.

(4) It is for the insurer to show that a qualifying misrepresentation was deliberate or reckless.

(5) But it is to be presumed, unless the contrary is shown—

(a) that the consumer had the knowledge of a reasonable consumer, and

(b) that the consumer knew that a matter about which the insurer asked a clear and specific question was relevant to the insurer.

Specific issues

6 Warranties and representations

(1) This section applies to representations made by a consumer—

(a) in connection with a proposed consumer insurance contract, or

(b) in connection with a proposed variation to a consumer insurance contract.

(2) Such a representation is not capable of being converted into a warranty by means of any provision of the consumer insurance contract (or of the terms of the

variation), or of any other contract (and whether by declaring the representation to form the basis of the contract or otherwise).

7 Group insurance

(1) This section applies where—

(a) a contract of insurance is entered into by a person ('A') in order to provide cover for another person ('C'), or is varied or extended so as to do so,

(b) C is not a party to the contract,

(c) so far as the cover for C is concerned, the contract would have been a consumer insurance contract if entered into by C rather than by A, and

(d) C provided information directly or indirectly to the insurer before the contract was entered into, or before it was varied or extended to provide cover for C.

(2) So far as the cover for C is concerned—

(a) sections 2 and 3 apply in relation to disclosure and representations by C to the insurer as if C were proposing to enter into a consumer insurance contract for the relevant cover with the insurer, and

(b) subject to subsections (3) to (5) and the modifications in relation to the insurer's remedies set out in Part 3 of Schedule 1, the remainder of this Act applies in relation to the cover for C as if C had entered into a consumer insurance contract for that cover with the insurer.

(3) Section 4(1)(b) applies as if it read as follows—

'(b) the insurer shows that without the misrepresentation, that insurer would not have agreed to provide cover for C at all, or would have done so only on different terms.'

(4) If there is more than one C, a breach on the part of one of them of the duty imposed (by virtue of subsection (2)(a)) by section 2(2) does not affect the contract so far as it relates to the others.

(5) Nothing in this section affects any duty owed by A to the insurer, or any remedy which the insurer may have against A for breach of such a duty.

8 Insurance on life of another

(1) This section applies in relation to a consumer insurance contract for life insurance on the life of an individual ('L') who is not a party to the contract.

(2) If this section applies—

(a) information provided to the insurer by L is to be treated for the purposes of this Act as if it were provided by the person who is the party to the contract, but

(b) in relation to such information, if anything turns on the state of mind, knowledge, circumstances or characteristics of the individual providing the information, it is to be determined by reference to L and not the party to the contract.

9 Agents

Schedule 2 applies for determining, for the purposes of this Act only, whether an agent through whom a consumer insurance contract is effected is the agent of the consumer or of the insurer.

10 Contracting out

(1) A term of a consumer insurance contract, or of any other contract, which would put the consumer in a worse position as respects the matters mentioned in subsection (2) than the consumer would be in by virtue of the provisions of this Act is to that extent of no effect.

(2) The matters are—

(a) disclosure and representations by the consumer to the insurer before the contract is entered into or varied, and

(b) any remedies for qualifying misrepresentations (see section 4(2)).

(3) This section does not apply in relation to a contract for the settlement of a claim arising under a consumer insurance contract.

Final provision

[. . .]

12 Short title, commencement, application and extent

(1) This Act may be cited as the Consumer Insurance (Disclosure and Representations) Act 2012.

(2) Section 1 and this section come into force on the day on which this Act is passed, but otherwise this Act comes into force on such day as the Treasury may by order made by statutory instrument appoint.

(3) An order under subsection (2) may not appoint a day sooner than the end of the period of 1 year beginning with the day on which this Act is passed.

(4) This Act applies only in relation to consumer insurance contracts entered into, and variations to consumer insurance contracts agreed, after the Act comes into force. In the case of group insurance (see section 7), that includes the provision of cover for C by means of an insurance contract entered into by A after the Act comes into force, or varied or extended so as to do so after the Act comes into force.

(5) Nothing in this Act affects the circumstances in which a person is bound by the acts or omissions of that person's agent.

(6) Apart from the provisions listed in subsection (7), this Act extends to England and Wales, Scotland and Northern Ireland.

(7) In section 11—

(a) subsection (3) extends to England and Wales and Scotland only;

(b) subsection (4) extends to Northern Ireland only.

SCHEDULE 1

INSURERS' REMEDIES FOR QUALIFYING MISREPRESENTATIONS

Section 4(3)

PART 1

CONTRACTS

General

1 This Part of this Schedule applies in relation to qualifying misrepresentations made in connection with consumer insurance contracts (for variations to them, see Part 2).

Deliberate or reckless misrepresentations

2 If a qualifying misrepresentation was deliberate or reckless, the insurer—

(a) may avoid the contract and refuse all claims, and

(b) need not return any of the premiums paid, except to the extent (if any) that it would be unfair to the consumer to retain them.

Careless misrepresentations—claims

3 If the qualifying misrepresentation was careless, paragraphs 4 to 8 apply in relation to any claim.

4 The insurer's remedies are based on what it would have done if the consumer had complied with the duty set out in section 2(2), and paragraphs 5 to 8 are to be read accordingly.

5 If the insurer would not have entered into the consumer insurance contract on any terms, the insurer may avoid the contract and refuse all claims, but must return the premiums paid.

6 If the insurer would have entered into the consumer insurance contract, but on different terms (excluding terms relating to the premium), the contract is to be treated as if it had been entered into on those different terms if the insurer so requires.

7 In addition, if the insurer would have entered into the consumer insurance contract (whether the terms relating to matters other than the premium would have been the same or different), but would have charged a higher premium, the insurer may reduce proportionately the amount to be paid on a claim.

8 'Reduce proportionately' means that the insurer need pay on the claim only X% of what it would otherwise have been under an obligation to pay under the terms of the contract (or, if applicable, under the different terms provided for by virtue of paragraph 6), where—

$$X = \frac{\text{Premium actually charged}}{\text{Higher premium}} \times 100$$

Careless misrepresentations—treatment of contract for the future

9—(1) This paragraph—

(a) applies if the qualifying misrepresentation was careless, but

(b) does not relate to any outstanding claim.

(2) Paragraphs 5 and 6 (as read with paragraph 4) apply as they apply where a claim has been made.

(3) Paragraph 7 (as read with paragraph 4) applies in relation to a claim yet to be made as it applies in relation to a claim which has been made.

(4) If by virtue of sub-paragraph (2) or (3), the insurer would have either (or both) of the rights conferred by paragraph 6 or 7, the insurer may—

(a) give notice to that effect to the consumer, or

(b) terminate the contract by giving reasonable notice to the consumer.

(5) But the insurer may not terminate a contract under sub-paragraph (4)(b) if it is wholly or mainly one of life insurance.

(6) If the insurer gives notice to the consumer under sub-paragraph (4)(a), the consumer may terminate the contract by giving reasonable notice to the insurer.

(7) If either party terminates the contract under this paragraph, the insurer must refund any premiums paid for the terminated cover in respect of the balance of the contract term.

(8) Termination of the contract under this paragraph does not affect the treatment of any claim arising under the contract in the period before termination.

(9) Nothing in this paragraph affects any contractual right to terminate the contract.

PART 2
VARIATIONS

10 This Part of this Schedule applies in relation to qualifying misrepresentations made in connection with variations to consumer insurance contracts.

11 If the subject-matter of a variation can reasonably be treated separately from the subject-matter of the rest of the contract, Part 1 of this Schedule applies (with any necessary modifications) in relation to the variation as it applies in relation to a contract.

12 Otherwise, Part 1 applies (with any necessary modifications) as if the qualifying misrepresentation had been made in relation to the whole contract (for this purpose treated as including the variation) rather than merely in relation to the variation.

PART 3
MODIFICATIONS FOR GROUP INSURANCE

13 Part 1 is to be read subject to the following modifications in relation to cover provided for C under a group insurance contract as mentioned in section 7 (and in this Part 'A' and 'C' mean the same as in that section).

14 References to the consumer insurance contract (however described) are to that part of the contract which provides for cover for C.

15 References to claims and premiums are to claims and premiums in relation to that cover.

16 The reference to the consumer is to be read—

(a) in paragraph 2(b), as a reference to whoever paid the premiums, or the part of them that related to the cover for C,

(b) in paragraph 9(4) and (6), as a reference to A.

PART 4
SUPPLEMENTARY

17 Section 84 of the Marine Insurance Act 1906 (return of premium for failure of consideration) is to be read subject to the provisions of this Schedule in relation to contracts of marine insurance which are consumer insurance contracts.

SCHEDULE 2
RULES FOR DETERMINING STATUS OF AGENTS

Section 9

1 This Schedule sets out rules for determining, for the purposes of this Act only, whether an agent through whom a consumer insurance contract is effected is acting as the agent of the consumer or of the insurer.

2 The agent is to be taken as the insurer's agent in each of the following cases—

(a) when the agent does something in the agent's capacity as the appointed representative of the insurer for the purposes of the Financial Services and Markets Act 2000 (see section 39 of that Act),

(b) when the agent collects information from the consumer, if the insurer had given the agent express authority to do so as the insurer's agent,

(c) when the agent enters into the contract as the insurer's agent, if the insurer had given the agent express authority to do so.

3—(1) In any other case, it is to be presumed that the agent is acting as the consumer's agent unless, in the light of all the relevant circumstances, it appears that the agent is acting as the insurer's agent.

(2) Some factors which may be relevant are set out below.

(3) Examples of factors which may tend to confirm that the agent is acting for the consumer are—

(a) the agent undertakes to give impartial advice to the consumer,

(b) the agent undertakes to conduct a fair analysis of the market,

(c) the consumer pays the agent a fee.

(4) Examples of factors which may tend to show that the agent is acting for the insurer are—

(a) the agent places insurance of the type in question with only one of the insurers who provide insurance of that type,

(b) the agent is under a contractual obligation which has the effect of restricting the number of insurers with whom the agent places insurance of the type in question,

(c) the insurer provides insurance of the type in question through only a small proportion of the agents who deal in that type of insurance,

(d) the insurer permits the agent to use the insurer's name in providing the agent's services,

(e) the insurance in question is marketed under the name of the agent,

(f) the insurer asks the agent to solicit the consumer's custom.

4—(1) If it appears to the Treasury that the list of factors in sub-paragraph (3) or (4) of paragraph 3 has become outdated, the Treasury may by order made by statutory instrument bring the list up to date by amending the sub-paragraph so as to add, omit or alter any factor.

(2) A statutory instrument containing an order under sub-paragraph (1) may not be made unless a draft of the instrument has been laid before and approved by a resolution of each House of Parliament.

PARTNERSHIPS (PROSECUTION) (SCOTLAND) ACT 2013
(2013, c 21)

PROSECUTION AFTER DISSOLUTION

1 Prosecution of dissolved partnership

(1) This section and sections 2 and 3 apply where—

(a) a partnership is dissolved, and

(b) an offence is alleged to have been committed by the partnership before dissolution.

(2) The partnership may be prosecuted, or continue to be prosecuted, for the offence as if it had not been dissolved.

(3) But it is not competent to commence proceedings against the partnership by virtue of subsection (2) if a period of more than 5 years has elapsed since the partnership was dissolved.

(4) For the purposes of subsection (3), proceedings are commenced on the date on which an indictment or, as the case may be, a complaint is served on the partnership.

(5) Subsection (3) is without prejudice to section 136 of the Criminal Procedure (Scotland) Act 1995 (time limit for certain offences).

(6) Where a partnership is convicted of an offence by virtue of subsection (2), any enactment or rule of law relating to the liability of partners on the conviction of a partnership applies as if the partnership had not been dissolved.

(7) But subsection (6) is subject to section 3 (which disapplies provisions restricting payment of fines to partnership assets).

2 Dissolution of partnership: proceedings against former partner or other person

(1) A person, who could have been prosecuted for the offence committed by the partnership had it not been dissolved, may be prosecuted, or may continue to be prosecuted, despite the dissolution.

(2) Subsection (1) applies irrespective of whether the partnership has been or is prosecuted for the offence but not where the partnership has been so prosecuted and acquitted.

(3) In proceedings against a person by virtue of subsection (1), evidence led may include evidence as to the commission of the offence by the partnership.

3 Payment of fine where dissolved partnership convicted

An enactment, in so far as it restricts to payment out of a partnership's assets the payment of a fine imposed on the partnership on its conviction of an offence, does not apply in the case of a partnership which has been dissolved.

PROSECUTION AFTER CHANGE IN MEMBERSHIP

4 Prosecution of partnership after change in membership

(1) This section and section 5 apply where—

(a) there is a change in the membership of a partnership,

(b) the partnership continues to carry on business after the change, and

(c) an offence is alleged to have been committed by the partnership before the change.

(2) The partnership may be prosecuted, or continue to be prosecuted, for the offence.

(3) For the purposes of this section and section 5, any enactment or rule of law, by virtue of which a change in membership of a partnership results in a new partnership being constituted, does not apply.

(4) In this section and section 5, there is a change in the membership of a partnership where—

(a) a partner dies or, if not an individual, ceases to exist,

(b) a partner resigns, retires or is expelled from the partnership, or

(c) a person is admitted as a partner into the partnership.

5 Change in membership of partnership: proceedings against partner or other person

(1) A person, who could have been prosecuted for the offence committed by the partnership had there not been a change in membership, may be prosecuted, or may continue to be prosecuted, for the offence despite the change in membership.

(2) Subsection (1) applies irrespective of whether the partnership has been or is prosecuted for the offence but not where the partnership has been so prosecuted and acquitted.

(3) In proceedings against a person by virtue of subsection (1), evidence led may include evidence as to the commission of the offence by the partnership.

GENERAL AND MISCELLANEOUS

7 Interpretation

In this Act—

(a) references to an offence, in relation to its commission or alleged commission by a partnership, are references to an offence that the partnership is, by virtue of an enactment or rule of law, capable of committing separately from its partners,

(b) 'enactment' includes an enactment contained—

(i) in subordinate legislation (within the meaning of the Interpretation Act 1978), or

(ii) in, or in an instrument made under, an Act of the Scottish Parliament.

8 Short title, commencement and extent

(1) This Act may be cited as the Partnerships (Prosecution) (Scotland) Act 2013.

(2) This Act comes into force on the day after the day on which this Act is passed.

(3) This Act applies where the partnership is dissolved or there is a change in the membership of the partnership on or after the day on which this Act comes into force.

(4) This Act (other than section 3)—

(a) applies irrespective of when the offence mentioned in section 1(1)(b) or 4 (1)(c) is alleged to have been committed,

(b) applies to any proceedings in relation to such an offence which are ongoing on the day this Act comes into force as it applies in relation to proceedings commenced after that day.

(5) This Act extends only to Scotland.

(6) But the amendment made by section 6(2), and any amendment made by an order under section 6(6), has the same extent as the enactment (or the relevant part of the enactment) to which it relates.

INSURANCE ACT 2015
(2015, c 4)

PART 1
INSURANCE CONTRACTS: MAIN DEFINITIONS

1 Insurance contracts: main definitions

In this Act (apart from Part 6)—

'consumer insurance contract' has the same meaning as in the Consumer Insurance (Disclosure and Representations) Act 2012;

'non-consumer insurance contract' means a contract of insurance that is not a consumer insurance contract;

'insured' means the party to a contract of insurance who is the insured under the contract, or would be if the contract were entered into;

'insurer' means the party to a contract of insurance who is the insurer under the contract, or would be if the contract were entered into;

'the duty of fair presentation' means the duty imposed by section 3(1).

PART 2
THE DUTY OF FAIR PRESENTATION

2 Application and interpretation

(1) This Part applies to non-consumer insurance contracts only.

(2) This Part applies in relation to variations of non-consumer insurance contracts as it applies to contracts, but—

(a) references to the risk are to be read as references to changes in the risk relevant to the proposed variation, and

(b) references to the contract of insurance are to the variation.

3 The duty of fair presentation

(1) Before a contract of insurance is entered into, the insured must make to the insurer a fair presentation of the risk.

(2) The duty imposed by subsection (1) is referred to in this Act as 'the duty of fair presentation'.

(3) A fair presentation of the risk is one—

(a) which makes the disclosure required by subsection (4),

(b) which makes that disclosure in a manner which would be reasonably clear and accessible to a prudent insurer, and

(c) in which every material representation as to a matter of fact is substantially correct, and every material representation as to a matter of expectation or belief is made in good faith.

(4) The disclosure required is as follows, except as provided in subsection (5)—

(a) disclosure of every material circumstance which the insured knows or ought to know, or

(b) failing that, disclosure which gives the insurer sufficient information to put a prudent insurer on notice that it needs to make further enquiries for the purpose of revealing those material circumstances.

(5) In the absence of enquiry, subsection (4) does not require the insured to disclose a circumstance if—

(a) it diminishes the risk,

(b) the insurer knows it,

(c) the insurer ought to know it,

(d) the insurer is presumed to know it, or

(e) it is something as to which the insurer waives information.

(6) Sections 4 to 6 make further provision about the knowledge of the insured and of the insurer, and section 7 contains supplementary provision.

4 Knowledge of insured

(1) This section provides for what an insured knows or ought to know for the purposes of section 3(4)(a).

(2) An insured who is an individual knows only—

(a) what is known to the individual, and

(b) what is known to one or more of the individuals who are responsible for the insured's insurance.

(3) An insured who is not an individual knows only what is known to one or more of the individuals who are—

(a) part of the insured's senior management, or

(b) responsible for the insured's insurance.

(4) An insured is not by virtue of subsection (2)(b) or (3)(b) taken to know confidential information known to an individual if—

(a) the individual is, or is an employee of, the insured's agent; and

(b) the information was acquired by the insured's agent (or by an employee of that agent) through a business relationship with a person who is not connected with the contract of insurance.

(5) For the purposes of subsection (4) the persons connected with a contract of insurance are—

(a) the insured and any other persons for whom cover is provided by the contract, and

(b) if the contract re-insures risks covered by another contract, the persons who are (by virtue of this subsection) connected with that other contract.

(6) Whether an individual or not, an insured ought to know what should reasonably have been revealed by a reasonable search of information available to the insured (whether the search is conducted by making enquiries or by any other means).

(7) In subsection (6) 'information' includes information held within the insured's organisation or by any other person (such as the insured's agent or a person for whom cover is provided by the contract of insurance).

(8) For the purposes of this section—

(a) 'employee', in relation to the insured's agent, includes any individual working for the agent, whatever the capacity in which the individual acts,

(b) an individual is responsible for the insured's insurance if the individual participates on behalf of the insured in the process of procuring the insured's insurance (whether the individual does so as the insured's employee or agent, as an employee of the insured's agent or in any other capacity), and

(c) 'senior management' means those individuals who play significant roles in the making of decisions about how the insured's activities are to be managed or organised.

5 Knowledge of insurer

(1) For the purposes of section 3(5)(b), an insurer knows something only if it is known to one or more of the individuals who participate on behalf of the insurer in the decision whether to take the risk, and if so on what terms (whether the individual does so as the insurer's employee or agent, as an employee of the insurer's agent or in any other capacity).

(2) For the purposes of section 3(5)(c), an insurer ought to know something only if—

(a) an employee or agent of the insurer knows it, and ought reasonably to have passed on the relevant information to an individual mentioned in subsection (1), or

(b) the relevant information is held by the insurer and is readily available to an individual mentioned in subsection (1).

(3) For the purposes of section 3(5)(d), an insurer is presumed to know—

(a) things which are common knowledge, and

(b) things which an insurer offering insurance of the class in question to insureds in the field of activity in question would reasonably be expected to know in the ordinary course of business.

6 Knowledge: general

(1) For the purposes of sections 3 to 5, references to an individual's knowledge include not only actual knowledge, but also matters which the individual suspected, and of which the individual would have had knowledge but for deliberately refraining from confirming them or enquiring about them.

(2) Nothing in this Part affects the operation of any rule of law according to which knowledge of a fraud perpetrated by an individual ('F') either on the insured or on the insurer is not to be attributed to the insured or to the insurer (respectively), where—

(a) if the fraud is on the insured, F is any of the individuals mentioned in section 4(2)(b) or (3), or

(b) if the fraud is on the insurer, F is any of the individuals mentioned in section 5(1).

7 Supplementary

(1) A fair presentation need not be contained in only one document or oral presentation.

(2) The term 'circumstance' includes any communication made to, or information received by, the insured.

(3) A circumstance or representation is material if it would influence the judgement of a prudent insurer in determining whether to take the risk and, if so, on what terms.

(4) Examples of things which may be material circumstances are—

(a) special or unusual facts relating to the risk,

(b) any particular concerns which led the insured to seek insurance cover for the risk,

(c) anything which those concerned with the class of insurance and field of activity in question would generally understand as being something that should be dealt with in a fair presentation of risks of the type in question.

(5) A material representation is substantially correct if a prudent insurer would not consider the difference between what is represented and what is actually correct to be material.

(6) A representation may be withdrawn or corrected before the contract of insurance is entered into.

8 Remedies for breach

(1) The insurer has a remedy against the insured for a breach of the duty of fair presentation only if the insurer shows that, but for the breach, the insurer—

(a) would not have entered into the contract of insurance at all, or

(b) would have done so only on different terms.

(2) The remedies are set out in Schedule 1.

(3) A breach for which the insurer has a remedy against the insured is referred to in this Act as a 'qualifying breach'.

(4) A qualifying breach is either—

(a) deliberate or reckless, or

(b) neither deliberate nor reckless.

(5) A qualifying breach is deliberate or reckless if the insured —

(a) knew that it was in breach of the duty of fair presentation, or

(b) did not care whether or not it was in breach of that duty.

(6) It is for the insurer to show that a qualifying breach was deliberate or reckless.

PART 3
WARRANTIES AND OTHER TERMS

9 Warranties and representations

(1) This section applies to representations made by the insured in connection with—

(a) a proposed non-consumer insurance contract, or

(b) a proposed variation to a non-consumer insurance contract.

(2) Such a representation is not capable of being converted into a warranty by means of any provision of the non-consumer insurance contract (or of the terms of the variation), or of any other contract (and whether by declaring the representation to form the basis of the contract or otherwise).

10 Breach of warranty

(1) Any rule of law that breach of a warranty (express or implied) in a contract of insurance results in the discharge of the insurer's liability under the contract is abolished.

(2) An insurer has no liability under a contract of insurance in respect of any loss occurring, or attributable to something happening, after a warranty (express or implied) in the contract has been breached but before the breach has been remedied.

(3) But subsection (2) does not apply if—

(a) because of a change of circumstances, the warranty ceases to be applicable to the circumstances of the contract,

(b) compliance with the warranty is rendered unlawful by any subsequent law, or

(c) the insurer waives the breach of warranty.

(4) Subsection (2) does not affect the liability of the insurer in respect of losses occurring, or attributable to something happening—

(a) before the breach of warranty, or

(b) if the breach can be remedied, after it has been remedied.

(5) For the purposes of this section, a breach of warranty is to be taken as remedied—

(a) in a case falling within subsection (6), if the risk to which the warranty relates later becomes essentially the same as that originally contemplated by the parties,

(b) in any other case, if the insured ceases to be in breach of the warranty.

(6) A case falls within this subsection if—

(a) the warranty in question requires that by an ascertainable time something is to be done (or not done), or a condition is to be fulfilled, or something is (or is not) to be the case, and

(b) that requirement is not complied with.

(7) In the Marine Insurance Act 1906—

(a) in section 33 (nature of warranty), in subsection (3), the second sentence is omitted,

(b) section 34 (when breach of warranty excused) is omitted.

11 Terms not relevant to the actual loss

(1) This section applies to a term (express or implied) of a contract of insurance, other than a term defining the risk as a whole, if compliance with it would tend to reduce the risk of one or more of the following—

(a) loss of a particular kind,

(b) loss at a particular location,

(c) loss at a particular time.

(2) If a loss occurs, and the term has not been complied with, the insurer may not rely on the non-compliance to exclude, limit or discharge its liability under the contract for the loss if the insured satisfies subsection (3).

(3) The insured satisfies this subsection if it shows that the non-compliance with the term could not have increased the risk of the loss which actually occurred in the circumstances in which it occurred.

(4) This section may apply in addition to section 10.

PART 4
FRAUDULENT CLAIMS

12 Remedies for fraudulent claims

(1) If the insured makes a fraudulent claim under a contract of insurance—

(a) the insurer is not liable to pay the claim,

(b) the insurer may recover from the insured any sums paid by the insurer to the insured in respect of the claim, and

(c) in addition, the insurer may by notice to the insured treat the contract as having been terminated with effect from the time of the fraudulent act.

(2) If the insurer does treat the contract as having been terminated—

(a) it may refuse all liability to the insured under the contract in respect of a relevant event occurring after the time of the fraudulent act, and

(b) it need not return any of the premiums paid under the contract.

(3) Treating a contract as having been terminated under this section does not affect the rights and obligations of the parties to the contract with respect to a relevant event occurring before the time of the fraudulent act.

(4) In subsections (2)(a) and (3), 'relevant event' refers to whatever gives rise to the insurer's liability under the contract (and includes, for example, the occurrence of a loss, the making of a claim, or the notification of a potential claim, depending on how the contract is written).

13 Remedies for fraudulent claims: group insurance

(1) This section applies where—

(a) a contract of insurance is entered into with an insurer by a person ('A'),

(b) the contract provides cover for one or more other persons who are not parties to the contract ('the Cs'), whether or not it also provides cover of any kind for A or another insured party, and

(c) a fraudulent claim is made under the contract by or on behalf of one of the Cs ('CF').

(2) Section 12 applies in relation to the claim as if the cover provided for CF were provided under an individual insurance contract between the insurer and CF as the insured; and, accordingly—

(a) the insurer's rights under section 12 are exercisable only in relation to the cover provided for CF, and

(b) the exercise of any of those rights does not affect the cover provided under the contract for anyone else.

(3) In its application by virtue of subsection (2), section 12 is subject to the following particular modifications—

(a) the first reference to 'the insured' in subsection (1)(b) of that section, in respect of any particular sum paid by the insurer, is to whichever of A and CF the insurer paid the sum to; but if a sum was paid to A and passed on by A to CF, the reference is to CF,

(b) the second reference to 'the insured' in subsection (1)(b) is to A or CF,

(c) the reference to 'the insured' in subsection (1)(c) is to both CF and A,

(d) the reference in subsection (2)(b) to the premiums paid under the contract is to premiums paid in respect of the cover for CF.

[PART 4A
LATE PAYMENT OF CLAIMS

[13A Implied term about payment of claims

(1) It is an implied term of every contract of insurance that if the insured makes a claim under the contract, the insurer must pay any sums due in respect of the claim within a reasonable time.

(2) A reasonable time includes a reasonable time to investigate and assess the claim.

(3) What is reasonable will depend on all the relevant circumstances, but the following are examples of things which may need to be taken into account—

(a) the type of insurance,

(b) the size and complexity of the claim,

(c) compliance with any relevant statutory or regulatory rules or guidance,

(d) factors outside the insurer's control.

(4) If the insurer shows that there were reasonable grounds for disputing the claim (whether as to the amount of any sum payable, or as to whether anything at all is payable)—

(a) the insurer does not breach the term implied by subsection (1) merely by failing to pay the claim (or the affected part of it) while the dispute is continuing, but

(b) the conduct of the insurer in handling the claim may be a relevant factor in deciding whether that term was breached and, if so, when.

(5) Remedies (for example, damages) available for breach of the term implied by subsection (1) are in addition to and distinct from—

(a) any right to enforce payment of the sums due, and

(b) any right to interest on those sums (whether under the contract, under another enactment, at the court's discretion or otherwise).]]

PART 5
GOOD FAITH AND CONTRACTING OUT

Good faith

14 Good faith

(1) Any rule of law permitting a party to a contract of insurance to avoid the contract on the ground that the utmost good faith has not been observed by the other party is abolished.

(2) Any rule of law to the effect that a contract of insurance is a contract based

on the utmost good faith is modified to the extent required by the provisions of this Act and the Consumer Insurance (Disclosure and Representations) Act 2012.

(3) Accordingly—

(a) in section 17 of the Marine Insurance Act 1906 (marine insurance contracts are contracts of the utmost good faith), the words from ', and' to the end are omitted, and

(b) the application of that section (as so amended) is subject to the provisions of this Act and the Consumer Insurance (Disclosure and Representations) Act 2012.

(4) In section 2 of the Consumer Insurance (Disclosure and Representations) Act 2012 (disclosure and representations before contract or variation), subsection (5) is omitted.

Contracting out

15 Contracting out: consumer insurance contracts

(1) A term of a consumer insurance contract, or of any other contract, which would put the consumer in a worse position as respects any of the matters provided for in Part 3 or 4 of this Act than the consumer would be in by virtue of the provisions of those Parts (so far as relating to consumer insurance contracts) is to that extent of no effect.

(2) In subsection (1) references to a contract include a variation.

(3) This section does not apply in relation to a contract for the settlement of a claim arising under a consumer insurance contract.

16 Contracting out: non-consumer insurance contracts

(1) A term of a non-consumer insurance contract, or of any other contract, which would put the insured in a worse position as respects representations to which section 9 applies than the insured would be in by virtue of that section is to that extent of no effect.

(2) A term of a non-consumer insurance contract, or of any other contract, which would put the insured in a worse position as respects any of the other matters provided for in Part 2, 3 or 4 of this Act than the insured would be in by virtue of the provisions of those Parts (so far as relating to non-consumer insurance contracts) is to that extent of no effect, unless the requirements of section 17 have been satisfied in relation to the term.

(3) In this section references to a contract include a variation.

(4) This section does not apply in relation to a contract for the settlement of a claim arising under a non-consumer insurance contract.

[16A Contracting out of the implied term about payment of claims: consumer and non-consumer insurance contracts

(1) A term of a consumer insurance contract, or of any other contract, which would put the consumer in a worse position as respects any of the matters provided for in section 13A than the consumer would be in by virtue of the provisions of that section (so far as relating to consumer insurance contracts) is to that extent of no effect.

(2) A term of a non-consumer insurance contract, or of any other contract, which would put the insured in a worse position as respects deliberate or reckless breaches of the term implied by section 13A than the insured would be in by virtue of that section is to that extent of no effect.

(3) For the purposes of subsection (2) a breach is deliberate or reckless if the insurer—

(a) knew that it was in breach, or

(b) did not care whether or not it was in breach.

(4) A term of a non-consumer insurance contract, or of any other contract, which would put the insured in a worse position as respects any of the other matters

provided for in section 13A than the insured would be in by virtue of the provisions of that section (so far as relating to non-consumer insurance contracts) is to that extent of no effect, unless the requirements of section 17 have been satisfied in relation to the term.

(5) In this section references to a contract include a variation.

(6) This section does not apply in relation to a contract for the settlement of a claim arising under an insurance contract.]

17 The transparency requirements

(1) In this section, 'the disadvantageous term' means such a term as is mentioned in section 16(2) [or 16A(4)].

(2) The insurer must take sufficient steps to draw the disadvantageous term to the insured's attention before the contract is entered into or the variation agreed.

(3) The disadvantageous term must be clear and unambiguous as to its effect.

(4) In determining whether the requirements of subsections (2) and (3) have been met, the characteristics of insured persons of the kind in question, and the circumstances of the transaction, are to be taken into account.

(5) The insured may not rely on any failure on the part of the insurer to meet the requirements of subsection (2) if the insured (or its agent) had actual knowledge of the disadvantageous term when the contract was entered into or the variation agreed.

18 Contracting out: group insurance contracts

(1) This section applies to a contract of insurance referred to in section 13(1)(a); and in this section—

'A' and 'the Cs' have the same meaning as in section 13,

'consumer C' means an individual who is one of the Cs, where the cover provided by the contract for that individual would have been a consumer insurance contract if entered into by that person rather than by A, and

'non-consumer C' means any of the Cs who is not a consumer C.

(2) A term of the contract of insurance, or any other contract, which puts a consumer C in a worse position as respects any matter dealt with in section 13 than that individual would be in by virtue of that section is to that extent of no effect.

(3) A term of the contract of insurance, or any other contract, which puts a non-consumer C in a worse position as respects any matter dealt with in section 13 than that person would be in by virtue of that section is to that extent of no effect, unless the requirements of section 17 have been met in relation to the term.

(4) Section 17 applies in relation to such a term as it applies to a term mentioned in section 16(2), with references to the insured being read as references to A rather than the non-consumer C.

(5) In this section references to a contract include a variation.

(6) This section does not apply in relation to a contract for the settlement of a claim arising under a contract of insurance to which this section applies.

[PART 6 amends the Third Parties (Rights Against Insurers Act 2010.]

PART 7
GENERAL

21 Provision consequential on Part 2

(1) The provision made by this section is consequential on Part 2 of this Act.

(2) In the Marine Insurance Act 1906, sections 18 (disclosure by assured), 19 (disclosure by agent effecting insurance) and 20 (representations pending negotiation of contract) are omitted.

(3) Any rule of law to the same effect as any of those provisions is abolished.

(4) *[Amends the Road Traffic Act 1988]*
(5) *[Applies to Northern Ireland]*
(6) In section 11 of the Consumer Insurance (Disclosure and Representations) Act 2012 (consequential provision), subsections (1) and (2) are omitted.

22 Application etc of Parts 2 to 5

(1) Part 2 (and section 21) and section 14 apply only in relation to—
(a) contracts of insurance entered into after the end of the relevant period, and
(b) variations, agreed after the end of the relevant period, to contracts of insurance entered into at any time.
(2) Parts 3 and 4 of this Act apply only in relation to contracts of insurance entered into after the end of the relevant period, and variations to such contracts.
(3) In subsections (1) and (2) 'the relevant period' means the period of 18 months beginning with the day on which this Act is passed.
[(3A) Part 4A applies only in relation to contracts of insurance entered into after that Part has come into force, and variations to such contracts.]
(4) Unless the contrary intention appears, references in Parts 2 to 5 to something being done by or in relation to the insurer or the insured include its being done by or in relation to that person's agent.

23 Extent, commencement and short title

(1) This Act extends to England and Wales, Scotland and Northern Ireland, except for—
(a) section 21(4), which does not extend to Northern Ireland; and
(b) section 21(5), which extends to Northern Ireland only.
(2) This Act (apart from Part 6 and this section) comes into force at the end of the period of 18 months beginning with the day on which it is passed.
(3) In Part 6—
(a) section 19 comes into force at the end of the period of two months beginning with the day on which this Act is passed; and
(b) section 20 and Schedule 2 come into force on the day appointed under section 21(2) of the Third Parties (Rights against Insurers) Act 2010 for the coming into force of that Act.
(4) This section comes into force on the day on which this Act is passed.
(5) This Act may be cited as the Insurance Act 2015.

SCHEDULE 1
INSURERS' REMEDIES FOR QUALIFYING BREACHES

Section 8(2).

PART 1
CONTRACTS

General

1 This Part of this Schedule applies to qualifying breaches of the duty of fair presentation in relation to non-consumer insurance contracts (for variations to them, see Part 2).

Deliberate or reckless breaches

2 If a qualifying breach was deliberate or reckless, the insurer—
(a) may avoid the contract and refuse all claims, and
(b) need not return any of the premiums paid.

Other breaches

3 Paragraphs 4 to 6 apply if a qualifying breach was neither deliberate nor reckless.

4 If, in the absence of the qualifying breach, the insurer would not have entered into the contract on any terms, the insurer may avoid the contract and refuse all claims, but must in that event return the premiums paid.

5 If the insurer would have entered into the contract, but on different terms (other than terms relating to the premium), the contract is to be treated as if it had been entered into on those different terms if the insurer so requires.

6—(1) In addition, if the insurer would have entered into the contract (whether the terms relating to matters other than the premium would have been the same or different), but would have charged a higher premium, the insurer may reduce proportionately the amount to be paid on a claim.

(2) In sub-paragraph (1), 'reduce proportionately' means that the insurer need pay on the claim only X% of what it would otherwise have been under an obligation to pay under the terms of the contract (or, if applicable, under the different terms provided for by virtue of paragraph 5), where—

$$X = \frac{\text{Premium actually charged}}{\text{Higher premium}} \times 100$$

PART 2
VARIATIONS

General

7 This Part of this Schedule applies to qualifying breaches of the duty of fair presentation in relation to variations to non-consumer insurance contracts.

Deliberate or reckless breaches

8 If a qualifying breach was deliberate or reckless, the insurer—

(a) may by notice to the insured treat the contract as having been terminated with effect from the time when the variation was made, and

(b) need not return any of the premiums paid.

Other breaches

9—(1) This paragraph applies if—

(a) a qualifying breach was neither deliberate nor reckless, and

(b) the total premium was increased or not changed as a result of the variation.

(2) If, in the absence of the qualifying breach, the insurer would not have agreed to the variation on any terms, the insurer may treat the contract as if the variation was never made, but must in that event return any extra premium paid.

(3) If sub-paragraph (2) does not apply—

(a) if the insurer would have agreed to the variation on different terms (other than terms relating to the premium), the variation is to be treated as if it had been entered into on those different terms if the insurer so requires, and

(b) paragraph 11 also applies if (in the case of an increased premium) the insurer would have increased the premium by more than it did, or (in the case of an unchanged premium) the insurer would have increased the premium.

10—(1) This paragraph applies if—

(a) a qualifying breach was neither deliberate nor reckless, and

(b) the total premium was reduced as a result of the variation.

(2) If, in the absence of the qualifying breach, the insurer would not have agreed to the variation on any terms, the insurer may treat the contract as if the variation was never made, and paragraph 11 also applies.

(3) If sub-paragraph (2) does not apply—

(a) if the insurer would have agreed to the variation on different terms (other than terms relating to the premium), the variation is to be treated as if it had been entered into on those different terms if the insurer so requires, and

(b) paragraph 11 also applies if the insurer would have increased the premium, would not have reduced the premium, or would have reduced it by less than it did.

Proportionate reduction

11—(1) If this paragraph applies, the insurer may reduce proportionately the amount to be paid on a claim arising out of events after the variation.

(2) In sub-paragraph (1), 'reduce proportionately' means that the insurer need pay on the claim only Y% of what it would otherwise have been under an obligation to pay under the terms of the contract (whether on the original terms, or as varied, or under the different terms provided for by virtue of paragraph 9(3)(a) or 10(3)(a), as the case may be), where—

$$Y = \frac{\text{Total premium actually charged}}{P} \times 100$$

(3) In the formula in sub-paragraph (2), 'P'—

(a) in a paragraph 9(3)(b) case, is the total premium the insurer would have charged,

(b) in a paragraph 10(2) case, is the original premium,

(c) in a paragraph 10(3)(b) case, is the original premium if the insurer would not have changed it, and otherwise the increased or (as the case may be) reduced total premium the insurer would have charged.

PART 3
Supplementary

Relationship with section 84 of the Marine Insurance Act 1906

12 Section 84 of the Marine Insurance Act 1906 (return of premium for failure of consideration) is to be read subject to the provisions of this Schedule in relation to contracts of marine insurance which are non-consumer insurance contracts.

. . .

CONSUMER RIGHTS ACT 2015
(2015, c 15)

PART 1
CONSUMER CONTRACTS FOR GOODS, DIGITAL CONTENT AND SERVICES

CHAPTER 1
Introduction

1 Where Part 1 applies

(1) This Part applies where there is an agreement between a trader and a consumer for the trader to supply goods, digital content or services, if the agreement is a contract.

(2) It applies whether the contract is written or oral or implied from the parties' conduct, or more than one of these combined.

(3) Any of Chapters 2, 3 and 4 may apply to a contract—

(a) if it is a contract for the trader to supply goods, see Chapter 2;

(b) if it is a contract for the trader to supply digital content, see Chapter 3 (also, subsection (6));

(c) if it is a contract for the trader to supply a service, see Chapter 4 (also, subsection (6)).

(4) In each case the Chapter applies even if the contract also covers something covered by another Chapter (a mixed contract).

(5) Two or all three of those Chapters may apply to a mixed contract.

(6) For provisions about particular mixed contracts, see—

(a) section 15 (goods and installation);

(b) section 16 (goods and digital content).

(7) For other provision applying to contracts to which this Part applies, see Part 2 (unfair terms).

2 Key definitions

(1) These definitions apply in this Part (as well as the definitions in section 59).

(2) 'Trader' means a person acting for purposes relating to that person's trade, business, craft or profession, whether acting personally or through another person acting in the trader's name or on the trader's behalf.

(3) 'Consumer' means an individual acting for purposes that are wholly or mainly outside that individual's trade, business, craft or profession.

(4) A trader claiming that an individual was not acting for purposes wholly or mainly outside the individual's trade, business, craft or profession must prove it.

(5) For the purposes of Chapter 2, except to the extent mentioned in subsection (6), a person is not a consumer in relation to a sales contract if—

(a) the goods are second hand goods sold at public auction, and

(b) individuals have the opportunity of attending the sale in person.

(6) A person is a consumer in relation to such a contract for the purposes of—

(a) sections 11(4) and (5), 12, 28 and 29, and

(b) the other provisions of Chapter 2 as they apply in relation to those sections.

(7) 'Business' includes the activities of any government department or local or public authority.

(8) 'Goods' means any tangible moveable items, but that includes water, gas and electricity if and only if they are put up for supply in a limited volume or set quantity.

(9) 'Digital content' means data which are produced and supplied in digital form.

CHAPTER 2
Goods

What goods contracts are covered?

3 Contracts covered by this Chapter

(1) This Chapter applies to a contract for a trader to supply goods to a consumer.

(2) It applies only if the contract is one of these (defined for the purposes of this Part in sections 5 to 8)—

(a) a sales contract;

(b) a contract for the hire of goods;

(c) a hire-purchase agreement;

(d) a contract for transfer of goods.

(3) It does not apply—

(a) to a contract for a trader to supply coins or notes to a consumer for use as currency;

(b) to a contract for goods to be sold by way of execution or otherwise by authority of law;

(c) to a contract intended to operate as a mortgage, pledge, charge or other security;

(d) in relation to England and Wales or Northern Ireland, to a contract made by deed and for which the only consideration is the presumed consideration imported by the deed;

(e) in relation to Scotland, to a gratuitous contract.

(4) A contract to which this Chapter applies is referred to in this Part as a 'contract to supply goods'.

(5) Contracts to supply goods include—

(a) contracts entered into between one part owner and another;

(b) contracts for the transfer of an undivided share in goods;

(c) contracts that are absolute and contracts that are conditional.

(6) Subsection (1) is subject to any provision of this Chapter that applies a section or part of a section to only some of the kinds of contracts listed in subsection (2).

(7) A mixed contract (see section 1(4)) may be a contract of any of those kinds.

4 Ownership of goods

(1) In this Chapter ownership of goods means the general property in goods, not merely a special property.

(2) For the time when ownership of goods is transferred, see in particular the following provisions of the Sale of Goods Act 1979 (which relate to contracts of sale)—

section 16: goods must be ascertained
section 17: property passes when intended to pass
section 18: rules for ascertaining intention
section 19: reservation of right of disposal
section 20A: undivided shares in goods forming part of a bulk
section 20B: deemed consent by co-owner to dealings in bulk goods

5 Sales contracts

(1) A contract is a sales contract if under it—

(a) the trader transfers or agrees to transfer ownership of goods to the consumer, and

(b) the consumer pays or agrees to pay the price.

(2) A contract is a sales contract (whether or not it would be one under subsection (1)) if under the contract—

(a) goods are to be manufactured or produced and the trader agrees to supply them to the consumer,

(b) on being supplied, the goods will be owned by the consumer, and

(c) the consumer pays or agrees to pay the price.

(3) A sales contract may be conditional (see section 3(5)), but in this Part 'conditional sales contract' means a sales contract under which—

(a) the price for the goods or part of it is payable by instalments, and

(b) the trader retains ownership of the goods until the conditions specified in the contract (for the payment of instalments or otherwise) are met;

and it makes no difference whether or not the consumer possesses the goods.

6 Contracts for the hire of goods

(1) A contract is for the hire of goods if under it the trader gives or agrees to give the consumer possession of the goods with the right to use them, subject to the terms of the contract, for a period determined in accordance with the contract.

(2) But a contract is not for the hire of goods if it is a hire-purchase agreement.

7 Hire-purchase agreements

(1) A contract is a hire-purchase agreement if it meets the two conditions set out below.

(2) The first condition is that under the contract goods are hired by the trader in return for periodical payments by the consumer (and 'hired' is to be read in accordance with section 6(1)).

(3) The second condition is that under the contract ownership of the goods will transfer to the consumer if the terms of the contract are complied with and—

(a) the consumer exercises an option to buy the goods,

(b) any party to the contract does an act specified in it, or

(c) an event specified in the contract occurs.

(4) But a contract is not a hire-purchase agreement if it is a conditional sales contract.

8 Contracts for transfer of goods

A contract to supply goods is a contract for transfer of goods if under it the trader transfers or agrees to transfer ownership of the goods to the consumer and—

(a) the consumer provides or agrees to provide consideration otherwise than by paying a price, or

(b) the contract is, for any other reason, not a sales contract or a hire-purchase agreement.

What statutory rights are there under a goods contract?

9 Goods to be of satisfactory quality

(1) Every contract to supply goods is to be treated as including a term that the quality of the goods is satisfactory.

(2) The quality of goods is satisfactory if they meet the standard that a reasonable person would consider satisfactory, taking account of—

(a) any description of the goods,

(b) the price or other consideration for the goods (if relevant), and

(c) all the other relevant circumstances (see subsection (5)).

(3) The quality of goods includes their state and condition; and the following aspects (among others) are in appropriate cases aspects of the quality of goods—

(a) fitness for all the purposes for which goods of that kind are usually supplied;

(b) appearance and finish;

(c) freedom from minor defects;

(d) safety;

(e) durability.

(4) The term mentioned in subsection (1) does not cover anything which makes the quality of the goods unsatisfactory—

(a) which is specifically drawn to the consumer's attention before the contract is made,

(b) where the consumer examines the goods before the contract is made, which that examination ought to reveal, or

(c) in the case of a contract to supply goods by sample, which would have been apparent on a reasonable examination of the sample.

(5) The relevant circumstances mentioned in subsection (2)(c) include any public statement about the specific characteristics of the goods made by the trader, the producer or any representative of the trader or the producer.

(6) That includes, in particular, any public statement made in advertising or labelling.

(7) But a public statement is not a relevant circumstance for the purposes of subsection (2)(c) if the trader shows that—

(a) when the contract was made, the trader was not, and could not reasonably have been, aware of the statement,

(b) before the contract was made, the statement had been publicly withdrawn or, to the extent that it contained anything which was incorrect or misleading, it had been publicly corrected, or

(c) the consumer's decision to contract for the goods could not have been influenced by the statement.

(8) In a contract to supply goods a term about the quality of the goods may be treated as included as a matter of custom.

(9) See section 19 for a consumer's rights if the trader is in breach of a term that this section requires to be treated as included in a contract.

10 Goods to be fit for particular purpose

(1) Subsection (3) applies to a contract to supply goods if before the contract is made the consumer makes known to the trader (expressly or by implication) any particular purpose for which the consumer is contracting for the goods.

(2) Subsection (3) also applies to a contract to supply goods if—

(a) the goods were previously sold by a credit-broker to the trader,

(b) in the case of a sales contract or contract for transfer of goods, the consideration or part of it is a sum payable by instalments, and

(c) before the contract is made, the consumer makes known to the creditbroker (expressly or by implication) any particular purpose for which the consumer is contracting for the goods.

(3) The contract is to be treated as including a term that the goods are reasonably fit for that purpose, whether or not that is a purpose for which goods of that kind are usually supplied.

(4) Subsection (3) does not apply if the circumstances show that the consumer does not rely, or it is unreasonable for the consumer to rely, on the skill or judgment of the trader or credit-broker.

(5) In a contract to supply goods a term about the fitness of the goods for a particular purpose may be treated as included as a matter of custom.

(6) See section 19 for a consumer's rights if the trader is in breach of a term that this section requires to be treated as included in a contract.

11 Goods to be as described

(1) Every contract to supply goods by description is to be treated as including a term that the goods will match the description.

(2) If the supply is by sample as well as by description, it is not sufficient that the bulk of the goods matches the sample if the goods do not also match the description.

(3) A supply of goods is not prevented from being a supply by description just because—

(a) the goods are exposed for supply, and

(b) they are selected by the consumer.

(4) Any information that is provided by the trader about the goods and is information mentioned in paragraph (a) of Schedule 1 or 2 to the Consumer Contracts (Information, Cancellation and Additional Charges) Regulations 2013 (SI 2013/3134) (main characteristics of goods) is to be treated as included as a term of the contract.

(5) A change to any of that information, made before entering into the contract or later, is not effective unless expressly agreed between the consumer and the trader.

(6) See section 2(5) and (6) for the application of subsections (4) and (5) where goods are sold at public auction.

(7) See section 19 for a consumer's rights if the trader is in breach of a term that this section requires to be treated as included in a contract.

12 Other pre-contract information included in contract

(1) This section applies to any contract to supply goods.

(2) Where regulation 9, 10 or 13 of the Consumer Contracts (Information, Cancellation and Additional Charges) Regulations 2013 (SI 2013/3134) required the trader to provide information to the consumer before the contract became binding, any of that information that was provided by the trader other than information about the goods and mentioned in paragraph (a) of Schedule 1 or 2 to the Regulations (main characteristics of goods) is to be treated as included as a term of the contract.

(3) A change to any of that information, made before entering into the contract or later, is not effective unless expressly agreed between the consumer and the trader.

(4) See section 2(5) and (6) for the application of this section where goods are sold at public auction.

(5) See section 19 for a consumer's rights if the trader is in breach of a term that this section requires to be treated as included in the contract.

13 Goods to match a sample

(1) This section applies to a contract to supply goods by reference to a sample of the goods that is seen or examined by the consumer before the contract is made.

(2) Every contract to which this section applies is to be treated as including a term that—

(a) the goods will match the sample except to the extent that any differences between the sample and the goods are brought to the consumer's attention before the contract is made, and

(b) the goods will be free from any defect that makes their quality unsatisfactory and that would not be apparent on a reasonable examination of the sample.

(3) See section 19 for a consumer's rights if the trader is in breach of a term that this section requires to be treated as included in a contract.

14 Goods to match a model seen or examined

(1) This section applies to a contract to supply goods by reference to a model of the goods that is seen or examined by the consumer before entering into the contract.

(2) Every contract to which this section applies is to be treated as including a term that the goods will match the model except to the extent that any differences between the model and the goods are brought to the consumer's attention before the consumer enters into the contract.

(3) See section 19 for a consumer's rights if the trader is in breach of a term that this section requires to be treated as included in a contract.

15 Installation as part of conformity of the goods with the contract

(1) Goods do not conform to a contract to supply goods if—

(a) installation of the goods forms part of the contract,

(b) the goods are installed by the trader or under the trader's responsibility, and

(c) the goods are installed incorrectly.

(2) See section 19 for the effect of goods not conforming to the contract.

16 Goods not conforming to contract if digital content does not conform

(1) Goods (whether or not they conform otherwise to a contract to supply goods) do not conform to it if—

(a) the goods are an item that includes digital content, and

(b) the digital content does not conform to the contract to supply that content (for which see section 42(1)).

(2) See section 19 for the effect of goods not conforming to the contract.

17 Trader to have right to supply the goods etc

(1) Every contract to supply goods, except one within subsection (4), is to be treated as including a term—

(a) in the case of a contract for the hire of goods, that at the beginning of the period of hire the trader must have the right to transfer possession of the goods by way of hire for that period,

(b) in any other case, that the trader must have the right to sell or transfer the goods at the time when ownership of the goods is to be transferred.

(2) Every contract to supply goods, except a contract for the hire of goods or a contract within subsection (4), is to be treated as including a term that—

(a) the goods are free from any charge or encumbrance not disclosed or known to the consumer before entering into the contract,

(b) the goods will remain free from any such charge or encumbrance until ownership of them is to be transferred, and

(c) the consumer will enjoy quiet possession of the goods except so far as it may be disturbed by the owner or other person entitled to the benefit of any charge or encumbrance so disclosed or known.

(3) Every contract for the hire of goods is to be treated as including a term that the consumer will enjoy quiet possession of the goods for the period of the hire except so far as the possession may be disturbed by the owner or other person entitled to the benefit of any charge or encumbrance disclosed or known to the consumer before entering into the contract.

(4) This subsection applies to a contract if the contract shows, or the circumstances when they enter into the contract imply, that the trader and the consumer intend the trader to transfer only—

(a) whatever title the trader has, even if it is limited, or

(b) whatever title a third person has, even if it is limited.

(5) Every contract within subsection (4) is to be treated as including a term that all charges or encumbrances known to the trader and not known to the consumer were disclosed to the consumer before entering into the contract.

(6) Every contract within subsection (4) is to be treated as including a term that the consumer's quiet possession of the goods—

(a) will not be disturbed by the trader, and

(b) will not be disturbed by a person claiming through or under the trader, unless that person is claiming under a charge or encumbrance that was disclosed or known to the consumer before entering into the contract.

(7) If subsection (4)(b) applies (transfer of title that a third person has), the contract is also to be treated as including a term that the consumer's quiet possession of the goods—

(a) will not be disturbed by the third person, and

(b) will not be disturbed by a person claiming through or under the third person, unless the claim is under a charge or encumbrance that was disclosed or known to the consumer before entering into the contract.

(8) In the case of a contract for the hire of goods, this section does not affect the right of the trader to repossess the goods where the contract provides or is to be treated as providing for this.

(9) See section 19 for a consumer's rights if the trader is in breach of a term that this section requires to be treated as included in a contract.

18 No other requirement to treat term about quality or fitness as included

(1) Except as provided by sections 9, 10, 13 and 16, a contract to supply goods is not to be treated as including any term about the quality of the goods or their fitness for any particular purpose, unless the term is expressly included in the contract.

(2) Subsection (1) is subject to provision made by any other enactment (whenever passed or made).

What remedies are there if statutory rights under a goods contract are not met?

19 Consumer's rights to enforce terms about goods

(1) In this section and sections 22 to 24 references to goods conforming to a contract are references to—

(a) the goods conforming to the terms described in sections 9, 10, 11, 13 and 14,

(b) the goods not failing to conform to the contract under section 15 or 16, and

(c) the goods conforming to requirements that are stated in the contract.

(2) But, for the purposes of this section and sections 22 to 24, a failure to conform as mentioned in subsection (1)(a) to (c) is not a failure to conform to the contract if it has its origin in materials supplied by the consumer.

(3) If the goods do not conform to the contract because of a breach of any of the terms described in sections 9, 10, 11, 13 and 14, or if they do not conform to the contract under section 16, the consumer's rights (and the provisions about them and when they are available) are—

(a) the short-term right to reject (sections 20 and 22);

(b) the right to repair or replacement (section 23); and

(c) the right to a price reduction or the final right to reject (sections 20 and 24).

(4) If the goods do not conform to the contract under section 15 or because of a breach of requirements that are stated in the contract, the consumer's rights (and the provisions about them and when they are available) are—

(a) the right to repair or replacement (section 23); and

(b) the right to a price reduction or the final right to reject (sections 20 and 24).

(5) If the trader is in breach of a term that section 12 requires to be treated as included in the contract, the consumer has the right to recover from the trader the amount of any costs incurred by the consumer as a result of the breach, up to the amount of the price paid or the value of other consideration given for the goods.

(6) If the trader is in breach of the term that section 17(1) (right to supply etc) requires to be treated as included in the contract, the consumer has a right to reject (see section 20 for provisions about that right and when it is available).

(7) Subsections (3) to (6) are subject to section 25 and subsections (3)(a) and (6) are subject to section 26.

(8) Section 28 makes provision about remedies for breach of a term about the time for delivery of goods.

(9) This Chapter does not prevent the consumer seeking other remedies—

(a) for a breach of a term that this Chapter requires to be treated as included in the contract,

(b) on the grounds that, under section 15 or 16, goods do not conform to the contract, or

(c) for a breach of a requirement stated in the contract.

(10) Those other remedies may be ones—

(a) in addition to a remedy referred to in subsections (3) to (6) (but not so as to recover twice for the same loss), or

(b) instead of such a remedy, or

(c) where no such remedy is provided for.

(11) Those other remedies include any of the following that is open to the consumer in the circumstances—

(a) claiming damages;

(b) seeking specific performance;

(c) seeking an order for specific implement;

(d) relying on the breach against a claim by the trader for the price;

(e) for breach of an express term, exercising a right to treat the contract as at an end.

(12) It is not open to the consumer to treat the contract as at an end for breach of a term that this Chapter requires to be treated as included in the contract, or on the grounds that, under section 15 or 16, goods do not conform to the contract, except as provided by subsections (3), (4) and (6).

(13) In this Part, treating a contract as at an end means treating it as repudiated.

(14) For the purposes of subsections (3)(b) and (c) and (4), goods which do not conform to the contract at any time within the period of six months beginning with the day on which the goods were delivered to the consumer must be taken not to have conformed to it on that day.

(15) Subsection (14) does not apply if—

(a) it is established that the goods did conform to the contract on that day, or

(b) its application is incompatible with the nature of the goods or with how they fail to conform to the contract.

20 Right to reject

(1) The short-term right to reject is subject to section 22.

(2) The final right to reject is subject to section 24.

(3) The right to reject under section 19(6) is not limited by those sections.

(4) Each of these rights entitles the consumer to reject the goods and treat the contract as at an end, subject to subsections (20) and (21).

(5) The right is exercised if the consumer indicates to the trader that the consumer is rejecting the goods and treating the contract as at an end.

(6) The indication may be something the consumer says or does, but it must be clear enough to be understood by the trader.

(7) From the time when the right is exercised—

(a) the trader has a duty to give the consumer a refund, subject to subsection (18), and

(b) the consumer has a duty to make the goods available for collection by the trader or (if there is an agreement for the consumer to return rejected goods) to return them as agreed.

(8) Whether or not the consumer has a duty to return the rejected goods, the trader must bear any reasonable costs of returning them, other than any costs incurred by the consumer in returning the goods in person to the place where the consumer took physical possession of them.

(9) The consumer's entitlement to receive a refund works as follows.

(10) To the extent that the consumer paid money under the contract, the consumer is entitled to receive back the same amount of money.

(11) To the extent that the consumer transferred anything else under the contract, the consumer is entitled to receive back the same amount of what the consumer transferred, unless subsection (12) applies.

(12) To the extent that the consumer transferred under the contract something for which the same amount of the same thing cannot be substituted, the consumer is entitled to receive back in its original state whatever the consumer transferred.

(13) If the contract is for the hire of goods, the entitlement to a refund extends only to anything paid or otherwise transferred for a period of hire that the consumer does not get because the contract is treated as at an end.

(14) If the contract is a hire-purchase agreement or a conditional sales contract and the contract is treated as at an end before the whole of the price has been paid, the entitlement to a refund extends only to the part of the price paid.

(15) A refund under this section must be given without undue delay, and in any event within 14 days beginning with the day on which the trader agrees that the consumer is entitled to a refund.

(16) If the consumer paid money under the contract, the trader must give the refund using the same means of payment as the consumer used, unless the consumer expressly agrees otherwise.

(17) The trader must not impose any fee on the consumer in respect of the refund.

(18) There is no entitlement to receive a refund—

(a) if none of subsections (10) to (12) applies,

(b) to the extent that anything to which subsection (12) applies cannot be given back in its original state, or

(c) where subsection (13) applies, to the extent that anything the consumer transferred under the contract cannot be divided so as to give back only the amount, or part of the amount, to which the consumer is entitled.

(19) It may be open to a consumer to claim damages where there is no entitlement to receive a refund, or because of the limits of the entitlement, or instead of a refund.

(20) Subsection (21) qualifies the application in relation to England and Wales and Northern Ireland of the rights mentioned in subsections (1) to (3) where—

(a) the contract is a severable contract,

(b) in relation to the final right to reject, the contract is a contract for the hire of goods, a hire-purchase agreement or a contract for transfer of goods, and

(c) section 26(3) does not apply.

(21) The consumer is entitled, depending on the terms of the contract and the circumstances of the case—

(a) to reject the goods to which a severable obligation relates and treat that obligation as at an end (so that the entitlement to a refund relates only to what the consumer paid or transferred in relation to that obligation), or

(b) to exercise any of the rights mentioned in subsections (1) to (3) in respect of the whole contract.

21 Partial rejection of goods

(1) If the consumer has any of the rights mentioned in section 20(1) to (3), but does not reject all of the goods and treat the contract as at an end, the consumer—

(a) may reject some or all of the goods that do not conform to the contract, but

(b) may not reject any goods that do conform to the contract.

(2) If the consumer is entitled to reject the goods in an instalment, but does not reject all of those goods, the consumer—

(a) may reject some or all of the goods in the instalment that do not conform to the contract, but

(b) may not reject any goods in the instalment that do conform to the contract.

(3) If any of the goods form a commercial unit, the consumer cannot reject some of those goods without also rejecting the rest of them.

(4) A unit is a 'commercial unit' if division of the unit would materially impair the value of the goods or the character of the unit.

(5) The consumer rejects goods under this section by indicating to the trader that the consumer is rejecting the goods.

(6) The indication may be something the consumer says or does, but it must be clear enough to be understood by the trader.

(7) From the time when a consumer rejects goods under this section—

(a) the trader has a duty to give the consumer a refund in respect of those goods (subject to subsection (10)), and

(b) the consumer has a duty to make those goods available for collection by the trader or (if there is an agreement for the consumer to return rejected goods) to return them as agreed.

(8) Whether or not the consumer has a duty to return the rejected goods, the trader must bear any reasonable costs of returning them, other than any costs incurred by the consumer in returning those goods in person to the place where the consumer took physical possession of them.

(9) Section 20(10) to (17) apply to a consumer's right to receive a refund under this section (and in section 20(13) and (14) references to the contract being treated as at an end are to be read as references to goods being rejected).

(10) That right does not apply—

(a) if none of section 20(10) to (12) applies,

(b) to the extent that anything to which section 20(12) applies cannot be given back in its original state, or

(c) to the extent that anything the consumer transferred under the contract cannot be divided so as to give back only the amount, or part of the amount, to which the consumer is entitled.

(11) It may be open to a consumer to claim damages where there is no right to receive a refund, or because of the limits of the right, or instead of a refund.

(12) References in this section to goods conforming to a contract are to be read in accordance with section 19(1) and (2), but they also include the goods conforming to the terms described in section 17.

(13) Where section 20(21)(a) applies the reference in subsection (1) to the consumer treating the contract as at an end is to be read as a reference to the consumer treating the severable obligation as at an end.

22 Time limit for short-term right to reject

(1) A consumer who has the short-term right to reject loses it if the time limit for exercising it passes without the consumer exercising it, unless the trader and the consumer agree that it may be exercised later.

(2) An agreement under which the short-term right to reject would be lost before the time limit passes is not binding on the consumer.

(3) The time limit for exercising the short-term right to reject (unless subsection (4) applies) is the end of 30 days beginning with the first day after these have all happened—

(a) ownership or (in the case of a contract for the hire of goods, a hirepurchase agreement or a conditional sales contract) possession of the goods has been transferred to the consumer,

(b) the goods have been delivered, and

(c) where the contract requires the trader to install the goods or take other action to enable the consumer to use them, the trader has notified the consumer that the action has been taken.

(4) If any of the goods are of a kind that can reasonably be expected to perish after a shorter period, the time limit for exercising the short-term right to reject in relation to those goods is the end of that shorter period (but without affecting the time limit in relation to goods that are not of that kind).

(5) Subsections (3) and (4) do not prevent the consumer exercising the short-term right to reject before something mentioned in subsection (3)(a), (b) or (c) has happened.

(6) If the consumer requests or agrees to the repair or replacement of goods, the period mentioned in subsection (3) or (4) stops running for the length of the waiting period.

(7) If goods supplied by the trader in response to that request or agreement do not conform to the contract, the time limit for exercising the short-term right to reject is then either—

(a) 7 days after the waiting period ends, or

(b) if later, the original time limit for exercising that right, extended by the waiting period.

(8) The waiting period—

(a) begins with the day the consumer requests or agrees to the repair or replacement of the goods, and

(b) ends with the day on which the consumer receives goods supplied by the trader in response to the request or agreement.

23 Right to repair or replacement

(1) This section applies if the consumer has the right to repair or replacement (see section 19(3) and (4)).

(2) If the consumer requires the trader to repair or replace the goods, the trader must—

(a) do so within a reasonable time and without significant inconvenience to the consumer, and

(b) bear any necessary costs incurred in doing so (including in particular the cost of any labour, materials or postage).

(3) The consumer cannot require the trader to repair or replace the goods if that remedy (the repair or the replacement)—

(a) is impossible, or

(b) is disproportionate compared to the other of those remedies.

(4) Either of those remedies is disproportionate compared to the other if it imposes costs on the trader which, compared to those imposed by the other, are unreasonable, taking into account—

(a) the value which the goods would have if they conformed to the contract,

(b) the significance of the lack of conformity, and

(c) whether the other remedy could be effected without significant inconvenience to the consumer.

(5) Any question as to what is a reasonable time or significant inconvenience is to be determined taking account of—

(a) the nature of the goods, and

(b) the purpose for which the goods were acquired.

(6) A consumer who requires or agrees to the repair of goods cannot require the trader to replace them, or exercise the short-term right to reject, without giving the trader a reasonable time to repair them (unless giving the trader that time would cause significant inconvenience to the consumer).

(7) A consumer who requires or agrees to the replacement of goods cannot require the trader to repair them, or exercise the short-term right to reject, without giving the trader a reasonable time to replace them (unless giving the trader that time would cause significant inconvenience to the consumer).

(8) In this Chapter, 'repair' in relation to goods that do not conform to a contract, means making them conform.

24 Right to price reduction or final right to reject

(1) The right to a price reduction is the right—

(a) to require the trader to reduce by an appropriate amount the price the consumer is required to pay under the contract, or anything else the consumer is required to transfer under the contract, and

(b) to receive a refund from the trader for anything already paid or otherwise transferred by the consumer above the reduced amount.

(2) The amount of the reduction may, where appropriate, be the full amount of the price or whatever the consumer is required to transfer.

(3) Section 20(10) to (17) applies to a consumer's right to receive a refund under subsection (1)(b).

(4) The right to a price reduction does not apply—

(a) if what the consumer is (before the reduction) required to transfer under the contract, whether or not already transferred, cannot be divided up so as to enable the trader to receive or retain only the reduced amount, or

(b) if anything to which section 20(12) applies cannot be given back in its original state.

(5) A consumer who has the right to a price reduction and the final right to reject may only exercise one (not both), and may only do so in one of these situations—

(a) after one repair or one replacement, the goods do not conform to the contract;

(b) because of section 23(3) the consumer can require neither repair nor replacement of the goods; or

(c) the consumer has required the trader to repair or replace the goods, but the trader is in breach of the requirement of section 23(2)(a) to do so within a reasonable time and without significant inconvenience to the consumer.

(6) There has been a repair or replacement for the purposes of subsection (5)(a) if—

(a) the consumer has requested or agreed to repair or replacement of the goods (whether in relation to one fault or more than one), and

(b) the trader has delivered goods to the consumer, or made goods available to the consumer, in response to the request or agreement.

(7) For the purposes of subsection (6) goods that the trader arranges to repair at the consumer's premises are made available when the trader indicates that the repairs are finished.

(8) If the consumer exercises the final right to reject, any refund to the consumer may be reduced by a deduction for use, to take account of the use the consumer has had of the goods in the period since they were delivered, but this is subject to subsections (9) and (10).

(9) No deduction may be made to take account of use in any period when the consumer had the goods only because the trader failed to collect them at an agreed time.

(10) No deduction may be made if the final right to reject is exercised in the first 6 months (see subsection (11)), unless—

(a) the goods consist of a motor vehicle, or

(b) the goods are of a description specified by order made by the Secretary of State by statutory instrument.

(11) In subsection (10) the first 6 months means 6 months beginning with the first day after these have all happened—

(a) ownership or (in the case of a contract for the hire of goods, a hirepurchase agreement or a conditional sales contract) possession of the goods has been transferred to the consumer,

(b) the goods have been delivered, and

(c) where the contract requires the trader to install the goods or take other action to enable the consumer to use them, the trader has notified the consumer that the action has been taken.

(12) In subsection (10)(a) 'motor vehicle'—

(a) in relation to Great Britain, has the same meaning as in the Road Traffic Act 1988 (see sections 185 to 194 of that Act);

(b) in relation to Northern Ireland, has the same meaning as in the Road Traffic (Northern Ireland) Order 1995 (SI 1995/2994 (NI 18)) (see Parts I and V of that Order).

(13) But a vehicle is not a motor vehicle for the purposes of subsection (10)(a) if it is constructed or adapted—

(a) for the use of a person suffering from some physical defect or disability, and

(b) so that it may only be used by one such person at any one time.

(14) An order under subsection (10)(b)—

(a) may be made only if the Secretary of State is satisfied that it is appropriate to do so because of significant detriment caused to traders as a result of the application of subsection (10) in relation to goods of the description specified by the order;

(b) may contain transitional or transitory provision or savings.

(15) No order may be made under subsection (10)(b) unless a draft of the statutory instrument containing it has been laid before, and approved by a resolution of, each House of Parliament.

Other rules about remedies under goods contracts

25 Delivery of wrong quantity

(1) Where the trader delivers to the consumer a quantity of goods less than the trader contracted to supply, the consumer may reject them, but if the consumer accepts them the consumer must pay for them at the contract rate.

(2) Where the trader delivers to the consumer a quantity of goods larger than the trader contracted to supply, the consumer may accept the goods included in the contract and reject the rest, or may reject all of the goods.

(3) Where the trader delivers to the consumer a quantity of goods larger than the trader contracted to supply and the consumer accepts all of the goods delivered, the consumer must pay for them at the contract rate.

(4) Where the consumer is entitled to reject goods under this section, any entitlement for the consumer to treat the contract as at an end depends on the terms of the contract and the circumstances of the case.

(5) The consumer rejects goods under this section by indicating to the trader that the consumer is rejecting the goods.

(6) The indication may be something the consumer says or does, but it must be clear enough to be understood by the trader.

(7) Subsections (1) to (3) do not prevent the consumer claiming damages, where it is open to the consumer to do so.

(8) This section is subject to any usage of trade, special agreement, or course of dealing between the parties.

26 Instalment deliveries

(1) Under a contract to supply goods, the consumer is not bound to accept delivery of the goods by instalments, unless that has been agreed between the consumer and the trader.

(2) The following provisions apply if the contract provides for the goods to be delivered by stated instalments, which are to be separately paid for.

(3) If the trader makes defective deliveries in respect of one or more instalments, the consumer, apart from any entitlement to claim damages, may be (but is not necessarily) entitled—

(a) to exercise the short-term right to reject or the right to reject under section 19(6) (as applicable) in respect of the whole contract, or

(b) to reject the goods in an instalment.

(4) Whether paragraph (a) or (b) of subsection (3) (or neither) applies to a consumer depends on the terms of the contract and the circumstances of the case.

(5) In subsection (3), making defective deliveries does not include failing to make a delivery in accordance with section 28.

(6) If the consumer neglects or refuses to take delivery of or pay for one or more instalments, the trader may—

(a) be entitled to treat the whole contract as at an end, or

(b) if it is a severable breach, have a claim for damages but not a right to treat the whole contract as at an end.

(7) Whether paragraph (a) or (b) of subsection (6) (or neither) applies to a trader depends on the terms of the contract and the circumstances of the case.

27 Consignation, or payment into court, in Scotland

(1) Subsection (2) applies where—

(a) a consumer has not rejected goods which the consumer could have rejected for breach of a term mentioned in section 19(3) or (6),

(b) the consumer has chosen to treat the breach as giving rise only to a claim for damages or to a right to rely on the breach against a claim by the trader for the price of the goods, and

(c) the trader has begun proceedings in court to recover the price or has brought a counter-claim for the price.

(2) The court may require the consumer—

(a) to consign, or pay into court, the price of the goods, or part of the price, or

(b) to provide some other reasonable security for payment of the price.

Other rules about goods contracts

28 Delivery of goods

(1) This section applies to any sales contract.

(2) Unless the trader and the consumer have agreed otherwise, the contract is to be treated as including a term that the trader must deliver the goods to the consumer.

(3) Unless there is an agreed time or period, the contract is to be treated as including a term that the trader must deliver the goods—

(a) without undue delay, and

(b) in any event, not more than 30 days after the day on which the contract is entered into.

(4) In this section—

(a) an 'agreed' time or period means a time or period agreed by the trader and the consumer for delivery of the goods;

(b) if there is an obligation to deliver the goods at the time the contract is entered into, that time counts as the 'agreed' time.

(5) Subsections (6) and (7) apply if the trader does not deliver the goods in accordance with subsection (3) or at the agreed time or within the agreed period.

(6) If the circumstances are that—

(a) the trader has refused to deliver the goods,

(b) delivery of the goods at the agreed time or within the agreed period is essential taking into account all the relevant circumstances at the time the contract was entered into, or

(c) the consumer told the trader before the contract was entered into that delivery in accordance with subsection (3), or at the agreed time or within the agreed period, was essential,

then the consumer may treat the contract as at an end.

(7) In any other circumstances, the consumer may specify a period that is appropriate in the circumstances and require the trader to deliver the goods before the end of that period.

(8) If the consumer specifies a period under subsection (7) but the goods are not delivered within that period, then the consumer may treat the contract as at an end.

(9) If the consumer treats the contract as at an end under subsection (6) or (8), the trader must without undue delay reimburse all payments made under the contract.

(10) If subsection (6) or (8) applies but the consumer does not treat the contract as at an end—

(a) that does not prevent the consumer from cancelling the order for any of the goods or rejecting goods that have been delivered, and

(b) the trader must without undue delay reimburse all payments made under the contract in respect of any goods for which the consumer cancels the order or which the consumer rejects.

(11) If any of the goods form a commercial unit, the consumer cannot reject or

cancel the order for some of those goods without also rejecting or cancelling the order for the rest of them.

(12) A unit is a 'commercial unit' if division of the unit would materially impair the value of the goods or the character of the unit.

(13) This section does not prevent the consumer seeking other remedies where it is open to the consumer to do so.

(14) See section 2(5) and (6) for the application of this section where goods are sold at public auction.

29 Passing of risk

(1) A sales contract is to be treated as including the following provisions as terms.

(2) The goods remain at the trader's risk until they come into the physical possession of—

(a) the consumer, or

(b) a person identified by the consumer to take possession of the goods.

(3) Subsection (2) does not apply if the goods are delivered to a carrier who—

(a) is commissioned by the consumer to deliver the goods, and

(b) is not a carrier the trader named as an option for the consumer.

(4) In that case the goods are at the consumer's risk on and after delivery to the carrier.

(5) Subsection (4) does not affect any liability of the carrier to the consumer in respect of the goods.

(6) See section 2(5) and (6) for the application of this section where goods are sold at public auction.

30 Goods under guarantee

(1) This section applies where—

(a) there is a contract to supply goods, and

(b) there is a guarantee in relation to the goods.

(2) 'Guarantee' here means an undertaking to the consumer given without extra charge by a person acting in the course of the person's business (the 'guarantor') that, if the goods do not meet the specifications set out in the guarantee statement or in any associated advertising—

(a) the consumer will be reimbursed for the price paid for the goods, or

(b) the goods will be repaired, replaced or handled in any way.

(3) The guarantee takes effect, at the time the goods are delivered, as a contractual obligation owed by the guarantor under the conditions set out in the guarantee statement and in any associated advertising.

(4) The guarantor must ensure that—

(a) the guarantee sets out in plain and intelligible language the contents of the guarantee and the essential particulars for making claims under the guarantee,

(b) the guarantee states that the consumer has statutory rights in relation to the goods and that those rights are not affected by the guarantee, and

(c) where the goods are offered within the territory of the United Kingdom, the guarantee is written in English.

(5) The contents of the guarantee to be set out in it include, in particular—

(a) the name and address of the guarantor, and

(b) the duration and territorial scope of the guarantee.

(6) The guarantor and any other person who offers to supply to consumers the goods which are the subject of the guarantee must, on request by the consumer, make the guarantee available to the consumer within a reasonable time, in writing and in a form accessible to the consumer.

(7) What is a reasonable time is a question of fact.

(8) If a person fails to comply with a requirement of this section, the enforce-

ment authority may apply to the court for an injunction or (in Scotland) an order of specific implement against that person requiring that person to comply.

(9) On an application the court may grant an injunction or (in Scotland) an order of specific implement on such terms as it thinks appropriate.

(10) In this section—

'court' means—

(a) in relation to England and Wales, the High Court or the county court,

(b) in relation to Northern Ireland, the High Court or a county court, and

(c) in relation to Scotland, the Court of Session or the sheriff;

'enforcement authority' means—

(a) the Competition and Markets Authority,

(b) a local weights and measures authority in Great Britain, and

(c) the Department of Enterprise, Trade and Investment in Northern Ireland.

Can a trader contract out of statutory rights and remedies under a goods contract?

31 Liability that cannot be excluded or restricted

(1) A term of a contract to supply goods is not binding on the consumer to the extent that it would exclude or restrict the trader's liability arising under any of these provisions—

(a) section 9 (goods to be of satisfactory quality);

(b) section 10 (goods to be fit for particular purpose);

(c) section 11 (goods to be as described);

(d) section 12 (other pre-contract information included in contract);

(e) section 13 (goods to match a sample);

(f) section 14 (goods to match a model seen or examined);

(g) section 15 (installation as part of conformity of the goods with the contract);

(h) section 16 (goods not conforming to contract if digital content does not conform);

(i) section 17 (trader to have right to supply the goods etc);

(j) section 28 (delivery of goods);

(k) section 29 (passing of risk).

(2) That also means that a term of a contract to supply goods is not binding on the consumer to the extent that it would—

(a) exclude or restrict a right or remedy in respect of a liability under a provision listed in subsection (1),

(b) make such a right or remedy or its enforcement subject to a restrictive or onerous condition,

(c) allow a trader to put a person at a disadvantage as a result of pursuing such a right or remedy, or

(d) exclude or restrict rules of evidence or procedure.

(3) The reference in subsection (1) to excluding or restricting a liability also includes preventing an obligation or duty arising or limiting its extent.

(4) An agreement in writing to submit present or future differences to arbitration is not to be regarded as excluding or restricting any liability for the purposes of this section.

(5) Subsection (1)(i), and subsection (2) so far as it relates to liability under section 17, do not apply to a term of a contract for the hire of goods.

(6) But an express term of a contract for the hire of goods is not binding on the consumer to the extent that it would exclude or restrict a term that section 17 requires to be treated as included in the contract, unless it is inconsistent with that term (and see also section 62 (requirement for terms to be fair)).

(7) See Schedule 3 for provision about the enforcement of this section.

32 Contracts applying law of [a country other than the UK]

(1) If—

(a) the law of a country or territory other than [the United Kingdom or any part of the United Kingdom] is chosen by the parties to be applicable to a sales contract, but

(b) the sales contract has a close connection with the United Kingdom,

this Chapter, except the provisions in subsection (2), applies despite that choice.

(2) The exceptions are—

(a) sections 11(4) and (5) and 12;

(b) sections 28 and 29;

(c) section 31(1)(d), (j) and (k).

(3) For cases where those provisions apply, or where the law applicable has not been chosen [. . .], see Regulation (EC) No 593/2008 of the European Parliament and of the Council of 17 June 2008 on the law applicable to contractual obligations [as that Regulation has effect as [assimilated direct] legislation (including that Regulation as applied by regulation 5 of the Law Applicable to Contractual Obligations (England and Wales and Northern Ireland) Regulations 2009 and regulation 4 of the Law Applicable to Contractual Obligations (Scotland) Regulations 2009), unless the case is one in respect of which Regulation (EC) No 593/2008 has effect by virtue of Article 66 of the EU withdrawal agreement, in which case see that Regulation as it has effect by virtue of that Article.]

CHAPTER 3
Digital content

What digital content contracts are covered?

33 Contracts covered by this Chapter

(1) This Chapter applies to a contract for a trader to supply digital content to a consumer, if it is supplied or to be supplied for a price paid by the consumer.

(2) This Chapter also applies to a contract for a trader to supply digital content to a consumer, if—

(a) it is supplied free with goods or services or other digital content for which the consumer pays a price, and

(b) it is not generally available to consumers unless they have paid a price for it or for goods or services or other digital content.

(3) The references in subsections (1) and (2) to the consumer paying a price include references to the consumer using, by way of payment, any facility for which money has been paid.

(4) A trader does not supply digital content to a consumer for the purposes of this Part merely because the trader supplies a service by which digital content reaches the consumer.

(5) The Secretary of State may by order provide for this Chapter to apply to other contracts for a trader to supply digital content to a consumer, if the Secretary of State is satisfied that it is appropriate to do so because of significant detriment caused to consumers under contracts of the kind to which the order relates.

(6) An order under subsection (5)—

(a) may, in particular, amend this Act;

(b) may contain transitional or transitory provision or savings.

(7) A contract to which this Chapter applies is referred to in this Part as a 'contract to supply digital content'.

(8) This section, other than subsection (4), does not limit the application of section 46.

(9) The power to make an order under subsection (5) is exercisable by statutory instrument.

(10) No order may be made under subsection (5) unless a draft of the statutory

instrument containing it has been laid before, and approved by a resolution of, each House of Parliament.

What statutory rights are there under a digital content contract?

34 Digital content to be of satisfactory quality

(1) Every contract to supply digital content is to be treated as including a term that the quality of the digital content is satisfactory.

(2) The quality of digital content is satisfactory if it meets the standard that a reasonable person would consider satisfactory, taking account of—

(a) any description of the digital content,

(b) the price mentioned in section 33(1) or (2)(b) (if relevant), and

(c) all the other relevant circumstances (see subsection (5)).

(3) The quality of digital content includes its state and condition; and the following aspects (among others) are in appropriate cases aspects of the quality of digital content—

(a) fitness for all the purposes for which digital content of that kind is usually supplied;

(b) freedom from minor defects;

(c) safety;

(d) durability.

(4) The term mentioned in subsection (1) does not cover anything which makes the quality of the digital content unsatisfactory—

(a) which is specifically drawn to the consumer's attention before the contract is made,

(b) where the consumer examines the digital content before the contract is made, which that examination ought to reveal, or

(c) where the consumer examines a trial version before the contract is made, which would have been apparent on a reasonable examination of the trial version.

(5) The relevant circumstances mentioned in subsection (2)(c) include any public statement about the specific characteristics of the digital content made by the trader, the producer or any representative of the trader or the producer.

(6) That includes, in particular, any public statement made in advertising or labelling.

(7) But a public statement is not a relevant circumstance for the purposes of subsection (2)(c) if the trader shows that—

(a) when the contract was made, the trader was not, and could not reasonably have been, aware of the statement,

(b) before the contract was made, the statement had been publicly withdrawn or, to the extent that it contained anything which was incorrect or misleading, it had been publicly corrected, or

(c) the consumer's decision to contract for the digital content could not have been influenced by the statement.

(8) In a contract to supply digital content a term about the quality of the digital content may be treated as included as a matter of custom.

(9) See section 42 for a consumer's rights if the trader is in breach of a term that this section requires to be treated as included in a contract.

35 Digital content to be fit for particular purpose

(1) Subsection (3) applies to a contract to supply digital content if before the contract is made the consumer makes known to the trader (expressly or by implication) any particular purpose for which the consumer is contracting for the digital content.

(2) Subsection (3) also applies to a contract to supply digital content if—

(a) the digital content was previously sold by a credit-broker to the trader,

(b) the consideration or part of it is a sum payable by instalments, and

(c) before the contract is made, the consumer makes known to the creditbroker (expressly or by implication) any particular purpose for which the consumer is contracting for the digital content.

(3) The contract is to be treated as including a term that the digital content is reasonably fit for that purpose, whether or not that is a purpose for which digital content of that kind is usually supplied.

(4) Subsection (3) does not apply if the circumstances show that the consumer does not rely, or it is unreasonable for the consumer to rely, on the skill or judgment of the trader or credit-broker.

(5) A contract to supply digital content may be treated as making provision about the fitness of the digital content for a particular purpose as a matter of custom.

(6) See section 42 for a consumer's rights if the trader is in breach of a term that this section requires to be treated as included in a contract.

36 Digital content to be as described

(1) Every contract to supply digital content is to be treated as including a term that the digital content will match any description of it given by the trader to the consumer.

(2) Where the consumer examines a trial version before the contract is made, it is not sufficient that the digital content matches (or is better than) the trial version if the digital content does not also match any description of it given by the trader to the consumer.

(3) Any information that is provided by the trader about the digital content that is information mentioned in paragraph (a), (j) or (k) of Schedule 1 or paragraph (a), (v) or (w) of Schedule 2 (main characteristics, functionality and compatibility) to the Consumer Contracts (Information, Cancellation and Additional Charges) Regulations 2013 (SI 2013/3134) is to be treated as included as a term of the contract.

(4) A change to any of that information, made before entering into the contract or later, is not effective unless expressly agreed between the consumer and the trader.

(5) See section 42 for a consumer's rights if the trader is in breach of a term that this section requires to be treated as included in a contract.

37 Other pre-contract information included in contract

(1) This section applies to any contract to supply digital content.

(2) Where regulation 9, 10 or 13 of the Consumer Contracts (Information, Cancellation and Additional Charges) Regulations 2013 (SI 2013/3134) required the trader to provide information to the consumer before the contract became binding, any of that information that was provided by the trader other than information about the digital content and mentioned in paragraph (a), (j) or (k) of Schedule 1 or paragraph (a), (v) or (w) of Schedule 2 to the Regulations (main characteristics, functionality and compatibility) is to be treated as included as a term of the contract.

(3) A change to any of that information, made before entering into the contract or later, is not effective unless expressly agreed between the consumer and the trader.

(4) See section 42 for a consumer's rights if the trader is in breach of a term that this section requires to be treated as included in a contract.

38 No other requirement to treat term about quality or fitness as included

(1) Except as provided by sections 34 and 35, a contract to supply digital content is not to be treated as including any term about the quality of the digital content or its fitness for any particular purpose, unless the term is expressly included in the contract.

(2) Subsection (1) is subject to provision made by any other enactment, whenever passed or made.

39 Supply by transmission and facilities for continued transmission

(1) Subsection (2) applies where there is a contract to supply digital content and the consumer's access to the content on a device requires its transmission to the device under arrangements initiated by the trader.

(2) For the purposes of this Chapter, the digital content is supplied—

(a) when the content reaches the device, or

(b) if earlier, when the content reaches another trader chosen by the consumer to supply, under a contract with the consumer, a service by which digital content reaches the device.

(3) Subsections (5) to (7) apply where—

(a) there is a contract to supply digital content, and

(b) after the trader (T) has supplied the digital content, the consumer is to have access under the contract to a processing facility under arrangements made by T.

(4) A processing facility is a facility by which T or another trader will receive digital content from the consumer and transmit digital content to the consumer (whether or not other features are to be included under the contract).

(5) The contract is to be treated as including a term that the processing facility (with any feature that the facility is to include under the contract) must be available to the consumer for a reasonable time, unless a time is specified in the contract.

(6) The following provisions apply to all digital content transmitted to the consumer on each occasion under the facility, while it is provided under the contract, as they apply to the digital content first supplied—

(a) section 34 (quality);

(b) section 35 (fitness for a particular purpose);

(c) section 36 (description).

(7) Breach of a term treated as included under subsection (5) has the same effect as breach of a term treated as included under those sections (see section 42).

40 Quality, fitness and description of content supplied subject to modifications

(1) Where under a contract a trader supplies digital content to a consumer subject to the right of the trader or a third party to modify the digital content, the following provisions apply in relation to the digital content as modified as they apply in relation to the digital content as supplied under the contract—

(a) section 34 (quality);

(b) section 35 (fitness for a particular purpose);

(c) section 36 (description).

(2) Subsection (1)(c) does not prevent the trader from improving the features of, or adding new features to, the digital content, as long as—

(a) the digital content continues to match the description of it given by the trader to the consumer, and

(b) the digital content continues to conform to the information provided by the trader as mentioned in subsection (3) of section 36, subject to any change to that information that has been agreed in accordance with subsection (4) of that section.

(3) A claim on the grounds that digital content does not conform to a term described in any of the sections listed in subsection (1) as applied by that subsection is to be treated as arising at the time when the digital content was supplied under the contract and not the time when it is modified.

41 Trader's right to supply digital content

(1) Every contract to supply digital content is to be treated as including a term—

(a) in relation to any digital content which is supplied under the contract and which the consumer has paid for, that the trader has the right to supply that content to the consumer;

(b) in relation to any digital content which the trader agrees to supply under the contract and which the consumer has paid for, that the trader will have the right to supply it to the consumer at the time when it is to be supplied.

(2) See section 42 for a consumer's rights if the trader is in breach of a term that this section requires to be treated as included in a contract.

What remedies are there if statutory rights under a digital content contract are not met?

42 Consumer's rights to enforce terms about digital content

(1) In this section and section 43 references to digital content conforming to a contract are references to the digital content conforming to the terms described in sections 34, 35 and 36.

(2) If the digital content does not conform to the contract, the consumer's rights (and the provisions about them and when they are available) are—

(a) the right to repair or replacement (see section 43);

(b) the right to a price reduction (see section 44).

(3) Section 16 also applies if an item including the digital content is supplied.

(4) If the trader is in breach of a term that section 37 requires to be treated as included in the contract, the consumer has the right to recover from the trader the amount of any costs incurred by the consumer as a result of the breach, up to the amount of the price paid for the digital content or for any facility within section 33(3) used by the consumer.

(5) If the trader is in breach of the term that section 41(1) (right to supply the content) requires to be treated as included in the contract, the consumer has the right to a refund (see section 45 for provisions about that right and when it is available).

(6) This Chapter does not prevent the consumer seeking other remedies for a breach of a term to which any of subsections (2), (4) or (5) applies, instead of or in addition to a remedy referred to there (but not so as to recover twice for the same loss).

(7) Those other remedies include any of the following that is open to the consumer in the circumstances—

(a) claiming damages;

(b) seeking to recover money paid where the consideration for payment of the money has failed;

(c) seeking specific performance;

(d) seeking an order for specific implement;

(e) relying on the breach against a claim by the trader for the price.

(8) It is not open to the consumer to treat the contract as at an end for breach of a term to which any of subsections (2), (4) or (5) applies.

(9) For the purposes of subsection (2), digital content which does not conform to the contract at any time within the period of six months beginning with the day on which it was supplied must be taken not to have conformed to the contract when it was supplied.

(10) Subsection (9) does not apply if—

(a) it is established that the digital content did conform to the contract when it was supplied, or

(b) its application is incompatible with the nature of the digital content or with how it fails to conform to the contract.

43 Right to repair or replacement

(1) This section applies if the consumer has the right to repair or replacement.

(2) If the consumer requires the trader to repair or replace the digital content, the trader must—

(a) do so within a reasonable time and without significant inconvenience to the consumer; and

(b) bear any necessary costs incurred in doing so (including in particular the cost of any labour, materials or postage).

(3) The consumer cannot require the trader to repair or replace the digital content if that remedy (the repair or the replacement)—

(a) is impossible, or

(b) is disproportionate compared to the other of those remedies.

(4) Either of those remedies is disproportionate compared to the other if it imposes costs on the trader which, compared to those imposed by the other, are unreasonable, taking into account—

(a) the value which the digital content would have if it conformed to the contract,

(b) the significance of the lack of conformity, and

(c) whether the other remedy could be effected without significant inconvenience to the consumer.

(5) Any question as to what is a reasonable time or significant inconvenience is to be determined taking account of—

(a) the nature of the digital content, and

(b) the purpose for which the digital content was obtained or accessed.

(6) A consumer who requires or agrees to the repair of digital content cannot require the trader to replace it without giving the trader a reasonable time to repair it (unless giving the trader that time would cause significant inconvenience to the consumer).

(7) A consumer who requires or agrees to the replacement of digital content cannot require the trader to repair it without giving the trader a reasonable time to replace it (unless giving the trader that time would cause significant inconvenience to the consumer).

(8) In this Chapter, 'repair' in relation to digital content that does not conform to a contract, means making it conform.

44 Right to price reduction

(1) The right to a price reduction is the right to require the trader to reduce the price to the consumer by an appropriate amount (including the right to receive a refund for anything already paid above the reduced amount).

(2) The amount of the reduction may, where appropriate, be the full amount of the price.

(3) A consumer who has that right may only exercise it in one of these situations—

(a) because of section 43(3)(a) the consumer can require neither repair nor replacement of the digital content, or

(b) the consumer has required the trader to repair or replace the digital content, but the trader is in breach of the requirement of section 43(2)(a) to do so within a reasonable time and without significant inconvenience to the consumer.

(4) A refund under this section must be given without undue delay, and in any event within 14 days beginning with the day on which the trader agrees that the consumer is entitled to a refund.

(5) The trader must give the refund using the same means of payment as the consumer used to pay for the digital content, unless the consumer expressly agrees otherwise.

(6) The trader must not impose any fee on the consumer in respect of the refund.

45 Right to a refund

(1) The right to a refund gives the consumer the right to receive a refund from the trader of all money paid by the consumer for the digital content (subject to subsection (2)).

(2) If the breach giving the consumer the right to a refund affects only some of the digital content supplied under the contract, the right to a refund does not extend to any part of the price attributable to digital content that is not affected by the breach.

(3) A refund must be given without undue delay, and in any event within 14 days beginning with the day on which the trader agrees that the consumer is entitled to a refund.

(4) The trader must give the refund using the same means of payment as the consumer used to pay for the digital content, unless the consumer expressly agrees otherwise.

(5) The trader must not impose any fee on the consumer in respect of the refund.

Compensation for damage to device or to other digital content

46 Remedy for damage to device or to other digital content

(1) This section applies if—

(a) a trader supplies digital content to a consumer under a contract,

(b) the digital content causes damage to a device or to other digital content,

(c) the device or digital content that is damaged belongs to the consumer, and

(d) the damage is of a kind that would not have occurred if the trader had exercised reasonable care and skill.

(2) If the consumer requires the trader to provide a remedy under this section, the trader must either—

(a) repair the damage in accordance with subsection (3), or

(b) compensate the consumer for the damage with an appropriate payment.

(3) To repair the damage in accordance with this subsection, the trader must—

(a) repair the damage within a reasonable time and without significant inconvenience to the consumer, and

(b) bear any necessary costs incurred in repairing the damage (including in particular the cost of any labour, materials or postage).

(4) Any question as to what is a reasonable time or significant inconvenience is to be determined taking account of—

(a) the nature of the device or digital content that is damaged, and

(b) the purpose for which it is used by the consumer.

(5) A compensation payment under this section must be made without undue delay, and in any event within 14 days beginning with the day on which the trader agrees that the consumer is entitled to the payment.

(6) The trader must not impose any fee on the consumer in respect of the payment.

(7) A consumer with a right to a remedy under this section may bring a claim in civil proceedings to enforce that right.

(8) The Limitation Act 1980 and the Limitation (Northern Ireland) Order 1989 (SI 1989/1339 (NI 11)) apply to a claim under this section as if it were an action founded on simple contract.

(9) The Prescription and Limitation (Scotland) Act 1973 applies to a right to a remedy under this section as if it were an obligation to which section 6 of that Act applies.

Can a trader contract out of statutory rights and remedies under a digital content contract?

47 Liability that cannot be excluded or restricted

(1) A term of a contract to supply digital content is not binding on the consumer to the extent that it would exclude or restrict the trader's liability arising under any of these provisions—

(a) section 34 (digital content to be of satisfactory quality),
(b) section 35 (digital content to be fit for particular purpose),
(c) section 36 (digital content to be as described),
(d) section 37 (other pre-contract information included in contract), or
(e) section 41 (trader's right to supply digital content).

(2) That also means that a term of a contract to supply digital content is not binding on the consumer to the extent that it would—

(a) exclude or restrict a right or remedy in respect of a liability under a provision listed in subsection (1),

(b) make such a right or remedy or its enforcement subject to a restrictive or onerous condition,

(c) allow a trader to put a person at a disadvantage as a result of pursuing such a right or remedy, or

(d) exclude or restrict rules of evidence or procedure.

(3) The reference in subsection (1) to excluding or restricting a liability also includes preventing an obligation or duty arising or limiting its extent.

(4) An agreement in writing to submit present or future differences to arbitration is not to be regarded as excluding or restricting any liability for the purposes of this section.

(5) See Schedule 3 for provision about the enforcement of this section.

(6) For provision limiting the ability of a trader under a contract within section 46 to exclude or restrict the trader's liability under that section, see section 62.

CHAPTER 4
Services

What services contracts are covered?

48 Contracts covered by this Chapter

(1) This Chapter applies to a contract for a trader to supply a service to a consumer.

(2) That does not include a contract of employment or apprenticeship.

(3) In relation to Scotland, this Chapter does not apply to a gratuitous contract.

[(3A This Chapter does not apply to anything that is governed by Regulation (EU) No 181/2011 of the European Parliament and of the Council of 16 February 2011 concerning the rights of passengers in bus and coach transport and amending Regulation (EC) No 2006/2004.]

(4) A contract to which this Chapter applies is referred to in this Part as a 'contract to supply a service'.

(5) The Secretary of State may by order made by statutory instrument provide that a provision of this Chapter does not apply in relation to a service of a description specified in the order.

(6) The power in subsection (5) includes power to provide that a provision of this Chapter does not apply in relation to a service of a description specified in the order in the circumstances so specified.

(7) An order under subsection (5) may contain transitional or transitory provision or savings.

(8) No order may be made under subsection (5) unless a draft of the statutory instrument containing it has been laid before, and approved by a resolution of, each House of Parliament.

What statutory rights are there under a services contract?

49 Service to be performed with reasonable care and skill

(1) Every contract to supply a service is to be treated as including a term that the trader must perform the service with reasonable care and skill.

(2) See section 54 for a consumer's rights if the trader is in breach of a term that this section requires to be treated as included in a contract.

50 Information about the trader or service to be binding

(1) Every contract to supply a service is to be treated as including as a term of the contract anything that is said or written to the consumer, by or on behalf of the trader, about the trader or the service, if—

(a) it is taken into account by the consumer when deciding to enter into the contract, or

(b) it is taken into account by the consumer when making any decision about the service after entering into the contract.

(2) Anything taken into account by the consumer as mentioned in subsection (1)(a) or (b) is subject to—

(a) anything that qualified it and was said or written to the consumer by the trader on the same occasion, and

(b) any change to it that has been expressly agreed between the consumer and the trader (before entering into the contract or later).

(3) Without prejudice to subsection (1), any information provided by the trader in accordance with regulation 9, 10 or 13 of the Consumer Contracts (Information, Cancellation and Additional Charges) Regulations 2013 (SI 2013/3134) is to be treated as included as a term of the contract.

(4) A change to any of the information mentioned in subsection (3), made before entering into the contract or later, is not effective unless expressly agreed between the consumer and the trader.

(5) See section 54 for a consumer's rights if the trader is in breach of a term that this section requires to be treated as included in a contract.

51 Reasonable price to be paid for a service

(1) This section applies to a contract to supply a service if—

(a) the consumer has not paid a price or other consideration for the service,

(b) the contract does not expressly fix a price or other consideration, and does not say how it is to be fixed, and

(c) anything that is to be treated under section 50 as included in the contract does not fix a price or other consideration either.

(2) In that case the contract is to be treated as including a term that the consumer must pay a reasonable price for the service, and no more.

(3) What is a reasonable price is a question of fact.

52 Service to be performed within a reasonable time

(1) This section applies to a contract to supply a service, if—

(a) the contract does not expressly fix the time for the service to be performed, and does not say how it is to be fixed, and

(b) information that is to be treated under section 50 as included in the contract does not fix the time either.

(2) In that case the contract is to be treated as including a term that the trader must perform the service within a reasonable time.

(3) What is a reasonable time is a question of fact.

(4) See section 54 for a consumer's rights if the trader is in breach of a term that this section requires to be treated as included in a contract.

53 Relation to other law on contract terms

(1) Nothing in this Chapter affects any enactment or rule of law that imposes a stricter duty on the trader.

(2) This Chapter is subject to any other enactment which defines or restricts the rights, duties or liabilities arising in connection with a service of any description.

What remedies are there if statutory rights under a services contract are not met?

54 Consumer's rights to enforce terms about services

(1) The consumer's rights under this section and sections 55 and 56 do not affect any rights that the contract provides for, if those are not inconsistent.

(2) In this section and section 55 a reference to a service conforming to a contract is a reference to—

(a) the service being performed in accordance with section 49, or

(b) the service conforming to a term that section 50 requires to be treated as included in the contract and that relates to the performance of the service.

(3) If the service does not conform to the contract, the consumer's rights (and the provisions about them and when they are available) are—

(a) the right to require repeat performance (see section 55);

(b) the right to a price reduction (see section 56).

(4) If the trader is in breach of a term that section 50 requires to be treated as included in the contract but that does not relate to the service, the consumer has the right to a price reduction (see section 56 for provisions about that right and when it is available).

(5) If the trader is in breach of what the contract requires under section 52 (performance within a reasonable time), the consumer has the right to a price reduction (see section 56 for provisions about that right and when it is available).

(6) This section and sections 55 and 56 do not prevent the consumer seeking other remedies for a breach of a term to which any of subsections (3) to (5) applies, instead of or in addition to a remedy referred to there (but not so as to recover twice for the same loss).

(7) Those other remedies include any of the following that is open to the consumer in the circumstances—

(a) claiming damages;

(b) seeking to recover money paid where the consideration for payment of the money has failed;

(c) seeking specific performance;

(d) seeking an order for specific implement;

(e) relying on the breach against a claim by the trader under the contract;

(f) exercising a right to treat the contract as at an end.

55 Right to repeat performance

(1) The right to require repeat performance is a right to require the trader to perform the service again, to the extent necessary to complete its performance in conformity with the contract.

(2) If the consumer requires such repeat performance, the trader—

(a) must provide it within a reasonable time and without significant inconvenience to the consumer; and

(b) must bear any necessary costs incurred in doing so (including in particular the cost of any labour or materials).

(3) The consumer cannot require repeat performance if completing performance of the service in conformity with the contract is impossible.

(4) Any question as to what is a reasonable time or significant inconvenience is to be determined taking account of—

(a) the nature of the service, and

(b) the purpose for which the service was to be performed.

56 Right to price reduction

(1) The right to a price reduction is the right to require the trader to reduce the price to the consumer by an appropriate amount (including the right to receive a refund for anything already paid above the reduced amount).

(2) The amount of the reduction may, where appropriate, be the full amount of the price.

(3) A consumer who has that right and the right to require repeat performance is only entitled to a price reduction in one of these situations—

(a) because of section 55(3) the consumer cannot require repeat performance; or

(b) the consumer has required repeat performance, but the trader is in breach of the requirement of section 55(2)(a) to do it within a reasonable time and without significant inconvenience to the consumer.

(4) A refund under this section must be given without undue delay, and in any event within 14 days beginning with the day on which the trader agrees that the consumer is entitled to a refund.

(5) The trader must give the refund using the same means of payment as the consumer used to pay for the service, unless the consumer expressly agrees otherwise.

(6) The trader must not impose any fee on the consumer in respect of the refund.

Can a trader contract out of statutory rights and remedies under a services contract?

57 Liability that cannot be excluded or restricted

(1) A term of a contract to supply services is not binding on the consumer to the extent that it would exclude the trader's liability arising under section 49 (service to be performed with reasonable care and skill).

(2) Subject to section 50(2), a term of a contract to supply services is not binding on the consumer to the extent that it would exclude the trader's liability arising under section 50 (information about trader or service to be binding).

(3) A term of a contract to supply services is not binding on the consumer to the extent that it would restrict the trader's liability arising under any of sections 49 and 50 and, where they apply, sections 51 and 52 (reasonable price and reasonable time), if it would prevent the consumer in an appropriate case from recovering the price paid or the value of any other consideration. (If it would not prevent the consumer from doing so, Part 2 (unfair terms) may apply.)

(4) That also means that a term of a contract to supply services is not binding on the consumer to the extent that it would —

(a) exclude or restrict a right or remedy in respect of a liability under any of sections 49 to 52,

(b) make such a right or remedy or its enforcement subject to a restrictive or onerous condition,

(c) allow a trader to put a person at a disadvantage as a result of pursuing such a right or remedy, or

(d) exclude or restrict rules of evidence or procedure.

(5) The references in subsections (1) to (3) to excluding or restricting a liability also include preventing an obligation or duty arising or limiting its extent.

(6) An agreement in writing to submit present or future differences to arbitration is not to be regarded as excluding or restricting any liability for the purposes of this section.

(7) See Schedule 3 for provision about the enforcement of this section.

CHAPTER 5
General and supplementary provisions

58 Powers of the court

(1) In any proceedings in which a remedy is sought by virtue of section 19(3) or (4), 42(2) or 54(3), the court, in addition to any other power it has, may act under this section.

(2) On the application of the consumer the court may make an order requiring specific performance or, in Scotland, specific implement by the trader of any obligation imposed on the trader by virtue of section 23, 43 or 55.

(3) Subsection (4) applies if—

(a) the consumer claims to exercise a right under the relevant remedies provisions, but

(b) the court decides that those provisions have the effect that exercise of another right is appropriate.

(4) The court may proceed as if the consumer had exercised that other right.

(5) If the consumer has claimed to exercise the final right to reject, the court may order that any reimbursement to the consumer is reduced by a deduction for use, to take account of the use the consumer has had of the goods in the period since they were delivered.

(6) Any deduction for use is limited as set out in section 24(9) and (10).

(7) The court may make an order under this section unconditionally or on such terms and conditions as to damages, payment of the price and otherwise as it thinks just.

(8) The 'relevant remedies provisions' are—

(a) where Chapter 2 applies, sections 23 and 24;

(b) where Chapter 3 applies, sections 43 and 44;

(c) where Chapter 4 applies, sections 55 and 56.

59 Interpretation

(1) These definitions apply in this Part (as well as the key definitions in section 2)—

'conditional sales contract' has the meaning given in section 5(3);

'Consumer Rights Directive' means Directive 2011/83/EU of the European Parliament and of the Council of 25 October 2011 on consumer rights, amending Council Directive 93/13/EEC and Directive 1999/44/EC of the European Parliament and of the Council and repealing Council Directive 85/577/EEC and Directive 97/7/EC of the European Parliament and of the Council;

'credit-broker' means a person acting in the course of a business of credit brokerage carried on by that person;

'credit brokerage' means—

(a) introducing individuals who want to obtain credit to persons carrying on any business so far as it relates to the provision of credit,

(b) introducing individuals who want to obtain goods on hire to persons carrying on a business which comprises or relates to supplying goods under a contract for the hire of goods, or

(c) introducing individuals who want to obtain credit, or to obtain goods on hire, to other persons engaged in credit brokerage;

'delivery' means voluntary transfer of possession from one person to another;

'enactment' includes—

(a) an enactment contained in subordinate legislation within the meaning of the Interpretation Act 1978,

(b) an enactment contained in, or in an instrument made under, a Measure or Act of the National Assembly for Wales,

(c) an enactment contained in, or in an instrument made under, an Act of the Scottish Parliament, and

(d) an enactment contained in, or in an instrument made under, Northern Ireland legislation;

'producer', in relation to goods or digital content, means—

(a) the manufacturer,

(b) the importer into [the United Kingdom], or

(c) any person who purports to be a producer by placing the person's name, trade mark or other distinctive sign on the goods or using it in connection with the digital content.

(2) References in this Part to treating a contract as at an end are to be read in accordance with section 19(13).

60 Changes to other legislation
Schedule 1 (amendments consequential on this Part) has effect.

PART 2
UNFAIR TERMS

What contracts and notices are covered by this Part?

61 Contracts and notices covered by this Part
(1) This Part applies to a contract between a trader and a consumer.
(2) This does not include a contract of employment or apprenticeship.
(3) A contract to which this Part applies is referred to in this Part as a 'consumer contract'.
(4) This Part applies to a notice to the extent that it—
(a) relates to rights or obligations as between a trader and a consumer, or
(b) purports to exclude or restrict a trader's liability to a consumer.
(5) This does not include a notice relating to rights, obligations or liabilities as between an employer and an employee.
(6) It does not matter for the purposes of subsection (4) whether the notice is expressed to apply to a consumer, as long as it is reasonable to assume it is intended to be seen or heard by a consumer.
(7) A notice to which this Part applies is referred to in this Part as a 'consumer notice'.
(8) In this section 'notice' includes an announcement, whether or not in writing, and any other communication or purported communication.

What are the general rules about fairness of contract terms and notices?

62 Requirement for contract terms and notices to be fair
(1) An unfair term of a consumer contract is not binding on the consumer.
(2) An unfair consumer notice is not binding on the consumer.
(3) This does not prevent the consumer from relying on the term or notice if the consumer chooses to do so.
(4) A term is unfair if, contrary to the requirement of good faith, it causes a significant imbalance in the parties' rights and obligations under the contract to the detriment of the consumer.
(5) Whether a term is fair is to be determined—
(a) taking into account the nature of the subject matter of the contract, and
(b) by reference to all the circumstances existing when the term was agreed and to all of the other terms of the contract or of any other contract on which it depends.
(6) A notice is unfair if, contrary to the requirement of good faith, it causes a significant imbalance in the parties' rights and obligations to the detriment of the consumer.
(7) Whether a notice is fair is to be determined—
(a) taking into account the nature of the subject matter of the notice, and
(b) by reference to all the circumstances existing when the rights or obligations to which it relates arose and to the terms of any contract on which it depends.
(8) This section does not affect the operation of—
(a) section 31 (exclusion of liability: goods contracts),
(b) section 47 (exclusion of liability: digital content contracts),
(c) section 57 (exclusion of liability: services contracts), or
(d) section 65 (exclusion of negligence liability).

63 Contract terms which may or must be regarded as unfair

(1) Part 1 of Schedule 2 contains an indicative and non-exhaustive list of terms of consumer contracts that may be regarded as unfair for the purposes of this Part.

(2) Part 1 of Schedule 2 is subject to Part 2 of that Schedule; but a term listed in Part 2 of that Schedule may nevertheless be assessed for fairness under section 62 unless section 64 or 73 applies to it.

(3) The Secretary of State may by order made by statutory instrument amend Schedule 2 so as to add, modify or remove an entry in Part 1 or Part 2 of that Schedule.

(4) An order under subsection (3) may contain transitional or transitory provision or savings.

(5) No order may be made under subsection (3) unless a draft of the statutory instrument containing it has been laid before, and approved by a resolution of, each House of Parliament.

(6) A term of a consumer contract must be regarded as unfair if it has the effect that the consumer bears the burden of proof with respect to compliance by a distance supplier or an intermediary with an obligation under any enactment or rule implementing the Distance Marketing Directive.

(7) In subsection (6)—

'the Distance Marketing Directive' means Directive 2002/65/EC of the European Parliament and of the Council of 23 September 2002 concerning the distance marketing of consumer financial services and amending Council Directive 90/619/EEC and Directives 97/7/EC and 98/27/EC;

'distance supplier' means—

(a) a supplier under a distance contract within the meaning of the Financial Services (Distance Marketing) Regulations 2004 (SI 2004/2095), or

(b) a supplier of unsolicited financial services within the meaning of regulation 15 of those regulations;

'enactment' includes an enactment contained in subordinate legislation within the meaning of the Interpretation Act 1978;

'intermediary' has the same meaning as in the Financial Services (Distance Marketing) Regulations 2004;

'rule' means a rule made by the Financial Conduct Authority or the Prudential Regulation Authority under the Financial Services and Markets Act 2000 or by a designated professional body within the meaning of section 326(2) of that Act.

64 Exclusion from assessment of fairness

(1) A term of a consumer contract may not be assessed for fairness under section 62 to the extent that—

(a) it specifies the main subject matter of the contract, or

(b) the assessment is of the appropriateness of the price payable under the contract by comparison with the goods, digital content or services supplied under it.

(2) Subsection (1) excludes a term from an assessment under section 62 only if it is transparent and prominent.

(3) A term is transparent for the purposes of this Part if it is expressed in plain and intelligible language and (in the case of a written term) is legible.

(4) A term is prominent for the purposes of this section if it is brought to the consumer's attention in such a way that an average consumer would be aware of the term.

(5) In subsection (4) 'average consumer' means a consumer who is reasonably well-informed, observant and circumspect.

(6) This section does not apply to a term of a contract listed in Part 1 of Schedule 2.

65 Bar on exclusion or restriction of negligence liability

(1) A trader cannot by a term of a consumer contract or by a consumer notice exclude or restrict liability for death or personal injury resulting from negligence.

(2) Where a term of a consumer contract, or a consumer notice, purports to exclude or restrict a trader's liability for negligence, a person is not to be taken to have voluntarily accepted any risk merely because the person agreed to or knew about the term or notice.

(3) In this section 'personal injury' includes any disease and any impairment of physical or mental condition.

(4) In this section 'negligence' means the breach of—

(a) any obligation to take reasonable care or exercise reasonable skill in the performance of a contract where the obligation arises from an express or implied term of the contract,

(b) a common law duty to take reasonable care or exercise reasonable skill,

(c) the common duty of care imposed by the Occupiers' Liability Act 1957 or the Occupiers' Liability Act (Northern Ireland) 1957, or

(d) the duty of reasonable care imposed by section 2(1) of the Occupiers' Liability (Scotland) Act 1960.

(5) It is immaterial for the purposes of subsection (4)—

(a) whether a breach of duty or obligation was inadvertent or intentional, or

(b) whether liability for it arises directly or vicariously.

(6) This section is subject to section 66 (which makes provision about the scope of this section).

66 Scope of section 65

(1) Section 65 does not apply to—

(a) any contract so far as it is a contract of insurance, including a contract to pay an annuity on human life, or

(b) any contract so far as it relates to the creation or transfer of an interest in land.

(2) Section 65 does not affect the validity of any discharge or indemnity given by a person in consideration of the receipt by that person of compensation in settlement of any claim the person has.

(3) Section 65 does not—

(a) apply to liability which is excluded or discharged as mentioned in section 4(2)(a) (exception to liability to pay damages to relatives) of the Damages (Scotland) Act 2011, or

(b) affect the operation of section 5 (discharge of liability to pay damages: exception for mesothelioma) of that Act.

(4) Section 65 does not apply to the liability of an occupier of premises to a person who obtains access to the premises for recreational purposes if—

(a) the person suffers loss or damage because of the dangerous state of the premises, and

(b) allowing the person access for those purposes is not within the purposes of the occupier's trade, business, craft or profession.

67 Effect of an unfair term on the rest of a contract

Where a term of a consumer contract is not binding on the consumer as a result of this Part, the contract continues, so far as practicable, to have effect in every other respect.

68 Requirement for transparency

(1) A trader must ensure that a written term of a consumer contract, or a consumer notice in writing, is transparent.

(2) A consumer notice is transparent for the purposes of subsection (1) if it is expressed in plain and intelligible language and it is legible.

69 Contract terms that may have different meanings

(1) If a term in a consumer contract, or a consumer notice, could have different meanings, the meaning that is most favourable to the consumer is to prevail.

(2) Subsection (1) does not apply to the construction of a term or a notice in proceedings on an application for an injunction or interdict under paragraph 3 of Schedule 3.

How are the general rules enforced?

70 Enforcement of the law on unfair contract terms

(1) Schedule 3 confers functions on the Competition and Markets Authority and other regulators in relation to the enforcement of this Part.

(2) For provision about the investigatory powers that are available to those regulators for the purposes of that Schedule, see Schedule 5.

Supplementary provisions

71 Duty of court to consider fairness of term

(1) Subsection (2) applies to proceedings before a court which relate to a term of a consumer contract.

(2) The court must consider whether the term is fair even if none of the parties to the proceedings has raised that issue or indicated that it intends to raise it.

(3) But subsection (2) does not apply unless the court considers that it has before it sufficient legal and factual material to enable it to consider the fairness of the term.

72 Application of rules to secondary contracts

(1) This section applies if a term of a contract ('the secondary contract') reduces the rights or remedies or increases the obligations of a person under another contract ('the main contract').

(2) The term is subject to the provisions of this Part that would apply to the term if it were in the main contract.

(3) It does not matter for the purposes of this section—

(a) whether the parties to the secondary contract are the same as the parties to the main contract, or

(b) whether the secondary contract is a consumer contract.

(4) This section does not apply if the secondary contract is a settlement of a claim arising under the main contract.

73 Disapplication of rules to mandatory terms and notices

(1) This Part does not apply to a term of a contract, or to a notice, to the extent that it reflects—

(a) mandatory statutory or regulatory provisions, or

(b) the provisions or principles of an international convention to which the United Kingdom [. . .] is a party.

(2) In subsection (1) 'mandatory statutory or regulatory provisions' includes rules which, according to law, apply between the parties on the basis that no other arrangements have been established.

74 Contracts applying law of [a country other than the UK]

(1) If—

(a) the law of a country or territory other than [the United Kingdom or any part of the United Kingdom] is chosen by the parties to be applicable to a consumer contract, but

(b) the consumer contract has a close connection with the United Kingdom, this Part applies despite that choice.

(2) For cases where the law applicable has not been chosen [. . .], see Regulation (EC) No 593/2008 of the European Parliament and of the Council of 17 June

2008 on the law applicable to contractual obligations [as that Regulation has effect as [assimilated direct] legislation (including that Regulation as applied by regulation 5 of the Law Applicable to Contractual Obligations (England and Wales and Northern Ireland) Regulations 2009 and regulation 4 of the Law Applicable to Contractual Obligations (Scotland) Regulations 2009), unless the case is one in respect of which Regulation (EC) No 593/2008 has effect by virtue of Article 66 of the EU withdrawal agreement, in which case see that Regulation as it has effect by virtue of that Article.]

75 Changes to other legislation
Schedule 4 (amendments consequential on this Part) has effect.

76 Interpretation of Part 2
(1) In this Part—
'consumer contract' has the meaning given by section 61(3);
'consumer notice' has the meaning given by section 61(7);
'transparent' is to be construed in accordance with sections 64(3) and 68(2).
(2) The following have the same meanings in this Part as they have in Part 1—
'trader' (see section 2(2));
'consumer' (see section 2(3));
'goods' (see section 2(8));
'digital content' (see section 2(9)).
(3) Section 2(4) (trader who claims an individual is not a consumer must prove it) applies in relation to this Part as it applies in relation to Part 1.

PART 3
MISCELLANEOUS AND GENERAL

CHAPTER 1
Enforcement etc

77 Investigatory powers etc
(1) Schedule 5 (investigatory powers etc) has effect.
(2) Schedule 6 (investigatory powers: consequential amendments) has effect.

78–80 [Amending provisions]

CHAPTER 2
Competition

81 Private actions in competition law
Schedule 8 (private actions in competition law) has effect.

[82 *Amends Enterprise Act 2002***]**

. . .

CHAPTER 5
Secondary ticketing

90 Duty to provide information about tickets
(1) This section applies where a person ('the seller') re-sells a ticket for a recreational, sporting or cultural event in the United Kingdom through a secondary ticketing facility.
(2) The seller and each operator of the facility must ensure that the person who buys the ticket ('the buyer') is given the information specified in subsection (3), where this is applicable to the ticket.
(3) That information is—
(a) where the ticket is for a particular seat or standing area at the venue for

the event, the information necessary to enable the buyer to identify that seat or standing area,

(b) information about any restriction which limits use of the ticket to persons of a particular description, and

(c) the face value of the ticket.

(4) The reference in subsection (3)(a) to information necessary to enable the buyer to identify a seat or standing area at a venue includes, so far as applicable—

(a) the name of the area in the venue in which the seat or standing area is located (for example the name of the stand in which it is located),

(b) information necessary to enable the buyer to identify the part of the area in the venue in which the seat or standing area is located (for example the block of seats in which the seat is located),

(c) the number, letter or other distinguishing mark of the row in which the seat is located,

(d) the number, letter or other distinguishing mark of the seat; and

[(e) any unique ticket number that may help the buyer to identify the seat or standing area or its location.]

(5) The reference in subsection (3)(c) to the face value of the ticket is to the amount stated on the ticket as its price.

(6) The seller and each operator of the facility must ensure that the buyer is given the information specified in subsection (7), where the seller is—

(a) an operator of the secondary ticketing facility,

(b) a person who is a parent undertaking or a subsidiary undertaking in relation to an operator of the secondary ticketing facility,

(c) a person who is employed or engaged by an operator of the secondary ticketing facility,

(d) a person who is acting on behalf of a person within paragraph (c), or

(e) an organiser of the event or a person acting on behalf of an organiser of the event.

(7) That information is a statement that the seller of the ticket is a person within subsection (6) which specifies the ground on which the seller falls within that subsection.

(8) Information required by this section to be given to the buyer must be given—

(a) in a clear and comprehensible manner, and

(b) before the buyer is bound by the contract for the sale of the ticket

(9) This section applies in relation to the re-sale of a ticket through a secondary ticketing facility only if the ticket is first offered for re-sale through the facility after the coming into force of this section.

91 Prohibition on cancellation or blacklisting

(1) This section applies where a person ('the seller') re-sells, or offers for resale, a ticket for a recreational, sporting or cultural event in the United Kingdom through a secondary ticketing facility.

(2) An organiser of the event must not cancel the ticket merely because the seller has re-sold the ticket or offered it for re-sale unless—

(a) a term of the original contract for the sale of the ticket—

(i) provided for its cancellation if it was re-sold by the buyer under that contract,

(ii) provided for its cancellation if it was offered for re-sale by that buyer, or

(iii) provided as mentioned in sub-paragraph (i) and (ii), and

(b) that term was not unfair for the purposes of Part 2 (unfair terms).

(3) An organiser of the event must not blacklist the seller merely because the seller has re-sold the ticket or offered it for re-sale unless—

(a) a term of the original contract for the sale of the ticket—

(i) provided for the blacklisting of the buyer under that contract if it was re-sold by that buyer,

(ii) provided for the blacklisting of that buyer if it was offered for re-sale by that buyer, or

(iii) provided as mentioned in sub-paragraph (i) and (ii), and

(b) that term was not unfair for the purposes of Part 2 (unfair terms).

(4) In subsections (2) and (3) 'the original contract' means the contract for the sale of the ticket by an organiser of the event to a person other than an organiser of the event.

(5) For the purposes of this section an organiser of an event cancels a ticket if the organiser takes steps which result in the holder for the time being of the ticket no longer being entitled to attend that event.

(6) For the purposes of this section an organiser of an event blacklists a person if the organiser takes steps—

(a) to prevent the person from acquiring a ticket for a recreational, sporting or cultural event in the United Kingdom, or

(b) to restrict the person's opportunity to acquire such a ticket.

(7) Part 2 (unfair terms) may apply to a term of a contract which, apart from that Part, would permit the cancellation of a ticket for a recreational, sporting or cultural event in the United Kingdom, or the blacklisting of the seller of such a ticket, in circumstances other than those mentioned in subsection (2) or (3).

(8) Before the coming into force of Part 2, references to that Part in this section are to be read as references to the Unfair Terms in Consumer Contracts Regulations 1999 (SI 1999/2083).

(9) This section applies in relation to a ticket that is re-sold or offered for re-sale before or after the coming into force of this section; but the prohibition in this section applies only to things done after its coming into force.

92 Duty to report criminal activity

(1) This section applies where—

(a) an operator of a secondary ticketing facility knows that a person has used or is using the facility in such a way that an offence has been or is being committed, and

(b) the offence relates to the re-sale of a ticket for a recreational, sporting or cultural event in the United Kingdom.

(2) The operator must, as soon as the operator becomes aware that a person has used or is using the facility as mentioned in subsection (1), disclose the matters specified in subsection (3) to—

(a) an appropriate person, and

(b) an organiser of the event (subject to subsection (5)).

(3) Those matters are—

(a) the identity of the person mentioned in subsection (1), if this is known to the operator, and

(b) the fact that the operator knows that an offence has been or is being committed as mentioned in that subsection.

(4) The following are appropriate persons for the purposes of this section—

(a) a constable of a police force in England and Wales,

(b) a constable of the police service of Scotland, and

(c) a police officer within the meaning of the Police (Northern Ireland) Act 2000.

(5) This section does not require an operator to make a disclosure to an organiser of an event if the operator has reasonable grounds for believing that to do so will prejudice the investigation of any offence.

(6) References in this section to an offence are to an offence under the law of any part of the United Kingdom.

(7) This section applies only in relation to an offence of which an operator becomes aware after the coming into force of this section.

93 Enforcement of this Chapter

(1) A local weights and measures authority in Great Britain may enforce the provisions of this Chapter in its area.

(2) The Department of Enterprise, Trade and Investment may enforce the provisions of this Chapter in Northern Ireland.

[(2A) The Competition and Markets Authority may also enforce the provisions of this Chapter.]

(3) Each of the bodies referred to in subsections (1)[, (2) and (2A)] is an 'enforcement authority' for the purposes of this Chapter.

(4) Where an enforcement authority is satisfied on the balance of probabilities that a person has breached a duty or prohibition imposed by this Chapter, the authority may impose a financial penalty on the person in respect of that breach.

(5) But in the case of a breach of a duty in section 90 or a prohibition in section 91 an enforcement authority may not impose a financial penalty on a person ('P') if the authority is satisfied on the balance of probabilities that—

(a) the breach was due to—

(i) a mistake,

(ii) reliance on information supplied to P by another person,

(iii) the act or default of another person,

(iv) an accident, or

(v) another cause beyond P's control, and

(b) P took all reasonable precautions and exercised all due diligence to avoid the breach.

(6) A local weights and measures authority in England and Wales may impose a penalty under this section in respect of a breach which occurs in England and Wales but outside that authority's area (as well as in respect of a breach which occurs within that area).

(7) A local weights and measures authority in Scotland may impose a penalty under this section in respect of a breach which occurs in Scotland but outside that authority's area (as well as in respect of a breach which occurs within that area).

(8) Only one penalty under this section may be imposed on the same person in respect of the same breach.

(9) The amount of a financial penalty imposed under this section—

(a) may be such as the enforcement authority imposing it determines, but

(b) must not exceed £5,000.

(10) Schedule 10 (procedure for and appeals against financial penalties) has effect.

(11) References in this section to this Chapter do not include section 94.

94 Duty to review measures relating to secondary ticketing

(1) The Secretary of State must—

(a) review, or arrange for a review of, consumer protection measures applying to the re-sale of tickets for recreational, sporting or cultural events in the United Kingdom through secondary ticketing facilities,

(b) prepare a report on the outcome of the review or arrange for such a report to be prepared, and

(c) publish that report.

(2) The report must be published before the end of the period of 12 months beginning with the day on which this section comes into force.

(3) The Secretary of State must lay the report before Parliament.

(4) In this section 'consumer protection measures' includes such legislation, rules of law, codes of practice and guidance as the Secretary of State considers relate to the rights of consumers or the protection of their interests.

95 Interpretation of this Chapter

(1) In this Chapter—

'enforcement authority' has the meaning given by section 93(3);

'operator', in relation to a secondary ticketing facility, means a person who—

(a) exercises control over the operation of the facility, and

(b) receives revenue from the facility,

but this is subject to regulations under subsection (2);

'organiser', in relation to an event, means a person who—

(a) is responsible for organising or managing the event, or

(b) receives some or all of the revenue from the event;

'parent undertaking' has the meaning given by section 1162 of the Companies Act 2006;

'secondary ticketing facility' means an internet-based facility for the re-sale of tickets for recreational, sporting or cultural events;

'subsidiary undertaking' has the meaning given by section 1162 of the Companies Act 2006;

'undertaking' has the meaning given by section 1161(1) of the Companies Act 2006.

(2) The Secretary of State may by regulations provide that a person of a description specified in the regulations is or is not to be treated for the purposes of this Chapter as an operator in relation to a secondary ticketing facility.

(3) Regulations under subsection (2)—

(a) are to be made by statutory instrument;

(b) may make different provision for different purposes;

(c) may include incidental, supplementary, consequential, transitional, transitory or saving provision.

(4) A statutory instrument containing regulations under subsection (2) is not to be made unless a draft of the instrument has been laid before, and approved by a resolution of, each House of Parliament.

CHAPTER 6
General

96 Power to make consequential provision

(1) The Secretary of State may by order made by statutory instrument make provision in consequence of this Act.

(2) The power conferred by subsection (1) includes power—

(a) to amend, repeal, revoke or otherwise modify any provision made by an enactment or an instrument made under an enactment (including an enactment passed or instrument made in the same Session as this Act);

(b) to make transitional, transitory or saving provision.

(3) A statutory instrument containing (whether alone or with other provision) an order under this section which amends, repeals, revokes or otherwise modifies any provision of primary legislation is not to be made unless a draft of the instrument has been laid before, and approved by a resolution of, each House of Parliament.

(4) A statutory instrument containing an order under this section which does not amend, repeal, revoke or otherwise modify any provision of primary legislation is subject to annulment in pursuance of a resolution of either House of Parliament.

(5) In this section—

'enactment' includes an Act of the Scottish Parliament, a Measure or Act of the National Assembly for Wales and Northern Ireland legislation;

'primary legislation' means—

(a) an Act of Parliament,

(b) an Act of the Scottish Parliament,
(c) a Measure or Act of the National Assembly for Wales, and
(d) Northern Ireland legislation.

97 Power to make transitional, transitory and saving provision

(1) The Secretary of State may by order made by statutory instrument make transitional, transitory or saving provision in connection with the coming into force of any provision of this Act other than the coming into force of Chapter 3 or 4 of this Part in relation to Wales.

(2) The Welsh Ministers may by order made by statutory instrument make transitional, transitory or saving provision in connection with the coming into force of Chapter 3 or 4 of this Part in relation to Wales.

98 Financial provision

There is to be paid out of money provided by Parliament—

(a) any expenses incurred by a Minister of the Crown or a government department under this Act, and

(b) any increase attributable to this Act in the sums payable under any other Act out of money so provided.

99 Extent

(1) The amendment, repeal or revocation of any provision by this Act has the same extent as the provision concerned.

(2) Section 27 extends only to Scotland.

(3) Chapter 3 of this Part extends only to England and Wales.

(4) Subject to that, this Act extends to England and Wales, Scotland and Northern Ireland.

100 Commencement

(1) The provisions of this Act listed in subsection (2) come into force on the day on which this Act is passed.

(2) Those provisions are—
(a) section 48(5) to (8),
(b) Chapter 3 of this Part in so far as it confer powers to make regulations,
(c) section 88(5) to (11),
(d) this Chapter, and
(e) paragraph 12 of Schedule 5.

(3) Chapters 3 and 4 of this Part come into force—

(a) in relation to England, on such day as the Secretary of State may appoint by order made by statutory instrument;

(b) in relation to Wales, on such day as the Welsh Ministers may appoint by order made by statutory instrument.

(4) Chapter 5 of this Part comes into force at the end of the period of two months beginning with the day on which this Act is passed.

(5) The other provisions of this Act come into force on such day as the Secretary of State may appoint by order made by statutory instrument.

(6) An order under this section may appoint different days for different purposes.

101 Short title

This Act may be cited as the Consumer Rights Act 2015.

. . .

SCHEDULE 2
CONSUMER CONTRACT TERMS WHICH MAY BE REGARDED AS UNFAIR

PART 1
LIST OF TERMS

1 A term which has the object or effect of excluding or limiting the trader's liability in the event of the death of or personal injury to the consumer resulting from an act or omission of the trader.

2 A term which has the object or effect of inappropriately excluding or limiting the legal rights of the consumer in relation to the trader or another party in the event of total or partial non-performance or inadequate performance by the trader of any of the contractual obligations, including the option of offsetting a debt owed to the trader against any claim which the consumer may have against the trader.

3 A term which has the object or effect of making an agreement binding on the consumer in a case where the provision of services by the trader is subject to a condition whose realisation depends on the trader's will alone.

4 A term which has the object or effect of permitting the trader to retain sums paid by the consumer where the consumer decides not to conclude or perform the contract, without providing for the consumer to receive compensation of an equivalent amount from the trader where the trader is the party cancelling the contract.

5 A term which has the object or effect of requiring that, where the consumer decides not to conclude or perform the contract, the consumer must pay the trader a disproportionately high sum in compensation or for services which have not been supplied.

6 A term which has the object or effect of requiring a consumer who fails to fulfil his obligations under the contract to pay a disproportionately high sum in compensation.

7 A term which has the object or effect of authorising the trader to dissolve the contract on a discretionary basis where the same facility is not granted to the consumer, or permitting the trader to retain the sums paid for services not yet supplied by the trader where it is the trader who dissolves the contract.

8 A term which has the object or effect of enabling the trader to terminate a contract of indeterminate duration without reasonable notice except where there are serious grounds for doing so.

9 A term which has the object or effect of automatically extending a contract of fixed duration where the consumer does not indicate otherwise, when the deadline fixed for the consumer to express a desire not to extend the contract is unreasonably early.

10 A term which has the object or effect of irrevocably binding the consumer to terms with which the consumer has had no real opportunity of becoming acquainted before the conclusion of the contract.

11 A term which has the object or effect of enabling the trader to alter the terms of the contract unilaterally without a valid reason which is specified in the contract.

12 A term which has the object or effect of permitting the trader to determine the characteristics of the subject matter of the contract after the consumer has become bound by it.

13 A term which has the object or effect of enabling the trader to alter unilaterally without a valid reason any characteristics of the goods, digital content or services to be provided.

14 A term which has the object or effect of giving the trader the discretion to decide the price payable under the contract after the consumer has become bound

by it, where no price or method of determining the price is agreed when the consumer becomes bound.

15 A term which has the object or effect of permitting a trader to increase the price of goods, digital content or services without giving the consumer the right to cancel the contract if the final price is too high in relation to the price agreed when the contract was concluded.

16 A term which has the object or effect of giving the trader the right to determine whether the goods, digital content or services supplied are in conformity with the contract, or giving the trader the exclusive right to interpret any term of the contract.

17 A term which has the object or effect of limiting the trader's obligation to respect commitments undertaken by the trader's agents or making the trader's commitments subject to compliance with a particular formality.

18 A term which has the object or effect of obliging the consumer to fulfil all of the consumer's obligations where the trader does not perform the trader's obligations.

19 A term which has the object or effect of allowing the trader to transfer the trader's rights and obligations under the contract, where this may reduce the guarantees for the consumer, without the consumer's agreement.

20 A term which has the object or effect of excluding or hindering the consumer's right to take legal action or exercise any other legal remedy, in particular by—

(a) requiring the consumer to take disputes exclusively to arbitration not covered by legal provisions,

(b) unduly restricting the evidence available to the consumer, or

(c) imposing on the consumer a burden of proof which, according to the applicable law, should lie with another party to the contract.

PART 2
SCOPE OF PART 1

Financial services

21 Paragraph 8 (cancellation without reasonable notice) does not include a term by which a supplier of financial services reserves the right to terminate unilaterally a contract of indeterminate duration without notice where there is a valid reason, if the supplier is required to inform the consumer of the cancellation immediately.

22 Paragraph 11 (variation of contract without valid reason) does not include a term by which a supplier of financial services reserves the right to alter the rate of interest payable by or due to the consumer, or the amount of other charges for financial services without notice where there is a valid reason, if—

(a) the supplier is required to inform the consumer of the alteration at the earliest opportunity, and

(b) the consumer is free to dissolve the contract immediately. Contracts which last indefinitely

23 Paragraphs 11 (variation of contract without valid reason), 12 (determination of characteristics of goods etc after consumer bound) and 14 (determination of price after consumer bound) do not include a term under which a trader reserves the right to alter unilaterally the conditions of a contract of indeterminate duration if—

(a) the trader is required to inform the consumer with reasonable notice, and

(b) the consumer is free to dissolve the contract.

Sale of securities, foreign currency etc

24 Paragraphs 8 (cancellation without reasonable notice), 11 (variation of contract without valid reason), 14 (determination of price after consumer bound) and 15 (increase in price) do not apply to—

(a) transactions in transferable securities, financial instruments and other products or services where the price is linked to fluctuations in a stock exchange quotation or index or a financial market rate that the trader does not control, and

(b) contracts for the purchase or sale of foreign currency, traveller's cheques or international money orders denominated in foreign currency.

Price index clauses

25 Paragraphs 14 (determination of price after consumer bound) and 15 (increase in price) do not include a term which is a price-indexation clause (where otherwise lawful), if the method by which prices vary is explicitly described.

SCHEDULE 3
ENFORCEMENT OF THE LAW ON UNFAIR CONTRACT TERMS AND NOTICES

Application of Schedule

1 This Schedule applies to—

(a) a term of a consumer contract,

(b) a term proposed for use in a consumer contract,

(c) a term which a third party recommends for use in a consumer contract,

or

(d) a consumer notice.

Consideration of complaints

2—(1) A regulator may consider a complaint about a term or notice to which this Schedule applies (a 'relevant complaint').

(2) If a regulator other than the CMA intends to consider a relevant complaint, it must notify the CMA that it intends to do so, and must then consider the complaint.

(3) If a regulator considers a relevant complaint, but decides not to make an application under paragraph 3 in relation to the complaint, it must give reasons for its decision to the person who made the complaint.

Application for injunction or interdict

3—(1) A regulator may apply for an injunction or (in Scotland) an interdict against a person if the regulator thinks that—

(a) the person is using, or proposing or recommending the use of, a term or notice to which this Schedule applies, and

(b) the term or notice falls within any one or more of sub-paragraphs (2), (3) or (5).

(2) A term or notice falls within this sub-paragraph if it purports to exclude or restrict liability of the kind mentioned in—

(a) section 31 (exclusion of liability: goods contracts),

(b) section 47 (exclusion of liability: digital content contracts),

(c) section 57 (exclusion of liability: services contracts), or

(d) section 65(1) (business liability for death or personal injury resulting from negligence).

(3) A term or notice falls within this sub-paragraph if it is unfair to any extent.

[. . .]

(5) A term or notice falls within this sub-paragraph if it breaches section 68 (requirement for transparency).

(6) A regulator may apply for an injunction or interdict under this paragraph in relation to a term or notice whether or not it has received a relevant complaint about the term or notice.

Notification of application

4—(1) Before making an application under paragraph 3, a regulator other than the CMA must notify the CMA that it intends to do so.

(2) The regulator may make the application only if—

(a) the period of 14 days beginning with the day on which the regulator notified the CMA has ended, or

(b) before the end of that period, the CMA agrees to the regulator making the application.

Determination of application

5—(1) On an application for an injunction under paragraph 3, the court may grant an injunction on such conditions, and against such of the respondents, as it thinks appropriate.

(2) On an application for an interdict under paragraph 3, the court may grant an interdict on such conditions, and against such of the defenders, as it thinks appropriate.

(3) The injunction or interdict may include provision about—

(a) a term or notice to which the application relates, or

(b) any term of a consumer contract, or any consumer notice, of a similar kind or with a similar effect.

(4) It is not a defence to an application under paragraph 3 to show that, because of a rule of law, a term to which the application relates is not, or could not be, an enforceable contract term.

(5) If a regulator other than the CMA makes the application, it must notify the CMA of—

(a) the outcome of the application, and

(b) if an injunction or interdict is granted, the conditions on which, and the persons against whom, it is granted.

Undertakings

6—(1) A regulator may accept an undertaking from a person against whom it has applied, or thinks it is entitled to apply, for an injunction or interdict under paragraph 3.

(2) The undertaking may provide that the person will comply with the conditions that are agreed between the person and the regulator about the use of terms or notices, or terms or notices of a kind, specified in the undertaking.

(3) If a regulator other than the CMA accepts an undertaking, it must notify the CMA of—

(a) the conditions on which the undertaking is accepted, and

(b) the person who gave it.

Publication, information and advice

7—(1) The CMA must arrange the publication of details of—

(a) any application it makes for an injunction or interdict under paragraph 3,

(b) any injunction or interdict under this Schedule, and

(c) any undertaking under this Schedule.

(2) The CMA must respond to a request whether a term or notice, or one of a similar kind or with a similar effect, is or has been the subject of an injunction, interdict or undertaking under this Schedule.

(3) Where the term or notice, or one of a similar kind or with a similar effect, is or has been the subject of an injunction or interdict under this Schedule, the CMA must give the person making the request a copy of the injunction or interdict.

(4) Where the term or notice, or one of a similar kind or with a similar effect, is or has been the subject of an undertaking under this Schedule, the CMA must give the person making the request—

(a) details of the undertaking, and

(b) if the person giving the undertaking has agreed to amend the term or notice, a copy of the amendments.

(5) The CMA may arrange the publication of advice and information about the provisions of this Part.

(6) In this paragraph—

(a) references to an injunction or interdict under this Schedule are to an injunction or interdict granted on an application by the CMA under paragraph 3 or notified to it under paragraph 5, and

(b) references to an undertaking are to an undertaking given to the CMA under paragraph 6 or notified to it under that paragraph.

Meaning of 'regulator'

8—(1) In this Schedule 'regulator' means—

(a) the CMA,

(b) the Department of Enterprise, Trade and Investment in Northern Ireland,

(c) a local weights and measures authority in Great Britain,

(d) the Financial Conduct Authority,

(e) the Office of Communications,

(f) the Information Commissioner,

(g) the Gas and Electricity Markets Authority,

(h) the Water Services Regulation Authority,

(i) the Office of Rail Regulation,

(j) the Northern Ireland Authority for Utility Regulation, or

(k) the Consumers' Association.

(2) The Secretary of State may by order made by statutory instrument amend sub-paragraph (1) so as to add, modify or remove an entry.

(3) An order under sub-paragraph (2) may amend sub-paragraph (1) so as to add a body that is not a public authority only if the Secretary of State thinks that the body represents the interests of consumers (or consumers of a particular description).

(4) The Secretary of State must publish (and may from time to time vary) other criteria to be applied by the Secretary of State in deciding whether to add an entry to, or remove an entry from, sub-paragraph (1).

(5) An order under sub-paragraph (2) may make consequential amendments to this Schedule (including with the effect that any of its provisions apply differently, or do not apply, to a body added to sub-paragraph (1)).

(6) An order under sub-paragraph (2) may contain transitional or transitory provision or savings.

(7) No order may be made under sub-paragraph (2) unless a draft of the statu-

tory instrument containing it has been laid before, and approved by a resolution of, each House of Parliament.

(8) In this paragraph 'public authority' has the same meaning as in section 6 of the Human Rights Act 1998.

Other definitions

9 In this Schedule—
'the CMA' means the Competition and Markets Authority;
'injunction' includes an interim injunction;
'interdict' includes an interim interdict.

The Financial Conduct Authority

10 The functions of the Financial Conduct Authority under this Schedule are to be treated as functions of the Authority under the Financial Services and Markets Act 2000.

. . .

BANKRUPTCY (SCOTLAND) ACT 2016
(2016, asp 21)

PART 1
APPLICATION OR PETITION FOR SEQUESTRATION

Applications and petitions

1 Sequestration
The estate of a debtor may be sequestrated in accordance with the provisions of this Act.

2 Sequestration of estate of living debtor

(1) The sequestration of the estate of a living debtor is—

(a) by debtor application made by the debtor, if subsection (2) or (8) applies to the debtor, or

(b) on the petition of—

(i) a qualified creditor, or qualified creditors, if the debtor is apparently insolvent,

[. . .] or

(iv) a trustee acting under a trust deed if a condition mentioned in subsection (7) is satisfied.

(2) This subsection applies to the debtor where—

(a) the debtor—

(i) has been assessed by the common financial tool as requiring to make no debtor's contribution, or

(ii) has been in receipt of payments, of a kind prescribed, for a period of at least 6 months ending with the day on which the debtor application is made,

(b) the total amount of the debtor's debts (including interest) at the date the debtor application is made is—

(i) not less than [such] amount as may be prescribed, and

(ii) not more than [£25,000] or such other amount as may be prescribed,

(c) the total value of the debtor's assets (leaving out of account any liabilities) on the date the debtor application is made does not exceed £2,000 or such other amount as may be prescribed,

(d) no single asset of the debtor has a value which exceeds £1,000 or such other amount as may be prescribed,

(e) the debtor does not own land,

(f) the debtor has been granted, within the prescribed period and in accordance with section 9, a certificate for sequestration of the debtor's estate,

(g) in the 10 years ending on the day before the day on which the debtor application is made or such other period as may be prescribed, no award of sequestration has been made against the debtor in pursuance of an application made by the debtor by virtue of this subsection, and

(h) in the 5 years ending on the day before the day on which the debtor application is made, no award of sequestration has been made against the debtor in pursuance of—

(i) an application made by the debtor other than by virtue of this subsection, or

(ii) a petition.

[(2A) For the purposes of subsection (2)(b), the amount of a loan made to the debtor is not to be regarded as a debt where the loan was made by virtue of regulations to which section 73B (regulations relating to student loans) of the Education (Scotland) Act 1980 applies.]

(3) For the purposes of subsection (2)(c) and (d)—

(a) any property of the debtor is not to be regarded as an asset if, under any provision of this or any other enactment, it would be excluded from vesting in AiB as trustee,

(b) if the debtor reasonably requires the use of a vehicle, any vehicle owned by the debtor the value of which does not exceed £3,000 or such other amount as may be prescribed is not to be regarded as an asset, and

(c) any other property of the debtor that is of a prescribed type is not to be regarded as an asset.

(4) For the purposes of subsection (2)(c) and (d), the Scottish Ministers may by regulations make provision about how the value of the debtor's assets is to be determined.

(5) The Scottish Ministers may by regulations modify subsection (2).

(6) Schedule 1 makes further provision about the application of certain provisions of this Act in relation to a debtor to whom subsection (2) applies.

(7) The conditions mentioned in subsection (1)(b)(iv) are—

(a) that the debtor has failed to comply—

(i) with an obligation imposed on the debtor under the trust deed, being an obligation with which the debtor reasonably could have complied, or

(ii) with an instruction reasonably given to, or requirement reasonably made of, the debtor by the trustee for the purposes of the trust deed, or

(b) that the trustee avers in the trustee's petition that it would be in the best interests of the creditors that an award of sequestration be made.

(8) This subsection applies to the debtor where—

(a) the total amount of the debtor's debts (including interest) at the date the debtor application is made is not less than £3,000 or such sum as may be prescribed,

(b) an award of sequestration has not been made against the debtor in the 5 years ending on the day before the date the debtor application is made,

(c) the debtor has obtained the advice of a money adviser in accordance with section 4(1),

(d) the debtor has given a statement of undertakings (including an undertaking to pay to the trustee, after the award of sequestration of the debtor's estate, an amount determined using the common financial tool), and

(e) the debtor—

(i) is apparently insolvent,

(ii) has been granted, within the prescribed period and in accordance with section 9, a certificate for sequestration of the debtor's estate, or

(iii) has granted a trust deed which, by reason of creditors objecting, or not agreeing, to it is not a protected trust deed.

(9) For the purposes of subsection (8)(e)(i), the debtor is not apparently insolvent by reason only of granting a trust deed or of giving notice to creditors as mentioned in section 16(1)(c).

(10) In subsection (8)(e)(ii), 'the prescribed period' means such period, ending immediately before the date the debtor application is made, as may be prescribed under section 9(4)(b).

3 Debt advice and information package

(1) No petition may be presented under section 2(1)(b)(i) unless the qualified creditor has, or qualified creditors have, provided the debtor, by such time prior to the presentation of the petition as may be prescribed, with a debt advice and information package.

(2) In this Act, 'debt advice and information package' means the debt advice and information package referred to in section 10(5) of the 2002 Act.

4 Money advice

(1) An application for the sequestration of a living debtor's estate may not be made unless the debtor has obtained from a money adviser advice on—

(a) the debtor's financial circumstances,

(b) the effect of the proposed sequestration,

(c) the preparation of the application, and

(d) such other matters as may be prescribed.

(2) In this Act, 'money adviser' means a person who—

(a) is not an associate of the debtor, and

(b) is of a prescribed description or falls within a prescribed class.

5 Sequestration of estate of deceased debtor

The sequestration of the estate of a deceased debtor is—

(a) by debtor application made by the executor, or a person entitled to be appointed as executor, on the estate,

(b) on the petition of a qualified creditor, or qualified creditors, of the deceased debtor,

[. . .] or

(e) on the petition of a trustee acting under a trust deed.

6 Sequestration of other estates

(1) The estate belonging to any of the following (or held for or jointly by, as the case may be, the trustees, partners or members of any of the following) may be sequestrated—

(a) a trust in respect of debts incurred by it,

(b) a partnership (including a dissolved partnership),

(c) a body corporate,

(d) an unincorporated body,

(e) a limited partnership (including a dissolved limited partnership) within the meaning of the Limited Partnerships Act 1907.

(2) But it is not competent to sequestrate the estate of any of the following—

(a) a company registered under the Companies Act 2006,

(b) a limited liability partnership, or

(c) any other entity if it is an entity in respect of which an enactment provides, expressly or by implication, that sequestration is incompetent.

(3) The sequestration of a trust estate in respect of debts incurred by the trust is—

(a) by debtor application made by a majority of trustees, with the concurrence of a qualified creditor or qualified creditors, or

(b) on the petition of—

[. . .]

(iii) a qualified creditor or qualified creditors, if the trustees as such are apparently insolvent.

(4) The sequestration of the estate of a partnership is—

(a) by debtor application made by the partnership where the partnership is apparently insolvent,

(b) by debtor application made by the partnership with the concurrence of a qualified creditor or qualified creditors, or

(c) on the petition of—

[. . .]

(iii) a trustee acting under a trust deed, or

(iv) a qualified creditor or qualified creditors, if the partnership is apparently insolvent.

(5) For the purposes of an application under subsection (4)(a), section 16(4) is to be read as if—

(a) the word 'either', and

(b) the words 'or if any of the partners is apparently insolvent for a debt of the partnership',

were omitted.

(6) A petition under subsection (4)(c) may be combined with a petition for the sequestration of the estate of any of the partners as an individual where that individual is apparently insolvent.

(7) The sequestration of the estate of a body corporate or of an unincorporated body is—

(a) by debtor application made by a person authorised to act on behalf of the body, with the concurrence of a qualified creditor or qualified creditors, or

(b) on the petition of—

[. . .]

(iii) a qualified creditor or qualified creditors, if the body is apparently insolvent.

(8) The application of this Act to the sequestration of the estate of a limited partnership is subject to such modifications as may be prescribed.

(9) Subsections (3)(a) of section 8 and (3) to (6) of section 10 apply for the purposes of this section as they apply for the purposes of their respective sections.

7 Qualified creditor and qualified creditors

(1) In this Act—

'qualified creditor' means a creditor who, at the date of the presentation of the petition, or as the case may be at the date the debtor application is made, is a creditor of the debtor in respect of relevant debts which amount (or of one such debt which amounts) to not less than [£5,000] or such sum as may be prescribed, and

'qualified creditors' means creditors who, at the date in question, are creditors of the debtor in respect of relevant debts which amount in aggregate to not less than [£5,000] or such sum as may be prescribed.

(2) In the definitions of 'qualified creditor' and 'qualified creditors' in subsection (1) 'relevant debts' means liquid or illiquid debts (other than contingent or future debts or amounts payable under a confiscation order) whether secured or unsecured.

(3) In subsection (2), 'confiscation order' means a confiscation order under Part 2, 3 or 4 of the Proceeds of Crime Act 2002.

(4) Paragraphs 1(1) and (3), 2(1)(a) and (2) and 5 of schedule 2 apply in order to ascertain the amount of the debt or debts for the purposes of subsection (1) as those paragraphs apply in order to ascertain the amount which a creditor is entitled to claim but as if for any reference to the date of sequestration there were

substituted a reference to the date of the presentation of the petition or, as the case may be, the date the debtor application is made.

8 Debtor applications: general

(1) Any debtor application must be made to AiB.

(2) A debtor application must—

(a) include a declaration by the money adviser who provided the advice referred to in section 4(1) that such advice has been given, and

(b) specify the name and address of the money adviser.

(3) The debtor must send to AiB along with the application—

(a) a statement of assets and liabilities, and

(b) a statement of undertakings.

(4) If the debtor—

(a) fails, in a statement of assets and liabilities sent to AiB in accordance with subsection (3)(a), to disclose a material fact, or

(b) makes in such a statement a material misstatement,

then the debtor commits an offence.

(5) A person who commits an offence under subsection (4) is liable on summary conviction to a fine not exceeding level 5 on the standard scale or to imprisonment for a term not exceeding 3 months or both to such fine and to such imprisonment.

(6) In any proceedings for an offence under subsection (4), it is a defence to show that the accused had a reasonable excuse for the failure in question or, as the case may be, for making the statement in question.

9 Certificate for sequestration

(1) A certificate for sequestration of the estate of a debtor is a certificate granted by a money adviser certifying that the debtor is unable to pay debts as they become due.

(2) A certificate may be granted only on the debtor applying for it.

(3) A money adviser must grant a certificate if, and only if, the debtor can demonstrate that the debtor is unable to pay debts as they become due.

(4) The Scottish Ministers may—

(a) by regulations make provision about certification by a money adviser, including—

(i) the form and manner in which a certification must be made,

(ii) the fee, if any, which a money adviser is entitled to charge for or in connection with granting a certificate,

(b) prescribe a period for the purpose of section 2(2)(f) or (8)(e)(ii).

10 Death or withdrawal

(1) Where, after a petition for sequestration is presented but before the sequestration is awarded, the debtor dies then, if the petitioner is a creditor, the proceedings are to continue in accordance with this Act so far as circumstances will permit.

(2) Where, after a debtor application is made but before the sequestration is awarded, the debtor dies then the application falls.

(3) Where, after a petition for sequestration is presented but before the sequestration is awarded, a creditor who is the petitioner withdraws or dies, there may be sisted in the place of that creditor any creditor who both was a qualified creditor at the date when the petition was presented and is a qualified creditor at the date of the sist.

(4) Where, after a petition for sequestration is presented but before the sequestration is awarded, a creditor who has lodged answers to the petition withdraws or dies, there may be sisted in the place of that creditor any other creditor.

(5) Where, after a debtor application is made but before the sequestration is

awarded, a creditor who concurs in the application withdraws or dies, any other creditor may, if the conditions mentioned in subsection (6) are met, notify AiB that the other creditor concurs in the application in place of the creditor who has withdrawn or died.

(6) The conditions are that the other creditor—

(a) was a qualified creditor at the date when the debtor application was made, and

(b) is a qualified creditor at the date of the notification.

11 Debtor application: provision of information

(1) Where a debtor application is made other than under section 5(a), the debtor must state in the application—

(a) whether or not the debtor's centre of main interests is situated in the United Kingdom or in [a member State (other than Denmark),] and

[(b) if the debtor's centre of main interests is situated in a member State (other than Denmark), whether or not the debtor possesses an establishment in the United Kingdom.]

(2) Where a debtor application is made by an executor under section 5(a) the executor must state in the application—

(a) whether or not the debtor's centre of main interests was situated in the United Kingdom or in [a member State (other than Denmark),] and

[(b) if the debtor's centre of main interests was situated in a member State (other than Denmark), whether or not the debtor possessed an establishment in the United Kingdom.]

[. . .]

12 Petition for sequestration of estate: provision of information

(1) A petitioner for sequestration of the estate of a debtor is, in so far as it is within the petitioner's knowledge, to state in the petition—

(a) whether or not the debtor's centre of main interests is situated in the United Kingdom or in [a member State (other than Denmark),] and

[(b) if the debtor's centre of main interests is situated in a member State (other than Denmark), whether or not the debtor possesses an establishment in the United Kingdom.]

[. . .]

13 Further provisions relating to presentation of petitions

(1) The petitioner is, on the day the petition for sequestration is presented under section 2, 5 or 6, to send a copy of the petition to AiB.

(2) A petition for the sequestration of the estate of a debtor (other than a limited partnership or a deceased debtor) may be presented—

(a) by a qualified creditor or qualified creditors only if the apparent insolvency founded on in the petition was constituted within 4 months before the date of presentation of the petition, or

(b) at any time by—

(i) a trustee acting under a trust deed,

[. . .]

(3) A petition for the sequestration of the estate of a limited partnership may be presented—

(a) by a qualified creditor or qualified creditors only if the apparent insolvency founded on in the petition was constituted within 4 months (or such other period as may be prescribed) before the date of presentation of the petition, or

(b) at any time by—

(i) a trustee acting under a trust deed,

[. . .]

(4) A petition for the sequestration of the estate of a deceased debtor may be presented—

(a) by a qualified creditor or qualified creditors—

(i) in a case where the apparent insolvency of the debtor founded on in the petition was constituted within 4 months before the date of death, at any time, and

(ii) in any other case (whether or not apparent insolvency has been constituted), not earlier than 6 months after the date of death, or

(b) at any time by—

(i) a person entitled to be appointed as executor of the estate, [or]

(ii) a trustee acting under a trust deed.

[. . .]

(5) The presentation of a petition for sequestration bars the effect of any enactment or rule of law relating to the limitation of actions.

(6) Where, before sequestration is awarded, it becomes apparent that a petitioning creditor was ineligible to petition, that person must withdraw, or as the case may be withdraw from, the petition; but another creditor may be sisted in that person's place.

14 Further provisions relating to debtor applications

(1) A debtor application may be made at any time; but this subsection is subject to subsections (2) and (3).

(2) A debtor application made in relation to the estate of a limited partnership may be made—

(a) at any time unless a time is prescribed, and

(b) if a time is prescribed, within that time.

(3) Any intromission by an executor with the deceased debtor's estate after the 12 months mentioned in subsection (4) is deemed an intromission without title unless, within that period, the executor—

(a) makes a debtor application under section 5(a), or

(b) petitions for the appointment of a judicial factor to administer the estate.

(4) The 12 months referred to in subsection (3) is the 12 months following the day on which the executor knew, or ought to have known, that the estate was absolutely insolvent and likely to remain so.

(5) The making of, or concurrence in, a debtor application bars the effect of any enactment or rule of law relating to the limitation of actions.

(6) Where, before sequestration is awarded, it becomes apparent that a creditor concurring in a debtor application was ineligible to concur, AiB must withdraw the ineligible creditor from the application.

(7) But another creditor may concur in place of the ineligible creditor; and if the other creditor does concur in place of the ineligible creditor, the other creditor must notify AiB of that fact.

[. . .]

[. . .]

Jurisdiction

15 Jurisdiction

(1) Where a petition is presented for the sequestration of the estate of a debtor (whether living or deceased), the sheriff has jurisdiction if, at the relevant time, the debtor—

(a) had an established place of business in the sheriffdom, or

(b) was habitually resident in the sheriffdom.

(2) AiB may determine a debtor application for the sequestration of the estate of a living or deceased debtor if, at the relevant time, the debtor—

(a) had an established place of business in Scotland, or

(b) was habitually resident in Scotland.

(3) Where a petition is presented for the sequestration of the estate of an entity which may be sequestrated by virtue of section 6, the sheriff has jurisdiction if the entity—

(a) had at the relevant time an established place of business in the sheriffdom, or

(b) was constituted or formed under Scots law and at any time carried on business in the sheriffdom.

(4) AiB may determine a debtor application for the sequestration of the estate of such an entity if the entity—

(a) had at the relevant time an established place of business in Scotland, or

(b) was constituted or formed under Scots law and at any time carried on business in Scotland.

(5) Even where a person (whether living or deceased) does not fall within subsection (1), the sheriff has jurisdiction in respect of the sequestration of that person's estate if—

(a) a petition has been presented for the sequestration of the estate of a partnership of which the person is, or was at the relevant time before dying, a partner, and

(b) the process of that sequestration is still current.

(6) Subsection (7) applies as regards any proceedings under this Act which—

(a) may be brought before a sheriff, and

(b) relate either to a debtor application or to the sequestration of a debtor's estate following any such application.

(7) The proceedings are to be brought before the sheriff who, under subsection (1) or (3), would have jurisdiction in respect of a petition for sequestration of the debtor's estate.

(8) References in this section to 'the relevant time' are to any time in the year immediately preceding (as the case may be)—

(a) the date of presentation of the petition,

(b) the date the debtor application is made, or

(c) the debtor's date of death.

[. . .]

Meaning of 'apparent insolvency'

16 Meaning of 'apparent insolvency'

(1) The apparent insolvency of a debtor is constituted, or where the debtor is already apparently insolvent again constituted, whenever—

(a) the debtor's estate is sequestrated,

(b) the debtor is adjudged bankrupt in England and Wales or in Northern Ireland,

(c) the debtor gives written notice to the debtor's creditors that the debtor has ceased to pay the debtor's debts in the ordinary course of business (but the debtor must not, at the time notice is so given, be a person whose property—

(i) is affected by a restraint order,

(ii) is detained under or by virtue of a relevant detention power, or

(iii) is subject to a confiscation or charging order),

[. . .]

(e) the debtor grants a trust deed,

(f) following the service on the debtor of a duly executed charge for payment of a debt, the days of charge expire without payment (unless the circumstances are shown to be such as are mentioned in subsection (2)),

(g) a decree of adjudication of any part of the debtor's estate is granted, either for payment or in security (unless the circumstances are shown to be such as are mentioned in subsection (2)),

(h) a debt constituted by a decree or document of debt, as defined in section 10 of the 2002 Act, is being paid by the debtor under a debt payment programme under Part 1 of that Act and the programme is revoked (unless the circumstances are shown to be such as are mentioned in subsection (2)), or

(i) a creditor of the debtor, in respect of a liquid debt which amounts to (or liquid debts which in aggregate amount to) not less than £1,500 or such sum as may be prescribed, serves on the debtor, by personal service by an officer of court, a demand in the prescribed form requiring the debtor either to pay the debt (or debts) or to find security for its (or their) payment and the condition set out in subsection (3) is met.

(2) The circumstances are—

(a) that at the time of the occurrence, the debtor was able and willing to pay the debtor's debts as they became due, or

(b) that, but for the debtor's property being affected by a restraint order or being subject to a confiscation order or charging order, the debtor would at that time have been able to pay those debts as they became due.

(3) The condition is that the debtor does not, within 3 weeks after the date of service—

(a) comply with the demand, or

(b) intimate to the creditor, by recorded delivery, that the debtor—

(i) denies that there is a debt, or

(ii) denies that the sum claimed by the creditor as the debt is immediately payable.

(4) The apparent insolvency of a partnership is constituted (or as the case may be again constituted) either—

(a) in accordance with subsection (1), or

(b) if any of the partners is apparently insolvent for a debt of the partnership.

(5) The apparent insolvency of an unincorporated body is constituted (or as the case may be again constituted) either—

(a) if a person representing the body is apparently insolvent for a debt of the body, or

(b) if a person holding property for the body in a fiduciary capacity is apparently insolvent for such a debt.

(6) Notwithstanding subsection (2) of section 6, the apparent insolvency of an entity such as is mentioned in that subsection may be constituted (or as the case may be again constituted) under subsection (1); and any reference to the debtor in subsections (1) to (3) and (7) is, except where the context otherwise requires, to be construed as including a reference to such an entity.

(7) The debtor's apparent insolvency continues—

(a) if constituted under paragraph (a) or (b) of subsection (1), until the debtor's discharge,

(b) if constituted under paragraph (c), (e), (f), (g), (h) or (i) of that subsection, until the debtor becomes able to pay the debtor's debts and pays them as they become due.

[. . .]

(8) In this section—

'charging order' means an order made under section 78 of the Criminal Justice Act 1988 or under section 27 of the Drug Trafficking Act 1994,

'confiscation order' means a confiscation order made under Part 2, 3 or 4 of the Proceeds of Crime Act 2002,

'liquid debt' does not include a sum payable under a confiscation order,

'relevant detention power' means section 44A, 47J, 47K, 47M, 47P, 122A, 127J, 127K, 127M, 127P, 193A, 195J, 195K, 195M or 195P of the Proceeds of Crime Act 2002, and

'restraint order' means a restraint order made under Part 2, 3 or 4 of that Act of 2002.

Concurrent proceedings

17 Concurrent proceedings for sequestration or analogous remedy

(1) If, in the course of sequestration proceedings (referred to in this section and in section 18 as the 'instant proceedings'), a person who is a petitioner for sequestration, the debtor, or a creditor concurring in a debtor application is or becomes aware of any of the circumstances mentioned in subsection (2), that person must as soon as may be take the action mentioned in subsection (3).

(2) The circumstances are that, notwithstanding the instant proceedings—

(a) a petition for sequestration of the debtor's estate is before a sheriff,

(b) such sequestration has been awarded,

(c) a debtor application has been made in relation to the debtor's estate,

(d) sequestration has been awarded by virtue of any such application,

(e) a petition for the appointment of a judicial factor on the debtor's estate is before a court,

(f) such a judicial factor has been appointed,

(g) a petition is before a court for the winding up of the debtor under Part 4 or 5 of the Insolvency Act 1986 or section 372 of the Financial Services and Markets Act 2000,

(h) an application for an analogous remedy in respect of the debtor's estate is proceeding, or

(i) such an analogous remedy is in force.

(3) The action is—

(a) where the instant proceedings are by petition for sequestration, to notify the sheriff to whom that petition was presented of the circumstances in question,

(b) where the instant proceedings are by debtor application, to notify AiB of those circumstances.

(4) A petitioner who fails to comply with subsection (1) may be made liable for the expenses of presenting the petition for sequestration.

(5) A debtor who fails so to comply commits an offence.

(6) A debtor who commits an offence under subsection (5) is liable on summary conviction to a fine not exceeding level 5 on the standard scale.

(7) A creditor concurring in a debtor application who fails so to comply may be made liable for the expenses of making the debtor application.

(8) In this section and in section 18, 'analogous remedy' means—

(a) in relation to England and Wales—

(i) an individual voluntary arrangement or bankruptcy order under the Insolvency Act 1986,

(ii) an administration order under section 112 of the County Courts Act 1984, or

(iii) a remedy having the like effect to any of those mentioned in sub-paragraphs (i) and (ii) or to sequestration, and

(b) in relation to Northern Ireland or to any other country, a remedy having the like effect as a remedy mentioned in paragraph (a).

18 Powers in relation to concurrent proceedings

(1) Where, in the course of instant proceedings (see section 17(1)) which are by petition, any of the circumstances mentioned in paragraphs (a) to (g) of section 17(2) exists, the sheriff to whom the petition in the instant proceedings was presented may, on the sheriff's own motion or at the instance of the debtor, of a creditor or of any other person having an interest—

(a) allow the petition to proceed,

(b) sist it, or

(c) dismiss it.

(2) Without prejudice to subsection (1), where, in the course of such instant proceedings, any of the circumstances mentioned in paragraph (a), (b), (e), (f) or

(g) of section 17(2) exists, the Court of Session may, on the Court's own motion or at the instance of the debtor, of a creditor or of any other person having an interest—

(a) direct the sheriff before whom the petition in the instant proceedings is pending or the sheriff before whom the other petition is pending, to sist or dismiss the petition in the instant proceedings or, as the case may be, the other petition, or

(b) order the petitions to be heard together.

(3) Without prejudice to subsection (1), where, in the course of such instant proceedings, any of the circumstances mentioned in paragraph (c) or (d) of section 17(2) exists, the sheriff to whom the petition in the instant proceedings was presented may, on the sheriff's own motion or at the instance of the debtor, of a creditor or of any other person having an interest, direct AiB to dismiss the debtor application.

(4) AiB must recall an award of sequestration if—

(a) the award was by virtue of a debtor application, and

(b) the sheriff directs AiB to dismiss the debtor application.

(5) The effect of the recall of an award of sequestration is, so far as practicable, to restore the debtor and any other person affected by the sequestration to the position the debtor or, as the case may be, the other person would have been in if the sequestration had not been awarded.

(6) A recall of an award of sequestration does not—

(a) affect the interruption of prescription caused by—

(i) the presentation of the petition for sequestration,

(ii) the making of the debtor application, or

(iii) the submission of a claim under section 46 or 122,

(b) invalidate any transaction entered into before such recall by the interim trustee, or by the trustee, with a person acting in good faith, or

(c) affect a bankruptcy restrictions order which has not been revoked under section 161(1)(a).

(7) Without delay after granting recall of an award of sequestration under subsection (4), AiB must send a certified copy of the decision to the Keeper of the Register of Inhibitions for recording in that register.

(8) Where, in the course of instant proceedings which are by debtor application, any of the circumstances mentioned in paragraphs (a) to (g) of section 17(2) exists, AiB may dismiss the debtor application in the instant proceedings.

(9) Subsection (10) applies where, in respect of the same estate—

(a) a petition for sequestration is pending before a sheriff, and

(b) an application for an analogous remedy (see section 17(8)) is proceeding or an analogous remedy is in force.

(10) The sheriff, on the sheriff's own motion or at the instance of the debtor, of a creditor or of any other person having an interest, may—

(a) allow the petition for sequestration to proceed,

(b) sist it, or

(c) dismiss it.

(11) Subsection (12) applies where, in respect of the same estate—

(a) a debtor application has been made and is not yet determined, and

(b) an application for an analogous remedy is proceeding or an analogous remedy is in force.

(12) AiB may proceed to determine the application or may dismiss it.

Creditor's oath

19 Creditor's oath

(1) Every creditor who is—

(a) a petitioner for sequestration,

(b) a creditor who concurs in a debtor application, or

(c) a qualified creditor who becomes sisted under subsection (3) of section 10 (or under that subsection as applied by section 6(9)),

must produce an oath, in the prescribed form, made by or on behalf of the creditor.

(2) The oath may be made—

(a) in the United Kingdom, before any person entitled to administer an oath there,

(b) outwith the United Kingdom, before—

(i) a British diplomatic or consular officer, or

(ii) any person authorised to administer an oath or affirmation under the law of the place where the oath is made.

(3) The identity of the creditor and the identity of the person before whom the oath is made, and their authority to make and to administer the oath respectively, are presumed to be correctly stated unless the contrary is established.

(4) Any seal or signature on the oath is presumed to be authentic unless the contrary is established.

(5) If the oath contains an error or has omitted a fact—

(a) the sheriff to whom the petition was presented, or

(b) in the case of a creditor concurring in a debtor application, AiB,

may at any time before sequestration is awarded allow another oath to be produced rectifying the original oath.

(6) This section applies to the making of that other oath as it applies to the making of the original oath.

(7) The creditor must produce, along with the oath—

(a) an account or voucher (according to the nature of the debt) which constitutes prima facie evidence of the debt, and

(b) if a petitioning creditor, such evidence as is available to the creditor to show the apparent insolvency of the debtor.

PART 2
SEQUESTRATION: AWARD AND RECALL

Incomplete or inappropriate debtor applications

20 Debtor application: incomplete application

(1) This section applies where a debtor application is made and AiB considers that—

(a) the application is incomplete,

(b) further information is required in relation to the application,

(c) further evidence is required to substantiate any fact relevant to the application, or

(d) any fee or charge applicable to the application is outstanding.

(2) AiB must specify by notice in writing to the debtor—

(a) any further information which must be provided,

(b) any further evidence which must be provided, and

(c) any fee or charge to be paid.

(3) Any information, evidence, fee or charge to be provided or paid under subsection (2) must be provided or paid within 21 days (or such greater number of days as may be specified by AiB) beginning with the day on which notice is sent under that subsection.

(4) AiB may refuse to award sequestration if, after the expiry of the days referred to in subsection (3), AiB considers that—

(a) the application remains incomplete,

(b) the debtor has provided insufficient information or evidence under subsection (2)(a) or (b), or

(c) any fee or charge applicable to the application remains outstanding.

21 Refusal of debtor application: inappropriate application

(1) This section applies where a debtor application is made and AiB considers that an award of sequestration may not be appropriate in the circumstances of the case.

(2) AiB must specify by notice in writing to the debtor—

(a) the reason why AiB considers the application may not be appropriate, and

(b) any further information which must be provided within 21 days (or such greater number of days as may be specified by AiB) beginning with the day on which notice is sent under this subsection.

(3) AiB may refuse to award sequestration if, after the expiry of the days referred to in subsection (2)(b), AiB remains of the view that an award of sequestration would be inappropriate in the circumstances of the case.

Award of sequestration

22 When sequestration is awarded

(1) Where a debtor application (other than an application under section 5(a)) is made and neither section 20 nor section 21 applies, AiB must award sequestration forthwith if satisfied—

(a) that the application is made in accordance with—

(i) this Act, and

(ii) any provisions made under this Act,

(b) that section [2(2) or (8)] applies to the debtor, and

(c) that the provisions of section 8(3)(a) have been complied with.

(2) Where a debtor application is made under section 5(a), AiB must award sequestration forthwith if satisfied—

(a) that the application has been made in accordance with this Act and with any provisions made under this Act, and

(b) that the provisions of section 8(3)(a) have been complied with.

(3) Where a petition for sequestration of the estate of a debtor is presented by—

(a) a creditor, or

(b) a trustee acting under a trust deed,

the sheriff must grant warrant to cite the debtor to appear before the sheriff on such date as is specified in the warrant to show cause why sequestration should not be awarded.

(4) Any date specified under subsection (3) must be—

(a) no fewer than 6, and

(b) no more than 14, days after the date of citation.

(5) The sheriff must forthwith award sequestration on that petition on being satisfied—

(a) if the debtor has not appeared, that proper citation has been made of the debtor,

(b) that the petition has been presented in accordance with this Act,

(c) that the provisions of section 13(1) have been complied with,

(d) that in the case of a petition by a trustee—

(i) at least one of the conditions in section 2(7)(a) applies, or

(ii) the petition includes an averment in accordance with section 2(7)(b), and

(e) that, in the case of a petition by a creditor, the requirements of this Act relating to apparent insolvency have been fulfilled.

(6) But subsection (5) is subject to section 23.

(7) In this Act, 'the date of sequestration' means—

(a) where a debtor application is made, the date on which sequestration is awarded,

(b) where the petition for sequestration is presented by a creditor, or by a trustee acting under a trust deed, and sequestration is awarded, the date on which the sheriff granted warrant under subsection (3) (or, where more than one warrant is so granted, the date on which the first warrant is so granted).

23 Circumstances in which sequestration is not to be awarded in pursuance of section 22(5)

(1) Sequestration must not be awarded in pursuance of section 22(5) if—

(a) cause is shown why sequestration cannot competently be awarded,

(b) the debtor forthwith pays or satisfies, or produces written evidence of the payment or satisfaction of—

(i) the debt in respect of which the debtor became apparently insolvent, and

(ii) any other debt due by the debtor to the petitioner and to any creditor concurring in the petition.

(2) Where the sheriff is satisfied that the debtor will, within 42 days beginning with the day the debtor appears before the sheriff, pay or satisfy the debts mentioned in sub-paragraphs (i) and (ii) of subsection (1)(b), the sheriff may continue the petition for no more than 42 days.

(3) The sheriff may continue the petition for such period as the sheriff thinks fit if satisfied—

(a) that a debt payment programme, under Part 1 of the 2002 Act, relating to the debts mentioned in sub-paragraphs (i) and (ii) of subsection (1)(b) has been applied for and has not yet been approved or rejected, or

(b) that such a debt payment programme will be applied for.

[23A Effect of sequestration on land attachment

(1) No land attachment of the heritable property of a debtor, created within the 6 months before the date of sequestration (whether or not subsisting at that date), is effectual to create a preference for the creditor.

(2) A creditor who creates a land attachment within the 6 months mentioned in subsection (1) is entitled to payment, out of the attached land or out of the proceeds of sale of it, of the expenses incurred—

(a) in obtaining the extract of the decree, or other document, containing the warrant for land attachment, and

(b) in serving the charge for payment, registering the notice of land attachment, serving a copy of that notice, and registering certificate of service of that copy.

(3) A notice of land attachment—

(a) registered on or after the date of sequestration against land forming part of the debtor's heritable estate (including any estate vesting under section 86(5) in the trustee in the sequestration) is of no effect,

(b) registered before that date and in relation to which, by that date, no land attachment is created is of no effect.

(4) It is not competent for a creditor to insist in a land attachment—

(a) created over the debtor's heritable estate before the beginning of the 6 months mentioned in subsection (1), and

(b) which subsists on the date of sequestration.

(5) But subsection (4) is subject to subsections (6) to (9).

(6) Where, in execution of a warrant for sale, a contract to sell the land has been concluded—

(a) the trustee must concur in and ratify the deed implementing that contract, and

(b) the appointed person must account for and pay to the trustee in the sequestration any balance of the proceeds of sale (being the balance which would, but for the sequestration, be due to the debtor) after disbursing those proceeds in accordance with section 116 of the Bankruptcy and Diligence etc (Scotland) Act 2007 (disbursement of proceeds of sale of attached land).

(7) Subsection (6) does not apply where the deed implementing the contract is not registered within 28 days beginning with the day on which—

(a) the certified copy of the order of the sheriff granting warrant is recorded, under subsection (1)(a) of section 26, in the Register of Inhibitions, or

(b) the certified copy of the determination of AiB awarding sequestration is recorded, under subsection (2) of that section, in that register.

(8) Where a decree of foreclosure has been granted but an extract of it has not been registered, the creditor may proceed to complete title to the land by registering that extract provided that the creditor does so before the expiry of the days mentioned in subsection (7).

(9) The Scottish Ministers may, as they think fit, prescribe a period in substitution for the days mentioned in subsection (7); and a different period may be prescribed for the purposes of subsection (8) than is prescribed for the purposes of subsection (7).

(10) Expressions used in this section which also occur in Chapter 2 of Part 4 of the Bankruptcy and Diligence etc (Scotland) Act 2007 have the same meanings in this section as they have in that Chapter.]

24 Effect of sequestration on diligence generally

(1) The order of the sheriff, or as the case may be the determination of the debtor application by AiB, awarding sequestration has, as from the date of sequestration, in relation to diligence done (whether before or after that date) in respect of any part of the estate of the debtor, the effect mentioned in subsection (2).

(2) The effect is of—

(a) a decree of adjudication of the heritable estate of the debtor for payment of debts duly recorded in the Register of Inhibitions on the date of sequestration,

(b) an arrestment in execution and decree of furthcoming,

(c) an arrestment in execution and warrant for sale, and

(d) an attachment,

in favour of the creditors according to their respective entitlements.

(3) Where an inhibition on the estate of the debtor takes effect within the 60 days before the date of sequestration, any relevant right of challenge vests, at the date of sequestration, in the trustee in the sequestration as does any right of the inhibitor to receive payment for the discharge of the inhibition.

(4) But subsection (3) neither entitles the trustee to receive any payment made to the inhibitor before the date of sequestration nor affects the validity of anything done before that date in consideration of such payment.

(5) In subsection (3), 'any relevant right of challenge' means any right to challenge a deed voluntarily granted by the debtor if it is a right which vested in the inhibitor by virtue of the inhibition.

(6) No arrestment, money attachment, interim attachment or attachment of the debtor's estate (including any estate vesting in the trustee under section 86(5)) executed—

(a) within the 60 days before the date of sequestration and whether or not subsisting at that date, or

(b) on or after that date,

is effectual to create a preference for the arrester or attacher.

(7) The estate so arrested or attached is, or any funds released under section 73J(2) of the Debtors (Scotland) Act 1987 (automatic release of funds) or the proceeds of sale of such estate are, to be handed over to the trustee.

(8) An arrester or attacher whose arrestment, money attachment, interim

attachment or attachment is executed within the period mentioned in subsection (6)(a) is entitled to payment, out of the arrested or attached estate or out of the proceeds of the sale of such estate, of the expenses incurred—

(a) in obtaining—

(i) warrant for interim attachment, or

(ii) the extract of the decree or other document on which the arrestment, money attachment or attachment proceeded,

(b) in executing the arrestment, money attachment, interim attachment or attachment, and

(c) in taking any further action in respect of the diligence.

(9) Nothing in subsections (6) to (8) applies to an earnings arrestment, a current maintenance arrangement, a conjoined arrestment order or a deduction from earnings order under the Child Support Act 1991.

25 Effect of sequestration on diligence: estate of deceased debtor

(1) [Sections 23A(1) and (2) and 24 apply] to the estate of a deceased debtor which—

(a) has been sequestrated within 12 months after the date of death, or

(b) was absolutely insolvent at that date and in respect of which a judicial factor has been appointed under section 11A of the Judicial Factors (Scotland) Act 1889 within 12 months after that date,

but with the modifications mentioned in subsection (2).

(2) The modifications are that—

(a) any reference to the date of sequestration is to be construed as a reference to the date of death, and

(b) any reference to the debtor is to be construed as a reference to the deceased debtor.

(3) It is not competent, on or after the date of sequestration, for any creditor [. . .] to be confirmed as executor-creditor on the estate.

(4) Subsections (5) and (6) apply where, within 12 months after the debtor's death—

(a) the debtor's estate is sequestrated, or

(b) a judicial factor is appointed under section 11A of the Judicial Factors (Scotland) Act 1889 to administer the debtor's estate and that estate is absolutely insolvent.

(5) No confirmation as executor-creditor on that estate at any time after the debtor's death is effectual in a question with the trustee or the judicial factor.

(6) But the executor-creditor is entitled—

(a) out of the estate, or

(b) out of the proceeds of sale of the estate,

to the expenses incurred by the executor-creditor in obtaining the confirmation.

26 Registration of warrant or determination of debtor application

(1) On the sheriff granting warrant under section 22(3) the sheriff clerk must forthwith send—

(a) a certified copy of the order granting the warrant to the Keeper of the Register of Inhibitions for recording in that register,

(b) a copy of that order to AiB, and

(c) where the debtor is taking part in a debt payment programme under Part 1 of the 2002 Act, a copy of that order to the DAS administrator ('DAS administrator' having the meaning given by regulation 2(1) of the Debt Arrangement Scheme (Scotland) Regulations 2011 (SSI 2011/141)).

(2) On awarding sequestration on a debtor application AiB must forthwith send a certified copy of AiB's determination of the application to the Keeper of the Register of Inhibitions for recording in that register.

(3) Recording under subsection (1)(a) or (2) has the effect, as from the date of sequestration, of an inhibition and of a citation in an adjudication of the debtor's

heritable estate at the instance of the creditors who subsequently have claims in the sequestration accepted under section 126.

(4) The effect mentioned in subsection (3) expires—

(a) on the recording by virtue of section 27(11)(a) of a certified copy of an order refusing to award sequestration or by virtue of section 30(9)(a) of a certified copy of an order recalling an award of sequestration,

(b) on the recording by virtue of section 18(7), 34(4) or 35(7) of a certified copy of a decision, or

(c) if the effect has not earlier expired by virtue of paragraph (a) or (b), at the end of 3 years beginning with the date of sequestration.

(5) But subsection (4)(c) is subject to subsections (6) and (7).

(6) The trustee may if not discharged send a memorandum, in a form prescribed by act of sederunt, to the Keeper of the Register of Inhibitions for recording in that register before the expiry of—

(a) the 3 years mentioned in subsection (4)(c), or

(b) a period for which the effect mentioned in subsection (3) has been renewed by virtue of subsection (7).

(7) The recording of a memorandum sent in accordance with subsection (6) renews the effect mentioned in subsection (3) for 3 years beginning with the expiry of—

(a) the 3 years mentioned in subsection (4)(c), or

(b) as the case may be, the period mentioned in subsection (6)(b).

(8) The trustee may, if appointed or reappointed under section 152, send a memorandum in a form prescribed by act of sederunt to the Keeper of the Register of Inhibitions for recording in that register before the expiry of that appointment.

(9) The recording of a memorandum sent in accordance with subsection (8) imposes the effect mentioned in subsection (3) for 3 years beginning with the day of notification in accordance with section 153(1).

27 Further matters in relation to award of sequestration

(1) On application the sheriff may, at any time after sequestration has been awarded, transfer the sequestration to any other sheriff.

(2) But subsection (1) is subject to subsection (3).

(3) The debtor may, with the leave of the sheriff, appeal to the Sheriff Appeal Court against such a transfer.

(4) Where the sheriff makes an order refusing to award sequestration, the petitioner may appeal against the order within 14 days after the date on which the order is made.

(5) If, following a debtor application, AiB refuses to award sequestration, the debtor or a creditor concurring in the application may apply to AiB for a review of the refusal.

(6) Any application under subsection (5) must be made within 14 days beginning with the day on which AiB refuses to award sequestration.

(7) If an application under subsection (5) is made, AiB must—

(a) take into account any representations made by an interested person within 21 days beginning with the day on which the application is made, and

(b) confirm the refusal, or award sequestration, within 28 days beginning with that day.

(8) If AiB confirms the refusal to award sequestration under subsection (7)(b), the debtor or a creditor concurring in the application may, within 14 days beginning with the day of that confirmation, appeal to the sheriff.

(9) An award of sequestration is not subject to review otherwise than by recall under—

(a) section 18(4),

(b) sections 29 and 30,
(c) section 34, or
(d) section 35.

(10) Subsection (9) is without prejudice to any right to bring an action of reduction of an award of sequestration.

(11) Where a petition for sequestration is presented by a creditor, or by a trustee acting under a trust deed, the sheriff clerk is—

(a) on the final determination or the abandonment of any appeal under subsection (4) in relation to the petition, or (if there is no such appeal) within the 14 days mentioned in that subsection, to send a certified copy of the order refusing to award sequestration to the Keeper of the Register of Inhibitions for recording in that register,

(b) to send forthwith a copy of that order to—

(i) AiB, and

(ii) where the debtor is taking part in a debt payment programme under Part 1 of the 2002 Act, the DAS administrator ('DAS administrator' having the meaning given by regulation 2(1) of the Debt Arrangement Scheme (Scotland) Regulations 2011 (SSI 2011/141)).

(12) Where sequestration has been awarded the process of sequestration is not to fall asleep.

28 Benefit from another estate

(1) Where a debtor learns, whether before or after the date of sequestration, that the debtor may derive benefit from another estate, the debtor must as soon as practicable after that date inform—

(a) the trustee in the sequestration, of that fact, and
(b) the person who is administering that other estate, of the sequestration.

(2) A debtor who fails to comply with subsection (1) commits an offence.

(3) A debtor who commits an offence under subsection (2) is liable, on summary conviction, to a fine not exceeding level 5 on the standard scale.

Recall of sequestration

29 Petitions for recall of sequestration

(1) A petition for recall of an award of sequestration may be presented to the sheriff by—

(a) the debtor,
(b) any creditor,
(c) any other person having an interest (whether or not a person who was a petitioner for, or concurred in a debtor application for, the sequestration),
(d) the trustee in the sequestration, or
(e) AiB.

(2) Such a petition may not be presented to the sheriff if the only ground is that the debtor has paid, or is able to pay, the debtor's debts in full.

(3) Subsection (2) does not apply where—

(a) sequestration was awarded following a petition of a qualified creditor or qualified creditors, and

(b) a petition for recall of the award of sequestration includes the ground that the debtor was not apparently insolvent.

(4) A copy of the petition, along with a notice stating that the recipient of the notice may lodge answers to the petition within 14 days after service of the notice, must be served by the petitioner on—

(a) the debtor [(where the debtor is not the petitioner)],
(b) any [other] person who was a petitioner for, or concurred in a debtor application for, the sequestration,
(c) the trustee [(where the trustee is not the petitioner)], and
(d) AiB [(where AiB is not the petitioner)].

(5) On service, under subsection (4), of a copy of the petition AiB must enter particulars of the petition in the register of insolvencies.
(6) A petition under this section may be presented at any time.
(7) But subsection (6) is subject to sections 114(3) and 115(3).
(8) Notwithstanding that a petition has been presented under this section, the proceedings in the sequestration are to continue as if the petition had not been presented until the recall is granted.
(9) But subsection (8) is subject to section 30(7).
(10) Subsection (11) applies where a petitioner under this section, or a person who has lodged answers to the petition, withdraws or dies.
(11) Any person—
(a) entitled to present, or
(b) entitled to lodge answers to,
a petition under this section may be sisted in place of the person who has withdrawn or died.

30 Recall of sequestration by sheriff

(1) The sheriff may recall the award of sequestration if satisfied that in all the circumstances of the case (including those arising after the date of the award) it is appropriate to do so.
(2) In particular, the sheriff may recall the award if satisfied—
(a) that the debtor has paid the debtor's debts in full [(including the payment of any interest payable on the debtor's debts and the payment of the outlays and remuneration of the interim trustee and of the trustee)],
(b) that a majority in value of the creditors reside in a country other than Scotland and that it is more appropriate for the debtor's estate to be administered in that other country, or
(c) that another award of sequestration of the estate, or of an analogous remedy, as defined in section 17(8), has (or other such awards have) been granted.
(3) Where another award of sequestration of the debtor's estate has been granted, the sheriff may, after such intimation as the sheriff considers necessary, recall an award (whether or not the award in respect of which the petition for recall was presented).
(4) Where the sheriff intends to recall an award of sequestration on the ground that the debtor has paid the debtor's debts in full, the order recalling the award may not—
(a) be made before the payment in full of [—
(i) any interest payable on the debtor's debts (see section 37A), and
(ii)] the outlays and remuneration of the trustee and of the interim trustee, or
(b) be subject to any conditions which are to be fulfilled before the order takes effect.
(5) On or before recalling an award of sequestration, the sheriff—
(a) must make provision for the payment of the outlays and remuneration of the trustee in the sequestration (see section 50(1)) and of any interim trustee (see section 53(1))—
(i) by directing that such payment must be made out of the debtor's estate, or
(ii) by requiring that a person who was a party to the petition for sequestration, or as the case may be to the debtor application, must pay the whole or any part of those outlays and remuneration,
(b) may direct that payment of the expenses of a creditor who was a petitioner for sequestration, or concurred in the debtor's application for sequestration, must be made out of the debtor's estate, and
(c) may make any further order the sheriff considers necessary or reasonable in all the circumstances of the case.
(6) Subsection (5)(b) is without prejudice to subsection (8).

(7) Where the sheriff considers that it is inappropriate to recall, or to refuse to recall, an award of sequestration forthwith, the sheriff may order that the proceedings in the sequestration are to continue but are to be subject to such conditions as the sheriff may think fit.

(8) The sheriff may make such order in relation to the expenses in a petition for recall as the sheriff thinks fit.

(9) The sheriff clerk must send—

(a) a certified copy of any order recalling an award of sequestration to the Keeper of the Register of Inhibitions for recording in that register, and

(b) a copy of any interim or final order recalling, or refusing to recall, an award of sequestration or a copy of any order under section 114(3)(b) or 115(3)(b)—

(i) to AiB, and

(ii) if AiB is not the trustee in the sequestration, to the trustee in the sequestration.

31 Application to Accountant in Bankruptcy for recall of sequestration

(1) An application for recall of an award of sequestration may be made to AiB on the ground that the debtor has paid or is able to pay the debtor's debts in full.

(2) An application may be made by—

(a) the debtor,

(b) any creditor (whether or not a person who was a petitioner for, or concurred in a debtor application for, the sequestration),

(c) the trustee (where AiB is not the trustee), or

(d) any other person having an interest (whether or not a person who was a petitioner for the sequestration).

(3) The person making an application must, at the same time as applying to AiB, give to the [other] persons mentioned in subsection (4)—

(a) a copy of the application, and

(b) a notice informing the recipient that the person has a right to make representations to AiB in relation to the application within 21 days beginning with the day on which the notice is given.

(4) The persons are—

(a) the debtor [. . .],

(b) any person who was a petitioner for, or concurred in a debtor application for, the sequestration, and

(c) the trustee [(where AiB is not the trustee)].

(5) Despite an application being made, the proceedings in the sequestration are to continue as if the application had not been made until a recall of an award of sequestration is granted[—

(a) where AiB is not the trustee,] under section 34(1) (subject to any conditions imposed under section 34(3)).

[(b) where AiB is the trustee, under section 35(6) (subject to any conditions imposed under section 35(6B)).]

(6) Where the applicant withdraws the application or dies, AiB may continue the application by substituting any person mentioned in subsection (2) for the applicant.

32 [Application under section 31: further procedure where Accountant in Bankruptcy is not trustee]

[(1) This section applies where—

(a) an application is made under section 31, and

(b) AiB is not the trustee.]

(2) The trustee must prepare a statement on the debtor's affairs so far as within the knowledge of the trustee.

(3) The trustee must submit the statement to AiB—

(a) at the same time as the trustee makes the application under section 31, or

(b) where that application is made by another person, within 21 days beginning with the day on which notice is given under section 31(3)(b).

(4) The statement must—

(a) indicate whether the debtor has agreed to—

(i) the interim trustee's claim for outlays reasonably incurred and for remuneration for work reasonably undertaken by the interim trustee (including any outlays and remuneration which are yet to be incurred), and

(ii) the trustee's claim for outlays reasonably incurred and for remuneration for work reasonably undertaken by the trustee (including any outlays and remuneration which are yet to be incurred),

(b) state whether or not the debtor's debts have been paid in full [, including the payment in full of—

(i) any interest payable on the debtor's debts (see section 37A),

(ii) the outlays and remuneration of the interim trustee and of the trustee,]

(c) where the debtor's debts have not been so paid—

(i) provide details of any debt which has not been paid, and

(ii) indicate whether, in the opinion of the trustee, the debtor's assets are likely to be sufficient to pay the debts in full (including the payment of [any interest payable on the debtor's debts and payment of] the outlays and remuneration of the interim trustee and of the trustee) within 8 weeks beginning with the day on which the statement is submitted, and

(d) provide details of any distribution of the debtor's estate.

(5) The trustee must notify every creditor known to the trustee that the application has been made—

(a) where it is made by the trustee, within 7 days beginning with the day on which it is made, and

(b) where it is made by a person other than the trustee, within 7 days beginning with the day on which notice is given under section 31(3)(b).

(6) If a creditor has not previously submitted a claim under section 46 or 122, the creditor must, in order to be included in the statement made by the trustee, submit a claim.

(7) That claim must be submitted—

(a) in accordance with section 46(2) to (4), and

(b) within 14 days beginning with the day on which notice is given under subsection (5).

(8) If any creditor submits a claim in accordance with subsection (7), the trustee must update and re-submit the statement within 7 days after the days mentioned in paragraph (b) of that subsection have expired.

(9) The trustee must update and re-submit the statement if—

(a) the statement previously submitted did not state in accordance with subsection (4)(b) that the debtor's debts have been paid in full, and

(b) before the day on which the application is determined by AiB, the trustee is able to make that statement.

33 Determination where amount of outlays and remuneration not agreed

(1) This section applies where—

(a) AiB receives an application under section 31 [. . .]

[(aa) AiB is not the trustee, and]

(b) the statement submitted by the trustee under section 32 indicates that the amount of the outlays and remuneration of the trustee is not agreed.

(2) The trustee must—

(a) at the same time as submitting the statement under section 32, provide AiB with—

(i) the trustee's accounts of the trustee's intromissions with the debtor's estate for audit, and

(ii) details of the trustee's claim for outlays reasonably incurred and for remuneration for work reasonably undertaken by the trustee (including any outlays and remuneration which are yet to be incurred), and

(b) provide AiB with such other information in relation to that claim as may reasonably be requested by AiB.

(3) AiB must, within 28 days after the days mentioned in section 32(7)(b) have expired, issue a determination fixing the amount of the outlays and of the remuneration payable to the trustee.

(4) AiB may, within the 28 days mentioned in subsection (3), determine the expenses reasonably incurred by a creditor who was a petitioner for, or as the case may be concurred in a debtor application for, sequestration.

(5) Subsections (2) to (4) of section 133 apply to AiB for the purpose of issuing a determination in accordance with subsection (3) as they apply to the commissioners or to AiB for the purpose of fixing an amount under that section.

34 [Recall of sequestration where Accountant in Bankruptcy is not trustee]

[(A1) This section applies where AiB is not the trustee.]

(1) AiB may recall an award of sequestration if—

(a) the trustee has notified AiB, in the statement submitted under section 32, that the debtor's debts have been paid in full[, including the payment in full of—

(i) any interest payable on the debtor's debts (see section 37A),

(ii) the outlays and remuneration of the interim trustee and of the trustee,] and

(b) AiB is satisfied that in all the circumstances it is appropriate to do so.

[(1A) Before recalling an award of sequestration AiB must take into account any representations made by an interested person within 21 days beginning with the day on which notice is given under section 31(3)(b).]

(2) AiB may not recall an award of sequestration after—

(a) where no appeal in made under section 37(5)(a), the day which is [9 weeks] after the day on which the statement was first submitted under section 32(3), or

(b) where such an appeal is made, such later day which is 14 days after the day on which the appeal is finally determined or abandoned.

(3) If AiB does not under subsection (1) recall an award of sequestration, the sequestration must continue but is to be subject to such conditions as AiB thinks fit.

(4) Without delay after granting recall under subsection (1), AiB must send a certified copy of the decision to the Keeper of the Register of Inhibitions for recording in that register.

35 [Recall of sequestration where Accountant in Bankruptcy is trustee]

(1) This section applies where AiB—

(a) is the trustee, and

(b) [either—

(i) receives an application under section 31, or

(ii)] considers recall of an award of sequestration [may] be granted on the ground that the debtor has paid, or is able to pay, the debtor's debts in full (including [the payment of any interest payable on the debtor's debts and the payment of] the outlays and remuneration of the interim trustee and the trustee).

(2) AiB must[—

(a) where an application under section 31 is received, notify every creditor known to AiB that the application has been made within 7 days beginning with the day on which the application is received,

(b) where AiB is acting on its own accord,] notify the debtor and every creditor known to AiB that AiB considers subsection (1) applies.

[(2A) At the same time as giving notice under subsection (2)(b), AiB must give to the persons mentioned in subsection (2B) a notice informing the recipient that the person has a right to make representations to AiB in relation to the notification within 21 days beginning with the day on which the notice is given.

(2B) The persons are—

(a) the debtor, and

(b) any person who was a petitioner for, or concurred in a debtor application for, the sequestration.]

(3) If a creditor has not previously submitted a claim under section 46 or 122, the creditor must, in order for the creditor's claim to a dividend out of the debtor's estate to be considered, submit a claim.

(4) The claim must be submitted—

(a) in accordance with section 46(2) to (4), and

(b) within 14 days beginning with the day on which notice is given under subsection (2).

(5) Before recalling an award of sequestration AiB must—

(a) take into account any representations made by an interested person within 21 days beginning with the day on which notice is given under [subsection (2A) or, as the case may be, section 31(3)(b)], and

(b) make a determination of AiB's fees and outlays calculated in accordance with regulations under section 205.

(6) AiB may recall an award of sequestration if satisfied that—

(a) the debtor has paid the debtor's debts in full[, including the payment in full of—

(i) any interest payable on the debtor's debts (see section 37A),

(ii) the outlays and remuneration of the interim trustee and of the trustee,]

(b) those debts were paid in full within 8 weeks after the days mentioned in subsection (5)(a) have expired, and

(c) in all the circumstances it is appropriate to recall it.

[(6A) AiB may not recall an award of sequestration after—

(a) where no appeal is made under section 37(5)(a), the day which is 9 weeks after the days mentioned in subsection (5)(a) have expired, or

(b) where such an appeal is made, such later day which is 14 days after the day on which the appeal is finally determined or abandoned.

(6B) If AiB does not under subsection (6) recall an award of sequestration, the sequestration must continue but is to be subject to such conditions as AiB thinks fit.

(6C) Despite notice being given under subsection (2)(b), the proceedings in the sequestration are to continue as if the notification had not been made until a recall of an award of sequestration is granted under subsection (6) (subject to any conditions imposed under subsection (6B)).]

(7) Without delay after recalling an award of sequestration under subsection (6), AiB must send a certified copy of the decision to the Keeper of the Register of Inhibitions for recording in that register.

36 Application for recall: remit to sheriff

(1) AiB may, at any time before deciding under section 34(1) whether to recall an award of sequestration, remit to the sheriff an application made under section 31.

(2) AiB may, at any time before deciding under section 35(6) whether to recall an award of sequestration, remit the case to the sheriff.

(3) If an application is remitted under subsection (1) or (2), the sheriff may dispose of the application or the case in accordance with section 30 as if it were a petition presented by AiB under section 29.

37 Recall of sequestration by Accountant in Bankruptcy: review and appeal

(1) A person mentioned in subsection (2) may apply to AiB for a review of—

(a) a decision of AiB under section 34(1) or 35(6) to recall, or refuse to recall, an award of sequestration, or

(b) a determination of AiB under section 33(4).

(2) The persons are—

(a) the debtor,

(b) any creditor,
(c) the trustee, and
(d) any other person having an interest.

(3) Any application under subsection (1) must be made within 14 days beginning with the day on which the decision or, as the case may be, the determination or requirement is made.

(4) If an application under subsection (1) is made, AiB must—

(a) take into account any representations made by an interested person within 21 days beginning with the day on which the application is made, and

(b) confirm, amend or revoke the decision, determination or requirement within 28 days beginning with that date.

(5) A person mentioned in subsection (2) may, within 14 days beginning with the day on which the decision, determination or requirement is made, appeal to the sheriff against—

(a) a determination of AiB under section 33(3) or 35(5)(b), or
(b) a decision of AiB under subsection (4)(b).

(6) Any decision of the sheriff on an appeal relating to a determination of AiB under section 33(3) or 35(5)(b) is final.

[37A Interest

(1) This section applies for the purpose of determining the amount of interest payable on the debtor's debts in relation to a recall of an award of sequestration.

(2) Interest, between the date of sequestration and the date of payment of the debt, is payable at the rate specified in section 129(10), unless subsection (3) applies.

(3) This subsection applies if the whole of the debt is paid in full within 6 months after the date of the award of sequestration, in which case interest is not payable on the debt.

(4) For the avoidance of doubt, if only part of the debt is paid within 6 months after the date of the award of sequestration, interest is payable on the whole of the debt (including any part of the debt already paid since the award) in accordance with subsection (2).]

38 Effect of recall of sequestration

(1) The effect of the recall of an award of sequestration is, so far as practicable, to restore the debtor and any other person affected by the sequestration to the position the debtor, or, as the case may be, the other person, would have been in if the sequestration had not been awarded.

(2) But subsection (1) is subject to subsection (3).

(3) A recall of an award of sequestration is not to—

(a) affect the interruption of prescription caused by—
(i) the presentation of the petition for sequestration,
(ii) the making of the debtor application, or
(iii) the submission of a claim under section 46 or 122,

(b) invalidate any transaction entered into before such recall by the interim trustee, or by the trustee in the sequestration, with a person acting in good faith, or

(c) affect a bankruptcy restrictions order which has not been revoked under section 161(1)(a).

PART 3
INITIAL STAGES OF SEQUESTRATION, STATUTORY MEETING AND TRUSTEE VOTE

Initial stages

39 Interim preservation of estate

(1) An interim trustee may, in pursuance of the function conferred by section 53(1), give general or particular directions to the debtor relating to the management

of the debtor's estate.

(2) In exercising the function so conferred, an interim trustee may—

(a) require the debtor to deliver up to the interim trustee—

(i) any money or valuables, or

(ii) any document relating to the debtor's business or financial affairs,

belonging to, or in the possession of, the debtor or under the debtor's control,

(b) place in safe custody anything mentioned in paragraph (a),

(c) require the debtor to deliver up to the interim trustee any perishable goods belonging to the debtor or under the debtor's control,

(d) arrange for the sale or disposal of such goods,

(e) make, or cause to be made, an inventory or valuation of any property belonging to the debtor,

(f) require the debtor to implement any transaction entered into by the debtor,

(g) effect or maintain insurance policies in respect of the business or property of the debtor, or

(h) carry on any business of the debtor or borrow money in so far as it is necessary for the interim trustee to do so to safeguard the debtor's estate.

(3) Section 111 applies to an interim trustee as it applies to a trustee.

(4) The sheriff, on the application of an interim trustee, may—

(a) on cause shown, grant a warrant authorising the interim trustee to enter the house where the debtor resides or the debtor's business premises and to search for and take possession of anything mentioned in subsection (2)(a) or (c) (if need be, by opening shut and lock-fast places), or

(b) make such other order to safeguard the debtor's estate as the sheriff thinks appropriate.

(5) Where AiB is the interim trustee, the debtor may apply to AiB for a review of a direction under subsection (1) on the ground that the direction is unreasonable.

(6) If an application under subsection (5) is made, AiB must—

(a) take into account any representations made by an interested person within 21 days beginning with the day on which the application is made, and

(b) confirm, amend or revoke the direction (whether or not substituting a new direction) within 28 days beginning with that day.

(7) The sheriff may, on an application made by the debtor made within 14 days beginning with the day on which AiB makes a decision under subsection (6)(b)—

(a) set aside a direction under subsection (1) or (6)(b) if the sheriff considers the direction to be unreasonable, and

(b) in any event, give such directions to the debtor regarding the management of the debtor's estate as the sheriff considers appropriate.

(8) The debtor must comply with a direction—

(a) under subsection (1) pending a decision by AiB under subsection (6)(b), and

(b) under subsection (6)(b) pending the final determination of any appeal (subject to any interim order of the sheriff).

(9) Where AiB is not the interim trustee, the sheriff, on an application by the debtor on the grounds that a direction under subsection (1) is unreasonable, may—

(a) set aside the direction if the sheriff considers it to be unreasonable, and

(b) in any event, give such directions to the debtor regarding the management of the debtor's estate as the sheriff considers appropriate.

(10) But, subject to any interim order of the sheriff, the debtor must comply with the direction appealed against pending the final determination of the appeal.

40 Offences in relation to interim preservation of estate

(1) If a debtor—

(a) fails without reasonable excuse to comply with a direction under subsection (1), (6)(b), (7)(b) or (9)(b), or a requirement under subsection (2)(a), (c) or (f), of section 39, or

(b) obstructs the interim trustee where the interim trustee is acting in pursuance of subsection (4)(a) of that section,

then the debtor commits an offence.

(2) A person who commits an offence under subsection (1) is liable—

(a) on summary conviction, to a fine not exceeding the statutory maximum, or—

(i) in a case where the person has previously been convicted of an offence inferring dishonest appropriation of property or an attempt at dishonest appropriation of property, to imprisonment for a term not exceeding 6 months, or

(ii) in any other case, to imprisonment for a term not exceeding 3 months,

or both to a fine not exceeding the statutory maximum and to such imprisonment as is mentioned, in relation to the case in question, in sub-paragraph (i) or (ii), or

(b) on conviction on indictment—

(i) to a fine, or

(ii) to imprisonment for a term not exceeding 2 years,

or both to a fine and to such imprisonment.

41 Statement of assets and liabilities etc

(1) Where a debtor has made a debtor application then, within 7 days after the appointment of the trustee in the sequestration under section 51 (where the trustee is not AiB), the debtor must send to the trustee such statement of assets and liabilities as was sent to AiB in pursuance of section 8(3)(a).

(2) Where a petitioner for sequestration is a creditor, or a trustee acting under a trust deed, then, within 7 days after having been notified by the trustee as mentioned in section 51(13) the debtor must send to the trustee a statement of assets and liabilities.

(3) If the debtor—

(a) fails to disclose any material fact in a statement of assets and liabilities sent to the trustee in accordance with subsection (1) or (2), or

(b) makes a material misstatement in any such statement,

then the debtor commits of an offence.

(4) A person who commits an offence under subsection (3) is liable on summary conviction to a fine not exceeding level 5 on the standard scale or to imprisonment for a term not exceeding 3 months (or both to such fine and to such imprisonment).

(5) In any proceedings for an offence under subsection (3), it is a defence for the accused to show that the accused had a reasonable excuse for the failure to disclose or for the making of the misstatement.

42 Duties on receipt of list of assets and liabilities

(1) As soon as practicable after a trustee has received a statement of assets and liabilities—

(a) the trustee must prepare a statement of the debtor's affairs so far as within the knowledge of the trustee, and

(b) if, in the trustee's opinion, the debtor's assets are unlikely to be sufficient to pay any dividend whatsoever in respect of the debts mentioned in section 129(1)(e) to (i) the trustee is so to indicate in the statement prepared under paragraph (a).

(2) Not later—

(a) than 4 days before the date fixed for the statutory meeting, or

(b) where the trustee does not intend to hold such a meeting, than 60 days after the date on which the sequestration is awarded,

the trustee must send to AiB the statement, copy statement and comments mentioned in subsection (3).

(3) The statement, copy statement and comments are—

(a) the statement of assets and liabilities (unless that statement has already been received by AiB by virtue of section 8(3)(a)),

(b) subject to subsection (4), a copy of the statement prepared under subsection (1)(a), and

(c) written comments by the trustee indicating what in the trustee's opinion are the causes of the insolvency and to what extent the conduct of the debtor may have contributed to the insolvency.

(4) The trustee need not send the copy mentioned in subsection (3)(b) if the trustee has, in accordance with section 108(1)(c), sent a copy of the inventory and valuation to AiB.

(5) The written comments made under subsection (3)(c) are absolutely privileged.

(6) Subsections (2) and (5) do not apply in any case where AiB is the trustee.

Statutory meeting

43 Statutory meeting

A meeting of creditors called under section 44 is referred to in this Act as 'the statutory meeting'.

44 Calling of statutory meeting

(1) The statutory meeting may be held at such time and place as the trustee in the sequestration may determine.

(2) But subsection (1) is subject to subsections (6) and (7).

(3) Not later than—

(a) 60 days after the date on which sequestration is awarded, or

(b) such greater number of days after that date as the sheriff may, on cause shown, allow,

the trustee must give notice to every creditor known to the trustee of whether or not the trustee intends to call the statutory meeting.

(4) A notice under subsection (3)—

(a) must be accompanied by a copy of the trustee's statement of the debtor's affairs, and

(b) where the trustee is notifying an intention not to hold the statutory meeting, must inform creditors of the effect of subsections (5) and (6).

(5) Within 7 days after the giving of notice under subsection (3), any creditor may request the trustee to call the statutory meeting.

(6) Where a request under subsection (5) is made (or requests under that subsection are made) by not less than ¼ in value of the debtor's creditors, the trustee must call the statutory meeting not later than—

(a) 28 days after the date on which notice is given under subsection (3), or

(b) such greater number of days after that date as the sheriff may, on cause shown, allow.

(7) Where the trustee gives notice under subsection (3) that the trustee intends to call the statutory meeting, that meeting must be called within 28 days after the date on which the notice is given.

(8) No fewer than 7 days before the date fixed for the statutory meeting, the trustee—

(a) must notify every creditor known to the trustee of the date, time and place of the meeting, and

(b) must in the notification—

(i) invite the submission of such claims as have not already been submitted, and

(ii) inform the creditors of the trustee's duties under section 48(4).

(9) The creditors may continue the statutory meeting to a date not later than—

(a) 7 days after the days mentioned in subsection (7) have expired, or

(b) such greater number of days after that expiry as the sheriff may, on cause shown, allow.

45 Procedure where no statutory meeting called

(1) Where the trustee in the sequestration does not call the statutory meeting and the 7 days mentioned in section 44(5) expire, the trustee must forthwith make a report to AiB on the circumstance of the sequestration.

(2) But subsection (1) does not apply if AiB is the trustee.

46 Submission of claims for voting purposes

(1) For the purposes of voting at the statutory meeting a creditor (in this section and in section 47 referred to as 'C') must, in accordance with this section, submit a claim to the trustee in the sequestration at or before the meeting.

(2) C submits a claim under this section by producing to the trustee—

(a) a statement of claim in the prescribed form, and

(b) an account or voucher (according to the nature of the debt) which constitutes prima facie evidence of the debt.

(3) But the trustee may dispense with any requirement under subsection (2) in respect of any debt or of any class of debt.

(4) Where C neither resides, nor has a place of business, in the United Kingdom, the trustee—

(a) must, if the trustee knows where C does reside or have a place of business and if no notification has been given to C under section 44(3), write to C informing C that C may submit a claim under this section, and

(b) may allow C to submit an informal claim in writing.

(5) If C has produced a statement of claim in accordance with subsection (2), C may at any time before the statutory meeting produce, in place of that statement of claim, another statement of claim specifying a different amount for C's claim.

(6) C may, in such circumstances as may be prescribed, state the amount of C's claim in foreign currency.

(7) The trustee must, on production of any document to the trustee under this section—

(a) initial the document,

(b) keep a record of it, stating the date on which it was produced to the trustee, and

(c) if requested by the person producing it, return it (if it is not a statement of claim) to that person.

(8) The submission of a claim under this section bars the effect of any enactment or rule of law relating to the limitation of actions.

(9) Schedule 2 has effect for determining the amount in respect of which C is entitled to claim.

47 Offences in relation to submission of claims for voting purposes

(1) Subsections (2) and (3) apply where C produces under section 46—

(a) a statement of claim,

(b) account,

(c) voucher, or

(d) other evidence,

which is false.

(2) C commits an offence unless C shows that C neither knew nor had reason to believe that the statement of claim, account, voucher or other evidence was false.

(3) The debtor commits an offence if the debtor—

(a) knew, or became aware, that the statement of claim, account, voucher or other evidence was false, and

(b) failed, as soon as practicable after acquiring such knowledge, to report to the trustee that the statement of claim, account, voucher or other evidence was false.

(4) A person who commits an offence under subsection (2) or (3) is liable—

(a) on summary conviction, to a fine not exceeding the statutory maximum, or—

(i) in a case where the person has previously been convicted of an offence inferring dishonest appropriation of property or an attempt at dishonest appropriation of property, to imprisonment for a term not exceeding 6 months, or

(ii) in any other case, to imprisonment for a term not exceeding 3 months,

or both to a fine not exceeding the statutory maximum and to such imprisonment as is mentioned, in relation to the case in question, in sub-paragraph (i) or (ii), or

(b) on conviction on indictment, to a fine, to imprisonment for a term not exceeding 2 years or both to a fine and to such imprisonment.

48 Proceedings before trustee vote

(1) At the commencement of the statutory meeting the trustee in the sequestration must chair the meeting and, as the person chairing it, is—

(a) for the purposes of subsection (3), to accept or reject in whole or in part the claim of each creditor (and if the amount of the claim is stated in foreign currency, to convert that amount into sterling, in such manner as may be prescribed, at the rate of exchange prevailing at the close of business on the date of sequestration),

(b) on that being done, to invite the creditors to elect one of their number to chair the meeting in place of the trustee,

(c) to preside over the election, and

(d) to arrange for a record to be made of the proceedings at the meeting.

(2) But, if no person is elected in pursuance of subsection (1)(b), the trustee must chair the statutory meeting throughout.

(3) The acceptance of a claim in whole or in part under paragraph (a) of that subsection is, subject to section 49(6), to determine the entitlement of a creditor to vote at the statutory meeting.

(4) On the conclusion of the proceedings under subsection (1)—

(a) the trustee must make available for inspection—

(i) the statement of assets and liabilities, and

(ii) the statement prepared under section 42(1),

(b) the trustee must answer to the best of the trustee's ability any questions,

(c) the trustee must consider any representations put to the trustee by the creditors which relate to the debtor's—

(i) assets and business or financial affairs, or

(ii) conduct in relation to such assets and affairs,

(d) after the trustee considers any such representations as are mentioned in paragraph (c) if, in the trustee's opinion, the debtor's assets are unlikely to be sufficient to pay any dividend whatsoever in respect of the debts mentioned in paragraphs (e) to (i) of section 129(1), the trustee is so to indicate,

(e) the trustee must determine whether it is necessary to revise the trustee's statement of the debtor's affairs, and

(f) if the trustee does so determine, the trustee must revise the statement either at, or as soon as may be after, the statutory meeting.

(5) Where the trustee does carry out such a revision, the trustee is as soon as possible after the statutory meeting to send a copy of the revised statement to every creditor known to the trustee.

Trustee vote

49 Trustee vote

(1) At the statutory meeting the creditors are, at the conclusion of the proceedings under section 48(4), to proceed to a vote at which they are—

(a) to confirm the appointment of the trustee appointed under section 51 (referred to in this section and in Part 4 as the 'original trustee'), or

(b) to elect another person as the trustee in the sequestration (referred to in this section and in that Part as the 'replacement trustee').

(2) The vote is referred to in this Act as a 'trustee vote'.

(3) None of the persons listed in subsection (5) is eligible for election as replacement trustee.

(4) No one who becomes a person so listed after being elected as replacement trustee is qualified to continue to act as trustee.

(5) The persons are—

(a) the debtor,

(b) a person not qualified to act as an insolvency practitioner,

(c) a person who, though qualified to act as an insolvency practitioner, is not qualified to act as such in relation to the debtor,

(d) a person who holds an interest opposed to the general interests of the creditors,

(e) a person who has not given an undertaking, in writing, to act as trustee, and

(f) AiB.

(6) None of the persons listed in subsection (7) is entitled to vote in the trustee vote.

(7) The persons are—

(a) anyone who, other than by succession, acquires after the date of sequestration a debt due by the debtor, and

(b) any creditor to the extent that the creditor's debt is a postponed debt.

(8) Where AiB is the original trustee, if no creditor entitled to vote in the trustee vote attends the statutory meeting or no replacement trustee is elected, AiB must—

(a) forthwith report the proceedings at the statutory meeting to the sheriff, and

(b) continue to act as the trustee.

(9) Where AiB is not the original trustee, if no creditor entitled to vote in the trustee vote attends the statutory meeting or no replacement trustee is elected, the original trustee must—

(a) forthwith—

(i) notify AiB accordingly, and

(ii) report the proceedings at the statutory meeting to the sheriff, and

(b) continue to act as the trustee in the sequestration.

PART 4
TRUSTEES AND COMMISSIONERS

Trustees

50 Functions of trustee

(1) In every sequestration there is to be a trustee, whose general functions are—

(a) to recover, manage and realise the estate of the debtor, whether situated in Scotland or elsewhere,

(b) to distribute the estate among the debtor's creditors according to their respective entitlements,

(c) to ascertain the reasons for the debtor's insolvency and the circumstances surrounding it,

(d) to ascertain the state of the debtor's liabilities and assets,

(e) to maintain, for the purpose of providing an accurate record of the sequestration process, a sederunt book during the trustee's term of office,

(f) to keep regular accounts of the trustee's intromissions with the debtor's estate, such accounts being available for inspection at all reasonable times by the commissioners, if there are any, the creditors and the debtor, and

(g) whether or not the trustee is still acting in the sequestration, to supply AiB with such information as AiB considers necessary to enable AiB to discharge AiB's functions under this Act.

(2) The trustee, in performing the trustee's functions under this Act, must have regard to advice offered to the trustee by the commissioners, if there are any.

(3) Where the trustee has reasonable grounds—

(a) to suspect that an offence has been committed in relation to a sequestration—

(i) by the debtor in respect of the debtor's assets, the debtor's dealings with them or the debtor's conduct in relation to the debtor's business or financial affairs, or

(ii) by a person other than the debtor in that person's dealings with the debtor, the interim trustee or the trustee in respect of the debtor's assets, business or financial affairs, or

(b) to believe that any behaviour on the part of the debtor is of a kind that would result in a sheriff granting, under section 156(1), an application for a bankruptcy restrictions order,

the trustee must report the matter to AiB.

(4) A report under subsection (3) is absolutely privileged.

(5) Subsections (1)(g) and (3) do not apply in any case where AiB is the trustee.

(6) Where AiB is the trustee, AiB may apply to the sheriff for directions in relation to any particular matter arising in the sequestration.

(7) The debtor, a creditor or any other person having an interest may, if dissatisfied with any act, omission or decision of the trustee, apply to the sheriff in that regard.

(8) On an application under subsection (7), the sheriff may confirm, revoke, or modify the decision in question, confirm or annul the act in question, give the trustee directions or make such order as the sheriff thinks fit.

(9) The trustee must comply with the requirements of subsections (1)(a) to (d) and (2) only in so far as, in the trustee's view, to do so would be—

(a) of financial benefit to the debtor's estate, and

(b) in the interests of the creditors.

51 Appointment of trustee

(1) Subsection (2) applies where the sheriff awards sequestration of the debtor's estate and the petition for the sequestration—

(a) nominates a person to be the trustee in the sequestration,

(b) states that the person—

(i) is qualified to act as an insolvency practitioner, and

(ii) has given an undertaking to act as the trustee in the sequestration, and

(c) has, annexed to it, a copy of the undertaking.

(2) The sheriff may, if—

(a) it appears to the sheriff that the person is so qualified and has given the undertaking, and

(b) no interim trustee is appointed under section 54(1),

appoint the person to be the trustee in the sequestration.

(3) Where the sheriff—

(a) awards sequestration of the debtor's estate,

(b) does not, under subsection (2), appoint a person to be the trustee in the sequestration, and

(c) no interim trustee is appointed under section 54(1),

the sheriff must appoint AiB to be the trustee in the sequestration.

(4) Subsections (5) and (7) apply where the sheriff—

(a) awards sequestration of the debtor's estate, and

(b) an interim trustee is appointed under section 54(1).

(5) The sheriff may appoint—

(a) the interim trustee, or

(b) subject to subsection (6), such other person as may be nominated by the petitioner,

to be the trustee in the sequestration.

(6) A person nominated under subsection (5)(b) may be appointed to be the trustee in the sequestration only if—

(a) it appears to the sheriff that the person is qualified to act as an insolvency practitioner and has given an undertaking to act as the trustee in the sequestration, and

(b) a copy of the undertaking has been lodged with the sheriff.

(7) Where the sheriff does not, under subsection (5), appoint a person to be the trustee in the sequestration, the sheriff must appoint AiB to be the trustee in the sequestration.

(8) Subsection (9) applies where AiB awards sequestration of the debtor's estate and the debtor application—

(a) nominates a person to be the trustee in the sequestration,

(b) states that the person—

(i) is qualified to act as an insolvency practitioner, and

(ii) has given an undertaking to act as the trustee in the sequestration, and

(c) has, annexed to it, a copy of the undertaking.

(9) AiB may, if it appears to AiB that the person is so qualified and has given that undertaking, appoint the person to be the trustee in the sequestration.

(10) But subsection (9) is subject to subsection (11).

(11) AiB is not to make an appointment under subsection (9) where—

(a) the debtor application is made by a debtor to whom section 2(2) applies, and

(b) AiB awards sequestration of the debtor's estate.

(12) Where AiB—

(a) awards sequestration of the debtor's estate, and

(b) does not, under subsection (9), appoint a person to be the trustee in the sequestration,

AiB is deemed to be appointed the trustee in the sequestration.

(13) Where a trustee is appointed in a sequestration for which the petition is presented by a creditor, or by a trustee acting under a trust deed, the appointee must, as soon as practicable, notify the debtor of the appointment.

(14) The trustee must, at the same time as notifying the debtor under subsection (13), send to the debtor for signature by the debtor a statement of undertakings in the form prescribed.

52 Application to Accountant in Bankruptcy by trustee for a direction

(1) This section applies where AiB is not the trustee in the sequestration.

(2) The trustee may apply to AiB for a direction in relation to any particular matter arising in the sequestration.

(3) Before giving any such direction, AiB may refer the matter to the sheriff by making an application for a direction in relation to the matter.

(4) The trustee may apply to AiB for a review of a direction given by AiB under this section.

(5) An application for a review under subsection (4) may not be made—

(a) by an interim trustee,

(b) after the expiry of 14 days beginning with the day on which notice of the direction by AiB is given to the trustee, or

(c) in relation to a matter on which AiB has applied to the sheriff for a direction under subsection (3).

(6) If an application for a review under subsection (4) is made, AiB must—

(a) take into account any representations made by the trustee, the debtor, any creditor or any other person having an interest, within 21 days beginning with the day on which the application is made, and

(b) confirm, amend or revoke the direction within 28 days beginning with that day.

(7) The trustee may, within 14 days beginning with the day of a decision of AiB under subsection (6)(b), appeal to the sheriff against that decision.

Interim trustees

53 Functions of interim trustee

(1) An interim trustee's general function is to safeguard the debtor's estate pending the determination of the petition for sequestration.

(2) An interim trustee, whether or not still acting in the sequestration, must supply AiB with such information as AiB considers necessary to enable AiB to discharge AiB's functions under this Act.

54 Appointment of interim trustee

(1) Where a petition for sequestration is presented by a creditor, or by a trustee acting under a trust deed, the sheriff may appoint an interim trustee before sequestration is awarded if—

(a) the debtor consents, or

(b) the trustee acting under the trust deed or any creditor shows cause.

(2) For the purposes of the appointment of an interim trustee under subsection (1)—

(a) where a person is nominated as mentioned in subsection (1)(a) of section 51 and the provisions of that subsection apply, the sheriff may appoint that person, and

(b) where such a person is not appointed, the sheriff must appoint AiB.

(3) Where an interim trustee is appointed under subsection (1), the appointee is, as soon as practicable, to notify the debtor of the appointment.

(4) The interim trustee must, at the same time as notifying the debtor under subsection (3), send to the debtor for signature by the debtor a statement of undertakings in the form prescribed.

55 Removal, resignation etc of interim trustee

(1) This section applies where—

(a) an interim trustee is appointed under section 54(1), and

(b) the petition for sequestration has not been determined.

(2) Where, under section 200(4) the sheriff removes an interim trustee from office the sheriff must, on the application of AiB, appoint a new interim trustee.

(3) Without prejudice to that section or to subsection (2), where the sheriff is satisfied—

(a) that the interim trustee is unable to act—

(i) for a reason mentioned in subsection (4), or

(ii) by, under or by virtue of any other provision of this Act, or

(b) that the interim trustee's conduct has been such that the interim trustee should no longer continue to act in the sequestration,

then, on the application of the debtor, a creditor or AiB, the sheriff must remove the interim trustee from office and appoint a new interim trustee.

(4) The reasons are—

(a) that the interim trustee is incapable (within the meaning of section 1(6) of the Adults with Incapacity (Scotland) Act 2000), or

(b) that the interim trustee has some incapacity by virtue of which the interim trustee is unable to act as interim trustee.

(5) An interim trustee (not being AiB) may apply to the sheriff for authority to resign office; and if the sheriff is, in respect of the applicant, satisfied as is mentioned in subsection (3), the sheriff must grant the application.

(6) Where, following an application under subsection (5) the interim trustee resigns office, the sheriff must appoint a new interim trustee.

(7) Where the interim trustee dies, the sheriff must, on the application of the debtor, a creditor or AiB, appoint a new interim trustee.

(8) A person (other than AiB) may not be appointed to act as interim trustee in a sequestration if the person is ineligible, by virtue of section 49(3), for election as a replacement trustee.

(9) An interim trustee who, by virtue of subsection (8), is prohibited from acting as such must forthwith make an application under subsection (5).

(10) Subsections (1) to (3) of section 51 apply as regards the appointment of an interim trustee under this section as if, for any reference—

(a) to the sheriff awarding sequestration of the debtor's estate, there were substituted a reference to the sheriff appointing a new interim trustee, and

(b) to the petition for sequestration, there were substituted a reference to the application under this section for the appointment of a new interim trustee.

56 Termination of interim trustee's functions where not appointed trustee

(1) This section applies where an interim trustee (not being AiB) is appointed under section 54(1) and the sheriff—

(a) awards sequestration and appoints another person as trustee under subsection (5) or (7) of section 51, or

(b) refuses to award sequestration.

(2) Where the sheriff awards sequestration and appoints another person as trustee in the sequestration, the interim trustee—

(a) must hand over to the other person everything in the interim trustee's possession which relates to the sequestration, and

(b) on that being done, must cease to act in the sequestration.

(3) The sheriff may make such order in relation to liability for the outlays and remuneration of the interim trustee as may be appropriate.

(4) Within 3 months after the sheriff awards, or refuses to award, sequestration the interim trustee must—

(a) submit to AiB—

(i) the interim trustee's accounts for intromissions (if any) with the debtor's estate,

(ii) a claim for outlays reasonably incurred by the interim trustee, and

(iii) a claim for remuneration for work reasonably undertaken by the interim trustee, and

(b) send a copy of the interim trustee's accounts and claims to—

(i) the debtor,

(ii) the petitioner, and

(iii) in a case where sequestration is awarded, the trustee and all creditors known to the interim trustee.

(5) On a submission being made under subsection (4)(a), AiB must—

(a) audit the accounts,

(b) issue a determination fixing the amount of the outlays and remuneration payable to the interim trustee,

(c) send a copy of the determination to—

(i) the interim trustee, and

(ii) the persons mentioned in subsection (4)(b), and

(d) where a trustee (not being AiB) is appointed in the sequestration, send a copy of the audited accounts and of the determination to the trustee.

(6) On receiving a copy of the determination sent under subsection (5)(c)(i), the interim trustee may apply to AiB for a certificate of discharge.

(7) The grant of a certificate of discharge under this section by AiB has the effect of discharging the interim trustee from all liability (other than any liability arising from fraud)—

(a) to the debtor,
(b) to the petitioner, or
(c) to the creditors,

in respect of any act or omission of the interim trustee in exercising the functions conferred on the interim trustee by this Act.

57 Appeal or review by virtue of section 56

(1) The interim trustee, or any person mentioned in subsection (4)(b) of section 56 may, within 14 days after the issuing of the determination under subsection (5)(b) of that section, appeal to the sheriff against the determination.

(2) The decision of the sheriff on an appeal under subsection (1) is final.

(3) The interim trustee must send to the persons mentioned in subsection (4)(b) of section 56 notice of any application under subsection (6) of that section and must inform them—

(a) that they may make written representations relating to it to AiB within 14 days after such notification, and

(b) of the effect mentioned in subsection (7) of that section.

(4) On the expiry of the 14 days mentioned in subsection (3)(a) AiB must, after considering any representations made to AiB—

(a) grant or refuse to grant the certificate of discharge, and

(b) notify accordingly the persons mentioned in section 56(4)(b).

(5) The interim trustee or any person mentioned in section 56(4)(b) may apply to AiB for a review of a determination under subsection (4).

(6) Any application under subsection (5) must be made within 14 days after the determination is issued.

(7) If an application under subsection (5) is made, AiB must—

(a) take into account any representations made by an interested person within 21 days beginning with the day on which the application is made, and

(b) confirm, amend or revoke the determination within 28 days beginning with that day.

(8) The interim trustee, or any person mentioned in subsection (4)(b) of section 56, may, within 14 days after a decision under subsection (7)(b), appeal to the sheriff against the decision.

(9) If, following an appeal under subsection (8), the sheriff determines that a certificate of discharge—

(a) which has been refused should be granted under section 56, the sheriff must order AiB to grant it,

(b) which has been granted should have been refused, the sheriff must revoke the certificate.

(10) Following any appeal under subsection (8), the sheriff clerk must send a copy of the decree of the sheriff to AiB.

(11) The decision of the sheriff on an appeal under subsection (8) is final.

58 Termination of Accountant in Bankruptcy's functions as interim trustee where not appointed trustee

(1) This section applies where AiB is appointed as interim trustee under section 54(1) and the sheriff—

(a) awards sequestration and appoints another person as trustee under section 51(5), or

(b) refuses to award sequestration.

(2) Where the sheriff awards sequestration and appoints another person as trustee in the sequestration, AiB—

(a) must hand over to the other person everything in AiB's possession which relates to the sequestration, and

(b) on that being done, must cease to act in the sequestration.

(3) The sheriff may make such order in relation to liability for the outlays and remuneration of AiB as may be appropriate.

(4) Within 3 months after the sheriff awards, or refuses to award, sequestration AiB must—

(a) send to the debtor and the petitioner—

(i) AiB's accounts for intromissions (if any) with the debtor's estate,

(ii) a determination of AiB's fees and outlays, calculated in accordance with regulations made under section 205, and

(iii) the notice mentioned in subsection (5), and

(b) in a case where sequestration is awarded, send a copy of those accounts, that determination and that notice to all creditors known to AiB.

(5) The notice is a notice in writing stating—

(a) that AiB has commenced procedure under this Act leading to discharge in respect of AiB's actings as interim trustee,

(b) that an application for a review may be made under section 59(1),

(c) that an appeal may be made to the sheriff under section 59(4), and

(d) that, in the circumstances mentioned in subsection (6), AiB is discharged from any liability incurred while acting as interim trustee.

(6) Subsection (7) applies where—

(a) the requirements of this section have been complied with, and

(b) either no appeal is made under section 59(4) or any such appeal is refused as regards the discharge of AiB.

(7) AiB is discharged from all liability (other than any liability arising from fraud)—

(a) to the debtor,

(b) to the petitioner, or

(c) to the creditors,

in respect of any act or omission of AiB in exercising the functions of interim trustee conferred on AiB by this Act.

59 Review or appeal by virtue of section 58

(1) The debtor, the petitioner or any creditor may apply to AiB for a review of the discharge of AiB in respect of AiB's actings as interim trustee.

(2) Any application under subsection (1) must be made within 14 days beginning with the day on which notice is sent under section 58(4)(a)(iii) or (b).

(3) If an application for a review under subsection (1) is made, AiB must—

(a) take into account any representations made, within 21 days beginning with the day on which the application is made, by an interested person, and

(b) confirm or revoke the discharge within 28 days beginning with that day.

(4) The debtor, the petitioner or any creditor may appeal to the sheriff within 14 days beginning with—

(a) the day on which notice is sent under section 58(4)(a)(iii) or (b), against the determination mentioned in section 58(4)(a)(ii), or

(b) the day of a decision by AiB under subsection (3)(b), against that decision.

(5) The sheriff clerk must, following an appeal under subsection (4), send a copy of the decree to AiB.

(6) The decision of the sheriff on an appeal under subsection (4) is final.

Replacement trustees

60 Appointment of replacement trustee

(1) This section applies where a replacement trustee is elected by virtue of a trustee vote.

(2) On the election of the replacement trustee the original trustee must immediately make a report of the proceedings at the statutory meeting—

(a) where the original trustee was not AiB, to AiB, or

(b) where the original trustee was AiB, to the sheriff.

(3) The debtor, a creditor, the original trustee, the replacement trustee or AiB may object to any matter connected with the election—

(a) in the case of an objection by a person other than AiB, by applying to AiB,

(b) in the case of an objection by AiB, by application to the sheriff.

(4) Any objection under subsection (3) must—

(a) specify the grounds on which the objection is taken, and

(b) be made within 4 days beginning with the day of the statutory meeting.

(5) If there is no timeous objection under subsection (3), AiB must without delay declare the elected person to be the trustee in the sequestration.

(6) No expense in objecting under this section is to fall on the debtor's estate.

61 Procedure in application to Accountant in Bankruptcy under section 60

(1) This section applies where an application is made to AiB under section 60(3)(a).

(2) AiB must—

(a) without delay give the original trustee, the replacement trustee, the objector and any other interested person an opportunity to make written submissions on the application, and

(b) make a decision.

(3) If AiB decides—

(a) to reject the objection in the application, AiB must without delay declare the elected person to be the trustee in the sequestration,

(b) to sustain the objection in the application, AiB must order the original trustee to arrange a new meeting at which a new trustee vote must be held.

(4) Sections 48, 49, 60 and 62, and this section, apply in relation to a meeting arranged by virtue of subsection (3)(b).

(5) The original trustee, the replacement trustee, the objector and any other interested party may apply to AiB for a review of a decision under subsection (2)(b).

(6) Any application under subsection (5) must be made within 14 days beginning with the day on which notice of the decision is given.

(7) If an application for a review under subsection (5) is made, AiB must—

(a) take into account any representations made by an interested party within 21 days beginning with the day on which the application is made, and

(b) confirm, amend or revoke the decision within 28 days beginning with that day.

(8) The trustee, the objector or any other interested party may, within 14 days beginning with the day of a decision of AiB under subsection (7)(b), appeal to the sheriff against that decision.

(9) No expense in objecting under this section is to fall on the debtor's estate.

62 Procedure in application under section 60, or appeal under section 61, to sheriff

(1) This section applies where there is—

(a) an application by AiB under section 60(3)(b), or

(b) an appeal under section 61(8).

(2) The sheriff must—

(a) without delay give the parties an opportunity to be heard on the application, and

(b) make a decision.

(3) If the sheriff decides—

(a) to reject an objection to the appointment of an elected person, the sheriff must without delay declare the elected person to be the trustee in the sequestration and make an order appointing the elected person to be the trustee in the sequestration, or

(b) to sustain such an objection, the sheriff must order the original trustee to arrange a new meeting at which a new trustee vote must be held.

(4) Sections 48, 49, 60, 61 and this section, apply in relation to a meeting arranged by virtue of subsection (3)(b).

(5) Any declaration, appointment or decision of the sheriff under this section is final.

63 Termination of original trustee's functions

(1) This section applies where—

(a) a replacement trustee is appointed under section 60, and

(b) the original trustee is not AiB.

(2) On the appointment of the replacement trustee, the original trustee—

(a) must hand over to the replacement trustee everything in the original trustee's possession which relates to the sequestration, including—

(i) the statement of assets and liabilities,

(ii) a copy of the statement of the debtor's affairs prepared under section 42(1)(a) (as revised under section 48(4)(f) if so revised), and

(iii) a copy of the written comments sent under section 42(2)), and

(b) on that being done, must cease to act in the sequestration.

(3) Within 3 months after the appointment of the replacement trustee, the original trustee must—

(a) submit to AiB—

(i) the original trustee's accounts for intromissions (if any) with the debtor's estate,

(ii) a claim for outlays reasonably incurred, and for remuneration for work reasonably undertaken, by the original trustee, and

(b) send to the replacement trustee a copy of what is submitted under paragraph (a).

(4) Where the original trustee was appointed under section 54(1) as the interim trustee in the sequestration, the original trustee's accounts and the claim referred to in subsection (3)(a)(ii) must include accounts and a claim for the period of the original trustee's appointment as interim trustee.

(5) On a submission being made under subsection (3)(a), AiB must—

(a) audit the accounts,

(b) issue a determination fixing the amount of the outlays and remuneration payable to the original trustee, and

(c) send a copy of—

(i) the determination to the original trustee, and

(ii) the audited accounts and the determination to the replacement trustee.

(6) The original trustee, the replacement trustee, the debtor or any creditor may appeal to the sheriff against the determination within 14 days after it is issued.

(7) The decision of the sheriff on an appeal under subsection (6) is final.

64 Accountant in Bankruptcy's intromissions in capacity of original trustee

(1) This section applies where AiB was the original trustee and some other person is appointed as replacement trustee under section 60.

(2) On the appointment of the replacement trustee AiB—

(a) must hand over to that person everything in AiB's possession—

(i) which relates to the sequestration, and

(ii) which AiB obtained in the capacity of original trustee (including the statement of assets and liabilities), and

(b) on that being done, must cease to act as trustee.

(3) AiB must, within 3 months after the appointment of the replacement trustee, supply to that person—

(a) AiB's accounts of AiB's intromissions (if any) as original trustee with the debtor's estate,

(b) a determination of AiB's fees and outlays calculated in accordance with regulations under section 205, and

(c) a copy of the notice mentioned in subsection (4)(b).

(4) AiB must send to the debtor and to all creditors known to AiB—
(a) a copy of the determination mentioned in subsection (3)(b), and
(b) a notice in writing stating—
(i) that AiB has commenced procedure under this Act leading to discharge in respect of AiB's actings as trustee,
(ii) that the accounts of AiB's intromissions (if any) with the debtor's estate are available for inspection at such address as AiB may determine,
(iii) that an application for a review may be made under subsection (5),
(iv) that an appeal may be made to the sheriff under subsection (8), and
(v) the effect of subsections (10) and (11).

(5) The replacement trustee, the debtor or any creditor may apply to AiB for a review of the discharge of AiB in respect of AiB's actings as trustee.

(6) Any application under subsection (5) must be made within 14 days beginning with the day on which notice is sent under subsection (4)(b).

(7) If an application under subsection (5) is made, AiB must—
(a) take into account any representations made by an interested person within 21 days beginning with the day on which the application is made, and
(b) confirm or revoke the discharge within 28 days beginning with that day.

(8) The replacement trustee, the debtor or any creditor may appeal to the sheriff within 14 days beginning with—
(a) the day on which notice is sent under subsection (4)(b), against the determination mentioned in subsection (3)(b), or
(b) the day of a decision of AiB under subsection (7)(b), against that decision.

(9) The decision of the sheriff on an appeal under subsection (8) is final.

(10) Subsection (11) applies where—
(a) the requirements of this section have been complied with, and
(b) either no appeal is made under subsection (8) or any such appeal is refused as regards the discharge of AiB.

(11) AiB is discharged from all liability (other than liability arising from fraud) to the creditors or to the debtor in respect of any act or omission of AiB in exercising the functions of trustee in the sequestration.

65 Discharge of original trustee

(1) On receiving a copy of the determination of AiB sent under section 63(5)(c)(i) the original trustee may apply to AiB for a certificate of discharge.

(2) The original trustee must send notice of the application to the debtor, to all creditors known to the original trustee and to the replacement trustee and must inform the debtor—
(a) that the debtor, the replacement trustee or any creditor may, in relation to the application, make written representations to AiB within 14 days after such notification,
(b) that the audited accounts of the original trustee's intromissions (if any) with the debtor's estate are available for inspection at the original trustee's office and that a copy of those accounts has been sent to the replacement trustee, and
(c) of the effect mentioned in subsection (11).

(3) On the expiry of the 14 days mentioned in subsection (2)(a) AiB must, after considering any representations duly made to AiB—
(a) grant or refuse to grant the certificate of discharge, and
(b) notify accordingly (in addition to the original trustee) the debtor, the replacement trustee and all creditors who have made such representations.

(4) The original trustee, the replacement trustee, the debtor or any creditor who has made representations by virtue of subsection (2)(a) may apply to AiB for a review of a determination under subsection (3).

(5) Any application under subsection (4) must be made within 14 days beginning with the day on which that determination is issued.

(6) If an application under subsection (4) is made, AiB must—

(a) take into account any representations made by an interested person within 21 days beginning with the day on which the application is made, and

(b) confirm, amend or revoke the determination (whether or not granting a certificate of discharge) within 28 days beginning with that day.

(7) The original trustee, the replacement trustee, the debtor or any creditor who has made representations by virtue of subsection (2)(a) may, within 14 days after a decision under subsection (6)(b), appeal to the sheriff against that decision.

(8) If, on such appeal, the sheriff determines that a certificate of discharge which has been refused should be granted the sheriff must order AiB to grant it.

(9) The sheriff clerk must send a copy of the sheriff's decree to AiB.

(10) The decision of the sheriff on an appeal under subsection (7) is final.

(11) The grant of a certificate of discharge under this section by AiB has the effect of discharging the original trustee from all liability (other than liability arising from fraud) to the creditors, or to the debtor, in respect of any act or omission of the original trustee in exercising the functions conferred on the original trustee by this Act.

(12) This section does not apply where AiB is the original trustee.

66 Replacement of trustee acting in more than one sequestration

(1) This section applies where a trustee acting as such in two or more sequestrations—

(a) dies,

(b) ceases, by virtue of section 49(4), to be qualified to continue to act as trustee, or

(c) becomes subject to the circumstances mentioned in subsection (2).

(2) The circumstances are that there is—

(a) a conflict of interest affecting the trustee, or

(b) a change in the personal circumstances of the trustee,

which prevents the trustee from carrying out the trustee's functions, or makes it impracticable for the trustee to carry out those functions.

(3) AiB may, in a case where subsection (1)(b) or (c) applies, determine that the trustee is removed from office in each sequestration in which the trustee has ceased to be qualified.

(4) AiB may appoint as the trustee in each sequestration in which the former trustee was acting a person—

(a) determined by AiB, and

(b) who consents to the appointment.

(5) A person may not be appointed under subsection (4) if the person is ineligible, by virtue of section 49(3), for election as a replacement trustee.

(6) If, in relation to any sequestration, AiB determines that no person is to be appointed under subsection (4), AiB is deemed to be the trustee in that sequestration.

(7) A determination or appointment under this section may be made—

(a) on the application of any person having an interest, or

(b) without an application, where AiB proposes to make a determination or appointment of AiB's own accord.

(8) The applicant must notify all interested persons where an application is made under subsection (7)(a).

(9) AiB must notify all interested persons where AiB proposes to make a determination or appointment by virtue of subsection (7)(b).

(10) A notice under subsection (8) or (9) must inform the recipient that the re-

cipient has a right to make representations to AiB, in relation to the application or to the proposed determination or appointment, within 14 days beginning with the day on which the notice is given.

67 Further provision as regards replacement under section 66

(1) Before making a determination or appointment under section 66, AIB must take into account any representations made by an interested person.

(2) AiB must notify any determination or appointment under section 66 to—

(a) the former trustee (or, where the former trustee has died, the former trustee's representatives),

(b) the debtor,

(c) the trustee appointed under section 66 (where the trustee appointed is not AiB), and

(d) each sheriff who awarded sequestration or to whom sequestration was transferred under section 27(1).

(3) The trustee appointed under section 66—

(a) must notify the determination or appointment under that section to every creditor known to the trustee,

(b) may require—

(i) delivery of all documents (other than the former trustee's accounts) relating to each sequestration in which the former trustee was acting and in the possession of the former trustee or of the former trustee's representatives,

(ii) delivery of a copy of the former trustee's accounts, and

(iii) the former trustee, or the former trustee's representatives, to submit the trustee's accounts for audit to the commissioners or, if there are no commissioners, to AiB.

(4) Where the trustee appointed under section 66 requires submission in accordance with subsection (3)(b)(iii), the commissioners or, as the case may be, AiB must issue a determination fixing the amount of the outlays and remuneration payable to the former trustee, or the former trustee's representatives, in accordance with section 132.

68 Review of determination or appointment under section 66

(1) A person mentioned in section 67(2)(a) or (b) or (3)(a) may apply to AiB for a review of any determination or appointment under that section.

(2) Any application under subsection (1) must be made within 14 days beginning with the day on which notice of the determination or appointment is given.

(3) If an application under subsection (1) is made, AiB must—

(a) take into account any representations made by an interested person within 21 days beginning with the day on which the application is made, and

(b) confirm, amend or revoke the determination or appointment within 28 days beginning with that day.

(4) A person mentioned in section 67(2)(a) or (b) or (3)(a) may, within 14 days beginning with the day of a decision of AiB under subsection (3)(b), appeal to the sheriff against that decision.

(5) AiB may refer a case to the court for a direction before—

(a) making any determination or appointment under section 66,

(b) issuing any determination under section 67(4), or

(c) undertaking any review under this section.

(6) Any appeal under subsection (4) or referral under subsection (5) must be made—

(a) by a single petition to the Court of Session where the appeal relates to two or more sequestrations and the sequestrations are, by virtue of section 15, in different sheriffdoms, and

(b) in any other case, to the sheriff.

Resignation or death of trustee

69 Resignation or death of trustee

(1) The trustee in the sequestration (in this section referred to as 'T') may apply to AiB for authority to resign office and AiB must grant the application where satisfied that—

(a) T is unable to act (whether by, under or by virtue of a provision of this Act or from any other cause), or

(b) T's conduct has been such that T should no longer continue to act in the sequestration.

(2) AiB may make the granting of an application under subsection (1) subject—

(a) to the election of a new trustee, and

(b) to such other conditions as AiB thinks appropriate in all the circumstances of the case.

(3) Where AiB grants an application under subsection (1), then—

(a) except where paragraph (b) applies, the commissioners, or if there are no commissioners AiB, must call a meeting of the creditors, to be held within 28 days after T resigns, for the election by the creditors of a new trustee, and

(b) if the application is granted subject to the election of a new trustee, T must call a meeting of the creditors, to be held within 28 days after the granting of the application, for such an election.

(4) Where the commissioners become, or if there are no commissioners AiB becomes, aware that T has died, they or as the case may be AiB are, as soon as practicable after becoming so aware, to call a meeting of creditors for the election by the creditors of a new trustee.

(5) The preceding provisions of this Part in relation to the election of a replacement trustee and the appointment of that trustee also apply, subject to any necessary modifications, in relation to the election and appointment of a new trustee in pursuance of subsections (1) to (3) or subsection (4).

(6) Where no new trustee is elected in pursuance of subsection (3) or (4), AiB may appoint as the new trustee in the sequestration—

(a) a person who applies to AiB within 14 days beginning with the day of the meeting arranged under subsection (3) or (4), or

(b) any other person as may be determined by AiB and who consents to the appointment.

(7) A person may not be appointed under subsection (6) if the person is ineligible, by virtue of section 49(3), for election as a replacement trustee.

(8) If, after the expiry of the days mentioned in subsection (6)(a), AiB determines that no person is to be appointed under subsection (6), AiB is deemed to be the new trustee in the sequestration.

(9) The new trustee (in this subsection and in [subsections (11) and (12)] referred to as 'NT') may require—

(a) delivery to NT of all documents relating to the sequestration and in the possession of T or T's representatives (except that, in the case of T's accounts, NT is entitled to delivery only of a copy),

(b) T or T's representatives to submit T's accounts for audit to the commissioners or, if there are no commissioners, to AiB.

(10) The commissioners are, or if there are no commissioners AiB is, to issue a determination fixing the amount of the outlays and remuneration payable to T or T's representatives in accordance with section 133.

(11) T or T's representatives, NT, the debtor or any creditor may within 14 days after a determination under subsection (10) is issued—

(a) by the commissioners, appeal against it to AiB,

(b) by AiB, appeal against it to the sheriff.

[(12) T or T's representatives, NT, the debtor or any creditor may, within 14 days beginning with the date of any decision of AiB in an appeal under subsection (11)(a), appeal to the sheriff against that decision.]

(13) The decision of the sheriff on an appeal under subsection (11)(b) or (12) is final.

Removal of trustee and appointment of new trustee

70 Removal of trustee other than where trustee is unable to act or should no longer continue to act: general

(1) The trustee in the sequestration (in this section and in sections 71 to 73 referred to as 'T') may be removed from office—

(a) by the creditors at a meeting called for the purpose if they also forthwith elect a new trustee, or

(b) by order made by AiB if AiB is satisfied that, on the basis of circumstances other than those mentioned in section 72(2), there are reasons to remove T from office.

(2) An order removing T in accordance with subsection (1)(b) may be made—

(a) on the application of—

(i) the commissioners, or

(ii) a person representing not less than ¼ in value of the creditors, or

(b) in any other case where AiB is satisfied as mentioned in that subsection.

(3) 'Creditors', in subsection (1)(a), does not include—

(a) anyone who, other than by succession, acquires after the date of sequestration a debt due by the debtor, or

(b) any creditor to the extent that the creditor's debt is a postponed debt.

(4) AiB must—

(a) order any application by a person mentioned in subsection (2)(a) to be served on T,

(b) enter particulars of the application in the register of insolvencies, and

(c) before deciding whether or not to make an order under subsection (1)(b), give T the opportunity to make representations.

(5) AiB may—

(a) in ordering, or

(b) instead of ordering,

the removal of T from office under subsection (1)(b), make such further or other order as AiB thinks fit.

(6) This section and sections 71 to 75 do not apply where AiB is the trustee in the sequestration.

(7) This section is without prejudice to section 200(4).

71 Removal of trustee other than where trustee is unable to act or should no longer continue to act: review, appeal and election of new trustee

(1) T, the commissioners or any creditor may apply to AiB for a review of any decision of AiB under section 70(1)(b) or (5).

(2) Any application under subsection (1) must be made within 14 days beginning with the day on which the decision is given.

(3) If an application under subsection (1) for a review is made, AiB must—

(a) take into account any representations made by an interested person within 21 days beginning with the day on which the application is made, and

(b) confirm, amend or revoke the decision within 28 days beginning with that day.

(4) T, the commissioners or any creditor may, within 14 days beginning with the day on which a decision of AiB under subsection (3)(b) is given, appeal to the sheriff against that decision.

(5) Subsection (6) applies where T has been removed from office—

(a) under section 70(1)(b),
(b) under section 200(4),
(c) following a review under subsection (1), or
(d) following an appeal under subsection (4).

(6) The commissioners (or if there are no commissioners AiB) must call a meeting of creditors, to be held within 28 days after the removal, for the election by the creditors of a new trustee.

(7) AiB may refer a case to the sheriff for a direction before—
(a) making an order under section 70(1)(b) or (5), or
(b) undertaking any review under this section.

(8) An application for a review under subsection (1) may not be made in relation to a matter on which AiB has applied to the sheriff for a direction under subsection (7).

72 Removal of trustee where trustee is unable to act or should no longer continue to act: general

(1) If AiB is satisfied that any of the circumstances mentioned in subsection (2) apply, AiB may—
(a) declare the office of trustee to have become, or to be, vacant, and
(b) make any necessary order—
(i) to enable the sequestration of the estate to proceed, or
(ii) to safeguard the estate pending the election of a new trustee.

(2) The circumstances are that—
(a) T is unable to act (whether by, under or by virtue of a provision of this Act or from any other cause whatsoever other than death), or
(b) T's conduct has been such that T should no longer continue to act in the sequestration.

(3) The declaration under subsection (1)(a), and any order under subsection (1)(b), may be made—
(a) on the application of the commissioners, of the debtor or of a creditor, or
(b) in any other case where AiB is satisfied as mentioned in subsection (1).

(4) AiB must order such intimation of an application by a person mentioned in subsection (3)(a) as AiB considers necessary.

(5) This section is without prejudice to section 200(4).

73 Removal of trustee where trustee is unable to act or should no longer continue to act: review, appeal and election of new trustee

(1) If AiB makes a declaration under section 72(1)(a), the commissioners (or if there are no commissioners AiB) must call a meeting of creditors, to be held within 28 days beginning with the day of the declaration, for the election of a new trustee by the creditors.

(2) T, the commissioners, the debtor or any creditor may apply to AiB for a review of any declaration made under section 72(1)(a) or of any order made under section 72(1)(b).

(3) Any application under subsection (2) must be made within 14 days beginning with the day of the declaration.

(4) If an application under subsection (2) is made, AiB must—
(a) take into account any representations made by an interested person within 21 days beginning with the day on which the application is made, and
(b) confirm, amend or revoke the declaration or order within 28 days beginning with that day.

(5) T, the commissioners, the debtor or any creditor may, within 14 days beginning with the day of any decision of AiB under subsection (4)(b), appeal to the sheriff against that decision.

(6) AiB may refer a case to the sheriff for a direction before—
(a) making any declaration or any order under section 72(1), or

(b) undertaking any review under this section.

(7) An application for a review under subsection (2) may not be made in relation to a matter on which AiB has applied to the sheriff for a direction under subsection (6).

74 Election or appointment of new trustee by virtue of section 71(6) or 73(1)

The preceding provisions of this Part in relation to the election of a replacement trustee and the appointment of that trustee also apply, subject to any necessary modifications, in relation to the election and appointment of a new trustee by virtue of section 71(6) or 73(1).

75 Further provision as regards election or appointment of new trustee

Subsections (6) to (13) of section 69 apply for the purposes of sections 70 to 74 as those subsections apply for the purposes of section 69.

Commissioners

76 Commissioners

In any sequestration [where AiB is not the trustee] there may be elected, in accordance with section 77, commissioners, whose general functions are—

(a) to supervise the intromissions of the trustee in the sequestration with the sequestrated estate, and

(b) to advise the trustee.

77 Election, resignation and removal of commissioners

(1) At the statutory meeting or at any subsequent meeting of creditors, the creditors (other than any such person as is listed in section 49(7)) may, from among the creditors or their mandatories, elect a commissioner or commissioners (or a new or additional commissioner or new or additional commissioners).

(2) No more than 5 commissioners are to hold office in any one sequestration at any one time.

(3) None of the persons listed in subsection (5) is eligible for election as a commissioner.

(4) Nor is anyone who becomes a person so listed after being elected as a commissioner entitled to continue to act as a commissioner.

(5) The persons are—

(a) any person listed in paragraph (a) or (d) of section 49(5), and

(b) a person who is an associate of the debtor or of the trustee in the sequestration.

(6) A commissioner may resign office at any time.

[(6A) A commissioner ceases to hold office if AiB is, or becomes, the trustee.]

(7) A commissioner may be removed from office—

(a) if the commissioner is a mandatory of a creditor (see paragraphs 14 to 16 of schedule 6), by the creditor recalling the mandate and intimating in writing to the trustee that it is recalled,

(b) by the creditors (other than any such person as is listed in section 49(7)) at a meeting called for the purpose, or

(c) by order of the sheriff if the sheriff is satisfied that the commissioner is no longer acting in the interests of the efficient conduct of the sequestration.

(8) An order under subsection (7)(c) may be made on the application of—

(a) AiB,

(b) a person representing not less than ¼ in value of the creditors, or

(c) the trustee.

(9) The sheriff must—

(a) order an application by a person mentioned in subsection (8) to be served on the commissioner,

(b) order that the application be intimated to every creditor who has given a mandate to the commissioner, and

(c) before deciding whether or not to make an order under subsection (7)(c), give the commissioner the opportunity to make representations.

(10) On an application under subsection (7)(c), the sheriff may—

(a) in ordering the removal of the commissioner from office, make such further order as the sheriff thinks fit, or

(b) instead of removing the commissioner from office, make such other order as the sheriff thinks fit.

(11) The trustee, AiB, any commissioner or any creditor may, within 14 days after a decision of the sheriff on an application under subsection (7)(c), appeal against that decision.

(12) Subsection (7) is without prejudice to section 200(4).

PART 5
VESTING ETC

Vesting

78 Vesting of estate at date of sequestration

(1) The whole estate of the debtor vests for the benefit of the creditors in the trustee in the sequestration, by virtue of the trustee's appointment, as at the date of sequestration.

(2) But subsection (1) is subject to section 88.

(3) It is not competent for—

(a) the trustee, or

(b) any person deriving title from the trustee,

to complete title, before the expiry of the period mentioned in subsection (4), to any heritable property in Scotland vested in the trustee by virtue of the trustee's appointment.

(4) The period is 28 days (or such other period as may be prescribed) beginning with the day on which the certified copy of—

(a) the order of the sheriff granting warrant is recorded under subsection (1)(a) of section 26 in the Register of Inhibitions, or

(b) the determination of AiB awarding sequestration is recorded under subsection (2) of that section in that register.

(5) The exercise by the trustee of any power conferred on the trustee by this Act, in respect of any heritable estate vested in the trustee by virtue of that person's appointment, is not challengeable on the ground of a prior inhibition.

(6) Where the debtor has an uncompleted title to any heritable estate in Scotland, the trustee may complete title to that estate either in the trustee's own name or in the name of the debtor.

(7) But completion of title in the name of the debtor does not validate by accretion any unperfected right in favour of a person other than the trustee.

(8) Moveable property in respect of which, but for this subsection—

(a) delivery or possession, or

(b) intimation of assignation,

would be required in order to complete title vests in the trustee, by virtue of the trustee's appointment, as if at the date of sequestration (as the case may be) the trustee had taken delivery or possession of the property or had made intimation of its assignation to the trustee.

(9) Any non-vested contingent interest which the debtor has vests in the trustee as if an assignation of that interest had been executed by the debtor (and intimation of assignation made) at the date of sequestration.

(10) Any non-vested contingent interest vested in the trustee by virtue of subsection (9) is, where it remains so vested as at the date which is 4 years after the date of

sequestration, re-invested in the debtor as if an assignation of that interest had been executed by the trustee (and intimation of assignation made) at that date.

(11) A person claiming a right to any estate claimed by the trustee may apply to the sheriff for the estate to be excluded from such vesting, a copy of the application being served on the trustee.

(12) The sheriff must grant the application if satisfied that the estate should not be so vested.

(13) Where any successor of a deceased debtor whose estate has been sequestrated has made up title to, or is in possession of, any part of that estate, the sheriff may on the application of the trustee order the successor to convey such estate to the trustee.

79 Provision supplementary to section 78 and interpretation of Part 5

(1) In subsection (1) of section 78, the 'whole estate of the debtor' means the debtor's whole estate at the date of sequestration (wherever situated) including—

(a) any income or estate vesting in the debtor on the date of sequestration,

(b) any property of the debtor title to which has not been completed by another person deriving right from the debtor, and

(c) the capacity to exercise and to take proceedings for exercising all such powers in, over or in respect of any property as—

(i) might have been exercised by the debtor for the debtor's own benefit as at, or on, the date of sequestration, or

(ii) might be exercised on a relevant date.

(2) But subsection (1) is subject to subsection (3) [. . .].

(3) The 'whole estate of the debtor' does not include any interest of the debtor as tenant under—

(a) a tenancy which is an assured tenancy within the meaning of Part 2 of the Housing (Scotland) Act 1988,

(b) a protected tenancy within the meaning of the Rent (Scotland) Act 1984 in respect of which, by virtue of Part 8 of that Act, no premium can lawfully be required as a condition of assignation,

(c) a Scottish secure tenancy within the meaning of the Housing (Scotland) Act 2001 [, or

(d) a private residential tenancy within the meaning of the Private Housing (Tenancies) (Scotland) Act 2016.]

(4) On the date on which the trustee serves notice to that effect on the debtor, the interest of the debtor as tenant under any of the tenancies referred to in subsection (3) forms part of the debtor's estate and vests in the trustee as if it had vested in the trustee under section 86(5).

(5) In this Part 'relevant date' means a date after the date of sequestration and before the date which is 4 years after the date of sequestration.

80 Property subject to restraint order

(1) Subsection (2) applies where—

(a) property is excluded from the debtor's estate by virtue of section 420(2)(a) of the Proceeds of Crime Act 2002 (property subject to a restraint order),

(b) an order under section 50, 67A, 128, 131A, 198 or 215A of that Act has not been made in respect of the property,

(c) the restraint order is discharged, and

(d) immediately after the discharge of the restraint order the property is not detained under or by virtue of section 44A, 47J, 122A, 127J, 193A or 195J of that Act.

(2) The property vests in the trustee in the sequestration as part of the debtor's estate.

(3) But subsection (2) does not apply to the proceeds of property realised by a management receiver under section 49(2)(d) or 197(2)(d) of that Act (realisation of property to meet receiver's outlays and remuneration).

81 Property released from detention

(1) Subsection (2) applies where—

(a) property is excluded from the debtor's estate by virtue of section 420(2)(b) of the Proceeds of Crime Act 2002 (property detained under certain provisions),

(b) no order is in force in respect of the property under section 41, 50, 120, 128, 190 or 198 of that Act, and

(c) the property is released.

(2) The property vests in the trustee in the sequestration as part of the debtor's estate.

82 Property in respect of which receivership or administration order is made

(1) Subsection (2) applies where—

(a) property is excluded from the debtor's estate by virtue of section 420(2)(c) of the Proceeds of Crime Act 2002 (property in respect of which an order for the appointment of a receiver or administrator under certain provisions of that Act is in force),

(b) a confiscation order is made under section 6, 92 or 156 of that Act,

(c) the amount payable under the confiscation order is fully paid, and

(d) any of the property remains in the hands of the receiver or administrator (as the case may be).

(2) The property vests in the trustee in the sequestration as part of the debtor's estate.

83 Property in respect of which realisation order is made

(1) Subsection (2) applies where—

(a) property is excluded from the debtor's estate by virtue of section 420(2)(d) of the Proceeds of Crime Act 2002 (property in respect of which an order has been made authorising realisation of the property by an appropriate officer),

(b) a confiscation order is made under section 6, 92 or 156 of that Act,

(c) the amount payable under the confiscation order is fully paid, and

(d) any of the property remains in the hands of the appropriate officer.

(2) The property vests in the trustee in the sequestration as part of the debtor's estate.

84 Property subject to certain orders where confiscation order discharged or quashed

(1) Subsection (2) applies where—

(a) property is excluded from the debtor's estate by virtue of section 420(2)(a), (b), (c) or (d) of the Proceeds of Crime Act 2002 (property excluded from debtor's estate),

(b) a confiscation order is made under section 6, 92 or 156 of that Act, and

(c) the confiscation order is discharged under section 30, 114 or 180 of that Act (as the case may be) or quashed under that Act or in pursuance of any enactment relating to appeals against conviction or sentence.

(2) Any such property vests in the trustee in the sequestration as part of the debtor's estate if it is in the hands of—

(a) a receiver appointed under Part 2 or 4 of that Act,

(b) an administrator appointed under Part 3 of that Act, or

(c) an appropriate officer (within the meaning of section 41A, 120A or 190A of that Act).

(3) But subsection (2) does not apply to the proceeds of property realised by a management receiver under section 49(2)(d) or 197(2)(d) of that Act (realisation of property to meet receiver's outlays and remuneration).

85 Vesting of income received by debtor after sequestration

(1) Any income, of whatever nature, received by the debtor on a relevant date, other than income arising from the estate which is vested in the trustee in the sequestration, is to vest in the debtor.

(2) But subsection (1) is subject to sections 90 to 97.

86 Further provision as regards vesting of estate

(1) Diligence in respect of a debt or obligation mentioned in subsection (2) is not competent against income vesting in the debtor under section 85.

(2) The debt or obligation is one in respect of which the debtor, if discharged under section 137, 138 or 140, would be discharged under section 145.

(3) For the purposes of subsection (1), diligence includes the making of a deduction from earnings order under the Child Support Act 1991.

(4) Subsection (5) applies where any estate, wherever situated—

(a) is acquired by the debtor on a relevant date, and

(b) would have vested in the trustee in the sequestration if it had been part of the debtor's estate on the date of sequestration.

(5) The estate vests in the trustee for the benefit of the creditors as at the date of acquisition.

(6) A person who holds estate vesting in the trustee under subsection (5) is, on production to the person of a copy of the order certified by the sheriff clerk, or as the case may be by AiB, appointing the trustee, to convey or deliver the estate to the trustee.

(7) But such a person incurs no liability to the trustee except to account for any proceeds of the conveyance which are in the person's hands if the person has, in good faith and without knowledge of the sequestration, conveyed the estate—

(a) to the debtor, or

(b) to anyone on the instructions of the debtor.

(8) The trustee is not entitled, by virtue of subsections (4) to (7), to any remedy against an appropriate bank or institution (in this section and in section 87(7) referred to as a 'bank') in respect of a banking transaction entered into before the receipt by the bank of a notice under subsection (9) (whether or not the bank is aware of the sequestration).

(9) Where the trustee knows, or becomes aware, of any estate vested in the trustee under section 78 or this section which comprises funds held by a bank, the trustee must serve a notice on the bank—

(a) informing the bank of the sequestration, and

(b) specifying reasonable detail in order to allow the bank to identify the debtor and the funds held.

(10) A notice under subsection (9)—

(a) must be in writing and may be sent—

(i) by first class post or by using a registered or recorded delivery postal service to the bank, or

(ii) in some other manner (including by electronic means) which the trustee reasonably considers likely to cause it to be delivered to the bank on the same or next day, and

(b) is deemed to have been received the day after it is sent.

(11) Subsections (4) to (8) are without prejudice to—

(a) section 85, and

(b) any right acquired in the estate in good faith and for value.

87 Dealings and circumstances of debtor after sequestration

(1) The debtor must immediately notify the trustee in the sequestration—

(a) of any assets acquired by the debtor on a relevant date, or

(b) of any other substantial change in the debtor's financial circumstances.

(2) A debtor who fails to comply with subsection (1) commits an offence.

(3) A debtor who commits an offence under subsection (2) is liable on summary conviction—

(a) to a fine not exceeding level 5 on the standard scale,

(b) to imprisonment for a term not exceeding 3 months, or

(c) both to such fine and to such imprisonment.

(4) Any dealing of, or with, the debtor and relating to the debtor's estate vested in the trustee under section 78 or 86 is of no effect in a question with the trustee.

(5) But subsection (4) does not apply where the person seeking to uphold the dealing establishes that the trustee—

(a) has abandoned to the debtor the property to which the dealing relates,

(b) has expressly or impliedly authorised the dealing, or

(c) is otherwise personally barred from challenging the dealing.

(6) Nor does subsection (4) apply where the person seeking to uphold the dealing establishes both—

(a) that the dealing is—

(i) the performance of an obligation undertaken before the date of sequestration by a person obliged to the debtor in the obligation,

(ii) the purchase from the debtor of goods for which the purchaser has given value to the debtor or is willing to give value to the trustee, or

(iii) one which satisfies the conditions mentioned in subsection (10), and

(b) that the person dealing with the debtor was, at the time when the dealing occurred, unaware of the sequestration and had at that time no reason to believe that the debtor's estate had been sequestrated or was the subject of sequestration proceedings.

(7) Nor does subsection (4) apply where the dealing is a banking transaction entered into before the receipt by the bank of a notice under section 86(9) (whether or not the bank is aware of the sequestration).

(8) Where the trustee has abandoned heritable property to the debtor, notice (in such form as may be prescribed) given to the debtor by the trustee is sufficient evidence that the property is vested in the debtor.

(9) Where notice is given under subsection (8), the trustee is as soon as reasonably practicable after giving it to record a certified copy of it in the Register of Inhibitions.

(10) The conditions are that—

(a) the dealing constitutes—

(i) the transfer of incorporeal moveable property, or

(ii) the creation, transfer, variation or extinguishing of a real right in heritable property,

for which the person dealing with the debtor has given adequate consideration to the debtor or is willing to give adequate consideration to the trustee,

(b) the dealing requires the delivery of a deed, and

(c) the delivery occurs during the period beginning with the date of sequestration and ending 7 days after the day on which—

(i) the certified copy of the order of the sheriff granting warrant is recorded in the Register of Inhibitions under section 26(1)(a), or

(ii) the certified copy of the determination of AiB awarding sequestration is recorded in that register under section 26(2).

Limitation on vesting

88 Limitation on vesting

(1) The following property of the debtor does not vest in the trustee in the sequestration—

(a) any property—

(i) kept outside a dwellinghouse, and

(ii) in respect of which attachment is, by virtue of section 11(1) of the 2002 Act, incompetent,

(b) any property—

(i) kept inside a dwellinghouse, and

(ii) not a non-essential asset for the purposes of Part 3 of that Act, and

(c) property held on trust by the debtor for any other person.

(2) The vesting of the debtor's estate in the trustee in the sequestration does not affect the right of hypothec of a landlord.

(3) Sections 78, 85 and 86 are without prejudice to the right of any secured creditor which is preferable to the rights of the trustee.

PART 6
DEBTOR'S CONTRIBUTION

Common financial tool

89 Assessment of debtor's contribution

(1) The Scottish Ministers may by regulations specify a method (the 'common financial tool') to be used to assess an appropriate amount of a living debtor's income (the 'debtor's contribution') to be paid to a trustee after the sequestration of the debtor's estate.

(2) Regulations under subsection (1) may in particular prescribe—

(a) a method for assessing a debtor's financial circumstances (including the debtor's assets, income, liabilities and expenditure),

(b) a method for determining a reasonable amount of expenditure for a debtor after the sequestration of the debtor's estate,

(c) the proportion of a debtor's income that is to constitute the debtor's contribution,

(d) that a method determined by another person must be used (with or without modification in accordance with regulations made under subsection (1)) as the common financial tool.

(3) The common financial tool must ensure that the amount of reasonable expenditure for a debtor is not less than the total amount of any income received by the debtor by way of guaranteed minimum pension (within the meaning of the Pension Schemes Act 1993).

(4) The common financial tool must ensure that an amount is allowed for—

(a) aliment for the debtor, and

(b) the debtor's relevant obligations.

(5) The 'debtor's relevant obligations' are any obligation of—

(a) aliment owed by the debtor ('obligation of aliment' having the meaning given by section 1(2) of the Family Law (Scotland) Act 1985),

(b) the debtor to make a periodical allowance to a former spouse or former civil partner, and

(c) the debtor to pay child support maintenance under the Child Support Act 1991.

(6) The amount allowed for the debtor's relevant obligations referred to in paragraphs (a) and (b) of subsection (5) need not be sufficient for compliance with a subsisting order or agreement as regards the aliment or periodical allowance.

Payments by debtor following sequestration

90 Debtor contribution order: general

(1) AiB must make an order fixing the debtor's contribution (a 'debtor contribution order')—

(a) in the case of a debtor application, at the same time as awarding sequestration of the debtor's estate,

(b) in the case of an award of sequestration following a petition under section 2(1)(b), after considering initial proposals for the debtor's contribution provided by the trustee.

(2) In a case referred to in subsection (1)(b), the trustee must send initial proposals for the debtor's contribution within [12] weeks beginning with the date of the award of sequestration.

(3) In making a debtor contribution order, AiB must use the common financial tool to assess the debtor's contribution.

(4) A debtor contribution order may fix the amount of the debtor's contribution as zero.

(5) A debtor contribution order may be made irrespective of sections 11 and 12 of the Welfare Reform and Pensions Act 1999.

(6) A debtor contribution order may provide that a third person must pay to the trustee a specified proportion of money due to the debtor by way of income.

(7) Where a third person pays a sum of money to the trustee in accordance with subsection (6), the third person is discharged from any liability to the debtor to the extent of the sum so paid.

(8) AiB must, immediately following the making of a debtor contribution order, give written notice of the order to—

(a) the debtor,

(b) the trustee, and

(c) any third person mentioned in the order.

(9) A debtor contribution order must not take effect on a date before the expiry of 14 days beginning with the day of notification of the order.

91 Debtor contribution order: payment period and intervals

(1) A debtor contribution order must contain provision requiring the debtor to pay the debtor's contribution (if not zero)—

(a) during the payment period, and

(b) at regular intervals determined by the person making or varying the order.

(2) In subsection (1)(a), 'payment period' means—

(a) the 48 months beginning with the date of the first payment,

(b) such shorter period as is determined by the person making or varying the order, or

(c) such longer period as is—

(i) determined by the trustee where there is a period during which the debtor did not pay an amount required under the debtor contribution order, or

(ii) agreed by the debtor and the trustee.

(3) The person making or varying the order may determine a shorter period under subsection (2)(b) only if, in the opinion of that person, the value of—

(a) the debtor's contribution during the shorter period, and

(b) any other estate of the debtor taken possession of by the trustee,

would be sufficient to allow a distribution of the debtor's estate to meet in full all of the debts mentioned in section 129.

(4) AiB must, when making a debtor contribution order—

(a) determine the date of the first payment, or

(b) in a case where the debtor's contribution is fixed as zero, determine the date which is to be deemed the date of the first payment under the order.

92 Debtor contribution order: review and appeal

(1) The debtor, the trustee or any other interested person may apply to AiB for a review of a debtor contribution order.

(2) An application under subsection (1) must be made within 14 days beginning with the day on which the order is made.

(3) If an application under subsection (1) is made, the order is suspended until the determination of that review by AiB.

(4) If an application under subsection (1) is made, AiB must—

(a) take into account any representations made by an interested person within 21 days beginning with the day on which the application is made, and

(b) confirm, amend or revoke the order within 28 days beginning with that day.

(5) The trustee or the debtor may, within 14 days beginning with the date of any decision of AiB under subsection (4)(b), appeal to the sheriff against that decision.

93 Effect of debtor contribution order

(1) The debtor must pay to the trustee any debtor's contribution (if not zero)—

(a) as fixed by AiB in making the debtor contribution order, or

(b) as varied in accordance with section 95.

(2) The requirement to pay the debtor's contribution applies irrespective of the debtor's discharge.

(3) If the value of the debtor's estate and income when taken possession of by the trustee is sufficient to allow a distribution of the debtor's estate to meet in full all of the debts mentioned in section 129, any debtor contribution order ceases to have effect.

94 Deductions from debtor's earnings and other income

(1) Subsections (2) to (6) apply where, under a debtor contribution order—

(a) the debtor is required to pay to the trustee an amount from the debtor's earnings or other income, or

(b) in accordance with section 90(6), a third person is required to pay to the trustee money otherwise due to the debtor by way of income.

(2) The debtor must give the person mentioned in subsection (3) an instruction to make—

(a) deductions of specified amounts from the debtor's earnings or other income, and

(b) payments to the trustee of the amounts so deducted.

(3) The person—

(a) in the case of an amount to be paid from the debtor's earnings from employment, is the person by whom the debtor is employed,

(b) in the case of an amount to be paid from other earnings or income of the debtor, is a third person who is required to pay the earnings or income to the debtor, and

(c) in the case mentioned in subsection (1)(b), is the third person who is required to pay the income to the trustee.

(4) The trustee may give the person mentioned in subsection (3) an instruction of the type mentioned in subsection (2) if the debtor fails—

(a) to comply with the requirements imposed by that subsection, and

(b) to pay the debtor's contribution in respect of 2 payment intervals applying by virtue of the debtor contribution order.

(5) A person mentioned in subsection (3) must comply with an instruction provided in accordance with subsection (2) or (4).

(6) Where the person by whom the debtor is employed or another third person pays a sum of money to the trustee in accordance with this section, that person is discharged from any liability to the debtor to the extent of the sum so paid.

(7) The Scottish Ministers may by regulations make provision about instructions to be provided under this section, including in particular—

(a) the form in which an instruction must be made,

(b) the manner in which an instruction provided in accordance with subsection (2) or (4) affects the recipient of that instruction, and

(c) the consequence of any failure of a recipient of an instruction provided in accordance with subsection (2) or (4) to comply with the duty imposed by subsection (5).

95 Variation and removal of debtor contribution order by trustee

(1) The trustee may vary or quash a debtor contribution order—

(a) on the application of the debtor, following any change in the debtor's circumstances,
(b) if the trustee considers it to be appropriate, following any such change, or
(c) if the trustee considers it to be appropriate when—
(i) sending a report to AiB under section 137(4), or
(ii) granting a discharge under section 138(2).
(2) In deciding whether to vary or quash a debtor contribution order, the trustee must use the common financial tool to assess the debtor's contribution.
(3) A decision by the trustee under subsection (1)(b) must not take effect before the expiry of 14 days beginning with the day on which the decision is made.
(4) The trustee must notify in writing the persons mentioned in subsection (5) immediately following—
(a) any variation or quashing of a debtor contribution order, or
(b) any refusal of an application as respects such an order.
(5) The persons are—
(a) the debtor,
(b) AiB (if the trustee is not AiB),
(c) any third person required to make a payment under the debtor contribution order or under section 94(5), and
(d) any other interested person.

96 Payment break
(1) The trustee may, on the application of the debtor, extend the payment period of a debtor contribution order by granting a payment break.
(2) A 'payment break' is a period not exceeding 6 months during which payments under the debtor contribution order are deferred.
(3) A debtor may apply for a payment break if—
(a) there has been a reduction of at least 50% in the debtor's disposable income (as determined using the common financial tool) as a result of any of the circumstances mentioned in subsection (4) arising in relation to the debtor, and
(b) the debtor has not previously applied for a payment break in relation to a debtor contribution order applying after the sequestration of the debtor's estate.
(4) The circumstances are—
(a) a period of unemployment or a change in employment,
(b) a period of leave from employment because of—
(i) the birth or adoption of a child, or
(ii) the need to care for a dependant,
(c) a period of illness of the debtor,
(d) a divorce,
(e) a dissolution of civil partnership,
(f) a separation from a person to whom the debtor is married or with whom the debtor is in civil partnership, and
(g) the death of a person who, along with the debtor, cared for a dependant of the debtor.
(5) An application for a payment break must specify the period during which the debtor wishes payments to be deferred.
(6) If, in the opinion of the trustee, a payment break is fair and reasonable, the trustee may grant it on such conditions and for such period as the trustee thinks fit.
(7) The trustee must notify in writing the grant of a payment break to—
(a) the debtor,
(b) AiB (if the trustee is not AiB), and

(c) any third person required to make a payment under the debtor contribution order.

(8) If the trustee decides not to grant a payment break, the trustee must notify the debtor of that decision and of the reasons for that decision.

(9) The payment period in a debtor contribution order is deemed to be varied by the addition to the period of any payment break granted under this section.

97 Sections 95 and 96: review and appeal

(1) The debtor or any other interested person may apply to AiB for a review of a decision by the trustee under section 95 or 96.

(2) Any application under subsection (1) must be made within 14 days beginning with the day on which the decision is made.

(3) If an application under subsection (1) relates to a decision by the trustee under section 95(1)(b), the decision is suspended until the determination of that review by AiB.

(4) If an application under subsection (1) is made, AiB must—

(a) take into account any representations made by an interested person within 21 days beginning with the day on which the application is made, and

(b) confirm, amend or revoke the decision within 28 days beginning with that day.

(5) The trustee or the debtor may, within 14 days beginning with the date of any decision of AiB under subsection (4)(b), appeal to the sheriff against that decision.

PART 7
SAFEGUARDING INTERESTS OF CREDITORS

Gratuitous alienations and unfair preferences

98 Gratuitous alienations

(1) Subsection (2) applies where—

(a) by an alienation (whether before or after the coming into force of this Act) by a debtor—

(i) any of the debtor's property has been transferred, or

(ii) any claim or right of the debtor has been discharged or renounced,

(b) any of the following has occurred—

(i) the debtor's estate has been sequestrated (other than, in the case of an individual, after the debtor has died),

(ii) the debtor has granted a trust deed which has become a protected trust deed,

(iii) the debtor has died and within 12 months after the date of death the debtor's estate has been sequestrated, or

(iv) the debtor has died, the debtor's estate was absolutely insolvent at the date of death and within those 12 months a judicial factor has been appointed under section 11A of the 1889 Act (see section 107) to administer that estate, and

(c) the alienation took place on a relevant day.

(2) The alienation is challengeable by—

(a) any creditor who is a creditor by virtue of a debt incurred on or before (as the case may be) the date of sequestration, the granting of the trust deed or the debtor's death, or

(b) (as the case may be) the trustee in the sequestration, the trustee acting under the trust deed or the judicial factor.

(3) For the purposes of paragraph (c) of subsection (1), the day on which an alienation takes place is the day on which the alienation becomes completely effectual.

(4) In that paragraph, 'relevant day' means, if the alienation has the effect of favouring—

(a) a person who is an associate of the debtor, a day not earlier than 5 years before, or

(b) any other person, a day not earlier than 2 years before,

(as the case may be) the date of sequestration, the granting of the trust deed or the date of death.

(5) On a challenge being brought under subsection (2), the court must grant decree—

(a) of reduction, or

(b) for such restoration of property to the debtor's estate, or such other redress, as may be appropriate.

(6) Except that the court is not to grant such decree if the person seeking to uphold the alienation establishes—

(a) that immediately, or at any other time, after the alienation the debtor's assets were greater than the debtor's liabilities,

(b) that the alienation was made for adequate consideration, or

(c) that the alienation was—

(i) a birthday, Christmas or other conventional gift, or

(ii) a gift made, for a charitable purpose, to a person who is not an associate of the debtor,

being a gift which, having regard to all the circumstances, it was reasonable for the debtor to make.

(7) Subsection [(5)] is without prejudice to any right acquired, in good faith and for value, from or through the transferee in the alienation.

(8) In subsection (6)(c)(ii), 'charitable purpose' means any charitable, benevolent or philanthropic purpose whether or not it is charitable within the meaning of any rule of law.

(9) For the purposes of subsections (1) to (8), an alienation in implementation of a prior obligation is deemed to be one for which there was no consideration, or no adequate consideration, to the extent that the prior obligation was undertaken for no consideration, or no adequate consideration.

(10) This section is without prejudice to the operation of section 2 of the Married Women's Policies of Assurance (Scotland) Act 1880 (which provides that a policy of assurance may be effected in trust for spouse, future spouse and children) including the operation of that section as applied by section 132 of the Civil Partnership Act 2004.

(11) A trustee in a sequestration, a trustee acting under a protected trust deed or a judicial factor appointed under section 11A of the 1889 Act has the same right as a creditor has under any rule of law to challenge an alienation of a debtor made for no consideration or for no adequate consideration.

99 Unfair preferences

(1) Subsection (5) applies to a transaction entered into (whether before or after the coming into force of this Act) by a debtor which has the effect of creating a preference in favour of a creditor to the prejudice of the general body of creditors, being a preference created not earlier than 6 months before—

(a) the date of sequestration of the debtor's estate (if, in the case of an individual, a date within the debtor's lifetime),

(b) the granting by the debtor of a trust deed which has become a protected trust deed,

(c) the debtor's death where, within 12 months after the date of death—

(i) the debtor's estate is sequestrated,

(ii) a judicial factor is appointed under section 11A of the 1889 Act to administer the debtor's estate and that estate was absolutely insolvent at the date of death.

(2) But subsection (5) does not apply to—

(a) a transaction in the ordinary course of trade or business,

(b) a payment in cash for a debt which when it was paid had become payable,

(c) a transaction by which the parties undertake reciprocal obligations (whether the performance by the parties of their respective obligations is to occur at the same time or at different times),

(d) the granting of a mandate by a debtor authorising an arrestee to pay over the arrested funds, or part of the arrested funds, to the arrester where—

(i) there has been a decree for payment or a warrant for summary diligence, and

(ii) the decree or warrant has been preceded by an arrestment on the dependence of the action or followed by an arrestment in execution.

(3) Paragraphs (b) and (c) of subsection (2) are to be disregarded if the transaction in question was collusive with the purpose of prejudicing the general body of creditors.

(4) For the purposes of subsection (1), the day on which a preference is created is the day on which it becomes completely effectual.

(5) The transaction is challengeable by—

(a) any creditor who is a creditor by virtue of a debt incurred on or before (as the case may be) the date of sequestration, the granting of the protected trust deed or the debtor's death, or

(b) (as the case may be) the trustee in the sequestration, the trustee acting under the protected trust deed or the judicial factor.

(6) On a challenge being brought under subsection (5) the court, if satisfied that the transaction challenged is a transaction to which that subsection applies, must grant decree—

(a) of reduction, or

(b) for such restoration of property to the debtor's estate, or such other redress, as may be appropriate.

(7) Subsection (6) is without prejudice to any right acquired, in good faith and for value, from or through the creditor in whose favour the preference was created.

(8) A trustee in a sequestration, a trustee acting under a protected trust deed or a judicial factor appointed under section 11A of the 1889 Act has the same right as a creditor has under any rule of law to challenge a preference created by a debtor.

Recall of certain orders

100 Recall of order for payment of capital sum on divorce or on dissolution of civil partnership

(1) This section applies where—

(a) a court has, under section 8(2) of the Family Law (Scotland) Act 1985 and whether before or after the coming into force of this Act, made—

(i) an order for the payment by a debtor of a capital sum,

(ii) an order for the transfer of property by the debtor, or

(iii) a pension sharing order,

(b) on the date of the making of the order the debtor was absolutely insolvent or was rendered so by implementation of the order, and

(c) within 5 years after the making of the order—

(i) the debtor's estate has been sequestrated other than on the death of the debtor,

(ii) the debtor has granted a trust deed which has (whether or not within the 5 years) become a protected trust deed,

(iii) the debtor has died and, within 12 months after the date of death, the debtor's estate has been sequestrated, or

(iv) the debtor has died and, within those 12 months, a judicial factor has been appointed under section 11A of the 1889 Act to administer the debtor's estate.

(2) The court, on the application of (as the case may be) the trustee in the sequestration, the trustee acting under the trust deed or the judicial factor, may make an order for recall of the order in question and—

(a) for the repayment to the applicant of the whole or part of any sum already paid under the order,

(b) for the return to the applicant of all or part of any property already transferred under the order, or

(c) (where such property has been sold) for payment to the applicant of all or part of the proceeds of sale.

(3) But before making an order under subsection (2), the court must have regard to all the circumstances including, in particular, the financial and other circumstances (in so far as made known to the court) of the person against whom the order would be made.

Excessive contributions

101 Recovery of excessive pension contributions

(1) Where a debtor's estate has been sequestrated and the debtor—

(a) has rights under an approved pension arrangement, or

(b) has excluded rights under an unapproved pension arrangement,

the trustee in the sequestration may apply to the court for an order under this section.

(2) Subsection (3) applies where the court is satisfied—

(a) that the rights under the arrangement are to any extent, and whether directly or indirectly, the fruits of relevant contributions, and

(b) that the making of any of the relevant contributions ('the excessive contributions') has unfairly prejudiced the debtor's creditors.

(3) The court may make such order as it thinks fit for restoring the position to what it would have been had the excessive contributions not been made.

(4) Subsection (5) applies where the court is satisfied that the value of the rights under the arrangement is, as a result of rights of the debtor under—

(a) the arrangement, or

(b) any other pension arrangement,

having at any time become subject to a debit under section 29(1)(a) of the 1999 Act (see section 107), less than it would otherwise have been.

(5) Where this subsection applies—

(a) any relevant contributions which were represented by the rights which became subject to the debit are, for the purposes of subsection (2), to be taken to be contributions of which the rights under the arrangement are the fruits, and

(b) where the relevant contributions represented by the rights under the arrangement (including those so represented by virtue of paragraph (a)) are not all excessive contributions, relevant contributions which are represented by the rights under the arrangement otherwise than by virtue of paragraph (a) are to be treated as excessive contributions before any which are so represented by virtue of that paragraph.

(6) In subsections (2) to (5), 'relevant contributions' means contributions to the arrangement or to any other pension arrangement—

(a) which the debtor has at any time made on the debtor's own behalf, or

(b) which have at any time been made on the debtor's behalf.

(7) The court must, in determining whether it is satisfied under subsection (2)(b), consider in particular—

(a) whether any of the contributions were made for the purpose of putting assets beyond the reach of, or of any of, the debtor's creditors, and

(b) whether the total amount of any contributions—

(i) made by or on behalf of the debtor to pension arrangements, and

(ii) represented (whether directly or indirectly) by rights under approved pension arrangements or excluded rights under unapproved pensions arrangements,

is an amount which is excessive in view of the debtor's circumstances when those contributions were made.

(8) For the purposes of this section and of sections 102 and 103, rights of a debtor under an unapproved pension arrangement are excluded rights if they are rights which are excluded from the debtor's estate by virtue of regulations under section 12 of the 1999 Act.

(9) In the recovery provisions (see section 103(7))—

'approved pension arrangement' has the same meaning as in section 11 of the 1999 Act, and

'unapproved pension arrangement' has the same meaning as in section 12 of that Act.

102 Orders under section 101

(1) Without prejudice to the generality of section 101(3), an order under that section may include provision—

(a) requiring the person responsible for the arrangement to pay an amount to the trustee,

(b) adjusting the liabilities of the arrangement in respect of the debtor,

(c) adjusting any liabilities of the arrangement in respect of any other person that derive, directly or indirectly, from rights of the debtor under the arrangement,

(d) for the recovery by the person responsible for the arrangement (whether by deduction from any amount which that person is ordered to pay or otherwise) of costs incurred by that person in complying in the debtor's case with any requirement under section 103(1) or in giving effect to the order.

(2) In subsection (1), references to adjusting the liabilities of the arrangement in respect of a person include, in particular, reducing the amount of any benefit or future benefit to which that person is entitled under the arrangement.

(3) In subsection (1)(c), the reference to liabilities of the arrangement does not include liabilities in respect of a person which result from giving effect to an order or provision falling within section 28(1) of the 1999 Act (pension sharing orders).

(4) The maximum amount which the person responsible for an arrangement may be required to pay by an order under section 101 is the lesser of—

(a) the amount of the excessive contributions, and

(b) the value of the debtor's rights under the arrangement (if the arrangement is an approved pension arrangement) or of the debtor's excluded rights under the arrangement (if the arrangement is an unapproved pension arrangement).

(5) An order under section 101 which requires the person responsible for an arrangement to pay an amount ('the restoration amount') to the trustee must provide for the liabilities of the arrangement to be correspondingly reduced.

(6) For the purposes of subsection (5), liabilities are correspondingly reduced if the difference between—

(a) the amount of the liabilities immediately before the reduction, and

(b) their amount immediately after the reduction,

is equal to the restoration amount.

(7) An order under section 101 in respect of an arrangement—

(a) is binding on the person responsible for the arrangement, and

(b) overrides provisions of the arrangement to the extent that they conflict with the provisions of the order.

103 Orders under section 101: supplementary

(1) The person responsible for—

(a) an approved pension arrangement under which a debtor has rights,

(b) an unapproved pension arrangement under which a debtor has excluded rights, or

(c) a pension arrangement under which a debtor has at any time had rights,

must, on the trustee in the sequestration making a written request, provide the trustee with such information about the arrangement and rights as the trustee may reasonably require for, or in connection with, the making of applications under section 101.

(2) Nothing in—

(a) any provision of section 159 of the Pension Schemes Act 1993 or section 91 of the Pensions Act 1995 (which prevent assignation and the making of orders that restrain a person from receiving anything which the person is prevented from assigning),

(b) any provision of any enactment (whether passed or made before or after the passing of the 1999 Act) corresponding to any of the provisions mentioned in paragraph (a), or

(c) any provision of the arrangement in question corresponding to any of those provisions,

applies to a court exercising its powers under section 101.

(3) Where any sum is required by an order under section 101 to be paid to the trustee, that sum is to be comprised in the debtor's estate.

(4) Regulations made by the Secretary of State may, for the purposes of the recovery provisions, make provision about the calculation and verification of—

(a) any such value as is mentioned in section 102(4)(b),

(b) any such amounts as are mentioned in section 102(6)(a) and (b).

(5) The power conferred by subsection (4) includes power to provide for calculation or verification—

(a) in such manner as may, in the particular case, be approved by a prescribed person, or

(b) in accordance with guidance from time to time prepared by a prescribed person.

(6) References in the recovery provisions to the person responsible for a pension arrangement are to—

(a) the trustees, managers or provider of the arrangement, or

(b) the person having, in relation to the arrangement, functions corresponding to those of a trustee, manager or provider.

(7) In this section and in section 101, 'the recovery provisions' means this section and sections 101 and 102.

(8) Regulations under subsection (4) may contain such incidental, supplemental and transitional provisions as appear to the Secretary of State necessary or expedient.

(9) In subsection (5), 'prescribed' means prescribed by the regulations.

104 Excessive contributions in pension-sharing cases: general

(1) For the purposes of section 98, a pension-sharing transaction is taken—

(a) to be a transaction, entered into by the transferor (in this section referred to as 'TR') with the transferee (in this section referred to as 'TE'), by which the appropriate amount is transferred by TR to TE, and

(b) to be capable of being an alienation challengeable under that section only so far as it is a transfer of so much of the appropriate amount as is recoverable.

(2) For the purposes of section 99, a pension-sharing transaction is taken—

(a) to be something (namely a transfer of the appropriate amount to TE) done by TR, and

(b) to be capable of being an unfair preference given to TE only so far as it is a transfer of so much of the appropriate amount as is recoverable.

(3) For the purposes of section 100, a pension-sharing transaction is taken—

(a) to be a pension sharing order made by the court under section 8(2) of the Family Law (Scotland) Act 1985, and

(b) to be an order capable of being recalled under that section only so far as it is a payment or transfer of so much of the appropriate amount as is recoverable.

(4) Subsection (5) applies where—

(a) an alienation is challenged under section 98,

(b) a transaction is challenged under section 99, or

(c) an application is made under section 100 for the recall of an order made in divorce proceedings.

(5) If any question arises as to whether, or the extent to which, the appropriate amount in the case of a pension-sharing transaction is recoverable, the question must be determined in accordance with subsections (6) to (10).

(6) The court is first to determine the extent, if any, to which TR's rights under the shared arrangement at the time of the transaction appear to have been, whether directly or indirectly, the fruits of contributions ('personal contributions') to the shared arrangement or any other pension arrangement—

(a) which TR has at any time made on TR's own behalf, or

(b) which have at any time been made on TR's behalf.

(7) Where it appears that those rights were to any extent the fruits of personal contributions, the court is then to determine the extent, if any, to which those rights appear to have been the fruits of personal contributions whose making has unfairly prejudiced TR's creditors ('the unfair contributions').

(8) If it appears to the court that the extent to which those rights were the fruits of the unfair contributions is such that the transfer of the appropriate amount could have been made out of rights under the shared arrangement which were not the fruits of the unfair contributions, then the appropriate amount is not recoverable.

(9) If it appears to the court that the transfer could not have been wholly so made, then the appropriate amount is recoverable to the extent to which it appears to the court that the transfer could not have been so made.

(10) In making the determination mentioned in subsection (7) the court must consider in particular—

(a) whether any of the personal contributions were made for the purpose of putting assets beyond the reach of TR's creditors or any of them, and

(b) whether the total amount of any personal contributions represented, at the time the pension sharing arrangement was made, by rights under pension arrangements is an amount which is excessive in view of TR's circumstances when those contributions were made.

(11) In this section and sections 105 and 106—

'appropriate amount', in relation to a pension-sharing transaction, means the appropriate amount in relation to that transaction for the purposes of section 29(1) of the 1999 Act (creation of pension credits and debits),

'pension-sharing transaction' means an order or provision falling within section 28(1) of that Act (orders and agreements which activate pension-sharing),

'shared arrangement', in relation to a pension-sharing transaction, means the pension arrangement to which the transaction relates,

'transferee' (or 'TE'), in relation to a pension-sharing transaction, means the person for whose benefit the transaction is made, and

'transferor' (or 'TR'), in relation to a pension-sharing transaction, means the person to whose rights the transaction relates.

105 Excessive contributions in pension-sharing cases: recovery orders

(1) In this section and section 106, 'recovery order' means, in any proceedings to which section 104 applies—

(a) a decree granted under section 98(5),

(b) a decree granted under section 99(6), or

(c) an order made under section 100(2).

(2) A recovery order may include provision—

(a) requiring the person responsible for a pension arrangement in which TE (see section 104(11)) has acquired rights derived directly or indirectly from the pension-sharing transaction (again see that section) to pay an amount to the trustee,

(b) adjusting the liabilities of the pension arrangement in respect of TE,

(c) adjusting any liabilities of the pension arrangement in respect of any other person that derive, directly or indirectly, from rights of TE under the arrangement,

(d) for the recovery by the person responsible for the pension arrangement (whether by deduction from any amount which that person is ordered to pay or otherwise) of costs incurred by that person in complying in the debtor's case with any requirement under section 106(1) or in giving effect to the order.

(3) Subsection (2) is without prejudice to the generality of section 98(5), 99(6) or 100(2).

(4) In subsection (2), references to adjusting the liabilities of a pension arrangement in respect of a person include, in particular, reducing the amount of any benefit or future benefit to which that person is entitled under the arrangement.

(5) The maximum amount which the person responsible for an arrangement may be required to pay by a recovery order is the smallest of—

(a) so much of the appropriate amount (see section 104(11)) as is recoverable in accordance with section 104,

(b) so much, if any, of the amount of the unfair contributions (within the meaning given by section 104(7)) as is not recoverable by way of an order under section 101 containing provision such as is mentioned in section 102(1)(a), and

(c) the value of the debtor's rights under the arrangement acquired by TE as a consequence of the transfer of the appropriate amount.

(6) A recovery order which requires the person responsible for an arrangement to pay an amount ('the restoration amount') to the trustee must provide for the liabilities of the arrangement to be correspondingly reduced.

(7) For the purposes of subsection (6), liabilities are correspondingly reduced if the difference between—

(a) the amount of the liabilities immediately before the reduction, and

(b) their amount immediately after the reduction, is equal to the restoration amount.

(8) A recovery order in respect of an arrangement—

(a) is binding on the person responsible for the arrangement, and

(b) overrides provisions of the arrangement to the extent that they conflict with the provisions of the order.

106 Recovery orders: supplementary

(1) The person responsible for a pension arrangement under which TE has, at any time, acquired rights by virtue of the transfer of the appropriate amount (see section 104(11)) is, on the trustee making a written request, to provide the trustee with such information about the arrangement and the rights under it of TR and TE as the trustee may reasonably require for, or in connection with, the making of an application for a recovery order.

(2) Nothing in the provisions mentioned in subsection (3) applies to a court exercising its power to make a recovery order (see section 105(1)).

(3) The provisions are—

(a) any provision of section 159 of the Pension Schemes Act 1993 or section 91 of the Pensions Act 1995 (which prevent assignation and the making of orders which restrain a person from receiving anything the person is prevented from assigning),

(b) any provision of any enactment (whether passed or made before or after the passing of the 1999 Act) corresponding to any of the provisions mentioned in paragraph (a), or

(c) any provision of the arrangement in question corresponding to any of those provisions.

(4) Regulations may, for the purposes of the recovery provisions, make provision about the calculation and verification of—

(a) any such value as is mentioned in section 105(5)(c),

(b) any such amounts as are mentioned in section 105(7)(a) and (b).

(5) The power conferred by subsection (4) includes power to provide for calculation or verification—

(a) in such manner as may, in the particular case, be approved by a prescribed person, or

(b) in accordance with guidance from time to time prepared by a prescribed person.

(6) References in the recovery provisions to the person responsible for a pension arrangement are to—

(a) the trustees, managers or providers of the arrangement, or

(b) the person having, in relation to the arrangement, functions corresponding to those of a trustee, manager or provider.

(7) In this section—

'prescribed' means prescribed by regulations,

'the recovery provisions' means this section and sections 98, 99, 100 and 105, and

'regulations' means regulations made by the Secretary of State.

(8) Regulations under the recovery provisions may contain such incidental, supplemental and transitional provisions as appear to the Secretary of State necessary or expedient.

107 References in Part 7 to 'the 1889 Act' and to 'the 1999 Act'

In this Part, references—

to 'the 1889 Act' are to the Judicial Factors (Scotland) Act 1889, and

to 'the 1999 Act' are to the Welfare Reform and Pensions Act 1999.

PART 8
ADMINISTRATION OF ESTATE BY TRUSTEE

General

108 Taking possession of estate by trustee

(1) The trustee in the sequestration must—

(a) for the purpose of recovering the estate of the debtor under section 50(1)(a), take possession as soon as may be after the trustee's appointment—

(i) of the debtor's whole estate so far as vesting in the trustee under sections 78 and 86, and

(ii) of any document in the debtor's possession or control relating to the debtor's assets or the debtor's business or financial affairs,

(b) make up and maintain an inventory and valuation of the estate, and

(c) forthwith thereafter send a copy of the inventory and valuation to AiB.

(2) Paragraph (a) of subsection (1) is subject to section 113.

(3) The trustee is entitled to have access to, and to make a copy of, any document relating to the assets or the business or financial affairs of the debtor—

(a) sent by or on behalf of the debtor to a third party, and

(b) in the third party's hands.

(4) If a person obstructs the trustee in the trustee's exercise, or attempted exercise, of a power conferred by subsection (3), the sheriff may, on the trustee's application, order the person to cease obstructing the trustee.

(5) The trustee may require delivery to the trustee of any title deed or other document of the debtor, even if a right of lien is claimed over it.

(6) Subsection (5) is without prejudice to any preference of the holder of the lien.

109 Management and realisation of estate

(1) The trustee in the sequestration, as soon as may be after the trustee's appointment, must consult with AiB concerning the exercise of the trustee's functions under section 50(1)(a).

(2) The trustee must comply with any general or specific directions given to the trustee (as the case may be)—

(a) by the creditors,

(b) on the application under this subsection of the commissioners, by the sheriff, or

(c) by AiB,

as to the exercise by the trustee of such functions.

(3) But subsection (2) is subject to subsections (4), (9) and (12).

(4) Subsections (1) and (2) do not apply where the trustee is AiB.

(5) The trustee may—

(a) carry on or close down any business of the debtor,

(b) bring, defend or continue any legal proceedings relating to the estate of the debtor,

(c) create a security over any part of the estate,

(d) where any right, option or other power forms part of the debtor's estate, make payments or incur liabilities with a view to obtaining, for the benefit of the creditors, any property which is the subject of the right, option or power,

(e) borrow money in so far as it is necessary for the trustee to do so to safeguard the debtor's estate, and

(f) effect or maintain insurance policies in respect of the business or property of the debtor.

(6) Any sale of the debtor's estate by the trustee may either be by public sale or by private bargain.

(7) The following rules apply to the sale of any part of the debtor's heritable estate over which a heritable security is held by a creditor or creditors if the rights of the secured creditor or creditors are preferable to those of the trustee—

(a) the trustee may sell that part only with the concurrence of every such creditor unless the trustee obtains a sufficiently high price to discharge every such security,

(b) the following acts are precluded—

(i) the taking of steps by a creditor to enforce the creditor's security over the part after the trustee has intimated to the creditor that the trustee intends to sell the part,

(ii) the commencement by the trustee of the procedure for the sale of the part after the creditor has intimated to the trustee that the creditor intends to commence the procedure for its sale,

(c) except that where the trustee or a creditor has given intimation under paragraph (b) but has unduly delayed in proceeding with the sale then, if authorised by the sheriff in the case of—

(i) sub-paragraph (i) of that paragraph, any creditor to whom intimation has been given may enforce the creditor's security, or

(ii) sub-paragraph (ii) of that paragraph, the trustee may sell the part.

(8) The function of the trustee under section 50(1)(a) to realise the debtor's

estate includes the function of selling, with or without recourse against the estate, debts owing to the estate.

(9) The trustee may sell any perishable goods without complying with any directions given to the trustee under subsection (2)(a) or (c) if the trustee considers that compliance with such directions would adversely affect the sale.

(10) The validity of the title of any purchaser is not challengeable on the ground that there has been a failure to comply with a requirement of this section.

(11) It is not competent for the trustee or an associate of the trustee, or for any commissioner, to purchase any of the debtor's estate in pursuance of this section.

(12) The trustee—

(a) must comply with the requirements of subsection (7) of this section, and

(b) may do anything permitted by this section,

only in so far as, in the trustee's view, it would be of financial benefit to the estate of the debtor, and in the interests of the creditors, to do so.

Contractual powers and money received

110 Contractual powers of trustee

(1) The trustee in the sequestration may, as respects any contract entered into by the debtor before the date of sequestration—

(a) adopt it (except where adoption is precluded by its express or implied terms) if the trustee considers that its adoption would be beneficial to the administration of the debtor's estate, or

(b) refuse to adopt it.

(2) But subsection (1) is subject to subsections (3) and (10).

(3) The trustee must, within 28 days after the receipt by the trustee of a request in writing from any party to a contract entered into by the debtor, adopt or refuse to adopt the contract.

(4) The 28 days mentioned in subsection (3) may be extended—

(a) in a case where AiB is the trustee, by the sheriff on the application of AiB, and

(b) in any other case, by AiB on the application of the trustee.

(5) The trustee may, within 14 days beginning with the day of the decision, apply to AiB for a review of a decision of AiB under subsection (4)(b).

(6) If an application for a review under subsection (5) is made, AiB must—

(a) take into account any representations made by an interested party within 21 days beginning with the day on which the application is made, and

(b) confirm, amend or revoke the decision within 28 days beginning with that day.

(7) The trustee may, within 14 days beginning with the day of the decision, appeal to the sheriff against a decision by AiB under subsection (6)(b).

(8) AiB may refer a case to the sheriff for a direction before—

(a) making a decision under subsection (4)(b), or

(b) undertaking any review under this section.

(9) An application for a review under subsection (5) may not be made in relation to a matter on which AiB has applied to the sheriff for a direction under subsection (8).

(10) If, within the 28 days mentioned in subsection (3) or as the case may be within the longer period allowed by virtue of subsection (4), the trustee does not reply in writing to a request under subsection (3), the trustee is deemed to have refused to adopt the contract.

(11) The trustee may enter into any contract where the trustee considers that to do so would be beneficial for the administration of the debtor's estate.

111 Money received by trustee

(1) All money received by the trustee in the sequestration in the exercise of the

trustee's functions must be deposited by the trustee in the name of the debtor's estate in an interest-bearing account in an appropriate bank or institution.

(2) But subsection (1) is subject to subsections (3) and (5).

(3) In any case where the trustee is AiB, all money received by AiB in the exercise of AiB's functions as trustee must be deposited by AiB in an interest-bearing account in an appropriate bank or institution—

(a) in the name of the debtor's estate, or

(b) in the name of the Scottish Ministers.

(4) But subsection (3) is subject to subsection (5).

(5) The trustee may at any time retain in the trustee's hands a sum not exceeding £200 or such other sum as may be prescribed.

Debtor's home

112 Debtor's family home

(1) This section applies where a debtor's sequestrated estate includes any right or interest in the debtor's family home.

(2) At the end of 3 years beginning with the date of sequestration, the right or interest—

(a) ceases to form part of the debtor's sequestrated estate, and

(b) is reinvested in the debtor (without disposition, conveyance, assignation or other transfer).

(3) Subsection (2) does not apply if—

(a) during the 3 years mentioned in subsection (2), the trustee in the sequestration—

(i) disposes of or otherwise realises the right or interest,

(ii) concludes missives for sale of the right or interest,

(iii) sends a memorandum to the Keeper of the Register of Inhibitions under section 26(6),

(iv) completes title in the Land Register of Scotland, or as the case may be in the Register of Sasines, in relation to the right or interest,

(v) commences proceedings to obtain the authority of the sheriff under section 113(1)(b) to sell or dispose of the right or interest,

(vi) commences proceedings in an action for division and sale of the family home,

(vii) commences proceedings in an action for the purpose of obtaining vacant possession of the family home,

(viii) enters with the debtor into an agreement such as is mentioned in subsection (4), or

(ix) commences an action under section 98 in respect of the right or interest, or

(b) the trustee in the sequestration—

(i) does not, at any time during the 3 years mentioned in subsection (2), know about the facts giving rise to a right of action under section 98, but

(ii) commences an action under that section reasonably soon after becoming aware of those facts.

(4) The agreement referred to in subsection (3)(a)(viii) is an agreement that the debtor is to incur a specified liability to the debtor's estate (with or without interest from the date of the agreement) in consideration of which the right or interest is to—

(a) cease to form part of the debtor's sequestrated estate, and

(b) be reinvested in the debtor (without disposition, conveyance, assignation or other transfer).

(5) If the debtor does not inform the trustee or AiB of the right or interest

within 3 months beginning with the date of sequestration then the 3 years mentioned in subsection (2) is to be taken—

(a) not to begin with the date of sequestration, but

(b) to begin instead with the date on which the trustee becomes aware of the right or interest.

(6) The sheriff may, on the trustee's application, substitute for the 3 years mentioned in subsection (2) a longer period—

(a) in prescribed circumstances, and

(b) in such other circumstances as the sheriff thinks appropriate.

(7) The Scottish Ministers may, by regulations—

(a) make provision for this section to have effect with the substitution, in such circumstances as may be specified in the regulations, of a shorter period for the 3 years mentioned in subsection (2),

(b) prescribe circumstances in which this section does not apply,

(c) prescribe circumstances in which a sheriff may disapply this section,

(d) make provision requiring the trustee to give notice that this section applies or does not apply,

(e) make provision about compensation,

(f) make such provision as they consider necessary or expedient in consequence of regulations made under paragraphs (a) to (e), or

(g) modify sub-paragraphs (i) to (viii) of subsection (3)(a) so as to—

(i) add or remove a matter, or

(ii) vary a matter,

referred to in that subsection.

(8) In this section, 'family home' has the same meaning as in section 113.

113 Power of trustee in relation to debtor's family home

(1) Before the trustee in the sequestration (in this section referred to as 'T'), or the trustee acting under the trust deed (in this section referred to as 'TU'), sells or disposes of any right or interest in the debtor's family home, T or TU must—

(a) obtain the relevant consent, or

(b) where unable to obtain that consent, obtain the authority of the sheriff in accordance with subsection (2) or as the case may be (3).

(2) Where T or TU requires to obtain the authority of the sheriff in terms of subsection (1)(b), the sheriff, after having regard to all the circumstances of the case including—

(a) the needs and financial resources of the debtor's spouse or former spouse,

(b) the needs and financial resources of the debtor's civil partner or former civil partner,

(c) the needs and financial resources of any child of the family,

(d) the interests of the creditors, and

(e) the length of the period during which (whether before or after the relevant date) the family home was used as a residence by any of the persons referred to in paragraphs (a) to (c),

may refuse to grant the application or may postpone the granting of the application for such period (not exceeding 3 years) as the sheriff may consider reasonable in the circumstances or may grant the application subject to such conditions as the sheriff may prescribe.

(3) Subsection (2) applies to an action brought by T or TU—

(a) for division and sale of, or

(b) for the purpose of obtaining vacant possession of,

the debtor's family home as that subsection applies to an application under subsection (1)(b).

(4) Before commencing proceedings to obtain the authority of the sheriff under

subsection (2) or (3), T or TU must give notice of the proceedings to the local authority in whose area the home is situated.

(5) Notice under subsection (4) must be given in such form and manner as may be prescribed.

(6) For the purposes of subsection (3), any reference in subsection (2) to the granting of the application is to be construed as a reference to the granting of decree in the action.

(7) In this section—

'family home' means any property in which, at the relevant date, the debtor had a right or interest (whether alone or in common with another person), being property which was occupied at that date as a residence—

(a) by—

(i) the debtor and the debtor's spouse or civil partner,

(ii) the debtor's spouse or civil partner,

(iii) the debtor's former spouse or former civil partner,

in any of those cases, whether with or without a child of the family, or

(b) by the debtor with a child of the family,

'child of the family' includes—

(a) any child or grandchild of either—

(i) the debtor, or

(ii) the debtor's spouse or civil partner (or former spouse or civil partner), and

(b) any person who has been brought up or accepted by either—

(i) the debtor, or

(ii) the debtor's spouse or civil partner (or former spouse or civil partner),

as if a child of the debtor, spouse, civil partner or former spouse or civil partner, (whatever age the child, grandchild or person may be),

'relevant consent' means, in relation to the sale or disposal of any right or interest in a family home—

(a) in a case where the family home is occupied by the debtor's spouse or civil partner (or former spouse or civil partner), the consent of the spouse or civil partner (or as the case may be former spouse or civil partner) whether or not the family home is also occupied by the debtor,

(b) where paragraph (a) does not apply, in a case where the family home is occupied by the debtor with a child of the family, the consent of the debtor, and

'relevant date' means the day immediately preceding the date of sequestration or, as the case may be, the day immediately preceding the date the trust deed was granted.

Rights of spouse or civil partner

114 Protection of rights of spouse against arrangements intended to defeat them

(1) Subsections (2) and (3) apply where a debtor's sequestrated estate includes a matrimonial home in respect of which—

(a) the debtor, immediately before the date the order was made appointing the trustee, was an entitled spouse, and

(b) the other spouse is a non-entitled spouse.

(2) Where the trustee in the sequestration knows—

(a) that the debtor is married to the non-entitled spouse, and

(b) where the non-entitled spouse is residing,

the trustee must inform the non-entitled spouse, within 14 days beginning with the date mentioned in subsection (1)(a), of the fact that sequestration of the debtor's estate has been awarded, of the right of petition which exists under section 29 and of the effect of subsection (3).

(3) On the petition under section 29 of the non-entitled spouse presented either

within 40 days beginning with the date mentioned in subsection (1)(a) or within 10 weeks beginning with the date of the award of sequestration the sheriff, if satisfied that the purpose of the petition for sequestration, or as the case may be the debtor application, was wholly or mainly to defeat the occupancy rights of the nonentitled spouse, may—

(a) under section 30, recall the sequestration, or

(b) make such order as the sheriff thinks appropriate to protect the occupancy rights of the non-entitled spouse.

(4) The reference in subsection (1)(a) to the date the order is made appointing the trustee is, in a case where more than one trustee is appointed in the sequestration, to be construed as a reference to the date the first order is made appointing a trustee.

(5) In this section—

'entitled spouse' and 'non-entitled spouse' are to be construed in accordance with section 6 of the Matrimonial Homes (Family Protection) (Scotland) Act 1981,

'matrimonial home' has the meaning given by section 22 of that Act, and

'occupancy rights' has the meaning given by section 1(4) of that Act.

115 Protection of rights of civil partner against arrangements intended to defeat them

(1) Subsections (2) and (3) apply where a debtor's sequestrated estate includes a family home in respect of which—

(a) the debtor, immediately before the date the order was made appointing the trustee, was an entitled partner, and

(b) the other partner in the civil partnership is a non-entitled partner.

(2) Where the trustee in the sequestration knows—

(a) that the debtor is in civil partnership with the non-entitled partner, and

(b) where the non-entitled partner is residing,

the trustee must inform the non-entitled partner, within 14 days beginning with the date mentioned in subsection (1)(a), of the fact that sequestration of the debtor's estate has been awarded, of the right of petition which exists under section 29 and of the effect of subsection (3).

(3) On the petition under section 29 of the non-entitled partner presented either within 40 days beginning with the date mentioned in subsection (1)(a) or within 10 weeks beginning with the date of the award of sequestration the sheriff, if satisfied that the purpose of the petition for sequestration, or as the case may be the debtor application, was wholly or mainly to defeat the occupancy rights of the non-entitled partner, may—

(a) under section 30, recall the sequestration, or

(b) make such order as the sheriff thinks appropriate to protect the occupancy rights of the non-entitled partner.

(4) The reference in subsection (1)(a) to the date the order is made appointing the trustee is, in a case where more than one trustee is appointed in the sequestration, to be construed as a reference to the date the first order is made appointing a trustee.

(5) In this section—

'entitled partner' and 'non-entitled partner' are to be construed in accordance with section 101 of the Civil Partnership Act 2004,

'family home' has the meaning given by section 135 of that Act, and

'occupancy rights' means the rights conferred by section 101(1) of that Act.

Account of state of affairs

116 Debtor's account of state of affairs

(1) This section applies to a debtor who—

(a) has not been discharged under this Act, or

(b) is subject to a debtor contribution order.

(2) The trustee in the sequestration must, at the end of—

(a) 6 months beginning with the date of sequestration, and

(b) each subsequent 6 months,
require the debtor to give an account in writing, in such form as may be prescribed, of the debtor's current state of affairs.

Financial education for debtor

117 Financial education for debtor

(1) The trustee must notify a living debtor that the debtor is required to undertake a prescribed course of financial education (a 'financial education course') specified by the trustee if, in the opinion of the trustee—

(a) any of the circumstances mentioned in subsection (2) applies, and

(b) undertaking the course would be appropriate for the debtor.

(2) The circumstances are—

(a) that in the 5 years ending on the date on which the sequestration was awarded—

(i) the debtor's estate was sequestrated,

(ii) the debtor granted a protected trust deed,

(iii) an analogous remedy (as defined in section 17(8)) was in force in respect of the debtor, or

(iv) the debtor participated in a debt management programme under which the debtor made regular payments,

(b) that the debtor is subject to, or under investigation with a view to an application being made for, a bankruptcy restrictions order,

(c) that the trustee considers that the pattern of the debtor's behaviour, whether before or after the award of sequestration, is such that the debtor would benefit from a financial education course, and

(d) that the debtor agrees to undertake a financial education course.

(3) The trustee must decide whether to issue a notification under subsection (1)—

(a) within 6 months beginning with the date of the award of sequestration, and

(b) in a case where section 143 applies, as soon as reasonably practicable after—

(i) the trustee ascertains the whereabouts of the debtor, or

(ii) the debtor makes contact with the trustee.

(4) A debtor must not be required to undertake or, as the case may be, complete the financial course specified by the trustee if, in the opinion of the trustee, the debtor—

(a) is unable to participate in the course as a result of the debtor's health (including by reason of disability or of physical or mental illness), or

(b) has completed a financial education course in the 5 years ending on the date on which the sequestration of the debtor's estate was awarded.

(5) Regulations under subsection (1) may in particular—

(a) prescribe the content, format and method of delivery of a course,

(b) prescribe different courses for different circumstances, or

(c) make provision for particular courses to be specified by a trustee where particular circumstances in subsection (2) apply.

(6) In subsection (2)(a)(iv), 'debt management programme' includes in particular a programme approved in accordance with section 2 of the 2002 Act.

PART 9
EXAMINATION OF DEBTOR

Private and public examination

118 Private examination

(1) The trustee in the sequestration may request—

(a) the debtor to appear before the trustee and to give information relating to the debtor's assets, the debtor's dealings with them or the debtor's conduct in relation to the debtor's business or financial affairs, or

(b) the debtor's spouse or civil partner, or any other person who the trustee believes can give such information to give that information.

(2) In this Act any such spouse, civil partner or other person is referred to as a 'relevant person'.

(3) The trustee may, if the trustee considers it necessary, apply to the sheriff for an order to be made under subsection (4).

(4) On an application under subsection (3), the sheriff may make an order requiring the debtor or a relevant person to attend for private examination before the sheriff on a date and at a time specified in the order.

(5) But subsection (4) is subject to section 120(3).

(6) A date specified in an order under subsection (4) must be not earlier than 8 days nor later than 16 days after the date of the order.

(7) A person who fails without reasonable excuse to comply with an order under subsection (4) commits an offence.

(8) A person who commits an offence under subsection (7) is liable, on summary conviction—

(a) to a fine not exceeding level 5 on the standard scale, or

(b) to imprisonment for a term not exceeding 3 months,

or both to such fine and to such imprisonment.

(9) Where the debtor is an entity whose estate may be sequestrated by virtue of section 6(1), the references, in this section and in sections 119 to 121, to the debtor are to be construed, unless the context otherwise requires, as references to a person representing the entity.

119 Public examination

(1) At least 8 weeks before the end of the first accounting period the trustee in the sequestration—

(a) may, or

(b) if requested to do so by AiB or by the commissioners (if any) or by ¼ in value of the creditors, must,

apply to the sheriff for an order for the public examination before the sheriff of the debtor, or of a relevant person, relating to the debtor's assets, the debtor's dealings with those assets or the debtor's conduct in relation to the debtor's business or financial affairs.

(2) Except that on cause shown such application may be made by the trustee at any time.

(3) On an application under subsection (1), the sheriff must make an order requiring the debtor or the relevant person to attend for examination before the sheriff in open court on a date and at a time specified in the order.

(4) But subsection (3) is subject to section 120(3).

(5) A date specified in an order under subsection (3) must be not earlier than 8 days nor later than 16 days after the date of the order.

(6) On the sheriff making an order under subsection (3), the trustee must—

(a) send to AiB a notice in such form, and containing such particulars, as may be prescribed,

(b) send a copy of the notice—

(i) to every creditor known to the trustee, and

(ii) where the order is in respect of a relevant person, to the debtor, and

(c) inform each person sent a copy under paragraph (b) that the person may participate in the examination.

(7) AiB must enter particulars of the notice sent under subsection (6)(a) in the register of insolvencies.

(8) A person who fails without reasonable excuse to comply with an order under subsection (3) commits an offence.

(9) A person who commits an offence under subsection (8) is liable, on summary conviction—

(a) to a fine not exceeding level 5 on the standard scale, or

(b) to imprisonment for a term not exceeding 3 months,

or both to such fine and to such imprisonment.

120 Provisions ancillary to sections 118 and 119

(1) If a debtor or relevant person is residing in Scotland, the sheriff may on the application of the trustee grant a warrant (which may be executed by a messenger-at-arms or sheriff officer anywhere in Scotland) to apprehend the debtor or relevant person and to have the apprehended person taken to the place of the examination.

(2) But a warrant under subsection (1) must not be granted unless the sheriff is satisfied that it is necessary to grant it to secure the attendance of the debtor or relevant person at the examination.

(3) If the debtor or relevant person is for any good reason prevented from attending for examination, the sheriff may grant a commission to take the examination of the debtor or relevant person (the commissioner being, in this section and in section 121, referred to as an 'examining commissioner').

(4) Subsection (3) is without prejudice to subsection (5).

(5) The sheriff or the examining commissioner may at any time adjourn the examination to such day as the sheriff or examining commissioner may fix.

(6) The sheriff or examining commissioner may order the debtor or a relevant person to produce for inspection any document—

(a) in the custody or control of the person so ordered, and

(b) relating to the debtor's assets, the debtor's dealings with those assets or the debtor's conduct in relation to the debtor's business or financial affairs,

and to deliver the document or a copy of the document to the trustee in the sequestration for further examination by the trustee.

Conduct of examination

121 Conduct of examination

(1) The examination, whether before the sheriff or an examining commissioner, must be taken on oath.

(2) At the examination—

(a) the trustee in the sequestration (or a solicitor or counsel acting on behalf of the trustee) and, in the case of public examination, any creditor may question the debtor or a relevant person, and

(b) the debtor may question a relevant person,

as to any matter relating to the debtor's assets, the debtor's dealings with those assets or the debtor's conduct in relation to the debtor's business or financial affairs.

(3) The debtor or a relevant person—

(a) is required to answer any question relating to the debtor's assets, the debtor's dealings with those assets or the debtor's conduct in relation to the debtor's business or financial affairs, and

(b) is not excused from answering any such question on the ground—

(i) that the answer may incriminate, or tend to incriminate, the person questioned, or

(ii) of confidentiality.

(4) Except that—

(a) a statement made by the debtor or a relevant person in answer to any such question is not admissible in evidence in any subsequent criminal proceedings against the person making it (except where the proceedings are in respect of a charge of perjury relating to the statement), and

(b) a person subject to examination is not required to disclose any information received from a person not called for examination if the information is confidential between the two persons.

(5) The rules relating to the recording of evidence in ordinary causes specified in the first schedule of the Sheriff Courts (Scotland) Act 1907 apply in relation to the recording of evidence at the examination before the sheriff or examining commissioner.

(6) The debtor's deposition at the examination must be subscribed by the debtor and by the sheriff (or, as the case may be, the examining commissioner).

(7) The trustee must send a copy of the record of the examination to AiB.

(8) A relevant person is entitled, as if the person were a witness in an ordinary civil cause in the sheriff court, to fees or allowances in respect of the person's attendance at the examination.

(9) Except that the sheriff may disallow or restrict the entitlement to such fees or allowances if the sheriff thinks it appropriate to do so in all the circumstances.

PART 10
CLAIMS, DIVIDENDS AND DISTRIBUTION ETC

Submission and adjudication of claims

122 Submission of claims to trustee

(1) A creditor must submit a claim in accordance with this section to the trustee in the sequestration in order to obtain an adjudication as to that person's entitlement—

(a) to vote at a meeting of creditors other than the statutory meeting, or

(b) (so far as funds are available) to a dividend out of the debtor's estate in respect of any accounting period.

(2) Where the claim is by virtue of—

(a) paragraph (a) of subsection (1), it must be submitted at or before the meeting,

(b) paragraph (b) of that subsection, it must be submitted in accordance with subsection (4).

(3) But subsection (1) is subject to subsections (4), (7) and (8) and to section 131(6) to (9).

(4) A creditor must, in order to obtain an adjudication as to the creditor's entitlement (so far as funds are available) to a dividend out of the debtor's estate, submit a claim to the trustee not later than the relevant day.

(5) The 'relevant day', in relation to a creditor, means—

(a) where notice is given to the creditor under section 44(3), the day which is 120 days after the day on which that notice is given,

(b) where no such notice is given, the day which is 120 days after the day on which the trustee gives notice to the creditor inviting the submission of claims.

(6) If a creditor submits a claim to the trustee after the relevant day, the trustee may, in respect of any accounting period, provide an adjudication as to the creditor's entitlement (so far as funds are available) to a dividend out of the debtor's estate if—

(a) the claim is submitted not later than 8 weeks before the end of the accounting period, and

(b) there were exceptional circumstances which prevented the claim from being submitted before the relevant day.

(7) Subsection (8) applies as regards a claim submitted by a creditor—

(a) under section 46 and accepted in whole or in part by the trustee for the purpose of voting at the statutory meeting, or

(b) under this section and not rejected in whole.

(8) The claim is deemed to have been re-submitted for the purpose of obtaining an adjudication as to the creditor's entitlement both to vote at any subsequent meeting and (so far as funds are available) to a dividend in respect of an accounting period or as the case may be of any subsequent accounting period.

(9) A creditor submits a claim under this section by producing to the trustee—

(a) a statement of claim in the prescribed form, and

(b) an account or voucher (according to the nature of the debt) which constitutes prima facie evidence of the debt.

(10) But the trustee, with the consent of the commissioners if any, may dispense with any requirement under subsection (9) in respect of any debt or of any class of debt.

(11) Where a creditor (in this subsection referred to as 'C') neither resides, nor has a place of business, in the United Kingdom, the trustee—

(a) must, if the trustee knows where C does reside or have a place of business and if no notification has been given to C under section 44(3), write to C informing C that C may submit a claim under this section, and

(b) may allow C to submit an informal claim in writing.

(12) Where a creditor has submitted a claim under this section (or under section 46 a statement of claim which has been deemed re-submitted as mentioned in subsection (8)), the creditor may at any time submit a further claim under this section specifying a different amount for the creditor's claim.

(13) But a secured creditor is not entitled to produce a further claim specifying a different value for the security at any time after the trustee requires the secured creditor to discharge, or convey or assign, the security under paragraph 4(3) of schedule 2.

123 Evidence as to validity or amount of claim

(1) The trustee in the sequestration, for the purpose of being satisfied as to the validity or amount of a claim submitted by a creditor under section 122, may require—

(a) the creditor to produce further evidence, or

(b) any other person who the trustee believes can produce relevant evidence to produce such evidence.

(2) If the creditor (or as the case may be the other person) refuses or delays to do so, the trustee may apply to the sheriff for an order requiring the creditor (or the other person) to attend for private examination before the sheriff.

(3) At any private examination under subsection (2)—

(a) a solicitor or counsel may act on behalf of the trustee, or

(b) the trustee may appear on the trustee's own behalf.

(4) Sections 118(4) to (7) and 121(1) apply, subject to any necessary modifications, to the examination of the creditor (or the other person) as they apply to the examination of a relevant person.

(5) References in subsections (1) and (4) to the creditor in a case where the creditor is an entity mentioned in section 6(1) are to be construed, unless the context otherwise requires, as references to a person representing the entity.

124 False claims etc

(1) Subsections (2) and (3) apply where a creditor produces under section 122 or 123—

(a) a statement of claim,

(b) account,

(c) voucher, or

(d) other evidence,

which is false.

(2) The creditor commits an offence unless it is shown that the creditor neither knew nor had reason to believe that the statement of claim, account, voucher or other evidence was false.

(3) The debtor commits an offence if the debtor—

(a) knew, or became aware, that the statement of claim, account, voucher or other evidence was false, and

(b) failed, as soon as practicable after acquiring such knowledge, to report to the trustee that the statement of claim, account, voucher or other evidence was false.

(4) A person convicted of an offence under subsection (2) or (3) is liable—

(a) on summary conviction, to a fine not exceeding the statutory maximum, or—

(i) in a case where the person has previously been convicted of an offence inferring dishonest appropriation of property or an attempt at dishonest appropriation of property, to imprisonment for a term not exceeding 6 months, or

(ii) in any other case, to imprisonment for a term not exceeding 3 months,

or both to a fine not exceeding the statutory maximum and to such imprisonment as is mentioned, in relation to the case in question, in sub-paragraph (i) or (ii), or

(b) on conviction on indictment—

(i) to a fine, or

(ii) to imprisonment for a term not exceeding 2 years,

or both to a fine and to such imprisonment.

125 Further provision as to claims

(1) A creditor may, in such circumstances as may be prescribed, state the amount of the creditor's claim under section 122 in foreign currency.

(2) The trustee in the sequestration must, on production of any document to the trustee for the purposes of any of sections 122 to 124—

(a) initial the document, and

(b) if requested by the person producing it, return it (if it is not a statement of claim) to that person.

(3) The submission of a claim under section 122 bars the effect of any enactment or rule of law relating to the limitation of actions.

(4) Schedule 2 has effect for determining the amount in respect of which the creditor is entitled to claim.

126 Adjudication of claims: general

(1) At the commencement of every meeting of creditors (other than the statutory meeting) the trustee in the sequestration must, for the purposes of section 128 so far as it relates to voting at the meeting, accept or reject the claim of each creditor.

(2) Subsection (3) applies where funds are available for payment of a dividend out of the debtor's estate in respect of an accounting period.

(3) For the purpose of determining who is entitled to such a dividend, the trustee—

(a) must, not later than 4 weeks before the end of the period, accept or reject every claim submitted (or deemed to have been re-submitted) to the trustee under this Act, and

(b) must, at the same time, make a decision on any matter required to be specified under paragraph (a) or (b) of subsection (7).

(4) The trustee must then, as soon as reasonably practicable, send a list of every claim so accepted or rejected (including its amount and whether it has been accepted or rejected) to the debtor and to every creditor known to the trustee.

(5) If the amount of a claim is stated in foreign currency, the trustee in adjudicating under subsection (1) or (3) on the claim must convert the amount into sterling, in such manner as may be prescribed, at the rate of exchange prevailing at the close of business on the date of sequestration.

(6) Where the trustee rejects a claim, the trustee must forthwith notify the claimant, giving reasons for the rejection.

(7) Where the trustee accepts or rejects a claim, the trustee must record the trustee's decision on the claim, specifying—

(a) the amount of the claim accepted by the trustee,

(b) the category of debt, and the value of any security, as decided by the trustee, and

(c) if the trustee is rejecting the claim, the trustee's reasons for doing so.

(8) Any reference in this section or in section 127 to the acceptance or rejection of a claim is to be construed as a reference to the acceptance or rejection of the claim in whole or in part.

127 Adjudication of claims: review and appeal

(1) The debtor or any creditor may apply to AiB for a review of—

(a) the acceptance or rejection of any claim, or

(b) a decision in respect of any matter requiring to be specified under section 126(7)(a) or (b).

(2) The debtor may make an application under subsection (1) only if the debtor satisfies AiB that the debtor has, or is likely to have, a pecuniary interest in the outcome of the review.

(3) Any application under subsection (1) must be made, in the case of a review relating to an acceptance or rejection—

(a) under subsection (1) of section 126, within 14 days beginning with the day of the decision to accept or reject the claim, and

(b) under subsection (3) of that section, within 28 days beginning with that day.

(4) If an application under subsection (1) is made, AiB must—

(a) take into account any representations made by an interested party within 21 days beginning with the day on which the application is made, and

(b) confirm, amend or revoke the decision within 28 days beginning with that day.

(5) The debtor or any creditor may, within 14 days beginning with the day of a decision by AiB under subsection (4)(b), appeal to the sheriff against that decision.

(6) The debtor may appeal under subsection (5) only if the debtor satisfies the sheriff that the debtor has, or is likely to have, a pecuniary interest in the outcome of the appeal.

Entitlement to vote and draw a dividend

128 Voting and drawing a dividend

(1) A creditor whose claim has been accepted in whole or in part by the trustee in the sequestration or on review or appeal under section 127 is entitled, in a case where the acceptance is under (or on review or appeal arising from)—

(a) section 126(1), to vote on any matter at the meeting of creditors for the purpose of voting at which the claim is accepted, or

(b) section 126(3), to payment out of the debtor's estate of a dividend in respect of the accounting period for the purposes of which the claim is accepted.

(2) But—

(a) paragraph (a) of subsection (1) is subject to sections 70(1)(a) and 77(1) and (7)(b), and

(b) the entitlement mentioned in paragraph (b) of that subsection arises only in so far as the estate has funds available, having regard to section 129, to make the payment in question.

(3) No vote may be cast, by virtue of a debt, more than once on any resolution put to a meeting of creditors.

[. . .]

Distribution

129 Priority in distribution

(1) The funds of the debtor's estate must be distributed by the trustee in the sequestration to meet the following debts in the order in which they are mentioned—

(a) the outlays and remuneration of an interim trustee in the administration of the debtor's estate,

(b) the outlays and remuneration of the trustee in the sequestration in the administration of the debtor's estate,

(c) where the debtor has died—

(i) deathbed and funeral expenses reasonably incurred, and

(ii) expenses reasonably incurred in administering the deceased's estate,

(d) the expenses reasonably incurred by a creditor who is a petitioner for, or concurs in a debtor application for, sequestration,

(e) ordinary preferred debts (excluding any interest which has accrued on those debts to the date of sequestration),

(f) secondary preferred debts (excluding any interest which has accrued on those debts to the date of sequestration),

(g) ordinary [non-preferential] debts (that is to say, debts which are neither secured debts nor debts mentioned in any other paragraph of this subsection),

[(ga) secondary non-preferential debts,

(gb) tertiary non-preferential debts,]

(h) interest, between the date of sequestration and the date of payment of the debt, at the rate specified in subsection (10) on—

(i) the ordinary preferred debts,

(ii) the secondary preferred debts, [. . .]

(iii) the ordinary [non-preferential] debts,

[(iv) the secondary non-preferential debts, and

(v) the tertiary non-preferential debts,]

(i) any postponed debt.

(2) In this Act—

'preferred debt' means a debt listed in Part 1 of schedule 3 of this Act,

'ordinary preferred debt' means a debt within any of paragraphs 1 to 6 of that Part, and

'secondary preferred debt' means a debt within [any of paragraphs 7 to 8A] of that Part.

(3) Part 2 of that schedule has effect for the interpretation of Part 1 of that schedule.

[(3A) In subsection (1), 'secondary non-preferential debts' and 'tertiary nonpreferential debts' have the meanings given by section 129A.]

(4) In this Act, 'postponed debt' means—

(a) a loan made to the debtor, in consideration of a share of the profits in the debtor's business, which is postponed under section 3 of the Partnership Act 1890 to the claims of other creditors,

(b) a loan made to the debtor by the debtor's spouse or civil partner, or

(c) a creditor's right to—

(i) anything vesting in the trustee by virtue of a successful challenge under section 98, or

(ii) the proceeds of sale of anything so vesting.

(5) A debt falling within any of paragraphs (c) to (i) of subsection (1) has the same priority as any other debt falling within the same paragraph and, where the funds of the estate are inadequate to enable the debts mentioned in the paragraph in question to be paid in full, those debts are to abate in equal proportions.

(6) Any surplus remaining after all the debts mentioned in this section have

been paid in full must be made over to the debtor or the debtor's successors or assignees.

(7) In subsection (6), 'surplus'—

(a) includes any kind of estate, but

(b) does not include any unclaimed dividend.

[. . .]

(9) Nothing in this section affects—

(a) any right of a secured creditor which is preferable to the rights of the trustee,

(b) any preference of the holder of a lien over a title deed, or other document, which has been delivered to the trustee in accordance with a requirement under section 108(5).

(10) The rate of interest referred to in paragraph (h) of subsection (1) is whichever is the greater of—

(a) the prescribed rate at the date of sequestration, and

(b) the rate applicable to that debt apart from the sequestration.

[129A Section 129: interpretation

(1) In this Act, 'secondary non-preferential debts' means non-preferential debts issued by a relevant financial institution under an instrument where—

(a) the original contractual maturity of the instrument is of at least one year,

(b) the instrument is not a derivative and contains no embedded derivative, and

(c) the relevant contractual documentation and where applicable the prospectus related to the issue of the debts explain the priority of the debts under this Act.

(2) In subsection (1)(b), 'derivative' has the same meaning as in Article 2(5) of Regulation (EU) No 648/2012.

(3) For the purposes of subsection (1)(b) an instrument does not contain an embedded derivative merely because—

(a) it provides for a variable interest rate derived from a broadly used reference rate, or

(b) it is not denominated in the domestic currency of the person issuing the debt (provided that the principal, repayment and interest are denominated in the same currency).

(4) In this Act, 'tertiary non-preferential debts' means all subordinated debts, including (but not limited to) debts under Common Equity Tier 1 instruments, Additional Tier 1 instruments and Tier 2 instruments (all within the meaning of Part 1 of the Banking Act 2009).

(5) In this section, 'relevant financial institution' means any of the following—

(a) a credit institution,

(b) an investment firm,

(c) a financial holding company,

(d) a mixed financial holding company,

[(da) an investment holding company,]

[(e) a financial institution which is—

(i) a subsidiary of an entity referred to in paragraphs (a) to (da), and

(ii) covered by the supervision of that entity on a consolidated basis by the Financial Conduct Authority in accordance with Part 9C rules or by the Prudential Regulation Authority in accordance with Regulation (EU) No 575/2013 of the European Parliament and of the Council of 26 June 2013 on prudential requirements for credit institutions and investment firms or CRR rules, or,]

(f) a mixed-activity holding company.

(6) The definitions in Article 4 of Regulation (EU) No 575/2013 apply for the purposes of subsection (5) [except for the definitions of 'consolidated basis' and 'consolidated situation'].

[(7) For the purposes of subsection (5)—

'on a consolidated basis' means on the basis of the consolidated situation;

'consolidated situation' means the situation that results from an entity being treated, for the purposes of Part 9C rules, Regulation (EU) 575/2013 or CRR rules (as appropriate), as if that entity and one or more other entities formed a single entity;

'CRR rules' has the meaning given in section 144A of the Financial Services and Markets Act 2000;

'Part 9C rules' has the meaning given in section 143F of the Financial Services and Markets Act 2000.]]

130 Accounting periods

(1) The trustee in the sequestration must make up accounts of the trustee's intromissions with the debtor's estate in respect of each accounting period.

(2) In this Act, 'accounting period' is to be construed as follows—

(a) the first accounting period is the period of 12 months, or such shorter period as may be determined or agreed in accordance with subsection (5), either period beginning with the date on which sequestration is awarded, and

(b) any subsequent accounting period is the period of 12 months beginning when its immediately preceding accounting period ends.

(3) But—

(a) paragraph (a) of subsection (2) is subject to subsection (4), and

(b) paragraph (b) of subsection (2) is subject to the exception that—

(i) in a case where AiB is not the trustee, the trustee and the commissioners (or, if there are no commissioners, the trustee and AiB) agree, or

(ii) in a case where AiB is the trustee, the trustee determines,

an accounting period is to be some other period beginning when its immediately preceding accounting period ends, it is that other period.

(4) Where the trustee was appointed under section 54(1) as interim trustee in the sequestration, the first accounting period is—

(a) the period—

(i) beginning with the date of the appointment as interim trustee, and

(ii) ending on the date 12 months after that on which sequestration is awarded, or

(b) such shorter period as may be determined or agreed in accordance with subsection (5).

(5) This subsection applies where the trustee considers that the funds of the debtor's estate are sufficient to pay a dividend in accordance with section 131(1) in respect of—

(a) in a case where the trustee is AiB, a shorter period of not less than 6 months determined by AiB, and

(b) in any other case, a shorter period of not less than 6 months agreed—

(i) between the trustee and the commissioners, or

(ii) if there are no commissioners, between the trustee and AiB.

(6) An agreement under sub-paragraph (i), or determination under subparagraph (ii), of subsection (3)(b)—

(a) may be made in respect of one accounting period or more,

(b) may be made before the beginning of the accounting period in relation to which it has effect and, in any event, is not to have effect unless made before the day on which that accounting period would, but for the agreement or determination, have ended, and

(c) may provide for different accounting periods to be of different duration.

131 Distribution in accordance with accounting periods

(1) The trustee in the sequestration must pay, under section 135(1), a dividend out of the estate in respect of each accounting period—

(a) if the funds of the debtor's estate are sufficient, and

(b) after making allowance for future contingencies.

(2) But subsection (1) is subject to the following subsections.

(3) The trustee may pay—

(a) the debts mentioned in paragraphs (a) to (d) of section 129(1), other than the trustee's own remuneration, at any time,

(b) the preferred debts at any time but only with the consent of the commissioners or, if there are no commissioners, of AiB.

(4) If, in respect of an accounting period, the trustee—

(a) is not ready to pay a dividend, or

(b) considers it would be inappropriate to pay a dividend because the expense of doing so would be disproportionate to the amount of the dividend,

the trustee may, with the consent of the commissioners or, if there are no commissioners, of AiB, postpone the payment to a date not later than the time for payment of a dividend in respect of the next accounting period.

(5) Where a review or appeal is made under section 127 as respects the acceptance or rejection of a creditor's claim, the trustee must, at the time of payment of dividends and until the review or appeal is determined, set aside an amount which would be sufficient, if the determination in the review or appeal were to provide for the creditor's claim being accepted in full, to pay a dividend in respect of that claim.

(6) Subsection (7) applies where a creditor—

(a) has failed to produce evidence in support of the creditor's claim earlier than 8 weeks before the end of an accounting period on being required to do so under section 123(1), and

(b) has given a reason for such failure which is acceptable to the trustee.

(7) The trustee must set aside, for such time as is reasonable to enable the creditor to produce that evidence or any other evidence that will enable the trustee to be satisfied under that section, an amount which would be sufficient, were the claim accepted in full, to pay a dividend in respect of that claim.

(8) Where a creditor submits a claim to the trustee later than 8 weeks before the end of an accounting period but more than 8 weeks before the end of a subsequent accounting period in respect of which, after making allowance for future contingencies, funds are available for the payment of a dividend, the trustee must, if the trustee accepts the claim in whole or in part, pay to the creditor—

(a) the same dividend as has, or dividends as have, already been paid to creditors of the same class in respect of any accounting period or periods, and

(b) whatever dividend may be payable to the creditor in respect of the subsequent accounting period mentioned above.

(9) Paragraph (a) of subsection (8) is without prejudice to any dividend which has already been paid.

(10) In the declaration of, and payment of, a dividend, a payment must not be made more than once by virtue of the same debt.

(11) Any dividend paid in respect of a claim must be paid to the creditor.

Procedure after end of accounting period

132 Submission of accounts and scheme of division

(1) Within 2 weeks after the end of an accounting period the trustee in the sequestration must, in respect of that period, submit to the commissioners (or, if there are no commissioners, to AiB))—

(a) the trustee's accounts of the trustee's intromissions with the estate of the debtor for audit and, where funds are available after making allowance for future contingencies, a scheme of division of the divisible funds, and

(b) a claim for the outlays reasonably incurred by the trustee and for the trustee's remuneration.

(2) Where documents mentioned in subsection (1) are submitted to the commissioners, the trustee must send a copy of them to AiB.

(3) All accounts in respect of legal services incurred by the trustee are, before they are paid by the trustee, to be submitted for taxation to the auditor of the court before which the sequestration is pending.

(4) But subsection (3) is subject to subsection (5).

(5) The trustee may pay the account without submitting it for taxation where—

(a) any such account has been agreed between the trustee and the person entitled to payment in respect of that account,

(b) the trustee is not an associate of that person, and

(c) the commissioners have (or, if there are no commissioners, AiB has) determined that the account need not be submitted for taxation.

(6) This section and sections 133 to 135 do not apply where AiB is the trustee in the sequestration.

133 Audit of accounts and determination as to outlays and remuneration payable to trustee

(1) Within 6 weeks after the end of an accounting period—

(a) the commissioners (or, as the case may be, AiB)—

(i) may audit the accounts, and

(ii) must issue a determination fixing the amount of the outlays and the remuneration payable to the trustee in the sequestration, and

(b) the trustee must make the audited accounts, scheme of division and that determination available for inspection by the debtor and the creditors.

(2) The basis for fixing the amount of the remuneration payable to the trustee may be a commission calculated by reference to the value of the debtor's estate which has been realised by the trustee.

(3) But there is in any event to be taken into account—

(a) the work which, having regard to that value, was reasonably undertaken by the trustee, and

(b) the extent of the trustee's responsibilities in administering the debtor's estate.

(4) In fixing the amount of such remuneration in respect of any accounting period, the commissioners (or, as the case may be, AiB) may take into account any adjustment which the commissioners or AiB may wish to make in the amount of remuneration fixed in respect of any earlier accounting period.

134 Appeal against determination as to outlays and remuneration payable to trustee

(1) Not later than 8 weeks after the end of an accounting period the trustee in the sequestration, the debtor or any creditor may appeal against a determination issued under section 133(1)(a)(ii)—

(a) to AiB where it is a determination of the commissioners, and

(b) to the sheriff where it is a determination of AiB.

(2) But subsection (1) is subject to subsection (4).

[(3) The trustee, the debtor or any creditor may, within 14 days beginning with the date of any decision of AiB in an appeal under subsection (1)(a), appeal to the sheriff against that decision.]

(4) The debtor may appeal under subsection (1) [or (3)] if, and only if, the debtor satisfies AiB, or as the case may be the sheriff, that the debtor has, or is likely to have, a pecuniary interest in the outcome of the appeal.

(5) Before the debtor or a creditor appeals under subsection (1) or (3), the debtor or, as the case may be, the creditor must give notice to the trustee of the intention to appeal.

[(6) The decision of the sheriff on an appeal under subsection (1)(b) or (3) is final.]

135 Further provision as to procedure after end of accounting period

(1) The trustee in the sequestration must pay to the creditors their dividends in accordance with the scheme of division on—

(a) the expiry of the 8 weeks mentioned in section 134(1), or

(b) if there is an appeal under that subsection, on the final determination of the last such appeal.

(2) There must be deposited by the trustee, in an appropriate bank or institution, any dividend—

(a) allocated to a creditor but not cashed or uplifted, or

(b) dependent on a claim in respect of which an amount has been set aside under subsection (5) or (7) of section 131.

(3) If a creditor's claim is revalued, the trustee may—

(a) in paying any dividend to that creditor, make such adjustment to it as the trustee considers necessary to take account of that revaluation, or

(b) require the creditor to repay to the trustee the whole or part of a dividend already paid to the creditor.

136 Procedure after end of accounting period where Accountant in Bankruptcy is trustee

(1) In any case where AiB is the trustee in the sequestration, AiB must at the end of each accounting period—

(a) prepare accounts of AiB's intromissions with the estate of the debtor, and

(b) make a determination of AiB's fees and outlays calculated in accordance with regulations under section 205.

(2) Such accounts and determination must be available for inspection by the debtor and the creditors by not later than 6 weeks after the end of the accounting period to which they relate.

(3) In making a determination as mentioned in subsection (1), AiB may take into account any adjustment which AiB may wish to make in the amount of AiB's remuneration fixed in respect of any earlier accounting period.

(4) Not later than 8 weeks after the end of an accounting period the debtor or any creditor may appeal to the sheriff against AiB's determination.

(5) But subsection (4) is subject to subsection (7).

(6) The decision of the sheriff on an appeal under subsection (4) is final.

(7) The debtor may appeal under subsection (4) if, and only if, the debtor satisfies the sheriff that the debtor has, or is likely to have, a pecuniary interest in the outcome of the appeal.

(8) Before the debtor or a creditor appeals under subsection (4), the debtor or as the case may be the creditor must give notice to AiB of the intention to appeal.

(9) On the expiry of the 8 weeks mentioned in subsection (4), AiB must pay to the creditors their dividends in accordance with the scheme of division.

(10) There must be deposited by AiB, in an appropriate bank or institution, any dividend—

(a) allocated to a creditor but not cashed or uplifted, or

(b) dependent on a claim in respect of which an amount has been set aside under subsection (5) or (7) of section 131.

(11) If a creditor's claim is revalued, AiB may—

(a) in paying any dividend to that creditor, make such adjustment to it as AiB considers necessary to take account of that revaluation, or

(b) require the creditor to repay to AiB the whole or part of a dividend already paid to the creditor.

PART 11
DISCHARGE

Discharge of debtor

137 Discharge of debtor where Accountant in Bankruptcy not trustee

(1) This section applies where AiB is not the trustee.

(2) AiB may, by granting a certificate of discharge in the prescribed form, discharge the debtor at any time after the date which is 12 months after the date on which sequestration is awarded.

(3) Before deciding whether to discharge the debtor under subsection (2), AiB must—

(a) consider the report provided by the trustee under subsection (4), and

(b) take into account any representations received during the 28 days mentioned in subsection (6)(b).

(4) The trustee must prepare and send a report to AiB—

(a) without delay after the date which is 10 months after the date on which sequestration is awarded, and

(b) if the debtor is not otherwise discharged, before sending to AiB the documentation referred to in section 148(1)(b)(i).

(5) The report must include—

(a) information about—

(i) the debtor's assets, liabilities, financial affairs and business affairs,

(ii) the debtor's conduct in relation to those assets, liabilities and affairs,

(iii) the sequestration, and

(iv) the debtor's conduct in the course of the sequestration,

(b) a statement of whether, in the opinion of the trustee, the debtor has as at the date of the report—

(i) complied with any debtor contribution order,

(ii) co-operated with the trustee in accordance with section 215,

(iii) complied with the statement of undertakings,

(iv) made a full and fair surrender of the debtor's estate,

(v) made a full disclosure of all claims which the debtor is entitled to make against any other persons, and

(vi) delivered to the trustee every document under the debtor's control relating to the debtor's estate, financial affairs or business affairs, and

(c) a statement of whether the trustee has, as at the date that the report is sent to AiB, carried out all of the trustee's functions in accordance with section 50.

(6) The trustee must, at the same time as sending a report to AiB under this section, give to the debtor and to every creditor known to the trustee—

(a) a copy of the report, and

(b) a notice informing the recipient that the recipient has a right to make representations to AiB in relation to the report within 28 days beginning with the day on which the notice is given.

(7) A discharge under this section is not to take effect before the expiry of 14 days beginning with the day of notification of the decision.

138 Discharge of debtor where Accountant in Bankruptcy trustee

(1) This section applies where AiB is the trustee.

(2) AiB may, by granting a certificate of discharge in the prescribed form, discharge the debtor at any time after the date which is 12 months after the date on which sequestration is awarded.

(3) AiB must, as soon as practicable after the date which is 12 months after the date on which sequestration is awarded—

(a) decide whether to discharge the debtor under subsection (2),

(b) notify the debtor and every creditor known to AiB of that decision, and

(c) send a report to those persons.

(4) The report must give an account of—

(a) the debtor's assets, liabilities, financial affairs and business affairs,

(b) the debtor's conduct in relation to those assets, liabilities and affairs,

(c) the sequestration, and

(d) the debtor's conduct in the course of the sequestration, including compliance with the statement of undertakings.

(5) Subsection (6) applies where—

(a) AiB refuses to discharge the debtor under subsection (2), and

(b) the debtor is not otherwise discharged.

(6) AiB must, as soon as practicable after the date which is 12 months after the date of the refusal—

(a) decide whether to discharge or refuse to discharge the debtor under subsection (2),

(b) notify the debtor and every creditor known to AiB of that decision, and

(c) send a report giving an account of the matters mentioned in subsection (4) to those persons.

(7) Discharge under this section is not to take effect before the expiry of 14 days beginning with the day of notification of the decision to discharge.

139 Discharge of debtor: review and appeal

(1) The trustee or the debtor may apply to AiB for a review of a decision to refuse to discharge the debtor under section 137(2) or 138(2).

(2) Any creditor may apply to AiB for a review of a decision to discharge the debtor under section 137(2) or 138(2).

(3) Any application under subsection (1) or (2) must be made within 14 days beginning with the day of the notification of the decision in question.

(4) If an application is made under subsection (2), the discharge is suspended until the determination of the review by AiB.

(5) If an application is made under subsection (1) or (2), AiB must—

(a) take into account any representations made by an interested person within 21 days beginning with the day on which the application is made, and

(b) confirm or revoke the decision within 28 days beginning with that day.

(6) The debtor, the trustee or any creditor may appeal to the sheriff, against any decision of AiB under subsection (5)(b), within 14 days beginning with the day of the decision.

140 Discharge of debtor to whom section 2(2) applies

(1) Where section 2(2) applies to a debtor, the debtor is discharged on the date which is 6 months after the date on which sequestration is awarded.

(2) A debtor may, following discharge, apply to AiB for a certificate of discharge in the prescribed form.

141 Deferral of discharge where debtor cannot be traced

(1) Subsection (2) applies where the trustee—

(a) having made reasonable inquiries, is unable to ascertain the whereabouts of the debtor, and

(b) as a result is unable to carry out the trustee's functions in accordance with section 50.

(2) The trustee must—

(a) notify the debtor by sending to the last known address of the debtor a deferral notice in the prescribed form,

(b) give a deferral notice to every creditor known to the trustee, and

(c) where the trustee is not AiB, apply in the prescribed form to AiB for a deferral.

(3) Any deferral application under subsection (2)(c) must be made by the trustee—

(a) no earlier than the date which is 8 months after the date on which sequestration is awarded, and

(b) no later than the date which is 10 months after the date on which sequestration is awarded.

(4) After receiving a deferral application, AiB must—

(a) take into account any representations made by an interested person within 14 days beginning with the day on which the application is made, and

(b) if satisfied of the matters mentioned in subsection (5), issue a certificate deferring discharge indefinitely.

(5) The matters are—

(a) that the trustee is unable to ascertain the whereabouts of the debtor, and

(b) it would not be reasonably practicable for the trustee to continue to search for the debtor.

(6) Where AiB is the trustee and has given a deferral notice in accordance with subsection (2)(b), AiB must—

(a) take into account any representations made by an interested person within 14 days beginning with the day on which the deferral notice is given, and

(b) if satisfied that it would not be reasonably practicable to continue to search for the debtor, issue a certificate deferring discharge indefinitely.

(7) Where a certificate is issued under subsection (4)(b) or (6)(b), AiB must make an appropriate entry in the register of insolvencies.

142 Debtor not traced: new trustee

(1) This section applies where a certificate is issued under section 141(4)(b).

(2) The trustee may apply to AiB, in the prescribed form, for authority to resign office.

(3) An application under subsection (2) must include details of every creditor known to the trustee.

(4) An application under subsection (2) may not be made—

(a) if, after the certificate is issued, the trustee ascertains the whereabouts of the debtor or the debtor makes contact with the trustee, or

(b) after the date which is 6 months after that on which the certificate is issued.

(5) Where an application is made under subsection (2), AiB must issue to the trustee who made the application a notice in the prescribed form granting the application.

(6) Where a notice is issued under subsection (5)—

(a) AiB is deemed to be the trustee,

(b) AiB must notify every creditor known to AiB that AiB is deemed to be the trustee,

(c) the former trustee is not entitled to recover, other than by a claim in the final distribution of the debtor's estate, outlays and remuneration payable under sections 132 and 133 [(there being no effect on any outlays and remuneration paid to the former trustee before the issue of the notice)], and

(d) subsections (9) to (13) of section 69 apply in relation to the appointment of AiB as the new trustee as they apply in relation to the appointment of a new trustee under that section.

143 Debtor not traced: subsequent debtor contact

(1) This section applies where—

(a) a certificate is issued under section 141(4)(b) or (6)(b), and

(b) the trustee ascertains the whereabouts of the debtor or the debtor makes contact with the trustee.

(2) Where AiB is the trustee, AiB may discharge the debtor at any time after the date which is 12 months after that on which—

(a) the whereabouts of the debtor were ascertained, or

(b) the debtor made contact with the trustee.

(3) Where AiB is not the trustee, the trustee must prepare and send a report to AiB without delay after the date which is 10 months after the earlier of—

(a) the date on which the whereabouts of the debtor were ascertained by the trustee, and

(b) the date on which the debtor made contact with the trustee.

(4) If the trustee sends a report to AiB under subsection (3)—

(a) the report must include the matters which, in a report sent to AiB, are included in accordance with subsection (5) of section 137, and

(b) subsection (6) of that section applies to a report sent under this section as it applies to a report sent in accordance with subsection (4) of that section.

(5) After receiving a report under subsection (3), AiB may discharge the debtor by granting a certificate of discharge in the prescribed form.

(6) Before deciding whether to discharge the debtor under subsection (5), AiB must—

(a) consider the report prepared under subsection (3), and

(b) take into account any representations received during the 28 days mentioned in subsection (6)(b) of section 137 (as applied in accordance with subsection (4)).

(7) Discharge under subsection (2) or (5) is not to take effect before the expiry of 14 days beginning with the day of notification of the decision to discharge.

(8) Discharge under subsection (2) or (5) is deemed for the purposes of section 145 to have been given under section 137(2).

144 Subsequent debtor contact: review and appeal

(1) The debtor may apply to AiB for a review of a decision under section 143(2) or (5) to refuse to discharge the debtor.

(2) Any creditor may apply to AiB for a review of a decision under section 143(2) or (5) to discharge the debtor.

(3) Any application under subsection (1) or (2) must be made within 14 days beginning with the day of notification of the decision in question.

(4) If an application for a review under subsection (2) is made, the discharge is suspended until the determination of that review by AiB.

(5) If an application for a review under subsection (1) or (2) is made, AiB must—

(a) take into account any representations made by an interested person within 21 days beginning with the day on which the application is made, and

(b) confirm or revoke the decision within 28 days beginning with the day on which the application is made.

(6) The debtor, the trustee or any creditor may appeal to the sheriff against any decision of AiB under subsection (5)(b) within 14 days beginning with the day of the decision.

145 Effect of discharge under section 137, 138 or 140

(1) On the discharge of the debtor under section 137, 138 or 140 the debtor is discharged of all debts and obligations contracted by the debtor, or for which the debtor was liable, at the date of sequestration.

(2) Subsection (1) is subject to subsections (3) and (5).

(3) The debtor is not discharged by virtue of subsection (1) from—

(a) any liability to pay a fine or other penalty due to the Crown,

(b) any liability to pay a fine imposed in a justice of the peace court (or a district court),

(c) any liability under a compensation order (within the meaning of section 249 of the Criminal Procedure (Scotland) Act 1995,

(d) any liability to forfeiture of a sum of money deposited in court under section 24(6) of the Criminal Procedure (Scotland) Act 1995,

(e) any liability incurred by reason of fraud or breach of trust,

(f) any obligation to pay—

(i) aliment, or any sum of an alimentary nature, under any enactment or rule of law, or

(ii) any periodical allowance payable on divorce by virtue of a court order or under an obligation, or

(g) the obligation imposed on the debtor by section 215.

(4) The obligations mentioned in paragraph (f) of subsection (3) do not include—

(a) aliment, or a periodical allowance, which could be included in the amount of a creditor's claim under paragraph 2 of schedule 2, or

(b) child support maintenance within the meaning of the Child Support Act 1991 which was unpaid in respect of any period before the date of sequestration of—

(i) any person by whom it was due to be paid, or

(ii) any employer by whom it was, or was due to be, deducted under section 31(5) of that Act.

(5) The discharge of the debtor under section 137, 138 or 140 does not affect any right of a secured creditor for an obligation in respect of which the debtor has been discharged, to enforce the security in respect of that obligation.

(6) In subsection (3)(a), the reference to a fine or other penalty due to the Crown includes a reference to a confiscation order made under Part 2, 3 or 4 of the Proceeds of Crime Act 2002.

(7) Nothing in this section affects regulations in relation to which section 73B of the Education (Scotland) Act 1980 (regulations relating to student loans) applies.

146 Discharge under section 140: conditions

(1) This section applies where a debtor is discharged under section 140.

(2) During the relevant period the debtor must comply with the condition in subsection (3) before the debtor, either alone or jointly with another person, obtains credit—

(a) to the extent of £2,000 (or such other sum as may be prescribed) or more, or

(b) of any amount where, at the time of obtaining credit, the debtor has debts amounting to £1,000 (or such other sum as may be prescribed) or more.

(3) The condition is that the debtor must inform the person who is providing credit to the debtor (or, as the case may be, jointly to the debtor and another person) that the debtor is required to comply with the conditions in this section.

(4) During the relevant period, the debtor must not engage (whether directly or indirectly) in a business under a name other than that to which the discharge relates unless the debtor complies with the condition in subsection (5).

(5) The condition is that the debtor must inform any person with whom the debtor enters into any business transaction of the name of the business to which the discharge relates.

(6) In this section, 'relevant period' means the 6 months beginning with the date of discharge.

147 Section 146: sanctions

(1) If a debtor fails to comply with the requirement imposed by subsection (2) or (4) of section 146, that section applies in relation to the debtor as if the relevant period were the 12 months beginning with the date of discharge.

(2) If a debtor fails to comply with the requirement imposed by subsection (2) or (4) of section 146 during the period when the section applies in relation to the debtor by virtue of subsection (1), the debtor commits an offence.

(3) A debtor who commits an offence under subsection (2) is liable on summary conviction—

(a) to a fine not exceeding the statutory maximum,

(b) to imprisonment for—

(i) a term not exceeding 3 months, or

(ii) if the person has previously been convicted of an offence inferring dishonest appropriation of property (or an attempt at such appropriation), a term not exceeding 6 months, or

(c) both to such fine and to such imprisonment.

(4) A debtor who commits an offence under subsection (2) is liable on conviction on indictment—

(a) to a fine,

(b) to imprisonment for a term not exceeding 2 years, or

(c) both to such fine and to such imprisonment.

[Failure of debtor to co-operate with trustee

147A Debtor fails to co-operate: Accountant in Bankruptcy appointment as new trustee

(1) This section applies where—

(a) AiB is not the trustee in the sequestration,

(b) the period of 5 years beginning with the date of sequestration of a debtor's estate has expired, and

(c) the debtor has not been discharged from that sequestration.

(2) The trustee in the sequestration may apply to AiB for authority to resign office on account of the debtor's failure to co-operate.

(3) An application under subsection (2) must be made in the prescribed form and include information about—

(a) the nature and the extent of the debtor's failure to co-operate with the trustee,

(b) the actions taken by the trustee to secure the debtor's co-operation,

(c) any other matters that the trustee considers relevant, and

(d) details of every creditor known to the trustee.

(4) Before making an application under subsection (2), the trustee must—

(a) notify the debtor by sending an intention to resign notice, and

(b) give an intention to resign notice to every creditor known to the trustee.

(5) An intention to resign notice must—

(a) be in the prescribed form, and

(b) include a statement informing the recipient that the recipient has a right to make representations to AiB in relation to the application within 14 days beginning with the day on which the application is made.

(6) After receiving an application under subsection (2), AiB must—

(a) take into account any representations made by an interested person within 14 days beginning with the day on which the application is made, and

(b) if satisfied of the matters mentioned in subsection (7), issue to the trustee who made the application a notice in the prescribed form granting the application.

(7) The matters are—

(a) that the debtor has failed to co-operate with the trustee to such an extent that the trustee is prevented from carrying out the trustee's functions under this Act,

(b) that the failure is likely to continue, and

(c) that the trustee has taken all reasonable steps to secure the debtor's co-operation.

(8) AiB—

(a) may request such further information from the trustee as AiB considers necessary to make a decision under subsection (6), and

(b) must notify the trustee, the debtor and every creditor known to AiB of its decision under subsection (6).

(9) Where a notice is issued under subsection (6)(b), 14 days after the notice is given—

(a) AiB is deemed to be the trustee,

(b) AiB must notify the debtor and every creditor known to AiB that AiB is deemed to be the trustee,

(c) AiB must make an appropriate entry in the register of insolvencies,

(d) the former trustee is not entitled to recover, other than by a claim in the final distribution of the debtor's estate, outlays and remuneration payable under sections 132 and 133 (there being no effect on any outlays and remuneration paid to the former trustee before the issue of the notice),

(e) subsections (9) to (13) of section 69 apply in relation to the appointment of AiB as the new trustee as they apply in relation to the appointment of a new trustee under that section,

(f) section 116 applies as if there were substituted for subsection (2)—

'(2) AiB may at any time before the discharge of the debtor require the debtor to give an account in writing, in such form as may be prescribed, of the debtor's current state of affairs.', and

(g) section 138 applies to the sequestration with the modifications in subsection (10).

(10) The modifications are—

(a) in subsection (2), the words 'after the date which is 12 months after the date on which sequestration is awarded' are omitted,

(b) in subsection (3), for 'must, as soon as practicable after the date which is 12 months after the date on which sequestration is awarded' substitute 'may, if the debtor co-operates with AiB to such an extent that AiB is able to carry out the trustee's functions under this Act',

(c) in subsection (6), for 'must, as soon as practicable after the date which is 12 months after the date of the refusal' substitute 'may, at any time after a refusal, if the debtor co-operates with AiB to such an extent that AiB is able to carry out the trustee's functions under this Act'.

147B Accountant in Bankruptcy appointment as new trustee: review and appeal

(1) The trustee may apply to AiB for a review of a decision under section 147A(6) to refuse an application.

(2) The debtor or any creditor may apply to AiB for a review of a decision under section 147A(6) to grant an application.

(3) Any application under subsection (1) or (2) must be made within 14 days beginning with the day of notification of the decision in question.

(4) If an application for review under subsection (2) is made, the grant of the application is suspended until the determination of that review by AiB.

(5) If an application for a review under subsection (1) or (2) is made, AiB must—

(a) take into account any representations made by an interested person within 21 days beginning with the day on which the application is made, and

(b) confirm or revoke the decision within 28 days beginning with the day on which the application is made.

(6) If, under subsection (5)(b), AiB—

(a) revoke a decision to grant an application, AiB must revoke the notice given under section 147A(6)(b) granting the application,

(b) revoke a decision to refuse an application, AiB must issue a notice under section 147A(6)(b) granting the application, or

(c) confirm a decision to grant an application, section 147A(9) applies as if for the words '14 days after the notice is given' there were substituted '14 days after the AiB decision under section 147B(5)(b)'.

(7) The debtor, the trustee or any creditor may appeal to the sheriff against any decision of AiB under subsection (5)(b) within 14 days beginning with the day of the decision.

(8) If an appeal relating to a decision mentioned in subsection (6)(b) or (c) is made, the grant of the application is suspended until the determination of that appeal.

(9) If, on an appeal under subsection (7), the sheriff determines that an application which has been refused should be granted—

(a) the sheriff must order AiB to issue a notice under section 147A(6)(b) granting the application, and

(b) section 147A(9) applies as if the words '14 days after the notice is given' were omitted.

(10) If, on an appeal under subsection (7), the sheriff determines that an application which has been granted should be refused, the sheriff must order AiB to revoke the notice given under section 147A(6)(b) granting the application.

(11) The sheriff clerk must send AiB a copy of the sheriff's decree.

(12) The decision of the sheriff on an appeal under subsection (7) is final.

147C Debtor fails to co-operate with AiB as trustee

(1) This section applies where—

(a) AiB is the trustee but was not appointed as trustee under section 147A,

(b) the period of 5 years beginning with the date of sequestration a debtor's estate has expired, and

(c) the debtor has not been discharged from that sequestration.

(2) AiB, if satisfied of the matters mentioned in subsection (3), may make a determination that the debtor has failed to co-operate.

(3) The matters are—

(a) that the debtor has failed to co-operate with AiB as trustee to such an extent that AiB is prevented from carrying out the AiB's functions as trustee under this Act,

(b) that the failure is likely to continue, and

(c) that AiB has taken all reasonable steps to secure the debtor's co-operation.

(4) If AiB makes a determination under subsection (2)—

(a) AiB must notify the debtor and every creditor known to AiB that AiB has made a determination under subsection (2), and

(b) section 116 applies as if there were substituted for subsection (2)—

'(2) AiB may at any time before the discharge of the debtor require the debtor to give an account in writing, in such form as may be prescribed, of the debtor's current state of affairs.', and

(c) section 138(6) applies as if for the words 'must, as soon as practicable after the date which is 12 months after the date of the refusal' there were substituted 'may, at any time after a refusal, if the debtor co-operates with AiB to such an extent that AiB is able to carry out the trustee's functions under this Act.'.]

Discharge of trustee

148 Discharge of trustee

(1) After the trustee in the sequestration has made a final division of the debtor's estate and has inserted the trustee's final audited accounts in the sederunt book, the trustee—

(a) must pay to AiB any unclaimed dividends and unapplied balances,

(b) on that being done—

(i) must send to AiB the sederunt book (in the format specified by subsection (2)) and a copy of the audited accounts, and

(ii) may at the same time apply to AiB for a certificate of discharge.

(2) The trustee must send an electronic version of the sederunt book in such format as AiB may from time to time direct.

(3) AiB must deposit any unclaimed dividends and any unapplied balances paid to AiB under subsection (1)(a) in an appropriate bank or institution.

(4) The trustee must send, to the debtor and to all the creditors known to the trustee, notice of any application under subsection (1)(b)(ii) and must inform the debtor and such creditors—

(a) that written representations relating to the application may be made by them to AiB within 14 days after the notification,

(b) that the sederunt book is available for inspection following a request made to AiB and contains the audited accounts of, and scheme of division in, the sequestration, and

(c) of the effect mentioned in subsection (7).

(5) On the expiry of the 14 days mentioned in subsection (4)(a), AiB, after examining the documents sent to AiB and considering any representations duly made to AiB, must—

(a) grant or refuse to grant the certificate of discharge, and

(b) notify accordingly—

(i) the trustee,

(ii) the debtor, and

(iii) all creditors who made such representations.

(6) Any certificate of discharge granted under subsection (5)—

(a) must take effect after the expiry of the 14 days mentioned in section 149(2), and

(b) has no effect if an application for review is made under section 149(1).

(7) The grant of a certificate of discharge under this section has the effect of discharging the trustee from all liability (other than any liability arising from fraud)—

(a) to the debtor, or

(b) to the creditors,

in respect of any act or omission of the trustee in exercising the functions conferred on the trustee by this Act (including, where the trustee was also the interim trustee, the functions of interim trustee).

(8) This section and section 149 do not apply in any case where AiB is trustee.

149 Further provision as regards discharge of trustee

(1) The trustee, the debtor or any creditor who has made representations under subsection (4)(a) of section 148 may apply to AiB for a review of a determination under subsection (5) of that section.

(2) Any application under subsection (1) must be made within 14 days beginning with the day of the determination.

(3) If an application for a review under subsection (1) is made, AiB must—

(a) take into account any representations made, within 21 days beginning with the day on which the application is made, by an interested person, and

(b) confirm, amend or revoke the determination (whether or not issuing a new certificate of discharge) within 28 days beginning with that day.

(4) Within 14 days after a decision under subsection (3)(b)—

(a) the trustee,

(b) the debtor, or

(c) any creditor who made representations under section 148(4)(a),

may appeal against the decision to the sheriff.

(5) If, on an appeal under subsection (4), the sheriff determines that a certificate of discharge which has been refused should be granted the sheriff must order AiB to grant it.

(6) The sheriff clerk must send AiB a copy of the sheriff's decree.

(7) The decision of the sheriff on an appeal under subsection (4) is final.

(8) Where a certificate of discharge is granted under section 148 or by virtue of this section, AiB must make an appropriate entry in—

(a) the register of insolvencies, and

(b) in the sederunt book.

(9) The provisions of this section apply (subject to any necessary modifications)—

(a) where a trustee has died, to the trustee's executor, or

(b) where a trustee has resigned office or been removed from office, to that trustee, as they apply to a trustee who has made a final division of the debtor's estate in accordance with the preceding provisions of this Act.

150 Unclaimed dividends

(1) Any person producing evidence of that person's right may apply to AiB to receive a dividend deposited under section 148(3) or 151(2), if the application is made not later than 7 years after the date of deposit.

(2) If AiB is satisfied of that person's right to the dividend, AiB must authorise the bank or institution in which the deposit was made to pay to the person the amount of the dividend and of any interest which has accrued on the dividend.

(3) AiB is, at the expiry of 7 years from the date of deposit of any unclaimed dividend or unapplied balance under section 148(3) or 151(2), to hand over the deposit receipt or other voucher relating to the dividend or balance to the Scottish Ministers who on that being done are entitled to payment of the amount due (principal and interest) from the bank or institution in which the deposit was made.

151 Discharge of Accountant in Bankruptcy

(1) This section applies where AiB has acted as the trustee in the sequestration.

(2) AiB must deposit any unclaimed dividends and any unapplied balances in an appropriate bank or institution.

(3) AiB must send to the debtor and to all creditors known to AiB—

(a) a determination of AiB's fees and outlays calculated in accordance with regulations under section 205,

(b) a notice in writing stating—

(i) that AiB has commenced the procedure under this Act leading to discharge in respect of AiB's actings as trustee,

(ii) that the sederunt book relating to the sequestration is available for inspection following a request made to AiB,

(iii) that an application for review may be made under subsection (4),

(iv) that an appeal may be made to the sheriff under subsection (7), and

(v) the effect of subsections (9) and (10).

(4) The debtor or any creditor may apply to AiB for review of the discharge of AiB in respect of AiB's actings as trustee.

(5) Any application under subsection (4) must be made within 14 days beginning with the day on which notice is sent under subsection (3)(b).

(6) If an application under subsection (4) is made, AiB must—

(a) take into account any representations made by an interested person within 21 days beginning with the day on which the application is made, and

(b) confirm or revoke the discharge within 28 days beginning with that day.

(7) The debtor or any creditor may, within 14 days beginning with the day on which a decision is made by AiB under subsection (6)(b), appeal to the sheriff against that decision.

(8) The decision of the sheriff on an appeal under subsection (7) is final.

(9) Subsection (10) applies where—

(a) the requirements of this section have been complied with, and

(b) no appeal is made under subsection (7) or such an appeal is made but is refused as regards the discharge of AiB.

(10) AiB is discharged from all liability (other than any liability arising from fraud)—

(a) to the debtor, or

(b) to the creditors,

in respect of any act or omission of AiB in exercising the functions of trustee in the sequestration (including, where the trustee was also the interim trustee, the functions of interim trustee).

PART 12
ASSETS DISCOVERED AFTER DISCHARGE OF TRUSTEE

152 Assets discovered after discharge of trustee: appointment of trustee

(1) This section applies where—

(a) the trustee is discharged—

(i) under section 148,

(ii) by virtue of section 149, or

(iii) under section 151, and

(b) after that discharge but within 5 years beginning with the date on which sequestration is awarded, the trustee or AiB becomes aware of any newly identified estate with a value of not less than £1,000 (or such other sum as may be prescribed).

(2) In this section, 'newly identified estate' means any part of the debtor's estate which—

(a) vested in the trustee in accordance with section 78 or 86, and

(b) was not, before the trustee was discharged, known to the trustee.

(3) AiB may—

(a) in a case where the trustee was discharged under section 148—

(i) on the application of the trustee who was discharged, reappoint that person as trustee on the debtor's estate, or

(ii) appoint AiB as trustee on that estate, or

(b) in a case where AiB was discharged under section 151, reappoint AiB as trustee on that estate.

(4) AiB may make an appointment or reappointment under subsection (3) only if, in the opinion of AiB, the value of the newly identified estate is likely to exceed the costs of—

(a) the appointment or reappointment, and

(b) the recovery, management, realisation and distribution of the newly identified estate.

(5) Where the trustee was discharged under section 148 and applies for reappointment under subsection (3)(a)(i), the discharged trustee must provide to AiB the information mentioned in subsection (8)(a) to (c).

(6) Where the trustee was discharged under section 148 and does not apply for reappointment under subsection (3)(a)(i), the discharged trustee must—

(a) provide AiB with details of any newly identified estate that the discharged trustee becomes aware of, where that estate has a value not less than the value mentioned in subsection (1), and

(b) if requested by AiB, provide AiB with the information mentioned in subsection (8)(b) and (c).

(7) Where AiB was discharged under section 151, AiB must record and consider the information mentioned in subsection (8).

(8) The information is—

(a) the estimated value of the newly identified estate,

(b) the reason why the newly identified estate forms part of the debtor's estate,

(c) the reason why the newly identified estate was not recovered,

(d) the estimated outlays and remuneration of the trustee following an appointment or reappointment under subsection (3), and

(e) the likely distribution under section 129 following such an appointment or reappointment.

(9) This section is without prejudice to any other right to take action following the discharge of the trustee.

153 Assets discovered after discharge of trustee: notice

(1) AiB must notify the debtor and any other person AiB considers to have an interest where—

(a) an application is made under section 152(3)(a)(i), or

(b) AiB proposes to make an appointment or reappointment under section 152(3)(a)(ii) or (b).

(2) A notice under subsection (1) must inform the recipient that the recipient has a right to make representations to AiB, within 14 days beginning with the day on which the notice is given, in relation to the application or the proposed appointment or reappointment.

(3) Before making an appointment or reappointment under section 152, AiB must take into account any representations made by an interested person.

(4) If AiB makes an appointment or reappointment under section 152, AiB must as soon as is practicable notify the debtor of the appointment or reappointment.

(5) Any notice under subsection (4) must include information in relation to the debtor's duty, under section 215, to co-operate with the trustee.

154 Assets discovered after discharge of trustee: appeal

Where AiB makes or refuses to make an appointment or reappointment under section 152, an interested person may, within 14 days after AiB's decision, appeal to the sheriff against that decision.

PART 13
BANKRUPTCY RESTRICTIONS ORDERS AND INTERIM BANKRUPTCY RESTRICTIONS ORDERS

Bankruptcy restrictions orders

155 Bankruptcy restrictions order

(1) Where sequestration of a living debtor's estate is awarded, an order (to be known as a 'bankruptcy restrictions order') in respect of the debtor may be made—

(a) by AiB, or

(b) on the application of AiB, by the sheriff.

(2) If AiB proposes to make a bankruptcy restrictions order, AiB must so notify the debtor.

(3) A notice under subsection (2) must inform the debtor that the debtor has a right to make representations to AiB in relation to the proposed bankruptcy restrictions order.

(4) Before making a bankruptcy restrictions order, AiB must take into account any representations made by the debtor.

156 Grounds for making bankruptcy restrictions order

(1) A bankruptcy restrictions order must be made if AiB, or as the case may be the sheriff, thinks it appropriate having regard to the conduct, whether before or after the date of sequestration, of the debtor.

(2) AiB, or as the case may be the sheriff, is in particular to take into account any of the following kinds of behaviour on the part of the debtor—

(a) failing to keep records which account for a loss of property—

(i) by the debtor, or

(ii) by a business carried on by the debtor,

where the loss occurred in the period beginning 2 years before the date of presentation of the petition for sequestration, or as the case may be the date the debtor application was made, and ending with the date of the application for a bankruptcy restrictions order,

(b) failing to produce records of that kind on demand by—

(i) AiB,

(ii) the interim trustee, or

(iii) the trustee in the sequestration,

(c) failing to supply accurate information to an authorised person for the purpose of the granting under section 9 of a certificate for sequestration of the debtor's estate,

(d) making a gratuitous alienation, or any other alienation, for no consideration or for no adequate consideration, which a creditor has, under any rule of law, right to challenge,

(e) creating an unfair preference, or any other preference, which a creditor has, under any rule of law, right to challenge,

(f) making an excessive pension contribution,

(g) failing to supply goods or services which were wholly or partly paid for, where the failure has given rise to a claim submitted by a creditor under section 46 or 122,

(h) trading at a time before the date of sequestration when the debtor knew, or ought to have known, that the debtor was unable to meet the debtor's debts,

(i) incurring, before the date of sequestration, a debt which the debtor had no reasonable expectation of being able to pay,

(j) failing to account satisfactorily to the sheriff, AiB, the interim trustee or the trustee, for—

(i) a loss of property, or

(ii) an insufficiency of property to meet the debtor's debts,

(k) carrying on any gambling, speculation or extravagance—

(i) which may have contributed materially to, or increased the extent of, the debtor's debts, or

(ii) which took place between the date of presentation of the petition for sequestration, or as the case may be the date the debtor application was made, and the date on which sequestration is awarded,

(l) neglect of business affairs, being neglect of a kind which may have contributed materially to, or increased the extent of, the debtor's debts,

(m) fraud or breach of trust,

(n) failing to co-operate with—

(i) AiB,

(ii) the interim trustee, or

(iii) the trustee in the sequestration.

(3) AiB, or as the case may be the sheriff, must in particular also consider whether the debtor—

(a) has previously been sequestrated, and

(b) remained undischarged from that sequestration at any time during the 5 years ending with the date of the sequestration to which the application relates.

(4) For the purposes of subsection (2)—

'excessive pension contribution' is to be construed in accordance with section 101, and

'gratuitous alienation' means an alienation challengeable under section 98.

157 Bankruptcy restrictions order: application of section 218(13)

(1) Where—

(a) AiB thinks it appropriate, AiB may, or

(b) as the case may be, the sheriff thinks it appropriate, the sheriff may, specify in a bankruptcy restrictions order that section 218(13) is to apply to the debtor, during the period the debtor is subject to the order, as if the debtor were a debtor within the meaning of section 219(2)(a).

(2) But for the purposes of subsection (1), section 219(2) has effect as if, for paragraph (c) of that section, there were substituted—

'(c) the 'relevant information' about the status of the debtor is the information that (as the case may be)—

(i) the debtor is subject to a bankruptcy restrictions order, or

(ii) where the debtor's estate has been sequestrated and the debtor has not been discharged, that fact.'.

158 Timing for making a bankruptcy restrictions order

(1) AiB must make, or apply to the sheriff for, any bankruptcy restrictions order within the period which begins with the date of sequestration and ends with the date on which the debtor's discharge becomes effective.

(2) But subsection (1) is subject to subsection (3).

(3) After the end of the period referred to in subsection (1), AiB may—

(a) make a bankruptcy restrictions order, or

(b) make an application for a bankruptcy restrictions order,

with the permission of the sheriff.

159 Duration of bankruptcy restrictions order and application for revocation or variation

(1) A bankruptcy restrictions order—

(a) comes into force when made, and

(b) ceases to have effect at the end of a day specified, for the purposes of this paragraph, in the order.

(2) The day specified under subsection (1)(b)—

(a) in the case of an order made by AiB—

(i) must not be before the expiry of 2 years beginning with the day on which the order is made, but

(ii) must be within 5 years beginning with that day, and

(b) in the case of an order made by the sheriff—

(i) must not be before the expiry of the 5 years beginning with the day on which the order is made, but

(ii) must be within 15 years beginning with that day.

(3) On an application by the debtor, the person mentioned in subsection (4) may—

(a) revoke a bankruptcy restrictions order, or

(b) vary it.

(4) The person is, in the case of a bankruptcy restrictions order —

(a) made by AiB, AiB, and

(b) made by the sheriff, the sheriff.

(5) If an application under subsection (3) is made to AiB, AiB must—

(a) take into account any representations made, within 21 days beginning with the day on which the application is made, by an interested person, and

(b) confirm, revoke or vary the order within 28 days beginning with that day.

(6) The debtor may appeal to the sheriff against any decision of AiB under subsection (5)(b) within 14 days beginning with the date of the decision.

(7) The sheriff may—

(a) in determining such an appeal, or

(b) otherwise on an application by AiB,

make an order providing that the debtor may not make another application under subsection (3) for such period as may be specified in the order.

(8) Variation under subsection (3)(b) may include providing for such an order to cease to have effect at the end of a day earlier than that specified under subsection (1)(b).

Interim bankruptcy restrictions orders

160 Interim bankruptcy restrictions orders

(1) Subsection (2) applies at any time—

(a) after AiB notifies the debtor under section 155(2) that AiB proposes to make a bankruptcy restrictions order, and

(b) before AiB decides whether to make the order.

(2) AiB may make an interim bankruptcy restrictions order if AiB thinks—

(a) that there are prima facie grounds to suggest that a bankruptcy restrictions order will be made, and

(b) that it is in the public interest to make such an order.

(3) Subsection (4) applies at any time between—

(a) the making of an application to the sheriff for a bankruptcy restrictions order, and

(b) the determination of that application.

(4) The sheriff may, on the application of AiB, make an interim bankruptcy restrictions order if the sheriff thinks—

(a) that there are prima facie grounds to suggest that the application for the bankruptcy restrictions order will be successful, and

(b) that it is in the public interest to make an interim bankruptcy restrictions order.

(5) An interim bankruptcy restrictions order—

(a) has the same effect as a bankruptcy restrictions order, and

(b) comes into force on being made.

(6) An interim bankruptcy restrictions order ceases to have effect—

(a) where it was made by AiB, on AiB deciding whether or not to make a bankruptcy restrictions order,

(b) where it was made by the sheriff, on the determination of the application for the bankruptcy restrictions order, or

(c) if the sheriff discharges it on the application of AiB or of the debtor.

(7) Where a bankruptcy restrictions order is made in respect of a debtor who is subject to an interim bankruptcy restrictions order, subsection (2) of section 159 has effect in relation to the bankruptcy restrictions order as if the reference in that subsection to the day the order is made were a reference to the day the interim bankruptcy restrictions order is made.

Effect of recall of sequestration

161 Bankruptcy restrictions orders and interim bankruptcy restrictions orders: effect of recall of sequestration

(1) Where an award of sequestration of a debtor's estate is recalled under section 30(1)—

(a) the sheriff may revoke any bankruptcy restrictions order or interim bankruptcy restrictions order in force in respect of the debtor, and

(b) no new bankruptcy restrictions order or interim bankruptcy restrictions order may be made in respect of the debtor.

(2) Where the sheriff refuses to revoke, under subsection (1)(a), a bankruptcy restrictions order or interim bankruptcy restrictions order the debtor may, within

28 days after the date on which the award of sequestration is recalled, appeal to the Sheriff Appeal Court against the refusal.

(3) The decision of the Sheriff Appeal Court on an appeal under subsection (2) is final.

(4) Where an award of sequestration of a debtor's estate is recalled under section 34(1) or 35(6)—

(a) AiB may revoke any bankruptcy restrictions order or interim bankruptcy restrictions order in force in respect of the debtor, and

(b) no new bankruptcy restrictions order or interim bankruptcy restrictions order may be made in respect of the debtor.

(5) Where AiB refuses to revoke under subsection (4) a bankruptcy restrictions order or interim bankruptcy restrictions order, the debtor may apply to AiB for a review of the refusal.

(6) Any application under subsection (5) must be made within 14 days beginning with the day on which the award of sequestration is recalled.

(7) If an application under subsection (5) is made, AiB must—

(a) take into account any representations made by an interested person within 21 days beginning with the day on which the application is made, and

(b) confirm the refusal or revoke the order within 28 days beginning with that day.

(8) The debtor may appeal to the sheriff against any decision of AiB under subsection (7)(b) within 14 days beginning with the day of the decision.

(9) The decision of the sheriff on an appeal under subsection (8) is final.

PART 14
VOLUNTARY TRUST DEEDS FOR CREDITORS

General

162 Voluntary trust deeds for creditors

Sections 163 to 193 and schedule 4 have effect in relation to voluntary trust deeds executed on or after the date on which this Part comes into force.

Protected trust deeds: protected status

163 Protected status: general

(1) A trust deed has protected status (and is to be known as a 'protected trust deed') where—

(a) the conditions set out in sections 164, 165, 166(2) (where it applies) and 167 to 170 are met, and

(b) the deed is registered under section 171(2) in the register of insolvencies.

(2) And it has that status from the date on which it is so registered (that date being, in this Part, referred to as the 'date of protection').

Conditions for protected status

164 Protected status: the debtor

(1) The debtor must be—

(a) a living individual who,

(b) a partnership which,

(c) a limited partnership (within the meaning of the Limited Partnerships Act 1907) which,

(d) a trust which,
(e) a corporate body which, or
(f) an unincorporated body which,
[has a sufficient connection to Scotland and] grants a trust deed for a single estate.

[(1A) For the purposes of subsection (1), a debtor has a sufficient connection to Scotland if—

(a) in the case of a debtor who is a living individual, the individual—

(i) was habitually resident in Scotland at any time in the year immediately preceding the date the trust deed is granted, or

(ii) had an established place of business in Scotland within that period,

(b) in the case of a debtor which is a body or entity of a kind mentioned in paragraphs (b) to (f) of subsection (1), the body or entity—

(i) had an established place of business in Scotland at any time in the year immediately preceding the date the trust deed is granted, or

(ii) was constituted or formed under Scots law and at any time carried on business in Scotland.]

(2) The debtor must not be—

(a) a debtor whose estate has been sequestrated if the trustee in the sequestration has not been discharged under section 148 or 151, or

(b) an entity referred to in section 6(2).

(3) The total amount of the debtor's debts (including interest) as at the date on which the debtor grants the trust deed must be not less than £5,000.

165 Protected status: the trustee

The trustee under the trust deed must be a person who would not be disqualified under section 49(3) to (5) from acting as the replacement trustee were the debtor's estate being sequestrated.

166 Exclusion of a secured creditor from trust deed

(1) The conditions set out in subsection (2) apply where a secured creditor is, by virtue of an agreement such as is mentioned in paragraph (b)(ii) of the definition of 'trust deed' in section 228(1) (in this Part referred to as 'the trust deed definition'), excluded from a trust deed.

(2) Before the debtor grants the trust deed—

(a) the trustee must provide the debtor and the secured creditor with a valuation, made by a chartered surveyor or other suitably qualified person, of the dwellinghouse (or part) which is to be excluded from the estate conveyed as mentioned in paragraph (b)(i) of the trust deed definition,

(b) the debtor must, in such form as may be prescribed for the purposes of this paragraph, request obtaining the secured creditor's agreement not to claim under the trust deed for any of the debt in respect of which the security is held, and

(c) any agreement so obtained must be set out in such form as may be prescribed for the purposes of this paragraph.

167 Statements in and advice regarding trust deed

(1) The trust deed must state—

(a) that, subject to any exclusion mentioned in paragraph (b)(i) of the trust deed definition, all of the debtor's estate (other than property listed in section 88(1) or which would be excluded under any other provision of this Act or of any other enactment from vesting in the trustee of a sequestrated estate) is conveyed to the trustee, and

(b) that the debtor agrees to convey to the trustee, for the benefit of creditors generally, any estate (wherever situated) which—

(i) is acquired by the debtor during the 4 years beginning with the date on which the trust deed is granted, and

(ii) would have been conveyed to the trustee by virtue of paragraph (a) had it been part of the debtor's estate on the date on which the trust deed was granted.

(2) Where the debtor's dwellinghouse, or part of the debtor's dwellinghouse, is excluded as mentioned in paragraph (b)(i) of the trust deed definition from the estate conveyed to the trustee, the trust deed must also include details—

(a) of any secured creditor who has agreed not to claim under the trust deed for any of the debt in respect of which the security is held, and

(b) of that debt.

(3) Before the debtor grants the trust deed—

(a) the trustee must advise the debtor that granting the deed may result—

(i) in the debtor's estate being sequestrated,

(ii) in the debtor's being refused credit, whether before or after the debtor's discharge under section 184,

(iii) subject to any exclusion mentioned in paragraph (b)(i) of the trust deed definition, in the debtor's not being able to remain in the debtor's current place of residence,

(iv) subject to any such exclusion, in the debtor's being required to relinquish property which the debtor owns,

(v) in the debtor's being required to make contributions from income for the benefit of creditors,

(vi) in damage to the debtor's business interests and employment prospects, and

(vii) in the fact of the debtor's having granted a trust deed becoming public information,

[(b) the trustee must provide the debtor with—

(i) a copy of a debt advice and information package, and

(ii) a copy of a trust deed information document,

(ba) the trustee must give the debtor adequate time to consider the advice and material provided under paragraphs (a) and (b),]

(c) the trustee and the debtor must both sign a statement to the effect that the trustee has fulfilled the duties referred to in this subsection.

[(4) For the purposes of subsection (3) a 'trust deed information document' means a document containing such information (including information regarding the consequences of granting a trust deed), and in such form, as the Scottish Ministers may determine.

(5) The trustee must have regard to any guidance issued by the Scottish Ministers about giving debtors adequate time to consider the advice and material provided under paragraphs (a) and (b) of subsection (3).

(6) The Scottish Ministers must publish any guidance issued under subsection (5).]

168 Payment of debtor's contribution

(1) The trust deed must state that the debtor is, during the payment period mentioned in subsection (2), to pay any contributions from income for the benefit of creditors (including, where the debtor is an individual, any contribution required by the common financial tool) at regular intervals.

(2) The payment period is—

(a) a period of 48 months beginning with the date on which the trust deed is granted,

(b) such period shorter than 48 months as is determined by the trustee, or

(c) such period longer than 48 months as is—

(i) determined by the trustee where there has been a period during which the debtor has not paid those contributions, or

(ii) agreed between the debtor and the trustee.

(3) The trustee may, under subsection (2)(b), determine a shorter payment period only if, in the trustee's opinion, payment of those contributions (from income or otherwise) during that period would allow distribution of the debtor's estate to meet in full the total amount, as at the date on which the debtor grants the trust deed, of the debtor's debts (including interest).

(4) Where the debtor is an individual, those contributions must be such as to result, over the payment period, in the payment of a sum less than the total amount, as at the date on which the debtor grants the trust deed, of the debtor's debts (including interest).

(5) In calculating those contributions for the purposes of subsections (1) and (4), the whole of the debtor's surplus income over the amount allowed for expenditure in the statement of the debtor's income and expenditure supplied under section 170(1)(d)(ii) must be applied.

169 Notice in register of insolvencies

After the trust deed has been delivered to the trustee, the trustee must without delay send a notice in such form as may be prescribed for the purposes of this section to AiB for publication by registration in the register of insolvencies.

170 Documents to be sent to creditors

(1) Not later than 7 days after the date of registration under section 169, the trustee must send to every creditor known to the trustee (other than any secured creditor who has, as mentioned in paragraph (b)(ii) of the trust deed definition, agreed not to claim under the trust deed for any of the debt in respect of which the security is held)—

(a) a copy of the trust deed,

(b) a copy of such form as may be prescribed for the purposes of a creditor making a statement of claim,

(c) a copy of the notice mentioned in section 169,

(d) a statement of the debtor's affairs, prepared by the trustee, containing—

(i) a list of the debtor's assets and liabilities,

(ii) a statement of the debtor's income and expenditure as at the date on which the trust deed was granted (being, where the debtor is a living individual, a statement in the [form prescribed for that purpose by the Protected Trust Deeds (Forms) (Scotland) Regulations 2016]),

(iii) a statement as to the extent to which those assets and that income will not vest in the trustee,

(iv) a statement as to whether, and if so on what basis, the [EU] insolvency proceedings regulation applies to the trust deed,

[. . .]

(vi) a statement as to whether the creditors are likely to be paid a dividend and the amount of the dividend that is expected to be paid,

(vii) if the case is one in which there is an exclusion such as is mentioned in paragraph (b)(i) of the trust deed definition, a statement by the trustee, on the basis of the information for the time being available to the trustee, as to what the effect of that exclusion is likely to be on any such dividend,

(viii) a statement that the trustee on request must provide a copy of any valuation held by the trustee which has been made by a third party and which relates to an asset of the debtor, any statement showing the amount due by the debtor under a security and any document showing the income for the time being of the debtor,

(ix) a copy of any agreement referred to in section 175(1),

(x) a statement explaining the conditions which require to be fulfilled before the trust deed will become a protected trust deed and the consequences of its so becoming,

(xi) details of any protected trust deed in respect of which, in the 6 months preceding publication of the notice provided for in section 169, the debtor has been discharged in terms of section 184(1) (or regulation 24(1) of the Protected Trust Deeds (Scotland) Regulations 2013 (SSI 2013/318)) or been refused a letter of discharge under section 184(8) (or regulation 24(8) of those regulations), and

(xii) where a secured creditor's agreement has been obtained by virtue of paragraph (b) of section 166(2), a statement containing the valuation made by virtue of paragraph (a) of that section and a statement of the amount owed, in respect of the security held, to that creditor, and

(e) a statement, in such form as may be prescribed for the purposes of this paragraph, of the trustee's anticipated realisations from the trust deed.

(2) The trust deed must be acceded to by the creditors to whom the trustee is required by subsection (1) to send documents (those creditors being in this Part referred to as 'the notified creditors') but is deemed to have been acceded to by them unless, within the relevant period, the trustee receives notification in writing from a majority in number, or no fewer than $\frac{1}{3}$ in value, of them that they object to the trust deed being granted protected status.

Registration for protected status

171 Registration for protected status

(1) As soon as reasonably practicable after the expiry of the relevant period (and in any event within 4 weeks after that expiry), the trustee must send to AiB for registration in the register of insolvencies—

(a) a copy of the trust deed,

(b) either—

(i) a copy of every form of agreement obtained by virtue of section 166(2)(c), or

(ii) a statement by the trustee that no such form of agreement has been obtained,

(c) a statement by the trustee that those creditors, if any, who have objected in writing to the trust deed during the relevant period do not constitute a majority in number, or $\frac{1}{3}$ or more in value, of the creditors,

(d) a copy of the statement referred to in section 167(3)(c),

(e) a copy of the statement referred to in section 170(1)(d),

(f) a copy of any agreement referred to in section 175(1),

(g) a statement, in the form prescribed for the purposes of section 170(1)(e), of the trustee's anticipated realisations from the trust deed,

(h) where the debtor, being a living individual, makes a contribution from income—

(i) a statement that the amount of the contribution is in accordance with the common financial tool as assessed by the trustee, and

(ii) any evidence or explanation required in applying the common financial tool.

[(i) a statement by the trustee, in the form prescribed for that purpose in the Protected Trust Deeds (Forms) (Scotland) Regulations 2016, that—

(i) the documents and statements required under paragraphs (a) to (h) of this subsection accompany the statement, and

(ii) the conditions set out in sections 164 to 170 have been met].

(2) AiB must register the trust deed in the register of insolvencies if—

(a) AiB has received all the documents required to be sent under subsection (1),

(b) [AiB is satisfied that] the conditions set out in sections 164 to 170 have been met, and

(c) AiB is satisfied, in accordance with the common financial tool, with the amount of the contribution determined.

(3) Subsection (4) applies where AiB notifies the trustee either—

(a) that the trust deed is registered in the register of insolvencies, or

(b) that such registration is refused.

(4) The trustee must, within 7 days after being so notified, notify the debtor and every creditor known to the trustee that the trust deed is so registered or refused.

[Removal of protected status where material error or irregularity

171A Removal of protected status where material error or irregularity

(1) If, within 3 months of the trust deed being registered in the register of insolvencies under section 171(2), the trustee becomes aware that any of the conditions set out in sections 164, 165, 166(2) (where it applied) or 167 to 170 were not met at the point of registration due to a material error or irregularity, the trustee must notify AiB.

(2) Where AiB is notified under subsection (1), AiB must decide whether the trust deed should cease to have protected status (see section 163).

(3) If AiB decides under subsection (2) that the trust deed should cease to have protected status AiB must, as soon as reasonably practicable, notify the trustee and the debtor in writing of that decision.

(4) Where the trustee receives a notification under subsection (3) the trustee must, as soon as reasonably practicable, notify every creditor known to the trustee (other than any secured creditor who has, as mentioned in paragraph (b)(ii) of the trust deed definition, agreed not to claim under the trust deed for any of the debt in respect of which the security is held).

(5) A notice under subsection (3) or (4) must state—

(a) the fact that a decision under subsection (2) has been made,

(b) the date on which the decision was made, and

(c) the ground or grounds for the decision.

(6) Where a notice is issued under subsection (3)—

(a) the trust deed ceases to have protected status 14 days after that notice is given (but see section 171B), and

(b) AiB must, as soon as reasonably practicable, remove the entry for the trust deed in the register of insolvencies.

171B Decision under section 171A: application to review

(1) The debtor, the trustee or a creditor may apply to AiB for a review of its decision under section 171A(2).

(2) An application under subsection (1) must be made within 14 days beginning with the date that decision was notified under section 171A(3).

(3) If an application for review under subsection (1) is made, AiB's decision under section 171A(2) is suspended until the determination of that review by AiB.

(4) If an application for a review under subsection (1) is made, AiB must—

(a) confirm or revoke the decision within 21 days beginning with the day on which the application is made, and

(b) notify the debtor, the trustee and (where relevant) the creditor who made the application under subsection (1) of the outcome.

(5) If, under subsection (4), AiB—

(a) confirms a decision, the decision takes effect 21 days after the day on which AiB notifies the debtor, the trustee and (where relevant) the creditor who made the application under subsection (1) of the outcome of its review,

(b) revokes a decision, the decision is of no effect.

(6) The trustee must, as soon as reasonably practicable following receipt of a notification under subsection (4), notify the outcome of the review to every creditor known to the trustee.

171C Effect of removal of protected status

A trust deed ceasing to have protected status by virtue of a decision under section 171A is not to—

(a) invalidate any acts of the trustee between the date the trust deed was registered and the date a decision under section 171A takes effect,

(b) prevent the trust deed from re-attaining protected status provided the conditions in sections 164–170, so far as applicable, are met, or

(c) prevent the debtor from—

(i) making a debtor application under section 2 or, as the case may be, 6,

(ii) applying for a moratorium under section 195 or, as the case may be, 196,

(iii) applying for a debt payment programme within the meaning of section 2 of the 2002 Act.]

Effect of protected status etc

172 Effect of protected status: general

(1) Where a trust deed has protected status then—

(a) subject to section 177, a creditor who (either or both)—

(i) is not a notified creditor, or

(ii) notified the trustee, during the relevant period, of objection to the trust deed,

has no higher right to recover the debt than a creditor who has acceded to, or been deemed by virtue of section 170(2) to have acceded to, the trust deed, and

(b) an application for sequestration of the debtor's estate may not be made by the debtor while the trust deed subsists.

(2) A creditor ceases to be deemed (by virtue of section 170(2)) to have acceded to a trust deed [if AiB agrees that the debtor should not be discharged from the trust deed under section 184A].

(3) Where a secured creditor's agreement has been obtained by virtue of section 166(2)(b) and the trust deed becomes a protected trust deed, that creditor is not entitled—

(a) to make a claim under the protected trust deed for any of the debt in respect of which the security is held,

(b) to do diligence against the assets conveyed to the trustee under the protected trust deed, or

(c) to petition for the sequestration of the debtor during the subsistence of the protected trust deed.

173 Effect of protected status on diligence against earnings

(1) This section applies where a trust deed has protected status.

(2) On the date of protection, any current earnings arrestment, maintenance arrestment, or, subject to subsection (3), conjoined arrestment order ceases to have effect.

(3) Any sum paid, before the date of protection, by the employer to the sheriff clerk under a conjoined arrestment order must be disbursed by the sheriff clerk under section 64 of the Debtors (Scotland) Act 1987 even if the date of disbursement is after the date of protection.

(4) A deduction from earnings order under that Act of 1987 is not competent after the date of protection to secure the payment of any amount due by the debtor under a maintenance calculation (within the meaning of that Act) in respect of which a claim could be made under the trust deed.

(5) The execution of an earnings arrestment or the making of a conjoined arrestment order is not competent, after the date of protection, to enforce a debt in respect of which the creditor is entitled to make a claim under the trust deed.

[173A Effect of protected status on essential supplies

(1) An insolvency-related term of a contract for the supply of essential goods or services to a debtor ceases to have effect if—

(a) a trust deed granted by the debtor is granted protected status, and

(b) the supply is for the purpose of a business which is or has been carried on by or on behalf of the debtor.

(2) An insolvency-related term of a contract does not cease to have effect by virtue of subsection (1) to the extent that—

(a) it provides for the contract or the supply to terminate, or any other thing to take place, because the individual becomes subject to an insolvency procedure other than a trust deed,

(b) it entitles a supplier to terminate the contract or the supply, or do any other thing, because the individual becomes subject to an insolvency procedure other than a trust deed, or

(c) it entitles a supplier to terminate the contract or the supply because of an event that occurs, or may occur, after a trust deed granted by the debtor is granted protected status.

(3) Where an insolvency-related term of a contract ceases to have effect under this section the supplier may—

(a) terminate the contract, if the condition in subsection (4) is met,

(b) terminate the supply, if the condition in subsection (7) is met.

(4) The condition in this subsection is that—

(a) the trustee under the trust deed consents to the termination of the contract,

(b) on application by the supplier the court grants permission for the termination of the contract, or

(c) any charges in respect of the supply that are incurred after the date of protection of the trust deed are not paid within the period of 28 days beginning with the day on which payment is due.

(5) An application by the supplier under subsection (4)(b) is to be made to the sheriff who, had a petition for sequestration of the estate been presented at the date the trust deed was granted, would have had jurisdiction to hear that petition in terms of section 15(1) or (3).

(6) The court may grant permission under subsection (4)(b) only if satisfied that the continuation of the contract would cause the supplier hardship.

(7) The condition in this subsection is that—

(a) the supplier gives written notice to the trustee under the trust deed that the supply will be terminated unless the trustee personally guarantees the payment of any charges in respect of the continuation of the supply after the date of protection of the trust deed, and

(b) the trustee does not give that guarantee within the period of 14 days beginning with the day the notice is received.

(8) For the purposes of securing that the interests of suppliers are protected, where—

(a) an insolvency-related term of a contract (the "original term") ceases to have effect by virtue of subsection (1), and

(b) a subsequent trust deed granted by the debtor is granted protected status, the contract is treated for the purposes of subsections (1) to (7) as if, immediately before the subsequent trust deed granted by the debtor is granted protected status, it included an insolvency-related term identical to the original term.

(9) A contract for the supply of essential goods or services is a contract for a supply mentioned in section 222(4).

(10) An insolvency-related term of a contract for the supply of essential goods or services to a debtor is a provision of the contract under which—

(a) the contract or the supply would terminate, or any other thing would take place, because a trust deed granted by the debtor is granted protected status,

(b) the supplier would be entitled to terminate the contract or the supply, or to do any other thing, because a trust deed granted by the debtor is granted protected status, or

(c) the supplier would be entitled to terminate the contract or the supply because of an event that occurred before a trust deed granted by the debtor is granted protected status.

(11) Subsection (1) does not have effect in relation to a contract entered into before 1st August 2017.]

174 Deductions by virtue of protected trust deed from debtor's earnings

(1) This section applies where—

(a) a debtor is required to pay to the trustee, by virtue of a protected trust deed, a contribution from income for the benefit of creditors,

(b) in respect of that contribution, an amount is required to be paid from the debtor's earnings from employment, and

(c) the debtor has failed on two consecutive occasions to pay that amount to the trustee.

(2) Following a request by the trustee, the debtor must give the debtor's employer an instruction, in such form as may be prescribed for the purposes of this section, to make—

(a) deductions of specified amounts from the debtor's earnings, and

(b) payments to the trustee of the amounts so deducted.

(3) The trustee may give the debtor's employer an instruction, in such form as may be prescribed for the purposes of this section (being a form to the same effect as is mentioned in subsection (2)), if the debtor fails to comply with the requirement imposed by that subsection.

(4) If agreed between the debtor and the trustee, the debtor may give the debtor's employer a variation to an instruction mentioned in subsection (2).

(5) The employer must comply with any instruction given in accordance with subsection (2) or (3) (or, if an instruction under subsection (2) is varied in accordance with subsection (4), with that instruction as so varied).

(6) The instruction having been delivered, the employer must, while it is in effect—

(a) deduct the sum specified in it on every pay day, and

(b) pay the sum deducted to the trustee as soon as it is reasonable to do so.

(7) Where an employer fails without good cause to make a payment due under an instruction, the employer is—

(a) liable to pay on demand by a trustee the amount that should have been paid, and

(b) not entitled to recover from a debtor the amount paid to the debtor in breach of the instruction.

(8) An employer may, on making a payment due under an instruction—

(a) charge a fee equivalent to the fee chargeable for the time being under section 71 (employer's fee for operating diligence against earnings) of the Debtors (Scotland) Act 1987, and

(b) deduct that fee from the balance due to the debtor.

(9) The trustee must, without delay after the discharge of a debtor under section 184, notify in writing any person who has received an instruction under subsection (2) or (3) (or an instruction under subsection (2) varied in accordance with subsection (4)) that the instruction is recalled.

175 Agreement in respect of debtor's heritable property

(1) Subject to the conditions in subsection (2), the trustee may, in such form as may be prescribed for the purposes of this section as at the date on which the trust deed is granted, agree—

(a) not to realise any specified heritable estate of the debtor which has been conveyed to the trustee,

(b) to relinquish the trustee's interest in respect of such heritable estate, and

(c) to recall any notice of inhibition in respect of such heritable estate in accordance with paragraph 3(3) of schedule 4.

(2) The conditions are that the debtor must—

(a) pay any amount determined by the trustee by a date so determined,

(b) pay a monthly amount so determined for a period so determined (being, in a case where there is a contribution from income, a period following the payment period applicable by virtue of section 168(2)), and

(c) co-operate with the administration of the trust.

(3) The amount of the debtor's payments under paragraphs (a) and (b) of subsection (2) must be determined in accordance with a valuation made by a chartered surveyor, or other qualified third party, of the debtor's heritable estate as at the date of grant of the trust deed.

(4) If the debtor fails to fulfil a condition mentioned in subsection (2), the trustee may withdraw from the agreement.

(5) The trustee must, as soon as is practicable, send a copy of the agreement (in the form mentioned in subsection (1)) to AiB and to every creditor known to the trustee other than any secured creditor who has, as mentioned in paragraph (b)(ii) of the trust deed definition, agreed not to claim under the trust deed for any of the debt in respect of which the security is held.

(6) This section does not apply to the debtor's dwellinghouse (or any part of that dwellinghouse) if the dwellinghouse or part is, by virtue of an exclusion such as is mentioned in paragraph (b)(i) of the trust deed definition, excluded from the estate conveyed to the trustee.

176 Dividend payments

(1) If the funds of the debtor's estate are sufficient, the trustee must pay a dividend out of it to the creditors no later than 6 weeks after the end of—

(a) a first dividend period of [12] months beginning with the date on which the trust deed is granted, and

(b) any subsequent dividend period of [3] months beginning with the end of the previous dividend period.

(2) The funds of the debtor's estate are 'sufficient' if, after—

(a) deduction of the trustee's fees and of any outlays payable under this Part, and

(b) making allowance for future contingencies,

a dividend may be paid to the creditors amounting to at least 5 pence for each pound sterling of the debtor's debt, as at the date of protection, under the trust deed.

177 Sequestration petition by qualified creditor

(1) A qualified creditor who is not a notified creditor or who has notified the trustee of objection to the trust deed within the relevant period may—

(a) not later than 5 weeks after the date of registration under section 169 of the notice mentioned in that section, or

(b) at any time if the creditor avers that the provision for distribution of the estate is, or is likely to be, unduly prejudicial to a creditor or class of creditors,

present a petition to the sheriff for sequestration of the debtor's estate.

(2) Subsection (1)(b) is subject to section 13(2)(a).

(3) The sheriff may award sequestration in pursuance of—

(a) subsection (1)(a), only if satisfied that to do so would be in the best interests of the creditors, and

(b) subsection (1)(b), only if satisfied that the creditor's averment is correct.

178 Creditor's application as respects intromissions of trustee

(1) A creditor who is not sent a copy of the notice mentioned in section 169 or who has notified the trustee of objection to the trust deed within the relevant period may apply to the sheriff under this section.

(2) Where on such an application the sheriff is satisfied, on grounds other than those on which a petition under section 177(1)(b) has been or could have been presented by the creditor, that the intromissions of the trustee with the estate of the debtor have been so unduly prejudicial to the creditor's claim that the creditor should not be bound by the trustee's discharge, the sheriff may order that the creditor is not to be so bound.

(3) On the sheriff making an order under subsection (2), the sheriff clerk must—

(a) send a copy of the order to the trustee, and

(b) send a copy of the order to AiB for registration in the register of insolvencies.

(4) Any application under subsection (1) must be made within 28 days after the registration in the register of insolvencies of the trustee's statement of realisation and distribution of estate under the protected trust deed, as mentioned in section 186(8)(b).

(5) The sheriff to whom the application may be made is the sheriff to whom a petition for sequestration would be brought in respect of the debtor by virtue of section 15(1) or (3).

Administration, accounting and discharge

179 Directions to trustee under protected trust deed

(1) AiB may give directions to the trustee under a protected trust deed as to how the trustee should conduct the administration of the trust.

(2) On a direction being issued by virtue of subsection (1) its terms must be intimated to the debtor and to all known creditors.

(3) The direction may be issued on the initiative of AiB or (at AiB's discretion) on the request of the trustee, the debtor or any creditor.

(4) The trustee must, unless subsection (5) applies, comply with the direction within 30 days beginning with the day on which the direction is given.

(5) Where the trustee has appealed under section 188(1)(c) and the appeal has been dismissed by the sheriff or withdrawn by the trustee, the trustee must comply with the direction within 30 days beginning with the day of dismissal or withdrawal.

(6) If it appears to AiB that the trustee has failed, without reasonable excuse, to comply with the direction, AiB may report the matter to the sheriff who, after hearing the trustee on the matter, may—

(a) censure the trustee, or

(b) make such other order as the circumstances of the case require.

180 Information and notification obligations of trustee under protected trust deed

(1) Where the trustee under a protected trust deed makes a determination to shorten or lengthen the payment period by virtue of section 168, the trustee must without delay notify the debtor accordingly.

(2) Whether or not still acting in the administration of the trust under a protected trust deed, the trustee must supply AiB with such information relating to the trust deed as AiB considers necessary to enable AiB to discharge AiB's functions under this Act.

(3) If it appears to AiB that the trustee has failed, without reasonable excuse, to supply information to AiB which is requested in accordance with subsection (2), AiB may report the matter to the sheriff who, after hearing the trustee on the matter, may—

(a) censure the trustee, or

(b) make such other order as the circumstances of the case require.

(4) On the trustee under a protected trust deed being replaced with a new trustee, the new trustee must without delay notify AiB accordingly.

181 Administration of trust under protected trust deed

(1) At intervals of not more than 12 months (the first such interval beginning with the date on which the trust deed was granted) and within 6 weeks after the end of each interval, the trustee under a protected trust deed must send the trustee's accounts of the trustee's intromissions with the debtor's estate in administering the trust during the period in question—

(a) to the debtor,

(b) to each creditor, and

(c) (unless they are sent under section 186) to AiB.

(2) At such intervals the trustee must send to AiB, the debtor and each creditor a report, in such form as may be prescribed for the purposes of this subsection, on the management of the trust during the period in question.

(3) Subsection (4) applies where—

(a) within 21 days after the date on which the report is sent, the trustee receives notification in writing from—

(i) a majority in number, or

(ii) no fewer than $^1/_3$ in value,

of the creditors that they object to a course of action recommended in the report, and

(b) the expected final dividend to ordinary creditors set out in the report is at least 20% lower than the expected dividend to ordinary creditors set out in the form prescribed for the purposes of section 170(1)(e).

(4) The trustee must request under section 179(3) a direction as to the administration of the trust.

(5) The debtor or any creditor may, within 14 days after receiving a statement by virtue of subsection (1), require AiB to exercise the function mentioned in section 200(1)(a) (in so far as relating to trustees under protected trust deeds) by carrying out an examination of the administration of the trust by the trustee.

(6) In determining the amount of any contribution from income to be made by the debtor—

(a) the trustee may take account of any social security benefit paid to the debtor, but

(b) any contribution must not include an amount derived from social security benefit.

182 Retention of documents by trustee under protected trust deed

The trustee under a protected trust deed must retain the following documents (or copies of those documents) for at least 12 months after the date of the trustee's discharge by the creditors under section 186—

(a) the trust deed,

(b) the statement mentioned in section 167(3)(c),

(c) the notice mentioned in section 169,

(d) the statement mentioned in section 170(1)(d),

(e) all statements of objection or accession received from creditors,

(f) the statement of anticipated realisations provided for in section 170(1)(e),

(g) any written agreement relating to the debtor's heritable estate and mentioned in section 175(1),

(h) all reports sent under section 181(2),

(i) any adjudication on a creditor's claim,

(j) any scheme of division among creditors,

(k) any circular sent to creditors with accounts,

(l) the debtor's discharge from the trust deed,

(m) the application to creditors for the trustee's discharge,

(n) the statement of realisation and distribution provided for in section 186(8)(b),

(o) any decree, interlocutory decree, direction or order granted by the court and relating to the administration of the trust, and

(p) any other document relating to the administration of the trust if it is a document which AiB, by notice to the trustee prior to the trustee's discharge, identifies as a document the trustee should retain.

183 Remuneration payable to trustee under protected trust deed

(1) For work done by the trustee in administering the trust, the trustee under a protected trust deed is entitled to remuneration consisting only of—

(a) a fixed fee which must be set out in a form prescribed for the purposes of this paragraph,

(b) an additional fee based on a percentage of the total assets and contributions realised by the trustee, being a fee set out in a form so prescribed, and

(c) outlays incurred—

(i) after the date on which the trust deed is granted, or

(ii) before that date on a single valuation of any item of the debtor's heritable estate specified or valued in such a valuation.

(2) In the event of unforeseen circumstances the fixed fee may by increased by—

(a) approval by a majority in value of the notified creditors, or

(b) approval by AiB (all notified creditors having first been asked to approve the increase).

(3) AiB must approve an increase in the fixed fee if satisfied—

(a) that a majority in value of the notified creditors have not refused to approve the increase, and

(b) that the increase is required for work to be completed by the trustee for the benefit of the creditors generally, being work which was not foreseen in submitting a form by virtue of section 170(1)(e).

(4) In deciding whether or not to grant the approval mentioned in subsection (2)(b), AiB may determine the amount of any increase in the fixed fee.

(5) The trustee is entitled to include work done in seeking to comply with section 166(2) (whether or not a secured creditor has agreed not to claim under the trust deed) in the fixed fee and any outlays incurred.

(6) Any debt due to a third party for work done before the granting of the trust deed does not rank higher than any other creditor's claim.

(7) The trustee is entitled to recover from the debtor's estate any audit fee charged by AiB under paragraph 1 or 2 of schedule 4 in accordance with such rate as may be prescribed under section 205.

(8) AiB may, at any time, audit the trustee's accounts and fix the outlays of the trustee in the administration of the trust.

184 Protected trust deed: discharge of debtor

(1) If the conditions set out in subsection (2) are met then, subject to subsections (6) and (9) and to section 185(1)—

(a) the debtor falls to be discharged from all debts and obligations —

(i) in terms of the protected trust deed, or

(ii) for which the debtor was liable as at the date that deed was granted, and

(b) the trustee under the protected trust deed must send—

(i) to AiB, an application for discharge of the debtor from the trust deed (being an application in such form as may be prescribed for the purposes of this paragraph), and

(ii) to the debtor, a copy of that application.

(2) The conditions are—

(a) that the trustee makes a statement (being a statement in such form as may be prescribed for the purposes of this paragraph) that, to the best of the trustee's knowledge, the debtor has—

(i) met the debtor's obligations in terms of the trust deed, and

(ii) co-operated with the administration of the trust, and

(b) any notice of inhibition under paragraph 3 of schedule 4 has been recalled or has expired.

(3) Subject to subsection (9), on receipt of the application referred to in subsection (1)(b)(i), AiB must register it in the register of insolvencies and the date of discharge is the date on which it is so registered.

(4) AiB must without delay notify the trustee of—

(a) the fact of registration, and

(b) the date of the debtor's discharge.

(5) The trustee must, within 7 days after receipt of the notification mentioned in subsection (4), notify the debtor and every creditor known to the trustee of the information set out in that notification.

(6) The letter of discharge does not—

(a) discharge the debtor from—

(i) any liability arising after the date on which the protected trust deed was granted,

(ii) any liability or obligation mentioned in section 145(3),

(iii) any liability for a debt in respect of which a security is held if the secured creditor has, as mentioned in paragraph (b)(ii) of the trust deed definition, agreed not to claim under the trust deed for any of the debt in respect of which the security is held, or

(b) affect the rights of a secured creditor.

(7) For the purposes of subsection (2)(a)(i), it is not a failure to meet the debtor's obligations for the debtor to refuse to —

(a) consent to the sale of the debtor's dwellinghouse (or of a part of that dwellinghouse) if the dwellinghouse or part is excluded, as mentioned in paragraph (b)(i) of the trust deed definition, from the estate conveyed to the trustee,

(b) give a relevant consent in terms of section 113(1)(a).

[. . .]

(9) AiB may refuse to register under subsection (3) an application sent under subsection (1)(b)(i) if not satisfied that the debtor has—

(a) met the debtor's obligations in terms of the trust deed, or

(b) co-operated with the administration of the trust.

(10) If AiB does so refuse, AiB must provide written notification of the refusal and of the reason for it to the trustee and the debtor.

(11) Within 7 days after the date on which the trustee receives any such notification as is mentioned in subsection (10), the trustee must send a copy of it to every creditor known to the trustee.

[184A Protected trust deed: refusal of debtor discharge

(1) If—

(a) the period for which payments are required under the trust deed has ended, and

(b) on request by the debtor, or where the trustee has not made a statement under section 184(2)(a) on the basis that the trustee considers that the debtor—

(i) has not met the debtor's obligations in terms of the trust deed, or

(ii) has not co-operated with the administration of the trust,

the trustee must as soon as reasonably practicable apply to AiB for agreement to refuse to discharge the debtor from the trust deed.

(2) If—

(a) the period for which payments are required under the trust deed has not ended,

(b) on request by the debtor, or where the trustee is satisfied that the debtor—

(i) has not met the debtor's obligations in terms of the trust deed, or

(ii) has not co-operated with the administration of the trust, and

(c) the trustee is satisfied that that failure to meet the debtor's obligations under the trust deed or to co-operate with the administration of the trust is likely to continue until the period for which payments are required under the trust deed ends,

the trustee must as soon as reasonably practicable apply to AiB for agreement to refuse to discharge the debtor from the trust deed.

(3) An application under subsection (1) or (2) must—

(a) be in the form prescribed for that purpose in the Protected Trust Deeds (Forms) (Scotland) Regulations 2016(1), and

(b) include details of the trustee's consideration under subsection (1) or, as the case may be, (2).

(4) Where AiB receives an application under subsection (1) or (2), and AiB agrees that the debtor should not be discharged from the trust deed, AiB must notify the trustee of that conclusion as soon as reasonably practicable.

(5) Where the trustee receives a notification from AiB under subsection (4), the trustee must—

(a) within 7 days, inform the debtor by notice in writing—

(i) of the fact and the reason for the refusal,

(ii) that the debtor is not discharged from the debtor's debts and obligations in terms of the trust deed, and

(iii) of the debtor's right to apply to the sheriff for a direction under section 189(1), and

(b) within 21 days of the date the notice is sent to the debtor under paragraph (a), send a copy of that notice to AiB.

(6) Where AiB considers that the debtor should be discharged from the trust deed, AiB must issue such direction to the trustee as it considers appropriate.

(7) Section 184(7) applies for the purposes of this section in the same way as it applies for the purposes of section 184(2)(a)(i).

(8) Nothing in this section prevents the trustee from being discharged under section 186.

184B Protected trust deed: early discharge in extenuating circumstances

(1) This section applies where the trustee considers that, due to extenuating circumstances affecting the debtor—

(a) the debtor can no longer meet their obligations under the trust deed,

(b) there is no reasonable prospect of the debtor being able to resume meeting their obligations under the trust deed, and

(c) the debtor should be discharged from the trust deed before the end of the period for which payments are required under the trust deed.

(2) The trustee must send a notice to each of the creditors of whom the trustee is aware.

(3) A notice under subsection (2) must—

(a) include details of the trustee's consideration under subsection (1), and

(b) seek agreement from the creditor that the debtor be discharged from the trust deed.

(4) The trustee must apply to AiB for the discharge of the debtor unless subsection (5) applies.

(5) This subsection applies if the trustee has, within 21 days of sending notices under subsection (2), received notification in writing from a majority in number, or no fewer than 1/3 in value, of the creditors that they object to the proposal to discharge the debtor.

(6) An application under subsection (4) must be in the form prescribed for that purpose by the Protected Trust Deeds (Forms) (Scotland) Regulations 2016.

(7) Before applying to AiB for the discharge of the debtor, the trustee must be satisfied that any notice of inhibition under paragraph 3 of schedule 4 has been recalled or has expired.

(8) On receipt of an application under subsection (4), AiB must register it in the register of insolvencies.

(9) Where AiB registers an application under subsection (4)—

(a) the debtor falls to be discharged from all debts and obligations—

(i) in terms of the protected trust deed, or

(ii) for which the debtor was liable as at the date that deed was granted,

(b) the date of discharge is the date on which the application is so registered, and

(c) AiB must without delay notify the trustee of—

(i) the fact of registration, and

(ii) the date of the debtor's discharge.

(10) The trustee must, within 7 days after receipt of the notification mentioned in subsection (8), notify the debtor and every creditor known to the trustee of the information set out in that notification.

(11) Section 184(6) applies to the notification of the debtor's discharge under subsection (9) in the same way as it applies to a letter of discharge under section 184.

184C Early discharge in extenuating circumstances: procedure where creditors object

(1) This section applies where—

(a) the trustee has, in accordance with section 184B(2) and (3), sought the agreement of the creditors to the early discharge of the debtor from a trust deed, and

(b) at the end of the period of 21 days beginning with the day on which notices are sent under section 184B(2), the trustee has received notification in writing from a majority in number, or no fewer than 1/3 in value, of the creditors that they object to the proposal to discharge the debtor.

(2) The trustee must apply to AiB for a review of the proposal that the debtor be discharged.

(3) An application for a review under subsection (2) must—

(a) include details of the trustee's consideration under section 184B(1),

(b) include details of the objections received from the creditors, and

(c) be made no later than 14 days beginning with the end of the period of 21 days referred to in subsection (1)(b).

(4) Where it receives an application under subsection (2), AiB must—

(a) determine whether it is satisfied that, taking into account all the circumstances, it is fair and reasonable for the debtor to be discharged from the trust deed, and

(b) notify the trustee of the outcome of that review.

(5) The trustee must, no later than 7 days after receiving a notification under subsection (4)(b), notify the outcome of AiB's review to—

(a) the debtor, and

(b) each creditor to whom notice was sent under section 184B(2).

(6) Where, after conducting a review under subsection (4), AiB determines that the debtor should be discharged from the trust deed—

(a) the trustee must apply to AiB for the discharge of the debtor, and

(b) on receipt of such an application, AiB must register it in the register of insolvencies.

(7) Where AiB registers an application under subsection (6)—

(a) the debtor falls to be discharged from all debts and obligations—

(i) in terms of the protected trust deed, or

(ii) for which the debtor was liable as at the date that deed was granted,

(b) the date of discharge is the date on which the application is so registered, and

(c) AiB must without delay notify the trustee of—

(i) the fact of registration, and

(ii) the date of the debtor's discharge.

(8) The trustee must, within 7 days after receipt of the notification mentioned in subsection (7)(c), notify the debtor and every creditor known to the trustee of the information set out in that notification.

(9) Section 184(6) applies to the notification of the debtor's discharge under subsection (7) in the same way as it applies to a letter of discharge under section 184.

(10) Where, after conducting a review under subsection (4), AiB determines that the debtor should not be discharged from the trust deed, AiB must issue a direction to the trustee.]

185 Student loans

(1) Section 184 does not affect the right to recover any debt arising from a student loan.

(2) In subsection (1), 'student loan' means a loan made by virtue of—

(a) section 73(f) of the Education (Scotland) Act 1980,

(b) section 1 of the Education (Student Loans) Act 1990,

(c) section 22 of the Teaching and Higher Education Act 1998, or

(d) Article 3 of the Education (Student Support) (Northern Ireland) Order 1998 (SI 1998/1760).

186 Protected trust deed: discharge of trustee

(1) This section applies where a trustee under a protected trust deed has made the final distribution of the trust estate among the creditors.

(2) Within 28 days after the date of final distribution, the trustee must apply for discharge to such of those creditors as have acceded (or are deemed to have acceded) to the trust deed.

(3) Any application under subsection (2) must be in such form as may be prescribed for the purposes of that subsection.

(4) The trustee must send AiB by the date of application—

(a) a copy of the application, and

(b) the accounts of the trustee's intromissions for the last period for which accounts must be sent under section 181(1).

(5) For the purposes of subsection (2), the 'date of final distribution' is the date on which all of the estate distributed has been placed beyond the control of the trustee.

(6) A creditor who does not respond to the application within 14 days after it is made is deemed to have agreed to the trustee's discharge.

(7) If a majority of the creditors in value consent to the application the trustee is discharged.

(8) On being discharged, the trustee must within 28 days of the discharge—

(a) inform AiB of the discharge,

(b) send AiB, for registration in the register of insolvencies, a statement of realisation and distribution of estate under the protected trust deed, and

(c) send AiB, where accounts submitted under subsection (4)(b) require to be revised, a copy of the revised accounts.

(9) A statement under subsection (8)(b) must be in such form as may be prescribed for the purposes of that subsection.

(10) Where the trustee's discharge is granted under this section, the discharge also applies as regards any previous trustee under the trust deed unless, under section 189, a person with an interest obtains an order to the contrary from the sheriff.

[186A Replacement of trustee in a protected trust deed

(1) AiB may, of its own accord or on the representation of any person, appoint itself as trustee in a protected trust deed where AiB is satisfied that—

(a) the trustee under a protected trust deed is unable to continue to act under that protected trust deed (including, for example, because the trustee is no longer authorised to act as an insolvency practitioner or because the trustee has died),

(b) all reasonable efforts have been made to appoint a replacement trustee but without success, and

(c) it is necessary, taking account of all the circumstances, for AiB to become the trustee in the protected trust deed.

(2) Before appointing itself as trustee under subsection (1), AiB must—

(a) take into account any representations made by an interested person,

(b) consider the public interest, and

(c) consider AiB's capacity and resources.

(3) Where AiB becomes the trustee in a protected trust deed by virtue of subsection (1), AiB must—

(a) notify—

(i) the debtor, and

(ii) each creditor of whom AiB is aware, and

(b) make an appropriate entry in the register of insolvencies.

186B Modification of this Part where Accountant in Bankruptcy becomes trustee in a protected trust deed

(1) Where AiB becomes the trustee in a protected trust deed by virtue of section 186A(1), this Part and schedule 4 apply to AiB as they apply to a trustee in a protected trust deed, subject to the following modifications.

(2) The following do not apply—

(a) section 165 (protected status: the trustee),

(b) sections 169 to 171,

(c) section 179 (directions to trustee under protected trust deed),

(d) section 184A (protected trust deed: refusal of debtor discharge),

(e) paragraphs 1 and 2 of schedule 4 (voluntary trust deeds for creditors).

(3) Section 171A (removal of protected status where material error or irregularity) is to be read as if—

(a) in subsection (1), for 'the trustee must notify AiB' there were substituted 'AiB must decide whether the trust deed should cease to have protected status (see section 163)',

(b) subsection (2) were omitted,

(c) in subsection (3)—

(i) for 'subsection (2)' there were substituted 'subsection (1)',

(ii) for 'the trustee and the debtor' there were substituted 'the debtor and every creditor known to AiB (other than any secured creditor who has, as mentioned in paragraph (b)(ii) of the trust deed definition, agreed not to claim under the trust deed for any of the debt in respect of which the security is held)',

(d) subsection (4) were omitted,

(e) in subsection (5)—

(i) 'or 4' were omitted,

(ii) in paragraph (a), for 'subsection (2)' there were substituted 'subsection (1)'.

(4) Section 171B (decision under section 171A: application to review) is to be read as if—

(a) in subsection (1)—

(i) ', the trustee' were omitted, and

(ii) for 'section 171A(2)' there were substituted 'section 171A(1)',

(b) in subsection (3), for 'section 171A(2)' there were substituted 'section 171A(1)',

(c) in subsection (4)(b), ', the trustee' were omitted,

(d) in subsection (5)(a), ', the trustee' were omitted.

(5) Section 180 (information and notification obligations of trustee under protected trust deed) is to be read as if subsections (2) to (4) were omitted.

(6) Section 181 (administration of trust under protected trust deed) is to be read as if—

(a) subsections (1)(c), (4) and (5) were omitted,

(b) in subsection (2), 'AiB' were omitted.

(7) Section 182 (retention of documents by trustee under protected trust deed) is to be read as if, in paragraph (p), for ', by notice to the trustee' to the end there were substituted 'identifies as a document that should be retained.'.

(8) Section 183 (remuneration payable to trustee under protected trust deed), is to be read as if subsections (2)(b), (3), (4), (7) and (8) were omitted.

(9) Section 184 (protected trust deed: discharge of debtor) is to be read as if—

(a) subsections (1)(b), (4) and (9) to (11) were omitted,

(b) for subsection (3) there were substituted—

'(3) AiB must record the fact and the date of the debtor's discharge in the register of insolvencies.',

(c) for subsection (5) there were substituted—

'(5) AiB must, within 7 days of recording the information referred to in subsection (3), notify the debtor and every creditor known to AiB of the fact and the date of the debtor's discharge.'.

(10) Section 184B (protected trust deed: early discharge in extenuating circumstances) is to be read as if—

(a) for subsection (4) there were substituted—

'(4) AiB must record the fact and the date of the debtor's discharge in the register of insolvencies unless subsection (5) applies.',

(b) subsections (6) and (8) were omitted,

(c) in subsection (7), 'Before applying to AiB for the discharge of the debtor' were omitted,

(d) in subsection (9)—

(i) for 'an application under subsection (4)' there were substituted 'the fact and the date of the debtor's discharge under subsection (4)',

(ii) paragraph (c) were omitted.

(11) Section 184C (early discharge in extenuating circumstances: procedure where creditors object) is to be read as if—

(a) for subsection (2) there were substituted—

'(2) AiB must review its proposal for the purpose of determining whether, taking account of all of the circumstances, it is fair and reasonable that the debtor be discharged.',

(b) subsections (3) and (4) were omitted,

(c) for subsection (5) there were substituted—

'(5) AiB must notify the outcome of its review to—

(a) the debtor, and

(b) each creditor to whom notice was sent under section 184B(2).',

(d) for subsection (6) there were substituted—

'(6) Where, after conducting a review under subsection (2), AiB determines that the debtor should be discharged from the trust deed, AiB must record the fact and the date of the debtor's discharge in the register of insolvencies.','

(e) in subsection (7)—

(i) for 'registers an application' there were substituted 'registers the debtor's discharge',

(ii) in paragraph (b), for 'the application' there were substituted 'the discharge',

(iii) in paragraph (c), for 'the trustee' there were substituted 'the debtor and every creditor known to AiB',

(f) subsections (8) and (10) were omitted.

(12) Section 186 (protected trust deed: discharge of trustee) is to be read as if—

(a) subsection (4) were omitted,

(b) in subsection (8)—

(i) paragraphs (a) and (c) were omitted,

(ii) in paragraph (b), for 'send AiB, for registration', there were substituted 'register'.

(13) Section 188 (protected trust deed: appeal) is to be read as if—
(a) subsections (1)(a) to (d) and (4) were omitted,
(b) in subsection (1)(e), for 'section 184C(4)' there were substituted '184C(2)'.]

[. . .]

Appeals and directions

188 Protected trust deed: appeal

(1) The persons mentioned in subsection (2) may appeal to the sheriff against—

(a) any refusal by AiB to register a trust deed if it is a refusal on the grounds that AiB is not satisfied as mentioned in section 171(2)(c),

(b) any determination by AiB fixing the remuneration payable to the trustee under a protected trust deed,

(c) any direction under section 179(1)[, 184A(6) or 184C(10)] to the trustee, [. . .]

(d) any refusal by AiB under section 184(9)[, or

(e) any determination by AiB under section 184C(4).]

(2) The persons are—

(a) the trustee,

(b) the debtor, if able to satisfy the sheriff that the debtor has, or is likely to have, a pecuniary interest in the outcome of the appeal, and

(c) any creditor, if able to satisfy the sheriff that the creditor has, or is likely to have any such interest in that outcome.

[(2A) The persons mentioned in subsection (2B) may appeal to the sheriff against the outcome of any review undertaken by AiB under section 171B.

(2B) The persons are—

(a) the trustee,

(b) the debtor,

(c) any creditor.

(2C) Where an appeal is brought under subsection (2A), AiB's determination on a review under section 171B is suspended until the determination of that appeal.]

(3) The trustee may appeal to the sheriff against a refusal by the creditors to grant the trustee's discharge under section 186(2).

(4) The debtor may appeal to the sheriff against a refusal by the trustee to [seek agreement from AiB to refuse to discharge the debtor under section 184A(1)].

(5) Any appeal under subsection (1) [or (2A)] must be made within 21 days after the refusal, determination or direction appealed against.

(6) The sheriff to whom any appeal under this section is to be made is the sheriff who, had a petition for the sequestration of the estate been presented at the date the trust deed was granted, would have had jurisdiction to hear that petition in terms of section 15(1) or (3).

(7) The decision of the sheriff on an appeal under this section is final.

189 Protected trust deed: sheriff's direction

(1) Any person with an interest may at any time apply to the sheriff for a direction as regards the administration of a trust under a protected trust deed.

(2) A direction by virtue of subsection (1) may include—

(a) any order the sheriff thinks fit to make in the interests of justice, or

(b) an order to cure any defect in procedure.

(3) The sheriff to whom any application under this section is to be made is the sheriff who, had a petition for the sequestration of the estate been presented at the date the trust deed was granted, would have had jurisdiction to hear that petition in terms of section 15(1) or (3).

[. . .]

193 Interpretation of Part 14

In this Part—

[. . .]

'the date of protection' has the meaning given by section 163(2),

'the notified creditors' has the meaning given by section 170(2),

'the relevant period' means the period of 5 weeks beginning with the date of registration of the notice referred to in section 169,

'remuneration' means reasonable fees and outlays, and

'the trust deed definition' has the meaning given by section 166(1).

194 Regulations modifying Part 14

(1) The Scottish Ministers may by regulations modify (or add to) the provisions of this Part but, subject to subsections (2) and (3), only in so far as corresponding modifications or additions might, before the coming into force of this Part, have been made by virtue of paragraph 5(1) of schedule 5 of the Bankruptcy (Scotland) Act 1985 to the Protected Trust Deeds (Scotland) Regulations 2013 (SSI 2013/318).

(2) Regulations under subsection (1) may make provision enabling applications to be made to the court.

(3) Regulations under subsection (1) may contain such modifications of the provisions of this Act as appear to the Scottish Ministers to be necessary in consequence of those regulations.

PART 15
MORATORIUM ON DILIGENCE

195 Moratorium on diligence: notice of intention to make debtor application under section 2(1)(a)

(1) A person may give written notice to AiB of the person's intention—

(a) to make a debtor application under section 2(1)(a),

(b) to seek to fulfil the conditions required in order for a trust deed granted by or on behalf of that person to be granted the status of protected trust deed, or

(c) to apply for the approval of a debt payment programme in accordance with section 2 of the 2002 Act.

(2) A person may not give notice under subsection (1) if that person has given such notice in the immediately preceding 12 months.

(3) AiB must, without delay after receipt of a notice under subsection (1), enter in the registers mentioned in subsection (4)—

(a) the name of the person who gave the notice, and

(b) such other information as AiB considers appropriate in relation to that person.

(4) The registers are—

(a) the register of insolvencies, and

(b) the register of debt payment programmes (in this Part referred to as the 'DAS register') established and maintained in accordance with section 7 of the 2002 Act.

196 Moratorium on diligence: notice of intention to make debtor application under section 6

(1) A person may give written notice to AiB of the person's intention to make a debtor application under section 6.

(2) A person may not give notice under subsection (1) in respect of an estate if any person has given such notice in respect of the same estate in the immediately preceding 12 months.

(3) AiB must, without delay after receipt of a notice under subsection (1), enter in the register of insolvencies—

(a) the name of the person who is the subject of the notice, and
(b) such other information as AiB considers appropriate in relation to that person.

197 Moratorium on diligence following notice under section 195(1) or 196(1)

(1) This section applies where a person gives notice under section 195(1) or 196(1).

(2) A moratorium on diligence applies in relation to the person who is the subject of the notice for the moratorium period determined in accordance with section 198.

(3) While a moratorium on diligence applies in relation to the person it is not competent—

(a) to serve a charge for payment in respect of any debt owed by the person, or

(b) to commence or execute any diligence to enforce payment of any debt owed by the person,

(c) to found on any debt owed by the person in presenting, or concurring in the presentation of, a petition for sequestration of the person's estate, or

(d) where an arrestment mentioned in subsection (1) of section 73J of the Debtors (Scotland) Act 1987 has been granted in respect of funds due to the person, to release funds to the creditor under subsection (2) of that section.

(4) The moratorium period applying in relation to the person must be disregarded for the purpose of determining the period mentioned in subsection (3) of that section 73J.

(5) Despite subsection (3)(b), it is competent to—

(a) auction an article which has been attached in accordance with the 2002 Act where—

(i) notice has been given to the debtor under section 27(4) of that Act, or

(ii) the article has been removed, or notice of removal has been given, under section 53 of that Act,

(b) implement a decree of furthcoming,

(c) implement a decree or order for sale of a ship (or of a share of a ship) or cargo, or

(d) execute—

(i) an earnings arrestment,

(ii) a current maintenance arrestment, or

(iii) a conjoined arrestment order,

which came into effect before the day on which the moratorium period in relation to the person began.

198 Period of moratorium

(1) The moratorium period applying in relation to a person is the period which—

(a) begins on the day on which an entry is made under section 195(3) or 196(3) in the register of insolvencies, and

(b) ends on—

(i) the day which is [6 months] after that day,

(ii) such earlier day as is mentioned in subsection (2), or

(iii) if subsection (3), (5) or (7) applies, such later day as is determined in accordance with subsection (4), (6) or (8).

(2) The earlier day is the day on which, in relation to the person who is the subject of the moratorium—

(a) an entry is made in the register of insolvencies recording the award of sequestration of the estate,

(b) an entry is made in the register of insolvencies recording that a trust deed granted by the person has been granted or refused protected status,

(c) an entry is made in the DAS register recording the approval of a debt payment programme in accordance with section 2 of the 2002 Act, or

(d) written notice is given to AiB—

(i) by the person withdrawing the notice given under section 195(1), or

(ii) by or on behalf of the person withdrawing the notice given under section 196(1).

(3) This subsection applies if, on the day which is [6 months] after the day on which the moratorium began under subsection (1)(a)—

(a) a debtor application has been made for sequestration of the estate of the person who is the subject of the moratorium,

(b) the moratorium has not ended by virtue of subsection (2)(a), and

(c) no decision has been made by AiB under section 27(7)(b).

(4) Where subsection (3) applies, the moratorium period ends on—

(a) the day on which an entry is made in the register of insolvencies recording the award of sequestration of the estate,

(b) in the case of refusal to award sequestration—

(i) the day of the expiry of the period applying by virtue of section 27(6) where no application for review is made under section 27(5), or

(ii) the day on which a decision is made by AiB under section 27(7)(b) where an application for review is made, or

(c) the day on which written notice is given to AiB—

(i) by the person withdrawing the notice given under section 195(1), or

(ii) by or on behalf of the person withdrawing the notice given under section 196(1).

(5) This subsection applies if, on the day which is [6 months] after the day on which the moratorium began under subsection (1)(a)—

(a) an entry has been made in the register of insolvencies recording an application for a trust deed granted by or on behalf of the person who is the subject of the moratorium to be granted the status of protected trust deed, and

(b) the moratorium has not ended by virtue of subsection (2)(b).

(6) Where subsection (5) applies, the moratorium period ends on—

(a) the day on which an entry is made in the register of insolvencies recording that the trust deed granted by or on behalf of the person has been granted the status of protected trust deed,

(b) where such an entry is not made, the day which is [7 weeks after the day on which the moratorium would have ended but for this subsection], or

(c) the day on which written notice is given to AiB by the person withdrawing the notice given under section 195(1).

(7) This subsection applies if, on the day which is [6 months] after the day on which the moratorium began under subsection (1)(a)—

(a) the person who is the subject of the moratorium has applied for approval of a debt payment programme under section 2 of the 2002 Act,

(b) the moratorium has not ended by virtue of subsection (2)(c), and

(c) the application has not been determined.

(8) Where subsection (7) applies, the moratorium period ends on—

(a) the day on which an entry is made in the DAS register recording the approval of the debt payment programme in accordance with section 2 of the 2002 Act,

(b) in the case of a rejection of a debt payment programme, the day on which an entry is made in the DAS register recording the rejection, or

(c) the day on which written notice is given to AiB by the person withdrawing the notice given under section 195(1).

[(9) The Scottish Ministers may by regulations modify this section so as to vary any of the periods specified in subsections (1)(b)(i), (3), (5), (6)(b) or (7).]

PART 16
ACCOUNTANT IN BANKRUPTCY

Appointment

199 Accountant in Bankruptcy

(1) The Accountant in Bankruptcy (in this Act referred to as 'AiB') is appointed by the Scottish Ministers and is an officer of the court.

(2) The Scottish Ministers may appoint a member of the staff of AiB—

(a) to be Depute Accountant in Bankruptcy, and

(b) as Depute Accountant in Bankruptcy, to exercise all the functions of AiB at any time when AiB is unable to do so.

Functions

200 Supervisory functions of Accountant in Bankruptcy

(1) AiB has, in the administration of sequestration and personal insolvency, the following general functions—

(a) as regards interim trustees (not being AiB), trustees in sequestrations (not being AiB), trustees under protected trust deeds and commissioners—

(i) supervision of the performance by them of the functions conferred on them by this Act, or by any other enactment or by any rule of law, and

(ii) the investigation of any complaints made against them,

(b) the determination of debtor applications,

(c) the maintenance of a register (in this Act referred to as the 'register of insolvencies'), in such form as may be prescribed,

(d) the preparation of an annual report, and

(e) such other functions as may from time to time be conferred on AiB by the Scottish Ministers.

(2) The register of insolvencies is to contain particulars of—

(a) persons who are the subject of notices under sections 195(1) and 196(1),

(b) estates which have been sequestrated,

(c) trust deeds sent to AiB for registration,

(d) bankruptcy restrictions orders and interim bankruptcy restrictions orders,

(e) the winding up and receivership of business associations which the Court of Session has jurisdiction to wind up, and

(f) any other document specified in regulations made under subsection (1) or any other enactment.

(3) The annual report must be presented to the Scottish Ministers and the Court of Session and must contain—

(a) statistical information relating to—

(i) the state of all sequestrations of which particulars have been registered in the register of insolvencies during the year to which the report relates,

(ii) the winding up and receivership of business associations of which particulars have been registered in the register of insolvencies during the year to which the report relates,

(b) particulars of trust deeds registered as protected trust deeds in that year, and

(c) particulars of the performance of AiB's functions under this Act.

(4) If it appears to AiB that a person mentioned in subsection (1)(a) has failed, without reasonable excuse, to perform a duty imposed on that person by any provision of this Act, or by any other enactment or by any rule of law, AiB must report the matter to the sheriff who, after hearing the person on the matter, may—

(a) remove the person from office,

(b) censure the person, or

(c) make such other order as the circumstances of the case may require.

(5) Subsection (6) applies where AiB has reasonable grounds to suspect that an offence has been committed—

(a) by a person mentioned in subsection (1)(a) in the performance of the person's functions under this Act or any other enactment or any rule of law,

(b) in relation to a sequestration, by the debtor in respect of the debtor's assets, the debtor's dealings with them or the debtor's conduct in relation to the debtor's business or financial affairs, or

(c) in relation to a sequestration, by a person other than the debtor in that person's dealings with the debtor, the interim trustee or the trustee in the sequestration in respect of the debtor's assets or the debtor's business or financial affairs.

(6) AiB must report the matter to the Lord Advocate.

(7) AiB must—

(a) make the register of insolvencies available for inspection at all reasonable times, and

(b) provide any person, on request, with a certified copy of an entry in the register.

(8) Regulations under subsection (1)(c) may in particular prescribe circumstances where information need not be in included in the register of insolvencies if, in the opinion of AiB, inclusion of the information would be likely to jeopardise the safety or welfare of any person.

(9) In subsections (2) and (3), 'business association' has the meaning given in section C2 of Part 2 of schedule 5 of the Scotland Act 1998.

201 Performance of certain functions of Accountant in Bankruptcy

(1) The functions of AiB, other than functions conferred by section 200, may be carried out on AiB's behalf by any member of AiB's staff authorised by AiB to do so.

(2) Without prejudice to subsection (1), AiB may appoint, on such terms and conditions as AiB considers appropriate, such persons as AiB considers fit to perform on AiB's behalf any of AiB's functions in respect of the sequestration of the estate of any debtor.

(3) A person appointed under subsection (2) must comply with such general or specific directions as AiB may from time to time give to such person as to the performance of those functions.

(4) AiB may pay a person so appointed such fee as AiB may consider appropriate.

202 Further duty of Accountant in Bankruptcy

AiB is, on receiving any notice under section 109(1) of the Insolvency Act 1986 in relation to a community interest company, to forward a copy of that notice to the Regulator of Community Interest Companies.

Directions to Accountant in Bankruptcy

203 Directions to Accountant in Bankruptcy

(1) The Scottish Ministers may, after consultation with the Lord President of the Court of Session, give AiB general directions as to the performance of AiB's functions under this Act.

(2) Directions under this section may be given in respect of—

(a) all cases, or

(b) any class or description of cases,

but are not to be given in respect of a particular case.

(3) AiB must comply with any directions given under this section.

Conduct of proceedings in the sheriff court

204 Conduct of proceedings in the sheriff court

(1) A person authorised by AiB may conduct civil proceedings in the sheriff court in relation to a function of AiB (including the functions listed in section 200).

(2) In subsection (1), 'civil proceedings' are proceedings which are not in respect of an offence.

Fees for Accountant in Bankruptcy

205 Fees for Accountant in Bankruptcy

(1) The Scottish Ministers may prescribe—

(a) the fees and outlays to be payable to AiB in respect of the exercise of any of AiB's functions under this Act,

(b) the time at or by which, and the manner in which, such fees and outlays are to be paid, and

(c) the circumstances, if any, in which AiB may allow—

(i) exemption from payment, or

(ii) the remission or modification of payment,

of any such fees or outlays.

(2) The Secretary of State may prescribe by regulations—

(a) the fees and outlays to be payable to AiB in respect of the exercise of any of AiB's functions under the Insolvency Act 1986,

(b) the time at or by which, and the manner in which, such fees and outlays are to be paid, and

(c) the circumstances, if any, in which AiB may allow—

(i) exemption from payment, or

(ii) the remission or modification of payment,

PART 17
MISCELLANEOUS

206 Liabilities and rights of co-obligants

(1) Where a creditor has an obligant bound to the creditor along with the debtor for the whole or part of the debt, the obligant is not freed or discharged from the obligant's liability for the debt by reason of the discharge of the debtor or by virtue of the creditor's voting or drawing a dividend or assenting to, or not opposing, the discharge of the debtor.

(2) Subsection (3) applies where—

(a) the creditor has had a claim accepted in whole or in part, and

(b) the obligant holds a security over any part of the debtor's estate

(3) The obligant must account to the trustee in the sequestration so as to put the estate in the same position as if the obligant had paid the debt to the creditor and thereafter had had the obligant's claim accepted in whole or in part in the sequestration after deduction of the value of the security.

(4) The obligant may require and obtain at the obligant's own expense from the creditor an assignation of the debt on payment of the amount of the debt and on that being done may in respect of the debt submit a claim, and vote and draw a dividend, if otherwise legally entitled to do so.

(5) Subsection (4) is without prejudice to any right, under any rule of law, of a co-obligant who has paid the debt.

(6) In this section, 'obligant' includes cautioner.

[. . .]

209 Extortionate credit transactions

(1) This section applies where—

(a) a debtor is, or has been, party to a transaction for, or involving, the provision of credit to the debtor, and

(b) the debtor's estate is sequestrated.

(2) The sheriff may, on the application of the trustee in the sequestration, make an order with respect to the transaction if the transaction—

(a) is, or was, extortionate, and

(b) was not entered into more than 3 years before the date of sequestration.

(3) For the purposes of this section a transaction is extortionate if, having regard to the risk accepted by the person providing the credit—

(a) the terms of the transaction are, or were, such as to require grossly exorbitant payments to be made (whether unconditionally or in certain contingencies) in respect of the provision of the credit, or

(b) the transaction otherwise grossly contravened ordinary principles of fair dealing.

(4) It is to be presumed, unless the contrary is proved, that a transaction with respect to which an application is made under this section is, or as the case may be was, extortionate.

(5) An order under this section with respect to a transaction may contain such one or more of the following as the sheriff thinks fit—

(a) provision setting aside the whole or part of any obligation created by the transaction,

(b) provision otherwise varying the terms of the transaction or varying the terms on which any security for the purposes of the transaction is held,

(c) provision requiring any person who is a party to the transaction to pay to the trustee any sums paid to that person, by virtue of the transaction, by the debtor,

(d) provision requiring any person to surrender to the trustee any property held by the person as security for the purposes of the transaction,

(e) provision directing accounts to be taken between any persons.

(6) Any sums required to be paid, or property required to be surrendered, to the trustee in accordance with an order under this section vest in the trustee.

(7) The powers conferred by this section are exercisable, in relation to a transaction, concurrently with any powers exercisable under this Act in relation to that transaction as a gratuitous alienation or unfair preference.

(8) In this section, 'credit' has the same meaning as in the Consumer Credit Act 1974.

210 Sederunt book and other documents

(1) Whoever by virtue of this Act for the time being holds the sederunt book must make it available for inspection at all reasonable hours by any interested party; but this subsection is subject to subsection (2).

(2) As regards any case in which the person on whom a duty is imposed by subsection (1) is AiB, the Scottish Ministers may by regulations—

(a) limit the period for which the duty is so imposed, and

(b) prescribe conditions in accordance with which the duty is to be carried out.

(3) The trustee must insert in the sederunt book the information listed in schedule 5.

(4) The Scottish Ministers may by regulations modify schedule 5.

(5) An entry in the sederunt book is sufficient evidence of the facts stated in that entry, (except where the entry is founded on by the trustee in the sequestration in the trustee's own interest).

(6) Notwithstanding any provision of this Act, the trustee is not bound to insert in the sederunt book a document of a confidential nature.

(7) The trustee is not bound to exhibit to a person other than a commissioner or AiB any document in the trustee's possession which is of a confidential nature.

(8) An extract from the register of insolvencies bearing to be signed by AiB is sufficient evidence of the facts stated in the extract.

211 Power of court to cure defects in procedure

(1) On the application of a person having an interest, the sheriff may—

(a) if there has been a failure to comply with a requirement of this Act (or of regulations under this Act), make an order—

(i) waiving the failure, and

(ii) so far as practicable, restoring any person prejudiced by the failure to the position that person would have been in but for the failure, or

(b) if for any reason anything required or authorised to be done in, or in connection with, the sequestration process cannot be done, make such order as may be necessary to enable the thing to be done.

(2) An order under subsection (1) may waive a failure to comply with a requirement mentioned in section 212(1)(a) or (b) only if the failure relates to—

(a) a document to be lodged with the sheriff,

(b) a document issued by the sheriff, or

(c) a time limit specified in relation to proceedings before the sheriff or a document relating to those proceedings.

(3) In an order under subsection (1), the sheriff may impose such conditions, including conditions as to expenses, as the sheriff thinks fit and may—

(a) authorise, or dispense with, the performance of any act in the sequestration process,

(b) appoint as trustee on the debtor's estate AiB or a person who would be eligible to be elected under section 49 (whether or not in place of an existing trustee),

(c) extend or waive a time limit specified in or under this Act.

(4) Subsection (5) applies where the sheriff, or as the case may be the Court of Session, considers that a remit from the sheriff to the Court of Session is desirable because of the importance or complexity of the matters raised by an application under subsection (1).

(5) The application—

(a) may at any time be so remitted—

(i) of the sheriff's own accord, or

(ii) on an application by a person having an interest, and

(b) must be so remitted, if the Court of Session so directs on an application by any such person.

212 Power of Accountant in Bankruptcy to cure defects in procedure

(1) AiB may make an order—

(a) correcting a clerical or incidental error in a document required by or under this Act, or

(b) waiving a failure—

(i) to comply with a time limit specified by or under this Act, and

(ii) for which no provision is made by or under this Act.

(2) An order under subsection (1) may be made—

(a) on the application of any person having an interest, or

(b) without an application if AiB proposes to correct or waive a matter mentioned in that subsection.

(3) The applicant must notify all interested persons where an application is made under subsection (2)(a).

(4) AiB must notify all interested persons where AiB proposes to make an order by virtue of subsection (2)(b).

(5) A notice under subsection (3) or (4) must inform the recipient that the recipient has a right to make representations to AiB in relation to the application or the proposed order within 14 days beginning with the day on which the notice is given.

(6) Before making an order under subsection (1), AiB must take into account any representations made by an interested person.

(7) An order under subsection (1) may—

(a) so far as practicable, restore any person prejudiced by the error or failure to the position that person would have been in but for the error or failure, and

(b) impose such conditions, including conditions as to expenses, as AiB thinks fit.

(8) After making an order under subsection (1) which affects a matter recorded in the Register of Inhibitions, AiB must without delay send a certified copy of the order to the keeper of that register for recording in that register.

213 Decision under section 212(1): review

(1) An interested person may apply to AiB for a review of a decision of AiB to make, or refuse to make, an order under section 212(1).

(2) Any application under subsection (1) must be made within 14 days beginning with the day of that decision.

(3) If an application under subsection (1) is made, AiB must—

(a) take into account any representations made by an interested person within 21 days beginning with the day on which the application is made, and

(b) confirm, amend or revoke the decision within 28 days beginning with the day on which the application is made.

(4) An interested person may appeal to the sheriff against a decision by AiB under subsection (3)(b) within 14 days beginning with the day of that decision.

(5) The decision of the sheriff on an appeal under subsection (4) is final.

214 Review of decision by Accountant in Bankruptcy: grounds of appeal

(1) For the avoidance of doubt, an appeal under a provision mentioned in subsection (2) may be made on—

(a) a matter of fact,

(b) a point of law, or

(c) the merits.

(2) The provisions are—

(a) section 27(8),

(b) section 37(5),

(c) section 52(7),

(d) section 57(8),

(e) section 59(4),

(f) section 61(8),

(g) section 64(8),

(h) section 65(7),

(i) section 68(4),

(j) section 71(4),

(k) section 73(5),

(l) section 92(5),

(m) section 97(5),

(n) section 110(7),

(o) section 127(5),

(p) section 139(6),

(q) section 144(6),

[(qa) section 147B(5),]

(r) section 149(4),

(s) section 151(7),

(t) section 161(8),

(u) section 213(4), and

(v) paragraph 3(9) of schedule 2.

215 Debtor to co-operate with trustee

(1) The debtor must take every practicable step (and in particular must execute any document) which may be necessary to enable the trustee in the sequestration to perform the functions conferred on the trustee by this Act.

(2) If the sheriff, on the trustee's application, is satisfied—

(a) that the debtor has failed to execute a document in compliance with subsection (1), the sheriff may authorise the sheriff clerk to do so, or

(b) that the debtor has failed to comply in any other respect with that subsection, the sheriff may order the debtor to do so.

(3) The execution, by virtue of paragraph (a) of subsection (2), of a document by the sheriff clerk has the like force and effect in all respects as if it had been executed by the debtor.

(4) If the debtor fails to comply with an order under subsection (2)(b) then the debtor commits an offence.

(5) If the debtor is convicted of an offence under subsection (4) then the debtor is liable—

(a) on summary conviction, to a fine not exceeding the statutory maximum, or—

(i) in a case where the debtor has previously been convicted of an offence inferring dishonest appropriation of property or an attempt at dishonest appropriation of property, to imprisonment for a term not exceeding 6 months, or

(ii) in any other case, to imprisonment for a term not exceeding 3 months,

or both to a fine not exceeding the statutory maximum and to such imprisonment as is mentioned, in relation to the case in question, in sub-paragraph (i) or (ii),

(b) on conviction on indictment—

(i) to a fine or to imprisonment for a term not exceeding 2 years, or

(ii) both to a fine and to such imprisonment.

(6) In this section, 'debtor' includes a debtor discharged under this Act.

216 Arbitration and compromise

(1) The trustee in the sequestration may (but if there are commissioners then only with their consent or with the consent of the creditors or of the sheriff)—

(a) refer to arbitration any claim or question, of whatever nature, arising in the course of the sequestration, or

(b) make a compromise with regard to any claim, of whatever nature, made against or on behalf of the sequestrated estate.

(2) Where a claim or question is referred to arbitration under this section, AiB may vary any time limit for carrying out a procedure under this Act.

(3) A decree arbitral on a reference under paragraph (a) of subsection (1), or a compromise under paragraph (b) of that subsection, is binding on the creditors and on the debtor.

217 Meetings of creditors and commissioners

Part 1 of schedule 6 has effect in relation to meetings of creditors other than the statutory meeting, Part 2 in relation to all meetings of creditors and Part 3 in relation to meetings of commissioners.

218 General offences by debtor etc

(1) Subsection (2) applies where, during the relevant period, a debtor makes a false statement in relation to the debtor's assets or financial or business affairs —

(a) to a creditor, or

(b) to a person concerned in the administration of the debtor's estate.

(2) Unless the debtor shows that the debtor neither knew nor had reason to believe that the statement was false, the debtor commits an offence.

(3) Subsection (4) applies where, during the relevant period, a debtor or some other person acting in the debtor's interest (whether or not with the debtor's authority)—

(a) destroys,
(b) damages,
(c) conceals,
(d) disposes of, or
(e) removes from Scotland,

any part of the debtor's estate or any document relating to the debtor's assets or business or financial affairs.

(4) Unless the perpetrator shows that it was not done with intent to prejudice the creditors, the perpetrator commits an offence.

(5) If, after the date of sequestration of the estate of a debtor, the debtor (being a person who is absent from Scotland) fails when required by the court to come to Scotland for any purpose connected with the administration of that estate, then the debtor commits an offence.

(6) Subsection (7) applies where, during the relevant period, a debtor or some other person acting in the debtor's interest (whether or not with the debtor's authority) falsifies any document relating to the debtor's assets or business or financial affairs.

(7) Unless the perpetrator shows that the perpetrator had no intention to mislead the trustee, a commissioner or any creditor, the perpetrator commits an offence.

(8) If a debtor whose estate is sequestrated—

(a) knows that a person has falsified a document relating to the debtor's assets or business or financial affairs, and

(b) fails, within one month of acquiring that knowledge, to report it to the trustee in the sequestration,

then the debtor commits an offence.

(9) Subsection (10) applies where, during the relevant period, a person (in this subsection and in subsection (10) referred to as 'P') who is absolutely insolvent—

(a) transfers anything to another person for an inadequate consideration, or
(b) grants an unfair preference to any of P's creditors.

(10) Unless P shows that it was not done with intent to prejudice P's creditors, P commits an offence.

(11) Subsection (12) applies where, at any time in the period of one year ending with the sequestration of the estate of a debtor who is engaged in trade or business, the debtor otherwise than in the ordinary course of the trade or business pledges or disposes of property which the debtor has obtained on credit and has not paid for.

(12) Unless the debtor shows that it was not done with intent to prejudice the debtor's creditors, the debtor commits an offence.

(13) If a debtor, either alone or jointly with another person, obtains credit—

(a) to the extent of £2,000 or such other sum as may be prescribed or more, *or*

(b) of any amount where, at the time the credit is obtained, the debtor has debts amounting to £1,000 or such other sum as may be prescribed or more,

without giving the person from whom the credit is obtained the relevant information about the debtor's status, then the debtor commits an offence.

219 General offences: supplementary and penalties

(1) For the purpose of calculating an amount of credit mentioned in subsection (13) of section 218 or of debts mentioned in paragraph (b) of that subsection, no account is to be taken of any credit obtained or, as the case may be, of any liability for charges in respect of—

(a) any of the supplies mentioned in section 222(4), and

(b) any council tax (within the meaning of section 99(1) of the Local Government Finance Act 1992.

(2) For the purposes of section 218(13)—

(a) 'debtor' means—

(i) a person whose estate has been sequestrated,

(ii) a person who has been adjudged bankrupt in England and Wales or in Northern Ireland, or

(iii) a person subject to a bankruptcy restrictions order, or a bankruptcy restrictions undertaking, made in England and Wales,

being, in the case of a person mentioned in sub-paragraph (i) or (ii), a person who has not been discharged,

(b) the reference to the debtor obtaining credit includes a reference to a case where goods—

(i) are hired to the debtor under a hire-purchase agreement, or

(ii) are agreed to be sold to the debtor under a conditional sale agreement, and

(c) the 'relevant information' about the status of the debtor is the information that (as the case may be)—

(i) the debtor's estate has been sequestrated and that the debtor has not been discharged,

(ii) the debtor is an undischarged bankrupt in England and Wales or in Northern Ireland, or

(iii) the debtor is subject to a bankruptcy restrictions order, or a bankruptcy restrictions undertaking, made in England and Wales.

(3) In section 218—

'the relevant period' means the period commencing one year immediately before the date of sequestration of the debtor's estate and ending with the debtor's discharge, and

references to intent to prejudice creditors include references to intent to prejudice an individual creditor.

(4) If a person does, or fails to do, in England and Wales or in Northern Ireland anything which if done, or as the case may be not done, in Scotland is an offence under section 218(2), (4), (7), (8), (10) or (12), then that person commits an offence under the subsection in question.

(5) A person convicted of an offence under section 218 is liable—

(a) on summary conviction, to a fine not exceeding the statutory maximum, or—

(i) in a case where the person has previously been convicted of an offence inferring dishonest appropriation of property or an attempt at dishonest appropriation of property, to imprisonment for a term not exceeding 6 months, or

(ii) in any other case, to imprisonment for a term not exceeding 3 months,

or both to a fine not exceeding the statutory maximum and to such imprisonment as is mentioned, in relation to the case in question, in sub-paragraph (i) or (ii), or

(b) on conviction on indictment, to a fine, or—

(i) in the case of an offence under section 218(2), (4), (7) or (12), to imprisonment for a term not exceeding 5 years, or

(ii) in any other case, to imprisonment for a term not exceeding 2 years,

or both to a fine and to such imprisonment as is mentioned, in relation to the case in question, in sub-paragraph (i) or (ii).

220 Summary proceedings

(1) Summary proceedings for an offence under this Act may be commenced at any time within 12 months after the date on which evidence sufficient in the opinion of the Lord Advocate to justify the proceedings comes to the Lord Advocate's knowledge.

(2) But such proceedings must not be commenced by virtue of this section more than 3 years after the commission of the offence.

(3) Section 136(3) of the Criminal Procedure (Scotland) Act 1995 (date of commencement of summary proceedings) has effect for the purposes of this section as it has for the purposes of that section.

(4) For the purposes of subsection (1), a certificate of the Lord Advocate as to the date on which the evidence in question came to the Lord Advocate's knowledge is conclusive evidence of the date on which it did so.

221 Outlays of insolvency practitioner in actings as interim trustee or trustee
The Scottish Ministers may, by regulations, provide for the premium (or a proportionate part of the premium) of any bond of caution or other security required, for the time being, to be given by an insolvency practitioner to be taken into account as part of the outlays of the practitioner in the practitioner's actings as an interim trustee or as trustee in the sequestration.

222 Supplies by utilities

(1) This section applies where on any day ('the relevant day')—

(a) sequestration is awarded in a case where a debtor application was made,

(b) a warrant is granted under section 22(3) in a case where the petition was presented by a creditor or by a trustee acting under a trust deed, or

(c) the debtor grants a trust deed.

(2) If a request falling within subsection (3) is made for the giving, after the relevant day, of any of the supplies mentioned in subsection (4), the supplier—

(a) may make it a condition of the giving of the supply that the office holder personally guarantee the payment of any charges in respect of the supply, and

(b) is not to make it a condition (or to do anything which has the effect of making it a condition) of the giving of the supply that any outstanding charges in respect of a supply given to the debtor before the relevant day are paid.

(3) A request falls within this subsection if it is made—

(a) by or with the concurrence of the office holder, and

(b) for the purposes of any business which is, or has been, carried on by or on behalf of the debtor.

(4) The supplies are—

(a) a supply of gas by a gas supplier, within the meaning of Part 1 of the Gas Act 1986,

[(aa) a supply of gas by a person within paragraph 1 of schedule 2A of the Gas Act 1986 (supply by landlords etc),]

(b) a supply of electricity by an electricity supplier, within the meaning of Part 1 of the Electricity Act 1989,

[(ba) a supply of electricity by a class of person within Class A (small suppliers) or Class B (resale) of schedule 4 of the Electricity (Class Exemptions from the Requirement for a Licence) Order 2001 (SI 2001/3270),]

(c) a supply of water by Scottish Water,

[(ca) a supply of water by a water services provider within the meaning of the Water Services etc (Scotland) Act 2005,

(cb) a supply of water by a person who has an interest in the premises to which the supply is given,]

(d) a supply of communications services by a provider of a public electronic communications service.

[(e) a supply of communications services by a person who carries on a business which includes giving such supplies, and

(f) a supply of goods or services mentioned in subsection (5A) by a person who carries on a business which includes giving such supplies, where the supply is for the purpose of enabling or facilitating anything to be done by electronic means.]

(5) In subsection (4)(d) 'communications services' do not include electronic communications services to the extent that they are used to broadcast, or otherwise transmit, programme services (within the meaning of the Communications Act 2003).

[(5A) The goods and services referred to in subsection (4)(f) are—
(a) point of sale terminals,
(b) computer hardware and software,
(c) information, advice and technical assistance in connection with the use of information technology,
(d) data storage and processing,
(e) website hosting.]
(6) In this section, 'the office holder' means, as the case may be—
(a) the interim trustee,
(b) the trustee in the sequestration, or
(c) the trustee acting under a trust deed.

223 Disqualification provisions: power to make regulations

(1) The Scottish Ministers may make regulations under this section in relation to a disqualification provision.
(2) A 'disqualification provision' is a provision, made by or under any enactment, which disqualifies (whether permanently or temporarily and whether absolutely or conditionally) a relevant debtor or a category of relevant debtors from—
(a) being elected or appointed to an office or position,
(b) holding an office or position, or
(c) becoming or remaining a member of a body or group.
(3) In subsection (2), the reference to a provision which disqualifies a person conditionally includes a reference to a provision which enables the person to be dismissed.
(4) Regulations under subsection (1) may repeal or revoke the disqualification provision.
(5) Regulations under subsection (1) may amend, or modify the effect of, the disqualification provision—
(a) so as to reduce the category of relevant debtors to whom the disqualification provision applies,
(b) so as to extend the disqualification provision to some or all natural persons who are subject to a bankruptcy restrictions order,
(c) so that the disqualification provision applies only to some or all natural persons who are subject to a bankruptcy restrictions order,
(d) so as to make the application of the disqualification provision wholly or partly subject to the discretion of a specified person, body or group.
(6) Regulations made by virtue of subsection (5)(d) may provide for a discretion to be subject to—
(a) the approval of a specified person or body,
(b) appeal to a specified person, body, court or tribunal.
(7) The Scottish Ministers may be specified for the purposes of subsection (5)(d) or (6)(a) or (b).
(8) In this section, 'bankruptcy restrictions order' includes—
(a) a bankruptcy restrictions order made under paragraph 1 of schedule 4A of the Insolvency Act 1986, and
(b) a bankruptcy restrictions undertaking entered into under paragraph 7 of that schedule.
(9) In this section, 'relevant debtor' means a debtor—
(a) whose estate has been sequestrated,
(b) who has granted (or on whose behalf has been granted) a trust deed,
(c) who has been adjudged bankrupt by a court in England and Wales or in Northern Ireland, or
(d) who, in England and Wales or in Northern Ireland, has made an agreement with the debtor's creditors—
(i) for a composition in satisfaction of the debtor's debts,
(ii) for a scheme of arrangement of the debtor's affairs, or
(iii) for some other kind of settlement or arrangement.

(10) Regulations under this section may make—
(a) provision generally or for a specified purpose only,
(b) different provision for different purposes, and
(c) transitional, consequential or incidental provision.

224 Regulations: applications to Accountant in Bankruptcy etc

(1) The Scottish Minsters may, by regulations, make provision in relation to the procedure to be followed in relation to—
(a) an application to AiB under this Act,
(b) an application to AiB for a review under this Act,
(c) any other decision made by AiB under this Act.

(2) In this section, 'decision' includes any appointment, determination, direction, award, acceptance, rejection, adjudication, requirement, declaration, order or valuation made by AiB.

(3) Regulations under subsection (1) may in particular make provision for, or in connection with—
(a) the procedure to be followed by the person making an application,
(b) the form of any report or other document that may be required for the purposes of an application or a decision,
(c) the form of a statement of undertakings that must be given by the debtor when making a debtor application,
(d) time limits applying in relation to the procedure,
(e) the procedure to be followed in connection with the production and recovery of documents relating to an application or a decision,
(f) the procedure to be followed (including provision about those entitled to participate) in determining an application or making a decision, and
(g) the procedure to be followed after an application is determined or a decision is made.

(4) Regulations under subsection (1) may—
(a) include such supplementary, incidental or consequential provision as the Scottish Minsters consider appropriate, or
(b) modify any enactment (including this Act).

(5) This section is without prejudice to section 194.

[224A Service of documents

(1) Where a provision of this Act or of any regulations made under it authorises or requires a document to be served on a person (whether the expression 'serve', 'give', 'send' or any other expression is used), the document may be served on the person—
(a) by being delivered personally to the person,
(b) by being sent to the proper address of the person—
(i) by a registered post service (as defined in section 125(1) of the Postal Services Act 2000), or
(ii) by a postal service which provides for the delivery of the document to be recorded, or
(c) by being transmitted to the person electronically.

(2) For the purpose of subsection (1)(b), the proper address of a person is—
(a) in the case of a body corporate, the address of the registered or principal office of the body,
(b) in the case of a partnership, the address of the principal office of the partnership,
(c) in any other case, the last known address of the person.

(3) Where a document is served as mentioned in subsection (1)(b) on an address in the United Kingdom it is to be taken to have been received 48 hours after it is sent unless the contrary is shown.

(4) For the purpose of subsection (1)(c)—

(a) electronic transmission of a document must be effected in a way that the recipient has indicated to the sender that the recipient is willing to receive the document,

(b) the recipient's indication of willingness to receive a document in a particular way may be—

(i) specific to the document in question or generally applicable to documents of that kind,

(ii) expressed specifically to the sender or generally (for example on a website),

(iii) inferred from the recipient having previously been willing to receive documents from the sender in that way and not having indicated unwillingness to do so again,

(c) the sender's uploading of a document to an electronic storage system from which the recipient is able to download the document may constitute electronic transmission of the document, where the recipient is sent a notification that the document has been uploaded in that way,

(d) a notice transmitted electronically is taken to have been received on the day of transmission unless the contrary is shown.

(5) This section does not apply where some other form of delivery is required by rules of court or by order of the court.]

PART 18
GENERAL

225 Regulations: general

(1) This section relates to regulations made under this Act by the Scottish Ministers.

(2) Such regulations may make different provision for different cases or classes of case.

(3) Subject to subsections (4) and (5), the regulations are subject to the negative procedure.

(4) Regulations under—

(a) section 2(4), (5) or (8)(a), 4(2)(b), 7(1), 9(4), 89(1), 94(7), 112(7)(g), 166(2)(b) or (c), 169, 170(1)(b) or (e), 174(2) or (3), 175(1), 181(2), 183(1)(a) or (b), 184(1)(b) or (2)(a), 186(3) or (9), 194(1) [, 198(9)] or 223,

(b) section 224(1) and containing provisions which add to, replace or omit any part of the text of an Act or of an Act of the Scottish Parliament, or

(c) paragraph 2(7) of schedule 1, are subject to the affirmative procedure.

(5) Regulations made under section 237(2) are not subject to the negative procedure or to the affirmative procedure.

[. . .]

227 Variation of references to time, money etc

For any reference in this Act to—

(a) a period of time,

(b) an amount of money, or

(c) a fraction,

there may be prescribed, in substitution, some other period or as the case may be some other amount or fraction.

228 Interpretation

(1) In this Act, unless the context otherwise requires—

'the 2002 Act' means the Debt Arrangement and Attachment (Scotland) Act 2002,

'Accountant in Bankruptcy' (or 'AiB') is to be construed in accordance with section 199, 'accounting period' is to be construed in accordance with section 130(2), 'apparent insolvency' and 'apparently insolvent' are to be construed in accordance with section 16,

'appropriate bank or institution' means—

(a) the Bank of England,

(b) a person who has permission under Part 4 of the Financial Services and Markets Act 2000 to accept deposits,

(c) an EEA firm of the kind mentioned in paragraph 5(b) of schedule 3 of that Act which has permission under paragraph 15 of that schedule (as a result of qualifying for authorisation under paragraph 12 of that schedule) to accept deposits, or

(d) a person who is exempt from the general prohibition in respect of accepting deposits as a result of an exemption order made under section 38(1) of that Act,

'associate' is to be construed in accordance with section 229,

'bankruptcy restrictions order' has the meaning given by section 155(1),

'business' means the carrying on of any activity, whether for profit or not,

'centre of main interests' has the same meaning as in the [EU] insolvency proceedings regulation,

'commissioner', except in the expression 'examining commissioner', is to be construed in accordance with section 76,

'common financial tool' has the meaning given by section 89(1),

'court' means Court of Session or sheriff,

[. . .]

'DAS register' has the meaning given by section 195(4)(b),

'date of sequestration' has the meaning given by section 22(7),

'debt advice and information package' has the meaning given by section 3(2),

'debtor' includes, without prejudice to the expression's generality, an entity whose estate may be sequestrated by virtue of section 6, a deceased debtor, a deceased debtor's executor or a person entitled to be appointed a deceased debtor's executor,

'debtor application' means an application for sequestration made to AiB under section 2(1)(a), 5(a) or 6(3)(a), (4)(b) or (7)(a),

'debtor contribution order' has the meaning given by section 90(1),

'debtor's contribution' has the meaning given by section 89(1),

[. . .]

'establishment' has the meaning given by [Article 2(10) of the EU] insolvency proceedings regulation,

['the EU insolvency proceedings regulation' means Regulation (EU) 2015/848 of the European Parliament and of the Council on insolvency proceedings [as it forms part of domestic law on and after exit day;]]

'examination' means a private examination under section 118 or a public examination under section 119,

'examining commissioner' is to be construed in accordance with section 120(3),

'interim bankruptcy restrictions order' is to be construed in accordance with section 160,

'interim trustee' is to be construed in accordance with sections 53 and 54,

[. . .]

'money adviser' has the meaning given by section 4(2),

[. . .]

'original trustee' is to be construed in accordance with section 49(1)(a),

'postponed debt' has the meaning given by section 129(4),

'preferred debt' has the meaning given by section 129(2),

'prescribed' means prescribed by regulations made by the Scottish Ministers,

'protected trust deed' is to be construed in accordance with section 163, 'qualified creditor' and 'qualified creditors' are to be construed in accordance with section 7(1),

'qualified to act as an insolvency practitioner' is to be construed in accordance with section 390 of the Insolvency Act 1986 (persons not qualified to act as insolvency practitioners),

'register of insolvencies' has the meaning given by section 200(1)(c),

'relevant person' has the meaning given by section 118(2),

'replacement trustee' is to be construed in accordance with section 49(1)(b),

[...]

'secured creditor' means a creditor who holds a security for a debt over any part of the debtor's estate,

'security' means any security, heritable or moveable, or any right of lien, retention or preference,

'sederunt book' means the sederunt book maintained under section 50(1)(e),

'sequestration proceedings' includes a debtor application (and analogous expressions are to be construed accordingly),

'statement of assets and liabilities' means a document (including a copy of a document) in such form as may be prescribed containing—

(a) a list of the debtor's assets and liabilities,

(b) a list of the debtor's income and expenditure, and

(c) such other information as may be prescribed,

'statement of undertakings' means the statement of debtor undertakings sent to the debtor under section 51(14) or 54(4) or, in the case of a debtor application, given by the debtor in making the application,

'statutory meeting' has the meaning given by section 43,

[...]

'trust deed' means—

(a) a voluntary trust deed granted by or on behalf of a debtor whereby the debtor's estate (other than such of that estate as would not, under any provision of this or any other enactment, vest in the trustee were that estate sequestrated) is conveyed to the trustee for the benefit of the debtor's creditors generally, and

(b) any other trust deed which would fall within paragraph (a) but for—

(i) the exclusion from the estate conveyed to the trustee of the whole or part of the debtor's dwellinghouse, where a secured creditor holds a security over it, and

(ii) the fact that the debtor's estate is not conveyed to the trustee for the benefit of creditors generally because the secured creditor has, at the debtor's request, agreed before the trust deed is granted not to claim under the trust deed for any of the debt in respect of which the security is held,

'trustee vote' is to be construed in accordance with section 49(1) and (2), and

'unfair preference' means a preference created as is mentioned in subsection (1) of section 99 by a transaction to which subsection (5) of that section applies.

(2) The expressions in the definition of 'appropriate bank or institution' in subsection (1) must be read with—

(a) section 22 of the Financial Services and Markets Act 2000,

(b) any relevant order under that section, and

(c) schedule 2 of that Act.

(3) In paragraph (b)(i) of the definition of 'trust deed' in subsection (1), 'the debtor's dwellinghouse' means a dwellinghouse (including any yard, garden, outbuilding or other pertinents) which, on the day immediately preceding the date the trust deed was granted—

(a) the debtor (whether alone or in common with any other person)—

(i) owned, or

(ii) leased under a long lease ('long lease' having the same meaning as in section 9(2) of the Land Registration etc (Scotland) Act 2012), and

(b) was the debtor's sole or main residence.

(4) For the purposes of subsection (3)(b), a dwellinghouse may be the debtor's sole or main residence irrespective of whether it is used, to any extent, by the debtor for the purposes of any profession, trade or business.

(5) Any reference in this Act to a debtor being absolutely insolvent is to be construed as a reference to the debtor's liabilities being greater than the debtor's assets; and any reference to a debtor's estate being absolutely insolvent is to be construed accordingly.

(6) Any reference in this Act to value of the creditors is, in relation to any matter, a reference to the value of their claims as accepted for the purposes of that matter.

(7) Any reference in this Act to 'the creditors' in the context of their giving consent or doing any other thing is, unless the context otherwise requires, to be construed as a reference to the majority in value of such creditors as vote in that context at a meeting of creditors.

(8) Any reference in this Act to any of the actings mentioned in subsection (9) barring the effect of any enactment or rule of law relating to the limitation of actions is to be construed as a reference to that act having the same effect, for the purposes of that enactment or rule of law, as an effective acknowledgement of the creditor's claim.

(9) The actings are—

(a) the presentation of a petition for sequestration,

(b) the concurrence in a debtor application, and

(c) the submission of a claim.

(10) Any reference in this Act to any such enactment as is mentioned in subsection (8) does not include a reference to an enactment which implements or gives effect to any international agreement or obligation.

(11) Any reference in this Act, however expressed, to the time when a petition for sequestration is presented is to be construed as a reference to the time when the petition is received by the sheriff clerk.

(12) Any reference in this Act, however expressed, to the time when a debtor application is made is to be construed as a reference to the time when the application is received by AiB.

229 Meaning of 'associate'

(1) For the purposes of this Act, any question whether a person is an associate of another person must be determined in accordance with the following provisions of this section.

(2) Subsection (1) is subject to section 230(1).

(3) And any reference, whether in the following provisions of this section or in regulations under section 230(1), to a person being an associate of another person is to be taken to be a reference to their being associates of each other.

(4) A person (in this subsection referred to as 'A') is an associate of a natural person (in this subsection referred to as 'B') if A is—

(a) B's spouse or civil partner,

(b) a relative of B or of B's spouse or civil partner, or

(c) the spouse or civil partner of such a relative.

(5) A person (in this subsection referred to as 'C') is an associate of any person (in this subsection referred to as 'D') with whom C is in partnership and of any person who is an associate of D.

(6) A firm is an associate of any person who is a member of the firm.

(7) For the purposes of this section, a person (in this subsection referred to as 'E') is a relative of a natural person (in this subsection referred to as 'F') if E is F's brother, sister, uncle, aunt, nephew, niece, lineal ancestor or lineal descendant treating any relationship of the half-blood as a relationship of the whole-blood and the stepchild or adopted child of someone (in this subsection referred to as 'S') as S's child.

(8) References in this section to a spouse or civil partner include references to a former spouse or civil partner and a reputed spouse or civil partner.

(9) A person (in this subsection referred to as 'G') is an associate of any person whom G employs or by whom G is employed.

(10) For the purposes of subsection (9), any director or other officer of a company is to be treated as employed by the company.

(11) A company is an associate of another company if—

(a) the same person has control of both, or if a person (in this subsection referred to as 'H') has control of one and persons who are H's associates have control of the other, or

(b) a group of two or more persons has control of each company and the groups either—

(i) consist of the same persons, or

(ii) could be regarded as consisting of the same persons by treating (in one case or more) a member of either group as replaced by a person of whom that member is an associate.

(12) A company is an associate of another person (in this subsection referred to as 'J') if—

(a) J has control of it, or

(b) J and persons who are J's associates together have control of it.

(13) For the purposes of this section, a person (in this subsection referred to as 'K') is taken to have control of a company—

(a) if the directors of the company, or of another company which has control of it, (or any of them) are accustomed to act in accordance with K's directions or instructions, or

(b) if K is entitled to exercise, or control the exercise of, $^1/_3$ or more of the voting power at any general meeting of the company or of another company which has control of the company.

(14) Where two or more persons together satisfy either of the conditions mentioned in subsection (13), they are taken to have control of the company.

(15) In subsections (10) to (14), 'company' includes any body corporate (whether incorporated in Great Britain or elsewhere).

230 'Associates': regulations for the purposes of section 229

(1) The Scottish Ministers may by regulations—

(a) amend section 229 so as to provide further categories of persons who, for the purposes of this Act, are to be associates of other persons, and

(b) provide that any or all of subsections (4) to (15) of that section (or any subsection added to that section by virtue of paragraph (a))—

(i) is to cease to apply, whether in whole or in part, or

(ii) is to apply subject to such modifications as they may specify in the regulations.

(2) The Scottish Ministers may in the regulations make such incidental or transitional provision as they consider appropriate.

[. . .]

232 Crown application

This Act binds the Crown as creditor only.

233 Re-enactment

Schedule 7, derived from Part 2 of schedule 7 of the Bankruptcy (Scotland) Act 1985 (and re-enacting sections 10 and 189 of the Bankruptcy (Scotland) Act 1913), has effect.

234 Modifications, repeals, savings, revocations and transitional provisions

(1) Schedule 8 makes provision for the modification of enactments.

(2) The enactments mentioned in schedule 9 are repealed, or as the case may be revoked, to the extent mentioned in the second column of that schedule.

(3) Nothing in this Act affects—

(a) any of the enactments repealed, revoked or amended by this Act in the enactment's operation in relation to—

(i) a sequestration as regards which the petition was presented, or the debtor application was made before, or

(ii) a trust deed executed before,

the coming into force of this Act, or

(b) any power to repeal, revoke or amend any such enactment, in so far as the power relates to such operation of the enactment.

(4) The apparent insolvency of a debtor may be constituted for the purposes of this Act even though the circumstance founded on for such constitution occurred on a date before the coming into force of this Act; and for those purposes the apparent insolvency is taken to have been constituted on the date in question.

(5) If a debtor whose estate is sequestrated after the coming into force of this Act is liable, by virtue of a transaction entered into before the date on which section 102 of the Bankruptcy (Scotland) Act 1913 was repealed, to pay royalties or a share of the profits to any person in respect of copyright, or interest in copyright, comprised in the sequestrated estate, then that section applies in relation to the trustee in the sequestration as it applied, before its repeal, in relation to any trustee in bankruptcy (within the meaning of that Act).

(6) Where sequestration of a debtor's estate is awarded under this Act a person—

(a) does not commit an offence under any provision of this Act in respect of anything done before the date of commencement of that provision, but

(b) instead commits an offence under the Bankruptcy (Scotland) Act 1985 (or as the case may be under the Bankruptcy (Scotland) Act 1913) in respect of anything so done which would have been an offence under that Act if the award of sequestration had been made under that Act.

(7) Unless the context otherwise requires, any reference in any enactment or document—

(a) to notour bankruptcy, or to a person being notour bankrupt, is to be construed as a reference to apparent insolvency, or to a person being apparently insolvent, within the meaning of section 16 of this Act,

(b) to a person's estate being sequestrated under the Bankruptcy (Scotland) Act 1913 or the Bankruptcy (Scotland) Act 1985 is to be construed as, or as including, a reference to its being sequestrated under this Act, and

(c) to a trustee in sequestration or to a trustee in bankruptcy, is to be construed as a reference to a trustee in a sequestration within the meaning of this Act,

(analogous references being construed accordingly).

(8) Unless the context otherwise requires, any reference in any enactment or document—

(a) to a 'gratuitous alienation' is to be construed as including a reference to an alienation challengeable under section 98(2), or

(b) to a 'fraudulent preference' or to an 'unfair preference' is to be construed as including a reference to an unfair preference within the meaning of this Act.

235 Continuity of the law

(1) The repeal and re-enactment of a provision by this Act does not affect the continuity of the law.

(2) Anything done, or having effect as if done, under (or for the purposes of or in reliance on) a provision repealed by this Act, being a provision in force or effective immediately before the coming into force of this Act, has effect after that coming into force as if done under (or for the purposes of or in reliance on) the corresponding provision of this Act.

(3) Any reference (express or implied) in this Act or in any other enactment or document to a provision of this Act is to be construed, so far as the context permits,

as including, as respects times, circumstances or purposes in relation to which the corresponding repealed provision had effect, a reference to that corresponding provision.

(4) Any reference (express or implied) in any enactment or document to a provision repealed by this Act is to be construed, so far as the context permits, as including, as respects times, circumstances or purposes in relation to which the corresponding provision of this Act has effect, a reference to that corresponding provision.

(5) Subsections (1) to (4) have effect in place of section 19(3) to (5) of the Interpretation and Legislative Reform (Scotland) Act 2010 (effect of repeal and reenactment); but nothing in this section affects any other provision of that Act.

(6) This section is without prejudice to section 234(3) and to any specific transitional provision or saving contained in this Act.

(7) References in this section to this Act include subordinate legislation made under or by virtue of this Act.

236 Sequestrations to which this Act applies

This Act applies to sequestrations as regards which the petition is presented, or the debtor application is made on or after the day on which this section comes into force.

237 Commencement

(1) This section and sections 225, 226, 228 to 230 and 238 come into force on the day after Royal Assent.

(2) The remaining provisions of this Act come into force on such day as the Scottish Ministers may by regulations appoint.

(3) Different days may, under subsection (2), be appointed for different purposes and for different provisions.

238 Short title

The short title of this Act is the Bankruptcy (Scotland) Act 2016.

SCHEDULE 1

(introduced by section 2(6))

DEBTOR TO WHOM SECTION 2(2) APPLIES: APPLICATION OF ACT

Modification of certain provisions of Act

1—(1) Where section 2(2) applies in relation to a debtor, this Act applies subject to the modifications mentioned in sub-paragraphs (2) to (6).

(2) Section 42 applies as if for subsection (1) there were substituted—

> '(1) This section applies where AiB receives by virtue of section 8(3)(a) the statement of assets and liabilities in relation to a debtor to whom section 2(2) applies.
>
> (1A) As soon as practicable, AiB must prepare a statement of the debtor's affairs, so far as within the knowledge of AiB, stating that, because 2(2) applies in relation to the debtor, no claims may be submitted by creditors under section 46 or 122.
>
> (1B) AiB must send a copy of the statement prepared under subsection (1A) to every known creditor of the debtor.'.

(3) Section 50(1) applies as if paragraphs (e) and (f) were omitted.

(4) Section 116 applies as if for subsection (2) there were substituted—

> '(2) AiB may at any time before the discharge of the debtor require the debtor to give an account in writing, in such form as may be prescribed, of the debtor's current state of affairs.'.

(5) Section 151 applies as if—
(a) subsections (2) to (6) and (9)(a) were omitted, and
(b) for subsection (7) there were substituted—
'(7) The debtor or any creditor may, within 14 days beginning with the day on which the debtor is discharged under section 140(1), appeal to the sheriff against the discharge of AiB in respect of AiB's actings as trustee.'.
(6) Sections 44, 46, 48, 49, 60, 63 to 65, 122, 131 and 210(3) do not apply.

Accountant in Bankruptcy's duty to consider whether paragraph 1 should cease to have effect

2—(1) This paragraph applies where paragraph 1 applies in relation to a debtor.
(2) If AiB considers that the circumstances mentioned in any of sub-paragraphs (3) to (6) apply in relation to the debtor, AiB must consider whether paragraph 1 should cease to have effect in relation to the debtor.
(3) The circumstances are that—
(a) AiB becomes aware the debtor application submitted under section 2 contains an error, and
(b) the nature of the error is such that the debtor was not at the time of application a debtor to whom section 2(2) applies.
(4) The circumstances are that—
(a) AiB becomes aware that the debtor application submitted under section 2 deliberately misrepresents, or fails to state, a fact that was the case at the time of application, and
(b) the nature of the misrepresentation or the omission of the fact is such that the debtor was not at that time a debtor to whom section 2(2) applies.
(5) The circumstances are that, at any time after the date on which the debtor application is made—
(a) the total value of the debtor's assets (leaving out of account any liabilities and any assets that, under section 88(1), would not vest in a trustee) exceeds £5,000 or such other sum as may be prescribed, or
(b) AiB assesses the debtor, under the common financial tool, as being able to make a contribution.
(6) The circumstances are that, at any time after the date of sequestration—
(a) AiB is not satisfied that the debtor has co-operated with the trustee, and
(b) AiB considers that if paragraph 1 were to cease to have effect it would be—
(i) of financial benefit to the estate of the debtor, and
(ii) in the interests of the creditors.
(7) The Scottish Ministers may by regulations modify this paragraph—
(a) by modifying the circumstances in which paragraph 1 ceases to have effect,
(b) in consequence of any modification made under sub-paragraph (7)(a).

Procedure where Accountant in Bankruptcy considers paragraph 1 should cease to have effect

3—(1) If AiB considers under paragraph 2(2) that paragraph 1 should cease to have effect in relation to a debtor, AiB must notify the debtor of that fact and of the matters mentioned in sub-paragraph (2).
(2) The matters are—
(a) the circumstances mentioned in paragraph 2 which AiB considers apply in relation to the debtor, and
(b) that the debtor may make representations to AiB within 14 days beginning with the giving of notification under sub-paragraph (1).
(3) On the expiry of the 14 days mentioned in sub-paragraph (2)(b) and after having taken into account any representations made by the debtor under that subparagraph, AIB must decide whether paragraph 1 should cease to have effect in relation to the debtor.

(4) If AiB decides that paragraph 1 should cease to have effect in relation to the debtor, AiB must, as soon as practicable after reaching that decision, give notice in writing to the debtor—

(a) of the decision, and

(b) of the effect of the decision.

Debtor's right of appeal against decision under paragraph 3

4—(1) This paragraph applies where AiB gives notice to a debtor under paragraph 3(4).

(2) The debtor may appeal to the sheriff against the decision.

(3) Any such appeal must be lodged within 14 days after the day on which the notice is given.

(4) If the sheriff grants the appeal, paragraph 1 continues to have effect in relation to the debtor.

(5) If the sheriff refuses the appeal, or if it is abandoned or withdrawn, paragraph 1 ceases to have effect in relation to the debtor.

Decision that paragraph 1 ceases to have effect: modification of certain provisions of Act

5—(1) Where paragraph 1 ceases to have effect in relation to a debtor, this Act applies subject to sub-paragraphs (2) to (4).

(2) The debtor must send to the trustee a statement of assets and liabilities—

(a) where no appeal is taken under paragraph 4, within 7 days beginning with the expiry of the period during which an appeal may be made under that paragraph, or

(b) where an appeal is refused or, as the case may be, abandoned or withdrawn, within 7 days beginning with—

(i) the day on which notice is given of the outcome of the appeal, or

(ii) as the case may be, its abandonment or withdrawal.

(3) Section 44 applies as if, in subsection (3)(a), for the words 'sequestration is awarded' there were substituted 'paragraph 1 of schedule 1 ceases to have effect in relation to the debtor'.

(4) Section 116 applies as if for subsection (2) there were substituted—

'(2) The trustee in the sequestration must require the debtor to give an account in writing, in such form as may be prescribed, of the debtor's current state of affairs—

(a) within 60 days beginning with the day on which paragraph 1 of schedule 1 ceases to have effect in relation to the debtor,

(b) on the expiry of 6 months beginning with the day on which the account is given under paragraph (a), and

(c) on the expiry of each subsequent 6 months.'.

SCHEDULE 2

(introduced by sections 7(4), 46(9) and 125(4))

DETERMINATION OF AMOUNT OF CREDITOR'S CLAIM

Amount which may be claimed generally

1—(1) Subject to the provisions of this schedule, the amount in respect of which a creditor is entitled to claim is the accumulated sum of principal and any interest which is due on the debt as at the date of sequestration.

(2) If a debt does not depend on a contingency but would not be payable but for the sequestration until after the date of the sequestration, the amount of the claim must be calculated as if the debt were payable on that date but subject to the deduction of interest at the rate specified in section 129(10) from that date until the date for payment of the debt.

(3) In calculating the amount of a creditor's claim, the creditor must deduct any discount (other than any discount for payment in cash) which is allowable by contract or course of dealing between the creditor and the debtor or by the usage of trade.

Claims for aliment and for periodical allowance on divorce or on dissolution of civil partnership

2—(1) A person entitled to aliment, however arising, from a living debtor as at the date of sequestration, or from a deceased debtor immediately before the debtor's death, is not entitled to include in the amount of the person's claim—

(a) any unpaid aliment for any period before the date of sequestration unless the amount of the aliment has been quantified by court decree or by any legally binding obligation which is supported by evidence in writing, and—

(i) in the case of spouses (or, where the aliment is payable to a divorced person in respect of a child, former spouses), or

(ii) in the case of civil partners (or, where the aliment is payable to a former civil partner in respect of a child after dissolution of a civil partnership, former civil partners),

they were living apart during that period, or

(b) any aliment for a period after the date of sequestration.

(2) Sub-paragraph (1) applies to a periodical allowance payable on divorce or on dissolution of a civil partnership—

(a) by virtue of a court order, or

(b) under any legally binding obligation which is supported by evidence in writing,

as it applies to aliment and as if, for sub-paragraphs (i) and (ii) of sub-paragraph (1)(a) and the word 'they' which immediately follows sub-paragraph (ii), there were substituted 'the payer and payee'.

Debts depending on contingency

3—(1) The amount which a creditor is entitled to claim does not include a debt in so far as its existence or amount depend on a contingency.

(2) But sub-paragraph (1) is subject to sub-paragraph (3).

(3) On an application by the creditor—

(a) to the trustee in the sequestration, or

(b) if there is no trustee, to AiB,

the trustee, or AiB, must put a value on the debt in so far as it is contingent.

(4) The amount in respect of which the creditor is then entitled to claim is that value but no more.

(5) And where the contingent debt is an annuity, a cautioner may not then be sued for more than that value.

(6) An interested person may apply to AiB for a review of a valuation under sub-paragraph (3) by the trustee.

(7) Any application under sub-paragraph (6) must be made within 14 days beginning with the day of the valuation.

(8) If an application under sub-paragraph (6) is made, AiB must—

(a) take into account any representations made by an interested person within 21 days beginning with the day on which the application is made, and

(b) confirm or vary the valuation within 28 days beginning with that day.

(9) An interested person may appeal to the sheriff against a decision by AiB under sub-paragraph (8)(b) within 14 days beginning with the day of the decision.

(10) AiB may refer a case to the sheriff for a direction before making a decision under sub-paragraph (8)(b).

(11) An appeal to the sheriff under sub-paragraph (9) may not be made in relation to a matter on which AiB has applied for a direction under sub-paragraph (10).

Secured debts

4—(1) A secured creditor, in calculating the amount of the secured creditor's claim, must deduct the value of any security as estimated by the secured creditor.

(2) But if the secured creditor surrenders, or undertakes in writing to surrender, a security for the benefit of the debtor's estate, the secured creditor is not required to make a deduction of the value of that security.

(3) The trustee in the sequestration may, at any time after the expiry of 12 weeks after the date of sequestration, require the secured creditor, at the expense of the debtor's estate, to discharge the security or convey or assign it to the trustee on payment to the creditor of the value specified by the creditor.

(4) The amount in respect of which the creditor is then entitled to claim is any balance of the creditor's debt remaining after receipt of the payment.

(5) A creditor whose security has been realised, in calculating the amount of the creditor's claim, must deduct the amount (less the expenses of realisation) which the creditor has received, or is entitled to receive, from the realisation.

Valuation of claims against partners for debts of the partnership

5—(1) Where a creditor claims, in respect of a debt of a partnership, against the estate of one of its partners, the creditor must estimate the value of—

(a) the debt to the creditor from the firm's estate where that estate has not been sequestrated, or

(b) the creditor's claim against that estate where it has been sequestrated,

and deduct that value from the creditor's claim against the partner's estate.

(2) The amount in respect of which the creditor is entitled to claim on the partner's estate is the balance remaining after that deduction is made.

SCHEDULE 3

(introduced by section 129(2) and (3))

PREFERRED DEBTS

Part 1
List of preferred debts

Contributions to occupational pension schemes etc

1 Any sum which is owed by the debtor and is a sum to which schedule 4 of the Pension Schemes Act 1993 (contributions to occupational pension scheme and state scheme premiums) applies.

Remuneration of employees etc

2—(1) So much of any amount which—

(a) is owed by the debtor to a person who is or has been an employee of the debtor, and

(b) is payable by way of remuneration in respect of the whole or any part of the 4 months which immediately precedes the relevant date,

as does not exceed the prescribed amount.

(2) An amount owed by way of accrued holiday remuneration, in respect of any period of employment before the relevant date, to a person whose employment by the debtor has been terminated (whether before, on or after that date).

(3) So much of any amount owed in respect of money advanced for the purpose as has been applied for the payment of a debt which, if it had not been paid, would have been a debt falling within sub-paragraph (1) or (2).

3 So much of any amount which—

(a) is ordered, whether before or after the relevant date, to be paid by the debtor under the Reserve Forces (Safeguard of Employment) Act 1985, and

(b) is so ordered in respect of a default made by the debtor before that date in the discharge of the debtor's obligations under that Act,

as does not exceed such amount as may be prescribed.

Levies on coal and steel production

4 Any sums due at the relevant date from the debtor in respect of—

(a) the levies on the production of coal and steel referred to in Articles 49 and 50 of the Treaty establishing the European Coal and Steel Community, or

(b) any surcharge for delay provided for in Article 50(3) of that Treaty and Article 6 of Decision 3/52 of the High Authority of that Community.

Debts owed to the Financial Services Compensation Scheme

5 Any debt owed by the debtor to the scheme manager of the Financial Services Compensation Scheme under section 215(2A) of the Financial Services and Markets Act 2000.

Deposits covered by Financial Services Compensation Scheme

6 So much of any amount owed at the relevant date by the debtor in respect of an eligible deposit as does not exceed the compensation that would be payable in respect of the deposit under the Financial Services Compensation Scheme to the person or persons to whom the amount is owed.

Other deposits

7 So much of any amount owed at the relevant date by the debtor to one or more eligible persons in respect of an eligible deposit as exceeds any compensation that would be payable in respect of the deposit under the Financial Services Compensation Scheme to that person or those persons.

8 An amount owed at the relevant date by the debtor to one or more eligible persons in respect of a deposit which—

(a) was made through a [non-UK] branch of a credit institution authorised by the competent authority of [the United Kingdom], and

(b) would have been an eligible deposit if it had been made through [a UK] branch of that credit institution.

[*Certain HMRC debts*

8A (1) Any amount owed at the relevant date by the debtor to the Commissioners in respect of—

(a) value added tax, or

(b) a relevant deduction.

(2) In sub-paragraph (1), the reference to 'any amount' is subject to any regulations under section 99(1) of the Finance Act 2020.

(3) For the purposes of sub-paragraph (1)(b) a deduction is 'relevant' if—

(a) the debtor is required, by virtue of an enactment, to make the deduction from a payment made to another person and to pay an amount to the Commissioners on account of the deduction,

(b) the payment to the Commissioners is credited against any liabilities of the other person, and

(c) the deduction is of a kind specified in regulations under section 99(3) of the Finance Act 2020.

(4) In this paragraph 'the Commissioners' means the Commissioners for Her Majesty's Revenue and Customs.]

Part 2
Interpretation of Part 1

Meaning of 'the relevant date'

9 In Part 1, 'the relevant date' means—

(a) in relation to a debtor other than a deceased debtor, the date of sequestration, and

(b) in relation to a deceased debtor, the date of death.

Amounts payable by way of remuneration

10—(1) For the purposes of paragraph 2, a sum is payable by the debtor to a person by way of remuneration in respect of any period if—

(a) it is paid as wages or salary (whether payable for time or for piece work or earned wholly or partly by way of commission) in respect of services rendered to the debtor in that period, or

(b) it is an amount falling within sub-paragraph (2) and is payable by the debtor in respect of that period.

(2) An amount falls within this sub-paragraph if it is—

(a) a guarantee payment under section 28(1) to (3) of the Employment Rights Act 1996 (entitlement to payment for workless day),

(b) a payment for time off under section 53(1) (looking for new employment or making arrangements for training for future employment) or 56(1) (antenatal care) of that Act,

(c) remuneration on suspension on medical grounds under section 64 of that Act,

(d) a payment for time off under section 169(1) of the Trade Union and Labour Relations (Consolidation) Act 1992 (trade union duties), or

(e) remuneration under a protective award made by an employment tribunal under section 189 of that Act (redundancy dismissal with compensation).

(3) For the purposes of paragraph 2(2), holiday remuneration is deemed, in the case of a person ('P') whose employment has been terminated by or in consequence of the award of sequestration of P's employer's estate, to have accrued to P in respect of a period of employment if, by virtue of P's contract of employment or of any enactment, that remuneration would have accrued in respect of that period if P's employment had continued until P became entitled to be allowed the holiday.

(4) In sub-paragraph (3), 'enactment' includes an order made or direction given under an enactment.

(5) Without prejudice to the preceding provisions of this paragraph—

(a) any remuneration payable by the debtor to a person in respect of a period—

(i) of holiday, or

(ii) of absence from work through sickness or other good cause,

is deemed to be wages, or as the case may be salary, in respect of services rendered to the debtor in that period, and

(b) references in this paragraph to remuneration in respect of a period of holiday include references to any sums which, if they had been paid, would have been treated for the purposes of the enactments relating to social services as earnings in respect of that period.

Meaning of 'prescribed'

11 In paragraphs 2 and 3, 'prescribed' means prescribed by regulations made by the Secretary of State.

Meaning of 'scheme manager'

12 In paragraph 5, 'the scheme manager' has the meaning given in section 212 (1) of the Financial Services and Markets Act 2000.

Meaning of 'eligible deposit'

13—(1) In paragraphs 6 to 8, 'eligible deposit' means a deposit in respect of which the person, or any of the persons, to whom it is owed would be eligible for compensation under the Financial Services Compensation Scheme.

(2) For the purposes of those paragraphs and of this paragraph, a 'deposit' means rights of the kind described in paragraph 22 of schedule 2 of the Financial Services and Markets Act 2000 (deposits).

(3) In paragraphs 7 and 8, 'eligible person' means—

(a) an individual, or

[(b) any micro, small or medium-sized enterprise, as defined with regard to the annual turnover criterion referred to in Article 2(1) of the Annex to Commission Recommendation 2003/361/EC.]

(4) In paragraph 8—

(a) 'credit institution' has the meaning given in Article 4.1(1) of the capital requirements regulation,

[(b) 'UK branch' means a branch, as defined in Article 4(1)(17) of the capital requirements regulation, which is established in the United Kingdom, and

(c) 'non-UK branch' means a branch, as so defined, which is established outside the United Kingdom.]

[(5) In sub-paragraph (4)(a) and (b), 'the capital requirements regulation' means Regulation (EU) No 575/2013 of the European Parliament and of the Council of 26 June 2013 on prudential requirements for credit institutions and investment firms and amending Regulation (EU) No 648/2012.]

Transitional provisions

14 Regulations under paragraph 2 or 3 may contain such transitional provisions as may appear to the Secretary of State necessary or expedient.

SCHEDULE 4

(introduced by section 162)

VOLUNTARY TRUST DEEDS FOR CREDITORS

Remuneration of trustee

1 Whether or not—

(a) provision is made in the trust deed for auditing the accounts of the trustee in the sequestration and for determining the method of fixing the trustee's remuneration, or

(b) the trustee and the creditors have agreed on such auditing and the method of fixing that remuneration,

the debtor, the trustee or any creditor may, at any time before the final distribution of the debtor's estate among the creditors, have the trustee's accounts audited by, and the trustee's remuneration fixed by, AiB.

Accountant in Bankruptcy's power to carry out audit

2 AiB may, at any time, audit the trustee's accounts and fix the trustee's remuneration.

Registration of notice of inhibition

3—(1) The trustee, from time to time after the trust deed is delivered to the trustee, may cause a notice in such form as is prescribed by act of sederunt to be recorded in the Register of Inhibitions.

(2) Such recording has the same effect as the recording in that register of letters of inhibition against the debtor.

(3) The trustee, after—

(a) the debtor's estate has been distributed finally among the debtor's creditors, or

(b) the trust deed has otherwise ceased to be operative,

must cause a notice in such form as is so prescribed to be recorded in that register recalling the notice recorded under sub-paragraph (1).

Lodging of claim to bar effect of limitation of actions

4 The submission to the trustee, acting under a trust deed, of a claim by a creditor bars the effect of any enactment or rule of law relating to limitation of actions.

Valuation of claims

5—(1) Unless the trust deed otherwise provides, schedule 2 applies in relation to a trust deed as it applies to a sequestration but subject to the following modifications.

(2) In paragraphs 1, 2 and 4, for the word 'sequestration', wherever it occurs, there is substituted 'granting of the trust deed'.

(3) In paragraph 3(3), for paragraphs (a) and (b) and the words 'the trustee or sheriff' which immediately follow paragraph (b) there is substituted 'the trustee'.

. . .

SCHEDULE 6

(introduced by section 217)

MEETINGS OF CREDITORS AND COMMISSIONERS

Part 1

Meetings of creditors other than the statutory meeting

Calling of meeting

1 The trustee in the sequestration must call a meeting of creditors if required to do so—

(a) by order of the sheriff,

(b) by 1/10 in number or 1/3 in value of the creditors,

(c) by a commissioner, or

(d) by AiB.

2 Any such meeting must be held not later than 28 days after—

(a) the issuing of the order under paragraph 1(a), or

(b) the receipt by the trustee of the requirement under paragraph 1(b), (c) or (d).

3 The trustee, or a commissioner who has given notice to the trustee, may at any time call a meeting of creditors.

4 The trustee, calling a meeting under paragraph 1 or 3, or a commissioner, calling a meeting under paragraph 3, is no fewer than 7 days before the date fixed for the meeting to notify—

(a) every creditor known to the trustee or, as the case may be, to the commissioner, and

(b) AiB,

of the date, time and place fixed for the holding of the meeting and of the meeting's purpose.

5 Where—

(a) a requirement has been made under paragraph 1, but
(b) no meeting has been called by the trustee,
AiB may, of AiB's own accord or on the application of any creditor, call a meeting of creditors.

6 AiB, calling a meeting under paragraph 5, is no fewer than 7 days before the date fixed for the meeting to take reasonable steps to notify the creditors of the date, time and place fixed for the holding of the meeting and of the meeting's purpose.

7 It is not necessary to notify under paragraph 4 or 6 any creditor whose accepted claim is less than £50 or such sum as may be prescribed, unless the creditor has in writing requested such notification.

Role of trustee at meeting

8 At the commencement of a meeting the trustee is to be the person chairing the meeting and as such is, after carrying out the trustee's duties under section 126(1)—
(a) to invite the creditors to elect one of their number to chair the meeting in the trustee's place, and
(b) to preside over the election.

9 If no person is elected in pursuance of paragraph 8, the trustee must chair the meeting throughout.

10 The trustee is to arrange for a record to be made of the proceedings at the meeting.

Appeals

11 The trustee, a creditor or any other person having an interest may, within 14 days after the date of a meeting called under paragraph 4 or 6, appeal to the sheriff against a resolution of the creditors at the meeting.

Part 2
All meetings of creditors

Validity of proceedings

12 No proceedings at a meeting are invalidated by reason only that a notice or other document relating to the calling of the meeting, being a notice required to be sent or given under a provision of this Act, has not been received by, or come to the attention of, any creditor before the meeting.

[*Holding of meeting*

13 Every meeting must be held either—
(a) in such place (whether or not in the sheriffdom) as is, in the opinion of the person calling the meeting, the most convenient for the majority of the creditors, or
(b) by such electronic means as would, in the opinion of the person calling the meeting, be most convenient to allow the majority of the creditors to participate in the meeting without being together in the same place.

13A Where a meeting is to be held in pursuance of paragraph 13(b), the references in paragraphs 4 and 6 to the place fixed for the holding of the meeting are to be read as references to the electronic means by which attendees are to be able to attend the meeting without being together in the same place.]

Mandatories

14 A creditor may authorise in writing a person to represent the creditor at a meeting.

15 A creditor must lodge with the trustee, before the commencement of the meeting, any authorisation given under paragraph 14.

16 Any reference in paragraph 8, or in the following provisions of this Part, to a creditor includes a reference to a person authorised under paragraph 14 by a creditor.

Quorum

17 The quorum at any meeting is one creditor.

Voting at meeting

18 Any question at a meeting is to be determined by a majority in value of the creditors who vote on that question.

Objections by creditors

19 At any meeting the person chairing it may allow or disallow any objection by a creditor, other than (if the person chairing the meeting is not the trustee) an objection relating to a creditor's claim.

20 A person aggrieved by the determination of the person chairing the meeting in respect of an objection may appeal to the sheriff against the determination.

21 If the person chairing the meeting is in doubt as to whether to allow or disallow an objection, the meeting must proceed as if no objection had been made, except that for the purposes of appeal the objection is to be deemed to have been disallowed.

Adjournment of meeting

22 If no creditor has appeared at a meeting by half an hour after the time appointed for its commencement, the person chairing the meeting may adjourn it to such other day as that person may appoint, being a day no fewer than 7, nor more than 21, days after that on which the meeting is adjourned.

23 The person chairing the meeting may, with the consent of a majority in value of the creditors who vote on a resolution to adjourn a meeting, adjourn the meeting.

24 Any adjourned meeting must be held at the same time [, and at the same place or by the same electronic means,] as the original meeting, unless [the resolution specifies otherwise].

Minutes of meeting

25 The minutes of every meeting must be signed by the person who chaired the meeting and within 14 days after the meeting must be sent to AiB.

Part 3
Meetings of commissioners

26 The trustee—

(a) may call a meeting of commissioners at any time, and

(b) must call such a meeting—

(i) on being required to do so by order of the sheriff, or

(ii) on being requested to do so by AiB or by any commissioner.

27 If the trustee fails to call a meeting of commissioners within 14 days after being required or requested to do so under paragraph 26, a commissioner may call a meeting of commissioners.

28 The trustee must give the commissioners at least 7 days' notice of a meeting called by the trustee unless the commissioners decide that they do not require such notice.

29 The trustee is to act as clerk at a meeting of commissioners.

30 If the commissioners are considering the performance of the functions of the trustee under any provision of this Act, the trustee must withdraw from the meeting if requested to do so by the commissioners and in such a case a commissioner must—

(a) act as clerk, and

(b) transmit a record of the deliberations of the commissioners to the trustee.

31 The quorum at a meeting of commissioners is one commissioner and the commissioners may act by a majority of the commissioners present at the meeting.

32 Any matter may be agreed by the commissioners without a meeting if such agreement—

(a) is unanimous, and

(b) is subsequently recorded in a minute signed by the commissioners.

SCHEDULE 7

(introduced by section 233)

RE-ENACTMENT OF SECTIONS 10 AND 189 OF THE BANKRUPTCY (SCOTLAND) ACT 1913

Arrestments and attachments

1—(1) Subject to sub-paragraph (2), all arrestments and attachments which have been executed within 60 days prior to the constitution of the apparent insolvency of the debtor, or within 4 months after its constitution, rank pari passu as if they had all been executed on the same date.

(2) Any such arrestment which is executed on the dependence of an action must be followed up without undue delay.

(3) A creditor judicially producing, in a process relative to the subject of such arrestment or attachment, liquid grounds of debt or decree of payment within the 60 days or 4 months referred to in sub-paragraph (1) is entitled to rank as if the creditor had executed an arrestment or an attachment.

(4) If, in the meantime—

(a) the first or any subsequent arrester obtains a decree of furthcoming and recovers payment, that arrester, or

(b) an attaching creditor carries through an auction or receives payment in respect of an attached article upon its redemption, that attaching creditor,

is accountable for the sum recovered to those who, by virtue of this Act, may eventually be found to have a ranking pari passu on the sum; and is liable in an action at their instance for payment to them proportionately, after allowing out of the fund the expense of such recovery.

(5) Arrestments executed for attaching the same effects of the debtor after the 4 months subsequent to the constitution of the debtor's apparent insolvency do not compete with those within the 60 days or 4 months referred to in sub-paragraph (1) but may rank with each other on any reversion of the fund attached in accordance with any enactment or rule of law relating to such ranking.

(6) Any reference in sub-paragraphs (1) to (5) to a debtor is to be construed as including a reference to an entity whose apparent insolvency may, by virtue of subsection (6) of section 16 of this Act, be constituted under subsection (1) of that section.

(7) This paragraph applies in respect of arrestments and attachments executed whether before or after the coming into force of this Act.

(8) Nothing in this paragraph applies to an earnings arrestment, a current maintenance arrestment or a conjoined arrestment order.

Exemptions from stamp or other duties for conveyances, deeds etc relating to sequestrated estates

2 Any—

(a) conveyance, assignation, instrument, discharge, writing or deed relating solely to the estate of a debtor which has been or may be sequestrated, under either this or any former Act, being estate which after the execution of the document in question is and remains the property of the debtor, for the benefit of the debtor's creditors, or of the trustee in the sequestration,

(b) discharge to the debtor,

(c) deed, assignation, instrument, or writing for reinvesting the debtor in the estate,

(d) article of roup or sale, or submission,

(e) other instrument or writing whatsoever relating solely to the estate of the debtor, and

(f) other deed or writing forming part of the proceedings ordered under such sequestration,

is exempt from all stamp duties or other Government duty.

MOVEABLE TRANSACTIONS (SCOTLAND) ACT 2023
(2023, asp 3)

PART 1
ASSIGNATION

CHAPTER 1
ASSIGNATION OF CLAIMS, PROTECTION OF DEBTORS AND RELATED MATTERS

Assignation of claims

1 Assignation of claims: general

(1) The assignation of a claim requires the execution or authentication of a document assigning the claim (an 'assignation document') by the person assigning it.

(2) The assignation document must identify the claim.

(3) But an assignation document which assigns a number of claims need not identify each claim separately provided that the document identifies the claims in terms of their constituting an identifiable class.

(4) It is competent to assign a claim which, at the time the assignation document is granted, is not held by the assignor (whether or not the claim yet exists at that time).

(5) For the purposes of subsection (2), the ways in which the claim can be identified in the assignation document include by making reference in the assignation document to another document, the terms of which are not reproduced.

[(6) This Part applies to the assignation of a claim as part of a financial collateral arrangement, within the meaning of regulation 3(1) of the Financial Collateral Arrangements (No 2) Regulations 2003 (SI 2003/3226), only under and in accordance with the Moveable Transactions (Scotland) Act 2023 (Financial Collateral Arrangements and Financial Instruments) (Consequential Provisions and Modifications) Order 2025 (SI 2025/275 (S 1)).]

2 Assignation of claim subject to a condition

(1) The assignation of a claim may be subject to a condition which must be satisfied before the claim is transferred.

(2) Any such condition must be specified in the assignation document.

(3) The condition may, for example—

(a) be the occurrence of a particular date,

(b) depend on something happening (whether or not it is certain that the thing will happen), or

(c) depend on a period of time elapsing during which something must not happen (whether or not it is certain that the thing will happen at some time).

(4) For the purposes of subsection (2), the ways in which the condition can be specified in the assignation document include by making reference in the assignation document to another document, the terms of which are not reproduced.

3 Transfer of claims

(1) A claim in respect of which an assignation document is granted is transferred on the requirements mentioned in subsection (2) all being met.

(2) Those requirements are that—

(a) the assignor is the holder of the claim,

(b) either—

(i) intimation of the assignation is effected under section 8(1), or

(ii) the assignation document is registered,

(c) the claim is identifiable as a claim to which the assignation document relates, and

(d) if the assignation is subject to a condition which must be satisfied before the claim is transferred, the condition is satisfied.

(3) For the purposes of subsection (1), if the claim is a claim such as is mentioned in section 1(4)—

(a) the requirement mentioned in subsection (2)(a) is met when the assignor becomes the holder of the claim, and

(b) any rule of law as to accretion does not apply in relation to the claim.

(4) Subsection (2)(b)(ii) is subject to section 27 (effective registration of assignation document) and, accordingly, the requirement of that subsection—

(a) is not met if the registration of the assignation document is ineffective in accordance with section 27(1), and

(b) is met if and when that registration becomes effective in accordance with section 27(3).

(5) Subsection (6) applies where—

(a) an assignor grants more than one assignation document in respect of the same claim,

(b) each of the purported assignations of the claim is to a different person, and

(c) the requirements of subsection (2) are all met in relation to each of the purported assignations at the same time by virtue of—

(i) the assignor becoming the holder of the claim,

(ii) the claim becoming identifiable as a claim to which the assignation document relates, or

(iii) where each of the purported assignations is subject to a condition which must be satisfied before the claim is transferred, those conditions being satisfied at the same time.

(6) The claim transfers under subsection (1) to the person to whom it is assigned by whichever of the purported assignations of the claim first met the requirement of subsection (2)(b).

(7) This section is subject to section 4 (assignation of claims: insolvency).

(8) The Scottish Ministers may by regulations prescribe types of claim in relation to which sub-paragraph (i) of subsection (2)(b) is to be disregarded.

[(9) See also article 4 (transfer of claim assigned as part of financial collateral arrangement) of the Moveable Transactions (Scotland) Act 2023 (Financial Collateral Arrangements and Financial Instruments) (Consequential Provisions and Modifications) Order 2025 (SI 2025/275 (S 1)).]

4 Assignation of claims: insolvency

(1) This section applies where—

(a) an assignation document is granted in respect of a claim such as is mentioned in section 1(4), and

(b) after the document is granted, the assignor becomes insolvent.

(2) The assignation is ineffective in relation to the claim if the assignor becomes the holder of the claim after becoming insolvent.

(3) But subsection (2) does not apply in relation to a claim in respect of income from property in so far as that claim—

(a) is not attributable to anything agreed to by, or done by, the assignor after the assignor became insolvent, and

(b) relates to the use of property in existence at the time the assignor became insolvent.

(4) Subsection (5) applies where—

(a) but for subsection (3), the assignation would be ineffective by virtue of subsection (2), and

(b) the assignor is discharged—

(i) under section 137, 138 or 140 of the Bankruptcy (Scotland) Act 2016, or

(ii) by virtue of section 184(3) of that Act.

(5) The assignation is ineffective, in relation to the claim, if by the time of discharge the assignor has not become the holder of the claim.

(6) For the purposes of this section—

(a) an assignor who is an individual, or the estate of which may be sequestrated by virtue of section 6 of the Bankruptcy (Scotland) Act 2016, becomes insolvent when—

(i) the assignor's estate is sequestrated,

(ii) the assignor grants a trust deed for creditors or makes a composition or arrangement with creditors,

(iii) the assignor is adjudged bankrupt,

(iv) a voluntary arrangement proposed by the assignor is approved, [or]

[. . .]

(vi) the assignor becomes subject to any other order or arrangement analogous to any of those mentioned in sub-paragraphs (i) to [(iv)] anywhere in the world, and

(b) an assignor other than is mentioned in paragraph (a) becomes insolvent when—

(i) a decision approving a voluntary arrangement entered into by the assignor has effect under section 4A of the Insolvency Act 1986 (the '1986 Act'),

(ii) the assignor is wound up under Part 4 or 5 of the 1986 Act or under section 367 of the Financial Services and Markets Act 2000,

(iii) an administrative receiver, as defined in section 251 of the 1986 Act, is appointed over all or part (being a part which includes the claim) of the property of the assignor,

(iv) the assignor enters administration ('enters administration' being construed in accordance with paragraph 1(2) of schedule B1 of the 1986 Act),

(v) an order under section 901F of the Companies Act 2006 sanctioning a compromise or arrangement entered into by the assignor comes into effect over all or part of the property of the assignor, or

(vi) the assignor becomes subject to any other order, appointment or arrangement analogous to any of those mentioned in sub-paragraphs (i) to (iv) anywhere in the world.

(7) The Scottish Ministers may by regulations modify—

(a) subsection (4),

(b) subsection (5),

(c) subsection (6).

5 Assignation in part

(1) A claim may be assigned in whole or in part.

(2) But if the claim is not a monetary claim, the claim may be assigned in part only if the claim is divisible and either—

(a) the debtor consents, or

(b) the assignation is not likely to result in the obligation to which it relates becoming significantly more burdensome for the debtor.

(3) Except in so far as the debtor agrees otherwise with the assignor, or agreed otherwise with a person who was previously the holder of the claim (when that person was the holder), the assignor is liable to the debtor for any expense incurred by the debtor which is attributable to the claim's being assigned in part rather than in whole.

6 Limitations as to assignability: general

(1) Nothing in this Part affects any other enactment, or any rule of law, by virtue of which the assignation of a claim is of no effect.

(2) But such an enactment or rule of law does not apply to an assignation if the grounds on which the assignation would be of no effect by virtue of that enactment or rule are grounds which this Part provides do not make the assignation of no effect.

(3) The assignation, in whole or in part, of a claim is of no effect if and in so far as, before the [relevant time]—

(a) the debtor and the holder of the claim had agreed that the claim was not to be so assigned, or

(b) the person whose unilateral undertaking gives rise to the claim had stated that the claim was not to be so assigned.

[(3A) For the purposes of subsection (3), the 'relevant time' is—

(a) where the claim is held by the holder immediately prior to the assignation document being granted in respect of the claim, the time at which the document is granted,

(b) where the claim is not held by the holder until after the assignation document is granted in respect of the claim, the time at which the claim would have otherwise transferred.]

(4) For the purposes of subsection (3)(a), it does not matter whether the holder of the claim became the holder of the claim after the agreement was made.

(5) Nothing in subsection (3) affects the operation of any other enactment concerning the effect of an agreement or statement such as is mentioned in that subsection.

7 Claim in respect of wages or salary

(1) It is not competent for an individual to assign a claim in respect of wages or salary payable to the individual.

(2) For the purposes of subsection (1), 'wages' and 'salary' include—

(a) any of the following which is referable to the individual's employment (whether or not payable under the individual's contract of employment)—

(i) a fee,

(ii) a bonus,

(iii) commission,

(iv) holiday pay, or

(v) any other emolument,

(b) any payment in respect of expenses incurred by the individual in carrying out that employment, and

(c) if the individual is dismissed from that employment by reason of redundancy, any payment referable to the redundancy.

(3) Nothing in subsection (1) affects the operation of any other enactment allowing the assignation of a claim such as is mentioned in that subsection in particular circumstances.

8 Intimation of the assignation of a claim

(1) For the purposes of section 3(2)(b)(i), intimation is effected only—

(a) by the assignor or the assignee serving notice of the assignation on the debtor, or

(b) on the occurrence either—

(i) of the debtor acknowledging to the assignee that the claim is assigned, or

(ii) of intimation to the debtor, in judicial proceedings to which the debtor is a party, that the assignation is founded on in the proceedings.

(2) Where there are co-debtors in respect of a claim, intimation as respects any one or more of them is, for the purposes of section 3(2)(b)(i), intimation to them all.

(3) A notice served under subsection (1)(a)—

(a) must—

(i) set out the name and address of both the assignor and the assignee,

(ii) provide details of the claim assigned, and

(iii) in the case of a claim assigned in part, provide details of the part assigned,

(b) must be in writing and consist of, or be contained within, one or more documents,

(c) need not be executed or authenticated, and

(d) if the claim is a monetary claim, may (but need not) be in such form (if any) as is prescribed for the purposes of this paragraph.

(4) Where a notice is served as mentioned in subsection (5)(c), paragraph (a) of subsection (3) may be satisfied by providing an electronic link to a website, or to a portal, in which the information mentioned in that paragraph is set out.

(5) For the purposes of subsection (1)(a), service of a notice must be by—
(a) delivering the notice personally to the debtor,
(b) sending it—
(i) by postal services, or
(ii) by any other service which conveys postal packets from one place to another,
either to the proper address of the debtor or to an address for postal communication provided to the assignor by the debtor, or
(c) transmitting it to an address for electronic communication so provided.
(6) But a determination (a 'determination as to method of service') may be made in accordance with subsection (7) that, as respects the claim (either or both)—
(a) only certain paragraphs and sub-paragraphs of subsection (5), as specified in the determination, are to apply for the purposes of section 3(2)(b)(i),
(b) subsection (5) is to apply as if for the closing words of paragraph (b) there were substituted a reference to a particular address as specified in the determination.
(7) A determination as to method of service is made in accordance with this subsection where it is made—
(a) by written agreement between the debtor and the holder of the claim, or
(b) where a unilateral undertaking gives rise to the claim, by a written statement (whether or not comprised within the undertaking) of the person whose undertaking it was.
(8) Where a determination as to method of service specifies an address as mentioned in subsection (6)(b)—
(a) the debtor may notify the holder of the claim of a different address to replace—
(i) the address so specified, or
(ii) an address previously notified under this paragraph, and
(b) an address notified under paragraph (a) is, until a further address is so notified, to be treated for the purposes of subsection (6)(b) as if it were specified in the determination.
(9) Where a notice is served—
(a) as mentioned in subsection (5)(b) (including, where relevant, as modified by subsection (6)(b)), and
(b) by being sent to an address in the United Kingdom,
it is to be taken to have been received 48 hours after it is sent unless it is shown to have been received earlier.
(10) Where a notice is served as mentioned in subsection (5)(c), it is to be taken to have been received 24 hours after it is transmitted unless it is shown to have been received earlier.
(11) In this section—
'holder of the claim' includes a person who becomes the holder of the claim after a determination is made,
'postal packet' and 'postal services' have the meanings given by section 27(1) and (2) of the Postal Services Act 2011,
'proper address of the debtor' means—
(a) in the case of a body corporate, the address of the registered or principal office of the body,
(b) in the case of a partnership, the address of the principal office of the partnership, and
(c) in any other case, the last known address of the debtor.
(12) Any reference in this section to—
(a) a notice being served on the debtor is to be construed as including a reference to its being served on a person authorised to receive such a notice on behalf of the debtor,

(b) the proper address of the debtor is, where a notice is served on a person so authorised, to be construed as a reference to the proper address of that person.

9 Warrandice implied in the assignation of a claim

(1) Subsections (2) to (5) apply except in so far as the assignor and the assignee agree otherwise.

(2) In granting, for value, an assignation document in respect of a claim, the assignor is taken to warrant to the assignee that—

(a) the assignor is entitled to, or (in the case of any such claim as is mentioned in section 1(4)) will be entitled to, transfer the claim to the assignee,

(b) the debtor is obliged to, or (when performance becomes due) will be obliged to, perform in full to the assignor, and

(c) the assignor has done nothing, and will do nothing, to prejudice the assignation.

(3) In granting, other than for value, an assignation document in respect of a claim, the assignor is taken to warrant to the assignee that the assignor will do nothing to prejudice the assignation.

(4) In granting an assignation document in respect of a claim (whether or not for value), the assignor is not taken to warrant to the assignee that the debtor will perform to the assignee.

(5) Subsections (2) to (4) apply in relation to providing, in a contract or unilateral undertaking, for the assignation of a claim as they apply in relation to the granting of an assignation document in respect of a claim.

Protection of debtors

10 Protection of debtor who performs in good faith

(1) Subsection (2) applies where, after a claim is transferred, the debtor, or any co-debtor, performs in good faith to the person last known to the debtor, or that co-debtor, to be the holder of the claim.

(2) The debtor, or (where there are two or more co-debtors) each of the co-debtors, is discharged from the claim to the extent of the performance.

(3) For the purpose of subsection (2), it is not to be taken that a debtor, or any co-debtor, has performed other than in good faith by reason only of (any or all of)—

(a) an assignation document's having been registered,

(b) the application of section 8(9),

(c) the application of section 8(10).

11 Further provision as to protection of debtor

(1) Subsection (2) applies where—

(a) the holder of a claim purports to assign the claim (or the same part of the claim) by means of more than one assignation document, each in favour of a different person,

(b) the claim (or part) is transferred to one of those persons,

(c) the debtor, or any co-debtor, receives notice of the purported assignation to the other (or, as the case may be, another) of those persons (the 'purported assignee'),

from the person who granted the purported assignation or from the purported assignee, in the manner mentioned in section 8(1)(a) or (b)(ii), and

(d) by virtue of that notice, the debtor, or any co-debtor, performs in good faith to the purported assignee.

(2) The debtor, or (where there are two or more co-debtors) each of the co-debtors, is discharged from the claim (or part) to the extent of the performance.

(3) Section 10(3) applies for the purposes of subsection (2) as it applies for the purposes of section 10(2).

12 Performance in good faith where claim assigned cannot be transferred by intimation

(1) Subsection (2) applies where—

(a) by virtue only of being of a type prescribed under section 3(8), a claim in respect of which an assignation document is granted is not transferred, and

(b) the debtor, or any co-debtor, performs in good faith to the assignee.

(2) The debtor, or (where there are two or more co-debtors) each of the co-debtors, is discharged from the claim to the extent of the performance.

(3) For the purposes of subsection (1)(b), a debtor, or co-debtor, is not to be taken to perform in good faith where that debtor or co-debtor knows—

(a) that the assignation document has not been registered, and

(b) that transfer of the claim requires registration.

13 Performance in good faith where claim assigned subject to condition

(1) Subsection (2) applies where—

(a) a claim in respect of which an assignation document is granted is subject to a condition which must be satisfied before the claim is transferred,

(b) the claim has not yet been transferred by virtue only of the condition not yet being satisfied, and

(c) the debtor, or any co-debtor, performs in good faith to the assignee.

(2) The debtor, or (where there are two or more co-debtors) each of the co-debtors, is discharged from the claim to the extent of the performance.

(3) Section 10(3) applies for the purposes of subsection (2) as it applies for the purposes of section 10(2).

14 Asserting defence or right of compensation

(1) Except in so far as the debtor and the assignor agree otherwise before [the relevant time], the debtor, or any co-debtor, may assert against the assignee any defence which the debtor, or co-debtor, would have had the right to assert against the assignor.

[(1A) For the purposes of subsection (1), the 'relevant time' is—

(a) where the claim is held by the assignor immediately prior to the assignation document being granted in respect of the claim, the time at which the document is granted,

(b) where the claim is not held by the assignor until after the assignation document is granted in respect of the claim, the time at which the claim is transferred.]

(2) Nothing in subsection (1) affects the operation of any other enactment which restricts or prevents the making of such an agreement.

(3) For the purposes of any enactment or rule of law concerning compensation, set-off, retention, balancing of accounts or counterclaims, a debtor is not to be treated as receiving notice of the assignation of a claim [by reason only of (any or all of)—

(a) an assignation document's having been registered in respect of the claim,

(b) the application of section 8(9),

(c) the application of section 8(10).]

15 Right to withhold performance until information as to assignation is provided

(1) A debtor on whom a notice of assignation of a claim is served under section 8(1)(a) by an assignee may request from the assignee reasonable evidence of the granting of an assignation document in respect of the claim.

(2) For the purposes of subsection (1), 'reasonable evidence' includes, for example, the written confirmation of an assignor that the assignor granted the document.

(3) Subsection (1) applies to a purported notice of assignation as it applies to a notice of assignation, and a reference in that subsection to an assignee includes a reference to a purported assignee.

(4) If evidence is requested under subsection (1), the debtor may withhold performance until—

(a) that evidence is received, or

(b) the debtor receives notification in writing from the purported assignee or the purported assignor that an assignation document has not been granted in respect of the claim.

(5) A debtor who, other than by virtue of section 8(1), has reasonable grounds to believe that an assignation document has been granted in respect of a claim may state those grounds to the supposed assignor and request that person to provide a written statement as to whether the document has been granted.

(6) If a written statement provided by virtue of subsection (5) is to the effect that the document has been granted, that statement must include the name and last known address of the assignee.

(7) If a written statement is requested under subsection (5), the debtor may withhold performance until that statement (conforming, where it is a statement to the effect mentioned in subsection (6), with the requirements of that subsection) is received.

(8) A debtor who knows that an assignation document has been granted in respect of a claim may request the assignor or the assignee to provide a written statement as to whether (either or both)—

(a) the assignation of the claim is subject to a condition,

(b) any such condition has been satisfied.

(9) If a written statement is requested under subsection (8), the debtor may withhold performance until that statement is received.

(10) Where a debtor who makes a request under subsection (1), (5) or (8) is a co-debtor, the reference in subsection (4) or (as the case may be) (7) or (9) to the debtor is to the debtor who made the request and does not include a reference to any co-debtor of that debtor.

Accessory security rights

16 Accessory security rights

(1) Subsections (2) and (3)—

(a) apply, and apply only, in relation to any claim assigned in whole, but

(b) are subject to any express provision to the contrary in the assignation document.

(2) Subject to anything which requires to be done under subsection (3), the assignee acquires, by virtue of the transfer of the claim, any security (in so far as the security is transferable) which relates to, and only to, the claim transferred.

(3) Where the performance of some act by the assignor is necessary for the security to transfer to the assignee, the assignor must—

(a) perform that act, and

(b) do so as soon as reasonably practicable after the claim is transferred.

(4) In this section, 'security' means both—

(a) a right in security, and

(b) the correlative right in respect of a cautionary obligation.

Abolition of certain rules of law

17 Abolition of certain rules of law

(1) The following rules of law are abolished insofar as they apply to an assignation of a claim to which this Part applies—

(a) any rule whereby a mandate may operate as an assignation of a claim,

(b) any rule whereby an assignation is rendered ineffective by an instruction to the debtor by an assignee of a claim that the debtor perform to the assignor,

(c) any rule whereby an assignee of a claim may sue in the name of an assignor, and

(d) any rule as to warrandice to be implied—

(i) in assigning a claim, or

(ii) in providing, in a contract or unilateral undertaking, for the assignation of a claim.

(2) But subsection (1)(c) does not affect the application of any enactment, or any rule of law, as respects subrogation.

Saving

18 Saving as respects International Interests in Aircraft Equipment (Cape Town Convention) Regulations 2015

(1) This Part is without prejudice to the application, as respects the assignment and acquisition of associated rights, of the International Interests in Aircraft Equipment (Cape Town Convention) Regulations 2015 (SI 2015/912).

(2) In subsection (1)—

'assignment' has the meaning given by regulation 5, as read with regulation 35, of those regulations, and

'associated rights' has the meaning given by regulation 5 of those regulations.

CHAPTER 2
Register of Assignations

Register of Assignations

19 The Register of Assignations

(1) There is to be a public register known as the Register of Assignations.

(2) The register is to be under the management and control of the Keeper.

(3) Subject to the provisions of this Act, the register is to be in such form as the Keeper thinks fit.

(4) The Keeper must take such steps as appear reasonable to the Keeper to protect the register from—

(a) interference,

(b) unauthorised access, and

(c) damage.

Structure and contents of the register

20 The parts of the register

The Keeper must make up and maintain, as parts of the register—

(a) the assignations record, and

(b) the archive record.

21 The assignations record

(1) An entry in the assignations record is to comprise—

(a) the assignor's name and address,

(b) where the assignor is an individual, the assignor's date of birth,

(c) any identifying number which the assignor has and which, by virtue of RoA Rules, must be included in the entry,

(d) the assignee's name and address,

(e) any identifying number which the assignee has and which, by virtue of RoA Rules, must be included in the entry,

(f) where the assignee is not an individual, an address (which may be an email address) to which any request for information regarding the assignation may be sent,

(g) such description of the claim as is required, or permitted, for the purposes of this subsection by RoA Rules,

(h) a copy of the assignation document,

(i) the registration number allocated under section 25(1)(b) to the entry,

(j) the date and time of registration of the assignation document,

(k) any other information that is required under any other section of this Act, and

(l) any other information that is specified for the purposes of this subsection by RoA Rules.

(2) The assignations record is the totality of all such entries.

22 The archive record

The archive record is the totality of—

(a) all entries and copy documents transferred from the assignations record under section 30(1)(a) or (2)(c),

(b) all copy documents included in the archive record under section 30(1)(c) or (2)(b),

(c) all copies of such other documents as the Keeper considers it appropriate to include in the archive record, and

(d) any other information that is specified for the purposes of this section by RoA Rules.

Registration process

23 Application for registration

(1) An assignee may apply to the Keeper for registration of an assignation document.

(2) The Keeper must deal with applications in the order in which they are received.

(3) The Keeper must accept the application if—

(a) it is submitted with a copy of the assignation document,

(b) it contains all the information the Keeper requires in accordance with section 21 to be able to make up an entry for the assignation document under section 25(1),

(c) it conforms to such RoA Rules as relate to the application, and

(d) either—

(i) such fee as is payable for the registration is paid, or

(ii) arrangements satisfactory to the Keeper are made for payment of that fee.

(4) If the requirements of subsection (3) are not satisfied, the Keeper must reject the application and inform the applicant accordingly.

24 Application for registration where claims assigned to different assignees

(1) Where an assignation document assigns different claims to different assignees, each assignee may apply to the Keeper for registration of the document only in so far as it assigns a claim to that assignee ('the applicant').

(2) A reference in this Part, in relation to an assignation document in respect of which such an application has been accepted by the Keeper, to—

(a) the registration of the document is a reference to the registration of the document in so far as it assigns a claim to the applicant,

(b) the assignee under the document is a reference to the applicant,

(c) a claim assigned by the document is a reference to a claim assigned by the document to the applicant.

25 Registration

(1) On accepting an application made under section 23, the Keeper must—

(a) make up an entry for the assignation document (from the assignation document, the information provided in the application and the circumstances of registration),

(b) allocate a registration number to the entry (based on the order in which applications are dealt with), and

(c) maintain the entry in the assignations record.

(2) An assignation document is taken to be registered on the date and at the time entered for it for the purpose of section 21(1)(j).

26 Verification statement

(1) After the registration of an assignation document under section 25, the Keeper must issue a written statement verifying the registration to—

(a) the assignor, and
(b) the assignee,
but only if and to the extent that the application made under section 23 contains an email address for those persons.
(2) That statement must—
(a) include—
(i) the date and time of the registration, and
(ii) the registration number allocated to the entry made up for the assignation document, and
(b) conform to such RoA Rules as relate to the statement.
(3) Where a statement is issued under subsection (1) and is received by the assignee but not the assignor, the assignor may request a copy of it from the assignee.
(4) Within 21 days beginning with the day a request is made under subsection (3), the assignee must supply the assignor with the copy requested.

Effective registration

27 Effective registration of assignation document

(1) The registration of an assignation document is ineffective if—
(a) the entry made up for the assignation document in the assignations record—
(i) does not include a copy of the assignation document, or
(ii) is, at the time of registration, seriously misleading as a result of an inaccuracy or inaccuracies in it, or
(b) the assignation document is invalid.
(2) But subsection (1)(a)(ii) is subject to section 28(1)(c) and (d).
(3) Where the registration of an assignation document is ineffective by virtue of subsection (1), it becomes effective if and when the entry is corrected.

28 Seriously misleading inaccuracies in the assignations record

(1) In determining for the purpose of section 27(1)(a)(ii) whether an entry in the assignations record is seriously misleading as a result of an inaccuracy or inaccuracies in it—
(a) the entry is seriously misleading where—
(i) any of subsections (2) to (5) apply, or
(ii) despite sub-paragraph (i) not being satisfied, the inaccuracy or inaccuracies are such that a reasonable person would be seriously misled by the entry,
(b) any inaccuracy is to be disregarded to the extent that it appears in the assignation document but is not replicated elsewhere in the entry,
(c) where the entry is seriously misleading in respect of only part of the assigned claim, that is not to be taken to affect the entry in its application to the rest of the claim,
(d) where the entry is seriously misleading in respect of a co-assignor or co-assignee but not in respect of both (or all) co-assignors or co-assignees, that is not to be taken to affect the entry in its application to a co-assignor or co-assignee in respect of whom the entry is not seriously misleading.
(2) This subsection applies where—
(a) the assignor is a person required by RoA Rules to be identified in the assignations record by an identifying number, and
(b) if a search of the record were to be carried out for that number, using the search facility provided under section 33, it would not disclose the entry.
(3) This subsection applies where—
(a) the assignor is not a person required by RoA Rules to be identified in the assignations record by an identifying number, and
(b) if a search of the record were to be carried out, using the search facility provided under section 33, for—

(i) the assignor's proper name at the date the application for registration was made, or

(ii) the assignor's proper name at that date together with the assignor's month and year of birth,

it would not disclose the entry.

(4) This subsection applies where the entry inaccurately reflects the assignee's proper name at the date the application for registration was made in such a way that a reasonable person would be seriously misled.

(5) This subsection applies where—

(a) there is a requirement, by virtue of section 21(1)(g), for an entry in the assignations record to specify the type of claim assigned, and

(b) the entry—

(i) describes the claim as being of a type that it is not, or

(ii) fails to allocate a type to the claim.

(6) In the application of this section to co-assignors and co-assignees—

(a) subsections (2) and (3) apply in relation to a co-assignor as they apply in relation to an assignor,

(b) subsection (4) applies in relation to a co-assignee as it applies in relation to an assignee.

(7) The Scottish Ministers may by regulations modify this section to make provision about what does, and what does not, make an entry seriously misleading for the purpose of section 27(1)(a)(ii) and how that is to be determined.

(8) In this section, the 'proper name' of an assignor or assignee means the person's name in the form determined in accordance with RoA Rules.

Corrections

29 Correction of the assignations record

(1) Where a court determines in any proceedings that the assignations record is inaccurate, the court—

(a) must direct the Keeper to correct the record, and

(b) may give the Keeper any further direction it considers necessary in connection with the correction.

(2) Where the Keeper becomes aware of a manifest inaccuracy in the assignations record, other than as a result of a direction under subsection (1)—

(a) the Keeper must correct the record if what is needed to correct it is manifest,

(b) otherwise, the Keeper must note the inaccuracy on the entry in question.

(3) There is an 'inaccuracy' in the assignations record where—

(a) the information included, by virtue of section 21(1), in an entry in the record is inaccurate or incomplete,

(b) an entry in the record—

(i) does not include a copy of the assignation document as required by paragraph (h) of that section, or

(ii) includes such a copy but the document copied is invalid, or

(c) an entry has incorrectly been removed from the record.

(4) A correction of the assignations record may involve—

(a) the removal of an entry,

(b) the removal of information included in an entry,

(c) the amendment of, or an addition to, the information, or replacement of a copy document, included in an entry,

(d) the restoration of information, or of a copy document, to an entry,

(e) the restoration of an entry (whether or not by transferring it from the archive record to the assignations record).

(5) A correction is taken to be made on the date and at the time entered for it in the register in pursuance of a provision of this Part.

30 Correction of the assignations record: procedure

(1) Where the Keeper corrects the assignations record by removing an entry from the assignations record, the Keeper must—

(a) transfer the entry to the archive record,

(b) note on the transferred entry—

(i) the subsection of section 29 by virtue of which the transfer is made, and

(ii) the details of the correction (including the date and time of the removal), and

(c) include in the archive record a copy of any document which discloses, or contributes to disclosing, the inaccuracy which is the subject of the correction.

(2) Where the Keeper corrects the record by restoring an entry, by restoring, removing or amending information included in an entry or by restoring or replacing a copy document, the Keeper must—

(a) note on the entry that it has been corrected and the details of the correction (including the date and time of the correction),

(b) include in the archive record a copy of any document which discloses, or contributes to disclosing, the inaccuracy which is the subject of the correction, and

(c) in the case of the replacement of the copy document, transfer the replaced copy to the archive record.

(3) Having corrected the record, the Keeper must notify the following persons (in so far as it is reasonable and practicable to do so) that the correction has been made—

(a) every person specified for the purposes of this subsection by RoA Rules, and

(b) any other person who appears to the Keeper to be affected by it materially.

(4) A failure to comply with subsection (1)(c), (2)(b) or (3) does not affect the validity of the correction of the record.

31 Proceedings involving the accuracy of the assignations record

The Keeper is entitled to appear and be heard in any civil proceedings, whether before a court or tribunal, in which—

(a) the accuracy of the assignations record, or

(b) what is needed to correct an inaccuracy in the record,

is put in question.

32 Power to make provision about applications for corrections

(1) The Scottish Ministers may by regulations modify this Part to make provision for or about applications to the Keeper for the correction of an entry in the assignations record.

(2) Regulations under subsection (1) may, in particular—

(a) make provision about—

(i) the persons, or descriptions of persons, who are entitled to make an application,

(ii) the circumstances in which an application is to be accepted (which may include consideration of whether there has been payment of a fee), and

(iii) the steps to be taken where an application is accepted,

(b) modify the Keeper's duty to act on becoming aware of a manifest inaccuracy in the assignations record to take account of the application process, and

(c) allow RoA Rules to make provision about the procedure in relation to applications for corrections.

Searches and extracts

33 Searching the assignations record

(1) The Keeper must provide a facility by which the assignations record may be searched.

(2) That search facility must allow the assignations record to be searched by reference to, and only by reference to—

(a) any of the following information in the entries contained in that record—

(i) the names of assignors, which must be capable of being searched with and without the months and years of birth of assignors who are individuals,

(ii) the identifying numbers of assignors required by RoA Rules to be identified in the assignations record by such a number,

(b) registration numbers allocated, under section 25(1)(b), to entries in that record, or

(c) any other factor, or characteristic, specified for the purposes of this paragraph by RoA Rules.

(3) Subject to any restrictions imposed under RoA Rules, a person may search the assignations record using the search facility provided under subsection (1) provided that either—

(a) such fee as is payable for the search is paid, or

(b) arrangements satisfactory to the Keeper are made for payment of that fee.

(4) But no fee is payable for a search of the assignations record which is carried out on behalf of an individual by a not-for-profit money adviser (being an adviser who does not charge individuals for the adviser's services).

(5) The Scottish Ministers may, by regulations, make further provision about the meaning of 'not-for-profit money adviser' for the purposes of subsection (4).

34 Admissibility and evidential status of search results

(1) A copy of a search result (in printed or electronic form) which relates to a search carried out by means of a search facility provided by the Keeper is admissible in evidence.

(2) In the absence of evidence to the contrary—

(a) where such a search result purports to show an entry in the assignations record, it is sufficient proof of—

(i) the registration of the assignation document to which the result relates,

(ii) where applicable, a correction of the entry in the assignations record to which the result relates, and

(iii) the date and time of such registration or, as the case may be, correction, and

(b) where such a search result purports not to show an entry in the assignations record, it is sufficient proof of an entry in the assignations record not being disclosed at the date and time of such search by means of the search carried out.

35 Extracts and their evidential status

(1) A person may apply to the Keeper for an extract of an entry in the register.

(2) The Keeper must issue the extract if—

(a) such fee as is payable for issuing it is paid, or

(b) arrangements satisfactory to the Keeper are made for payment of that fee.

(3) But if, on application under subsection (1), the applicant requests an extract as at a specific date and time, the Keeper need comply with the request only to the extent that it is reasonably practicable to do so.

(4) The Keeper may validate the extract as the Keeper considers appropriate.

(5) The Keeper may issue the extract as an electronic document unless the applicant requests that it be issued as a traditional document.

(6) The extract is to be accepted for all purposes as sufficient evidence of the contents of the entry as at—

(a) in the case of an extract requested as mentioned in subsection (3), the date and time to which the extract relates (being a date and time specified in the extract), and

(b) in any other case, the date on which and the time at which the extract is issued (being a date and time specified in the extract).

Requests for information

36 Assignee's duty to respond to request for information

(1) An entitled person may ask the person identified in an entry in the assignations record as the assignee (the 'registered assignee') to provide the entitled person with a written statement as to whether—

(a) a claim specified by the entitled person is assigned by the assignation document,

(b) the registered assignee has granted a further assignation document in respect of the claim, or

(c) a condition specified by the entitled person and to which the assignation is subject has been satisfied.

(2) The following are entitled persons for the purposes of this section—

(a) in relation to a request under subsection (1), a person who (depending on who holds the claim) may have a right to execute diligence against the claim, or

(b) a person not mentioned in paragraph (a) but who has the consent of the person identified in the entry as the assignor to make a request under subsection (1).

(3) For the purposes of subsection (2)(a), a person who may have a right to execute diligence against the claim includes a person authorised to execute a charge for payment who (depending on who holds the claim) may have a right to execute diligence against the claim if and when the days of charge expire without payment.

(4) The registered assignee must, within 21 days beginning with the day of receiving a request under subsection (1), comply with it unless—

(a) it is manifest that the registration is ineffective in relation to the assignation of the claim to which the request relates,

(b) in the case of a request made under subsection (1)(a), it is manifest from the entry for the assignation that the claim specified is not assigned by the assignation document,

(c) both—

(i) the registered assignee has, within the period of 3 months ending with the day of receipt of the request, complied with a request under the same paragraph of subsection (1) from the same person and in relation to the same claim, and

(ii) the information contained in the statement issued in relation to the earlier request remains correct.

(5) The registered assignee may recover from the entitled person any costs reasonably incurred in complying with the request.

(6) On the application of the registered assignee, the court may by order—

(a) exempt the registered assignee from complying with a request under subsection (1) or such part of the request as it specifies in the order, or

(b) extend the period within which the registered assignee must comply with the request by such number of days as it specifies in the order,

if satisfied that in all the circumstances it would be reasonable to do so.

(7) If, on the application of the entitled person, the court is satisfied that the registered assignee has, without reasonable excuse, failed to comply with subsection (4), it may by order require the registered assignee to comply with the request within 14 days or such other period (which may be longer or shorter than 14 days) as the court considers appropriate.

(8) The Scottish Ministers may by regulations modify this section so as to specify further persons, or descriptions of persons, who are entitled persons for the purposes of this section.

Entitlement to compensation

37 Liability of Keeper

(1) A person is entitled to be compensated by the Keeper for loss suffered in consequence of—

(a) an inaccuracy in the assignations record to the extent that it is attributable to the making up, maintenance or operation of the register (including an attempted correction of it),

(b) the issue, under section 26(1), of a written statement which is incorrect,

(c) the service, under section 30(3), of a notification which is incorrect,

(d) a search result which—

(i) relates to a search of the assignations record carried out by means of a search facility provided by the Keeper,

(ii) ought (as a result of the search terms used) to reflect accurately the contents of the assignations record at the time the search was made, and

(iii) does not accurately reflect those contents,

(e) the issue, under section 35, of an extract which is not a true extract,

(f) an application being accepted or rejected in error,

(g) an attempt to make an application, which the Keeper would otherwise have accepted, failing as a result of an error in the system the Keeper has for accepting applications, or

(h) applications being dealt with otherwise than in the order in which they are received.

(2) But the Keeper has no liability under subsection (1)—

(a) in so far as the person's loss could have been avoided had the person taken measures which it would have been reasonable for the person to take,

(b) in so far as the person's loss was not reasonably foreseeable, or

(c) for non-patrimonial loss.

(3) For the avoidance of doubt, an inaccuracy in information included in an entry in the assignations record when that entry is made up under section 25(1)(a) or corrected under section 29 does not fall within subsection (1)(a) to the extent that the Keeper—

(a) has been misled into making the inaccuracy, and

(b) reasonably believed the information to be accurate.

(4) For the purposes of subsection (3), the circumstances where the Keeper is entitled to reasonably believe information to be accurate include those where it is provided—

(a) in connection with an application to which the entry relates, or

(b) by the court.

38 Liability of certain other persons

(1) A person ('P') is entitled to be compensated in the following circumstances—

(a) where P suffers loss in consequence of an inaccuracy in an entry in the assignations record then, to the extent that it is not attributable to the Keeper, P is entitled to be compensated for that loss by—

(i) the person who made the application for registration which gave rise to the inaccurate entry if that person failed to take reasonable care in making it, or

(ii) where the inaccurate entry arises from the attempted correction of an apparent inaccuracy, the person who notified the Keeper of the apparent inaccuracy if that person failed to take reasonable care in doing so,

(b) where P suffers loss in consequence of an inaccuracy in information supplied in response to a request under section 36(1), P is entitled to be compensated for that loss by the person who supplied the information if that person failed to take reasonable care in supplying it, or

(c) where P suffers loss in consequence of a failure, without reasonable excuse, to comply with a request in accordance with section 36(4), P is entitled to be compensated for that loss by the person whose failure it was.

(2) But a person has no liability under subsection (1)—

(a) in so far as P's loss could have been avoided had P taken measures which it would have been reasonable for P to take,

(b) in so far as P's loss was not reasonably foreseeable, or

(c) for non-patrimonial loss.

Rules

39 Rules

(1) The Scottish Ministers may by regulations make rules ('RoA Rules')—

(a) about the making up and keeping of the register,

(b) about the procedure in relation to applications for registration under section 23(1),

(c) about searches in the register and the results of those searches,

(d) about the required form and content of any document or information to be used in relation to the register,

(e) requiring there to be entered in the assignations record or the archive record such information as is specified in the rules, or

(f) regarding other matters in relation to registration under this Part, being matters for which the Scottish Ministers consider it necessary or expedient to provide in order to give full effect to the purposes of this Part.

(2) RoA Rules under subsection (1) may, in particular, include provision—

(a) about the identification, in any application and in the register, of any person or claim, including—

(i) how the proper form of a person's name is to be determined, and

(ii) where the person has an identifying number (whether of numerals or of letters and numerals) allocated to the person, whether that number must be used in identifying the person,

(b) about the nature of the address of the assignor or the assignee to be included in an entry in the register,

(c) about the degree of precision with which time is to be recorded in the register,

(d) about information which, though contained in an assignation document, need not be included in a copy of that document submitted with an application under section 23(1),

(e) about whether a signature contained in an assignation document need be included in a copy of that document so submitted,

(f) about information which, though contained in the register, is not to be—

(i) available to persons searching it, or

(ii) included in any extract issued under section 35,

(g) about when the register is open for—

(i) registration,

(ii) searches.

[(3) Before making RoA Rules under subsection (1), the Scottish Ministers must consult the Keeper.]

CHAPTER 3
Miscellaneous and Interpretation of Part 1

Miscellaneous

40 Repeal of Transmission of Moveable Property (Scotland) Act 1862

The Transmission of Moveable Property (Scotland) Act 1862 is repealed.

Interpretation of Part 1

41 Interpretation of Part 1

(1) In this Part (except where the context requires otherwise)—

'the archive record' is to be construed in accordance with section 22,

'assignation' means assignation of a claim,

'assignation document' has the meaning given by section 1(1),

'the assignations record' is to be construed in accordance with section 21(2),
'assignee' means the person to whom a claim is assigned,
'assignor' means the person by whom a claim is assigned,
'claim'—

(a) means a right to the performance of an obligation (including an obligation not to do something), but

(b) does not include a non-monetary right relating to land or a negotiable instrument,

'correction', in relation to the assignations record, is to be construed in accordance with section 29(4),
'debtor' means the person against whom a claim may be enforced,
'holder', in relation to a claim, means the person who has the right to performance of an obligation under the claim,
'inaccuracy', in relation to the assignations record, is to be construed in accordance with section 29(3),
'the register' means the Register of Assignations,
'right in security'—

(a) means a right in security over property (including a floating charge), but

(b) does not include a right to execute diligence,

'RoA Rules' has the meaning given by section 39(1).

(2) Where two or more persons are co-assignors or co-assignees in relation to a claim, any reference in this Act to the assignor or assignee (as the case may be) is, unless the context requires otherwise, a reference to all of those persons.

(3) A reference (however expressed) in this Part to—

(a) an assignation document having been granted in respect of a claim is to be construed as a reference to the document having been executed or authenticated,

(b) an assignation document being registered is to be construed as a reference to the Keeper's carrying out, in respect of the document, the duties imposed on the Keeper by section 25(1)(a) and (b).

PART 2
SECURITY OVER MOVEABLE PROPERTY

CHAPTER 1
Pledge

Pledge, secured obligation and encumbered property

42 Pledge

(1) A pledge is created in accordance with this section.

(2) Where a pledge is to be created over moveable property which is corporeal only, the pledge is created—

(a) by delivery of the property to the secured creditor, provided that the property is the provider's at the time of delivery,

(b) in a case where the property is not the provider's at the time of such delivery, on the property becoming the provider's subsequent to such delivery, or

(c) by registration in accordance with section 48 or 49.

(3) Where a pledge is to be created over moveable property which is—

(a) incorporeal only, or

(b) both corporeal and incorporeal,

the pledge is created by registration in accordance with section 48 or 49.

(4) A pledge created by registration in accordance with section 48 or 49 is to be known as a 'statutory pledge'.

(5) Nothing in this section affects any rule of law which existed prior to the commencement of this section whereby a pledge may be created over a negotiable

instrument, and nothing in this Part applies in relation to any pledge created in accordance with such a rule.

[(6) See also Part 3 of the Moveable Transactions (Scotland) Act 2023 (Financial Collateral Arrangements and Financial Instruments) (Consequential Provisions and Modifications) Order 2025 (SI 2025/275 (S 1)).]

43 Secured obligation and encumbered property

(1) The obligation secured by a pledge ('the secured obligation')—

(a) may be any obligation owed, or which will or may become owed, to or by any person, and

(b) includes ancillary obligations owed (for example, to pay interest, damages and the reasonable expense of extra-judicial recovery of interest or damages).

(2) The property over which a pledge is created and in respect of which the pledge subsists ('the encumbered property') includes, except in so far as the provider and the secured creditor agree otherwise, the natural fruits of the property but not its incorporeal fruits.

(3) At the time the pledge is created, the property which is to be the encumbered property must be transferable (whether or not its transferability is restricted in some way).

Possessory pledge

44 Delivery

(1) For the purposes of section 42(2)(a) and (b), delivery must be carried out—

(a) by physically handing over, or giving control of, the property to the relevant person,

(b) by giving control of the premises in which the property is located to the relevant person,

(c) by instructing another person who has direct possession or custody of the property to hold the property on behalf of the relevant person, or

(d) by delivering a bill of lading representing the property to the relevant person (and where that bill is to the order of a particular person, by procuring the endorsement of the bill in favour of the secured creditor).

(2) Property which, at the time agreement is reached on the creation of the pledge, is already in the direct possession or custody of the relevant person is deemed to have been delivered to the secured creditor for the purposes of section 42(2)(a) or, as the case may be, (b).

(3) In this section, 'relevant person' means—

(a) the secured creditor, or

(b) a person authorised to accept delivery on behalf of the secured creditor or, where subsection (2) applies, authorised to hold the property on behalf of the secured creditor.

(4) This section is without prejudice to section 2 of the Factors Act 1889.

Statutory pledge

45 Constitutive document

(1) A statutory pledge requires a constitutive document.

(2) The constitutive document must—

(a) be executed or authenticated by the provider,

(b) identify the property which is to be the encumbered property, and

(c) identify the obligation which is to be the secured obligation.

(3) If the encumbered property is to consist of more than one item, the constitutive document must—

(a) identify each item separately, or

(b) identify the items in terms of their constituting an identifiable class.

(4) The property identified (whether separately or as a class) as the property which is to be the encumbered property may be either property of, or property to be acquired by, the provider.

(5) For the purposes of subsections (2) and (3), the ways in which the encumbered property or the secured obligation can be identified in the constitutive document include by making reference in the constitutive document to another document, the terms of which are not reproduced.

46 Competence of individual acting as provider of a statutory pledge

(1) It is not competent for an individual to be the provider of a statutory pledge unless—

(a) the individual is acting in the course of—

(i) the individual's business,

(ii) the activities of a charity of which the individual is a trustee, or

(iii) the activities of an unincorporated association (other than a charity) of which the individual is a member, and

(b) the encumbered property is a permitted asset, or consists only of permitted assets.

[(1A) But see also article 6 (competence of individual acting as provider of statutory pledge over financial instrument) of the Moveable Transactions (Scotland) Act 2023 (Financial Collateral Arrangements and Financial Instruments) (Consequential Provisions and Modifications) Order 2025 (SI 2025/275 (S 1)).]

(2) For the purpose of subsection (1)(b), an asset is a 'permitted asset' if—

(a) it is (as the case may be)—

(i) used, or to be used, wholly or mainly for the purposes of the individual's business,

(ii) an asset of the charity, or

(iii) owned by the individual on behalf of, or jointly with the other members of, the association, and

(b) in the case of corporeal property, it has a monetary value exceeding £3,000 immediately before the document under which it will become encumbered property is granted.

(3) The Scottish Ministers may by regulations—

(a) modify subsection (2)(b) so as to modify the amount for the time being specified there,

(b) modify this section so as to specify types of property which are or are not permitted assets.

(4) For the purposes of this section—

(a) 'charity' means—

(i) a charity within the meaning of section 106 of the Charities and Trustee Investment (Scotland) Act 2005, or

(ii) an organisation managed or controlled wholly or mainly outwith Scotland and which is registered in a register equivalent to the Scottish Charity Register (kept under section 3 of that Act) for the purposes of the country in which it operates,

(b) a trustee of a charity is one of the persons having the general control and management of the administration of the charity.

47 Competence of creating statutory pledge over certain kinds of property

(1) It is not competent to create a statutory pledge over corporeal property which is—

(a) an aircraft in respect of which it is competent to register a mortgage in the register of aircraft mortgages kept by the Civil Aviation Authority,

(b) an aircraft object (as defined in regulation 5 of the International Interests in Aircraft Equipment (Cape Town Convention) Regulations 2015 (SI 2015/912)), or

(c) a ship (or a share in a ship) in respect of which it is competent to register a mortgage in the register of British ships maintained for the United Kingdom under section 8 of the Merchant Shipping Act 1995.

(2) It is not competent to create a statutory pledge over incorporeal property unless that property is—

(a) intellectual property, or

(b) an application for, or licence over, intellectual property.

[(2A) But see also article 5 (competence of creating statutory pledge over financial instrument) of the Moveable Transactions (Scotland) Act 2023 (Financial Collateral Arrangements and Financial Instruments) (Consequential Provisions and Modifications) Order 2025 (SI 2025/275 (S 1)).]

(3) The Scottish Ministers may by regulations modify this section so as to specify further kinds of incorporeal property over which it is competent to create a statutory pledge.

48 Creation of statutory pledge by registration: general

(1) A statutory pledge is created over property which is identified in a constitutive document in accordance with section 45 on the requirements mentioned in subsection (2) all being met.

(2) Those requirements are that—

(a) the property is the provider's,

(b) the statutory pledge is registered, and

(c) the property is identifiable as property to which the constitutive document relates.

(3) Subsection (2)(b) is subject to section 91 (effective registration of statutory pledge) and, accordingly, the requirement of that subsection—

(a) is not met if the registration of the constitutive document is ineffective in accordance with section 91(1), and

(b) is met if and when that registration becomes effective in accordance with section 91(3).

(4) This section is subject to section 50 (creation of statutory pledge: insolvency).

49 Creation of statutory pledge over added property

(1) Where a statutory pledge is amended so as to add property to the encumbered property by means of an amendment document under section 58, a statutory pledge is created over the added property on the requirements mentioned in subsection (2) all being met.

(2) Those requirements are that—

(a) the added property is the provider's,

(b) the amendment is registered, and

(c) the added property is identifiable as property to which the amendment document relates.

(3) Subsection (2)(b) is subject to section 92 (effective registration of amendment to statutory pledge) and, accordingly, the requirement of that subsection—

(a) is not met if the registration of the amendment document is ineffective in accordance with section 92(1), and

(b) is met if and when that registration becomes effective in accordance with section 92(3).

(4) This section is subject to section 50 (creation of statutory pledge: insolvency).

50 Creation of statutory pledge: insolvency

(1) This section applies where—

(a) the property identified (whether separately or as a class) as the property which is to be the encumbered property under a statutory pledge is or includes property to be acquired by the provider, and

(b) after the pledge is granted, the provider becomes insolvent.

(2) The statutory pledge is not created over any property which, though identified by the constitutive document or by an amendment document as property to be encumbered, is acquired by the provider after becoming insolvent.

(3) For the purposes of subsection (2)—

(a) a provider who is an individual, or the estate of which may be sequestrated by virtue of section 6 of the Bankruptcy (Scotland) Act 2016, becomes insolvent when—

(i) the provider's estate is sequestrated,

(ii) the provider grants a trust deed for creditors or makes a composition or arrangement with creditors,

(iii) the provider is adjudged bankrupt,

(iv) a voluntary arrangement proposed by the provider is approved, [or]

[. . .]

(vi) the provider becomes subject to any other order or arrangement analogous to any of those mentioned in sub-paragraphs (i) to [(iv)] anywhere in the world, and

(b) a provider other than is mentioned in paragraph (a) becomes insolvent when—

(i) a decision approving a voluntary arrangement entered into by the provider has effect under section 4A of the Insolvency Act 1986 ('the 1986 Act'),

(ii) the provider is wound up under Part 4 or 5 of the 1986 Act or under section 367 of the Financial Services and Markets Act 2000,

(iii) an administrative receiver, as defined in section 251 of the 1986 Act, is appointed over all or part (being a part to which the constitutive document or any amendment document relates) of the property of the provider,

(iv) the provider enters administration ('enters administration' being construed in accordance with paragraph 1(2) of schedule B1 of the 1986 Act),

(v) an order under section 901F of the Companies Act 2006 sanctioning a compromise or arrangement entered into by the provider comes into effect over all or part of the property of the provider, or

(vi) the provider becomes subject to any other order, appointment or arrangement analogous to any of those mentioned in sub-paragraphs (i) to (v) anywhere in the world.

(4) The Scottish Ministers may by regulations modify subsection (3).

Property encumbered by statutory pledge: effect of transfer by provider

51 Property encumbered by statutory pledge: transfer by provider

(1) If the provider of a statutory pledge transfers the encumbered property (or any part of it) to a third party, the transferred property remains encumbered by the pledge unless—

(a) the consent mentioned in subsection (2) is obtained,

(b) the third party acquires the property unencumbered under any of sections 53 to 55, or

(c) the pledge is otherwise extinguished by the transfer, in whole or in relation to the transferred property, under section 52, 93 or 108.

[(1A) See also article 8 (acquisition of financial instrument encumbered by statutory pledge in the ordinary course of trading) of the Moveable Transactions (Scotland) Act 2023 (Financial Collateral Arrangements and Financial Instruments) (Consequential Provisions and Modifications) Order 2025 (SI 2025/275 (S 1)).]

(2) The consent referred to in subsection (1)(a)—

(a) is the prior written consent of the secured creditor—

(i) to the particular transfer, and

(ii) to the property in question being transferred unencumbered by the pledge, and

(b) does not include consent granted more than 14 days before the day of the particular transfer.

(3) Whether to grant or withhold the consent mentioned in subsection (2) must remain at the discretion of the secured creditor (that is, the secured creditor may not agree in advance how that discretion will be exercised).

(4) The Scottish Ministers may by regulations—

(a) modify subsection (2) (including by specifying further descriptions of consent by reference to which subsection (1) is to apply),

(b) modify this section so as to specify further matters relevant to the granting or withholding of consent.

52 Extinction of statutory pledge where dealings inconsistent with a fixed security

If a secured creditor acquiesces, expressly or impliedly, in a provider's transfer of encumbered property (or any part of it) to a third party, other than by means of granting the consent mentioned in section 51(2), the statutory pledge under which the property (or part) was encumbered is extinguished [(but see also article 11(3) (restriction, discharge or extinction of unregistered statutory pledge over financial instrument) of the Moveable Transactions (Scotland) Act 2023 (Financial Collateral Arrangements and Financial Instruments) (Consequential Provisions and Modifications) Order 2025 (SI 2025/275 (S 1))).]

53 Acquisition in good faith from seller acting in ordinary course of business

(1) A purchaser of corporeal property which is encumbered property under a statutory pledge acquires it unencumbered by the statutory pledge, despite the consent mentioned in section 51(2) not having been obtained, if—

(a) the person from whom the property is acquired is acting in the ordinary course of that person's business, and

(b) at the time of acquisition, the purchaser is in good faith.

(2) For the purposes of subsection (1)(b), a purchaser is not to be taken to be other than in good faith by reason only of the statutory pledge having been registered.

54 Acquisition in good faith for personal, domestic or household purposes

(1) An individual who acquires corporeal property which is encumbered property under a statutory pledge acquires it unencumbered by the statutory pledge, despite the consent mentioned in section 51(2) not having been obtained, if—

(a) the property is wholly or mainly acquired for personal, domestic or household purposes,

(b) the acquirer gives value for the property acquired, and

(c) at the time of acquisition, the acquirer is in good faith.

(2) For the purposes of subsection (1)(c), an acquirer is not to be taken to be other than in good faith by reason only of the statutory pledge having been registered.

(3) The Scottish Ministers may by regulations modify subsection (1) so as to—

(a) limit its application to cases where the value of all that is acquired does not, at the time of acquisition, exceed a specified amount, and

(b) modify the amount for the time being specified there by virtue of paragraph (a).

55 Acquisition in good faith of motor vehicles

(1) Subsections (2) to (4) apply where—

(a) there is a sale agreement (including a conditional sale agreement) or a hire-purchase agreement in respect of a motor vehicle,

(b) the motor vehicle is encumbered property under a statutory pledge,

(c) at the time of entering into the agreement, the purchaser or hirer is not a person carrying on a business described in section 29(2) of the Hire-Purchase Act 1964, and

(d) the purchaser or hirer is, at that time, in good faith.

(2) On the motor vehicle being transferred to the purchaser or hirer in accordance with the agreement, that person acquires it unencumbered by the statutory pledge despite the consent mentioned in section 51(2) not having been obtained.

(3) And the statutory pledge is not to be enforced against the motor vehicle before the motor vehicle is transferred to the purchaser or hirer in accordance with the agreement.

(4) But if the transferor is, at the time the agreement is entered into, a person carrying on a business described in section 29(2) of the Hire-Purchase Act 1964, the secured creditor is entitled to receive from the transferor the lesser of—

(a) the amount outstanding in respect of the secured obligation, and

(b) the amount received, or to be received, by the transferor in respect of the acquisition.

(5) Where the secured creditor receives a sum under subsection (4)—

(a) the provider's liability to the secured creditor under the secured obligation is reduced by the same amount, but

(b) the transferor has a right of relief against the provider in respect of the sum.

(6) For the purposes of subsection (1)(d), a purchaser or hirer is not to be taken to be other than in good faith by reason only of the statutory pledge having been registered.

(7) In this section, 'conditional sale agreement', 'hire-purchase agreement' and 'motor vehicle' have the meanings given by section 29(1) of the Hire-Purchase Act 1964.

(8) The Scottish Ministers may by regulations specify classes of motor vehicles to which subsections (1) to (7) do not apply.

(9) Regulations under subsection (8) may modify sections 53 and 54 to provide that either or both of those sections do not apply to some or all of the classes of motor vehicle specified under subsection (8).

Rights relating to matrimonial or family home where relevant to a statutory pledge

56 Occupancy and other rights in family home following grant of statutory pledge

(1) The Matrimonial Homes (Family Protection) (Scotland) Act 1981 ('the 1981 Act') and the Civil Partnership Act 2004 ('the 2004 Act') are amended in accordance with this section.

(2) After section 2(8) of the 1981 Act and section 102(8) of the 2004 Act, insert—

'(8A) In subsection (1)(a), 'secured loan' includes secured obligation (construed in accordance with section 43(1) of the Moveable Transactions (Scotland) Act 2023).'.

(3) In section 3 of the 1981 Act and section 103 of the 2004 Act, at the end of subsection (2) insert 'or the rights of any secured creditor in relation to the non-performance of a secured obligation.'.

(4) After section 3(8) of the 1981 Act, insert—

'(9) In subsection (2)—

'secured creditor' has the meaning given by section 113(1) of the Moveable Transactions (Scotland) Act 2023, and

'secured obligation' is to be construed in accordance with section 43(1) of the Moveable Transactions (Scotland) Act 2023.'.

(5) After section 103(9) of the 2004 Act, insert—

'(10) In subsection (2)—

'secured creditor' has the meaning given by section 113(1) of the Moveable Transactions (Scotland) Act 2023, and

'secured obligation' is to be construed in accordance with section 43(1) of the Moveable Transactions (Scotland) Act 2023.'.

(6) In section 6(2) of the 1981 Act and section 106(2) of the 2004 Act, in the definition of 'dealing', after the words 'heritable security' insert ', the grant of a statutory pledge'.

(7) In section 8 of the 1981 Act, after subsection (2B) insert—

'(2C) For the purposes of subsection (2A) above, the time of granting a security, in the case of a statutory pledge, is—

(a) the date of delivery of the constitutive document of the statutory pledge, or

(b) where the statutory pledge is granted in an amendment document, the date of delivery of that document.'.

(8) In section 108 of the 2004 Act, after subsection (4) insert—

'(5) For the purposes of subsection (3), the time of granting a security, in the case of a statutory pledge, is—

(a) the date of delivery of the constitutive document of the statutory pledge, or

(b) where the statutory pledge is granted in an amendment document, the date of delivery of that document.'.

(9) The title of section 8 of the 1981 Act and section 108 of the 2004 Act becomes 'Interests of creditors'.

Assignation, amendment, restriction or extinction of statutory pledge

57 Assignation of statutory pledge

(1) Except in so far as the provider and the secured creditor agree otherwise, a statutory pledge may be assigned.

(2) A statutory pledge is assigned only by the secured creditor executing or authenticating a document assigning the pledge.

(3) Subject to the provisions of that document, the assignation conveys to the assignee entitlement to the benefit of any notice served, or enforcement procedure commenced, by the assignor in respect of the statutory pledge before the assignation (to the effect that the assignee may proceed as if the assignee served that notice or commenced those procedures).

[(4) See also article 9 (assignation of unregistered statutory pledge over financial instrument) of the Moveable Transactions (Scotland) Act 2023 (Financial Collateral Arrangements and Financial Instruments) (Consequential Provisions and Modifications) Order 2025 (SI 2025/275 (S 1)).]

58 Amendment of statutory pledge

(1) Subject to section 59(a), a statutory pledge may be amended only by means of a document (an 'amendment document') executed or authenticated by the secured creditor and the provider.

(2) But an amendment document which relates only to the addition of property to the encumbered property need not be executed or authenticated by the secured creditor.

[(2A) See also article 10 (amendment of unregistered statutory pledge over financial instrument) of the Moveable Transactions (Scotland) Act 2023 (Financial Collateral Arrangements and Financial Instruments) (Consequential Provisions and Modifications) Order 2025 (SI 2025/275 (S 1)).]

(3) An amendment document which relates to the addition of property to the encumbered property must identify the property to be added.

(4) If the property to be added consists of more than one item, the amendment document must—

(a) identify each item separately, or

(b) identify the items in terms of their constituting an identifiable class.

(5) The property identified (whether separately or as a class) as the property which is to be the added property may be either property of, or property to be acquired by, the provider.

(6) Where an amendment increases the extent of the statutory pledge—

(a) the statutory pledge is amended to give effect to the increase only when the amendment is registered effectively (see section 92), and

(b) subject to any agreement to the contrary by the parties to the amendment document, any other amendments to the statutory pledge made by the amendment document also take effect at the time mentioned in paragraph (a).

(7) For the purposes of subsection (6), an amendment increases the extent of the statutory pledge where—

(a) the amendment adds property to the encumbered property, or

(b) both—

(i) the extent of the secured obligation is determinable from the terms alone of the entry for it in the statutory pledges record, and

(ii) the amendment increases that extent.

(8) For the purposes of subsections (3) and (4), the ways in which property added can be identified in the amendment document include by making reference in the amendment document to another document, the terms of which are not reproduced.

59 Restriction or discharge of statutory pledge

A statutory pledge may be—

(a) restricted to only part of the encumbered property, or

(b) discharged,

by means of a written statement by the secured creditor [(but see also article 11 (restriction, discharge or extinction of unregistered statutory pledge over financial instrument) of the Moveable Transactions (Scotland) Act 2023 (Financial Collateral Arrangements and Financial Instruments) (Consequential Provisions and Modifications) Order 2025 (SI 2025/275 (S 1))).]

Ranking of pledges etc.

60 Ranking

(1) Subject to the provisions of this section and of any other enactment, the priority in ranking of—

(a) any two pledges, or

(b) a pledge and a right in security other than a pledge,

is determined according to their creation, the earlier created having priority over the later.

(2) Where a provider grants two or more statutory pledges over property which is not the property of the provider at the time the pledges are granted, the priority in ranking of the pledges is determined according to the dates on which and times at which they are registered effectively (see sections 91 and 92), the earlier having priority over the later.

[(2A) But see also article 13 (ranking of statutory pledges over financial instruments) of the Moveable Transactions (Scotland) Act 2023 (Financial Collateral Arrangements and Financial Instruments) (Consequential Provisions and Modifications) Order 2025 (SI 2025/275 (S 1)).]

(3) Where property is subject both to a pledge and to a security arising by operation of law, the security arising by operation of law has priority over the pledge.

(4) The priority in ranking of a pledge is the same irrespective of whether the secured obligation is an obligation owed or is an obligation which will or may become owed.

(5) As between any two pledges, or as between a pledge and a right in security other than a pledge, the secured creditors or (as the case may be) the secured creditor and the holder of that other right may set out in a written agreement—

(a) that there is no priority in ranking, or

(b) that any priority in ranking is to be determined in a way other than would be the case in the absence of such an agreement.

(6) An agreement under subsection (5)—

(a) has effect only as between the parties to it and their successors, and

(b) is not registrable in the register.

61 Amendment of Companies Act 1985 and Insolvency Act 1986

Both in section 486(1) of the Companies Act 1985 and in section 70(1) of the Insolvency Act 1986, in the definition of 'fixed security'—

(a) the words from 'a heritable security' to '1970' become paragraph (a) of the definition, and

(b) after that paragraph insert '; or

(b) a statutory pledge within the meaning given by section 113(1) of the Moveable Transactions (Scotland) Act 2023;'.

62 Effect of diligence on pledge

(1) Subsection (2) applies where diligence is executed in respect of property which is, or any part of which is, encumbered by a pledge.

(2) The pledge has, in respect of the property or (as the case may be) the part, priority in ranking over the diligence except in relation to any part of the secured obligation which consists of a sum—

(a) advanced after execution of the diligence, and

(b) not required to be advanced by—

(i) a contractual agreement entered into before execution of the diligence, or

(ii) an undertaking entered into before execution of the diligence.

(3) Subsection (4) applies where a pledge is created over property in respect of which, or in respect of part of which, diligence has been executed.

(4) The diligence has, in respect of the property or (as the case may be) the part, priority in ranking over the pledge.

Enforcement of pledge

63 The expression 'pledge' in sections 64 to 77

In sections 64 to 77, the expression 'pledge' does not include a pledge as defined in section 189(1) of the Consumer Credit Act 1974 (that is to say, does not include a pawnee's rights over an article taken in pawn).

64 Enforcement of pledge: general

(1) A pledge is enforceable only in accordance with the provisions of this Part.

(2) A pledge may be enforced—

(a) in such circumstances as are agreed between the provider and the secured creditor, or

(b) subject to any such agreement, where there has been a failure to perform the secured obligation.

(3) Any agreement under subsection (2)(a) must be in writing.

(4) In enforcing a pledge, a secured creditor must conform to reasonable standards of commercial practice.

(5) Subsection (2) is subject to sections 55(3), 65 and 66.

65 Pledge enforcement notice

(1) Before taking any other steps to enforce a pledge, the secured creditor must serve a notice in, or as nearly as may be in, the form prescribed for the purposes of this subsection (to be known as a 'pledge enforcement notice') on—

(a) the provider,

(b) the debtor in the secured obligation (if a person other than the provider),

(c) the holder of any other right in security over all or part of the encumbered property,

(d) any creditor who has executed diligence against all or part of the encumbered property, and

(e) in the case of a statutory pledge over property which is capable of being occupied, any occupier of all or part of the property (if a person other than the provider).

(2) But—

(a) paragraph (c) of subsection (1) is to be disregarded if the secured creditor does not know, and cannot reasonably be expected to know, of the right in security mentioned in that paragraph, and

(b) paragraph (d) of that subsection is to be disregarded if the secured creditor does not know, and cannot reasonably be expected to know, of the diligence executed as mentioned in that paragraph.

(3) If, by virtue of subsection (1)(e) of section 87 of the Consumer Credit Act 1974, a default notice must be served on the provider, the requirements of that section and of section 88 of that Act must be satisfied before a pledge enforcement notice is served.

(4) The Scottish Ministers may by regulations modify this section so as to specify—

(a) further persons, or descriptions of persons, on whom the secured creditor must serve a pledge enforcement notice (being persons who have statutory duties in relation to the provider's estate),

(b) cases when the requirement to serve a notice on a person specified by virtue of paragraph (a) is to be disregarded.

66 Whether court order required for enforcement

(1) A court order is required for enforcing a pledge only—

(a) as mentioned in subsections (2) and (3),

(b) where taking possession of, or steps in relation to, encumbered property in accordance with section 67(3) or (4).

[(1A) But see also article 14 (whether court order required for enforcement) of the Moveable Transactions (Scotland) Act 2023 (Financial Collateral Arrangements and Financial Instruments) (Consequential Provisions and Modifications) Order 2025 (SI 2025/275 (S 1)).]

(2) In a case where the provider of a pledge is an individual, a court order is required for enforcing the pledge if the provider is a sole trader and enforcement is against property used wholly or mainly for the purposes of the provider's business.

(3) A court order is required for enforcing a statutory pledge in respect of property which is the sole or main residence of an individual unless, after the pledge becomes enforceable by virtue of section 64(2), the following persons agree in writing to its being enforced without such an order—

(a) the secured creditor,

(b) the provider, and

(c) the individual whose sole or main residence is the property in question (if a person other than the provider).

(4) The court is not to grant an order required by subsection (3) unless satisfied that enforcement is reasonable having had regard to all the circumstances of the case.

(5) Those circumstances include—

(a) the nature of, and reason for, the default by virtue of which authority to enforce is sought,

(b) whether the person in default has the ability to remedy the default within a reasonable time,

(c) whether the secured creditor has done anything to help the person in default remedy the default,

(d) where it is, or was, appropriate for the person in default to take part in a debt payment programme approved under Part 1 of the Debt Arrangement and Attachment (Scotland) Act 2002, whether that person is taking part, or has taken part, in such a programme, and

(e) whether reasonable alternative accommodation is available for (or can be expected to be available for) the individual whose sole or main residence is the property in question.

67 Secured creditor's right to take possession of, or steps in relation to, corporeal property

(1) This section applies in relation to corporeal property in respect of which a secured creditor in a statutory pledge has served a pledge enforcement notice.

(2) Subject to any court order that is required under section 66, the secured creditor is entitled to—

(a) take possession of the property, and

(b) take any reasonable steps necessary to ensure, whether or not by immobilising the property, that it is not disposed of or used in an unauthorised way,

but only in accordance with subsection (3) or, as the case may be, subsection (4).

(3) Where the property is in the possession of a relevant person, the secured creditor may take possession or steps under subsection (2)—

(a) with the consent of the relevant person,

(b) with the consent of the court, through the agency of an authorised person, or

(c) personally, if authorised to do so by the court.

(4) Where the property is not in the possession of a relevant person, the secured creditor may take possession or steps under subsection (2)—

(a) with the consent of—

(i) the provider, given after the pledge becomes enforceable, and

(ii) any third party who for the time being either is in direct possession, or has custody, of the property,

(b) through the agency of an authorised person, or

(c) personally, if authorised to do so by the court.

(5) For the purposes of subsections (3) and (4), a 'relevant person' is a person who, in respect of the property or of any part of it—

(a) has a right in security which has priority in ranking over, or ranks equally with, the pledge to which the pledge enforcement notice relates, or

(b) has executed diligence which has priority in ranking over, or ranks equally with, that pledge.

(6) In taking possession of the property under subsection (2)(a), the secured creditor is entitled to remove any individual from that property, but only through the agency of an authorised person.

(7) In this section, 'authorised person' means a messenger-at-arms or sheriff officer.

(8) The Scottish Ministers may by regulations modify this section so as to specify further persons, or descriptions of persons, who are authorised persons for the purposes of this section.

68 Secured creditor's right to sell

(1) Where a pledge enforcement notice has been served in respect of property, the secured creditor is, subject to any court order that is required under section 66, entitled to sell all or any of that property.

(2) In selling property by virtue of subsection (1), the secured creditor must take all reasonable steps to ensure that the price obtained is the best reasonably obtainable.

(3) The secured creditor is entitled to purchase all or any of the property but only—

(a) in a sale by public auction, and

(b) for a price no lower than one which bears a reasonable relationship to market value.

[(3A) But see also article 16 (secured creditor's right to sell financial instrument) of the Moveable Transactions (Scotland) Act 2023 (Financial Collateral Arrangements and Financial Instruments) (Consequential Provisions and Modifications) Order 2025 (SI 2025/275 (S 1)).]

(4) Any proceeds obtained by virtue of subsection (1) are to be held in trust by the secured creditor until applied under section 77.

69 Sale: unencumbered acquisition

(1) This section applies where a secured creditor sells property by virtue of section 68(1) and transfers the property to the purchaser.

(2) The purchaser acquires the property unencumbered by—

(a) the pledge which was the subject of the pledge enforcement notice, and

(b) any right in security, or any diligence, ranking equally with or postponed to the pledge.

(3) The purchaser acquires the property unencumbered by—

(a) any right in security which has priority in ranking over the pledge, or

(b) any diligence which has priority in ranking over the pledge,

only if the holder of the right in security or, as the case may be, the creditor who executed the diligence consented to the sale.

70 Secured creditor's right to let

(1) A secured creditor who, by virtue of section 68(1), is entitled to sell corporeal property is entitled to let all or any of that property.

(2) In letting property by virtue of subsection (1), the secured creditor must take all reasonable steps to ensure that the income obtained is the best reasonably obtainable.

(3) Any rental income obtained by virtue of subsection (1) is to be held in trust by the secured creditor until applied under section 77.

(4) The provider and the secured creditor may agree, whether before or after the pledge becomes enforceable by virtue of section 64(2), that subsection (1) is not to apply in relation to the corporeal property or some part of it.

(5) Any such agreement must be in writing.

71 Secured creditor's right to grant licence over intellectual property

(1) A secured creditor who, by virtue of section 68(1), is entitled to sell intellectual property is entitled to grant a licence over all or any of that property, but only if and to the extent that the provider is entitled to grant such a licence.

(2) In granting a licence by virtue of subsection (1), the secured creditor must take all reasonable steps to ensure that the income obtained is the best reasonably obtainable.

(3) Any income obtained by virtue of subsection (1) is to be held in trust by the secured creditor until applied under section 77.

(4) The provider and the secured creditor may agree, whether before or after the pledge becomes enforceable by virtue of section 64(2), that subsection (1) is not to apply in relation to the intellectual property or some part of it.

(5) Any such agreement must be in writing.

72 Secured creditor's right to protect and manage the property

(1) A secured creditor who, by virtue of section 68(1), is entitled to sell property is entitled to take reasonable steps to—

(a) protect, maintain and manage it, and

(b) preserve its value.

(2) The right under subsection (1) includes, for example, the right of the secured creditor to—

(a) effect or maintain an insurance policy in relation to the property,

(b) settle any liability in relation to the property,

(c) bring, defend or continue legal proceedings in relation to the property,

(d) take such other steps as the provider has agreed (whether before or after the pledge becomes enforceable by virtue of section 64(2)) may be taken by the secured creditor.

[(2A) See also article 17 (secured creditor's right to protect and manage financial instrument) of the Moveable Transactions (Scotland) Act 2023 (Financial Collateral Arrangements and Financial Instruments) (Consequential Provisions and Modifications) Order 2025 (SI 2025/275 (S 1)).]

(3) Subsection (1) is without prejudice to section 67(2)(b).

73 Secured creditor's right to appropriate

(1) Where a pledge enforcement notice has been served, the secured creditor is entitled to appropriate any or all of the encumbered property in accordance with section 74 or (as the case may be) 75 in satisfaction, in whole or in part, of the secured obligation.

(2) But it is not competent to appropriate by virtue of subsection (1)—

(a) corporeal property, unless that property is in the possession of the secured creditor, or

(b) property with a value which exceeds the total of—

(i) the amount for the time being remaining due under the secured obligation, and

(ii) such expenses as have reasonably been incurred by the secured creditor in enforcing the pledge,

unless a sum of money equivalent to the amount by which that total is exceeded is set aside by the secured creditor and held in trust until applied under section 77.

[(3) See also article 18 (secured creditor's right to appropriate financial instrument) of the Moveable Transactions (Scotland) Act 2023 (Financial Collateral Arrangements and Financial Instruments) (Consequential Provisions and Modifications) Order 2025 (SI 2025/275 (S 1)).]

74 Appropriation with prior agreement

(1) A provider and a secured creditor may, before a pledge becomes enforceable by virtue of section 64(2), agree that the secured creditor is entitled to appropriate by virtue of section 73(1)—

(a) the encumbered property, or

(b) any part of that property.

(2) Any agreement under subsection (1) must be in writing.

(3) Property may only be appropriated in accordance with that agreement if it is property in relation to which the provider and the secured creditor have, in the agreement, set out a method of readily determining a reasonable market price.

(4) Property appropriated in accordance with that agreement is appropriated only for the value, at the date of appropriation, of the property's market price as determined as mentioned in subsection (3).

(5) Before exercising a right to appropriate property by virtue of subsection (1), the secured creditor must serve a notice on—

(a) the provider,

(b) the debtor in the secured obligation (if a person other than the provider),

(c) the holder of any other right in security over all or part of the property, and

(d) any creditor who has executed diligence against all or part of the property.

(6) But—

(a) paragraph (c) of subsection (5) is to be disregarded if the secured creditor does not know, and cannot reasonably be expected to know, of the right in security mentioned in that paragraph, and

(b) paragraph (d) of that subsection is to be disregarded if the secured creditor does not know, and cannot reasonably be expected to know, of the diligence executed as mentioned in that paragraph.

(7) A notice under subsection (5) must—

(a) identify the property to be appropriated,

(b) specify the amount for the time being remaining due under the secured obligation,

(c) specify the amount expected to be obtained by the appropriation, and

(d) state that—

(i) the recipient (if a person other than the provider or the debtor) may give a written statement to the secured creditor objecting to the appropriation, and

(ii) if such a statement is received by the secured creditor within 14 days beginning with the day that the person objecting received the notice, the appropriation is not to proceed.

(8) If, within the period specified in sub-paragraph (ii) of subsection (7)(d), the secured creditor receives a written statement as mentioned in that subsection from a recipient of a notice other than the provider or the debtor—

(a) the appropriation is not to proceed, and

(b) the secured creditor must, by written statement and without delay, inform each of the other recipients of the notice that the appropriation is not proceeding.

[(8A) See also article 19 (appropriation of financial instrument with prior agreement) of the Moveable Transactions (Scotland) Act 2023 (Financial Collateral Arrangements and Financial Instruments) (Consequential Provisions and Modifications) Order 2025 (SI 2025/275 (S 1)).]

(9) The Scottish Ministers may by regulations modify this section so as to—

(a) specify—

(i) further persons, or descriptions of persons, on whom the secured creditor must serve a notice (being persons who have statutory duties in relation to the provider's estate),

(ii) cases when the requirement to serve a notice on a person specified by virtue of sub-paragraph (i) is to be disregarded,

(b) require a notice under subsection (5) to be in, or as nearly as may be in, such form as is for the time being prescribed (and may in consequence remove any requirements in this section as to what such a notice must contain).

75 Appropriation without prior agreement

(1) This section applies in respect of property in relation to which the provider and the secured creditor have not reached agreement under section 74(1).

(2) Property may only be appropriated by virtue of section 73(1) if the amount obtained by the appropriation bears a reasonable relationship to the market value of the property appropriated on the date of the appropriation.

(3) Before exercising a right to appropriate property by virtue of section 73(1), the secured creditor must serve a notice on—

(a) the provider,

(b) the debtor in the secured obligation (if a person other than the provider),

(c) the holder of any other right in security over all or part of the property, and

(d) any creditor who has executed diligence against all or part of the property.

(4) But—

(a) paragraph (c) of subsection (3) is to be disregarded if the secured creditor does not know, and cannot reasonably be expected to know, of the right in security mentioned in that paragraph, and

(b) paragraph (d) of that subsection is to be disregarded if the secured creditor does not know, and cannot reasonably be expected to know, of the diligence executed as mentioned in that paragraph.

(5) Any notice served under subsection (3) must—

(a) identify the property to be appropriated,

(b) specify the amount for the time being remaining due under the secured obligation,

(c) specify the amount expected to be obtained by the appropriation, and

(d) state that—

(i) the recipient may give a written statement to the secured creditor objecting to the appropriation, and

(ii) if such a statement is received by the secured creditor within 14 days beginning with the day that the person objecting received the notice, the appropriation is not to proceed.

(6) If, within the period specified in sub-paragraph (ii) of subsection (5)(d), the secured creditor receives a written statement as mentioned in that subsection from a recipient of a notice—

(a) the appropriation is not to proceed, and

(b) the secured creditor must, by written statement and without delay, inform each of the other recipients of the notice that the appropriation is not proceeding.

(7) The Scottish Ministers may by regulations modify this section so as to—

(a) specify—

(i) further persons, or descriptions of persons, on whom the secured creditor must serve a notice (being persons who have statutory duties in relation to the provider's estate),

(ii) cases when the requirement to serve a notice on a person specified by virtue of sub-paragraph (i) is to be disregarded,

(b) require a notice under subsection (3) to be in, or as nearly as may be in, such form as is for the time being prescribed (and may in consequence remove any requirements in this section as to what such a notice must contain).

76 Appropriation: unencumbered acquisition

Where a secured creditor appropriates property by virtue of section 73(1), the secured creditor acquires the property unencumbered by any right in security or any diligence.

77 Application of proceeds from enforcement of pledge

(1) Any proceeds arising from the enforcement of a pledge are to be applied—

(a) firstly, in payment of all expenses reasonably incurred by the secured creditor in connection with the enforcement (including any incurred under section 67(2) or 72), and

(b) secondly, in payment of the amount due to—

(i) the holder of any right in security over the property from which the proceeds arose, and

(ii) any creditor who has executed diligence against that property, and

(c) with the residue (if any) from the proceeds being paid to the provider.

(2) Any payment made by virtue of subsection (1)(b) is to be made in conformity with the ranking of the right in security or, as the case may be, of the diligence.

(3) But no such payment is to be made to—

(a) the holder of a right in security which has priority in ranking over the pledge enforced, or

(b) any creditor who has executed diligence which has such priority,

unless that holder or creditor consented to the enforcement in question.

(4) Where payment falls to be made, by virtue of subsection (1)(b), to more than one person with the same ranking but the proceeds are inadequate to enable those persons to be paid in full, their payments are to abate in equal proportions.

(5) Where a question arises regarding to whom a payment under this section is to be made, the secured creditor must—

(a) consign the amount of the payment (so far as ascertainable) in court for the person appearing to have the best right to that payment, and

(b) lodge in court a statement of the amount consigned.

(6) Where a consignation is made in pursuance of subsection (5)(a)—

(a) it operates as a payment of the amount due, and

(b) a certificate of the court is sufficient evidence of that payment.

(7) The secured creditor must, as soon as reasonably practicable after applying the proceeds arising from the enforcement, issue the persons mentioned in subsection (8) with a written statement of how the proceeds have been applied under this section.

(8) The persons referred to in subsection (7) are—

(a) the provider,

(b) the debtor in the secured obligation (if a person other than the provider), and

(c) any person who both—

(i) is mentioned in subsection (1)(b), and

(ii) has consented to the enforcement in question.

(9) In a case where—

(a) all or any of the property is let by the secured creditor by virtue of section 70(1), or

(b) the secured creditor grants a licence over all or any of it by virtue of section 71(1),

subsection (7) applies in relation to any proceeds of the letting or licensing as if, for the words 'as soon as reasonably practicable after applying the proceeds arising from the enforcement', there were substituted 'every month beginning with the month after the first proceeds arising from the enforcement are received'.

(10) The Scottish Ministers may by regulations modify this section so as to specify further persons, or descriptions of persons, to whom the secured creditor must issue a written statement (being persons who have statutory duties in relation to the provider's estate).

78 Mandatory application for removal of an entry from the statutory pledges record

(1) This section applies where a statutory pledge which has been registered is extinguished by virtue of—

(a) the enforcement of the statutory pledge,

(b) the enforcement of another right in security over the encumbered property of the statutory pledge, or

(c) the enforcement of diligence against the encumbered property of the statutory pledge.

(2) The secured creditor must, as soon as reasonably practicable after the enforcement of the statutory pledge or, as the case may be, becoming aware of the event mentioned in paragraph (b) or (c) of subsection (1), make an application under section 96(1) for removal of the entry for the statutory pledge from the statutory pledges record.

Liability for loss due to enforcement

79 Liability for loss suffered by virtue of enforcement

(1) A person ('P') is entitled to be compensated by a secured creditor for loss suffered in consequence of the secured creditor's failure to comply with any obligation imposed on the secured creditor by any provision of sections 64 to 78.

(2) But the secured creditor has no liability under subsection (1)—

(a) in so far as P's loss could have been avoided had P taken measures which it would have been reasonable for P to take, or

(b) in so far as P's loss was not reasonably foreseeable.

Service of documents for purposes of this Chapter

80 Service of documents for purposes of this Chapter

(1) In relation to the service of documents for the purposes of this Chapter, the provider and the secured creditor may agree (either or both)—

(a) that the document may or must be served on a person by being sent to an address specified in the agreement (being an address other than is mentioned in subsection (4) of section 26 of the Interpretation and Legislative Reform (Scotland) Act 2010),

(b) that service is to be by a method mentioned in subsection (2) of that section and specified in the agreement.

(2) The agreement need not refer expressly to that section or to any provision of that section.

(3) Any such agreement must be in writing.

(4) Where there is such an agreement but service cannot be effected in accordance with it, the agreement is to be disregarded in applying section 26 of that Act of 2010 for the purposes of this Chapter.

CHAPTER 2
Register of Statutory Pledges

Register of Statutory Pledges

81 The Register of Statutory Pledges

(1) There is to be a public register known as the Register of Statutory Pledges.

(2) The register is to be under the management and control of the Keeper.

(3) Subject to the provisions of this Act, the register is to be in such form as the Keeper thinks fit.

(4) The Keeper must take such steps as appear reasonable to the Keeper to protect the register from—

(a) interference,

(b) unauthorised access, and

(c) damage.

Structure and contents of the register

82 The parts of the register

The Keeper must make up and maintain, as parts of the register—

(a) the statutory pledges record, and

(b) the archive record.

83 The statutory pledges record

(1) An entry in the statutory pledges record is to comprise—

(a) the provider's name and address,

(b) where the provider is an individual, the provider's date of birth,

(c) any identifying number which the provider has and which, by virtue of RSP Rules, must be included in the entry,

(d) the secured creditor's name and address,

(e) any identifying number which the secured creditor has and which, by virtue of RSP Rules, must be included in the entry,

(f) where the secured creditor is not an individual, an address (which may be an email address) to which any request for information regarding the statutory pledge may be sent,

(g) such description of the encumbered property as is required, or permitted, for the purposes of this subsection by RSP Rules,

(h) a copy of the constitutive document of the statutory pledge,

(i) the registration number allocated under section 87(1)(b) to the entry,

(j) where the statutory pledge has been amended in pursuance of section 58(6), a copy of the amendment document,

(k) the date and time of registration of—

(i) the statutory pledge, and

(ii) any amendment to the statutory pledge,

(l) any other information that is required under any other section of this Act, and

(m) any other information that is specified for the purposes of this subsection by RSP Rules.

(2) The statutory pledges record is the totality of all such entries.

84 The archive record

The archive record is the totality of—

(a) all entries and copy documents transferred from the statutory pledges record under section 102(2)(a) or (3)(c) or by virtue of section 95(1)(a),

(b) all copy documents included in the archive record under section 102(2)(c) or (3)(b),

(c) all copies of such other documents as the Keeper considers it appropriate to include in the archive record, and

(d) any other information that is specified for the purposes of this section by RSP Rules.

Registration process

85 Order in which applications are to be dealt with

The Keeper must deal with—

(a) applications for registration of a statutory pledge under section 86, and

(b) applications for registration of an amendment to a statutory pledge under section 88,

in the order in which they are received.

86 Application for registration of statutory pledge

(1) A secured creditor may apply to the Keeper for registration of a statutory pledge.

(2) The Keeper must accept the application if—

(a) it is submitted with a copy of the constitutive document,

(b) it contains all the information the Keeper requires in accordance with section 83 to be able to make up an entry for the statutory pledge under section 87(1),

(c) it conforms to such RSP Rules as relate to the application, and

(d) either—

(i) such fee as is payable for the registration is paid, or

(ii) arrangements satisfactory to the Keeper are made for payment of that fee.

(3) If the requirements of subsection (2) are not satisfied, the Keeper must reject the application and inform the applicant accordingly.

87 Registration of statutory pledge

(1) On accepting an application made under section 86, the Keeper must—

(a) make up an entry for the statutory pledge (from the constitutive document, the information provided in the application and the circumstances of registration),

(b) allocate a registration number to the entry (based on the order in which applications are dealt with), and

(c) maintain the entry in the statutory pledges record.

(2) A statutory pledge is taken to be registered on the date and at the time entered for it for the purposes of section 83(1)(k)(i).

88 Application for registration of amendment

(1) A secured creditor may apply to the Keeper for registration of an amendment to a statutory pledge to increase the extent of the statutory pledge within the meaning of section 58(7).

(2) The Keeper must accept the application if—

(a) it is submitted with a copy of the amendment document,

(b) it contains all the information the Keeper requires in accordance with section 83 to be able to revise the entry to which the application relates,

(c) it conforms to such RSP Rules as relate to the application, and

(d) either—

(i) such fee as is payable for the registration is paid, or

(ii) arrangements satisfactory to the Keeper are made for payment of that fee.

(3) If the requirements of subsection (2) are not satisfied, the Keeper must reject the application and inform the applicant accordingly.

89 Registration of amendment

(1) On accepting an application made under section 88, the Keeper must revise the entry for the statutory pledge to which the application relates in accordance with the application.

(2) An amendment to a statutory pledge is taken to be registered on the date and at the time entered for the amendment for the purposes of section 83(1)(k)(ii).

90 Verification statement as to registration of statutory pledge or amendment

(1) After the registration of a statutory pledge under section 87 or an amendment to a statutory pledge under section 89, the Keeper must issue a written statement verifying the registration to—

(a) the secured creditor, and

(b) the provider,

but only if and to the extent that the application made under section 86 or (as the case may be) section 88 contains an email address for those persons.

(2) That statement must—

(a) include—

(i) the date and time of the registration, and

(ii) the registration number allocated to the entry to which the application relates, and

(b) conform to such RSP Rules as relate to the statement.

(3) Where a statement is issued under subsection (1) and is received by the secured creditor but not the provider, the provider may request a copy of it from the secured creditor.

(4) Within 21 days beginning with the day a request is made under subsection (3), the secured creditor must supply the provider with the copy requested.

Effective registration

91 Effective registration of statutory pledge

(1) The registration of a statutory pledge is ineffective if—

(a) the entry made up for the statutory pledge in the statutory pledges record—

(i) does not include a copy of the constitutive document, or

(ii) is, at the time of registration, seriously misleading as a result of an inaccuracy or inaccuracies in it, or

(b) the constitutive document is invalid.

(2) But subsection (1)(a)(ii) is subject to section 94(1)(c) and (d).

(3) Where the registration of a statutory pledge is ineffective by virtue of subsection (1), it becomes effective if and when the entry is corrected.

92 Effective registration of amendment to statutory pledge

(1) The registration of an amendment to a statutory pledge is ineffective if—

(a) the entry for the statutory pledge in the statutory pledges record—

(i) does not include a copy of the amendment document, or

(ii) is, in consequence of the amendment, seriously misleading as a result of an inaccuracy or inaccuracies in it, or

(b) the amendment document is invalid.

(2) But subsection (1)(a)(ii) is subject to section 94(1)(c) and (d).

(3) Where the registration of an amendment to a statutory pledge is ineffective by virtue of subsection (1), it becomes effective if and when the entry as amended is corrected.

93 Supervening inaccuracies: protection of third parties

(1) Subsection (5) applies where, at some time after a statutory pledge is registered effectively—

(a) a person acquires, for value, in good faith and exercising reasonable care—

(i) property which is encumbered under the pledge, or

(ii) a right in such property, and

(b) at the time the person acquires that property or right ('the acquired property'), any one of condition A, condition B or condition C is met.

(2) Condition A is that the entry for the pledge in the statutory pledges record has been incorrectly removed from the statutory pledges record (whether or not on transfer of that entry to the archive record) and remains incorrectly absent from the record.

(3) Condition B is that—

(a) the acquired property does not have an identifying number which, by virtue of RSP Rules, must be used in identifying it, and

(b) the entry for the pledge in the statutory pledges record is seriously misleading in respect of the acquired property.

(4) Condition C is that—

(a) the acquired property has an identifying number which, by virtue of RSP Rules, must be used in identifying it, and

(b) if a search of the statutory pledges record were to be carried out for that number using the search facility provided under section 104, it would not disclose the entry.

(5) On the acquisition, the statutory pledge is extinguished in relation to the acquired property.

(6) For the purposes of subsection (1)(a), the circumstances in which a person will not be taken to be in good faith and exercising reasonable care include where the person fails to carry out a search of the statutory pledges record in respect of the acquisition.

94 Seriously misleading inaccuracies in the statutory pledges record

(1) In determining for the purposes of sections 91(1)(a)(ii), 92(1)(a)(ii) and 93(3) whether an entry in the statutory pledges record is seriously misleading as a result of an inaccuracy or inaccuracies in it—

(a) the entry is seriously misleading where—

(i) any of subsections (2) to (6) apply, or

(ii) despite sub-paragraph (i) not being satisfied, the inaccuracy or inaccuracies are such that a reasonable person would be seriously misled by the entry,

(b) any inaccuracy is to be disregarded to the extent that it appears in the constitutive document, or in any amendment document, but is not replicated elsewhere in the entry,

(c) where the entry is seriously misleading in respect of only part of the encumbered property, that is not to be taken to affect the entry in its application to the rest of the property,

(d) where the entry is seriously misleading in respect of a co-provider or co-secured creditor but not in respect of both (or all) co-providers or co-secured creditors, that is not to be taken to affect the entry in its application to a co-provider or co-secured creditor in respect of whom the entry is not seriously misleading.

(2) This subsection applies where—

(a) the provider is a person required by RSP Rules to be identified in the statutory pledges record by an identifying number, and

(b) if a search of the record were to be carried out for that number, using the search facility provided under section 104, it would not disclose the entry.

(3) This subsection applies where—

(a) the provider is not a person required by RSP Rules to be identified in the statutory pledges record by an identifying number, and

(b) if a search of the record were to be carried out, using the search facility provided under section 104, for—

(i) the provider's proper name, or

(ii) the provider's proper name together with the provider's month and year of birth,

it would not disclose the entry.

(4) This subsection applies—

(a) for the purposes of sections 91(1)(a)(ii) and 92(1)(a)(ii) only, and

(b) where the entry inaccurately reflects the secured creditor's proper name at the date the application for registration was made in such a way that a reasonable person would be seriously misled.

(5) This subsection applies where—

(a) the encumbered property is or includes property required by RSP Rules to be identified in the statutory pledges record by an identifying number, and

(b) if a search of the record were to be carried out for that number, using the search facility provided under section 104, it would not disclose the entry.

(6) This subsection applies where—

(a) there is a requirement, by virtue of section 83(1)(g), for an entry in the statutory pledges record to specify the type of property encumbered, and

(b) the entry—

(i) does not describe the property as being of a type that it is, or

(ii) fails to allocate a type to the property.

(7) In the application of this section to co-providers and co-secured creditors—

(a) subsections (2) and (3) apply in relation to a co-provider as they apply in relation to a provider,

(b) subsection (4) applies in relation to a co-secured creditor as it applies in relation to a secured creditor.

(8) The Scottish Ministers may by regulations modify this section to make provision about what does, and what does not, make an entry seriously misleading for the purposes of sections 91(1)(a)(ii), 92(1)(a)(ii) and 93(3) and how that is to be determined.

(9) In this section, the 'proper name' of a provider or secured creditor means the person's name in the form determined in accordance with RSP Rules.

Duration

95 Power of Scottish Ministers in relation to duration of statutory pledge

(1) The Scottish Ministers may by regulations—

(a) specify a period from the creation or renewal of an entry in the statutory pledges record at the end of which the statutory pledge to which the entry relates will be extinguished and the entry removed, unless during that period the entry has been—

(i) renewed by virtue of paragraph (b), or

(ii) removed, and

(b) enable an application to be made by the secured creditor for the renewal of an entry which would otherwise fall to be removed by virtue of paragraph (a).

(2) Before laying a draft of a Scottish statutory instrument containing regulations under subsection (1) before the Scottish Parliament, the Scottish Ministers must consult the Keeper.

Corrections

96 Application by secured creditor for correction of statutory pledges record

(1) A relevant person may apply to the Keeper for an entry in the statutory pledges record to be corrected.

(2) The Keeper must accept the application if—

(a) it conforms to such RSP Rules as relate to the application, and

(b) either—

(i) such fee as is payable for the correction is paid, or

(ii) arrangements satisfactory to the Keeper are made for payment of that fee.

(3) If the requirements of subsection (2) are not satisfied, the Keeper must reject the application and inform the applicant accordingly.

(4) For the purposes of subsection (1), 'relevant person'—

(a) means the person who is the secured creditor in relation to the entry (whether or not identified as such in the entry), and

(b) where the statutory pledge has been assigned, also includes the person who was the secured creditor before the assignation.

97 Correction of record in response to application under section 96

(1) On accepting an application made under section 96, the Keeper must correct the entry in the statutory pledges record accordingly.

(2) After the correction of an entry under subsection (1), the Keeper must issue a written statement verifying the correction to—

(a) the applicant, and

(b) the provider,

but only if and to the extent that the application contains an email address for those persons.

(3) That statement must—

(a) include—

(i) the date and time of the correction, and

(ii) the registration number allocated to the entry to which the correction relates, and

(b) conform to such RSP Rules as relate to the statement.

(4) Where a statement is issued under subsection (2) and is received by the applicant but not the provider, the provider may request a copy of it from the applicant.

(5) Within 21 days beginning with the day a request is made under subsection (4), the applicant must supply the provider with the copy requested.

98 Demand that application for correction be made under section 96

(1) A person may, where the conditions in subsection (2) or (3) are met, issue a demand to the person identified in an entry in the statutory pledges record as the secured creditor (the 'registered creditor') that the registered creditor apply to the Keeper under section 96 for the entry to be corrected.

(2) The conditions in this subsection are that the person—

(a) is identified as the provider, or as a co-provider, of the statutory pledge in the entry, and

(b) either—

(i) claims not to be either the provider, or a co-provider, of the statutory pledge, or

(ii) considers that all or part of the property identified as the encumbered property in the entry is not encumbered property.

(3) The conditions in this subsection are that the person—

(a) has a right in property identified as the encumbered property in the entry, and

(b) considers that all or part of the property is not encumbered property.

(4) A demand issued under subsection (1) must—

(a) be in a prescribed form, and

(b) specify a period (being a period of not less than 21 days after it is received) within which compliance with it is sought.

(5) A registered creditor may not charge a fee for compliance with a demand under subsection (1).

(6) If the registered creditor fails to comply with the demand within the period specified by virtue of subsection (4)(b), the person who made the demand may apply to the Keeper for the statutory pledges record to be corrected.

99 Response to application for correction under section 98(6)

(1) The Keeper must accept an application made under section 98(6) if—

(a) it conforms to such RSP Rules as relate to the application, and

(b) either—

(i) such fee as is payable for the application is paid, or

(ii) arrangements satisfactory to the Keeper are made for payment of that fee.

(2) If the requirements of subsection (1) are not satisfied, the Keeper must reject the application and inform the applicant accordingly.

(3) On accepting an application made under section 98(6), the Keeper must—

(a) serve a notice on the registered creditor stating that the Keeper intends to correct the statutory pledges record on a date specified in the notice (being a date no fewer than 21 days after the date of the notice),

(b) note on the entry to which the application relates that the application has been received and include in that note—

(i) the details of the correction sought, and

(ii) the date on which the application was received,

(c) issue a written statement to the applicant verifying that the application has been received, and

(d) notify the person identified in the entry as the provider (if a different person from the applicant) that the notice mentioned in paragraph (a) has been served on the registered creditor.

(4) The registered creditor—

(a) may, before the date specified under subsection (3)(a), apply to the court opposing the making of the correction, and

(b) on making any such application, must notify the Keeper accordingly.

(5) Where the registered creditor is not the secured creditor in relation to the statutory pledge in the entry—

(a) the registered creditor must, in so far as it is reasonable and practicable to do so, promptly notify the secured creditor of the notice received under subsection (3)(a), and

(b) subsection (4) applies to the secured creditor as it applies to the registered creditor.

(6) On an application under subsection (4)(a), the court may—

(a) if satisfied that the correction is not justified, direct that no change be made to the record in consequence of the application under section 98(6), or

(b) if satisfied that the correction is justified in whole or in part, direct that the record be corrected accordingly.

(7) But the court is not to make a direction under subsection (6) unless satisfied that, before the date specified by virtue of subsection (3)(a), the Keeper received notification under subsection (4)(b) of the application to the court.

(8) If the Keeper does not receive, before the date specified by virtue of subsection (3)(a), notification under subsection (4)(b) of an application to the court, the Keeper is on that date to make the correction.

(9) In this section, 'registered creditor' has the same meaning as in section 98.

100 Correction of the statutory pledges record at instance of the court or the Keeper

(1) Where a court determines in any proceedings that the statutory pledges record is inaccurate, the court—

(a) must direct the Keeper to correct the record, and

(b) may give the Keeper any further direction it considers necessary in connection with the correction.

(2) Subsection (3) applies where the Keeper becomes aware of a manifest inaccuracy in the statutory pledges record other than—

(a) as a result of a direction under subsection (1),

(b) where an application has been made under section 96(1) or 98(6) in respect of the inaccuracy, or

(c) where the Keeper considers that—

(i) such an application could reasonably be made in respect of the inaccuracy, and

(ii) the inaccuracy is not attributable to the Keeper.

(3) The Keeper must—

(a) correct the record if what is needed to correct it is manifest,

(b) if what is needed to correct it is not manifest, note the inaccuracy on the entry in question.

101 Meaning of 'inaccuracy' and how a correction is made

(1) There is an 'inaccuracy' in the statutory pledges record where the record misstates what the position is, in law or in fact, in relation to a statutory pledge.

(2) A correction of the statutory pledges record—

(a) may relate to an inaccuracy—

(i) which has existed since an entry in the record was made up, or

(ii) which has arisen due to circumstances that have occurred since the submission of the application in respect of which the entry was made up, and

(b) may involve—

(i) the removal of an entry,

(ii) the removal of information included in an entry,

(iii) the amendment of, or an addition to, the information, or replacement of a copy document, included in an entry,

(iv) the restoration of information, or of a copy document, to an entry,

(v) the restoration of an entry (whether or not by transferring it from the archive record to the statutory pledges record).

(3) A correction is taken to be made on the date and at the time entered for it in the register in pursuance of a provision of this Part.

102 Correction of the statutory pledges record: procedure

(1) This section applies where the Keeper corrects the statutory pledges record by virtue of section 97(1), 99(6)(b) or (8) or 100(1)(a) or (3)(a).

(2) Where the Keeper corrects the statutory pledges record by removing an entry from the statutory pledges record, the Keeper must—

(a) transfer the entry to the archive record,

(b) note on the transferred entry—

(i) the section by virtue of which the transfer is made, and

(ii) the details of the correction (including the date and time of the removal), and

(c) include in the archive record a copy of any document which discloses, or contributes to disclosing, the inaccuracy which is the subject of the correction.

(3) Where the Keeper corrects the record by restoring an entry, by restoring, removing or amending information included in an entry or by restoring or replacing a copy document, the Keeper must—

(a) note on the entry that it has been corrected and the details of the correction (including the date and time of the correction),

(b) include in the archive record a copy of any document which discloses, or contributes to disclosing, the inaccuracy which is the subject of the correction, and

(c) in the case of the replacement of the copy document, transfer the replaced copy to the archive record.

(4) Having corrected the record other than by virtue of section 97(1), the Keeper must notify the following persons (in so far as it is reasonable and practicable to do so) that the correction has been made—

(a) every person specified for the purposes of this subsection by RSP Rules, and

(b) any other person who appears to the Keeper to be affected by it materially.

(5) A failure to comply with subsection (2)(c), (3)(b) or (4) does not affect the validity of the correction of the record.

103 Proceedings involving the accuracy of the statutory pledges record

The Keeper is entitled to appear and be heard in any civil proceedings, whether before a court or tribunal, in which—

(a) the accuracy of the statutory pledges record, or

(b) what is needed to correct an inaccuracy in the record,

is put in question.

Searches and extracts

104 Searching the statutory pledges record

(1) The Keeper must provide a facility by which the statutory pledges record may be searched.

(2) That search facility must allow the statutory pledges record to be searched by reference to, and only by reference to—

(a) any of the following information in the entries contained in that record—

(i) the names of providers, which must be capable of being searched with and without the months and years of birth of providers who are individuals,

(ii) the identifying numbers of providers required by RSP Rules to be identified in the statutory pledges record by such a number,

(iii) if RSP Rules require the encumbered property to be identified (whether by an identifying number or in some other way), by reference to such identification,

(b) registration numbers allocated, under section 87(1)(b), to entries in that record, or

(c) any other factor, or characteristic, specified for the purposes of this paragraph by RSP Rules.

(3) Subject to any restrictions imposed under RSP Rules, a person may search the statutory pledges record using the search facility provided under subsection (1) provided that either—

(a) such fee as is payable for the search is paid, or

(b) arrangements satisfactory to the Keeper are made for payment of that fee.

(4) But no fee is payable for a search of the statutory pledges record which is carried out on behalf of an individual by a not-for-profit money adviser (being an adviser who does not charge individuals for the adviser's services).

(5) The Scottish Ministers may, by regulations, make further provision about the meaning of 'not-for-profit money adviser' for the purposes of subsection (4).

105 Admissibility and evidential status of search results

(1) A copy of a search result (in printed or electronic form) which relates to a search carried out by means of a search facility provided by the Keeper is admissible in evidence.

(2) In the absence of evidence to the contrary—

(a) where such a search result purports to show an entry in the statutory pledges record, it is sufficient proof of—

(i) the registration of the statutory pledge, or an amendment to the entry in the statutory pledges record, to which the result relates,

(ii) where applicable, a correction of the entry in the statutory pledges record to which the result relates, and

(iii) the date and time of such registration or, as the case may be, correction, and

(b) where such a search result purports not to show an entry in the statutory pledges record, it is sufficient proof of an entry in the statutory pledges record not being disclosed at the date and time of such search by means of the search carried out.

106 Extracts and their evidential status

(1) A person may apply to the Keeper for an extract of an entry in the register.

(2) The Keeper must issue the extract if—

(a) such fee as is payable for issuing it is paid, or

(b) arrangements satisfactory to the Keeper are made for payment of that fee.

(3) But if, on application under subsection (1), the applicant requests an extract as at a specific date and time, the Keeper need comply with the request only to the extent that it is reasonably practicable to do so.

(4) The Keeper may validate the extract as the Keeper considers appropriate.

(5) The Keeper may issue the extract as an electronic document unless the applicant requests that it be issued as a traditional document.

(6) The extract is to be accepted for all purposes as sufficient evidence of the contents of the entry as at—

(a) in the case of an extract requested as mentioned in subsection (3), the date and time to which the extract relates (being a date and time specified in the extract), and

(b) in any other case, the date on which and the time at which the extract is issued (being a date and time specified in the extract).

Requests for information

107 Secured creditor's duty to respond to request for information

(1) An entitled person may ask the person identified in an entry in the statutory pledges record as the secured creditor (the 'registered creditor') to provide the entitled person with the following—

(a) if the registered creditor is the secured creditor, with a written statement as to whether or not property specified by the entitled person is, or is part of, the encumbered property,

(b) if the registered creditor is no longer the secured creditor, with—

(i) information to that effect,

(ii) the name and address of the person to whom the registered creditor assigned the statutory pledge, and

(iii) where relevant and in so far as known, the names and addresses of subsequent assignees, or

(c) if the registered creditor has never been the secured creditor, with information to that effect.

(2) The following are entitled persons for the purposes of this section—

(a) a person who has a right in the property so specified,

(b) a person who has a right to execute diligence against the property so specified (or who is authorised to execute a charge for payment and will have the right to execute diligence against that property if and when the days of charge expire without payment), and

(c) a person who is not mentioned in paragraph (a) or (b) but who has the consent of the person identified in the entry as the provider to make a request under subsection (1).

(3) The registered creditor must, within 21 days beginning with the day of receiving a request under subsection (1), comply with it unless—

(a) it is manifest that the registration is ineffective in relation to the statutory pledge to which the request relates,

(b) it is manifest from the entry for the statutory pledge that the property specified under subsection (1) by the entitled person is not encumbered by the pledge, or

(c) both—

(i) the registered creditor has, within the period of 3 months ending with the day of receipt of the request, complied with a request under subsection (1) from the same person and in relation to the same property, and

(ii) the information contained in the statement issued in relation to the earlier request remains correct.

(4) The registered creditor may recover from the entitled person any costs reasonably incurred in complying with the request.

(5) On the application of the registered creditor, the court may by order—

(a) exempt the registered creditor from complying with a request under subsection (1) or such part of the request as it specifies in the order, or

(b) extend the period within which the registered creditor must comply with the request by such number of days as it specifies in the order,

if satisfied that in all the circumstances it would be reasonable to do so.

(6) If, on the application of the entitled person, the court is satisfied that the registered creditor has, without reasonable excuse, failed to comply with subsection (3), it may by order require the registered creditor to comply with the request within 14 days or such other period (which may be longer or shorter than 14 days) as the court considers appropriate.

(7) This section applies in relation to any person whose name and address have been provided to an entitled person by virtue of subsection (1)(b) as it applies to the registered creditor.

(8) The Scottish Ministers may by regulations modify this section so as to specify further persons, or descriptions of persons, who are entitled persons for the purposes of this section.

108 Acquisition of property confirmed by creditor not to be encumbered property

(1) Subsection (2) applies where a person who is an entitled person for the purposes of section 107—

(a) makes a request under subsection (1) of that section,

(b) receives a response from the person of whom the request was made, in the form of a statement of the type mentioned in paragraph (a) of that subsection, advising that the property specified under that subsection by the entitled person is neither the encumbered property nor part of that property, and

(c) within 3 months beginning with the date of being so advised acquires in good faith—

(i) the property so specified (or any part of it), or

(ii) a right in that property (or part).

(2) On that acquisition, the statutory pledge is extinguished in relation to the property (or part).

Entitlement to compensation

109 Liability of Keeper

(1) A person is entitled to be compensated by the Keeper for loss suffered in consequence of—

(a) an inaccuracy in the statutory pledges record to the extent that it is attributable to the making up, maintenance or operation of the register (including an attempted correction of it),

(b) the issue, under section 90(1) or 97(2), of a written statement which is incorrect,

(c) the service, under section 102(4), of a notification which is incorrect,
(d) a search result which—
(i) relates to a search of the statutory pledges record carried out by means of a search facility provided by the Keeper,
(ii) ought (as a result of the search terms used) to reflect accurately the contents of the statutory pledges record at the time the search was made, and
(iii) does not accurately reflect those contents,
(e) the issue, under section 106, of an extract which is not a true extract,
(f) an application being accepted or rejected in error,
(g) an attempt to make an application, which the Keeper would otherwise have accepted, failing as a result of an error in the system the Keeper has for accepting applications, or
(h) applications being dealt with otherwise than in the order in which they are received.
(2) But the Keeper has no liability under subsection (1)—
(a) in so far as the person's loss could have been avoided had the person taken measures which it would have been reasonable for the person to take,
(b) in so far as the person's loss was not reasonably foreseeable, or
(c) for non-patrimonial loss.
(3) For the avoidance of doubt, an inaccuracy in information included in an entry in the statutory pledges record when that entry is made up under section 87(1)(a), revised under section 89(1) or corrected by virtue of section 97(1), 99(6)(b) or (8) or 100(1)(a) or (3)(a) does not fall within subsection (1)(a) to the extent that the Keeper—
(a) has been misled into making the inaccuracy, and
(b) reasonably believed the information to be accurate.
(4) For the purposes of subsection (3), the circumstances where the Keeper is entitled to reasonably believe information to be accurate include those where it is provided—
(a) in connection with an application to which the entry relates, or
(b) by the court.

110 Liability of certain other persons
(1) A person ('P') is entitled to be compensated in the following circumstances—
(a) where P suffers loss in consequence of an inaccuracy in an entry in the statutory pledges record then, to the extent that it is not attributable to the Keeper, P is entitled to be compensated for that loss by—
(i) the person who made the application for registration which gave rise to the inaccurate entry if that person failed to take reasonable care in making it, or
(ii) where the inaccurate entry arises from the attempted correction of an apparent inaccuracy, the person who notified the Keeper of the apparent inaccuracy if that person failed to take reasonable care in doing so,
(b) where P suffers loss in consequence of an inaccuracy in information supplied in response to a request under section 107(1), P is entitled to be compensated for that loss by the person who supplied the information if that person failed to take reasonable care in supplying it, or
(c) where P suffers loss in consequence of a failure, without reasonable excuse, to comply with a request in accordance with section 107(3), P is entitled to be compensated for that loss by the person whose failure it was.
(2) But a person has no liability under subsection (1)—
(a) in so far as P's loss could have been avoided had P taken measures which it would have been reasonable for P to take,
(b) in so far as P's loss was not reasonably foreseeable, or
(c) for non-patrimonial loss.

Rules

111 Rules

(1) The Scottish Ministers may by regulations make rules ('RSP Rules')—

(a) about the making up and keeping of the register,

(b) about the procedure in relation to—

(i) applications for registration under section 86(1) or 88(1), or

(ii) applications for corrections under section 96(1) or 98(6),

(c) about searches in the register and the results of those searches,

(d) about the required form and content of any document or information to be used in relation to the register,

(e) requiring there to be entered in the statutory pledges record or the archive record such information as is specified in the rules, or

(f) regarding other matters in relation to registration under this Part, being matters for which the Scottish Ministers consider it necessary or expedient to provide in order to give full effect to the purposes of this Part.

(2) RSP Rules under subsection (1) may, in particular, include provision—

(a) about the identification, in any application and in the register, of any person or property, including—

(i) how the proper form of a person's name is to be determined, and

(ii) where the person or property has an identifying number (whether of numerals or of letters and numerals) allocated to the person or property, whether that number must be used in identifying the person or property,

(b) about the nature of the address of the provider or the secured creditor to be included in an entry in the register,

(c) about the degree of precision with which time is to be recorded in the register,

(d) about information which, though contained in a constitutive document or amendment document, need not be included in a copy of that document submitted with an application under section 86(1) or 88(1),

(e) about whether a signature contained in a constitutive document or amendment document need be included in a copy of that document so submitted,

(f) about information which, though contained in the register, is not to be—

(i) available to persons searching it, or

(ii) included in any extract issued under section 106,

(g) about when the register is open for—

(i) registration,

(ii) searches.

[(3) Before making RSP Rules under subsection (1), the Scottish Ministers must consult the Keeper.]

CHAPTER 3

Miscellaneous and Interpretation of Part 2

Miscellaneous

112 Competence of creating an agricultural charge

On the coming into force of this section, it ceases to be competent to create an agricultural charge ('agricultural charge' having the meaning given by section 5 of the Agricultural Credits (Scotland) Act 1929).

Interpretation of Part 2

113 Interpretation of Part 2

(1) In this Part (except where the context requires otherwise)—

'amendment document' has the meaning given by section 58(1),

'the archive record' is to be construed in accordance with section 84,
'corporeal moveable property' does not include money,
'correction', in relation to the statutory pledges record, is to be construed in accordance with section 101(2),
'encumbered property' has the meaning given by section 43(2),
'inaccuracy', in relation to the statutory pledges record, is to be construed in accordance with section 101(1),
'money' has the meaning given by section 175(1) of the Bankruptcy and Diligence etc. (Scotland) Act 2007,
'pledge', in sections 64 to 77, is to be construed in accordance with section 63,
'pledge enforcement notice' has the meaning given by section 65(1),
'provider'—
(a) means the person who grants a pledge, and
(b) includes or, as the case may be, consists of any successor in title, or representative, of a provider (unless the successor or representative is a person who, by virtue of Chapter 1, had acquired the encumbered property unencumbered by the statutory pledge in question),
'the register' means the Register of Statutory Pledges,
'right in security'—
(a) means a right in security over property (including a floating charge), but
(b) does not include a right to execute diligence,
'RSP Rules' has the meaning given by section 111(1),
'secured creditor'—
(a) means the person in whose favour a pledge is granted, and
(b) includes or, as the case may be, consists of any successor in title, or representative, of a secured creditor,
'secured obligation' is to be construed in accordance with section 43(1),
'statutory pledge' has the meaning given by section 42(4), and
'the statutory pledges record' is to be construed in accordance with section 83(2).

(2) Where two or more persons are co-providers or co-secured creditors in relation to a statutory pledge, any reference in this Act to the provider or secured creditor (as the case may be) is, unless the context requires otherwise, a reference to all of those persons.

(3) A reference in this Part—
(a) to a statutory pledge being registered (however expressed) is to be construed as a reference to the Keeper's carrying out, in respect of the pledge, the duties imposed on the Keeper by section 87(1)(a) and (b),
(b) to an amendment to a statutory pledge being registered (however expressed) is to be construed as a reference to the Keeper's carrying out, in respect of the amendment, the duty imposed on the Keeper by section 89(1).

PART 3
MISCELLANEOUS AND GENERAL

Computer system

114 Automated computer system

(1) The Keeper may, by means of an automated computer system under the Keeper's management and control, carry out the duties imposed on the Keeper under Chapter 2 of Part 1 and Chapter 2 of Part 2.

(2) The power under subsection (1) includes, for example, the power to enable—
(a) the electronic generation and communication of applications under this Act,
(b) automated registration under this Act, and

(c) the creation of electronic documents.

(3) The Keeper may impose reasonable conditions for using any computer system provided for the purposes of subsection (1).

Registration of electronic documents

115 Competence of registration of electronic documents

Section 9G(1)(d) of the Requirements of Writing (Scotland) Act 1995 (registration and recording of electronic documents) does not apply in relation to the registration of a document by the Keeper under this Act.

Good faith

116 Good faith

(1) This section applies in relation to any provision made in this Act as respects good faith.

(2) If there is a dispute as to whether a person was in (or acted in) good faith, the burden of proof lies on whoever asserts that the person was not in (or did not act in) good faith.

Review of the Act

117 Review of Act

(1) The Scottish Ministers must, as soon as reasonably practicable after the end of the review period—

(a) undertake a review of the operation of this Act, and

(b) prepare a report on that review.

(2) The report must, in particular, set out—

(a) an assessment of—

(i) the impact of allowing the debtor to waive the right to assert defences as provided for in section 14(1), and

(ii) how well the provisions regarding statutory pledges are working in relation to sole traders and small businesses, and

(b) the steps (if any) that the Scottish Ministers propose to take as a result of the findings of the review.

(3) The Scottish Ministers must, as soon as reasonably practicable after preparing the report—

(a) publish the report, and

(b) lay the report before the Scottish Parliament.

(4) For the purposes of this section, 'the review period' is the period of 5 years beginning with the day on which sections 1 and 42 come into force or, if they come into force on different days, the earlier of those days.

General

118 Regulations

(1) Any power of the Scottish Ministers to make regulations under this Act includes the power to make—

(a) incidental, supplementary, consequential, transitional, transitory or saving provision,

(b) different provision for different purposes.

(2) Regulations under any of the following sections are subject to the affirmative procedure: section 3(8), 4(7), 28(7), 32(1), 36(8), 46(3), 47(3), 50(4), 51(4), 54(3), 55(8), 65(4), 67(8), 74(9)(a), 75(7)(a), 77(10), 94(8), 95(1), 107(8) or 120(3).

(3) Regulations under section 74(9)(b), 75(7)(b) or 119 which add to, replace or omit any part of the text of an Act are subject to the affirmative procedure.

(4) Any other regulations under this Act are subject to the negative procedure.
(5) This section does not apply to regulations under section 121.

119 Ancillary provision

(1) The Scottish Ministers may by regulations make any incidental, supplementary, consequential, transitional, transitory or saving provision they consider appropriate for the purposes of, in connection with or for giving full effect to this Act or any provision made under it.

(2) Regulations under this section may modify any enactment (including this Act).

120 Interpretation of Act

(1) In this Act (except where the context requires otherwise)—

'court' means Court of Session or sheriff,

'electronic document' has the meaning given by section 9A of the Requirements of Writing (Scotland) Act 1995,

'electronic signature' has the meaning given by section 12(1) of the Requirements of Writing (Scotland) Act 1995,

'the Keeper' means the Keeper of the Registers of Scotland,

'prescribed' means prescribed by regulations made by the Scottish Ministers,

'registration number' means a unique identifier consisting of numerals or of letters and numerals, and

'traditional document' has the meaning given by section 1A of the Requirements of Writing (Scotland) Act 1995.

(2) In this Act, a reference (however expressed) to—

(a) the authentication of a document by a person is a reference to the electronic signature of that person—

(i) being incorporated into, or logically associated with, the electronic document, and

(ii) having been created by that person,

(b) the execution of a document is a reference to the document's being subscribed as a traditional document in compliance with section 2(1) of the Requirements of Writing (Scotland) Act 1995.

(3) The Scottish Ministers may by regulations modify (either or both) paragraph (a) or paragraph (b) of subsection (2).

(4) Where, under or by virtue of a provision of this Act, however expressed, a person ('P') is required or permitted to proceed in some way, the provision is to be construed as if any reference in it to P includes a reference to any person authorised by P to proceed in such a way on P's behalf.

121 Commencement

(1) This section and sections 118, 119 and 122 come into force on the day after Royal Assent.

(2) The other provisions of this Act come into force on such day as the Scottish Ministers may by regulations appoint.

(3) Regulations under this section may—

(a) include transitional, transitory or saving provision,

(b) make different provision for different purposes.

122 Short title

The short title of this Act is the Moveable Transactions (Scotland) Act 2023.

ELECTRONIC TRADE DOCUMENTS ACT 2023
(2023, c 38)

1 Definition of 'paper trade document'

(1) A document is a 'paper trade document' for the purposes of this Act if—

(a) it is in paper form,

(b) it is a document of a type commonly used in at least one part of the United Kingdom in connection with—

(i) trade in or transport of goods, or

(ii) financing such trade or transport, and

(c) possession of the document is required as a matter of law or commercial custom, usage or practice for a person to claim performance of an obligation.

(2) The following are examples of documents that are commonly used as mentioned in subsection (1)(b)—

(a) a bill of exchange;

(b) a promissory note;

(c) a bill of lading;

(d) a ship's delivery order;

(e) a warehouse receipt;

(f) a mate's receipt;

(g) a marine insurance policy;

(h) a cargo insurance certificate.

2 Definition of 'electronic trade document'

(1) This section applies where information in electronic form is information that, if contained in a document in paper form, would lead to the document being a paper trade document.

(2) The information, together with any other information with which it is logically associated that is also in electronic form, constitutes an 'electronic trade document' for the purposes of this Act if a reliable system is used to—

(a) identify the document so that it can be distinguished from any copies,

(b) protect the document against unauthorised alteration,

(c) secure that it is not possible for more than one person to exercise control of the document at any one time,

(d) allow any person who is able to exercise control of the document to demonstrate that the person is able to do so, and

(e) secure that a transfer of the document has effect to deprive any person who was able to exercise control of the document immediately before the transfer of the ability to do so (unless the person is able to exercise control by virtue of being a transferee).

(3) For the purposes of subsection (2)—

(a) a person exercises control of a document when the person uses, transfers or otherwise disposes of the document (whether or not the person has a legal right to do so), and

(b) persons acting jointly are to be treated as one person.

(4) Reading or viewing a document is not, of itself, sufficient to amount to use of the document for the purposes of subsection (3)(a).

(5) When determining whether a system is reliable for the purposes of subsection (2), the matters that may be taken into account include—

(a) any rules of the system that apply to its operation;

(b) any measures taken to secure the integrity of information held on the system;

(c) any measures taken to prevent unauthorised access to and use of the system;

(d) the security of the hardware and software used by the system;

(e) the regularity of and extent of any audit of the system by an independent body;

(f) any assessment of the reliability of the system made by a body with supervisory or regulatory functions;

(g) the provisions of any voluntary scheme or industry standard that apply in relation to the system.

3 Possession, indorsement and effect of electronic trade documents

(1) A person may possess, indorse and part with possession of an electronic trade document.

(2) An electronic trade document has the same effect as an equivalent paper trade document.

(3) Anything done in relation to an electronic trade document has the same effect (if any) in relation to the document as it would have in relation to an equivalent paper trade document.

(4) An electronic trade document is to be treated as corporeal moveable property for the purposes of any Act of the Scottish Parliament relating to the creation of a security in the form of a pledge over moveable property.

4 Change of form

(1) A paper trade document may be converted into an electronic trade document, and an electronic trade document may be converted into a paper trade document, if (and only if)—

(a) a statement that the document has been converted is included in the document in its new form, and

(b) any contractual or other requirements relating to the conversion of the document are complied with.

(2) Where a document is converted in accordance with subsection (1)—

(a) the document in its old form ceases to have effect, and

(b) all rights and liabilities relating to the document continue to have effect in relation to the document in its new form.

5 Exceptions

(1) If an intention that section 3 should not apply in relation to an electronic trade document appears in, or can reasonably be inferred from, the document or terms that have effect in relation to the document—

(a) that section does not apply in relation to the document, and

(b) section 4 also does not apply in relation to it.

(2) Sections 1 to 4 do not apply in relation to—

(a) an uncertificated unit of a security that is transferable by means of a relevant system in accordance with the Uncertificated Securities Regulations 2001 (SI 2001/3755), or

(b) a document or instrument of a type specified in regulations made by the appropriate authority.

(3) The Secretary of State may by regulations amend this section so as to amend or remove the exception conferred by subsection (2)(a).

(4) The Secretary of State must consult the Scottish Ministers before making regulations under subsection (2)(b) that contain provision that is to have effect in relation to Scotland.

(5) Subsection (4) does not apply if the regulations are to be made by the Secretary of State and the Scottish Ministers acting jointly.

(6) Regulations under this section may include incidental, consequential, transitional or saving provision.

(7) 'The appropriate authority', in relation to regulations under subsection (2)(b), means—

(a) in any case, the Secretary of State or the Secretary of State and the Scottish Ministers acting jointly;

(b) in a case in which all of the provision made by the regulations is within Scottish devolved competence, the Scottish Ministers.

(8) Provision is within Scottish devolved competence if it is provision which would be within the legislative competence of the Scottish Parliament if contained in an Act of that Parliament.

6 Regulations under section 5

(1) Any power to make regulations under section 5, so far as exercisable by the Secretary of State acting alone or by the Secretary of State and the Scottish Ministers acting jointly, is exercisable by statutory instrument.

(2) For regulations made under section 5 by the Scottish Ministers acting alone, see section 27 of the 2010 Act (Scottish statutory instruments).

(3) A statutory instrument containing regulations made under section 5 by the Secretary of State acting alone, or by the Secretary of State and the Scottish Ministers acting jointly, may not be made unless a draft of the instrument containing the regulations has been laid before and approved by a resolution of each House of Parliament.

(4) Regulations made under section 5 by the Scottish Ministers acting alone, or by the Secretary of State and the Scottish Ministers acting jointly, are subject to the affirmative procedure (see section 29 of the 2010 Act).

(5) Where regulations are made under section 5 by the Secretary of State and the Scottish Ministers acting jointly—

(a) section 29 of the 2010 Act (affirmative procedure) applies in relation to the regulations as it applies in relation to devolved subordinate legislation (within the meaning of Part 2 of that Act) which is subject to the affirmative procedure, but as if references to a Scottish statutory instrument were to a statutory instrument, and

(b) section 32 of the 2010 Act (laying) applies in relation to the laying before the Scottish Parliament of the statutory instrument containing the regulations as it applies in relation to the laying before that Parliament of a Scottish statutory instrument (within the meaning of Part 2 of that Act).

(6) In this section 'the 2010 Act' means the Interpretation and Legislative Reform (Scotland) Act 2010 (asp 10).

7 Consequential provision

(1) In section 89B(2) of the Bills of Exchange Act 1882 (instruments to which section 89A applies), at the end insert 'or to anything that is an electronic trade document for the purposes of the Electronic Trade Documents Act 2023 (see section 2 of that Act).'

(2) In section 1 of the Carriage of Goods by Sea Act 1992 (shipping documents etc), omit subsections (5) and (6).

8 Extent, commencement and short title

(1) This Act extends to England and Wales, Scotland and Northern Ireland, except that section 3(4) extends only to Scotland.

(2) This Act comes into force at the end of the period of two months beginning with the day on which it is passed.

(3) Sections 3 and 4 do not apply in relation to a paper trade document or an electronic trade document issued before the day on which this Act comes into force.

(4) This Act may be cited as the Electronic Trade Documents Act 2023.

PART II
STATUTORY INSTRUMENTS

COMMERCIAL AGENTS (COUNCIL DIRECTIVE) REGULATIONS 1993 (SI 1993/3053)

PART I
GENERAL

2 Interpretation, application and extent

(1) In these Regulations—

'commercial agent' means a self-employed intermediary who has continuing authority to negotiate the sale or purchase of goods on behalf of another person (the 'principal'), or to negotiate and conclude the sale or purchase of goods on behalf of and in the name of that principal; but shall be understood as not including in particular:

(i) a person who, in his capacity as an officer of a company or association, is empowered to enter into commitments binding on that company or association;

(ii) a partner who is lawfully authorised to enter into commitments binding on his partners;

(iii) a person who acts as an insolvency practitioner (as that expression is defined in section 388 of the Insolvency Act 1986) or the equivalent in any other jurisdiction;

'commission' means any part of the remuneration of a commercial agent which varies with the number or value of business transactions;

['EEA Agreement' means the Agreement on the European Economic Area signed at Oporto on 2nd May 1992 as adjusted by the Protocol signed at Brussels on 17th March 1993;

'member State' includes a State which is a contracting party to the EEA Agreement;]

'restraint of trade clause' means an agreement restricting the business activities of a commercial agent following termination of the agency contract.

(2) These Regulations do not apply to—

(a) commercial agents whose activities are unpaid;

(b) commercial agents when they operate on commodity exchanges or in the commodity market;

(c) the Crown Agents for Overseas Governments and Administrations, as set up under the Crown Agents Act 1979, or its subsidiaries.

(3) The provisions of the Schedule to these Regulations have effect for the purpose of determining the persons whose activities as commercial agents are to be considered secondary.

(4) These Regulations shall not apply to the persons referred to in paragraph (3) above.

(5) These Regulations do not extend to Northern Ireland.

PART II
RIGHTS AND OBLIGATIONS

3 Duties of a commercial agent to his principal

(1) In performing his activities a commercial agent must look after the interests of his principal and act dutifully and in good faith.

(2) In particular, a commercial agent must—

(a) make proper efforts to negotiate and, where appropriate, conclude the transactions he is instructed to take care of;

(b) communicate to his principal all the necessary information available to him;

(c) comply with reasonable instructions given by his principal.

4 Duties of a principal to his commercial agent

(1) In his relations with his commercial agent a principal must act dutifully and in good faith.

(2) In particular, a principal must—

(a) provide his commercial agent with the necessary documentation relating to the goods concerned;

(b) obtain for his commercial agent the information necessary for the performance of the agency contract, and in particular notify his commercial agent within a reasonable period once he anticipates that the volume of commercial transactions will be significantly lower than that which the commercial agent could normally have expected.

(3) A principal shall, in addition, inform his commercial agent within a reasonable period of his acceptance or refusal of, and of any non-execution by him of, a commercial transaction which the commercial agent has procured for him.

5 Prohibition on derogation from regulations 3 and 4 and consequence of breach

(1) The parties may not derogate from regulations 3 and 4 above.

(2) The law applicable to the contract shall govern the consequence of breach of the rights and obligations under regulations 3 and 4 above.

PART III
REMUNERATION

6 Form and amount of remuneration in absence of agreement

(1) In the absence of any agreement as to remuneration between the parties, a commercial agent shall be entitled to the remuneration that commercial agents appointed for the goods forming the subject of his agency contract are customarily allowed in the place where he carries on his activities and, if there is no such customary practice, a commercial agent shall be entitled to reasonable remuneration taking into account all the aspects of the transaction.

(2) This regulation is without prejudice to the application of any enactment or rule of law concerning the level of remuneration.

(3) Where a commercial agent is not remunerated (wholly or in part) by commission, regulations 7 to 12 below shall not apply.

7 Entitlement to commission on transactions concluded during agency contract

(1) A commercial agent shall be entitled to commission on commercial transactions concluded during the period covered by the agency contract—

(a) where the transaction has been concluded as a result of his action; or

(b) where the transaction is concluded with a third party whom he has previously acquired as a customer for transactions of the same kind.

(2) A commercial agent shall also be entitled to commission on transactions concluded during the period covered by the agency contract where he has an exclusive right to a specific geographical area or to a specific group of customers and where the transaction has been entered into with a customer belonging to that area or group.

8 Entitlement to commission on transactions concluded after agency contract has terminated

Subject to regulation 9 below, a commercial agent shall be entitled to commission on commercial transactions concluded after the agency contract has terminated if—

(a) the transaction is mainly attributable to his efforts during the period covered by the agency contract and if the transaction was entered into within a reasonable period after that contract terminated; or

(b) in accordance with the conditions mentioned in regulation 7 above, the order of the third party reached the principal or the commercial agent before the agency contract terminated.

9 Apportionment of commission between new and previous commercial agents

(1) A commercial agent shall not be entitled to the commission referred to in regulation 7 above if that commission is payable, by virtue of regulation 8 above, to the previous commercial agent, unless it is equitable because of the circumstances for the commission to be shared between the commercial agents.

(2) The principal shall be liable for any sum due under paragraph (1) above to the person entitled to it in accordance with that paragraph, and any sum which the other commercial agent receives to which he is not entitled shall be refunded to the principal.

10 When commission due and date for payment

(1) Commission shall become due as soon as, and to the extent that, one of the following circumstances occurs:

(a) the principal has executed the transaction; or

(b) the principal should, according to his agreement with the third party, have executed the transaction; or

(c) the third party has executed the transaction.

(2) Commission shall become due at the latest when the third party has executed his part of the transaction or should have done so if the principal had executed his part of the transaction, as he should have.

(3) The commission shall be paid not later than on the last day of the month following the quarter in which it became due, and, for the purposes of these Regulations, unless otherwise agreed between the parties, the first quarter period shall run from the date the agency contract takes effect, and subsequent periods shall run from that date in the third month thereafter or the beginning of the fourth month, whichever is the sooner.

(4) Any agreement to derogate from paragraphs (2) and (3) above to the detriment of the commercial agent shall be void.

11 Extinction of right to commission

(1) The right to commission can be extinguished only if and to the extent that—

(a) it is established that the contract between the third party and the principal will not be executed; and

(b) that fact is due to a reason for which the principal is not to blame.

(2) Any commission which the commercial agent has already received shall be refunded if the right to it is extinguished.

(3) Any agreement to derogate from paragraph (1) above to the detriment of the commercial agent shall be void.

12 Periodic supply of information as to commission due and right of inspection of principal's books

(1) The principal shall supply his commercial agent with a statement of the commission due, not later than the last day of the month following the quarter in which the commission has become due, and such statement shall set out the main components used in calculating the amount of the commission.

(2) A commercial agent shall be entitled to demand that he be provided with all the information (and in particular an extract from the books) which is available to his principal and which he needs in order to check the amount of the commission due to him.

(3) Any agreement to derogate from paragraphs (1) and (2) above shall be void.

(4) Nothing in this regulation shall remove or restrict the effect of, or prevent reliance upon, any enactment or rule of law which recognises the right of an agent to inspect the books of a principal.

PART IV
CONCLUSION AND TERMINATION OF THE AGENCY CONTRACT

13 Right to signed written statement of terms of agency contract

(1) The commercial agent and principal shall each be entitled to receive from the other, on request, a signed written document setting out the terms of the agency contract including any terms subsequently agreed.

(2) Any purported waiver of the right referred to in paragraph (1) above shall be void.

14 Conversion of agency contract after expiry of fixed period

An agency contract for a fixed period which continues to be performed by both parties after that period has expired shall be deemed to be converted into an agency contract for an indefinite period.

15 Minimum periods of notice for termination of agency contract

(1) Where an agency contract is concluded for an indefinite period either party may terminate it by notice.

(2) The period of notice shall be—

(a) 1 month for the first year of the contract;

(b) 2 months for the second year commenced;

(c) 3 months for the third year commenced and for the subsequent years;

and the parties may not agree on any shorter periods of notice.

(3) If the parties agree on longer periods than those laid down in paragraph (2) above, the period of notice to be observed by the principal must not be shorter than that to be observed by the commercial agent.

(4) Unless otherwise agreed by the parties, the end of the period of notice must coincide with the end of a calendar month.

(5) The provisions of this regulation shall also apply to an agency contract for a fixed period where it is converted under regulation 14 above into an agency contract for an indefinite period subject to the proviso that the earlier fixed period must be taken into account in the calculation of the period of notice.

16 Savings with regard to immediate termination

These Regulations shall not affect the application of any enactment or rule of law which provides for the immediate termination of the agency contract—

(a) because of the failure of one party to carry out all or part of his obligations under that contract; or

(b) where exceptional circumstances arise.

17 Entitlement of commercial agent to indemnity or compensation on termination of agency contract

(1) This regulation has effect for the purpose of ensuring that the commercial agent is, after termination of the agency contract, indemnified in accordance with paragraphs (3) to (5) below or compensated for damage in accordance with paragraphs (6) and (7) below.

(2) Except where the agency [contract] otherwise provides, the commercial agent shall be entitled to be compensated rather than indemnified.

(3) Subject to paragraph (9) and to regulation 18 below, the commercial agent shall be entitled to an indemnity if and to the extent that—

(a) he has brought the principal new customers or has significantly increased the volume of business with existing customers and the principal continues to derive substantial benefits from the business with such customers; and

(b) the payment of this indemnity is equitable having regard to all the circumstances and, in particular, the commission lost by the commercial agent on the business transacted with such customers.

(4) The amount of the indemnity shall not exceed a figure equivalent to an indemnity for one year calculated from the commercial agent's average annual remuneration over the preceding five years and if the contract goes back less than five years the indemnity shall be calculated on the average for the period in question.

(5) The grant of an indemnity as mentioned above shall not prevent the commercial agent from seeking damages.

(6) Subject to paragraph (9) and to regulation 18 below, the commercial agent shall be entitled to compensation for the damage he suffers as a result of the termination of his relations with his principal.

(7) For the purpose of these Regulations such damage shall be deemed to occur particularly when the termination takes place in either or both of the following circumstances, namely circumstances which—

(a) deprive the commercial agent of the commission which proper performance of the agency contract would have procured for him whilst providing his principal with substantial benefits linked to the activities of the commercial agent; or

(b) have not enabled the commercial agent to amortize the costs and expenses that he had incurred in the performance of the agency contract on the advice of his principal.

(8) Entitlement to the indemnity or compensation for damage as provided for under paragraphs (2) to (7) above shall also arise where the agency contract is terminated as a result of the death of the commercial agent.

(9) The commercial agent shall lose his entitlement to the indemnity or compensation for damage in the instances provided for in paragraphs (2) to (8) above if within one year following termination of his agency contract he has not notified his principal that he intends pursuing his entitlement.

18 Grounds for excluding payment of indemnity or compensation under regulation 17

The [indemnity or] compensation referred to in regulation 17 above shall not be payable to the commercial agent where—

(a) the principal has terminated the agency contract because of default attributable to the commercial agent which would justify immediate termination of the agency contract pursuant to regulation 16 above; or

(b) the commercial agent has himself terminated the agency contract, unless such termination is justified—

(i) by circumstances attributable to the principal, or

(ii) on grounds of the age, infirmity or illness of the commercial agent in consequence of which he cannot reasonably be required to continue his activities; or

(c) the commercial agent, with the agreement of his principal, assigns his rights and duties under the agency contract to another person.

19 Prohibition on derogation from regulations 17 and 18

The parties may not derogate from regulations 17 and 18 to the detriment of the commercial agent before the agency contract expires.

20 Restraint of trade clauses

(1) A restraint of trade clause shall be valid only if and to the extent that—

(a) it is concluded in writing; and

(b) it relates to the geographical area or the group of customers and the geographical area entrusted to the commercial agent and to the kind of goods covered by his agency under the contract.

(2) A restraint of trade clause shall be valid for not more than two years after termination of the agency contract.

(3) Nothing in this regulation shall affect any enactment or rule of law which imposes other restrictions on the validity or enforceability of restraint of trade clauses or which enables a court to reduce the obligations on the parties resulting from such clauses.

PART V
MISCELLANEOUS AND SUPPLEMENTAL

21 Disclosure of information

Nothing in these Regulations shall require information to be given where such disclosure would be contrary to public policy.

22 Service of notice etc

(1) Any notice, statement or other document to be given or supplied to a commercial agent or to be given or supplied to the principal under these Regulations may be so given or supplied:

(a) by delivering it to him;

(b) by leaving it at his proper address addressed to him by name;

(c) by sending it by post to him addressed either to his registered address or to the address of his registered or principal office;

or by any other means provided for in the agency contract.

(2) Any such notice, statement or document may—

(a) in the case of a body corporate, be given or served on the secretary or clerk of that body;

(b) in the case of a partnership, be given to or served on any partner or on any person having the control or management of the partnership business.

23 Transitional provisions

(1) Notwithstanding any provision in an agency contract made before 1st January 1994, these Regulations shall apply to that contract after that date and, accordingly any provision which is inconsistent with these Regulations shall have effect subject to them.

(2) Nothing in these Regulations shall affect the rights and liabilities of a commercial agent or a principal which have accrued before 1st January 1994.

THE SCHEDULE

Regulation 2(3)

1 The activities of a person as a commercial agent are to be considered secondary where it may reasonably be taken that the primary purpose of the arrangement with his principal is other than as set out in paragraph 2 below.

2 An arrangement falls within this paragraph if—

(a) the business of the principal is the sale, or as the case may be purchase, of goods of a particular kind; and

(b) the goods concerned are such that—

(i) transactions are normally individually negotiated and concluded on a commercial basis, and

(ii) procuring a transaction on one occasion is likely to lead to further transactions in those goods with that customer on future occasions, or to transactions in those goods with other customers in the same geographical area or among the same group of customers, and

that accordingly it is in the commercial interests of the principal in developing the market in those goods to appoint a representative to such customers with a view to the representative devoting effort, skill and expenditure from his own resources to that end.

3 The following are indications that an arrangement falls within paragraph 2 above, and the absence of any of them is an indication to the contrary—

(a) the principal is the manufacturer, importer or distributor of the goods;

(b) the goods are specifically identified with the principal in the market in question rather than, or to a greater extent than, with any other person;

(c) the agent devotes substantially the whole of his time to representative activities (whether for one principal or for a number of principals whose interests are not conflicting);

(d) the goods are not normally available in the market in question other than by means of the agent;

(e) the arrangement is described as one of commercial agency.

4 The following are indications that an arrangement does not fall within paragraph 2 above—

(a) promotional material is supplied direct to potential customers;

(b) persons are granted agencies without reference to existing agents in a particular area or in relation to a particular group;

(c) customers normally select the goods for themselves and merely place their orders through the agent.

5 The activities of the following categories of persons are presumed, unless the contrary is established, not to fall within paragraph 2 above—

Mail order catalogue agents for consumer goods.

Consumer credit agents.

FINANCIAL SERVICES AND MARKETS ACT 2000 (REGULATED ACTIVITIES) ORDER 2001
(SI 2001/544)

[CHAPTER 14A
REGULATED CREDIT AGREEMENTS

The activities

[60B Regulated credit agreements

(1) Entering into a regulated credit agreement as lender is a specified kind of activity.

(2) It is a specified kind of activity for the lender or another person to exercise, or to have the right to exercise, the lender's rights and duties under a regulated credit agreement.

(3) In this article—

['credit agreement'—

(a) in relation to an agreement other than a green deal plan, means an agreement between an individual or relevant recipient of credit ('A') and any other person ('B') under which B provides A with credit of any amount;

(b) in relation to a green deal plan, has the meaning given by article 60LB;]

['exempt agreement' means a credit agreement which is an exempt agreement under articles 60C to 60H, but where only part of a credit agreement falls within a provision of articles 60C to 60H, only that part is an exempt agreement under those articles];

['regulated credit agreement' means—

(a) in the case of an agreement entered into on or after 1st April 2014, any credit agreement which is not an exempt agreement; or

(b) in the case of an agreement entered into before 1st April 2014, a credit agreement which—

(i) was a regulated agreement within the meaning of section 189(1) of the Consumer Credit Act 1974 when the agreement was entered into; or

(ii) became such a regulated agreement after being varied or supplemented by another agreement before [1st April 2014,

and would not be an exempt agreement pursuant to article 60C(2) on 21st March 2016 if the agreement were entered into on that date.]]

[60C Exempt agreements: exemptions relating to the nature of the agreement

(1) [A] credit agreement is an exempt agreement for the purposes of this Chapter in the following cases.

[(2) A credit agreement is an exempt agreement if—

(a) by entering into the agreement as lender, a person is or was carrying on an activity of a kind specified by article 61(1) (entering into regulated mortgage contracts);

(b) by entering into the agreement as home purchase provider, a person is or was carrying on an activity of a kind specified by article 63F(1) (entering into regulated home purchase plans) [; or

(c) [. . .] by administering the agreement on 21st March 2016 a person is carrying on an activity of a kind specified by article 61(2) (administering regulated mortgage contracts).].

(3) A credit agreement is an exempt agreement if—

(a) the lender provides the borrower with credit exceeding £25,000, and

(b) the agreement is entered into by the borrower wholly or predominantly for the purposes of a business carried on, or intended to be carried on, by the borrower.

(4) A credit agreement is an exempt agreement if—

(a) the lender provides the borrower with credit of £25,000 or less,

(b) the agreement is entered into by the borrower wholly for the purposes of a business carried on, or intended to be carried on, by the borrower, and

[(c) the agreement is a green deal plan made in relation to a property that is not a domestic property (as defined by article 60LB).]

[(4A) A credit agreement is an exempt agreement if—

(a) the lender provides the borrower with credit of £25,000 or less,

(b) the agreement is entered into by the borrower wholly for the purposes of a business carried on, or intended to be carried on, by the borrower, and

(c) the agreement is entered into by the lender and the borrower under the Bounce Back Loan Scheme.

(4B) For the purposes of paragraph (4A), 'Bounce Back Loan Scheme' means the scheme of that name operated from 4th May 2020 by the British Business Bank plc on behalf of the Secretary of State.

(4C) An agreement exempt under paragraph (4A) may not also be an article 36H agreement by virtue of paragraph (4) of that article.]

(5) For the purposes of paragraph (3), if an agreement includes a declaration which—

(a) is made by the borrower,

(b) provides that the agreement is entered into by the borrower wholly or predominantly for the purposes of a business carried on, or intended to be carried on, by the borrower, and

(c) complies with rules made by the FCA for the purpose of this article,

the agreement is to be presumed to have been entered into by the borrower wholly or predominantly for the purposes specified in sub-paragraph (b) unless paragraph (6) applies.

(6) This paragraph applies if, when the agreement is entered into—

(a) the lender (or, if there is more than one lender, any of the lenders), or

(b) any person who has acted on behalf of the lender (or, if there is more than one lender, any of the lenders) in connection with the entering into of the agreement,

knows or has reasonable cause to suspect that the agreement is not entered into by the borrower wholly or predominantly for the purposes of a business carried on, or intended to be carried on, by the borrower.

(7) Paragraphs (5) and (6) also apply for the purposes of paragraph (4) but with the omission of the words 'or predominantly'.

(8) A credit agreement is an exempt agreement if it is made in connection with trade in goods or services—

(a) between the United Kingdom and a country outside the United Kingdom,

(b) within a country [outside the United Kingdom], or

(c) between countries outside the United Kingdom, and

the credit is provided to the borrower in the course of a business carried on by the borrower.]

[60D Exempt agreements: exemption relating to the purchase of land for non-residential purposes

(1) A credit agreement is an exempt agreement for the purposes of this Chapter if, at the time it is entered into, any sums due under it are secured by a legal [or equitable] mortgage on land and the condition in paragraph (2) is satisfied.

(2) The condition is that less than 40% of the land is used, or is intended to be used, as or in connection with a dwelling—

(a) by the borrower or a related person of the borrower, or

(b) in the case of credit provided to trustees, by an individual who is a beneficiary of the trust or a related person of a beneficiary.

(3) For the purposes of paragraph (2)—

(a) the area of any land which comprises a building or other structure containing two or more storeys is to be taken to be the aggregate of the floor areas of each of those stories;

(b) 'related person' in relation to a person ('B') who is the borrower or (in the case of credit provided to trustees) a beneficiary of the trust, means—

(i) B's spouse or civil partner,

(ii) a person (whether or not of the opposite sex) whose relationship with B has the characteristics of the relationship between husband and wife, or

(iii) B's parent, brother, sister, child, grandparent or grandchild.

[(4) This article does not apply to an agreement if—

(a) the agreement is entered into on or after 21st March 2016,

(b) under the agreement a mortgage creditor grants or promises to grant a credit in the form of a deferred payment, loan or other similar financial accommodation,

(c) the credit is granted or promised to an individual who is acting for purposes outside those of any trade, business or profession carried on by the individual,

(d) the purpose of the agreement is to acquire or retain property rights in land or in an existing or projected building, and

(e) the agreement does not meet the conditions in paragraphs (i) to (iii) of article 61(3)(a) (regulated mortgage contracts).

(5) A reference in paragraph (4)(d) to any land or building—

(a) in relation to an agreement entered into before [IP completion day], is a reference to any land or building in the United Kingdom or within the territory of an EEA State;

(b) in relation to an agreement entered into on or after [IP completion day], is a reference to any land or building in the United Kingdom.]]

[60E Exempt agreements: exemptions relating to the nature of the lender

(1) A credit agreement is an exempt agreement for the purposes of this Chapter in the following cases.

(2) [Subject to article 60HA, a relevant credit agreement] relating to the purchase of land is an exempt agreement if the lender is—

(a) specified, or of a description specified, in rules made by the FCA under paragraph (3), or

(b) a local authority.

(3) The FCA may make rules specifying any of the following for the purpose of paragraph (2)—

(a) an authorised person with permission to effect or carry out contracts of insurance;

(b) a friendly society;

(c) an organisation of employers or organisation of workers;

(d) a charity;

(e) an improvement company (within the meaning given by section 7 of the Improvement of Land Act 1899);

(f) a body corporate named or specifically referred to in any public general Act;

(g) a body corporate named or specifically referred to in, or in an order made under, a relevant housing provision;

(h) a building society (within the meaning of the Building Societies Act 1986);

(i) an authorised person with permission to accept deposits.

(4) Rules under paragraph (3) may—

(a) specify a particular person or class of persons;

(b) be limited so as to apply only to agreements or classes of agreement specified in the rules.

(5) [Subject to article 60HA, a relevant credit agreement] is an exempt agreement if it is—

(a) secured by a legal [or equitable] mortgage on land,

(b) that land is used or is intended to be used as or in connection with a dwelling, and

(c) the lender is a housing authority.

(6) A credit agreement is an exempt agreement if—

(a) the lender is an investment firm or a [qualifying] credit institution, and

(b) the agreement is entered into for the purpose of allowing the borrower to carry out a transaction relating to one or more financial instruments.

(7) In this article—

'housing authority' means—

(a) in England and Wales, the Homes and Communities Agency, the Welsh Ministers [, a company which is a wholly-owned subsidiary of the Welsh Ministers, a registered social landlord within the meaning of Part 1 of the Housing Act 1996,] or a private registered provider (within the meaning of Part 2 of the Housing and Regeneration Act 2008);

(b) in Scotland, the Scottish Ministers or a registered social landlord (within the meaning of the Housing (Scotland) Act 2010;

(c) in Northern Ireland, the Northern Ireland Housing Executive [or a housing association within the meaning of Part 2 of the Housing (Northern Ireland) Order 1992];

'relevant credit agreement relating to the purchase of land' means—

(a) a borrower-lender-supplier agreement financing—

(i) the purchase of land, or

(ii) provision of dwellings on land,

and secured by a legal [or equitable] mortgage on that land,

(b) a borrower-lender agreement secured by a legal [or equitable] mortgage on land, or

(c) a borrower-lender-supplier agreement financing a transaction which is a linked transaction in relation to—

(i) an agreement falling within sub-paragraph (a), or

(ii) an agreement falling within sub-paragraph (b) financing—

(aa) the purchase of land,

(bb) the provision of dwellings on land,

and secured by a legal [or equitable] mortgage on the land referred to in subparagraph (a) or the land referred to in paragraph (ii);

'relevant housing provision' means any of the following—

(a) section 156(4) or 447(2)(a) of the Housing Act 1985,

(b) section 156(4) of that Act as it has effect by virtue of section 17 of the Housing Act 1996 (the right to acquire), or

(c) article 154(1)(a) of the Housing (Northern Ireland) Order 1981

[(7A) In paragraph (7), in the definition of 'housing authority', in paragraph (a), 'wholly-owned subsidiary' has the same meaning as in section 1159 (meaning of 'subsidiary' etc) of the Companies Act 2006.

(7B) For the purpose of paragraph (7A), the Welsh Ministers are to be treated as a body corporate.]

(8) For the purposes of the definition of 'relevant credit agreement relating to the purchase of land', a transaction is, unless paragraph (9) applies, a 'linked transaction' in relation to a credit agreement ('the principal agreement') if—

(a) it is (or will be) entered into by the borrower under the principal agreement or by a relative of the borrower,

(b) it does not relate to the provision of security,

(c) it does not form part of the principal agreement, and

(d) one of the following conditions is satisfied—

(i) the transaction is entered into in compliance with a term of the principal agreement;

(ii) the principal agreement is a borrower-lender-supplier agreement and the transaction is financed, or to be financed, by the principal agreement;

(iii) the following conditions are met—

(aa) the other party is a person to whom paragraph (10) applies,

(bb) the other party initiated the transaction by suggesting it to the borrower or the relative of the borrower, and

(cc) the borrower or the relative of the borrower enters into the transaction to induce the lender to enter into the principal agreement or for another purpose related to the principal agreement or to a transaction financed or to be financed by the principal agreement.

(9) This paragraph applies if the transaction is—

(a) a contract of insurance,

(b) a contract which contains a guarantee of goods, or

(c) a transaction which comprises, or is effected under—

(i) an agreement for the operation of an account (including any savings account) for the deposit of money, or

(ii) an agreement for the operation of a current account, under which the customer ('C') may, by means of cheques or similar orders payable to C or to any other person, obtain or have the use of money held or made available by the person with whom the account is kept.

(10) The persons to whom this paragraph applies are—

(a) the lender;

(b) the lender's associate;

(c) a person who, in the negotiation of the transaction, is represented by a person who carries on an activity of the kind specified by article 36A (credit broking) by way of business who is or was also a negotiator in negotiations for the principal agreement;

(d) a person who, at the time the transaction is initiated, knows that the principal agreement has been made or contemplates that it might be made.]

[60F Exempt agreements: exemptions relating to number of repayments to be made

(1) A credit agreement is an exempt agreement for the purposes of this Chapter in the following cases.

(2) A credit agreement is an exempt agreement if—

(a) the agreement is a borrower-lender-supplier agreement for fixed-sum credit[, other than a green deal plan],

(b) the number of payments to be made by the borrower is not more than [twelve],

(c) those payments are required to be made within a period of 12 months or less (beginning on the date of the agreement),

(d) the credit is—

(i) secured on land, or

(ii) provided without interest or other [. . .] charges, and

(e) [neither paragraph (7) nor paragraph (7A) (taken with paragraph (7B)) applies to the agreement].

(3) A credit agreement is an exempt agreement if—

(a) the agreement is a borrower-lender-supplier agreement for running-account credit,

(b) the borrower is to make payments in relation to specified periods which must be, unless the agreement is secured on land, of 3 months or less,

(c) the number of payments to be made by the borrower in repayment of the whole amount of credit provided in each such period is not more than one,

(d) the credit is—

(i) secured on land, or

(ii) provided without interest or other significant charges, and

(e) paragraph (7) does not apply to the agreement.

(4) [Subject to article 60HA, a credit agreement] is an exempt agreement if—

(a) the agreement is a borrower-lender-supplier agreement financing the purchase of land,

(b) the number of payments to be made by the borrower is not more than four, and

(c) the credit is—

(i) secured on land, or

(ii) provided without interest or other charges.

(5) A credit agreement is an exempt agreement if—

(a) the agreement is a borrower-lender-supplier agreement for fixed-sum credit,

(b) the credit is to finance a premium under a contract of insurance relating to land or anything on land,

(c) the lender is the lender under a credit agreement secured by a legal [or equitable] mortgage on that land,

(d) the credit is to be repaid within the period (which must be 12 months or less) to which the premium relates,

(e) in the case of an agreement secured on land, there is no charge forming part of the total charge for credit under the agreement other than interest at a rate not exceeding the rate of interest from time to time payable under the agreement mentioned at sub-paragraph (c),

(f) in the case of an agreement which is not secured on land, the credit is provided without interest or other charges, and

(g) the number of payments to be made by the borrower is not more than twelve.

(6) A credit agreement is an exempt agreement if—

(a) the agreement is a borrower-lender-supplier agreement for fixed-sum credit,

(b) the lender is the lender under a credit agreement secured by a legal [or equitable] mortgage on land,

(c) the agreement is to finance a premium under a contract of whole life insurance which provides, in the event of the death of the person on whose life the contract is effected before the credit referred to in sub-paragraph (b) has been repaid, for payment of a sum not exceeding the amount sufficient to meet the amount which, immediately after that credit has been advanced, would be payable to the lender in respect of that credit (including interest from time to time payable under that agreement),

(d) in the case of an agreement secured on land, there is no charge forming part of the total charge for credit under the agreement other than interest at a rate not exceeding the rate of interest from time to time payable under the agreement mentioned at sub-paragraph (b),

(e) in the case of an agreement which is not secured on land, the credit is provided without interest or other charges, and

(f) the number of payments to be made by the borrower is not more than twelve.

(7) This paragraph applies to—

(a) agreements financing the purchase of land;

(b) agreements which are conditional sale agreements or hire-purchase agreements;

(c) agreements secured by a pledge (other than a pledge of documents of title or of bearer bonds).

[(7A) This paragraph applies to agreements entered into on or after the regulatory commencement date which are not secured on land—

(a) where—

(i) the lender and the supplier are not the same person; and

(ii) paragraph (7B) does not apply to the agreement; or

(b) made in the following way—

(i) a person ('the principal supplier') offers to supply goods or services to a consumer ('the consumer') financed by a credit agreement provided by another person ('the lender');

(ii) the lender, under a pre-existing arrangement with that principal supplier, purchases the goods or services from the principal supplier, for supply to the consumer; and

(iii) the lender is, in relation to the credit agreement with the consumer mentioned in sub-paragraph (i), also the supplier of the goods or services to that consumer.

(7B) This paragraph applies to—

(a) agreements to finance premiums under contracts of insurance;

(b) agreements where—

(i) the borrowers are employees; and

(ii) the agreements result from an arrangement between the lender or supplier and—

(aa) the borrowers' employer, or

(bb) an undertaking which is a member of the same group as the borrowers' employer;

(c) agreements to finance the provision of goods or services offered by a registered social landlord (as defined by article 36FA(4)) to—

(i) its tenants,

(ii) its leaseholders, or

(iii) persons with whom the registered social landlord has entered a shared ownership agreement within the meaning of section 83(3) of the Housing (Scotland) Act 2001.

(7C) In paragraph (7A), 'regulatory commencement date' has the meaning given in article 1(3) of the Financial Services and Markets Act 2000 (Regulated Activities etc.) (Amendment) Order 2025.]

[(8 In this article, 'payment' means any payment which comprises or includes—

(a) the repayment of capital, or

(b) the payment of interest or any other charge which forms part of the total charge for credit.]]

[60G Exempt agreements: exemptions relating to the total charge for credit

(1) A credit agreement is an exempt agreement for the purposes of this Chapter in the following cases.

(2) A credit agreement is an exempt agreement if—

(a) it is a borrower-lender agreement, [. . .]

(b) the lender is a credit union and the rate of the total charge for credit does not exceed 42.6 per cent[, and

(c) paragraph (2A) applies to the agreement.]

[(2A) This paragraph applies to the agreement if—

(a) the agreement is not [one to which subsection (2) of section 423A of the Act applies]

(b) the agreement is [one to which that subsection applies] and—

(i) the agreement is [one to which subsection (3) of that section applies,]

(ii) the agreement is a bridging loan [. . .], or

(iii) in relation to the agreement—

(aa) the borrower receives timely information on the main features, risks and costs of the agreement at the pre-contractual stage, and

(bb) any advertising of the agreement is fair, clear and not misleading] [; or
(c) the agreement was entered into before 21st March 2016.]

(3) [Subject to paragraph (8), a credit agreement] is an exempt agreement if—

(a) it is a borrower-lender agreement,

(b) it is an agreement of a kind offered to a particular class of individual or relevant recipient of credit and not offered to the public generally,

(c) it provides that the only charge included in the total charge for credit is interest,

(d) interest under the agreement may not at any time be more than the sum of one per cent and the highest of the base rates published by the banks specified in paragraph (7) on the date 28 days before the date on which the interest is charged, and

(e) paragraph (5) does not apply to the agreement.

(4) [Subject to paragraph (8), a credit agreement] is an exempt agreement if—

(a) it is a borrower-lender agreement,

(b) it is an agreement of a kind offered to a particular class of individual or relevant recipient of credit and not offered to the public generally,

(c) it does not provide for or permit an increase in the rate or amount of any item which is included in the total charge for credit,

(d) the total charge for credit under the agreement is not more than the sum of one per cent and the highest of the base rates published by the banks specified in paragraph (7) on the date 28 days before the date on which the charge is imposed, and

(e) paragraph (5) does not apply to the agreement.

(5) This paragraph applies to an agreement if—

(a) the total amount to be repaid by the borrower to discharge the borrower's indebtedness may vary according to a formula which is specified in the agreement and which has effect by reference to movements in the level of any index or other factor, or

[(b) the agreement—

(i) is not—

(aa) secured on land, or

[(bb) offered by a lender to a borrower as an incident of the borrower's employment with the lender or with an undertaking in the same group as the lender;] and

(ii) does not meet the general interest test.]

(6) For the purposes of [paragraphs (5) and (8)], an agreement meets the general interest test if—

(a) the agreement is offered under an enactment with a general interest purpose, and

(b) the terms on which the credit is provided are more favourable to the borrower than those prevailing on the market, either because the rate of interest is lower than that prevailing on the market, or because the rate of interest is no higher than that prevailing on the market but the other terms on which credit is provided are more favourable to the borrower.

(7) The banks specified in this paragraph are—

(a) the Bank of England;
(b) Bank of Scotland;
(c) Barclays Bank plc;
(d) Clydesdale Bank plc;
(e) Co-operative Bank Public Limited Company;
(f) Coutts & Co;
(g) National Westminster Bank Public Limited Company;
(h) the Royal Bank of Scotland plc.

[(8) A credit agreement [to which subsection (2) of section 423A of the Act applies] [which is entered into on or after 21st March 2016] is an exempt agreement pursuant to paragraph (3) or (4) only if—

(a) the agreement meets the general interest test;

(b) the borrower receives timely information on the main features, risks and costs of the agreement at the pre-contractual stage; and

(c) any advertising of the agreement is fair, clear and not misleading.

[(9) In this article 'bridging loan' means a mortgage agreement that—

(a) is of no fixed duration or is due to be repaid within 12 months, and

(b) is used by a consumer, within the meaning given by section 423A(4) of the Act, as a temporary financing solution while transitioning to another financial arrangement for the immovable property concerned.]]]

[60H Exempt agreements: exemptions relating to the nature of the borrower

[(1)] [A] credit agreement is an exempt agreement for the purposes of this Chapter if—

(a) the borrower is an individual,

(b) the agreement is either—

(i) secured on land, or

[(ii) for credit which exceeds £60,260 and [, if entered into on or after 21st March 2016,] is for a purpose other than—

(aa) the renovation of residential property,

[. . .]]

(c) the agreement includes a declaration made by the borrower which provides that the borrower agrees to forgo the protection and remedies that would be available to the borrower if the agreement were a regulated credit agreement and which complies with rules made by the FCA for the purposes of this paragraph,

(d) a statement has been made in relation to the income or assets of the borrower which complies with rules made by the FCA for the purposes of this paragraph,

(e) the connection between the statement and the agreement complies with any rules made by the FCA for the purposes of this paragraph (including as to the period of time between the making of the statement and the agreement being entered into), and

(f) a copy of the statement was provided to the lender before the agreement was entered into.

[(1A) Article 4(4B) does not apply to an agreement which is exempt under paragraph (1), the purpose of which is to acquire or retain property rights in land or in an existing or projected building, and—

(a) a declaration has been made by the borrower which either—

(i) provides that the borrower is UK resident, or

(ii) provides that the borrower is treated as present in the United Kingdom,

(b) a copy of that declaration was provided to the lender before the agreement was entered into, and

(c) the agreement is entered into on or after 21st July 2022.

(1B) For the purposes of paragraph (1A), a borrower is 'UK resident' if—

(a) the borrower is present in the United Kingdom on at least 183 days during the continuous period of 365 days ending with the date the agreement is entered into, or

(b) the spouse or civil partner of the borrower—

(i) is living with the borrower on the date the agreement was entered into, and

(ii) is present in the United Kingdom on at least 183 days during the continuous period of 365 days ending with the date the agreement is entered into.

(1C) For the purposes of paragraph (1A), a borrower is treated as present in the United Kingdom if, on the date the agreement was entered into, the borrower—

(a) is in Crown employment, and

(b) is present in a country or territory outside the United Kingdom for the purpose of performing activities in the course of that employment, or

(c) is the spouse or civil partner of an individual who—

(i) is in Crown employment,

(ii) is present in a country or territory outside the United Kingdom for the purpose of performing activities in the course of that employment, and

(d) is living with their spouse or civil partner.

(1D) References in this article to a borrower being present in the United Kingdom on a day are to the borrower being present in the United Kingdom at the end of that day.

(1E) Individuals who are married to, or are civil partners of, each other are treated, for the purposes of this article, as living together unless—

(a) they are separated under an order of a court of competent jurisdiction,

(b) they are separated by deed of separation, or

(c) they are in fact separated in circumstances in which the separation is likely to be permanent.

(1F) For the purposes of this article, 'Crown employment' means employment under or for the purposes of a government department or any officer or body exercising on behalf of the Crown functions conferred by a statutory provision.]

[. . .]]

[60HA Exempt agreements: [provision qualifying articles [60E and 60F]

(1) A credit agreement [entered into on or after 21st March 2016] is not an exempt agreement pursuant to article 60E(2) or (5) [or 60F(4) if it is a mortgage agreement to which paragraph (2) does not apply.]

(2) This paragraph applies [to an agreement] if—

[. . .]

(b) the agreement is a bridging loan within the meaning [given by article 60G(9)] or

(c) the agreement is a restricted public loan in respect of which—

(i) the borrower receives timely information on the main features, risks and costs at the pre-contractual stage; and

(ii) any advertising is fair, clear and not misleading.

(3) In paragraph (2)(c) 'restricted public loan' means a credit agreement that is—

(a) offered to a particular class of borrower and not offered to the public generally;

(b) offered under an enactment with a general interest purpose; and

(c) provided on terms which are more favourable to the borrower than those prevailing on the market, because it meets one of the following conditions—

(i) it is interest free;

(ii) the rate of interest is lower than that prevailing on the market; or

(iii) the rate of interest is no higher than that prevailing on the market but the other terms on which credit is provided are more favourable to the borrower.]

Exclusions

[60I Arranging administration by authorised person

A person ('A') who is not an authorised person does not carry on an activity of the kind specified by article 60B(2) in relation to a regulated credit agreement where A—

(a) arranges for another person, who is an authorised person with permission to carry on an activity of that kind, to exercise or to have the right to exercise the lender's rights and duties under the agreement, or

(b) exercises or has the right to exercise the lender's rights and duties under the agreement during a period of not more than one month beginning with the day on which any such arrangement comes to an end.]

[60J Administration pursuant to agreement with authorised person
A person who is not an authorised person does not carry on an activity of the kind specified by article 60B(2) in relation to regulated credit agreement if that person exercises or has the right to exercise the lender's rights and duties under the agreement pursuant to an agreement with an authorised person who has permission to carry on an activity of the kind specified by article 60B(2).]

[. . .]

60K [Other exclusions]
Article 60B is also subject to [the exclusions in articles [. . .] 72G (local authorities) and 72I (registered consumer buy-to-let mortgage firms)].

Supplemental

[60L Interpretation of Chapter 14A etc
(1) In this Chapter—
'assignment', in relation to Scotland, means assignation;
'associate' means, in relation to a person ('P')—
(a) where P is an individual, any person who is or who has been—
(i) P's spouse or P's civil partner;
(ii) a relative of P, of P's spouse or of P's civil partner;
(iii) the spouse or civil partner of a relative of P or P's spouse or civil partner;
(iv) if P is a member of a partnership, any of P's partners and the spouse or civil partner of any such person;
(b) where P is a body corporate—
(i) any person who is a controller ('C') of P, and
(ii) any other person for whom C is a controller;
'borrower' means [(except in relation to green deal plans: see instead article 60LB)] a person who receives credit under a credit agreement or a person to whom the rights and duties of a borrower under a credit agreement have passed by assignment or operation of law;
'borrower-lender agreement' means—
(a) a credit agreement—
(i) to finance a transaction between the borrower and a person ('the supplier') other than the lender, and
(ii) which is not made by the lender under pre-existing arrangements, or in contemplation of future arrangements, between the lender and the supplier,
(b) a credit agreement to refinance any existing indebtedness of the borrower, whether to the lender or another person, or
(c) a credit agreement which is—
(i) an unrestricted-use credit agreement, and (ii) not made by the lender—
(aa) under pre-existing arrangements between the lender and a person other than the borrower ('the supplier'), and
(bb) in the knowledge that the credit is to be used to finance a transaction between the borrower and the supplier;
'borrower-lender-supplier agreement' means—
(a) a credit agreement to finance a transaction between the borrower and the lender, whether forming part of that agreement or not;
(b) a credit agreement—
(i) to finance a transaction between the borrower and a person ('the supplier') other than the lender, and

(ii) which is made by the lender under pre-existing arrangements, or in contemplation of future arrangements, between the lender and the supplier, or

(c) a credit agreement which is—

(i) an unrestricted-use credit agreement, and

(ii) made by the lender under pre-existing arrangements between the lender and a person ('the supplier') other than the borrower in the knowledge that the credit is to be used to finance a transaction between the borrower and the supplier;

'conditional sale agreement' means an agreement for the sale of goods or land under which the purchase price or part of it is payable by instalments, and the property in the goods or land is to remain with the seller (notwithstanding that the buyer is to be in possession of the goods or land) until such conditions as to the payment of instalments or otherwise as may be specified in the agreement are fulfilled;

'credit' includes a cash loan and any other form of financial accommodation;

['credit agreement'—

(a) in relation to an agreement other than a green deal plan, has the meaning given by article 60B;

(b) in relation to a green deal plan, has the meaning given by article 60LB;]

'credit union' means a credit union within the meaning of—

(a) the Credit Unions Act 1979;

(b) the Credit Unions (Northern Ireland) Order 1985;

'deposit' (except where specified otherwise) means any sum payable by a borrower by way of deposit or down-payment, or credited or to be credited to the borrower on account of any deposit or down-payment, whether the sum is to be or has been paid to the lender or any other person, or is to be or has been discharged by a payment of money or a transfer or delivery of goods or other means;

'exempt agreement' has the meaning given by article 60B;

'finance' includes financing in whole or in part, and 'refinance' is to be read accordingly;

'fixed-sum credit' means a facility under a credit agreement whereby the borrower is enabled to receive credit (whether in one amount or by instalments) but which is not running-account credit;

'hire-purchase agreement' means an agreement—

(a) which is not a conditional sale agreement,

(b) under which goods are bailed or (in Scotland) hired to a person ('P') in return for periodical payments by P, and

(c) the property in the goods will pass to P if the terms of the agreement are complied with and one or more of the following occurs—

(i) the exercise by P of an option to purchase the goods;

(ii) the doing by any party to the agreement of any other act specified in the agreement;

(iii) the happening of any event specified in the agreement;

'legal [or equitable] mortgage' includes [a legal or equitable] charge and, in Scotland, a heritable security;

'lender' means [(except in relation to green deal plans: see instead article 60LB)]—

(a) the person providing credit under a credit agreement, or

(b) a person who exercises or has the right to exercise the rights and duties of a person who provided credit under such an agreement;

'payment' (except in article 60F) means a payment comprising or including an amount in respect of credit;

'regulated credit agreement' has the meaning given by article 60B;

'relative' means brother, sister, uncle, aunt, nephew, niece, lineal ancestor or lineal descendent;

'relevant recipient of credit' means—

(a) a partnership consisting of two or three persons not all of whom are bodies corporate, or

(b) an unincorporated body of persons which does not consist entirely of bodies corporate and is not a partnership;

'restricted-use credit agreement' means a credit agreement—

(a) to finance a transaction between the borrower and the lender, whether forming part of that agreement or not,

(b) to finance a transaction between the borrower and a person ('the supplier') other than the lender, or

(c) to refinance any existing indebtedness of the borrower's, whether to the lender or another person;

'running-account credit' means a facility under a credit agreement under which the borrower or another person is enabled to receive from time to time from the lender or a third party cash, goods or services to an amount or value such that, taking into account payments made by or to the credit of the borrower, the credit limit (if any) is not at any time exceeded;

'security' in relation to a credit agreement, means a mortgage, charge, pledge, bond, debenture, indemnity, guarantee, bill, note or other right provided by the borrower or at the implied or express request of the borrower to secure the carrying out of the obligations of the borrower under the agreement;

'total charge for credit' has the meaning given in rules made by the FCA under article 60M;

'total price' means the total sum payable by the debtor under a hire-purchase agreement, including any sum payable on the exercise of an option to purchase but excluding any sum payable as a penalty or as compensation or damages for a breach of the agreement;

'unrestricted-use credit agreement' means a credit agreement which is not a restricted use credit agreement.

[(1A) For the purposes of this Chapter, a credit agreement that is a green deal plan is to be treated as—

(a) a borrower-lender-supplier agreement falling within paragraph (a) of the definition of 'borrower-lender-supplier agreement';

(b) a restricted-use credit agreement falling within paragraph (a) of the definition of 'restricted-use credit agreement'].

(2) For the purposes of the definition of 'restricted-use credit agreement'—

(a) a credit agreement does not fall within the definition if the credit is in fact provided in such a way as to leave the borrower free to use it as the borrower chooses, even though certain uses would contravene that or any other agreement; and

(b) an agreement may fall within paragraph (b) of the definition even though the identity of the supplier is unknown at the time the agreement is made.

(3) For the purposes of the definition of 'borrower-lender agreement' [and the definition of 'borrower-lender-supplier agreement'], a credit agreement is, subject to paragraph (6), entered into under pre-existing arrangements between a lender and a supplier if it is entered into in accordance with, or in connection with, arrangements previously made between the lender (or the lender's associate) and the supplier (or the supplier's associate) unless the arrangements fall within paragraph (5).

(4) For the purposes of the definition of 'borrower-lender agreement' [and the definition of 'borrower-lender-supplier agreement'], a credit agreement is entered into in contemplation of future arrangements between a lender and a supplier if it is entered into in the expectation that arrangements will subsequently be made between the lender (or the lender's associate) and the supplier (or the supplier's associate) for the supply of cash, goods or services to be financed by the credit agreement unless the arrangements fall within paragraph (5).

(5) Arrangements fall within this paragraph if they are—

(a) for the making, in circumstances specified in the credit agreement, of payments to the supplier by the lender ('L') and L indicates that L is willing to make, in such circumstances, payments of the kind to suppliers generally, or

(b) for the electronic transfer of funds from a current account held with an authorised person with permission to accept deposits (within the meaning given by article 3).

(6) If a lender is an associate of the supplier's, the credit agreement is to be treated as entered into under pre-existing arrangements between the lender and the supplier unless the lender can show that this is not the case.

(7) For the purposes of the definition of 'running-account credit', 'credit limit' means, as respects any period, the maximum debit balance which, under a credit agreement, is allowed to stand on the account during that period, disregarding any term of the agreement allowing that maximum to be exceeded on a temporary basis.

(8) For the purposes of this Chapter, a person by whom goods are bailed or (in Scotland) hired to an individual or relevant recipient of credit under a hire-purchase agreement is to be taken to be providing that individual or person with fixed-sum credit to finance the transaction of an amount equal to the total price of the goods less the aggregate of the deposit (if any) and the total charge for credit.

(9) For the purposes of this Chapter, where credit is provided otherwise than in sterling, it is to be treated as provided in sterling of an equivalent amount.

[(10) For the purposes of this Chapter, where a provision specifies an amount of credit, running-account credit shall be taken not to exceed the amount specified in that provision ('the specified amount') if—

(a) the credit limit does not exceed the specified amount; or

(b) the credit limit exceeds the specified amount, or there is no credit limit, and—

(i) the borrower is not enabled to draw at any one time an amount which, so far as it represents credit, exceeds the specified amount; or

(ii) the agreement provides that, if the debit balance rises above a given amount (not exceeding the specified amount), the rate of the total charge for credit increases or any other condition favouring the lender or the lender's associate comes into operation; or

(iii) at the time the agreement is made it is probable, having regard to the terms of the agreement and any other relevant considerations, that the debit balance will not at any time rise above the specified amount.

(11) For the purposes of this Chapter, an item entering into the total charge for credit is not to be treated as credit even though time is allowed for its payment.]

[60LA Meaning of consumer etc

(1) For the purposes of sections 1G, 404E and 425A(18) of the Act (meaning of 'consumer'), in so far as those provisions relate to a person ('A') carrying on a regulated activity of the kind specified by—

(a) article 60B (regulated credit agreements), or

(b) article 64 (agreeing to carry on specified kinds of activity) in so far as that article relates to article 60B,

a person who is treated by A as a person who is or has been the borrower under a regulated credit agreement is to be treated as a 'consumer'.

(2) For the purposes of section 328(8) of the Act (meaning of 'clients') in so far as that provision relates to a person ('A') carrying on a regulated activity of the kind specified by—

(a) article 60B (regulated credit agreements), or

(b) article 64 (agreeing to carry on specified kinds of activity) in so far as that article relates to article 60B,

a person who is treated by A as a person who is or has been the borrower under a regulated credit agreement is to be treated as a 'client'.

(3) In this article, 'borrower' includes (in addition to those persons included in the definition in article 60L [or, where the credit agreement is a green deal plan, article 60LB])—

(a) any person providing a guarantee or indemnity under a regulated credit agreement, and

(b) a person to whom the rights and duties of a person falling within sub-paragraph (a) have passed by assignment or operation of law.]

[60LB Green deal plans

(1) A green deal plan is to be treated as a credit agreement for the purposes of this Order if (and only if)—

(a) the property in relation to the plan is a domestic property at the time when the plan is commenced, or

(b) if sub-paragraph (a) does not apply, the occupier or owner of the property who makes the arrangement for the plan is an individual or relevant recipient of credit.

(2) In the application of this Order to a green deal credit agreement—

(a) the lender is to be treated as being—

(i) the green deal provider (within the meaning of Chapter 1 of Part 1 of the Energy Act 2011) for the plan, or

(ii) a person who exercises or has the right to exercise the rights and duties of the green deal provider under the plan,

(b) credit is to be treated as advanced under the agreement of an amount equal to the amount of the improvement costs, and

(c) the advance of credit is to be treated as made on the completion of the installation of the energy efficiency improvements to the property (but this sub-paragraph is subject to any term of the green deal plan providing that part of the advance is to be treated as made on completion of any part of the installation).

(3) A reference in a provision of this Order listed in the first column of the table in Schedule 4A to the borrower is, in the application of the provision in relation to a green deal credit agreement, to be read as a reference to—

(a) a person who at the relevant time falls (or fell) within the description or descriptions specified in the corresponding entry in the second column of the table, or

(b) if more than one description is specified and at the relevant time different persons fall (or fell) within the descriptions, each of those persons,

and except as provided by this paragraph, a person is not and is not to be treated as the borrower in relation to the agreement.

(4) References in Schedule 4A to the 'improver', 'first bill payer', 'current bill payer' and 'previous bill payer' are to be read as follows—

(a) a person is the 'improver' if the person—

(i) is the owner or occupier of the property, and

(ii) is the person who makes (or has made or proposes to make) the arrangement for the green deal plan;

(b) a person is the 'first bill payer' if the person is liable to pay the energy bills for the property at the time when the green deal plan is commenced;

(c) a person is the 'current bill payer' if the person is liable by virtue of section 1(6)(a) of the Energy Act 2011 to pay instalments under the plan as a result of being for the time being liable to pay the energy bills for the property;

(d) a person is a 'previous bill payer' if, as a result of previously falling within sub-paragraph (c) for an earlier period, the person has an outstanding payment liability under the plan in respect of that period.

(5) In this article—

'domestic property' means a building or part of a building that is occupied as a dwelling or (if not occupied) is intended to be occupied as a dwelling;

'energy bill' has the same meaning as in section 1 of the Energy Act 2011;

'energy efficiency improvements' has the meaning given by section 2(4) of the Energy Act 2011;

'green deal credit agreement' means a green deal plan that is to be treated as a credit agreement for the purposes of this Order by virtue of paragraph (1);

'improvement costs', in relation to a green deal plan, are the costs of the energy efficiency improvements to the property which are to be paid by instalments under the plan after the time when credit is to be treated as being advanced by virtue of paragraph (2) (but ignoring any interest or other charges for credit in determining those costs);

'occupier' and 'owner' have the same meanings as in Chapter 1 of Part 1 of the Energy Act 2011;

'property', in relation to a green deal plan, means the property to which the energy efficiency improvements under the plan are or are intended to be made.

(6) For the purposes of this article—

(a) a green deal plan is commenced when—

(i) the occupier or owner of the property signs in the prescribed manner a document in relation to the plan in accordance with section 61(1) of the Consumer Credit Act 1974 (requirements as to form and content of regulated agreements)(1), or

(ii) if the occupier or owner of the property does not sign such a document, the green deal plan is made;

(b) a person is liable to pay the energy bills for a property at any time if the person would be treated as the bill payer for the property at that time for the purposes of Chapter 1 of Part 1 of the Energy Act 2011 (see section 2(3) and (10)).]

[60M Total charge for credit

(1) The FCA may make rules specifying how the total charge for credit to the borrower under a credit agreement is to be determined for the purposes of this Chapter.

(2) Rules made under paragraph (1) may in particular—

(a) specify how the total charge for credit to a person who is, or is to become, the borrower under a credit agreement is to be determined;

(b) specify what items are to be included in determining the total charge for credit and how the value of those items is to be determined;

(c) specify the method of calculating the rate of the total charge for credit;

(d) provide for the whole or part of the amount payable by the borrower or a relative of the borrower under a linked transaction (within the meaning given by article 60E(8)) to be included in the total charge for credit, whether or not the lender is a party to the transaction or derives a benefit from it.]

[CHAPTER 14B
REGULATED CONSUMER HIRE AGREEMENTS

The activities

[60N Regulated consumer hire agreements

(1) Entering into a regulated consumer hire agreement as owner is a specified kind of activity.

(2) It is a specified kind of activity for the owner or another person to exercise, or to have the right to exercise, the owner's rights and duties under a regulated consumer hire agreement.

(3) In this Chapter—

'consumer hire agreement' means an agreement between a person ('the owner') and an individual or relevant recipient of credit ('the hirer') for the bailment or, in Scotland, the hiring, of goods to the hirer which—

(a) is not a hire-purchase agreement, and

(b) is capable of subsisting for more than three months;

'exempt agreement' means a consumer hire agreement which is an exempt agreement under articles 60O to 60Q;

'owner' means—

(a) the person who bails or, in Scotland, hires, goods under a [. . .] consumer hire agreement, or

(b) a person who exercises or has the right to exercise the rights and duties of a person who bailed or, in Scotland, hired, goods under such an agreement;

['regulated consumer hire agreement' means—

(a) in the case of an agreement entered into on or after 1st April 2014, any consumer hire agreement which is not an exempt agreement; or

(b) in the case of an agreement entered into before 1st April 2014, a consumer hire agreement which—

(i) was a regulated agreement within the meaning of section 189(1) of the Consumer Credit Act 1974 when the agreement was entered into; or

(ii) became such a regulated agreement after being varied or supplemented by another agreement before 1st April 2014.]]

[60O Exempt agreements: exemptions relating to nature of agreement

(1) An agreement is an exempt agreement for the purposes of this Chapter if—

(a) the hirer is required by the agreement to make payments exceeding £25,000, and

(b) the agreement is entered into by the hirer wholly or predominantly for the purposes of a business carried on, or intended to be carried on, by the hirer.

(2) For the purposes of paragraph (1), if an agreement includes a declaration which—

(a) is made by the hirer,

(b) provides that the agreement is entered into by the hirer wholly or predominantly for the purposes of a business carried on, or intended to be carried on, by the hirer, and

(c) complies with rules made by the FCA for the purposes of this article,

the agreement is to be presumed to have been entered into by the hirer wholly or predominantly for the purpose in sub-paragraph (b) unless paragraph (3) applies.

(3) This paragraph applies if, when the agreement is entered into—

(a) the owner (or, if there is more than one owner, any of the owners), or

(b) any person who has acted on behalf of the owner (or, if there is more than one owner, any of the owners), in connection with the entering into of the agreement,

knows or has reasonable cause to suspect that the agreement is not entered into by the hirer wholly or predominantly for the purposes of a business carried on, or intended to be carried on, by the hirer.

(4) For the purposes of this article, where credit is provided otherwise than in sterling, it is to be treated as provided in sterling of an equivalent amount.]

[60P Exempt agreements: exemptions relating to supply of essential services

An agreement is an exempt agreement for the purposes of this Chapter if—

(a) the owner is a body corporate which is authorised by or under an enactment to supply gas, electricity or water, and

(b) the subject of the agreement is a meter or metering equipment which is used (or is to be used) in connection with the supply of gas, electricity or water.]

[60Q Exempt agreements: exemptions relating to the nature of the hirer

An agreement is an exempt agreement for the purposes of this Chapter if—

(a) the hirer is an individual,

(b) the agreement includes a declaration made by the hirer which provides that the hirer agrees to forgo the protection and remedies that would be available to the hirer if the agreement were a regulated consumer hire agreement and which complies with rules made by the FCA for the purposes of this paragraph,

(c) a statement has been made in relation to the income or assets of the hirer which complies with rules made by the FCA for the purposes of this paragraph,

(d) the connection between the statement and the agreement complies with any rules made by the FCA for the purposes of this paragraph (including as to the period of time between the making of the statement and the agreement being entered into), and

(e) a copy of the statement was provided to the owner before the agreement was entered into.]

Exclusion

[60R [Other exclusions]
Article 60N is subject to [. . .] the exclusion in article 72G (local authorities)].]

[Supplemental

[60S Meaning of consumer etc

(1) For the purposes of sections 1G, 404E and 425A of the Act (meaning of 'consumer'), in so far as those provisions relate to a person ('A') carrying on a regulated activity of the kind specified by—

(a) article 60N (regulated consumer hire agreements), or

(b) article 64 (agreeing to carry on specified kinds of activity) in so far as that article relates to article 60N,

a person who is treated by A as a person who is or has been the hirer under a regulated consumer hire agreement is to be treated as a 'consumer'.

(2) For the purposes of section 328(8) of the Act (meaning of 'clients') in so far as that provision relates to a person ('A') carrying on a regulated activity of the kind specified by—

(a) article 60N (regulated consumer hire agreements), or

(b) article 64 (agreeing to carry on specified kinds of activity) in so far as that article relates to article 60N,

a person who is treated by A as a person who is or has been the hirer under a regulated consumer hire agreement is to be treated as a 'client'.

(3) In this article, 'hirer' includes (in addition to those persons defined as 'the hirer' in the definition of 'consumer hire agreement' in article 60N(3))—

(a) any person providing a guarantee or indemnity under a consumer hire agreement, and

(b) a person to whom the rights and duties of a person falling within subparagraph (a) have passed by assignment or operation of law.]]

LIMITED LIABILITY PARTNERSHIPS REGULATIONS 2001 (SI 2001/1090)

PART VI
DEFAULT PROVISION

7 Default provision for limited liability partnerships
The mutual rights and duties of the members and the mutual rights and duties of the limited liability partnership and the members shall be determined, subject to the provisions of the general law and to the terms of any limited liability partnership agreement, by the following rules:

(1) All the members of a limited liability partnership are entitled to share equally in the capital and profits of the limited liability partnership.

(2) The limited liability partnership must indemnify each member in respect of payments made and personal liabilities incurred by him—

(a) in the ordinary and proper conduct of the business of the limited liability partnership; or

(b) in or about anything necessarily done for the preservation of the business or property of the limited liability partnership.

(3) Every member may take part in the management of the limited liability partnership.

(4) No member shall be entitled to remuneration for acting in the business or management of the limited liability partnership.

(5) No person may be introduced as a member or voluntarily assign an interest in a limited liability partnership without the consent of all existing members.

(6) Any difference arising as to ordinary matters connected with the business of the limited liability partnership may be decided by a majority of the members, but no change may be made in the nature of the business of the limited liability partnership without the consent of all the members.

(7) The books and records of the limited liability partnership are to be made available for inspection at the registered office of the limited liability partnership or at such other place as the members think fit and every member of the limited liability partnership may when he thinks fit have access to and inspect and copy any of them.

(8) Each member shall render true accounts and full information of all things affecting the limited liability partnership to any member or his legal representatives.

(9) If a member, without the consent of the limited liability partnership, carries on any business of the same nature as and competing with the limited liability partnership, he must account for and pay over to the limited liability partnership all profits made by him in that business.

(10) Every member must account to the limited liability partnership for any benefit derived by him without the consent of the limited liability partnership from any transaction concerning the limited liability partnership, or from any use by him of the property of the limited liability partnership, name or business connection.

8 Expulsion

No majority of the members can expel any member unless a power to do so has been conferred by express agreement between the members.

CONSUMER CREDIT (DISCLOSURE OF INFORMATION) REGULATIONS 2010 (SI 2010/1013)

1 Citation, commencement and interpretation

(1) These Regulations may be cited as the Consumer Credit (Disclosure of Information) Regulations 2010 and shall come into force on 30th April 2010.

(2) In these Regulations—

'the Act' means the Consumer Credit Act 1974;

'advance payment' includes any deposit and in relation to a regulated consumer credit agreement includes also any part-exchange allowance in respect of any goods agreed in antecedent negotiations [. . .] to be taken by the creditor in part exchange but does not include a repayment of credit or any insurance premium or any amount entering into the total charge for credit;

'ancillary service' means a service that relates to the provision of credit under the agreement and includes in particular an insurance or payment protection policy;

'the APR' means the annual percentage rate of charge for credit determined in accordance with Schedule 2 to these Regulations and the [total charge for credit rules];

'cash price' in relation to any goods, services, land or other things means the price or charge at which the goods, services, land or other things may be purchased by, or supplied to, the debtor for cash account being taken of any discount generally available from the dealer or supplier in question;

'credit intermediary' has the same meaning as in [section 61A] of the Act; 'distance contract' means any regulated agreement made under an organised

distance sales or service-provision scheme run by or on behalf of the creditor who, in any such case, for the purpose of that agreement makes exclusive use of one or more means of distance communication up to and including the time at which the agreement is made. For this purpose, 'means of distance communication' means any means which, without the simultaneous physical presence of the creditor or a person acting on behalf of the creditor and of the debtor, may be used for the making of a regulated agreement between the parties to that agreement;

'excluded pawn agreement' means a pawn agreement—

(a) where the debtor is not a new customer of the creditor (see [paragraph (6)]), and

(b) where, before the agreement is made, the creditor has not received a request from the debtor for the pre-contract credit information (see regulation 9);

'linked credit agreement' means a regulated consumer credit agreement which—

(a) serves exclusively to finance an agreement for the supply of specific goods or the provision of a specific service or land, and

(b) (i) where the supplier or service provider himself finances the credit for the debtor, or if it is financed by a third party, where the creditor uses the services of the supplier or service provider in connection with the preparation or making of the credit agreement, or

(ii) where the specific goods or land or the provision of a specific service are explicitly specified in the credit agreement;

'pawn agreement' means a consumer credit agreement under which the creditor takes an article in pawn;

'pre-contract credit information' means the information specified in regulation 3(4);

'total amount of credit' means the credit limit or the total sums made available under a consumer credit agreement;

'total amount payable' means the sum of the total charge for credit and the total amount of credit payable under the agreement as well as any advance payment;

'total charge for credit' means the total charge for credit determined in accordance with the [total charge for credit rules] and the Schedule to these Regulations; ['the total charge for credit rules' means rules made by the Financial Conduct Authority under article 60M of the Financial Services and Markets Act 2000 (Regulated Activities) Order 2001 for the purposes of Chapter 14A of Part 2 of that Order;]

(3) In these Regulations, a reference to a repayment is a reference to—

(a) a repayment of the whole or any part of the credit,

(b) a payment of the whole or any part of the total charge for credit, or

(c) a combination of such repayments and payments.

(4) In these Regulations, a reference to rate of interest is a reference to the interest rate expressed as a fixed or variable percentage applied on an annual basis to the amount of credit drawn down.

(5) In these Regulations, a reference to an agreement includes a reference to a prospective agreement.

(6) For the purposes of the definition of 'excluded pawn agreement' and regulation 8 the debtor is a new customer if the debtor has not entered into a pawn agreement with the creditor in the three years preceding the start of the negotiations antecedent to the agreement.

[. . .]

2 Agreements to which these Regulations apply

(1) These Regulations apply in respect of a regulated consumer credit agreement, except as provided for in paragraphs (2) to (4).

(2) These regulations do not apply to an agreement to which section 58 of the Act (opportunity for withdrawal from prospective land mortgage) applies.

(3) These Regulations do not apply to an authorised non-business overdraft agreement which is—

(a) for credit which exceeds £60,260 [unless it is a residential renovation agreement], or

(b) secured on land.

(4) Except as provided for in paragraph (5) these Regulations do not apply to an agreement—

(a) under which the creditor provides the debtor with credit exceeding £60,260 [unless it is a residential renovation agreement],

(b) secured on land,

(c) entered into by the debtor wholly or predominantly for the purposes of a business also carried on, or intended to be carried on, by him, or

(d) made before 1st February 2011.

(5) These Regulations apply to an agreement mentioned in paragraph (4) (which is not also an agreement mentioned in paragraph (2) or (3)) where a creditor or, where applicable a credit intermediary, discloses or purports to disclose the pre-contract credit information in accordance with these Regulations rather than in accordance with the Consumer Credit (Disclosure of Information) Regulations 2004 or the Financial Services (Distance Marketing) Regulations 2004 (as the case may be).

[(6) Article 60C(5) and (6) of the Financial Services and Markets Act 2000 (Regulated Activities) Order 2001 applies for the purposes of paragraph (4)(c).]

3 Information to be disclosed: agreements other than telephone contracts, non-telephone distance contracts, excluded pawn agreements and overdraft agreements

(1) This regulation applies to an agreement other than—

[(a) an agreement made by voice telephone communication where it is a distance contract and the debtor consents to the disclosure of the information referred to in regulation 4(2);

(aa) an agreement made by voice telephone communication where it is not a distance contract (see regulation 4(3));]

(b) an agreement made using a means of distance communication other than a voice telephone communication, which does not enable the provision of the pre-contract credit information before the agreement is made (see regulation 5);

(c) an excluded pawn agreement;

(d) an authorised non-business overdraft agreement (see regulations 10 and 11).

(2) In good time before the agreement is made, the creditor must disclose to the debtor, in the manner set out in regulation 8, the pre-contract credit information.

(3) Paragraph (2) does not require a creditor to disclose the pre-contract credit information where it has already been disclosed to the debtor by a credit intermediary in a manner which complies with paragraph (2).

(4) For the purposes of these Regulations, the pre-contract credit information comprises—

(a) the type of credit,

(b) the identity and geographical address of the creditor and, where applicable, of the credit intermediary,

(c) the total amount of credit to be provided under the agreement and the conditions governing the draw down of credit. In the case of an agreement for running-account credit, the total amount of credit may be expressed as a statement indicating the manner in which the credit limit will be determined where it is not practicable to express the limit as a sum of money,

(d) the duration or minimum duration of the agreement or a statement that the agreement has no fixed or minimum duration,

(e) in the case of—

(i) credit in the form of deferred payment for specific goods, services or land, or

(ii) a linked credit agreement,

a description of the goods, services or land and the cash price of each and the total cash price,

(f) the rate of interest charged, any conditions applicable to that rate, where available, any reference rate on which that rate is based and any information on any changes to the rate of interest (including the periods that the rate applies, and any conditions or procedure applicable to changing the rate),

(g) where different rates of interest are charged in different circumstances the creditor must provide the information in paragraph (f) in respect of each rate,

(h) the APR and the total amount payable under the agreement illustrated (if not known) by way of a representative example mentioning all the assumptions used in order to calculate that rate and amount,

(i) the amount (expressed as a sum of money), number (if applicable) and frequency of repayments to be made by the debtor and, where appropriate, the order in which repayments will be allocated to different outstanding balances charged at different rates of interest,

(j) in the case of an agreement for running-account credit, the amount of each repayment is to be expressed as (a) a sum of money; (b) a specified proportion of a specified amount; (c) a combination of (a) or (b); or (d) in a case where the amount of any repayment cannot be expressed in accordance with (a), (b) or (c), a statement indicating the manner in which the amount will be determined,

(k) if applicable, any charges for maintaining an account recording both payment transactions and draw downs, unless the opening of an account is optional, and any charge payable for using a method of payment in respect of payment transactions or draw downs,

(l) any other charges payable deriving from the credit agreement and the conditions under which those charges may be changed,

(m) if applicable, a statement that fees will be payable by the debtor to a notary on conclusion of the credit agreement,

(n) the obligation, if any, to enter into a contract for ancillary services relating to the consumer credit agreement, in particular insurance services, where the conclusion of such a contract is compulsory in order to obtain the credit or to obtain it on the terms and conditions marketed,

(o) the rate of interest applicable in the case of late payments and the arrangements for its adjustment, and, where applicable, any charges payable for default,

(p) a warning regarding the consequences of missing payments (for example, the possibility of legal proceedings and the possibility that the debtor's home may be repossessed),

(q) where applicable, any security to be provided by the debtor or on behalf of the debtor,

(r) the existence or absence of a right of withdrawal,

(s) the debtor's right of early repayment under section 94 of the Act, and where applicable, information concerning the creditor's right to compensation and the way in which that compensation will be determined,

(t) the requirement for a creditor to inform a debtor in accordance with section 157(A1) of the Act that a decision not to proceed with a prospective regulated consumer credit agreement has been reached on the basis of information from a credit reference agency and of the particulars of that agency,

(u) the debtor's right to be supplied under section 55C of the Act on request and free of charge, with a copy of the draft agreement except where—

(i) the creditor is at the time of the request unwilling to proceed to the making of the agreement, or

(ii) the agreement is an agreement referred to in regulation 2(4)(a) to (c) or a pawn agreement,

(v) if applicable, the period of time during which the creditor is bound by the pre-contract credit information, [and

(w) where the agreement references a benchmark, as defined in point 3 of Article 3(1) of Regulation EU 2016/1011 of the European Parliament and of the Council of 8 June 2016 on indices used as benchmarks in financial instruments and financial contracts or to measure the performance of investment funds and amending Directives 2008/48/EC and 2014/17/EU and Regulation (EU) No 596/ 2014, the name of the benchmark and of its administrator and the potential implications on the debtor and of its administrator.]

(5) For the purpose of the representative example referred to in paragraph (4) (h)—

(a)(i) where the debtor has informed the creditor or credit intermediary of one or more components of his preferred credit, such as the duration of the consumer credit agreement or the total amount of credit, and

(ii) where the creditor would in principle agree to offer credit on such terms,

the creditor or credit intermediary must take those components into account when calculating the representative APR and the total amount payable;

(b) where the creditor uses the assumption set out in [the total charge for credit rules] the creditor must indicate that other draw down mechanisms for this type of consumer credit agreement may result in a higher APR;

(c) subject to paragraph (a), in the case of an agreement for running-account credit, where the credit limit is not known at the date on which the pre-contract credit information is disclosed, the total amount of credit is to be assumed to be £1,200 or in a case where credit is to be provided subject to a maximum credit limit of less than £1,200, an amount equal to that maximum limit.

(6) In the case of a consumer credit agreement under which repayments do not give rise to an immediate reduction in the total amount of credit advanced but are used to constitute capital as provided for under the agreement or under an ancillary agreement, the creditor or credit intermediary must provide a clear and concise statement that such agreements do not provide for a guarantee of repayment of the total amount of credit drawn down under the credit agreement unless such a guarantee is given.

4 Information to be disclosed: telephone contracts

(1) This regulation applies to an agreement (other than an authorised non-business overdraft agreement) made by way of a voice telephone communication (whether or not it is a distance contract).

(2) Where the agreement is a distance contract and where the debtor explicitly consents, the creditor must disclose the following information before the agreement is made—

(a) the identity of the person in contact with the debtor and that person's link with the creditor,

(b) a description of the main characteristics of the credit agreement which includes the information set out in regulation 3(4)(c), (d), (e), (f), (g), (h), (i) [, (j) and (w)],

(c) the total price to be paid by the debtor to the creditor for the credit including all taxes paid via the creditor or, if an exact price cannot be indicated, the basis for the calculation of the price enabling the debtor to verify it,

(d) notice of the possibility that other taxes or costs may exist that are not paid via the creditor or imposed by the creditor,

(e) whether or not there is—

(i) a right to withdraw under section 66A of the Act, or

(ii) a right to cancel under regulation 9 of the Financial Services (Distance Marketing) Regulations 2004 and, where there is such a right, its duration and the conditions for exercising it, including information on the amount which the consumer may be required to pay in accordance with regulation 13 of those Regulations, as well as the consequences of not exercising that right,

(f) that other information is available on request and the nature of that information.

(3) Where the agreement is not a distance contract the creditor must disclose the information in paragraph (2)(b) before the agreement is made.

(4) The creditor must disclose the pre-contract credit information in the manner set out in regulation 8 immediately after the agreement is made.

5 Information to be disclosed: non-telephone distance contracts

(1) This regulation applies to an agreement (other than an authorised nonbusiness overdraft agreement) made—

(a) at the debtor's request, and

(b) using a means of distance communication other than a voice telephone communication which does not enable the provision before the agreement is made of the pre-contract credit information.

(2) The creditor must disclose the pre-contract credit information in the manner set out in regulation 8 immediately after the agreement is made.

6 Information to be disclosed: distance contracts for the purpose of a business

(1) This regulation applies to an agreement that is a distance contract entered into by the debtor wholly or predominantly for the purposes of a business carried on, or intended to be carried on by him.

(2) Where the agreement is an agreement to which [regulations 3, 4 or 5] would otherwise apply the creditor may comply with those regulations by disclosing the pre-contract credit information immediately after the agreement is entered into.

[(3) Article 60C(5) and (6) of the Financial Services and Markets Act 2000 (Regulated Activities) Order 2001 applies for the purposes of paragraph (1).]

7 Information about contractual terms and conditions: [regulations 3, 4 and 5]

(1) This regulation applies to an agreement which is—

(a) a distance contract to which [regulations 3, 4 or 5] applies, and

(b) which is not entered into by the debtor wholly or predominantly for the purposes of a business carried on, or intended to be carried on, by him.

(2) The creditor must ensure that—

(a) the information provided to the debtor pursuant to [regulations 3, 4 or 5] includes the contractual terms and conditions, and

(b) the information provided to the debtor in relation to the contractual obligations which would arise if the distance contract were made accurately reflects the contractual obligations which would arise under the law presumed to be applicable to that contract.

[(3) Article 60C(5) and (6) of the Financial Services and Markets Act 2000 (Regulated Activities) Order 2001 applies for the purposes of paragraph (1).]

8 Manner of disclosure

(1) The pre-contract credit information must be disclosed by means of the form contained in Schedule 1.

(2) The form must be—

(a) in writing, and

(b) of a nature that enables the debtor to remove it from the place where it is disclosed to him.

(3) The form must be completed as specified in this paragraph—

(a) the relevant pre-contract credit information is to be provided in the appropriate row,

(b) the form is to be completed in accordance with the notes to that form,

(c) the asterisks and notes may be deleted,

(d) gridlines and boxes may be omitted, and

(e) any information contained in the form must be clear and easily legible.

(4) Any additional information relating to the credit which is provided in writing by the creditor to the debtor must be provided in a separate document to the form.

(5) Where a consumer credit agreement is a multiple agreement containing more than one part for the purposes of section 18 of the Act, the pre-contract credit information in respect of each part may be provided in the same form provided that—

(a) information that is not common to each part of the agreement is disclosed separately within the relevant section of the form, and

(b) it is clear which information relates to which part.

[(6) Where a consumer credit agreement references a benchmark, the name of the benchmark and of its administrator and the potential implications for the debtor shall be provided by the creditor, or where applicable, by the credit intermediary, to the debtor in a separate document, which may be annexed to the form in Schedule 1.]

9 Information to be disclosed: pawn agreements

(1) This Regulation applies to a pawn agreement.

(2) In good time before a pawn agreement is made (unless the debtor is a new customer), the creditor must inform the debtor of his right to receive the pre-contract credit information in the form contained in Schedule 1, free of charge, on request.

10 Information to be disclosed: overdraft agreements

(1) This regulation applies to an agreement which is an authorised nonbusiness overdraft agreement.

(2) In good time before an authorised non-business overdraft agreement is made, the creditor must disclose to the debtor, the information in paragraph (3) in the manner set out in regulation 11.

(3) The information referred to in paragraph (2) is as follows—

(a) the type of credit,

(b) the identity and geographical address of the creditor and, where applicable, of the credit intermediary,

(c) the total amount of credit,

(d) the duration of the agreement,

(e) the rate of interest charged, any conditions applicable to that rate, any reference rate on which that rate is based and any information on any changes to the rate of interest (including the periods that the rate applies, and any conditions or procedure applicable to changing the rate),

(f) where different rates of interest are charged in different circumstances the creditor must provide the information in paragraph (e) in respect of each rate,

(g) the conditions and procedure for terminating the agreement,

(h) where applicable, an indication that the debtor may be requested to repay the amount of credit in full on demand at any time,

(i) the rate of interest applicable in the case of late payments and the arrangements for its adjustment, and, where applicable, any charges payable for default,

(j) the requirement for a creditor to inform a debtor in accordance with section 157(A1) of the Act that a decision not to proceed with a prospective regulated consumer credit agreement has been reached on the basis of information from a credit reference agency and of the particulars of that agency,

(k) the charges, other than the rates of interest, payable by the debtor under the agreement (and the conditions under which those charges may be varied),

(l) if applicable, the period of time during which the creditor is bound by the information set out in this paragraph.

(4) Paragraph (2) does not apply to—

(a) an agreement made by a voice telephone communication (whether or not it is a distance contract),

(b) an agreement made at the debtor's request using a means of distance communication, other than a voice telephone communication, which does not enable the provision of the information required by paragraph (2) before the agreement is made, or

(c) an agreement that does not come within sub-paragraph (a) or (b) but where the debtor requests the overdraft be made available with immediate effect.

(5) In the case of an agreement that falls within paragraph (4)(a) that is also a distance contract, where the debtor explicitly consents the creditor must disclose the following information before the agreement is made—

(a) the identity of the person in contact with the debtor and that person's link with the creditor,

(b) a description of the main characteristics of the financial service including at least the information in paragraph (3)(c), (e), (f), (h) and (k),

(c) the total price to be paid by the debtor to the creditor for the credit including all taxes paid via the creditor or, if an exact price cannot be indicated, the basis for the calculation of the price enabling the debtor to verify it,

(d) notice of the possibility that other taxes or costs may exist that are not paid via the creditor or imposed by the creditor,

(e) whether or not there is a right to cancel under regulation 9 of the Financial Services (Distance Marketing) Regulations 2004 and where there is such a right, its duration and the conditions for exercising it including information on the amount which the consumer may be required to pay in accordance with regulation 13 of those regulations, as well as the consequences of not exercising that right, and

(f) that other information is available on request and the nature of that information.

[(5A) In the case of an agreement that falls within paragraph (4)(a) that is also a distance contract, where the debtor does not explicitly consent to the disclosure of the information in paragraph (5), the creditor must disclose the information in paragraph (3) to the debtor before the [agreement] is made.]

(6) In the case of an agreement that falls within paragraph (4)(a) that is not a distance contract the creditor must disclose the information in paragraph (5)(b) before the agreement is made.

(7) In the case of an agreement that is a distance contract to which this regulation applies the creditor must ensure that the information he provides to the debtor pursuant to this regulation regarding the contractual obligations which would arise if the distance contract were concluded, accurately reflects the contractual obligations which would arise under the law presumed to be applicable to that contract.

(8) In the case of an agreement that falls within paragraph (4)(c), the creditor must disclose the information in paragraph (3)(c), (e), (f), (h), and (k) to the debtor before the agreement is made in the manner set out in regulation 11.

(9) Where a current account is an agreement for two or more debtors jointly the creditor may comply with paragraphs (5), [(5A),] (6) or (8) by disclosing the information to one debtor provided that each of the debtors have given the creditor their consent that the creditor may not comply in each debtor's case with the relevant paragraph.

11—(1) Where regulation 10(2) applies, the creditor must comply with that regulation by—

(a) disclosing the information by means of the [. . .] form set out in Schedule 3 to these Regulations and as specified in paragraph (2), or

(b) disclosing the information in writing so that all information is equally prominent.

(2) The specifications referred to in paragraph (1)(a) are that—

(a) the relevant information must be provided in the appropriate row,

(b) the form must be completed in accordance with the notes to that form,

(c) the asterisks and notes may be deleted,

(d) gridlines and boxes may be omitted, and

(e) any information contained in the form must be clear and easily legible.

(3) Where regulation 10(8) applies, the creditor may provide the information orally.

12 Modifying agreements

(1) Subject to paragraphs (2) to (4), these Regulations apply to a modifying agreement which varies or supplements an earlier agreement and which is, or is treated under section 82(3) of the Act as, a regulated agreement.

[(2) Where a modifying agreement modifies an earlier consumer credit agreement, the requirements of regulations 3, 4 and 10 will be deemed to be satisfied if—

(a) in good time before the modifying agreement is made—

(i) the information specified by regulations 3(4) and 10(3) is disclosed to the debtor in respect of any provision of the earlier agreement which is varied or supplemented, and

(ii) the creditor informs the debtor in writing that the other information in the earlier agreement remains unchanged, and

(b) where the Financial Services (Distance Marketing) Regulations 2004 apply, the creditor complies with regulations 7 and 8 of those Regulations.]

(3) Where a modifying agreement is made in a manner that does not allow the creditor to comply with the requirement in [paragraph (2)(a)(ii)], the creditor is deemed to have complied with that requirement if—

(a) before the agreement is made the creditor informs the debtor orally that the other information in the earlier agreement remains unchanged, and

(b) this is confirmed to the debtor in writing immediately after the agreement is made.

(4) This regulation does not apply to an excluded pawn agreement.

Regulation 8(1) SCHEDULE 1

PRE-CONTRACT CREDIT INFORMATION

[. . .]

1. Contact details

Creditor. Address. Telephone Number(s).* E-Mail Address.* Fax Number.* Web address.*	[Identity.] [Geographical address of the creditor to be used by the debtor.]
If applicable Credit intermediary. Address. Telephone number(s).* E-mail address.* Fax number.* Web address.*	 [Identity.] [Geographical address of the credit intermediary to be used by the debtor.]

* This information is optional for the creditor. The row may be deleted if the information is not provided.

Wherever "if applicable" is indicated, the creditor must give the information relevant to the credit product or, if the information is not relevant for the type of credit considered, delete the respective information or the entire row, or indicate that the information is not applicable.

Indications between square brackets provide explanations for the creditor and must be replaced with the corresponding information.

2. Key features of the credit product

The type of credit.	
The total amount of credit. This means the amount of credit to be provided under the proposed credit agreement or the credit limit.	[The amount is to be expressed as a sum of money. In the case of running-account credit, the total amount may be expressed as a statement indicating the manner in which the credit limit will be determined where it is not practicable to express the limit as a sum of money.]
How and when credit would be provided.	[Details of how and when any credit being advanced is to be drawn down.]
The duration of the credit agreement.	[The duration or minimum duration of the agreement or a statement that the agreement has no fixed or minimum duration.]
Repayments. If applicable: Your repayments will pay off what you owe in the following order.	[The amount (expressed as a sum of money), number (if applicable) and frequency of repayments to be made by the debtor. In the case of an agreement for running-account credit, the amount may be expressed as a sum of money or a specified proportion of a specified amount or both, or in a case where the amount of any repayment cannot be expressed as a sum of money or a specified proportion, a statement indicating the manner in which the amount will be determined. [The order in which repayments will be allocated to different outstanding balances charged at different rates of interest.]
The total amount you will have to pay. This means the amount you have borrowed plus interest and other costs.	[The amount payable by the debtor under the agreement (where necessary, illustrated by means of a representative example). The total amount payable will be the sum of the total amount of credit and the total charge for credit payable under the agreement as well as any advance payment where required. In the case of running account credit, where it is not practicable to express the limit as a sum of money, a credit limit of £1200 should be assumed. In a case where credit is to be provided subject to a maximum credit limit of less than £1200, an amount equal to that maximum limit. The total charge for credit is to be calculated using the relevant APR assumptions set out in Schedule 2 to the Consumer Credit (Disclosure of Information) Regulations 2010 and the Total Charge for Credit Regulations, and where appropriate the relevant components of the debtor's preferred credit.]

If applicable [The proposed credit will be granted in the form of a deferred payment for goods or service.] or [The proposed credit will be linked to the supply of specific goods or the provision of a service.] Description of goods/services/land (as applicable). Cash price.	[A list or other description] [Cash price of goods or service.] [Total cash price.]
If applicable Security required. This is a description of the security to be provided by you in relation to the credit agreement.	[Description of any security to be provided by or on behalf of the debtor.]
If applicable Repayments will not immediately reduce the amount you owe.	[In the case of a credit agreement under which repayments do not give rise to an immediate reduction in the total amount of credit advanced but are used to constitute capital as provided by the agreement (or an ancillary agreement a clear and concise statement) where applicable, that the agreement does not provide for a guarantee of the repayment of the total amount of credit drawn down under the credit agreement.]

3. Costs of the credit

The rates of interest which apply to the credit agreement	[Details of the rate of interest charged, any conditions applicable to that rate, where available, any reference rate on which that rate is based and any information on changes to the rate of interest (including the periods that the rate applies, and any conditions or procedure applicable to changing the rate). Where different rates of interest are charged in different circumstances, the creditor must provide the above information in respect of each rate.]
Annual Percentage Rate of Charge (APR). This is the total cost expressed as an annual percentage of the total amount of credit. The APR is there to help you compare different offers.	[% if known. If the APR is not known a representative example (expressed as a %) mentioning all the necessary assumptions used for calculating the rate (as set out in Schedule 2 to the Consumer Credit (Disclosure of Information) Regulations 2010, the Total Charge for Credit Regulations and, where appropriate, the relevant components of the debtor's preferred credit). Where the creditor uses the assumption set out in [. . .] the Total Charge for Credit Regulations, the creditor shall indicate that other draw down mechanisms for this type of agreement may result in a higher APR.]

If applicable In order to obtain the credit or to obtain it on the terms and conditions marketed, you must take out: —an insurance policy securing the credit, or —another ancillary service contract. If we do not know the costs of these services they are not included in the APR.	[Nature and description of any insurance or other ancillary service contract required.]
Related costs	
If applicable You must have a separate account for recording both payment transactions and drawdowns.	[Details of any account or accounts that the creditor requires to be set up in order to obtain the credit together with the amount of any charge for this.]
If applicable Charge for using a specific payment method.	[Specify means of payment and the amount of charge.]
If applicable Any other costs deriving from the credit agreement. If applicable Conditions under which the above charges can be changed.	[Description and amount of any other charges not otherwise referred to in this form.] [Details of the conditions under which any of the charges mentioned above can be changed.]
If applicable You will be required to pay notarial fees.	[Description and amount of any fee.]
Costs in the case of late payments	Either [A statement that there are no charges for late or missed payments.] Or [Applicable rate of interest in the case of late payments and arrangements for its adjustment and, where applicable any charges payable for default.]
Consequences of missing payments.	[A statement warning about the consequences of missing payments, including: —a reference to possible legal proceedings and repossession of the debtor's home where this is a possibility, and —the possibility of missing payments making it more difficult to obtain credit in the future.]

4. Other important legal aspects

Right of withdrawal.	Either: [A statement that the debtor has the right to withdraw from the credit agreement before the end of 14 days beginning with the day after the day on which the agreement is made, or if information is provided after the agreement is made, the day on which the debtor receives a copy of the executed agreement under sections 61A or 63 of the Consumer Credit Act 1974, the day on which the debtor receives the information required in section 61A(3) of that Act or the day on which the creditor notifies the debtor of the credit limit, the first time it is provided, whichever is the latest.] Or [There is no right to withdraw from this agreement—if there is a right to cancel the agreement this should be stated.](**a**) [If the right to cancel is under the Financial Services (Distance Marketing) Regulations 2004 refer to section 5 of the form.]
Early repayment. If applicable Compensation payable in the case of early repayment.	[A statement that the debtor has the right to repay the credit early at any time in full or partially.](**b**). [Determination of the compensation (calculation method) in accordance with section 95A [(and, where applicable, section 95B)] of the Consumer Credit Act 1974.]
Consultation with a Credit Reference Agency(**c**).	[A statement that if the creditor decides not to proceed with a prospective regulated consumer credit agreement on the basis of information from a credit reference agency the creditor must, when informing the debtor of the decision, inform the debtor that it has been reached on the basis of information from a credit reference agency and of the particulars of that agency.]
Right to a draft credit agreement(**d**).	[A statement that the debtor has the right, upon request, to obtain a copy of the draft credit agreement free of charge, unless the creditor is unwilling at the time of the request to proceed to the conclusion of the credit agreement.]
If applicable The period of time during which the creditor is bound by the pre-contractual information.	[This information is valid from [—] until [—].] or [Period of time during which the information on this form is valid.]

(**a**) i.e. If there is a cancellation right in respect of an agreement involving credit in excess of £60,260.

(**b**) The words "or partially" may be excluded in the case of agreements secured on land.

(**c**) This requirement does not apply in the case of agreements secured on land.

(**d**) This requirement does not apply in the case of agreements secured on land, agreements for credit agreements exceeding £60,260, pawn agreements and business purpose agreements.

If applicable

5. Additional information in the case of distance marketing of financial services

(a) concerning the creditor	
If applicable The creditor's representative in [the United Kingdom.] Address. Telephone number(s). E-mail address.* Fax number.* Web address.*	[i.e. where different from section 1.] [Identity.] [Geographical address to be used by the debtor.]
If applicable Registration number.	[The Firm Reference Number (FRN) (if any) or Interim Permission Number (if any), and any other relevant registration number of the creditor. [(For 90 days, starting on the day that a creditor is given an FRN, either the FRN or any Interim Permission Number valid immediately before the start of this 90 day period may be provided.)]]
If applicable The supervisory authority.	[The [Financial Conduct Authority] or any other relevant supervisory authority or both.]
(b) concerning the credit agreement	
If applicable(**a**) Right to cancel the credit agreement.	[Practical instructions for exercising the right to cancel indicating, amongst other things, the period for exercising the right, the address to which notification of exercise of the right to cancel should be sent and the consequences of nonexercise of that right.]
If applicable The law taken by the creditor as a basis for the establishment of relations with you before the conclusion of the credit agreement. If applicable The law applicable to the credit agreement and/or the competent court. If applicable Language to be used in connection with the credit agreement.	[English/other law] [A statement concerning the law which governs the contract and the courts to which disputes may be referred.] [Details of the language that the information and contractual terms will be supplied in and used, with your consent, for communication during the duration of the credit agreement.]
(c) concerning redress	
Access to out-of-court complaint and redress mechanism.	[Whether or not there is an out-of-court complaint and redress mechanism for the debtor and, if so, the methods of access to it.]

* This information is optional for the creditor. The row may be deleted if the information is not provided.

(**a**) If the right to withdraw referred to in section 4 does not apply.

Regulation 1(2) SCHEDULE 2

PROVISIONS RELATING TO CALCULATION AND DISCLOSURE OF THE TOTAL CHARGE FOR CREDIT AND APR

1. Assumptions about running-account credit

(a) In the case of an agreement for running-account credit, the assumption in paragraph (b) shall have effect for the purpose of calculating the total charge for credit and any APR in place of any assumptions in [the total charge for credit rules] that might otherwise apply—

(b) in a case where the credit limit applicable to the credit is not known at the time the pre-contract credit information is disclosed but it is known that it will be subject to a maximum limit of less than £1,200, the credit limit shall be assumed to be an amount equal to that maximum limit.

2. Permissible tolerances in disclosure of an APR

For the purposes of these Regulations, it shall be sufficient compliance with the requirement to show an APR if there is included in the pre-contract credit information—

(a) a rate which exceeds the APR by not more than one,

(b) a rate which falls short of the APR by not more than 0.1, or

(c) in a case to which paragraph 3 or 4 of this Schedule applies, a rate determined in accordance with those paragraphs or whichever of them applies to that case.

3. Tolerance where repayments are nearly equal

In the case of an agreement under which all repayments but one are equal and that one repayment does not differ from any other repayment by more whole pence than there are repayments of credit, there may be included in the precontract credit information a rate found under [the total charge for credit rules] as if that one repayment were equal to the other repayments to be made under the agreement.

4. Tolerance where interval between relevant date and first repayment is greater than interval between repayments

In the case of an agreement under which-

(a) three or more repayments are to be made at equal intervals, and

(b) the interval between the relevant date and the first repayment is greater than the interval between the repayments,

there may be included in the pre-contract credit information a rate found under [the total charge for credit rules] as if the interval between the relevant date and the first repayment were shortened so as to be equal to the interval between repayments.

SCHEDULE 3 Regulation 11(1)

[PRE-CONTRACT CONSUMER CREDIT INFORMATION (OVERDRAFTS)]

1. Contact details

Creditor. Address. Telephone number(s).* E-mail address.* Fax number.* Web address.*	[Identity.] [Geographical address of the creditor to be used by the debtor.]
If applicable Credit intermediary. Address. Telephone number(s).* E-mail address.* Fax number.* Web address.*	 [Identity.] [Geographical address of the credit intermediary to be used by the debtor.]

*This information is optional for the creditor. The row may be deleted if the information is not provided.

Wherever "if applicable" is indicated, the creditor must give the information relevant to the credit product or, if the information is not relevant for the type of credit considered, delete the respective information or the entire row or indicate that the information is not applicable.

Indications between square brackets provide explanations for the creditor and must be replaced with the corresponding information.

2. Description of the main features of the credit product

The type of credit.	
The total amount of credit. This means the amount of credit to be provided under the agreement or the credit limit.	[The amount is to be expressed as a sum of money. In the case of running account credit, the total amount may be expressed as a statement indicating the manner in which the credit limit will be determined where it is not practicable to express the limit as a sum of money.]
The duration of the credit agreement.	[The duration or minimum duration of the agreement or a statement that the agreement has no fixed or minimum duration.]
If applicable Repayment of the credit.	[A statement informing the debtor that the debtor may be required to repay the amount of credit in full on demand at any time.]

3. Costs of the credit

The rates of interest which apply to the credit agreement.	[Details of the rates of interest charged, any conditions applicable to that rate, where available any reference rate on which that rate is based and any information on changes to the rate of interest (including the periods that the rate applies and any conditions or procedure applicable to changing the rate). Where different rates of interest are charged in different circumstances, the creditor must provide the above information in respect of each rate.]
If applicable Costs. If applicable The conditions under which those costs may be changed.	[The costs applicable from the time the credit agreement is concluded.]
Costs in the case of late payments.	Either [A statement that there are no charges for late or missed payments.] Or [Applicable rate of interest, in the case of late payments and arrangements for its adjustment and, where applicable, any charges payable for default.]

4. Other important legal aspects

Termination of the credit agreement.	[The conditions and procedure for termination of the credit agreement.]
Consultation with a credit reference agency.	[A statement that if the creditor decides not to proceed with a prospective regulated consumer credit agreement on the basis of information from a credit reference agency the creditor must, when informing the debtor of that decision, inform the debtor that it has been reached on the basis of information from a credit reference agency and of the particulars of that agency.]
If applicable The period of time during which the creditor is bound by the pre-contractual information.	[This information is valid from [—] until [—] or [Period of time during which the information on this form is valid.]

If applicable

5. Additional information to be given in the case of distance marketing of financial services

(a) concerning the creditor	
If applicable The creditor's representative in [the UK.] Address. Telephone number.* E-mail address.* Fax number.* Web address.*	[i.e. where different from section 1.] [Identity.] [Geographical address to be used by the debtor.]
If applicable Registration number.	[The Firm Reference Number (FRN) (if any) or Interim Permission Number (if any), and any other relevant registration number of the creditor. [(For 90 days, starting on the day that a creditor is given an FRN, either the FRN or any Interim Permission Number valid immediately before the start of this 90 day period may be provided.)]]
If applicable The supervisory authority.	[The [Financial Conduct Authority] or any other relevant supervisory authority or both.]
(b) concerning the credit agreement	
If applicable The law taken by the creditor as a basis for the establishment of relations with you before the conclusion of the credit contract.	[English/other law.]
If applicable The law applicable to the credit agreement and/or the competent court.	[A statement concerning the law which governs the contract and the courts to which disputes may be referred.]
If applicable Language to be used in connection your agreement.	[Details of the language that the information and contractual terms will be supplied in and used, with the debtor's consent, for communication during the duration of the credit agreement.]
(c) concerning redress	
Access to out-of-court complaint and redress mechanism.	[Whether or not there is an out-of-court complaint and redress mechanism for the debtor who is party to the distance contract and, if so, the methods of access to it.]

*This information is optional for the creditor. The row may be deleted if the information is not provided.

CONSUMER CONTRACTS (INFORMATION, CANCELLATION AND ADDITIONAL CHARGES) REGULATIONS 2013 (SI 2013/3134)

PART 1
GENERAL

1 Citation and commencement

(1) These Regulations may be cited as the Consumer Contracts (Information, Cancellation and Additional Charges) Regulations 2013 and come into force on 13th June 2014.

(2) These Regulations apply in relation to contracts entered into on or after that date.

2 Regulations superseded

The following do not apply in relation to contracts entered into on or after 13th June 2014—

(a) the Consumer Protection (Distance Selling) Regulations 2000;

(b) the Cancellation of Contracts made in a Consumer's Home or Place of Work etc Regulations 2008.

3 Review

(1) The Secretary of State must before the end of each review period—

(a) carry out a review of these Regulations,

(b) set out the conclusions of the review in a report, and

(c) publish the report.

[. . .]

(3) The report must in particular—

(a) set out the objectives intended to be achieved by these Regulations,

(b) assess the extent to which those objectives have been achieved, and

(c) assess whether those objectives remain appropriate and, if so, the extent to which they could be achieved in a way that imposes less regulation.

(4) A review period is—

(a) the period of 5 years beginning with the day on which these Regulations come into force, and

(b) each successive period of 5 years.

4 'Consumer' and 'trader'

In these Regulations—

'consumer' means an individual acting for purposes which are wholly or mainly outside that individual's trade, business, craft or profession;

'trader' means a person acting for purposes relating to that person's trade, business, craft or profession, whether acting personally or through another person acting in the trader's name or on the trader's behalf.

5 Other definitions

In these Regulations—

'business' includes the activities of any government department or local or public authority;

'business premises' in relation to a trader means—

(a) any immovable retail premises where the activity of the trader is carried out on a permanent basis, or

(b) any movable retail premises where the activity of the trader is carried out on a usual basis;

'CMA' means the Competition and Markets Authority;

'commercial guarantee', in relation to a contract, means any undertaking by the trader or producer to the consumer (in addition to the trader's duty to supply goods that are in conformity with the contract) to reimburse the price paid or to replace, repair or service goods in any way if they do not meet the specifications or any other requirements not related to conformity set out in the guarantee statement or in the relevant advertising available at the time of the contract or before it is entered into;

'court'—

(a) in relation to England and Wales, means the county court or the High Court,

(b) in relation to Northern Ireland, means a county court or the High Court, and

(c) in relation to Scotland means the sheriff court or the Court of Session;

'delivery' means voluntary transfer of possession from one person to another;

'digital content' means data which are produced and supplied in digital form;

'distance contract' means a contract concluded between a trader and a consumer under an organised distance sales or service-provision scheme without the simultaneous physical presence of the trader and the consumer, with the exclusive use of one or more means of distance communication up to and including the time at which the contract is concluded;

'district heating' means the supply of heat (in the form of steam or hot water or otherwise) from a central source of production through a transmission and distribution system to heat more than one building;

'durable medium' means paper or email, or any other medium that—

(a) allows information to be addressed personally to the recipient,

(b) enables the recipient to store the information in a way accessible for future reference for a period that is long enough for the purposes of the information, and

(c) allows the unchanged reproduction of the information stored; 'functionality' in relation to digital content includes region coding, restrictions incorporated for the purposes of digital rights management, and other technical restrictions;

'goods' means any tangible moveable items, but that includes water, gas and electricity if and only if they are put up for sale in a limited volume or a set quantity;

'off-premises contract' means a contract between a trader and a consumer which is any of these—

(a) a contract concluded in the simultaneous physical presence of the trader and the consumer, in a place which is not the business premises of the trader;

(b) a contract for which an offer was made by the consumer in the simultaneous physical presence of the trader and the consumer, in a place which is not the business premises of the trader;

(c) a contract concluded on the business premises of the trader or through any means of distance communication immediately after the consumer was personally and individually addressed in a place which is not the business premises of the trader in the simultaneous physical presence of the trader and the consumer;

(d) a contract concluded during an excursion organised by the trader with the aim or effect of promoting and selling goods or services to the consumer;

'on-premises contract' means a contract between a trader and a consumer which is neither a distance contract nor an off-premises contract;

'public auction' means a method of sale where—

(a) goods or services are offered by a trader to consumers through a transparent, competitive bidding procedure run by an auctioneer,

(b) the consumers attend or are given the possibility to attend in person, and

(c) the successful bidder is bound to purchase the goods or services;

'sales contract' means a contract under which a trader transfers or agrees to transfer the ownership of goods to a consumer and the consumer pays or agrees to pay the price, including any contract that has both goods and services as its object;

'service' includes—

(a) the supply of water, gas or electricity if they are not put up for sale in a limited volume or a set quantity, and

(b) the supply of district heating;

'service contract' means a contract, other than a sales contract, under which a trader supplies or agrees to supply a service to a consumer and the consumer pays or agrees to pay the price.

6 Limits of application: general

(1) These Regulations do not apply to a contract, to the extent that it is—

(a) for—

(i) gambling within the meaning of the Gambling Act 2005 (which includes gaming, betting and participating in a lottery);

(ii) in relation to Northern Ireland, for betting, gaming or participating lawfully in a lottery within the meaning of the Betting, Gaming, Lotteries and Amusements (Northern Ireland) Order 1985; [or

(iii) participating in a lottery which forms part of the National Lottery within the meaning of the National Lottery etc Act 1993;]

(b) for services of a banking, credit, insurance, personal pension, investment or payment nature;

(c) for the creation of immovable property or of rights in immovable property;

(d) for rental of accommodation for residential purposes;

(e) for the construction of new buildings, or the construction of substantially new buildings by the conversion of existing buildings;

(f) for the supply of foodstuffs, beverages or other goods intended for current consumption in the household and which are supplied by a trader on frequent and regular rounds to the consumer's home, residence or workplace;

[(g) which is a package travel contract within the meaning of the Package Travel and Linked Travel Arrangements Regulations 2018;

(h) which is a regulated contract within the meaning of the Timeshare, Holiday Products, Resale and Exchange Contracts Regulations 2010.]

(2) These Regulations do not apply to contracts—

(a) concluded by means of automatic vending machines or automated commercial premises;

(b) concluded with a telecommunications operator through a public telephone for the use of the telephone;

(c) concluded for the use of one single connection, by telephone, internet or fax, established by a consumer;

(d) under which goods are sold by way of execution or otherwise by authority of law.

(3) Paragraph (1)(b) is subject to regulations 38(4) (ancillary contracts) and 40(3) (additional payments).

PART 2
INFORMATION REQUIREMENTS

Chapter 1
Provision of information

7 Application of Part 2

(1) This Part applies to on-premises, off-premises and distance contracts, subject to paragraphs (2), (3) and (4) and regulation 6.

(2) This Part does not apply to contracts to the extent that they are—

(a) for the supply of a medicinal product by administration by a prescriber, or under a prescription or directions given by a prescriber;

(b) for the supply of a product by a health care professional or a person included in a relevant list, under arrangements for the supply of services as part of the health service, where the product is one that, at least in some circumstances is available under such arrangements free or on prescription.

(3) This Part, except for regulation 14(1) to (5), does not apply to contracts to the extent that they are for passenger transport services.

(4) This Part does not apply to off-premises contracts under which the payment to be made by the consumer is not more than £42.

(5) In paragraph (2)—

'health care professional' and 'prescriber' have the meaning given by regulation 2(1) of the National Health Service (Pharmaceutical and Local Pharmaceutical Services) Regulations 2013;

'health service' means—

(a) the health service as defined by section 275(1) of the National Health Service Act 2006 or section 206(1) of the National Health Service (Wales) Act 2006,

(b) the health service as defined by section 108(1) of the National Health Service (Scotland) Act 1978, or

(c) any of the health services under section 2(1)(a) of the Health and Social Care (Reform) Act (Northern Ireland) 2009;

'medicinal product' has the meaning given by regulation 2(1) of the Human Medicines Regulations 2012;

'relevant list' means—

(d) a relevant list for the purposes of the National Health Service (Pharmaceutical and Local Pharmaceutical Services) Regulations 2013, or

(e) a list maintained under those Regulations.

8 Making information etc available to a consumer

For the purposes of this Part, something is made available to a consumer only if the consumer can reasonably be expected to know how to access it.

9 Information to be provided before making an on-premises contract

(1) Before the consumer is bound by an on-premises contract, the trader must give or make available to the consumer the information described in Schedule 1 in a clear and comprehensible manner, if that information is not already apparent from the context.

(2) Paragraph (1) does not apply to a contract which involves a day-to-day transaction and is performed immediately at the time when the contract is entered into.

[(3) If the contract is for the supply of digital content other than for a price paid by the consumer—

(a) any information that the trader gives the consumer as required by this regulation is to be treated as included as a term of the contract, and

(b) a change to any of that information, made before entering into the contract or later, is not effective unless expressly agreed between the consumer and the trader.]

[. . .]

10 Information to be provided before making an off-premises contract

(1) Before the consumer is bound by an off-premises contract, the trader—

(a) must give the consumer the information listed in Schedule 2 in a clear and comprehensible manner, and

(b) if a right to cancel exists, must give the consumer a cancellation form as set out in part B of Schedule 3.

(2) The information and any cancellation form must be given on paper or, if the consumer agrees, on another durable medium and must be legible.

(3) The information referred to in paragraphs (l), (m) and (n) of Schedule 2 may be provided by means of the model instructions on cancellation set out in

part A of Schedule 3; and a trader who has supplied those instructions to the consumer, correctly filled in, is to be treated as having complied with paragraph (1) in respect of those paragraphs.

(4) If the trader has not complied with paragraph (1) in respect of paragraph (g), (h) or (m) of Schedule 2, the consumer is not to bear the charges or costs referred to in those paragraphs.

[(5) If the contract is for the supply of digital content other than for a price paid by the consumer—

(a) any information that the trader gives the consumer as required by this regulation is to be treated as included as a term of the contract, and

(b) a change to any of that information, made before entering into the contract or later, is not effective unless expressly agreed between the consumer and the trader.]

[. . .]

(7) This regulation is subject to regulation 11.

11 Provision of information in connection with repair or maintenance contracts

(1) If the conditions in paragraphs (2), (3) and (4) are met, regulation 10(1) does not apply to an off-premises contract where—

(a) the contract is a service contract,

(b) the consumer has explicitly requested the trader to supply the service for the purpose of carrying out repairs or maintenance,

(c) the obligations of the trader and the consumer under the contract are to be performed immediately, and

(d) the payment to be made by the consumer is not more than £170.

(2) The first condition is that, before the consumer is bound by the contract, the trader gives or makes available to the consumer on paper or, if the consumer expressly agrees, on another durable medium—

(a) the information referred to in paragraphs (b) to (d), (f) and (g) of Schedule 2,

(b) an estimate of the total price, where it cannot reasonably be calculated in advance, and

(c) where a right to cancel exists, a cancellation form as set out in part B of Schedule 3.

(3) The second condition is that, before the consumer is bound by the contract, the trader gives or makes available to the consumer the information referred to in paragraphs (a), (l) and (o) of Schedule 2, either on paper or another durable medium or otherwise if the consumer expressly agrees.

(4) The third condition is that the confirmation of the contract provided in accordance with regulation 12 contains the information required by regulation 10(1).

(5) For the right to cancel where this regulation applies, see in particular—

(a) regulation 28(1)(e) and (2) (cases where cancellation excluded: visit requested for urgent work);

(b) regulation 36 (form of consumer's request, and consequences).

12 Provision of copy or confirmation of off-premises contracts

(1) In the case of an off-premises contract, the trader must give the consumer—

(a) a copy of the signed contract, or

(b) confirmation of the contract.

(2) The confirmation must include all the information referred to in Schedule 2 unless the trader has already provided that information to the consumer on a durable medium prior to the conclusion of the off-premises contract.

(3) The copy or confirmation must be provided on paper or, if the consumer agrees, on another durable medium.

(4) The copy or confirmation must be provided within a reasonable time after the conclusion of the contract, but in any event—

(a) not later than the time of the delivery of any goods supplied under the contract, and

(b) before performance begins of any service supplied under the contract.

(5) If the contract is for the supply of digital content not on a tangible medium and the consumer has given the consent and acknowledgement referred to in regulation 37(1)(a) and (b), the copy or confirmation must include confirmation of the consent and acknowledgement.

13 Information to be provided before making a distance contract

(1) Before the consumer is bound by a distance contract, the trader—

(a) must give or make available to the consumer the information listed in Schedule 2 in a clear and comprehensible manner, and in a way appropriate to the means of distance communication used, and

(b) if a right to cancel exists, must give or make available to the consumer a cancellation form as set out in part B of Schedule 3.

(2) In so far as the information is provided on a durable medium, it must be legible.

(3) The information referred to in paragraphs (l), (m) and (n) of Schedule 2 may be provided by means of the model instructions on cancellation set out in part A of Schedule 3; and a trader who has supplied those instructions to the consumer, correctly filled in, is to be treated as having complied with paragraph (1) in respect of those paragraphs.

(4) Where a distance contract is concluded through a means of distance communication which allows limited space or time to display the information—

(a) the information listed in paragraphs (a), (b), (f), (g), (h), (l) and (s) of Schedule 2 must be provided on that means of communication in accordance with paragraphs (1) and (2), but

(b) the other information required by paragraph (1) may be provided in another appropriate way.

(5) If the trader has not complied with paragraph (1) in respect of paragraph (g), (h) or (m) of Schedule 2, the consumer is not to bear the charges or costs referred to in those paragraphs.

[(6) If the contract is for the supply of digital content other than for a price paid by the consumer—

(a) any information that the trader gives the consumer as required by this regulation is to be treated as included as a term of the contract, and

(b) a change to any of that information, made before entering into the contract or later, is not effective unless expressly agreed between the consumer and the trader.]

[. . .]

14 Requirements for distance contracts concluded by electronic means

(1) This regulation applies where a distance contract is concluded by electronic means.

(2) If the contract places the consumer under an obligation to pay, the trader must make the consumer aware in a clear and prominent manner, and directly before the consumer places the order, of the information listed in paragraphs (a), (f), (g), (h), (s) and (t) of Schedule 2.

(3) The trader must ensure that the consumer, when placing the order, explicitly acknowledges that the order implies an obligation to pay.

(4) If placing an order entails activating a button or a similar function, the trader must ensure that the button or similar function is labelled in an easily legible manner only with the words 'order with obligation to pay' or a corresponding unambiguous formulation indicating that placing the order entails an obligation to pay the trader.

(5) If the trader has not complied with paragraphs (3) and (4), the consumer is not bound by the contract or order.

(6) The trader must ensure that any trading website through which the contract is concluded indicates clearly and legibly, at the latest at the beginning of the ordering process, whether any delivery restrictions apply and which means of payment are accepted.

15 Telephone calls to conclude a distance contract

If the trader makes a telephone call to the consumer with a view to concluding a distance contract, the trader must, at the beginning of the conversation with the consumer, disclose—

(a) the trader's identity,

(b) where applicable, the identity of the person on whose behalf the trader makes the call, and

(c) the commercial purpose of the call.

16 Confirmation of distance contracts

(1) In the case of a distance contract the trader must give the consumer confirmation of the contract on a durable medium.

(2) The confirmation must include all the information referred to in Schedule 2 unless the trader has already provided that information to the consumer on a durable medium prior to the conclusion of the distance contract.

(3) If the contract is for the supply of digital content not on a tangible medium and the consumer has given the consent and acknowledgment referred to in regulation 37(1)(a) and (b), the confirmation must include confirmation of the consent and acknowledgement.

(4) The confirmation must be provided within a reasonable time after the conclusion of the contract, but in any event—

(a) not later than the time of delivery of any goods supplied under the contract, and

(b) before performance begins of any service supplied under the contract.

(5) For the purposes of paragraph (4), the confirmation is treated as provided as soon as the trader has sent it or done what is necessary to make it available to the consumer.

17 Burden of proof in relation to off-premises and distance contracts

(1) In case of dispute about the trader's compliance with any provision of regulations 10 to 16, it is for the trader to show that the provision was complied with.

(2) That does not apply to proceedings—

(a) for an offence under regulation 19, or

(b) relating to compliance with an injunction, interdict or order under regulation 45.

18 Effect on contract of failure to provide information

Every contract to which this Part applies is to be treated as including a term that the trader has complied with the provisions of—

(a) regulations 9 to 14, and

(b) regulation 16.

Chapter 2
Offences

19 Offence relating to the failure to give notice of the right to cancel

(1) A trader is guilty of an offence if the trader enters into an off-premises con-

tract to which regulation 10 applies but fails to give the consumer the information listed in paragraph (l), (m) or (n) of Schedule 2 in accordance with that regulation.

(2) A person who is guilty of an offence under paragraph (1) is liable on summary conviction to a fine not exceeding level 5 on the standard scale.

20 Defence of due diligence

(1) In any proceedings against a person (A) for an offence under regulation 19 it is a defence for A to prove—

(a) that the commission of the offence was due to—

(i) the act or default of another, or

(ii) reliance on information given by another, and

(b) that A took all reasonable precautions and exercised all due diligence to avoid the commission of such an offence by A or any person under A's control.

(2) A person is not entitled to rely on the defence provided by paragraph (1) without leave of the court unless—

(a) that person has served on the prosecutor a notice in writing giving such information as was in that person's possession identifying or assisting in the identification of the other person; and

(b) the notice is served on the prosecutor not less than 7 days before the hearing of the proceedings or, in Scotland, 7 days before the intermediate diet or 14 days before the trial diet, whichever is earlier.

21 Liability of persons other than the principal offender

Where the commission by a person of an offence under regulation 19 is due to the act or default of another person, that other person is guilty of the offence and may be proceeded against and punished whether or not proceedings are taken against the first person.

22 Offences committed by bodies of persons

(1) Where an offence under regulation 19 committed by a body corporate is proved—

(a) to have been committed with the consent or connivance of an officer of the body corporate or

(b) to be attributable to any neglect on the part of an officer of the body corporate,

the officer, as well as the body corporate, is guilty of the offence and liable to be proceeded against and punished accordingly.

(2) In paragraph (1) a reference to an officer of a body corporate includes a reference to—

(a) a director, manager, secretary or other similar officer; and

(b) a person purporting to act as a director, manager, secretary or other similar officer.

(3) Where an offence under regulation 19 committed in Scotland by a Scottish partnership is proved—

(a) to have been committed with the consent or connivance of a partner, or

(b) to be attributable to any neglect on the part of a partner,

that partner, as well as the partnership shall be guilty of the offence and liable to be proceeded against and punished accordingly.

(4) In paragraph (3) a reference to a partner includes a person purporting to act as a partner.

23 Duty to enforce

(1) Subject to paragraphs (2) and (3)—

(a) it is the duty of every weights and measures authority in Great Britain to enforce regulation 19 within its area; and

(b) it is the duty of the Department of Enterprise, Trade and Investment in Northern Ireland to enforce regulation 19 within Northern Ireland.

(2) No proceedings for an offence under regulation 19 may be instituted in England and Wales except by or on behalf of an enforcement authority.

(3) Nothing in paragraph (1) authorises any weights and measures authority to bring proceedings in Scotland for an offence.

[. . .]

PART 3
RIGHT TO CANCEL

27 Application of Part 3

(1) This Part applies to distance and off-premises contracts between a trader and a consumer, subject to paragraphs (2) and (3) and regulations 6 and 28.

(2) This Part does not apply to contracts to the extent that they are—

(a) for the supply of a medicinal product by administration by a prescriber, or under a prescription or directions given by a prescriber;

(b) for the supply of a product by a health care professional or a person included in a relevant list, under arrangements for the supply of services as part of the health service, where the product is one that, at least in some circumstances is available under such arrangements free or on prescription;

(c) for passenger transport services.

(3) This Part does not apply to off-premises contracts under which the payment to be made by the consumer is not more than £42.

(4) In paragraph (2)(a) and (b), expressions defined in regulation 7(5) have the meaning given there.

28 Limits of application: circumstances excluding cancellation

(1) This Part does not apply as regards the following—

(a) the supply of—

(i) goods, or

(ii) services, other than supply of water, gas, electricity or district heating,

for which the price is dependent on fluctuations in the financial market which cannot be controlled by the trader and which may occur within the cancellation period;

(b) the supply of goods that are made to the consumer's specifications or are clearly personalised;

(c) the supply of goods which are liable to deteriorate or expire rapidly;

(d) the supply of alcoholic beverages, where—

(i) their price has been agreed at the time of the conclusion of the sales contract,

(ii) delivery of them can only take place after 30 days, and

(iii) their value is dependent on fluctuations in the market which cannot be controlled by the trader;

(e) contracts where the consumer has specifically requested a visit from the trader for the purpose of carrying out urgent repairs or maintenance;

(f) the supply of a newspaper, periodical or magazine with the exception of subscription contracts for the supply of such publications;

(g) contracts concluded at a public auction;

(h) the supply of accommodation, transport of goods, vehicle rental services, catering or services related to leisure activities, if the contract provides for a specific date or period of performance.

(2) Sub-paragraph (e) of paragraph (1) does not prevent this Part applying to a contract for—

(a) services in addition to the urgent repairs or maintenance requested, or

(b) goods other than replacement parts necessarily used in making the repairs or carrying out the maintenance, if the trader supplies them on the occasion of a visit such as is mentioned in that sub-paragraph.

(3) The rights conferred by this Part cease to be available in the following circumstances—

(a) in the case of a contract for the supply of sealed goods which are not suitable for return due to health protection or hygiene reasons, if they become unsealed after delivery;

(b) in the case of a contract for the supply of sealed audio or sealed video recordings or sealed computer software, if the goods become unsealed after delivery;

(c) in the case of any sales contract, if the goods become mixed inseparably (according to their nature) with other items after delivery.

29 Right to cancel

(1) The consumer may cancel a distance or off-premises contract at any time in the cancellation period without giving any reason, and without incurring any liability except under these provisions—

(a) regulation 34(3) (where enhanced delivery chosen by consumer);
(b) regulation 34(9) (where value of goods diminished by consumer handling);
(c) regulation 35(5) (where goods returned by consumer);
(d) regulation 36(4) (where consumer requests early supply of service).

(2) The cancellation period begins when the contract is entered into and ends in accordance with regulation 30 or 31.

(3) Paragraph (1) does not affect the consumer's right to withdraw an offer made by the consumer to enter into a distance or off-premises contract, at any time before the contract is entered into, without giving any reason and without incurring any liability.

30 Normal cancellation period

(1) The cancellation period ends as follows, unless regulation 31 applies.

(2) If the contract is—

(a) a service contract, or

(b) a contract for the supply of digital content which is not supplied on a tangible medium,

the cancellation period ends at the end of 14 days after the day on which the contract is entered into.

(3) If the contract is a sales contract and none of paragraphs (4) to (6) applies, the cancellation period ends at the end of 14 days after the day on which the goods come into the physical possession of—

(a) the consumer, or

(b) a person, other than the carrier, identified by the consumer to take possession of them.

(4) If the contract is a sales contract under which multiple goods are ordered by the consumer in one order but some are delivered on different days, the cancellation period ends at the end of 14 days after the day on which the last of the goods come into the physical possession of—

(a) the consumer, or

(b) a person, other than the carrier, identified by the consumer to take possession of them.

(5) If the contract is a sales contract under which goods consisting of multiple lots or pieces of something are delivered on different days, the cancellation period ends at the end of 14 days after the day on which the last of the lots or pieces come into the physical possession of—

(a) the consumer, or

(b) a person, other than the carrier, identified by the consumer to take possession of them.

(6) If the contract is a sales contract for regular delivery of goods during a defined period of more than one day, the cancellation period ends at the end of 14 days after the day on which the first of the goods come into the physical possession of—

(a) the consumer, or

(b) a person, other than the carrier, identified by the consumer to take possession of them.

31 Cancellation period extended for breach of information requirement

(1) This regulation applies if the trader does not provide the consumer with the information on the right to cancel required by paragraph (l) of Schedule 2, in accordance with Part 2.

(2) If the trader provides the consumer with that information in the period of 12 months beginning with the first day of the 14 days mentioned in regulation 30(2) to (6), but otherwise in accordance with Part 2, the cancellation period ends at the end of 14 days after the consumer receives the information.

(3) Otherwise the cancellation period ends at the end of 12 months after the day on which it would have ended under regulation 30.

32 Exercise of the right to withdraw or cancel

(1) To withdraw an offer to enter into a distance or off-premises contract, the consumer must inform the trader of the decision to withdraw it.

(2) To cancel a contract under regulation 29(1), the consumer must inform the trader of the decision to cancel it.

(3) To inform the trader under paragraph (2) the consumer may either—

(a) use a form following the model cancellation form in part B of Schedule 3, or

(b) make any other clear statement setting out the decision to cancel the contract.

(4) If the trader gives the consumer the option of filling in and submitting such a form or other statement on the trader's website—

(a) the consumer need not use it, but

(b) if the consumer does, the trader must communicate to the consumer an acknowledgement of receipt of the cancellation on a durable medium without delay.

(5) Where the consumer informs the trader under paragraph (2) by sending a communication, the consumer is to be treated as having cancelled the contract in the cancellation period if the communication is sent before the end of the period.

(6) In case of dispute it is for the consumer to show that the contract was cancelled in the cancellation period in accordance with this regulation.

33 Effect of withdrawal or cancellation

(1) If a contract is cancelled under regulation 29(1)—

(a) the cancellation ends the obligations of the parties to perform the contract, and

(b) regulations 34 to 38 apply.

(2) Regulations 34 and 38 also apply if the consumer withdraws an offer to enter into a distance or off-premises contract.

34 Reimbursement by trader in the event of withdrawal or cancellation

(1) The trader must reimburse all payments, other than payments for delivery, received from the consumer, subject to paragraph (10).

(2) The trader must reimburse any payment for delivery received from the consumer, unless the consumer expressly chose a kind of delivery costing more than the least expensive common and generally acceptable kind of delivery offered by the trader.

(3) In that case, the trader must reimburse any payment for delivery received from the consumer up to the amount the consumer would have paid if the consumer had chosen the least expensive common and generally acceptable kind of delivery offered by the trader.

(4) Reimbursement must be without undue delay, and in any event not later than the time specified in paragraph (5) or (6).

(5) If the contract is a sales contract and the trader has not offered to collect the goods, the time is the end of 14 days after—

(a) the day on which the trader receives the goods back, or

(b) if earlier, the day on which the consumer supplies evidence of having sent the goods back.

(6) Otherwise, the time is the end of 14 days after the day on which the trader is informed of the consumer's decision to withdraw the offer or cancel the contract, in accordance with regulation [32].

(7) The trader must make the reimbursement using the same means of payment as the consumer used for the initial transaction, unless the consumer has expressly agreed otherwise.

(8) The trader must not impose any fee on the consumer in respect of the reimbursement.

(9) If (in the case of a sales contract) the value of the goods is diminished by any amount as a result of handling of the goods by the consumer beyond what is necessary to establish the nature, characteristics and functioning of the goods, the trader may recover that amount from the consumer, up to the contract price.

(10) An amount that may be recovered under paragraph (9)—

(a) may be deducted from the amount to be reimbursed under paragraph (1);

(b) otherwise, must be paid by the consumer to the trader.

(11) Paragraph (9) does not apply if the trader has failed to provide the consumer with the information on the right to cancel required by paragraph (l) of Schedule 2, in accordance with Part 2.

(12) For the purposes of paragraph (9) handling is beyond what is necessary to establish the nature, characteristics and functioning of the goods if, in particular, it goes beyond the sort of handling that might reasonably be allowed in a shop.

(13) Where the provisions of this regulation apply to cancellation of a contract, the contract is to be treated as including those provisions as terms.

35 Return of goods in the event of cancellation

(1) Where a sales contract is cancelled under regulation 29(1), it is the trader's responsibility to collect the goods if—

(a) the trader has offered to collect them, or

(b) in the case of an off-premises contract, the goods were delivered to the consumer's home when the contract was entered into and could not, by their nature, normally be returned by post.

(2) If it is not the trader's responsibility under paragraph (1) to collect the goods, the consumer must—

(a) send them back, or

(b) hand them over to the trader or to a person authorised by the trader to receive them.

(3) The address to which goods must be sent under paragraph (2)(a) is—

(a) any address specified by the trader for sending the goods back;

(b) if no address is specified for that purpose, any address specified by the trader for the consumer to contact the trader;

(c) if no address is specified for either of those purposes, any place of business of the trader.

(4) The consumer must send off the goods under paragraph (2)(a), or hand them over under paragraph (2)(b), without undue delay and in any event not later

than 14 days after the day on which the consumer informs the trader as required by regulation 32(2).

(5) The consumer must bear the direct cost of returning goods under paragraph (2), unless—

(a) the trader has agreed to bear those costs, or

(b) the trader failed to provide the consumer with the information about the consumer bearing those costs, required by paragraph (m) of Schedule 2, in accordance with Part 2.

(6) The contract is to be treated as including a term that the trader must bear the direct cost of the consumer returning goods under paragraph (2) where paragraph (5)(b) applies.

(7) The consumer is not required to bear any other cost of returning goods under paragraph (2).

(8) The consumer is not required to bear any cost of collecting goods under paragraph (1) [unless the trader has offered to collect the goods and the consumer has agreed to bear the costs of the trader doing so.]

36 Supply of service in cancellation period

(1) The trader must not begin the supply of a service before the end of the cancellation period provided for in regulation 30(1) unless the consumer—

(a) has made an express request, and

(b) in the case of an off-premises contract, has made the request on a durable medium.

(2) In the case of a service other than supply of water, gas, electricity or district heating, the consumer ceases to have the right to cancel a service contract under regulation 29(1) if the service has been fully performed, and performance of the service began—

(a) after a request by the consumer in accordance with paragraph (1), and

(b) with the acknowledgement that the consumer would lose that right once the contract had been fully performed by the trader.

(3) Paragraphs (4) to (6) apply where a contract is cancelled under regulation 29(1) and a service has been supplied in the cancellation period.

(4) Where the service is supplied in response to a request in accordance with paragraph (1), the consumer must (subject to paragraph (6)) pay to the trader an amount—

(a) for the supply of the service for the period for which it is supplied, ending with the time when the trader is informed of the consumer's decision to cancel the contract, in accordance with regulation 32(2), and

(b) which is in proportion to what has been supplied, in comparison with the full coverage of the contract.

(5) The amount is to be calculated—

(a) on the basis of the total price agreed in the contract, or

(b) if the total price is excessive, on the basis of the market value of the service that has been supplied, calculated by comparing prices for equivalent services supplied by other traders.

(6) The consumer bears no cost for supply of the service, in full or in part, in the cancellation period, if—

(a) the trader has failed to provide the consumer with the information on the right to cancel required by paragraph (l) of Schedule 2, or the information on payment of that cost required by paragraph (n) of that Schedule, in accordance with Part 2, or

(b) the service is not supplied in response to a request in accordance with paragraph (1).

37 Supply of digital content in cancellation period

(1) Under a contract for the supply of digital content not on a tangible medium, the trader must not begin supply of the digital content before the end of the cancellation period provided for in regulation 30(1), unless—

(a) the consumer has given express consent, and

(b) the consumer has acknowledged that the right to cancel the contract under regulation 29(1) will be lost.

(2) The consumer ceases to have the right to cancel such a contract under regulation 29(1) if, before the end of the cancellation period, supply of the digital content has begun after the consumer has given the consent and acknowledgement required by paragraph (1).

(3) Paragraph (4) applies where a contract is cancelled under regulation 29(1) and digital content has been supplied, not on a tangible medium, in the cancellation period.

(4) The consumer bears no cost for supply of the digital content, in full or in part, in the cancellation period, if—

(a) the consumer has not given prior express consent to the beginning of the performance of the digital content before the end of the 14-day period referred to in regulation 30,

(b) the consumer gave that consent but did not acknowledge when giving it that the right to cancel would be lost, or

(c) the trader failed to provide confirmation required by regulation 12(5) or 16(3).

38 Effects of withdrawal or cancellation on ancillary contracts

(1) If a consumer withdraws an offer to enter into a distance or off-premises contract, or cancels such a contract under regulation 29(1), any ancillary contracts are automatically terminated, without any costs for the consumer, other than any costs under these provisions—

(a) regulation 34(3) (where enhanced delivery chosen by consumer);

(b) regulation 34(9) (where value of goods diminished by consumer handling);

(c) regulation 35(5) (where goods returned by consumer);

(d) regulation 36(4) (where consumer requests early supply of service).

(2) When a trader is informed by a consumer under regulation 32(1) or (2) of a decision to withdraw an offer or cancel a contract, the trader must inform any other trader with whom the consumer has an ancillary contract that is terminated by paragraph (1).

(3) An 'ancillary contract', in relation to a distance or off-premises contract (the 'main contract'), means a contract by which the consumer acquires goods or services related to the main contract, where those goods or services are provided—

(a) by the trader, or

(b) by a third party on the basis of an arrangement between the third party and the trader.

(4) Regulation 6(1)(b) (exclusion of financial services contracts) does not limit the contracts that are ancillary contracts for the purposes of this regulation.

PART 4
PROTECTION FROM INERTIA SELLING AND ADDITIONAL CHARGES

39 Inertia selling

Before regulation 28 of the Consumer Protection from Unfair Trading Regulations 2008 (and in Part 5 of those Regulations) insert—

'27A Inertia selling

(1) This regulation applies where a trader engages in the unfair commercial practice described in paragraph 29 of Schedule 1 (inertia selling).

(2) The consumer is exempted from any obligation to provide consideration for the products supplied by the trader.

(3) The absence of a response from the consumer following the supply does not constitute consent to the provision of consideration for, or the return or safe-keeping of, the products.

(4) In the case of an unsolicited supply of goods, the consumer may, as between the consumer and the trader, use, deal with or dispose of the goods as if they were an unconditional gift to the consumer.'.

40 Additional payments under a contract

(1) Under a contract between a trader and a consumer, no payment is payable in addition to the remuneration agreed for the trader's main obligation unless, before the consumer became bound by the contract, the trader obtained the consumer's express consent.

(2) There is no express consent (if there would otherwise be) for the purposes of this paragraph if consent is inferred from the consumer not changing a default option (such as a pre-ticked box on a website).

(3) This regulation does not apply if the trader's main obligation is to supply services within regulation 6(1)(b), but in any other case it applies even if an additional payment is for such services.

(4) Where a trader receives an additional payment which, under this regulation, is not payable under a contract, the contract is to be treated as providing for the trader to reimburse the payment to the consumer.

41 Help-line charges over basic rate

(1) Where a trader operates a telephone line for the purpose of consumers contacting the trader by telephone in relation to contracts entered into with the trader, a consumer contacting the trader must not be bound to pay more than the basic rate.

(2) If in those circumstances a consumer who contacts a trader in relation to a contract is bound to pay more than the basic rate, the contract is to be treated as providing for the trader to pay to the consumer any amount by which the charge paid by the consumer for the call is more than the basic rate.

[. . .]

PART 6

ENFORCEMENT

44 Complaints

(1) It is the duty of an enforcement authority to consider any complaint made to it about a contravention of these Regulations, unless—

(a) the complaint appears to the authority to be frivolous or vexatious, or

(b) another enforcement authority has notified the CMA that it agrees to consider the complaint.

(2) If an enforcement authority has notified the CMA as mentioned in paragraph (1)(b), that authority is under a duty to consider the complaint.

(3) The following are enforcement authorities for the purposes of these Regulations—

(a) every local weights and measures authority in Great Britain;

(b) the Department of Enterprise, Trade and Investment in Northern Ireland.

45 Orders to secure compliance

(1) An enforcement authority may apply for an injunction, or in Scotland an interdict or order of specific implement, against any person who appears to the authority to be responsible for a contravention of these Regulations.

(2) The court on an application under this regulation may grant an injunction, interdict or order on such terms as it thinks fit to secure compliance with these Regulations.

46 Notification of undertakings and orders to the CMA

An enforcement authority must notify the CMA—

(a) of any undertaking given to it by or on behalf of any person who appears to it to be responsible for a contravention of these Regulations;

(b) of the outcome of any application made by it under regulation 45, and of the terms of any undertaking given to the court or of any order made by the court;

(c) of the outcome of any application made by it to enforce a previous order of the court.

Regulation 9(1)

SCHEDULE 1
INFORMATION RELATING TO ON-PREMISES CONTRACTS

The information referred to in regulation 9(1) is—

(a) the main characteristics of the [goods, services or digital content], to the extent appropriate to the medium of communication and to the [goods, services or digital content];

(b) the identity of the trader (such as the trader's trading name), the geographical address at which the trader is established and the trader's telephone number;

(c) the total price of the [goods, services or digital content] inclusive of taxes, or where the nature of the [goods, services or digital content] is such that the price cannot reasonably be calculated in advance, the manner in which the price is to be calculated;

(d) where applicable, all additional delivery charges or, where those charges cannot reasonably be calculated in advance, the fact that such additional charges may be payable;

(e) where applicable, the arrangements for payment, delivery, performance, and the time by which the trader undertakes to deliver the goods[, to perform the service or to supply the digital content];

(f) where applicable, the trader's complaint handling policy;

(g) in the case of a sales contract, a reminder that the trader is under a legal duty to supply goods that are in conformity with the contract;

(h) where applicable, the existence and the conditions of after-sales services and commercial guarantees;

(i) the duration of the contract, where applicable, or, if the contract is of indeterminate duration or is to be extended automatically, the conditions for terminating the contract;

(j) where applicable, the functionality, including applicable technical protection measures, of digital content;

(k) where applicable, any relevant compatibility of digital content with hardware and software that the trader is aware of or can reasonably be expected to have been aware of.

Regulations 10(1) and 13(1)

SCHEDULE 2
INFORMATION RELATING TO DISTANCE AND OFF-PREMISES CONTRACTS

The information referred to in regulations 10(1) and 13(1) is (subject to the note at the end of this Schedule)—

(a) the main characteristics of the [goods, services or digital content], to the extent appropriate to the medium of communication and to the [goods, services or digital content];

(b) the identity of the trader (such as the trader's trading name);

(c) the geographical address at which the trader is established and, where available, the trader's telephone number, fax number and e-mail address, to enable the consumer to contact the trader quickly and communicate efficiently;

(d) where the trader is acting on behalf of another trader, the geographical address and identity of that other trader;

(e) if different from the address provided in accordance with paragraph (c), the geographical address of the place of business of the trader, and, where the trader acts on behalf of another trader, the geographical address of the place of business of that other trader, where the consumer can address any complaints;

(f) the total price of the [goods, services or digital content] inclusive of taxes, or where the nature of the [goods, services or digital content] is such that the price cannot reasonably be calculated in advance, the manner in which the price is to be calculated,

(g) where applicable, all additional delivery charges and any other costs or, where those charges cannot reasonably be calculated in advance, the fact that such additional charges may be payable;

(h) in the case of a contract of indeterminate duration or a contract containing a subscription, the total costs per billing period or (where such contracts are charged at a fixed rate) the total monthly costs;

(i) the cost of using the means of distance communication for the conclusion of the contract where that cost is calculated other than at the basic rate;

(j) the arrangements for payment, delivery, performance, and the time by which the trader undertakes to deliver the goods[, to perform the services or to supply the digital content];

(k) where applicable, the trader's complaint handling policy;

(l) where a right to cancel exists, the conditions, time limit and procedures for exercising that right in accordance with regulations 27 to 38;

(m) where applicable, that the consumer will have to bear the cost of returning the goods in case of cancellation and, for distance contracts, if the goods, by their nature, cannot normally be returned by post, the cost of returning the goods;

(n) that, if the consumer exercises the right to cancel after having made a request in accordance with regulation 36(1), the consumer is to be liable to pay the trader reasonable costs in accordance with regulation 36(4);

(o) where under regulation 28, 36 or 37 there is no right to cancel or the right to cancel may be lost, the information that the consumer will not benefit from a right to cancel, or the circumstances under which the consumer loses the right to cancel;

(p) in the case of a sales contract, a reminder that the trader is under a legal duty to supply goods that are in conformity with the contract;

(q) where applicable, the existence and the conditions of after-sale customer assistance, after-sales services and commercial guarantees;

(r) the existence of relevant codes of conduct, as defined in regulation 5(3)(b) of the Consumer Protection from Unfair Trading Regulations 2008, and how copies of them can be obtained, where applicable;

(s) the duration of the contract, where applicable, or, if the contract is of indeterminate duration or is to be extended automatically, the conditions for terminating the contract;

(t) where applicable, the minimum duration of the consumer's obligations under the contract;

(u) where applicable, the existence and the conditions of deposits or other financial guarantees to be paid or provided by the consumer at the request of the trader;

(v) where applicable, the functionality, including applicable technical protection measures, of digital content;

(w) where applicable, any relevant compatibility of digital content with hardware and software that the trader is aware of or can reasonably be expected to have been aware of;

(x) where applicable, the possibility of having recourse to an out-of-court complaint and redress mechanism, to which the trader is subject, and the methods for having access to it.

Note: In the case of a public auction, the information listed in paragraphs (b) to (e) may be replaced with the equivalent details for the auctioneer.

Regulations 10 and 13

SCHEDULE 3

INFORMATION ABOUT THE EXERCISE OF THE RIGHT TO CANCEL

A. Model instructions for cancellation

Right to cancel

You have the right to cancel this contract within 14 days without giving any reason.

The cancellation period will expire after 14 days from the day [See Note 1]. To exercise the right to cancel, you must inform us [See Note 2] of your decision to cancel this contract by a clear statement (eg a letter sent by post, fax or e-mail). You may use the attached model cancellation form, but it is not obligatory. [See Note 3]

To meet the cancellation deadline, it is sufficient for you to send your communication concerning your exercise of the right to cancel before the cancellation period has expired.

Effects of cancellation

If you cancel this contract, we will reimburse to you all payments received from you, including the costs of delivery (except for the supplementary costs arising if you chose a type of delivery other than the least expensive type of standard delivery offered by us).

We may make a deduction from the reimbursement for loss in value of any goods supplied, if the loss is the result of unnecessary handling by you.

We will make the reimbursement without undue delay, and not later than—

(a) 14 days after the day we receive back from you any goods supplied, or

(b) (if earlier) 14 days after the day you provide evidence that you have returned the goods, or

(c) if there were no goods supplied, 14 days after the day on which we are informed about your decision to cancel this contract.

We will make the reimbursement using the same means of payment as you used for the initial transaction, unless you have expressly agreed otherwise; in any event, you will not incur any fees as a result of the reimbursement. [See Note 4].

[See Note 5]

[See Note 6]

Notes on instructions for completion:

1. Insert one of the following texts between inverted commas:
   (a) in the case of a service contract or a contract for the supply of digital content which is not supplied on a tangible medium: 'of the conclusion of the contract.';
   (b) in the case of a sales contract: 'on which you acquire, or a third party other than the carrier and indicated by you acquires, physical possession of the goods.';
   (c) in the case of a contract relating to multiple goods ordered by the consumer in one order and delivered separately: 'on which you acquire, or a third party other than the carrier and indicated by you acquires, physical possession of the last good.';
   (d) in the case of a contract relating to delivery of a good consisting of multiple lots or pieces: 'on which you acquire, or a third party other than the carrier and indicated by you acquires, physical possession of the last lot or piece.';
   (e) in the case of a contract for regular delivery of goods during a defined period of time: 'on which you acquire, or a third party other than the carrier and indicated by you acquires, physical possession of the first good.'.

2. Insert your name, geographical address and, where available, your telephone number, fax number and e-mail address.

3. If you give the option to the consumer to electronically fill in and submit information about the consumer's cancellation from the contract on your website, insert the following: 'You can also electronically fill in and submit the model cancellation form or any other clear statement on our website [insert Internet address]. If you use this option, we will communicate to you an acknowledgement of receipt of such a cancellation on a durable medium (eg by e-mail) without delay.'.

4. In the case of sales contracts in which you have not offered to collect the goods in the event of cancellation insert the following: 'We may withhold reimbursement until we have received the goods back or you have supplied evidence of having sent back the goods, whichever is the earliest.'.

5. If the consumer has received goods in connection with the contract

   (a) insert:

   —'We will collect the goods.'; or,

   —'You shall send back the goods or hand them over to us or ... [insert the name and geographical address, where applicable, of the person authorised by you to receive the goods], without undue delay and in any event not later than 14 days from the day on which you communicate your cancellation from this contract to us. The deadline is met if you send back the goods before the period of 14 days has expired.'

   (b) insert:

   —'We will bear the cost of returning the goods.';

   —'You will have to bear the direct cost of returning the goods.';

   —If, in a distance contract, you do not offer to bear the cost of returning the goods and the goods, by their nature, cannot normally be returned by post: 'You will have to bear the direct cost of returning the goods, ... [£] [insert the amount].'; or if the cost of returning the goods cannot reasonably be calculated in advance: 'You will have to bear the direct cost of returning the goods. The cost is estimated at a maximum of approximately ... [£] [insert the amount].'; or

—If, in an off-premises contract, the goods, by their nature, cannot normally be returned by post and have been delivered to the consumer's home at the time of the conclusion of the contract: 'We will collect the goods at our own expense.'; and,

(c) insert

—'You are only liable for any diminished value of the goods resulting from the handling other than what is necessary to establish the nature, characteristics and functioning of the goods.'

6. In the case of a service contract insert the following: 'If you requested to begin the performance of services during the cancellation period, you shall pay us an amount which is in proportion to what has been performed until you have communicated us your cancellation from this contract, in comparison with the full coverage of the contract.'.

B. Model cancellation form

To [here the trader's name, geographical address and, where available, fax number and e-mail address are to be inserted by the trader]:

I/We [*] hereby give notice that I/We [*] cancel my/our [*] contract of sale of the following goods [*]/for the supply of the following service [*],

Ordered on [*]/received on [*],

Name of consumer(s),

Address of consumer(s),

Signature of consumer(s) (only if this form is notified on paper),

Date

[*] Delete as appropriate.

INDEX OF STATUTES